King's Navy

Fleet Admiral Ernest J. King
and the Rise of American Sea Power
1897–1947

David Kohnen

Schiffer
Military History

4880 Lower Valley Road
Atglen, PA 19310

Other Schiffer books on related subjects

*United States Naval Vessels: The Official United States Navy Reference Manual
Prepared by the Division of Naval Intelligence, 1 September 1945*
Samuel Loring Morison
978-0-7643-0090-5

Reaping the Whirlwind: The U-boat War off North America during World War I
Dominic Etzold
978-0-7643-6704-5

Designed by Molly Shields
Cover design by Christopher Bower
Type set in Charter/Times New Roman

ISBN: 978-0-7643-6837-0
Printed in India

Published by Schiffer Publishing, Ltd.
4880 Lower Valley Road
Atglen, PA 19310
Phone: (610) 593-1777; Fax: (610) 593-2002
Email: Info@schifferbooks.com
Web: www.schifferbooks.com

For our complete selection of fine books on this and related subjects, please visit our website at www.schifferbooks.com. You may also write for a free catalog.

Schiffer Publishing's titles are available at special discounts for bulk purchases for sales promotions or premiums. Special editions, including personalized covers, corporate imprints, and excerpts, can be created in large quantities for special needs. For more information, contact the publisher.

We are always looking for people to write books on new and related subjects. If you have an idea for a book, please contact us at proposals@schifferbooks.com.

For the people and things that went before . . .

CONTENTS

Part III
"Make Best with What You Have"

Foreword
by Andrew Lambert

For Ernest J. King, history was the fundamental guide for those attempting to navigate the uncharted waters of the future. Ruthlessly ambitious and completely dedicated to the service, King had as many rivals as admirers within the ranks of the US Navy. His sharp intellect and aggressive approach to the business at hand, securing and promoting the vital interests of his country, and the Navy that he believed would be critical in the coming war, outpaced his contemporaries. King remained steadfastly fixed on doing his duty, developing the new American "sea power." He would become the embodiment of the service, and the spokesman for its interests, his powerful presence in the higher councils of war shaped by the education he received serving at sea and ashore between the administrations of America's most navally minded presidents, Theodore and Franklin Roosevelt. Rising from relative obscurity, the son of Scots-Irish immigrants, wartime service in European waters in 1917–18 brought him into contact with the dominant Royal Navy, at the height of its powers. Learning the lessons of that war and mastering new technologies equipped him for the supreme command when America went to war in December 1941, working with the Royal Navy to win the Second World War, paving the way for an American peace and the era of the United Nations.

The recorded experience the Dutch and English sea power states directly influenced the intellectual development of American notions of "sea power." The Roosevelts, descended from Dutch settlers, exercised a unique influence on American naval culture during King's service. King attended the Naval Academy with Henry Latrobe Roosevelt, and they remained friends after Roosevelt left the Naval Academy to join the Marines during the Spanish-American War. Such personal connections built personal links with that singularly maritime American clan—the Roosevelts of New England.

Influential patrons oversaw King's progress through the ranks of the naval service in peace and war: because wise patrons pick out the rising stars—those who will add luster to their careers. King was an outstanding student of his profession. In an age of dynamic technological change, King wisely framed his understanding of the future by seeking perspectives from the history-based teachings of the critical maritime thinkers, John Knox Laughton, Stephen B. Luce, and Alfred Thayer Mahan. Admirals William S. Sims and Henry T. Mayo helped shape King's strategic understanding of multinational naval strategy. Mayo and Sims facilitated King's rapid promotion from the junior officer ranks, which inspired envious observers to refer to him as the "boy captain" during the First World War era.

King's experiences as a young officer shaped his development into a global commander. He existed within a bureaucratic-tribal culture where admirals acted as chieftains at sea and in the higher levels of administration. Civil servants enabled the uniformed branch to focus on the daily operations of the regimentally organized formations ashore and on board ship. While American military doctrine has emphasized the hierarchical benefits of "unity of command," during operations—in peace or war—blind adherence to hierarchy has often proved counterproductive.

Having grappled with this question in the first two decades of his naval service, King studied the great captains of the past and concluded that the best of them won the day by fostering teamwork in command, without undue emphasis upon the superficialities of rank. King perfected his understanding of command by serving on the staffs of flag officers like Sims and Mayo, who worked together with their staffs to attain what King called "unity of effort." During the First World War, Mayo and Sims relied on King to coordinate fleet operations on both sides of the Atlantic. He served as a personal representative of Adm. Mayo—commuting between the Atlantic Fleet, the Navy Department, and the London Flagship organizations in Europe and America. King frequently interacted with the "Historical Section" of the Imperial War Staff.

Wartime service as a staff officer broadened King's education in grappling with problems of combined and joint command. Naval professionals frequently failed to understand the nuanced relationships between differing national policies and the administration of strategy. At the front in Europe, King gained an appreciation for the British way of war. His friend Capt. Dudley W. Knox introduced King to Sir Julian Corbett and the analysts in the Historical Section. By 1918, this organization provided an administrative means to fuse historical analysis with the applied purposes of supporting operations. As the American fleet representative, King worked with many notable British officers at the Admiralty. King befriended Dudley Pound, Andrew Cunningham, Alfred Dewar, Bertram Ramsay, and Roger Keyes. These officers envisioned a future "League Navy" in which the anglophone maritime powers cooperated under the common cause to mitigate global threats from the dominant continental powers. King also harbored hopes for the League Navy idea, as did the wartime assistant secretary of the Navy, Franklin D. Roosevelt. In 1918–19, King accompanied Roosevelt at the European front.

Personal associations blossomed into actual friendships and later provided keys to victory when the Anglo-American navies converged for a second time to combat common enemies in the global maritime arena. King's experience in the First World War and association with British naval thinkers remained a powerful influence. In the 1920s he qualified in submarines and naval aviation, critical steps in preparing himself for the three-dimensional warfare of the next war. In the early 1930s he gained critical experience commanding the battle-cruiser hulled aircraft carrier USS *Lexington*. Having completed the Naval War College for a third time, King received the call for an early promotion into the flag ranks when President Franklin D. Roosevelt took office. From 1933 Roosevelt instituted peace time policies that later anchored American sea power in wartime. Roosevelt quietly encouraged King, since he upset the bureaucratic routines of the Navy Department when he served as chief of the Bureau of Aeronautics. Notably, King used his position to foster civil-military alliances between industry and the naval services.

Service in the peacetime Navy Department of the 1930s enabled King to win the requisite peacetime battles to prepare for the unfortunate realities of war. Old associations between the Roosevelt family and King enabled America to navigate a turbulent era of peace and war. By 1937, Roosevelt earmarked King for high command. Having read Mahan's *The Influence of Sea Power* series, Roosevelt linked the hard-driving King with the historical example of Admiral Sir John Jervis, Earl St. Vincent—another officer with character and determination to win the day, as a fleet commander or a shore-based commander in chief, whatever the circumstances.

In the 1930s British and American naval officers considered the strategic potential of future transatlantic collaboration. Japan's decision to end the Washington Naval Treaty process in 1936 inspired more-focused informal discussions among gentlemen including

King. Japan's imperial aggression in China coincided with the ominous rise of Nazi Germany and Fascist Italy, aggressive ambitious military powers in Europe. Soviet Russia and Communist ideology further complicated the global discussions among Anglo-American policymakers and military staffs in the months preceding the outbreak of the Second World War in September 1939. King was among the architects of what became the "two-ocean navy," which reflected the global aims of the Roosevelt administration—using American sea power to enforce the Pan-American Neutrality Zone. In 1940 and 1941, King was far in advance of his contemporaries, recognizing that solving the old Mahanian "problem of Asia" would require America to begin by helping to solve what may also be characterized as the "problem of Europe."

King used classroom studies and the gaming floors of the Naval War College to inform a globalist maritime strategic perspective. He was one of the few who recognized that the oceanic front was a singular environment, one in which airpower had a limited capacity for sustained operations along vast lines of communications. In his view, armies always functioned as tactical organizations. Consequently, he emphasized the development of auxiliary logistical forces, marine expeditionary doctrines, and what he called "balanced" fleet appropriations. Any ship built on King's watch would have the capacity to perform multiple technical functions while also having the capacity to operate on any oceanic front. Having witnessed the Royal Navy methods of supply in the First World War, King fostered the expansion of the "fleet train" organization to connect the "producer logistics" from America with the "consumer logistics" of maritime forces operating far from shore bases.

Roosevelt encouraged King to prepare American sea power to win the war in the global maritime arena. The Japanese attack on Pearl Harbor provided the president with the mandate to appoint King to the supreme command—first as commander in chief, US Fleet, and then as the chief of naval operations. As an experienced aircraft carrier commander, King had simulated the attack on Pearl Harbor multiple times before the Japanese attack, a "*tactical* masterpiece" that he believed revealed the bankruptcy of Japanese strategy in the Pacific. King emphasized that the combined efforts of the Anglo-American sea power could subject their common enemies to a strategy of "unremitting pressure" through simultaneous operations on all global fronts—not focusing on a specific European or Asian front without mitigating the ability of the enemy to regain an advantage elsewhere.

Few other officers on active service offered the unique combination of practical experience and intellectual originality that King used to balance American policy interests with an Allied transatlantic strategy. Experiences in Europe during the "Great War" defined his global approach as a supreme commander during the second global conflict of the twentieth century. No American did more to achieve what Winston S. Churchill called the "special relationship" between the navies of Britain and America—once Roosevelt set the course to establish the United Nations under the leadership of the "four policemen," the continental powers of the Soviet Union and China and the maritime nations of the British Empire and United States. Under Roosevelt's vision, King committed absolutely to the strategy of using Anglo-American sea power to win the global front by enabling Soviet and Chinese armies to whither common Axis enemies ashore. King believed in the singular potential of sea power, operating in close combination with aviation and special-operations forces—a point that is perhaps best illustrated in King's personal effort to wage a different kind of war in China, using proxies to fix the Japanese on the Asian continent while enabling sea power to take hold on the global stage.

This book is a critical contribution to our understanding of the world wars of the twentieth century. It examines the career and achievements of Fleet Admiral Ernest King within a comprehensive analysis of larger historical trends and global affairs, highlighting the critical role of individuals in shaping and driving the critical "special relationship" of the twentieth century that secured victory at sea, not once but twice, a relationship that continues to shape the maritime world of the twenty-first century. This book is based on a wealth of detailed research in the widest range of original sources, analyzed with a range of relevant tools, from strategic theory to intelligence, to explain how the "King's Navy" of Britannia progressively amalgamated with King's American fleets into the Second World War and beyond.

There is much in this book that is new, and it will be essential reading for naval, academic, and general audiences alike. David Kohnen uses a broadly humanistic approach to examine the idea of transatlantic collaboration—not cooperation—as King's navy evolved from the classically British sea power state to an American continentalist vision of "sea power"—a combination that provided context for the leviathan that evolved out of the depths of history to shape the maritime world of the twenty-first century. Rather than examining the world wars as arbitrarily defined discrete chronological events, Kohnen stresses long-term trends, human interaction, and the synergy of interests that brought two major powers, which had many reasons to disagree—not least their history—into alignment, delivering a combined war effort that proved far greater than the sum of its parts.

This book will be a landmark among twentieth-century studies, an enduring classic that future historians cannot ignore. Kohnen's conclusions challenge popular portrayals of King—getting beneath the rough, salty caricature to reveal a truly remarkable maritime thinker, one whose ideas need to be recovered and reexamined by those who face the increasingly complex demands of the twenty-first century. The historiography of the world wars has much to offer those who shape policy today and tomorrow, not least the importance of long-term planning, for strategy, policy, and career development. Where should we look for a future King? What skill sets will they require, and how well do peacetime career paths, at sea and ashore, equip future commanders for the test of war?

King's Navy is at once a superb study of high command in total war, and a textbook for the critical element in naval service—the career-long self-education that prepares great leaders for the most-demanding tasks. It was no accident that Ernest J. King passed the stern test of war: he had been preparing for it all his professional life. Nor is it an accident that this superb book has developed through exhaustive, rigorous scholarship, combined with fresh questions and a refusal to accept old explanations and arguments. *King's Navy* serves our collective purpose by charting a new course as we face the twenty-first century and beyond.

Andrew Lambert, FKC
Laughton Professor of Naval History
Kings College London

Acknowledgments

History has already happened, and historians generally understand the book is never actually written in history. The past and future are likewise inventions of the mind. Historians are just like anyone else, as we navigate the uncharted waters of the present in anticipation of the unwritten future. Thus, this book serves as a snapshot in time for readers to consider in examining the questions of empire and American sea power during the first fifty years of the twentieth century. Having begun my research on what I am calling "King's navy" in the 1990s, I have since been able to gather information about our topic in various other books, archival collections, and documents still in the possession of descendants of many key personalities featured in this study. As this book is now presented, it shall serve only as a point of reference for future historians to continue building upon what we have collectively been able to understand in reconstructing the strategic trends and personality dynamics that shaped the past.

The oceanic world provided context for King's navy to evolve from the demise of historical empires. This history may thus inform our collective future, as we consider our futures in the maritime environments of inner and outer space. Just as the islands served as landmarks along the oceanic highways of the past, the stars provide means for us to pursue new discoveries and perhaps recognize that we are all just sailors in an unchained voyage. Indeed, when I began writing this book, I certainly had no idea what awaited me along the paths to discovery. From this experience, I have concluded that the phosphorescent wake of history may perhaps illuminate our collective understanding of what may await us all just over the horizon and beyond.

In my personal voyages through the maritime past, I have discovered many waypoints and previously uncharted regions of history. Along the way, many friends and colleagues have guided me to discoveries in archives that I may never have made without their help. My study of *King's Navy* originates with the work I completed during studies at the Naval War College and then at University of London, King's College. Along the way, Andrew Lambert taught me that history is never actually written. Lambert taught me to recognize that the purpose of studying the past centered on the basic question of *why* people acted as they did *at the time* in history. He further emphasized the fundamental purpose of historians.

Rather than reciting old sagas, historians must constantly seek new understanding through applied research in original documentary sources. Wild ideas are the foundation for research, and original sources serve as the key to unlocking the past in our collective quest to win the future. Following my service ashore in Iraq and into my residency as a naval officer, John Hattendorf influenced my perception of the Naval War College as the historical epicenter of American "sea power." Earlier in my studies, Carl Boyd pushed me to focus on the largely uncharted strategic connections between operations and intelligence. The late Craig M. Cameron inspired me to challenge popular myths by revisiting original documentary sources. My friend and literary agent, the late Jim Hornfischer, reminded me to use original historical sources to attract general audiences in seeking new adventures in the largely uncharted waters of maritime history.

The solitary art of researching and writing about history also requires historians to assist each other. For this reason, I am indebted to a very large list of mentors, colleagues, and friends. The Pritzker Military Library and Museum provided key support for my research, as did the granddaughter of US Navy captain Charles H. Maddox, Pamela Ribby. I feel particularly obliged to acknowledge the selfless assistance of Steve Kornatz, Jon Scott Logel, Mark Fiorey, John T. Kuehn, Richard B. Frank, Craig Symonds, Al Nofi, Christopher Bell, Philips Payson O'Brian, Stephen Phillips, Larry Brown, James W. E. Smith, Benjamin Armstrong, Claude Berube, Tracie Logan, Paul Engelstad, Adam Kane, Rick Russell, Robert von Maier, and Tom and Trent Hone. Rear Admiral Katsuya Yamamoto and Captain Riyuji Honmyo of the Historical Section of the Japanese Naval Staff College, along with Professors Sadeo Asada and Naoyuki Agawa, provided instrumental assistance in my research of American naval experiences in Japan. Given the work of all hands as we pulled together in producing this book, I cannot sufficiently express my gratitude to Pete Schiffer, John Stone, Carey Massimini, Bob Biondi, and my friends at Schiffer Publishing for your encouragement and kindness.

Many great friends have selflessly shared their knowledge and access to previously unseen documentary sources. Among others, Nicholas Jellicoe and Dr. Nathaniel Sims helped me recognize the friendly interconnections among between their great naval families. Sims donated previously unseen family papers to the Naval War College, which revealed fresh information about the close connections he maintained with protégés, like King, among many others. Similarly, the grandsons of Cdre. Dudley W. Knox, North and Peter Sturtevant, provided materials previously held unseen from the Knox family archives. Similarly, I am indebted to the families of individuals who silently served behind closed doors and kept their vows of secrecy after the war. I appreciate the assistance I have received from the families of Capt. Rodger Winn, Capt. Kenneth A. Knowles, and Cmdr. John B. McDiarmid. For this, I particularly wish to thank Kenneth Knowles Jr., David Parsons, Judy Parsons, and Kate Lloyd. In addition, the late Sammuel B. Livecci and Rene Chevalier helped to understand the operations and intelligence functions of the wartime CominCh organization in ways that remain opaque in original documentary sources.

Future historians shall have much to discover in these still largely untapped documentary collections at the Naval War College. Unfortunately, access to these truly unique records has been made more difficult by the president of the Naval War College. Since the COVID-19 pandemic, the historical and administrative records of the institution have disappeared into deep storage. Despite appeals filed with the director of naval history by this author, nothing has been done to recover these records. Meanwhile, the federal government pays contractors to store these priceless national treasures, which sit idly in boxes—making it rather difficult for historians to practice their art. Under these circumstances, the author is moved to encourage all in the cause of winning the future in suggesting, "Historians of the world—UNITE!"

Having myself qualified on the deck as a naval officer, I have visited the same places and traversed the same waters as Sims and King. Along the way, I grew interested in understanding the interpersonal networks among notable personalities to develop fresh conclusions about the history of American sea power. Like the Sims family, King's descendants graciously shared their time and interest in assisting my work. I am especially grateful to retired Commander Janvier King Smith and his wife, Maureen. Nikki and

Egerton van den Berg provided insight to their grandfather. Meg van den Berg also shared key insights about her father. I also thank King's granddaughter Elizabeth and her husband, Harry Slaughter III, for their ongoing interest in my work. Tom and Ellie Savage and Steven Savage provided great encouragement—sharing unique insights and access to papers and other historical materials unique to the King family. Indeed, I followed the advice of Admirals Sims and King while writing this book—their mottos being "Remain cheerful" and "Make best with what you have."

I have frequently been reminded to check the phosphorescent wake of history in our collective effort to navigate the uncharted waters just beyond the horizon. Since long voyages require all hands to participate in the adventure, I am compelled to offer my deepest thanks to my wife, Dr. Sarah Goldberger, and our daughters, Elisabeth and Katherine. Among other things, Sarah has supported my research while "enduring freedom" after September 11, 2001, as a navy wife. Having survived this most recent era of American adventurism, Sarah has anchored my US naval career and my work as a historian in museums. Without the support of Sarah and our daughters, this book would not have been written.

THE SIDE NUMBER

Before the First World War, the US Navy developed administrative systems for categorizing vessel classes and functional types. The "USS" initialism preceded the individual warship name, followed by a parenthetical reference to the vessel class or type, and then an individual numerical reference. For example, the Navy Department registered warships as follows, USS *Nevada* (Battleship No. 36). Under General Order 541 of 1920, the US Navy simplified the reference to appear as USS *Nevada* (BB-36). For the purposes of simplicity, this book employs the parenthetical classification as outlined in General Order 541 in the first references to individual American warships.

Prologue: The Triple Threat

The glow of Christmas illuminated the New England shoreline along the inky-black waters in the Narragansett Bay. From Point Judith and all along the coast, lighthouses beckoned in the peaceful silence under the stars. Snowflakes peppered the watery surface as a brisk chill cut across the bow on the cruiser USS *Augusta* (CA-31)—at anchor off the Naval War College along the shores of Rhode Island. The dim incandescence of cigarettes occasionally appeared where sailors gathered on the decks just before dawn. Above, the four-star flag of Admiral Ernest J. King appeared from the topmast. With the clang of a bell and the sound of a boatswain's whistle, the Atlantic Fleet flagship came alive as the admiral stepped onto the deck. The rising sun cast over the new day, as the Stars and Stripes broke freely at the fantail. Bugles roused the sailors to look aloft as King rendered a crisp salute. King then returned to his flag cabin to review the morning radio traffic. It was just another slow-rolling Sunday on December 7, 1941.

Shipboard routines intermixed with ancient naval traditions when King traversed the wooden decks. Armored steel defined the American fleet, and all hands understood King's role in building it. With Nazi marauders awaiting farther out to sea, Atlantic Fleet sailors had already experienced the consequences of what King called "waging peace."[1] King expected his men to go into harm's way with convoys and beyond the declared lines of demarcation within the Pan-American Neutrality Zone. American sailors on board USS *Reuben James* (DD-245) paid the price—going to their watery grave under the starry skies of Halloween night—just a few weeks earlier as King pondered the war-warning message on that morning in December 1941.[2]

The phosphorescent wake of torpedoes illuminated lines between life and death for sailors traversing the Atlantic abyss. Pressing the limits, King and his fellow sailors sailed far beyond the horizon to defend American neutrality—often without headlines or public fanfare. The rigors of naval service in peacetime always resembled war on the cruel sea. History followed in the wake of American warships in the global maritime arena. Influenced by the Naval War College, King's navy studied the works of the Prussian general, Carl von Clausewitz, through the extrapolations of US Army theorists like brevet brigadier general Emory Upton. The continentalist theories of British thinkers like Halford MacKinder and the American, Frederick Jackson Turner, also shaped the ideas of the younger generation at the dawn of the twentieth century. In naval affairs, the maritime vision of Sir John Knox Laughton and RAdm. Stephen B. Luce also provided additional foundation for the theories of Alfred Thayer Mahan.

British concepts of sea power directly influenced the views of the new generation of American naval professionals in the era of Theodore Roosevelt. Given the works of Mahan, American naval thinkers progressively embraced the teachings of Sir Julian Corbett. Applied historical studies enabled thinkers, like King, to reject the principles of continental warfare to argue that "armies are essentially redundant in peace-time [and] navies always have a job to do in winning the sustainable end of war."[3] King coldly warned that "war is force—force to the utmost—to compel the enemy to do your will, and it isn't anything else, but machines don't do it."[4]

King fully understood the role of technology in naval operations, although he placed higher priority on the human dimension. He warned that "we hear a great deal in these days of machines—machines do this, and machines do that and we have some very remarkable machines [but] the important thing is not the machines, but the men who man them and give them life."[5] He thought that the "men who win are the men whose morale is high because they believe in what they are fighting for and because the folks at home believe in what they are fighting for."[6] In the effort to win the future, King always operated within the historical nexus between peace and war. King explained this outlook to his flag secretary, Lt. George L. Russell, that "there always has been a twilight zone, and there will always be such a zone."[7]

American sailors joined King in the oceanic twilight zone between peace and war, quietly enduring the routine hardships of chipping rust from the bulkheads and swabbing the saltwater off the deck. Younger sailors tended to fade into the gray bulkheads, whereas the old hands often traded off-color comments with their commander. King regularly appeared on the deck, sometimes rewarding his men with a wry smirk. King coached his men to be happy in their work by invoking the motto of his old mentor, Adm. William S. Sims—"Remain cheerful."[8]

Carrying the traditions of a bygone era into the windy seas and the wireless wars of the future, King inspired his men to recognize themselves as being part of an elite class in American culture. The naval service provided opportunity for sailors of all ethnic backgrounds and social stations to pull together as a team. King fostered the seagoing spirit by including sea stories about the heroic exploits of such heroes as Lord Horatio Nelson and Cdre. John Paul Jones in the shipboard newspapers. History—even if partially true—provided another means for King and his men to endure the cruel sea. He always gave all in providing the example for others to follow. Setting the tone in 1941, King issued formal orders to the Atlantic Fleet with his motto, "Make best with what you have."[9]

Knowing the ebbs and flows of naval operations within the nexus between peace and war, King always acted as though the enemy lurked just over the horizon. He directed the skipper on *Augusta*, Capt. Carleton H. Wright, to maintain a constant radio watch to ensure the landline connection with the telephone relay station at nearby Conanicut Island in Jamestown. On that chilly morning of December 7, King enjoyed a light breakfast with his staff and then smoked a cigarette with a cup of coffee while awaiting the arrival of his barge. Every day at 08:00, King usually went ashore to Coaster's Harbor Island for other morning meetings with his friend of more than four decades, RAdm. Edward C. Kalbfus—then serving in his second tour as president of the Naval War College.[10]

Kalbfus mentored King along their long voyage together from the era of President Theodore Roosevelt through the administration of Franklin Delano Roosevelt and beyond. Their association within the ranks proved vital in both peace and war. Kalbfus stood among many unsung heroes framing King's strategic conclusions. Twice presiding over the education of fellow naval officers in Newport, Kalbfus also shaped King's delineation between army concepts in military doctrine and the broader naval definitions for attaining control within the global maritime arena. In 1941, King grappled with the problems during staff discussions between the British and American commands. He explained the agreement defining the "term 'joint' was applied to the operations of one country [and] the term 'combined' to British and US."[11]

King credited Kalbfus for writing the book on how to win the sustainable end of war in the global maritime arena. The 1936 edition of *Sound Military Decision*, as compiled by Kalbfus, also served as the basis for King's Atlantic Fleet staff in orchestrating naval operations during the undeclared quasi-war within the Pan-American Neutrality Zone.[12] Kalbfus and King met on an almost daily basis in the Communications Annex next to the Naval War College. From within the makeshift submarine-tracking room inside the Communications Annex, the Atlantic Fleet intelligence officer, Lt. Robert Weeks, monitored the global situation for King.

Weeks tracked Nazi provocations by plotting the latest reports from the Admiralty, which usually marked the locations of British naval forces and lost merchant vessels. Among other qualities, Weeks held qualifications for assignment to future command in destroyers and submarines. He specialized in wireless communications and cryptography. Before reporting to King in the Atlantic Fleet, Weeks worked alongside British cryptanalysts at Bletchley Park before serving in the submarine- tracking room at the Operational Intelligence Center (OIC) in London.[13] Having dodged German bombs during the blitz, Weeks accompanied King to reestablish the Atlantic Fleet. Through associates in the Office of Naval Communications at the Navy Department, Weeks fully understood the strategic situation in the Pacific. The role of Weeks in shaping events that followed thereafter faded into secretive netherworld of his own making within the intelligence community, which evolved from a world seemingly always at war.[14]

Having reunited against common enemies in the First World War, the British Empire weathered the gathering storm with the rise of American sea power. Characterizing the situation as it existed in the undeclared quasi-war of 1941, King struggled to balance British uncertainty against American indifference by explaining that in "Germany there were the Nazis and in Italy there were the Fascists; I don't know what particular name could be given to the ideology in Japan, but it was just as vicious."[15] He explained, "Things that we naval officers are taught at the Naval War College [were] to estimate the situation."[16] King noted that our "British friends have the same thing, but of course they have a different name for it, so they call it 'appreciation.'"[17] King always found humor in the British view of American "immaturity" in maritime affairs. Always loyal to their collective cause, King firmly appreciated the British way of war while setting the new course for American sea power into the Second World War and beyond.

King stood among the few to recognize the British Empire as the fundamental historical influence upon future American sea power. The ongoing European war and the old problems of Asia converged against ongoing American efforts to hold the peace in the global maritime arena.[18] King characterized the situation in 1941 that "Britain was fighting for her life and that was an immediate factor."[19] He noted that "Russia was in a bad way and needed munitions and more munitions."[20] Always keeping the American naval neutrality strategy at center of focus, King lamented that "Russia had unlimited manpower, but very limited capacity to manufacture munitions [and] China had unlimited manpower and no munitions."[21] King taught that "you have got to go into every situation and size it up on its merits and make what seems to be the best decision, looking to ultimate victory."[22] Whether in peace or war, King warned that "there are no thumb rules that will work."[23]

King recognized the advantages of collaboration among the Anglo-American maritime powers in efforts to enable the armies of China and Russia to defeat common enemies ashore in Asia and Europe. For this reason, King rejected the military maxim that "if you are dealing and fighting against two allies, decide which is the weaker and knock him out."[24] Comparing the capabilities of German and Italian forces in Europe, King noted that "it would seem that Japan was relatively the weaker."[25] In 1941, King argued that the "situation in Europe was too immediate [and] had to be dealt with."[26] In his estimate, "Japan can't afford to go south with her fleet, because the British fleet could handle their warships, and her islands would be left unguarded from action by the American fleet."[27] King assumed that Japan "couldn't go after the United States because that would lay Japan open to attack by the British."[28] Under the circumstances, King thought, "Japan is not going to move anyplace, for a while anyway."[29]

King expected the Japanese focus on the ongoing war in China, although he worried about keeping lines of communications open with the distant American imperial outpost in the Philippines. The greater threat seemed to exist in Europe, as the British struggled to hold the oceanic lines of communications open in the Atlantic. King discussed these problems with journalists in the fall of 1941. In the vividly titled exposé "Stormy Man, Stormy Weather," King stood indefatigable. "In the Navy," the tale begins, "there are only two opinions of Ernest Joseph King—that he is a great fellow and a great sailorman [or] that he is a no-good, ring-tailed son-of-the-bilge."[30] The salty image suited King, as *Time* magazine editors noted, "On occasion he can be graceful and charming [but] there is a storm within him . . . at sea he is at his best."[31]

Seeking to catch a juicy story for a headline above the fold, journalists closely monitored key American commanders and their families. Among others, Glenn C. H. Perry had monitored King's naval career since the First World War and into the 1920s "as a four-striper in charge of raising sunken submarines."[32] Perry noted, "Franklin D. Roosevelt had been Assistant Secretary of the Navy [and] during that time formed a respect for King that kept on growing [to] full flower."[33] The Second World War rumbled beyond the east and west horizons in the Pan-American Neutrality Zone. King stood among the few Americans to recognize the gathering storm, warning that the "First World War was a breeze in comparison."[34] He made these remarks at the time to trusted journalists among the "Arlington County Commandos."[35]

King rarely harbored secrets, always finding means to tell the unvarnished truth in convincing others to follow. Among the Arlington County Commandos, Phelps Adams admitted that King "never failed to astonish me—and I think the others of our group—was the uninhibited disclosure of highly sensitive information."[36] Trusted journalists recognized that "Ernie King was—above all—a realist [and] did not indulge in wishful thinking or close his eyes to unpleasant problems in the hope that they would go away."[37] In the November 27 issue of *Life* magazine, Joseph J. Thorndike shared a similar impression under the confident title "King of the Atlantic: America's Triple-Threat Admiral Is the Stern, Daring Model of a War Commander."[38] On the same day that *Life* magazine featured the story of King, American commanders received the communiqué from the chief of naval operations (CNO), Adm. Harold R. Stark, that "negotiations with Japan looking toward stabilization of conditions in the Pacific have ceased and an aggressive move by Japan is expected within the next few days."[39]

Another global war boiled over from foreign shores of Asia and Europe to threaten the future of American sea power. Roosevelt balanced his diplomatic policies to enable his admirals to hold the peace as long as possible in the American hemisphere. King understood the mission, placing the warships of the Atlantic Fleet in harm's way to defend American interests against foreign threats. King and his Atlantic Fleet staff existed at the center of turmoil and uncertainty. For this reason, King always kept a predictable routine by which his subordinates managed the stresses of an undeclared war.

War seamlessly intermixed with the peacetime functions of the American sea services within the global maritime arena. Whether at peace or at war, King always understood the realities inherent with leading sailors to overcome the difficulties of the cruel sea. King regularly left his staff to manage operations on board *Augusta*—always at the ready to steam to battle. He frequently went ashore to review incoming message traffic with his fleet intelligence officer, Weeks, inside the Communications Annex at the Naval War College. Whenever time allowed, King sometimes appeared in civilian clothing for the morning briefing in the Communications Annex. Keeping his predictable schedule, King took his ritualistic walk along the historic streets of Newport. "Skirting the harbor front," King walked "rapidly through the town and [stopped] in at the Reading Room, an ancient club of the town, for a glass of sherry, thus making one of his rare contacts with local society."[40]

Newport elites frequently gathered at the Reading Room for an early-afternoon luncheon before adjourning to the parlor. Overstuffed leather sofas and an eclectic selection of classic books intermixed with the daily newspapers for Reading Room patrons.[41] The faded smells of pipe smoke lingered, as King quietly enjoyed brunch and then sipped on an afternoon coffee in the corner by the fireplace. King ritualistically enjoyed wasting Sunday afternoons—glancing the latest headlines while scrutinizing the box scores. As war loomed over the horizons in the Atlantic and Pacific in the winter of 1941, King sought refuge in the traditions and old ghosts of such historic places.[42]

The historic waters surrounding Coaster's Harbor Island in the Narragansett Bay always inspired King's confidence about the future. Fully anticipating another unfortunate world war just beyond the horizon, King had trained his Atlantic Fleet staff to understood their responsibility to act on his authority in the event of any unforeseen surprise. Just down the hill from the Reading Room at the Communications Center by the Naval War College, King's man Capt. Francis S. Low remembered the moment when the "attack on Pearl Harbor was flashed to us at Newport about 1:00 p.m."[43]

The warships and merchants that sailed under the Stars and Stripes damned the torpedoes of Nazi submarines in the Atlantic. Still neutral in the global war at sea, American sea power girded for the brewing storm over Europe. When the message flashed about Pearl Harbor, Low immediately telephoned the Navy Department to confirm reports incoming from the Pacific. Low confirmed the report about Pearl Harbor with Lt. Cmdr. William R. Smedberg III, flag secretary with Stark at the epicenter of global operations in Washington, DC.[44] Smedberg advised Low about the decision to initiate immediate offensive operations against imperial Japan. Thus, the Atlantic Fleet stood cleared for action to wage war—to include unrestricted submarine warfare—against Japanese-flagged vessels in the Atlantic. Low sent the duty officer, Russell, to deliver the message to King.[45]

As Low attempted to get a telephone connection from the Naval War College, Russell carried the message heralding the Japanese attack at Pearl Harbor up the hill to the Reading Room in downtown Newport. Russell found the Reading Room somewhat surreal. He recalled that the sound of silence was deafening. The heels of his shoes resonated on the creaky wooden floors inside the old boy's club on Bellevue Avenue. Russell found King among a small group near the radio in the gaming room. Russell handed King the slip of paper. King glanced at him to acknowledge his subordinate and calmly adjusted his glasses to read the text, "as though it was just another routine message."[46] King seemed nonplused. He simply told Russell to "keep me apprised." Russell recalled that King then "just went back to what he was doing."[47]

Having studied the problem of past wars in history, King had already fought the battles to come on the fictional battlefields on Naval War College gaming floors and solved peacetime fleet problems. At sixty-three years of age, King immediately recognized the fundamental flaw in enemy strategy. King stood fully confident about future victory—even while American sea power settled into the muddy shallows of Pearl Harbor. With a beer in hand and a cigarette in the other, King calmly told friends that "Pearl Harbor came as a terrible shock [not] because it happened, but because of where it happened."[48] The audacious Japanese gamble deeply impressed King, describing the airstrike at Pearl Harbor as a "tactical masterpiece."[49]

Imperial Japan gambled upon American greed and childish indifference about the future in the global maritime arena. As the Roosevelt administration shifted from neutrality policy to call the grand bluff, King also received summons to the White House. Roosevelt knew what to expect from King. In past meetings involving the British, Roosevelt had observed King. Unlike others, King demonstrated a singular understanding in articulating the cultural and strategic context. From studies at the Naval War College, King concluded that the British home isles and Formosa stood as the key terrestrial "citadels" by which to hold—or seize—maritime access to Europe and Asia from the Americas.[50]

King understood the historical trends, perceiving the ongoing wars in Europe and Asia as being interconnected with the global focus of American sea power. The key to winning in Asia always hinged upon securing stability ashore in Europe first. From the War of American Independence through the First World War, American strategy always followed the prevailing winds out of Europe first; for King, the only solution for what retired rear admiral Alfred Thayer Mahan perceived as the "problem of Asia."[51] He also warned against imperial strategies for fixing American sea power to the futures of foreign regimes. First World War experience inspired King to recognize the paramount objective of Europe first.

Looking outward, King set the clear *offensive* course for American sea power to sustain the British while reducing common enemies ashore through maritime assistance to the associated armies of the Soviet Union and China.[52] In so doing, he seized a place among the most consequential figures in history by encouraging fellow Americans to "grasp the nettle firmly."[53] With forty years on active service, King knew the triumphs and tragedies to come. Foreign partners struggled for strategic control, as Roosevelt empowered King to orchestrate the strategy for "waging peace" into the Second World War.[54] Following Roosevelt's flag into embattled waters and over to foreign shores, King marshaled the strategy and placed a steady hand on the tiller to win the future under the United Nations. To this end, King orchestrated operations with intelligence to enable American sea power to attain unprecedented supremacy within the global maritime arena.

PART I
"REMAIN CHEERFUL"

CHAPTER 1

The Uses of Adversity

The spectacular disaster by the pier sides in Pearl Harbor provided a clear mandate for King's navy to become second to none. American sea power lingered peacefully in the global hurricane of war. The doldrums of peacetime routine quickly evaporated, with the Japanese attacking on multiple Pacific fronts. King understood the ramifications on December 8, 1941, as he listened intently to the radio address by the president. Roosevelt unslipped the Shakespearian hounds of war by describing the Japanese as a "dastardly and unprovoked attack [on] a date which will live in infamy."[1] Congress immediately ratified Roosevelt's call to war against imperial Japan. Then, just two days later, Nazi Germany and Fascist Italy declared war on the United States. Old dreams of a future "Imperial Federation" also reappeared in what Roosevelt described as the "United Nations."[2][3]

The British Empire stood upon the proverbial hinge of fate, as American sea power slowly shifted peace to war. Exploiting the opportunity to influence transatlantic policy, Winston S. Churchill characterized relations with the Americas as a "grand alliance."[4] The great sorcerer in the British way of war, Churchill, also twisted historical facts to celebrate the imperial past among the "English-speaking peoples."[5] In response, the political war-lock, Roosevelt, conjured an alternative future in which historical empires held no future under his vision for the United Nations. The Axis tripartite—and certainly not the Roosevelt administration—thrust the United States into the bull's-eye. However, Churchill and Roosevelt never actually rectified their differing outlooks, as the pair grappled with the consequences of Pearl Harbor.[6]

Churchill and Roosevelt demonstrated magical skills in penetrating the enigmatic circumstances of being in a global war of completely unforeseeable scale. Past global wars followed in the technological chronology of human destruction on an industrial scale by the First World War. In the wireless world, intercepted communications failed to reveal evidence of serious coordination among the Axis tripartite of imperial Japan, Nazi Germany, and Fascist Italy. From Pearl Harbor to Singapore, the war also unfolded in the "war rooms" of London and Washington.[7] When Churchill and Roosevelt met under the soft glimmer of Christmas on December 22, 1941, intelligence provided the means to unify the efforts of Britain and America against common rivals.

Behind the darkened curtains and the smoke-filled rooms within the White House, the fuzzy illumination of Christmas intermixed with flowing spirits to inspire the cheerful exchanges between Churchill and Roosevelt. These two characters immediately recognized their role in the global war. Churchill cast himself as the unflinching British bulldog, whereas Roosevelt took the role of master in the kennel. Churchill sought future empires, whereas Roosevelt talked about the "four freedoms."[8] In their previous seaborne agreement under the Atlantic Charter, the Anglo-American navies stood together to ensure the ancient principle of "freedom of the seas."[9] In earlier meetings at sea on the flagship, *Augusta*, Churchill fully understood the meaning of Roosevelt when first being introduced to his favorite pet, Murray the Outlaw of Falahill—or FALA. Both Churchill and Roosevelt shared a distant ancestral connection with the sixteenth-century Scottish "outlaw" John Murray. The feisty Scotch terrier customarily barked at Churchill during meetings with Roosevelt—both remaining cheerful for the media.[10]

The bleak realities of war forced Churchill and Roosevelt together in an imperfect friendship. Both ably represented their respective regimes while presenting a unified façade on the public stage. Churchill modeled himself after his ancestor the Duke of Marlborough, while also celebrating his mother's American heritage. Roosevelt likewise took pride in his ancient Dutch imperial heritage and revered his opium-dealing New England merchant grandfather Warren Delano. Unslipping his American hounds, Roosevelt relied upon his salty Scots-Irish attack dog, King. Never upset when breaking glass, King nurtured his popular image as a "formidable old crustacean."[11] Roosevelt also groomed the caricature of King—referring to him as "blowtorch."[12] Roosevelt also amused himself by addressing the admiral as "Ernie," just to watch King's reaction.[13]

THE ANGLOPHOBE

Roosevelt embraced the historical dream of American sea power, which King shared in formulating practical strategies to win the future. Roosevelt recognized King as the only real choice for the job of putting American sea power back on course in the aftermath of disaster. King's abrasive style upset many peacocks in the swampy political battleground of Washington. King rarely cowered whenever he stood alone in debates of strategic perspective. In December 1941, King had expected to retire within roughly nine months.[14] Always weary of Roosevelt's reputation for using people to attain political ends, King used his impending retirement to destroy bureaucratic barriers within the Navy Department.

King unflinchingly carried the banner of American sea power into the global maritime arena. He had no intention of ceding the bureaucratic high ground in this historic quest to win the future. In this respect, Roosevelt and King shared similar challenges among the big personalities on the Washington battlefield. King's dueling partners in the War Department—like Generals Douglas MacArthur and George C. Marshall—used King to wage their own political battles within the War Department. The ancient bureaucratic fight for resources between the Department of War and the Navy Department frequently inspired childish behavior among the key personalities within these rival feudal empires on the Washington battlefield. The former secretary of state and twice-serving secretary of war, Henry L. Stimson, mused about King and his associates in memoirs. Stimson lambasted naval officers for acting as though the navy represented the "only true church."[15.] Stimson carried the analogy further in describing the "high priests of this Church were a group of men [known] as 'the Admirals.'"[16] Stimson believed that the "'the Admirals' had never been given their comeuppance."[17]

Old vendettas among the upper echelons between the Departments of War and Navy created difficulties for the Roosevelt administration. In managing these rivalries, Roosevelt accepted the role of being the final authority for any given decision. On the other hand, he too used his subordinates to keep the balance among all the key partners. Roosevelt used King as his proverbial queen on the chessboard of war. For this reason, King became a favorite target for the British. When the Admiralty pushed for full control over convoy operations in the Atlantic, King refused to relinquish control—knowing from First World War experience the strategic ramifications for the future of American sea power beyond the Second World War.

King viewed the world wars as being interconnected with past world wars in an ongoing competition for control in the global maritime arena. The British Empire always served as the foundation for what King recognized as a future for American sea power. He acted accordingly in the ongoing tug-and-pull between London and Washington in defining the transatlantic alliance at sea. Few of his immediate counterparts fully grasped the complexities of King's way of "looking outward" on questions of global command.[18] King understood the ancient troubles of Asia as inextricably intertwined with those ashore in Europe and America.[19] British traditions of maritime supremacy intermixed with the politics inherent with negotiating *unity of command* within the coalition, as King's navy conversely maneuvered to achieve transatlantic *unity of effort* along multiple fronts within the global maritime arena.

King accepted his duty to serve Roosevelt's vision in shaping Anglo-American strategy. Detractors unfairly mischaracterized King for being "slow to take action, believing that ships would be safer sailing independently than in weakly defended convoys."[20] American critics, like Ralph Ingersoll, parroted the myth that "King is said to have opened the first meeting of the Combined Chiefs of Staff by announcing flatly that he had served under the British in the last war and now wanted it understood [that] he would never serve under them again, or permit any of his ships to serve under them 'if he could help it.'"[21] Upon reading this passage, King barked that "I never said or <u>thought</u> these remarks about the Royal Navy."[22] King told the historian Samuel Eliot Morison that Ingersoll's portrayal "is wildly inaccurate."[23]

The real war unfolded on the maps on walls and tables behind closed doors, more than in the turrets of tanks and battleships in the global maritime arena. King arguably stood above all others in those epic battles. He traded verbal attacks with devastating verbal perries in the unresolved fight to win the future—always balancing differing British and American policies to strike common strategic objectives.[24] King firmly rejected theoretical arguments as presented by RAF and USAAF counterparts about the success of strategic bombing. He warned against bombing civilian industrial targets for the practical reason that "<u>we</u> are going to have to rebuild it <u>when</u> we win."[25] He rejected the tactical assertions of airpower theorists by seizing the higher strategic argument, which emphasized the requirements for postwar reconstruction. King instead pressed RAF and USAAF counterparts to focus on enemy naval bases, logistical hubs, and tactical ground support for Allied forces ashore.[26]

King served as a convenient foil for blurring the strategic differences between Churchill and Roosevelt, as British and American strategists struggled to frame coherent global objectives. In heated debates among Allied commanders, King recalled the moment when "Mr. Churchill sat with a big cigar and pencil in his hand, and we came to the place when something was said about continuing the effort against German submarines."[27] Churchill boomed, "I would like to note an exception—would you mind changing that to German U-boat?"[28] Churchill explained, "To my mind the submarine is a term that applies to our gallant fellows and yours that go out to sink the villainous German shipping [while] 'U-boat' applies to those rascals, those villains that sink your shipping and ours."[29]

Army and air force failures to concentrate strategic bombing efforts against enemy naval bases ashore loomed over the unresolved debates of transatlantic command. British and American policies for future reconstruction similarly stalled at the crossroads between imperial traditions and utopian dreams. Pondering the strategic consequences as the British Empire foundered in the global maritime arena, King admitted that "he cannot understand how they make mistake after mistake."[30] His remarks inspired journalists to joke about "HMS *Ridiculous* [and] a whole new Royal Navy, such as HMS *Impossible*, HMS *Improvident*, HMS *Spurious*, and so on down the line of battle."[31] British observers failed to appreciate the American point of view. Field Marshal Alan Brooke described King as a "tough sixty-three-year-old salt of strong views and uncompromising temper who had grown up with the American navy and was intensely jealous of its independence."[32] Conversely, Brooke applauded King for telling fellow leaders immediately after Pearl Harbor to "toss defensive talking and thinking overboard, our days of victory are in the making—we will win this war."[33]

THE ANGLOPHILE

While others among the Anglo-American high command debated the priorities for global operations, King stood among the very few to push immediate global offensive operations on all oceanic fronts. Above all, he understood the full potential of American sea power. British observers portrayed King to as a "very forceful character, devoted to his service and determined that it should not again play second fiddle to the Royal Navy."[34] Royal Navy captain Stephen Roskill addressed the problem of Anglo-American collaboration in his history *Naval Policy between the Wars*. Roskill lamented the "tendency by historians to underplay, if not actually ignore, the serious differences of opinion and the rivalry in many fields which arise between the two nations during the inter-war period."[35] Roskill refuted the notion that

> King was anti-British, though very prevalent at the time, is certainly an oversimplification of his attitude, and possibly an unfair stigmatism of a man who did, after all, repeatedly send help to the Royal Navy. It is probably nearer to the truth to say that in his heart he admired the other service's traditions and fighting record but was determined that it should not deprive the United States Navy, in whose creation he himself played such a great part, of the glory of victories which he felt to be its right.[36]

Sharing a similar perspective, Royal Navy vice-admiral Sir John M. Mansfield wryly remarked that "King thinks everybody has as much brains as he has [that] we write instructions for the boneheads—there is a lot of bone in the world."[37]

The past always shaped King's perspective in framing the mission of American sea power in the global maritime arena in both peace and war. History provided basis for King to examine trends leading into the unwritten future. The maritime policies of President Theodore Roosevelt served as an early foundation for King's strategic development. Roosevelt made an indirect reference to the Colt .45 pistol in his speech "Our Peacemaker, the Navy."[38] Roosevelt also considered the "navy of the United States [as] the right arm of the United States and is emphatically the peacemaker."[39] "Woe to our country," Roosevelt warned, "if we permit that right arm to be palsied or even to become flabby and inefficient!"[40]

Roosevelt's ideas resonated within the minds of younger naval officers among King's immediate circle. Having served in Teddy's Great White Fleet four decades earlier, King indeed personified the idealized image of American sea power. With four decades' experience on the deck, King's uniform hung efficiently from his wiry torso as he stood 6 feet with a slim 33-inch waist at 159 pounds.[41] American journalists called him "Triple Threat," for holding credentials in surface, subsurface, and aviation operations.[42] In the media, King personified Roosevelt's "two-ocean navy."[43] After the disaster at Pearl Harbor, King thus became "an alluring target [for] his enemies in the press, Congress, and the navy rubbed their hands and warmed to the task of giving him the deep six."[44]

When disaster struck in the Pacific, the Roosevelt administration pulled King from the Atlantic to lend a hand in the transition from peace to war. Roosevelt and King also calculated opportunities to unify British and American sea power against common enemies.[45] In the winter of 1941, King fully expected to retire upon reaching age sixty-four within a few months immediately following Pearl Harbor.[46] Having earlier served on the General Board, King also understood the existing war plans to focus on winning victory in Europe first. Synchronization with foreign allies stood among the highest strategic priorities. For this reason, King first recommended the merger of CNO and CinCUS to replicate the authorities held by the chief of staff of the Army, Marshall. He further suggested five-star ranks for the temporal purposes of synchronizing the relationships between British Joint Staff and American JCS. Unlike in the First World War, the British would have *no* authority to command American forces without first negotiating unanimous JCS approval.[47]

Lessons learned from the Civil War through the First World War influenced Marshall and King to present a unified front in dealings with foreign counterparts. King explained that the "Constitution provides for essential coordination and correlation between the government and the armed forces by making the President, executive head of the government, and as commander-in-chief of the Army and Navy."[48] Roosevelt occasionally asked King to explain his reluctance to indulge foreign partners. In turn, King asked for clarification on American policy. Roosevelt understood King's implication about their roles in shaping global strategy. King explained their relationship "as when a lawyer's client leaves his lawyer to conduct his case in court or a doctor's patient leaves to the doctor the conduct of the necessary treatment."[49] Roosevelt had the constitutional responsibility to set policy, which set course for King to synchronize operations in the global maritime arena.

Roosevelt and King also shared similar views, as defined by their common understanding of history. Both traded notes about past world wars from the era of Oliver Cromwell and Samuel Pepys through the Napoleonic Wars and the Civil War. Roosevelt consulted George Washington and Abraham Lincoln, whereas King drew inspiration from the memoirs of Ulysses S. Grant, as given for his tenth birthday as a gift in 1888. King also kept inscribed copies of works by Mahan—including *The Gulf and Inland Waters*, *From Sail to Steam*, *The Problem of Asia*, and *Naval Administration*. King regularly reread Mahan's *Types of Naval Officers*. King's old British friend, Admiral Roger Keyes, 1st Baron Keyes of Zeebrugge and Dover, gave him an inscribed copy of *Amphibious Warfare and Combined Operations*.[50]

King's well-worn copies of books from his personal library featured neatly underlined paragraphs. Margin annotations appear in small print, as King used history to deal with circumstances he faced in the moment. King's extensive personal library continued growing throughout his long career from the wooden decks of sailing ships to those of oil-fired warships of steel and steam. Long before he dove into the depths with Neptune and then flew into the wild blue yonder as an aviator, King's generation kept looking outward and beyond the horizon of American sea power. Mahan's study *The Problem of Asia* profoundly influenced King in recognizing the importance of China and the Middle East in American relations with Europe.[51] King's bookshelf similarly included copies of Sir Julian Corbett's biography of Sir Francis Drake along with such classics as *England in the Seven Years War* and *Principles of Maritime Strategy*. Churchill's inscription for King's copy of *While England Slept* read, for King, "with all good wishes for our lion of the sea."[52]

King read history with an applied purpose, always seeking means to gain the competitive advantage under any circumstance. Contrary to many portrayals, King harbored great respect for British maritime traditions. King took time to request genealogical information from the Public Records Office in London.[53] His request prompted a detailed response from the registrar general in Edinburgh, Scotland.[54] Far from an Anglophobe, King modeled himself after Royal Navy admiral John Jervis, Earl of St. Vincent.[55] Known for his sharp discipline and equally sharp mind, St. Vincent inspired King to recognize that there are two basic kinds of naval officers, "good guys and S.O.B.s, and the quicker you learn to be an S.O.B. the better off you will be."[56] His rivals noted an explosive temper, although one subordinate noted, "King could be gentle with a competent man who was trying hard."[57]

King used Navy Regulations like a boarding axe in the pugilistic battles of bureaucracy within the service. Admirals Hugo Osterhaus and William S. Sims groomed King to understand the fine art of pushing the limits. Adm. Henry T. Mayo then groomed King for future flag rank. Osterhaus enjoyed a beer, although Sims and Mayo favored the tee-totaling culture. Such mentors collectively broke wild horses like King, thereby driving him to achieve his full potential as a naval professional. For more than five decades on the deck, King always relied upon his devoted spouse, Mattie, in setting the standard by which other navy families followed.[58]

Outside the family lifelines, King presented the façade of an unflinching seagoing commander. Conversely, members of his personal staff remembered that King's business-like manner disappeared at the transom at home. He seemed prone to acting with old fashioned propriety among friends. For King, the uniform served as a suit of armor. At home, King customarily changed out of his uniform, put on comfortable clothes, and closed the day with a good book. He relaxed with a glass of beer, or an occasional nightcap with a dram of scotch or sherry. Safe at home, King frequently asked his bride to dance to their favorite Felix Arndt ditty, "Nola."[59.] Ernest and Mattie King raised six happy daughters and a son—and then fourteen grandchildren and one adopted grandchild. King's daughters simply called him "Daddy."[60]

King nurtured the reputation as a serious naval professional, which centered on an understanding of the social expectations of the service. Using Navy Regulations as both a guide and a bureaucratic tool, he set the example by which subordinates struggled to meet his higher standards. Close observers noted his approach that "when some erring officer appeared before him, he asked just two questions: What did you do? [and that] was the easy one, setting up the second."[61] Those familiar with King's ritualistic interrogation style described the follow-up question, "which was one word long: Why? [and] that was the zinger that reduced strong men to quivering hulks."[62] King explained his approach that "leadership is easy, once you learn how to act the part."[63]

King developed his own unique façade by studying villains and heroes of the past, taking an applied approach when reading history. He recognized that great leaders always succeeded—or otherwise won glory in defeat—by believing in "some basic principles of personal honor, and the willingness to do your duty at any price to serve some greater purpose."[64] King warned Americans that "we, as a people, are prone to think well of ourselves and whatever is ours."[68] King often paraphrased Naval War College teachings. RAdm. Stephen B. Luce inspired King that "all naval operations are strategic, whether in peace or war."[65] King noted that "our purpose has always been of not taking an aggressive attitude, even when war is coming."[66]

The historical empires of Europe and Asia loomed over the horizons in the American hemisphere when King joined the ranks. Having seen combat in the Spanish-American War, King fully agreed with Mahan that "land powers will try to reach the sea and to utilize it for its own ends, while the sea power must obtain support on land, through the motives it can bring to bear upon the inhabitants."[69] Mahan used the British Empire as a reference for American readers. Mahan explained, "I am frankly an imperialist, in the sense that I believe that no great nation should henceforth maintain the policy of isolation which fitted our early history."[70]

The teachings of Mahan burned like glowing coals on every page among the other masterworks on display upon the bookshelves in King's personal library. He pontificated about seeking knowledge from the past in asking his contemporaries, "Why should we not make as much effort to win the peace as we do to win the war?"[71] The condescension of knowing the secrets of history inspired King to accuse fellow Americans of indulging insufferably in "sentimentalism (sometimes called polly-anna-ism) which is our chief characteristic."[72] King argued that "historically it is traditional (and habitual) for us to be inadequately prepared." He lambasted American confidence in their exceptionality and for trying to

> make everyone believe he knows it all; the preponderance (inherent in democracy) of people whose real interest is in their own welfare as individuals; the glorification of our victories in war and the corresponding ignorance of our defeats (and disgraces) and of their basic causes; the inability of the average individual (the man on the street) to understand the interplay of cause and effect not only in foreign but in domestic affairs, as well as his lack of interest in such matters.[73]

King certainly looked down upon the collective ignorance of fellow human beings—because he admittedly stood among us. Having joined the ranks without a penny in his pocket in 1897, he always drew from his working-class roots the insatiable will to win for the next five decades on the deck. By the time he hauled down his five-star flag in 1947, American sea power stood second to none in the global maritime arena. The US Navy would never be the same after he left the fleet—when American sea power faded into the hazy horizons of strategic airpower.[74]

WORKING-CLASS HERO

The simplicity of King's personality reflected his singular aspiration to earn a place among the brightest stars in maritime history. The past always chased King throughout his seagoing life of adventure with the American fleet during the pivotal era in the first fifty years of the twentieth century. The son of immigrants, King always knew about the mud on his shoes when telling friends salty tales about familial connections with the ancient Scottish clans. He claimed to hold ancient ancestral ties with Royal Navy admiral Sir Richard King, 1st Baron King. Such uncommon historical figures had almost nothing in common with King's family. In fact, his Scottish father, James, and his Irish mother, Elizabeth Keam-King, both fled the privations of old Europe. Poverty drove the Kings abroad to the Americas, as the Union fought the Confederacy in the Civil War. The King family eventually settled on the rusty northern shores of Lake Erie in Lorain, Ohio.

Rapid industrialization defined the American experience for many recent immigrant families. Jim Crow laws quickly derailed the promise of Reconstruction after the Civil War, as another American aristocracy took form among the old money in the Gilded Age. Always the prodigal Buckeye son, King grew up to the sounds of steam trains rolling through his backyard and the siren songs from ships traversing the Great Lakes. Born on November 23, 1878, King had nothing to lose as the eldest son. He was never alone from the very beginning—always part of home team. He shared his room with his younger brothers, Norman and Percy, in a modest home with his two sisters, Maude and Mildred.

Hardworking experiences as a youth enabled King to attain a rudimentary understanding of steam-powered engines and metalworking. Adversity struck the King family when his sister Maude died at age six. The hardships continued when typhoid fever struck the King family. King's father endured the hardships of raising children with stoic determination.[75] King observed the heroism of his father after he hired a recent immigrant from Canada, Anna M. Braun, to nurse his ailing wife and children. She taught King to develop a working knowledge in German and French languages. Braun tutored the King children in mathematics and literature during his convalescence at home. Braun also introduced King's father to his second wife, Amelia, as the pair helped raise the King children. King repaid Braun by mentoring her son, Boynton, during future adventures at sea.[76]

King escaped the monotonous existence of life among the lower working classes by spending his free time on intellectual voyages to history. He reveled in heroic tales of George Washington and John Paul Jones, and the glory of Lord Horatio Nelson. King's personal library also included Stephen Crane's literary warning to young readers, *The Red Badge of Courage*.

The glories of war intermixed with dreams of escaping the working-class doldrums of northern Ohio, as King drew pictures of uniforms and battle scenes. He also marshaled an army of toy soldiers cast from a lead mold given to him by his father. For fun, King and his brother reenacted battles from Agincourt to the Alamo. Native American culture also fascinated King, as did their triumph at the Battle of Little Big Horn. King thought that General George Custer's last stand "should be studied by anybody who thinks they are a military genius."[77]

History provided an escape for King to indulge youthful dreams of future glory on the battlefield. Civil War veterans inspired his young mind. Early in his upbringing, King took full responsibility in seeking a path in life. The untimely deaths of his mother and sister placed the King family in a terrible position. To the chagrin of his father, King dropped out from school to work in the shipyards and railroad repair shops. Children worked alongside their elders along the rusty shores of northern Ohio upon the Great Lakes. The railroad paid just enough for a beer at the end of a long day. Lakeshore shipyards provided just a bit more. King's father intervened when he attempted to sign onto a steamer—pulling him back from the brink and pushing him back into the classroom. Having gained an appreciation for hard work, King graduated first in the class of 1897. King's high school valedictory speech, "The Uses of Adversity," warned fellow Americans to avoid the pitfalls of laziness and self-pity.[78]

King's father put a fire in the bellies of his sons, earning him a reputation for being a hardworking family man with a strong sense of duty to the community. He won the respect of local city leaders the Lorain area, which provided opportunities. King's father wanted his boys to benefit from being born American. Following in his father's footsteps, King pushed his family and his close associates to understand that "things come 'right' the more one is steadfast in the belief that they will—and never gives up the belief, no matter what delays discouragements may intervene."[79] King's father drove his boys to seek opportunities to climb the social ladders in American society through the enlightened confidence attained through practical education. Seeing the chance to put his boys ahead of others, King's father successfully lobbied Republican congressman Winfield S. Kerr to make the arrangements for the US Naval Academy in Annapolis, Maryland. The sea services served as a unique crucible of American culture. The maritime and naval services provided practical education in civilian trades, somewhat more than the rigidly military engineering focus of the army indoctrination provided at West Point in New York or such equivalents as the Virginia Military Institute (VMI) or the Citadel.

Continental conquest influenced the military engineering focus of West Point, since the old lost cause of the Confederacy remained alive among other such institutions in the southern states. Naval innovators like Luce and Mahan conversely recognized opportunities for Americans to seize an alternative future by taking their place among the great sea powers within the global maritime arena.[79] To this end, the Navy Department actively recruited from industrialized cities and midwestern farming communities in landlocked states. White Anglo-Saxon Protestant traditions intermixed with older Yankee entrepreneurial maritime influences of New England, which inspired Luce to spearhead the naval propaganda campaign from within the seagoing ranks of the late nineteenth century. Following Luce and his naval protégés, the assistant secretary of the Navy, Theodore Roosevelt, set policies by which the Navy Department recruited prospective naval officers from midwestern working classes—providing the requisite opening for King.[80]

Given the opportunity, King embraced American dreams of sea power much like young novices joined religious orders in the ancient monastic cultures of Asia and old

Europe.[81] The aristocratic façade, as fueled by the prevailing White Anglo-Saxon Protestant culture within the ranks, also somewhat contrasted with the industrial realities and hardtack lifestyle on board ship.[82] Youngsters earned the chance to compete for a brighter future on the yard at the Naval Academy along the historic shores of the Severn River. King recalled that his proud father gave him a round-trip train ticket from Lorain to Annapolis. King kept the return ticket as a good-luck charm.[83] Among the naval cadets of 1897, King quickly embraced the naval culture. Within the Class of 1901, King recognized opportunities to earn a place among the future stars of the fleet. Friends also noted that "Ernest King might just as well have grown up in Renfrewshire as in Ohio [as] he went to the Naval Academy in identically the spirit that has sent many an ambitious young Scot to Edinburgh with little beyond a sack of oatmeal and an unswerving determination to excel in his profession."[84]

MY EDUCATION WAS DEFECTIVE

The quest to win personal glory in combat inspired King to indulge dreams of an adventurous future on the high seas. King joined the naval cadet volunteers to earn a ribbon in combat during the Spanish-American War. Among other naval cadet pals, King joined Rufus F. Zogbaum to talk their way into the "cod fish patrol" in the North Atlantic—on board the cruiser USS *San Francisco*. Within weeks, King arrived in Cuban waters on *San Francisco*. There, King's other buddy, Passed-Midshipman Dudley W. Knox, claimed to command a flotilla of tugboats out of Key West. After the Spanish-American War, Knox joked, "I could call myself a commodore before I earned my appointment as an ensign."[85]

Annapolis failed to measure against the practical education King obtained through voluntary service in wartime. Among other naval cadets, he proudly sported his campaign ribbon for combat service in the Spanish-American War. He faced few opportunities to earn his glory from the enemy. Still, King earned a reputation for being steady and reliable among observant senior mentors. Lt. Hugo Osterhaus took note of King in Cuban waters, which later proved important in his progression up the fleet ladder.[86] After service in the "splendid little war," he returned to studies at the Naval Academy with shoulder tattoos of an anchor and a dagger. King secretly identified with the Scottish pirate and Yankee mercenary John Paul Jones. Still, King understood the rules imposed by the white Anglo-Saxon Protestant elders among the top ranks within the US naval service.[87]

Old traditions intermixed with technological innovation and professional standards under the still-evolving vision of American sea power. With the Class of 1901, King stood among the last to receive formal training in traditional windpowered sailing ships. King concluded that "my education was defective."[88] Steam propulsion required sailors trained in the technical fundamentals, which drove the Naval Academy curriculum. He strongly criticized the curriculum at the Naval Academy for its "concentration on fractions."[89] He thought that the "average midshipman, reluctant to admit his ignorance, would stand at the blackboard chewing chalk rather than ask a question."[90]

The intellectual rust of hierarchical orthodoxy among flag officers intermixed with outdated doctrine, which frequently quashed creativity among the younger ranks.[91] King joined fellow naval cadets William S. Pye and Caspar Goodrich Jr. in the quest to revise the outdated doctrinal assumptions, which prevailed within the hierarchical bureaucratic culture of the Navy Department and generally extended to the seagoing forces. Raging against the administrative machinery of the service, King and Pye and remained very close after they collaboratively designed a prize-winning gadget to improve accuracy in naval gunnery.[92]

King and his fellow naval cadets also ignored regulations when filing a patent for their gunnery mechanism. The Bureau of Ordnance (BuOrd) subsequently claimed all subsequent royalties.[93] Lt. William S. Sims won King's respect by speaking out against the myopia of BuOrd. Sims wrote an open letter to President Theodore Roosevelt about the fact that "foreigners are keenly alive to these defects in our ships."[94] In June 1901, Lt. Albert P. Niblack noted that "everyone is 'mum'" about serious problems in American warship design and gunnery."[95] Sims cared nothing about the controversy, claiming to stand among the secret "Society for Repression of Ignorant Assumptions."[96] Younger officers, like King, enjoyed hearing stories about Sims "because he had the will and sense of duty required in getting his ideas to the very top whenever circumstances required immediate action."[97]

The US naval service enabled young professionals of King's generation to revel in Age of Sail traditions while operating on the technological cutting edge. The Naval Academy placed King into a completely different social circle. He developed lifelong associations with Henry Latrobe Roosevelt during their studies together at the Naval Academy. Through this association, King befriended Theodore Roosevelt Jr. Among other Roosevelt connections, King regularly interacted with the Roosevelt family. Among others, King served with Franklin's cousin, Lt. Harvey Delano—the son of RAdm. Francis H. Delano. Marine captain Frederick H. Delano also maintained lifelong ties with King.[98]

The Naval Academy provided opportunities for King to win a place among the captains of American industry and the upper class. Old money intermixed with new blood on the yard in Annapolis. King remembered feeling special about receiving an invitation to join a Naval Academy clique in which the sons of wealthy families intermixed with working-class heroes like King. One morning, he found a handwritten invitation to join the exclusive club with fellow naval cadets, known as the "Fine Gentlemen."[99] The group smuggled liquor and cigars onto the yard for reading-group discussions of poetry and Age of Sail heroes. The Fine Gentlemen in King's immediate orbit included Pye, Rufus Zogbaum, John V. Babcock, Walter N. Vernou, and Casper Goodrich Jr. Another classmate, Adolphus Andrews, presided over a separate circle, which largely comprised sons with ties to the old Confederacy. Initially, Andrews and King shared a room. Andrews recited tales of Texas and the glorious lost cause, which riled King's Buckeye sensibilities. King frequently lost his temper with Andrews. Among the Class of 1901, King characterized Andrews as an outcast by suggesting that "no one liked him at all."[100]

Tunes of glory loomed over the relationship of Andrews and King among the brigade in Annapolis. On board the barkentine USS *Monongahela*, Andrews stood the guns and King checked the charts as cadet navigator when a Black deck seaman, Sam Tines, showed King the lines while telling tales of glory on the high seas. The naval cadets also visited the typical sailorly haunts during their summer cruise to Britain and Portugal in 1899. Andrews and King failed to gel during these experiences together. King described Andrews as "very intelligent and a very ambitious man."[101]

PIRATE KING

The Naval Academy defined the careers of King's generation in the brave new era of steel and steam. King demonstrated his superior skills as a navigator under the supervision of Lt. Harry Kimmel on board the steam frigate USS *Chesapeake* during the summer cruise with the Class of 1901. The skipper on the rival training ship, USS *Newport*, Lt. Cmdr. Austin M. Knight gave superior marks for Andrews. This extra push from above enabled Andrews to win the first leg in the race up the fleet ladder within the Class of 1901— graduating first among sixty-seven. Falling to fourth in the class, King won the higher honor as cadet lieutenant commander—standing at the front within the brigade. King also held the honor of being elected as second in the class as "court beauty" and the top competitor in the "Almost Married Man's Club."[102] Classmates described King's pale laugh to be "as rosy as his cheeks," and characterized his temperament by saying, "Don't fool with nitroglycerin."[103]

The personal rivalry of Andrews and King became the stuff of legends among the naval ranks. Fellow cadets also followed in King's wake to the highest levels of global command for the next four decades, to include Harold R. Stark, Chester W. Nimitz, and William F. "Bill" Halsey Jr.[104] Career-minded younger officers sought senior-ranking patrons to establish themselves within the American military monoculture. In this, King benefited from the mentoring hand of Midshipman Halsey's father, Lt. Cmdr. William F. Halsey Sr. Before graduation exercises at the Naval Academy in 1901, the elder Halsey encouraged King to break from the traditional paths to glory within the battleship ranks by instead joining the crew of an auxiliary yacht—then preparing to conduct a routine charting expedition in the Caribbean. King reported with the rank of passed midshipman to Lt. Cmdr. Samuel W. B. Diehl on the steam yacht USS *Eagle*.

Diehl appointed King to assume duties of significant responsibility, as aide with collateral duties as the operations and navigation officer on *Eagle*. Diehl immediately impressed King. Nearly forty years earlier, Diehl participated in the transition from sailing ships to coal-fired steam. He experienced major Civil War combat in the riverine battles within the inland waterways. Diehl then fought pirates in the Asiatic. He razed villages and killed civilians during the punitive expedition to Korea in 1871. Diehl drew from experience to help organize the Office of Naval Intelligence (ONI) in 1882. He assisted the Naval War Board during operations during the 1898 Spanish-American War. By 1901, Diehl took his mission as being focused upon educating the next generation about war. He offered King the coveted position of navigation officer along with two warrant officers and sixty-three sailors after a brief interview on board *Eagle* at the shipyard in Portsmouth, New Hampshire.[105]

On a long naval expedition to Caribbean waters, Diehl gave homework for the younger naval officers to lead wardroom discussions about naval tactics. Diehl often broke out the charts to discuss the maritime geography. He told sea stories about great captains in history. Diehl also stocked the wardroom with the works of Mahan and Robert Southey's biography *The Life of Horatio Lord Nelson*. Diehl used these works as textbooks to inspire discussion among the officers of *Eagle*. He educated the wardroom, sharing personal opinions that victory from the War of Independence through the Civil War and Spanish-American War reflected American strategy in relations with Europe first.[106] Diehl shared the outlook of his friend Mahan that American sea power had the capacity to foster the "common good of Europe and Asia [not] for the subversion of Asiatic genius, but the quiet introduction of European leaven."[107]

Diehl taught younger naval thinkers among King's generation to think broadly about the differences between armies and navies. On this point, Mahan's work sparked discussions about the differences between military and naval operations. Mahan mused about the "conflict" between "naval and military strength, where the ocean touches or penetrates the land."[108] He emphasized, "Land power is modified by proximity of the sea; and correspondingly, whenever the ocean touches the land, the circumstance at once conditions sea power."[109] Mahan warned naval thinkers to heed the "resultant, dependent in character upon the contrasted strengths of opposing forces."[110]

Navies guarded peacetime commercial stability before determining the strategic outcomes of past wars, whereas armies existed simply to fight battles, in Mahan's analysis. Having heard Mahan during his studies in Annapolis, King reveled in the seagoing schoolhouse wherein the skipper, Diehl, assumed the role of headmaster. The nautical environment on board *Eagle* with Diehl on the deck truly set an inspirational example for King. Leading shore parties on surveys of remote coves, King scrutinized old Spanish and British charts, which proved surprisingly accurate.[111] Diehl approved when King s experimented with Age of Sail tactics.

King maneuvered *Eagle* into the shallows, sometimes brushing the keel with the bottom, having monitored the rhythm of winds, tides, and currents. These adventures also carried a practical wartime purpose. Spain remained an influence in Cuba, and foreign warships threatened from Caribbean ports under the French, Dutch, and British.[112]

Cuba stood among the keys to the oceanic waterways leading into the Caribbean and the lucrative natural resources of South America. Cuba also provided a strategic anchorage for the US Navy to patrol the routes leading around the Cape of Good Hope to the Pacific and beyond to Asia.[113] Plodding the white sands along Caribbean shores, King retraced the steps of conquistadores and pirates. This experience deeply influenced King for the remainder of his career at sea. For a job well done, Diehl gave young King a copy of *A General History of the Pyrates*. As originally published in 1724, the volume given by Diehl to King included an inscription, "An officer must first know what is known to discover what is yet to be explored."[114]

King discovered means by which to operate smaller warships from clandestine pirate coves throughout the Caribbean. He supervised the navigational surveys completed on *Eagle*. The ship stood out to sea as King led a shore party to explore the remote inlets near Cienfuegos. In performing the beach survey, his eyes progressively became damaged by the sun. Concerned, Diehl ordered King to report for treatment by US Army physicians at Rowell Barracks, near the Naval Station at Guantánamo Bay. The army doctors recommended treatment in the United States, since King had essentially gone blind because of sun glare. Diehl released King from *Eagle*. He hitched a ride on a packet ship and reported for medical convalescence to the Naval Hospital in Brooklyn. During his convalescence, King proposed to Mattie Rankin Egerton, and in 1903 they announced their engagement to the newspapers.

King faced the potential medical diagnosis of being found unfit for sea duty and the premature death of his naval career. He wanted to escape the prodding eye of navy doctors to return to sea as quickly as possible. King strained to pass the requisite eye exam. Over time, he made a full recovery before reporting for duty on the battleship USS *Illinois*

(BB-7). Diehl sent a commendation letter with a recommendation for King. With this endorsement, Capt. George A. Converse appointed King for the coveted position of "captain" of turret 1 on *Illinois*. Converse also paired King with Lt. Orton Porter Jackson. In the patriarchal ranks of the fleet, Converse initially took a shine to King during the voyage to the Mediterranean.[115]

Formative experiences together on *Illinois* seasoned King and Jackson in their handling of more-senior-ranking officers. Converse treated King and Jackson as a protégés—assigning them for duty as personal liaisons to the embarked staff of RAdm. Arthur S. Crowninshield. King violated protocol by asking Crowninshield for an assignment to the Asiatic Fleet without first discussing the move with Converse. The impetuousness of King violated rules of protocol. Converse exploded on King that "*your* needs are irrelevant to the needs of the service [and] *you* are needed here now and not there and then!"[116] Although frustrated, Converse rewarded King with positive remarks in his detaching report from *Illinois*.[117]

ADVENTURES ON *CINCINNATI*

Having jumped ship upon returning to Hampton Roads, King traveled by train to the West Coast. Upon arriving, King immediately blew off steam ashore while awaiting transportation to meet USS *Cincinnati* (CL-7). He reported to the ship just before getting underway to join the Asiatic Fleet. During the long voyage, King developed many close friends among the officers and enlisted crewmen on board *Cincinnati*. Traversing the shores of Asia along the congested shipping routes along the Chinese coast, King also enjoyed blowing off steam with his enlisted men. King earned a reputation for heavy steaming along with his classmate Roe Vincent. Vincent and King proved to be exemplary naval officers at sea, but not on liberty ashore—both earning reputations for partying as hard as they worked. Decades later, King mused that whenever "Vincent went ashore, he usually wore a special vest [and] when we saw him thus attired, we knew he was underway for a drinking party and more than that."[118] King recalled, "Vincent's division was always a perfect hurly-burly [but] always won in any competition."[119]

The deployment of *Cincinnati* to the Asiatic Fleet coincided with and reflected the American strategy for the region. Among the Anglo-Dutch and French flags, the Stars and Stripes on American vessels in Asian ports reflected centuries of imperial exploitation. The burgeoning presence of Japanese flags on ships further intensified the global competition among seagoing powers. The skipper on *Cincinnati*, Capt. Newton E. Mason, explained the stakes to his younger officers. He also considered King a very promising officer. Mason endorsed the appointment for King to assume rank as an ensign. Mason added the loaded observation by describing King as "technically excellent and will do well to remain at sea."[120] Another shipmate noted, "Any seaman who did a good job for Ernie King, as far as he was concerned, was as good as the highest-ranking admiral because he was good at what he was doing."[121]

Seeking adventure in the Asiatic Fleet, King was the ringleader among a group of junior officers from *Cincinnati*. He gained a reputation for carousing. King finally exceeded the limits after a visit to the pre-*Dreadnought* battleship HMS *Jupiter*. The Royal Marines on *Jupiter* challenged King to a drinking competition on the Fourth of July. Ens. Edward C. Kalbfus joined King in defending the honor of *Cincinnati*. King and Kalbfus won the alcoholic battle.[122] During service together on *Cincinnati*, Kalbfus worked with

King in a pseudo-laboratory setting in their state room as they developed a concoction known as the "King's Peg"—involving the mixture of "three parts champagne, brandy, and a dash of port wine."[123]

Among fellow officers in the *Cincinnati* wardroom, King rebelliously cracked jokes about the ridiculous tendencies of naval bureaucracy. He broke the cardinal rule by carousing with his enlisted men in tattoo parlors and pubs. King especially enjoyed drinking with British sailors during his early adventures. In Singapore, King joined a boozy group of British and American sailors for a drinking competition at the Tanglin Club. King consumed "stingers"—a potent cocktail featuring brandy mixed with crème de menthe.[124] He toasted the King's navy and celebrated the memory of Horatio Nelson with Royal Navy sailors. Following an epic party at the Tanglin Club, King nearly missed the departure of his ship.

The steam-powered siren of *Cincinnati* beckoned the end of liberty for the American sailors ashore. The skipper had already issued orders to shift colors and secure all lines, as King sauntered aboard to the sounds of the boatswain's whistle and fellow crewmen pulling up the gangway. Drunk and missing his cap upon appearing at the quarterdeck with his collar undone, the executive officer on *Cincinnati*, Lt. Cmdr. Hugh Rodman, threatened to see King dismissed from the service.[125] Rodman barked an angry series of insults, which prompted King to respond impertinently—much to the enjoyment of fellow sailors. Rodman's rage and King's indifference provided ample comedy relief for the hangover of getting underway again for the crew of *Cincinnati*.

Youthful indiscretions on deployment with the Asiatic Fleet defined the reputation of King among many senior-ranking officers and their associates. The outgoing skipper, Mason, documented King's bad behavior in fitness reports. Mason berated King to the incoming *Cincinnati* skipper, Cmdr. Hugo Osterhaus. Recognizing the wild horses yet to be broken among the wardroom officers, Osterhaus used Naval Regulations as the foundation for creative leadership. He forcefully held King on course and away from the rocks and shoals. Unlike Mason's literal interpretation, Osterhaus used regulations as a common point for adaptation.

Osterhaus kept a firm hand on the tiller to guide King in looking outward to a brighter future. Osterhaus described the difficulties in handling King. Fitness reports indicated that "Ensign King failed to return to the ship in time for his duty."[126] In another, Osterhaus reported that "King became slightly under the influence of liquor at an entertainment on board and was unfit for duty."[127] The executive officer on *Cincinnati*, Rodman, recommended stiff punishment for King. Under the circumstances, Osterhaus acknowledged that King "made disrespectful answers to the Executive Officer."[128] Osterhaus acted as a referee among the duelists—Rodman and King—noting that "Young King is a promising officer, and it would be unjust to him to overlook an offense of this nature."[129]

Recognizing the dangers inherent with leaving sailors to their fates ashore, Osterhaus placed responsibility upon Kalbfus for keeping King on course. Unlike the skipper and executive officer, the first among equals, Kalbfus, had the ability to mitigate the rebellious proclivities of King. Their relationship remained unchanged for the next five decades. King's reputation for hard-driving behavior ashore had impressed the enlisted men, in particular. The chief petty officers on *Cincinnati* understood the potential consequences—collectively deciding to lend a hand in teaching King the proper way of having fun under the harshest possible circumstances.

The opium dens and brothels attracted weary sailors far from home to seek refuge in the seedy culture ashore. Having nearly lost himself on liberty in Asiatic waters, King went ashore to rescue a group of his sailors from a public house in Tsingtao. King then defended them in the quasi-legal rituals of captain's mast. Osterhaus usually allowed subordinates like King to determine the appropriate remedy for the guilty sailors. Chief Charles A. Focht described King as "strict but fair."[130] Focht characterized King as a "wonderful man [who] always appreciated something you did for him; if you were in his division, 'you were in.'"[131] Chief Charles Boylen told King that "you've been strict, but you've also been very fair."[132]

King attained a broader perspective through interactions with the Indigenous populations of Asia. He often visited the historic sights in the area surrounding Yokosuka and Yokohama in Japan. King reveled in the culture. Just fifty years after Cdre. Matthew Perry established ties with Japan, King never forgot feeling perturbed after an enjoyable visit to the Daibutsu of Kamakura, "when he found that his pocketbook had been stolen."[133] The incident left a lasting impression. King recalled the loss of his pocketbook as an unfortunate "first unpleasant encounter with the Japanese."[134] He later equated the theft of his pocketbook in Japan in 1903 with the "impersonal nature [of] modern warfare."[135]

CHAPTER 2
The Love Feast

King certainly gained a perspective of American sea power while immersed in the cross-roads of imperial competition along Asian shores. Having nearly lost himself in the seedy sailor haunts ashore, King thrived during operations at sea. Osterhaus provided the ideal example for King to follow in handling other insubordinate scoundrels—with potential. Osterhaus mentored King to make the life-determining leap from the rank of ensign to lieutenant. King earned perfect scores on the test for promotion. He had the opportunity to circumvent the intermediary one-and-a-half-line rank of lieutenant (junior grade). King qualified too for the full two-stripe bar of line lieutenant. Osterhaus recommended King for a full lieutenancy, with following assignments leading to faster future promotions. The executive officer, Rodman, conversely voiced concerns about King in letters to the Bureau of Navigation (BuNav).

Osterhaus failed to provide an endorsement for Rodman's letter, which implied disagreement between the two about King. Osterhaus saw great potential in King. To the contrary, Rodman wanted King unceremoniously drummed out. The future teetered in the bureaucratic balance for King. With his promotion pending approval at the Navy Department, King received a summons from BuNav to report to the president of the Naval War College, RAdm. Charles H. Stockton. As the chair on the Navy Retention Board, Stockton also had the reputation for being a hanging judge—strictly by the book.[1] Osterhaus advised King to stand confident in facing the proverbial guillotine, or to prepare himself for a far more difficult future on the deck. With these thoughts in mind, King hitched the transpacific ride on USS *Solace* (AH-2), reporting as ordered to the Navy Department.[2]

Unfavorable reports from his previous skippers and from Rodman resonated in negative terms for King with the retention board. His career appeared over. During the proceedings, Stockton forced King to read his fitness reports aloud. Stockton then subjected King to a series of pointed questions. Like a prosecutor in a courtroom, Stockton treated King as the perpetrator of despicable deeds. Stockton then asked King to judge his own performance and to make recommendations for prospective action. Stockton kept a grim face in delivering the final verdict. Stockton then shifted to congratulatory remarks in announcing King's temporary promotion to the rank of lieutenant. Stockton demonstrated a sense of humor in arranging orders for King to serve as officer in charge of discipline at the Naval Academy.[3]

Awaiting the vacancy to open at the Naval Academy, King reported for temporary duty at the Navy Department. His old skipper, Converse, controlled officer assignments. Converse subjected King to friendly grilling before directing him to Capt. William H. Reeder for temporary duty on battleship USS *Alabama* (BB-8). Reeder assigned King to command the admiral's barge. In this role, King frequently interacted with the embarked staff of RAdm. Charles H. Davis Jr. During service on *Alabama*, King worked with the admiral's staff, including Lieutenants Frank H. Clark Jr., Harry E. Yarnell, and Dudley W. Knox.[4] At that time, these young officers witnessed the moment when the Atlantic Squadron formally transitioned into the Atlantic Fleet on January 1, 1906.[5] The Pacific Fleet formed four months later. During the reorganization, the Asiatic *Fleet* became the Asiatic *Squadron*.

For the sake of keeping the peace with the imperial navies of Europe and Asia, the Americans sailed proudly among the distant outposts and inland waters from Panay to Hong Kong and Incheon. American warships in distant waters along the China coast still operated as before within the Asiatic Squadron. Debates concerning task organizational functions and the associated bureaucratic definitions of terms like "fleet" and "squadron" thereafter defined careers in King's generation. Divergent organizational concepts with military organizations ashore influenced debates concerning rank equivalencies and interservice command relationships. In these discussions, King spent many decades examining the issue to conclude that the army and navy should unify under the vision of American sea power into a global "Security Force that is available in the whole world [and] no other service in the world can offer better capabilities for that purpose, that is, the preservation of World peace."[6]

FACING THE ABYSS

Administrative changes within the fleet reflected the grander debates within American society about the question of sea power. Imperial possessions, such as the Philippines, increasingly appeared unnecessary to naval professionals during the transition from coal to oil propulsion.[7] Looking outward to the petroleum-fueled future, President Theodore Roosevelt anticipated the future by envisioning the withdrawal of American military forces ashore in distant imperial outposts in the Philippines and beyond to Asia.[8] Roosevelt also advocated for commercially focused maritime alliances with regional powers, to include China and imperial Japan.[9] He further clarified strategic differences between the warlike mission of American military forces ashore and the peacekeeping mission of naval forces afloat.[10] Roosevelt viewed imperial Japan as a maritime partner in protecting American interests in Asia.[11]

Service in foreign waters from the Mediterranean to the Asiatic Fleet defined the views of American naval professionals. Having the requisite tattoos to show for his youthful adventures in the fleet, King dedicated himself to earning a place among the stars in flag rank. Knowing the expectations of the service, King asked Martha "Mattie" Rankin Egerton for assistance in escaping the "Almost Married Man's Club."[12] The Egerton family network centered on the greater Baltimore region, with old historical extensions to the *Mayflower* pilgrims and the British aristocracy. Mattie's family held high standing in the best social circles. Her father kept ties with both Roosevelt families at Oyster Bay and Hyde Park. Her mother's Virginia cousins included the future president Woodrow Wilson; they had ancestral relationships to the Egerton baronet of England. Mattie's family heritage added to King's attraction. He intended to add his name to Mattie's family tree. In the fall of 1905, King married Mattie in the historic chapel at the Military Academy at West Point in New York.[13]

Familial interconnections within the army and navy frequently determined the balance between success and failure. King understood the unspoken rules within the American armed services. Upon his marriage to Mattie, the Kings stood among the brightest young couples in uniform. Mattie's sister, Florence, served as maid of honor and her husband, US Army second lieutenant Walter D. Smith, served as King's best man. King first met Smith during Army-Navy football matchups as rival cadets. On the gridiron, Smith dazzled the likes of John Heisman and George Halas while playing for Army. Smith and King became very close friends, which later proved decisive in both peace and war. As a wedding gift, Smith gave King an inscribed copy of US Army colonel Arthur L. Wagner's *Organization and Tactics*. King described the book as a revelation for "certain military concepts which he subsequently made applicable to naval service."[14] Friends recalled that King "spent many of his leaves touring the Civil War battlefields [and he] was an expert in this field."[15] King recalled "three years duty at the Naval Academy, [where] he read military and naval history voraciously."[16]

Renewed by his marriage to Mattie to win his own place in history, King also understood the consequences of failure. King admitted, "As a young ensign he early realized that he had a tendency to be 'soft' and that he knew, if he was to progress in the navy, he would have to get a grip on himself."[17] The Kings maneuvered from the fields of West Point through the watery seascapes of Hampton Roads before setting the anchor outside the Naval Academy gates. Following duty on *Alabama*, King reported to the Naval Academy superintendent, RAdm. James H. Sands. Having transformed into the image of a perfect naval professional with a family, King put the midshipmen on notice—setting the highest standards for them to meet. In Annapolis, King also developed close friendships to the aide to the superintendent, Lt. Arthur MacArthur III, whose brother, Douglas, served in the army. King characterized Arthur as a "very able officer and very different in personality and temperament from his brother."[18]

HOME IN ANNAPOLIS

King focused upon developing his reputation to exceed the US Naval ideal of a gentleman and professional. His classmates Pye and Vernou teamed with King to teach the next generation by setting the highest example of professionalism. Service reputation became intertwined with antiquated concepts of chivalry. With Mattie expecting their first of seven children, King set anchor in Annapolis by purchasing a home at 45 Franklin Street—just down the hill from the Maryland state capitol and outside the South Gate on the yard of the Naval Academy. Purchasing a home in Annapolis symbolically established the King family among other Naval Academy social circles.[19] Midshipman Charles D. Griffen dated one of King's daughters. He later attained flag rank under King. Reflecting upon the family, Griffen noted that "Mrs. King was one of the most charming and delightful people I've ever known and, with all his children, really did keep the 'home fires burning.'"[20]

Lifelong personal connections among naval professionals proved vital in both peace and war. King supervised the educations of his future subordinates. Among others, he set the example for John S. McCain, Henry Kent Hewitt, Raymond A. Spruance, Richmond Kelly Turner, Thomas C. Kinkaid, and Richard S. Edwards. Other associations with the younger generation included Frank Jack Fletcher—the nephew of RAdm. Frank Friday Fletcher. Midshipman William E. Ferrell, whose family lived next to the King family on Franklin Street in Annapolis, fell behind in his studies after suffering an injury. King later assisted Ferrell in securing an appointment in the naval rank of professor of aeronautics in the Mathematics Department at the Naval Academy.[21]

The fraternal connections among established officers and aspirant midshipmen provided foundation for future success in both peace and war. Like the "Fine Gentlemen" of King's Class of 1901, the midshipmen under his mentorship after 1905 also formed their own secret society, known as the "Green Bowlers."[22] This secretive group pulled together in traversing the slippery fleet ladder during their careers beyond the regular surface line, as the US Navy bridged the wireless world with submarines and aviation.[23] Through this and other fraternal groups within the ranks, King kept ties with then midshipmen Willis A. "Ching" Lee, Roland M. Brainard, Theodore Wilkinson, Leo Thebaud, Dewitt Ramsey, Charles P. Snyder, Tully Shelly, Lynde McCormick, and Marc A. Mitscher—all later becoming trusted members of King's inner circle.[24]

The assignment to supervise midshipmen at the Naval Academy placed King into the role of mentor for many fellow travelers. The future of American sea power centered on those most steeped in the visionary historical musings of such luminaries as Luce and Mahan. The patronage system within the ranks also shaped King's circle of trusted associates. For example, Midshipman Charles S. "Savvy" Cooke Jr. graduated earlier from the University of Alabama. His uncle, RAdm. Stephen B. Luce, pushed Cooke to seek his future in the naval service. The familial connection with Luce also inspired King's interest in helping Cooke throughout his career. King certainly idolized Luce, whose "name must always be venerated by officers who take their profession seriously."[25]

Embracing his mission with religious fervor on the staff of the Naval Academy, King seemed "to be a very military figure who by his presence and every action personified what the average midshipman felt he would like to be when he 'grew up.'"[26] In addition to Luce and Mahan, the president of the Naval War College, RAdm. Casper F. Goodrich, also confided in King about his nephew—Midshipman Alan Goodrich Kirk—as he faced possible dismissal for earning poor grades. Adm. Goodrich knew King through his son, Casper, both having graduated with the Class of 1901. Casper died when his turret exploded on board USS *Georgia* (BB-15) during exercises off Cape Cod in 1907.

Following the accident on *Georgia*, Adm. Goodrich focused upon Kirk with hopes of keeping the family line alive within the naval ranks. Goodrich asked King to lend a hand with Kirk. Personal connections between King and younger officers, like Kirk, later proved decisive in war.[27] Service on the Naval Academy staff enabled King to refine his image as a serious professional. King also used the assignment to redefine his image and personal reputation within the ranks. Many years later, Francis S. Low recalled that "my first knowledge that there was an E. J. King in the Navy came on my entrance to the Naval Academy."[28] Low explained that King "had just finished a tour at the Academy as drill officers and they had left the brigade of midshipmen somewhat stunned and exhausted."[29]

King understood that professional interconnections within the ranks often extended to family within the semimonastic ranks of the American military. Married with children, King developed a reputation as a well-anchored family man of Annapolis. Riding the bureaucratic waves in the Great White Fleet era, Cmdr. William S. Sims took an interest in King. Sea stories about King's antics with the Asiatic Fleet contrasted with his new image as the model American naval professional. Curious to know more, Sims established first contact with King. The naval inspector for gunnery and as naval aide to President Theodore Roosevelt, Sims first introduced King to the military aide, US Army captain Douglas MacArthur.[30]

The Roosevelt family set the course for American sea power in the global maritime arena. Familial connections with Britain, and particularly Teddy's Confederate uncles, shaped the Roosevelt view of sea power.[31] The historical works by Mahan further fueled American maritime policy, as did Franklin's uncle, Harvard University professor James R. Soley.[32] Having served as assistant secretary of the Navy, Soley also served on the staff at the Naval War College in Newport.[33] Under the influence of Teddy and "Uncle James," Franklin followed in their wake as the assistant Navy secretary after 1914.[34] The Roosevelts envisioned American sea power with an oil-fired US Navy as "second to none."[35] Theodore's natural boldness held equal consequences by comparison with Franklin's passive-aggressive approach.[36] Theodore administered by charging ahead and damning the bureaucratic torpedoes, whereas Franklin used "honeying and consoling words that would return to plague him later."[37]

Foreign ideas influenced debates within the American government about the future military policy of the United States. When Theodore approved the War Department proposal to establish the Army General Staff System, critics within Congress accused the Roosevelt administration of violating constitutional checks and balances. From his perch at Princeton University, Woodrow Wilson lectured Americans about the "menace of Prussianism."[38] The debates ongoing on the Washington battlefield ultimately stunted the bureaucratic revolution, which happened within the lifelines of the Navy Department. As a result, the Departments of State and Navy failed to develop the hierarchical Christmas tree models of administration and unified command. The president of the Naval War College, RAdm. Charles Sperry, amplified the teachings of Mahan in advising the Roosevelt administration to concentrate American sea power under clear lines of seagoing fleet staffs.[39]

Looking to the future, Roosevelt used past precedence to unify seagoing efforts by consolidating US naval warships under the singular responsibility of individually designated fleet commanders with associated staffs. Although elder officers celebrated the move, Mahan also complained that Roosevelt "should think the Presidency enough of a fulltime job without trying to be Secretary of the Navy as well."[40] Change followed the winds and tides in the wake of Theodore and other key members of the Roosevelt family—to include his sons, cousins, and many likeminded in-laws. Confederate relatives also had a major hand in developing the organizational framework of the Navy Department into the US Navy of the twentieth century.

The past always informed the maritime polices of the Roosevelts, although history served only as the anchor point for tethering the future of American sea power. When Theodore established fleet staffs in 1906, many Civil War veterans aspired to secure higher rank. Many also lingered without actual purpose among the upper ranks. To clear the decks for younger leaders to advance, Roosevelt influenced legislation in Congress to promote Civil War–era veterans to higher rank with immediate assignment to the retired list. For example, retired captains like Mahan became rear admirals in the Navy Register. Retired lieutenant William McCarty Little held the appointment in the *naval rank* of professor at the Naval War College. For this reason, McCarty Little received direct promotion from retired lieutenant—skipping the ranks of lieutenant commander and commander—to the tombstone rank of captain by act of Congress in 1906. Similarly, Mahan received honorary tombstone status as a flag officer, although he continued using his permanent rank of captain.[41]

Roosevelt provided graceful means for old fogies to walk the planks leading to comfortable retirements. Tombstone promotions enabled Roosevelt to rebuild the ranks with younger officers. He wanted officers on active service to look the part of being an elite, for naval officers to stand above as an elite within an elite, and for all hands to lose their "desk bellies." To these ends, officers of the "Army and Navy were required to walk fifty miles in three days, or ride horseback seventy-five miles, or ride a bicycle one hundred miles."[42]

Roosevelt further transformed the US Navy by making the pivotal strategic decision to shift from coal- to oil-fired battleships. The decision followed the "Battleship Conference," which Sims helped arrange at the Naval War College in 1908.[43] Given ongoing maritime policy debates among civilian policymakers, American naval thinkers continued looking outward. Mahan worried about the historical trends that seemingly indicated future conflicts just beyond the horizons within the global maritime arena. Mahan predicted a future role for American sea power. Looking beyond the future in 1910, Mahan warned that Germany "will be decidedly stronger at sea than we in the United States expect to be and we have over her no military check [such as] the interests of Canada [to] impose upon Great Britain."[44] Mahan considered Europeans prone to the "excitement of drink, liable to excess in demonstration, and misdirection and ultimate collapse in energy."[45]

DANGEROUS PRECEDENTS

Roosevelt built upon the Great White Fleet to advance the cause of American sea power with the transition from coal to petroleum fuels. The strategic innovations of submarine and aviation technologies also coincided with the revolutionary influence of wireless communications. Following these futuristic trends, the historical rivalries that shaped the transatlantic relationship between the British Empire and the United States faded under the optimistic vision of renewed collaboration among naval powers at the dawn of the twentieth century. Having left office, Roosevelt accepted an invitation to speak about the future of Anglo-American collaboration at the Guildhall in central London on May 31, 1910. Roosevelt voiced his personal support for the British.[46] His speech ultimately set the stage for controversy when the American fleet sailed into European waters later that year.

Roosevelt earlier installed loyalists within the ranks to positions of future influence among the seagoing line. Circumventing the normal routines, Roosevelt ordered BuNav, retired RAdm. John E. Pillsbury, to remove the captain slated for the assignment to put Sims in command on the pre-*Dreadnought* USS *Minnesota* (BB-22)—an assignment usually reserved for officers of a higher lineal seniority, or already holding rank as captain.[47] At the time, Sims held the lower rank of commander, with relatively junior lineal standing. In frustration, Capt. William S. Benson warned that the navy had "established a dangerous precedent of giving battleships to Commanders."[48] Similarly, Capt. Joseph Strauss described the problem that "Sims' dominance had reached the captains (all his superiors in rank and age) and there was a scarcely concealed hostility to him and all his works."[49]

Roosevelt's patronage of Sims inspired many envious rivalries among more-senior-ranking officers. Benson outright disliked Sims. Conversely, Strauss respected Sims for being capable and yet fundamentally flawed by hubris and a bombastic demeanor.[50] In this respect, Sims shared similar personality traits with many others among Roosevelt's closer associates. Unlike many other American naval officers, Sims also took a cosmopolitan view of maritime policy and naval strategy. Among his many foreign friends, Royal Navy

Rear-Admiral Sir John Jellicoe congratulated Sims about the appointment to *Minnesota*. Jellicoe recognized an American ally in writing Sims, "I hope if you do come over [to Britain] I shall see you."[51]

Revolutionary myths evolved with the historical trends between the British Empire and United States in the global maritime arena. Setting a clear course toward closer collaboration, Roosevelt fostered friendly associations through Confederate relatives in Britain. The incoming administration of President William H. Taft also envisioned American sea power as part of a global consortium of naval powers Setting the agenda for Taft to execute, Roosevelt spoke about the future to welcome the Great White Fleet home to Hampton Roads. Roosevelt spoke from the barbette by the big guns of *Connecticut*. Among the onlooking sailors, Sims stood with a Vandyke mustache and fore-and-aft cap. Lt. Ernest J. King stood behind Sims near Ens. John S. McCain. All separately recalled Roosevelt explaining the "big stick" policy.[52]

In anticipation of the cruise to European waters, *Minnesota* sailed at the honorary position to lead the American line of battle. The flag of RAdm. Hugo Osterhaus flew from the mastheads over *Minnesota*, denoting the presence of the commander of the Third Battleship Division, Atlantic Fleet. Sims carried the honor of being skipper in the flagship. With Osterhaus on the embarked staff, King also sailed with his classmate Pye on *Minnesota*. During their workups in the Caribbean, Sims congratulated King and Pye on their gunnery contraption—by highlighting the flaws.[53]

King accepted a friendly challenge from Sims during their voyage together. Although assigned to the embarked staff, King went belowdecks to assist efforts to attain a few more knots from the engines of *Minnesota*. In the race for liberty ashore in Guantánamo, *Minnesota* edged ahead of battleship USS *New Hampshire* (BB-25). After their voyage to the Caribbean on *Minnesota*, King often characterized Sims with double-edged praise for winning a battleship command "before he was normally due for it [and] older officers scarcely cared for this deviation in routine, but Sims was a go-getter."[54]

Following the wake of Fiske within the senior ranks, Sims used *Minnesota* as a platform for educating younger officers about the bureaucratic ways of the Navy Department. Elder officers like Fiske and Sims greatly influenced the views of younger guns like King.[55] In reflection, King observed that "no one but the Secretary himself had any authority over the bureaus and they had none over each other."[56] King thought that "there is good evidence that where there is diversification of function, a horizontal organization is best."[57] King explained that a stopgap solution emerged when four naval aides received appointments as direct advisers to the Navy secretary in 1909.[58] Having adopted the outlook of Fiske and Sims on questions of civil-military command, King complained that the naval aides "were authorized to sign 'by direction,' they were not interposed between Bureau Chiefs and the Secretary, and the organization remained as horizontal as ever."[59]

Imperial competitions in Europe and Asia inspired the entrepreneurial views of Mahan in efforts to define the future of American sea power. To this end, Osterhaus and Sims planned to put on a great show for their European counterparts during the Atlantic Fleet cruise to the North Sea and English Channel waters. Lending a hand, King and Pye coordinated arrangements with the Departments of Navy and State to set timetables for port calls in the British Isles and France. During their previous visit to the British Isles with the Class of 1901, King and Pye provided recommendations for sailors to enjoy liberty ashore. Notably, Osterhaus hauled down his flag on *Minnesota* upon the arrival of RAdm.

Joseph B. Murdock in March 1910. At that time, King also detached for duty as assistant chief engineer on *New Hampshire*. Thus, Murdock relied very heavily upon Sims in executing their plans for the European cruise in the fall of 1910.

Royal Navy warships sailed with American battleships in the North Sea during gunnery exercises and high-speed maneuvers. Imperial German and French warships maintained a respectful distance observing the Americans in action. From *Minnesota*, Sims put the other battleships on their paces during gunnery exercises in the North Sea. King trailed on *New Hampshire*, sailing in company with *Vermont*, *Mississippi*, *Idaho*, *North Dakota*, *Delaware*, and *Connecticut*. The silhouettes of American warships then turned southward along the horizon along the northern German coast without making a gesture of goodwill. Failing to visit German ports, the Americans instead pulled into ports in Cherbourg, Weymouth, and Gravesend. At anchor in the Thames estuary, *Minnesota* led the procession as the other American battleships arrived shortly before Thanksgiving of 1910.

The British made special arrangements to entertain their American guests with Thanksgiving turkeys and comradery in launching the holiday season. Awaiting to welcome the Americans in London, Adm. Sir John "Jacky" Fisher and his protégé, Jellicoe, focused their friendly overtures on Sims. Among the other Americans, King joined his classmate Lt. John V. Babcock at the Whitehead torpedo factory. Then, Royal Navy captain Mark Kerr and the crew of HMS *Invincible* hosted Babcock and King for dinner. King described Kerr as a "great scholar of the Battle of Trafalgar and talked fascinatingly on that subject."[60]

The British subjected the Americans to an action-packed calendar of celebratory events and mandatory fun. The American entrepreneur in London, Harry Gordon Selfridge, sponsored a series of dinners—helping the British foster personal connections with the visiting American sailors. Selfridge and other American expatriates joined the fun, as Jellicoe sat with Sims with the *Minnesota* crew for a special turkey feast at the Savoy Hotel.[61] During the proceedings, King and Babcock sat at another table to hear the formal announcement of Jellicoe's promotion and appointment as the Royal Navy commander in chief, Atlantic Fleet.[62] King also recalled meeting Cmdr. Dudley Pound for the first time while visiting British warships in 1910.[63] King kept mental notes, which he duly reported. The Bureau of Steam Engineering later commended King for supplying the "excellent information that he had received from the British during this visit."[64]

With trouble brewing on the far horizons, the London newspapers celebrated newly rekindled friendships with the Americans. Fattened up for the final goodbye feast after nearly two boozy weeks ashore, the British hosted the American sailors for closing events at the Guildhall in December 1910. The echoes of Roosevelt's remarks six months earlier must have resonated when Sims added his voice within the historic chambers of Guildhall. The lord mayor of London, Sir Thomas Veazey Strong, hosted the American sailors.[65] During the festivities, Sims sat with the "Battalion from Ships at Gravesend" at table 13 and King sat with the gang from the "Battalion from Ships at Weymouth" at table 17.

American policy influenced the strategy of deploying Atlantic Fleet battleships for operations in European waters. British hosts celebrated their American guests during the proceedings at Guildhall. The Christmas spirits dininished when Sims overlooked the presence of Fleet Street journalists. His British hosts cheered as Sims spoke in glowing terms about transatlantic collaboration. He recalled:

I spoke slowly and distinctly, and I pronounced every word carefully [that] if ever the integrity of the British Empire should be seriously threatened by external enemy, they might count upon the assistance of every man, every ship, every dollar, and every drop of blood, from their kinsmen across the seas.[66]

Having participated in the Atlantic Fleet cruise to European waters, the controversial headlines surrounding the events at Guildhall later influenced King to observe, "Sims always had a talent for speaking above his rank."[67]

Following the Guildhall celebrations, the British accepted the Atlantic Fleet invitation to attend a formal dinner on *Minnesota*. At anchor at Gravesend on the Thames, Murdock directed Sims to "stock the wine mess and have our men fully polished."[68] Sims hosted his mother-in- law, Margaret (Collier) Hitchcock, with other visiting family member during the formal dinner on the *Minnesota*.[69] Jellicoe and his wife, Florence, invited Hitchcock and the Sims family to stay at their home.[70] The following day, Sims and *Minnesota* set sail.

British newspapers highlighted the Guildhall proceedings as clear evidence of Anglo-American solidarity. In the United States and imperial Germany, newspapers highlighted official complaints from the imperial German ambassador, Bernstorff. The Guildhall remarks placed Sims at the center of an international political crisis.[71] Journalists para-phrased an American naval officer who witnessed the Guildhall remarks that if that "speech had been made by any other officer below the rank of captain in the Atlantic Fleet, except Sims, [and] I'll bet you dollars to doughnuts that no attention would have been paid to it but coming from Sims, who despite his rank and youth is one of the best[-]known officers in the service, made it different."[72] The *New York Times* then worsened the situation by referring to Guildhall as the "Love Feast."[73]

Sims stood completely oblivious when muckraking headlines alleged secret alliances between the British Empire and the United States after Guildhall Sims thought nothing about Guildhall. As he traversed the English Channel for similar celebrations for Christmas with the Atlantic Fleet in France, newspapers twisted the Guildhall statements into being a statement of national policy on the part of Sims. In essence, Sims bumbled into the cold war among empires within the global maritime arena. Given the previous address of Roosevelt, the remarks by Sims caused trouble for the secretary of state, Philander Knox. Taft initially dismissed the controversy. However, on December 17, 1910, the secretary of the Navy, George von L. Meyer, requested an immediate report from the ambassador in London, Whitelaw Reid. In turn, Reid telegrammed Adm. Murdock in Brest. Murdock shared the telegram with Sims. In a joint statement, Murdock and Sims reported that his speech was "entirely extemporaneous [and that] he had no copy of it."[74]

The Guildhall controversy exploded just in time for Americans to debate questions concerning the future of an Anglo-American alliance. As they celebrated the holidays with French navy rear-admiral Ferdinand de Bon and his staff in Brest, Murdock and Sims collaborated in drafting their report.[75] Reid then included the Guildhall report with other diplomatic papers in the fast-sailing Cunard steamer RMS *Lusitania*, which set the record by completing two Atlantic crossings in only fourteen days—just in time to be featured in the headlines of the *New York Times*.

Political competition among Democratic hopefuls and Republican incumbents further amplified the Guildhall controversy in American newspapers. The aspirant future president, Woodrow Wilson, used Guildhall to criticize the Roosevelt and Taft administrations. Americans tended to indulge the mythology of "splendid isolationism," which Wilson exploited for a future run for the White House.[76] The war with Spain followed by the American liberation of the Philippines sparked an insurgency. The "open door" policy in Asia essentially thrust Americans into the fight for control in the global maritime arena. Mahan's advocacy for transatlantic collaboration between the old naval powers of Europe and the new American upstart also divided American voters between those looking outward and those seeking to escape the problems of Europe and Asia.[77]

Wilson warned Americans about the dangers of becoming too heavily involved with foreign affairs. American newspapers meanwhile abandoned previous jingoistic support for military adventurism. Journalists highlighted the ugly military tactics employed against Filipino nationalist forces, which forever stained the Stars and Stripes in the region. Wilson exploited these facts to reassert old myths about American principles of freedom and democracy. Native American tribal leaders certainly recognized the fallacies of Wilsonian idealism, as did Black people in the Jim Crow South. Wilson's pacifistic musings still held appeal among Americans. Divisions among recent immigrant populations unified under the Wilsonian dream of isolation as wars brewed over the horizon on foreign shores.[78]

The Roosevelt administration loomed over the succeeding Taft administration when Sims mused about Anglo-American solidarity at Guildhall. Remarks previously made at the Guildhall by Roosevelt in May 1910 also set the stage for an inadvertent controversy about those of Sims in December. Missing in the media portrayals, both Roosevelt and Sims strongly believed in American independence in shaping relations with the imperial coalitions of Asia and Europe. Both believed that the "United States was sufficiently powerful so that by independent and parallel action the United States could preserve a balance as between the coalitions which would maintain the peace and further American objectives."[79]

The Taft administration completely overcompensated in response to the Guildhall controversy. Taft publicly condemned the Guildhall remarks by Sims. Navy Department bureaucrats also removed Sims from command on *Minnesota*, which created additional speculation. Taft privately consoled Sims about these moves. Then the muckraking media had a heyday, making Taft look even more incompetent when Sims coincidentally appeared on the list for automatic promotion to the rank of captain, based on his Naval Academy year group and lineal seniority in the Naval Register. At that time, the Navy Department did not have a system of "promotion by selection."[80]

Sims had already completed a seagoing assignment and fully qualified for the promotion in accordance with the criteria for the Navy retention board. Admiral of the Fleet Dewey chaired, with RAdm. Bradley Fiske serving as the recording secretary. Dewey and Fiske protected Sims in full accordance with Navy Regulations. Yet, Sims received assignment to the experimental "Long Course" of thirty-six months' duration. Sims felt exiled, characterizing the Naval War College as an assignment where misfits "could be kept for a year, with the hope that a turn in his health or the ceaseless pruning of the Selection Boards would eliminate him as a detailing problem."[81] Sims considered his career to be over after his assignment to Newport.[82]

CHAPTER 3
Grape Juice Wars

Sims considered the Naval War College an unimportant diversion from the primary seagoing mission of the American fleet. His sudden assignment also served as an implied warning for younger practitioners, like King. Newspaper accounts highlighted the juicy infighting within the ranks after Sims settled into his splendid exile in Newport. After witnessing the relatively innocent remarks made by Sims at the Guildhall, King took heed of the bureaucratic consequences for drifting out of place within the line officer ranks. King observed that for Sims, "all matters were clear white or dead black."[1] King thought that Sims "generally sounded off about them in a manner [that] was not in good taste."[2] Having witnessed the radical transition from wind to steam, Sims and King anticipated the technological shift from coal to oil during their visit to European waters.

Torpedo boats and submarines provided early means to develop procedures for liquid-fueled warships. During conversations with British counterparts before Guildhall, Sims and King recognized the unique challenges the European navies faced in shifting from coal- to oil-fired battleships and cruisers. Sims kept an eye on King from afar, always monitoring the pulse of the fleet by recognizing talent among the up-and-coming generation. King likewise impressed influential elders during service in European waters on *New Hampshire*. Capt. James Slidell Rodgers assisted King with endorsements from Admirals Osterhaus and Murdock. With their collective endorsements, King reported as the executive officer with Capt. Thomas W. Kinkaid at the Engineering Experiment Station in Annapolis. There, Kinkaid inspired King to accept the philosophy that their work "will never be completed [and] there will always be progress."[3] Kinkaid described the mission as discerning "what is progress—and what is not."[4] At that time, King joined Lt. Cmdr. Henry C. Dinger in his efforts to develop oil-fired warships.[5] At higher levels of administration, the Standard Oil Company concurrently pushed the Navy Department to build oil-fired warships. At that time, Sims advised King to focus on smaller warships—like submarines and destroyers—as being "where the future is."[6]

WHERE THE FUTURE IS

European experimentation in petroleum fuels carried extreme consequences in the grander competition among empires within the global maritime arena. The fight for control in Asia and the Middle East further accentuated tensions among the Europeans. Americans, by contrast, enjoyed the relative luxury of two oceanic barriers. Anticipating the future in an oil-fired fleet, Sims experimented with new concepts of American fleet organization on the gaming floors and classroom debates at the Naval War College on the shores of the Narragansett. His essays informed King's approach in supervising practical experimentation ongoing along the shores of the Severn at the Engineering Experimentation Station in Annapolis.

Sims worked with King in developing procedures for transferring oil between ships and for subsurface and surface operations in conjunction with new trends in wireless communications and aviation technology.[7] In the race to win the future, USS *Paulding* (DD-22) paved the way for newer "standard-type" Nevada-class battleships after 1910. Standardization in design and operational doctrine provided means by which to attain unity of effort among the seagoing forces. Having taken his first dive ten years earlier, King coordinated electronic-communications tests with Lt. Chester W. Nimitz in the submarine *E-1* in 1912. As the officer in charge, King supervised wireless communications experiments from below the surface. Electronic communications provided means by which to operate surface ships and aircraft in conjunction with submarines. King and Nimitz agreed that future submarines "will advance more rapidly than for surface craft; we find that submarine craft rank equally well, if not better than surface craft."[8]

Submarines and aviation loomed over the big-gun surface fleet, as the younger generation embraced electrified atmosphere in an era increasingly transformed by wireless-communications technology.[9] Newspapers highlighted headlines surrounding the sinking of RMS *Titanic* when King supervised the first successful wireless transmission between warships and aircraft. Nimitz lurked below the surface when Ens. Charles Maddox flew in a wireless-rigged Wright Flyer above King in the torpedo boat USS *Stringham*. Aviator lieutenants John Rodgers and Patrick Bellinger also volunteered to pilot the aircraft used during these test flights along the shores of the Severn.[10] During the wireless experiments, King observed from *Stringham* when a Wright Flyer flown by Lt. John H. Towers crashed into the Severn River. Nonplused by the experience of surviving a crash, Towers challenged King to accompany him on another experimental flight. In the wintery cold of December, Towers piloted King's first flight on a naval aircraft. Towers and King remained friendly, although both indulged in a heated personal competition to claim their place in aviation history.[11]

Aviation and wireless-communications technologies stood in the earliest phases of development, as King assisted efforts to develop practical procedures for gaining the technical advantage in fleet operations. During his assignment at the Experimentation Station, King developed close ties with Lawrence Sperry. Among other innovations, Sperry perfected the mechanisms for autopilot and artificial-horizon technologies. King accompanied Sperry on test flights to refine the mechanisms for use at sea. Observing from above, King also recognized the potential of aviation for use against—and in support of—battleship fleets. King articulated his perspective in lectures and in articles published in the Naval Institute's *Proceedings*. He provided ideas for developing doctrinal procedures for integrating surface with subsurface and aerial forces at sea. His mentor, Kinkaid, later rewarded King for this work by noting in a fitness report that King possessed "excellent executive ability."[12]

King held the bureaucratic keys to secure choice assignments on board battleships and cruisers. Instead, King requested orders to secure a seagoing command of his own—in destroyers, "where the future is."[13] Destroyer and torpedo boat sailors took pride in referring to their warships as "flivvers"—adapting from the nickname associated with the Ford Model T in reference to their tin-can destroyers.[14] King saw his future away from the routines of the regular surface line, since flivvers operated with relative independence under the big guns of the fleet. Looking outward for a clear path among the stars of the fleet, King stood at the crossroads between the historical dominance of big-gunned warships and the future below and above the surfaces of the sea.

Heated debates among the elders about the future focus of warship design and fleet organization created subdivisions among the lower ranks within the US naval hierarchy. RAdm. French E. Chadwick initiated serious discussions about the organization of smaller warships within fleet organizations, as established in the Atlantic, Pacific, and Asiatic. Chadwick had also traded veiled insults with Mahan about the role of strategic headquarters ashore. Mahan had served on the Naval War Board during the Spanish-American War. This experience soured his views about the Joint Army-Navy Board, which nullified the Naval General Board by fusing the functions with those of the Army General Staff.

Nobody really had control over the civilian bureaucracies within the Departments of War and Navy. Thus, RAdm. Bradley Fiske merged functions to establish the chief of naval operations (CNO) as an equivalent to the Army chief of staff. In Fiske's view, the CNO theoretically served as the global coordinator for the fleet organizations and seagoing forces. He asked pointed questions for the land-focused continentalists. Fiske also engaged American taxpayers with the rhetorical question "What is the navy for?"[15] He asked readers to consider what "principles should be followed in designing, preparing, and operating [our Navy] in order to get the maximum return for the money expended?"[16]

Fiske pressed US naval professionals to understand the purpose of fighting wars centered on the attainment of clear and sustainable peacetime ends. Unlike the army, Fiske portrayed the maritime mission of American sea power as being fundamental to any great entrepreneurial society in history. His ideas rekindled debates between the civil-military stakeholders within the Departments of War, Navy, and State. Civilian bureau chiefs within the Navy Department fought Fiske and other supporters of his reorganization agenda. War Department bureaucrats similarly maneuvered to fortify their control by attempting to seize control over training the state naval militias under the Militia Acts. Within this context, Fiske fought withering bureaucratic wars between the various uniformed service branches.

The fundamental principle of civilian control loomed over the policy debates, which shaped the strategic course of American sea power. Fiske and his associates openly challenged the traditional authorities of the Navy secretary and civilian bureau chiefs. Upon entering office as Navy secretary, Josephus Daniels and his assistant secretary, Roosevelt, worked the lines to mitigate Fiske's zealous campaign to bring order to the bureaucratic chaos as the first aide for naval operations.[17] Daniels withheld civilian control over naval operations, which riled Fiske and his associates. Naval professionals openly pushed the limits. In 1914, Daniels muzzled opinionated professionals—like Fiske—by invoking restrictions articulated in Navy regulations.[18] In response, Fiske used Daniels as the example for explaining problems inherent with civilian control within the Navy Department. Fiske's protégé, Sims, followed in the wake—zeroing in the guns to sink the reputation of Daniels from within the ranks of the US Navy.[19]

Fleet commanders and warship skippers similarly continued following old traditions of acting first before requesting formal permission from the Navy Department. Given the advantages inherent with electronic communications, naval officers generally strived to act as Nelson or John Paul Jones may have done under certain tactical circumstances—often with strategic consequences for the future of American foreign policy. To empower naval officers to act with utmost freedom within the context of fleet operations, Fiske supervised the establishment of flotillas comprising smaller warships under the command of a commodore with a staff. In so doing, Fiske also expanded the number of seagoing commanders within the fleet—which by extension expanded the administrative infrastructure of the shore establishment.

Although the Navy secretary retained overall control on paper, the task increasingly proved impossible for an individual civilian appointee to manage, much less lead. Technological changes in the petroleum-fueled fleet of the future compelled changes in the command relationships between the civilian Navy secretary and the seagoing professionals within the Navy Department.[20] Successive Navy secretaries acquiesced as uniformed professionals asserted their expertise. Such was the price of progress after 1910, as Fiske used the flotilla system to develop new procedures in smaller oil-fired warships that later served as the basis for use on board the larger oil-fired battleships under construction. The Naval General Board provided the mandate for Fiske to empower commodores to hold autonomous flotilla commands over destroyers and torpedo boats, submarines, and other support forces by 1914.[21] Elder officers, like Sims, served as commodores—in captain's rank—to pioneer an alternate route up the fleet ladder to the flag ranks. Younger officers, like King, likewise had the chance to earn the coveted numerical annotation for command qualification in the Naval Register. [22]

Fiske arranged orders for Sims to organize the Destroyer and Torpedo Boat Flotilla within the Atlantic Fleet. In this role, Sims served in the rank of four-stripe captain but carried the title of commodore. He had the ability to form a staff with Cmdr. William V. Pratt as chief of staff, Lt. Cmdr. Dudley W. Knox as aide, and Lt. John V. Babcock as secretary. Sims sought younger officers to join the flotilla as skippers. To these ends, Sims wrote to King that "you should consider coming to the flotilla to lend us a hand in the schemes we are trying to develop."[23] King hedged his response to Sims in articulating preference to stay with the expedition to Mexican waters in the spring of 1914.

OF ALL THE GODDAMNED THINGS

American sea power lingered in the dead calm between peace and war when the Wilson administration took the decks of the White House. With trouble brewing along the southern border with Mexico, US Army major general Leonard Wood joined with RAdm. Bradley Fiske and Admiral of the Fleet George Dewey to make the case for expanding the army and navy ranks. The bureaucratic triumvirate invoked studies prepared by the Joint Board. Unimpressed, Wilson burst into a lecture about civil-military traditions. Wilson issued gag orders to silence armed-service leaders as precursors to war brewed beyond the horizon in Europe and Asia.[24] Wilson's pacifism failed to thwart prospective enemies. British and German spies openly operated among American immigrant populations.[25] Then, the Germans ham-handedly threw another gauntlet down along the southern border.

American border security operations in Mexico fell into the broader context of strategic competitions among foreign empires. The Wilson administration muddled into the hazy waters of diplomatic intrigue and American entrepreneurialism by sending forces to Mexico. In complete violation of American policy, the Remington Arms Company sold weapons to a Russian intermediary working on behalf of Mexican forces. The cargo departed New England to arrive in Germany on board the American-flagged merchant ship

SS *Brinkhorn*. Then, German longshoremen transferred the American-made weapons to the Hamburg-American Line steamer SS *Ypiranga*. In clear violation of Wilson administration policies, *Yapringa* steamed under the command of a reserve imperial German naval officer to deliver the arms to Mexican forces. This information filtered through US naval intelligence channels to enable American warships to intercept *Ypiranga* in the approaches to Veracruz on April 21, 1914.[26]

The strategic stakes quickly escalated, as *Ypiranga* carried auxiliary status as an imperial German navy warship, which further complicated the strategic calculus.[27] Rebellion in Mexico provided opportunity for entrepreneurial outlaws like Pancho Villa to earn a place in the heroic mythology of the Americas. Rallying the impoverished population to stand up against government corruption and foreign meddling in Mexican affairs, Villa also challenged American claims along the border. Within this confused civil-military organization, the policies of the Wilson administration remained in a constant state of change as American service professionals rushed to seek contact with a largely undefined Mexican enemy. The crisis escalated when Mexican locals arrested American sailors ashore in Tampico. The on-scene commander, RAdm. Henry T. Mayo, demanded satisfaction. When the Mexican authorities apologized, Mayo responded with a series of punitive provisions. Having learned the ropes in an era before wireless and electronic communications, Mayo acted without first securing guidance from the Navy Department. As a result, Americans stood surprised about the developing drama along the border—when headlines heralded the "Tampico Affair."[28]

The Wilson administration scrambled to meet the challenges inherent with balancing peacetime policy against preplanned provisions for operations in Mexico, as articulated in military terms within War Plan GREEN. In addition, Mayo earlier served as the personal aide to Navy secretary Meyer. The policies of the Roosevelt and Taft administrations intermixed with provisions found in army plans, which Mayo studied during his six-week preparation for prospective squadron commanders at the Naval War College. His combat experiences in suppressing rebellions from Asia to the Caribbean further shaped Mayo's decisions off Veracruz.[29] Once Mayo issued an ultimatum to the Mexican authorities in Tampico, the Wilson administration focused on "face-saving" through military escalation.[30]

Wilson overreacted by mobilizing American forces for warlike operations along the Mexican border and surrounding waters. He conversely hoped to avoid a major war with a show of American force. Wilson's philosophical approach to policymaking failed to provide firm foundations for sound military strategy, as the secretaries of war and navy—Newton D. Baker and Josephus Daniels—struggled to define their roles in shaping operational command. Largely out of bureaucratic momentum, American army troops fell under the expeditionary command of the brevet one-star brigadier John J. Pershing. Ashore, Pershing relied heavily upon Capt. George S. Patton to coordinate operations during adventures to hunt Pancho Villa. These operations around the southwestern desert often unfolded like a strange comedy.[31] Army authorities ended at the shoreline, where the two-star admiral Mayo held command over naval expeditionary forces.

The Wilson administration ordered American military and naval forces to close the Mexican boarder and blockade the surrounding waters. In turn, Navy secretary Daniels acted in close consultation with Admirals Dewey and Fiske. The president of the Naval War College, RAdm. Austin M. Knight, served as a close adviser with the General Board of the Navy.[32] Fleet commanders in the Asiatic, Pacific, and Atlantic coordinated operations to support Mayo in Mexican waters. Like many other younger officers, King requested orders to the front.[33] Just four days after the seizure of weapons on board *Ypiranga*, Navy secretary Daniels endorsed orders detaching King from duty in Annapolis to "proceed immediately to Galveston, Texas, to report to the commander, Second Division, Torpedo Flotilla, Atlantic Fleet."[34] He made his own way to Texas by train, only to find his entire chain of command already departed. King found the destroyer USS *Terry* (DD-25) awaiting at the pier. At this time, King assumed his first seagoing command as the skipper.

The situation off Tampico sparked the Navy Department bureaucrats to mobilize the reserve fleet, which relied upon locally based naval militia personnel. Within the Atlantic Fleet, *Terry* sailed among the Reserve Flotilla with an enlisted crew of civilian naval militia. The civilian volunteer warriors embarked before King arrived. Regular navy officers trickled in from other commands to serve under King on temporary duty in the Reserve Flotilla. King selected Lt. Claude B. Mayo as executive officer and navigator. Lt. Robert A. Theobald took charge as the engineer. Lt. (j.g.) Paul H. Bastedo served as the training officer. All later served with King at highest levels of command three decades later.

The reserve flotilla served as a crucible for younger skippers to cut their teeth within the battleship fleet. As a promising young lieutenant, King and the *Terry* crew gained experience escorting convoys along the coast while dodging bullets in waters close to shore. Having recently tested the procedure during earlier service at the Experiment Station in Annapolis, King experimented with procedures for transferring oil without stopping. King later claimed to have refueled *Terry* while sailing in trail behind the naval auxiliary ship USS *Arethusa* (AO-7).[35.] With only the volunteers among the crew to tell tales, the professional officers with King likely felt free to act with gumption at the front.

The Tampico affair and associated operations off Veracruz interrupted the blissful mythology of American isolationism. As the troops chased their glory in combat ashore, American sailors improvised means to assert control along the Mexican shoreline and into the strategic approaches to the Panama Canal Zone.[36] The adventurous experience of military operations in Mexico also proved formative in the careers of younger officers like King. Among others, US Army captain Douglas MacArthur also commandeered a train to find his way to the front. The American journalist and ardent peace activist John K. Turner negotiated with various Mexican factions to release the wayward sailors. The Wilson administration then struggled to negotiate Turner's release after his arrest by Mexican forces.[37] His brother, US Navy lieutenant Richmond Kelly Turner, coincidentally arrived on the gunboat USS *Marietta* (PG-15) with the American fleet off Mexico.

The excitement of going to war contrasted with the deflating experience of actual operations. King later described the Mexican sojourn as the "Grape Juice War."[38] Having served on *Terry* for fewer than two months, King received a surprise offer from Sims to join the Atlantic Fleet Destroyer Flotilla in June 1914. Sims advised King to expect orders to report as skipper on the destroyer USS *Cassin* (DD-43) in Boston. Upon receiving the formal orders, King dutifully left *Terry* under the command of a friend, Lt. Cmdr. Arthur L. Bristol Jr., while awaiting the new skipper, Lt. Cmdr. Aubrey Fitch.[39]

King relinquished command on *Terry* with a train ticket to Annapolis for a short visit with his family. Typically, Sims sent a telegram to report without delay from Texas to Rhode Island without stopping for leave. Sims advised King that their mutual friend,

Knox, collapsed from exhaustion on board the flotilla flagship USS *Dixie* (AD-1). Knox fell as he supervised dockyard workers while reconfiguring USS *Birmingham* (CL-2) as the new flotilla flagship.[40] Navy doctors discovered ulcers, which resulted in the reassignment of Knox to a convalescent home in New Hampshire. From those quiet surroundings, Knox sent the recommendation that inspired Sims to appoint King as the aide on the staff.[41]

Sims asked King to accept duty as the interim aide by finding another sufficiently experienced officer as a prospective replacement for Knox. King demurred, reasoning that "I have taken a personal and selfish view of this matter of command, but I have wanted command of a destroyer for many years."[42] Sims explained that the needs of the service required King to relinquish seagoing command as a temporary replacement for Knox on the flotilla staff.[43] Under the circumstances, King wrote, "I am professionally in need of destroyer command experience but am ready to give up command if [my] services are needed."[44] Sims responded that "I quite understand your desire to get some experience of command of such a fine boat as the Cassin, or any of the destroyers, for that matter, and I will try to find a man to take Knox's place."[45] Sims added, "As the efficiency of the whole flotilla of course comes ahead of one boat or individual, I may have to ask you to help us out, for a time at least."[46] King formally relieved Lt. Cmdr. Harris Laning as skipper on Cassin in Boston on July 23, 1914.

The American fleet quietly wallowed in the calm waters of peacetime routine, unlike the Sims flotilla. King assumed duty as aide to Sims on the flotilla staff on August 9—five days after German forces launched offensive operations in Europe. Sims and his skippers also studied the ships and tactical procedures of Nelson's navy to examine then-current trends, examine the possibilities, and conceptualize future warship designs.[47] Within the battleship fleet, the Sims flotilla moved like a school of fish between the various coastal ports along the Atlantic coast. Sims maneuvered fast-running "flivvers" of roughly 800 tons in swarming tactics against larger warships. King recommended destroyers of approximately 1,000 tons that had greater speed, range, and firepower—albeit less maneuverable.

Sims haughtily accused King of being overconfident in his technical assertions. After this exchange, Sims compromised by splitting the differences with King to produce a design of 900 tons. The skippers presented Sims with their concept on board his flagship, *Dixie*. The skippers jokingly christened their innovative destroyer deign as USS *Sims*.[48] The Sims Flotilla informed the development of future American destroyer designs. For example, Sims failed to file the requisite paperwork with the Navy Department before installing wireless-communications equipment on board his warships. Sims also took his skippers by surprise. King recalled when the flotilla radio officer, Lt. (j.g.) Robert Lavender, "came on board *Cassin* and without saying anything to anybody went into the radio room and told the radio man to cut this out and to do that."[49] Upon discovering these unauthorized modifications, King immediately took a launch to the newly christened flotilla flagship *Birmingham* and demanded an explanation from Lavender, who thought that "line officers could use radio only if radio officers agreed and approved."[50] Witnesses stood in awe of King as he fumed, "Of all the goddamned things I have ever heard of!"[51]

King's wrath reflected the frustrations of many seagoing professionals in relations with technical specialists within the line. Sims watched from the flying bridge as King subjected Lavender to a vicious tirade. Finally, Sims sent Babcock to the rescue. King later learned from Babcock that Sims thought that "I might throw young Lavender over-board for the fish."[52] King also reeled against the increased flow of superfluous messages from Sims and the flotilla staff. Messages from curious civilians with wireless sets at sea and ashore also greatly annoyed King. Above all, he considered queries for status reports as demeaning. "If we had been able to say, 'You can use only seven radio messages a day[,]' everything would have been simplified," King believed that radio "logs are full of unimportant matters—only five percent of what they contain is important."[53]

FLYING CIRCUS

Sims groomed the destroyer flotilla skippers for higher command with a mixture of tradi-tion and applied historical reasoning. Operating in the uncharted waters of the wireless world, Sims inspired King to complete the correspondence courses in strategy and tactics by 1915. King then completed the six-week-long "Staff Course" during evening sessions at the Naval War College, which set him in the running for a prospective assignment to a four-star fleet staff by 1916. These studies coincided with the Sims vision of creating a "War College afloat."[54] Fostering innovation, Sims used the open "conference method" as perfected at the Naval War College. Another witness, Pratt, recalled Sims listened intently to the freewheeling debates among subordinates, wherein "dissent and argument became the rule of the conference until consensus occurred." Sims then provided the ultimate ruling on any given issue and would then expect all to demonstrate "complete loyalty to the operating plan."[55]

King firmly embraced the War College Afloat concept of Sims, setting the example for fellow officers in the flotilla to follow.[56] During off-hours, King attended lectures at the Naval War College.[57] The skippers under Sims developed a pack mentality about the oil-fired future electrified US Navy. King performed double duty with Babcock and Lt. Cmdr. Emory S. Land.[58] Until Knox returned from extended medical convalescence, King per-formed double duty on the flotilla staff and simultaneously as the skipper on *Cassin*. Sims kept the destroyers at anchor in the basin close to the Naval War College—frequently at-tending the evening lectures in the North Annex rotunda, where wine and cheese followed with cigars.[59] Sims referred to his destroyer men as a "band of brothers."[60] His delivery was always punctuated with dramatic flare. King thought that "Captain Sims himself was an officer of extraordinary energy but given to speaking with exaggeration."[61]

The Sims flotilla worked up the procedures for refueling multiple warships simultane-ously by sailing together in close formation. In 1915 and 1916, the Sims flotilla perfected the concept. With Sims supervising the effort, King served as officer in charge during the first documented transfers of petroleum fuel involving two destroyers running simultane-ously alongside USS *Jason* (AC-12). The tests, conducted under the shadows of the Naval War College in the Narraganset Bay, served as the basis for procedures later employed in combat.[62] Side-by-side petroleum-refueling procedures set American warships apart from other navies, later proving decisive in war.[63] As a reward for a job well done, Sims recognized King as the top gun among flotilla skippers—among other future stars to in-clude Joel R. P. Pringle, Hutch I. Cone, Harry E. Yarnell, Harold R. Stark, Joseph K. Taussig, Arthur L. Bristol Jr., and William F. "Bill" Halsey Jr.[64]

Skippers among the Sims flotilla developed into a close team, which fueled friendly competition among their crews. Sims pushed his skippers to compete for the honor of sailing at the head and the rear in formation. He commissioned Tiffany to forge a silver trophy for the top-performing warship. Sims also presented an inscribed cigarette case to the top-performing skipper. King recalled the spirit that permeated the Sims flotilla. "Stark's crew were always in clean shirts and had their ship in top condition," King recalled. "You could always eat off her decks." Stark painted a red stripe on the funnels and at the waterline of USS *Patterson* (DD-36). In describing the jaunty mix of colors of *Patterson*, King called the ship "Stark's showboat."[65] In the friendly spirit of competition, King responded by painting blue and gold rings to trim the tops on the funnels of *Cassin*. He recalled that *Jarvis* under Halsey featured a center funnel ringed by "little green shamrocks."[66] Akin to Baron Manfred von Richthofen's "flying circus," the destroyer skippers in the Sims flotilla developed lasting personal ties. Sims flotilla veterans used the phrase "Remain cheerful" as their parting salutation among their elite club.[67]

King learned about the importance of teamwork under Sims while plying the Narragansett Bay and along the Atlantic coast. King had individually gained a reputation as an outstanding officer. On the other hand, Sims taught King to succeed as a member of a team. King initially thought Sims "did not like him any too well."[68] However, King later recognized Sims as a critical figure in the development of modern American sea power. King considered Sims a mentor. Sims shocked King by giving him the honor of breaking his own pennant as commander of Destroyer Division 6 at the lead of four other ships commanded by members of his Naval Academy class.[69]

Always running on the edges of technological innovation, Sims balanced futuristic notions and theoretical debates on questions of strategy by using historical case studies to examine problems of modern focus. He expected subordinates, like King, to take an applied approach in attaining an appreciation for history. Among his favorites, Sims arranged for King to serve as secretary-treasurer for the Naval Institute. With assistance from King, the modern-day point appeared clear in a historical essay published by Knox in *Proceedings*, "The Great Lesson from Nelson for Today." The professional alliance of King and Knox blossomed on the fertile grounds of maritime history.

King used history with an applied view in examining strategic developments with a modern purpose. The Panama Canal presented fresh strategic problems for the Americans to consider. For example, King translated the German text of an article by Professor Dr. Fritz Zedow of the University of Greifswald. From this text, King highlighted Zedow's warning that the "Japanese Empire presents an obvious war danger [and that] progress of the United States in carrying out its present-day paramount imperialistic policy will soon be the cause of a tremendous conflict."[70] King improved his linguistic skills by translating foreign texts on subjects in history and maritime affairs.

King focused on past disasters to identify means by which to avoid future strategic debacles. He used history to secure the advantage when navigating the unwritten future. In discussions with his friend Knox, King frequently referred to the 1757 execution of Royal Navy admiral John Byng "for not conducting battle prescribed in regulations; a striking contrast occurred forty years later when [Horatio] Nelson's initiative at the Battle of St. Vincent was heartily approved by [Admiral] Sir John Jervis."[71] In selecting heroes, King aspired to follow in the wake of Jervis. American naval myths, like John Paul Jones, also inspired King to adopt the motto "Make the best with what you have."[72] Friendly observers, like Knox, noted how King mimicked heroes of the past as a commander. Knox thought that King followed the rule of "never do[ing] anything himself that he can get anyone else to do for him."[73]

Service with Sims in the destroyer flotilla provided firm foundations for King to maneuver up the fleet ladder to positions of higher responsibility and command. Sims drove King and the flotilla skippers to push beyond existing doctrine and technological limits. Sims also seemed overly abrupt and unfriendly to King. Much to his surprise, King received a glowing fitness report. Sims described King as "one of the ablest officers of his grade of my acquaintance."[74] Sims then presented King with an inscribed Tiffany cigarette case with the silhouette of *Cassin* with pennant flying from the masthead. In the wooden presentation case, Sims also gave King a matching cigarette holder. He used the cigarette holder in two world wars—later passing it along with other cherished keepsakes held within the King family.[75]

THE "CHEER UP" SHIP

Naval War College teachings always inspired discussion among practitioners within the military and naval services. Sims used historical foundations to drive the American fleet over the technological horizon and beyond to future uncharted waters. He faced many difficulties in bringing the oil-burning battleship USS *Nevada* (BB-36) to the fleet. He continued rallying a team spirit by overlooking all the technical problems. Building confidence among the crew, he referred to *Nevada* as the "Cheer Up Ship" to earn status as the best-performing warship in the Atlantic Fleet.[76] In the same year, he challenged fellow seagoing commanders to embrace their task in professional *naval* education in his essay "Cheer Up!! There Is No Naval War College."[77]

Navy Department bureaucrats and the old-salt horses among the admirals of the fleet tended to discount the strategic value of the Naval War College. Many perceived the institution as a vast waste of time and treasure. The costs involved with keeping the Naval War College inspired significant debate within the seagoing ranks. Always stirring the pot, Sims wrote and self-published a pamphlet, "The Practical Character of the Naval War College." Sims encouraged subordinates to pursue future assignments ashore to the Naval War College. Sims inspired King to think that "it was at the Naval War College that Capt. A. T. Mahan wrote his great works on sea power [and] the ablest officers were all anxious to take the course at the War College, even though there were still a few die-hards who fought against it."[78]

Taking on the role of Bolshevik with a manifesto to pass around, Sims advocated for the Naval War College. He argued that the institution provided means by which naval professionals could escape the distractions of the fleet. Sims firmly believed that the "history of naval warfare is in no sense a theoretical proceeding, but essentially a practical one that is entirely indispensable as a preparation for actual conflict."[79] Given their shared affinity for the institution, Sims thought King should consider taking a "foreign assignment as a special intelligence officer [since] it might do you some good to get away from the humdrum of the navy for a while."[80] Sims warned King to avoid becoming "beguiled by the sea."[81]

The war in Europe shaped the peacetime focus of American peacekeeping operations, as the Atlantic Fleet maneuvered between ports along the eastern sea frontier and into Caribbean waters. British and French warships frequently interrupted the peace, hunting for German targets. The commerce raiders *Kronprinz Wilhelm* and *Prinz Eitel Friedrich* caused significant havoc before their internment at Hampton Roads in 1915. That same year in May, a German submarine sank the passenger steamer RMS *Lusitania* off the Irish coast. American casualties intermixed with the names of mothers and children, which sparked debates about the European war in the United States.

The Atlantic Fleet staff monitored the ominous presence of foreign warships in American waters. American voters stood divided. Those of German and Irish heritage viewed the European conflict with significant skepticism.[82] Though the Wilson administration clearly favored the Anglo-French, Italian, and imperial Russian *Entente*, diplomatic neutrality defined American engagement with Central Powers of imperial Germany, Austria-Hungary, and the Ottoman Empire. Twisting international protocols to the extreme, the German High Command sent the "merchant" submarine SM *U-Deutschland* to Baltimore and New London. Then, in anticipation of reinstating unrestricted submarine warfare in European waters, the attack submarine SM *U-53* appeared unannounced at the symbolic center of American sea power—at the Naval War College in October 1916.[83]

American neutrality complicated the strategic competition among the continental empires of Europe and Asia. Americans studied the clashes off Tsingtao in the Marshall Islands, Guam, and beyond to the Falkland Islands, which set the stage for the dramatic adventures of German commerce raiders—like SMS *Seeadler* and SMS *Emden*. The operations of SMS *Dresden* and SMS *Karlsruhe* drew similar attention in conjunction with those of the auxiliary cruisers *Kronprinz Wilhelm* and *Prinz Eitel Friedrich* in American waters. When Sims detached for a battleship command, King continued operating his Destroyer Division in aggressive patrols along the American sea frontier. On occasion, he sailed into the crosfire. King recalled closing with a German-flagged merchant ship in the approaches to New York. Suddenly, a British warship appeared mists. The British warship sailed at high speed and nearly collided with King's destroyers on course to intercept the German vessel. Following the incident, King joked that the "British were very nice to us [to] let us use the high seas."[84]

The fog of war swept over American coastal waters, where foreign-flagged warships interacted in the merchant sea-lanes with US naval patrols. The Wilson administration sought to offset war with the Navy Second to None—using American sea power as a counterforce against foreign competitors. Within this context, the Bureau of Construction and Repair (BuC&R) held significant influence within the Navy Department. BuOrd and BuNav likewise controlled personnel by setting career milestones up the fleet ladder to higher command within the seagoing ranks.

Professional officers served brief terms as bureau chiefs, leaving civilian bureaucrats to dominate within the Navy Department. Constitutional questions about civilian control dominated the thoughts of ranking service professionals. Behind closed doors, Admirals Luce, Mahan, and Fiske stood among the more vocal advocates for clarifying the command relationships between civilian policymakers and service professionals. Fiske conspired with Representative Richmond P. Hobson, a former naval officer, to pass legislation creating the Office of CNO in 1915 with verbiage describing a naval

> officer on the active list of the Navy appointed by the president from among the officers of the Line of the Navy, *not below the grade of Captain* for a period of four years, who shall under the direction of the SecNav be charged with the operations of the fleet, and with the preparation and readiness of plans for its use in war.[85]

Having won the bureaucratic battle through subterfuge, Fiske immediately transferred to the retired list and happily spent his waning years helping the staff at the Naval War College. Fiske proudly counted among his greatest accomplishments the creations of CNO and its associated Operations Navy (OpNav) planning staff.[86]

Civilian officials within the Navy Department circled bureaucratic wagons to consolidate power. Of the twenty-six admirals on active service, eight others stood in waiting for promotion. Daniels overlooked flag officers to nominate Capt. William S. Benson as the first prospective CNO. In 1915, Benson stood thirtieth on the list of eighty-nine captains and served as commandant of the Philadelphia Naval Shipyard. Appointed to the two-star rank in May, Benson assumed duty as CNO with collateral duty as an ex officio member of the General Board of the Navy, under the chairmanship of admiral of the fleet, Dewey. Benson also stood two-stars subordinate to the commanders of the seagoing fleets in the Atlantic, Pacific, and Asiatic—Admirals Fletcher, Cameron Winslow, and Albert Winterhaler. In three-stars, Adm. Henry T. Mayo served as second in command of the Atlantic Fleet.

Other flag officers treated the CNO as an unnecessary appendage to preexisting fleet command organizations. As the first to hold the offices, Benson also lacked sufficient personnel to organize his staff. From the Naval War College, Fiske and Sims helped Benson. Loyalists of Sims, Pratt, and Knox volunteered for duty on the fledgling OpNav staff.[87] Benson struggled to balance the upper levels of bureaucracy, and his staff managed the daily grind of creating an organization out of nothing.[88] Meanwhile, Navy secretary Daniels wrestled for control over the future civil-military relationship within the Navy Department. Annoyed by his naysayers within the ranks, Daniel issued a series of directives to reassert control over the policy debates ongoing within the ranks. Daniels focused on Fiske and like-minded associates like Sims in reasserting the Navy Regulation that "no person belonging to the Navy or plotted under the Navy Department shall attempt, directly or indirectly, to influence legislation in respect to the Navy without the express authority and approval of the Department."[89]

Restrictions imposed by Daniels upon the professional debates ongoing within the ranks failed to stop the progressive erosion of civilian control within the Navy Department. Among the key middlemen in balancing the policies of Daniels against the strategic vision of Fiske, the assistant Navy secretary, Roosevelt, habitually waited for opportunities to circumvent bureaucratic restrictions by "calling up his friends to ask if there was anything he could do for them as acting secretary."[90] Behind closed doors, Roosevelt shook the bureaucratic routines that drove the administrative patronage system within the Navy Department. As a civilian bureaucrat, Roosevelt treated the naval services much like his cousin Theodore—as a personal project for which only he had a solution. He took a possessive view of American sea power, which sometimes riled naval professionals and at other times made him a favorite hero within the ranks of the service. For example, Roosevelt claimed credit for establishing competitive selection boards in 1915. Good performance—rather than longevity—thereafter defined the requirements for promotion in the race up the fleet ladders to higher command.[91]

Roosevelt successfully convinced Daniels to view the new competitive promotion system as a mechanism for pruning prospective rebels among the seagoing ranks. Conversely, Roosevelt also assured old innovators—like Luce, Mahan, Dewey, and Fiske—to embrace the new promotion system. He won the trust of senior service leaders when Roosevelt's favorite old-salt horse, Sims, became the first officer to be selected for flag rank through merit promotion. Command of *Nevada* propelled Sims to the top for the promotion board in 1916. Sims expected to receive following orders for duty as the commandant of Narragansett Bay Naval Station, in anticipation of assuming flag rank as president of the Naval War College by the spring of 1917.

The visionary influence of Luce upon the global maritime views of Theodore and Franklin followed in conjunction with the ebbs and flows of the Naval War College, which served as the forum wherein military and naval professionals sharpened their professional understanding. Luce and Mahan had also worked alongside with Fiske on the staff, with Franklin Roosevelt's uncle James Soley. Knowing the Naval War College as the gateway to influence higher American policy to achieve strategic ends, Sims asked King to join the team in Newport as the flag aide. King respectfully declined the assignment after his other mentor, Osterhaus, wrote that "you can never go wrong if you are on the deck of a warship."[92] Although Sims set an example for pushing bureaucratic limits, King accepted an assignment with Mayo in the Atlantic Fleet.

Sims and Mayo shared many similar ideas, although their command personalities stood at opposite ends of the bureaucratic extremes. Sims frequently sermonized with haughty parables and bombastic conclusions. His predictive logic often proved to be correct—after the fact. By contrast, Mayo quietly performed his duty in strict accordance with Navy Regulations. Mayo had mastered the art of using overlapping directives to nullify administrative barriers, adapt to circumstances, and win the day without having to explain the decisions made in attaining the desired end objectives—whether in peace or war. Under Mayo in the Atlantic Fleet, King came to recognize the value of allowing actions to speak more loudly than words as American sea power joined the fight for future empires in what later became known as the First World War.

CHAPTER 4
Fleets in Being

Under the Constitution, the Navy secretary held formal authority to command seagoing fleet organizations. The CNO had an ambiguous role in relations with fleet headquarters. For this reason, many officers declined orders to the office of CNO. In addition, the Atlantic and Pacific Fleets became four-star commands in 1915.[1] The relationships among higher American naval commanders remained in an unsettled state when the Wilson administration faced the grim decision between shifting from peace to war. In January 1917, the German foreign secretary, Arthur Zimmermann, transmitted a message to the German consulate in Mexico. In the message, he outlined an outlandish plan to reintroduce unrestricted submarine warfare in conjunction with a plot to instigate Mexican and Japanese attacks on the United States.

German aggression on the high seas intermixed with headlines about atrocities against women and children on the embattled shores of Europe. American newspapers pushed readers to question the Wilson administration's neutrality policy. Adding fuel to the fire, British cryptographers solved the Zimmermann telegram on January 17, 1917. The First Sea Lord, Jellicoe, shared the information with the American ambassador, Walter Hines Page, on February 23.[2] In turn, Page encouraged the Wilson administration to make a strong stand in response to the Zimmermann telegram.[3] Within five days, Wilson released the full text of to the American media.[4]

Congress pressured the Wilson administration for a clear policy in response to the Zimmermann telegram. Wilson also faced pressure from within his own administration. Meanwhile, Marxists, labor activists, and various other pacifist movements pulled the Wilson administration in the opposite polar direction. Suffragettes and Teetotalers also added a voice of support for the first female member of Congress, Republican representative Jeanette Rankin of Montana. She strongly condemned fellow Americans for pushing the Wilson administration to abandon neutrality. German American organizations stood divided over the question of war, some following the lead of former president Theodore Roosevelt, others seeking neutrality, and others actively declaring their full support for the German and Austria-Hungarian empires. Few understood the Ottoman connection with the Central Powers. Americans also failed to understand the Anglo-French, Italian, Japanese, and Russian Entente.[5]

The Wilson administration struggled to repurchase time for the neutrality policy to regain support among American voters. In the interim, the US Navy quietly scrambled to strategic coastal defensive positions in American waters and in the Panama Canal Zone. The CNO, Benson, ordered fleet and naval district commanders to act under Plan BLACK.[6] Fleet commanders understood their broader strategic guidance as being defensive in focus.[7] Embarked on the recently commissioned flagship USS *Pennsylvania* (BB-38), Mayo issued orders to the Atlantic Fleet to assemble in the waters off "Base 2" near Yorktown, Virginia.[8] Within the Chesapeake Bay, battleships stood safely at anchor near the railhead and shipyards in Hampton Roads offered sufficient facilities to support operations along the eastern sea frontier from Canadian waters to the Caribbean.

In the absence of a clear American strategy or formal declaration of war, Daniels and Benson sought a suitable liaison to represent the Navy Department in London. The First Sea Lord, Jellicoe, amplified concurrent requests from Page and the US naval attaché, Capt. William B. McDougall, for an American flag officer with sufficient authority to coordinate prospective tactical operations in European waters. Initially, Benson asked Capt. Henry Braid "Nobby" Wilson to "aid the [Navy] Department in putting into immediate effect the cooperation with the Allies which we were planning."[9] He held command on the flagship *Pennsylvania.* Mayo likely influenced Wilson to hold fast with the fleet in Hampton Roads.

The Wilson administration vacillated about policy, which hindered Daniels in framing the strategic focus for American operations in the global maritime arena. The assistant CNO in the Navy Department, Pratt, observed that the OpNav staff performed "work assumed backbreaking proportions because of the inability of Daniels and Benson to act quickly."[10] Given the situation, he perceived Benson as being overly "conservative, too deliberative in his decision making, and decidedly Anglophobic."[11] The Wilson administration adopted the policy of seeking "peace without victory."[12] The Germans then embarrassed Wilson by reengaging unrestricted submarine warfare tactics, prompting the American cessation of diplomatic relations with the court of Kaiser Wilhelm II in January 1917.

PLAN BLACK

Wilson faced the crossroads in framing policies designed to preserve peace at all costs while the winds of war gathered inescapable momentum. The Joint Board pushed the administration to take appropriate steps to mobilize forces in the event of war. Under Plan BLACK, the time required for mobilization already seemed inadequate by the spring of 1917. When Admirals Bradley Fiske and Benson pushed Wilson to make strategic decisions in preparing for the likelihood of war, Wilson "angrily ordered that proposals should go into the wastebasket."[13] Horrified by the indecisiveness of Wilson and his associates, assistant Navy secretary Roosevelt took charge. Shakespeare's portrayal of Lord Thomas Cromwell in handling the whims of King Henry VIII served as an analogy for Roosevelt's performance as a Navy Department insider.

Risking all for the good of the regime, Roosevelt followed in the footsteps of his cousin in managing the ambiguities of policy to clarify the strategic necessities for fleet operations in anticipation of war. Roosevelt later admitted that "he had committed enough illegal acts to put him in jail for 999 years and that he would have been undoubtedly impeached had he made wrong guesses."[14] Roosevelt argued that the "navy was still unprepared and I spent forty millions for guns before Congress gave me or anyone permission to spend the money."[15] He claimed full credit for selecting Sims "as the head of the Inter-allied fleet in March, 1917."[16] Roosevelt received the request from the British Admiralty to send over one of our Admirals so that he could become acquainted with conditions over there. I conveyed this information to President Wilson in the presence of Secretary Daniels. President Wilson turned to Mr. Daniels and asked, 'who shall we send?' Mr. Daniels said there were several men that could be sent over and he suggested that he be given a few days to make a selection.[17]

Within the ranks existed "four or five different explanations of how Sims received his appointment."[18] However, Roosevelt clearly made the final decision to send Sims.[19]

Mayhem within the Navy Department influenced problems among the seagoing forces, particularly in the Atlantic Fleet. King credited Roosevelt for taking charge, as Daniels and Benson hesitated to calculate the political ramifications. King explained that Roosevelt "resorted to keeping crucial papers in his desk until Mr. Daniels was out of town, so as to sign them himself and get matters under way."[20] "Daniels would either forget that he had approved it, or at least would not change his mind if he did remember," King explained, "since the matter would already be under way and working in good shape."[21] Daniels and Benson dithered with politics in Washington, which hindered the seagoing forces. Observing with disgust, King wryly observed that the office of CNO, "in the form passed by Congress, represented the ashes of a once good idea."[22]

"SINK US"

The CNO struggled to define the focus of American strategy, as the Army-Navy Board emphasized continental defenses. Tactical debates about land operations overshadowed serious discussions of maritime strategy. Under the mobilization plan promulgated by Daniels on March 21, 1917, Mayo expected to assume control over seagoing forces as the commander in chief, US Fleet (CinCUS).[23] On the same day, Sims received orders to assume the two-star rank of rear admiral.[24] Concurrently, Daniels advised Sims to make preparations to execute a secret fact-finding mission to London, "not because of your Guildhall speech, but in spite of it."[25] "Don't let the British pull the wool over your eyes," Benson reputedly warned Sims. "We would as soon fight them as the Germans."[26] Benson denied the remark but admitted telling Sims to make sure "his feelings toward the British did not lead him to any indiscretion."[27]

Laboring over the decision to declare war against imperial Germany, the Wilson administration failed to empower subordinate commanders to take appropriate action. Daniels and Benson vested Sims with no seagoing command—restricting his role to that of a simple liaison between the Admiralty and Navy Department.[28] In the confusion, the acting director in BuNav, RAdm. Leigh C. Palmer, requested details from Sims.[29] By the time Palmer sent the message, Sims was already gone. Leaving their uniforms in Newport as ordered, Sims and Babcock traveled in civilian clothes from Kingston by train to New York Harbor and embarked SS *New York* on March 31, 1917. Wilson subsequently requested the formal war declaration against imperial Germany on April 6, 1917. He referred to the American relationship with the Entente as an "associated power" and *not* as an "ally."[30]

Under such conditions, nobody in the American command understood the strategy for establishing a workable partnership to coordinate operations in conjunction with the

Entente. Three days after the declaration of war against Germany, Daniels also refused to follow the sequence of Plan BLACK. Daniels instead used Benson as a middleman in dealings with the key fleet commanders. Mayo prodded for clear direction while sitting idly with the Atlantic Fleet at Base 2 in Hampton Roads.[31] Mayo stood surprised when Sims arrived with Babcock—without their uniforms—for initial meetings with the First Sea Lord, Jellicoe, at the Admiralty on April 10. Daniels later reasoned that they "worked in such close cooperation with the British fleet and I sent a younger admiral [Sims] as commander of it."[32] The CNO, Benson, also failed to provide clear decisions—leaving Mayo and Sims to carry the burdens of mitigating the bureaucratic disaster of American wartime command after 1917.

Sims stopped asking for permission from Washington and simply acted upon requests from the Admiralty. Jellicoe provided top cover for Sims by making separate requests between the Admiralty and Navy Department. By the time a decision came from Washington, Sims usually had already solved the original problem. Mayo dutifully acted upon dispatches from Sims without asking permission in advance. Jellicoe influenced Sims to pull together with "Allied Governments by which our ships can put into any of their naval bases and obtain urgent supplies just as if they belonged to the Navy of the country."[33] British handlers orchestrating American strategy, the media portrayed Sims as the supreme commander for future US naval operations in European waters.[34]

Navy Department bureaucrats abused their prerogative to transmit wireless communications to the fleet.[35] The CNO, Benson, used wireless to micromanage seagoing forces.[36] For this reason, King strongly criticized Benson for running "everything himself, and in his concern over detail would lose control over the general situation."[37] King explained, "Dispositions were arranged in Washington without Adm. Mayo being consulted or informed of the probable use of the ships for which he was, as commander in chief, responsible."[38] Thus, Mayo appointed King to serve as aide and "Strategical Officer" on the Atlantic Fleet staff, with the specified duty of coordinating the American mobilization, transatlantic planning, and US naval operations at the front.[39]

WAR IS NOT SIMPLY FIGHTING

The Wilson administration decided to synthesize policy objectives for individual American commanders to execute global strategy. During the First World War, foreign partners treated the Americans as subordinates—filling gaps on widely dispersed fronts. American forces sailed for widely ignored adventures from the Mediterranean to Siberia and beyond to China. Frustrated by the experience, Mayo lectured the Atlantic Fleet staff to understand that "war is not simply fighting; it is for the attainment of a definite purpose [since] each act of war should be in harmony with the general purpose, [and] it is evident that there must be a supreme control to direct the act of war."[40] Mayo grew deeply frustrated by the increasing volume of conflicting orders emanating from the Navy Department. At that time, Mayo met Anglo-French representatives at the Chamberlain Hotel, overlooking the approaches to Hampton Roads, four days following the American war declaration on April 10—the same day Sims arrived in London.[41]

Sims and Mayo held concurrent meetings with British and French emissaries in London and at Hampton Roads. Among other observers at the Chamberlain Hotel meetings, Sir William Wiseman advised the British War Cabinet that "there still remains a strong feeling of mistrust of Great Britain [as] inherited from the days of the War of Independence and fostered by the ridiculous history books still used in national schools of America."[42] The British carefully co-opted the revolutionary mythology of American independence during preliminary naval staff talks in Hampton Roads. The Atlantic Fleet anchorage at "Base 2" in the James River stood near the spot where Lord Charles Cornwallis surrendered to General George Washington at Yorktown during the War for Independence.[43]

For the first time since the Battle of the Virginia Capes, British and French warships squared off in close formation. The British and French battle ensigns flew from the topmasts with American flags under US Navy escort into the Atlantic Fleet anchorage at Hampton Roads.[44] The Yorktown Victory memorial loomed ashore when Anglo-French and American fleet commanders converged in the historic waters where Washington's triumph occurred just over a century earlier. The British commander in chief, North America and West Indies Station, Vice-Admiral Sir Montague Edward Browning, sailed on HMS *Leviathan* accompanied by his French counterpart, Rear-Admiral Maurice Ferdinand Albert Grasset, on the light cruiser *Gloire* for meetings with Benson and Mayo on the flagship *Pennsylvania*.[45] Sailing from the Navy Yard in Washington on the yacht *Sylph*, Benson lacked clear authority to act without first securing approvals from the Navy Department.[46] Observing from the corners, King noted that "Benson seemed scantly cooperative [so] the conference migrated to Washington the following day, for Vice-Admiral Browning felt that his instructions required him to see the Secretary of the Navy."[47]

The critical decision by Mayo to send the destroyers occurred *before* a request conveyed by Sims through telegraph and wireless communiqués, which filtered through State Department channels to the Navy Department.[48] Given these facts, Mayo directed King to coordinate the procurement of spare parts and assist the destroyer skippers planning the transatlantic voyage.[49] He traveled by train to coordinate logistics in US naval shipyards along the eastern sea frontier.[50] On April 19, 1917, King received orders to "return to the port in which the Flag Ship of the Atlantic Fleet might be."[51]

The Navy Department frequently truncated the command relationship by circumventing the Atlantic Fleet staff. To Mayo's chagrin, the CNO staff transmitted orders on Benson's authority without prior coordination with the Atlantic Fleet staff. Navy secretary Daniels often convoluted the situation by sending duplicate orders. He also sent contradictory directives, which caused further confusion along the waterfront. Mayo stood completely by surprise when Cmdr. Joseph K. Taussig received direct orders to sail from Yorktown to refuel in New York before taking on supplies in Boston. Taussig logged that "things are very much upset at headquarters [and] we must continue to expect to be buffeted around in all manner of ways."[52] He sailed on April 28 with sealed orders to report to the senior Royal Navy commander in Queenstown (Cobh) Ireland. The British media highlighted Taussig and Jellicoe's long friendship.[53] Having witnessed the meetings in Yorktown three weeks before, Taussig sailed with five other American destroyers on *Wadsworth* into Queenstown. He set anchor by the Royal Navy headquarters on Haulbowline Island.[54]

British propagandists noted the Germanic surname to portray Taussig as the quintessential American ally. The youthful appearance of Taussig provided the perfect juxtaposition with the Irish surname of Royal Navy commander of western approaches, Rear-Admiral Sir Lewis Bayly.

Keeping British traditions alive on the occupied shores of Ireland, Bayly welcomed Taussig ashore with an invitation that evening to Admiralty House, overlooking the harbor, to "dine in undress, no speeches."[55] According to British accounts, Bayly asked when the American destroyers would be ready for action, to which Taussig reportedly replied that "we are ready now, sir."[56] On May 8, 1917, Taussig and his fellow destroyer skippers accepted a lifetime membership at the Royal Cork Yacht Club near Admiralty House on the Queenstown waterfront. The Royal Cork subsequently served as the designated US Navy Officers Club in Queenstown.[57]

READY NOW?

Cheerful relations among Royal Navy and US Navy personnel contrasted with the underlying tensions among the Irish population. The Irish had fought a losing battle against British oppressors during the Easter Uprising the year before, as American allies arrived on the European front.[58] On May 28, Sims coincidentally received authority to assume temporary three-star rank.[59] Sims initially took the title of "Commander, US Naval Destroyers Operating from British Bases."[60] Benson modified the title by designating Sims as "Commander, US Navy Destroyers in European Waters" on June 8, 1917.[61] Between May and August 1917, Benson took the role of an unnecessary middleman in relations between Mayo and Sims. Acting upon requests from London, Mayo stayed with the fleet in Hampton Roads. He put King in charge of coordinating the pivotal refueling operations on USS *Maumee* (AO-2) and USS *Jupiter* (AC-3). King earlier experimented with transferring petroleum between ships during operations off Veracruz. His peacetime experience proved useful in the early phases of American naval operations in the First World War.[62]

The experimental tactic of side-by-side refueling had happened six months earlier in the Narragansett Bay. Given personal experience in these operations, King had a key role in the successful refueling operations of *Maumee* and *Jupiter* during combat operations. Acting on the authority of Mayo to support Atlantic Fleet destroyers, King worked directly with the crews of *Maumee* and *Jupiter* to execute these operations. Notably, King worked directly with the executive officer on *Maumee*, Lt. Cmdr. Chester W. Nimitz, to prepare the procedures for side-by-side refueling—without stopping—in combat operations during the transatlantic voyages of destroyers headed to the European front in the spring of 1917. Sailing to a designated rendezvous, *Maumee* loitered in position as the destroyers converged. Conversely, *Jupiter* made the transatlantic crossing with a cargo on board, a US naval aviation detachment, and two destroyers in tow. *Jupiter* replenished the destroyers during the voyage to a designated rendezvous point off Bordeaux.[63]

Orders originating from the Navy Department to individual warships caused major confusion among the Atlantic Fleet. In turn, Mayo and Sims struggled to coordinate transatlantic operations to have a regular rotation of liaison personnel between the Atlantic Fleet and the US Naval Headquarters, later known as the "London Flagship."[64] Sims received orders to "assume command of all American destroyers operating from

British bases, including tenders and auxiliaries thereto which may be sent later."[65] The amplified role of Sims riled other American flag officers—including the CNO, Benson. In radio messages, he also abbreviated his signature by signing off as "SimsADUS" or "Sims, Admiral, Destroyers, US Navy."[66]

Sims acted in accordance with the mission in London by asserting command in the absence of a clear American policy, or coherent strategic plan. Navy secretary Daniels muddled along, allowing his assistant, Roosevelt, to manage the war effort. The CNO, Benson, also issued directives without first coordinating with Daniels or Roosevelt. As a result, Sims stood in between as the ranking American commander in Europe—without clear authority to assert command over warships technically assigned to the Atlantic Fleet, under Mayo. Confusion reigned supreme within the American high command. Under the circumstances, Mayo supported Sims by championing his formal appointment within the Navy Department hierarchy as the commander, US Naval Forces in Europe, with collateral duty—under Mayo—as the commander, Atlantic Fleet Destroyer Flotilla, in European waters. In these double roles, Sims kept his headquarters in what became known as the "London Flagship" while simultaneously flying his command pennant from the masts of his actual flagship, *Melville*, in Queenstown.[67]

Mayo coincidentally rigged the lines in close collaboration with foreign partners to unify naval efforts against common rivals within the global maritime arena. The First Sea Lord, Jellicoe, clearly influenced Mayo in efforts to establish Sims as the public face of transatlantic collaboration in the First World War. Jellicoe unleashed the British propaganda campaign to portray Sims as the overall commander of US naval forces in Europe. For five days, between June 18 and 23, Sims assumed command in Queenstown. "The British Admiralty merely took this way of showing a great courtesy to the American Navy," Sims later explained, "emphasizing to the world the excellent relations that existed between the two services."[68]

For the first time in British naval history, Sims assumed full status as the first American to hold command over Royal Navy forces. Jellicoe had arranged leave for Bayly and then installed Sims as the temporary commander, western approaches, in Queenstown. Jellicoe placed Sims at center stage in the media when Royal Navy sailors lowered Bayly's flag and concurrently broke the three-star flag of Sims at Admiralty House, which overlooked the approaches to Queenstown and over Spike Island—where the British kept Irish prisoners in horrific conditions.[69]

Jellicoe masterfully amplified the importance of Sims as the most preferred American liaison between the Admiralty and Navy Department. The British essentially forced the Wilson administration to formally designate Sims as "Commander, US Naval Forces in Europe" with additional duty as US naval attaché in London.[70] With the fleet at Hampton Roads, Mayo focused on the fleet, enabling Sims to nurture relationships as the American liaison to the Allied Naval Council in Europe. King recalled the philosophy of Mayo that the "Fleet should be in a true sense of the word a 'Fleet' and not a collection of more or less independent forces."[71] Mayo worked to "instill into the Fleet the proper realization of 'decentralization of authority' and 'initiative of the subordinate.'"[72] Drawing perspective from observing his mentors in action, King applauded Mayo for placing "trust in his subordinates, but to require of them due performance of their proper responsibilities."[73]

REVOLUTIONARY HISTORY AND PROPAGANDA

The Atlantic Fleet stood majestically at anchor in the muddy inland waterways of Hampton Roads. American civilians visited the fleet for dances, YMCA reading groups, and other social gatherings. Civilians cheered the sailors during baseball and football tournaments on the same fields upon which General George Washington commanded combined French and American forces against the British armies and naval forces of Lord Charles Cornwallis roughly one hundred years earlier. Coincident with the Fourth of July 1917, Adm. Browning returned with a British naval delegation to the Atlantic Fleet anchorage at Hampton Roads on July 4, 1917. In a symbolic gesture of transatlantic reconciliation and respect, Browning returned to Yorktown for the specific purposes of visiting the hallowed grounds and historic Revolutionary War landmarks in the area.

King accompanied the admirals up the hill to the victory monument, upon which the heroic narrative of Washington's victory over Cornwallis was chiseled in stone. The Yorktown monument loomed above, as Browning cheerfully read aloud the heroic portrayals of Washington's victory. Browning's gesture greatly impressed King.[74] Not to be outdone by the British in Yankee relations, the French responded with a charm offensive featuring Marshal Joseph Joffre. After visiting Washington's tomb at Mount Vernon, Joffre took a train—dubbed the "Lafayette Special"—to the Yorktown battlefield. Hosting Joffre fell upon King to coordinate. On board the Atlantic Fleet flagship, *Pennsylvania*, Joffre insisted upon crawling into a turret with 14-inch guns. King recalled Joffre struggled with "his substantial figure making it impossible."[75] King intervened in time to avoid the "undignified spectacle of a Marshal of France getting stuck in a space too small for him!"[76]

In the confused weeks following the American declaration of war against imperial Germany, other foreign emissaries arrived for discussions concerning the focus of future strategy in the war at sea. Having first met with Jellicoe and Sims in London, imperial Russian admiral Alexandr Kolchak sailed to the United States. The provisional regime in Russia struggled to hold power when Kolchak visited American aristocrats in the gilded mansions of Newport in the summer of 1917. Kolchak delivered a lecture about the situation in Russia at the Naval War College.[77] He then flew over the Naval War College on a sightseeing trip over the Narragansett Bay. King rendezvoused with Kolchak in Washington during meetings with Secretary Daniels and the CNO at the Navy Department. Representing the Atlantic Fleet staff, King accompanied Kolchak to meet with Mayo and visit the fleet at Hampton Roads.

Kolchak encouraged the Americans to lend a hand in restoring the czarist regime in imperial Russia. Bolshevik insurgents earlier toppled the Russian monarchy, which threatened monarchial order of Europe. Kolchak noted historical connections, such as the purchase of Alaska from Russia to encourage Americans join the counterrevolution. Kolchack invoked common strategic interests to defend the Trans-Siberian Railway.[78] Having made his best argument on the East Coast, Kolchak traveled across America to circumnavigate his way to Siberia through Japan. Ultimately, he failed in glorious form. Bolsheviks summarily executed Kolchak on the snowy wastelands of Siberia.[79]

Given appeals by foreign partners, the US Navy lacked a clear strategy to inform operational plans under development. Observing from within the Atlantic Fleet, King grew frustrated with the mismanagement of American forces. Experience in the First World War shaped his perspective, as the Admiralty used the US Navy to fill gaps within the broader context of allied operations in Europe and beyond to Asia.[80] Having centuries of experience in such matters, the Admiralty exploited American ignorance. Service with the Royal Navy at the front progressively inspired US naval practitioners to envision their future role. The dream of an Imperial Federation between the British Empire and the United States seemed appropriate. Within the Navy Department, all agreed that it "would be directly against the interests of humanity to have the two great Anglo-Saxon speaking nations [pitted] against each other."[81]

The Admiralty stood at the center of a maritime empire with the rudimentary electronic-communications linkages to naval bases running from Europe through India and beyond to Asia and the Americas. With the arrival of American warships, the Admiralty had greater ability to allocate forces to safeguard the wider interests of Britannia.[82] Out of convenience, the Admiralty provided their American partners with administrative assistance, general strategic priorities, and operational support at the tactical level. Wartime service as Mayo's trusted liaison in Europe influenced King to reject doctrinal definitions of "unity of command."[83] Sims favored amalgamation among seagoing forces. By intermixing British with American warships, Sims hoped to draw the best ideas from allies for future application in American strategy.

Policy differences between the Imperial War Staff in London and their equivalents in Washington contrasted with the cheery strategic image of Anglo-American solidarity within the global maritime arena. Having run an empire for nearly three centuries, the British asserted "unity of command" and, in so doing, inspired American naval thinkers, like King, to fight instead for sovereignty under the principle of "unity of effort."[84] Experiences working with foreign allies in European waters during the war and into an era of unsettled peace also deeply influenced King on questions of global strategy and naval command—whether in peace or war.

Muddling along in the absence of a clear American policy in relations with European partners, the weight of making strategic decisions often fell to Sims. By implication, or by default, Sims accepted responsibility for American naval command.[85] Further complicating the situation for Sims in June 1917, US Army general John J. Pershing suddenly arrived in London without significant notice with the rarified title of commander, Allied Expeditionary Force (AEF).[86] Meeting the challenge of joint army-navy command, Sims also synthesized coalition strategy by establishing the "Naval Planning Section" within the London headquarters.[87] For this task, Sims purposely requested officers with war college experience to form the Planning Section.[88]

As forces trickled across the Atlantic, Sims progressively expanded the American naval presence ashore in Europe. He asserted higher command over US Navy captain Joel R. P. Pringle and also assumed rank in the rolls of the Royal Navy as the chief of staff to the commander of the western approaches, Bayly.[89] Symbolically, Sims designated the destroyer tender in Queenstown, USS *Melville* (AD-2), as his flagship. On the other hand, Pringle also reported to Mayo. The CNO frequently transmitted directives to Pringle without including Mayo or Sims. In transatlantic relations, the British often exploited the chaos of American command. Both Sims and Pringle formally appeared in the rolls of the Admiralty chain of command, which greatly upset American sensitivities.[90]

COMMANDER IN CHIEF, US FLEET

Differences within the bureaucratic culture of the American land and sea services caused major confusion during operations at the front. In examining problems of American command after 1917, Sims reported to the Department of State as a naval attaché and concurrently to Navy secretary Daniels as the designated Navy Department liaison in London. More confusingly, Sims stood as the senior operational commander in European waters, which conversely rendered him subordinate to the overall Atlantic Fleet command of Mayo.[91] Acting the part of middleman, King advised Sims—speaking with the full authority of Mayo. Such First World War experiences shaped King's outlook on issues of command and organization.[92]

Under Plan BLACK, Mayo held clear strategic authority over all American naval operations in European waters. His paramount duty centered on defense in American waters. For this reason, Mayo chose to stay anchored at Base 2 in Hampton Roads. He therefore empowered Sims, leaving him free to focus on the tactical operations in Europe. Under Plan BLACK, Mayo carried the functions of CinCUS. Mayo personally pronounced the acronym as "Com-Inch." Most others verbalized the term as "sink us."[93] The Atlantic Fleet staff referred to Mayo as the "CominCh"—being the spoken means to pronounce the phrase "commander in chief."[94]

Fearing the prospective challenge to civilian control in wartime, Daniels failed to issue the order to empower Mayo as the CinCUS in accordance with Plan BLACK.[95] The confused decisions of SecNav Daniels and CNO Benson also complicated the evolving command organization under Mayo.[96] In 1917, Benson regularly issued orders directly to warship skippers without first advising the Atlantic Fleet chain of command.[97] Taking his position under Plan BLACK at Hampton Roads, Mayo had no clear authority to offer recommendations to Sims in handling the complexities of combined Anglo-French and American maritime collaboration.[98] As Atlantic Fleet warships sailed individually to European waters, Mayo organized the staff to assist operations in coordination with Sims in London.[99]

Wilson administration policies failed to synchronize with the strategic realities of war in Europe. With fewer than five personnel, Sims relied heavily upon Babcock to assemble an American naval staff around the naval attaché, McDougall, and the paymaster, Lt. Edward C. Tobey. Another American, Tracy Barrett Kittredge, joined Sims as a civilian volunteer. He earlier participated in the California Naval Militia as a student at the University of Berkeley before he attended Oxford University for his graduate studies in history and the classics. He then served under Herbert Hoover with the Belgian Relief Commission.[100] Such experience proved very useful.[101]

Before the American declaration of war, Kittredge moved with relative freedom among headquarters on the European front. His marriage to the daughter of an Italian nobleman, Olympia Scalzi, opened doors for Kittredge.[102] He recalled hearing about the American declaration of war during a meeting with associates on the German General Staff in Berlin. Kittredge thought that the "Germans tried to be decent, but at that they did not succeed very well [as we] were escorted without difficulties to the Swiss border."[103]

Kittredge served as the intelligence officer for Sims in establishing the American naval headquarters at the European front. His associates from earlier studies at Oxford included Frank Birch, Nigel de Gray, and Alastair Denniston—all serving as Royal

Navy Volunteer Reserve officers assigned to the Admiralty inside the Naval Intelligence Division. After a few weeks of working together, Sims summarily commissioned Kittredge as a lieutenant (junior grade) in the US Navy Volunteer Reserve Force (USNVRF).[104] He accepted the appointment and acquired a uniform in the rank of lieutenant.[105] Kittredge became the trusted intermediary between the Admiralty intelligence subdivisions and Sims's London Flagship.

Jellicoe entrusted Sims with the most-sensitive strategic information available to the Admiralty. Jellicoe encouraged Sims to act beyond his formal authority in organizing US Navy operations on the European front.[106] On paper, Sims held the two-star assignment as president of the Naval War College, with collateral duty as the commandant, Narragansett Bay Naval Station. His temporary promotion to three-star rank in June only complicated American strategy when Sims determined that the "only effective way to throw the weight of the US Navy into the war without delay was to use its available units to strengthen the weak spots in other Navies."[107]

Mayo likewise improvised to overcome confusion about the future course of American strategy. Frustrated with Daniels and Benson, Mayo politely requested their acceptance of Atlantic Fleet staff liaisons to coordinate operations with OpNav staff in Washington and Sims in London. Benson disapproved the recommendation without providing an explanation. This bureaucratic insult riled Mayo to send liaisons without asking.[108] Assistant Navy secretary Roosevelt provided top cover by issuing a directive to the fleet commanders to maintain a regular rotation of staff liaisons. Thereafter, Atlantic Fleet liaisons regularly visited the Pacific and Asiatic fleets, under Admirals William B. Caperton and Knight.

Saving his best men for the most-challenging assignments, Mayo sent an all-star Atlantic Fleet team to coordinate with Sims in Europe. The Atlantic Fleet chief of staff, Capt. Orton P. Jackson, along with his loyal subordinates, King and Pye, sailed together to investigate the situation at the front.[109] Upon arrival in London, King found Sims and his small staff of fewer than five personnel completely worn out. His Naval Academy classmate Babcock had collapsed from a "nervous breakdown."[110] Babcock continued progressing in the ranks, although his future among the stars also remained tied with the fate awaiting his strongest supporter—Sims.[111]

Mayo attempted to act as a buffer, simultaneously protecting Sims from the politics of the Navy Department while enabling American forces to organize for maritime operations leading onto far shores of the European front. American military forces lacked experience in such large-scale campaigns. For this reason, Mayo twice sent his staff for extended coordination assignments to the European front, the first beginning in August 1917 through January 1918 and then the second phase from August 1918 through April 1919. During both deployments, King played the key role as the intermediary for Mayo in relations with Sims.[112]

British handlers certainly played Sims against his superiors inside the Navy Department and within the Atlantic Fleet. Sims never fully trusted his immediate superior, Mayo. Past bad blood with Benson also soured the relationships between Sims and Daniels. Quietly holding things together, Roosevelt and Mayo enabled the American naval command to attain administrative equilibrium long enough to avoid complete disaster. This is reflected in the observations compiled by King in "Estimate of the Situation with Regard to the Efficient Development of Operations of the Atlantic Fleet."[113]

Between luncheons and dinner parties with British colleagues, Sims allowed himself to become paranoid about his exact position in the grander malaise of American naval command. From an Atlantic Fleet perspective, Jackson and King pulled no punches in explaining the situation that "Allied difficulties have mostly been caused by lack of foresight."[114] After reading their report, Sims wrote his wife, Anne, that "Jackson and King 'knifed' me as soon as they returned from their trip."[115] "I wrote to Benson last week and told him very plainly that my position would be quite impossible if [Mayo] were sent over here," Sims complained. "I should ask to be relieved."[116]

What Sims failed to understand at the time was that Mayo could not abandon his responsibilities to defend American waters under Plan BLACK. At any moment, Mayo also expected to receive authorization to assume global responsibility as the CinCUS. Protecting his authority as CNO, Benson thwarted Mayo's appointment to assume the functions of CinCUS under Plan BLACK. Making the best of a terrible situation, Mayo used his Atlantic Fleet staff as though he was the CinCUS. Because Mayo accepted his role as the unacknowledged hero of the First World War, Sims inadvertently found himself in the role of being the face of American sea power thereafter. Holding Roosevelt's full support, Sims also received reinforcements for the London Flagship.

Within a six-month period, Roosevelt and Mayo provided Sims with means to expand his headquarters from one assistant and the naval attaché into an organization more than 400 uniformed naval personnel with an additional unknown number of civilian assistants.[117] Always the navy man, Sims maintained his flagship afloat, *Melville*, which technically fell under Mayo for the purposes of supporting Atlantic Fleet operations. Mayo also sent the destroyer tender *Dixie* to augment *Melville*. Capt. Dudley W. Knox recalled walking up the brow during a visit to *Dixie* in Queenstown. At the quarterdeck, Knox noticed a sign characterized the situation. "Yes, you can have it," read the sign—followed by these caveats:

If we haven't got it—we'll get it,
If we can't get it—we'll make it
What is it?[118]

As one of the logistical problems that beset the American flotilla at Queenstown and at other bases in Europe, Sims and the staff in London struggled to negotiate supply issues within the Admiralty. Simultaneously, Sims subjected Navy secretary Daniels and the CNO to an unrelenting bureaucratic barrage of messages, which caused additional controversy in Washington.[119]

DIRECT CONNECTIONS

The Royal Navy educated the US Navy about the strategic interconnections between operations and intelligence.[120] As a liaison to Mayo in Europe, King assisted Knox following his arrival for duty in London at Christmas in 1917. King also assisted Knox in organizing the American Naval Planning Section in London.[121] Through the Planning Section, British concepts for coordinating global operations with intelligence extended through the wireless network running through the London headquarters of Sims.[122] The intelligence officer inside the headquarters, Kittredge, described "a direct telephonic communication between the British and French Admiralties."[123] In addition, the Americans had full access to the Admiralty, which "includes a highly efficient Intelligence Division."[124] The connection between Sims and the Admiralty featured "special telephone and telegraph wires [that] have been installed between the Admiralty and the US Navy Headquarters."[125]

The British fully recognized history as a foundational element in organizing the various analytical methods and technical subfunctions of intelligence. Experience with the British inspired Knox and King to recognize the practical purpose of having eccentric minds—willing to challenge naval dogma—on their team. Among other such figures within the Imperial War Staff, Sir Julian Corbett had a profound influence upon Knox and King. Under Corbett's leadership, the "Historical Section" provided strategic analysis to augment the daily deluge of tactical intelligence, which filtered from the front.[126]

British methods for implementing strategy through administrative command organizations influenced the Americans to learn the art of winning without having to commit forces to the tactical task. The key to winning centered on seizing free access to natural resources—using entrepreneurial means to gain strategic control rather than actual force. These revelations became apparent for King through his close wartime interactions with Royal Navy Rear-Admiral Sir Roger Keyes and Captains Sir Dudley Pound, Sir James Somerville, and Sir Charles Little, who were on the Admiralty planning staff. Royal Navy commodore James Graham, 6th Duke of Montrose, provided Mayo and King a tour of the aircraft carrier HMS *Argus*. Such engagements among British and American naval officers formed the foundations for future collaboration.[127]

Few Americans had the ability to gain such an interesting strategic perspective on the problems inherent with Anglo-American command. As Mayo's trusted agent in relations with Sims and other key commanders in Europe, King witnessed all the problems associated with combined and joint operations at sea and ashore.[128] He was there on that auspicious date on December 7, 1917, when the British formally reorganized the Grand Fleet to include the "Sixth Battle Squadron" under US Navy rear admiral Hugh Rodman. Through significant bureaucratic effort, King managed the arrangements for the Grand Fleet to absorb the coal-fired battleships of the Ninth Battleship Division of the Atlantic Fleet.[129]

Wilson previously rejected recommendations from Sims in reaching the labored decision to commit battleships and the associated elements of the fleet to fight in Europe. Daniels wavered when the CNO, Benson, fought against the idea outright. Through the smoky haze in mirrored rooms from behind the curtains of bureaucratic atrophy, Roosevelt and Mayo quietly enabled the right decisions to become apparent for all involved. The First Sea Lord, Jellicoe, also had a key role in working the lines with Sims and in direct communications with Mayo. With Jellicoe's role obscured by the grandeur of the moment, his successor in command of the Grand Fleet, Royal Navy admiral Sir David Beatty, cast himself in the role of leading the symbolic unification of British and American sea power.[130] The experience of falling under British naval command held significant consequences for the future of American sea power.

CHAPTER 5

The League of Peace and a Free Sea

The British relied upon American resources, which required collaboration at the highest levels of command within the Admiralty and Navy Department. For example, coal from the Scottish North and Wales and the trains carrying the coal to the Grand Fleet became known colloquially as the "Jellicoe Express." Conversely, petroleum proved scarce in the British home islands. The Royal Navy had oil-fired super-dreadnoughts, such as HMS *Queen Elizabeth.*

Given petroleum shortages, Mayo initially withheld the oil-fired battleships in American waters. Mayo coordinated these efforts with RAdm. Albert Gleaves as the commander, Cruiser and Transport Force. Mayo empowered Gleaves to run the convoy system, which complicated relations with Sims in London.[1]

British handlers exploited the petty personality dynamics when American commanders on the European front generally ignored directives emanating from Sims in London. To restore some level of control over American strategy, Mayo acted the part of referee in disputes between Sims and his fellow subordinates. By 1918, Mayo also adopted a special communications cipher to obscure the infighting and to assert direct control among American naval commands at the front.[2] Cmdr. Russell Willson, the Atlantic Fleet communications officer, invented a device designed to double-encrypt communications among US naval forces. British code breakers attempted to solve American communications, as encrypted in the Naval Cipher Box (NCB). The British failed to advise their American friends about their effort to solve these communications, and Willson's design remained the standard. US naval cryptanalysts later learned about British efforts to solve American codes and cyphers, which frustrated discussions concerning future collaboration between the Admiralty and Navy Department.[3]

THE "BOY CAPTAIN"

Transatlantic collaboration tilted upon the question of trust between the British and American governments, which hinged upon mutual interests in relations with other allies among the Entente powers. From his interactions with the Admiralty staff, King progressively understood American sea power as the key to solving the enigma of war in the global maritime arena. He recognized the struggles of the Royal Navy as directly tied to their nostalgic dreams of keeping the imperial system in place. Mentors like Sims and Mayo further influenced King to foster closer collaboration between the fleets deployed to European waters. He respected the British naval tradition, although he stood particularly impressed by the Imperial Japanese Navy officers and sailors. Given this experience at the front, King agreed with the vision articulated by Corbett in pamphlet form in 1917, "The League of Peace and a Free Sea."[4]

Old ideas of Imperial Federation helped shape the British concept of creating the future League of Nations. As an extension of this vision, Jellicoe also envisioned an amalgamated fleet consisting of warships from the major naval powers operating together in both peace and war. The concept of a "League Navy" progressively dominated wardroom discussions on board American warships. The idea also loomed over Jellicoe's invitation to Mayo, as relayed by Sims and separately by King, to inspect the Grand Fleet and other key ports on the European front in the fall of 1917. Royal Navy captain Sir Bertram Ramsay issued similar overtures to Mayo to join the expedition to the Belgian coast in the flagship, HMS *Broke*. Jellicoe and Ramsay hosted Sims and Mayo for their adventure to observe the bombardment of German coastal fortifications at Ostend.[5]

Jellicoe and Ramsay exploited the traditions and popular image of British sea power to put on a show for the Americans. Off Ostend, Ramsay demonstrated his ability to maneuver *Broke* close—a skill that served him very well in planning similar operations roughly two decades later off Normandy.[6] Just as he would nearly two decades later along the shores of Normandy, Ramsay kept the strategic goal in focus during the bombardment of Ostend in 1917. German artillery provided the appropriate backdrop when Ramsay ordered the battle flags of Britania and Columbia to fly at an equal altitude from the mastheads. King stood proud when Jellicoe's flag broke simultaneously alongside Mayo's four-star flag.[7]

Genuine gestures of respect helped solidify the strategic connections between the Royal Navy and US Navy. Experience at the front in Europe inspired King to look outward to consider the future of American sea power.[8] King later described the role of strategic planning as being intertwined with the movement of supplies for operations, which required a clearly designated logistical "commander to control and direct their movements (logistics) and their supply (administration)."[9] Touring the front with Mayo and other members of the Atlantic Fleet staff, the chief of staff, Jackson, suffered severe injuries in a car accident in the French countryside in October 1917.[10] Mayo immediately replaced Jackson with King.[11] At age thirty-nine, King earned positional rank associated with being chief of staff to the Atlantic Fleet commander. For this reason, King earned the nickname "Boy Captain."[12]

Mayo pushed King into the unfamiliar arena of coordinating operational relationships among foreign partners at the front. The meeting with French field marshal Ferdinand Foch during a luncheon in Paris stood out among other occasions. Sims and Mayo sat at the head of the table with Foch, as King took mental notes. King had a working knowledge of French, as did Sims and Mayo. Yet, even the translators experienced a "good deal of difficulty understanding Foch."[13] Sims later joked with King about Foch's accent, saying that it was influenced by too much wine. Following the visit to Paris, King accompanied Mayo through the Italian Alps and Rome. During the tour, King befriended Italian colonel Pietro Badoglio. Notably, King kept in contact after meetings with Captain Suzuki Kantarō on board the Imperial Japanese Navy flagship of Admiral Kōzō Sato, on the cruiser *Akashi*.[14] Roughly two decades later, King's connections with Badaglio and Kantarō helped negotiations concerning the futures of Italy and Japan.

King recognized the interconnections of diplomacy and strategy through the cosmopolitan experience in Europe. Within the context of Grand Fleet, the Royal Navy added Rodman to the rolls along with the American officers of Battle Division 9. Within the Grand Fleet, British commanders honored the Americans by placing them at the rear among the line of battle formation—with designation as the Sixth Battle Squadron. Such symbolic gestures of friendship carried an underlying message about the future relationship with the Americans. US naval officers generally accepted their subordinate role while striving to "remain cheerful."[15]

The Anglo-American forces of the Grand Fleet set a bad precedence for future Royal Navy collaboration with the US Navy. Rodman's flag lieutenant, Jonas H. Ingram, and the gunnery officer, Lt. Roland H. Brainard, filtered reports outlining problems within the American battleship squadron that failed to appear in reports.[16] King included these details within reports submitted separately to Mayo. Rodman never figured out the secret to Mayo's clairvoyance, as articulated in directives transmitted from the Atlantic Fleet. The troubles associated with sailors infected by flu also failed to appear in reports from Rodman.

Mayo knew exactly when to intervene in requesting additional medical reinforcements to lend a hand at the Grand Fleet anchorage in Scapa Flow.[17] He knew that the British always acted as though the "sun never sets" upon the empire in framing partnerships with the Americans.[18] Theodore Roosevelt also warned fellow Americans to tread carefully. Coalitions historically proved difficult, which Roosevelt explained. He warned Americans about the Europeans that "[our] superior virtue in the face of the war-worn nations of the Old World will not make us more acceptable as mediators among them."[19]

CROSSING THE "T"

Centuries of British imperial triumph and maritime tradition left an impression upon American naval officers. Indeed, the British viewed their American cousins as somewhat comedic, overly direct, and overconfident. The British sometimes looked down upon their American cousins.[20] Assistant Secretary of the Navy Franklin D. Roosevelt told the *Daily Mail* that the "United States has no intention of challenging anybody's supremacy [and] there is not a sane person in the United States who thinks of constructing a Fleet for the purpose of disputing Britain's position at sea."[21] Even the Anglophile Sims warned British counterparts to avoid making too many assumptions about American inclinations to lend a hand.[22] Similarly, King noted that the "British have been managing world affairs for well over three hundred years [since] the defeat of the Spanish Armada in 1588."[23] King observed, "History demonstrates [that] we can always do better."[24]

Personality dynamics fueled deep divisions among the American army and navy commanders on the European front. Their ability to cooperate only worsened in the heat of combat. The 1918 spring offensives on the western front and the Bolshevik uprisings shocked the Entente. Pershing's army suffered unnecessarily in counterattacking German storm troopers through the poisoned malaise of gas, machine guns, and mud. Assistant Navy secretary Roosevelt worried about all the American casualties. He insisted upon making a fact-finding visit to Europe in July. In turn, Mayo assigned King as Roosevelt's escort at the front. After Ireland, King sailed with Roosevelt to visit forces in England and up to Scotland before heading to London for meetings with Sims.[25]

Roosevelt first recognized Sims as the right choice for the task of establishing the administrative foothold in the transatlantic relationship. As the coalition evolved, Sims noticeably adopted the British point of view—sometimes at American expense. Roosevelt recognized that the time had arrived for a change. Roosevelt advised Sims to anticipate possible promotion to four-star rank. In January 1918, Sims wrote his wife that "I might be offered Chief of Naval Operations, but [I] would rather have the fleet."[26] Sims thought, "I have worked enough and had better make room for the younger men."[27] Typically, Sims demurred by suggesting that the "law is rigged [CNO] is no good."[28]

The question of American naval command stood among many left unanswered among the associated powers of Europe. Making matters worse, the divisions among British and French forces also fueled problems within the AEF. After meetings in London, Roosevelt and King went to Paris for additional meetings with Pershing and Lejeune. At that time, King split for surprise visits with his brother-in-law, brevet one-star brigadier Walter D. Smith. The sounds of German artillery barrages added to the drama of sitting in the bunker, as King and Smith shared a bottle of wine. King and Smith smoked cigars and told tall tales before visiting the field headquarters of Brig. Gen. Douglas MacArthur. At the front, King approached a group of German prisoners. He smoked cigarettes with the enemy. King found the discipline impressive among German prisoners.[29]

Touring the western front and along the Riviera, King noted the personality dynamics among strategic commanders. Within the multinational context of command on the western front and in European waters, the AEF operated in a subordinate role, as other Allied forces engaged the enemy more closely on the western front. American troops and supplies sat idly as the French and British armies continued to carry the weight. Maj. Gen. John A. Lejeune consolidated Marine regiments to form the Fourth Brigade under the US Army's Second Division, which maneuvered under the AEF at the European front after July 1918. Simultaneously, Lejeune assisted Pershing in efforts to coordinate operations with the "Rainbow Division" under MacArthur. This amalgamation of National Guard regiments struggled in the face of a well-entrenched and combat-seasoned enemy.[30]

In conversations with AEF troops at the front, King noted logistical bottlenecks along the roads leading to the trenches. Poor logistical planning hindered the AEF. King noted this shortfall. During a visit to Brest, King discovered evidence of mismanagement under Rear Admiral Henry Braid Wilson. King accused Wilson of failing to understand the consequences of failure. Wilson ordered King to falsify his reports to Mayo. Shocked, King told Wilson in direct terms that he served "overseas on duty for Admiral Mayo, to whom he would tell the truth, and not what he was *asked* to tell."[31]

Given the troubles surrounding Wilson in France, other commanders struggled to decipher the exact chain of command in Europe. King recalled that "Sims and Wilson couldn't agree on anything in Brest [and] always hated each other."[32] Sims also tangled with RAdm. Joseph Strauss, the commander of the Mine Forces in the North Sea. Meanwhile, Sims struggled to coordinate operations with Niblack at Gibraltar. In dealings with European partners at the front, Anglo-French commanders exploited problems of American organization. Observing from below, King drew lessons from First World War experiences to frame his own ideas about the future of coalition operations and American sea power.

THE LEAGUE NAVY

The Entente allies courted their American counterparts to join in the vision of a future coalition of navies. Strategic negotiations between London and Paris with Washington influenced multinational operations at the front in the First World War, as the British and French empowered the Americans to lead combined efforts in Siberia, the

Mediterranean and Adriatic Seas, and beyond in East Asia and the Pacific.[33] Indeed, the British concept of Imperial Federation gained momentum through the efforts of Lord Arthur Balfour.[34] As foreign secretary, Balfour harbored dreams of regaining influence among the lost dominions in the Americas. He envisioned the establishment of a League of Nations and an associated "League of Nations Navy."[35] The idea sparked debates within the US Navy. Sims and Pratt strongly endorsed the vision of a "League Navy." King also joked with British friends that the "capitol of the reunited British Empire would be in Washington, DC."[36]

King George V joined the diplomatic charm offensive to spark a lasting alliance between the British Empire and America. For the first time in the century after the War of Independence, the British monarchy formally recognized the Fourth of July as a holiday worthy of celebrating American sovereignty. The king then attended the baseball game between the US Army and US Navy teams at the football stadium at Stamford Bridge on the outskirts of London. Before the ballgame on the Fourth of July 1918, the minister of munitions, Winston S. Churchill, delivered an oration in the ancient grandeur of Central Hall at Westminster. Sims represented the Americans as the guest of honor. Capt. Ernest J. King sat in the balcony overlooking the proceedings, as Churchill took to the podium. He referred to the rebellion of Oliver Cromwell before naming such American luminaries as Benjamin Franklin and George Washington. Then, Churchill artfully suggested that the

> Declaration of Independence is not only an American document; it follows on Magna Carta and the Petition of Right as the third of the great title deeds on which the liberties of the English-speaking race are founded. By it we lost an Empire, but by it we also preserved an Empire.[37]

Sims later described the Churchill's delivery as "being one of the most eloquent speeches I have ever heard."[38] Sims gushed that Churchill "will have considerable influence upon our relations in the future [and] there is no doubt about the intellectual capacity of this man."[39] When asked to speak after Churchill, Sims recognized that he would "have to be very careful not to make one of my customary indiscreet remarks" as he had at Guildhall.[40] Instead of extemporaneous remarks, Sims read from a carefully crafted speech, as prepared by his staff, and as vetted by King in conjunction with Mayo. Later that afternoon, King joined Sims in observing the moment when King George V signed a baseball for the winning US Navy team.[41]

The ballgame at Stamford Bridge appeared in British media as a happy gesture, whereas American newspapers characterized the event as a final victory. British onlookers set aside past rivalries with the Americans to mark the centenary of George Washington's success during the War of Independence.[42] An estimated 70,000 fans observed King George V walking with Sims to home plate. The king then accepted a clean white Spalding baseball featuring red and bluish stitches. The king signed the American baseball "George, R.I., July 4th 1918." George V had acquiesced to sign an American baseball, though the "R.I." after his signature still referred to his traditional status as the "Rex Imperator." American newspapers described the baseball signed by the king as the "instrument of surrender."[43]

British and American commanders on the European front struggled to navigate underlying differences of doctrine and tradition. Drawing from wartime experiences in Europe, King developed clear opinions about the Admiralty and the Royal Navy during the yearly Grand Fleet exercises of 1918. The Grand Fleet commander, Beatty, explained the scenario for the exercises to Sims and Mayo at the London Flagship. In a gesture of collaboration, Beatty invited King and Pye to sail as exercise observers on board the flagship, HMS *Queen Elizabeth*. King took a dim view of Beatty as a commander but recognized his genius as a showman.

Beatty planned to replicate his earlier performance at Jutland, maneuvering the Grand Fleet into position to surprise the opposing force. The destroyers and aerial scouting forces, under Vice-Admiral Sir Frederick Doveton Sturdee, replicated the Imperial German High Seas Fleet during the Grand Fleet maneuvers. As he had during the Battle of the Falklands three years earlier, Sturdee used the weather to obscure his force—catching Beatty off guard. In a feat akin to that of Nelson in the 1797 Battle of the Nile, Sturdee cornered Beatty's force from two directions. Sturdee then proceeded to "Cross the T," systematically dividing Beatty's line of battle. The Grand Fleet had been humiliated in this simulated battle. Beatty acted as though his mistake had been part of an elaborately planned ruse.[44] Beatty maintained a commanding presence throughout the embarrassing spectacle, which inspired King and Pye to chuckle. Beatty later complained to Mayo about the behavior of King and Pye.[45] Although humiliated, Beatty simply cinched his hat to a jaunty angle and stuffed his hands in his pockets. He then confidently walked off the bridge with bravado and complimentary words about the excellent maneuvers. The vanity of Beatty appeared comedic, as King and Pye raised practical concerns about operating warships within the context of a fleet. First World War experiences inspired King to develop a "very strong (personal) opinion [against] 'mixed forces.'"[46]

Service in Europe similarly propelled King into other influential circles within the American government and naval organization. Wartime requirements had opened the ranks for younger officers to secure promotions at a faster pace than in peacetime. Already serving under Mayo as the temporary chief of staff in the Atlantic Fleet, King also received the positional temporary promotion to the rank of captain in October 1918. Mayo put King at center stage in negotiations with the Entente, in relations with Sims, with Pershing, and with the various secretaries of state, war, and Navy—all before King's fortieth birthday. Mayo's mentoring approach also groomed King for future high command in the global maritime arena.

Among the younger associates of Sims and Mayo, American naval officers developed a completely new understanding of global strategy. Friendships blossomed among the younger naval professionals within the European and American fleets. Joining other Atlantic Fleet veterans, King participated in the transatlantic fraternity of British and American naval officers within the Queenstown Association. The organization convened for black-tie dinners and associated events for many decades after the war. Jellicoe and Bayly customarily participated in the Queenstown Association. Other prominent American members included Sims, Mayo, Pringle, Taussig, Knox, Stark, and Halsey. British naval officers fostered lasting friendships with their American counterparts through such fraternal organizations as the Queenstown Association after the First World War.[47] The British also extended honorary reciprocal memberships in the global network of gentlemen's clubs for their American friends.[48]

The spirit of collaboration ran high among British and American naval officers, which fueled the vision for an ongoing special connection between the navies of Britannia and Columbia. By pooling fleet resources, the British attempted to convince like-minded Americans to participate in an Anglo-American naval partnership in Asiatic waters. In 1918, King witnessed the conversation when Roosevelt and Sims discussed plans to refine the American command organization in Europe. Roosevelt suggested that Sims "should be prepared to accept a promotion."[49] King overheard Roosevelt musing about Sims having the opportunity to become the CNO or, possibly, a seagoing fleet commander in four-star rank. Sims demurred, preferring to secure a seagoing fleet command. At that point, Roosevelt floated the idea of nominating Sims as prospective relief for Adm. Austin M. Knight, the commander, Asiatic Fleet. As Jellicoe had gone down under to coordinate British affairs in Asiatic waters, Roosevelt thought the assignment of Sims to the same region fit the circumstances of 1918.

Stars seemed to come into alignment as Sims emerged as the most likely choice for the mission of setting the foundations for an Anglo-American naval alliance to safeguard common interests in Asia. The armistice of November 11, 1918, frustrated the plan to send Sims to Asia, as US naval forces drifted beyond Europe and into the confused waters of Bolshevik revolution.[50] While inspecting the Imperial German High Seas Fleet at Scapa Flow, King witnessed the arguments between Anglo-French and American leaders.[51] As negotiations between the Entente and Central Powers proceeded, Anglo-French and American diplomats stood divided about the focus of war reparations, restoring the imperial order, and the future distribution of interned enemy warships. Imperial German warships sat idly at anchor under Anglo-French and American guns at Scapa Flow, which caused heated debates between Paris, London, and Washington.[52]

The Wilson administration struggled to navigate the uncharted waters in the nexus between peace and war at Versailles. In efforts to impose peace upon the Central Powers, the British and French pushed for major military expeditions in the eastern Mediterranean—thereby reducing the imperial footprints of Austro-Hungary and the Ottomans. The Americans took the alternate view of concentrating all efforts in European waters from the British Isles, with military forces ashore positioned to drive from the French countryside into the heart of Germany. The American troops standing watch on the Rhine loomed like a bayonet at the throat of greater Germany. Anglo-French differences with the Americans in solving the continental problems of Europe remained unresolved during the world wars and throughout the twentieth century. The debate deeply influenced younger American naval thinkers of King's generation.[53]

Wine-and-cheese experiences with the chateau generals and monarchs of Europe proved formative for the Americans. Mentors like Sims and Mayo also provided an example for King in considering problems of multinational command in wartime. During the negotiations at Versailles, King participated in the promotion ceremony when Sims received four-star rank on December 18, 1918. Coincident with this development, Mayo finally received designation of CinCUS to augment his influence during the Versailles negotiations in January 1919, "which caused a good deal of confusion at the time."[54] In relations with other fleet commanders, Mayo "did not in any way act differently than before."[55] However, Sims and Mayo stood oddly out of place with the arrivals of Benson and Daniels at Versailles.

The British vision of the Imperial Federation intermixed with the fundamental problem of American sea power, which stood in the balance when the Wilson administration grappled with the effort to negotiate with foreign regimes in the smoky mirrored rooms of Versailles. Wilson also repackaged the message of H. G. Wells in *The War to End War*, to seek an equitable "peace without victory."[56] Wilson modified the vision of American sea power, which coincided with the deaths of past luminaries, Admiral Mahan in 1914 and then Admirals Luce and Dewey in 1917. The guns then stood silent in the First World War when the negotiations at Versailles commenced. Coincidentally, the former president, Roosevelt, died in January 1919. "Theodore Roosevelt is dead," Sims wrote a friend. "I have been able to think of nothing else for days."[57]

A SICK PEACE

The death of Roosevelt upset many American naval professionals, as the influenza pandemic loomed over negotiations at Versailles. During the period of uncertainty in the spring of 1919, Mayo and King traveled extensively throughout Europe. King recalled the humming sounds of wireless equipment and the huge antennae at the "Lafayette Radio" station in Bordeaux. Commanders Leigh Noyes and Russell Willson, the communications specialists on the Atlantic Fleet staff, reveled in the power of the transatlantic signal. King then accompanied Mayo along the Riviera to Rome before making the round trip back to Versailles and onward to London. King toured the German submarine SM *U-155*, and then the American warships at Rosyth and up to Scapa Flow. Considering the future of an Anglo-French and American maritime alliance in the Atlantic, the dreamy vision of a similar transpacific coalition with imperial Japan appeared possible to some US naval thinkers.

Problems bubbled beneath the surface of the friendly façade among the Anglo-French and associated American powers. Before making the historic journey to appear at Versailles, President Wilson bartered the future of American sea power. British policies, as advocated by Prime Minister David Lloyd George, along with the British concept of Imperial Federation intermixed with the impractically American utopian dream of Wilson's "fourteen points" and a future "League of Nations." Conversely, the British naturally maneuvered to retaining future supremacy in the global maritime arena—especially in shaping relations with the Americans and the Japanese. The illusion of solidarity faded into the ethereal debates concerning the efforts to organize the future "League Navy."[58]

The League Navy concept also provided means by which to mitigate tensions among these key naval powers, as Anglo-American and French diplomats quietly worried about the rising influence of imperial Japan in Asia. The vision of a multinational naval alliance among the seagoing powers held significant appeal among the associates of Jellicoe and Sims. In 1919, King George V created the 1st Earl of Jellicoe, Admiral of the Fleet John Jellicoe, in anticipation of his Empire Naval Mission to the Pacific. With his newly minted title, Jellicoe embraced the general concept of a future League Navy. Jellicoe joined Sims in efforts to convince other Americans about the merits of naval coalitions in peacetime, along with imperial Japanese admiral Funakoshi Kaijishiro.[59]

Historical alliances among multinational coalitions frequently failed under the weight of conflicting national policies and dissimilar cultural dynamics. Among other examples, King recalled the exploits of Nelson during the Trafalgar campaign. During the epic battle of 1805, Nelson exploited the divisions between the French and Spanish fleets by "driving the British force through the enemy line of battle and crossing the 'T' with full broadsides . . . confusion on the enemy ships won the day more than the actual destruction of the enemy fleets [and] this is the real lesson of Trafalgar."[60]

Confusion about the differing policies among the Entente powers similarly influenced the steady collapse of the Central Powers. Under the circumstances, the Anglo-French, Japanese, and American naval staffs also struggled to unify strategic differences under a coherent command organization. The Allied Naval Council provided one means to achieve the collective strategic end, although the Wilson administration refused to allow Sims the requisite freedom to act as a fully vested participant in the ongoing strategic conversations among the Entente powers. The European problems also extended to Asia, as the Wilson administration scurried to maintain the "Open Door" to China.

Recognizing the stakes, assistant Navy secretary Roosevelt uniquely understood the importance of having a place at the tables of discussion within the Allied Naval Council. Roosevelt made preliminary arrangements to send Sims to the Asiatic Fleet in four-star rank. With Jellicoe already heading to the region, Funakoshi and Sims also shared common views about the League Navy concept. The Jellicoe-Sims-Funakoshi cabal soon faced resistance from within the Allied Naval Council. British overtures rang hollow among Wilson administration skeptics—and especially Daniels and Benson—in negotiations concerning future fleet construction among the major sea powers at Versailles.[61]

The League Navy seemed fiendishly *British* among the Anglophobic ranks of the Wilsonadministration, rendering Anglophiles like Roosevelt and Sims to suffer in frustration about the raging debates concerning the future League of Nations. The British dream of an Imperial Federation inspired Balfour to press the Wilson administration to embrace the quasi-American vision for the League of Nations. In the spirit of transatlantic collaboration, the First Sea Lord, Wemyss, failed to recognize the bubbling tensions below the happy façade of Anglo-American collaboration as the delegates gathered at Versailles.

Wemyss developed close friendships with Sims and Mayo, which transcended the combined ranks of the Royal Navy and US Navy in European waters. When the Wilson administration sent representatives to participate in negotiations at Versailles, Wemyss stood completely shocked by the openly hostile attitude of his immediate American counterpart, Benson.[62] During what Daniels later called the "Naval Battle of Paris," Wemyss and Benson dueled over the future. Wemyss spoke in proper King's English to Benson—like a frustrated teacher educating his slow-minded student. In response, Benson burst into a foul tirade, as punctuated by sailorly language. Benson diverted negotiations into the gutter at Versailles.[63] Wilson administration officials stood silent when Benson acted the part of an American bull in the Hall of Mirrors at Versailles. The vision of a League Navy was reflected in the shattered shards at the feet of Daniels when he then snubbed Roosevelt—refusing without explanation to make the announcement to name Sims as the prospective commander of the Asiatic Fleet.

Roosevelt's carefully maneuvered chess pieces all stood in place for the League Navy concept, as envisioned under the nascent alliance among the associated Jellicoe-Sims-Funakoshi naval cabal. Standing in four-star rank with nowhere else to go and with five years to serve before mandatory retirement, Sims also represented a clear path to establish a future League Navy for that brief fleeting moment in the spring of 1919.[64] Sims earlier directed the Planning Section of Knox to conceptualize the League Navy and means by which to employ American forces under the vision.[65] Mayo similarly employed King in coordinating the studies ongoing under Pratt.[66] At that time, Sims told Pratt that "I think your dope about Japan is about right [and] I do not think we will have anything to fear from them."[67]

The global balance hinged upon cooperation among the European and Asian navies in conjunction with military reductions among the armies ashore. Such measures proved increasingly difficult. The Bolshevik Revolution pulled American forces to Siberia, as did coincidental problems in the Balkans and Levant.[68] Burgeoning revolutions on the far shores of Asia further complicated negotiations concerning the future character and organization of the League Navy.[69] The Armistice loomed over labored deliberations at Versailles, like the flu pandemic lingering over America at that time.[70] The Wilson administration likewise lost interest as the various foreign delegations at Versailles fought over the German High Seas Fleet. With the Treaty of Versailles concluded in June 1919, the Germans scuttled their own fleet at Scapa Flow. In so doing, the Germans inadvertently settled disputes among the Entente powers—leaving the Americans to spinoff into a decade of peacetime decadence of the Prohibition.[71]

FLEETS IN BEING

Morale blossomed for war volunteers and reservists seeking to return to their civilian careers upon their return to America. Conversely, the spirits dried up among US naval professionals when Daniels announced plans to reorganize the seagoing fleets for the purposes of reducing the number of four- and three-star commands. Daniels ignored Roosevelt and Sims by naming RAdm. Robert Coontz as prospective Asiatic Fleet commander. Daniels further humiliated Sims by nominating his wartime subordinates to hold four-star fleet commands in the Pacific and Atlantic, with Rodman slated for four-star fleet command as the prospective relief for Knight in the Pacific and with Wilson as the relief for Mayo in the Atlantic.

Daniels bumbled efforts to appease the divergent opinions of Roosevelt and Benson with inartful decisions about future command appointments. Subordinates of Sims received the key assignments, leaving him to feel the velvet stiletto of Benson as delivered by the muddling hands of Daniels. From December 1918 to April 1919, Sims stood in four-star rank while awaiting orders to the Asiatic Fleet. Benson also menaced the effort, as Roosevelt pushed Daniels to announce Sims as the CNO or as a prospective replacement for Mayo as the CinCUS. The four-star office of CinCUS also lapsed in the absence of a clear declaration of war after Mayo reported to the General Board on June 30, 1919.[72] The League Navy faded with the falling stars when Sims requested immediate reassignment to his position—in two-star rank—president of the Naval War College. Sims wryly mused about relieving Daniels "from the embarrassment of not knowing what to do with me."[73]

The departure of Sims from negotiations at Versailles for the self-inflicted exile to Newport marked the beginning of another chapter in his revolutionary career. Sims predicted the future by thwarting efforts by the army to unify American sea power through the backchannels of the Joint Board. By seeking the heroes' welcome in Newport, Sims accepted the associated reduction from four-star rank as a *promotion* to a more useful purpose in two stars as president of the Naval War College. Daniels failed to recognize the rage bubbling behind the stoic façade when Sims used his nomination for the newly established Distinguished Service Medal as an opportunity to rage against the bureaucratic machine within the Navy Department.

Daniels and Sims inadvertently opened opportunities for competitors within the Departments of War and State to seek bureaucratic control over American sea power.

Indeed, Daniels inadvertently made matters worse by correctly portraying Sims as the face of the future—largely ignoring the role of Mayo as the actual hero of American sea power in the First World War. Rivals in the War Department meanwhile seized the opportunity to exploit the controversy. In September 1919, Pershing received the unprecedented promotion of four gold stars as general of the armies—equating him in popular stature to General George Washington.[74]

War Department propaganda centered on the chiseled mythos of Pershing, among other historical generals from Washington to Grant. Recognizing the army challenge, Roosevelt pushed Sims to accept a ceremonial rank to replicate the functions previously performed by the late admiral Dewey on the Navy General Board. Daniels, in turn, lauded Sims as the living embodiment of historic naval heroes John Paul Jones, David Glasgow Farragut, and Dewey.[75] Unwilling to play along, Sims developed a long list of grievances against the Pictorial Bureau within the Navy Department. Daniels became the focus of Sims's ire.[76]

Daniels further enraged Sims with proposals to unify the army and naval war colleges by shuttering the original institution and symbolic home of American sea power. Daniels wanted to move the war college from Rhode Island to Washington, DC. Daniels earlier riled Sims with musing about ambitions to "make the Navy a great university [with] college extensions afloat and ashore."[77] He described every warship as a "school [where] every enlisted man and petty and warrant officer should receive the opportunity to improve his mind, better his position and fit himself for promotion."[78] Daniels seemed utterly childlike to Sims.[79] He completely dismissed the idea of amalgamating the army and naval war colleges in noting that the "clouds are not trees, dirt is not water, and deserts are not seas."[80]

Wartime paths to glory inspired Sims to ponder whether the question of responsibility fell to civilian policymakers or to service practitioners. Sims had returned from Europe on a mission to win the peace during his second tenure as the president of the Naval War College.[81] His wife, Anne, considered Sims as completely changed from the cheerful warrior she had loved before the war. Anne thought Sims suffered from a "spiritual loneliness that, I believe, increased with him from that time until his death."[82] She recalled that after "weeks went on he realized that the time had come to 'set his face toward Jerusalem' [and] he finally spoke to me about the pile of manuscripts on his desk."[83]

CRUSADING FOR THE ONLY TRUE CHURCH

Reckoning with the unbridled carnage of war in the wireless world of competition in an era of unsettled peace inspired American naval practitioners to reconsider the future of sea power. The propaganda of Daniels also annoyed King, as Mayo humbly sat in the shadows when the Pictorial Bureau cast Sims as the navy equivalent to Pershing. The humility exhibited by Mayo inspired King, as the limelight fell upon Pershing and Sims.[84] Pershing nurtured the myth, whereas Sims could not be had—by anyone and especially Daniels.[85] To contrast with the heroic image of Pershing in American memory, Sims followed the difficult path of righteous rebellion in articulating his disgust for politics and war. Sims also criticized fellow naval professionals for making the "assumption that an officer must kill a lot of people in order to gain distinction."[86]

Pershing embraced the stoic image of being the modern equivalent to Washington and Grant, whereas naval officer equivalents sought a brighter horizon. Mayo focused on taking care of veterans after service on the General Board. With two Medals of Honor and a Brevet Medal, Maj. Gen. Smedley D. Butler also stood with the disenchanted First World War veterans during the Prohibition era. Unlike Mayo's quiet Vermonter approach, Butler vocally broke ranks to advocate for the working classes by indicting the wealthy industrialists and profiteers of war in his treatise *War Is a Racket*. Taking a similar tack, Sims engaged in a backchannel battle with Daniels through muckraking interlocutors in the media, including Henry Reuterdahl, Burton Hendrick, and John Ratham.[87]

The schism between Daniels and Sims proved deeply detrimental with coinciding headlines about the Newport sex scandal. Salacious accounts of sailors snorting cocaine while dressed in drag at the local YMCA delighted the muckraking media—as taxpayers pondered the future of American sea power.[88] Meanwhile, assistant Navy secretary Roosevelt played all political sides of the scandal. At first, he condemned the sailors involved. Roosevelt then intervened on behalf of the accused. During this period, King remarked that "one ought to be suspicious of anyone who won't take a drink or doesn't like women."[89]

Congress launched a very public investigation of Daniels and the Navy Department, largely on the basis of a letter written by Sims that leaked into the media.[90] King accused Sims of being a "show[-]off."[91] King explained that "because of Sims's temperament [and] while admiring many of his ideas, [he] was never one of the group of Sims's devoted disciples and followers."[92] This disingenuous statement by King contrasted with his characterization of Sims as the "man who changed the navy."[93] Just as any master is often surpassed by a former pupil, Sims set an example that King struggled to avoid. King identified that Mayo "was the man for me."[94] King also agreed with the sentiments of Capt. William D. Leahy that "Admiral Sims provides a splendid example of what not to do."[95]

CHAPTER 6
Eclipse

Having served in close quarters with Sims and Mayo in navigating the hazards of combined command in Europe, the younger generation of King drew lessons from the chaotic experience in coordinating differing strategic objectives among multinational forces within the context of US naval operations. Older officers, like Rear Admirals Rodman and Wilson, belittled the wartime upstarts, like thirty-nine-year-old King—calling him the "boy captain."[1] Rodman and Wilson seemed myopic and outdated to King. Following the flag of Sims into the postwar reckoning, King further agreed that the "Naval War College should be made one of the principal assets of the Naval Service."[2] Amplifying the point, Sims recommended decommissioning warships to expand the Naval War College, to "avoid decreasing the efficiency of the education of our officers."[3]

Naval practitioners returned from war with looming questions concerning the future focus of American sea power. Following their return from Versailles, Sims and Mayo focused on improving the quality of professional naval education. King took orders as the officer in charge of the Naval Postgraduate School in Annapolis. Knox joined Sims in Newport as chief of staff in the Strategy and Operations Department. Pringle and Taussig also joined reserve lieutenant Tracy Barrett Kittredge, to Newport.[4] In 1919, Knox and Kittredge organized the "Historical Section"—following the example of Sir Julian Corbett.[5] Among other veterans of the London Flagship, Knox and Kittredge recruited reserve lieutenant Philip B. Whelpley to serve with a yearly general service civilian appointment with a salary of $2,900.00 within the Historical Section of the Naval War College.[6]

Fighting the political crosswinds and prevailing undercurrents, the Historical Section concept provided a means by which to use the past as a relatively benign mechanism for examining problems of modern focus. Already suffering from early symptoms of polio, Assistant Secretary Roosevelt later used his influence to arrange an assignment for Knox to build upon his work at the Naval War College as the officer in charge within a coequal "Historical Section," as later designated Op-16-E within ONI.[7] Knox rekindled his previous intellectual partnership with Pye to shape arguments articulated by Capt. Harry E. Yarnell and Lt. Holloway H. Frost in their report titled "The Conduct of an Overseas Naval Campaign."[8] Looking outward, they used history as the foundation for expanding the futuristic vision of American sea power within the global maritime arena.[9]

The Naval War College provided the forum within which Sims fused the past with the future vision of American sea power. In an article, "Naval War College," Sims outlined peacetime purposes for naval professionals to continue fighting for the definitive end of war. In lectures and published works, Sims voiced strong support for the League of Nations and the associated creation of an international naval peacekeeping force among the key seagoing powers.[10] Despite the abortive effort to organize the League Navy as a strategic network of seagoing powers, Sims still believed in the capacity of American sea power to attain the sustainable end of war in the global maritime arena. History provided means by which Sims framed the future.[11]

Rallying the younger generation to this cause, Sims used the ongoing debates concerning the future of American sea power to influence the military policy of the United States. Differences between military tactics in operations ashore provided an opportunity for Sims to advance the cause of professional *naval* education. Sims fostered an ally to the cause after reading an essay published by King in the *Proceedings* under the title "Some Ideas about the Effects of Increasing the Size of Battleships."[12] Sims congratulated King on the essay. Typically, Sims also warned King about the still-unrealized potential of submarines and aviation in the new wireless world of battleships. Sims also hoped to recruit King as an ally, given his assignment to reopen the Naval Postgraduate School in Annapolis in 1919.[13]

Sims acted behind bureaucratic curtains to rally the younger generation to pull together under the cause of professional *naval* education. With Knox and Kittredge researching the problem from within the Historical Section at the Naval War College, Sims also recruited King into the discussion at the Postgraduate School. Knox and King also brought Pye into the deliberations, since his position at ONI provided access to key policy documents inside the Navy Department. By the summer of 1919, they compiled the Knox-Pye-King (K-P-K) Report. After they submitted their preliminary findings to BuNav, the K-P-K Report mysteriously disappeared. One of King's spies at BuNav, Capt. Hayne Ellis, advised that several senior officers took deep exception upon reading the K-P-K Report assertion that ranking naval officers had only been, "educated to the lowest commissioned grade."[14] The elders responded in kind after the publication of the K-P-K Report. Among their first targets, Knox faced the likelihood of reverting to a lower rank.

Knox stood too junior in lineal standing to hold his temporary wartime appointment to the accelerated rank of captain. He also faced the pruning process within the Medical Retention Board. Knox faced the likelihood of being transferred to the retired list. Under the circumstances, Sims made a last-ditch effort to preempt the retention board by arranging orders for Knox to a seagoing command, with the added title honorific functions as commodore on the flagship USS *Brooklyn*, which carried designation as the flagship for Destroyer Flotilla in the Pacific Fleet. Sims also gave Knox the missionary task of serving as the first—and only—president of the Naval War College in San Diego, California. Just as Knox gained headway, *Brooklyn* appeared on the decommissioning list—along with its skipper, Knox. Deemed unfit for sea duty by the Bureau of Naval Medicine (BuMed), Knox embraced his fate, using his naval rank throughout his forced retirement.

Navy Department allies provided opportunity for Knox to work his way to the highest levels of influence on the public stage and within the ranks of the federal civil service. As a tombstone captain on the retired list, Knox parlayed past naval experience to secure work as a journalist. He used his naval rank in retirement as chief editor at the *Army and Navy Journal*. Working in civilian attire while covering the Washington Naval Conference, Knox recognized the proceedings as a historical turning point.[15] He condemned the delegates for creating conditions that inevitably undercut chances for future peace in the global maritime arena. He criticized the agreements concluded at the Washington Naval

Conference as a betrayal, in noting that the "wastage of men and wealth during the World War was so great, and the process of reconstruction so slow afterward, that there was still serious danger of world bankruptcy three years after the Armistice."[16]

INTO THE BLACK CHAMBER

Anglo-American collaboration with imperial Japan held the potential to blossom under the stunted dream of a League of Nations Navy.[17] Backchannel deals and cryptologic cheating on the part of the Americans doomed negotiations during the Washington Naval Conference. The 5-5-3 ratio favored the Anglo-American fleets and placed the Japanese at a mathematical disadvantage.[18] The lopsided peacetime arrangements struck between the Europeans and Americans put the Asian empires on course for a future war. During the Washington Naval Conference, the American cryptologist Herbert O. Yardley monitored the message traffic between the various foreign participants.

British and American cryptographers anticipated the negotiation authorities governing the Japanese delegation at the Washington Naval Conference. Having served as a US Army cryptologist with William F. Friedman in the First World War, Yardley fused information within the "Black Chamber" to provide information from within the War Department to the Departments of Navy and State. Yardley's team read the secret communications between Tokyo and the Japanese negotiators.[19] However, Secretary of State Henry L. Stimson dismissed Yardley by stating that "gentlemen do not read each other's mail."[20]

Unemployed and without means, Yardley began writing a memoir about his service as a US Army intelligence officer. He then talked about his work in the State Department in *The American Black Chamber*.[21] With bridges burned south of the border, Yardley left for Canada. He found work in the burgeoning Canadian intelligence bureaucracy, which further frustrated diplomatic relations between the British Empire and the United States. Yardley later faded into the opium dreamworld and debauchery on the wild western frontiers of Asia.[22]

Competing for control in the Asiatic, imperial Japan ended the collaborative naval relationships with the British and Americans. Similar to Yardley, the British journalist Hector C. Bywater described a future naval conflict of unprecedented scale in the fictional *Great Pacific War: A History of the American-Japanese Campaign of 1931–33*.[23] Published shortly after the Washington Naval Conference and the conclusion of the Five-Power Treaty of 1923, the *Great Pacific War* reads like the script of a tabletop naval war game. He used *Jane's All the World's Fighting Ships* to provide accurate orders of battle, basing his characters on actual personalities and actual geography.[24] Bywater exploited contacts within the ranks of the Royal Navy and US Navy to spin provocative tales of future fictional wars.[25]

Bywater and Yardley abandoned the gentlemanly constraints that governed the protocols of secrecy by publishing details of intelligence activities, which general readers had no actual need to know. On the literary battlefields, Sims also won the battle of public opinion upon receiving a Pulitzer Prize for his ghostwritten indictment as articulated in his purposely ironic title *The Victory at Sea*. His most poisonous condemnations of Daniels appeared between the lines of Kittredge's *Naval Lessons of the Great War*. Readers applauded Sims and Kittredge for setting the historical record straight, at least from their points of view. Joining the debate, Knox further indicted the terms concluded by the

Washington Naval Treaty within the text of *Eclipse of American Sea Power*. Knox invoked Republican senator Henry Cabot Lodge and the Democratic Franklin D. Roosevelt to explain his "professional interpretation [about] the wisdom of Secretary Roosevelt's advice [that] under the new conditions the United States must keep up her 'Treaty Navy' if the great experiment is to succeed."[26]

Roosevelt used the image of American sea power to portray the naval services as a unifying element in American culture. Sailors of all economic classes pulled together with those of all racial backgrounds, although the internal divisions between officers and deckhands seemed to mimic the relationships between aristocrats and slaves. Naval service required all hands to pull together—all sharing equal responsibility in facing the judgment of the cruel sea. The service reflected the nation for Roosevelt—adding his voice to Navy League efforts to push the first "Navy Day" in 1922. Sims and Knox also helped set the date to coincide with Theodore Roosevelt's birthday of October 27.[27]

The Roosevelt family rekindled the candles in resurrecting the religious fervor about the future of American sea power. Working from both sides of the political aisles of Congress, the Roosevelts rallied the disciples of Luce and Mahan. Joining the cause, Sims and Knox worked with Roosevelt's cousin—the assistant secretary of the Navy, Theodore Douglas Robinson, in refining the familiar slogan "Join the Navy and *See* the World." Robinson changed it to "Join the Navy and *Show* the World."[28] His predecessor and cousin, Franklin, later floated the slogan "Join the Navy and *Free* the World."[29] He later changed the slogan to "Join the Navy and *Save* the World."[30]

HIS OWN LITTLE YACHTING CLUB

The cutthroat bureaucratic battles between the army pilots and naval aviators inspired Moffett and his acolytes to form their administrative phalanx to ward off attacks from within the Departments of War and Navy. Aviation and submarine technologies influenced the decisions of many US naval professionals. Younger officers tended to seek earlier command opportunities outside the ranks beyond the clubhouse organization among the battleship fleet. Middle-ranking officers, like King, quit the big-gun fraternity upon reaching the crossroads between the old and new. Having attained his captaincy early, King had also checked the prerequisites for attaining flag rank. Youth counted against chances for another early promotion as the stars lined up against him. King anticipated the bureaucratic undercurrents when the US Navy dissolved the geographically fixed fleets of the Pacific and Atlantic to form the single United States Fleet.

On paper, the Navy secretary retained full control over the shore establishment and seagoing fleets, with the CNO acting as an adviser. Under General Order 94 of December 8, 1922, the CinCUS reemerged from the conceptual bureaucratic depths of the Joint Board. The CNO lost control over seagoing forces with the dissolution of the Atlantic and Pacific Fleets. After 1923, the CNO remained tied to the Washington battlefield while the CinCUS had actual four-star *seagoing* command over the Battle Fleet and the Scouting Fleet, which later evolved into the "Battle Forces" and "Scouting Forces." CinCUS controlled the warships and global operations, although the CNO had superior authority over the four-star commander in the Asiatic Fleet.

Efficiencies gained through electronic communications conversely added layers of administration, which rarely affected the on-the-spot decisions of naval commanders of the past. Centralization under the Navy secretary also amplified the bureaucratic processes for making decisions within the seagoing ranks. Technology reduced the traditional geographic distances such that flag officers and warship skippers lamented that the "laying of cables spoiled the Asiatic Station."[31] Seagoing professionals lamented their new role of being "a damned errand boy at the end of a telegraph wire."[32]

Rivalries among the staffs of four- and three-star flag officers continued as before, although the number of two-star headquarters also expanded. Flag officers filled jobs previously performed by lieutenants, tripling the number of flag officers. Younger officers had few options in the surface fleet. In 1919, the Naval Register listed twenty-five permanently appointed flag officers with the baseline two-stars—with roughly thirty in temporary positional rank. Two decades later, the Naval Register listed seventy-seven flag officers, with eleven in waiting for a billet to open. Calculating the odds, King faced many years of backstabbing and feudal interservice rivalry in the quest to win promotion into the flag ranks.

Very few American taxpayers paid attention to the peacetime infighting among military and naval service professionals. Observing from within the surface line, King viewed many fellow naval officers with utter contempt. His old roommate from the Naval Academy, Capt. Adolphus Andrews, was among the most hated. He earned a backstabbing reputation for standing "against his classmates just because they were his classmates."[33] King lambasted Andrews after he secured command of the presidential yacht USS *Mayflower* (PY-1). King criticized Andrews for openly declaring his support for the Democratic Party and then shifting his loyalties to the Republican Party. Such violations of the old rule of maintaining an apolitical façade also set Andrews apart from others within the ranks. King described Andrews as an "apple polisher of the first order [who] treated the service as his own little yachting club."[34]

TRAINING ADMIRALS

The politics of demobilization extended to the ongoing debates about the future of American sea power in the global maritime arena. With a growing family and in anticipation of marking twenty-four years in the ranks, King contemplated leaving active service in 1919.[35] At that time, the Navy Register listed 241 captains on the active list. King was among 131 officers with temporary wartime appointments in that rank. At age forty, King held the lineal standing of 226 among all the other temporary-grade captains on active service. Under the circumstances, he expected to lose his captaincy. With the associated postwar reductions in force, King worried about being stuck in bureaucratic amber in the lower rank and pay grade of commander.[36]

King again stood at the crossroads in considering the fleeting professional opportunities outside the service. Mattie carried significant responsibility in the King household. Their eldest daughter, Elizabeth, entered middle school at twelve years of age, and their five other daughters helped care for Mildred—the baby, born in 1920. Professional aspirations intermixed with family responsibilities. With five daughters already in tow, Mattie became pregnant with another daughter soon after King returned from Europe. Under the circumstances, King pondered lucrative opportunities among the civilian captains of American industry.

Facing a future of gray paint and steel decks with twenty years logged on the deck, King had nothing more to prove as a naval officer. His campaign ribbons served as evidence of King's preparedness for peace, after service in the Spanish-American War, Philippines, Mexico, Haiti, and then the First World War. Much to his surprise, King then received a Navy Cross Medal in the most undignified manner. Mattie expected to see new orders upon signing the certified-mail delivery from the Navy Department. The plain manila envelope contained documents and a cardboard box.[37] King chuckled upon reading the citation, which highlighted his service on the Atlantic Fleet <u>staff</u>. King mused that "the Navy Cross should be a medal given when the deeds done are worthy of both the Navy and the Cross."[38]

The Navy Cross carried double edges for King, since the newly established decoration equated to comparable European medals and high honors. Conversely, the proliferation of medals and meaningless decorations disgusted King. Rank and proximity to power apparently determined the distribution of medals and associated honors within the Navy Department of Secretary Daniels. The old American tradition of keeping the military free of superfluous baubles and other such monarchist pomposities faded with the creation of medals like the Navy Cross, Distinguished Service Medal, and Silver Star. After the First World War, the Medal of Honor also attained a strangely un-American importance.[39]

Navy secretary Daniels unashamedly showered medals and choice assignments upon political allies and personal favorites. He personally authorized fifty-five Medals of Honor to naval personnel for service in Mexico. Among them, he approved the medals for Ensigns Theodore Wilkinson, Jonas Ingram, and Frank Jack Fletcher. Notably, Wilkinson had graduated first in his Naval Academy class, Ingram had been a star Naval Academy football player, and Fletcher was the nephew of the commander in chief, Atlantic Fleet. Daniels issued direct orders to force the son of an influential congressman, Marine major Smedley Butler, to wear a second Medal of Honor. In disgust, Butler argued that the "Medal of Honor is the prize for which all of us soldiers strive and risk our lives and to have it thrown around broad cast is an unutterably foul perversion of Our Country's greatest gift."[40]

Politics defined the criteria for civilian officials and uniformed power brokers within the ranks in determining an individual's worthiness for medals and choice assignments. The resulting civil-military conflict prompted many service professionals to believe that "honors and preferment went, not to the most capable or deserving, but to the most pliant, and the most subservient, among the officers of the Navy [and] nothing more destructive of morale can be imagined."[41] King observed that "Secretary Daniels from time to time would order to the Atlantic Fleet certain flag officers who were not entirely qualified for their duties."[42]

Dumb controversies about policy on the public stage overshadowed actual strategic problems within the ranks. Bureaucratic infighting among superiors inspired King to consider transfer to the retired list in his *temporary* rank of captain. In this way, he could retain his temporary rank in "tombstone status" without reverting to his lower *permanent* rank of commander.[43] Classmates from the Naval Academy had already left the service to pursue their fortunes in business and politics. Among others, John M. Caffrey offered King a very lucrative job with the Columbia Sugar Company in Louisiana. Caffrey held significant influence within the Democratic Party.[44] Given the opportunity, he balanced his options as he faced an inevitable shift from his temporary four-stripe rank as a captain and back to his permanent rank of three-stripe commander.[45] With another newborn in the household, King also understood what he needed to do to win future promotions in the peacetime ranks of the US Navy.

Decorations issued by Daniels carried double meaning among many naval service professionals. Although the Medal of Honor and Purple Heart decorations dated to an earlier era, foreign decorations issued to American servicemen also sparked significant debate within Congress.[46] Controversy followed when Daniels decorated Sims with the newly established Distinguished Service Medal. Daniels previously denied permission for Sims to accept decorations from the various Entente powers. Daniels then allowed Sims to accept the honors, but then denied permission for Sims to wear them. In the process, Daniels seemed to suffer from clownlike incompetence—at least among Sims and his closer associates.[47] Refusing to play along with the Daniels agenda, Sims publicly declined the Navy Distinguished Service Medal, "for the good of the service."[48]

The divisive controversy between Daniels and Sims trickled down through the ranks of the US Navy. Loyalists stood divided by their affiliations with either Daniels or Sims. Many also seized neutral ground—fighting to stay out of the politically charged fray. During heated testimony on Capitol Hill, Sims and Daniels competed to win the support of younger officers—like King. Sharing their cause on questions of naval education. Daniels groomed King by introducing him to influential entrepreneurs like Charles M. Schwab, Daniel Guggenheim, Vincent Astor, and Arthur Curtis James. More importantly, Daniels put King in the same political circles with Congressman Carl Vinson in 1920. This association later proved important in King's career.[49]

GENERATIONAL EBBS AND FLOWS

The civil-military question of command and the American system of checks and balances always fascinated King. Civilian "parvenues" amused King. The common vernacular term "quack" seemed appropriate when King referred to those "who professes specialty [without] adequate and suitable education and training in the fundamentals."[50] Though he believed firmly in civilian control under the Constitution, King rarely deferred to the ignorance of politicians and parvenus outside the uniformed ranks. Sims similarly courted King by rallying their mutual interests to support the future by educational means at the Naval War College and the Naval Postgraduate School. The K-P-K recommendations, for example, reflected the backchannel influence of Sims and Mayo in the ongoing dialogue between the Naval War College and General Board on the question of naval education, which naturally influenced the views of King after 1919.

War experiences further inspired King's evolution as a very savvy naval thinker in his own right by mimicking the arguments of others. Having met Sir Julian Corbett and Spenser Wilkinson in London during the war, King drew heavily from Corbett's *Some Principles of Maritime Strategy* and *Seven Years War*. Wilkinson's *Brain of the Navy* and *Command of the Sea* provided inspiration.[51] King studied Sir Edward Hamley's *Operations of War* and drew additional perspective on the tenets of leadership from Mahan's *Types of Naval Officers*, Winston S. Churchill's *River War*, and John T. Headley's *Napoleon and His Marshals*.[52]

In formulating the image of being a naval strategist second to none, King closely studied the historical texts for ideas. The example of Marshal Bon-Adrien Jeannot de Moncey captivated King. At ninety-one years of age in December 1840, Moncey sat invalid in a chair in the chapel of Saint-Jerôme in Paris when a cadre of the Old Guard escorted the mummy of Napoleon into the temporary crypt. Moncey suddenly rose from his chair, saluted, and then fell back into his chair.[53] For King, the example of Moncey illustrated the fundamental problem of blind obedience in military affairs. King noted that the "great weakness of the Napoleonic system was that it required the detailed supervision of Napoleon."[54]

Civil-military debates concerning the character and culture of the armed services lingered without clear resolution in King's busy mind. Since the Civil War era, the US Navy maintained relative course and speed with American society on such divisive questions as racial integration. Skippers earlier staffed their wardrooms with slaves to tend to the officers, which progressively set the stage for change in the Reconstruction Era. Black sailors, along with other religious and racial minorities, enjoyed relative freedom to serve among the enlisted ranks of the seagoing line through the First World War. In 1920, Daniels then issued the dictum that turned back the cultural clock for another two decades.[55]

Discrimination policies within the naval services tended to reflect trends in American society. Within the Wilson administration, nostalgic memories of the Old South intermixed with the progressive spirit of industrialization and professionalization among the white Anglo-Saxon Protestant monoculture of the US Navy. King took a practical view in navigating the extremes of naval service culture. He viewed the policies of the Navy Department as a foundation for adaptation, taking a practical view in recognizing that Black sailors had a role in shaping the future of American sea power. King never challenged the regulations, although healways sought to achieve utmost efficiency in efforts to make all hands happy in their work.[56]

King strongly disliked naval officers whose superior rank seemed to be beyond their lower intellectual capacity. Young guns, like King, bemoaned the quiet oppression of "cackling crows just peck[ing] and caw[ing] about the 'good old days' when we have actual work to do."[57] King used his position at the Postgraduate School to rage against the machine of the Navy Department. Notwithstanding elder examples from Luce to Mahan and from Sims to Mayo, most superior-ranking officers struck King as being "old fogies."[58]

Navy Department demobilization policies set the pace for resetting the ranks for peacetime operations. King faced the inevitable reduction in rank from captain to his permanent grade of commander, due to budgetary reductions in force after 1919. His deadline for submitting a request for transfer to the retired list as a captain also loomed. In 1920, he stood too junior among captains for a major warship command, and too senior among those holding temporary wartime appointments for a flotilla command. He nearly submitted his retirement papers when his old nemesis, Adm. "Nobby" Wilson, received orders to Annapolis as the superintendent of the Naval Academy. Unwilling to serve under Wilson at the Postgraduate School, King called the director of Gun Exercises and Engineering Personnel in BuOrd, Capt. William D. Leahy, who told King that this "was a hell of a time to ask for sea duty."[59]

Officers of higher rank and lineal standing dominated the slate for major warship commands among the regular line. Leahy explained the situation when King asked about the process for transferring to the retired list. Leahy baited King to stay on active service to command an auxiliary ship in the Fleet Train, which King lovingly called his "beef boat."[60] In June 1921, King reported as skipper on the refrigerator ship USS *Bridge* (AF-1). His brother Norman also joined the ship for a visit.[61]

BEEF BOATS AND FRENCH BRAID

King enjoyed the freedom of standing at the key crossroads between remaining on watch with the American fleet or, alternatively, beginning a lucrative civilian career within the burgeoning civil-military industrial complex. He still had time to decide to retire in the tombstone rank of captain. Upon assuming command on *Bridge*, King always referred to himself as captain regardless of his actual lower permanent rank in the Navy Register. Yet, fate always carried a double edge. By taking command on *Bridge*, King inadvertently placed himself in the crosshairs of another higher-ranking nemesis—Rodman—whose colorfully disingenuous leadership style always bothered King. The salty Kentuckian Rodman often lectured sailors about the teetotaling benefits of drinking coffee. Among other quirks, Rodman kept a flask in his pocket and openly doused his coffee with Kentucky whiskey.[62]

Past interactions with the old Kentuckian added heat to the bubbling rage within the Buckeye spirit of King. For more than two decades, Rodman upset King's Scotch Irish sensibilities. Always using Navy Regulations for the purposes of upsetting administrative routines, King enjoyed goading Rodman into making a fool of himself. Rodman required all hands to wear the newer British reefer-style jacket as the uniform prescribed on warships and naval facilities in Hampton Roads. During the period of transition from one style to another, King specifically wore the obsolete high-collar tunic—much to the chagrin of Rodman.

The phased introduction of British styles within the American ranks also riled the Scotch Irish spirit in King after the First World War. He clung to his American-styled high-collar tunic. Sack coats with ties seemed too British for King. Having recently been promoted to the temporary rank of captain during service in Europe before Versailles, King had purchased new uniforms in that rank at the best bespoke tailor shops of Paris and London. He continued to wear the older high-collar styles during the transition to the new Royal Navy double-breasted cuts of US naval uniforms. King paid extra expense for the silver-and-gold-embroidered bullion insignia. Upon taking the deck as skipper on *Bridge*, King continued wearing his obsolete high-collared uniform and refused to purchase the new reefer jacket. King used the uniform to demonstrate his rebellious sense of organizational protocol. The postwar US Navy uniform regulations required broader-crowned caps with "English braid." Instead, King kept wearing the smaller-crowned captain's hat, featuring "French braid," while on sea duty on *Bridge*.[63]

The esoteric nuances of Naval Regulations and uniform fashions provided opportunity for King to play games with his old nemesis Rodman. Upon receiving orders to remote to the lower permanent rank of commander, King dutifully removed the eagles and one of the stripes to pin on the silver oak leaves and three-stripe insignia. The shadows of his higher-ranking insignia appeared on his uniform, and a "tarnished and weather-beaten appearance of his cap."[64] Whenever *Bridge* pulled into Hampton Roads, King went out of his way to pass by the offices of the base commander, Rodman. Shaking in anger, Rodman subjected King to a foul tirade: "I won't have such a cap on board my base!"[65] However, the phased transition from older-styled uniforms to newer British cuts allowed for American naval officers to continue wearing French braid "in place of English braid."[66] Rodman himself wrote the instruction, which King noted. In response, Rodman barked, "You go to hell."[67] King described the missive as "Rodman's customary way of ending a lost argument."[68]

The older generation lingered among the surface fleet, as younger regular line officers pursued their futures in the specialized ranks of aviation and submarines. Another old nemesis, RAdm. Louis R. de Steiger, disliked King since their service together on *Illinois* in China two decades earlier. King described the demeanor of de Steiger as unnecessarily "very strict in every way."[69] Commanding the Fleet Train frustrated de Steiger to view the mission as the "kind of penance that had to be borne."[70] De Steiger disliked his job, which required him to balance fleet requirements against the unionized civilian cabals that controlled naval shipyards and seaports.

Service in the Fleet Train concurrently provided opportunity for naval professionals to sharpen their strategic understanding of civil-military realities. Service with the Fleet Train certainly defined King's perspective of fixed supply bases ashore and the responsibilities carried by seagoing skippers. Unwilling to defer to anyone unworthy, King conversely referred to civilians as "amateur sailors."[71] His reputation for haranguing civilian pilots became the inspiration for many sea stories among the sailorly culture along the East Coast. On one epic occasion, King humiliated a civilian pilot when he nearly ran the ship aground in the approaches to Hampton Roads. King always followed the rules of the road. He emphasized that the "mark of a great shiphandler is never getting into situations that require great shiphandling."[72]

Civilians customarily failed to accept the rigorous traditions of order and discipline, which set naval service professionals apart among the tribal ranks of the American waterfront. King broke many bureaucratic rice bowls by indirectly insulting the civilian commodore of Hampton Roads tugboats, "Cap'n Jim" McAllister. Whenever maneuvering *Bridge* into Hampton Roads, King habitually assumed personal control of the deck when maneuvering into the channel. Civilian pilots complained about King to de Steiger. Putting on a show for McCallister's representatives, de Steiger verbally admonished King. Conversely, de Steiger reported, "Commander King has maintained and operated a very efficient vessel [and] in unusually efficient condition."[73]

For the time being, King successfully escaped the bureaucratic realities of peacetime combat operations by running down to the sea in ships. Command on *Bridge* provided the foundation for King to ease into assignments on the fringes of the surface line. He gained firsthand experience in the civil-military black art of logistics.[74] King also followed the example of Sims by expecting his subordinates to participate. The entire wardroom on *Bridge* followed King in completing Naval War College correspondence courses. He also employed his officers as tutors for enlisted sailors in anticipation of promotion exams. Admirers characterized King while skipper on *Bridge* that "he spent much time on deck watching other ships through glasses—'practicing to be an admiral'—it was said."[75] On the other hand, King also recognized the ebbing traditions of the Nelsonial ideal among the shifting tides of history and technological innovation in the shore-based wireless world of the twentieth century.

HOT AIR

Debates concerning future administration within American armed services reflected the global trends. The Versailles Treaty loomed over the failure of the American government in forming the League of Nations. The subsequent Treaty of Rapallo between the Soviet Union and the Weimar Democracy in Germany also set the stage for future troubles, later culminating in the rise of the National Socialists and Fascists of Europe. Japanese disgust about the subsequent naval treaties concluded in Washington, London, and Paris also set the stage for trouble over the horizon. In these pugilistic peacetime battles among international powers, RAdm. William A. Moffett emerged from the depths of Navy Department bureaucracy as the first chief of the Bureau of Aeronautics (BuAer) by 1919.

Moffett possessed the unique capacity to handle command at sea with equal alacrity in navigating the rocky political shoals within the Navy Department. Having earned fame within the ranks as a big-gun battleship sailor, Moffett wore the distinctive Medal of Honor for service at Veracruz in 1914, during which he witnessed the first tactical air support operations of US naval aviators in combat. The experience inspired Moffett to create the rudimentary foundations of an aviation training school while in command at Great Lakes Naval Training Station near Chicago. By 1919, he commanded battleship USS *Mississippi* (BB-41). His mentor, Fiske, also influenced the assistant secretary, Roosevelt, to rig the lines to organize BuAer under Moffett.

British innovations in the development of aircraft carriers coincidentally inspired Moffett to recognize the future of naval aviation. Roosevelt elevated the bureaucratic stature of BuAer by arranging two-star rank for Moffett by 1921.[76] After the departure of Roosevelt and with the fading influence of other allies within the Wilson administration, Moffett also fought successive Republican Party efforts to enact the forced "unification" of the Departments of War and Navy.[77] The internationalist agenda of the Wilson administration concurrently faded under the incoming administration of President Warren G. Harding.[78] Despite past proposals to unify the Departments of War and Navy, Harding reopened old scabs by acting upon proposals by a Republican representative from Wisconsin, Florian Lampert, to create the "Department of Defense, with Under Secretaries of the Army, the Navy, and the Air."[79]

The future of American sea power stood in the balance when Harding turned inward to capitalize on postwar dividends. Prodded by his political advisers and personal business associates, Harding attempted to reorganize the constitutional authorities under the executive branch—reducing bureaucratic checks and balances under the divisions established under the Constitution. Harding wanted to consolidate military and naval missions under federal and state governance for the purposes of simplifying policies and procurement processes. Within the Departments of War and Navy, the specter of unification appeared as a "threat to free government."[80]

Harding muddled into the bureaucratic tar pits of federal administration, often consciously knowing about the sleezy arrangements being struck under his name among members of the administration. Profiteers also made inroads to Congress in efforts to exploit oil deposits and other natural resources on federally controlled territory.[81] Helium and other natural-gas reserves fell among key commodities of immediate strategic concern to the Navy. Given the role of zeppelins in the First World War, naval experimentation in aviation also hinged upon control over key helium deposits at Teapot Dome in Wyoming.[82] Helium proved vital to the future vision for naval aviation, as Moffett focused on developments in"lighter than air" (LTA) zeppelin technology while the director of Military Aeronautics, Col. William L. "Billy" Mitchell, concentrated on "heavier than air" (HTA) land-based aviation platforms.[83]

Like other prophetic figures in history, Mitchell and Moffett rode the technological trends to attain popular status as visionaries. Mitchell and Moffett both played games and occasionally pushed the limits of truth in their advocacy. In examining the aviation trends on the gaming floors of the Naval War College, Sims accused Mitchell of being "guilty as sin" in falsifying facts about the capabilities and limitations of aviation technology.[84] Recalling the airpower debates of the 1920s, King thought, "Sims talked in declarations and often sounded screwy to people who didn't know him."[85] King compared Mitchell in stipulating that "Sims sounded off too much [but] was the better man."[86]

Following a series of bombing tests off Hampton Roads, Mitchell eventually faced the verdict of expounding upon the truth during his subsequent court-martial. The finger-prints of many American naval officers likely appeared upon the dagger that resulted in the bureaucratic martyrdom of Mitchell.[87] Indeed, the cadre within BuAer had become informally known as the "Moffett mafia" within the Navy Department.[88] Following the death of President Harding in 1923, President Calvin Coolidge pushed the Billy Mitchell controversy out of the headlines. He used the proven tactic of forming a blue-ribbon commission for the strategic purposes of ignoring the fundamental problems of policy.[89]

Military requirements ashore frequently failed to measure against equivalent functions for airpower among the naval forces afloat. Unwilling to learn about the differences between military and naval functions, Coolidge assembled a bipartisan extragovernmental commission by appointing an old friend, Dwight Morrow, to examine the air services of the army and navy.[90] When the zeppelin USS *Shenandoh* (LZ-1) crashed, the newspaper controversy also provided a mandate for Coolidge to use the "Morrow Board" as the vehicle for striking a series of compromises. In essence, the Morrow Board accommodated Mitchell's acolytes by creating the US Army Air Corps as a coequal branch to the infantry and artillery under the general staff. Concurrently the Morrow Board tabled efforts to unify military and naval aviation.[91]

The unsettled hot air intermixed with the cold waters of future American maritime policy for seagoing strategic thinkers within the fleet. Successive Republican presidential administrations pushed the vision of a future "Department of National Defense."[92] Politically driven unification proposals inspired debates about equally controversial issues in the *Proceedings* of the Naval Institute, alongside titles like "Airphobia," "Ships That Are No More," "Limitation of Naval Armament," "Law and War," and "Government's New Radio Policy." The British theorist Hector Bywater provided a counterpoint with his essay "The Battleship and Its Uses" alongside that of RAdm. William V. Pratt's "Some Aspects of Our Air Policy."[93] From these ongoing debates between the land and sea services, King operated on the cutting edges of technological innovation to recognize the interconnections between subsurface explorations of inner space and the longer horizons leading to outer space—himself finding his own path to the stars among the ranks of American sea power in the 1920s and 1930s.

CHAPTER 7
King of the Wolves

King was committed to enduring the grueling obscurity of low pay and the long-haul hardships inherent with the seagoing lifestyle within the cloistered naval service ranks. Coincident with the birth of his sixth daughter, King received a summons to detach from *Bridge* for temporary duty at the Navy Department to preside over a criminal investigation of the Electric Boat Company.[1] Navy Department procedure required King to put on the façade of being completely beyond reproach as the lead inquisitor during investigations of Electric Boat. In preparation for this work, King studied mistakes made in efforts to build upon German submarine technology. During this period, King regularly consulted experienced submariners like Commanders Chester W. Nimitz and Francis J. Cleary. Having earlier lost his ring finger in the line of duty, Nimitz endured far less physical hardship as compared with Cleary—who lost his leg to the machine.[2]

Officials at the Electric Boat Company and Submarine Boat Company avoided public scrutiny by lodging separate legal accusations against the Navy Department for criminal fraud and abuse. Behind the scenes, the litigation teams of Henry R. Sutphen at Electric Boat worked with Henry R. Carse at the Submarine Boat Company.[3] The Navy secretary, Edwin Denby, also maintained friendly ties with Sutphen and Carse. Such cozy relationships among civilian policymakers and private industrialists carried potential consequences. Journalists like Glen C. H. Perry of the *Washington Sun* specialized in examining the internal affairs of the Navy Department.[4] For this reason, Denby directed the CNO, Adm. Robert E. Coontz, to delegate the investigation to the General Board.

The General Board provided strategic means for the Navy Department to handle administrative problems, which held significant potential for creating controversy on the public stage.[5] Upon receiving the assignment from Coonz, the General Board delegated the investigation to RAdm. David W. Taylor. In turn, he formed an investigative subcommittee. Taylor specifically requested King to supervise the investigation.[6] The assignment provided two potential outcomes for King. On one path, King had the opportunity to fix the problem and become the bureaucratic hero. On the other, King faced the prospective burden of becoming the perfect patsy.

King had no obvious affiliation with any of the parties involved with the Electric Boat Company in the dispute with the Navy Department. On June 3, 1922, King received orders to wear the temporary rank of captain for the purposes of the investigation, with temporary duty on the staff of Taylor in the flagship of the submarine flotillas on board USS *Chewink* (AM-39), at anchor in New London, Connecticut.[7] On July 14, 1922, King formally took charge—with Capt. Thomas C. Hart and Cmdr. Chester W. Nimitz providing expert assistance. Taylor also approved King's request for additional investigators, including Capt. Frederick D. Berrien and Lt. Francis S. "Frog" Low.[8] During the investigations, he sailed in several recently commissioned submarines. King determined that "we were just repeating the same mistakes as the Germans did."[9]

Former German enemies carried the blame for all the problems besetting American submarine designs, according to King. In his findings, King provided an opportunity for Electric Boat to sell much-bigger—and more expensive—long-range submarines. Much to the chagrin of the "big-gun" surface line cadre, the Navy Department faced few options in approving recommendations to scrap smaller submarines in favor of building future fleet-type designs.[10] In the wake of the investigation, King received high marks in his fitness report as an "officer of exceptional ability and most conscientious in his efforts to improve the service."[11] RAdm. Chester Welles endorsed the assessment by characterizing King as an "earnest and effective officer [who should] be considered for important commands."[12]

THE COMPANY MAN

The Electric Boat investigation served as an opportunity for King to regain his position at the head of the pack in the race to control the future of American sea power. He received orders to take command on *Chewink* in the permanent rank of four-stripe captain. In this assignment, King also held the honor of commanding the flagship of the submarine flotillas based in New London. Meanwhile, King commanded *Chewink* while transporting mines from the North Sea Mine Barrage between ports in New England and the ordnance depot at Yorktown, Virginia. During these operations, King fell under the temporary command of Capt. Charles B. McVay Jr. In evaluating King and the excellent performance of the *Chewink* crew, McVay awarded King the top superior performance ratings across all nineteen categories of fitness, including the areas of conduct, professional qualification, and military bearing. Returning the favor, King also mentored the younger son, Lt. Charles B. McVay III.[13]

Interconnections among navy families reflected a common sense of loyalty to the greater vision of American sea power. Close familial ties among service families also reflected the tribal culture of the US Navy. To succeed, King understood the importance of setting the example, meeting the high ideals of the service, and maintaining good order and discipline on the home front. As King focused on being the best naval officer in the service, Mattie helped by taking uncontested command in running the crew at home. When King received orders to submarine duty, Mattie rented the King family home in Annapolis and moved their six daughters into the senior officer's quarters next to those of the base commander and flag officers in New London. She was pregnant during the move from Annapolis to New London.

King nurtured relationships with the Electric Boat Company in anticipation of resettling the family to New England. Shortly after arriving with their six daughters in tow, the King family ranks expanded when Mattie delivered their seventh child, Ernest J. King Jr., in 1922. His promotion to the permanent grade of captain finally forced King to decide upon his future. King had to accept mandatory time on active service to accept the promotion, subject to the needs of the navy—thereby restricting him from pursuing opportunities beyond the bureaucratic clutches of the service. King accepted the promotion with following orders to take command in Submarine Division 11 of the Atlantic Fleet. In this role, King assumed the temporal title of "commodore" upon breaking his pennant on the submarine *S-20* in September 1922.

Balancing the responsibilities of command with those of keeping a family, King spent his off-hours completing the prerequisites for assignment to the resident curriculum in the senior course of the Naval War College. King had earned a reputation for being a vocal advocate for the Naval War College and for the practical mission of naval education. Setting the example for his subordinates, King organized a study group for fellow officers to complete the Naval War College correspondence courses.[14] Some of the junior officers participated primarily for the purposes of meeting King's elder daughters. Among others, Lieutenants Francis S. Low and Alan R. McCann developed early connections with King during service in submarines in New London. Later, King relied heavily upon Low and McCann while coordinating global antisubmarine operations with intelligence.[15]

PULLING HIS BEATTY

King used the new double-breasted uniform to reinvent himself as the imposing commodore of the submarine flotilla. His friend Knox described the transformation of King from being a skipper into being a commander of fleets. In a personal letter to the naval historian Samuel Eliot Morison, Knox described the cartoonish image of King "pulling his Beatty."[16] Knox told Morison that "Beatty knew how to play the part of a winner after Jutland." King viewed Beatty with skepticism as a naval commander. Conversely, King recognized showmanship as part of the success of Beatty. For this reason, Knox explained that King "pulled his Beatty [by] stuffing his hands into his pockets and cap synched [sic] down at an angle just above the eyes."[17] Knox also noted that King added his own touch to the look by incorporating the chivalrous hint of a white handkerchief to the upper left pocket—just below his decorations.[18]

The traditional divisions between commissioned officers and enlisted sailors blurred within the ranks of the submarine force. Out of necessity, all hands carried an equal share of the workload. King fully embraced this element in submarine culture. He especially respected the expertise provided by seasoned enlisted sailors. King assembled his flotilla staff with officers promoted from the ranks—otherwise known colloquially as "mustangs."[19] Having served in the Asiatic Fleet as a young officer, King spun the yarn that the term "mustang" originated from an ancient Chinese reference to the "sages of the Kingdom of Low."[20] Among his favorites, King nurtured the careers of enlisted sailors Frank Crilley, Thomas Eadie, Richard E. Hawes, and Charles F. Grisham.[21] Within the specialized community of navy divers—including Edward Ellsberg, Charles "Swede" Momsen, and Alan R. McCann—King also developed key connections with Richard S. Edwards and Charles A. Lockwood. The heroic leadership of Lt. Charles "Savvy" Cooke Jr., the skipper of USS *S-5*, drew King's attention.[22]

Divers and submariner associates of King pioneered innovations in undersea warfare technology and doctrine. Crilley and Eadie received Medals of Honor for their service as salvage divers. King later selected Grisham to command the flagship of the US fleet, USS *Dauntless* (PG-61). Hawes—very reluctantly—accepted the order from King to take a commission. Hawes later retired in two-star rank. According to legend, King and his close circle designed the golden dolphin insignia of the US Navy submarine force. In fact, he held a competition for his sailors to submit designs. King approved the design for submission to the Navy Department.[23] He stipulated that the "insignia should only be worn after an officer has completed full qualification and only when the recipient is assigned to sea duty in submarines."[24]

Specialized qualifications by line officers required the individual to remove their insignia upon the regular rotation to surface assignments. King completed all the prerequisites and earned full qualifications to command in submarines. He helped secure official approval for officers to wear the submarine insignia by 1923. On principle, King never wore the insignia during subsequent service as the base commander ashore at New London.[25] Reflecting upon early experiences in submarines, Francis S. Low observed that service with King in New London required a "proper sense of humor and of the ridiculous."[26]

Playing to win at all costs, King used his authority to stack the ranks of the New London command baseball team. He pulled ringers from the crews of individual submarines to assemble a New London baseball team worthy of playing the very best among local civilian clubs, YMCA teams, and semiprofessional barnstormers.[27] King ignored complaints from individual submarine skippers. As a result, Taylor overruled King in forcing sailors to return to primary duties on board submarines. Following the decision, Low recalled seeing King in a rage.[28] Low explained that

Admiral Taylor, a delightful, gruff old bachelor, [. . .] said, "Low transfer [King's baseball team] all to sea duty." This I did, over my own signature, and thereby sowed a small whirlwind. Taylor's flagship was anchored in New London at the time and early the following morning along came Captain King, breathing fire. He brushed me aside when I met him at the gangway and practically ran up to Admiral Taylor's cabin. He emerged in about half an hour and excited as he entered. Taylor sent for me and said, "Low, the order stands." I thought to myself how well I had selected a first-class enemy for the future. I did not see him again until 1939.[29]

King and Low shared a common appreciation for baseball, since both followed the statistics listed in the newspapers. As commander of the naval base in New London, King arranged junkets for his sailors to attend games at Yankee Stadium and Fenway Park.[30]

Baseball enabled individual commanders to stand out among the higher levels in the grander competition. King treated all the various sports as a form of war. He regularly ran boxing "smokers" between the various ships and base headquarters. King held individual skippers accountable for keeping their sailors engaged in athletic activities. Above all sports, King took particular interest in baseball—perhaps because of the yearly meetings of the United States Fleet for simulated seagoing combat and joint army-navy exercises.[31] The glory of winning the CinCUS trophy in all sports loomed large. Winning the CinCUS trophy for baseball was, however, the equivalent to winning a World Series pennant. Being the winner always required the will to win, as far as King believed. He expected his men to fight for every triumph—even on the baseball diamonds and boxing rings of the fleet. Low observed that King viewed failures by his subordinates as a reflection of his performance as a leader. He always supported his subordinates whenever they did all they could to do to win—even in defeat—using setbacks as the basis for improvement in anticipation of the future contests of life.[32]

Teetotalers and glad-handers among the civilian population ashore always riled King whenever the reputation of the service came into question on the public stage. Restrictions imposed upon the consumption of alcohol seemed farcical. King and Mattie maintained a personal stash of Canadian liquor. His superiors likewise kept liquor for parties held among officers behind secured doors within the sanctuary of the naval base at New London. As base commander, King regularly rescued drunken sailors from the local police.[33] Occasionally, he had to rescue officers for walking around in public with alcohol on their breath. One wayward officer resisted arrest. King intervened, telling the policeman that he had no jurisdiction over a federally appointed naval officer. King then took the officer in question into custody and deposited him with his skipper for further rendering. At that time, the officer protested. King sternly retorted, "Anything happens that reflects on the Navy, it is my business!"[34]

King embraced the function of being the senior-ranking representative of the US Navy at New London and recognized the importance of maintaining discipline within the household and in the public eye. King had rented his home in Annapolis to establish temporary residence with his pregnant wife and six daughters on base in New London.[35] Having served with King in the 1920s, McCann remembered a story that "King lined his six girls up before their beds every morning after breakfast for inspection . . . that would be typical of King."[36] In managing the crew at home, King disagreed with Mattie for encouraging their daughters to date sailors under his command. Their daughter Elizabeth kept King busy during their time in New London. In a rehearsed act, King glared at her suitors over the top of his newspaper until they looked away—never saying a word. She later characterized King's demeanor as a carefully rehearsed act: "He is the most even-tempered man I know [and] he is always in a rage."[37]

King rarely held subordinates accountable for mistakes resulting from circumstances beyond their immediate control. Whenever he lost his temper unjustly, King exhibited humility in admitting mistakes. McCann recalled that "King was a real taskmaster [and] one day shortly after 13:00 King came to my office and gave me a terrible chewing out in the presence of my staff [and] spared no words whatsoever."[38] McCann attempted to explain, but King's "face turned white as a sheet [and] he continued to castigate me."[39] McCann finally had enough and walked away "rip-roaring mad."[40]

The abusive tirade by King proved completely embarrassing for all present when McCann calmly saluted and walked away. In reflection, King realized he had gone too far. He went to McCann's office to apologize. McCann came immediately to attention. He later recalled that whenever "King told somebody to 'sit down' in his presence you knew everything was all right."[41] McCann explained that "King walked into my office and spoke to everyone there[,] saying, '[L]adies and gentlemen[,] I apologize for everything that I said in this office about an hour ago [and] I was wrong and I am sorry.'"[42] This incident loomed large for McCann, later observing that it "took a big man to do that. [I] never knew King to be unfair to any man and if he did he would apologize for it."[43]

Subordinates recalled the distant personality of King, which overshadowed his underlying fairness. McCann recalled an incident when serving as skipper on USS *S-46*. As he maneuvered into port, the currents carried *S-46* into hitting a submerged foundation marking the former spot of a navigational light in the Narragansett Bay. McCann expected to be relieved after the collision. He recalled King advising "to think nothing of it."[44] King then sent a scathing memorandum to the base commander for failing to clear the channel.[45] McCann thought there "was Ernie King again, as fair and square as he could be." McCann admitted that "I became rather fond of the old man."[46] McCann summarized King as being a "rather cold person [with] a very, very strong character who did not make friends very easily."[47]

King earned the loyalty of subordinates by backing them up in the face of bureaucratic stupidity or naked injustice. When the Navy Department issued the directive restricting Black sailors to serving as messmen and steward's mates, King quietly issued his own directive that all hands must qualify to stand operational watches in the bridge and engineering on board submarines. "About the only time I ever saw King really smile," McCann recalled of an incident involving a "black first[-]class machinist's mate who was one of my best sailors."[48] McCann continued, "In those days one had to go before the mast in order to request [permission] to get married."[49] McCann witnessed the meeting with King, during which the sailor explained that "he had been living for twenty years with one woman and they had six children and he felt that it was time that he ought to get married [and] it was the only time I've ever seen King really laugh—he absolutely went into stitches."[50]

By fostering disciplined leadership at all levels of command, King drew from his experience in battleships and destroyers to transform the submarine service into an elite branch of the US Navy. King emphasized teamwork as the key to success while commanding Submarine Divisions 11 and 3 during Fleet Problem I off the Panama Canal in February 1923. Experimenting with ideas first gained on the floors of the Naval War College, King commanded a task force of sixteen submarines during Fleet Problem I. He studied the ideas published by other submariners and then used tactics employed in surface torpedo boats to demonstrate the potential of submarine group tactics during the exercises—roughly a decade before the German navy reconstituted their submarine forces to organize into "wolf packs."[51]

The submariners under King's command disliked operating in such close quarters for the unproven group attack operations. He later noted that "submarine officers at that time were so obsessed with the possible danger of collision that they were unreasonably opposed to operating in close order."[52] Drawing from earlier techniques employed in the Sims destroyer flotilla, King coordinated the submarine group tactics with electronic communications. He organized three divisions of four submarines to form into groups, such that with "adequate training, submarine squadrons should be able to operate effectively in formation even when submerged.[53] During Fleet Problem I, King staged a simulated series of submarine group attacks against the surface forces. He demonstrated the vulnerability of the Panama Canal with a simulated submarine attack against the locks.[54] Such superior performance inspired the commander of submarines, Taylor, to characterize King as "thoroughly reliable . . . painstaking and trustworthy . . . holds certificate for completion War College Correspondence Course."[55]

FROM THE DEPTHS

King believed in the strategic mission of professional education and set the example by excelling as a student of the naval profession. He enjoyed reading history while listening to the radio in his office, or sitting in his favorite chair with a drink on the table in the corner of the living room of the family home. Outsiders often misunderstood King's demeanor, which inspired occasional jokes among subordinates. When riled, King's wrath seemed overly severe to those who did not know him.[56] He occasionally appeared in the stands for the games with Mattie and his family. The eldest of his six daughters were in their teens, and Mattie had baby Joe in tow in New London. King stood out as the model US naval professional on the public stage.[57]

King inadvertently earned international fame for supervising efforts to rescue submariners from the bottom of the sea. On September 25, 1925, USS *S-51* sank within a minute to settle at a depth of roughly 130 feet after a collision with the merchant ship SS *City of Rome*, in the approaches to the Narragansett Bay off Block Island. King recalled the shock borne by the King family upon receiving news of the sinking of one of *his* submarines. He recalled taking leave from duty for a quick vacation with Mattie in the Berkshire Mountains. Upon their return to New London, their daughter Elizabeth ran out to the car. She asked with emotion, "Daddy, wasn't it awful about the loss of *S-51*?"[58] King explained that he and Mattie "had seen no newspapers."[59] Elizabeth gave King the initial details about the *S-51* sinking, as derived from newspaper accounts and from the rumors circulating around New London. Hers was the first report that King had heard of that tragic sinking.[60] He knew many of the thirty-six crewmen personally, and only three from the bridge team survived the sinking of *S-51*.

The crew of *S-51* showed signs of life from within the stricken submarine at the bottom of the sea. King personally knew the skipper, Lt. Rodney Hiram Dobson, as an attentive naval officer. Dobson served as an aide to King with Submarine Squadron 11 on board *Chewink* before taking command on *S-51*. King knew some of the ballplayers among the crew of *S-51*.[61] He organized a memorial service and wrote out the speech. As he prepared to deliver the remarks, his boss, RAdm. Harley H. Christie, arrived for the memorial after working over the wreck site. King dutifully passed his script to Christie, and the memorial service drew major media attention. With Christie on scene to handle the press at the memorial, King recalled that he "listened to, rather than gave, his own address!"[62]

The loss of an American combatant in peacetime reflected poorly on the reputation of the US Navy under any circumstances. Just two years earlier and in the months following the frustrating announcement of the Washington Naval Treaty, nine destroyers sank, with two others sustaining heavy damage, during fleet maneuvers off Point Honda along the California coast. Submarine mishaps drew significant media attention in the past. Yet, the collision of *S-51* with a merchant ship held potential for fueling popular perceptions of the US Navy. Merchant sailors frequently complained about the poor seamanship of US naval professionals.[63] Given the stakes, King participated in the investigation of the incident.[64]

King exonerated the dead and mitigated the political fallout by placing full blame on the configuration of the running lights. The civilian merchant sailors on board *City of Rome* stood blameless, since the low profile of *S-51* obscured their actual position. The *S-51* crew stood similarly unable to work out the proximity of *City of Rome* because of the positioning of the running lights. Heavy weather and seas stood out as the key factor, which placed *City of Rome* on a collision course with the doomed *S-51*. The US Coast Guard had also declared the presence of rumrunners, which the crew of *S-51* expected to find. Having observed a dim light in the distance on a low-profile vessel, the merchant skipper on *City of Rome*, John H. Diehl, also identified the small silhouette of *S-51* as a rumrunner. He maneuvered appropriately to avoid contact with what he thought was a rumrunner, as did the skipper of *S-51*.

Disaster unfolded as both skippers reacted appropriately to the nonexistent ghost of a rumrunner, when *City of Rome* T-boned *S-51* amidships to port and just ahead of the conning tower. The skipper, Dobson, was killed instantly. The submarine sank like a brick. An oil slick appeared on the surface to mark the watery grave of *S-51*.[65] The politics surrounding the question of blame propelled King into the spotlight on the global media stage. As the commodore responsible for training the *S-51* crew, King also stood out among the list of potential scapegoats for the Navy Department. He fully understood the stakes when leading the investigation into the sinking of *S-51*.

By faulting the lighting configuration of *S-51* and the nonexistent threat of rumrunners, King enabled naval investigators to exonerate all hands after the collision with *City of Rome*. Admirals Claude C. Bloch and Charles P. Plunkett immediately concurred with the findings, which served as an elegant means of exonerating the sailors on both *City of Rome* and *S-51*. The media conversely took greater interest in relitigating the conclusions offered in the preliminary investigation. Having influenced the findings concerning the configuration of running lights on American submarines, King recognized the twisted logic of the navy upon receiving orders to command the salvage operations surrounding the wreck of *S-51*. He initially demurred about the offer from Plunkett. However, Christie convinced King to take the job.[66]

The divers focused on the problem, and King provided the bureaucratic top cover to pull the sunken submarine out of the muddy depths of the sea. Having earlier served with King in the Atlantic Fleet, Cmdr. Lynde McCormick characterized King as the "only guy who could do the job right [and] the guy who also knew how to take it for the team if it got all fouled up."[67] One of his friends, retired Capt. Dudley W. Knox, later described King's unique capacity to grasp the basics of a given problem. More importantly, King knew how to make a clear decision. In so doing, King empowered subordinates to complete a given job with minimal supervision. Knox suggested that King "never does anything himself that he can get anyone else to do for him."[68] Submarine salvage operations highlighted the unique ability of King to manage and lead teams of subject matter experts under the most-challenging circumstances.[69]

Behind the scenes, King participated in efforts to frame the official narrative of the *S-51* salvage for the purposes of influencing the media narrative. He also assumed command of the *S-51* salvage with Lieutenants Crilley, Edward Ellsberg, and Henry Hartley. Boatswain Richard E. Hawes assumed command of the small boats and Thomas Eadie fell in with the other divers, as King supervised the whole operation from USS *Falcon* (AM-28).[70] Heavy seas thwarted their efforts and drove the team to the extreme limits of endurance—which King considered "as rigorous mentally and physically as combat."[71] In the February 1927 edition of the Naval Institute's *Proceedings*, King proudly highlighted the supreme performance of the navy divers under his command in "Salvaging USS *S-51*." For their performance, the Distinguished Service Medal was issued to King, Ellsberg, and Hartley. Eadie initially received a Navy Cross. King supported an upgrade for Eadie to receive the Medal of Honor.[72]

Publicity surrounding the dramatic salvage of *S-51* provided opportunities for King to secure an assignment leading to the possibility of an early promotion. All the admirals directly involved showered King with official letters of commendation. The chief of BuOrd, Bloch, chose to issue a special fitness report for King. The report issued by Bloch enhanced future chances for King to secure choice assignments. The commander of the Third Naval District in New York City, Plunkett, described King as a "superior officer in his grade [and] fully qualified to perform the duties of the next higher grade."[73] Christie provided the icing on the cake by characterizing King as an "efficient, capable and ambitious officer with a high sense of duty."[74] Christie envisioned that King would be speedily promoted to flag rank, as a "bold type of officer who is not afraid of responsibility [and] qualified for promotion when due."[75]

The tragic loss of *S-51* faded into the shadows of the heroic story of King and the navy divers. Newspaper accounts cast King in the role of the fictional Captain Nemo from Jules Verne's classic *20,000 Leagues under the Sea*. Images captured during the salvage operations featured King at the center of action, wearing his navy cap squarely, with a civilian-styled sea jacket and high-laced boots. Media accounts featured references to his six daughters and son.[76] Given the successful salvage of *S-51*, King seized the opportunity to lobby for early orders to a major warship command. In turn, Leahy offered King command on USS *Henderson* (AP-1). In Fleet Exercise III, *Henderson* operated with the aircraft carrier *Langley* to stage a simulated amphibious assault against the Panama Canal. Although the vessel sailed in the auxiliary forces, Leahy sweetened the offer by telling King about plans to send *Henderson* to the Asiatic Fleet as the flagship for expeditionary operations in Chinese waters.[77]

Leahy managed the assignments for senior-ranking personnel within BuOrd, which set the slate within BuNav for major warship commands. He maintained files on individual officers, their families, and their associates. In making command decisions, Leahy certainly weeded out those officers who failed to meet the high standards of the naval service, traditions of honor, and the unending pursuit of excellence along the fleet ladder to positions of higher rank and responsibility. Leahy recognized King as a model naval officer. By offering *Henderson*, Leahy was attempting to place King on the fast track to higher rank as skipper of the warship designated to become the flagship of the Asiatic Fleet.

The prospective assignment to the Asiatic Fleet seemed too far off the course King envisioned among the ranks of the surface line. King declined *Henderson* and pressed Leahy for the opportunity to commission the new light cruiser USS *Raleigh* (CL-7). In response, Leahy told King that "you are too junior to have a cruiser at this time[,] as cruiser commands are presently reserved for officers below the classes of 1898 and 1899."[78] Leahy then suggested orders to the aviation tender USS *Wright* (AV-1), noting that "Babcock is in command there and Yarnell is well situated with Moffett."[79] King subsequently made an overture to Moffett by writing a personal letter to his assistant, Capt. Alfred W. Johnson, that "I suppose that Bill Leahy has told you of my strenuous desire to get command in one of the scouts."[80]

Age requirements for duty with aviation forces in the Scouting Fleet stood among the key bureaucratic obstacles for King to navigate. Working behind the scenes, Leahy and Johnson placed King on track to fly higher within the ranks of the US Navy. Working the ropes at the Navy Department, Moffett sought senior-ranking officers, like King, for potential duty on the cutting edges of aviation technology. Captains already on track for such duty included Joseph M. Reeves, Harry E. Yarnell, Frederick Horne, Frederick D. Berrien, and Frank R. McCrary. Given King's well-established reputation in the surface and submarine fleets, Moffett recognized an opportunity to capitalize on the heroic story of *S-51*.

Moffett summoned King for an interview at the Navy Department, which culminated in a verbal offer for an aircraft carrier command on *Lexington*. Moffett then changed his mind as King handled the final details surrounding the postmortem investigation of

S-51. With some disappointment, King accepted orders to command *Wright*.[81] King subsequently assisted his relief, Andrews, in learning the ropes of the submarine force before relinquishing command in New London. Unlike King, Andrews failed to qualify in submarines during his tenure. Chasing King up the fleet ladder to the top, Andrews subsequently failed to qualify as an aviator. Naval Academy associates from the Class of 1901 recognized King as their pacesetter in the race to the stars within the ranks of American sea power.

CHAPTER 8
King of Aviators

King stood out as the personification of American sea power on the international stage and within the ranks of the US naval services. The dramatic salvage of *S-51* set King's popular image as a naval officer second to none in the American media. His celebrity status also extended to his family. Newspapers covered the activities of his daughters. When his eldest announced her engagement to a US Army pilot, journalists spun tales about "mutiny" in the King family.[1] Always watching for an opportunity, RAdm. William F. Moffett summoned King for a meeting at the Navy Department. Moffett offered King the chance to earn qualifications as a naval aviator. Moffett also dangled before him the promise of an accelerated promotion to flag rank—possibly as the next chief of BuAer. Age restrictions posed a potential hurdle, since King had far exceeded the limits imposed by BuMed. At age forty-seven, King solicited the orders for naval flight training. His initial request subsequently disappeared into the bureaucracy at BuNav. Moffett told King to "fret not, I have a friend or two who owe me."[2]

Moffett worked the lines in the Navy Department and among friends in Congress to enlist King in the bigger fight for air. The War Department threatened to overtake the Navy Department with such heroes as Charles Lindbergh and Jimmy Doolittle. Naval aviators like Cmdr. Harold Grow also captivated the public.[3] Yet, given the bureaucratic martyrdom of Billy Mitchell, Moffett worried about the prospective unification of army and naval aviation under a separate air force. Moffett recognized King as an ideal ally to help the cause of naval aviation under the political circumstances on the Washington battle-field of the late 1920s and into the 1930s.[4]

Pulling the requisite bureaucratic strings, Moffett arranged first orders for King to serve as skipper on *Wright*. The assignment served as a gateway to flight training in Pensacola, Florida. Having relieved his friend Babcock as skipper on *Wright*, King focused on earning the distinctive pin worn by naval aviators—featuring golden anchor with wings as fashioned after the Royal Air Force insignia during the First World War. US naval aviators considered themselves an elite branch, having earned the specialized qualifications for aviation duty. Older officers, like King, stood out among the younger aviators—most of them being lieutenants in their late twenties and early thirties.[5]

King exploited his prerogatives as the skipper on *Wright* by violating Navy Department safety regulations. On his personal authority, aviators assigned under his command provided King with tutorials about aviation theory and basic techniques in maneuver, as an initial preparation for formal flight training. King failed to request permission before he took to the air. Although he stood as the skipper in command on board *Wright*, Captains Harry E. Yarnell and John J. Raby technically held the superior authority for aviation operations. At that time, *Wright* served as the flagship for Yarnell as the commander of

Air Squadrons, Scouting Fleet. Raby served as his chief of staff. Thus, Yarnell and Raby technically held authority over King when he took to the skies in one of the seaplanes embarked with *Wright*.

Navy Regulations empowered seagoing commanders to assert their authority as they deemed necessary. By extension, rules of tradition superseded BuMed. As skipper on *Wright*, King violated BuMed age restrictions to begin flying lessons as an observer on his own. King took the aviators embarked on *Wright* by complete surprise by appearing in flight gear. He walked to the front of the wardroom and quietly sat down in a chair to hear the preflight briefing. King then acted with complete nonchalance by following the aviators of *Wright*. He then failed to request permission before climbing into the forward cockpit of an N-9H seaplane, as piloted by Lt. Carlton McGauley. Lt. Abel T. Bidwell recalled that King "just climbed into the cockpit and looked at McGauley with a dumb smirk."[6]

The commodore who was embarked, Yarnell, turned a blind eye when King began his unauthorized escapades in the air. On board *Wright*, King indeed ruled over the waves while Yarnell waived the rules. Yarnell acted surprised when King nearly lost control of a seaplane while landing. The incident forced Yarnell to push King to submit the proper paperwork. Yarnell then wrote an endorsement letter for King to enroll in flight training. Yarnell justified the waiver to ignore age restrictions by noting the impressive number of hours that King had already logged in off the record flights with McGauley.[7] With Yarnell's recommendation, Raby stated, "I presume it is the Department's desire to have some captains qualify as naval aviators [and] I believe there is no better candidate than Captain King [and] as a matter of principle I think that all personnel actually performing flight duty should be officially designated therefore."[8]

Moffett personally endorsed the request from King to receive formal designation as an aviator under instruction. Running against the prevailing winds of the Navy Department, Moffett upset the bureaucrats in the BuMed and BuNav by nullifying the administrative restrictions and age limit prerequisites for flight training. Moffett characterized King's request as "not only desirable but commendable, particularly in view of his age."[9] Moffett argued that it was "urgently recommended that Captain King be given orders to duty involving flying."[10] Moffett further pushed bureaucratic limits by suggesting that "in view of the great amount of flying that he is doing in connection with his present duty, that he be issued orders to duty involving flying in lieu of designation as a student naval aviator."[11]

SETTING PRECEDENTS

King exploited overlapping guidelines within Navy Regulations to circumvent the administrative hurdles of BuMed and BuNav. RAdm. Edward R. Stitt, BuMed, found King to be physically and psychologically qualified for aviation duty, "except for age which exceeds the specified age set forth in Article E-1202, BuNav Manual, 1925, in which this bureau ·concurs."[12] At forty-eight years of age, King's actions represented a direct threat to the existing system. The chief of BuNav, RAdm. William B. Shoemaker, concurred with the recommendation of Capt. Thomas R. Kurtz that "Captain King has shown that regardless of whether he has flying orders or not[,] he is spending considerable time in the air, considerably more than the minimum necessary in the case of officers with flight orders to draw flight pay."[13] Kurtz attempted to stop King in noting that "as a precedent would be established in this case, I recommend that his request to be designated a student aviator be disapproved."[14] Of note, Kurtz perhaps hoped to keep King from getting too far ahead among the Class of 1901 in the race up the fleet ladder to the stars.

Moffett and Yarnell encouraged King to continue flying, which greatly upset Shoemaker at the BuNav. King worked with Capt. John R. Y. Blakely to coordinate temporary duty orders to leave *Wright* during overhauls in drydock. Having qualified as an aerial observer, Capt. Frederick C. Horne subsequently took temporary command on *Wright* to enable King to complete formal aviation training. At that time, King earned the distinction of being the oldest to receive formal orders to duty as an aviator under instruction. Before Shoemaker had the chance to stop Moffett from approving the temporary-duty orders, King had already reported to Capt. Frank B. Upham at the Naval Air Station in Pensacola.

In the fight for control over officer assignments and appropriations, Moffett and Shoemaker feuded over the precedent set by King. As he flew over the sunny shores of Florida, Moffett and Shoemaker fought for control in Washington. BuAer sought more vacancies and to expand the number of qualified aviators, whereas BuNav struggled to keep the surface forces fully manned. Navy secretary Wilbur directed the director of Fleet Training, RAdm. Montgomery Taylor, to form a committee to assist the General Board in preparing recommendations to resolve the problem. Having earlier handled the controversies with Electric Boat Company, Taylor ably balanced the expectations of the bureau chiefs. The first "Taylor Board" fell short of Moffett's expectations, which prompted Taylor to form another board. In the aggregate, Taylor helped Moffett in expanding the aviation ranks.[15]

Aviation and submarines operated on the fringes of the prevailing mission, as supporting forces to the surface fleet. Insignia denoting specialized qualifications created tensions, since those wearing the golden dolphins of the submarine force and the anchored-wing insignia of naval aviation stood apart from their counterparts among the regular surface forces of the fleet. Upon reporting for duty in 1926, Lt. Joseph James "Jocko" Clark recalled his first meeting with Capt. Thomas C. Hart on *Mississippi*. He held submarine qualifications and had logged some hours in aircraft. Yet, as a battleship skipper, Hart followed the tradition of *not* wearing his specialized qualification insignia while serving outside the ranks of the submarine service.

The original purpose of specialized insignia centered on recruiting personnel from the regular line into the unproven ranks of the submarine and aviation functions of the fleet. Like King and other elders, Hart refused to allow submariners and aviators to presume supremacy over their shipmates of the regular line. Clark recalled that Hart barked about major personnel shortfalls among junior-ranking line officers throughout the fleet. Hart complained that "we got too goddamned many aviators on this ship already."[16] Ranting about the intrusion of aviators in the daily routines of battleship operations, Hart barked, "I can take you up to my quarterdeck and show you oil marks where the aviators have spilled oil."[17] "I can also show you Irish pennants hanging from the planes," and Hart exclaimed that "aviators are just not seamen!"[18]

Aviators presumed to hold status as an elite among the ranks of the American sea services. Regular sailors generally resented aviators for failing to pull together with the rest of the crew. Unlike the standard service uniforms worn by officers of the regular line, aviators stood out with green uniforms resembling those worn by the US Marine

Corps. Aviators further separated themselves from regular seamen by wearing distinctive insignia, flight suits, leather jackets, and silk scarves. Squadron logos worn on their jackets and painted on the sides of aircraft further separated the aviators as being somehow above their shipmates on board. Aviators took over the best spaces inside the ship, carving out their own hangouts in squadron wardrooms and marking their messroom tables with squadron logos.[19]

The unhealthy competition and resentment of surface sailors in their relations with submariners and aviators reflected similar divisions within the halls of the Navy Department. Moffett encroached upon the authority held by his counterparts among the bureau chiefs. The CNO frequently served as referee in the bureaucratic battles between the bureau chiefs. With Moffett attempting to create naval aviation as a fleet within a fleet, the chief of the BuNav, Shoemaker, retained control over the assignments of officers, and aviators stood subordinate to the overarching mission of the fleet. Battleships frequently sailed shorthanded. Younger officers with qualifications in submarines or aviation upset the hierarchical culture of the surface forces when serving in the seagoing line.

Many senior-ranking officers abandoned the established route up the fleet ladder within the surface fleet. Submarines and aviation provided an outlet for senior officers willing to take the riskier paths up the fleet ladder to flag rank. King followed Hart into submarines and then King followed Yarnell into aviation. In so doing, King stood among the few to hold qualifications for seagoing command in the surface line, submarines, and aviation. King attended flight school in Pensacola with two other officers of senior rank, Capt. Alva D. Bernhard and Commander Richmond Kelly Turner.

WRITTEN IN BLOOD

Aviation technology evolved with the winds, since wood and canvas airframes handled very much like kites with their underpowered engines. Flying from the open cockpits with crude instruments required aviators to always keep their wits. The daredevil spirit of many aviators helped in refining the design of aircraft. Safety regulations tended to reflect the lessons derived from past disasters. During ground school at Pensacola, Lt. Marshall R. Greer took charge as the instructor for the senior officers. He educated the prospective aviators to anticipate problems in the air, keep an eye on the horizon, and know that flight manuals were "written in blood." Flying as a wingman with King, Lt. (j.g.) Daniel V. Gallery Jr. helped the elder officers during training. Greer and Gallery had graduated with the same class at the Naval Academy—nearly two decades after King.

Having previously established credentials among the battleship and submarine ranks, King lacked the youthful spirit of fellow prospective aviators at Pensacola. Gallery recalled that King "was pretty old when he went through."[20] Gallery explained the divisions between the "black shoe" battleship sailors and "brown shoe" ranks of naval aviation.[21] "There was a very distinct division of the Navy between black shoes and the brown shoes," and Gallery observed that the "black shoes saw the battleship as being the backbone of the fleet."[22] "So we were glad," he continued, "to get any senior black shoes into our ranks by pinning wings on them."[23]

Gallery sought wings in his twenties, while King insisted on doing the same training in his forties. Gallery flew as wingman to King at Pensacola, which enabled the pair to develop an understanding. Senior naval officers attended Pensacola for the primary purposes of gaining familiarity with aviation. Officers in the ranks of commander and captain had the option to bow out of stunt flying and complicated flight maneuvers. Old hands, like King, held higher rank and frequently acted the part of "Johnny come lately."[24] Gallery changed his view of King when hearing him tell their flight instructor, "I'll take the stunt check the same as everyone else."[25]

Elder aviation candidates frequently failed to grasp the requisite avionic theories or master basic flight procedures. King recalled the difficulties experienced by his contemporary, Bernhard, during ground school in Pensacola. King vividly recalled Bernhard sitting alone in a chair in the barracks room. King described Bernhard as "this unhappy man practicing landings, seated in one chair, and attempting to move another according to the instruction manual that lay open on a third." King found out that Bernhard had "never driven a car or played tennis, pool, or any game that required timing of movement, and as he was over forty, his chances of learning seemed very poor." King characterized Bernhard as a "fine and outstanding officer [who] was determined to be a naval aviator or nothing."[26]

King set the pace among the elders, since Bernhard and Turner agreed to complete the same training as all their younger classmates in flight school. King described Turner as the top gun of the class at Pensacola. Turner helped King and Bernhard in keeping up with the academic requirements, since he kept excellent notes during the lectures at ground school. Turner had no trouble in the cockpit, whereas King struggled with developing the finesse required for more-complicated maneuvers. Bernhard struggled to get the swing of flying and washed out. The elder officers had the option of earning aviation observer (AO) qualifications, which also provided a pathway to command in aircraft carriers, zeppelins, and aviation auxiliaries and at naval air stations. Following King's lead, Bernhard refused to quit—earning the full qualification as a naval aviator in a following class.

Gallery watched King in action, progressively gaining a vivid perspective upon the individual personality. "He was a very austere and reserved sort of character," Gallery observed, noting that King eventually "loosened up and became one of the boys."[27] Comparing the older officers, Gallery thought "King [was] distant at first, but soon became one of the gang [while] 'Terrible' Turner just snarled at us." Gallery flew alongside King during a long-distance training flight from Pensacola to a remote airfield in Wilmington, North Carolina. "King and I and another officer slept together in the same bed," Gallery recalled; King "slept at the position of attention."[28] "King was a real lone wolf," Gallery thought. "I don't know that he had any close friends—I think I was eventually as close as anyone of my time."[29] Gallery thought King "was hard to know, but easy to love."[30]

King similarly learned to respect the inherent dangers of aviation, which required a daredevil's willingness to take measured risks within the existing limits of technology. He never "pushed the envelope" too far.[31] At Pensacola, Lt. Cmdr. Felix Baker and Lt. George van Deurs supervised King's training as an aviator. Van Deurs recalled receiving letters from fellow naval officers that said that King was a "horse's so-and-so, you don't want him in your outfit or any other, don't let him get by."[32] Van Deurs described King as being a complete teetotaler. With Prohibition being the law of the land, the younger officers of the squadron went to great lengths to hide their liquor in King's presence, though "every bunk [had] a three-gallon keg of shinny under it."[33] Van Deurs thought that "Ernie never saw any signs of liquor [since] we had been warned."[34]

The instructors at Pensacola required their senior-ranking students to meet the same high academic and physical standards as their younger naval aviation trainees. Baker recalled that "I had no 'personal' difficulties with him, but he was a hard student to teach."[35] "He was mechanical [and] by the numbers," Baker recalled; King "did not have the 'feel' of the airplane, but he was safe, calculating, and careful."[36] Baker explained:

> I reached the conclusion that, because of his large family he felt that he should take no unnecessary risks. He positively did not show personal fear, did not have any tendency to freeze at the controls or in any other way indicate fear when I was in the plane with him . . . there was never the slightest insertion of his superiority of rank.[37]

Younger aviators understood the role of elder officers like King. As a young lieutenant, Gallery explained that "it was impossible to get real aviators jumped way ahead of their time in rank to take the big jobs." Gallery thought that the "old timers didn't learn anything about flying [but] learned a lot about Naval aviation."[38] Gallery explained that the "older officers certainly had no resentment to[ward] the younger officers who were their instructors. [The] youngsters knew how to fly, and the oldsters didn't—so that was that."[39]

Memories of youthful skepticism about elder naval officers remained alive in King, which influenced his relationships with the junior-ranking upstarts among the submarine and aviation ranks. He failed to see himself as the elder among the new young turks of the fleet. In this respect, Gallery recalled how King always radiated confidence, since "it was just his natural way."[40] Van Deurs recalled that King also adapted to circumstances as required. Prohibition loomed over the party when King accidentally walked in on Gallery, van Deurs, and other younger aviators in training. Van Deurs recalled that "Ernie was just standing there looking silly with a glass in his hand before he knew what had happened."[41]

King immediately shifted his demeanor from being the senior officer present to that of an old-fashioned gentleman. He joined the party with grace and discipline. In so doing, King won the respect of the younger student aviators in Pensacola. He told his fellow aviators that he normally spent his "Saturday nights in his room while everybody else was down at the country club or the hotel just raising hell with a big dance." King remained all about business during the duty day throughout the week, although van Deurs noted that King purchased a membership in the country club and that thereafter "Ernie was the first guy there on Saturdays from then on." Many decades later, van Deurs thought that King "joined the club because actually he was a great guy with the ladies and liquor both."[42]

Quotations attributed to King associates like van Deurs have muddied the waters in considering the behavioral dynamics within the naval monoculture. When a statement is taken out of its original context, van Deurs may have implied bad behavior on the part of King. When it is placed into an objective historical context along with the rest of what van Deurs had to say, King clearly set the highest standards for other naval professionals to follow. Van Deurs clearly respected King for being an honorable naval officer. Van Deurs also grew to become a trusted friend of the King family. Taking the decades in between events into consideration, van Deurs characterized King as being "rough and tough as anybody ever said he was, but he was a helluva lot more human than most people give him credit for."[43]

Danger always chased the aviators at sea and ashore as they pressed the limits of existing technology. Among the aviators and in the seagoing ranks of the fleet, the peacetime stakes for sailors often proved fatal. Trailing behind King and Gallery on one training mission in a formation check flight over Pensacola, two aircraft collided in midair. Lieutenants William J. McCord and Edward R. Frawley corkscrewed to their deaths. Six other aviators in King's class at Pensacola died in subsequent training flights. Given the dangers, Gallery observed that King "sailed right through."[44] Gallery later recalled, "After we had finished the course and gotten our wings and went back in the fleet, he became E. J. King again."[45]

NAVAL AVIATOR NO. 3368

Aviator wings opened the doors for King to charge from the depths of the submarine force and surpass the humdrum of the surface fleet to achieve new highs within the ranks of the US Navy. Upon completing aviation training in Florida on May 26, 1927, at forty-eight years of age, King held pending status for six months because of the ongoing dispute between Moffett and Shoemaker at the Navy Department. Technically, he was still the skipper on *Wright* while he completed training on temporary orders to Pensacola. Summarizing King's performance as an aviator, Upham issued a fitness report that upset Shoemaker at the BuNav. Calling him a "Superior type of Line Officer," Upham explained that "Captain King is a qualified Naval Aviator and has set high standards for other Captains."[46]

Seagoing command on *Wright* enabled King to circumvent the existing bureaucratic barriers in his efforts to earn wings and take flight within the ranks of the US Navy. Further emphasizing the point after King returned to command *Wright* after completing formal flight qualifications, Raby issued additional endorsements. Raby described King as having "good material for Chief of BuAer [and] very forceful." [47] Raby recognized King as a prospective successor to Moffett as the future top aviator in the navy. Raby recommended King for future assignment to command in aircraft carriers. Yet, King waited for nearly six months to receive formal authorization from the Navy Department to wear the pin denoting his qualification as an aviator. Finally, after Moffett intervened, King received his formal designation as "Naval Aviator No. 3368" on December 8, 1927.[48]

Moffett promised King a future assignment to command an aircraft carrier, although his qualification had upset the lineup of other officers seeking the same duty. Too many senior-ranking officers sought orders for only three available aircraft carrier commands in the fleet. However, Moffett lacked enough qualified aviators for flight duty.[49] The US Navy competed with the US Army Air Corps for enough airframes to fill the hangars on board the aircraft carriers. Given other major challenges, the US Navy surface forces coveted the sailors on assignment for duty in aircraft carriers. Specialized qualifications for enlisted aviators sapped the surface fleet of able seamen.[50]

Within the aviation ranks of the joint services, King elbowed into the fight for the future of American sea power. Moffett gladly accepted King as a trusted adviser, although he had promised other well-qualified and seasoned aviators an aircraft carrier command. Administratively, King held the advantage of a higher lineal number and rank seniority by five years to Capt. John H. Towers. Given their earlier friendship, King and Towers indulged in a heated competition to reign supreme over naval aviation. King faced competition from Cmdr. Richmond Kelly Turner, Cmdr. John H. Hoover, Cmdr. John S. McCain, Cmdr. Leigh Noyes, and Cmdr. Patrick Bellinger. All were well qualified for command, but Moffett stood in the middle of multiple bureaucratic battles for air within the Navy Department, in relations with the War Department and with the Department of Commerce. The ratification of the Air Commerce Act of 1926 further complicated the bureaucratic calculus, particularly after the US Army Air Corps initiated discussion to carry the mail with the Postal Office Department.[51]

The accidental sinking of a submarine provided Moffett with an opportunity to maneuver King out of the bureaucratic crossfire in Washington. USS *S-4* sank with all hands following an accidental collision with the US Coast Guard cutter *Paulding* shortly before Christmas 1927. In the shallows off the New England coast, USS *S-4* settled into the mud with at least six of the forty crewmen still alive. Botched salvage efforts surrounding USS *S-4* represented a major public-relations disaster for the US Navy.[52] Under the circumstances, King received surprise orders to take charge of the salvage effort three months after the initial sinking. King reassembled his dream team of navy divers, Crilley, Eadie, and Hawes. Just as they had two years earlier with USS *S-51*, they successfully raised the wreck of USS *S-4* from the depths. King and his navy divers then supervised the grisly work of recovering the bodies of his fellow US Navy sailors entombed in USS *S-4*.[53] For his work, King again received letters of commendation from multiple admirals. He later received a Distinguished Service Medal for his role in salvaging USS *S-4*. Having previously earned Medals of Honor for their salvage work USS *S-51*, Crilley and Eadie received Navy Crosses for USS *S-4*. Another Medal of Honor sailor, Chief George Cregan, also received a Navy Cross for the the USS *S-4* salvage.[54]

Journalists portrayed King as an undersea hero comparable to the mythical Captain Nemo from the popular science fictions of Jules Verne. Exploits in subsurface operations also carried below the surface of popular narratives about King on the cutting edges of the futuristic image of naval aviation technology. He hitched a ride on board the newly commissioned *Lexington* on the way home from New England to Hampton Roads. The skipper, Berrien, gave King the flag officer's stateroom and the run of the ship. Much to his chagrin, King inadvertently entrapped himself with a Hollywood film crew.

Civilian journalists pestered King for gory details about the dead sailors recovered from the submarines he helped salvage. Greatly annoyed by the joyriders on board *Lexington*, King sicced the civilians away to instead harass US Army reserve colonels Charles A. Lindbergh and Billy Mitchell. Hounded by the journalists, Lindbergh looked with snake eyes upon King—much to his amusement as he peered from his perch on the flying bridge overlooking the flight deck along "vulture's row."[55]

King considered the media presence unsettling for the crew on *Lexington*, since the frenzy surrounding Lindbergh and Mitchell concurrently distracted from regular naval routines. Lindbergh embraced stardom, and Mitchell acted his part as the martyr of American airpower. In a calculated media stunt, Lindbergh and Mitchell caroused on the decks of *Lexington* to press the army vision of unification among the aviation branches of the land and sea services. King recalled, "Mitchell had a stain on his shirt, his tie was backwards and too short, and his dirty white socks could be seen because his pants were also too short."[56] King thought that Mitchell "looked like a traveling salesman."[57]

Lindbergh had just completed the first successful transatlantic flight. On board *Lexington*, King thought that "Lindy would have been a good one [and] just impressed the hell out of everybody."[58]

Petty rivalries among army and naval aviators reflected underlying problems of organization and competing political agendas within the American government. Airpower advocates within the army shrewdly used the American media to generate excitement about the futuristic vision of the wild blue yonder. Building from the heroic image of dashing aviators of the First World War, Col. Henry A. "Hap" Arnold championed efforts to recruit unemployed barnstormers while using US Army resources to support the delivery of airmail on behalf of the US Postal Service.

The civil-military legislative question of using military personnel to carry the mail sparked controversy in Congress. Shaping the image of the army air corps as an elite group, wartime aces like Eddy Rickenbacker were joined by barnstormers like Jimmy Doolittle and Charles Lindbergh to fly the mail.[59] The concept impressed naval aviators like Moffett. The mail delivery mission represented an important opportunity to develop long-range airframes. King credited Arnold for pushing the limits of constitutional restraints on civil-military relationships. King observed that "Arnold was a likable fellow, though not too much in the way of brains." King explained that his nickname, "'Happy,' was appropriate [because] he was always willing to say, 'me too.'"[60]

STRONG MEN

Burgeoning rivalries between the pilots of the US Army and aviators of the US Navy coincided with struggles for resources between the Departments of War and Navy. Propaganda reflected the fight for air among the aviation branches of the armed services. Moffett countered army propaganda by highlighting the dashing uniforms and colorful image of naval aviation at air shows. He pushed aviators to extreme limits by sending them on long flights over the oceans to reach the shores of Asia and Europe. Moffett used the media to rally support among taxpayers. Among his biggest weapons in the propaganda war, zeppelins captivated onlookers. Aviation—and smaller warships among the scouting forces—also stood out as being means to circumvent the somewhat toothless diplomatic restrictions as imposed upon global navies under such provisions as the Treaty of Paris, or alternatively the Kellogg-Briand Pact of 1928.

Politics always intermixed with American naval strategy in framing the future priorities for fleet operations in both peace and war. The majestic image of zeppelins flying gracefully among the clouds over American cities drew popular interest in naval aviation. While impressive, zeppelins proved impractical for actual fleet operations. RAdm. Joseph Reeves joined King in the chorus in making the forceful argument against the zeppelin program. Reeves and King advocated for future expenditures in aircraft carrier construction.[61] Moffett disregarded naysayers in debates surrounding the zeppelin program, or LTA, while others sought HTA airframes for use with warships among the fleet.

The specter of service unification loomed over the internal fights concerning the vision of a separate national civil-military air service. Like the fabled tale of Icarus, Mitchell had flown too close to the political sun in pushing the idea of strategic airpower. Yet, as Mitchell accepted his place as a bureaucratic martyr on the public stage, Moffett quietly worked the lines to protect the future of naval aviation. Moffett's two-pronged focus on

LTA and HTA conversely divided the ranks of BuAer. Zeppelins consistently failed to prove their worth under operational conditions, inspiring efforts to focus on aircraft carriers.[62] King added his voice to those of Reeves and Towers in pushing future fleet construction priorities for USS *Langley* (CV-1) and the newer aircraft carriers of the fleet, USS *Lexington* (CV-2) and USS *Saratoga* (CV-3).

Zeppelins loomed large in the propaganda of naval aviation, whereas aircraft carriers stood out as an unproven novelty within the context of the battleship fleet. Grappling with the question of strategic airpower, Moffett and King agreed on the importance of delineating the differences between land and sea operations. Moffett pressed the LTA vision of vast fleets of zeppelins flying majestically over the fleet. The dramatic flights of US Navy zeppelins inspired Philip F. Nowlin in creating the popular science fictions of Buck Rogers, which resonated among American youth. Moffett shrewdly exploited the popularity of such futuristic visions to generate public support for his naval aviation agenda. King agreed with Moffett in shaping the functions of aviation as being an "integral part of the navy."[63]

Airships competed with battleships in shaping the futuristic image of the US Navy in popular media. Moffett used zeppelins as the counterargument against US Army concepts of strategic airpower. The spectacle and drama of massive airships flying overhead proved successful, as smaller fighter aircraft flew like bees around the hive, hovering aloft. During operations, naval aviators orbited in smaller fighter aircraft around zeppelins. Audiences reveled in watching film footage of aircraft being recovered with hooks and then hoisted into the hangars fitted within the larger zeppelin. King recognized the propaganda value of zeppelins although concluded that the technology "had no practical value and are a waste of resources." "Zeppelins excited the public, but are too vulnerable," King argued. "Zeppelins have no real use in war."[64]

Moffett and King disagreed about the role of zeppelins, although they shared a common view about the importance of aircraft carriers. "Admiral Moffett was a strong man," King recalled, "[and] apparently I was too."[65] Running against Moffett on the question of naval air power, King risked opportunities for future assignment to an aircraft carrier command. Among other points of contention, King criticized Moffett for using zeppelins "tactically when their proper use was strategically, for scouting."[66] Unable to hold his tongue with Moffett in debating priorities during service in the BuAer, King rankled the other bureau chiefs within the Navy Department while filling in for Moffett during his junket overseas as a delegate to the London Disarmament Conference in 1929.

The key policymakers within the Navy Department left for London with their assistants in Washington. Like a fox in a henhouse, King seized the opportunity to set policy by exercising his *acting* authority in the absence of Moffett. Navy secretary Curtis D. Wilbur prepared to depart office after the arrival of his successor, Charles Francis Adams III. The discussions in London dominated the thoughts of Wilbur and Adams—leaving the assistant Navy secretary, Henry Latrobe Roosevelt, to take the helm of the Navy Department. Roosevelt empowered King to completely reorganize BuAer during Moffett's absence. Roosevelt and King also discussed the problem of focusing too heavily on the functions and capabilities of individual ships and aircraft—both agreeing about the importance of keeping the broader strategic purposes to developing the "balanced fleet" wherein all the individual assets operated in unison to achieve clear and discernable ends, whether in peace or war.[67]

Roosevelt and King pressed the limits of their *acting* authorities to enact policies without first asking their superiors for permission. For example, Moffett placed high priority on expanding the ranks of naval aviation, although he sought to achieve this objective by creating pressure on Congress through public affairs. He kept several celebrities on the books for the purposes of creating a certain image, perhaps at the ultimate expense of naval aviation. King personally disliked many in Moffett's inner circle. King referred to them as "'prima donna' aviators—Al Williams, the speed king, [Carleton] C. Champion, a top altitude flyer, and Dick Byrd, the arctic explorer."[68] Given the opportunity with the *acting* authority as chief of BuAer, King conspired with his classmate Kurtz and RAdm. Richard H. Leigh in the BuNav. King arranged sea-duty orders for Williams, Champion, and Byrd.[69] Williams resigned in protest, which riled Moffett.

The question of strategic airpower loomed over the discussions concerning the focus of future priorities. President Herbert Hoover enacted policies designed to reduce budgets by cutting the armed services. Already struggling to fill existing requirements in the fleet, Moffett countered the army propaganda campaign by portraying naval aviation as an elite service within the already established context of the selective ranks of the American fleet. Moffett countered the heroic aura surrounding figures like Lindbergh and Doolittle of the army with the equally impressive exploits of William, Champion, and Byrd of the navy. The zeppelin program stood as a centerpiece in the Moffett propaganda agenda. To the chagrin of many naval aviators, the Army Air Corps masterfully used propaganda and "out-Moffetted Moffett."[70]

RAGTIME

Upon King's return from London, Moffett and King squared off for a major showdown about their differences concerning the future of naval aviation. Moffett ultimately shared King's concerns and recognized the importance of aircraft carriers, although the two essentially failed to work together in meeting their common objectives in the air. In memoirs, King explained that "words passed."[71] Moffett lost patience with King. "Possibly one or the other had a bad night, but the fur flew," King recalled about losing faith in his boss when "Moffett suggested sarcastically that he should quit so that King could be chief of the BuAer."[72] In frustration, King requested any available orders for an immediate assignment to sea duty.

Moffett banished King to voluntary exile at sea, far from the bureaucratic dramas of the Navy Department. Moffett kept King on track to become a future successor as chief of BuAer. Moffett characterized King's service as the assistant chief of the BuAer. Moffett described King as a true professional of the highest "personal and military character."[73] Moffett then alluded to the ongoing fight between the BuAer and BuNav by mentioning King's "tact in handling personnel."[74] "Captain King had been selected for and actually been ordered in command of the carrier USS *Lexington*." Moffett explained that King accepted the "natural disappointment at losing command of a carrier [with] the greatest cheerfulness and has shown the most marked attention to duty."[75]

King received an additional second assignment as skipper on *Wright* along with collateral command responsibility ashore in command of naval airfields in Hampton Roads. Moffett verbally reaffirmed promises about a future command on *Lexington*—upon the detachment of the skipper, Capt. Frank D. Berrien. Moffett failed to tell other aspirant aviators, like Towers, about the fact that the fix had already been arranged for King to have *Lexington*. Among the aviation ranks, Towers stood out as being one of the guys, whereas King held popular status as an old fogie—an outcast among elder battleship sailors. All bets centered on Towers as the most likely successor to Berrien as the future skipper of *Lexington*.

Having traversed the fleet ladder together, King and Berrien had completely different leadership styles in relations with their subordinates. Berrien played the role of being a friend to every sailor. Berrien allowed the aviators on *Lexington* to mimic the white scarf and leather jacket look of Lindbergh. Many painted or pinned the distinguishing wings of gold on their leather jackets. Brown shoes and humorous squadron insignia further set the aviators apart from the regular line officers and deck seamen. King found the elitism among many naval aviators deeply problematic. He thought that aircraft of any design should always serve the tasks for which the airframe could best perform a given purpose. In the context of the fleet, King viewed aircraft as nothing more than manned equivalents to the shells fired from battleship guns.[76]

King insisted upon following the established rule of never wearing an insignia unless assigned on flight status. Thus, he never wore the submarine pin. However, King made special efforts to continue wearing naval aviation insignia by maintaining the hourly requirements for keeping flight status. King's demeanor and seemingly quirky fixation on regulations reflected his personality. Many of his contemporaries within the ranks viewed King as a lone wolf with antisocial tendencies. Brown-shoe aviators of the younger generation likewise viewed King as a misfit. He greatly upset the naval aviators embarked on *Lexington* by making black shoes the required footwear for all hands. Aviators disliked the order, since it directly undercut the elitist assumptions of brown-shoe culture.

Rumors among the crew preceded the arrival of King, which amplified the desired effect in setting the tone on board *Lexington*. Commissioned just two years earlier in December 1927, *Lexington* gained the reputation as the showboat of the fleet. Shakedowns followed the standard process employed in regular surface ships.[77] Without enough aviators and airframes to conduct major flight operations, *Lexington* sailed majestically along the coast between major cities for the purposes of rallying American taxpayers to support the fleet. Upon assuming command, Berrien embraced his role as a spokesman for the navy. The *Lexington* crew settled into their mission of presenting a future vision of the US Navy on the high seas and skies above.[78] As Berrien cheerfully played the role of the good cop, the executive officer, Cmdr. John H. Hoover, took the role of bad cop in relations with the crew.

Berrien proved very popular among the crew, although Hoover had earned the reputation for being a complete martinet with the reputation for dressing down officers in the presence of their men. Berrien played the role of good cop, always cheerfully encouraging the crew and playing the role of fatherly figure. Hoover earned the wry nickname "Genial John," for his appearance. He always dressed impeccably and, while he struck fear among the crew, Hoover earned the reputation for being fair.[79] With the pending detachment of Berrien as skipper, he and Hoover began preparing the *Lexington* crew for the arrival of King. Lending a hand, the old salts spread rumors about their youthful antics with King in the Asiatic Fleet. Sea stories about King enhanced the mystique and fearsome reputation of King as a person.

Shipboard newspaper stories appeared, setting the stage for the arrival of King as the prospective skipper. One yarn told the tale of "Neptune's Son," and another warned the *Lexington* crew to keep a lookout for "Ahab's Ghost." Berrien clearly helped in shaping the expectations of the *Lexington* crew in anticipation of the combination punch of King and Hoover.[80]

The crew assembled to form on the flight deck as Berrien and King appeared. Hoover stood at the head of the formation. Berrien and King walked briskly to the podium. Berrien waxed poetic and delivered a flowery speech with honest emotion before reading his detachment orders to the crew. He then shook hands with King as he walked up to the podium. In his deep midwestern drawl, King read his orders to assume command.

The *Lexington* crew stood with their counterparts from the aviation detachment while King delivered a short speech. He had delivered variations of the same speech many times before when taking command. Perhaps King sympathized with the sailors in formation. Knowing that their feet perhaps hurt after hearing the long prose of their former skipper, King set a completely different tone. "There are no shortcuts," King mused. "All hands are expected to do their part—the sharks do not care about your rank."[81] Stories about his terse speech resonated in the folklore among aviators. Nearly a year after King took command, Jocko Clark remembered fellow aviators lamenting the departure of Berrien and mimicking King's gruff conclusion: "Different skippers, different long splices. Carry on!"[82]

Immediately following the change of command, King and Hoover strode off the deck to the island on the starboard side of the flight deck. Berrien simultaneously requested permission to disembark from the officer of the deck (OOD); he then saluted the colorsand traversed the companion ladder, and, as his gig departed, the claxon on *Lexington* rang for general quarters. The stunned sailors of *Lexington* stood there shocked. When the old hands broke for their battle stations, the younger sailors scurried to action—many dressed in their white dress uniforms. King sat at his perch on the flying bridge as Hoover stood by. Too slow! Hoover harangued the *Lexington* crew through the tin-sounding speakers on the 1 Main Circuit (1 MC). Upon securing from battle stations, almost immediately the claxon for General Quarters rang and the trumpets blared in the backdrop of the standard instructions, as broadcasted through the 1 MC.[83]

With the detachment of Berrien, *Lexington* quickly transformed to reflect the personality of King. In contrast, Berrien focused on surface operations and largely delegated the functions associated with flight operations to the squadron commanders. He ran the ship and allowed the aviators free rein in the air. Berrien allowed aviators to perform stunts during operations. Worse still, he turned a blind eye when aviators occasionally took joy rides for overnight visits with girlfriends ashore. As a result, *Lexington* had acquired a reputation as a "slack and ragtime ship."[84] Gallery recalled the moment immediately after Berrien relinquished command, traded salutes with the new skipper, and traversed the companion ladder for duty ashore. Within minutes, King's voice boomed over the loudspeakers. He called the *Lexington* officers and embarked squadron commanders to the conference room immediately adjacent to his stateroom. "When they were all assembled," Gallery explained,

King strode out of his stateroom into the cabin with the US Navy regulations under his arm . . . he glared at the assembled officers for a few moments then took the book from his arm and slammed it on the table and said, "[F]rom now on we run this a ship according to this book . . . that is all[,] gentlemen."[85]

The officers stood in shock until someone broke the tenuous silence with a dirty joke. "King was a cold[-]blooded and aloof individual, very difficult to be intimate with," Gallery recalled, continuing that King "expected you to do a good job and his attitude was 'don't expect to get a medal for doing it, that's what you are paid for.'"[86] "He was a man of few words," Gallery noted. "When things were going to his satisfaction, he would just grunt [but] when things were going wrong he had plenty to say and it was emphatic, profane, and to the point—but he was not unreasonable."[87]

King set high standards for the *Lexington* crew in driving them to seek status as the best of the fleet. Having graduated from the Naval Academy in the Class of 1929, Ens. Robert A. Heinlein hoped to earn wings as a naval aviator. He initially served under Barrien as a gunnery officer and earned a temporary-duty assignment to refine his skills in New York City. Having lived the bohemian lifestyle in Greenwich Village, he rejoined the ship in Hampton Roads shortly after Berrien transferred command to King. Upon returning to *Lexington*, Heinlein immediately recognized major changes in the personality of the crew. He knew King from previous interactions as a close friend of his daughters. Heinlein fully understood King, knowing the sharp contrasts between the environment ashore in Annapolis and the mission afloat on *Lexington*. Heinlein knew King as a devoted family man from visits to his home in Annapolis. Heinlein knew King's reputation for being relentless as a seagoing naval officer.[88]

Heinlein drove the initial conversation with King by claiming to hold aspirations to attend the Navy Postgraduate School. Heinlein enrolled in the Naval War College correspondence course. By discussing his professional aspirations, Heinlein avoided talking about his recent divorce. He knew that King viewed divorced naval officers as being somehow defective. Having failed in marriage, Heinlein clearly drew the interest of King. Placed in charge of preparing the shipboard newspaper, Heinlein carried the unspoken duty of entertaining King and crew with weekly stories in his column, "The Neighborhood News (With Malice for All and Charity for None)." The experience proved definitive in shaping the futuristic vision of Heinlein, since King later provided the key inspiration for the science fiction character "Captain Yancey" in the Heinlein novel *Space Cadet*, and, by extension, King inspired the character of "Commodore Christopher Pike" in the literature of *Star Trek*.[89]

CHAPTER 9

Johnny Come Lately

The crusty traditions of a bygone era seeped into the shipboard culture among the crew on *Lexington.* The sleek lines of the cruiser hull and massive flight deck towering above suggested the future, although King adopted the briny persona of a sea captain from another time. He rarely betrayed a subordinate with a smile or unwarranted praise. King seemed distant to most of the *Lexington* crew, although a few of the old timers on board amplified his commanding aura with sea stories and tall tales. Among many of the junior officers, King initially seemed maniacal, humorless, and downright mean. Others saw through the act. For example, Heinlein later used the personality of King to write science fiction adventure stories. As the publisher of the shipboard newspaper, *The Observer*, King also became the first formal editor in Heinlein's early career as an author. During service together on *Lexington*, King inspired Heinlein to see the future of American sea power—over the blue seas, below the darkest depths, and beyond to the brightest stars of space.[1]

King hit *Lexington* like an armor-piercing enemy bomb by setting their sights on fixing the divisions between aviators and regular seamen. With this basic goal in mind, King used his executive officer, Hoover, as the hatchet man. King and Hoover shared the duty of being the proverbial "bad cops" in whipping the *Lexington* crew into shape. They also refused to allow elitist cliques among the aviators to persist on board *Lexington.* Before King and Hoover arrived, the black-shoe sailors carried the heavy burdens of maintaining the ship and handling the dangerous duty of managing the flight deck. Brown-shoe aviators tended to fade into the clubhouse atmosphere of their wardrooms below decks before and after flight operations. King and Hoover recognized the divisions between black-shoe sailors and brown-shoe aviators as detrimental to overall good order and discipline.

King and Hoover left the warrant officers and chief petty officers to the task of whipping the deck seamen into shape. In turn, King and Hoover worked in tandem to break the aviators of their elitist assumptions. Aviators also tended to operate in packs, which King and Hoover addressed by forcing them to fly in different types of aircraft rather than specializing in any single type of airframe. He further upset routines by placing aviators on regular seagoing watch schedules, which had to be balanced against the rigorous rotation of flight operations. Squadron commanders lodged formal complaints and invoked safety concerns, which King simply rejected without explanation. For many brown-shoe aviators, his approach fueled his reputation among the brown-shoe aviators as a "Johnny come lately."[2]

King created a major stir among aviators by issuing orders for all hands to wear the standard uniform of the day for the surface fleet. He required all hands to wear black shoes on board *Lexington.* King and Hoover issued fines for aviators found in brown shoes. Flight suit coveralls also became off-limits for aviators unless they were walking between their briefing rooms and the cockpit.[3] Anyone on the flight deck required a reason for being there. King refused to allow sailors to simply stand around on his flight deck. On one occasion, he witnessed a pair of aviators wafting around and smoking cigarettes. The pair attempted to hide under the fight deck up near the bow. King saw a puff of cigarette smoke. From the crow's nest, King barked at the two and directed them to report to the bridge. His voice carried over the flight deck.[4] The two aviators vanished. When nobody reported to the bridge, King ordered squadron commanders to collect all cigarettes, issue them only when the smoking lamp was lit, and log the consumption of cigarettes by the serial numbers of each aviator.[5]

Like the tactics employed by the fictional Captain Queeg in naval literature, King issued an order for squadron commanders to sign and submit a weekly report for the number of cigarettes consumed by each aviator on board *Lexington*. Squadron commanders held personal responsibility to prepare the reports for initial review by the executive officer, Hoover. In turn, King reviewed the reports. Occasionally, he returned the reports to the squadron commanders with annotations directing reductions in the consumption of cigarettes by each of the individual aviator serial numbers.[6] Thus, King never knew the actual identity of the persons affected.

As the lords of discipline on board *Lexington*, King and Hoover set a new tone for sailors and aviators to develop together as a singular team. As the aide to the skipper, Heinlein had a unique perspective on the tactics employed by King and Hoover. During service on *Lexington*, Heinlein regularly later wrote about King's tactics to his Naval Academy classmate Lt. (j.g.) Caleb "Cal" Laning—the nephew of the president of the Naval War College, RAdm. Harris Laning.[7] Among other initiatives, King organized study groups for junior officers, like Heinlein, to complete their Naval War College correspondence courses for prerequisite screening for future assignment to assignments leading to promotion. The numerical annotation for completing the Naval War College curriculum provided inroads for individuals, like Heinlein, to compete for higher marks on fitness reports and for choice assignments.[8]

King operated *Lexington* as a cruiser, and he considered the aviation wing embarked as nothing more than long-range gun projectiles. Aviation squadron commanders conversely acted as though their wings qualified them as being somehow superior to the traditional line of battle mentality of the fleet. Aviators on *Lexington* initially disliked King for insisting on adhering to what they believed were antiquated spit-and-polish traditions. For example, aviation squadron commanders customarily referred to themselves in the navy vernacular as "skippers." King asserted his role by insisting that only he held the prerogative to use the titles of "captain" or "skipper."[9] King tolerated no special privileges, or call signs for aviators. King bruised the egos of aviation squadron commanders by grouping them with all the other subordinates. He addressed them only by their rank, functional title, or surname. He rankled squadron executive officers—all holding status as senior lieutenants or lieutenant commanders—by grouping them with all the other officers on board. He addressed officers below the rank of commander as "mister."[10] Heinlein recalled, "Aviators used to rant about this 'slur' in private—but they had centuries of tradition against them; there can be only one captain in a ship underway."[11]

King methodically established himself as being the one and only captain on board *Lexington*. He drew from archaic British naval traditions to whip the crew into shape. King confused many by referring to the "Marine Guard captain as [the higher rank of] 'Major.'"[12] King always requested permission to enter the spaces assigned to the marine detachment.

Although he held the prerogative to go wherever he desired to go as the skipper, King requested permission to enter spaces assigned to the chief petty officer's mess. More confusingly to many of the officers on *Lexington*, King always treated the warrant officers as though they held equal rank. He traded jokes and spoke in an informal manner by the first name with warrant officers, although he generally referred to the higher enlisted ratings as "chief."[13]

PLAY BALL

King expected aviators to act in accordance with the higher traditions of naval service, always being prepared to stand the watch. Heinlein recalled that the "aviators in particular bitched about it."[14] King's relentless drilling of aviators included making them "get up so early just for practice."[15] Heinlein recalled that aviators "particularly resented the days on which planes were warmed before daybreak but not flown—insufficient gasoline allotment to fly."[16] Heinlein explained that King forced aviators to simulate battle, "manning his plane, then sat in for an hour, ready to fly, then hears the bugler sound 'secure from battle stations.'"[17] Heinlein remembered many occasions when aviators became "particularly surly about 'that bastard on the bridge'—since, by King's policy, no one but he himself knew whether or not the planes would actually be ordered into the air."[18]

King took firm control of the helm by enforcing the hierarchical chain of command to instill good order and discipline. Like Nelson's band of brothers, King expected his officers to work hard and exceed standards of performance and personal conduct. Enlisted personnel faced dire consequences for failure. Using Navy Regulations as the tool, he punished bad conduct or poor performance with swiftness and clarity. Through these measures, King ultimately instilled a sense of confidence among the crew. He used profanity, just as "Mozart is played." Witnesses recalled King's "command voice—pitched just loud enough for me to hear it said in flat tones."[19]

King frequently surprised the crew by appearing unannounced in places normally ignored in the bowels of the ship. In so doing, he won the trust of many old salts among the regular ship's company on *Lexington* by rejecting the cockiness among many of the aviators and enlisted personnel assigned from the squadrons. King used baseball as an analogy to explain his leadership philosophy to the *Lexington* crew. His philosophy appeared in notes taken by Heinlein in the shipboard newspaper, *The Observer*. "We will assume that the ship is akin to a baseball team," King mused, and that the "crew [is] the team [and] the Commanding officer [is] the umpire."[20] He continued that the "umpire requires all men to be in proper uniform and in their places at the command "Play Ball" [and] each man must be ready to take his turn at bat and be ready to "Hit the Ball."[21] King explained that the "same procedure holds true with the ship."[22] King emphasized that the "Commanding Officer expects everyone to be in proper uniform and ready to 'Turn To' and "Hit the ball' on time—let us show good sportsmanship BE ON TIME AND READY TO HIT THE BALL."[23]

Baseball and boxing matches provided informal opportunities for King participate in the social culture on board *Lexington*. All hands individually had a job to do, and, together, all hands shared in the collective success of *Lexington*. Taking the role of the ship's league commissioner, King monitored the baseball teams of each of the individual divisions and squadrons to identify the most-talented ringers for *his* ship's all-star team. Before a baseball grudge match against the *Saratoga* team, King told his handpicked roster of *Lexington* baseball stars that the "ship has not fallen down on anything since I came aboard[, and it] makes little difference in most activities if you do it—it generally gets done."[24] Pressing his point, King told his ballplayers that the

> important consideration is how you do it, in what style. Talking about style gets one nowhere. In the doing of many things, one develops style. It must become the desire, the will of everyone who has the ship's interest at heart to do things in a manner that will maintain and build up what we would like to call "*Lexington* Style."[25]

Playing to win, King enabled his ballplayers time to refine their skills. His mechanics built a pitching machine and rigged a batting cage in the repair spaces on the hangar deck. Pitchers regularly tossed balls through a spare tire. One sailor with previous experience as a semiprofessional ballplayer, Howard Mills, joined *Lexington* while King stood in command. Mills discovered that *Lexington* ballplayers enjoyed extra free time to refine their skills—all for the purposes of dominating opposing teams from other ships in fleet tournaments.[26] King expected his team to win by any means necessary with respect for the game and for the opposing team. He used the same approach in war. He expected his sailors to do the right thing as members of *his* team—even when unsupervised.

King regularly conducted formal inspections on a rotating schedule between the various departments and subdivisions. He kept to the schedule to enable the *Lexington* crew to anticipate inspections. King knew about the gambling rings, dirty magazines, and other sailorly activities under the polished surface of shipboard culture. Warships, in the end, required the human factor to enable the machine to operate in harmony. Being an old hand himself, King knew all the hiding places for illicit liquor in the overheads and under hatches. Unlike other sea captains of his generation, King kept to the "Fleet-wide unwritten rule: DON'T GET CAUGHT."[27]

Heinlein observed how King recognized higher performance by allowing individuals to perform their assigned tasks without close supervision. Through his approach, King influenced the sailors of *Lexington* to work harder and play together as a close-knit team and not as a "ragtime" collection of individuals doing their own thing.[28] Occasionally, King found evidence of alcohol being consumed on board. He monitored the individuals in question and acted only when their performance became problematic. King regularly held court at the head of his wardroom table with the squadron commanders and their equivalents from the various departmental subdivisions.

Through such traditional rituals, King greatly upset the routines already established on board *Lexington*. His friend and predecessor in command, Berrien, had allowed the squadron commanders to keep their own separate routines and watch rotations. Lt. Jocko Clark joined *Lexington* as skipper in Fighting Squadron 2 (VF-2) shortly after King assumed command. Clark described, "*Lexington* was by far the cleanest ship on which I ever served."[29] Similarly, he characterized King as being like a sea captain of a bygone era "with a deceptive twinkle in his eye."[30] Clark explained the secret to working under King. "If a man knew his business, it was easy enough to get along with Ernie King."[31]

King whipped the *Lexington* crew into walking with a swagger, which by extension served as a reflection of *his* reputation among other warship commanders. "Within a few months after he took command," Heinlein described that the "Lady Lex was the tautest—and happiest—ship in the fleet and winning every sort of competition."[32] King encouraged

Heinlein to write accounts of the *Lexington* with pizzazz. King told Heinlein to write fictional stories for the entertainment of the crew in *The Observer*, which kept the readers guessing about the next exciting episode in the story line. King directed Heinlein to write stories about naval history that applied to the operations being performed by the crew on *Lexington*. Heinlein drew some inspiration from Buck Rogers in crafting his weekly fictions. Historical sea stories about familiar heroes from Horatio Nelson to John Paul Jones appeared with stories of pirates, sea shanties, and mermaids. Heinlein thought, "We were a band of brothers (in Nelson's words), and Uncle Ernie was our inspiration and mentor."[33]

THE OBSERVER

King reviewed Heinlein's earliest writings as the publisher of the shipboard weekly newspaper, *The Observer*. King recognized Heinlein's talent for writing. King gave Heinlein responsibility for producing the column "Weekend Watch." As the assistant editor of *The Observer*, Heinlein developed a biweekly serial about a detective—based directly on the personality of their skipper and senior officers. Heinlein worked with King in the editing process. Thus, the Heinlein stories served as another way for King to communicate to the crew.[34] Heinlein later built upon the experience in writing the "Heinlein Juveniles" of science fiction, including the bestseller *Starship Troopers*.[35]

King used the shipboard newspaper and the creative writings of contributors like Heinlein as an alternative means to foster the community dynamic on board *Lexington*. Together, King and Hoover used the shipboard newspaper as an informal means to turn *Lexington* into a true community. Heinlein wrote humorous articles interspersed with lighthearted prose, which conveyed serious direction from the higher command. One headline, "Plan Folding Planes for Subs," highlighted experiments for using submarines to attack the Panama Canal with aircraft. In the same issue, Heinlein used salty humor to soften the seriousness of the work performed on *Lexington*. Heinlein reported that "Soapy Davis says his mother wanted him to study abroad, so he joined the Navy and has been studying them in various ports of call."[36]

Operations in close quarters on board an experimental warship under the steady command of King defined the futuristic perspective of Heinlein. The salty "old man" King seemed to come from a completely different planet than Heinlein, as the past intertwined with the future of American sea power. Heinlein explained that "I have found that among officers old enough to remember King and had served under him," and that there existed "just two sorts: those who think he was wonderful, and those who hate his guts."[37] Having unique access to King as the editor of the *Lexington* newspaper, Heinlein prepared all the reports as aide to King. In addition to his duties as assistant communications officer (pronounced as "COMMO"), Heinlein stood bridge watch as assistant navigation officer (or "NAV") and qualified junior officer of the deck (or "J"–"O"–"O"–"D").[38] Heinlein reviewed all the message traffic arriving, or sent, from *Lexington*. King directed Heinlein to hold collateral duty as defense lawyer during "captain's mast" rituals.[39]

King exhibited unique capacity for using the chain of command while simultaneously communicating to all the sailors throughout the ship. He mastered the art of exploiting the scuttlebutt culture of the ship. Heinlein observed King handling the crew with the masterful grace of a horseman mounted on a well-trained steed. Heinlein explained that King treated the crew with "utter fairness at all times [and] he never missed a shortcoming—but I never knew him to use other than a quiet, neutral voice in correcting one."[40] Heinlein observed that King "was equally quick to note excellence, to remark on it, at once and in louder voice."[41] "If he ever gave an officer a royal chewing-out," Heinlein explained, "it was in his cabin with the door closed . . . any word of it that got out came from the victim himself, not from King."[42] Heinlein used the phrase "training admirals" in describing King's approach to command.[43] "One way or another," Heinlein observed, King "always got rid of the misfits. Heinlein thought, "King taught by example rather than by precept."[44]

King fostered an aura of mystery about the purposes behind some of the tasks he assigned to the crew. "Familiarity breeds contempt," King wrote to a friend. "The service demands us to do what we are required to do in the rank and time our duty demands us to do so."[45] Many wondered about his strange practice of mixing up the uniforms of the day. For example, he ordered the *Lexington* crew turned out in his "Russian uniform." White jackets and blue trousers with blue caps became a trademark of King. King indirectly influenced the daily routine of every sailor by mixing up his selections of uniforms as they attempted to guess the prescribed uniform for the following day. Heinlein replicated the experience in prose:

All hands, now hear this! The uniforms for inspection will be—1st Division, dungarees; 2nd Division, blue dress with flat hats; 3rd Division, undress whites; fourth division, undress blue with wet weather gear and bare feet; M Division, undress blue, pea coats, and watch caps (that one might cause some fast scurrying around as the black gang may be lax about having watch caps), B Division, white dress with white hats; E Division, white undress trousers, undershirts, white hats; A Division, undress blue, white hats; V Division, flight-deck khaki for flight-deck personnel, summer flight suits, C Division, dress for all those holding flight orders; Marine Guard, first platoon, combat dress with packs and all weapons, second platoon, blue full dress with white gloves, white belts, and medals; S Division white working clothes with cooks and bakers in uniform chef's caps, others in white hats; C Division, N Division and band, blue full dress.[46]

King expected officers to set the example for enlisted sailors, standing in formation with their men—regardless of their status as ship's company or aviation squadron or flag staff. King used the uniform inspections as an opportunity for comedy, as he indulged in a friendly game with Lt. Abraham DeSomer.

King demonstrated an acute sense of humor, which many observers among the crew began to celebrate. He loudly razzed DeSomer—a former enlisted man—about being having "poor judgement for accepting his demotion as a commissioned officer." Having received the Medal of Honor for earlier service as an enlisted sailor at Veracruz, DeSomer outright refused to wear the decoration for the daily uniform inspections as conducted by King. Observing by his side as the aide, Heinlein recalled King putting on a theatrical show and "would always stop, speak to him by name, note that he was not wearing it, tell him that he was out of uniform, order him to wear it next time and always receive 'aye-aye, captain!' in answer."[47] This ritual became an ongoing joke among the *Lexington* crew. Heinlein explained that the "next time [DeSomer] would again not be wearing it and again they would go through the same solemn little ritual almost in the same words." "King never seemed to get angry about it," Heinlein remembered. "I think King enjoyed the little game these two old veterans played."[48]

Setting the tone as the ultimate authority on board *Lexington*, King emphasized the hierarchical order of functions within the chain of command to inspire subordinates to be happy in their work. From the top, he relied heavily upon Hoover to focus on the administration. Meanwhile, King concentrated on the operations of *Lexington*—relying equally as heavily upon Cmdr. Lewis Comstock, the senior navigation officer on *Lexington*.[49] Observing the relationships among the senior officer, Heinlein described Comstock as "dressed in China Station uniforms that looked cheap, skimpy, and one size too small—he looked like an unmade bed even at inspections." "He was foul-mouthed and habitually snarled at his juniors for no reason," Heinlein explained, but that Comstock "was unsurpassed as a navigator."[50]

King and Comstock frequently traded personal insults, which initially seemed serious among the bridge team. Heinlein later realized that the relationship of King and Comstock ran deeper and that the banter between the two old salts served the purposes of keeping the bridge team focused and—simultaneously—well entertained. Heinlein wrote comedic stories for the entertainment of the *Lexington* crew featuring two cartoonish sailor characters. The old seagoing captain, the executive officer, and the ship's master in the fictional sea stories resembled the craggy personalities of King, Hoover, and Comstock.

King drove *Lexington* to earn formal recognition for being the top-performing warship in the US Navy. He encouraged sailors to work as hard as possible, particularly during fleet exercises. "During something over three days King was on the bridge every time and all the time that I was there," Heinlein recalled. "I sometimes snatched forty winks on the transom in the charthouse."[51] King never announced his departure from the bridge or allowed his subordinates to "see him horizontal save possibly his Marine orderly fetching him an urgent dispatch."[52] This created the myth among the *Lexington* crew that King always stood watch and "never slept at all."[53] King set the tone, and the pace, for junior officers to follow. At fifty years of age, he energetically whipped the *Lexington* crew into a well-oiled machine. Like King, *Lexington* always stood ready for action.

King used *Lexington* as a floating laboratory to develop independent aircraft carrier strike tactics. All hands had their role in advancing the future of naval aviation and, by extension, American sea power. King understood the doctrinal foundations and procedures in executing the traditional responsibilities of naval command at sea, and yet, simultaneously, he demonstrated unique willingness to abandon protocols, take risks, and set new standards of success. Sailing on the cutting edge of the future, King rode the prevailing currents under the flag of RAdm. Joseph M. Reeves, the Battle Force commander (Air).

Known for his tall frame and goatee, Reeves had a key role in setting future priorities for naval aviation. He took a very skeptical view of army concepts of strategic airpower, and he ultimately discounted the zeppelins of the US Navy as ineffective. During planning conferences held in San Diego before fleet problems, King recalled that Reeves observed that "Zeppelins excited the public, but are too vulnerable in actual combat."[54] To prove their shared conclusions, Reeves and King used the fleet exercises to showcase the capabilities of aircraft carriers. Reeves and King grappled with the questionable capacity for LTA airships to operate in conjunction with HTA forces among the warships of the fleet.

Reeves and King shared long experience in the traditional surface line, which informed their view of aircraft carriers. Turreted guns straddled the bridge superstructure on the flight deck, providing means to operate like battle cruisers. In exercises, *Lexington* operated under the overall command of another salt from the traditional line, RAdm. Clarence S. Kempff. King recalled that "Kempff was a great talker [and] he appeared somewhat ineffective to those who did not know him, but he always had the situation in the hollow of his hand."[55]

Existing US naval doctrine fell short in balancing the differences between missions performed by aviators and those of surface commanders. The black-shoe line officers of the surface fleet generally discounted their brown-shoe-wearing counterparts in naval aviation. For this reason, Kempff allowed Reeves and King to use *Lexington* as a test bed for new doctrinal ideas. Reeves and King drew from their historical studies and firsthand experience to develop the future role of aircraft carriers in fleet operations. King drove his aviators to experiment with new methods for maneuvering squadrons between multiple flight decks during operations with *Saratoga*. These tactics later proved decisive in war.

BLACK, BROWN, AND BLUE

Fleet problems and joint army-navy exercises drew significant media interest, which amplified the importance of demonstrating the full potential of American sea power for American taxpayers. In every year in the 1920s and 1930s, simulated battles at sea and ashore replicated the realities and dangers of actual combat. In anticipation of fleet problems scheduled for 1930, Reeves and Kempff held a series of conferences with their key commanders in San Francisco and San Diego. Reeves provided the broader aviation strategy for the friendly "blue" fleet, as King and McCrary developed a roving offensive plan to use the aircraft carriers in a roving operation designed to defend the Panama Canal against an enemy "black" fleet, under Admiral Frank H. Schofield, and a simulated enemy "brown" fleet, which reflected the presence of Royal Navy warships in the Caribbean, such as the battleship HMS *Nelson*. With three turrets configured ahead of the pilothouse and stack, *Nelson* cut a very strange profile.

The aviation strategy for the fleet exercises incorporated zeppelins operating in conjunction with aircraft carriers and other surface escort forces. Overhead floated USS *Los Angeles* (ZR-3) with Lt. Cmdr. Vincent R. Clark in command. Planning their operations for Fleet Problems XI, XII, and XIII, King worked together with his Naval Academy classmate and fellow aircraft carrier skipper, Capt. Frank R. McCrary, on USS *Saratoga* (CV-3). Reeves encouraged King and McCrary to press the limits of aircraft carrier doctrine during the Caribbean fleet problems in the spring of 1931.

Reeves and King shared a common understanding about the future potential of aircraft carriers. In efforts to prove his theories about the potential of aircraft carriers, King relied heavily upon the assistance of Commanders Victor Herbster, the air operations officer assigned with ship's company on *Lexington*, and Forrest Sherman, the squadron operations officer embarked. Later, King requested Herbster as the prospective relief of Hoover in anticipation of his detachment as the executive officer on *Lexington*. Herbster developed procedures to enable King and McCrary to launch aircraft from one carrier and landing on another—extending the tactical range of the fleet by maneuvering the other carrier beyond the horizon for aircraft to rendezvous at a predetermined point. Submarines positioned along the line of flight provided additional support.

For King, aviators and submariners shared similar roles on the fringes of the regular line of battle in concentrated fleet operations at sea. During the fleet problems, King and McCrary faced off against their formidable adversary, Capt. John H. Towers—the staunch brown-shoe skipper in the former aircraft carrier *Langley*. Although his ship still had half of a flight deck on the stern, Towers stood deeply frustrated about being relegated to command *Langley*, rather than *Lexington* or *Saratoga*.[56] Adding salt to the wounded ego of Towers, the *Langley* sailed with a shortened flight deck and carried the downgraded status as an aircraft tender in accordance with the London Naval Treaty of 1930.

Old rivalries among the ranking aircraft carrier commanders played out in simulated battles at sea. King had a difficult relationship with Towers,since both competed for the same jobs within the context of naval aviation.[57] King kept the black-shoe mentality in regulating the brown-shoe culture of naval aviation. All centered on the seagoing traditions of the regular line.[58] Towers took the opposite view among the brown shoes, seeking means to develop aviation as an altogether separate branch of the sea services.[59] King and Towers squared off as adversaries—with *Langley* operating in the simulated role of an enemy aircraft carrier. In simulated battle, King maneuvered *Lexington* to sail alongside *Langley* to exchange visual signals with Towers. Airmen from *Lexington* surprised Towers during maneuvers and simulated a devastating attack on *Langley*. Heinlein recalled King gloated in defeating Towers. Heinlein sent the signal, which resulted in Towers sending a dirty joke in response. King simply waved goodbye to Towers with "a wry smile."[60]

Fleet problems provided opportunities for aspirant admirals to demonstrate their competence as seagoing commanders. Among other innovations, King and his team developed procedures for rotating aircraft on the flight deck and by a continuous combat air patrol (CAP) umbrella over *Lexington*.[61] Such tactics later proved vital in actual combat. King also pushed the limits by conducting flight operations in dusky conditions with the sun rising and setting over the horizon. Sailing behind *Lexington* during night flight experiments, Lt. Cmdr. John L. McCrea, the skipper on USS *Trever* (DD-339), worked with King to develop procedures for rescuing aviators after mishaps during flight operations.[62] Working in close quarters, McCrea observed that King "was austere—ramrod straight and carried himself with dignity."[63] King had the ability to convey his expectations in clear terms, as McCrea noted, "There was never any doubt as to what he said or wanted."[64] McCrea concluded that King "was everything a naval officer should have been."[65]

King expanded the scouting ranges by integrating the flight schedules of aircraft launched from cruisers with those of the aircraft carriers. King drew from experience in surface ships to employ aircraft carriers in tandem with the fleet, rather than tying them down as part of the standard surface line of battle. King used his experience in surface ships to develop tactics for aircraft by using the base course method to expand the range of flight. By establishing a set bearing for all to follow, warship skippers had freedom of maneuver along that course. The same applied for aircraft. King proved the concept during simulated battle. He launched all aircraft in the hunt for *Langley* in Galápagos waters after the return of one formation of aircraft, with thirty-one aircraft still unaccounted for as dusk settled over *Lexington*.

King worked the lines to find his missing aviators, just as the errant *Lexington* aircraft located *Langley*. Lt. (j.g.) Albert "Buddy" Scoles diverted from the planned flight path to score a simulated sinking against *Langley*. Back on board *Lexington*, Heinlein recalled the impressive image of King. Chain-smoking in silence on the bridgewing, he simply allowed his team to do their job of locating the missing squadrons. Heinlein used a newly installed radio direction finder to get a bearing on the communications between Scoles and his fellow aviators. Heinlein eventually picked up the signal of one of the aircraft. On the basis of the weather conditions and differences of illumination between the location of the aircraft and *Lexington*, Heinlein deduced the optimal course for a rendezvous. Heinlein remembered that King sprang from his chair and rang up to full speed.[66]

The prospect of losing so many aircraft in peacetime loomed over the situation, as King calmly managed a solution. Having expended fuel reserves during the attack on *Langley*, Scoles and the aviators pressed the wind to find refuge on *Lexington*. Under the circumstances, King ordered the engine room to make smoke to give away his location. Setting aside the tactical rules of the exercise, King focused on the strategic objective by ordering all the flight deck lights to be turned on. King used spotlights to enable weary flight crews to locate *Lexington* at a distance and land safely on the flight deck.[67]

The spotlights on *Lexington* appeared akin to the dazzling spectacle of a Hollywood movie premiere, according to Scoles. As the weary aviators balanced the stress of fuel gauges indicating empty tanks within eyeshot of safety on board their ship, Scoles loitered until the last aircraft in his air wing safely landed. When Scoles followed, his engine ran completely out of fuel and cut out just as his aircraft rolled to a stop.[68] US Army pilot observers embarked as referees for the exercise stood in complete awe of King's leadership. One asked him about his technique for keeping cool in a bad situation. "Hell, I was too busy to worry about how I felt [because] what I had to do was to figure out how to get those damn planes back on board."[69]

King immediately returned *Lexington* to full battle readiness and the simulated combat operations within the context of the exercises. When the weary squadron commanders reported to King to debrief their attack on *Langley*, he cut to the chase by asking, "Where the hell have you been."[70] King always focused on the central task of enabling his sailors to survive for the purposes of fighting another day. As the aviators revved their engines before sunrise, King illuminated the deck lights of *Lexington*. For this maneuver, King received a reprimand from exercise observers. Heinlein witnessed as King "exploded, using these censored words:"

> deleted censored blank <u>blank</u>! I will not allow myself to be forced to have to write to the mother of some blank kid and explain to her how he got his censored head chopped off by a deleted prop of a blank plane he couldn't see in the dark and was too inexperienced to know how to avoid! No, by blank, I will <u>not</u>! . . . I won't have my men killed just for realism in a blank blank blankety drill![71]

Heinlein continued, "I wish I had a recording of that speech; his rhetoric and command of improper language was superb."[72] Heinlein later used the incident as the basis for a fictional short story about a blind girl using musical skills to see her way to safety after crashing on the moon. He wrote a variation of the story for the entertainment of the crew in the *Lexington* newspaper, later rehashing the narrative under the title "Searchlight."[73] Operating on the edges of existing technology required King to draw from decades of practical experience as a naval officer. Heinlein recalled that "King turned on every light on the flight deck and kept them on until the last plane was in the air." Continuing, Heinlein explained that "an extra squadron aboard made that deck a tight jungle, difficult enough with your parachute on your tail, crawling under wings, trying to find your own plane, in an endless hazard of props turning up, even with deck lights on."[74.] The *Lexington* crew "was <u>proud</u> of the Old Man that night, [in that] he showed his bravery and basic humanity—with his flag almost in sight."[75]

Taking the calculated risk to guide the aviators home to the pitching decks of *Lexington* greatly enhanced the reputation of King among the ship's crew and the aviators. The following morning, aircraft from *Saratoga* suddenly appeared over *Lexington*—resulting in a simulated sinking.[76] Reeves signaled, "King is but a man, as I am."[77] Reeves later applauded King for demonstrating the potential of aircraft carriers. Reeves endorsed King's recommendations for operating carriers at the center of fleet formations, using maneuver to strike, and operating in the darkness of early night. Reeves endorsed King's recommendation that the "ship and squadrons must be tied together."[78] The tactics demonstrated in exercises under King later paid significant dividends in such future battles as those in the Coral Sea and off Midway roughly a decade later.

CHAPTER 10

Wars among Stars

Simulated wars at sea and ashore enabled the joint services of the army and navy similar opportunities for practitioners to shine. Traversing the fleet ladder up to the stars of flag rank in peacetime, American service practitioners treated the simulated wars of the 1920s and 1930s as seriously as actual war.[1] The exercises conducted ashore and afloat in actual maneuvers reflected the theoretical experimentation and tabletop discussions of the Naval War College, Marine Corps Schools, and Army War College. Aspirant admirals, like King, treated the fleet problems as opportunities to gain the attention of flag officers of both the army and navy, civilian bureaucrats, and politicians. Politics influenced the competition to win promotion on selection boards. Command on *Lexington* put King at center in writing the rules of the game.

King frequently received orders between exercises to sail *Lexington* between major ports along the American coast. He understood the effect on sailor morale whenever illuminated skylines ashore appeared in the distance. For this reason, King always sailed far out to sea. He then rang up battle stations to simulate high-speed tactical approaches in entering port—as though conducting an airstrike. "King could be highly independent," Lt. Cmdr. Malcolm Schoeffel explained, "sometimes arrogantly so."[2] After the conclusion of the exercises, Schoeffel recalled the "whole Battle Fleet was tidily lined up and waiting for the signal to go home."[3] "With two black balls hoisted," *Lexington* suddenly cut ahead of the line of ships "at high speed right through the train at the center of the disposition, scattering tenders right and left."[4] Schoeffel recalled feeling consternation as *Lexington* steamed passed through the fleet. He recalled, "Without saying 'excuse me,' King just went right over the horizon."[5]

These breeches of seagoing protocol angered the regular line skippers of the surface forces, which fueled the flames of indignation against King and the aviators of the fleet. As the aviation aide to Reeves on *Saratoga*, Schoeffel read the message traffic and heard the complaints about King and other shenanigans by *Lexington* during exercises. From the flagship, *Pennsylvania*, the CinCUS, Adm. David S. Sellers, witnessed as King "crossed the 'T'" in the battle line. Sellers sent a signal to Reeves asking, "What goes on?"[6] Schoeffel recalled that "'Reeves was more amused than otherwise' by responding that the fleet 'was maneuvered magnificently.'"[7] At that time, Schoeffel knew King only by reputation. Later having the opportunity to sail under his command, Schoeffel later used the phrase employed by others in examining the behavior of King as "training future admirals for war."[8]

Fleet problems and joint army-navy exercises ashore frequently occurred within the grander strategic context of events unfolding on the distant shores of Europe and Asia.

In the spring of 1931, imperial Japan flooded north from the Korean border to conquer Manchuria.[9] The commander of the Asiatic Fleet, Adm. Charles B. McVay Jr., was completely taken aback by the Japanese offensive. He requested immediate reinforcements to augment the Asiatic Fleet in the Philippines. In turn, Pratt issued secret orders to the Battle Force to prepare for war. Aircraft carrier skippers received authorization to load live ordnance and make immediate preparations to sail to Asiatic waters. Heinlein described the eeriness of undeclared war:

> We arrived there after dark—no liberty for crew, no shore leave for officers, officers were forbidden to make telephone calls, and armed Marines on the dock made it impossible for men to do so . . . we worked all night and into the next morning unloading target ammo and practice war heads, taking aboard war ammo of all sorts and real war heads, extra supplies, topped off our oil, water, and aviation gas tanks, and took aboard another squadron of planes, pilots and plane crews over our complement (120 planes instead of 90)—and at once got underway, then went to full speed for Hawaii, under radio silence and condition "B" once clear of the Bay, then at darken ship that night and every night. Shortly we were in formation with what had to be a large task force (the entire Battle Fleet in fact, plus units of Scouting Fleet then in the Pacific). The mystery, the speed, the extra planes, etc., made it clear to the greenest enlisted man that we were headed somewhere, loaded for bear, and expecting to fight. This crisis never did get into the public news [and] I have never seen a word of print about it. But our Quaker "pacifist" President, Mr. Hoover, had handed the emperor a war ultimatum.[10]

Hoover muddled through with a demoralized navy operating at half pay.[11] The secretary of state, Henry Stimson, frequently challenged his counterparts in the Departments of War and Navy to justify their purposes in peacetime. Along with other members of the Republican Party, Stimson strongly supported the idea of a unified Department of National Defense during his tenure as secretary of state in the Hoover administration.[12]

Stimson's views about proposals to unify military and naval administration in conjunction with efforts to frame separate air services reflected the political trends. Given the foreign air forces as one model, Stimson also disliked the emergence of the CNO, Pratt, as the spokesman for American naval policy during the hazy circumstances of 1931—when Americans nearly went to war for the future of Asia. Navy secretary Charles Adams also struggled against health issues while grappling with the bigger strategic challenges, leaving Pratt to fill the administrative void. With the vacillations of the Hoover administration on the policy for Asia, Pratt "supplanted the secretary as the Navy's chief spokesman in politico-military matters."[13]

Old bureaucratic conflicts between the Departments of State and Navy influenced Stimson's perspective on Pratt. Given problems unfolding on far-off foreign shores, Stimson and Pratt also faced significant policy challenges in formulating diplomatic strategies in South America and in relations with Canada, which also extended to Europe. Criminal activity along the southern border with Mexico provided additional distractions for the Hoover administration.[14] American military and maritime forces meanwhile stretched the limits to interdict the unwinnable battle to stop the flow of Canadian liquor into Mafia-run speakeasies in the United States.

Pratt stood among the most consequential naval officers in efforts to advance the cause of American sea power in a widely misunderstood era of unsettled peace. The lingering ramifications of the First World War failed to halt the pace of vicious political fights on the Washington battlefield. On the brink of war with Japan in 1931, Stimson worried about his ebbing influence over questions of diplomatic policy when the ailing Navy secretary, Adams, allowed Pratt to lead strategic decisions during joint meetings with army and naval leaders on the West Coast. During these meetings, Pratt listened to the plans as presented by Yarnell and King.

Pacific lines of strategic communications extended well beyond the tactical capacity of American sea power for offensive operations against Japanese forces in Asia. The Philippines garrisons ashore also lacked means to sustain defensive operations, which also hindered the abilities of the Asiatic Fleet to support similar operations in China. In the event of war, American forces in the Asiatic faced dire circumstances—well beyond the immediate control of anyone in positions of command responsibility at that time. Should the Japanese make the opening moves with a first shot, King emphasized fundamental vulnerabilities of such islands as Wake, Midway, and Hawaii. Both strongly emphasized the strategic importance of holding the strongpoints between Hawaii-Guam-Kiska to control the oceanic area known as the "North Pacific Triangle."[15] For King, Hawaii stood out as the ultimate key to defending the West Coast of the United States and the Panama Canal long enough to retake the strategic initiative in offensive operations across the Pacific.[16]

LIBERTY SECURED

King's chance to face the Imperial Japanese Navy in combat as an aircraft carrier skipper fizzled from the headlines. Having readied for battle in 1931, the *Lexington* crew felt the elation in preparing for glory. The afterglow faded quickly after King announced orders to secure live ordnance, with following orders to account for all weapons during offloading operations at Bremerton Naval Shipyard. *Lexington* then turned south for a brief kiss at its homeport in San Pedro. King granted brief liberty ashore for all hands in anticipation of sailing *Lexington* through the Panama Canal for simulated combat in the Caribbean. The departure of American aircraft carriers with the seagoing battle forces also provided a diplomatic signal for Japan, which clarified the military policy of the United States.

The empires of Europe and Asia kept close watch over American fleet maneuvers, which similarly drew global media interest. For the exercises of 1931 and 1932, Panama served as the Philippines, Jamaica as Formosa, Puerto Rico as Okinawa, Haiti as Kyūshū, and Cuba as Honshū. The northern coast of South America served as the geographic transposition to replicate operations in Chinese waters.[17] King also used the conflict in China to emphasize the seriousness of the fleet exercises in the Caribbean. King conversely allowed the shipboard newspaper to publish recipes for rum drinks, which implied a possible liberty call for the *Lexington* crew. The promise of fun on the beaches and bars of Cuba loomed within eyeshot, as King dropped anchor.

King gained a reputation for racing other skippers in the sailing competition to beat the fleet into port. Upon setting the lines and completing docking, King issued the liberty call for the *Lexington* crew long before the rest of the fleet. His gig crew prepared for port as the deck crews secured the aircraft, boatswains set the lines, and engineers secured power. Heinlein recalled that King always rewarded his crew for excellent performance. Setting anchor off Cuba on March 31, 1931, King began inspecting the white uniforms of the *Lexington* crew as the boatswains prepared to deploy the liberty boats. Up in the bridge, Heinlein listened to a Mexican radio broadcast. Although he struggled to understand Spanish, Heinlein understood something disastrous had occurred.

Heinlein continued monitoring the broadcast when a radioman delivered an official report providing details about a major earthquake off Nicaragua. He recalled telling King about the disaster. Without hesitation, King canceled liberty and ordered the *Lexington* crew to stoke boilers and prepare to sail. He restricted freshwater consumption and put the *Lexington* condensers to use in making more. "In less than forty minutes we were standing out and proceeded at flank speed (about 39.6 knots) once clear of the harbor," Heinlein recalled. "No preparation, no waiting to take special supplies aboard."[18] "Sixteen boilers at flank speed used up the fresh water awfully fast," Heinlein explained. "We were ordered not to bathe until further notice and to be sparing in the use of fresh water for any purpose."[19] Upon reaching the outer limits of range, King launched aircraft "with blankets, landing force tents, medical supplies, and food; King stripped the ship of all but bare necessities to get us to Panama."[20]

King sailed at top speed to the scene of the disaster without first asking permission from higher-level command. Meanwhile, he put his bridge team to work. Heinlein recalled studying all the available charts and maps with King. The information depicted on the charts proved unreliable. However, King drew from his own youthful adventures on *Eagle*—when he went temporarily blind while surveying the area. Heinlein recalled King telling tales about the experience. Heinlein remembered King claiming that "he could see better after he went blind."[21] His knowledge of the ancient pirate coves and shallows in the waters off Nicaragua proved useful as *Lexington* maneuvered to support the humanitarian relief mission ashore.[22]

King used *Lexington* as a command ship after he took personal command of the humanitarian mission at the scene off Nicaragua. On his own authority, King deployed medical personnel with marine security forces to assist the Nicaraguan authorities. The earthquake caused significant devastation in Managua, with an estimated 5,000 civilians killed. As other forces arrived at the scene, *Lexington* received orders to depart for liberty in Panama City—then proceed back into the Pacific through the Panama Canal. Anchored off port, King noted that the HMS *Nelson* "scraped all along one side so badly as to require ten days['] repair work."[23] For this reason, King refused to relinquish command to pilots provided by Panama Canal authorities. Breaking from protocol, he retained the right to issue all commands to the *Lexington* crew during transits in the Panama Canal and other hazardous navigational areas.

King expected officers to set standards of performance, although he provided some leeway for those serving in the enlisted ranks. Heinlein explained that King ran an "extremely taut and very happy ship, with a very high score in reenlistment to stay."[24]

King trained the crew to recognize that a warship was more than "merely an inanimate assembly of wood and metal; to him it was a living thing with a soul that one could love."[25] Heinlein described "King's meticulous courtesy in respecting the private sphere of his subordinates lives," and Heinlein explained that King frequently "restated the truism that a warship was a home as well, and often the only home a bachelor had—he not only stated this cliché, he lived by it."[26]

The businesslike atmosphere fostered by King as the skipper on *Lexington* at sea persisted whenever relaxing with his sailors. Concurrently, he modified his approach to provide mentoring advice to those among the crew willing to approach him. While in Panama City, Heinlein recalled finding King sipping a bottle of Dewar's White Label whiskey in a bar.

Heinlein had the courage to socialize with King. Taking mental notes, Heinlein observed that King "could drink at least one fifth of Scotch unassisted without getting drunk after a man-killing ordeal [but] he did not drink to excess (for him) and never at the wrong time."[27] Ultimately, King followed the rule of thumb that a "naval officer never drinks—if he drinks, he doesn't get drunk; if he gets drunk, he doesn't stagger—if he staggers, he doesn't fall; if he falls, he falls flat on his face with his arms under him so no one can see his stripes."[28]

Service on *Lexington* enabled Heinlein to develop unique perceptions of King's personality. Recalling their visit to Panama, Heinlein challenged the popular myth of King's Anglophobia. Rather, he bought drinks for a Royal Navy acquaintance from the First World War—along with sailors from HMS *Nelson*. King joined the British sailors in their traditional cheer to the health of King George V. In a separate part of the barroom, King held court with the *Lexington* officers at a private table.[29] "Not once did anyone else drink from King's private bottle," Heinlein explained; when King ordered, "the waiter fetched it from the bar."[30] "The Captain was cold sober, erect, and speech unslurred," Heinlein explained, "after more than half a fifth plus a couple more drinks while I soaked up a rum, gum, and lime."[31] After several drinks, King advised his officers to "stir around and have fun—we go back to work in a couple of days."[32]

King allowed the crew to replenish their courage ashore and took time for himself to recalibrate in anticipation of simulated war at sea. Heinlein explained the method King employed in holding disciplinary "mast" in issuing punishments to the crew: "He was strict but never petty." Heinlein described preparing the prosecutions for "a ship with 2,000 and up men in her has a large mast, almost daily in port, a couple times a week even at sea, very large after a weekend on R&R [I] prepared a mast list of fifty or more—all guilty save for a rare exception."[33] Holding collateral duty as the "sea lawyer" for the defense, Heinlein explained the theater as King appeared, with "cap squared and looking like an American eagle with every feather groomed [he was] the living embodiment of the presence of command."[34]

King allowed sailors to explain themselves at mast, listening intently to every word with the sternness of a hanging judge. "Then he would throw the book at them," Heinlein recalled, "all accompanied by a oral chewing out, each of which was a literary gem."[35] Methodically, King subjected the guilty to verbal renderings with "no profanity, no salty slang, all just loud enough to be heard by everyone present—always grammatical, never repetitious—words that cut like the strokes of the cat [or whip]."[36] Heinlein recalled being called to review the punishments awarded after proceedings, always finding King

> seated at his desk, cap off and bald head in view, deep worry lines in his face and looking ten or fifteen years older—old, and tired, and worried, and bent under the load he carried and could not put down. I disliked being forced to see him right after he had held mast; it was painful to me to see how hard he took it. No loss of sleep, no grueling physical ordeal, ever seemed to affect him. But holding mast—punishing his own children—always wrung him out.[37]

The theater of mast carried a practical purpose, which never centered on punishment. Rather, King used mast to restore order and discipline in the aftermath of liberty. King never allowed other officers to leaf through individual service records during the proceedings. Heinlein carried the responsibility to handle the records under sealed lock and key. In performing this duty, Heinlein "would carry a sidearm (not his sword but a loaded forty-five)."[38]

Marines armed with loaded weapons performed the judicial responsibility of handling official paperwork. Heinlein served the simultaneous roles as bailiff, lead prosecutor, and public defender on *Lexington*. "Publicly he 'threw the book," Heinlein remembered, "and that was the word that got on the grapevine."[39] Conversely, Heinlein explained, "King handed out extremely gentle sentences, ones that rarely marred a man's official record enough to slow up his promotions."[40] Heinlein concluded that the "real punishments lay in those scorching oral spankings."[41] King quickly shifted the crew from lingering over spilled beer and barroom brawls by reinstituting the calm associated with disciplined shipboard routines. The bell chimes marking the end and the beginning of the three-section watch usually followed with the reassuring sounds of the boatswain's pipe after the expected announcements as listed in the plan of the day.[42]

DAT OL' DEBBIL SEA

King recalibrated the *Lexington* crew for operations in simulated battle by diverting southward on an unplanned reconnaissance ahead of the fleet. Upon traversing into the Pacific, the crew had expected to sail from the Panama Canal to home ports in California. Simulating actual war, King kept the *Lexington* crew engaged with unscheduled drills and flight operations to replicate the presence of enemy forces along the West Coast of South America outward to the Galápagos Islands. Running *Lexington* southward to the equator, King seemed to grow more and more angry about something. The chiefs on board had issued preliminary orders to the *Lexington* crew to prepare for the arrival of King Neptune and his court.

Having never crossed the equator, King grew annoyed upon seeing signs of the traditional shellback rituals. Approaching the equator, King planned a skirting course to the north to avoid the humiliation of appearing among the "pollywogs" in anticipation of evolving into a "shellback" during the traditional line-crossing court of honor. Knowing the situation, Reeves ordered King to press southward on a course to cross the equator. His angry attitude suddenly shifted upon receiving new orders to detach from exercises when Vice President Charles Curtiss requested the aircraft carriers to serve as backdrops for an election year speech to be delivered in San Pedro, California. In the shipboard newspaper, Heinlein wrote that "wogs await Polly as she lay on her back for the shell to fire—Beware of Propellers and Send the *Observer* Home."[43]

King anticipated media attention upon receiving orders to maneuver *Lexington* back to home port. He received a letter of commendation from Navy secretary Adams for the earthquake relief effort in Nicaragua. King congratulated the *Lexington* crew for setting the fleet standard for superior performance in exercises and in actual humanitarian operations. On the way to home port, however, King left absolutely no time for unnecessary relaxation—running at high speed from the Panama Canal to recover aircraft incoming from the Nicaraguan relief efforts. He put the crew back to work holystoning wooden flight decks and scraping the rust before painting bulkheads. Notably, he had metal fittings painted—not only to reduce the fire hazards associated with chemicals and cleaning supplies but also to reduce the time wasted with the unnecessary rituals of polishing the brass. By the time *Lexington* reached Long Beach, the warship appeared newly commissioned.

King anticipated the presence of the media, which customarily covered the dramatic return of the fleet. Rather than face questions from journalists ashore, he decided to continue the charade of replicating wartime conditions upon entering the approaches to port. He allowed the navigation team to plot the course without his immediate supervision. As the sun set on the horizon, King took a position on the bridgewing as the helmsmen and navigation team quietly maneuvered *Lexington* toward the illuminated shoreline surrounding the welcoming piers at Long Beach. Given limited visibility, King calmly sipped coffee and smoked a cigarette from his chair on the bridgewing.

King's confidence proved premature, since his navigation team mistakenly put *Lexington* in the channel leading into the shallows of the submarine anchorage. Interrupting the serenity of the moment, spotters reported contact with a stationary target right in front of *Lexington*. As the massive ship closed, the skipper in the submarine USS *Bonita* (SS-165)—sitting at anchor—transmitted a frantic message to order *Lexington* to divert course. The sender was King's former subordinate Lt. Cmdr. Alan McCann. In response, King directed McCann to maneuver *Bonita* and make way. The submarine stood defiantly as the massive aircraft carrier closed and McCann confidently advised King to recheck his charts. McCann recalled that after a brief silence, *Lexington* suddenly turned. McCann received no apology from King, just the signal "Carry on."[44]

According to Heinlein, the *Lexington* bridge team stood terrified in anticipation of an epic outburst from King. To their surprise, King very calmly instructed the navigation team about their mistakes. Heinlein later discovered that King carried his own sextant, took his own readings, and annotated the correct information next to the mistakes recorded in the official navigational log of *Lexington*. "You'll never get into trouble," he told one erstwhile navigator, "if you clearly mark the appropriate fathom curve and constantly note the fathometer readings."[45] Officers with close experience in the bridge with King described him as a "wizard with a chart and a pencil."[46]

Age of Sail traditions merged with the practical purposes of ensuring navigational accuracy, which King expected from his subordinates. As the skipper, he always carried the burden of full responsibility in the event of disaster. King strived to empower subordinates without micromanaging them in performing their assigned task. However, he struggled with a series of four replacements following the detachment of the navigation officer, Comstock, in July 1930.[47] Rather than destroy their careers, he simply reassigned them other duties on board *Lexington*. Without Comstock to ensure high quality as chief navigation officer, King struggled for another year to find a suitable replacement. King assumed personal responsibility for training the junior officers to understand the art and science of navigation. Lt. Cmdr. Homer W. Graf later attained flag rank, as did Lieutenants Harry L. Dodson and Oliver W. Gaines. After an exasperating period of having to worry about the navigation team, King recruited an associate from the previous service in submarines, Cmdr. Joseph M. Deem. Joining King in June 1931, Deem brought order to the chaos among the navigation team on *Lexington*.

The freewheeling tactics associated with destroyers and submarines intermixed with the vision of naval aviation, as King devised schemes to change the character of surface fleet operations. Recalling the situation, van Deurs explained that the "black-shoe boys decided to put Ernie King where he couldn't mess anything up [since] he had pulled surprises on them in a couple of fleet problems and spoiled their battleship game."[48] Making best with what he had within the context of the fleet problem, King worked together with Commander Forrest Sherman to devise plans to maneuver *Lexington* and *Saratoga* as an aircraft carrier task force—separate from the main line of battle. King joined McCrary to brief their plan in San Francisco during predeployment conferences with Adm. Harry Yarnell. Another participant in these discussions, Towers, falsely claimed full credit for proposing the idea of conducting an attack on Pearl Harbor during Fleet Problem XII, which coincided with the Grand Army-Navy Exercise No. 4 from January to March 1932.[49]

Breaking from the prescribed constraints of the fleet problem, Yarnell approved the plan for an unscripted aircraft carrier raid on the rival force battleships at anchor in Pearl Harbor. Nine years before an actual attack, King maneuvered *Lexington* in company with *Saratoga* to a position approximately 100 nautical miles north of Oahu.[50] The rules of the fleet problem provided means by which King achieved complete surprise against his opposition. Stormy seas covered their movements, as King maneuvered behind a weather front to obscure the high-speed movements of *Lexington* and *Saratoga*.[51] Inching into position, *Lexington* and *Saratoga* awaited the moment to launch as planned on the morning of Sunday, February 7. Heinlein recalled King standing in foul-weather gear with a cigarette dangling from his mouth. "Visibility was poor, but we had the comforting presence of the captain, who stayed out in the rain just as we did," Heinlein explained. "We stood there for an eternity in silence—when King surprised me by saying to me, 'Dat ol' Debbil Sea is angry with us today.'"[52]

A REAL GEM

King exploited the weather to evade detection by the enemy scouting forces at sea and the land-based army reconnaissance forces ashore in Hawaii. Service rivalries underscored elations, since joint exercises provided opportunities for army and navy commanders to score political points in the grander bureaucratic competition for strategic control. Army pilots struggled to operate over water, consistently failing to locate naval targets.[53] On board *Saratoga*, Yarnell coordinated with the commanders of the surface and amphibious forces to execute the landings in Oahu in conjunction with the simulated strikes against Pearl Harbor and the army base facilities at Hickam and Wheeler airfields.

King commanded the task group. He selected Lt. Cmdr. Jocko Clark to lead the strike formation.[54] Lt. Dan Gallery accompanied him as a fighter escort group leader.[55]

Catching the army garrison defenses by complete surprise, the naval aviators of *Lexington* and *Saratoga* launched just before dawn and flew from multiple lines of attack. Concurrently, *Lexington* and *Saratoga* maneuvered to an alternate position—just over the horizon—to recover the returning aircraft. Army umpires stood completely chagrined and questioned the "'legality' of attacking on a Sunday morning."[56] RAdm. Joel R. P. Pringle, in contrast, characterized the operations of *Lexington* and *Saratoga* as "a real gem."[57]

The operations of *Lexington* and *Saratoga* highlighted the potential of aircraft carriers, which concurrently highlighted the fundamental vulnerability of fixed bases ashore and warships at anchor in port. Islands appeared particularly vulnerable to aircraft-carrier-supported amphibious forces. The CNO, Pratt, and the CinCUS, Schofield, drew key conclusions from Fleet Problem XII and the associated joint army-navy exercises ashore in Hawaii, as well as those conducted simultaneously on the West Coast of the United States.[58] In the ongoing struggles for future bureaucratic control and resources, Pratt and Schofield correctly identified the fundamental and unanswered question of strategic responsibility in shaping future relationships within the Departments of State, Navy, and War.[59] In addition, the US Army claimed control over all land-based aviation, base security, and major aviation support facilities. Navy warships in port therefore fell under the overall responsibility of the army territorial defense authorities. The army controlled all landline communications, which represented an untenable vulnerability for the naval force commanders.[60]

Peacetime fleet problems provided means by which King waged war against fellow skippers. Envious rivals among the surface line stood humiliated when King's team on *Lexington* received the coveted letter of commendation from the secretary of the Navy for their performance during the fleet problems. King also accepted the trophy on behalf of *Lexington* for winning the designation as best ship in the United States Fleet.[61] King proved himself worthy of promotion into the flag ranks during the operations of *Lexington* and *Saratoga* in anticipation of an American election year. Congressional leaders bickered over the costs associated with keeping the fleet in peacetime. The performance of King and the aircraft carriers proved the value of naval aviation—for the time being—as Congressman Carl Vinson successfully thwarted the "shotgun marriage" of the Departments of War and Navy after the crises of 1931 and 1932.[62]

PETUNIA'S DADDY

The political embers remained hot in the decade following King's original surprise attack against the American fleet anchorage at Pearl Harbor. He later replicated the same surprise in fleet exercises and again on the gaming floors of the Naval War College. The ongoing civil war in China coincided with the invasion of the Asian continent by imperial Japan. Under the circumstances, the Hoover administration shuttered under the barrage of critiques from the aspirant president, Roosevelt. Given his past service in the Navy Department, his childlike affinity for the US naval services also provided convincing justifications for revisiting the dream of American sea power. Economic depression inspired the taxpaying American public to embrace the civil-military industrial relationships. By rebuilding the US Navy into a two-ocean force, American shipyards—as connected with the railroads—provided opportunities for creating new and good-paying jobs for all Americans, recent immigrants, and migrant populations.[63]

Roosevelt highlighted the future of American sea power in a speech delivered at Long Beach, with *Lexington* and *Saratoga* tied together at the pier as a backdrop. King listened intently to the speech and later introduced Roosevelt to Mattie, his daughters, and his son. Roosevelt declined an invitation to join the *Lexington* crew for ballroom dancing at the Hotel Majestic in Long Beach. Four times each year while he served in command, King and Mattie supervised planning for the quarterly ballroom party for the *Lexington* crew and music provided by the ship's band. As recounted by an anonymous writer—most likely Heinlein—the first in the series of *Lexington* balls set the highest standard, as held at the Majestic Ballroom in Long Beach with a reported 2,500 in attendance.[64]

King always set the tone with cheerful smiles and while dancing with the wives and girlfriends of his men. Accounts found in the shipboard newspaper highlight the point that whenever the skipper danced with the date, the individual sailor considered it a personal honor while dancing with "Mrs. King."[65] "Masquerade hats, colored lights, and lighting effects, horns and rattles," an *Observer* newspaper described, and a "general spirit of fun and good fellowship lent a carnival air to the festivities." Among other highlights, the "event of the evening was a grand march led by our Commanding Officer, Captain E. J. King, and Mrs. J. F. Matthews [and] following them were our Chief Storekeeper, J. F. Matthews, and Mrs. King."[66]

King and his wife regularly attended the weekly dances as organized by the individual divisions on *Lexington*. The events happened whenever the ship stood idle in port. Official business always stood off-limits for discussion at *Lexington* social events.[67] Mattie played her role as the matriarch of the *Lexington* family, keeping tabs on younger officers' wives. King's daughters did their part. Heinlein held a trusted place in the King family. He frequently socialized with King's daughters during port visits in Long Beach and Seattle. King's daughters just referred to him as "daddy."[68] As an outside observer of the King family, Heinlein characterized the "King girls [as] pretty, vivacious, good dancers, fun to be around[,and] well worth forgetting that they were too closely related to my C.O."[69]

Heinlein regularly called upon the Kings' home in Long Beach, gaining another firsthand perspective on the character of King himself. Mattie clearly held command as the skipper in home, although King silently asserted command by fostering an inescapable presence—usually to be seen sitting in his corner chair while reading the newspaper, with the radio providing background noise. His side table featured a silver Tiffany cigarette box and an ashtray, as presented to him by the sailors on board *Wright*. He generally had a cup of coffee on the table during the day, and in the evenings he enjoyed a mug of beer, a glass of sherry, or a dram of scotch. "He seemed to me to be a normal family man," and Heinlein also described King as a "Navy man who always lived at home when opportunity permitted."[70] "Mrs. King was pleasant but most quiet, as quiet as he was," and Heinlein also observed that she always "received me most cordially into their home."[71]

Heinlein described King as being a devoted family man and a strong father figure in dealings with navy subordinates. Heinlein occasionally accompanied his friend Lt. Caleb "Cal" Laning for evenings with King's daughters Martha and Claire. Whenever Heinlein visited, Mattie cheerfully welcomed Heinlein with small talk. Heinlein inevitably heard the familiar low tones of King's unique command voice. Without dropping his newspaper, King customarily advised Heinlein to bring the daughters "home by nine, or you are not going home."[72] Heinlein recalled bringing Martha and Claire home after the designated hour:

> There is about one chance in ten thousand that she somehow managed to sneak in and reach her room without its being noticed that she had been out all night. And she must have had a bootleg-corn-liquor breath on her that could knock over a dog.[73]

Reporting the next morning on board *Lexington*, Heinlein expected to be punished. He delivered the daily message traffic to King. To Heinlein's surprise, King said nothing about the previous evening. As Heinlein walked out of the office, King said, "'I think you are an officer with promise." Heinlein stood stunned until King said, "That is all."[74]

Having decades of experience on the deck, King fully understood the perspective of junior officers. He had sown his wild oats and nearly lost his career during service in the Asiatic Fleet. King provided the same mentorship he had received from such mentors as Osterhaus, Sims, and Mayo. Having run close to the wind, Heinlein observed that King had a special touch in nurturing junior officers to follow his example. Above all, King and the King clan "appeared to be a happy family, rather more than usually close."[75] Heinlein's partner in crime on board *Lexington,* Lieutenant Robert Clark, similarly noted that King basically "kept to himself, but really was a softie when it came to his family."[76]

Largely following orders from Mattie in managing the crew within the household, King presided within a stable and happy home. King's daughters always enjoyed the attention of aspiring military and naval officers. He sometimes provided close tactical support. The third daughter, Martha, occasionally used King as a strategic weapon to evade the more persistent suitors. One aspiring naval officer asked Martha for her name during a social mixer. Uninterested, she lied about her name being "Petunia." Having coordinated their counterattack, Martha later used her father to ward off the enemy when the young gentleman knocked on the door. "Good morning, sir, I am here to see Petunia," to which King gruffly advised with full honesty that there "is nobody here by that name."[77]

Comfortably settled in their home in California, King and the *Lexington* crew received disappointing orders to set sail for an extended period in drydock at the Puget Sound Naval Shipyard, near Seattle. King received his orders in anticipation of detachment as the skipper on *Lexington*. His superior performance while in command on board *Lexington* provided placed King in line for early promotion to flag rank. To this end, King accepted orders to the resident course of the Naval War College. As a final task before detachment, King received orders to take *Lexington* from Long Beach to Puget Sound.

Uncharacteristically, King allowed the crew to host visitors and families for the voyage north. He allowed them to embark their automobiles and some household goods on board *Lexington*. Upon reaching the approaches to Puget Sound, Heinlein recalled a risky plan devised by King to navigate without tugboats through the narrows of Puget Sound to reach Bremerton Naval Shipyard. "King planned that passage with the navigator in great detail," Heinlein explained, "using a specially prepared blowup of the chart, a template in scale of the ship, and plotted positions, times, currents expected."[78] Every variable being considered, King supervised the *Lexington* crew to monitor "orientations with bearings pre-plotted for bridge, eyes, and fantail for every available fixed landmark and paired range markers."[79] Heinlein recalled, "I had a chance to study that plot ahead of time and was dazzled by it."[80]

Heinlein considered King a virtuoso at maneuvering *Lexington*, setting standards for others to follow. Heinlein recalled that "I grabbed a spot on the flag bridge where I could see the navigator moving his template around on that plot on a jury-rigged plotting board outside the wheelhouse [where] the bridge was very quiet." He continued:

All that could be heard was the navigator calling out his plot to the captain, and Captain King's still lower but always crisply clear voice, giving orders to engine room and wheel. At the very last, when it was clear that we had made it without touching, there was a long sigh, not loud—a soft sigh but quite audible as it came from so many people. King did not seem to hear it.

Following this performance, King simply walked to perch on the portside flying bridge overlooking the *Lexington* flight deck like a "passenger enjoying the pleasant sight of a scenic channel."[81] Heinlein received straight top rankings from King. In a parting fitness report, Heinlein shed a tear when reading King's endorsements, which included the highest praise, "completed War College Correspondence Course."[82]

In his later career as writer of popular American fiction, Heinlein consistently drew from his adventures with King to craft exciting stories about the future. After service on *Lexington*, Heinlein kept very close ties with Martha and the King family. King's son-in-law Freddy also fed into Heinlein's futuristic adventures.[83] Among others within King's close circle, Heinlein considered King the "most nearly perfect military officer I have ever known."[84] Refuting the mythology and rumors of bad behavior, Heinlein rushed to note that "King's reputation as a martinet was undeserved [and] comes solely from those who failed to meet his standards . . . a strict disciplinarian but never petty."[85]

The award-winning crew of *Lexington* grew deeply fond of King, most lamenting the impending departure of their fearsomely efficient skipper. Before his change of command, the officers, crew, and their wives planned a series of celebrations to offer their farewells to King and his family. On one occasion, Heinlein brought King's daughters Martha and Claire for a party at "Stone Acres"—a farm on the outskirts of Seattle where the officers of *Lexington* established an informal officer's club and crash pad. Heinlein described the place as

a raunchy setup so secluded that a massacre would have gone unnoticed and was the site of an endless drunken brawl from about 1645 each day to about

0740 the next morning, and from just after 1200 on Saturdays until about 0740 on Mondays. My messmates had furnished it sparsely with 3rd hand or salvage chairs, cots, couches, beds, a card table or two, and had modified the piping so that the spigot in the kitchen sink dispensed moonshine cougar milk from a barrel in the attic then dubbed it "Stone Acres" and underlined the pun by hanging two cocoanut shells as their road sign at the gate.[86]

King found out about Stone Acres from his daughters but never rendered the place off-limits. In his final days as skipper on *Lexington*, the officers held an informal party for King at Stone Acres—amplified by liquor smuggled in from Canada. During the proceedings, the *Lexington* officers presented King a large sheepskin scroll embossed with hand-inscribed portrayals of their collective achievements. King later recalled that if they had "tried for years to discover what he would most treasure, they could not have had a happier thought."[87]

Having enjoyed a relaxed celebration with his officers, King joined the rest of the *Lexington* crew for a formal ball at the Olympic Hotel in downtown Seattle. Local dignitaries wore black ties, and the crew all wore their best uniforms. Among those in attendance, Chief Quartermaster Stanley Dynkowski spoke with liquor fueling his words. Heinlein witnessed the moment that "Chief Ski was very drunk indeed, put his arms around King's neck[,] and said, 'Cap'n King, what am I going to do when you leave?"[88] Enlisted sailors encircled the pair and cheered King as cheerful tears appeared in the corners of his eyes. Later, King told his biographer about the jovial sailors begging to receive appropriate punishments. One of the sailors screamed to King that "if you are not going to put me in the brig, all I can say is, the Navy has gone to hell!"[89]

Having created a band of brothers on *Lexington*, King reluctantly recognized the value of departing quickly upon completing command. On the day following the party at the Olympic Hotel, all hands nursed hangovers in their white uniforms on the flight deck of *Lexington*. King suddenly appeared with his relief, Capt. Charles A. Blakely, and walked past each of the sailors for inspection. King then walked to the podium and read his detachment orders before rendering the obligatory salute and walking off the deck. Heinlein recalled that King quietly "left in mufti [and] seemed smaller in civilian clothes, older, and slightly stooped [and] carrying an overnight bag and that did not look right, either."[90] King requested permission to leave the ship, saluted the colors, and walked briskly away from *Lexington* without looking back. Heinlein recalled feelings of happiness intermixed with disappointment as "I watched him walking down the dock."[91]

King won numerous simulated wars in peacetime command on board *Lexington*, which provided inroads for possible early promotion into the flag ranks. Success followed in his wake as he looked upward to the stars. Confident in the future, King drove with Mattie and their family across the country to the familiar shores of New England.[92] He was among only four other aviators with a legitimate chance of competing for the eventual appointment to replace Moffett. King understood the stakes as his Class of 1901 entered the zone to participate in the annual beauty contest for prospective flag officers. Having successfully completed his seagoing command on *Lexington*, King stood eligible for the flag selection board in 1932.

Competitive selection boards operated under the precepts issued by the secretaries of war and Navy, although the number of authorized promotions always hinged upon the budgetary restrictions imposed by Congress under the Constitution. Pratt and Schofield also advised King to anticipate extended orders leading to the potential promotion path from captain to the two-star functions of president of the Naval War College.[93] Fifty years after the institution first appeared on the books of the US Navy, King reentered the old building wherein Luce and Mahan first developed their vision of American sea power. Having known Luce and Mahan as a junior officer, King also rekindled his connection with Sims. As a forum, the Naval War College still carried significant historical influence as the "directional authority of a weathercock on the roof of a New England barn."[94]

CHAPTER 11
"Citizen Fixit"

Professor Sir John Knox Laughton used history as the platform for teaching British naval professionals about the unwritten future. From his lecture halls at the University of London–King's College, Laughton also inspired the Americans. He assisted Luce and Mahan in their efforts to organize the Naval War College—roughly forty years before King returned to Newport for the resident course for senior-ranking officers. Twice before, he completed the war college certification, first for the staff course and then by setting the example for his subordinates by taking the correspondence course. Superior performance as the *Lexington* skipper had also placed King on the fast track for promotion to the flag ranks. While waiting for the selection board, King relished the opportunity to ponder Pratt's characterization of an "intimate connection between the Fleet in being and the War College, the home of thought."[1]

King was among the most seasoned and technically qualified officers on active service. Among 245 captains on active service in 1932, King competed for early promotion. Timing was everything in the calculus to fill one of the few potential vacancies expected to open among the fifty-nine admirals on active service. The most senior admiral on the active list had entered service in 1883, and the most junior in 1895. King knew his record exceeded many other competitors for promotion to flag rank. However, he competed against the more senior standing graduates of the Naval Academy classes of 1896 to 1900. As a member of the Class of 1901, King hoped to earn flag rank during the 1932 selection board. Should he be selected, he also held the perfect position to become the natural relief for the outgoing president of the Naval War College, RAdm. Harris Laning, in the spring of 1933.[2]

Among the saltiest naval officers in the fleet, King stood among the most qualified officers on active service. Beyond his demonstrated success in submarines and aviation, King also held the firm confidence of the CinCUS, Schofield, and the CNO, Pratt. Two stars appeared upon King's professional horizon at the Naval War College. For this reason, King purchased another home on 37 Kay Street in Newport. His old mentor, retired admiral Sims, lived just around the corner with his family at 73 Catherine Street. Sims and King frequently haunted the Newport Reading Room on 29 Bellevue Avenue—up the street from their homes in Newport.[3] Meanwhile, King rented their home at 45 Franklin Street in Annapolis. His lawyer, Cornelius Bull, also assisted King in managing properties in Georgetown, New London, and Long Beach.[4]

The future potential for submarines and aircraft carriers in the wireless-communications era of seagoing fleet operations loomed among many open questions. Logistics and intelligence functions also festered below the surface of debates concerning hierarchically driven command relationships between staffs ashore and naval forces operating on multiple seagoing fronts. The older policy debates about unification also filled the air within the classrooms of the war colleges and staff schools. The Joint Board further muddied the waters in conjunction with the unresolvable conflicts between the Departments of War and Navy in setting future procurement priorities. During studies in Newport, King examined the politics of procurement and the Byzantine process for managing the funding debates within Congress.[5]

The ongoing fights for control in the air placed the Army General Staff at odds with their counterparts in OpNav. Army commanders sought unity of command to coordinate aviation forces against targets ashore, whereas naval doctrine required ships to maneuver along with aviation and submarines. Under the circumstances, the Army chief of staff, Gen. Douglas MacArthur, accepted a gentleman's agreement with the CNO, Pratt. Together, MacArthur and Pratt informally concluded that the future

> Naval Air Force will be based on the fleet and move with it as an important element in solving the primary missions confronting the fleet. The Army Air Forces will be land-based and employed as an essential element to the Army in the performance of its mission to defend the coasts at home and in our overseas possessions, thus assuring the fleet absolute freedom of action without any responsibility for coast defense.[6]

The arrangements established by bureaucratic handshake between MacArthur and Pratt served as a temporary measure to enable the services to safeguard their budgetary interests *at the time*.[7] MacArthur claimed control over all military airfields ashore, and Pratt reserved the right to control air operations involving naval forces operating in conjunction with warships.[8]

The airpower debates reflected budget constraints under the economic-austerity policies of the Hoover administration. Half pay for the armed services seemed appropriate for Hoover. Government housing for officers and barracks for enlisted personnel seemed sufficient for Hoover, since servicemen seemingly had better conditions than most American taxpayers. Enlisted sailors also lived on board ships, receiving access to state-of-the-art training in all the key industrial trades. Hoover administration policies seemed whacky to his Democratic Party challenger, Roosevelt, during the 1932 election season. He seized the opportunity to foster ties with union laborers following the Hoover administration decision to close American factories associated with the construction of warships in the Midwest and naval shipyards on the coasts.

Roosevelt set a clear agenda to reinvigorate the American economy through peacetime naval reconstruction and civil-maritime industrialization policies. His global oceanic outlook also stood at odds with the continentalist mindset that defined the Hoover administration. Army officers like Pershing and MacArthur openly favored Hoover. Both held celebrity status, which transcended the idealized image of American servicemen. Naval officers like Pratt and Schofield also tended to favor the grand old traditions of Teddy Roosevelt and the Republican Party. Conversely, naval officers understood the nuanced maritime outlook of Franklin Roosevelt, given their past experiences with him as assistant Navy secretary. Since his departure from the Navy Department, Roosevelt used the economic depression as a platform for highlighting the problematic record of the Hoover administration.

Naval procurement debates rumbled behind the scenes on the Washington battlefield when Roosevelt rallied Americans to the cause of creating jobs through warship construction. His calls to reopen naval shipyards also coincided with the arrival of the Bonus Army. The Hoover administration appeared heavy handed when the Army chief of staff, MacArthur, squared off against the retired Marine major general Smedley Butler on the streets of Washington.[9] The Hoover administration condemned Butler as a traitorous Bolshevik. Indeed, Butler pulled no punches in criticizing Republican and Democratic politicians for their greedy partnerships with civilian industrialists.[10]

Civil-military debates raged in conjunction with the presidential race ongoing between Hoover and Roosevelt. Still uncertain about the future military policy of the United States, the Naval War College staff encouraged discussions about the potential strategic ramifications beyond the election of 1932. In these efforts, history provided a common point of reference for contemporaneous analysis. Given technological variables, King recalled that many fellow practitioners struggled to understand the interrelationship between the past and present. He noted Mahan's critique of naval professionals suffering from the "vague feeling of contempt for the past, supposed to be obsolete, [that] combines with natural indolence to blind men even to those permanent strategic lessons which lie close to the surface of naval history."[11]

For King, history provided the secrets for winning verbal battles in the classroom setting and beyond to the unwritten future. As a primer for considering historical fundamentals, King drew heavily from the two-volume primer, as previously compiled by Stark, under the title *Extracts from Books Read in Connection with War College Reading Courses*.[12] This remarkable document captured the essence of literary works by great military thinkers from Clausewitz to Corbett and from Mahan to Sims.

Never satisfied with the editorial pruning of others, King progressively gravitated to the complete texts. He devoured the books provided by the Naval War College, many of which featured handwritten annotations made by previous readers. King soon expanded his personal library with pristine copies of the key masterworks featured in the Naval War College curriculum of the day. He parroted the ideas in his own words—using his acquired genius as a weapon in the classroom battlefield of the Naval War College. King also used his historical knowledge to trump doctrinal arguments as presented by the instructors and fellow practitioners in the classroom setting and gaming floors. For King, the Naval War College always operated with a clear operational purpose—using sea power to attain the sustainable strategic end of war.[13]

KING'S BOYS

King earlier completed the correspondence courses of the Army and Navy War Colleges to set the example for others to follow within the ranks. Mattie ran the ship within the King family—all in accordance with the basics outlined in the manual published by their old friend Anne Briscoe Pye, the wife of King's pal Capt. William S. Pye, within the text of a manual for new spouses, *The Navy Wife*.[14] Anne Pye and Mattie King followed the implied rules for navy spouses in running the operations at home, thereby enabling their seafaring husbands to focus on their careers. The race to succeed within the ranks of the US Navy always involved the families, which required navy wives to accept their roles as the keepers of the personal shore establishment of individual naval officers on the rise.[15]

Feudal competitions among graduates of the Military Academy at West Point and the Naval Academy in Annapolis were frequently combined with those of military and maritime schools like Virginia Military Institute and the locally established maritime academies along the coasts of America. Whenever service families intermarried, the match often featured in local newspaper headlines. For example, when Mattie agreed to marry King, their engagement featured in the *Army-Navy Journal*. Decades later, in 1932, three of King's daughters had married US Army officers, and it featured prominently in *Life* magazine that "one of them did marry an Annapolis graduate [but others] are married to Army men [and] King has taken a good deal of ribbing on the subject of his six daughters who are often referred to as 'King's boys.'"[16]

Bureaucratic debates concerning the character and organization of the army and naval services frequently followed the ebbs and flows of family interconnections within the ranks. For this reason, the King family drew the attention of the American media. Many journalists took a very personal interest in service personalities. One media exposé noted that "it was not until King was forty-four that his seventh child turned out to be a boy."[17] Journalists noted that an English friend of the King family joked that his son's name "should have been Ernest Endeavor!"[18] Between the lines of standard narratives about King, the King family had a very important role in shaping his development as a flag officer with the requisite connections to influence efforts to unify the bureaucracies of the War Department and Navy Department. Indeed, King sat at the center of a very extensive family network, which also extended to their friends and associates within the ranks of civilian industry, the military, and federal government.[19]

Army officers won the hearts of King's daughters and progressively overwhelmed the naval ranks of the family. The eldest, Elizabeth, married US Army captain Oliver Wolcott van den Berg—of an established old New England family with famed connections to the Sons of Liberty and the American founding fathers in the War of Independence. The second daughter, Eleanor, married a West Point graduate and army pilot, Lt. Edward B. Hempstead. King's daughters Martha and Claire kept King busy as they followed the family traditions of marrying servicemen. Claire married Ens. John M. B. Howard after he graduated from the Naval Academy. Much to his disappointment, Howard received orders for immediate transfer to the retired list. As the American services weathered half pay in the Depression era, Howard joined his Naval Academy classmate Draper Kauffman in requesting immediate assignment to the retired list to pursue opportunities in the merchant marine.[20] Howard and Kauffman both accepted jobs with Esso Oil Company.[21]

The King family ranks reflected the close connections among the households of American armed-service professionals. Having moved into their new home in Newport in June 1932, King gave away his daughter Martha to US Army lieutenant Frederic H. "Freddy" Smith Jr., of the US Army Air Corps. Friends of the King family told reporters, "I never saw a man give away a bride so gracefully."[22] Unrelated to Frederic but sharing the same surname, US Army colonel Walter D. Smith stood among the joint ranks of the extended King family. Nearly twenty-five years earlier, he stood in as best man for King when he married Mattie at the Military Academy at West Point. Smith had earned fame as a football player before he married Mattie's sister Florence Egerton. By 1932, Smith supervised the Historical Section of the Army War College. Matriarchs of their military families, the sisters Mattie and Florence enabled King and Smith to focus on their careers while running the home.[23]

The ranks of the King family proved comparably more substantial than those of the American military and naval services. His brother-in-law Smith earned brigadier rank in command of the reserve cadre formations of the 82nd Infantry Division. Military culture defined the King family, which bonded as a particularly tight-knit organization under the skipper at home—Mattie. One granddaughter described King and Mattie as "charismatic" and as the "core of the family." "She was the rock," adding that King "sent letters regularly to his wife and (children)."[24] King's grandson Van described King as a "great gentleman with a commanding presence and a calming voice—granddad had that special quality."[25]

King seemed like a towering hero as he captivated his grandchildren with tales of adventure on the high seas. Van recalled receiving a "neat little Hawaiian god statue that I had with me that granddad sent for good luck when I went to West Point."[26] Van often wore his fine bespoke suits on dates and special occasions.[27] As with his sailors, King's wrath could be terrifying. His eldest daughter, Elizabeth, once skipped school. Upon receiving notice from the headmaster, Mattie reported the infraction to King. Elizabeth later recalled the ramifications for skipping school. She remembered hiding under the bed and hearing him walk up the steps. When King walked into the room, Elizabeth "saw his black shoes under the dust ruffle [and] all he had to do was just stand there, not saying a word."[28]

The social scene in Newport provided many opportunities for service professionals to rekindle their relationships with family and friends. King used the assignment to the Naval War College to nurture ties with the future stars of the army and navy. Mattie similarly developed close friendships with the wives of such future admirals as Spruance, Turner, Hewitt, and Kirk.[29] In addition, King rekindled his connections with older mentors like Sims and Mayo during service in Newport. King and Mattie regularly hosted Admiral and Mrs. Sims for afternoon discussions over tea and sandwiches. King also remembered discussing strategic trends with his old mentor Sims during lunches in their home. The intimate connections between the older generation and the younger guns of the American fleet provided continuity as the past faded into the wake of the future in the classrooms and gaming floors of the Naval War College.[30]

REFLECTING UPON THE PAST AND FUTURE

Civilian academics from such universities as Yale and Harvard frequently delivered special lectures to the staff and practitioners attending the Naval War College. Robert G. Albion spoke broadly about maritime culture, Samuel E. Morison considered the age of exploration, and Edward Meade Earle of Princeton talked on the theoretical connections between policy and strategy. Serving in retired status at the ONI as the officer in charge of the Navy Library and Archives, Capt. Dudley W. Knox frequently traveled from Washington to Newport to deliver lectures on naval history.[31] He and others delivered lectures about the League of Nations, army-navy procurement problems, questions of future strategy, and other trends.[32]

Service at the Naval War College provided opportunity for service practitioners to let their hair down and take time to think. The curriculum of the Naval War College focused on the patterns between history and the challenges of the present. King studied the methods employed by the great captains of the past—from Admiral Horatio Nelson to David Dixon Porter. In retirement, Sims delivered lectures about his experiences to extrapolate about issues of current interest. The staff at the Naval War College balanced the debate by supervising students' written work.[33] During his studies in Newport, King rekindled friendships with William F. Halsey Jr., Charles R. Train, Morton Deyo, and Donald P. Moon. The Naval War College staff included Captain Wilbur R. Van Auken and Commanders Raymond A. Spruance, Alan G. Kirk, Richmond Kelly Turner, Henry Kent Hewitt, and Charles Maddox. Notably, Cmdr. Roscoe C. McFall lectured about the gaming experiments conducted with King's class on the use of circular formations in fleet operations. Such tactics represented a clear break from the existing doctrine and surface line traditions.[34]

Fleet operations defined strategic discussions about the future of aviation and sub-surface technology at the Naval War College. Logistics and intelligence also required an understanding of the wireless world of electronic communications. Keeping the debate lively during Prohibition, US Navy destroyers maintained a steady flow of Canadian liquor to facilitate cheerful studies at the Naval War College.[35] The staff kept the illicit booze locked in the basement of the North Annex, two floors below the portraits of Admirals Luce and Mahan in the rotunda. During visits to the Naval War College, Capt. William D. Leahy enjoyed participating in the social culture of Newport. He particularly enjoyed drinking with the Naval War College staff during evening cigars under the rotunda of the North Annex.[36]

Prohibition failed to stop the flow of beer and liquor behind the cloistered walls of the Naval War College. King kept his office in room E-13, on the eastern corner of the Naval War College—with windows facing the original building and overlooking the picturesque seascapes of the Narragansett Bay. He regularly joined the mess discussions for the evening gatherings in the North Annex, wherein the staff and attending practitioners continued discussing the trends of the day. The room featured the historic rotunda with a portrait of Luce overlooking the fireplace. Historic artifacts and archival files provided inspiration for discussion. King recalled taking the "time to browse in the excellent library, to reflect upon past and future service, and to consider the world situation, particularly in those aspects that appeared to be leading toward war."[37]

The transatlantic relationship between Europe and the Americas likewise influenced King's views about the problem of Asia. During his studies, King rekindled friendships with British friends serving on the battleship HMS *Marlborough* and cruiser HMS *Danae* during their port calls to Newport. Having studied the maneuvers of *Marlborough* in the Jutland war game, King regretted leaning about the plan to scrap the venerable warship during his tour on board. During the visit to *Danae*, Capt. Charles H. Knox-Little shared fond memories of Anglo-American collaboration with King. Another friend from the First World War, the British naval attaché Capt. Patrick McNamara, emphasized the prospect of Royal Navy and US Navy collaboration—and particularly in strategic relations with the Imperial Japanese Navy.[38] King sympathetically noted that American sea power "virtually reduced Great Britain to second place."[39] He continued that "Great Britain must be considered a potential enemy . . . not in questions of security, but as to matters involving our foreign trade, financial supremacy, and our dominant position in world affairs."[40]

TURNING INWARD WHILE LOOKING OUTWARD

Given social dynamics in American society, the Naval War College provided a broad stage for scholars to expose practitioners to various perspectives. In a series of lectures, scholars associated with Harvard and Princeton Universities examined the political influence of Communist ideology, international diplomacy, and race. Professor William Starr Meyers of Princeton examined the philosophy of government. Providing a practical perspective from the State Department, John D. Hickerson explained American policy in relation to the British Commonwealth of Nations. Professor George H. Blakeslee then joined fellow Harvard University historians Bruce C. Hopper and the white supremacist Theodore Lothrop Stoddard to present lectures on the influence of communism in Russia and China.[41]

Racial politics influenced questions of future American sea power on the Naval War College lecture stage. Stoddard drew heavily from eugenics theory in his published works. Stoddard proudly stood among the ranks of the Ku Klux Klan. Stoddard waxed poetic about the specter of Bolshevism with polished words about the "Rising Menace of the Under-Man" and the "Rising Tide of Color." The works by Stoddard resonated among American readers, which influenced the National Socialist definition of the German term *Untermenschen*. At the Naval War College, Stoddard presented a lecture called "Racial Aspiration as Influencing National Policy."[42] Interestingly, the staff removed his file from other lectures from 1932 and 1933. The Stoddard file eventually surfaced among other administrative files kept by the Office of the President of the Naval War College more than a decade later.

Placing the question of race into the broader context of culture within the US Navy, shipboard realities forced skippers at sea to make accommodations to keep good order and discipline among the races. Racial lines also influenced relationships between officers and enlisted ratings.[43] Given the legacies of Jim Crow politics in American society, King notably opened the ranks of the sea services for women and racial minorities roughly a decade later.[44] King was aware of the debate between Stoddard and Black historian William E. B. DuBois. Just a few months earlier, DuBois masterfully portrayed Stoddard as a charlatan during a debate held in Chicago, Illinois. Advertisements for the debate appeared like a cinematic blockbuster, the World Series, or perhaps a major prize fight in the arena of public opinion. Using historical evidence as a counterpoint, DuBois systematically eviscerated Stoddard and his racist views. DuBois famously used humor to refute the wild theories of Stoddard and his racist fellow traveler Madison Grant.[45]

The poisonous mix of racial social theory and the quackery of eugenic science concerned practitioners attending the Naval War College. Considering the political aspects, Stoddard maintained close ties within the ranks of the Republican Party. The Harding and Coolidge administrations also publicly endorsed the theories of Stoddard, which became an issue for Hoover during the 1932 race. The Democratic Party contender, Franklin D. Roosevelt, publicly dismissed the paranoid theories of Stoddard and other racist scholars. As an open issue in an election year, the Naval War College provided the forum wherein King could grapple with the strategic questions inherent within cultural politics and American society.[46]

Racism stood out as a major problem of strategic concern within the ranks of the American armed services. From the Philippines to the Caribbean, US Army regiments maintained strict separation between officers and enlisted personnel, which also extended to the racial divisions between individual units and troops. Unlike the military culture ashore, the American sea services always reflected the cosmopolitan influence of global culture. Since his earliest training at sea as a naval cadet, King had consistently served in close quarters with Black sailors and fellow shipmates from other ethnic origins. He rode the waves of racial policy alongside his shipmates throughout his career. Racial issues frequently originated from outdated regulations and misguided interpretations of history, in King's mind at least.[47]

Misguided racial theories coincided with the menaces of extreme militarism and Communist ideology, which King addressed within the open forum of the Naval War College. He also examined the role of propaganda and the psychological vulnerabilities associated with collective ignorance.[48] King attended the Naval War College lecture by Harvard professor Gordon Allport titled "Psychology of Propaganda in Peace and War."[49] Allport relied heavily upon the teachings of Sigmund Freud, using imagery from newspapers and magazines to demonstrate the use of sexual imagery for the purposes of influencing the masses into thinking alike. Taking the primary group discussion to another level, Sevellon Brown of the *Providence Journal* explained various investigative tricks employed by journalists in "Collection and Dissemination of News."[50]

King thought that the greatest threat existed in the influence of external manipulators and the eclectic character of the American political system. The ancient problems of economic class and race fueled the tensions of the times, which King keenly observed with an objective apolitical lens. As the Republican and Democratic Parties raced to political extremes to win control in the 1932 election year, King progressively gravitated to the view of Franklin D. Roosevelt's trusted adviser Harold Ickes. Responding to critics of the New Deal platform, Ickes observed that "Communism is merely a convenient Bugaboo." Ickes continued to suggest that the "Fascist-minded men of America [are] the real enemies of our institutions through their solidarity and willingness to turn the wealth of America against the welfare of America."[51]

King's personal views appear between the lines in papers written during his residency at the Naval War College. Given the trends in American politics, King examined the interconnections with Europe and Asia. Writing in 1932, King considered the oceanic barriers fundamental to American defense. He observed that "Germany is subdued but resentful of her status and apparently determined to resume her prewar standing and influence." He reasoned, "Italy is at present aggressive towards other European nations but is not likely to cause us any serious trouble." He identified a more ominous threat: "Russia, under its present Soviet regime[,] is a menace in its determined and energetic endeavors to change the political character of every nation." King characterized the Soviet regime as "so aggressive and so unscrupulous."[52] The prospect of future war centered in Asia, which King identified as the region of convergence in the imperial competition for strategic resources. He considered that the "Philippines are a serious strategical liability in that Japan is likely to seize them as an opening move . . . in their evident intention to seize and hold a dominating position in Asia."[53] Under the circumstances, King predicted that the strategic trends "point very definitely to Japan as a potential enemy, which will be satisfied to seize and hold and then defy us to change the situation."[54] King described racism and restrictive American immigration policies as being the counterproductive diplomatic "barrier against Oriental peoples."[55] He predicted Japanese retaliation in "any available way, such as in trade relations, Chinese questions, or the promotion of unrest in the Philippines."[56]

American arrogance fueled other strategic problems, as King considered the ramifications for the future military policy of the United States. He somewhat agreed with the critique of Soviet leaders about American notions of being culturally exceptional, ideologically superior, or fundamentally peaceful.[57] King criticized fellow Americans for indulging in "our national altruism, our belief in our own capacity to do well at anything we undertake, together with our childlike trust and faith in our destiny." He lamented the ignorance of Americans for failing to understand the peacetime role of the sea services such that "we appear to be unable to appreciate preparedness even when, as individuals, we carry fire insurance on our houses and collision insurance on our cars."[58]

King worried about the weakness of the League of Nations without participation of the United States. He identified the British Empire and imperial Japan as the most-significant threats. King envisioned the potential of an Anglo-Japanese alliance, the inadequacy of international law, and the potential failure of the League of Nations. Should an American rival decide to pursue military action in the future, King predicted that an enemy "may be expected to resort to war to keep what he has or get what he wants."[59] Having seen the carnage of the First World War, King paraphrased the nineteenth-century observations of Clausewitz to argue how, in the twentieth century,

> war is so costly in all respects—as to human life, money, disruption of trade and of industry as examples—that a government's first care in waging war is to consider and to determine the nature of the war. It is obvious that the means should, as a matter of common sense, be adapted to the end in view, so that war is carried on only in such manner and in such degree as will procure the object for which the war is entered.[60]

During advanced studies at the Naval War College, King anticipated the loss of access to land bases in any potential war involving an adversary in either Europe or Asia. In relations with the British Empire, King lamented equal inadequacy of American sea power to compensate for the "inferiority of our Fleet and of our shipping (lack of 'ways and means')." Looking outward, King predicted, "Japan will take such steps as to compel us to overseas operations [by] attacks on the Philippines or even on Hawaii as a potent handicap to our overseas operations."[61]

King recognized the limits of diplomacy in considering the strategic consequences of an inadequate navy. He reached the pragmatic conclusion that "international law is not law in the usual sense [but] a growth by secretion of customs and practices of long standing and of specific or general agreements among a majority of nations."[62] Continuing, he observed that the League of Nations "aspires to permanency and has a covenant of rights, duties, and obligations which are binding upon adhering nations."[63] The British Empire seemed to be a natural ally for the United States. As King noted, "Japan will assume the offensive initially to acquire an advantage where she can assume the defensive and defy us to alter the situation—not that her defensive attitude will be in any degree passive, it will not."[64]

The problems of Asia appeared intertwined with those of Europe, as the naval powers of Japan and Britain approached the crossroads between peace and war. Examining the possibilities, King emphasized the maneuverability of naval forces over the static defense of positions ashore.[65] He warned about the pitfalls of imperial strategy. King observed that Americans dabbled in strategy, failing to understand how "our altruism and our strong inclination to play 'Citizen Fixit' have combined to involve us much more deeply than is necessary or desirable, even though initially not intended."[66]

Sustained logistics and superior airpower provided means to enable the US Navy to maneuver against prospective enemies on multiple fronts. For King, American garrisons deployed to distant bastions ashore appeared as major strategic liabilities in case of an attack by a foreign enemy. He considered the prospect of surprise attack, particularly against strategic positions in the Philippines, Guam, Hawaii, Alaska, and the Panama Canal. King noted that the

> most striking difference between land and naval warfare is the relative mobility of land and naval forces. The advantage of navies in this respect is, however, offset by the limitations imposed by fuel expenditures. An army can stop and hold; a navy must, relatively, be able to move in order to hold. An army campaign or battle may require, respectively, months and days whereas a naval campaign or battle will usually require, respectively, weeks and hours. An army reverse may be counter-acted; a naval reverse usually is final.[67]

Naval air forces provided greater maneuverability, as compared with land-based air forces. For these reasons, King reached strong conclusions about strategy. He drew clear distinctions between land and sea operations in considering organizational relationships among army and naval commanders—particularly as related to the tactical use of airpower.[68]

Given examples provided by foreign counterparts, King rejected the idea of unifying American air forces under a separate military branch. King noted the demise of aviation in the Royal Navy after the establishment of the Royal Air Force, which essentially consolidated airpower under the land-oriented thinkers of the British army. For these reasons, he rejected the arguments of Mitchell and his followers in the US Army. King thought, "Army aviation should end at the shoreline."[69] Given broad concepts in strategy and tactics, King embraced the ethereal advantages of wireless, intelligence, and logistics. He emphasized these points by observing that "often the determining element in naval strategy is logistics . . . naval strategy is concerned and emphasizes the importance of what are known as lines of communication."[70] He further emphasized "conditions which have arisen from time to time by reason of the evolution of weapons and the advent of new degrees of mobility in maneuver."[71] He warned of the "false assumption about progress in technology."[72]

The parochial differences between armies and navies hinged on the question of common sense in examining the distinctions between land and sea operations. King characterized naval officers as being "broadly educated about the seas and the stars, but army pilots are just trained to look down upon all of us who walk upon the ground [and] they always have trouble navigating over water where the airfield is always moving."[73]

Aircraft carrier operations required special training for aviators to survive the rigors of the oceanic landscape. Fixed fortifications ashore required garrisons with sufficient supplies to hold ground, whereas naval forces used the fluidity of the maritime environment to influence outcomes ashore.[74]

RED, ORANGE, AND BLUE

King thrived in Newport, studying the past to consider options for application in simulated battles waged on the gaming floors of the Naval War College. Customarily, the president of the Naval War College, Laning, and his executive officer, Andrews, acted as umpires in conducting the simulated battles. During the gaming experiments, the Naval War College staff derived strategic situations from the joint war plans—such as RED (British Empire) and ORANGE (Japan).[75] CRIMSON-delineated navies were associated with the British. YELLOW and JADE represented navies associated with Japan. BROWN represented navies of South America and neutral forces.[76] In characterizing joint army-navy color plans, King's protégé, Van Deurs, recalled their impressions of Plan ORANGE when "we began reading it to see what we were supposed to do [and] finally we all got laughing so hard that it was hard to keep reading . . . [we] were taking turns reading out of this thing and it was just like reading the funny papers."[77]

The operational focus of games frequently reflected the then-current concerns of the times. Naval officers perceived the color plans for what they were—army plans that were aspirational in purpose or, alternatively, "completely ridiculous."[78] In the aftermath of the London Naval Conference, the staff at the Naval War College used the joint color plans for the simple purpose of providing foundations for fictitious scenarios on the gaming floor. These were not plans that anybody in the naval ranks considered as being useful for operations in an actual war. During the final gaming exercise, held in the spring of 1933, King took command BLUE (United States) in a simulated global war against the imperial forces of RED and ORANGE.[79]

Games conducted on the floors of the Naval War College followed a logical process, which provided inspiration for producing analytical written studies. In setting the pieces, King first identified common trade interests as the point of mutual vulnerability for the RED/ORANGE alliance. In examining the gambit, King assumed that the "Philippines were to be overrun, we knew that Australia was menaced, and that New Zealand was menaced, but there was not enough to go around, and you had to decide what to do with what you had and get busy making more."[80]

King understood the importance of buying sufficient time for American industry to build requisite munitions and mobilize the nation to meet the global challenges from foreign shores. Only when Americans stood united, "why you might be able to shift the balance."[81] During his initial setup for the purposes of gaming analysis at the Naval War College, King chose to maintain a small and mobile defensive force in the Atlantic to thwart RED.[82] The greater threat appeared clear, since the RED/ORANGE scenario pitched American forces against the combined strength of the Royal Navy, Commonwealth forces, and Imperial Japanese Navy.

Cultural divides within the British Commonwealth forces of RED and CRIMSON provided means by which King intended to exploit strategic fissures within the enemy coalition. He firmly discounted the scenario in which RED had acquiesced to an alliance with ORANGE. King thought that Japan's primary focus of evicting European and American forces from Asia also ran against any prospective alliance with Britain, as RED, or the United States, as BLUE.[83] For this reason, King proposed an offensive drive through the central Pacific—using BLUE aircraft carriers and submarines in advance of battleships and amphibious forces to seize key islands in the Marshall and Caroline Islands.[84]

King framed plans to divide the RED and ORANGE alliance by severing lines of communication to the British home islands in the Atlantic. Ceding the Philippines to the enemy, King planned to create a strategic vacuum designed to overextend the combined forces of RED and ORANGE. [85] He envisioned BLUE surface forces as the centerpiece in defending the American hemisphere while employing submarines and aircraft carrier forces in an unrelenting offensive against the enemy. The Panama Canal provided means to maneuver between RED and ORANGE. King further emphasized the role of logistics and intelligence functions in operations.[86]

War games provided food for thought in analyzing battles of the past and in considering ideas for potential application in the future. King employed BLUE naval forces in a campaign centered on maneuvering task forces at high speed to conduct coastal raids and aerial strikes in a widely dispersed offensive strategy.[87] He identified the decisive point that "we shall oblige Great Britain in an overseas offensive which should impose on her the handicap inherent in the necessity to establish and secure lines of overseas communication for the supply of her fleet and the transport of supply of troops."[88] By drawing RED to commit forces in support of the alliance with ORANGE, King intended to use BLUE naval task forces to clear the way for decisive amphibious thrusts leading across the central Pacific into the heart of YELLOW (China) and JADE (French and Dutch Indochina).

King considered the island strongholds of the United Kingdom and imperial Japan particularly vulnerable to the influence of American sea power. He identified British and Japanese trade as an Achilles heel for both empires. King thought that "Japan is likely to be without allies except possibly impressed forces from China or considerable assistance from Soviet Russia as to munitions and other supplies."[89] On the other hand, King realistically predicted that the greatest weakness for American forces centered on the "initial handicap of inadequate 'ways and means,' to expend much blood and treasure to overcome this handicap (if we can finally overcome it), and gain the victory."[90]

Having earned the opportunity through written analysis of the RED-ORANGE enemy, King received command of the BLUE fleet. Tossing a spanner in the works, the Naval War College president, Laning, frustrated King by requiring his BLUE strategy to conform to the established script. King faced few options other than to follow the "school solution."[91] On aviation issues in particular, King advised Laning in examining the strategic trends in efforts to improve the curriculum in Newport.[92] His studies of the problem solidified his convictions about focusing strategic naval operations on the routes running between the west coast along the islands of the central Pacific to Formosa. The three existing aircraft carriers in the American fleet seemed insufficient to the task. Budget cuts further hindered future aircraft carrier hulls, such as USS *Ranger* (CV-4). As a cost-savings measure, the US Navy tinkered with hybrid designs for "flight deck cruisers."[93]

Hybrid designs for adapting existing warships for other purposes inspired discussions at the Naval War College. Debates among younger officers similarly fueled the wild ideas of King's former subordinate on *Lexington*, Heinlein, and his classmate Cal Laning. When

King later held supreme command in wartime, the younger generation of Heinlein and Laning developed means to enable the US Navy to gain supremacy in electronic communications, intelligence, and naval operational doctrine. Heinlein and Laning drew inspiration from the science fiction writings of Dr. E. E. Smith. The *Skylark* and *Lensmen* fictions of Smith inspired Heinlein and Laning. In framing fleet operations, the wild ideas of Heinlein and Laning filtered into the innovative decisions of King during the peacetime voyages of *Lexington* and beyond to the classroom discussions and gaming floors of the Naval War College.[94]

Strategic debates concerning the future of fleet operations conversely revealed problems in the curriculum at the Naval War College. Battle studies of Trafalgar and Jutland provided means to examine transcendent historical trends in the curriculum organized by Sims after the First World War. By 1932, King used these historical battles as the basis for examining future contingencies, using the traditional battle line as the basis for submarine, aircraft carrier, and amphibious operations in a wireless world. Happy for the chance to carve out his own place in future history, King bought another house in Newport with the full expectation of becoming president of the Naval War College after his residency in the classroom.[95]

Old mentors influenced the careers of upwardly mobile competitors in the generation of King and Andrews. Having retired from the General Board to serve as governor of the Philadelphia Naval Hospital, Mayo occasionally visited the Naval War College. In the summer of 1932, Mayo visited King in Newport. He discussed the problems of joint and combined command during operations in the First World War.[96] Sims spoke plainly and in provocative terms that "the battleship is dead."[97] Never shirking in the face of controversy, he recommended reducing the focus on battleship construction to build "an airplane carrier of thirty-five knots and carrying one hundred planes." Refuting the ideas of Mitchell and other airpower enthusiasts in the US Army, Sims admonished Congress to recognize battleships as outdated by describing aircraft carriers as a "capital ship of much[-]greater offensive power than any battleship."[98]

Always willing to charge into a bureaucratic debate, Sims definitively rejected the role of zeppelins in future fleet operations. He emphasized how aircraft carriers would be the key to the future of naval aviation. Sims and King stood together in making the argument for aircraft carriers, which rankled Moffett.[99] Having vested interest in continuing the LTA program, Moffett encouraged King to take a familiarization flight on USS *Akron* (ZRS-4) in November 1932.[100] *Akron*'s skipper, Cmdr. Frank McCord, gave King a special experience—flying over New York City before maneuvering to the Narragansett Bay. McCord maneuvered *Akron* at low altitude to enable King to climb a ladder onto the decks of a ferry. He then sailed into the Narragansett to fleet landing, going ashore at the Naval War College.[101]

King flew over the historic campus of the Naval War College with a firm appreciation of the interrelationship of historical trends. Looking down from the skies above, King anticipated orders to replace Laning as president of the Naval War College. The CNO, Pratt, reaffirmed the idea with King. According to the plan, he expected to stay in Newport for roughly two years.

Then, he hoped to be on track for a three-star command at sea in his late fifties. King could then compete for a four-star assignment at just about the right time before reaching mandatory retirement at age sixty-four. In the spring of 1933, Pratt charted the stars for

King to follow to be in the right position to reach the highest levels of command within six years after completing the senior residency in Newport.[102] King liked the idea of matriculating to the two-star flag rank as president of the Naval War College to develop his ideas for applied purposes in peacetime fleet problems. By 1935, he could then compete for a three-star assignment and then win four stars by 1939. Looking outward to the next ten years on active service beyond Newport, King planned his career path to mandatory retirement—culminating in 1942.[103]

NEW DEALS

Airpower debates between the Departments of War and Navy loomed over the classroom discussions and war game experiments of the Naval War College. In handwritten notes, King's brother-in-law in the US Army and his son-in-law in the Air Corps provided the bureaucratic intelligence for King to state, "I am reliably informed that the Army and Army Air Force seriously propose [that] there be a 'new deal' wherein functions are to be based on the premise that the Army alone deals with land objectives, the Navy is limited to the sea, and the present Army forces control all air."[104] He argued that the army vision of bureaucratic unification among the American air forces of land and sea seemed "unrealistic—not to say arbitrary, even dangerous—oversimplification, and from the Navy view it is, in effect, a straight-jacket."[105] Fighting for the future, King explained, "I am further reliably informed that existing—tried and proven agreements be thrown overboard, among them that part of 'Joint Action of the Army and Navy' as approved by the Joint Board."[106]

King warned about the arbitrary decision to place responsibility upon the War Department to control land-based aviation. Taking his cause to the bureaucratic limits, King lectured the chief of staff of the US Army, MacArthur, and the chief of the Air Corps, Brig. Gen. Benjamin Foulois, about the differences between land and sea by emphasizing the fact that the "fleet has requirements for reconnaissance and maneuver, which requires specialized training for aviators."[107] King predicted disaster looming beyond the horizon, as the Hoover administration cut peacetime budgets for the Departments of War and Navy. Lacking an understanding of the broader maritime context, Hoover closed shipyards, reduced the fleet to half pay, and decommissioned warships without contracts for replacements. Under the circumstances, King anticipated improvements when the "man of the hour"—Franklin D. Roosevelt—won the presidency in 1932.

PART II
"WAGING PEACE"

CHAPTER 12
Heavier Than Air

The election of another president from the Roosevelt family marked a major waypoint in the development of American sea power. When Franklin took the oath of office to begin his singular reign from the White House, he quickly implemented the "Good Neighbor Policy" and pushed the future concept of a Pan-American Neutrality Zone. Roosevelt envisioned the general withdrawal of American military forces from the imperial stage. Leftover military acquisitions of an earlier era, like the Philippines, seemed strategically unnecessary for Roosevelt. The oil-fired American fleet provided sufficient foundation for Roosevelt to seek global stability through diplomatic means. He followed the basic principles of the Monroe Doctrine and Roosevelt Corollary to consolidate strategic control as the industrial and economic powerhouse in the American hemisphere.[1]

Always making ready for future battle in peacetime, King used the Naval War College as the forum for navigating the uncharted waters of policy under the Roosevelt administration. Given the vision for a Pan-American Neutrality Zone, King recognized the potential of long-range scouting forces in fleet operations.[2] King's predictive approach in examining the wireless world of submarines and aviation ran against the undercurrents within the so-called gun club of the traditional surface line within the US Navy.[3] King further riled the gunnery clique and the aviators by reminding them of the broader strategic purposes of American sea power during an election year.[4]

Unification loomed over the internal debates among military and naval officers about the unproven theory of strategic airpower. As these debates raged in the war colleges and planning staffs in 1932, the Republican senator William H. King of Utah nearly closed the debate by pushing legislation to unify the Departments of War and Navy. His proposal failed when the outgoing Navy secretary, Adams, successfully argued that a single defense department stood to become a "job too big for any man to handle."[5] The CNO, Pratt, also joined forces with his counterpart, MacArthur, to thwart the effort. Having studied these debates from the solitude of Newport, King set his course by the prevailing winds of the incoming Roosevelt administration.

King held firm to an apolitical oath to the Constitution, always recusing himself from the right of all American citizens to participate in the election process by voting. On a personal level, however, he shrewdly maintained friendships with such Republicans as Wendell Willkie and Thomas Dewey while simultaneously fostering personal alliances with Democratic Party power brokers like Carl Vinson. During studies in Newport, King's emergence from the depths of the submarine force into the wild blue ranks of naval aviation also coincided with the rise—and eventual decline—of the Roosevelt administration after 1933.[6] Although the pair were *not* close friends, Roosevelt had known King for nearly thirty years. Roosevelt often joked among friends that the "only living man he feared was [Admiral] Ernest J. King."[7]

FEAR ITSELF

The election of another Roosevelt marked the beginning of another renaissance in the history of American sea power. When he delivered his first inaugural speech on March 4, 1933, Roosevelt rallied Americans to recognize that the "only thing we have to fear is fear itself."[8] On that date, King listened to Roosevelt's speech from his home on Kay Street in Newport. He expected to stay in Newport with his family in anticipation of completing the senior residency at the Naval War College. Pratt and Schofield had already advised King about his candidacy for prospective assignment in the rank of captain for the two-star appointment as president of the Naval War College. The Class of 1901 had just become eligible for consideration under the precepts governing the decisions of the Selection Board for fiscal year 1933.

The outgoing Hoover administration naturally had a lingering influence upon the upper levels of American command, as the incoming Roosevelt administration set an alternative course. King was perfectly positioned to claim no loyalty to any given political party. His assignment to the Naval War College proved especially fortuitous. From his studies in Newport, King fully understood that "history teaches us that the outcome of more than one great campaign has hinged upon some seemingly minor omission or error in human execution."[9] American naval practitioners learned to "work out a plan to a detailed perfection matched only by the Germans and then, as the situation changes, throw it out."[10] The curriculum emphasized that the *task* of planning that served the *purpose* of achieving the "harmonious exercise of command through unity of thought and effort is the aim of the War College."[11]

Sitting between the key cities of Boston and New York, the Naval War College provided an ideal location for King to nurture key connections on the political fringes of the Washington scene. He planned to remain in Newport, with hopes of becoming the president of the Naval War College. In a sudden twist of fate, Moffett went down with the airship when the *Akron* crashed in a storm off New Jersey in April 1933. Moffett's untimely death, among other developments in a series of unpredictable events, propelled King into the flag ranks earlier than expected. Immediately following the *Akron* crash, the CNO and CinCUS, Admirals Pratt and Schofield, worked behind the scenes to install King as the successor to Moffett. In turn, Navy secretary Charles F. Adams approved special arrangement to detach King early from the resident course of the Naval War College—with temporary promotion to two-star rank—as the *interim* chief of BuAer.

The race to claim control over the air defined King's tenure as chief of BuAer within the Navy Department. Civilian administrators and various bureau chiefs scrambled to seize the helm in BuAer.[12] The competition to seize control over BuAer reflected the dysfunction of BuC&R, BuOrd, and Bureau of Engineering (BuEng), falling under Rear Admirals Emory S. Land, Edgar Larimer, and Samuel B. Robinson, respectively. Under duress, Capt. Arthur B. Cook manned the bureaucratic battle stations on behalf of King within BuAer. Cook allied with the chief of BuNav, RAdm. Frank B. Upham, to install King as chief of BuAer.

The death of Moffett created significant bureaucratic turmoil within the Navy Department. The power vacuum within BuAer also created a major vulnerability in the fight for the future of naval aviation. Army air enthusiasts plotted to seize their claim on the naval aviation mission. In taking command at BuAer, King's brother-in-law and his sons-in-law in the US Army Air Corps also shared information about the gossip circulating among aviators. King used this information to stay ahead of prospective attacks from within BuAer. Given his earlier bureaucratic service in Washington, King stood out as an outsider in the minds of Moffett's acolytes. Towers and Bellinger viewed King as a "Johnny come lately."[13]

Observing from the bureaucratic high ground, Pratt viewed the venomous infighting for bureaucratic power within the Navy Department as a disgusting spectacle. He sought an outsider to bring sanity to the chaos within BuAer. Pratt also anticipated other bureaucratic storms concerning the future of airpower. Moffett had run BuAer like a clubhouse. Towers and Bellinger were among Moffett's favorites. Pratt understood that Moffett disliked other potential candidates, like Reeves and King, for having alternative views about the future of naval aviation. Pratt chose King to break up the cliquish culture among naval aviators. On April 21, 1933, Pratt issued dispatch orders for King to report to the Navy Department. Two days later, King reported to Pratt and then joined him for interviews with the secretary of the Navy, Claude Swanson, and President Roosevelt.[14]

King allowed his actions to speak in the place of words by issuing directives specifically designed to change the stale routines of BuAer. He framed new policies to synchronize with those of the Roosevelt administration agenda. Upon occupying Moffet's former office, King wore the temporary rank of two-stars as though his permanent appointment had already been adjudicated by Congress. King knew he could easily be "remoted" to his lower permanent rank of captain. The fleeting opportunity to speak with two-stars inspired King to abandon the vision of Moffett during interviews for the permanent appointment as chief of BuAer. He suggested that naval aviation "should not be a separate service onto itself within the Fleet."[15] King further argued that BuAer held relevance only among "shore activities necessary to support the Fleet."[16]

US Army pilots blurred the lines between military and maritime missions in the grander quest to amalgamate US naval aviation under a future unified airpower bureaucracy. Uniforms served as a powerful weapon in King's fight for air. He greatly upset Towers and Bellinger by requiring them to cease wearing aviation-green uniforms with brown shoes on the grounds of the Navy Department. King initially wore the green and khaki uniforms like other naval aviators. He eventually found these uniforms to be counterproductive for naval aviation—appearing somewhat too analogous with those of the US Army, the Civilian Conservation Corps, and the National Park Service.[17] Soon after his ascension to the top aviator functions within BuAer, King forced Towers and Bellinger to wear black shoes with traditional service dress blue or whites within the boundaries of Washington, DC.[18]

10,455 POUNDS OF HOUSEHOLD GOODS

The bureaucratic battles within the Navy Department increasingly centered on the question of King's future. King eventually purchased an apartment in Georgetown during service at BuAer. During weekend visits to Newport, King often joined Mattie for meetings with their neighbors next door on Kay Street—Admiral and Mrs. Sims. "As might have been expected, Sims did most of the talking," King recalled, "knowing Sims so well that he simply sat back and listened."[19] Very likely, Sims had a hand in advising the CNO, Pratt, about the potential selection of King to receive the permanent appointment as chief of BuAer.

Considering all the potential candidates, Pratt advised Secretary of the Navy Claude Swanson about King as follows:

a) He is highly intelligent

b) He is extremely active and energetic

c) He is very forceful

d) He is a flyer and a pilot

e) He is a man of great decision and character

f) He is a good strategist and tactician

g) He is not as tactful as some men but is very direct

h) He is trustworthy[20]

With such glowing endorsements, Swanson approved the temporary promotion of King to two-star rank with a provisional appointment to serve as chief of BuAer. His temporary two-star-rank assignment was subject to formal review under the regulations governing promotion and medical boards. The two-star rank coincided with the politically charged "unification" debates and the associated administrative uncertainties about the future of naval aviation.[21]

Major bureaucratic infighting between army and naval aviators fueled the ongoing vicious battles among civilian power brokers and the admirals inside the Navy Department. Anticipating the ugly administrative battles to come, King admitted at the time that "I hope I shall be able to carry out, approximately, the expectations of all my friends—that will be some job!"[22] The King family rallied to enable him to focus on meeting career goals and service expectations within the ranks. The arrival of his first grandchildren coincided with his temporary appointment to take charge in BuAer. King and Mattie also worked together to raise his teenage daughters and ten-year-old son.

Accepting the rigors inherent with the service lifestyle, King focused on the job of fighting the peacetime bureaucratic battles of the US Navy. Mattie arguably had the equally difficult—if not heroically unsung—and arduous duty of manning the watch on the home front. On April 27, 1933, she carried the burden of supervising the movers in shipping 10,455 pounds of household goods from Kay Street in Newport to the other King home on Franklin Street in Annapolis.[23] Always the shrewd entrepreneur, King rented his home in Newport to fellow naval officers. He also purchased a flat in Georgetown, within walking distance to his office inside the Navy Department. King visited the family on weekends, sometimes tossing a baseball with his young son on the Naval Academy yard near their homestead on Franklin Street in Annapolis.[24]

Having established residence in Newport for the long term, King was uniquely educated and prepared for the unique bureaucratic culture of Washington and the ugly knife fights ongoing within the Navy Department. Upon hearing the news from Pratt concerning the future of the BuAer, the skipper in the battleship USS *Idaho* (BB-42), Capt. Harold Earle Cook, wrote King that "you would have my vote for any job that you might desire but here is an appointment that no one could say that the best man did not get."[25] Discounting Towers for being partisan, Cook told King that "your appointment increases my faith in things as they should be [but] I hope the War College will not 'bilge' you if you leave there before the end of the semester and final exams."[26] Cook had heard rumors of possible skullduggery on the part of Capt. Adolphus Andrews, who was then serving as the interim president of the Naval War College.

Interpersonal rivalries among individuals, as exemplified by Andrews and King, reflected the tribal culture and group dynamics that characterized affairs within the ranks. Andrews and King always acted cordially in public. Behind the scenes, the pair rallied subordinates in an ongoing and vicious competition. Andrews and King traded flowery compliments and joked with one another. Conversely, King characterized Andrews as untrustworthy, vain, and selfish.[27] Among fellow Naval Academy graduates from the Class of 1901, Andrews earned the reputation for undercutting his closest running mates among the ranks.

Andrews attained a reputation for bootlicking, particularly after he commanded the Presidential Yacht. He maintained closed ties within the Republican Party, having befriended Warren G. Harding and Herbert Hoover. Andrews used his influence to win key assignments.[28] Later, King conceded that Andrews was "very intelligent and a very ambitious man."[29] Others among the Class of 1901, like Pye, described Andrews "as a suave Texan who spoke loudly and carried a small stick."[30] Babcock disliked Andrews for being "smart about greasing the decks with his palms."[31] King recalled that Andrews "never came to our reunions [and] was always a friend, but only to himself."[32] King concluded that "no one liked him at all [and] he would be against them because they were his classmates."[33] King enviously mused about the dog-eat-dog race to the top of the fleet ladder that Andrews "stepped on many knuckles along the way."[34]

Andrews attempted to thwart King from receiving full credit for completing the resident curriculum in the senior course of the Naval War College. He reasoned that King failed to complete the game as prescribed in the curriculum. His early detachment from Newport to Washington resulted in King failing to complete the final battle problem. King then submitted his final thesis in pencil, which violated the protocol of submitting a final typewritten version. King dutifully decided to have the final version typed and submitted by his Naval Academy classmate Babcock.[35] "I am assured that the War College will give me a diploma if I 'come and get it.'" King planned to "be on hand when they serve them out!"[36] On May 26, 1933, King sat next to the governor of Rhode Island, Theodore F. Greene, and the assistant secretary of the Navy, Henry Latrobe Roosevelt. The acting president, Andrews, however, omitted King when calling out the names of others receiving certificates for completing the course.[37] Behind the scenes, Capt. Wilbur Van Auken filed the paperwork crediting King with completing the Naval War College residency in 1933. At age fifty-three, King had roughly ten years to reach four-star rank before facing mandatory retirement.

TWO-OCEAN NAVY

Naval War College credentials provided scant advantages for King in the viciously political arenas of Washington. He entered the fray with confidence, much like how gladiators of the past faced their uncertain fortunes within the colosseums of ancient Rome. King utterly lacked the suave personality and, perhaps, the vision of Moffett. As the chief of BuAer, King characteristically "grasped the nettle firmly."[38] He sought the strategic advantage by shifting priorities within BuAer. He immediately challenged army claims on heavy aircraft by focusing future procurement priorities on long-range flying boats. King also focused on the development of remote advanced bases, which connected with the civil-military questions concerning oceanic travel by air.[39]

Debates concerning the establishment of advanced bases for sustained oceanic operations intertwined with the development of logistical doctrine. Base facilities ashore always grounded maritime policies, which informed the strategies by which seagoing forces always tethered to the flag of any given naval power in history. The "fleet train" concept in the era of the great white fleet informed the works of American naval officers in the First World War era and into the era of petroleum-fueled fleets. In the 1920s and 1930s, retired captain Dudley W. Knox used his semicivilian status to make the case for planning future logistics around advanced bases. In 1934, he argued, "Bases mean ships," to make the key point in sustaining army garrisons—and airfields—for the purpose of sustained naval operations in the global commons. Knox worked as the de facto publicist for the Navy Department. Knox could say things that serving naval officers, like King, could not.[40]

Naval officers spoke in empirical terms about the realities of logistics and capabilities, which often placed them at odds with their counterparts among the army and burgeoning air force ranks.[41] Although he always kept an apolitical façade, King was caught between the warring factions—with his brother-in-law firmly entrenched on the Army General Staff and with his Army Air Corps sons-in-law seeking their futures beyond the wild blue yonder. King also transcended the political parties through such personal friendships as those of Wendell Willkie of the Republican Party and Carl Vinson of the Democrats.

Despite his reputation for being difficult and petty, King worked the lines as a very savvy politician behind closed doors. As his close friend Knox noted, King "more often than not had already worked out the plan with his bosses before anyone else knew what the plan was going to be." Given this personality trait, King found a kindred spirit on the Washington battlefield after the inauguration of President Franklin D. Roosevelt. Together, Roosevelt and King harbored a shared vision for the future "two-ocean navy."[42]

The policies implemented by previous presidents provided the platform upon which the Roosevelt administration justified the restoration of American sea power. His predecessor, Hoover, closed several naval shipyards to reduce budgets. As a result, many American taxpayers lost good-paying shipyard jobs. Hoover inadvertently set the table for Roosevelt to make the case for rebuilding the American sea services. His message resonated with voters as naval construction engaged the nascent capacity of American industry. Having studied his own familial connections to the problem of Asia, Roosevelt worried about the Japanese war in China. He also hoped to reduce the likelihood of another world war between Japan and the European and American naval powers. To this end, Roosevelt focused his domestic agenda on the old ideas of his cousin Teddy in pursuing national unity through "Our Navy, the Peacemaker."[43]

Roosevelt focused American maritime policy upon the historical foundations provided in the Monroe Doctrine. He also exploited his cousin's concept of the Roosevelt Corollary by consolidating continental control in the American hemisphere. Unlike Teddy's impetuous delivery, Franklin articulated the Roosevelt maritime view with the soft-tongued explanation of American sea power as an interrelated element of economic prosperity. American taxpayers responded with successive reelections of the Roosevelt administration, and the future naval vision of peace and stability under the Stars and Stripes ranging far and wide upon the high seas. To achieve this end, Roosevelt had also kept detailed notes about the various tribes within the ranks of the American army and navy.

Knowing the strengths and weaknesses of key officers within the ranks of the army and navy, Roosevelt masterfully manipulated the merit promotion system to install loyalists at the tops of the military and naval hierarchies on the peacetime Washington battlefield. Roosevelt likewise fostered alliances with key personalities in Congress. Representative Carl Vinson helped the cause. The former president, Hoover, also held opinions in confidence when the Roosevelt administration began the delicate bureaucratic process of easing out the proverbial American Caesar from his throne—the Army chief of staff, Gen. Douglas MacArthur.

Roosevelt counted MacArthur among the most-dangerous political figures in American history. Having known his famous father and late brother, US Navy captain Arthur MacArthur II, Roosevelt understood the heroic myth of the MacArthur family. The historical connections between the associated clans always bubbled beneath the surface of decisions during the Roosevelt administration. Considering the politics after the Bonus Army debacle, the ongoing debates concerning the future of aviation between the Departments of War and Navy coincided with generational shifts at the higher levels of command. With the retirement of Pratt as the CNO in 1933, the informal agreement he had negotiated with MacArthur also lapsed.

The gentleman's agreement between Pratt and MacArthur was literally bureaucratically up in the air, as the Roosevelt administration set an alternative course to build the American economy around domestic lines of communication and beyond into the global commons. Sea power provided the broader context for pursuing the interstate highway system, building the inland waterways, and creating jobs for all taxpaying hands. Confident in the naval vision of Roosevelt, the new CNO, Standley, failed to renew the agreement with MacArthur, and the strategic debates concerning command relationships between sea and land forces intensified. Fighting for air, MacArthur frequently leveled personal insults at the CNO, Standley, and the new chief of BuAer, King.

As to the question of long-range aviation, MacArthur claimed full control over land bases whereas Standley remained equally firm in protecting *naval* aviation. Standley acted upon advice from King regarding controlling the future of aviation in the oceanic commons. Island outposts in the vast oceanic areas of the Pacific became a topic of heated bureaucratic contention.[44] MacArthur harangued counterparts in the Navy

Department for brokering deals with aircraft manufacturers to develop seaplanes. Long-range reconnaissance requirements provided justification for King to convince Standley to approve procurement contracts with Consolidated Aircraft Corporation to build flying boats. These massive aircraft had the capability to operate on either land or sea. King described the Consolidated design as bringing "distinctly naval weapons for use over the sea against naval objectives."[45]

From within the Navy Department, King warned about Army efforts to claim control over aircraft capable of long-range flights over oceanic areas. He had inside information about the War Department perspective from his brother-in-law on the Army staff and his sons-in-law in the US Army Air Corps. King warned his counterparts in the Navy Department that the land services had the advantage in the procurement and development of long-range airframes. King understood the grander importance of American taxpayers. He explained that the US Army Air Corps specifically focused on the development of larger aircraft to "appeal to the popular imagination."[46] King understood the politics of aviation in long-range procurement planning. He warned Standley that the army "will beat the Navy to its development."[47]

BEAT ARMY

King framed the question of aviation procurement policy by pursuing a strategy designed to meet the operational requirements of American sea power. King developed a strategy designed to serve the broader mission of the armed services—both ashore and afloat.[48] Among other challenges, King faced resistance within the Navy Department in his efforts to solve the fundamental problems of recruiting and retaining naval aviation personnel. To these ends, King fostered a bureaucratic alliance with the chief of the BuNav, RAdm. William D. Leahy. Knowing the routines of Roosevelt in making decisions, Leahy encouraged King to join afternoon discussions over martinis at the White House during their tour together as bureau chiefs at the Navy Department. Leahy advised King to remember that "nobody knows better than you, but you need to learn how to make them feel like they know better than you."[49]

Leahy and King used the informality of the White House cocktail sessions to influence the policies of the Roosevelt administration. Others sipped martinis with Roosevelt, whereas King preferred a glass of beer. Clearly, Roosevelt observed the behavior of his guests—likely taking mental notes about them. Leahy had the ability to soften King's standoffish demeanor.[50] Leahy frequently set the table for King to provide important facts within the context of casual conversations with Roosevelt. In general, King avoided small talk and spoke to Roosevelt only when asked specific questions. Whenever the president cracked a joke—sometimes at King's expense—King joined in the game with an appropriately humorous response. He knew the pitfalls of becoming too closely associated with any given administration in American politics. For this reason, King kept to his no-nonsense reputation in dealings with Roosevelt.[51]

American tradition required King to accept a different kind of uniform on the Washington battlefield. Service personnel traditionally wore civilian attire. Exceeding all expectations, King purchased a closet full of bespoke suits from Brooks Brothers in New York, as he moved with his family from Newport to Washington. Committed to attain the highest levels of command inside the Navy Department, King signed the contract to build a large family home at 2919 43rd Street Northwest—on the outskirts of central Washington, DC. King recognized the area as a good investment as the city expanded.[52] He paid for the new home with assistance from his attorney, Cornelius H. "Nellie" Bull. Together, King and Bull handled the whole transaction without direct bank involvement.

The special relationship of King and Bull ultimately provided useful inroads to influential journalists on the Washington scene. King failed to understand the role of public affairs, although Bull had the talent for working behind closed doors to shape the media narrative. Glen Perry of the *Washington Sun* characterized Bull as a charming personality "who played a delightful guitar."[53] Bull earlier served in the trenches of the First World War and "was wounded and invalided." Perry described Bull as a political conservative with an intense "detestation of the New Deal."[54] On the other hand, Bull supported the Roosevelt administration policies to expand the peacetime capacities of the American sea services. Perry explained that Bull maintained close ties with a "whole slew of naval officers."[55] Perry also told his editor that "King is alright [*sic*]."[56] Perry knew about public smear tactics as employed by King's rivals. Perry warned editors that "if you hear stories running down King . . . don't believe 'em."[57]

Given connections within Washington press circles, Bull coached King in developing an understanding of political strategy making on the Washington battlefield. Bull tutored King in played the part required to win in the vicious games of bureaucracy and dealmaking. King deeply disliked the backchannel dealings and underhandedness that characterized the ongoing bureaucratic infighting within the Main Navy Building in the shadow of the Washington Monument on Constitution Avenue. Newspaper reporters characterized King as an "admiral who regards land as a foreign element—a nice place to visit but he wouldn't want to live there."[58] Although he always denied his Washington network, King had the reputation for being "a personal friend since Mr. Roosevelt was assistant secretary of the Navy during the last war."[59] "He was not as has sometimes been reported a close personal friend," King noted; "F.D.R. always had two strings in his bow."[60] King characterized the tactics of Roosevelt that "he liked to tease people and kept them in check."[61] "If F.D.R. asked me a question," King explained, "I would tell him straight out what I thought about it whether he liked it or not."[62]

FIXERS AND BLIND AMBITION

King navigated the crosscurrents in avoiding the political rocks and shoals of Washington by taking clear positions on key questions of policy and strategy. He avoided cocktail discussions and earned the reputation for being a cold fish. King rejected the image of aviators as being somehow an elite over other branches of the armed services. He considered aviation to be a function subordinate to the broader menu of missions ashore and at sea. Fighting against airpower enthusiasts inside the War Department, King fought the naval aviator clique inside the Navy Department. He emphasized the multiple functions of the regular line, adaptability, and the practical attainment of clearly defined goals. He disliked the games among the political culture of Washington. He derided participants in the backchannel culture as being "fixers."[63]

King occasionally lost his cool whenever he was presented with a question he considered to be outright stupid. Congressmen and their staffers grew frustrated whenever King answered queries with sarcasm, or simple disdain. In one *Time* magazine exposé, journalists described King as being known to "fly into ugly, inarticulate rage."[64] He saw through the plainspoken persona of the Democratic senator from Missouri, Harry S Truman. In verbal duels, King and Truman used their midwestern drawls to great effect while performing on the theatrical stages of Congress. Truman frequently used the tactic of leading his target by providing the answer before delivering a question. In response, King answered Truman with empirical facts laced with backhanded compliments. King kept the banter going by asking Truman probing questions of his own—and frequently with a bit of sarcasm.[65]

King fought against the bureaucratic winds of Washington as the top aviator within BuAer. His affinity for service traditions and the black-shoe culture of the regular line set him at odds with the upstarts within the brown-shoe ranks of naval aviation. He focused on the fundamental requirements of the mission first. To these ends, King placed priority upon securing funding for training. He then focused on recruiting future aviation personnel from within the sea services.[66] The CNO, Standley, and his assistant, RAdm. Joseph K. Taussig, delayed King in his efforts to expand the ranks of naval aviation. The surface line and gunnery specialists among the flag ranks failed to embrace King's prediction that the "day is coming when the aviators and submariners will run this Navy[;it's] just logical."[67]

The seagoing fleet lacked sufficient funding and trained personnel for traditional mission areas. The submarine and aviation forces sapped resources from the surface fleet, which upset the surface line culture, in which officers just "sit around the wardroom and drink coffee."[68] Having spent his formative years in the surface line, King focused on the future by rousing the younger officers out of the wardroom and into the air, down into the depths, and out to sea. Focusing on his mission, King demonstrated his own abilities as a "fixer."[69] King haggled with Leahy and Land in BuNav and BuC&R. Together, they devised the schemes to recruit future aviation personnel from the ranks of civilian universities and aviation technical schools—to include those with Black students.[70]

The plan held potential for reducing the costs for aviation by reducing the number of aviation personnel on active service by expanding the numbers among the junior ranks of the naval reserves. Civilians with naval aviation training provided means for rapid expansion in the event of a war.[71] King also required naval aviators and submariners to remain tied to the surface line—expecting them to seek any opportunity to command in the regular surface line.[72] Working behind closed doors, King circumvented reluctant civilian bureaucrats and a succession of bureau chiefs to quietly assign promising younger naval officers to aviation and submarine duty—working with the assistant chief of the BuNav, Capt. Chester W. Nimitz, to fill gaps in the line by expanding the naval reserves.[73]

King similarly collaborated with Leahy and Nimitz to recruit qualified commanders from the seagoing ranks for service in naval aviation. For example, the BuMed rejected Halsey for assignment to aviation duty because he suffered from poor eyesight.[74] Undaunted, King and Nimitz circumvented the system while Halsey attended the Naval War College in Newport and then the Army War College in Washington, DC. Having secured clearance for aviation duty from another doctor, Halsey subsequently earned his wings as a naval aviator at Pensacola.[75] He then continued up the fleet ladder as the skipper on *Saratoga*. In a similar case, King and Nimitz saved the career of Capt. John Towers after the BuMed found him ineligible for flight duty on the grounds of poor eyesight.[76] "It was arranged for Towers to get a lens to wear over one of his eyes which would meet the doctor's requirements," King recalled. "Towers would not use the damned thing."[77] King never told Towers about his role in negotiating with the BuMed. King and Towers always kept a friendly rivalry. Nimitz later surprised Towers by explaining King's role in saving his career.[78]

Aviation and submarines provided opportunities for senior officers to escape the stratified hierarchy of the surface fleet. The CNO, Standley, reacted by attempting to subordinate King. In his quest to expand the number of qualified naval aviators, King simply went around Standley in making direct appeals to the secretary of the Navy, Swanson, and the assistant secretary, Henry Latrobe Roosevelt. Technically, the chiefs of bureaus had the traditional authority to deal directly with the civilian authorities in setting policy—thereby circumventing the CNO. In this way, King demonstrated the ability to swim with the most-vicious political sharks of Washington. Still uncomfortable in civilian clothes as a bureau chief, he exploited personal connections with his former Naval Academy classmate Roosevelt to influence the decisions of his distant cousin—President Roosevelt. King became a master of such backchannel tactics, which is among the many reasons why he later instituted strict procedures about holding the bureaus subordinate to the CNO.[79]

Standley frequently learned about actions taken after the fact by the various bureau chiefs of the Navy Department. Standley accused King and Leahy of insubordination. Shocked by the behavior of Standley and his implications of mutiny, King argued that any "bureau chief worth his salt deserved to be treated as a member of the team, which Standley showed little inclination to do."[80] The spectacular bureaucratic battles between Standley and King shook the foundations of the Navy Department. As King fought the battle, Leahy quietly worked with Nimitz to create aviation billets in memoranda submitted to Congress. Leahy impressed King with such bureaucratic magic. He similarly recalled that Nimitz "would frequently use some circumlocution to avoid saying unpleasant things."[81] King thought, "Like Leahy, and other officers who served in BuNav, Nimitz was essentially a 'fixer.'"[82]

Standley worked the orders for Andrews to replace Leahy, which hindered King inside the Navy Department. King and Andrews continued their epic competition, which provided the bureaucratic cover for Nimitz to examine the records of 250 lieutenants for competing promotion in 1936. He convinced Andrews to stack the deck by opening opportunities for seagoing lieutenants from the surface fleet to secure promotion in the expanded ranks. The Naval Air Force provided means to advance more personnel to the next-higher grade. Fully complicit in the scheme, King described functionaries like Nimitz as having "what is known as 'pull' in the United States[, which] is known as 'interest' in Great Britain." "In England a man of 'interests' is one who has friends that will help him along," King observed. "No matter what you call it, it is the same thing."[83]

Interdepartmental feuds ongoing under Standley coincided with the steady collapse of the Pratt and MacArthur armistice in the airpower feud on the Washington battlefield. Standley was caught by surprise by the US Army Air Corps when Maj. Gen. Frank M. Andrews seized control over debates concerning strategic airpower theory. Andrews envisioned fleets of bombers in the air under a joint army-navy air force. Service unification concepts ironically fueled efforts by the army to control naval aviation assets in the global maritime arena.[84] The bureaucratic games between the Departments of War and Navy hindered efficiency in the development of American civil-military aviation policy. Recruiting aviators into the services proved equally difficult. Army pilots carried the image of the swashbuckling aces of the First World War.

Sailors always had to face the unforgiving rigors of the sea, which also extended to the air. Civilian airlines also provided greater pay and perks, which far exceeded the incentive to join the ranks of the army and navy. Retaining trained aviators proved equally difficult. Synchronizing the construction of warships with the development and maintenance of aviation squadrons proved nearly impossible within the Navy Department. Under the circumstances, King and Leahy collaborated to secure procurement priorities for the fourth aircraft carrier to join the fleet, *Ranger*—with Capt. John S. McCain in command.[85]

King proposed radical schemes to shake up the routines of the Navy Department in an effort to expand the aviation ranks. His assistant in BuAer, Joy Bright Hancock, drew from previous service as a yeomanette. She drafted the memo when King suggested opening aviation to racial minorities. Hancock developed close ties with King as a trusted secretary—running the administration within the office of the chief of BuAer. In this role, Hancock kept King apprised of the gossip circulating around the various subdivisions of the Navy Department. On the bureaucratic battlefields of Washington, Hancock maintained a sophisticated network of friends and professional associates. Her assistance proved vital in King's peacetime successes in BuAer. Her future husband, Cmdr. Ralph Oftsie, also defined priorities at BuAer under King.[86]

Native Americans and sailors of Pacific Island and Filipino descent had already broken bureaucratic barriers within the ranks of the officer corps. For example, Cmdr. "Jocko" Clark—of the Cherokee Nation—fell within King's orbit among naval aviators.[87] Given the racial policies of the time, King proposed opening the aviation ranks for Black sailors. He had earlier served with Black Americans in surface warships and submarines in the past. King considered the exclusion of any able-bodied seaman for duty in aviation as a waste of precious human resources. He took an aloof approach in balancing cynical bureaucratic procedures and racial restrictions against immediate practical requirements for executing the aviation mission with suitably trained personnel.[88]

At the time, King understood that the idea of opening the aviation ranks for Black Americans held very little prospect for success. However, he shrewdly used the racial restrictions within the ranks to make the alternative point about fulfilling future aviation requirements. He wrote about "regrets that the Navy did not make as good of use of the Negroes in other fields."[89] Using existing racial policy as a political gambit to expand the aviation ranks, King nevertheless had an instrumental role in later efforts to open the ranks of the US Navy to women and racial minorities.[90] His efforts in peacetime were precursors to later changes in navy policy under wartime circumstances.[91]

King fought the bureaucratic war to break down peacetime tribal dynamics within the line ranks of the US Navy. The earlier public-relations disasters for the BuAer smoldered in the wreckage of the airships *Shenandoah* and then *Akron*. Under the circumstances, King relied upon an old family friend, Ward Van Orman, to execute the public-affairs stunt of reaching the outer limits of the stratosphere. The Van Orman family had once looked after King as a teenager after his mother died in Lorain, Ohio. Van Orman earned a heroic reputation for his inventions and his exploits in zeppelin and balloon racing. He worked for Goodyear Tire Company in developing means to reach unprecedented altitudes in balloons.

King and Van Orman pooled the resources of Goodyear and of the Navy Department to launch a joint army-navy flight to the stratosphere. Cmdr. Thomas G. W. "Tex" Settle commanded the flight with the assistance of Maj. Chester L. Fordney, US Army Air Corps. Reaching an estimated altitude of more than 60,000 feet, Settle and Fordney reached the edges of space to set the record in November 1933. King and Van Orman trumpeted the feat, which helped the sales of Goodyear Tires. King diverted funds to his friend Van Orman in efforts to develop the rubber Goodyear blimp designs for reconnaissance, rescue at sea, and antisubmarine operations. He later noted that he "disliked the contemptuous way in which they were often dismissed as 'gasbags' or 'pigbags' for he felt that any weapon that had been the object of so much experimentation [also] deserved at least serious consideration."[92]

King recognized blimps as another means to circumvent the War Department in the procurement fight. King's brother-in-law, Col. Walter D. Smith, and his unrelated son-in-law of the same surname, Freddy, kept King apprised of US Army Air Corps initiatives. The younger Smith worked on the staffs with Maj. Gen. Benjamin D. Foulois and Brig. Gen. Henry A. "Hap" Arnold in organizing the Army Air Corps Mail Operation (AACMO).[93] Such civil-military partnerships as AACMO opened prospective doors for greater investment in the development of long-range airframes for civilian and military purposes.

Land-based airframes lacked the range to fly globally without access to airfields ashore, which provided opportunity for naval aviators to make their case for long-range maritime air routes along key island chains leading to the major continents. With AACMO attaining mixed results in the air, King requested $70 million for the purposes of developing the Consolidated Aircraft Company designs for the "Catalina" flying boat. Pushing the limits of his BuAer authority, King also claimed full control over the procurement process. Army pilots were helpless when King approved designations for Catalina airframes to receive the "VP" designation—with the "V" referring to the HTA category and the "P" delineating the aircraft for use in long-range patrol.[94]

King initiated efforts to organize VP squadrons to operate under the overall control of the scouting forces within the context of the Battle Fleet organization under CinCUS. He used the argument to focus on VP squadrons to reduce expenditures on the LTA program—essentially killing the airship program by demonstrating that BuAer could procure twenty-six long-range Catalina flying boats for the same costs associated with the construction of an airship.[95] King kept an open mind about the blimp program, which kept the peace with civilian industrialists at Goodyear and Michelin. However, King placed future procurement priorities on HTA options.[96]

Army planners saw the Catalina program and the VP squadrons as a direct threat, since King held the advantage in claiming the prerogative for long-range flights over oceanic areas. The US Army competed against the US Navy to design future long-range airframes. Boeing fought Consolidated and the upstart Bell Aircraft Company for lucrative contracts with the Departments of War and Navy. In the race to win the long-range mission, King joined Orville Wright and Ward Van Orman to observe the first prototype of a Boeing model 299. Arnold trumpeted the potential of the aircraft before the first flight. After a successful takeoff, the aircraft crashed on the strip at Wright Field, near Dayton, Ohio, in 1935.[97] Despite this unfortunate setback, the airframe later evolved into the symbol of strategic airpower as the B-17 "Flying Fortress." However, the initial failure of the "Flying Fortress" represented a significant setback for the War Department. Sensing the opportunity, King exploited the mishap by pressing for funding of the Catalina program and for the development of the associated VP squadrons.[98]

CHAPTER 13

Render unto Caesar

The future of aviation at sea and over the horizons ashore and beyond defined bureaucratic relations between the Departments of War and Navy. Visions of a separate air force, like those in Europe, influenced American aspirations for the future in the air. The fledgling American aviation industry also sought government contracts. Civilian entrepreneurs focused on the development of fast and reliable airframes. Competing with railroads and shipping lines, commercial aviation entrepreneurs increasingly focused on developing larger aircraft with powerful engines and a large cargo capacity. Oceanic flights to Europe and Asia held great potential for massive profits. Under these circumstances, King placed priority on the Catalina after 1934. The move frustrated the airpower clique within the US Army ranks. The policies of the Roosevelt administration also inspired critics in the army and air corps to refer to the White House as a naval "wardroom."[1]

The Roosevelt administration focused on sparking the American economy through domestic investment and an interconnected maritime agenda. American sea power defined the diplomatic policies of Roosevelt. In speeches and offhand remarks to the media, Roosevelt frequently upset MacArthur and his associates in Congress. Roosevelt admitted, "Let me tell you that from the bottom of my heart [pause] not only as the Commander in Chief of the United States, but as one who can only say unofficially [pause] but who does say to you unofficially that I love the United States Navy more than any other branch of our government."[2]

Roosevelt upset MacArthur by making such brash statements about the primacy of the American sea services. American traditions of civilian control stood in the balance when MacArthur challenged Roosevelt. On numerous occasions, MacArthur spoke in a condescending tone to Roosevelt. On at least one memorable occasion, Roosevelt barked, "You must not talk that way to the President!"[3] Taking his place as one of the most dangerous military figures in American history, MacArthur openly challenged the constitutional traditions of civilian rule. Roosevelt finally had enough. Working the lines, Roosevelt abruptly dismissed MacArthur during a meeting, after which he recalled that "I just vomited on the steps of the White House."[4]

Politics always loomed over the question of command, since the Roosevelt administration viewed MacArthur as a Hoover loyalist and Republican Party sympathizer. Caught in the middle between two personal friends, retired captain Dudley W. Knox acted as an intermediary between Roosevelt and MacArthur. Knox was the brother-in-law of the late captain Arthur MacArthur II and kept close contact with his brother, Doug, during the ongoing peacetime battles of peacetime Washington. At that time, Knox served as the officer in charge of the Historical Section in the ONI. In this role, Knox worked closely with his old friend King from within the Navy Department. Roosevelt and Knox shared keen interests in naval history and nautical lore. Roosevelt acted upon recommendations from Knox in navigating relations with MacArthur.[5]

The aviation appropriations fight between the Departments of War and Navy provided the justification that Roosevelt needed to arrange a new assignment for MacArthur. In exasperation, Roosevelt plotted to push MacArthur into early retirement with a promotion to an exalted position in exile. In the past, American military personnel occasionally accepted diplomatic appointments among the ranks of foreign armies and naval services. For example, Adm. Sims had appeared in the rolls of the Royal Navy during the First World War, as did VAdm. Joel R. P. Pringle.[6] US naval linguists on assignment with ONI often received honorary rank from their host countries. Seeking brighter horizons as a civilian, US Navy lieutenant William J. Sebald resigned in 1930 and later established a law practice in Japan.[7] In the interests of transpacific collaboration, he failed to request formal Navy Department approval upon accepting an honorary appointment in the Imperial Japanese Navy from Emperor Hirohito in 1935.[8] In the interests of building Pan-American collaboration, Capt. William S. Pye held similar rank as a rear admiral in the Peruvian navy.[9]

Looking outward to avoid future wars on the other side of the planet in Asia, Roosevelt defanged MacArthur with a double-edged mission to organize the Philippine National Army. Roosevelt specifically directed MacArthur to plan for an American withdrawal from the Philippines within ten years. Roosevelt encouraged MacArthur to vacate his position as Army chief of staff to accept his diplomatic appointment as field marshal in the yet-to-be-organized Philippine National Army. By implication, Roosevelt encouraged MacArthur to recognize the Philippines as an opportunity for him to mold the new nation in his own image.[10] Roosevelt told MacArthur to develop the Philippines to serve as a peaceful counterforce against the militant trends in the greater Asiatic.[11] Having signed the Philippine Liberation Act into law the previous year, Roosevelt also clarified the "hands- off policy" to govern MacArthur's actions, such that Americans "had no intention of going to war with China or Japan."[12]

MacArthur accepted the Philippines assignment as an opportunity to escape the Washington battlefield. He essentially withdrew to win another day—perhaps looking to launch his own presidential campaign. Being too young to retire at the impending conclusion of his tour as the Army chief of staff, MacArthur remained on the active list of the US Army until his transfer to the retired list in 1936—in four stars. Technically, he reverted to his permanent rank of two stars upon receiving the honorary "tombstone" rank in four stars. He also retained the four-star insignia, but only in his honorary status as a field marshal in the Philippine National Army. MacArthur thus played the role of an American Caesar.[13] MacArthur's presence in the Philippines also still enhanced American diplomatic efforts in the greater Asiatic.[14]

LOOKING FOR A TOMBSTONE

The departure of MacArthur from the Washington battlefield enabled airpower advocates within the Navy Department to pursue an aggressive maritime agenda. Under his authority as chief of BuAer, King expanded efforts to establish remote island bases to support long-range amphibian airframes under development by the Boeing and Consolidated Aircraft Corporations. King also arranged funding for the work of Carl Norden and the Sperry

Corporation, enabling the development of gyro mechanisms for what became the Norden bombsight. Navy Department contracts, as enacted under King's authority, later paid great dividends for the US Army Air Corps. As King prepared to detach as chief of BuAer, the US Navy essentially sailed on a steady course to control the future of American sea power—in the air. By 1936, King carried aviation to the fleet upon relieving RAdm. J. Frederick Horne as the commander, Base Force (Air), in 1936.

King forced numerous bureaucratic changes in the organization of the Navy Department in the closing weeks of service at the helm of BuAer. During his final weeks at BuAer, King submitted a proposal to enhance the authority of the CNO by clarifying lines of command with the operational forces, which fell under the CinCUS. King shared his ideas with the various bureau chiefs and the president of the Naval War College, RAdm. Edward C. Kalbfus, and his successor, Capt. Charles P. Snyder.[15] King solicited the perspectives of his mentors Sims and Pratt, and other trusted friends within the Navy Department— including retired captain Dudley W. Knox.[16]

The bureau system within the Navy Department ashore seemed unnecessarily focused on bureaucratic promulgations of overlapping administrative processes, which tended to bog down the seagoing ranks of the fleet. King initiated a personal quest to push sweeping changes. First, he refused to enact procedures for which only the bureaucrats ashore could explain a purpose. Second, King instituted procedures—under existing Navy Regulations—that nullified those requirements for which only the bureaucrats ashore had a reason for imposing upon the fleet. Finally, King worked below and above the bureaucratic center to reorganize the ranks of the seagoing forces to center on clearly defined tasks and finite end objectives.

For the purposes of efficiency in operations at sea, King proposed major overhauls to the seagoing bureaucracy of the Battle Force. In 1936, the number of US Navy admirals capped at sixty-three, with an additional six captains sitting in waiting for a vacancy to promote to flag rank. Of the sixty-three permanent-grade two-star admirals on active service, fewer than ten opportunities existed for naval officers to earn additional stars beyond the permanent grade of two stars within the ranks of the US Navy and US Marine Corps.[17] The CNO and CinCUS held precedence as the key four-star assignments. Two other four-stars served as commanders of the Asiatic Fleet and Battle Force. Only three held three stars. Under Naval Regulations, four-star commanders had the temporal authority to spot-promote a two-star to the higher grade as strategic requirements and tactical circumstances dictated.

King vocally pushed for reductions in the number of senior officers on active service, with coinciding expansions for the number of billets for the fleet retired list and the federally administered Naval Reserve. King also floated the idea of reestablishing state-managed naval militias.[18] King furthermore rejected false bureaucratic separations between the US Navy and the other branches of the American sea services. With four individuals holding four stars on their shoulders on the active list of the US Navy in 1936, the commandants of the US Marine Corps and Coast Guard lacked proper authority in relations with their equivalent three- and four-star counterparts of the other services. The civilians involved with setting policy for the US Merchant Marine focused primarily on the commercial functions—often at the expense of planning for shipping requirements in war.

Corbett's philosophical writings on maritime strategy and naval history deeply impressed King. In his own studies of history, King took heed in pondering the warning that "our best minds cramp their strategical view by assuming unconsciously that the sole purpose of a fleet is to win battles at sea."[19] The disjointed organization of the US Navy further amplified administrative problems in efforts to set policy and frame collaborative strategy with other armed services. King considered past problems of command in the First World War era in order to warn others about the obvious inefficiencies of the OpNav staff and bureau system.

The CNOs essentially were toothless to fix problems among the operational units of the Battle Force, Base Force, and Scouting Force—all of which fell squarely under the control of the CinCUS. King noted that the CNO and CinCUS organizations suffered from clear duplications of two-star rank among the various commands of the shore establishment, as well as those seagoing "type commands" within the surface, submarine, and aviation forces.[20] The director of war plans, Capt. William S. Pye, endorsed King's campaign to reorganize the Scouting Forces.[21] He understood that King very likely saw himself in the three-star role. The CNO, Standley, killed the King proposal upon passing the idea for General Board review.[22]

Congress governed the number of flag officers on the active lists of the army and naval services. Individuals with previous service at a higher grade had the ability to transfer to the retired list at their earlier "tombstone" rank of three or four stars.[23] Andrews thwarted King from attaining three stars in 1936. The CNO, Standley, rejected King's recommendation at the behest of Andrews. As a result, King reported in two-star rank to relieve Horne as commander, Base Force (Air). King later stood chagrined in two stars when Andrews appeared in three-star rank as commander, Scouting Forces.[24]

King's family stayed behind in Washington when King broke his two-star flag on the ship he earlier commanded, *Wright*. He placed top priority upon integrating the VP squadrons into the Base Force. The first shipments of Catalina flying boats inspired King to experiment with long-range aviation reconnaissance. To assist this work, he assembled a handpicked staff to assist in these efforts. Among others, Lt. Cmdr. Paul Pihl tutored King about the capabilities of the Catalina flying boat.[25] The massive wing design enabled the aircraft to loiter for long periods. Although the hull design seemed bulky in appearance, the Catalina proved highly maneuverable. The aircraft proved to be forgiving for elder aviators like King.[26]

King and Pihl worked together in developing tactics designed to extend the range of Catalina aircraft by pre-positioning refueling ships in remote locations. Having earlier served as skipper, King chose *Wright* as his flagship during maneuvers in the North Pacific Triangle between Alaska, Hawaii, and San Francisco.[27] King then transferred his flag to the former aircraft carrier *Langley* to scout out the remote islands of Alaska—right up to the outer limits of imperial Japanese–claimed territory. King refined the tactics for pre-positioning refueling ships. He targeted the islands and reefs, such as French Frigate Shoals, to demonstrate the potential of Catalinas to perform long-range reconnaissance in advance of the fleet. King experimented with using submarines in conjunction with Catalinas based in Hawaii.[28]

King took personal risks by flying along on missions ranging farther than the designed capacity of the Catalina. Using the auxiliary ships and tenders of the Base Force to support the long-range flights, King pushed the limits of the Catalina in the same manner as Queen Elizabeth I used her ships to map the farthest reaches of the sea. King and his aviators charted new islands and identified reefs of interest that might serve as logistical points in future conflicts in the Pacific and Atlantic. From French Frigate Shoals to Puerto Rico,

King sought means for Catalinas to cover the American hemisphere and provide reconnaissance for the fleet.

King's aviators conducted routine mapping missions in the same way as sailors charted new discoveries in the past. Just as he had done thirty years earlier as a passed midshipman on *Eagle*, King participated in the mapping operations. He usually took the role of navigator during long-range reconnaissance flights in Catalinas. On one excursion, King suffered minor injuries on one trip from San Diego to Acapulco, after a swell sheered the pontoon off the wing of the Catalina upon hitting the surface of the water. The aircraft diverted off course, broke up, and sank. King and the aircrew survived, largely unscathed. Yet, Drew Pearson, the muckraking journalist, accused King of being too old to fly, in his syndicated column "Washington Merry Go Round."[29] King's attorney, Bull, considered filing a libel suit against Pearson. At that time, King told Bull, "[Pearson] needs to join polite society, or just shut the hell up."[30]

King focused on the mission of aviation in the future operations of the fleet, which frequently drew media interest. Having scouted out the remote islands of the Pacific during his early months in command with the Base Forces, King and his staff provided support for the search for Amelia Earhart in July 1937. Surveys conducted by King the previous year provided the most up-to-date information about the key islands within the huge search area surrounding the Howland, Baker, and Canton Islands.[31] King's Catalinas flew out to support the search efforts. His old command, *Lexington*, served as the flagship for the search, which proved futile.[32] However, the Earhart search conversely provided unique opportunities for the US Navy to collect additional data on foreign island outposts, maritime activity, and encrypted tactical communications among foreign naval forces in the region—to include those of the British, French, Dutch, and Japanese.[33] Journalists and amateur sleuths fueled various outlandish myths about Earhart, which persisted in popular memory.[34]

American naval aviators gained excellent experience by scouting the remote reaches of the Pacific and Atlantic. Catalinas replaced zeppelins as the futuristic platform to symbolize naval aviation, along with the dashing youthful image associated with fixed-wing aircraft carrier aviation. King used the massive Catalinas for display purposes at fairs and aviation expositions. In November 1936, King met Brig. Gen. George C. Marshall for the first time in Portland, Oregon. King later described Marshall as "an affable enough guy, but really very dense[, a] real mudshoe."[35]

Naval aviators demonstrated the full potential of Catalinas to operate with heavy electronics equipment and weapons. The chief budgeting officer within the Navy Department, RAdm. Claude Bloch, provided top cover for King in efforts to build the Catalina fleet. Bloch championed King's efforts to expand the role of long-range aviation reconnaissance forces in fleet operations. Armed with torpedoes and bombs, the Catalina received designation as patrol bombers, with the addition of a "Y" to distinguish the aircraft as being part of the HTA fleet. Although known as the Catalina, the naval initialism "PBY" became a general term for flying boats. Part and parcel of PBY, Bloch supported King's emphasis on developing airfields on advanced bases that were interconnected by the "Fleet Train."

A NAVY FAMILY

Submariners and aviators always operated under the guns of the surface fleet with their elder champion, King. He encouraged the younger guns to act as an elite within the elite ranks of the naval service. King fostered a familial relationship with fellow aviators on his staff. King frequently dined with Pihl and his wife of sixteen years, Charlotte, at their home in California. She first introduced King to her brother, Indiana senator Wendell Willkie, during a dinner gathering.[36] King earned the reputation for being a fatherly figure among the aviators by winning the hearts of many of their children—including the Pihls, as well as Lieutenants Stanton "Stan" Dunlap, Alfred "Dick" Matter, Logan C. Ramsey, Bertram "Bert" Prueher, and Daniel "Dan" Gallery Jr.[37] Continuing, Gallery explained that King "was known to the whole Navy as 'Uncle Ernie,' but he could be a Dutch uncle if the occasion demanded."[38]

Among prospective naval aviators, King infused the best traditions of the battleship navy with the optimistic vision of the future below the waves and beyond to the skies over the horizon. Gallery described King as a "hard-boiled, two-fisted seafaring, flying and fighting man."[39] At one point, Gallery asked King about statements attributed to him that when the "going gets tough, they always send for the sons of bitches."[40] King retorted with a wry smile, saying, "My dear mother never used such language and should never be described like that."[41] Gallery explained, "I've known [King] for a long time, and I would rather not serve directly under him, except in battle."[42] Adding to the explanation, Gallery thought that King "is rather unreasonable about expecting other people to be as good as he is."[43]

King drew strength from the youthful spirit among lower-ranking sailors and his close circle of family and trusted friends. At his advanced rank and age, King acted as the surrogate "sea daddy" for officers far younger than he. He took care of them as though part of the King family. On the home front, King hired a Black domestic assistant, Lena Bunch, to assist Mattie. Following a heart attack, Mattie required an extra hand to keep pace with grandchildren living in the home.[44] Old neighbors from the Annapolis social scene, the Ferrell family, also remained very close to the King family. Operating in shared social circles, Nan Ferrell—along with Abby Dunlap and Betsy Matter—assisted with the matriarch of the King family.[45] In personal correspondence, Mattie also traded cooking recipes and advice to the younger Abby and Betsy. King's daughters maintained close and friendly ties within their naval family circle along with the Pihls, Matters, and Dunlaps.[46]

Loyalty to the high ideals and social expectations of the US Navy always defined the character of King and his close circle of trusted associates. His immediate family understood their role in shaping the career of the patriarch, as much as King always stayed true to the matriarch and their children, their extended families, and associated friends. Among his many favorites was Lt. Boynton L. Braun, who had a particularly special connection to King on a personal level. Braun's mother cared for King, his brother, and his sisters after their mother died. King likewise fostered Braun's career in the navy. Upon graduating from the Naval Academy with the Class of 1921, Braun sailed with King on *Lexington* and stayed close to King, Mattie, and the family. Braun later pioneered efforts to use smaller escort carriers in conjunction with amphibious forces.[47]

TRINITY OF STARS

King anticipated the likelihood of a war involving European and imperial Japanese forces in the Pacific. The ongoing war in China resulted in Americans being killed in the crossfire.[48] At age fifty-nine in 1937, he recognized that the younger generation faced the likelihood of another major war. King recognized the strategic implications after imperial Japanese forces in China sank USS *Panay* (PR-5) in embattled waters of the Yangtse River.[49] With the *Panay* sinking, Lord Phillip Kerr of Lothian, British ambassador to the United States, approached Roosevelt about prospective Anglo-American collaboration in Asia.[50] Following a series of secret meetings between British and American staffs, the Roosevelt administration convinced Congress to pass the Two-Ocean Navy Act. In 1936, Roosevelt also directed the Joint Board to examine requirements associated with defending the American hemisphere against foreign aggressors. He gave the Navy General Board the task of examining the problems of future fleet organization and command.[51] In so doing, Roosevelt prepared plans to reorganize geographic fleets during his second term in the White House.

War loomed over the horizons on the distant shores of Europe and Asia, which many Americans ignored. Conflicts unfolding abroad conversely caused significant concern among the upper echelons of the Departments of State and Navy. The commander of the Battle Force, Kalbfus, told King to prepare US naval aviation forces for an attack against Japan. In response, King recommended caution. Kalbfus acted with bravado in telling King to "forget it—all we've got to do is send a couple of carriers over and burn up Tokio [*sic*]."[52] The CNO, Leahy, shared similar plans—to blockade Japan with American sea power to "check the Tokyo bandits' ideas of conquest, possibly even without a war."[53]

The problems of Asia loomed over the question of transatlantic collaboration with the British Empire and the other European powers. The revolutionary vision of Bolshevism contrasted with the hypermilitarized rise of fascism in Europe. The two ideologies clashed in the bloody battles of the Spanish Civil War. In response, the US Navy quietly formed "Squadron 40-Tare" under Cdre. Charles Courtney, with headquarters afloat off Lisbon.[54] The operations of Squadron 40-Tare provided momentum for broader diplomatic discussions among the major European powers. Courtney regularly sent American warships for friendly-port visits to all the key ports of Europe—including those of Nazi Germany and Fascist Italy. The presence of US naval warships and aircraft in embattled waters signaled American resolve to defend interests in Europe and Asia.

King anticipated the underlying currents in navigating the uncertainties of peace while operating naval forces at full readiness for war. He broke his three-star flag as commander of the Battle Force (Air). King then rotated between his favorite ship, *Lexington*, the sister ship USS *Saratoga* (CV-3), and the other two carriers during the major fleet exercises. King advised aviators to embrace their role as the leading force at the head of the offensive seagoing line.[55] Sailing in *Saratoga* and *Lexington* in Carrier Division 1, King relied on Capt. John S. McCain to maneuver the first warship designed specifically as an aircraft carrier on *Ranger*.

Cocky young aviators and submariners took pride in their "Johnny come lately" elders, which transformed the surface-focused culture of the regular line. Having recently earned aviator's wings at age fifty-one, RAdm. William F. Halsey Jr. fell in as commander, Carrier Division 2. He handled the newest carriers, USS *Yorktown* (CV-5) and USS *Enterprise*

(CV-6), with Captains Donald B. Duncan and Miles R. Browning developing tactics designed to maintain a constant rotation of CAP, moving aircraft between carriers, integrating fighters with bombers for strike missions, and with simultaneous carrier launch operations. King and his team perfected "deck-load launch" procedures, enabling aircraft to fly in a rhythm designed to maximize the strike time on targets.[56]

Naval War College discussions informed King's applied approach in developing aircraft carrier doctrine. Throughout 1938, King and his staff jumped between the carriers *Saratoga* and *Lexington.* Fleet problems and military training amplified the diplomatic counterforce of American sea power.[57] Roosevelt embraced the vision of Walter Lippmann in seeking the construction of a "nuclear alliance" system. Lippmann told American readers to "know our limitations and our place in the scheme of things."[58] Roosevelt and Lippmann engaged in an open discussion about American interests. In their public exchanges, the pair used the media to educate the American public about trends. Roosevelt progressively expanded his vision of a Pan-American Neutrality Zone. Roosevelt characterized American sea power as power in which "we shall no longer exhort mankind to build castles in the air while we build our own defenses in sand."[59]

Roosevelt asked the Joint Board to provide recommendations for organizing American forces for a two-front campaign to defend the hemisphere against simultaneous adversaries in Asia and Europe. The request naturally shifted the balance in relations between the planners on the Army General Staff and the naval War Plans Division. Analysis performed under the authority of the Navy General Board on the gaming floors of the Naval War College provided an oceanic context for prospective military operations on the far shores of Asia and Europe. King's assertions about the "citadels" of Formosa and the British Home Islands, as he previously articulated in his writings at the Naval War College, also resonated in the halls of the Departments of War and Navy.

King emphasized the offensive primacy of American sea power in efforts to reduce the likelihood of foreign-enemy attacks. He pushed the planning staffs to focus on the requirements inherent in seizing advanced base facilities to support logistical requirements for sustained naval operations on the global stage. Island outposts ostensibly connected with deepwater ports, which ostensibly served as the key nodes for sustained military operations ashore. To examine these requirements in 1938 and 1939, the joint army-navy Exercises and associated fleet problems replicated the unlikely scenario of an alliance between imperial Japan and the British Empire—using the army plans to simulate simultaneous threats from ORANGE and RED.[60]

The actual conflicts in Asia and Europe provided a realistic backdrop to the simulated battles of Fleet Problem XIX. Always looking outward to the next election year, Roosevelt also used the maneuvers to ponder the future leadership of the armed services. In 1938, retired general John J. Pershing strongly endorsed *Brigadier* George C. Marshall to replace Craig as Army chief of staff. Roosevelt also anticipated replacements for the CNO, Leahy, and the CinCUS, Bloch. Testing the waters, Roosevelt directed Fleet Problem XIX to commence with an unannounced flash message to all shore establishments and seagoing forces—requiring ships to initiate operations from a cold start.[61]

The scenario called for an alliance between ORANGE and RED, which culminated in simultaneous surprise attacks against BLUE from the Pacific and Atlantic. From the army staff, Marshall worked closely with Lt. Col. Dwight D. Eisenhower to anticipate the requirements to buy time for the American fleet to rescue American outposts in the

Philippines while simultaneously defending against the unlikely scenario of an enemy naval campaign from Canada and South America. Leahy and Bloch supervised the naval maneuvers, which unfolded in a simulated global war in the North Pacific Triangle off Hawaii and in the Caribbean. Admiral James O. "Jo" Richardson fought against the simulated enemy fleet of Kalbfus.

Richardson concentrated on main lines of oceanic communication between the West Coast and Hawaii, simultaneously maneuvering assets into the Panama Canal Zone to protect critical shipping lanes along the East Coasts of North and South America. To exploit the gaps in Richardson's defensive plan, Kalbfus maneuvered his forces to simulate enemy attacks by targeting major coastal cities, military garrisons, airfields, and fleet concentration areas. Kalbfus unleashed his commander of the Battle Force (Air), and King simulated the functions of an Imperial Japanese Navy aircraft carrier task force commander and embarked with *Lexington*, under the command of his former executive officer, Capt. John H. Hoover. Operating in tandem with *Lexington*, Halsey embarked as a subordinate task group commander on *Saratoga*, with Captain John H. Towers as skipper. On board *Ranger*, McCain augmented the aircraft carrier task forces.

Richardson and Kalbfus conspired to demonstrate the inability of army forces to defend warships in port. To these ends, King and Halsey also acted in conjunction with the Scouting Forces, under RAdm. Joseph K. Taussig, to coordinate aviation strikes with submarines. On Taussig's embarked staff on the cruiser USS *Chicago* (CA-29), King's old protégé McCann coordinated submarine movements under the immediate supervision of Capt. Henry Kent Hewitt. During their planning conferences, Kalbfus empowered King and Taussig to use their forces to keep the enemy guessing while simulated US Marine amphibious forces maneuvered against enemy targets. To observe the maneuvers, Stark embarked King's flagship, *Lexington*.

The ghost of Sims embarked with Stark as King and Halsey developed their schemes for maneuvering their warships in conjunction with those of Taussig and Yarnell against the main line of Richardson's battle fleet. Akin to spring training in baseball or on the football pitch, the veterans of the old Sims Flotilla now held positions to apply their wildest ideas as flag officers. King recalled that "Stark would go down into the shaft alleys and all over the ship [but was] always on hand to learn anything there was to learn."[62] "We had some great discussions," King recalled, when hanging out with his old friend Stark, "on the starboard veranda near our sea cabin."[63]

Recommendations derived from discussions in the classrooms and practical experiments conducted on the gaming floors of the war colleges influenced innovation in the fleet problems conducted ashore and afloat. During Fleet Problem XIX, King surprised the umpires by breaking from scripted events to exploit a weather front. To cover their actions, King's staff devised an internal communication code. The forces ashore and afloat lost track of King's aircraft carriers. The weather front further obscured the movements of *Lexington* and *Saratoga* to launch positions approximately 100 nautical miles north of Hawaii. For the second time in peacetime exercises, King highlighted the vulnerability of island anchorages such as Pearl Harbor and fixed army garrisons ashore—like those in Hawaii—during Fleet Problem XIX.[64]

BOMBED AGAIN

American naval officers understood the logistical difficulties associated with sustained maritime operations in waters as distant as those surrounding remote island outposts, such as the relatively tiny target of Hawaii. Immediately following the fleet problems of 1938, Lt. Cmdr. Logan C. Ramsey published his *Proceedings* article "Aerial Attacks on Fleets at Anchor."[65] In a similar narrative, Lt. Stephen Jurika Jr. published an essay in the *Saturday Evening Post* with the title "Pilots, Man Your Planes."[66] King reviewed and approved the publications of both articles by Ramsey and Jurika. Ramsey flew the lead aircraft. Jurika helped plan the operations as part of King's staff.

The young guns among the naval aviation ranks celebrated the virtuoso demonstrations of aircraft carrier capabilities by King. Having embarrassed the surface force commanders of the simulated enemy in Fleet Problem XIX in the Pacific, King returned with his carriers to the West Coast to coordinate plans for Fleet Problem XX in the Caribbean. He kept with the fictional scenario in transitioning from Fleet Problem XIX and into Fleet Problem XX. *Saratoga* sailed along the West Coast to cover simulated amphibious landings at San Clemente Island. King supervised the operations of the commander of Task Force 7, RAdm. Chester W. Nimitz, to conduct the straddling technique of refueling between two large warships.[67] Having studied the tactics during earlier studies at the Naval War College, King's task forces demonstrated the viability of dispersing warships in circular formations.[68]

The circular-formation tactics reflected the collaboration of many practitioners at the Naval War College. The circular formation had evolved from the ideas first developed under Sims during his second tenure as president of the Naval War College—when Nimitz attended and when King completed the correspondence course. Popular myths surrounding the origin of such tactics center on Nimitz, since he received primary credit for developing the circular formation in fleet operations.[69] He *incorrectly* credited Cmdr. Roscoe C. MacFall for the concept.[70] Although MacFall certainly had a role in developing the tactics, King used the circular formation with carriers at the center in gaming experiments conducted during his resident studies at the Naval War College.[71] The actual use of circular formations at sea during the fleet problems of 1938 and 1939 ultimately proved the value of such tactics.[72]

Fleet problems and joint army-navy exercises concurrently revealed significant problems in military and naval doctrine. King based his tactics on his studies of the historical battles at Port Arthur and Tsushima Straits during the Russo-Japanese War. The Cuxhaven raid in the First World War also provided inspiration during the fleet problems.[73] Operations ongoing along the West Coast simulated the persistent presence of the Japanese, as King maneuvered on *Lexington* and *Ranger* through the Panama Canal and into the Caribbean.[74]

The stakes ran high for aspirant four-star admirals as the fleet maneuvered from the Pacific to the Caribbean. During Fleet Exercise XX in February 1939, King once again demonstrated his capacity to shake the doctrinal foundations of the US Navy during Fleet Problem XX. Notably, President Franklin D. Roosevelt joined the fleet on board USS *Houston* (CA-30) in the Caribbean—observing his admirals in action while making final decisions about the future four-star replacements for Leahy and Bloch as CNO and CinCUS.[75] Roosevelt pretended to be on a fishing trip on board *Houston*—carousing around with enlisted sailors and gleefully telling jokes while teasing their superiors.[76] As he observed from the teakwood decks of *Houston*, King took center stage as the aircraft carrier task force commander.

Roosevelt certainly noted King's masterful performance in handling aircraft carrier forces against simulated enemy fleets and shore positions. King divided his carrier forces into two primary groups to provide simultaneous coverage over the key maritime lines of communication along the East and West Coasts—using submarines in conjunction with surface and air forces. During tactical maneuvers held in the Caribbean, King sailed with *Lexington* and *Ranger* to coordinate operations with Halsey on the newly commissioned USS *Yorktown* and USS *Enterprise* (CV-6). King's aviators maneuvered to hit garrisons ashore while limiting enemy maneuverability over critical maritime lines of communication. His aircraft carriers also simulated tactical air support during Fleet Landing Exercise (FLEX) 5 at Puerto Rico, thus demonstrating the prospective role of Marine amphibious forces' seizure of islands.

Roosevelt very likely earmarked King for future command within the seagoing ranks of the fleet. King clearly outclassed other admirals in the heat of simulated battle during Fleet Problem XX. His submarine qualifications and more-recent service as an aircraft carrier admiral stood second to none in the surface fleet. Yet, King famously lacked the political finesse for a peacetime assignment ashore. Roosevelt and King also shared an understanding of the global situation in anticipation of an unprecedented run for a third term in the White House. During exercises in the Caribbean, Roosevelt very likely told King about his vision for reorganizing the US Navy after the election, given the plans already on the drawing boards of the Joint Board and Naval General Board for future "Fleet Organization and Command."[77]

Roosevelt certainly had King in mind for future assignment to high command, given the situation unfolding in the global maritime arena. Imperial Japanese propagandists claimed to fight a war of liberation in China under the slogan "Asia for the Asians."[78] The Nazis envisioned the full unification of Europe under their twisted dream of a "Greater Germany." All agreed about the pernicious threat of Soviet ideology, although Roosevelt never fully rejected the philosophical concept of communism. Meanwhile, *Panay* provided impetus for the British to rekindle transatlantic connections with the Americans.[79] With Roosevelt charting the way ahead, King stood at the ready to execute the task of "waging peace."[80] Together, Roosevelt and King also shared the strategic understanding that the attainment of sustainable peacetime ends is always the determining factor for victory in wars—in the past and in the future.

CHAPTER 14

Second to None

Fleet problems provided opportunities for Roosevelt to observe commanders in simulated combat. He kept personal tabs on the seventy-four flag officers on active service. Roosevelt understood the interpersonal dynamics among his admirals.[1] In 1938, the competition among US naval practitioners further intensified. The duplicative functions between the CNO and CinCUS created unnecessary divisions and inflated the rank structure of the US Navy, which potentially held significant consequences in the event of an enemy attack. King explained that the "bill establishing the CNO, in the form passed by Congress, represented the ashes of a once[-]good idea."[2] King knew the politics in calculating his chances to be CNO, or CinCUS, which rested with "Congressmen, the President, the Secretary of the Navy and kibitzers in his offices [who] generally have had a hand in choosing subordinate commanders for duty with the fleets."[3]

Roosevelt needed to fill the prospective vacancies of CNO and CinCUS with the right types of naval officers to fit the peacetime circumstances. In 1938, Roosevelt weighed his options carefully in discussions with the chief of BuNav, RAdm. James O. "Jo" Richardson, and his assistant, Capt. Frank Jack Fletcher.[4] Standing out among the herd, King was among only four with "triple threat" qualifications in battleships, submarines, and aviation. Conversely, King seemed like a misfit with a reputation for being a cold fish.[5] King explained, "For about fifteen years there had been a clique centering around [sic] the BuOrd." He described the "Gun Club, consisting of Bloch, Stark, Leahy—a clique that kept closely together—Richardson was on the fringes, although not actually in it."[6]

Roosevelt recognized King as the type of naval officer required for defeating prospective enemies in combat. Roosevelt had studied the official records of King, as J. Edgar Hoover and the Federal Bureau of Investigation scrutinized the potential nominees for appointment to four-star rank in the US Navy. King nurtured ties with Republicans, like Willkie, while keeping friendly connections with Roosevelt's allies and fellow Democrats like Carl Vinson, Harry Hopkins, and Edward R. Stettinius. Facing another election cycle, Roosevelt recognized King as the type of naval officer fit for war at a time when Americans most desired peace.[7] Yet, King's unvarnished approach failed to resonate with many key players in Washington, DC. One loyal subordinate, Gallery, explained that King suffered from being "scrupulously honest."[8]

Politics always influenced the promotion board processes and selective assignments for American armed-service professionals. Competence rarely served as the primary justification for promotion, which King fully understood in calculating the probabilities for future four-star assignment. Mandatory retirement loomed for King. His friend RAdm. Arthur B. Cook also warned King about the bureaucratic intrigues of Towers and Bellinger. Apart from other aviators, King stood alone within the cliquish culture of BuAer. Cook and Mitscher stood neutral as Towers and Bellinger undercut their competitors among the "Johnny come lately" aviators like King, Cook, Horne, Yarnell, Halsey, Noyes, Hoover, and McCain.[9]

King faced few prospects, with nowhere to go further up the standard fleet ladder to higher rank within naval aviation. As he approached the end of his three-star tour as commander, Battle Force (Air), another close friend, Kalbfus, nominated King for prospective four-star assignment as the commander, Battle Force.[10] King immediately discounted the prospect of filling the shoes of Kalbfus. Still, King hoped to become CNO or CinCUS. The only other possible assignment to four stars existed far over the horizon in the Asiatic Fleet. In personal correspondence, Kalbfus lowered King's expectations by writing, "Our flags will be hauled down in a few days."[11] Kalbfus praised King in noting, "I wish to take this means of conveying to you my deep appreciation [and] my considered opinion that you have made a great contribution to the Fleet and, therefore, to the Country."[12]

Within the Roosevelt administration, the Asiatic Fleet had a unique place in the global hierarchy of American sea power. Since the era of Theodore Roosevelt, the commander of the Asiatic Fleet operated with significant autonomy in advancing the military policy of the United States. The sun seemed to be rising within the ranks of the US Navy when Adm. Harry E. Yarnell opened a channel for future aviators to serve in four-star rank as the commander of the Asiatic Fleet. In this capacity, Yarnell also operated with the authority of the CNO as commander, Naval District 16 (Com16). As Yarnell prepared to retire, King was among the most technically qualified to command American naval forces in the region.[13]

The Asiatic Fleet sailed in close quarters with European warships and with imperial Japanese forces looming just over the horizon. Under the circumstances, Roosevelt considered the idea of placing MacArthur and King together in the same proximity as far beyond the horizon as the Philippines "utterly ridiculous."[14] The Asiatic Fleet required tact, which King seemingly failed to offer. Roosevelt consulted trusted friends about King, including Leahy and Stark. As decisions progressively unfolded, Stark asked King, "Why the hell didn't you start getting along in the Gun Club?"[15] In response, King explained that they "had their chance several years ago and they didn't take it—so the hell with them."[16]

Roosevelt watched approvingly as King's aircraft carrier task groups maneuvered circles around the opposing surface forces and fixed army garrisons ashore. At the close of the fleet exercises, Roosevelt held court following the debriefings by the umpires and key commanders of the Battle Force.[17] He took special note of King's golden aviator wings above his Navy Cross ribbon over the left top pocket of his white, heavily starched choker uniform. As the admirals gathered on board *Houston* for a social gathering, President Roosevelt held court on February 28, 1939. King sat next to the president. With a wry smile—while lighting a cigarette—King asked Roosevelt whether he had "caught any fish." Earlier in the day, Roosevelt caught a shark while fishing off the fantail of *Houston*. King's wisecrack prompted Roosevelt to burst into laughter as he glanced at all the admirals. King recalled that Roosevelt said, "I am still fishing."[18]

King respectfully responded to Roosevelt's humor, which often carried an implied double meaning. Roosevelt chided King about his reputation for being the "triple threat" and "blowtorch."[19] Roosevelt also asked King in all seriousness, with a drink in hand, whether "you cut your toenails with a torpedo net cutter."[20] On these occasions, Roosevelt customarily burst out into a boisterous laughter as King respectfully stood in stoic silence.

With the fleeting chance to make four-star rank just over the horizon, King recalled the scene on board *Houston* that "President Roosevelt was in high spirits, for he loved the Navy and always visibly expanded when at sea."[21] Orbiting Roosevelt as he held court, King recalled the ritualistic protocol among fellow admirals that "as the admirals greeted him, he would have some pleasant, half-teasing personal message for each."[22] Roosevelt firmly shook hands with King and, "after a brief chat, admonished King, in his bantering way, to watch out for the Japanese and the Germans."[23]

Roosevelt's quip about the Japanese or the Germans perhaps spoke volumes about his thinking as relating to King. While Roosevelt failed to make his decisions clear, King felt relatively confident about his future.[24] Following a very brief meeting with Roosevelt on board *Houston*, Bloch brushed aside the other aspirant admirals to push King back into the circle around Roosevelt. Bloch asked King, "Why don't you go [back] over and speak to the President?"[25] King looked at the pathetic spectacle and told Bloch that "if the president wishes to ask me anything, I am right here."[26]

Roosevelt calculated with a clear political agenda in considering the various contestants for the key four-star nominations. He relied heavily upon the recommendations of Leahy making key appointments. Roosevelt advised Leahy, "'If we have a war, you're going to be right back here helping me run it."[27] Keeping his friends close, Roosevelt promised Leahy the lucrative opportunity to serve as governor of Puerto Rico—where he had many close friends in the sugar and rum industry.[28] Roosevelt set the foundations for installing Leahy as the future Navy secretary. Meanwhile, Roosevelt also maneuvered Bloch to bring order to the chaos of naval administration in the Pacific. Roosevelt rotated Bloch out of the four-star CinCUS billet to reorganize the shore establishment in the two-star duty as commander, Naval District 14 (Com14) in Hawaii.[29]

Roosevelt made predictable decisions about the future CNO and CinCUS in anticipation of another election cycle. Notwithstanding the politics, Leahy and Bloch dutifully provided Roosevelt with their recommendations for their impending reliefs. King appeared among the top contenders for either the CNO or the CinCUS positions. Within the fleet, officers generally understood that "BuOrd had the CNO position locked up and the CinCUS usually went to the secretary's budget officer."[30] This rule clearly continued under Roosevelt.[31] At that time, King also knew about Roosevelt's vision for unifying the Navy Department.[32] Unsurprisingly, the chief of BuOrd, Stark, and the budget officer, Richardson, held the traditional advantages associated with their positions in the order of peacetime successions for the CNO and CinCUS.[33]

TEARS IN THE BEER?

Roosevelt recognized King as among the most technically qualified naval officers in the history of American sea power. Anticipating the future, King made clear his desires to close his naval career as CNO, preferring the "top post in the Navy [for] which he had consciously been training over a number of years on the chance that he might be singled out."[34] Under prevailing political circumstances at that time, King discounted the likelihood of winning a four-star appointment. The Asiatic Fleet seemed too far beyond the political horizon, and the surface gunnery sailors still controlled the pathways to CinCUS, Battle Force, and CNO. Among these, CNO seemed remotely possible, but King "had little conviction that it would fall to him."[35]

Roosevelt anticipated significant difficulties within Congress and among the political factions of Washington, given King's previous success in pushing the aviation agenda within the Navy Department. In his brief conversation with Roosevelt on *Houston*, King mused about the possibilities of closing his career in the traditionally rarified assignments of president of the Naval War College or as superintendent of the Naval Academy.[36] Having had his audience with Roosevelt on the decks of *Houston*, King went ashore to the officer's club in Culebra to await the arrival of his gig on the way back to *Lexington*. He watched the sunset over *Houston*.[37] As King sipped on his beer at the officer's club at Culebra, he fully understood that the "Gun Club that maintained practically a monopoly of the top posts both in the Navy Department and at sea, to the exclusion of others including naval aviators."[38]

Naval exercises coincided with the politics of the Roosevelt administration and the uses of American sea power in fostering the etherical Pan-American Neutrality Zone. British and French outposts intermixed with those of the Dutch and old Spain along the old pirate haunts, which King reveled in revisiting during the fleet problems. King shifted his three-star flag between *Lexington* and *Saratoga*—often for the simple purposes of being seen by his sailors but also for the ulterior motives of having fun. In Barbados, King re-introduced himself to Royal Navy commodore James Graham, 6th Duke of Montrose. King organized a formal dinner on board *Lexington* during which he happened to have a biography about the Montrose family. King claimed to have an ancient family connection with the Duke of Montrose, a claim in which the duchess took great interest. King gave the book to the Duke and Dutchess of Montrose before departing the scene on *Lexington*.[39]

King's future among the stars of the fleet remained uncertain when disaster unfolded among the line of battleships in the approaches to the Panama Canal. Trailing in line, *Lexington* and *Saratoga* followed the battleships when USS *Idaho* (BB-42) lurched out of control. The new skipper, Capt. Alexander Sharp, was on board with the outgoing skipper, Capt. Harvey Delano, when *Idaho* broke formation. Capt. Delano had familial connections with Roosevelt. Following the freak grounding of *Idaho*, King received the unwelcome duty of leading the investigation and sustained serious damage to the rudder. King also carried the burden of chairing the court-martial proceedings for Delano in Balboa. Once again demonstrating mastery of Navy Regulations, King was "glad that the court was finally able to locate a thoroughly concealed defective screw in the rudder control mechanism that had been incorrectly installed when the ship was built more than twenty years before."[40]

Delano was officially deemed blameless for the *Idaho* mishap, as King's artful handling of the investigation kept the reputations of all hands completely intact. Delano's public standing as a battleship captain also reflected the competence of the US Navy as an institution from King's personal perspective. He handled the court-martial by framing the technical evidence with the logical outcome, which coincidentally kept fellow naval officers—especially one with connections to Roosevelt—from being blamed for the damage sustained on *Idaho*. In the strategic interests of American sea power, King absolved Delano by finding an obscure technical glitch in the rudder system that had existed for nearly two decades. Delano subsequently failed to achieve flag rank upon requesting an early transfer to the retired list, as his successor on *Idaho* later retired in three stars as a vice admiral.

The broken hearts and fallen stars of the fleet understood the rules of lineal seniority and politics, which always determined the ultimate selections for the highest ranks of the armed services. Technical competence had rarely propelled service professionals to the very top in peacetime.[41] Coincident with the verdict of the *Idaho* court-martial in Balboa, King received a surprise summons from the president of Panama, Juan Demóstenes Arosemena. Along with other members of the court-martial, King received the Order of Balboa from Arosemena. At that time, foreign decorations required approvals from the White House and Congress under Naval Regulations. Under these circumstances, Roosevelt very likely lurked in the backdrop when King received the Order of Balboa.[42]

The impending retirement of Leahy and anticipated departure of Bloch for duty in Hawaii loomed over the Caribbean. When King arrived with *Lexington* off Guantánamo, aviators and submariners placed their longshot bets on King to become the CinCUS. When the dice finally tumbled to a verdict, Lt. Cmdr. Malcolm Schoeffel sat next to King at the officer's club when "another admiral remarked to King, 'what do you think about Stark being made CNO?'"[43] At that pregnant moment, Stark also appeared at the bar. Stark immediately told King that "you are the man that should have had this job."[44] With a smirk, King stood up and firmly shook hands with Stark—buying a round for all hands in the club to lead in a celebratory toast for the newly appointed CNO.[45]

King completely understood the logic when Stark won the appointment to replace Leahy as CNO with the simultaneous nomination of Richardson to relieve Bloch as CinCUS. Snyder simultaneously relieved Kalbfus in the Battle Force. Roosevelt selected the elder salt RAdm. Thomas C. Hart for the Asiatic Fleet. Among other junior-ranking witnesses, Schoeffel recalled that "King was sitting at the bar when another young aviator remarked look at the old man, he's finished."[46] From across the bar, King stood up straight as an arrow and barked, "MISTER—check your speed—you are in the presence of a fleet commander."[47]

Roosevelt made relatively predictable choices in selecting battleship sailors for the CinCUS and Battle Force commands. In selecting Stark as the CNO, Roosevelt symbolically conjured the ghost of Sims and popular memories of transatlantic collaboration, the widely forgotten League Navy concept, and lost Corbettian dreams of "The League of Peace and a Free Sea."[48] Roosevelt also took heed in King's contemporaneous estimate, "Naval Strategy and Tactics," in which the strategic ideas of Corbett most strongly resonated above those of other familiar luminaries of the past.[49] Roosevelt wanted to keep King close to the helm while navigating the uncharted waters within the nexus between peace and war after 1938.[50] King also understood the rationale for filling other potential assignments when Kalbfus received orders for a second tenure as president of the Naval War College and Adm. David F. Sellars received the sunset assignment in Annapolis.[51]

Roosevelt maneuvered his flag officers like chessmen, castling King with the General Board for the time being in anticipation of placing future enemies in check. King had *not* been crying in his beer about being overlooked for the nomination to a four-star command in 1938, as has been alleged ever since. Indeed, Roosevelt also entrusted King with assignment to the General Board: "Because of the increased importance of naval aviation [it] became necessary to settle the question whether the fleet should be organized by types of ships or by the task to be performed."[52] For nearly fifteen years, the Naval War College had highlighted the problems of joint army-navy command on the gaming floors and in the classroom setting. The General Board used these studies to push changes in the relationships between military and naval staffs within the deliberations of the Joint Board.

With his assignment to Washington, King joined efforts already ongoing within the General Board to reorganize geographic fleet staffs under the clear control of the CNO.

Roosevelt intended to nullify the functions of CinCUS as early as 1937.[53] Naval War College studies informed the decisions of Roosevelt making his selections to "Beat Hitler first." [54] In framing the future strategic priorities of fleet priorities to attain this objective, King stood ready for action after his remotion from three stars to two with the General Board. In personal correspondence, Halsey prophetically wrote, "Dear Ernie, I thank you for your patience of me personally and for the professional lessons you have given me."[55] Halsey added that "I should be proud to serve under you any time—anywhere and under any conditions [and] here's hoping for more stars afloat."[56]

FIGHTING FOR PEACE

American journalists kept taxpayers informed about the rotations of flag officers within the military and naval services. The armed services also competed for favor on Capitol Hill. Before King detached from command in three-star rank, the Navy Department directed his aircraft carriers to assist the production of the movie *Dive Bomber* starring Errol Flynn and Fred McMurray.[57] Among other chores, King and his staff assisted the production during fleet problems conducted off the West Coast. The annual convention of the American Legion in Los Angeles provided another stage upon which to rally support for naval aviation. During the filming, King joined Halsey on *Saratoga* to observe rehearsals for an aerial parade involving 330 aircraft, which resulted in tragedy off the coast of California.

Fleet problems and joint exercises proved exceedingly realistic in replicating the conditions of war. Many anonymous service personnel died in simulated combat. Their contributions in peacetime later enabled victory in war. Flying with Fighting Squadron 3 from *Saratoga*, Lt. William S. Pye Jr. flew the lead aircraft in a close formation of younger aviators during training exercises. Another aircraft collided with Pye's, and the pair corkscrewed into the ocean. The aviators went down with their aircraft into the depths. The father, RAdm. William S. Pye, commanded the search-and-rescue operations. He had no information about the identities of the aviators and found no evidence of their survival. King first learned the identity of the downed airmen. He accepted the burden of informing his friend about the tragic truth about the death of his eldest son.[58]

Simulated wars enabled military and naval forces to improve coordination in operations ashore and at sea. Foreign observers used the exercises to foster friendly relations and take note of new developments. King invited Royal Navy vice admiral Robert Raikes, commander in chief, South Atlantic, to San Pedro for simulated dive-bombing attacks on the anchorage. Raikes and his staff "were greatly impressed."[59] King used the opportunity to demonstrate the full potential of aircraft carriers against static targets, such as enclosed anchorages and naval base facilities ashore. King wrote the memo outlining means to augment friendly foreign naval efforts in Asia by operating American warships between Hawaii, Kiska, Midway, and Guam.[60]

Training provided convenient cover for neutrality operations in anticipation of possible American involvement in actual combat. Fleet exercises also provided cover for British and American officers to compare notes. Setting the foundations for future negotiation, the appointments of Gen. George C. Marshall as Army chief of staff and of Stark as CNO reflected the obvious choices for Roosevelt, basing his decisions on past First World War experience in navigating the uncharted waters of collaboration after 1939.[61]

Burgeoning naval thinker Stephen B. Luce looking intently on board the steam frigate USS *Hartford,* likely before the Civil War. *US Navy photograph*

Haunted by the Civil War and inspired by General Carl von Clausewitz, Brevet Brig. Gen. Emory Upton, author of *Military Policy of the United States. US Navy photograph*

The Clausewitz of the maritime realm, Sir John Knox Laughton of King's College London, who inspired RAdm. Stephen B. Luce to organize naval education as a fundamental function of American strategy after the Civil War. *Courtesy of King's College London*

The American Neptune, RAdm. Stephen B. Luce.
Library of Congress

The past as prologue on the technological cutting edge
at Coaster's Harbor Island, as sailor trainees muster on
the historic grounds of the Naval War College seen on
the horizon. *US Navy photograph*

Martha Rankin Egerton with a member of the "married man's club" of the Class of 1901, naval cadet Ernest J. King, near the Naval Academy in Annapolis, ca. 1900. *Courtesy of Thomas King Savage and the King family*

Always on the cutting edge, King used money saved during deployment with the Asiatic Fleet after he married Mattie to purchase a new car and buy the family home at 45 Franklin Street—nearby the yard on board the Naval Academy in Annapolis, Maryland. *Courtesy of Thomas King Savage and the King family*

President Theodore Roosevelt addressing his sailors upon the return of the Great White Fleet to Hampton Roads, during which he noted that the US Navy has "falsified every prediction of the prophets of failure." *US Navy photograph*

King   Sims

Lt. King (*looking to* his right) with Cmdr. Sims (*looking outward*) to hear President Roosevelt's inspired vision of "sea power" as a unifying element in American society and the future of "Our Navy, the Peacemaker." *US Navy photograph*

Cmdr. William S. Sims on board USS *Minnesota*, underway in 1910. *Courtesy of Dr. Nathaniel Sims and family*

Visions of the future war in Europe, as articulated in historical terms in Mahan's "warning" pamphlet in anticipation of the First World War. *Author's collection*

BRITAIN AND THE
GERMAN NAVY
ADMIRAL MAHAN'S WARNING

Price One Halfpenny
Reprinted from The Daily Mail.

Curtiss sea plane operating with the Atlantic Fleet
Torpedo Boat and Destroyer Flotilla in Mexican waters
in 1914. *US Navy photograph*

Naval War College correspondence courses and wardroom gaming competitions provided opportunities for younger naval professionals to impress their elders on board ship. *US Navy photograph*

Cmdr. King shortly after completing the Naval War College staff course, as the chief engineering officer and strategical officer with Adm. Mayo and the Atlantic Fleet. *National Archives and Records Administration*

Cmdr. Nimitz as executive officer in the purpose-built petroleum refueler *Maumee*, following North Atlantic operations during which he employed procedures earlier perfected by Sims and the skippers of the Atlantic Fleet Destroyer Flotilla. *US Navy photograph*

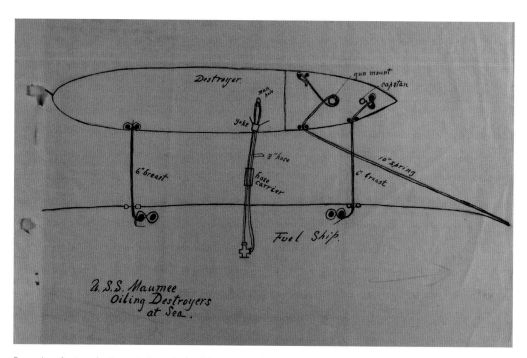

Procedure for transferring petroleum fuels with two ships running abeam, as first executed by Sims and the Atlantic Fleet Destroyer Flotilla between 1914 and 1916. *National Archives and Records Administration*

Adm. Henry T. Mayo on board the Atlantic Fleet flagship, USS *Pennsylvania*—of note, Cmdr. William S. Pye and temporary captain Ernest J. King sit to the far left with the staff. Later, King prominently displayed this picture in the CominCh headquarters of the Second World War. *Courtesy of Janvier King Smith and the King family*

Gen. John Pershing (*left*) upon arriving in London with American ambassador Walter H. Page, RAdm. William S. Sims, Edward Stanley 17th Earle of Derby, and Field Marshal Sir John French on June 6, 1917. *US Navy photograph*

US naval headquarters of Adm. Sims in the "Little America" area of central London, near the Admiralty and closely linked to British intelligence. *US Navy photograph*

Adm. William S. Benson shortly after assuming duty as chief of naval operations with his aides, Commanders Charles Belknap Jr. and Worral Carter. Belknap served as the censor in the Navy Department and then the Navy Overseas Transportation Service. He resigned from the navy to become the president of Monsanto Chemical Company. During the Second World War, Belknap assisted King as Carter supervised logistics in the Pacific. *US Navy photograph*

Navy secretary Daniels with the Earl Jellicoe, during the American leg of his global Empire Mission in conjunction with efforts to establish a future League Navy. *Library of Congress*

THE OFFICIAL NAVAL HISTORIAN OF THE WAR: SIR JULIAN CORBETT.

Britannia's oracle and the visionary of a "League of Peace and Free Sea," Professor Sir Julian Corbett ran the "Historical Section" of the Imperial War Staff, which operated in conjunction with the intelligence subdivisions of the Admiralty. *Courtesy of King's College London*

Capt. Dudley W. Knox as officer in charge of the American Naval Planning Section in London, later being the prime mover in organizing the "Historical Section" as the chief of staff for strategy at the Naval War College. *Courtesy of Dr. Nathaniel Sims and family*

International man of intrigue, Lieutenant Tracy Barrett Kittredge, USNRF, secretly linked the intelligence functions of the Admiralty and US naval forces in Europe during two world wars, as a founding member of the "Historical Section" at the Naval War College, and then as a civilian expatriate with the International Red Cross in Switzerland. *Courtesy of Branden Little*

British sailors hailing the arrival of the US Navy warships
of Battleship Division 9, Atlantic Fleet, on December 7,
1917—many of which proved the vulnerability of
battleships roughly two decades hence at Pearl Harbor.
US Navy art collections

Franklin D. Roosevelt, assistant secretary of the Navy,
greeting American naval officers during the voyage to
European waters in 1918. *US Navy photograph*

American newspapers described the
baseball, as signed by King George
V, as the "instrument of surrender"
after the Navy team captain, Yeoman
"Minooka" Mike McNally, accepted
at Stamford Bridge Football Stadium
on July 4, 1918. From *Souvenir of the
Anglo-American Baseball League,
author's collection*

The past and future as seen with the converted collier USS *Langley*, joining the Battle Fleet as an aircraft carrier with the German-inspired designs featured in the American submarine *S-42* after the First World War. *US Navy photograph*

No 5.
U.S. Naval War College
Game board not of sufficient size to permit the playing of such a tactical problem as that of the Battle of Jutland

Gaming the past with an applied purpose at the Naval War College, using the Battle of Jutland as the basis for decision analysis and strategic experimentation in the 1920s. *US Navy photograph*

Rebels with a singular cause, RAdm. William S. Sims and
Lt. Col. William "Billy" Mitchell reached completely
different conclusions about future army and naval
requirements for airpower. *US Navy photograph*

The converted collier *Langley* as an aircraft carrier at the head of the battle fleet and scouting forces during Fleet Problems in the 1920s. *US Navy photograph*

"I began to learn the intimate connection between the fleet in being and the War College, the home of thought," as Cdre. William V. Pratt stands second from the left to perfect ideas first developed in the classrooms and gaming floors of Newport during Fleet Problems in the 1920s. *US Navy photograph*

King (*far left*) on the deck supervising salvage operations surrounding USS *S-51. US Navy photograph*

Design for submarine qualification insignia, as submitted by King to the Bureau of Navigation. *National Archives*

At age forty-nine, Capt. King stands at center with Cmdr. Richmond Kelly Turner standing third from left, and junior Lt. Daniel V. Gallery Jr. sitting second from left during naval aviation training at Pensacola in 1927. *Courtesy of Janvier King Smith and King family*

Having served as Pershing's confidant, Marshall understood the problems inherent with fusing European and American strategy ashore. London Flagship experience with Sims similarly prepared Stark to understand the British point of view in framing American naval strategy. Roosevelt also put King on the General Board, given his seasoning under both Sims and Mayo, to assist in framing means by which to fuse transatlantic strategy to defend the American hemisphere and offset prospective enemies along the divided maritime fronts of the Pacific and Atlantic.[62]

WHY ENGLAND SLEPT

Asia always loomed over the horizon in strategic debates concerning the future focus of American sea power within the global maritime arena. European and American forces in the region occasionally fell into the crossfire of the imperial Japanese war against the Chinese. During the Hainan landings in February 1939, Vice-Admiral Kondō Nobutake hoped to avoid another *Panay* incident with the US Navy, as Lt. Cmdr. Milton E. "Mary" Miles monitored the battle ashore under the flag of American neutrality as the skipper on USS *John D. Edwards* (DD-216). He grew disgusted and ordered the ship to general quarters. Miles then maneuvered at top speed toward the Japanese forces while flying a large pennant that read "??? !!! ***," meaning "What the Hell!"[63] For such bravado, King earmarked Miles as someone worthy of watching for the future.[64]

Operations in close quarters to war influenced the political debates ongoing in London and Washington. Unwilling to muddle into another world war, Prime Minister Neville Chamberlain shared similar concerns to Roosevelt about the aggressive character of the Axis Tripartite. Chamberlain and Roosevelt quietly encouraged collaboration among the navies of Britain and America. Reading tea leaves, Winston S. Churchill accused Chamberlain of provoking a war through weak-kneed diplomatic compromises. In his 1938 indictment, *While England Slept*, Churchill warned about threats from Hong Kong to Baghdad to Berlin.[65] King took note of Churchill's treatise *While England Slept*.[66] Playing on the Churchillian message, the son of the ambassador in London, John F. Kennedy, also warned fellow Americans to prepare for war in his study *Why England Slept*.

American taxpayers preferred to focus on the baseball box scores and superfluous political dramas in the headlines, rather than the wars happening on foreign shores. In a letter of September 11, 1939, Roosevelt lamented the tragedy of another war in Europe—adding reassurance for the British prime minister, Chamberlain, about American resolve to support high democratic principles of freedom. *On the same day*, Roosevelt sent another letter to the first lord of the Admiralty, Churchill. Roosevelt reflected upon his earlier service as assistant secretary of the Navy in noting, "Because you and I occupied similar positions in the World War I want you to know how glad I am that you are back again in the Admiralty."[67] Roosevelt shrewdly hedged his bets, as the Chamberlain government collapsed and opened the political debates culminating in the rise of another government.

Roosevelt received personal overtures from key political leaders on all sides of the wars of Asia and Europe. Emperor Hirohito and Adolf Hitler separately engaged Roosevelt through their diplomatic intermediaries. Chiang Kai-shek and Josef Stalin operated on the fringes.[68] Among the rich cast of characters, Churchill emphasized the importance of the British Empire. Roosevelt responded by delivering speeches about dreams of liberty and unity among all nationalities. American naval forces operated under the Neutrality

Acts of 1935, 1936, 1937, and 1939.[69] Roosevelt then influenced Congress to declare a Pan-American Security Zone in October 1939.[70] This unprecedented boundary extended well into the Atlantic and along the eastern coasts from Iceland in the North Atlantic to Cape Horn in South America. In so doing, he provided opportunities for the British to exploit the umbrella of American neutrality.[71]

The Pan-American Security Zone provided a route through which merchant shipping sailed under the general protection of US Navy patrols. This strategy began paying dividends by December 1939, as Royal Navy forces used US Navy bearings to locate and capture the Norddeutscher Lloyd passenger liner SS *Columbus* as the vessel departed the Mexican port at Vera Cruz.[72] Royal Navy warships benefited from US Navy broadcasts reporting contact with the German pocket battleship *Admiral Graf Spee*.[73] Between August and December, Atlantic Squadron warships reported contacts with German and Italian vessels—including the *Admiral Graf Spee* and its affiliated auxiliary vessels. Such information proved very useful for the Royal Navy.

British forces exploited American information to locate and intercept rival warships and merchant vessels. Unfiltered contact reports broadcasted by radio enhanced the picture depicted on the maps and within plotting rooms of the Admiralty. Families huddled under German bombs in the railway tunnels of the Underground. Meanwhile, analysts at the Admiralty endured similar toils inside the dank Citadel bunker complex in central London. The ugly cement bunker complex upset the architectural landscape of the Admiralty Old Building (OB) and the Horse Guards Parade. Analysts serving therein referred to the bunker as "Lenin's Tomb."[74] Naval planners worked together with analysts to locate enemy targets from within the Operational Intelligence Centre (OIC).

Working inside the OIC in London required nerves of steel, since the conditions were often comparable to the environment inside a bunker close to the enemy front. Fusing radio intercepts with firsthand reports from the forces at sea, the analysts within the OIC in London often participated directly in combat. Intercepted enemy communications enabled the OIC to locate the enemy. In one dramatic example, the OIC proved its worth by enabling British forces to neutralize the German pocket battleship *Admiral Graf Spee*.[75] Sympathetic American neutrals also provided information, which enabled the Royal Navy to systematically locate and destroy the supply ships affiliated with *Admiral Graf Spee*. Then, by December 1939, the warship sank in dramatic form when the crew scuttled at the mouth of the river Plate within the approaches to Montevideo in Uruguay. Among the first warships to reach the scene, USS *Helena* (CL-50) sent a boarding party with Ens. Richard D. Sampson to inspect the wreck. He sent a detailed report to ONI in February 1940.[76] This information also filtered through backchannels to the British. Recalling the significance of *Graf Spee*, Churchill mused that the incident "warmed the very cockles of the British heart."[77]

The Roosevelt administration hastened efforts to improve hemispheric defenses with American sea power. To this end, the acting secretary of the Navy, Charles Edison, put King on the task of working up plans with the naval architect William Francis Gibbs. Among other key issues, King wanted Gibbs to help the General Board make the case for smaller-caliber antiaircraft guns. These weapons ran against BuOrd, which emphasized larger-caliber guns and special antiaircraft shells fitted with proximity fuses. King refuted BuOrd, since the complicated fuses never functioned in simulated combat conditions during fleet problems and joint exercises. Bureau chiefs earned the reputation for riding "their own hobby horses and carry[ing] out projects of interest to no one else, to experiment, sometimes wastefully, sometimes creatively, without fear of interference from doubting superiors."[78] Edison gave King tacit "carte blanche to improve the antiaircraft defenses of all of our ships."[79]

King forcibly pushed the Navy Department into making sound military decisions about trends in technology and future warship design. King joined forces with Gibbs to compel the bureaucrats into abandoning proximity fuses for antiaircraft weapons. Rather, King and Gibbs favored the installation of quadruple-mounted 40 mm and double 20 mm Bofors, and Oerlikon designs seemed most promising against aircraft at higher altitudes. In addition, he recommended the installation of .50-caliber Browning machine guns anywhere decks could accommodate the mounts. King frequently undercut the bureau chiefs. His assistant, Low, recalled that King "cut completely across the usual channels [and,] in point of fact, got the job started in about three months instead of two or three years."[80] Low explained that King upset the civilian bureaucrats within the bureaus "who had been for many years in the habit of advising, suggesting and vetoing, but rarely doing anything quickly."[81]

The General Board members were among the key consumers of information provided by ONI, as amplified by studies conducted by the Naval War College. Reports submitted by various naval attachés worldwide also provided useful insights on foreign technological innovations and tactical procedures. King ran the younger assistants on the General Board at a pace akin to seagoing operations. As secretary, Capt. Oscar C. Badger kept apace with King. Working on the problems of submarine design and antisubmarine weaponry, King relied heavily upon Commanders Bernhard Bieri, Ruthven E. Libby, and Low. Later, Low explained that for "three months, mornings, or afternoons, and often on Saturday mornings [we] sweated over drawing boards containing the plans of every major ship in the Navy down to and including destroyers."[82]

King used his perch on the General Board to divert resources to develop the war-winning workhorses of the US Navy. Together, they advocated for the shallow-draft boats and landing-craft "sled" designs of Andrew Higgins. King worked closely with the naval architect John C. Niedermair to study photographs of imperial Japanese designs for landing craft. The imagery filtered through ONI, after Marine major Victor H. Krulack took snapshots of Japanese troops landing ashore in China. Pooling this information with British and German designs, the Americans developed Landing Ship–Vehicle and Personnel (LCVP), Landing Ship–Infantry (LCI), and Landing Ship–Tank (LST). Additionally, King pushed the development of floating drydocks for sustained operations in the global commons, supported by remote island Advanced Base facilities—which included the anticipated construction of future deepwater ports and airfields.[83]

The merger of the BuEng with BuC&R, as suggested by the General Board, culminated in the establishment of the BuShips. The bureaucratic consolidation on the OpNav staff also streamlined the work of the General Board. Given his role, King established key connections that later proved decisive in war. King expanded his personal network within the Electric Boat Company under John Jay Hopkins, and its Elco subsidiary influenced King to take notice of the innovative Motor Torpedo Boat designs of Henry Sutphen, Irwin Chase, Bill Fleming, and Glenville Tremaine.

Service on the General Board placed King among the inner circles of the Roosevelt administration. The retirement of Leahy as the CNO shortly after his sixty-fourth birthday in the summer of 1939 provided indications and warnings about the future. Following a reception held at the White House, Leahy sat as the guest of honor held at the Mayflower Hotel. Among the elites of Washington, he sat with King, Stark, Nimitz, and Ingersoll at the head table overlooking the large audience—all dressed in white formal attire.[84] Leahy then left for a civil service appointment as governor of the unincorporated territory of Puerto Rico. Meanwhile, King and Stark continued the hard peacetime work of overhauling the US Navy within the context of another world war. His former Naval War College associate, Capt. Raymond Spruance, joined Leahy. As territorial governor, Leahy relied upon the assistance of the naval district commander, Spruance, in patrolling the waters surrounding Puerto Rico.[85]

American journalists continued following King after news of his assignment to the General Board percolated among the barrooms and gossip clubs of Washington. Notably, King earned the title of "Triple Threat," as coined in the popular media in 1939.[86] Indeed, the General Board clearly was *not* a backwater, nor did it become a tombstone assignment for King.[87] Glenn Perry of the *Washington Sun* explained that King was "reputed to be ice-cold, hard as steel, emotionless, [and] disagreeable, turned out on closer inspection to be a man who loves to laugh, a man with a keen sense of humor, and a quick wit."[88] In fact, King's assignment to the General Board reflected the immediacy of the global situation. With the world at war, Roosevelt wanted King to be close to the peacetime battlefield of Washington, DC. The assignment provided opportunity for King to write his own ticket to the topmasts of the Roosevelt administration.[89] In considering King's tenure, the official Navy Department historian, Robert Greenhagh Albion, explained that the General Board served as the gateway to future four-star commands. Albion explained that the General Board "ordinarily was 'no dead end.'"[90]

CHAPTER 15
Somewhere, over the RAINBOW

Wars on foreign shores failed to impress many taxpayers and their congressional representatives, which greatly frustrated efforts by the Roosevelt administration. Roosevelt knew that the US Navy stood unprepared to fight simultaneous wars on multiple oceanic fronts.[1] Roosevelt needed help in fixing the broken relationships on the Joint Board and the various bureaucratic subdivisions within the Navy Department.[2] He thought changing "anything in the Na-a-vy is like punching a feather bed . . . you punch it with your right and you punch it with your left until you are finally exhausted, and then you find the damn bed just as it was before you started punching."[3] Roosevelt knew that King packed a heavy bureaucratic punch. Given the situation in 1940, Roosevelt administration officials observed King thriving on the "General Board to become a hard-bitten and aggressive leader who had the attributes needed [for all] wartime contingencies."[4]

The Roosevelt administration provided a mandate for the recommissioning and refitting of mothballed warships. The "red lead" destroyers then stood ready for action. Through the good offices of the secretary of state, Cordell Hull, the Roosevelt administration used mothballed warships to clear the books while using the Neutrality Acts as the basis for supporting foreign partners. The move also cleared the way for the Roosevelt administration to establish mandates for future fleet construction. Close coordination between the Department of State and the Joint Board coincided with detailed planning within the General Board of the Navy to facilitate the "Destroyers for Bases" scheme and the "Cash and Carry" policies of the Roosevelt administration. With the British as the primary beneficiary, King played the key role in reflagging outdated "four-pipe" destroyers of the Wickes, Clemson, and Caldwell classes during service on the General Board in 1940.[5]

Roosevelt enhanced the strategic position of Britain in meeting emergent threats from continental Europe. At the same time, the older warships of the American fleet lacked the capacity to meet the emergent challenges of the Imperial Japanese Navy.[6] In all the key warship categories, the Americans lacked means to counter newer Japanese designs of faster speeds, superior armor protection, and greater destructive potential. Logistically, the Japanese were also demonstrating the nascent ability to sustain offensive operations along the shores of China.[7] Unlike American forces operating on a constant rotation from Asiatic waters to other areas of the Pacific, those assigned to the Atlantic followed a relatively comfortable peacetime routine along the American coast.[8]

American sailors celebrated their liberty as polished brass and fresh paint obscured the underlying rust that characterized the warships assigned to the Atlantic Squadron. Commander Francis S. Low explained that warships assigned to the Atlantic were "jokingly referred to as 'flower squadron' because of its social obligations."[9] In theory, the

Atlantic Squadron provided means to establish a "fleet in being" strategy in relations with Europe. Having specialized in battleships, Rear Admiral Hayne Ellis commanded the Atlantic Squadron. Given immediate responsibility to orchestrate the Neutrality Patrols in the Atlantic as the commander, Atlantic Squadron, Ellis operated under the immediate authority of Stark. Simultaneously, Ellis performed the duties of commander, Patrol Force, under Richardson. Overlapping commands among the shore establishment hindered Ellis in synthesizing maritime policy with strategy in coordinating peacetime operations at sea.[10]

Ellis set the tone for the Atlantic Squadron, breaking his flag on the battleship USS *New York* (BB-34). The syndicated journalist Drew Pearson lambasted Ellis as an indirect means to challenge the naval policies of the Roosevelt administration. In his newspaper column,

> "Washington Merry-Go-Round," Pearson portrayed Ellis as a dilettante. Pearson wrote that "Ellis is the smartest appearing admiral in the navy [but] no intellectual giant—in a battle he might fire all his guns at once, but never haul down his flag. To the very end he would go down a laughing, blustering fighter."[11]

Ellis focused on rebuilding American confidence in the capabilities of the US Navy in the Atlantic. To these ends, he broke his flag afloat in the aging battleship USS *Texas* (BB-35), although more frequently he rotated to the aircraft carrier *Ranger*. Elements of the First Marine Brigade, under Brigadier Holland M. Smith, embarked warships under Ellis. Together, Ellis and Smith created the First Joint Training Force, comprising personnel of the army, navy, and the coast guard. Ellis and Smith based the organization on the operations of the first US Navy flag officer from the Civil War, Adm. David G. Farragut. Thus, Ellis and Smith set aside their familial ties to the Confederacy by rechristening the Atlantic Squadron as the "Farragut Attack Force."[12]

Ellis and Smith successfully rallied the Atlantic Squadron to shift from routine operations along the American coast in anticipation of operations farther afield. Ellis changed the mentality of the "Flower Squadron." The "Farragut Attack Force" implied that the Atlantic Squadron stood ready to win in combat. The wars in Europe and Asia provided a point of reference for Ellis and Smith to rally the Farragut Attack Force to operate at full wartime readiness in training. With time running short, Ellis faced mandatory retirement upon reaching age sixty-four. Roosevelt wanted a commander with firsthand experience at coordinating aviation and submarine operations to support surface task groups. To these ends, Roosevelt turned to King on the General Board to rig the fleet for aggressive peacetime operations in the Atlantic.[13]

THE TRIPLE THREAT

The Roosevelt administration used the Neutrality Acts to clear the books of old warships while expanding the mandate to build the future American fleet. On the General Board, King shaped the future of the US Navy. As war clouds gathered on the horizon, King possibly anticipated a future in retirement as a civilian business executive. During service on the General Board, King reaffirmed close friendships with the captains of American industry, including Henry Ford. Shipbuilders Henry J. Kaiser and Homer L. Ferguson rekindled their friendship with King during his tenure on the General Board. Similarly, he met frequently with the key entrepreneurs and designers of the American aviation industry, including Artemis L. Gates, Allan Lockheed, and Glenn L. Martin.[14]

Gates introduced King to an Ivy League network of influential industrialists and politicians. The lawyer and journalist Frank Knox held significant sway. He earlier served with Theodore Roosevelt in the Rough Riders. Knox maintained Republican Party affiliations. His assistant, James N. Forrestal, earned millions on Wall Street. His ties with Roosevelt also dated to the First World War. As a former US naval volunteer reservist of the First World War, Forrestal qualified to fly with the Royal Canadian Navy before earning bureaucratic wings with Roosevelt inside the Navy Department. The politician Forrestal interacted like oil against the saltwater character of the old salt King. The pair never overcame personality differences, which later proved disastrous to their shared understanding of American sea power.[15]

Knox and Forrestal influenced discussions concerning future appropriations for the Navy Department, which extended to debates about the future priorities for fleet construction. Assistant Navy secretary Edison advised King in the art of handling civilian bureaucrats. Edison attempted to prepare King for the vicious bureaucratic battles to come, as King broke from the standard narrative of the Joint Board and Navy General Board to identify critical strategic gaps within the fleet. King pushed fellow board members to take the broader view in discussions of specific warship types—always emphasizing the strategic goal of producing a fully integrated "balanced fleet" for the future task organization under the CNO—ships that could rotate to various geographic areas and still succeed in performing any given mission. To this end, King championed Iowa-class battleships, Fletcher-class destroyers, and Gato-class submarines. Most importantly, King advocated for the construction of auxiliaries to augment the planned network of advanced bases.

Sustained operations in the global maritime arena required naval thinkers to concentrate on the large areas of oceanic terrain, as highlighted in hues of blue rather than green. King forced the General Board to follow in his wake to build warships designed with larger fuel bunkers, stainless-steel interiors, long-range wireless transmitters, and ice cream machines. King also thought that each sailor west of Hawaii should receive a regular supply of at least two beers per day at sea, as were provided during liberty ashore every sixty days—in essence, 120 cans of beer every two months.[16] For King, the sailorly task of relaxing always carried the discernable purpose of sustaining long-range fleet operations. His quest for efficiency also extended to the seemingly superfluous question of uniforms.

King always pushed sailors to keep clean ships, although he never embraced the spit-and-polish traditions of the US Navy. Shiny brass and white paint on gray hulls only seemed to cover the sleepless rust beneath the surfaces of the fleet. On the General Board, King warned about the paints and polishes required to keep ships looking good in port. Such materials seemed an unnecessary fire hazard. King complained about fore-and-aft caps, with epaulettes, and the requirement for officers to carry swords with multiple variations of service dress uniforms. He suggested and sketched a Scottish-styled dirk with a sharkskin hilt and emblazoned with the US Naval crest to replace naval swords. Seeking to reduce the variety of naval uniforms, King recommended only the service dress blues for duty ashore. Along the waterfront and at sea, King proposed gray jumpsuits—like the aviator flight suit—for all hands.[17]

Service on the General Board enabled King to indulge pet ideas, some of which carried significant consequences for the future of American sea power. He drove major changes in the organization and configuration of the fleet. He placed higher priorities on submarine construction, cruiser development, and aircraft carriers. King directly participated in the development of the Iowa-class battleships. He advocated the Princeton-class "flying deck cruisers." He pressed for greater antiaircraft gunnery protection in surface ships. Logistic auxiliaries, such as floating drydocks, received top priority under King.[18]

American warships frequently sailed into the crossfire of battles ongoing abroad between the empires of Europe and Asia. King had special access to all the reports submitted from the oceanic fronts. For example, American naval observers in China took pictures and careful notes on Japanese methods for amphibious assault. US Marine captain Victor H. Krulak photographed Japanese amphibious operations. He noted that the shallow-draft vessels featured flat keels. Trapdoor bows enabled Japanese troops to storm ashore quickly. Having witnessed the swiftness of Japanese amphibious tactics, Krulak offered recommendations for improving upon the Japanese design. Andrew Higgins seized upon the idea, mobilizing his shipyard to begin constructing prototypes of American landing craft and motor torpedo boats for littoral operations close to shore.[19]

Wars in Asia and Europe inspired journalists to focus on key personalities in the top tiers of the Departments of War and Navy. The conclusion of the Axis Tripartite Pact was followed by other dramatic headlines, as Nazi forces invaded Poland in September 1939. Hitler's détente with Stalin seemingly placed the American hemisphere on another planet from the rest of the world. Americans generally remained oblivious when, from behind closed doors on the General Board, King advised Roosevelt to understand that "it is essential to consider now—and to prepare now—the 'ways and means' wherewith to expedite the seizure and occupation of bases westward of the 180th meridian."[20] Anticipating logistical challenges to get over the horizon, King pushed to organize "primary advanced base units."[21] King advised Roosevelt to pre-position older battleships in Hawaii to facilitate the rapid relief of the Philippines in "accordance with current war plans."[22]

The General Board provided opportunity for King to exercise intellectual flexibility in anticipation of prospective American participation in future wars at sea. Unbound by the traditional responsibilities of command, King pressed Roosevelt to replicate the design of the US Coast Guard Hamilton class for potential use in future antisubmarine operations. King provided similar recommendations for amphibious warship construction. King further warned the Roosevelt administration to augment the existing six aircraft carriers in service with an additional three under development. King warned about the lack of trained personnel for sustained operations at sea.[23] In making this point, King traded notes with his brother-in-law, Gen. Smith, and son-in-law Maj. Smith, inside the War Department. In 1940, King recommended using the army as a gateway for recruiting sailors and airmen into the naval and aviation services. His understanding reflected the influence of his familial network of spies, which extended to the inner sanctum of the US Army Air Corps.[24]

HAOLE TSUNAMI

Airpower loomed over the broad Pacific horizons in coordinating maritime strategy and in positioning forces to attain the "fleet in being" effect in conjunction with Roosevelt administration policies to mitigate tensions between imperial Japan and the United States.

After 1939, Stark and King worked collaboratively in revising existing army defensive plans to reflect offensive naval strategies, which focused on achieving sustainable peacetime ends. At the recommendation of the General Board, Stark established the Hawaiian Training Detachment of the US Fleet.[25] Notably, the aircraft carrier USS *Enterprise* (CV-6) initially had been designated as the flagship in Hawaii. The CinCUS, Richardson, and his staff found *Enterprise* unsuitable, shifting their flag to familiar confines on the flagship *Pennsylvania*. King described Richardson as having "brains and ability, but something missing about him."[26]

The Hawaiian Training Detachment referred to the shore headquarters that functioned to facilitate logistical support for the *occasional* presence of mainline battleships and related auxiliaries of the Battle Force. Under the plan, warships rotated from West Coast ports for temporary service at Pearl Harbor. Individual sailors carried the burden of being deployed to the relatively remote realities of Hawaii. The only workable port also lacked infrastructure for the associated tsunami of military personnel pulling in with the fleet. Native Hawaiians and the local "haole" population of recent white immigrants to the island also enjoyed the solitude—sparking complaints about the expected influx of sailors.[27]

Tensions between the local populations in Hawaii stood among many other strategic considerations, which complicated the final decision to position American warships in the islands. Past military adventures by American forces intermixed with recent memories of the scandalous behavior of Lt. Thomas Massie during the exercises of 1931 and 1932. Allegations of rape and murder surrounded the young officer, which caused major problems during what became known as the "Massie Affair."[28] Just seven years later, many Hawaiians recalled the scandal when the Roosevelt administration announced plans to deploy the fleet to Pearl Harbor.

Navy Regulations created additional problems for the CinCUS staff in planning the fleet rotation plans for warships to maneuver between the West Coast for temporary duty with the Hawaii Training Detachment.[29] Enlisted sailors generally lived on board their warships while in port. Sailors below the rank of first-class petty officer generally required permission to marry. Married sailors and chiefs had the option of requesting quarters ashore, which often required the additional justification of having a spouse with whom to live. Officers above the rank of lieutenant had the ability to request quarters for their families on a very limited basis. By implication, officers in the ranks of ensign and lieutenant (junior grade) generally stayed with their men on board ship—or at the discretion of individual skippers.[30]

Given the inherent challenges of rotating the fleet to Hawaii, the Roosevelt administration attempted to achieve the "fleet in being" effect in relations with imperial Japan and the European navies of the Pacific. Under the Destroyers for Bases policy, foreign ports also became available for the regular rotation of American warships. With this added advantage, King supervised General Board studies and Naval War College gaming analysis to develop an operational schedule for rotating warships between British protectorates in the Atlantic and Pacific. These plans extended to the Atlantic Squadron task force 40-Tare. Operating in European waters during the Spanish Civil War, American warships rotated between the Azores to Gibraltar and from Madeira to Morocco before turning to the wine-and-cheese ports of England, France, and Italy.[31]

The Farragut Attack Force in the Atlantic used training as the justification for expanding peacetime operations at sea. From Argentia to Bermuda and into the Panama Canal Zone, the Special Service Squadron further expanded operations in South American waters."[32] The Roosevelt administration explained that the seagoing mission was for promoting "friendly relations and to contribute to the growth of understanding in all respects between the United States and other republics of the western hemisphere."[33] Election year politics always influenced Roosevelt in explaining the operations of American seagoing forces.[34] During this period, Roosevelt also asked King for advice. In turn, King produced a thirty-page study, "Naval Strategy and Tactics."[35] King submitted the paper on July 30, 1940.

King highlighted the differences between military operations ashore and those of naval forces afloat. In particular, he emphasized that the "important and often[-]determining element in naval strategy is <u>logistics</u>, which is an all-inclusive term involving locations and distances (time and space) translated into fuel endurance, and of supplies, munitions, food[,] and other essential stores."[36] King advised that "it may be said that the combatant ships of a fleet can operate to a distance of about 2,000 miles from a base, or for a period of about fifteen days."[37] King pushed the point about the importance of advanced bases. He explained that logistics "necessarily takes account of the number, distribution[,] and capacities of naval bases, whether permanent or temporary, where the materials of logistics are available to the fleet."[38]

Logistics dominated the future course of American sea power, as King outlined the requirements for operations far beyond the horizon in European and Asian waters. He emphasized the point by describing the art of logistics as the "essential factor" that "tracks clear back into the mine, the farm, and the factory before you get it all hooked up."[39] King placed highest priority on "safeguarding and making effective our own lines of communication [and] do our utmost to cripple and to cut the enemies' lines of communication."[40]

With King as a member of the General Board, his star certainly began rising to another level inside the Roosevelt administration. King advised Stark and the OpNav staff during secret discussions between Washington and London. King also collaborated with the assistant CNO, RAdm. Royal E. Ingersoll, and the aide CNO, Smedberg.[41] Logistical requirements inspired King to initiate discussions between the General Board and the War Plans Division. He asked about prospective access to foreign naval bases in conjunction with negotiations between the Admiralty and Navy Department in 1940. However, the director of war plans, Ghormley, initially refused to release full details about the RAINBOW series. He kept the actual plans under lock and key—failing to provide full access to the seagoing commanders. King explained that Ghormley "was a good man [and] was the best planning officer in the navy."[42] King conversely thought that "Ghormley never told anybody about what he was planning, so nobody knew what he wanted them to do."[43]

King complained about the restrictions imposed on discussions concerning the RAINBOW plans. He asked Kalbfus the strategic question "How the hell are we supposed to know our task if we don't have a clear understanding of our ultimate purposes?"[44] King told Stark that "if we keep fiddling around about fighting RED and CRIMSON, how would War Plans [Ghormley] propose <u>working with</u> [the British] in managing ORANGE, BLACK, GRAY, and BLUE right now?"[45] Observing helplessly from the General Board of the Navy, King pressed about the ultimate goals of transatlantic collaboration between the British Empire and United States.[46] King worried about the Destroyers for Bases deal, which cleared the decks of outdated warships and simultaneously sapped the emergency reserve.[47]

Warships unmanned and in mothballs still had strategic value for the purposes of sustaining the "fleet in being" effect. Advising the Roosevelt administration from the General Board, King took the opportunity to recommend the construction of two new warships for every mothballed vessel lost under the Destroyers for Bases and the Lend-Lease arrangements. King also assisted Stark in organizing the strategy for maintaining the Pan-American Neutrality Zone on both coasts. These moves also coincided with grander diplomatic efforts, as the Roosevelt administration reinforced friends and attempted to mitigate the prospects for another global war of unprecedented scale. From the CinCUS headquarters in San Francisco, Richardson quipped about the "considerable body of opinion in Washington [that the] Japanese could be 'bluffed.'"[48]

ALONG FOR THE RIDE

Richardson disagreed with the Roosevelt administration concept of concentrating mainline battleships in Hawaii. Despite the sound military decisions behind the plan to *rotate* surface combatants between the West Coast and the North Pacific triangle, the policies of the Roosevelt administration fell out of sync with Richardson's particular strategic perspective. He felt compelled an offer an honest—albeit contrary—point of view. Roosevelt himself took Richardson's ideas into consideration, although made final decisions open to further discussions. Becoming paranoid in the process, Richardson thought King ovestepped by arguing that that the CNO, Stark, "should by implication hold overall authority for US Navy operations."[49]

Political trends within the Roosevelt administration set the stage for major strategic reorganization in the relationships between the Departments of War and Navy. From the General Board, King correctly identified the lopsided authorities between Army chief of staff and those of the CNO as being a fundamental vulnerability.[50] Richardson agreed with King on this point but felt nullified when Navy secretary Edison arrived by surprise with King in Hawaii.[51] Richardson mused that "I believe that Stark thought King should have the CinCUS billet at the time that it was given to me."[52] Richardson thought that "it seemed an unusual thing to me that King should be attached to the secretary's party as an observer, by Stark."[53] Richardson spoke tersely to King in Hawaii. Later, King recalled Richardson barking, "What the hell was I doing there?"[54] Taken aback, King turned with a squared-off jaw and a squinted eye to reply, "I went along for the ride."[55]

Edison recognized King as the type of naval officer required for implementing the naval neutrality strategy of the Roosevelt administration. King likewise described Edison as a "straight thinker who took nothing for granted."[56] King recalled that Edison "wished to carry on as Secretary of the Navy, but was sent off to run as governor of New Jersey, and so resigned and was succeeded by Frank Knox."[57] Edison wrote a parting recommendation to Roosevelt that "I take the liberty of bringing to your attention the need for shaking the service out of a peace-time psychology [to] throw off a routine state of mind requires leadership of the Jervis type."[58] In closing, Edison tossed Richardson overboard to advise the following:

I believe that Rear Admiral E. J. King, USN, is outstandingly of this type and that his appointment as Commander in Chief of the United States Fleet would do wonders for the fleet and the service. I earnestly recommend his appointment [and] this is to be considered in no way a reflection upon Admiral Richardson's performance of duty.[59]

Edison delivered the velvet stiletto to Richardson, opening the path for an erstwhile Jervis to rig the fleet for battle.

Roosevelt took heed of Edison's advice as they prepared for another election year campaign against the Republican Party. Edison successfully carried the Democratic Party banner as governor of New Jersey. Edison also advised Roosevelt in selecting the newspaperman Frank Knox as the incumbent Navy secretary. Forty-two years earlier, he served with Roosevelt's cousin Teddy as a member of the "Rough Riders" during the Spanish-American War. His "Bull Moose" Republican credentials propelled Knox into the spotlight with Alf Landon on the Republican Party ticket against Roosevelt in 1936.

Chuffed by the opportunity, Knox set aside politics to join the Roosevelt administration as Navy secretary. As a newspaperman, Knox also did as the Roosevelt administration expected him to do—talk in glowing terms about the navy. King explained that Knox "kept telling all the newspaper men about what we were trying to do [so] we just stopped telling Knox anything."[60] Secrets still leaked on a regular basis from the rotten bureaucratic confines of the Navy Department. King found the leak. He explained that Undersecretary Forrestal "was as tricky as he could be."[61]

Forrestal had the oily personality of a professional politician, which caused friction in the saltwater relationship with the no-nonsense demeanor of King. Since their first meeting in the First World War, the pair shared an intense dislike for each other. Forrestal served briefly in the US Naval Volunteer Reserve Force and qualified with the Royal Canadian Air Force as an aviator. He never landed on board the pitching decks of a warship. Forrestal claimed to know about naval aviation. King found Forrestal a dangerous political parvenu or, alternatively, an "empty shirt in an expensive suit with a cheap tie and scuffed shoes."[62] King recalled how Forrestal always "wanted a yes man in the job."[63] King thought that "Forrestal kibitzed without understanding what he was doing [but] FDR at least listened to my advice too."[64]

Behind closed doors, King applauded the Republican Party ideals of fiscal conservatism while embracing the vision of American sea power, as championed by the Democratic Party under Roosevelt. Politics always became intertwined with strategic considerations, from King's perspective. He also strived to keep an open mind in navigating the prevailing political trends and strategic undercurrents—always seeking the safest course.[65] Cmdr. Paul and Charlotte Pihl had introduced King to Charlotte's brother Wendell Willkie. During the election of 1940, King understood the stakes. He kept an open mind and apolitical outlook. King avoided taking a clear position on the ongoing debates between Willkie and Roosevelt.[66]

King kept a professional distance from potential political allies within the halls of Congress and the White House. Keeping the needs of the navy at center focus, service on the General Board enabled King to gain unique insights into the political battlefields of Washington. Among other developments of interest to King, it became impossible to overlook the influx of British personnel inside the Navy Department. After 1940, British accents intermixed with Yankee over drinks in the smoky mirrored rooms of the Army-Navy Club and other watering holes of Washington. Royal Navy captain Arthur Wellesley Clarke drew interest, as the Duke of Wellington also came to King's curious mind. With the clandestine establishment of the British Admiralty Delegation (BAD) in Washington, Clarke influenced policy decisions of the Roosevelt administration.[67] Clarke usually knew more about American policy than his US Navy counterparts. Clarke proved masterful at being the unnoticed spider in the corner of rooms during important strategic discussions.[68]

THIS IS GOING TO BE UGLY

The ghosts of Jellicoe and Sims loomed in the corners of the Admiralty and Navy Department, as their protégés reanimated strategic collaboration between the Royal Navy and US Navy. Four decades after the Seymour Expedition in China and two decades after American forces arrived in European waters in the First World War, British and American naval officers again appeared together in the halls of the Admiralty and Navy Department in anticipation of American operations in the Second World War. The First Sea Lord, Pound, rekindled collaboration in regular correspondences with trusted American friends like Stark, Knox, and King. On the fringes of the seagoing ranks, Alistair Denniston and Frank Birch at Bletchley Park rekindled past friendships with Americans like Tracy Barrett Kittredge and Angus MacLean Thuermer.

American civilians with ties to the Navy Department provided means by which to monitor the pulse of strategic affairs on foreign shores. Humanitarian work placed Kittredge in regular contact with key leaders in Berlin and Rome. Kittredge met regularly with the naval attaché in London, Kirk. Operating on similar fringes, MacLean Thuermer similarly enjoyed unique access as a freelance reporter on the continent.[69] Having met Hitler and other major Nazi figures, MacLean Thuermer shared his notes with the American naval attaché in Berlin, Capt. Paul Pihl. In his reports filed with Knox at ONI, Pihl noted, "This is going to be an ugly war here in Europe."[70] Another journalist, Edgar Snow, similarly warned the American naval attaché in China, Capt. James M. McHugh, about the likelihood of disaster in Asia. In turn, McHugh dutifully reported the trends, as compiled by Knox and his Historical Section, or "Op-16-E" at ONI.[71]

Americans generally ignored the rise of the Axis Tripartite and the Communist ideology of the Soviet Comintern. Fearing the consequences, Knox quietly advised the Roosevelt administration to reopen transatlantic communications channels from within the "Historical Section" at ONI.[72] Knox advised Roosevelt that the "British conception of 'national defense' is much broader than ours."[73] "They fight with rates of exchange, loans, mercantile shipping, commercial treaties," he continued, "all correlated with international politics, military and naval action."[74] In the early stages of reengaging the special relationship between London and Washington, Knox provided Roosevelt with a backchannel for transatlantic communication.[75]

Knox used the Historical Section as a conduit for negotiation by using the past as means to frame the future of transatlantic collaboration at sea. He recommended creating equivalencies between the British organization in advising the Roosevelt administration that "co-ordination is needed."[76] Citing the British model, Knox first observed that the

War Cabinet held no executive authority and provided advice only to the prime minister. "It is not a super-department," and Knox also observed that the British committee system "in no way modifies or limits control and responsibility of existing agencies."[77] Secondarily, he found "elasticity" in the British model with "no fixed composition [and] the head (prime minister) selects and varies members called on to consider particular cases, as he likes."[78] "Personally," Knox offered as a caveat, "I would interchange 'committee' and 'council' in the organization terminology."[79]

In this way, Knox hoped to make a distinction between the existing British system and the prospective American establishment of a civil-military joint staff. Knox advised Roosevelt to replicate the British model by reorganizing the closest American equivalent—the Joint Board. In turn, Roosevelt quietly worked with the chief of staff of the US Army, Gen. George Marshall, and the CNO, Stark, to press the limits of constitutional authority in synthesizing the functions of the Joint Board. Members of the Army General Staff and the Navy General Board lacked actual authority over global strategy as *advisers* to the presidential administration. The Joint Board had *no* authority to provide strategic directives for operations.

King had full access to information derived from sensitive intelligence sources, which provided additional context in considering the observations found in reports submitted by American emissaries on foreign shores. Naval attachés in Europe and Asia provided regular updates. From Berlin, Pihl coordinated information with his counterpart in Rome, Capt. Thomas C. Kinkaid, keeping apprised of the Axis Tripartite in Europe.[80] Cmdr. Henri Smith-Hutton and Lt. Stephen Jurika likewise provided insight to ongoing debates within the imperial Japanese army and naval staffs. In addition, Smith-Hutton received highly sensitive access to the banking and business activities of key Japanese officials from a Naval Academy classmate, William J. Sebald.[81]

The information provided by naval attaches proved crucial to the development of an Anglo-American maritime alliance. Information provided by the naval attaché in London, Kirk, proved particularly decisive in efforts to synthesize Royal Navy with US Navy operations during the period of American neutrality. Nearly forty years earlier, King ensured that Kirk completed the prerequisite mathematical exams to join the ranks of the service. By the spring of 1940, he stood in particularly good standing within the British government. In particular, the deputy chief of the Naval Staff at the Admiralty, Rear-Admiral Tom Phillips, approached Kirk with an offer to open Royal Navy shipyard facilities to US Navy warships of the Asiatic Fleet.

Coincident with discussions concerning their common problems of Asia, Phillips advised Kirk of plans to expand the Royal Navy diplomatic mission in Washington. Phillips introduced Kirk to the Royal Navy liaison to the War Cabinet, Clarke, and from the Admiralty, Captain Cecil Perry. In this way, Phillips entrusted Clarke, Perry, and Kirk with the mission of reconstructing the transatlantic alliance between the Admiralty and Navy Department. After meeting Kirk in London, Clarke arrived in Washington as a secret BAD liaison to the Navy Department. In this role, Clarke lacked clear authority to "convey any particular views or thoughts."[82] Clarke described his orders to Washington as "purely verbal [and] deliberately vague."[83]

Essentially, Clarke carried the authority to execute British policy on his own—limited only by the understanding that the British government reserved the right to deny its role in shaping the transatlantic relationships in America. British satellites in New York City connected with branch offices throughout the United States. The visitors speaking the King's English indicated their affiliation with the British Joint Staff Mission in Washington.[84] Recalling the experience, Clarke reported such difficulties as having "no provision for housing missions[,] and officers were forced to exist on their bare pay[; we] were in effect asking USA to present us with munitions free of charge."[85] Royal Navy observers understood that US Navy officials, like King, always faced being "torn between the desire to meet us and the knowledge that if he did he was liable to be grilled on Capitol Hill."[86]

Royal Navy personnel operated with extreme caution to avoid bringing attention to their activities inside the United States. "It is impossible to assess exactly what we lost in those early days by being thus debarred from joining Clubs, etc. and in fact living the ordinary life of US Officers of equivalent rank." One report advised that "most Americans think highly of being asked to one's 'home' as opposed to formal entertainment in hotels."[87] The administrative restrictions on Royal Navy personnel seemed so counterproductive that "being debarred from setting up house[,] one lost many opportunities of gaining confidence."[88] Liaisons inside the United States followed the basic rule of avoiding "direct dealings with the American press [since] some sections of the press would have been only too glad to use British opinions as a stick to beat the [Roosevelt] Administration or some other political object."[89] At the same time, Royal Navy liaisons thought, "In dealings with the press it was found safest to strike a note of profound admiration of all American institutions [and that] undue reserve is abhorred by Americans."[90]

STONE FRIGATES

To facilitate relations, the Admiralty carefully modified administrative restrictions on Royal Navy personnel assigned to the United States. Among the first to appear in the halls of the Navy Department, Clarke discreetly compiled a list of hotels near major port facilities throughout the United States. He anticipated an influx of Royal Navy personnel in the spring of 1941. Clarke negotiated an ongoing contract for rooms at the Hotel Grafton in Washington.[91] He secured an additional lease to install the official "Military Mission" inside a mansion located in Dupont Circle—in the private home of Roosevelt's naval aide, Capt. Paul H. Bastedo, at 3055 Whitehaven Street. The mansion stood conveniently adjacent to the British embassy on Massachusetts Avenue in Washington. Clark's connection with Bastedo also provided a direct backchannel to Roosevelt.

Clarke and Bastedo negotiated a private lease, enabling the British to use Bastedo House with utmost discretion as a satellite facility in downtown Washington. In advance, Bastedo secured permission from the assistant CNO, Ingersoll, at the Navy Department.[92] In the following years, British officials frequently rented the personal properties of ranking American naval officers, like King, in the Washington, DC, area. Among other examples, Bastedo House became the most visible hub of Royal Navy activity in the United States. The Admiralty kept traditions of billeting Royal Navy personnel with orders to "stone frigates." Under British law, Royal Navy personnel were subject to discipline onlywhen assigned to warships.[93] Thus, many Royal Navy personnel carried orders to the HMS *Asbury* while residing in Bastedo House.

The Admiralty practice of assigning personnel to buildings named after historic warships became the norm within the British and affiliated Commonwealth naval services. In general, Royal Navy personnel assigned to the United States carried orders to the warships HMS *Saker* or HMS *Asbury*. Since these historic warships did not actually exist in 1940, and the administrative assignment to the stone frigates *Saker* and *Asbury* often confused uninitiated US Navy officers, this antiquated tradition provided discreet means for the Admiralty to assign personnel for duty ashore within the United States. British naval liaisons in Washington—all apparently assigned to warships—sometimes confused the Americans by claiming association with the stone frigates *Saker* and *Asbury*.[94]

Behind closed doors, British operatives in America set critical administrative foundations for transatlantic collaboration. In addition to the work of Sir Henry Tizard—using British technical innovations to barter with the Americans—the Admiralty also fostered gentlemanly ties by trading inside information.[95] Formal collaboration among the bureaucratic subdivisions of intelligence progressively spliced the future British Empire and the United States—as characterized by Churchill as the "special relationship."[96] In his *History of the English-Speaking Peoples*, Churchill also made many assumptions about the future by manipulating historical tales about the "vast dominions secured in the New World and in India, and the first British Empire came into being."[97] Churchill's flowery historical musings often ran flat with Roosevelt and many other key Americans, like King, as the gathering storm loomed over the horizons of Asia and Europe.

CHAPTER 16
British Invasion

Churchill naturally fought to preserve British imperial traditions, although the Roosevelt administration struggled to avoid direct American military involvement in another imperial war within the global maritime arena. Admiralty liaisons in Washington advised their superiors in London of serious differences between the focus of Royal Navy and US Navy strategy. Stark entrusted Clarke with details of War Plan No. 46 (WPL-46), which carried the designation RAINBOW 5 (WPL-46/RAINBOW 5). During the afternoon of November 20, 1940, Clarke reviewed the US Navy plan to focus on supporting future operations in Europe—at the expense of simultaneous efforts in Asia. Clarke said, "He was not allowed to take the Plan away," and Clarke also reported unique access that was "specifically authorized by the Chief of Naval Operations to study it at his leisure and to let the First Sea Lord know of its contents."[1] Clarke was appalled by the concept that the US Navy plan "might take up to two years before Japan itself was struck[, and] virtually disregarded the vulnerability of the South-West Pacific and did not envisage any worthwhile strengthening of the United States Asiatic Fleet."[2]

The transatlantic alliance hinged on resolving differences between the British and American strategies. Clarke explained that "it was about this time it began to be apparent [that] the two parties had divergent views of some moment in regard to the Naval strategy that should be pursued against Japan."[3] In discussions of Royal Navy strategy, Stark encouraged Clarke to convey the US Navy "Estimate of the World Situation."[4] Stark discouraged Clarke from making assumptions about US Navy collaboration by giving special access to key documents of the War Plans Division. Clarke discovered that the Royal Navy "strategic concept for the war against Japan differed materially from that held by the Navy Department."[5] He reported that the basic American strategy "pre-supposed the abandonment of the Philippines and other American outposts in the Western Pacific [and] envisaged an American Navy on the defensive in the preliminary stages of the war, with a subsequent step-by-step advance to the offensive across the central Pacific."[6] Clarke recalled that the

only transitory fly in the ointment in consequence of a return to the charge by the Admiralty on the Singapore issue, as a consequence of which the Chief of Naval Operations [Stark] stated that "unless we were prepared to drop the question of American reinforcement to the Far East, no useful purpose would be served in having staff conversations at all."[7]

For Clarke, the US Navy position on the question of Singapore was "virtually an ultimatum and in consequence the [British] Naval Representatives to come from the United Kingdom were briefed to be accordingly wary."[8]

Observing from his perch on the General Board, King participated in discussions between the British and American staffs for the purposes of providing clear strategic recommendations to the Roosevelt administration. He regularly provided direct advice to the CNO, Stark, and to his subordinates on the OpNav staff—and particularly the directors of communications, intelligence, and war plans—Captains Leigh Noyes, Alan G. Kirk, and Robert Ghormley. In the fall of 1940, Noyes, Kirk, and Ghormley all passed their work to their reliefs, respectively being Captains Joseph R. Redman, Theodore S. "Ping" Wilkinson, and Richmond Kelly "Terrible" Turner. Behind closed-door deliberations with British emissaries, Redman and Turner spoke very strongly about placing the higher priority on American strategic interests.[9]

Anglo-American staff discussions coincided with the ongoing strategic deliberations within the Roosevelt administration. Under the neutrality policies, the planning staffs of the armed services struggled to adapt the War Department "color" plans to fit within the context of a broader global strategy. With conflicts ongoing on the separate fronts of Europe and Asia, army planners joined their naval counterparts to amalgamate the continental focus of existing military plans with the oceanic mission of the naval service. As a key member of the General Board, King directly contributed to efforts to develop the Navy Department revisions of the army "color" into the RAINBOW series.[10] In these efforts, King regularly worked with the president of the Naval War College, Kalbfus, to game the various possibilities, identify strategic opportunities, and advise counterparts in the Navy Department.[11]

British observers struggled to understand the American system of overlapping bureaucracies in shaping strategic relationships. The naval neutrality policies of the Roosevelt administration further complicated ongoing discussions between the Royal Navy and US Navy. Stark asked for recommendations to address the problem from the former CNO, Pratt, and the president of the Naval War College, Kalbfus.[12] Captains Robert Ghormley and then Richmond Kelly Turner concurrently coordinated the RAINBOW plans to synthesize the policies of the Roosevelt administration with the practical strategic objective of using foreign intermediaries as the buffer against possible attack by common enemies of the Axis Tripartite and Soviet Comintern. In evaluating the various RAINBOW options, Stark provided Roosevelt a menu framed within subcategories listed alphabetically as A, B, C, and D.

DOGS OF WAR

Roosevelt and Stark always considered the British Empire as the key element in framing the RAINBOW plans. Stark explained that "if Britain wins decisively against Germany, we can win everywhere; but if she loses the problem confronting us would be very great."[13] He thought, "Should the British Isles then fall we would find ourselves alone and at war with the rest of the world [and] we would be thrown back on our haunches."[14] Stark concluded, "While we might not lose everywhere, we might, possibly, not win anywhere."[15] This prediction became the basis for his recommendation to adopt option "D," which, in navy vernacular, Stark called "PlanDog."[16] Within the Navy Department, WPL-46/

RAINBOW 5 became known unofficially as "Base Plan 1" or "Plan Dog."[17] In essence, Plan Dog set course to "go on the offensive in the Atlantic (against Germany and Italy) while remaining on the defensive in the Pacific."[18]

Stark afforded Clarke special access to secret US Navy plans, which reflected encouraging progress in transatlantic relations. The director of the War Plans Division, Ghormley, received a temporary promotion to three-star rank as the special naval observer in London. Captains Richmond Kelly Turner and Charles "Savvy" Cooke Jr. subsequently handled the delicate chores of planning transatlantic strategy.[19] In dispatches to London, Clarke described Turner as a dangerously overconfident figure. Clarke reported being harangued for nearly two hours during a "monologue by Captain Turner on his views of how the Naval war should be conducted."[20] Others characterized Turner as "the navy's Patton [who] possessed that amalgam of military brilliance, opinionated paranoia, and instinctive courage that leads men into enemy gunfire; but their immoderate self-assertion soured cooperation down the ladder of command."[21]

Stark surprised Richardson with the orders to shift forces to the Atlantic from the Pacific and by concentrating battleship forces in Hawaii. Richardson considered the fleet vulnerable and "out of balance."[22] Richardson insulted Stark in the presence of Roosevelt during meetings held in the White House. "I believed then, and believe now," Richardson thought, that Stark lacked the capacity to serve as CNO "under conditions then existing."[23] Richardson lectured Roosevelt on the inadequacies of Pearl Harbor as a naval port.[24] Richardson directly insulted Roosevelt in a verbal diatribe. Richardson later recalled, "When the President heard my statement, he looked and acted completely crushed. He *was* shocked."[25] Richardson recalled that King "never volunteered any advice or opinion."[26] Still, King recalled barking at Richardson that the "facilities of Pearl Harbor are key to operations beyond Hawaii, and this is exactly why we cannot <u>now</u> sustain operations beyond Midway for any reasonable period of time."[27]

SPARK OF A BLOWTORCH

The challenge in Europe centered on negotiating means to collaborate with the British on American terms. Given the German submarine menace in the Atlantic, the Imperial Japanese Navy threat in the Pacific could not be ignored in shaping the focus of Anglo-American naval collaboration.[28] For King, the path from Hawaii to the Marshall Islands and beyond held equal importance to the oceanic routes leading through Guam to the Solomons and beyond to Australia.[29] The northern routes along Alaska carried lesser strategic importance from a military perspective. Conversely, the islands off Alaska and the West Coast of Canada carried significant political importance from an American perspective.

King considered the oceanic areas between Hawaii and Guam and northward to Kiska as being the key to holding the advantage in the Pacific. He believed that the fleet should conduct operations in the "North Pacific Triangle" between Hawaii, Midway, and Kiska. King recommended rotating forces between Hawaii, the Philippines, and Guam.[30] Through constant operations in the Pacific, the US Navy had the flexibility to augment the Asiatic Fleet or defend the Panama Canal, as required.[31] On the looming question of command, King believed that Richardson had the "brains and ability, but something missing about him."[32] Stark asked King what he thought about Richardson's ideas. In response, King stated that "he himself did not care for them—Betty, you are absolutely right."[33] King finally stated authoritatively that the "fleet should stay in Hawaii, and you should shift ships to and fro as required."[34]

Richardson's personal insults against Stark and emotional outbursts against Roosevelt highlighted the problem of command within the US Navy in very clear terms. Richardson failed to understand the bigger policies, which undermined his ability to implement strategy. At Roosevelt's request, Stark asked the General Board to examine the problem. King subsequently assisted in drafting General Order 143, "Assignment of Units in the Organization of the Seagoing Forces of the US Navy."[35] The order reestablished the Atlantic Fleet and Pacific Fleet, with the Asiatic Fleet all falling squarely under the CNO as "administrative and task organizations."[36] The order further subordinated CinCUS as "an administrative organization for *training purposes only*."[37] CinCUS had authority to exist only when "two or more fleets are concentrated, or are operating in conjunction with each other, the senior Commander in Chief is responsible to the Chief of Naval Operations for joint operations."[38]

Richardson again failed to see the soundly framed policy that informed the strategic intent of General Order 143. Instead, he took the order as a personal insult. He angrily resigned as the CinCUS. Roosevelt acted completely taken aback and asked Richardson to reconsider. Roosevelt asked Richardson to stay on active service and serve as a personal adviser as a member of the General Board. Richardson dutifully accepted—still harboring a grudge against Roosevelt and Stark. In coordinating his departure as CinCUS, Richardson recalled, "Stark had told me that he thought the two best officers in our Navy at the time [were] King and Kimmel."[39] Richardson agreed but added, "Because of his seniority, I thought King should relieve me."[40]

Stark had already coordinated with Nimitz to arrange the new rotation of admirals under General Order 143. Kimmel's appointment to CinCUS produced the desired effect when Adm. Charles P. Snyder, commander of Battleship Forces, submitted his resignation. King later explained, "Snyder was able to stand being subordinate to Richardson, of the Class of 1902, but not to Kimmel, of the Class of 1903."[41] Snyder held four-star rank while serving as commander, Battle Force. Upon transfer, Snyder served on the General Board in two-star rank.[42] Stark nominated Pye to replace Snyder in three-star rank by January 1941.[43] The reduction of the Battle Force to three-star rank enabled the appointment of King to four-star rank as the prospective commander, Atlantic Fleet.

The ongoing Japanese war in Asia coincided with the Nazi and Fascist assaults in Europe, which drove the British and Americans into secret discussions to coordinate strategy in the global maritime arena. Secret meetings between British and American naval staffs set the foundations for prospective collaboration. By 1941, the reestablishment of standing geographical fleet commands in the Pacific and Atlantic signaled American reluctance to reinforce the Asiatic Fleet in the Philippines. The assistant CNO, Ingersoll, and Rear Admiral Russell Willson participated in secret discussions to establish a special communications link between London, Singapore, and Washington.[44] King later noted that Ingersoll "did not like the British."[45] Ingersoll recalled his orders to make "preliminary arrangements, if we could, with the British for joint action in case of war with Japan."[46] Ingersoll reported that the "exchange of information by informal agreement is now taking place [and] the British believe this should be extended."[47]

From within the General Board, King was among the few to recognize the strategic situation in the Pacific as being interconnected with the emergent challenges in the

Atlantic. Cmdr. Malcolm Schoeffel recalled a discussion with King during service in the Ships Movements Division at that time. Schoeffel remembered that King had differing views about the employment of air forces in the Atlantic.[48] King frequently ran afoul of army aviators. He also questioned some of the decisions of Ellis in maneuvering American submarines and aircraft carriers in the Atlantic. In observing the differences between Ellis and King on the question of airpower, Schoeffel noted, "I vividly recall King smiling very kindly [that] you'll have to admit my experience in this matter has been broader than his."[49]

Monitoring the ongoing debates from afar, Roosevelt asked King to explain the differences between military and naval concepts of strategy and tactics. King drew heavily from the works of Sir Julian Corbett in explaining that "history records all too many instances where political objectives have conflicted in time or in space with the correct military (naval) objective."[50] He explained that

> such unfortunate circumstances are usually due to lack of community of ideas and of comprehension between the political leaders and the heads of fighting forces, not infrequently because of excluding the latter from council on the one hand, or on the other, reluctance to speak out without invitation even when present in council.[51]

Seeking assistance in framing neutrality as the peacetime policy by which to frame strategy, Roosevelt embraced the views of King—a polarizing personality widely known among friends and enemies as the "blowtorch."[52] This reputation was etched into a large brass crowbar, inscribed with the words "toothpick for blowtorch."[53]

Roosevelt empowered Stark to overhaul the ranks of the US Navy in anticipation of waging peace operations on multiple war fronts within the global maritime arena. Given the myriad of challenges from Asia to Europe, the German submarine menace in the Atlantic loomed over the broader transatlantic discussion. Under the circumstances, Roosevelt agreed with Stark that "King belonged in the Atlantic [and] Ingersoll might take command of the Pacific Fleet, and Nimitz go to the Asiatic Fleet to relieve Hart."[54] King recalled, "Kimmel's name had been left out, which shows in itself what Stark thought of Kimmel."[55]

ICING ON THE CAKE

Roosevelt orchestrated the bureaucratic nullification of the CinCUS through a slow reorganization of the seagoing fleets. The First World War–era precedence for geographically oriented fleets in the Pacific and Atlantic provided a basis for Roosevelt to reestablish similar organizations to serve as coequal headquarters with the Asiatic Fleet, all falling subordinate to the global authority of the CNO. Working the lines of administration, Stark and Nimitz quietly manipulated the rotation of flag officers through the good offices of BuNav to cut the orders for the incumbent commanders of the nascent establishment of the Pacific and Atlantic fleets. In September 1940, Nimitz informed King of his assignment as the prospective commander, Atlantic Squadron, with an effective date to be determined by December.

Rather than signaling the end of a long seagoing career, the General Board had served as a waypoint for King to await the opportunity to assist in reestablishing the geographic fleet commands. With over forty years on active service and at sixty-two years age at that time (1940), King had two more years to command at sea before facing mandatory retirement.[56] In addition to the Atlantic Squadron, King's name appeared on the slate for the concurrent duty in two-star rank as the commander, Patrolling Forces.[57] In this role, King technically fell under the CNO. However, he also fell under the immediate responsibility of the commander of the Scouting Forces—recently upgraded to three-star status under VAdm. Adolphus Andrews.

By implication, Andrews held technical seniority to King under the organization as it existed when his assignment appeared on the flag rotation roster as the prospective relief for Ellis in the Atlantic Squadron. In a friendly gesture, Andrews wrote King a congratulatory note upon his appointment to command seagoing forces in the Atlantic that "I think we can accomplish much together."[58] King took the congratulatory note as a backhanded way for Andrews to assert his dominance in their relationship. Andrews and other flag officers in positions associated with the CinCUS organization had little information about the yet-unannounced plans to establish the Pacific and Atlantic Fleets under the CNO. King explained that when "I took over this job [the] command now bares [sic] the awkward and unpleasing title, 'Patrol Force, US Fleet,' which I hope to see changed before long to the more appropriate, 'Atlantic Force.'"[59]

Unlike the sunny culture of the West Coast, the East Coast always fell under the stormy shadows of the Washington and New England bureaucratic establishment ashore. Sailors assigned to warships in the Atlantic tended to seek means to maneuver as quickly as possible to the Pacific. Clarifying their task with a clear purpose, King recalibrated his sailors to recognize their mission in the Atlantic as the most important effort in the history of American sea power. On December 17, 1940, Ellis introduced their new commander to the sailors of the flagship *Texas* over the ship's intercom.

Ellis ably prepared the foundations for King to clarify speculation among the sailors of the Atlantic Squadron. On cue, King gruffly warned in his midwestern monotone that "all hands should be prepared for war."[60] King explained that the "youngest and most inexperienced sailor on board is just as important as I am—and the sharks do not care about rank—so I assure you that I shall do my part and you are expected to do yours with equal zest—that is all."[61] With these words, King dared his men to keep up. Indeed, his reputation had already had an effect among the sailors of *Texas*. Elder sailors welcomed the disciplined clarity of King's command style. For the uninitiated, the elders told sea stories about King's sailorly exploits ashore and at sea—striking fear among many shavetail officers and the new boots. In this way, King's speech produced the desired effect of placing all hands on unambiguous notice—to toe the line. The executive officer on *Texas*, Cmdr. Thomas Inglis, later described King as a "tough commander, but one whose strength of character and professional competence reassured us that we were going into a war with a LEADER."[62]

King wore two-star rank upon relieving Ellis in the Atlantic, which fell subordinate to the three- and four-star commanders under the functions of CinCUS. To clarify lines of command, Roosevelt approvingly observed from afar as Stark manipulated the slate—with assistance from Nimitz—to elevate King to a higher rank. Of the eighty-four admirals in the navy of 1941, only four held four-star rank. General Order 143 vested the CNO with clear preeminence over the CinCUS, the commander of the Battle Force, and the Asiatic Fleet.[63] In correspondence, Nimitz directed King to assume the title of [commander,]

Atlantic Fleet, with an effective date of January 11, 1941. Nimitz continued, "This will make it possible for you to be appointed a Vice Admiral on or about 1 February."[64] He explained that the

> President's directive came as a complete surprise to me on 6 January, after we had prepared the various orders incident to the changes in the slate recently directed by the President. You can well imagine that we had to do a considerable amount of work under pressure, which will account for this late letter advising you of the changes, which will affect your future.[65]

Nimitz wrote, "Stark joins me in best wishes and congratulations."[66] In a separate handwritten memorandum affixed to the official letter, Nimitz advised King, "You will need to tell the tailor to add another stripe to your uniform—congratulations."[67] King wrote his friend William Francis Gibbs to explain the circumstances. Thanks to Nimitz fixing the slate, King told Gibbs that his anticipated promotion to four-star rank "was the icing on the cake."[68] Navy secretary Knox concurrently wrote King that "I am still a great deal of a novice in this Navy business [and] I am depending upon you men to help me along in my education."[69]

King held the mandate to employ American sea power in the Atlantic, as part of the broader naval neutrality strategy. The Pan-American Security Zone provided clear lines of demarcation to contain the wars of Europe and Asia. Roosevelt bifurcated the sphere of American military interest at the 180th meridian. In the Pacific, the strategic lines roughly followed the oceanic routes between Kiska, Hawaii, and Guam. In the Atlantic, King stood before the Atlantic Fleet staff with a globe.[70] He dramatically drew a line from Newfoundland to Bermuda and beyond to St. Paul's Rocks southward to the Falkland Islands, around the Horn, and north to the Galápagos, leading to the Revillagigedo Islands on the Pacific approaches to the Panama Canal. King advised the staff that vessels and aircraft "other than those powers having sovereignty over territory in the Western Hemisphere is to be viewed as possibly actuated by an unfriendly interest toward shipping or territory in the Western Hemisphere."[71]

The British were chagrined about the policies of the Roosevelt administration, following clear proclamations concerning the Pan-American Neutrality Zone. Roosevelt publicly rejected the prospect of committing American ground forces to another foreign war. Conversely, he reaffirmed commitments to defend foreign interests with American sea power. From a British perspective, Clarke experienced major difficulties in "reconciling divergent views upon the strategy which should be pursued in the Far East."[72] Clarke explained that the compromise in effect was that "the Americans were not prepared to augment the strength of their Asiatic Fleet from the main Pacific Fleet based upon Hawaii, they did undertake to put increased naval Forces into the Atlantic and so in turn enable us to strengthen our Far Eastern Fleet when the time came, at the expense of our European Naval strength."[73]

Clarke's report prompted the Admiralty to press the Navy Department to focus on Asia. "It is interesting to speculate," Clarke later mused, "how different the situation would have been if the Americans had been prepared to dispatch a portion of their Pacific Fleet to the Far East."[74] "In the interest of secrecy," Clarke noted, "it was not considered possible for Dominion Representatives to attend the actual meetings."[75] Clarke complained about

American secrecy concerning their plans to Royal Australian Navy commander Henry M. Burrell and Royal Canadian Navy commander Philip B. "Barry" German.

British assumptions of supremacy frequently proved counterproductive in shaping strategic relations with the Americans. During informal meetings at Bastedo House, Clarke kept Burrell and German fully apprised throughout 1941.[76] Working purely from memory, Clarke drew up duplicate copies of American plans for Burrell and German, "which they ultimately took back with the form for the information of their Chiefs of Staff."[77] The British campaign to influence American sea power centered on London and Washington, extending to Singapore and Hong Kong. All efforts centered on the Naval Intelligence Division at the Admiralty. Under the shadow of Nelson's statue in Trafalgar Square, the director of naval intelligence, Rear-Admiral Sir John H. Godfrey, pushed his American liaison, US Navy captain Alan Goodrich Kirk, to toe the line. Godfrey took the characteristically British view of Americans. Godfrey treated Americans as affable amateurs in running global maritime affairs.[78]

The past always followed in the wake of ongoing British efforts to bring former colonial interests back under the benevolent rule of Britannia. Godfrey had a tendency to upset Yankee sensibilities, as Kirk recalled that "there was never really any real warmth of friendship between him and me, or between him and most of his officers."[79] Kirk noted that the British "way is to tell everybody exactly what they are supposed to do [and] this is the result of wireless or radio."[80] Kirk characterized Godfrey as "highly strung[,] which made him unnecessarily combative."[81] Given nuances of personality and naval rank, Godfrey annoyed Kirk about English grammar and proper speech. In responding to a question, Kirk recalled saying, "I think I should 'mull' it over."[82] Horrified by the violation of the King's English, Godfrey scolded Kirk by stating that is a "word we do not use."[83] Godfrey frequently employed the "royal we," which greatly annoyed the Yankee sensibilities of Kirk.[84]

The relationship between Godfrey and Kirk reflected the differences of British and American perspective. Godfrey attempted to use intelligence exchanges as an inroad to *influence* American strategy. Kirk accepted the information to *inform* American strategy. His replacement as US naval attaché in London, Capt. Charles H. Lockwood, continued the discussions. He carried the relationship further by requesting a submarine-qualified officer to serve as a liaison to the OIC. Soon thereafter, Lt. Lewis D. Follmer arrived for duty as an assistant naval attaché. After 1940, Lockwood assigned Follmer to serve as an observer within the submarine-tracking rooms of the Admiralty in London and those connecting in the network down in Portsmouth and up in Liverpool.[85]

Service on the General Board placed King at the center of strategic efforts to fuse British collaboration with American neutrality policy. Royal Navy rear-admiral Charles C. Little rekindled previous associations with King, Stark, Knox, and many other American naval officers in the Washington area. In July 1941, Little reported that the "number of British in Washington [exceeded] the numbers that were here in 1814 when we burned the capitol."[86] Little observed that the "US Navy are not in the mood to openly take advice from us."[87] British Admiralty Delegation (BAD) liaisons, like Royal Navy rear-admiral James W. S. Dorling, warned British counterparts to understand that Americans "are not English, they are proud of being American; that they delight in frankness and openness, they detest and suspect reserve or any hint of condescension."[88]

The imperial mindset of British observers in Washington provided an advantage in relations with the entrepreneurial dynamics of American culture. Dorling noted that

Americans "are very susceptible to generous praise and that a word of praise will pave the way for a helpful suggestion or comment."[89] Dorling used transactional diplomacy. He considered the Americans as vulnerable to a "good bargain."[90] Dorling described Americans as susceptible to offers for assistance in noting that "if help is required[,] one must try to help them."[91] In the broadest terms, Dorling suggested, "It is personal contacts and friendship that count most in the long run."[92]

The transatlantic negotiations between London and Washington proceeded behind closed doors and in the absence of sufficient coordination with other key stakeholders. The America-Britain-Canada-1 (ABC-1) discussions happened in the absence of representatives sufficiently empowered to speak for such key partners as Australia and New Zealand. Following the ABC-1 discussions of March 1941, British representatives with the "Military Mission" assumed a new title as members of the "Joint Staff Mission in Washington."[93] Later, the Royal Navy subsection of the Joint Staff Mission adopted the title of British Admiralty Delegation. Members of BAD had strict orders to operate "under cover."[94] Under ABC-1, the BAD established the Mid-Ocean Meeting Point (MOMP) in accordance with the Pan-American Security Zone. "I have to say that although the ABC-1 plan had been developing from early January 1941," King later recalled, "I wasn't able to see the plan (believe it or not); anything I knew about these plans I picked up casually."[95]

Secrecy concerning transatlantic strategy hindered efforts to synthesize British operations with the American neutrality strategy. Under ABC-1, the Canadian prime minister, Mackenzie King, similarly lacked full details of the arrangements between Churchill and Roosevelt. Excluded from the ABC-1 discussions in Washington, the Canadian prime minister outright rejected the strategic concept of dividing the Atlantic Ocean between European, Asiatic, and American spheres of responsibility.[96] To soothe relations with the Canadian government, the First Sea Lord, Pound, created the Mid-Ocean Escort Force (MOEF). Under this arrangement, Royal Navy and Royal Canadian Navy forces fell under the strategic control of the US Navy within the Pan-American Neutrality Zone out to the oceanic Change of Operations Point (CHOP) lines, such as MOMP.[97]

CANADIAN CHILL

Given past imperial connections with London, the major American naval commands in Ottawa and Washington struggled for control over the transatlantic relationship. Traditional ties with the Royal Navy created false assumptions about the relationship with the Royal Canadian Navy. As chief of the Naval Staff, RAdm. Percy Nelles claimed the right to control operations in the Northwest Atlantic. He used the Naval Service Headquarters (NSHQ) in Ottawa to coordinate Royal Canadian Navy efforts. Through his emissaries in London and Washington, Nelles expected equal partnership in the grander scheme of global Allied command.

Canadians took a very chilly view of the British, seeking to foster closer ties with American cousins to the south. Embedded with the BAD in Washington, Cmdr. Barry German relied upon the assistance of Royal Navy captain Clarke in following the ABC-1 negotiations with their American counterparts.[98] This arrangement fell under the British caveat that the Royal Canadian Navy would operate in "waters and territories in which Canada assumes responsibility for the strategic direction of military forces, *as may be* defined in United States–Canada joint agreements."[99] In related correspondence, Pound invited Nelles to establish the Newfoundland Escort Force (NEF).[100]

Pound allowed the Navy Department to claim strategic control over maritime operations within the broadly framed Pan-American Neutrality Zone. He simultaneously encouraged Nelles and the Royal Canadian Navy to negotiate separate regional command relationships with the US Navy in American waters. This provision established grounds for the Joint Canadian–United States Base Defense Plan (BP-1), which defined basic provisions for US Navy ships to operate from Canadian ports in Nova Scotia and New Brunswick. The complex arrangements with Canada and the Navy Department became further complicated as the War Department stipulated that the US Army controlled land and air forces within the American sphere of influence. The US Army chief of staff, Marshall, claimed "paramount command in sea areas or along coastal frontiers."[101] King retorted, "I can only fall back on the basic premise that if the area is primarily 'sea-going'—which includes island areas—it is <u>Navy</u>."[102]

The focus of US Navy operations in the Northwest Atlantic hinged on air and surface escort coverage within the primary shipping lanes. In January 1941, King requested RAdm. Arthur L. Bristol to assume command in Canadian waters. Concurrently, the Tenth Naval District commander, RAdm. Raymond A. Spruance, flew to Washington from Puerto Rico. King designated Spruance as the commander, Caribbean Patrol, "because I can make good use of him and, as well, have him feel that he is an integral member of the 'sea forces' in the Caribbean."[103] By March, Spruance assumed his new role in Puerto Rico, as Bristol broke his flag at Hampton Roads in the destroyer-tender USS *Prairie* (AD-15). King vested Bristol with the title "Commander, Atlantic Support Force." Bristol then sailed in *Prairie* to Newfoundland and established headquarters facilities ashore in Argentia.[104] King designated Bristol as commander, Task Force 24 (TF-24).[105] Bristol's mission somewhat upset relations among Canadian naval commanders.

Convoy escort operations involving Canadian warships fell under the immediate control of NSHQ in Ottawa. Cdre. Leonard W. Murray established NEF headquarters at St. John's in Newfoundland. In operations at sea, Murray retained full freedom to operate independently for offensive operations while working together with the US Navy through "command by cooperation."[106] Under the circumstances, Bristol and Murray worked in the spirit of collaboration—at the center of a complicated relationship between the Admiralty, NSHQ, and the Navy Department. The tactical guidelines appeared within the Atlantic Convoy Instructions (ACI), providing detailed instructions for merchant skippers to operate within the context of a convoy formation.

The Admiralty frequently installed retired naval officers to keep fellow merchant seamen in line as convoy commodores. Having knowledge of Royal Navy procedures, the convoy commodores used the ACI as a basis for collaborating with escort group (EG) and support group (SG) commanders. The ACI generally required EG skippers to establish a defensive bubble surrounding merchant convoys. The SG skippers operated independently from convoys on "hunter-killer" operations against enemy targets.[107] Royal Navy and Royal Canadian Navy commanders developed "exhaustion" tactics against enemy submarines.[108]

THE CRUEL SEA

Convoy operations were among the most complex administrative naval missions to coordinate in examining the relationship between headquarters ashore and the skippers at sea. The influx of civilians within the rigid ranks of the British navy created friction between "long-service officers and ratings[, who] were called 'the caretakers' by their 'hostilities-only' shipmates." Royal Navy professionals struggled with the "delicate balance between stifling orthodoxy and ineffective amateurism."[109] Drawing from personal experience in convoy operations during 1941, reserve lieutenant Nicholas Monserrat lambasted the reports received from the Admiralty, which indicated the limits of intelligence. Monserrat described "the chinks in their armor to safeguard against so many circling enemies."[110] Monserrat recalled the frustration of receiving information late. "'There are nine U-boats in your area,' said the Admiralty at dusk that night," Monserrat noted, with a wry sense of Merseyside irony, "as generous as ever."[111]

In convoy operations, Royal Navy doctrine encouraged convoy escort commanders to attack enemy contacts. Cmdr. Donald MacIntyre explained the relationship between the OIC in London and escort operations in the North Atlantic. He acknowledged that Allied antisubmarine efforts hinged on the "U-boat tracking room at the Admiralty, under the direction of Rodger Winn."[112] "Time and again information was passed out to convoys giving the position of U-boats with amazing accuracy," McIntyre explained, "far greater than the originators themselves ever claimed for their estimates."[113] Hunter-killer escort tactics indeed followed in the "true nature of the 'Nelsonial' spirit."[114] Like MacIntyre, other escort skippers, like Captain Johnny Walker and Commander Peter Gretton, drew from their personal combat experience to refine Royal Navy convoy doctrine.[115] Royal Navy vice-admiral Sir T. Hugh Binney argued that "the best position for anti-submarine vessels is in company with a convoy . . . every anti-submarine vessel with sufficiently good sea-keeping qualities should be employed with convoys rather than dispersed in hunting units."[116]

The Royal Navy developed new procedures for escort commanders to mitigate offensive submarine group tactics. Evaluating experience from multiple convoy battles, Sir Patrick Blackett used methods in operational research (OR) and decision analysis to offer conclusions, which suggested that the hunter-killer tactics proved counterproductive.[117] Blackett influenced the Admiralty decision to route convoys on evasive courses. As a result, the Royal Navy adopted the principle of the "safe and timely" arrival of convoys, as described in the Western Approaches Convoy Instructions (WACIs).[118]

Admiralty directives conflicted with those employed within the Navy Department and among the seagoing forces of the US Navy. Capt. Lewis Denfeld submitted a scathing analysis of the Royal Navy convoy system. Denfeld drafted the report from experiences in London and afloat with Royal Navy warships in the Atlantic. Among his many critiques, Denfeld found that the Admiralty placed "too many ships in convoy [and that the] size of convoys vary from 30 to as many as 90 ships."[119] "This tends to cut down speed of convoy as a whole and makes convoys very unwieldy, especially when only a few escort ships are available." He continued that the "round about route taken to reach final destination causes loss of so many ship days that the same result is obtained by the Axis powers that would be reached if more ships were sunk."[120] Denfeld further suggested that the Admiralty method of "safe and timely" arrival by rerouting ships wasted fuel and time. "It took thirteen days," he argued, to "make what would normally in peacetime be a seven-day trip."[121] Denfeld criticized the Royal Navy tactic of evasive routing that "it is realized that the British have a hard task to perform, and their Navy is spread very thin [but] it is essential that the largest number of ships possible reach the British Isles in the shortest possible time."[122]

CHAPTER 17
King's Speech

British and Canadian forces struggled to coordinate wartime operations with American associates under the neutrality policies of the Roosevelt administration. Clarifying the strategic objectives for 1941, King recommended "'radical' [and] 'drastic' action—by the British—with our help NOW."[1] Given the ongoing undeclared war at sea, King admitted that "I'm afraid the citizenry will have to learn the bitter truth that war is not waged with words or promises, or vituperation vide Winston Churchill's 'blood sweat and tears.'" King coldly believed that "there are grim facts to be faced [and] the sooner the better."[2] With these unhappy views about the task at hand for the Atlantic Squadron, King wore temporary three-star rank by January 1941. Having received the insignia worn by his late mentor Adm. Mayo from Mayo's son, King appeared in four-star rank upon reestablishing the Atlantic Fleet under the big guns of the battleship *Texas* on February 1, 1941.

King and the General Board quietly set the administrative cornerstones for the restoration of geographic fleets in the Pacific and Atlantic, thereby enabling neutrality policies to align with Roosevelt's global strategy with American sea power. With his four-star flag flying above, King read his orders and then mused, "Some twenty years ago, the United States Atlantic Fleet ceased to exist as such."[3] King noted that the "significance of the fact that there is again a United States Atlantic Fleet should be a matter of satisfaction and pride in the fleet that its commander-in-chief is to fly a four-star flag."[4] He stipulated that this "new status and these new honors require of all hands—from admiral to seaman— renewed and continued efforts shall be a fleet in fact as well as in name."[5] King emphasized that "we must all realize that we are no longer in a peacetime status and have no time to lose in preparing our ships and ourselves to be ready in every way for the serious work that is close aboard."[6] In a parting shot, King described the First Marine Division "as an integral and important part of the Atlantic Fleet."[7]

King understood the military task of waging peace by placing sailors on full battle readiness to enforce American neutrality in the global maritime arena. The fallacy of peace always faded into the backdrop of maritime wars on the unrelenting oceanic commons whenever foreign conflicts unfolded ashore. Under the circumstances, King issued the Atlantic Fleet directive "Making the Best of What We Have" to calibrate sailors for the mission. King explained, "*When* [the] existing emergency becomes intensified—develops into a state of war—all of us will accept cheerfully and willingly the difficulties and discomforts as well as the hazards and the dangers with which we shall then be confronted."[8] He directed them to stop the practice of using white paint on the boatswain's lace (macramé) adorning the rails and ladders. King issued orders to reduce the variety of paint colors and other solvents, noting the potential fire hazards in combat conditions. King ordered ships to run in radio silence, restricting wireless communications to single-sentence directive transmissions to King, only when any given situation required *him* to take personal action.[9]

American warships operated at the nexus of peace and war, as King rallied the Atlantic Fleet to recalibrate with an equal sense of purpose. King summarily reassigned individual skippers for issuing "orders to subordinates to follow orders."[10] His aide, Lt. John R. Topper, observed King's methods from close quarters. Topper described King as a "seagoing man at heart [and he] concisely spelled out the duties and responsibilities of members of his staff."[11] Topper explained that King "was a Naval Officer first and last." Topper thought the "glimpse of a smile from King was equal to a real belly laugh from the average person, yet those around him knew when he was pleased, and the world knew when he was displeased."[12] Topper explained that King "never became chummy with anyone [and he] hated signs of stupidity and could be vitriolic in his expressions."[13]

King took his visible place on the deck to govern the forward progress of the Atlantic Fleet, empowering his trusted circle of subordinates on the staff to act on his personal authority. Individual skippers fully understood King's approach, using the staff to manage the seagoing operations of the fleet. Topper developed special rapport with King in conversations about issues of common historical interest. History provided a neutral place for King to enjoy informal conversations with subordinates without violating the hierarchical traditions of rank and seniority. Topper explained that King "could repeat the minutest details of naval and land battles fought centuries ago [and] discuss the leaders of history almost from the beginning, touching on their main strength and especially their weaknesses."[14] In reflection, Topper celebrated King as the "greatest naval officer of all time[, and] I wish there were some naval hero in history to compare, American or foreign, with this unusual man [but] I know of no one."[15]

King ran a very taut ship, although he understood that the art of command centered on the intangible human factor. Topper described King as a "man of destiny[,] and his goals were set to prepare himself fully for whatever that destiny proved to be."[16] Topper explained that King "had steeled himself to be tough and properly disciplined himself to meet any situation."[17] King told Topper that "one should keep his social and official life well separated."[18] Members of his inner circle knew King as a family man—deeply devoted to his wife and large family of seven children and fourteen grandchildren. He also kept close company with his brother-in-law and sons-in-law in the US Army. Among others known within the ranks as "King's men," Lt. Wallis Morris Beakley, described King as a true family man. Beakley explained, "I knew them better than the Admiral."[19]

King expected subordinates to follow the example by making informed decisions without first asking for permission. "God pity the staff member or Task Commander who did not show initiative and fully carry out his responsibilities," Topper warned.[20] He then explained that the "quickest way to get the Admiral perturbed was to more or less *ask* him *how* to carry out an assignment."[21] The chief of staff, Capt. Oscar C. Badger, managed King's expectations until his detachment to command USS *North Carolina* (BB-55). Capt. Olaf M. Hustvedt then assumed the duty of running the staff. Topper described the role of the chief of staff under King as being the "'good cop,' so that King could be the 'bad cop' and not the other way around."[22]

Topper observed King's role as being the task master among the various personalities on the Atlantic Fleet staff. According to Topper, the chief of staff had the duty of being the "'glad hander' who was to ease the pain if the Admiral had to do a bit of lashing."[23]

Topper recalled explaining this perception to King, who then "smiled a little and said, 'We must have one non-sundowner on the staff, and I have made that person my Chief of Staff.'"[24] Unlike other seagoing commanders, King kept his Atlantic Fleet staff small—to embark any ship at any time. Low recalled that service as the operations officer under King required "proper sense of humor and of the ridiculous [since] King had a keen sense of such matters."[25]

King trained Atlantic Fleet sailors to take appropriate action and adapt to surprises. He used routines to replicate the possibility of an enemy attack at anytime. Embracing his role as the crazy man in the bridge, King played the old trick of mixing up the daily routine with uniform inspections, which became legendary among Atlantic Fleet sailors. King ordered the "Cossack Uniform" with white tops and blue trousers to show "who can prescribe the uniform."[26] Having read about the development of khaki uniforms in the Royal Navy in the Age of Sail, King experimented with using coffee to adapt the working white uniforms of the US Navy.[27] He ordered the crew on *Texas* to dye their uniforms in coffee, which resulted in the sailors turning out in a wide spectrum of different shades of brown. Just as Royal Navy captain William Bligh directed the crew of HMAV *Bounty* to dance every morning during their infamous voyage of 1789, pettiness served a practical purpose for King in preparing the Atlantic Fleet for war in 1941.[28]

King expected his subordinates to act without asking permission, in accordance with their mission. Procedures provided order to the chaos of shipboard operations. The implied tasks always dictated the expectations of King. Journalists covering King's performance as Atlantic Fleet commander noted that whenever "something has been done wrong, King has simply to call the offender, ask him to tell exactly what he did, and then utter one icy word, 'why?'" An enlisted sailor told Joseph J. Thorndike of *Life* magazine that "King is never unjust or unreasonable . . . he bears down hard on faults of negligence or laziness [but] if an officer has done his best, even though a poor best, he is not blamed."[29] Sailors thought of King as "a good man to a good man [and] we gets along fine."[30]

Thorndike perceptively noted the traditions of the service and other historical influences upon King. Sailors embraced his quirks, which always carried a practical purpose. Thorndike explained that King "likes funny movies and Napoleon."[31] On movie nights, he sat with sailors and, whenever the comedy failed to meet their high standards, King led the way by being first to leave. King also showed himself as a "great student of military history and can out-argue many a general on the battles of the Civil War."[32] King reveled in the Napoleonic era, which *Life* journalists highlighted in glowing detail. History served the purpose of inspiring sailors to act in accordance with the high expectations and example of their commander, as King told sea stories about Jervis and Nelson. Sailors understood the point when King told an especially animated story about Jervis when giving the order for "mutineers to be strung up."[33]

King fostered unity of effort among the captains and individual sailors of the fleet by setting an example, which resonated with all hands. Thorndike reported in *Life* that "everything he uses has four stars [as] rigidly fixed by Navy protocol[,] and Admiral King is a stickler for strict observance."[34] As a fly on the bulkhead, Thorndike also recognized the role of King's staff in creating the aura of command. Hustvedt and Low carried the brunt in daily relations with King, although Commanders Donald B. Duncan and Ruthven Libby assisted in coordinating air and surface operations of the Atlantic Fleet, along with Lt. Cmdr. Stanton B. Dunlap. Standing out among the submariners and aviators on the staff of eleven officers, the fleet Marine officer, Maj. Oman T. Pfeiffer, coordinated amphibious planning on the staff, later admitting, "Admiral King was very partial towards Marines."[35]

Duty with King always focused on seagoing operations, since he expected the Atlantic Fleet to perform with utmost efficiency as if at war. Topper recalled how King instructed warship skippers to maintain full readiness while tied to the pier with "fuel, supplies and ammunition, and have a crew on board at all times sufficient to take the ship to sea."[36] His staff rarely went ashore to relax while in port, always ready to go into battle. King kept morale by indirect means. He empowered the chief steward, Narisco Arce, to use his connections with Filipino cousins to ensure the Atlantic Fleet staff always had the best mess facilities. First Class Steward George Perry, a Black sailor, held the special trust of King. Low observed that Perry and King shared a common sense of humor. His US Marine orderlies, like Pvt. Roger C. Friend, helped keep King on his daily schedule.[37]

The Atlantic Fleet staff matured into an efficient bureaucratic machine, which enabled King to implement his will through subordinate commanders. He drew from personal experiences in the First World War to orchestrate operations with intelligence. Helping to evaluate the dispatches, the fleet intelligence officer of the Atlantic Fleet, Lt. Robert Weeks, and his assistants, Lieutenants Charles B. Lanman and George Russell, kept King apprised of the latest intelligence developments.[38] Among all the intelligence officers on active service in the US Navy in the spring of 1941, Weeks stood out as being among the most knowledgeable on questions concerning the sources and methods of British intelligence.

Weeks understood the nuances of strategic collaboration between the Admiralty and Navy Department. He carried the added burden of keeping King apprised of any major developments in the undeclared quasi war at sea. Just before reporting for duty with King in the Atlantic Fleet, Weeks briefly visited the British cryptographic center on the grounds of Bletchley Park. Weeks held responsibility as the senior representative with the assistance of reserve lieutenant (j.g.) Prescott Currier. Weeks and Currier traveled with US Army captains Abraham Sinkov and Frank Rowlett. However, Weeks and Currier reported to Ghormley, SpeNavO, and they *did not* hold the same mission as their army counterparts during their coincidental visit to Bletchley Park.[39] The US Navy specifically *did not* establish a stable presence on the grounds of Bletchley Park, unlike the US Army.[40]

Weeks and Currier traced the connections leading from Bletchley Park to the OIC in London. The pair worked closely with British analysts in the convoy-routing subdivision and the adjacent submarine-tracking room. British methods for synthesizing naval operations with intelligence informed the recommendations provided by Weeks. Beyond analytical aspects, he similarly understood the technological aspects in evaluating British information as derived from German naval communications. Weeks had received detailed briefings from British cryptographers before returning from the European front with a paper copy of the German naval Enigma cipher machine.[41] In the spring of 1941, Weeks similarly educated King and the Atlantic Fleet staff about the nuances of German naval communications procedures and submarine tactics. Weeks explained British convoy-routing and antisubmarine tactics. Having qualifications for command in submarines, Weeks worked closely with Low on the Atlantic Fleet staff to coordinate American submarine and surface escort operations.[42] Weeks established a rudimentary OIC equivalent for the Atlantic Fleet inside the Communications Annex on the grounds of the Naval War College.[43]

The Atlantic Fleet operated on intelligence cues provided by the Admiralty and through the war rooms of the Navy Department. The BAD liaison in Washington, Clarke, regularly coordinated with Weeks in Newport to synthesize operations with intelligence within the seagoing Atlantic Fleet staff. Every morning, Weeks reviewed incoming message traffic and official correspondence within the offices provided ashore at the Naval War College. King relied heavily upon the administrative support and unique resources provided by the Naval War College. His longtime friend and former superior four-star commander, RAdm. Edward C. Kalbfus, reverted in rank to two-star status for a second tour as president.

The staffs of King and Kalbfus worked together in the communications center of the Naval War College. Weeks and Low kept a regular Atlantic Fleet presence at a desk in the plotting room on the second floor of the wooden building, which overlooked the approaches to the Narragansett Bay. With the staff embarked in the flagship, the Naval War College also served as the administrative headquarters of the Atlantic Fleet ashore. King kept an aircraft reserved at the Quonset Naval Air Station, and the train station at Kingston provided efficient means for King to travel from Rhode Island to Washington whenever circumstances required. King always kept the Atlantic Fleet ready to sail into harm's way. Between port calls in Newport, King kept a regular rotation between Argentia and Cuba while coordinating the quasi war in the Atlantic. The Naval War College staff augmented the Atlantic Fleet to aid in planning operations with intelligence. King routinely used the campus on Coaster's Harbor Island, and he still had access to his home ashore in Newport. Still, King lived with his sailors on board his flagship.

King earlier requested the battleship *Pennsylvania* for service as the flagship of the Atlantic Fleet. His recollections of Mayo and the First World War served as one symbolic justification for his request, in conjunction with ongoing transatlantic discussions between the Admiralty and Navy Department. The request to release *Pennsylvania* from its function as the flagship for operations in the Pacific was denied, so King accepted the recently overhauled cruiser *Augusta* as the replacement for *Texas* as the flagship of the Atlantic Fleet. Fresh from a major refit after being damaged by Japanese artillery fire in Chinese waters, *Augusta* appeared majestic as the newly designated flagship of the Atlantic Fleet under King—at anchor in the Narragansett Bay. Seeing the warship from his office on Coaster's Harbor Island, the president of the Naval War College asked in a radio signal, "At what time may Rear Admiral Kalbfus call upon Admiral King." In a gesture of mutual respect, Kalbfus received the response that "Admiral King will call upon the President of the Naval War College at whatever time it is convenient for the President to receive him."[44]

Tradition inspired the unwritten rules of service protocol as practiced by seagoing practitioners of King's navy. The president of the Naval War College carried the distinction of carrying forward the illuminated history and futuristic vision of Luce. In the historical mind of King, the future always centered on studying the past with an applied purpose. For this reason, he always viewed the educational functions of the War College as fundamental to the operations of the fleet in both peace and war. The honor of carrying the legacy of Luce likewise established the president of the Naval War College as being among the most important jobs in the American fleet. The vision of sea power always required an understanding that "ships are inanimate tools without men working the lines or handling the helm[, and] war college is where the apprentice may mature into the master tradesman."[45]

Kalbfus and King frequently discussed the strategic challenges involved with employing naval forces in peacetime with the desired operational objective of avoiding war. [46] Since the "fundamental principle of war," as defined by Kalbfus in *Sound Military Decision*, focused on the "attainment of an end," King evaluated Atlantic Fleet plans with these "rules of thumb":

1. Suitability of the end in view, as determined by the factor of the appropriate effect desired

2. Feasibility of the effort required, as determined by the means available and opposed, influenced by the factor of the physical conditions prevailing in the field of action

3. Acceptability of the results of the effort involved, as determined by the factor of the consequences as to costs, which factors are in turn dependent on each other[47]

Unlike the emphasis US Army planners placed upon the various "Principles of War," the doctrinal ideas of Kalbfus centered on attaining clear results.[48] US naval thinkers had singular focus in attaining the *fundamental* end goal.[49]

King embraced methodology prescribed by Kalbfus in *Sound Military Decision* in planning Atlantic Fleet operations. King drew from his readings of history, taking note of the works compiled by his friend, retired Capt. Dudley W. Knox, which highlighted the strategic lessons of the "quasi-wars" of the past.[50] He kept the home port of the Atlantic Fleet close to the action at the Naval War College. The position provided excellent access to the North Atlantic with the railheads between Boston and New York close by from Kingston station. An assistant with the Atlantic Fleet staff, Lt. Dashiell L. Madeira, remembered that King maintained his flight status by flying solo from the Naval Air Station in Quonset, Rhode Island. Madeira recalled King griping, "I've got to go to Washington again [to] straighten out those dumb bastards once more."[51]

BRANDISHING SWORDS

The Roosevelt administration pursued an aggressive diplomatic strategy by amplifying the influence of American sea power. By 1941, the outdated "color plans," such as ORANGE, had been superseded by the RAINBOW series. Coincident arrangements made in Singapore during the American-Dutch-British (ADB) meetings failed to synchronize with agreements made under ABC-1.[52] Given these complexities, none of the American commanders in the Philippines—or their British counterparts in Singapore and China—had full understanding of the changes made under the RAINBOW series. Only on the authority of Stark as the CNO did the director of war plans, Turner, allow access to changes made to plans associated with the RAINBOW series in keeping with the secret aspects of ABC-1 and ADB discussions in the spring of 1941.[53]

The defunct provisions of War Plan ORANGE centered on defending the Philippines by withdrawing ground forces to establish strategic bastions and reinforced tactical positions to await reinforcement from the US Navy. In the Asiatic Fleet, Admirals Harry E. Yarnell and his successor, Thomas C. Hart, lacked a full understanding of the changes made under the RAINBOW plans. Making matters more complex, Hart inherited the challenge of working with retired two-star general Douglas MacArthur in his ambiguous role as Roosevelt's representative to the Philippine national government. MacArthur regularly invoked his former US Army status while wearing his hat with formal rank as a field marshal in the Philippine National Army.[54]

Imperial Japanese aggression in Asia inspired transatlantic discussions to coordinate Royal Navy and US Navy operations in the region. In April 1941, the Soviet-Japanese Neutrality Pact complicated the strategic calculus. In June, the invasion by Nazi Germany and Fascist Italy into the Soviet Union caught imperial Japanese strategists by surprise. The failure of the Axis Tripartite to develop into a mature alliance appeared within the subtext when Roosevelt invited his friend Ambassador Kichisaburō Nomura for drinks at the White House on July 24, 1941. Roosevelt invited the retired CNO, Pratt, to participate in the discussion. Roosevelt and Pratt had befriended Nomura when he served in admiral's rank as the Japanese naval attaché in Washington during the First World War.[55]

Roosevelt considered Nomura to be an honest broker in negotiations with Emperor Hirohito and the imperial Japanese regime. The former CNO, Pratt, participated in the discussions with Nomura.[56] In their discussions, Nomura agreed that "after some years the Navies of Japan and of the United States would be cooperating against Hitler as a common enemy."[57] In response, Roosevelt proposed a transpacific partnership between imperial Japan and the United States.[58] Roosevelt explained that the "policy of the United States in allowing oil to go to Japan had succeeded in keeping war out of the South Pacific, 'for our own good, for the good of the defense of Great Britain, and the freedom of the seas.'"[59]

Roosevelt invited Stark to explain the US Navy shift from the Pacific to the Atlantic in the discussions with Nomura. In explaining the rationale for the move, Roosevelt mused about the opportunity to form a naval alliance among Japan, Britain, and America. Over cocktails, Roosevelt told Nomura that the "average American citizen could not understand why his government was permitting Japan to be furnished with oil in order that such oil might be utilized by Japan in carrying on her purposes of aggression."[60] Nomura offered an encouraging response that "he who continuously brandishes the sword eventually kills himself."[61]

The meeting between Roosevelt and Nomura sparked additional efforts to use American sea power as a stabilizing influence. On the day after the meetings at the White House, King received a surprise telephone summons to meet Roosevelt at his New York residence in Hyde Park on July 25, 1941. "Secrecy remained a major factor," King later recalled, "for the chief consideration was to keep any knowledge of the meeting from the Axis powers, at least until the participants were safely on their way home."[62] King delegated the task of coordinating tactical plans to the Atlantic Fleet staff. Low and Weeks coordinated the operation with intelligence in sailing Roosevelt in complete secrecy on board *Augusta* to the enclosed anchorage at Argentia.[63] The British Imperial Staff and Joint Chiefs stood in unison with their American counterparts standing behind the chairs of Churchill and Roosevelt on HMS *Prince of Wales*.

The historical legacies of the British Empire influenced the future policy objectives of the Roosevelt administration. King understood the objective of American sea power as being centered on avoiding actual war and using peacetime operations to prepare for winning any future war as quickly and decisively as possible. To these ends, British and American sailors mingled and danced together to music provided by the ship's bands. The lively swing music still failed to obscure the somber purpose of the Argentia meetings between Churchill and Roosevelt.[64] Given the spirit of transatlantic unity, Churchill and Roosevelt failed to extend an invitation to their counterpart in Canada, Prime Minister Mackenzie King.

STANDING IN THE SHADOWS OF NELSON

The absence of Commonwealth and Dominion representatives at the historic seaborne meeting of Churchill and Roosevelt symbolized other problems bubbling below the cheery façade of the transatlantic relationship. Churchill calculated Anglo-American strategy against the balance of Parliament, just as Roosevelt faced the domestic politics that fueled debates in Congress. His contentious relationship with the Supreme Court also loomed over the Roosevelt administration. The civil-military divides baked into the Constitution defined American defensive preparations among various state and local authorities in American coastal areas in the hot summery months of 1941.[65]

The differences between land forces ashore and seagoing forces appeared within the subtext of problems at the topmost tiers of the American command.[66] King described the situation as being "all fowled [sic] up."[67] He confided in journalists that he "was disgusted with [the] stupidity of the British Navy."[68] King grew weary of British assumptions of past supremacy, but also of the "messed-up situation in Washington."[69] King attempted to bring order to the chaos by consolidating overlapping chains of command.

Further complicating the relationships for King, the naval district commander controlled the Naval Reserve and seagoing Auxiliary Forces of the Atlantic Fleet.[70] Among other competitors for command, Andrews remoted to two stars as the commander, North Atlantic Naval Coastal Frontier—with headquarters located in downtown New York City. King asserted his four-star rank in relations with Andrews. Similarly, he claimed control over seagoing forces of Admirals Raymond A. Spruance and James L. Kauffman—as the respective Naval District commanders of Puerto Rico and the Gulf Coast Frontier.

King framed the mission of the Atlantic Fleet as being focused first on implementing neutrality policies within the Pan-American Neutrality Zone. By implication, King placed the Atlantic Fleet on course to support British, Dutch, and Free French forces while simultaneously guarding lines of communications in American waters. In 1941, the Danes invited American forces to establish a neutral presence in Iceland. In turn, King appointed his friend Kauffman to command Task Force 19, with Capt. Allan G. Kirk in charge of the convoy operations to Iceland. Kirk carried responsibility for the amphibious landings of the First Provisional Brigade under US Marine colonel John Marston.[71] The operation under King set new precedents for the US Marines in amphibious operations.[72] In the summer of 1941, King also directed Kirk to develop plans to support an expedition to Africa. The ambassador to Vichy France, Leahy, initiated negotiations to deploy American neutrality forces to bases along North Africa.[73]

British naval escorts provided overall coverage to enable American amphibious forces to land without significant difficulty in Iceland. King selected Kauffman to command the operations in Iceland for strategic purposes. His son, Draper, earned a heroic reputation as an RNVR officer during the London Blitz. On July 4, 1941, the younger Kauffman appeared in RNVR uniform under the statues of Nelson and Washington in Trafalgar Square. Given his background, the younger Kauffman's words carried great significance when he declared that "it seems to me that it is we [Americans] who should be grateful to [Britain] for the wonderful way they are mending the Anglo-American front line and keeping a barrier between the Huns and ourselves."[74] Having spoken on behalf of the British, the younger Kauffman subsequently resigned his RNVR commission to join the reserve ranks of the US Navy.

The American outpost in Iceland provided an ideal launch point for US naval aviators to establish a constant presence over maritime lines of communication. King empowered the elder Kauffman to employ American surface and air forces in Iceland to operate in the "Black Gap" of the North Atlantic. US naval aviators reported contacts with German submarines in open communications. Such information enabled British and American forces to work in tandem against Axis vessels in the Atlantic.[75] King trusted his subordinates to use their best judgment in performing their mission.[76] RAdm. David McDougal LeBreton assumed command over the battleships. Journalists described him as a "greying, bandy-legged bantam . . . disparagers say that he is adept at polishing topside apples."[77] King selected RAdm. Arthur B. Cook to command the aircraft carrier division, which centered on USS *Ranger* (CV- 4) and the newly commissioned USS *Wasp* (CV-7). Rotating between the Pacific and Atlantic, *Lexington* and *Saratoga* maintained station in the Caribbean and off Hampton Roads.

Neutrality policies set the strategic focus for waging peace operations in the Atlantic seascapes, which nominally fell to the responsibility of King. Military District commanders and civilian officials regularly ignored King, just as their Naval District and commercial merchant constituencies did in relations with the Atlantic Fleet. The thankless responsibility of waging peace required all hands and for King to keep a stiff upper lip.[78]

Roosevelt and Stark provided top cover for King to execute the unambiguous neutrality mission of the Atlantic Fleet. Looking outward to the wars ongoing abroad, King worked very closely with the chairman of the US Maritime Commission, retired rear admiral Emory S. Land, to expand the US Naval Reserve with civilian Merchant Mariners.[79] King concurrently established close ties with the commandant of the Coast Guard, RAdm. Russell Waesche.[80] Working in tandem, King and the Atlantic Fleet supported Waesche in executing the "Ice Patrol" operations under US Coast Guard commodore Edward H. "Iceberg" Smith.[81] Having earned a PhD in oceanography at Harvard, he coordinated Coast Guard ice patrol operations as a cover story to interdict Nazi weather ships and the associated stations ashore in Arctic waters.[82]

King worked in tandem with the Royal Navy by hindering German surface and submarine commerce raiders with the neutrality patrol operations of the Atlantic Fleet. RAdm. Robert "Ike" Giffen commanded the cruiser flotilla of the Atlantic Fleet, working closely with RAdm. Ferdinand Reichmuth as the commander of the two primary destroyer flotillas of the Atlantic Fleet. Atlantic Fleet submarines under RAdm. Richard S. Edwards conducted aggressive surveillance operations to locate and identify Axis-flagged shipping, broadcasting the contact reports for the benefit of other forces in the area. Bristol coordinated operations with Canadian forces on behalf of King at Argentia. From the outset, King pressed his forces in the Atlantic to prepare for wartime operations—to include efforts to synthesize merchant shipping with air and sea escort operations.[83] Yet, King still lacked the requisite authority and resources to meet the enemy threat as it existed *at the time*.[84]

CHAPTER 18
A Tactical Masterpiece

The bureaucratic center of transatlantic strategy progressively shifted from the embattled streets of London to the bustling halls of Washington. King used American neutrality as a weapon in orchestrating the undeclared war of the Atlantic Fleet. He positioned warships to thwart prospective enemies—using the "fleet in being" concept to use neutrality under the Stars and Stripes as a *counterforce* to constrain prospective enemies.[1] Through preliminary arrangements such as ABC-1, the Royal Navy and Royal Canadian Navy received "Red Lead" warships from the US Navy. Under the Destroyers for Bases arrangement and "Cash and Carry" policies of the Roosevelt administration, the British Purchasing Commission in New York City produced paperwork on the promise of future payment.[2] Under the scheme, British sailors received special training from Americans.[3] Royal Navy and Royal Canadian Navy escort skippers exploited the presence of US Navy warships of the same classes and appearance.[4]

The differences between a Union Jack and the Stars and Stripes ensign blurred through the salt-encrusted lenses of binoculars and periscopes. In several incidents, German naval forces attacked vessels registered under the neutrality protections of the United States.[5] The sinking of the American merchant ship SS *Robin Moor* by a German submarine then provided the justification for Roosevelt to warn Congress that "such methods are fully in keeping with the methods of terrorism hitherto employed by the present leaders of the German Reich."[6] "We must take it that notice has now been served upon us," Roosevelt suggested, and that "no American ship or cargo on any of the seven seas can consider itself immune from acts of piracy."[7]

Roosevelt referred to past quasi wars of the US Navy to explain American policy for maintaining freedom of the seas. He explained that "we have striven and fought in defense of freedom of the seas for our own shipping, for the commerce of our sister Republics, for the rights of all Nations to use the highways of world trade."[8] Roosevelt warned listeners that "some people seem to think that we are not attacked until bombs actually drop in the streets of New York or San Francisco or New Orleans or Chicago."[9] He warned that the "Battle of the Atlantic now extends from the icy waters of the North Pole to the frozen continent of the Antarctic [sinking] merchant ships in alarming and increasing numbers by Nazi raiders or submarines [and] even of ships carrying neutral flags."[10] He then declared an "unlimited national emergency."[11]

King operated on the fringes of American neutrality by placing Atlantic Fleet forces on the edges of harm's way in the North Atlantic shipping lanes. For example, he supervised the Atlantic Fleet staff in efforts to help contain the German battleship *Bismarck* in May 1941. From the flagship *Augusta* during the hunt for the German battleship *Bismarck*, Navy secretary Knox stood with King, as the delicate balance between peace and war overshadowed American naval involvement in the hunt for *Bismarck*. Recalling the experience, Low explained that

> we were still neutral, but King deployed all long-range Naval aircraft in a search pattern with orders, of course, not to participate in anything but the search. He specifically told his aviation officer to be certain that none of these aircraft landed in Narragansett Bay. In spite of this, some did, but his aviation officer, thinking perhaps to soften the coming blow on those who had returned to Narragansett Bay, said to him nervously "Admiral, there must be a Narragansett Bay in Newfoundland." To this King replied, "there better be."[12]

The Royal Navy ultimately sank *Bismarck* with direct US Navy involvement in every facet of the operation. Atlantic Fleet personnel on assignment to SpeNavO in London directly participated in the destruction of *Bismarck*. Working from the OIC in London, US Navy commander Frank T. Watkins assisted in pinpointing *Bismarck*. British colleagues at the OIC provided full access to intercepted wireless messages and other key sources to Watkins.[13]

The hunt culminating in the sinking of *Bismarck* provided an important propaganda victory for the British, which coincidentally enhanced the spirit of collaboration with the Americans. Among many others, Ens. Leonard B. Smith had the most recognizable role in the operations. He flew an American-built PBY "Catalina" when he observed *Bismarck* on May 27, 1941. Smith transmitted the coordinates to Royal Navy forces in the area, as two other US Navy aviators, Joe Johnson, and Carl W. Rinehart, joined Smith in their PBYs. Flying in British markings, the American-built PBYs sealed the fate of *Bismarck*. The following day, US Navy lieutenant commander Joseph H. Wellings plotted the target on HMS *Rodney*. He observed the falling shells as Royal Navy forces surrounded *Bismarck*.[14]

Operations culminating in the sinking of *Bismarck* provided ample evidence of the central role of intelligence collaboration between the Admiralty and Navy Department. King used the Atlantic Fleet as a barrier in the race to sink *Bismarck*. Throughout these operations, the director of naval intelligence in Washington, Kirk, provided cues to the Atlantic Fleet intelligence officer, Weeks. In turn, he provided the information required for King to maneuver his task forces in the Atlantic to block *Bismarck*—enabling the Royal Navy to close in for the final kill.[15] All of these efforts unfolded behind closed doors and without fanfare. Recalling his abbreviated tenure as the director of naval intelligence in 1941, Kirk found that "everybody sort of thought Naval Intelligence was striped pants, cookie-pushers, going to parties and so on."[16]

Salt horses still dominated the top tiers of the Admiralty and Navy Department bureaucracies. Among the operational staffs, the functions associated with intelligence and logistics always held a secondary place. The more nuanced subfunctions, such as cryptography, fell into the bureaucratic mires of administrative culture and basic—usually self-inflicted—ignorance. Serving as the aide to Stark at the Navy Department, Smedberg recalled that the "communications setup in Washington was terrible[; we] had no communication with our commander in chief in the Pacific, we had to use Army communications."[17] Under the circumstances, the director of war plans, Capt. Richmond Kelly Turner, formed an operational tracking room with retired captain Martin Kellogg Metcalf presiding.

Capt. Frank T. Leighton supervised "Op-38-W"; the tracking room itself was better known as the "Chart Room" or alternatively as the "War Room." This organization served as the basis for what became the Combat Intelligence Division.[18]

Intelligence provided means by which to anticipate prospective enemy intentions, thereby providing means to navigate the future course of American sea power. Stark relied upon old comrades from the London Flagship in the Sims era. Retired captain Dudley W. Knox and reserve lieutenant Tracy Barrett Kittredge provided firsthand information about the strategic trends. Living in Europe, Kittredge worked from Switzerland for the International Red Cross and then with the Rockefeller Foundation in Europe. His second wife, Elanor Hayden, networked with many prominent wives of key leaders inside the Third Reich—including Annaleis von Ribbentropp. Her husband, Joachim, stood among the inner circle as Hitler's foreign minister. Kittredge provided regular updates to Knox, who then passed the word to Stark and Roosevelt.[19]

Kittredge had the ability to blend into the wallpaper at social events and in the halls of European governments. His personal connections with Frank Birch and Alastair Denniston proved useful for the British intelligence services. Kittredge kept his trusted associates well informed of meetings with all the key leaders of Europe. As the British and American navies opened communications at higher levels of command, the informal friendships among key subordinates provided useful connections between the Historical Sections of the Naval Intelligence Division of the Admiralty and the ONI at the Navy Department.[20] The director of the Historical Section at ONI, Knox, recruited reserve lieutenant commander Charles F. Baldwin to assist these efforts. Within documents, Knox frequently used the cryptic title of "Op-16-E" while Baldwin carried the administrative title of "Op-16-B/8."

Baldwin offered significant experience, having earlier served on assignment with the SpeNavO organization in London. He studied the submarine-tracking methods of Winn during his temporary assignment at the Admiralty, inside Section 8S of the OIC.[21] Baldwin attempted to replicate the organization within the ONI.[22] However, Knox and Baldwin ran afoul of their counterparts in the War Plans Division of the CNO for criticizing the efforts of Leighton.[23] Having served with Baldwin on temporary duty inside the Admiralty OIC in 1941, Cmdr. Arthur McCollum referred to the Leighton organization as a "chart room with buttons to move around for ships and locations, but they got so bemused with different shapes of buttons that they couldn't see the woods for the trees."[24]

The Admiralty OIC provided inspiration for Stark to develop the rudimentary framework for a similar organization inside the Navy Department. The aide to the CNO, Smedberg, with Cmdr. George C. Dyer, supervised the daily routines among the various subdivisions associated with the war room under Leighton within Stark's headquarters on the third deck of the Navy Department—inside room 3459. Cmdr. Charles H. Murphy held the esponsibility to maintain the "strategic plot" inside the adjacent rooms 3060 and 3062. Dyer described the room as "directly above Convoy and Routing[,] which was still under CNO[;] a circular stairway connected the two."[25] King also explained to his task force commanders that the "Admiralty in London appears to insist on knowing where each and every one of our ships are at every hour of the day and night, and the Navy Department seems to acquiesce to this 'curiosity.'"[26] In September 1941, King informed admirals Arthur B. Cook and Jonas Ingram that

Leighton (OpNav) is keeping a score board and card index on the whereabouts of each and every ship at all hours of the day and night. He is the one who is continuously "pestering" you and Cook and me about these matters, so that he can keep his little toys and other play things in order. Again, Admiral Stark sees daily a chart on which is indicated the location of our own and British forces in the Atlantic—he has commented to me several times on the scarcity of your detachments at sea, as well as those of Cook's.[27]

King established procedures designed to minimize the flow of radio communications to support the requirements established by Leighton. From the fall of 1941, King directed Cook and Ingram to supply daily reports to the Atlantic Fleet headquarters. King explained that Leighton appeared to suffer from the "'mania' to be able [to] plot the whereabouts of every ship at sea [but] to what end—except possibly, to justify the existence of the plotters."[28]

King occasionally took out his frustrations on subordinates whenever operations failed to produce desired outcomes. Low recalled suffering a vicious dressing down "so unwarranted and unfair that I retired to a wing of the bridge to nurse my pride."[29] King continued haranguing Low on the bridgewing. Having had enough, Low then barked back that "there is not one goddam thing you can do to me I can't take."[30] At that point, King stopped the verbal attack. He stood quietly on the bridgewing, smoking a cigarette. King broke the uncomfortable silence when leaving Low alone on the bridgewing with orders to "carry on."

FLEXING

Seagoing commanders grew annoyed about the requirement to transmit situation updates to the plotting rooms ashore. King leaned heavily upon the Atlantic Fleet staff while coordinating warlike operations without a formal declaration of war.[31] Low observed that "King was highly respected, but I don't think much beloved."[32] "I have always suspected that some of his contemporaries," Low explained, "wished him no good or were jealous of his capabilities."[33] Low recalled, "I have repeatedly seen [King] allow unit commanders and captains of private ships to work themselves into situations from which there seemed to be little hope of extrication and then turn his back when they sought help."[34] At the same time, he added, "I never saw one case where the individual was not able to work himself out of his troubles."[35] Above all, Low noted that "King himself lived exactly the sort of life he [exemplified] and required it of all of his commanders and of his staff." He expected leaders to take charge by training their replacements in nurturing teamwork through the "initiative of the subordinate."[36]

The Atlantic Fleet synthesized operations with intelligence in realistic simulations of combat. Actual experience in antisubmarine operations added to the reality during peacetime neutrality operations in the Atlantic. Between operations, King used exercises to keep his men ready for action in war. For example, he used novel tactics in coordinating naval aviation forces in close support of amphibious forces during exercises conducted in the Caribbean. Studies conducted at the Naval War College in Newport influenced doctrinal development efforts by Marine Corps Schools in Quantico, Virginia.[37] Serving at the side of King on the Atlantic Fleet staff, Marine major Oman T. Pfeiffer recalled,

"King was very partial to the Marines."[38] In coordinating amphibious operations, King frequently crossed swords with Brig. Gen. Holland M. Smith during Fleet Landing Exercise 7 (FLEX 7).

The FLEX 7 maneuvers enabled King and Smith to develop and refine the command relationships between amphibious commanders at sea and ashore. King held overarching command of the amphibious forces at sea and ashore, as Smith assumed tactical control for the forces embarked ashore. King directed Smith to run night landings, coastal raids, and scouting expeditions into Puerto Rico and the remote pirate lairs of St. John Island.[39] The commandant of the Tenth Naval District, Capt. Raymond A. Spruance, simulated the role of an enemy defender ashore in Puerto Rico against Smith's landing forces. Spruance's Caribbean Patrol Forces also provided an opportunity for King to refine the doctrine for amphibious force commanders. Ultimately, King demonstrated the importance of attaining overwhelming control in contested waters to support naval expeditionary forces ashore. The FLEX 7 exercises simulated actual combat conditions, thereby setting the tone for future innovation in American naval operations and amphibious doctrine.[40]

Advance base problems and amphibious FLEX operations enabled the US Navy and Marine Corps to experiment in the absence of a true enemy foil. The realistic character of training under King likewise simulated the heat of actual combat. Spruance ably challenged the landing forces, which sparked the fiery personality of Smith during FLEX 7. Observing from the bridgewings in King's flagship, Topper recalled that as the amphibious operations went awry over and again, Smith "could not contain himself!"[41] Topper described King with an approving smirk on his face as "Smith showed he was under considerable pressure—quite nervous—chewing on his cigar like it was Juicy Fruit Gum."[42] When King left the bridge, Smith suddenly subjected Topper to a stream of "abusive language."[43] In response, Topper used humor to defuse Smith by warning that you "might burst a blood vessel or have a heart attack—or possibly have to change his skivvies and trousers."[44]

Topper explained that the best way to deal with Smith's temper tantrums was by laughing at him.[45] Topper later recalled the moment when Smith "came to his senses and realized he was making a complete ass of himself."[46] Finally realizing King had left the bridge, Smith apologized to Topper for the unnecessary personal insults. In turn, Topper warned Smith to avoid showing such signs of weakness to King. As the FLEX 7 exercises came to an end, Topper delivered a personal note of congratulations from King to Smith. Upon reading the note, Topper recalled how Smith "cried just like a baby."[47]

King and Smith refined the tactics and doctrinal procedures that progressively defined US naval operations in both peace and war. Both saw the future of amphibious warfare and the US Marine Corps. Others involved with the FLEX 7 maneuvers included Captains Daniel Barbey and Donald P. Moon. Captains Louis Denfeld and Alan Goodrich Kirk joined the Atlantic Fleet, helping King to coordinate reconnaissance, close escort, and gunnery operations. Spruance simulated the enemy as the defending commander ashore on Puerto Rico.

King compared notes with all the key commanders to refine procedures for future amphibious operations. Following the FLEX 7 maneuvers, King accompanied Marine major Victor H. Krulak ashore for meetings with Spruance and Leahy in Puerto Rico. Krulak convinced King to ride ashore in an experimental Higgins-type Landing Vehicle–Transport (LVT). As they approached the beach, Krulak was horrified when the LVT struck a reef and the engine flooded. Making the situation worse, King "had to crawl over the side of that damned machine and wade in his white uniform, water up to his waist."[48]

OFFENSIVE ACTION AGAINST U-BOATS

King consistently acted as though at war while seeking opportunities to support the British with American sea power. King used Atlantic Fleet forces to locate German supply vessels and survey potential submarine rendezvous sites. At one point, King received a proposal from the RAdm. Richard S. Edwards to use American submarines in clandestine attacks against German targets. King approved the idea and directed Edwards to prepare a study with Low and Capt. Bernard H. Bieri on the Atlantic Fleet staff. Edwards and his team recommended three groups comprising between three and five submarines to focus on Axis submarine-refueling areas, surface raiders, and blockade-running merchants. He reasoned that the "Germans would more likely than not assume that the British had done the job."[49]

Stark rejected King's offensive proposal for covert American submarine operations against Axis forces in the Atlantic. Willing to push the limits, King demonstrated his skill as a commander, working to *enforce* American neutrality. The preliminary plan for the operation, "Offensive Action Against U-Boats," proposed clandestine US Navy submarine operations against German naval forces in the Atlantic.[50] "I have just OK'd Edwards" proposal re[garding] 'submarine sanctuaries,'" King reported to Stark. "The general subject of submarine vs. submarine need not be abandoned—it should merely be held over for later consideration."[51] King emphasized, "As to communications [I] continue to think over the 'vital subject,' we discussed last week—I continue to be appalled at the dearth of first-class material!"[52] King explained:

> Roosevelt, during 1941, didn't think very much of building escort vessels which we didn't need at that time. The best available source on that point is Admiral Stark as he was Chief of Naval Operations during 1941 and the point will be seen in due time from his own records, perhaps. Although Admiral Stark asked several months before, the President would not agree saying at that time that congress didn't want any war but they might help with money to build new large warships which were really important and then in due time they would give us (the Navy) enough money to build escort ships, but he seemed to have forgotten that there would be no time when we got into the war (or any war) to just say "presto" and then to see, "overnight," that we had hundreds of escort ships ready to go to sea![53]

The Atlantic Fleet lacked sufficient forces to support the Royal Navy and enforce the Neutrality Patrols. "We do not have <u>now</u> any vessels to spare," King complained in November 1941.[54] In personal correspondence, King asked Stark to support "separate submarine[-]hunting groups."[55]

The Atlantic Fleet stood in a constant state of wartime readiness with the primary mission of preserving peace. King encouraged the sailors of the Atlantic Fleet to embrace their difficult duty of holding the first lines of American oceanic defenses. King's men sustained casualties in the fall of 1941. German torpedoes seriously damaged USS *Greer* (DD-145) and USS *Kearny* (DD-432) in the Atlantic shipping lanes in September.[56]

Running in ballast on a return voyage from Iceland, USS *Salinas* (AO-19) sustained damage after another German submarine encounter. Marines of the Atlantic Fleet stood watch ashore in Iceland to enable King's seagoing forces to enforce American neutrality against German surface raiders and submarines in the transatlantic shipping lanes. His amphibious forces, under Capt. Alan Goodrich Kirk at Little Creek in Virginia, prepared for expeditions in anticipation of war.[57]

The bloody red flag of Nazism loomed over the horizon of the Atlantic and beyond to the embattled shores of Europe. Under the flag of American neutrality, Roosevelt empowered King and the Atlantic Fleet to "shoot on sight" upon contacting German naval forces after September 1941. "It is a fair assumption," journalists noted, that King and the Atlantic Fleet "ha[ve] been operating regularly about one speech ahead of the President."[58] Damning the torpedoes, King drove the Atlantic Fleet to the brink—operating near convoys and beyond the declared lines of demarcation in the Pan-American Neutrality Zone. In the stormy seas south of Iceland, the phosphorescent wake of torpedoes appeared in the inky waters. American sailors on board USS *Reuben James* (DD-245) paid the price of innocence—going to their watery grave under the starry skies of Halloween night.[59]

Roosevelt condemned the blatant Nazi aggression and then authorized the US Navy to respond with equal force in defense of American neutrality. In the week following the loss of *Reuben James*, King's navy tracked down and captured the German blockade runner MV *Odenwald*.[60] As events unfolded in the Atlantic on November 23, 1941, King attended his sixty-third birthday party with his family in their home in Washington, DC. The following day, Roosevelt hosted King for lunch at the White House to discuss the situation in the Atlantic. Under the circumstances in 1941, King firmly argued that "submarines must come to the convoys to attack and so come readily within the attacking scope of the escorts—which is rather better than the 'needle-in-the-haystack' method!"[61] King advised, "I need every ship I can get that displaces over 600 tons—can maintain 12 knots at sea—and can steam 3,000 miles or more!"[62]

Roosevelt agreed with King about the immediacy of the situation in the Atlantic, although other competing priorities and political considerations constrained efforts to mobilize forces in anticipation of direct American intervention ashore in Europe. The sinking of *Reuben James* prompted the natural tendency of Navy Department bureaucrats to begin processing paperwork. Among others, Undersecretary Forrestal suggested the posthumous awards of the Navy Cross medal for the late skipper, Lt. Heywood L Edwards, and similar recommendations for other members of the *Reuben James* crew.

King rejected the idea of issuing medals and awards for sound strategic reasons, under the impending circumstances of war. Recalling the media debates surrounding the Sims-Daniels fights about decorations and then the more recent questions surrounding the issuance of Navy Cross medals for *Panay* sailors in Chinese waters, King explained, "I suggest that we 'go slow' in this matter of making 'heroes' out of [the *Reuben James* crew]."[63] Decorating the dead always carried political overtones. Decorations, in general, also tended to appear on the uniforms of personnel "whose actual performance often stood subject to scrutiny." King recognized the demoralizing effect of medals and decorations among regular sailors as they quietly performed their duty. Speaking in plain terms from the embattled peacetime decks of the Atlantic Fleet, King warned that incidents involving German submarines "can be expected to become commonplace."[64] Conjuring the ghost of Sims in closing his correspondence, King encouraged Stark to "Remain Cheerful!"[65]

German and Italian aggression in the Atlantic and Mediterranean threatened to sever the vital oceanic lines of communication that connected the British home islands with the critical resources provided by the imperial Dominions and Commonwealth. In anticipation of direct US Navy involvement in the Atlantic, Roosevelt solicited the opinions of US Navy strategists at the White House in the fall of 1941. The Atlantic Fleet operations officer, Low, witnessed the moment when Roosevelt listened to King outline the sequence of strategy for conducting the "coming war not only so clearly and precisely as to be impressive, but so presciently in its foresight that it differed only in detail from the way matters actually happened."[66] "I have no doubt," Low concluded, that this "one encounter with F.D.R. had a considerable bearing on King's later appointment to our highest naval post."[67] Peacetime battles in the Atlantic loomed over King's warning to Roosevelt that "any campaign in the Pacific will require time, personnel[,] and equipment, which will require time, personnel[,] and equipment for the build-up."[68]

THIS IS NO DRILL

Without involving Roosevelt directly, Stark acted on his own authority as the CNO to contain prospective enemies while helping foreign partners under the banner of American neutrality in the global war at sea. He designated the facilities ashore—not islands themselves—as neutral American naval facilities. American citizens serving under the Navy Department as construction contractors also received protections under Naval Regulations. Stark empowered RAdm. Ben Morrell, chief of the Bureau of Yards and Docks, to coordinate these peacetime operations on foreign soil.[69] On at least one occasion, Stark signed a document to take full responsibility to enable Morrell to violate existing federal law in order to get the job done.[70]

War remained a distant rumble over the horizons in Asia, unlike the boiling conflict unfolding in the Atlantic between American and European forces. The German and Italian offensive into the Soviet Union appeared to coincide with imperial Japanese interest in seizing Singapore, King told journalists that "Japan can't afford to go south with her fleet, because the British fleet could handle their warships, and her islands would be left unguarded from action by the American fleet."[71] King reasoned that Japan "couldn't go after the United States because that would lay Japan open to attack by the British."[72] Thus, he reassured journalists by suggesting that "Japan is not going to move anyplace, for a while anyway."[73] When pressed by the media to predict Japanese intentions, King bluntly admitted that "he didn't know."[74] The quasi war in the Atlantic influenced American strategy in the Pacific, since "expectation in Washington was that the Japanese declaration of war would take the form of an attack in the Philippines."[75]

The Roosevelt administration anticipated an imperial Japanese offensive against European and American outposts in Asia. To enable collaboration between London and Washington, Roosevelt approved the recommendations of Stark by authorizing the deployment of US naval vessels to protect the delivery of civilian construction teams on remote island outposts in the Pacific. Churchill and Roosevelt placed highest priority on establishing a high-grade link between Singapore, Melbourne, Manila, and Honolulu. For the mission, the fleet communications officer of the Pacific Fleet, Capt. Charles Maddox, embarked USS *Antares* (AG-10) to lead the expedition to Christmas and Canton Islands in October 1941.

The US Navy lacked sufficiently trained personnel to construct the infrastructure required for close coordination among various British and American headquarters in the global maritime arena. In 1941, a New York construction man, Willard G. Triest, advised King in his efforts to build or expand naval bases in Iceland and other Atlantic ports. King overruled BuMcd restrictions to appoint Triest with a reserve commission in the rank of lieutenant commander. Triest barely fit into his naval uniform but had the gumption to get the job done. He reported on board *Antares* for the expedition to Christmas and Canton Islands with an army of recently recruited reservists with civilian construction worker experience to build a network of relay stations to enable British and American officials to share special intelligence.[76]

Given the highly secretive nature of the mission, the *Antares* expedition caused significant disagreement among British and American officials. British commanders worried about their responsibility for defending the islands against potential Japanese attacks. In such an event, an attack against British islands implied the prospect of an inadvertent attack against American civilians.[77] The Commonwealth governments of Australia and New Zealand, along with the Free French Government in Exile, worried about the prospect of a land grab by the United States. The French outright rejected American requests to establish a relay station in New Caledonia.[78]

Maddox successfully delivered the American communications experts along with construction supplies at Canton Island. He subsequently sailed on *Antares* for Pearl Harbor, arriving on the morning of December 7, 1941. Maddox awaited clearance to enter Pearl Harbor in *Antares* when his bridge team spotted the unmistakable silhouette of a midget submarine conning tower in the wash behind an American warship. Maddox immediately reported the sighting, which prompted USS *Ward* (DD-139) to open fire at roughly 0645 in Hawaii. Roughly an hour later, Japanese aircraft appeared over Diamond Head—achieving a complete and devastating surprise attack against the battleships berthed in the enclosed shallows of Pearl Harbor. Cmdr. Logan C. Ramsey had highlighted the vulnerability of the anchorage after service with King in the patrol squadrons. Still, Ramsey was surprised by the brazen Japanese attack. Keeping his head, Ramsey transmitted the signal "Air raid on Pearl Harbor, this is no drill."[79]

"TACTICAL MASTERPIECE"

Public hysteria followed the imperial Japanese attack, as the battleships of the Pacific Fleet smoldered in the shallows of Pearl Harbor. Political enemies of Roosevelt immediately began circulating rumors—while simultaneously demanding explanations after a series of major disasters.[80] Further complicating matters within the Roosevelt administration, local civilian authorities reported enemy submarine sightings with Nazi agents wading ashore to meet treasonous Americans of German descent.[81] Other false reports about a German zeppelin raid on New York City coincided with headlines concerning an actual Japanese submarine attack off the coast of California. Within days following the raid at Pearl Harbor, land-based Japanese aircraft sank the battleships HMS *Repulse* and HMS *Prince of Wales* off Singapore.[82] Coincident with these losses, American forces on Guam surrendered and the rescue mission to Wake Island fizzled in the face of the Japanese.

American naval thinkers, including King, discounted the prospect of an imperial Japanese attack against Hawaii. In conversations with journalists following the attack,

King credited the Japanese for pulling off the surprise. Among others, Glenn Perry of the *Washington Sun* remembered that "Pearl Harbor came as a terrible shock [not] because it happened, but because of where it happened."[83] King later explained that "we did our best to keep our powder dry [as the] president did what he could to shelter the American hemisphere with the combination of diplomatic slight [*sic*] of hand and the fleet in being."[8]

Keeping calm and carrying on in the aftermath of disaster, King simply reacted to the bad news with confidence. King received initial reports about Pearl Harbor while having lunch at the Newport Reading Room. His aide Russell remembered delivering the message to King. He then continued reading the newspaper. King knew nothing could be done immediately. He set the tone for the staff by acting decisively—with clarity and calmness. King simply directed the Atlantic Fleet chief of staff, Capt. Olaf Hustvedt, to cancel all liberty and to get sailors matched up with their warships for offensive operations. He ordered the staff to coordinate with their counterparts in Washington to determine whether Atlantic Fleet warships needed to deploy to the Pacific. An aide thought, "I honestly think the word 'pressure' was foreign to him."[85]

King knew the politics of Pearl Harbor, which required the Roosevelt administration to deliver an immediate response against imperial Japan.[86] In the flow of messages between Washington and the seagoing fleet commanders, King received a summons to the Navy Department. King left his classmate and trusted friend RAdm. Arthur B. Cook in temporary command of the Atlantic Fleet. He then departed with his aide Sanders to travel by train from Kingston Station in Rhode Island. From the same train station as Sims just twenty-four years before, the pair traveled incognito clothes to Union Station in Washington on December 9, 1941. Sanders was having trouble with the ticket vendor. Finally, Sanders was able to "reserve two chairs in the parlor car on the afternoon Boston–Washington express."[87] Sanders remembered King acting as though their journey was just another business trip. Upon arriving at Union Station in the early evening, Sanders went to the Army-Navy Club and "King went immediately to his home."[88]

King spent the evening with his family, discussing the scope of the war and the likely costs in American lives. With his various sons-in-law already serving in uniform, his only son, Joe, served as a midshipman at the Naval Academy. After a discussion with his family on the likelihood of a major war, King drove the family car to retrieve Sanders on the way to the Navy Department. Sanders described the scene at Main Navy asappearing like an "ant hill with the top kicked off."[89] Corroborating the situation as it existed at the time, Captain Forrest Sherman recalled the moment when King arrived in Stark's office: "I shall never forget the emotions evidenced by the face of Admiral King[:] an initial expression of sorrow, with some moisture visible in his eyes, followed immediately by an expression of cold determination."[90] Setting aside these emotions, King coldly described the imperial Japanese campaign as a "tactical masterpiece."[91]

CHAPTER 19
Citadels on the "Far Shore"

The attack on Pearl Harbor upset the peacetime routines for all Americans, although King recognized the fundamental flaw in the enemy plan. Coincident with the initial attacks, Navy secretary Knox approved Stark's recommendation to initiate "unrestricted air and submarine warfare against Japan—inform army—inform British and Dutch."[1] Pearl Harbor provided clear justification for the Roosevelt administration to unify all the various branches and subbranches of the United States government. Roosevelt worked behind closed doors to negotiate with rivals within both the Republican and Democratic Parties to gain their support for him to assert full constitutional responsibility as the unambiguous commander in chief of the Army and Navy. Just as in 1917, the Republican representative from Montana, Rankin, courageously spoke the honest convictions of American pacifists in December 1941—taking her place in history as the only member of Congress to make the symbolic gesture of voting against the American war declaration against imperial Japan.[2]

Among Roosevelt's most important first moves, he ostensibly used the Pan-American Neutrality Zone as the basis for setting future strategy for *offensive* operations in the global maritime arena. To these ends, Roosevelt sent Secretary Knox to inspect the damage at Pearl Harbor and held Stark by his side in Washington. Working behind the scenes, Roosevelt summoned King for a series of meetings during the four days following December 9. At this time, King strongly reasserted his support for Stark's "Europe First" concept. Under WPL- 46/RAINBOW 5, CCS and JCS staffs soon began referring in oblique terms to enemy held territory as the "far shore."[3] Always focused on the strategic horizons of Europe and Asia, King sought to impose unremitting pressure on the enemy on all fronts. Building from war college studies, King focused plans on the "citadels" of Formosa and Britain—the gateways to Asia and Europe.[4]

King characterized the British Empire as an important adjunct to the main line of American effort, which centered on enabling the armies of the Soviet Union and China to carry the burden of defeating the Axis Tripartite ashore.[5] In setting the stage for decisive operations on the Atlantic front, King pushed for a series of immediate surprise jabs against the enemy in the Pacific. He understood the strategic imperative of putting the enemy on their heels—referring to these initial operations as the "Pearl Harbor in Reverse."[6] King then returned to Newport by December 13, only to receive another summons from Roosevelt on December 16. The following day, King found Navy secretary Knox waiting in the passageway leading to Stark's offices on the third deck of Main Navy.[7] Knox preempted Stark, who had already recommended King for duty as an ideal relief for duty as the CNO. At that time, Knox informed King of plans to enhance the functions of CNO with the reestablishment of the CinCUS.[8]

Roosevelt shrewdly calculated the political appearances of replacing key commanders closest to the political battleground in Washington. Keeping card-carrying Republicans like Stimson and Knox as the respective secretaries of war and Navy, Roosevelt also managed the potential critiques from Republican-leaning retired flag officers like Pershing and Pratt. MacArthur always stood out as a major concern, as Roosevelt navigated uncharted political hazards by holding Marshall in place as chief of staff of the Army and Stark as the CNO. Working his political magic, Roosevelt quietly manipulated the inner workings of the armed service staffs by his masterful handling of Stimson and Knox.

Roosevelt kept his immediate circle of strategic advisers unchanged in the immediate aftermath of Pearl Harbor. Working the lines for future battles to come, Roosevelt asked Marshall and Stark for recommendations in reorganizing the military and naval staffs. In turn, Marshall requested Maj. Gen. Joseph T. McNarney, and Stark requested King. Roosevelt coincidentally advised Marshall and Stark to prepare plans for enhancing efforts by Strong and Ghormley in London. During this period, McNarney also returned from London to assist Marshall in reorganizing the Army General Staff in close collaboration with Generals Lesley McNair, Brehon B. Somervell, and Henry A. Arnold.[9]

The changes already happening within the War Department coincided with the comparably difficult bureaucratic revolution from above at the Navy Department. Roosevelt managed the politics, as Stark continued to pull King into the circle of trust with the provisions to reestablish CinCUS to perform the following functions:

- Make available for evaluation all pertinent information and naval intelligence
- Prepare and execute plans for current war operations
- Conduct operational duties
- Effect all essential communications
- Direct training essential to carrying out operations
- Serve as personal aides [for seagoing commands]

Roosevelt approved these measures, keeping Stark as the CNO responsible for governing the subordinate functions of CinCUS in accordance with General Order 143. Under these circumstances, King refused to accept the traditional acronym CinCUS, or "sink us" in US Navy vernacular. He noted that the title "seemed a little too inappropriate in sound after Pearl Harbor."[10] King offered the subtle change of creating a new acronym, "CominCh."[11] Recalling experiences during the First World War, King explained that the Royal Navy used "initial <u>letters</u>" while the US Navy used "abbreviations composed of initial <u>syllables</u>."[12] King recalled, "CominCh came as a natural to designate Mayo."[13]

King understood the importance of defining clear lines of responsibility in clarifying the strategic chain of command within the Navy Department and among seagoing forces. Roosevelt considered fusing the functions of CNO and CominCh under King with the title of "Commander in Chief, <u>US Navy.</u>"[14] The CNO, Stark, endorsed the idea of merging the functions of CNO with those of CinCUS under the concept of a future "CinCUSN."[15] The former CNO, Pratt, endorsed the idea in personal correspondence and in commentary published in the media. Roosevelt agreed with the idea of fusing the functions of CNO and CinCUS under a singular command, although he understood the likelihood of a political backlash from within Congress. King later warned about the temptation of creating a "superman" to serve as "chief of staff of all the armed forces as an infringement on the prerogatives of the President of the United States as Commander in Chief of the armed forces."[16]

Roosevelt installed King by using the existing legal provisions to resurrect the traditional concept of CinCUS. The separate functions of CNO and CinCUS continued in accordance with existing congressional legislation.[17] While Stark lingered on the public stage as the CNO after Pearl Harbor, the announcement designating King as CinCUS immediately improved morale within the embattled seagoing ranks of the fleet. For example, Lt. Cmdr. Henry E. Eccles wrote that the "appointment of Ernie King as Commander in Chief, US Fleet, [is] a splendid shift and I know that we will have a well[-]thought[-] out and aggressive campaign."[18]

Roosevelt withheld Stark as the CNO to enable King to focus on conducting the war at sea as the CominCh. King left RAdm. Arthur B. Cook in temporary command in the Atlantic Fleet. King also formally changed his title from being CinCUS to CominCh following a brief ceremony chaired by Navy secretary Knox on December 20. On Christmas Day, King brought Edwards, Libby, and Low to report for duty in CominCh. RAdm. Russell Willson reported from the Naval Academy to assume duty with CominCh as chief of staff. King appointed RAdm. Frederick Horne to serve as the CominCh liaison to the CNO staff of Stark. King recruited Lieutenants Charles Lanman and George Russell to serve as flag secretaries, reporting after the new year.

All these moves happened without the standard peacetime administrative routines of the Navy Department. Given their positions when Pearl Harbor unfolded, Marshall and Stark performed their duty in fulfilling their roles as senior commanders during the troubled months following the attack. They also held their ground in anticipation of the arrival of Churchill and the British Joint Staff for emergency meetings during the holidays. Navy secretary Knox impatiently told King to ignore Stark altogether and "get going!"[19] In full deference to his immediate superiors, King retorted, "Aye-aye—with what?"[20] Among trusted members of the Arlington County Commandos, King chuckled about the joke, as retold by journalist Glenn Perry, "Knock Knox, who's there?"[21]

Within this confused context, King claimed to have had no previous knowledge concerning the appointment of Nimitz as the relief for Kimmel in the Pacific Fleet. Journalists surprised Stark and King with questions about the newly appointed commanders in the Pacific.[22] US Army Air Force lieutenant general Delos Emmons took command in Hawaii, coincident with Roosevelt's decision to send Nimitz to assume command of the Pacific Fleet.[23] For his part, Nimitz had expected to relieve Hart as the Asiatic Fleet commander. Just five days preceding the attack on Pearl Harbor, Nimitz also explained, during a speech he delivered at the Naval War College, major challenges in efforts to expand the ranks of the peacetime navy to exceed one million personnel. Coincidentally, Roosevelt refused to open the ranks of the naval services for draftees. Roosevelt also lambasted Nimitz for talking nonsense about future personnel requirements with "milky way figures like that."[24]

Joint Board and Naval General Board estimates for strategic requirements provided foundation for the predictive assertions of Nimitz. His immediate superiors, Stark and King, were the real authors of those wild figures, which later proved completely accurate. In the immediate aftermath of Pearl Harbor, Stark and King also voiced serious reservations about Nimitz—preferring to send Ingersoll to the Pacific. Stark had expected to send Nimitz to the Asiatic or, alternatively, as commander of American submarine forces.

Similarly, King worried that Nimitz "is a kibitzer and never made a decision by himself."[25] King strongly preferred to send the director of war plans, Turner, to command the Pacific Fleet.[26] However, Roosevelt personally selected Nimitz for the Pacific Fleet. Navy secretary Knox also played intermediary. Roosevelt told King in a private luncheon about shared reservations about Nimitz. Playing to the ego of his singular audience, Roosevelt asked King to "help Nimitz along." Continuing, Roosevelt told King that "I expect you to hold our course in this goddamned war."[27]

CHRISTMAS AT THE WHITE HOUSE

Roosevelt asserted his full command authority as the skipper in the ship of state, giving King the equivalent responsibility for holding control over the wheel and rudder for the purposes of winning the sustainable peacetime end of war in the global maritime arena. Having reached an understanding, Roosevelt also used King to cast an optimistic view over the gloomy headlines following Pearl Harbor. Roosevelt exploited the cheerful rituals of the Christmas holidays to relaunch the hopeful American principles of freedom and democracy. When Churchill arrived with the British Joint Staff and they presented themselves to Roosevelt at the White House, the pair issued an optimistic holiday message in a combined statement. Churchill and Roosevelt reassured their listeners to expect significant hardships along the inevitable path to future victory.

Behind the image of solidarity, Churchill and Roosevelt fundamentally disagreed about their future conceptions of victory. Churchill looked to the past to inform his policy to restore order under the imperial mythology of Britannia and the historical connections among English-speaking peoples. Roosevelt drew from the past to outline an alternative vision in which his fundamental concept of Four Freedoms might thrive under the utopian dream of the United Nations. Behind closed doors, British members of the Joint Staff meanwhile fought raging bureaucratic battles with their American counterparts in efforts to strike common strategic ground. Churchill relentlessly hounded Field Marshal Sir John Dill, Air Marshall Sir Charles Portal, and the First Sea Lord, Admiral of the Fleet Sir Dudley Pound. Similarly, Roosevelt stood firm about his basic policies in discussions with his cabinet secretaries; the Army chief of staff, Marshal; the CNO, Stark; and the CominCh, King.

The joint army-navy board remained in place while Roosevelt forcibly established equivalencies between the British Joint Staff and dissimilar American equivalents. Decisions made during the Christmas meetings of 1941 and 1942 later carried the designation ARCADIA, which arguably stood among the most consequential moments in American naval history—perhaps as important as the appointment of General George Washington by decree of the Continental Congress.[28] Historical precedent provided foundations upon which Roosevelt adapted American traditions to the new strategic realities of 1942. The principles of civilian command over American policy also evolved within the context of transatlantic strategic collaboration under the brave new vision for the future United Nations.

As the president sculpted the future transatlantic alliance, Lincoln's example from the Civil War also inspired Roosevelt's novel use of his executive powers. He circumvented legislative and judiciary oversight while undercutting his civilian secretaries of war and Navy by promulgating direct "Military Orders" to his subordinate generals and admirals.[29] Republican and Democratic Party naysayers worked quietly during the months of uncertainty after Pearl Harbor—when Roosevelt stood alone with the singular authority of war powers granted by Congress—as the one and only commander in chief of the Army and Navy. Challenges from within Congress and the American media later provided fodder for enemy propaganda, as Roosevelt and his trusted generals and admirals focused on their task of winning the sustainable peacetime end of war as quickly as possible after 1942.

The Joint Staff organization of the British directly influenced deliberations among the Americans. In early January 1942, Stark and King suggested the establishment of a single army-navy staff to advise Roosevelt on maritime strategy. Stark and King used Knox to fend off Stimson's moves to place Marshall and the General Staff of the War Department in command over American strategy. Roosevelt took heed and acted on King's recommendations during the ARCADIA discussions.[30] Mutual historical interests provided a basis for understanding between Roosevelt and King. During the Civil War, Lincoln created the rank of admiral in the US Navy to stop US Army commanders from asserting undue authority over naval forces.

Roosevelt set the course and speed as King pulled the lines and followed the rudder orders from the bridge with his CominCh staff on the third deck of the Navy Department. Such measures enabled Roosevelt to use King as the hatchet man in framing combined and joint policy, which set the strategic course for global offensive operations.[31] During preliminary meetings in Washington, the differences between British and American systems of rank were the first challenges. The First Sea Lord, Pound, carried the equivalent of five-star rank, as did his counterparts on the British Joint Staff. After Pearl Harbor, Stark continued as CNO and King nominally held two roles—commanding forces in the Atlantic with additional responsibility by executive order for global operations as the CominCh.[32]

Memories of the First World War's imbalance between British and American organizations and hierarchies complicated the question of divided US naval command. Under the circumstances, King proposed the idea of creating equivalencies with British ranks—or essentially a five-star American rank.[33] Churchill and Roosevelt left the idea up for discussion. Politically, Roosevelt allowed the idea of five-star promotions to linger. With the ships still resting in the mud of Pearl Harbor, Roosevelt tabled the five-star idea as an option for the future.[34] Roosevelt assumed control over his generals and admirals. He sometimes pitted his generals against his admirals. On the public-affairs front, War Department centralization sometimes overwhelmed the decentralized character of the Navy Department—sometimes leaving the admirals to fend for themselves in managing the propaganda war. On this front, King utterly failed to understand the role of public opinion in educating taxpayers about the stunning success of American sea power in keeping the peace—and then winning it—after Pearl Harbor.[35]

Keeping friends close and potential political enemies closer, Roosevelt set the policies by which King dutifully drove strategy in the global maritime arena. Balancing politics against strategic realities, Roosevelt also kept King on a long bureaucratic leash. With less than ten months on active service before mandatory retirement, King anticipated the appointment of a younger replacement. Uncorroborated rumors of impending change circulated among journalistic circles. Glenn Perry of the *Washington Sun* noted King's "enemies in the press, Congress[,] and the navy rubbed their hands and warmed to the task of giving him the deep six."[36] Within this politically spiced stew, King focused on the task at hand and simply did his duty. He always expected to be relieved during the war.

Roosevelt used King as the heavyweight for equalizing the delicate strategic balances in the transatlantic relationship. Emergency executive powers provided means by which Roosevelt changed the American system of overlapping checks and balances. He replicated the British example of the "Joint Staff" by establishing the American "Joint Chiefs of Staff" (JCS). This decision reflected the previous decision to form an Anglo-American "Combined Chiefs of Staff" (CCS). King explained his role, which Bull recorded in contemporaneous notes that

> Admiral King and General Marshall act as agents for the Joint Chiefs of Staff and this, in turn, derives its powers from the President who is the Commander in Chief of the Army and Navy. This is the best way of exercising command where several men are concerned and who must act in concert. In no instance does the President interfere in military strategy or in military operations. A free hand is given the military men on the Joint Chiefs of Staff.[37]

King told journalists in secret meetings to recognize the British as an ally with an agenda, which placed the Americans at a disadvantage throughout 1942. He complained that "Congress has now appropriated money for a Two-Ocean Navy."[38] Still recovering from the shock of Pearl Harbor, King warned, however, that the "Navy is not in being [now] we are paying the penalty."[39]

The smiling faces of Churchill and Roosevelt provided the false appearance of complete solidarity, as the British sought to retain power and the Americans struggled to protect their future interests. Roosevelt recalled his experience in the First World War, in anticipation of direct American involvement in the Second World War, that "I have always disliked [Churchill] since the time I went to England [but] I'm willing to help them as much I can, but don't want them to play me for a sucker."[40] Ultimately, Churchill and Roosevelt fought for their particular visions—one seeking the restoration of the British Empire and the other fighting for something more consistent with American traditions.

Lincoln inspired Roosevelt in setting the wartime agenda for American sea power in the global maritime arena. He preferred to act on his own authority—customarily undecutting his civilian secretaries of state, Navy, and war. Looking beyond the constitutional checks and balances, Roosevelt intended to end militaristic imperial traditions through the globalization of American principles under the "Four Freedoms" and the United Nations.[41] To attain this end objective, Roosevelt used the CCS to force consensus among the key Allied leaders. On paper, the CCS also subdivided into separate joint staffs within the British and American commands.

The CCS operated under the authority of Churchill and Roosevelt with handshakes and informal gentlemen's agreements. The JCS operated in the same way. King explained that the earlier concept of the Joint Board "is still in the books, but its functions were taken over by the JCS, which has a smaller and consequently more workable membership."[42] He noted that the JCS "never had a written charter [but] its functions and responsibilities paralleled those of the CCS and those of the CCS were written out."[43] King explained that "Army, Navy, and air representatives had their differences of opinion

[and]so did United States and British representatives when they got together [and] decisions by 'majority vote' were not permitted."[44] King considered "it 'far fetched' to say that 'unanimous decisions' were required."[45] The JCS required constant "'give and take' [since] the military leaders did not want to be running to the President or Prime Minister to resolve every argument."[46]

The Anglo-American competition to control tangible strategic resources in pursuit of differing priorities similarly divided the CCS and JCS in managing the secret aspects of operations and intelligence. The British used intelligence to orchestrate American naval operations in the First World War. With this in mind, King walked into the White House room in which Churchill "maintained his 'war room' with all maps and charts [showing] where every vessel in the British Navy was at all times."[47] King considered such micro-management "silly."[48] He criticized the British for wasting time on minutia to "minutest detail and with pinpoint accuracy every minute."[49] Staying out of the politics, King argued that "obviously, with so many participants in the war, the decisions could not be made with 'a show of hands' for nothing could be accomplished by this means."[50]

Churchill inspired Roosevelt to reorganize the Cabinet Room at the White House into an ersatz global command headquarters. Roosevelt placed his naval aide, Capt. John L. McCrea, in charge of what became the White House "Map Room."[51] In turn, he appointed the Hollywood movie star and reserve lieutenant (j.g.) Robert Montgomery to run the daily routines of the Map Room. McCrea and Montgomery handled the most-sensitive sources of intelligence.

British ULTRA classifications intermixed within the American "MAGIC Book," which Montgomery maintained in the Map Room at the White House.[52] Despite the best efforts of the CCS and JCS, the actual definitions of such caveats—and the associated procedures for handling information derived from special intelligence sources—failed to follow any given British or American administrative standard.[53]

Among the critical decisions reached at ARCADIA, Churchill and Roosevelt agreed to follow the general strategic principle of requiring unanimous consent by the CCS to set key objectives for major campaigns. The WPL-46/RAINBOW 5 concept for winning in Europe first always stood chiseled in administrative stone while Chuchill and Roosevelt initially agreed to follow the principle of providing the "essential minimum" to fix enemy forces in Asia.[54] Roosevelt added pressure upon his naval commanders—King especially— to keep equivalent focus on attaining an ultimate victory in Asia. As the war unfolded, King's insistence on balancing European operations against those ongoing in Asia likely shortened the timelines for victory, thereby keeping the CCS and JCS focused on ultimate war aims—saving lives by focusing on sustainable peacetime ends in war.[55]

The CCS framed uniform procedures to coordinate the policies of Churchill and Roosevelt, which enabled cohesion between the Joint Staff and JCS in setting the strategic schedule for the war. Synchronization in the oceanic commons to enable offensive action ashore was among the key priorities. All operations required unanimous CCS approval.[56] For the Americans, the JCS always required unanimous consent, and all operations required execution dates to set procurement and logistical priorities.[57] The standardized designation of "Dog Day," or "D-day," became the chronological basis for retroactive planning for future operations. D-day later became a term synonymous with the Europe First principle, which overshadowed the phased grander strategy to solve the problem of Asia in pursuit of Roosevelt's American dream of the United Nations.[58]

SOLD DOWN THE RIVER

Roosevelt placed a steady hand on the tiller in addressing innumerable challenges of strategy and command. The media sought an explanation for the devastation at Pearl Harbor. Coincident with these tumultuous events, Navy secretary Knox flew to Hawaii to assess the damage. Meanwhile his counterpart in the War Department, Stimson, recommended the immediate dismissals of Kimmel and the US Army commander Lt. Gen. Walter C. Short. The media also called for bureaucratic blood, but Roosevelt hesitated until Knox returned to add his endorsement to the Stimson recommendation to relieve Kimmel and Short. Roosevelt finally issued the directive on December 17. Two days later, Associate Justice Owen Roberts assembled a joint army-navy committee to inform the congressional investigations surrounding the disaster at Pearl Harbor. The controversy never fully settled in popular media.[59]

King strongly disagreed with the decision to summarily relieve the commanders at the scene in Pearl Harbor. Marshall and Arnold guiltily failed to intervene when Roosevelt accepted the recommendations from Secretaries Stimson and Knox to summarily relieve the commander at the scene in Hawaii. In protest, Stark instead offered his resignation to Roosevelt. King felt the same way, although he failed to defend Short and Kimmel as vociferously as he did about about his old friend Pye. Having taken temporary command in the Pacific Fleet after Pearl Harbor, Pye muddled operations to relieve the beleaguered American garrison at Wake Island—just as Nimitz flew from Washington to fill the vacuum of Pacific Fleet command on December 22, 1941. American defenders on Wake Island eventually surrendered. Media reports later highlighted the vicious tactics of the imperial Japanese forces—featuring grisly tales about the slaughtered American garrison of Wake Island.

Pye's decision to hold the fleet at sea coincided with the delayed arrival of Nimitz as the new Pacific Fleet commander. While Pye accepted full responsibility for the disaster at Wake, he also exhibited sound military decision-making by allowing time for the actual fleet commander to take charge of the situation in the Pacific. In the ambiguous days of Pye's tenure in temporary command, Nimitz flew across the American continent to arrive in Hawaii—just in time to join Kimmel and Pye for a very subdued Christmas Eve. Observing helplessly from afar, Stark and King understood Pye's strategic reasoning in handling a tactically superior enemy force during operations surrounding Wake Island. King later credited Pye for marshaling the initial attempt at relieving the garrison at Wake and for "undoubtedly taking the broader viewpoint[, but] he still missed an opportunity."[60]

Short and Kimmel followed the fate of the venerable battleship *Arizona*, as the attack on Pearl Harbor faded into simplistic heroic American myths and popular memories of infamy. The humiliations subsequently endured by Short and Kimmel—along with Pye— also seemed deeply unfair to King. In the aftermath of disaster, King attempted to console Kimmel that "no one thought the Jap[anese] would strike—or even that they were ready to strike!"[61] King later branded Kimmel and Short as "scapegoats to satisfy popular demand for fixing the responsibility for Pearl Harbor."[62] King thought Kimmel and Short had been "'sold down the river' as a political expedient."[63]

War secretary Stimson had a major role in flaming the fires of controversy in the aftermath of Pearl Harbor. His impetuous recommendation to sacrifice Kimmel and Short, as subsequently endorsed by Knox, also failed to stop the damage from spreading in the minds of the American public. When Stimson goaded Roosevelt and Knox to add Stark's name to the list of those responsible for the disaster, King responded by highlighting equal responsibilities held by Marshall and Arnold in the months culminating in the surprises of December 1941. King highlighted then-existing agreements between the Departments of War and Navy, which unambiguously placed responsibility upon the US Army for defending ships in coastal waters and in port at American naval base facilities. Characteristically, King spoke with empirical confidence in criticizing Marshall and Arnold for providing "inadequate defensive power against an air attack on the fleet base at Pearl Harbor."[64] King pressed the fact by stating that "Stark's position in relation to the Pearl Harbor attack was less responsible than that of General Marshall as Chief of Staff of the Army."[65]

Vicious bureaucratic infighting among key commanders contrasted with the optimistic façade, which Churchill and Roosevelt heroically constructed for public consumption. The situation unfolding in the Pacific also coincided with apparent failures of British forces in the Atlantic and North Africa. Parliamentary rivals subjected Churchill to face a vote of confidence, as Roosevelt struggled to marshal congressional support for a long series of emergency wartime measures to rig Americans for global war. Under the earlier ABC-1 and ADB staff agreements, Churchill and Roosevelt empowered their subordinates to act in the absence of a truly mature combined transatlantic policy. British discussions of strategy progressively attained a Yankee accent in efforts to cajole the Americans during the ARCADIA meetings in Washington.

Arrangements negotiated in peacetime frequently provided foundation for strategic improvisation in the absence of an actual plan. Out of necessity, the embattled forces of the British and Dutch joined the Americans of the Asiatic Fleet to form ABDA Command (ABDACom). Facing overwhelming odds in the Philippines, Hart acted in accordance with the ABD staff agreement to embark the submarine USS *Shark* (SS-174). He sailed for Surabaya to report under the overall command of British army general Sir Archibald Wavell. On Christmas Day 1941, Wavell formally designated Hart as the senior naval commander within the hastily organized ABDACom. Hart failed to offer an encouraging response in stating, "Hell, I'm too tired [and] too old."[66] British observers immediately lost faith by describing, "Poor old Hart . . . quite unfitted for the job, he has no kick in him at all."[67]

Memories of past wartime partnerships with the British intermixed with American preconceptions. In characterizing the complexities, observers at the time noted the British tendency of characterizing American procedures as "immature," and conversely the Americans regarded British assumptions of supremacy as being "obsolete."[68] British bumbling also riled the Americans. In the mayhem associated with the evacuation of Singapore, withdrawing British forces misplaced the PURPLE device earlier provided by the US Army.[69] Thus, British haughtiness on questions of security appeared completely unjustified to American commanders. Ultimately, the failure of ABDACom highlighted strategic problems requiring immediate action on the part of the CCS and JCS during the early months of 1942.

BALLADS OF A THIN MAN

War justified the extralegal authorities bestowed upon the CCS and JCS by Churchill and Roosevelt. The ad hoc character of the CCS and JCS never resolved differences of British strategy, or American command. Often in conjunction with British prompting, Marshall undercut King by making public statements about the need for creating a "Supreme Commander over all the armed forces."[70] From the outset, Marshall's views overshadowed King's strong conviction that it "would be 'folly' to substitute the judgement of a 'super-man' for the combined judgement of a panel of experienced leaders representing all the services."[71] Alluding to the policies of the Roosevelt administration, King explained the functions of the CCS and JCS as being interconnected democratic forums to define "what the conduct of the war meant to the future of the world."[72]

Journalists on the Washington battlefield lauded Marshall's diplomatic acumen and towering image as a great leader. By contrast, King seemed like a "dead duck about to be fired."[73] Throughout the first months of 1942, Stark and King stood together in efforts to synthesize the functions of CNO and CominCh. Concurrently, Stark was somewhat surprised when the assistant CNO, Ingersoll, personally lobbied King for reassignment to a seagoing command. Stark had promised Ingersoll the Pacific Fleet, as previously arranged by Nimitz. Surprises unfolding in the immediate aftermath of Pearl Harbor frustrated these plans. Under the circumstances, King nominated Ingersoll as the incumbent to command the Atlantic Fleet.[74] King remembered that "Ingersoll was somewhat miffed that he did not become commander in chief Pacific Fleet rather than the Atlantic."[75] King also noted that Ingersoll "never came to Washington unless we sent for him."[76]

References to the higher authority of the CNO still appeared in message traffic, although the CominCh acronym progressively attained greater significance in communications transmitted to global forces at the front. From humble beginnings, the acronym soon became the shorthand reference to King personally. By implication, messages released under the term became widely understood as a direct order from the "Thin Man" himself.[77] Newly minted as the CominCh, King directed Ingersoll to concentrate on the North Atlantic convoy routes to Britain. Concurrently, King directed Nimitz to follow the principle that "all your objectives are hereby condensed into two: hold the Hawaiian Islands and maintain communications with the United States [and] hold the Hawaii-Samoa line and extend it to Australia."[78]

King faced unprecedented challenges in navigating uncharted political waters while coordinating multinational strategic priorities within the CCS and JCS. The mandatory retirement age of sixty-four years appeared just over the horizon as King participated in a staged ceremony with Navy secretary Knox on December 30, 1941. For publicity purposes, King reenacted his oath of office as the CominCh. Simultaneously, Ingersoll formally assumed command under the shadow of the Naval War College as the new Atlantic Fleet commander on board the historic decks of the frigate *Constellation*. On the other side of the globe, Nimitz concurrently read his orders for a small audience on the quarterdeck of USS *Grayling* (SS-209) at Pearl Harbor.[79] Stark dutifully held his station as the CNO when King publicly appeared on center stage as the CominCh.[80]

Bringing order to the chaos of the CCS and JCS, King placed top priority on fixing the internal bureaucratic problems of the Navy Department. Among his first concerns upon taking control as CominCh, King noted that the "Pearl Harbor disaster has a terrible smell [and] something went completely wrong with our intelligence activities."[81] While organizing the CominCh headquarters, Edwards recalled finding "King enthroned in the most disreputable office I have ever seen [and that] someone had moved out in a hurry, taking the furniture with him, but not the dirt."[82] Edwards then "liberated a flat[-]top desk from somewhere and a couple of chairs."[83] He recalled that King "sat on one side of the desk, opposite him sat Russell Willson."[84] Edwards and Low augmented everything by stealing a "broken[-]down table from a friend who was out to lunch and set up shop in a corner of [King's] office."[85] "I recall thinking," Edwards concluded, "that as the head-quarters of the greatest navy in the world it fell somewhat short of being impressive."[86]

King configured the CominCh staff as a small organization capable of embarking his flagship at any time. Although tied to the pier, he maintained seagoing watches and routines for the CominCh staff. He initially occupied the flagship, USS *Vixen* (PG-53)—berthed at the Washington Navy Yard. He concurrently appropriated the steam yacht *Delphine* to serve as a flagship for the CominCh staff. In January 1942, King selected Cmdr. George F. Grisham to supervise the conversion of *Delphine*. Having earlier served as an enlisted man under King at New London in the 1920s, Grisham knew the expectations of his boss. During overhauls in Detroit, Grisham transformed *Delphine* into the flagship of the US Navy, USS *Dauntless*. For the duration of the war, *Dauntless* stood ready to sail at the pier on the Washington Navy Yard.

The bureaucratic routines of the Navy Department greatly frustrated King, particularly as superficial organizational hurdles undercut efforts to manage the strategic priorities. Mobilization and procurement issues further hindered progress in King's campaign to synthesize operations with intelligence. Edwards explained:

> Joint planning between Army and Navy never took the form of a lot of Army and Navy offices getting together in one room for joint planning. First, one got the general concept of what was desired. Then, the Army plan was gotten up. Then the Navy plan in rough was gotten up. Then, Army and Navy planners got together and adjusted their rough plans so that an integral plan for the whole business would come out.[87]

Turner and Edwards managed the effort to unify the strategic administration functions of OpNav with the operational-planning and tactical-command functions of CominCh. Turner and Edwards synthesized "war room" analysis under Cmdr. George C. Dyer. Across the hallway, Cmdr. Charles H. Murphy assisted by organizing the "strategic plot," which included information derived from intercepted enemy messages.[88]

THINGS WOULD BE ALL RIGHT

King concentrated on major policy issues while empowering Edwards to manage the creativity among the underlings within the various subdivisions of the CNO and CominCh staffs. Initially, King accepted British overtures to lead efforts ongoing in the Atlantic and within ABDACom. Indeed, an alternative assessment of early successes by enemy sub-marines in the Atlantic also reflected critical shortcomings within the British organization during the early phases of 1942—when American forces muddled through mindboggling challenges that far exceeded the personal authorities of any given individual, including

Roosevelt and King. During this period of uncertainty, King expected the seagoing professionals of the American sea services to accept significant risks to buy time for building new warships, perfecting new weapons, and concurrently train fresh recruits.[89] Demonstrating great creativity, King's men proposed the wild idea of using army bombers to stage a long-range aircraft carrier strike against Tokyo. King signed off on the preliminary proposal, as presented for JCS consideration on January 4, 1942.[90]

The seemingly outlandish idea of launching army bombers from aircraft carriers had a longer history. The concept had been the subject of many barroom discussions among army and naval aviators for more than two decades. Under the circumstances following Pearl Harbor, the idea literally took off with the plans submitted by Captains Donald B. Duncan and Low. During discussions between Churchill and Roosevelt, King gained the requisite permissions for Duncan and Low to work up the concept into an actual operation.[91] The air operations officer on board the newly commissioned USS *Hornet* (CV-8), Lt. Cmdr. Stephen Jurika, helped develop the tactical target list, phases of the operation, and the scheme of maneuver. Jurika offered intimate knowledge of Japan from his previous service as a language officer assigned as an assistant naval attaché in Tokyo. Jurika knew the best targets to achieve maximum psychological effects against the Japanese.[92]

Jurika assisted Low and Duncan in framing the plan to deploy an aircraft carrier task force in a surprise attack against the Japanese home islands. The outlandish scheme was the launching of army bombers from an aircraft carrier. King asked Marshall to borrow B-25 Mitchell bombers for the mission. Two-star major general Henry "Hap" Arnold resisted the idea of releasing army aircraft to the navy. Roosevelt ultimately approved the operation, then known as the "Joint Army-Navy Bombing Project." Roosevelt directed Marshall to share army aircraft with the navy, and King compromised by accepting Lt. Col. James H. Doolittle to lead army pilots in the attack against Japan.[93] King supervised the work of Low and Duncan from within the CominCh headquarters. On the basis of their recommendations, King placed Halsey in overall command as the task force commander on USS *Enterprise* (CV-6), and Capt. Marc A. Mitscher carrying Doolittle and his bombers on *Hornet*.

In the dim morning light over the pitching decks, *Hornet* turned into the wind as sailors guided Doolittle's B-25 into position for launch. Cleared for takeoff, the bomber initially hovered precariously over the misty gray sea. Doolittle's men followed the lead aircraft into the rising sun over Japan. American diplomats meanwhile awaited their fate from within the embassy in Tokyo. Having earlier supervised Jurika during their service together as naval attachés, Capt. Henri Smith-Hutton remembered how the Japanese guards surrounding the American embassy always rendered proper salutes while avoiding eye contact.[94] Following Pearl Harbor, Smith-Hutton also continued regular meetings with his friendNakamura Katsuhira, an Imperial Japanese Navy captain. In reflection, Smith-Hutton described Nakamura as

> rather sad because I think he was really a friend of the United States. He said, 'Yes, the report was true [but that] he had just learned about it himself and could verify it. As to the declaration of war, he couldn't say, because that would have to come from the Foreign Ministry and was not a Navy Department matter.[95]

The Kampetei maintained an ominous presence at the embassy.[96] Ambassador Joseph C. Grew encouraged Smith-Hutton to organize miniature golf tournaments in the hallways of the American embassy. Four months following Pearl Harbor, Smith-Hutton remembered seeing red dots painted on the wings of low-flying bombers over Tokyo. Smith-Hutton witnessed the so-called Doolittle Raid from the ground, and his experiences later proved vital after his repatriation and subsequent service as King's intelligence officer.[97]

Stark progressively ceded the functions of the CNO to meld with those carried by King within the CominCh headquarters. To assist, Edwards reported from the Atlantic simultaneously with the arrival of Cooke from the Pacific. Edwards had impressed King by employing US Navy submarines in the Atlantic. Cooke had survived the Pearl Harbor attack as skipper on the Pacific Fleet flagship, *Pennsylvania*.[98] "Edwards and Cooke knew that they were part of my staff," King later explained, and that they "were never trying to fix things up for themselves."[99] Edwards and Cooke enabled King to run the circus by encouraging "free and uninhibited debate until he had absorbed all points of view." Edwards recalled that King "would then come forth with a clear-cut scheme, usually so obviously applicable as to cause all concerned to wonder why they had not thought of it themselves."[100] King recalled that "Dick and Savvy are salty—once I had them, I knew things would be alright [*sic*]."[101]

CHAPTER 20
The Fixers

Churchill and Roosevelt set the tone for transatlantic maritime policy, as the CCS and JCS developed means by which to synthesize combined strategy. Throughout 1942, King kept the CominCh staff focused on coalition priorities for Europe First while simultaneously managing to keep the imperial Japanese from consolidating offensive gains in Asia. He told trusted journalist friends that "every theatre of the war is linked with every other, and success in one theater may profoundly affect the struggle in the other."[1] Similar to the grander war effort, King lamented the peacetime practices of promoting "doogooders and politicians."[2] King blamed service academies and the "fixers" in BuNav for nurturing the wrong types of naval officers in peacetime.[3] Recalling the first months of the war, King lamented that the "best of the bunch had to be called home and relieved after six days."[4]

King perceived Nimitz as indecisive in performing the fundamental responsibility of managing personnel. King furthermore worried about the growing size of the joint organization and associated Pacific Fleet staff in Hawaii, which surrounded Nimitz. King explained his view of Nimitz by recalling a series of wartime exchanges concerning his request for an aviation-qualified admiral. King considered the qualification unnecessary for commanding aircraft carriers in the Pacific. In attempting to fulfill the Nimitz request, King listed eligible candidates as Horne, Towers, Noyes, Turner, Halsey, and McCain.[5] Of this number, Towers, Halsey, and McCain already held commands in the Pacific Fleet. King's former chief of staff, RAdm. Leigh Noyes, served as skipper in the newly commissioned USS *Wasp* (CV-7). King lamented that Noyes "had trouble in making decisions."[6] Under the circumstances, King offered Nimitz three alternatives—with Horne as the top choice, followed by Turner, and then Towers.[7]

Observing from within the CominCh headquarters, Edwards advised King on matters concerning the assignments of key commanders. As the deputy CominCh, Edwards noted that King "saw the president very frequently [in] 1942, several times a week if not every day."[8] He always acted with confidence in selecting commanders. Edwards explained that King named commanders "after exchange of ideas at CominCh-CinCPAC conferences[,] with exchange of suggestions from SecNav and President often entering in."[9] Recalling the challenges of 1942, Edwards explained that the "Solomons campaign was not a campaign but rather a desperate 'reasoned risk' and felt that it rather than Midway was the actual turning point of the war."[10] Continuing, Edwards reasoned that Nimitz had a minimal role in this ultimate success, since the Japanese "still had a strong Navy after Midway but did not after the Solomons."[11] In examining the willingness to take such strategic risks, Edwards thought that "it was extremely fortunate in having men of the caliber of King and Marshall at the helm from the very beginning instead of having to blunder around before finally finding adequate leaders."[12]

Given overlapping responsibilities to pursue victory in Europe first, King faced few alternatives in allowing Nimitz to operate as autonomously as possible in executing the strategy for Asia. When King offered to send Horne and Turner to assist, Nimitz rejected Horne for holding seniority in lineal standing, and Turner for having too many personal enemies among the CinCPAC staff. King considered the rejection of Horne as a sign of weakness on the part of Nimitz.[13] In frustration, King gave Nimitz the devil's choice between the strong personalities of Turner and Towers. Nimitz again annoyed King by rejecting both Turner and Towers.[14] Edwards recalled King's silent rage whenever Nimitz forced an ongoing back-and-forth exchange in making decisions. Edwards waited as King "quietly chewed on his cigarette holder, sipped on his coffee, and the vein on his forehead began to pulse vigorously."[15]

King always respected Nimitz for being a very competent engineer with significant experience in submarines and surface operations. King also worried about the easygoing touch of Nimitz. Given the situation in the spring of 1942, King overruled Nimitz and sent Turner to plan the early offensive responses to the Japanese. King's deputy, Edwards, explained that "Turner planned the Solomons invasion [and] was sent out to carry it out."[16] Given concerns about the command organization in the Pacific, King initiated a rigorous schedule to hold face-to-face meetings with Nimitz roughly every sixty days in either San Francisco or Hawaii. King frequently flew to the other side of the Atlantic for similar meetings with Stark in London—and beyond for gatherings of the CCS and JCS on the other side of the planet.[17]

"THE NUMBER ONE MAN, PRESENT"

Like the great captains of the past who maneuvered on horseback or took a prominent place in the cockpit with the sailors in combat, King used electronic communications and airplanes to engage his enemies more closely. His towering personal presence also shaped strategic deliberations within the CCS and JCS.[18] Observing from the corners, Edwards explained that King and Churchill "got along well together, as they were entirely frank and determined[; though] they collided from time to time they understood each other."[19] Recalling the dynamics within the CCS and JCS, King admitted that "with a group like that, we argued about this, that[,] and the other."[20] King admitted that "I was never a yes man and I knew that sometimes Marshall was firmly against some ideas of FDR."[21] RAdm. Julius Furer observed that "one was ever left in doubt as to where King stood on any question [and] Roosevelt changed the subject when he saw the color rising in Ernie's face."[22]

British and American representatives on the CCS and JCS universally criticized the hardheaded nature of King. In defense of his boss, Edwards explained that King fully "agreed (and always had) that it was necessary to knock out Germany first [and keeping] his policy of never letting the Japanese get consolidated anywhere."[23] Counterparts on the CCS and JCS credited King for keeping the wider perspective in framing Allied strategy.[24] His counterparts within the Allied high command frequently grew frustrated with King, particularly Brooke and Arnold. Recalling experiences with the BAD in Washington and then as First Sea Lord, Cunningham observed that King "had a rooted antipathy to placing United States naval forces under British command, though he raised no objection to British forces and units being under United States command wherever he thought it fit and proper."[25]

Churchill drove the British members of the Joint Staff to stand firm in negotiations with American counterparts in the CCS. In dealings with the British, King stated that "Sir Dudley Pound was a very sound man."[26] King explained that Air Marshal Charles Portal "had real brains, and understood strategy [and] very much broader in his views than Arnold." King thought Portal "had the damnedest beak of a nose that anyone had ever seen [but] Arnold was not in the same class as Portal as to brains and abilities."[27] King greatly respected Field Marshal Sir John Dill but equally disliked Field Marshal Sir Alan Brooke.[28] "Brooke talked so damned fast," King complained, that "you could not understand what he was talking about!"[29] King noted that "it became a bit of a joke between Marshall and me because Alan Brooke talked so fast that they just named him Alanbrooke."[30]

Stark and King worked well together in overcoming these problems of combined strategy and global naval command. During the first four months after Pearl Harbor, King explained that "Stark managed the meetings, and was the Number One man present."[31] Stark and King drove strategic decisions. King explained that "I caused a chart to be made up [showing] two items that loom largely and count most in the conduct of war—manpower and munitions."[32] He emphasized, "We never had enough ships [and] we built ships all over the place and we never had too many."[33] King considered that shipping "was the machinery through which the President and Prime Minister exercised their control over grand strategy."[34] King explained that "you had to decide what to do with what you had and get busy about making more[,] and maybe three months from now, why you might be able to shift the balance."[35] King stipulated, "Remember again, please, we always had to be looking six months, eight months ahead, but all we could decide was what would happen in the next three or four months, but we could have a look ahead and anticipate what we might be able to do in eight or nine months or a year." He concluded, "So we just stepped along as circumstances permitted—or could be made to permit."[36]

Differing policy objectives between Churchill and Roosevelt caused extra work for the strategic planners on the CCS and JCS. King recalled that "we usually had one or more cover plans, and we sometimes tried not to be too careful about the cover plans, so that the enemy got hold of part of them and thought he knew what we were going to do [and] that would suit us just fine."[37] King then quoted words attributed to "Stonewall Jackson: 'Mystify, mislead, and surprise the enemy."[38] Logistical planning thus intermixed with deception planning. Looking outward in planning combined strategy within the CCS and JCS, King always held the priorities for postwar reconstruction as the center focus for coordinating the demise of the Axis Tripartite. For King, global priorities fell under the overall strategy of "Europe First and Asia too."[39]

Unwilling to relinquish the future of the British Empire to the Americans, Churchill pressed his admirals to replicate the First World War relationship between the Admiralty and Navy Department. Roosevelt quietly provided the foundation for King to play his strategic role—as the counterforce against British efforts to subordinate American sea power in the Second World War. Reflecting upon the circumstances during the first four months of 1942, King recalled, "Sir Dudley Pound, the First Sea Lord, offered me twenty coal[-]burning trawlers to help out [and] I took 'em and was glad to get them."[40] In addition, the Royal Navy loaned the US Navy the HMS *Victorious,* which sailed under an American flag as USS *Robin* for operations in the Pacific. As King's vision for the American fleet remained in an early stage of development, pooling resources provided means by which the Anglo-American fleets held the line in 1942.[41]

German naval operations in the Atlantic and into the Indian Ocean frequently overwhelmed British naval capacity, requiring the diversion of American resources from other fronts. Similarly, Japanese forces represented a real threat in the Pacific. Taking a personal role in setting the course for American sea power, Roosevelt also inspired American naval officers to complain, "I wish to God [Roosevelt] get absorbed in the Army for a change."[42] The official wartime chronicler of the Navy Department, Dr. Robert G. Albion observed that King "wielded unprecedented professional power both in policy-making and operational control."[43] Albion also noted that Roosevelt's "love for the navy was possessive."[44]

Roosevelt empowered King to institute radical changes in the organization of the US Navy. At King's request, Roosevelt recalled retired rear admiral Emory S. Land for active service with rank as a (three-star) vice admiral. Land reorganized the peacetime Maritime Commission into the War Shipping Administration (WSA), which became the central civil-military organization involved with merchant and warship production.[45] King and Land set priorities for American industrial requirements to rapidly expand the merchant and naval fleets. Both shared the common vision of building ships to perform specific tasks, working together to overcome bureaucratic atrophy among the various bureaus of the Navy Department. King and Land drove the civilian captains of industry, like William Francis Gibbs, Henry J. Kaiser, and Andrew Higgins.[46]

Civilians traditionally controlled the course and speed of change within the Navy Department. Roosevelt vested King with supercharged authority to break traditions for the purposes of achieving the full wartime potential of American sea power. Simultaneously with efforts to institute military order within the chaos of the Navy Department, King also kept unrelenting pressure on himself to execute the full scope of the WPL 46/ RAINBOW 5 strategy—which he himself helped develop during previous peacetime service with the General Board—to win victory in Europe first. King reasoned that "if the British had the Atlantic and the Americans had the Pacific as separate fronts, the CCS would never have been able to synchronize offensive priorities on all fronts."[47] King concluded that "defensive people are always chasing the enemy on their terms [but] I always like to make the enemy fight on my terms."[48] King referred to the US Navy manual on conducting "smokers" for boxing tournaments on board ship and explained that "sometimes you have to take a few punches before you can knock 'em out with just the one that they didn't see coming."[49]

The CominCh headquarters in Washington slowly evolved into the strategic center of American strategy under King. As a result, the preexisting OpNav staff under the CNO progressively followed the trends. Taking an increasingly distant role in coordinating efforts as the CNO, Stark wrote several letters to King with the phrase "from one sitting on the sidelines."[50] In one particular memo, Stark then suggested that King should "shut down the Naval War College as an educational institution; make it the US Strategic Planning center; and transmit its output to the Joint Planners here in Washington."[51] King flatly told Stark that "I am not in sympathy with the views of the 'one sitting on the sidelines.'"[52] On February 13, 1942, King rejected the idea as "totally unrealistic and unsound."[53] Continuing, King told Stark that "it seems to me that any endeavor to separate strategic planning from operations categorically is a serious misconception of the realities of conducting a war program."[54] King argued against efforts to "technically sub-divide the functions of command [since] they are all parts of an indivisible whole."[55]

The ghosts of Luce and Sims hovered in the corners of King's mind as he framed the administrative intersections between the functions of CNO and CominCh. Stark directly participated in the reorganization, as implemented by King. From their studies of staff organization at the Naval War College, Stark and King fused the staffs—delineating administrative functions within the CNO subsections of OpNav with the established delineation of "Op," whereas the newly reconfigured CominCh staff carried the "F" to denote a seagoing "fleet" staff assignment.[56] Many individuals carried both the "Op" and "F" designations.[57] Notably, anyone holding the "F" designation received sea pay. King thought that "<u>differentiation</u> (not separation) between the functions of this job and that of the Chief of Naval Operations is still indeterminate and will take time to work out." King told Cooke that "it seems to me that differentiation should hinge on a distinction between 'projects' and 'plans.'"[58]

The fleet organization concepts instituted under Stark and King originated from within the General Board. By 1942, the ideas developed over five years culminated in the reestablishments of the geographic fleets and the consolidation of authorities under the CNO. The fusion of CNO with CominCh during the first four months after Pearl Harbor also followed a methodically executed timeline in which Stark actively participated in enabling the empowerment of King as both CNO and CominCh. Admirals Richardson and Snyder unfortunately harbored personal grudges against Stark. In memoirs, Richardson alleged that Stark had "utterly failed to display loyalty downward that every subordinate has a right to expect from his superior officer."[59] Richardson put words in the mouth of Roosevelt that he "did not give a damn what happened to Stark so long as he was gotten out of Washington as soon as practicable."[60] Richardson mischaracterized the circumstances surrounding the promulgation of Executive Order 9096 (EO 9096) by smearing Stark.

King provided an account that corresponded more closely with the original documentation concerning the development and implementation of EO 9096.[61] Knowing the political ramifications after Pearl Harbor, King rushed to hold Stark in place as the CNO—since his role in the JCS centered on building the transatlantic relationships between the Admiralty and Navy Department. As CominCh, King's focused on global strategy and operations. He had enough on his plate in meeting the multifront challenges of 1942. King also thought that the "CNO should be the top man."[62] In a memorandum, King asked Richardson to explain the "paramount duty" clause in the draft signed by Roosevelt in EO 9096. Richardson ignored King and passed the buck to Navy secretary Knox. Before anyone told Stark about his position being nullified by the clause, Knox told King that "we understand you like Stark very well, but we have decided now to change things."[63] King then explained, "I was saddled with the job of telling Admiral Stark."[64]

Having had a hand in writing the ultimate outcome as the CNO, Stark firmly agreed with the verbiage of EO 9096. In many respects, the administrative merger of the CNO and CominCh under the singular authority of King also originated under Leahy in 1937. Whenever Roosevelt pushed the limits of constitutional authority, Stark also assumed full responsibility as the CNO after 1939. He also had a hand in writing the verbiage of EO 9096 in March 1942, which effectively placed King in full command of American sea power. In reflection, King observed that "Stark is a damned good man and I'll never forgive the Army for not taking at least part of the blame for Pearl Harbor."[65]

From King's perspective, the politics of Pearl Harbor always posed an unnecessary distraction during the war. The wartime media also smeared the public reputation of naval officers like Kimmel and Stark, while army officers like Marshall and Arnold somehow escaped the humiliation of having to explain their more direct responsibility for problems that influenced the disaster of Pearl Harbor.[66] For this reason, among others, King thought his army counterparts—and the airpower propaganda machine of the War Department—specifically soiled Stark's good name to undercut the Navy Department as part of a broader postwar army-navy unification strategy.[67] King told journalists about feeling "not too happy about the Army's part in the Pearl Harbor affair."[68]

Roosevelt fully recognized the political ramifications of Pearl Harbor and withheld Stark as CNO as long as practicable before singing EO 9096. Roosevelt then orchestrated a soft landing for Stark. With camera lightbulbs flashing inside the Oval Office, Roosevelt decorated Stark with a second Distinguished Service Medal. Roosevelt applauded Stark for "building and administering the largest peacetime navy in the history of this country."[69] Roosevelt lionized Stark for exhibiting "exceptional qualities of leadership and outstanding ability to effect a high state of training for war and the building of a two-ocean navy."[70] Roosevelt also conjured the spirit of Sims in announcing the decision to elevate the mission in London from three to four stars, with Stark assigned to the newly established role of commander, US Naval Forces in Europe (ComNavEu).

By no means was Stark sent to the critical front in Europe as a form of bureaucratic purgatory after Pearl Harbor, especially when examined within the context of the burgeoning battles for control over the transatlantic alliances between London and Washington. King relieved Stark as the CNO on March 27, 1942, which established him among the most consequential Americans in maritime history—perhaps adjacent to George Washington or Sims, since King stood as the only officer to hold the unified duties of CNO and CominCh as well as his associated functions as the senior American naval member of the CCS and JCS.

The administrative nuances of high command often appear between the lines of bureaucratic minutia. Notably, the former CNO, Stark, retained the number 1 ranking as the most senior flag officer on the active list as ComNavEu. His symbolic seniority also measured against his singular function to unify the efforts of British and American sea power. Although Stark fell subordinate to the CNO/CominCh in strategy and operations, King held lineal standing as the number 2–ranking flag officer on active service. When Leahy later joined the mix, Stark and King still stood supreme on the CCS and JCS. Until the closing months of the war, Leahy always served on temporary duty on retired status—but only at Roosevelt's pleasure.

Civilian bureaucrats within the Navy Department were absolutely horrified by the authorities vested in the admirals. Secretaries Hull and Stimson voiced strong protests about Roosevelt's extraordinary measures under EO 9096, although Navy secretary Knox kept his powder dry. Behind closed doors, Knox supported King against the loud protests of Undersecretary Forrestal. To preserve civilian control within the Navy Department, Forrestal also used backchannels with Missouri senator Harry S Truman. The supercharged wartime authorities bestowed upon King under EO 9096 remained an open debate for the remainder of the war.[71] The personality clashes between Forrestal and King rambled behind closed doors within the Navy Department for the remainder of their lives.[72]

Roosevelt always held the final responsibility for defining the authorities carried by Marshall and King. King blamed Marshall and Arnold for failing to defend the fleet in accordance with joint army-navy agreements, as imposed by the War Department upon their navy counterparts. To mitigate the personality dynamics among the JCS, Roosevelt used trusted confidants, like Leahy, to monitor the relationship. Capt. John L. McCrea meanwhile provided regular updates to King about conversations between Roosevelt and Leahy. Well placed to know details, McCrea ran the Map Room at the White House.[73] Knowing the difficulties inherent with coalition warfare, McCrea once asked King about rumors in the media that when "they get in trouble they always send for the sons of bitches."[74] "No, John," King explained, "I didn't say it, but I wish I had."[75]

YOU LOOK UNHAPPY

Intelligence collaboration proved analogous to the oakum between the holystoned decks of the grand Anglo-American naval armada, which executed the combined strategies of the British Empire and United States. Unlike in the previous world war, however, Roosevelt took firm control over negotiating policy with other multinational counterparts. Following the ARCADIA meetings and the establishments of the CCS and JCS, Roosevelt specifically empowered King to be the staunch advocate for the future of American sea power under EO 9096. Roosevelt fully understood the requirements—always reliant upon King to serve up the hard realities in deliberations among the CCS and JCS. Knowing the remarkable extraconstitutional responsibilities inherent with EO 9096, the president of the Naval War College, Kalbfus, congratulated King that "from the earliest days [my] thought for you has always been '<u>more</u> power to you.'"[76] Kalbfuls wrote King that "in offering my congratulations on your latest step upward, I now am changing my slogan to '<u>All</u> power to you.'"[77]

The Naval War College served as the prerequisite for officers assigned to the headquarters of Sims in the previous war. This rule also applied for King in selecting leaders to enact his will within his headquarters.[78] Naval War College credentials proved difficult to find alongside the names of many officers below the rank of captain on the active list. Making best with what he had, King shanghaied war-college-certified veterans of the Atlantic Fleet staff to unify the staffs of CNO and ComInCh. His trusted "henchmen" from the Atlantic Fleet, Bieri and Low, identified bureaucratic holdouts and assisted in the reorganization of the CNO and ComInCh headquarters.[79] At Stark's recommendation, King placed Smedberg in temporary command of the "war room." Also at Stark's recommendation, King recalled Dyer from sea duty as the executive officer on USS *Indianapolis* (CA-35) to relieve Smedberg.[80]

The regular bureaucratic processes for detailing personnel to key assignments proved inadequate to meet wartime necessities. Stark helped King build his team inside the burgeoning global headquarters on the third deck of Main Navy. Seagoing officers stood deeply frustrated upon receiving flash orders to leave the front for duty ashore. For example, King personally released the order "relief immediate—Dyer proceeds ComInCh Washington."[81] Adding to the point, King directed Dyer that "you will consider yourself immediately detached from duty on board [and] any delay counts as leave."[82] The skipper on *Indianapolis*, Capt. Edward W. Hanson, told Dyer, "Ernie never asks, so you better get going."[83] A few days later, Dyer reported to King. "You look unhappy," King said to Dyer, and to which he responded, "I *am* unhappy."[84] Dyer complained, "I was executive officer of a fine cruiser in the war zone and I find myself ordered to Washington."[85] King explained to Dyer that "I was told by an officer for whose judgement I have great respect [Stark] that 'if I wanted an officer who would spit in my eye *when* it was necessary to spit, I should send for you.'"[86]

King directed Dyer to fix the organization within operations and intelligence subdivisions of the Navy Department. Dyer explained that the "F-35 War Room was something of a dummy room, with relatively low order of security [and] for people entitled to see <u>something</u>."[87] Continuing, Dyer noted that the "F-11 Chart Room was on a higher level, with [an] admittance list initially less than 12."[88] Dyer said that the "plot room represented the lowest level of all [whereas] it should have had all the information."[89] Dyer explained:

> The most immediate problem was the submarine, so a section was set up for [the] tracking of German submarines and [the] detour of merchant shipping around them. A/S [antisubmarine] was the principal business of F-35: "operational information" and providing "information of ships" movements (Op-38-W had not dealt in A/S business. Capt. Leighton kept a record of where ships were, new ships going into commission, limited information on foreign navies). F-35 provided official weather forecasts in code, and submarine warnings (as soon as [the] submarine [was] physically sighted, fact broadcast to all merchant ships). Communications deserves high praise for their speed and efficiency in these warnings: within ten minutes of receipt of SOS they would often have a warning out on the air.[90]

Information derived from cryptanalysis flowed freely among the analysts. In the spring of 1942, British critiques of security prompted King to stipulate that the "number of officers who have access to this Chart Room must be kept to a <u>low minimum</u>."[91]

Civilian bureaucrats dominated the routines of the Navy Department, which hindered progress. Dyer explained that the "naval appropriations acts had always limited the number of enlisted personnel on duty in Washington [so] even in the War Plans Division civilians were used."[92] Dyer recalled that civil servants lacked the right mindset for war, "work[ing] from 0650 to 2100 a normal routine." "At their usual quitting time," Dyer chuckled, "civilians calmly walked off."[93] An associate of Dyer remembered incredulously that while "our ships were getting torpedoed, these old retreads and civil servants would watch the clock until quitting time, stop what they were doing, get up from their desk, and walk out."[94] Dyer recalled the orders issued by King in February 1942, directing to have the "civilians out [in] 30 days."[95]

Civilian bureaucrats on the Washington battlefield reacted to King's reorganization directives in a manner akin to their shock after Pearl Harbor. Walking the decks of the Navy Department, King overhauled the culture within Main Navy as he had on the aircraft carrier *Lexington* ten years earlier. He customarily entered offices unannounced, introduced himself, and then questioned civil servant employees about their age and whether they had prior service. Dyer and another aide, Russell, accompanied King on the daily patrols. King often lulled targets in trite conversations before lowering the boom. Russell recalled that the "following day[,] many of them received orders [and] some of the old retreads wanted to put on their old rank, which King generally accepted."[96] He usually rejected civilian requests for direct appointments to higher naval ranks. Older retirees and reservists frequently served under younger officers on the active list of King's navy of the Second World War.[97]

The singular authorities of EO 9096 enabled King to transform the bureaucratic culture of the Navy Department. Recalling experience with Sims and the London Flagship, King kept the CominCh organization small. Initially, Dyer recommended plans to renovate the Navy Department to accommodate "an eventual staff of 400, requiring five wings of third deck."[98] He based the projected figure "on the fact that as Admiral Sims had 400 in London in 1918, at least that number would be required here."[99] Although the Sims headquarters of the First World War provided a good point of reference, King rejected the idea of building such a large organization. "King has always been very loathed to add personnel," Dyer explained, and that "King constantly made efforts to reduce, rather than add."[100] Dyer later recalled that King would be "damned if he was going to have a staff of more than fifty as CominCh."[101]

King cleared the Navy Department of unnecessary bureaucrats and formed the CominCh headquarters around a few carefully chosen loyalists. Having become seasoned in the bureaucratic monoculture among civil servants, King observed that one should not "be too hard on the civil service-people—they are a lot of 'red tape' wielders who merely 'slave' at their jobs and have no discretion but to fulfill the rules to the letter."[102] He also explained the key to success in combating bureaucrats was that "my experience in life has been that things come 'right' the more one is steadfast in the belief that they will—and never gives up the belief—no matter what delays and discouragements may intervene." Continuing, King advised, "Don't let anything get you down—hold fast to the belief that you'll get what you want if you stick to it—work for it—plan for it—and don't take 'no' for an answer."[103]

The spartan façade of King immediately set the tone for new members of the CominCh staff. The underlying sense of fear mixed with pride for those serving under King. Having earned his doctoral credentials in history at the University of London before joining the Naval Reserves, Lieutenant Walter Muir Whitehill characterized the experience of joining the staff in the CominCh headquarters as follows:

> I occupied a desk in their crowded office, Room 3047, across the corridor, I had come to know the thoughts and personality of Admiral King through his papers, including those formidable yellow chits with a very few penciled words followed by the initial "K," which were capable of setting mighty events in motion, but I was entirely without personal knowledge of him. Just as a pair of footprints or a vacant chair served to represent the Buddha in the earliest Buddhist art, so the sound of a buzzer summoning the Flag Secretary to room 3048 was the only symbol of Admiral King in room 3047, yet his unseen presence dominated the room.[104]

The example set by King inspired "practically every officer on his staff [to be] fiercely loyal to him."[105] To reduce duplication between the CNO and CominCh, King unified the operations and intelligence-plotting functions. King formed CominCh around three primary divisions—F-1 for Plans, F-2 for Readiness, and F-3 for Operations. The Plans/F-1 occupied parts of the sixth and seventh wings, Readiness/F-2 worked in another half of the seventh wing, and Operations/F-3 was nearest to King's office off the seventh wing.

Coincident with the arrival of German submarines in American waters, King endorsed the recommendation of Dyer to subdivide the war room into a clearly defined Pacific Section and Atlantic Section.[106] Among the personnel assigned to the F-35 tracking room, Dyer placed a fellow submariner, Lt. George H. Laird, in charge of submarine tracking. Before the Pearl Harbor disaster, Laird earlier completed temporary-duty assignments inside the Admiralty OIC in London and CinCWA in Liverpool. Having similar experience with British methods, Lt. Donald E. Lane became the tracking officer for the Pacific. Merchant mariners joined F-35, mobilized from the US Naval Reserve.[107] Having worked as merchant mariners in civilian ships, Eugene E. Husting and Paul N. Culp joined the F-35 plotting room as reserve naval officers.[108] Merchant mariners offered an intimate understanding of shipping routes—thereby providing means to predict the most-likely areas of enemy operations.

Fleet commanders struggled in establishing collaborative relationships with the combined area commanders of MacArthur in the Asiatic and Stark in Europe. Once King instituted changes within the Navy Department, he also noted that "no coordinating agency exists for submarine tracking and antisubmarine operations among district and fleet organizations."[109] King directed Low and Dyer to fix these disconnections between the operations and intelligence organizations of the shore establishment and seagoing forces. In April 1942, Low recruited an old shipmate, retired lieutenant commander Kenneth A. Knowles, to join the team at CominCh. His prior service in the Asiatic Fleet informed his work as the civilian chief editor of *Our Navy* magazine. Knowles had the right analytical mindset with the ability to reach logical conclusions.[110]

Personal connections influenced the decision to bring Knowles into the CominCh headquarters. Having first enlisted in the US Marines, he graduated with the US Naval Academy Class of 1927. Knowles then served in the Asiatic Fleet on a variety of warships and native junks, patrolling the waters of the Philippines and into China. During service on the destroyer USS *Paul Jones* (DD-230), he won the lasting respect of the executive officer, Lt. Cmdr. Francis S. Low.[111] Knowles drew the attention of the Asiatic Fleet intelligence officer, Lt. Cmdr. Henri Smith-Hutton.[112] After service with Captains Russell Willson and Charles "Savvy" Cooke, Knowles joined the flagship *Pennsylvania*—where he gained an early appreciation for the role of fleet intelligence officers at sea by working with Lt. Cmdr. Joseph J. Rochefort during the fleet problems of 1936 and 1937.[113]

Familial connections among military and naval personalities further amplified the potential for Knowles in efforts to synthesize operations with intelligence from within the Navy Department. He had the intangible advantage of being a first cousin to the Army chief of staff, Marshall. In addition to his exemplary naval service record, Knowles earlier made an impression with King during Fleet Problem XVII. During events conducted off the West Coast near the Panama Canal, Knowles helped King develop tactical procedures for coordinating antisubmarine operations.[114] In the peacetime logic of the Navy Department, Knowles received orders to transfer to the retired list upon failing to screen for sea duty with BuMed. In the era before radar, poor eyesight disqualified Knowles from service in the fleet. He fought vigorously in an unsuccessful bureaucratic battle to change the ruling of BuMed, although he ended up on the retired list in 1937.[115]

Former shipmates close to King pulled together on behalf of Knowles in rigging the lines of bureaucracy within the Navy Department. Low prepared the package of paper endorsements from Willson and Cooke. Then, Low wrote the talking points for King's telephone call to BuNav. Cleared for sea duty with CominCh, Knowles received orders to report immediately from his duty station with the ROTC in Texas. Knowles left his wife and children the following morning, reporting to Dyer in the "war room" of CominCh headquarters.[116] He fit in well with the others in the small clique of Asiatic Fleet veterans. Knowles described them as "S.O.B.'s as far as operations went, they were pretty strict on performance and so was I." Knowles thought we "fitted together pretty well."[117] The seagoing atmosphere of the CominCh headquarters inspired Knowles to request orders for sea duty. In the spring of 1942, King arranged orders for Low to command on USS *Wichita* (CA-45). Expecting to command during the amphibious landings in North Africa, Low asked Knowles to join *Wichita* as navigation officer. BuMed refused to allow Knowles to proceed with Low to *Wichita*.

Fate again intervened to place Knowles on an unexpected course up the fleet ladder on the future track to command global antisubmarine operations with intelligence. King's chief of staff, Edwards, sent Knowles as the CominCh liaison to the OIC in London. Reflecting upon the circumstances, Knowles believed that his "availability was more important than any attributes that I might bring."[118] When Knowles arrived in the CominCh headquarters, he had no idea that he would become a key linchpin in the special relationship between the OIC in London, as its equivalents coincidentally evolved in Ottawa, Hawaii, Melbourne, Kilindini, and Colombo. First studying the British way of war, Knowles progressively became the key to global antisubmarine victory. Within the context of King's navy, Knowles quietly stood among the most significant architects in designing the transatlantic alliance to operate with intelligence within the global maritime arena in both war and the inevitable peace.

CHAPTER 21
Alcoholic Luncheon

King understood the global naval war as an interconnected whole, rather than focusing on various widely separated individual theaters. He used the word "enemy" as the singular reference for the individual factions associated with the Axis Tripartite.[1] King always considered the British to be vital to American global interests, along with the Soviet Union and China. He referred to them as "allies" (lowercase "a"), although he preferred to refer to these wartime alliances as being bound under Roosevelt's vision of a future "United Nations."[2] Roosevelt set the policy by which King framed his global strategy. For most of his career, the Europe First concept always defined American thinking in efforts to solve the Mahanian "problem of Asia." Future American interests within the global maritime arena always defined King's strategy for collective operations among the naval powers.

Sound military decision-making required all hands to follow King in securing the collective attainment of sustainable peacetime ends, always in accordance with the policies set by the Roosevelt administration. Despite the assertions of many critics, King never digressed from the overarching task of achieving strategic stability in Europe first for the purpose of achieving similar ends in Asia. To these ends, King constantly pressed the CCS and JCS to pull together. Taking the broad view of operations, King consistently emphasized the priority of defeating Japan as being a coequal prerequisite for defeating common enemies among the Axis powers of Europe. He weathered severe criticism from the British and from counterparts in the War Department. Congressional inquiries, such as those associated with the investigation of Pearl Harbor, also harassed King's navy—sometimes as ferociously as the Axis enemy   in conjunction with efforts to synthesize operations on multiple naval fronts at sea and ashore.

Rivals of the Roosevelt administration used the German submarine menace to criticize the Navy Department. German submarines and Nazi surface marauders appeared in familiar form in British and American propaganda. Horrific tales about piratical Nazis on the high seas stood in contrast to the actual capabilities of the German navy. King stuck to his guns. Over six-packs of beer, King reassured journalists that "we shall have the answer and are working on it."[3] King admitted that the Germans were "training crews all the time and, as usual, the German makes a very good U-boat sailor."[4] He thought that the "U-boat problem is still far from being solved and we are a long way from whipping them."[5] He told the Arlington County Commandoes that the "answer to the U-boat is [aviation] and escort vessels and it takes time to build these weapons."[6] King explained that the director of naval intelligence at the Admiralty, Godfrey, pushed the notion that "British officers should work actually in the Navy Department at Washington [not] as liaison officers and observers, but as actual working members of the British and American teams."[7]

Churchill worried about the rising supremacy of their American counterparts. The German submarine menace provided means by which to negotiate transatlantic checks and balances with King's navy. Working behind closed doors at the Admiralty, Godfrey hoped to retain strategic control over operational forces by regulating the flow of intelligence to the front. During the first eight months of 1942, German and Italian submarines claimed nearly 700 vessels along American shores.[8] During the same period, Allied forces sank fewer than seven German submarines off the coast.[9] Channeling Godfrey's mindset, Royal Navy Volunteer Reserve lieutenant-commander Patrick Beesly conveniently blamed the disasters of 1942 on King.

The British feared the demise of centuries of maritime tradition as the familiar German submarine bogeyman appeared in the faint backdrop of antiaircraft balloons and searchlight beams. German bombs naturally left deep scars in the minds of many British city dwellers. Frustrated by the ravages of war, the British found a convenient American target in their critique of King. For example, Beesly clearly harbored an agenda by suggesting "if not actually anti-British[, King] was certainly not over-receptive to ideas and suggestions by the Admiralty." Beesly suggested that German submarine operations in American waters came as

no surprise to the British Admiralty. Nor can it have been entirely unexpected by the American Navy Department. Some such attack should in any case have been anticipated as an obvious result of Germany's declaration of war, but with the information available in O.I.C., the gist of which was passed to Washington, it seems inconceivable now that the Americans could have been so completely and totally unprepared as was in fact in the case.[10]

Along with many other erroneous assertions, Beesly also mischaracterized King's actual authority to act within the context of the American bureaucracy as it existed *at that time*.[11]

The inability to synthesize operations with intelligence caused major problems between the Admiralty and Navy Department. For this reason, Godfrey sent Cmdr. Rodger Winn on a missionary visit to push the British agenda in America. British superiors described Winn as "not gifted with the best of health, but this handicap has no effect on his zeal and devotion to duty."[12] Commodore (First Class) Sir Edmund Rushbrooke considered Winn as "most reliable and conscientious, [and that he] has an exceptional memory, a quick grasp of essentials[,] and the ability to draw sound conclusions."[13]

Beesly assumed control in the submarine-tracking room at the Admiralty while Winn reported on temporary duty in America. The head of BAD, Admiral Sir Percy Noble, met with Winn for preliminary meetings in Washington. Noble advised Winn to be careful. Winn recalled Nobles exact words that "If you fail," said Sir Percy in his most charming manner, "I shall have no hesitation in throwing you to the dogs."[14] Winn also misspoke by referring to the "Tenth Fleet," which *did not* actually exist at the time of his visit to Washington. Winn's recollections reflected a clear British agenda in characterizing their American counterparts.[15]

Looking down from the airy elevations of glorious British tradition, the historical supremacy of the Royal Navy failed to impress the practical realities within the American camp. Revolutionary myths still inspired the Annapolites within the US Navy, as retold in fables about the buccaneer Scottish commodore John Paul Jones. The conflicting narratives of Nelson and Jones also reflected the very real differences of perspective between British and American policies, which extended to the strategic divides between the Admiralty and Navy Department throughout the difficult summer of 1942.

Despite the best British efforts to replicate the relationships of the previous world war, the Americans simply proved unwilling to follow the same course to the future. The myth of Nelson perhaps hindered Winn's initial effort to bring the Admiralty a solution to the Navy Department problem. He wore his Royal Navy uniform with great pride in the halls of the American naval headquarters—wherein he intended to *tell* King's navy the solution for solving the enigma of global antisubmarine operations. Obviously advancing the British narrative about the Americans, Beesly characterized the US Navy "as more rank-conscious and far less tolerant of its reserve officers than the Royal Navy had become," and considered that

> anyone representing the majesty of the British Admiralty had no need for a large number of stripes on his sleeve. When, a year later, it was proposed to send [Beesly] on a visit to Ottawa and Washington, Winn suggested that [Beesly] be given the acting rank of Lieutenant Commander. The recommendation was rejected on the grounds that any Lieutenant in His Majesty's Navy who was incapable of keeping his end up with American Admirals, Canadian Air Marshals, or indeed anyone in the whole wide world, was quite unfit to hold the rank of Lieutenant.[16]

Winn employed the King's English to strategic effect while lecturing the Americans within the CominCh headquarters. Winn's assistant, Beesly, later recalled that British overtures tended to create difficulties in closing the lines of communication with their American cousins.

Winn wrote vivid recollections of the Navy Department, describing US naval counterparts with anecdotes akin to the Hollywood movie portrayals of American cowboys. In a tacit mischaracterization of the American perspective, Winn claimed that Edwards thought that the "Americans had plenty of ships they could afford to lose."[17] Winn claimed to bark back at the American admiral that the Royal Navy was "not prepared to sacrifice men and ships [because of] your bloody incompetence and obstinacy."[18]. Clearly, tensions must have run very high when Edwards invited Winn for lunch at the Washington Army and Navy Club. Winn told full details to Edwards about Bletchley Park, the role of special intelligence, and the Admiralty OIC concept. Winn mused that "I then threw in a hint [that] we might have better information to impart if we could be sure how it would be handled."[19] Winn and Edwards haggled over the details during an "alcoholic luncheon and [we] returned mellow."[20]

Spirits enhanced collaborative discussions as Winn and Edwards discussed means to share information about the enemy. In his report, Winn recalled that King "received me cordially if not to say effusively."[21] Winn "assured" King that US Navy submarine-tracking-room "personnel and organization were excellent and at least as good as my own room."[22] "Whilst he was digesting this with genuine pleasure," Winn recalled, "I added a remark that some men had a knack of saving ships from submarines and others, whilst most excellent in other jobs, were useless or even dangerous in this work."[23] Winn characterized US Navy leaders as overly confident. Winn later lambasted King as "a facade, without much behind him [but he] knew how to make a decision, and stick to it, and he could inspire fear in his subordinates."[24] Winn recalled, "After my interview with Ernie King, Edwards said to me somewhat sheepishly[,] 'I want you to go to New York.'"[25]

Winn grew frustrated with the inability of American naval officers to collaborate on the simplest aspects involved with convoy and antisubmarine operations. Winn likely lacked an understanding of the personalities when Edwards asked, "I want you to explain to CinC East Coast [Andrews] that the submarine war must be controlled from Washington."[26] Drawing conclusions from speculation, Winn described Andrews as a "friend of Admiral Leahy[,] and a direct order from King would have been taken to the highest level with great uncertainty as to the result."[27] Once again, Winn provided recollections that failed to fit the actual facts of 1942. At the time of his visit to Washington, Leahy still held his status as a retired admiral with additional duty as an ambassador at large on assignment to the Department of State. Leahy had not yet reported for duty with King on the JCS.

Despite the nuances in Winn's recollections, the administrative dysfunction within the Navy Department appeared to represent a clear strategic problem. Above all, Winn disliked King personally and the methods employed by his immediate staff. Winn explained that "I got no impression of a really first-rate mind."[28] He called King "insanely vain and a megalomaniac."[29] Winn blamed King for fostering the "interplay of personalities and the odd ramifications of intrigue, which played their part at the higher levels of the United States Navy Department."[30] Winn described King as being culpable for allowing the leading officer within the Convoy and Routing Division of CominCh, Metcalf, to take an Anglophobic view in managing combined operations at sea. "Metcalf was animated by intense anti-British feeling, and that professionally he was obstructive." Winn further observed that Metcalf "was an old teammate and close friend of Admiral King."[3] Actually, King and Metcalf had served together under Mayo in the Atlantic Fleet during the First World War.

"SLIGHTLY DEAF"

King embraced his role as a favorite British scapegoat for the steady success of American sea power. Past experiences with the British certainly informed American actions immediately following Pearl Harbor. Congressional inquiries focused on the key victims of the attack—the US Navy. The sea power agenda of the Roosevelt administration before the attack drew greater scrutiny on the naval services by his political enemies. The merger of the CNO and CominCh under EO 9096 served as an expedient measure to empower King to change the bureaucratic culture of the Navy Department. Upon taking full command as CominCh/CNO, King supported the assignment of Stark to relieve Ghormley as the SpeNavO. In June 1942, Stark retained his four-star rank as ComNavEu. King subsequently empowered Stark to select a core group of US Navy officers, including reserve lieutenant Tracy Barrett Kittredge.

The ghost of Sims influenced discussions of Anglo-American solidarity in transatlantic affairs, as King and Stark organized US naval operations in Europe. Among other tangible reminders of the past, William S. "Billy" Sims Jr. reported for duty under Stark in the ComNavEu headquarters.[32] His brother-in-law, reserve lieutenant Elting S. Morison, served under retired captain Dudley W. Knox in the Historical Section of the Navy Department. King personally approved the publication of Morison's biography of Sims in the summer of 1942. Morison's famous cousin, Lt. Cmdr. Samuel Eliot Morison, also performed similar work as a roving historian. His American son, Royal Naval Volunteer Reserve lieutenant Peter G. Morison, served in the Historical Section of the Naval Intelligence Division at the Admiralty. After 1942, Morison worked with Billy Sims and Elting Morison to produce an official history of the American headquarters in London.[33]

Memories of collaboration between the Admiralty and the London Flagship of Sims provided a foundation for continued transatlantic collaboration. The legacies of Sims set the tone for Stark to fill a similar role. In a personal letter of May 18, 1942, the First Sea Lord, Pound, wrote to King that "we are all very glad to have Betty Stark here[,] and I am endeavoring to keep him in the picture as much as possible."[34] To assist the mission in London, King ordered Capt. Alan Goodrich Kirk to serve as the chief of staff in setting up the ComNavEu headquarters. Kirk recalled that Stark suffered from being "under quite a cloud after the Pearl Harbor episode."[35] Kirk quoted Stark:

> Alan, the President only gave me two directives when I came over here, [first] have the office open at 9 o'clock every morning even though the British didn't open theirs till 10. Second, he told me I was never to have tea at 5 o'clock. Those are the orders of the President of the United States to his Senior Naval Commander European Theatre.[36]

King recognized the overwhelming task carried by Stark, and sent Kirk for the purposes of fostering collaboration within the British command.[37] Stark and Kirk progressively built ComNavEu to serve as the European equivalent to the Nimitz headquarters on the Asian front.[38] King recognized the British home islands as the advanced base for the inevitable amphibious campaign against the Axis of Europe.

The Europe First principle placed the British Isles at the top on the list of hierarchical priorities, with the Asiatic gateways of Formosa falling to a close second for the Americans. Roosevelt and King clearly agreed on these priorities. Both considered China and the Soviet Union to be the primary means by which to win in Asia and Europe, an idea supported primarily by the combined maritime strength of Britannia and Columbia. Coincident with planning future amphibious efforts on the European front, Formosa stood out as the key to solving the problem of Asia. King's men, Edwards and Cooke, envisioned operations to secure the China coast—from Singapore to Inchon and north to Port Arthur and the approaches of Vladivostok. The maritime connections between Europe and Asia appeared within the context of planning logistics for simultaneous amphibious campaigns within the global maritime arena.

Looking beyond Europe to Asia, RAdm. Richmond Kelly Turner proposed to conduct a war of attrition by providing advisers and supplies to operate with Chinese forces against the Japanese.[39] His assistants, Capt. Willis A. "Ching" Lee and Cmdr. Milton "Mary" Miles, developed basic plans for naval operations in Chinese waters and beyond to continental Asia. In close consultation with Capt. Alan Goodrich Kirk and Cmdr. Arthur McCollum in ONI, Lee and Miles organized War Plans Division efforts to help the Chinese in defeating imperial Japan. All also maintained old associations with key figures in China, including many former associates of the Chinese nationalist Sun Yat Sen.

The restoration of China as a future ally defined American strategy in the Pacific, since King wanted to "use the manpower of China and her geographic position, against Japan."[40] He noted that "all of this had to be set up a long time ahead [and] we didn't know enough about how things would turn out in Europe, how much we were going to be able to spare, so it took an awful lot of foresight."[41] With China on his mind, King ordered Miles to organize US naval operations ashore at Chungking in April 1942.[42] The Roosevelt administration placed high priority on the effort, as King championed Miles's effort to establish the Sino-American Cooperation Organization (SACO). King designated Miles to the temporary grade of two-star rear admiral as commander, US Naval Forces in China.[43]

HAPPY VALLEY

Miles acted under the immediate authority of King in making strategic preparations for the arrival of the US Navy in China. Making his way to China, Miles and his team completed specialized training with reserve commander Draper Kauffman.[44] Proceeding to the front, Miles arrived in China by May 1942. He subsequently acted as King's man in relations with the Chinese National Army of Generalissimo Chiang Kai-shek. Lieutenant General Dai Li of the Kuomintang befriended Miles. Ultimately, Miles became a power broker in Chiang's wartime collaboration with the Chinese Communist forces of Mao Tse-Tung. The strange interconnections between Miles and Chinese leaders proved effective against imperial Japanese forces in China. Conversely, Miles stood at the crossroads of Allied struggles in Asia.[45]

King empowered Miles to drive American strategy in Asia from remote-operations bases in China. He resurrected the pennant he earlier displayed on *John D. Edwards* to fly over the "Happy Valley" training camp near the Chinese coast. His teams wore shoulder patches with the distinctive insignia "??? !!! ***" [meaning "What the Hell"].[46] His sailors operated with Chinese allies to collect the information required to predict the winds and tides of the Pacific. Such information greatly enhanced US Navy planning in the Pacific, which enabled tactical commanders to anticipate the most-favorable conditions for attacking the enemy. Although imperfect, the weather reports from Miles in China enabled King's navy to achieve greater success in the Pacific.[47]

Miles reported directly to King and operated SACO as a satellite organization of the CominCh headquarters. Logistics always required coordination by the CCS and JCS to support operations in China. However, Miles carried no direct operational responsibility to foreign allies, MacArthur, or Nimitz. In framing future operations in the Pacific, King drew the line south from the equator to the Solomon Islands in establishing the Pacific Ocean Area (POA) as the scope-of-command responsibility for Nimitz on March 31, 1942. A few days later, MacArthur secured the authority to establish the South-West Pacific Area (SWPA) in Australia. The purpose of clarifying lines of command centered on the personality of MacArthur and his overbearing approach. "Nimitz was a good sound man," King thought, "but he wasn't even in the same class to be pitted with MacArthur."[48]

King knew Nimitz as a cerebral problem solver with the added advantages of having an easygoing manner. King thought Nimitz might have been better suited for assignment on the European front. Since Navy secretary Knox had made the decision to send Nimitz to the Pacific, King somewhat worried whether Nimitz had the ability to make clear decisions as CinCPac/POA. King drew from decades of knowing Nimitz to help him succeed.

Nimitz similarly understood King.[49] During meetings held in San Francisco in April 1942, King directed Nimitz to consolidate the communications and intelligence organizations within the Pacific Fleet headquarters.[50]

The British system of fusing operations with intelligence under an OIC inspired King to insist upon the establishment of a similar system among the key American commands. Nimitz kept most of Kimmel's team on board, including Capt. Charles H. "Soc" McMorris as the war plans officer and Lt. Cmdr. Edwin T. Layton as the fleet intelligence officer. At his recommendation, Nimitz formally absorbed Cmdr. Joseph Rochefort into the Pacific Fleet staff—still holding double duty as the naval district communications officer. Nimitz resisted the idea of reorganizing his staff, given the dissenting opinions of his intelligence officer, Layton, and his lead cryptographer, Rochefort.[51] In April 1942—in the week preceding the Battle of Midway—King warned Nimitz about the "delicacy of the dissemination of intelligence."[52] King discussed the problem with Nimitz as "On the one hand the effort is to prevent drying up information sources, while on the other hand the effort is to give information to those who can use it in time."[53]

Organizational changes within the Navy Department influenced the personality dynamics among the seagoing fleets in the Atlantic and Pacific. Given the strategic challenges of multinational coordination with the British in operations and intelligence, King frequently annoyed his subordinate Nimitz. By empowering CominCh to direct tactical operations among task forces in the Pacific, King also pushed Nimitz to reorganize the CinCPac/POA headquarters in Hawaii for the purposes of establishing a worldwide network of Joint Intelligence Centers (JIC).[54] King's directive seemed like an imposition to Nimitz. At the tactical levels, King further annoyed Nimitz by pushing for the development of Advanced Intelligence Centers (AIC).[55] King shared his vision with Nimitz in San Francisco between April 25 and 27, 1942.

Working for King at that time, Cmdr. Arthur McCollum accompanied Nimitz to explain the concept to the staff in Hawaii. Under previous informal arrangements, the British supplied information derived from European sources in exchange for American information derived from similar high-grade material from Asia.[56] McCollum earlier served on temporary assignment with SpeNavO in London and fully understood the relationships between the cryptanalytic functions of Bletchley Park and the coordinating mission of the OIC in London. He championed the idea of replicating the OIC system within the US Navy. McCollum explained that the "concept was warmly received by Rochefort, if less so by Nimitz's fleet intelligence officer, Layton."[57] Rochefort and Layton had settled into a routine and resisted making precipitous changes of organization while simultaneously coordinating operations with intelligence in the Pacific during April 1942.[58]

King pushed Nimitz to merge the relevant subdivisions of the Pacific Fleet and Pacific Ocean Area headquarters. The equivalent sections of the naval district, under Bloch, and those of the army and air force liaison with Nimitz merged within the consolidated context of the Intelligence Center, Pacific Ocean Areas (ICPOA), in Hawaii.[59] Although the functions already existed, the ICPOA formally organized in May 1942.[60] ICPOA struggled in an early stage of organization in Hawaii, as King refined procedures for the CominCh headquarters to serve as a clearinghouse for disseminating information derived from high-grade Anglo-American intelligence sources.

Foreign allies frequently criticized American counterparts as being either inept or bumbling fools. British, Dutch, and French observers had criticized Nimitz. Australian and New Zealand liaisons worried, since Nimitz appeared unprepared for the rigors of war. The director of naval intelligence for the Royal New Zealand Navy, Lieutenant-Commander F. M. Beasly, reported, "I was disappointed with Admiral Nimitz, who struck me as being an old man, slow, and perhaps slightly deaf."[61] King thought Nimitz struggled to make hard decisions without first asking permission. King said, "I cannot make his back stiff."[62] King derided Nimitz for tending to "go soft when action is required."[63]

The early aircraft carrier operations of the US Navy in the Pacific demonstrated the potential of King's navy to win in combat. Intelligence also enabled his staff in Washington to coordinate operations with their counterparts in Hawaii. In April 1942, information derived from enemy communications enabled King and Nimitz to stage a surprise attack against the enemy.[64] RAdm. Frank Jack Fletcher held overall command of the *multinational* task forces at Coral Sea, as Royal Navy rear admiral John Crace also joined the fray. His presence proved significant, since his Australian heritage also highlighted the operations at Coral Sea as a combined operation in British and American propaganda.[65]

Coral Sea proved significant because the Imperial Japanese Navy faced the rare experience of accepting the humiliation of failure. The confused battle also marked the first time in which warships failed to make direct contact in combat. The entire exchange primarily happened in the air, or under the surface in submarines. During the battle, *Lexington* delivered a series of devastating blows against the enemy under the command of Capt. Frederick C. Sherman, King's friend. Having previously served together in submarines and aviation, King and Sherman shared a clear understanding of their task. Sherman lost his command when an enemy submarine torpedoed *Lexington*, much to King's chagrin. Although both deeply lamented the loss of their ship on a personal level, King rewarded Sherman with an assignment as an assistant chief of staff in the CominCh headquarters before sending him back to the front as commander of Carrier Division 2—with temporary two-star rank.

King ultimately rewarded all the key commanders involved at Coral Sea with assignments leading to higher rank and positions of critical wartime responsibility. This fact has often been overlooked, since many considered King's decision to reassign Fletcher from combat command premature. Later, rumors within the ranks suggested that King removed Fletcher for losing *Lexington*.[66] This is patently untrue. In fact, King worried about the physical and mental condition of Fletcher following many unbroken months of service in sustained seagoing combat.[67] King progressively grew weary of Nimitz for failing to rotate Fletcher from command in the weeks preceding the Battle of Midway.[68]

The worrisome situation in the Pacific added to King's ongoing challenges in negotiating the priorities of combined strategy in the Atlantic. The annoying presence of German submarines in American waters forced King to make major changes of organization along the sea frontiers on both coasts of the United States. King vested Ingersoll with overarching authority in the Atlantic. Admirals Andrews and Kauffman fell subordinate to Ingersoll under the mergers of naval districts into the Eastern Sea Frontier and Gulf Sea Frontiers. In the South Atlantic, Ingersoll also held seniority over Vice Admiral Jonas Ingram.

King circumvented military and naval district commanders to assert direct command over civilian authorities and paramilitary organizations. The Civil Air Patrol (CAP) operated as an adjunct of the US Army Air Force. King's reorganization of naval coastal forces greatly upset CAP leaders, as well as the airpower clique inside the War Department.[69] Combating the enemy submarine threat required strategic coordination from the highest levels of command, which placed the army airpower clique in direct conflict with King's navy. Given British concepts of strategic airpower, War secretary Stimson severely criticized King for failing to set up an organization based on the RAF Coastal Command concept.

Churchill similarly used the enemy submarine menace to prod Roosevelt into using British solutions for American problems of command. King served as a convenient villain in these debates. After EO 9096 placed full responsibility upon King, Assistant Secretary of the Navy Forrestal used the enemy submarine problem to discredit King. Recalling the situation, King explained that "Forrestal put Secretary Knox up to the idea that King should only be CominCh, and that Admiral [Frederick] Horne should be Chief of Naval Operations."[70] "Forrestal really wanted to manage everything about material himself and leave me to the fighting part." King explained, "Forrestal hated like hell that I had both jobs."[71]

The ambiguous victory of the US Navy at the Battle of Coral Sea sparked concerns about the organization in the Pacific. King recalled the circumstances, saying, "Knox sent for me shortly before the Battle of Midway [to say] you'd better go to sea and manage that battle."[72] King described feeling "astounded." He refused to go after saying, "Nimitz is doing all right!"[73] King retained overall strategic command. Nimitz held operational responsibility for operations surrounding Midway. With Halsey out of action and in the hospital under doctor's orders, King strongly endorsed the nomination of Spruance to serve as the tactical commander in Task Force 16. King acquiesced to Fletcher's retaining command in Task Force 17.

Orchestrating strategy with intelligence, King directed Nimitz to position US naval forces to engage simultaneously on the oceanic lines running between the potential targets of Kiska and Midway. King had prodded Nimitz to organize ICPOA for the purposes of synthesizing the flow of information from Washington to Hawaii and related headquarters ashore and afloat.[74] In the grander scheme, Midway seemed a bridge too far for the enemy to hold.

King understood, according to Low, the "Japanese military mind, which one keen observer once remarked was frequently beset by 'mental indigestion.'"[75] King identified the Japanese fleet as the key, rather than the island of Midway itself. King made his strategic desires clear, empowering Nimitz and his staff to coordinate tactical operations.

The prospective occupation of Midway seemed almost acceptable to King, as the enemy progressively overextended already stretched oceanic lines of communications. The exchanges between King and Nimitz in anticipation of Midway reveal many complexities of command. Exchanges between the Admiralty and CominCh headquarters also reflected the scale of coordination in advance of operations surrounding Midway. King directed Ghormley to tell the "First Sea Lord in person that [the] indicated imminence of enemy attacks on Midway and Alaska [and] perhaps Hawaii has required withdrawal of carrier cruiser groups from South Pacific."[76] King explained plans to use "cruisers and destroyers but no carrier wherewith to work against enemy activities in Coral Sea."[77] King then asked his old friend Pound, "Will Admiralty entertain request for carrier from Eastern Fleet to join up with [Rear Admiral Herbert F.] Leary temporarily[?]"[78] King continued, "If so[,] move had best be made at once [as] alternative suggest consideration of coordinated Eastern Fleet and British shore[-]based air raids on Rangoon or Andaman Islands and line of communication between Rangoon and Singapore."[79] King directed Nimitz to bring "his ships away from stations along the Australian route."[80] King placed priority on the "defense of Hawaii, along the Midway route."[81]

King placed all their bets on the defense of the Midway-Hawaii-Kiska triangle by repositioning forces away from the defense of the South Pacific. The move had significant connotations within the context of relations with the British. King told journalists at the time that Midway "was a risky thing to do[,] for should the Japanese suddenly swing south across the supply lines to Australia, we would find our fleet in the wrong place and at the wrong time."[82] Notably, King told journalists that "two days before the Midway battle our information went blotto!"[83] Meeting in secret with journalists, King explained the situation in that "the Battle of Midway resulted in a complete victory."[84] Reflecting on the actions, King recalled that Japanese "timing was perfect [but] we did know that the Jap[anese] were on the move, we did not know exactly where they planned to strike nor when the blow would be delivered." After the battle, King explained that the "Japanese fleet just faded into oblivion."[85]

CHAPTER 22
TOP SECRET

Intelligence analysts served behind closed doors to examine events unfolding on maps with pins and string. Photographs and intercepted messages from various sources provided means to gain the enemy perspective, which often provided decisive advantages for the key commanders. Strategic battles often failed to appear beneath the headlines and tactical recitals of heroism in combat. After the battle, the actual events often failed to appear in full form. As a result, the initial stories—as told in wartime propaganda and then repeated for other purposes in official postwar histories—continued to influence popular memories of past victories and the anguishing consequences of defeat. Just as the British viewed Washington's victory at Yorktown somewhat differently than American historians have repeated the narrative, stories surrounding epic battles like those of the Atlantic and Pacific often fell into the backdrop of glory above and upon the continents of Europe and Asia in the Second World War.

Looking outward from the past, historians shall still find new discoveries by examining the once-classified details of intelligence. For example, British narratives about the Battle of the Atlantic often appeared somehow disconnected from such battles as those at Coral Sea and Midway, North Africa and Guadalcanal, or Normandy and Saipan. Taking the popular narratives into consideration, the facts frequently appeared just beneath the surface of history. The intangible truth often went to the graves of those most directly involved with the actual decisions, which shaped events on the battlefields of the global maritime arena.

Intelligence has always existed in the cluttered minds of politicians and strategic commanders, whether in peace or war. The sources and methods used in the production of intelligence are frequently obscure for the uninitiated. On the other hand, popular media accounts and official histories still provide the proverbial breadcrumbs required for navigating the densely packed forests—or the carefully pruned fields—that define the challenges of researching original documentary sources.

The epic tales of Nelsonial triumph at the Battle of Trafalgar officially coincided with the mythology found in American stories of glory at the Battle of Midway. Fifty years after the fact, the US Navy directed all hands to cut cakes and celebrate the mythology of Midway. Among the greatest myths, the failures of intelligence before Pearl Harbor appeared between the lines of equally mythologized tales of victory after the Battle of Midway in 1942. Indeed, details about the quality of US naval intelligence appeared on the front page under the headline "Jap Fleet Smashed by US—2 Carriers Sunk at Midway" in the *Chicago Tribune* as early as June 7. Below the headline, the byline declared, "US Navy Knew in Advance All About Jap Fleet."[1]

With the politics unfolding in conjunction with transatlantic negotiations at the time, the strategic consequences of celebrating victories on the battlefield seemed outright dangerous in the singular view of King. Shocked by the stupidity of his subordinates in the fleet, King issued orders to find the culprits responsible for leaking high-grade sources of intelligence to the media. As a result of the investigations after Midway, King issued detailed procedures for handling information with terms like RESTRICTED, CONFIDENTIAL, and SECRET. The term TOP SECRET required special authority.[2] Looking outward to foreign shores for a solution, King used the British system to synthesize American processes for high-grade intelligence sources in 1942.

British overtures to amalgamate Americans into combined operations resonated within the intelligence subdivisions within the War Department. In contrast, King had no intention of replicating the First World War relationships that had proven so counterproductive in the aftermath. Essentially, King intended to synthesize operations with intelligence with a distinctly American purpose in mind. He knew about the British organization from the detailed reports provided by past American liaisons to include Baldwin, Follmer, and Weeks.[3] In addition, King acted on the recommendation of Royal Navy captain Eric S. Brand, a British officer serving as the director of Naval Intelligence at the NSHQ in Ottawa.

Brand complained to King about the system for sending raw information initially collected in Canada to Britain for analysis.[4] Then, the OIC in London often spun the intelligence before retransmitting the information back to Canada.[5] Brand considered the transatlantic organization of British naval intelligence administratively nonsensical. His views also reflected those of Royal Canadian Navy captain Jean Maurice Barbé Pougnet "Jock" de Marbois, then presiding in the Foreign Intelligence branch of the OIC within NSHQ in Ottawa. Under the circumstances of 1942, the Canadians shared the views of King's American navy in shaping the future transatlantic relationships with their embattled cousins within the global maritime arena.[6]

THE CONFUSION OF IT ALL

British habits frequently roused strong feelings among skeptical Americans, as experienced by Winn after visits to the Canadian and American headquarters. On the other hand, King *did* coordinate with his British and Canadian counterparts to synthesize naval operations— first within the American hemisphere and then beyond to other global naval fronts. Never unwilling to claim credit for a good idea, King acted on the recommendations of Low and Cooke to send Knowles to the Admiralty OIC in the fall of 1942. King provided no clear orders for Knowles. Having no actual experience as an intelligence analyst, Knowles also considered his assignment to London as an unfortunate diversion from his quest to return to the seagoing line.[7]

British naval intelligence organizations struggled to adapt under the tsunami of uninitiated novices from America. With the arrival of Knowles in London, the Canadian NSHQ issued orders for Royal Canadian Navy Volunteer Reserve lieutenant John B. McDiarmid. Having volunteered as a citizen of the United States, McDiarmid held a PhD in classics from Johns Hopkins University. McDiarmid subsequently repaid tuition debts by working in Great Lakes cargo ships. He then answered the call to fight the Nazis by taking his commission in the Canadian ranks with following assignment to the flagship of Atlantic convoy Escort Group B1, HMS *Hurricane* (H-06).[8]

Previous merchant sailor experience provided the foundation for McDiarmid's Atlantic convoy operations. German submarines harassed the convoy as McDiarmid performed the duties of assistant navigation officer in the destroyer HMS *Hurricane* (H-06) during their crossing.[9] In Liverpool, German bombers chanced to damage *Hurricane* in port. Stranded in Liverpool, McDiarmid received temporary assignment to the Western Approaches Headquarters in Derby House along the Merseyside in Liverpool. He met Winn for the first time while assisting with efforts to track submarines and maneuver convoys in Liverpool. He then returned to *Hurricane* for convoy escort duty at sea. In the summer of 1942, McDiarmid received orders to detach for assignment to the Admiralty OIC. He reported to London at the same time as Knowles.[10]

Winn unhesitatingly absorbed McDiarmid and Knowles into the submarine-tracking team in London. Winn's assistant, Beesly, recalled that the "burden still had to be borne by the four original watchkeepers, Majolier, Finlaison, Whittal, and Wilmot-Stilwell (the latter's death during the war was certainly hastened by over-strain."[11] McDiarmid similarly recalled the "slight claustrophobic effect of dungeons, the urgent running to and fro, the cautious jingling of telephone calls, and the clatter of teleprinters, and the apparent 'confusion of it all.'"[12]

Just as the King's English influenced American variants, British terminology infused with Yankee definitions for fusing naval operations with intelligence. Admiralty OIC personnel used the phrase "Special Intelligence" (or "SI") in reference to information gleaned from enemy radio transmissions, with "Very Special Intelligence" being reserved for specific cryptologic subcategories.[13] Beesly explained in memoirs written many decades later that "in the Navy, at least, it [ULTRA] was only applied to outgoing signals and documents as a security grading and the actual information itself was always referred to as 'Special Intelligence.'"[14]

The terminology employed within the Anglo-American submarine-tracking organizations entered new phases of evolution as the transatlantic special relationship became real. Collective efforts to destroy enemy submarines provided the mandate for future collaboration after 1942. Winn taught McDiarmid and Knowles about the alchemistic art of tracking submarines. "At the time we were not receiving any ULTRA," Knowles recalled, who also remembered spending "a good ten hours every day in the tracking room [and] absorbed, by osmosis at least, a great deal of experience in tracking."[15] Knowles made clear technical distinctions between cryptography and the broader operational tasks inherent with the analytical functions of intelligence. He never considered himself an intelligence officer when emphasizing that "we were operational [and] I was operations entirely, and that was my field."[16]

Knowles rejected the administrative divisions of operations and intelligence functions in characterizing the limitations of key informational sources about the enemy. He warned about the assumption that "once an enemy's cipher is broken, there is little need for a tracking room [and] it might be the case if we could read the enemy's cipher continuously and if the enemy sent out operational information by radio."[17] Knowles explained:

Unfortunately, neither of these conditions prevail very often. During periods of unreadable enemy traffic and when U/Boats are operating on special missions, pursuant to special unsolved ciphers, or under radio silence, U/Boat tracking becomes increasingly important. Even when the enemy's cipher is broken, there are many times when the navigational positions are still unreadable due to their being disguised by means of grid positions. Furthermore, tracking is necessary even when all the enemy U/Boat traffic is being read for the latter must be supplemented by other intelligence, principally contacts and sightings, in order to maintain a satisfactory U/Boat estimate.[18]

The illusion of intelligence supremacy always affected efforts to hold an advantage in operations against committed enemies within the global maritime arena.[19] The pressures of performing this type of secretive work also took significant tolls upon those most closely engaged against elusive enemies. During combat within the tracking rooms on all fronts, the analysts quietly suffered stresses analogous to those experienced by troops at the front.

Food rationing added to the bleakness of mindless destruction on the once-majestic streets of London. The mental stresses inherent with fighting for survival added to the pressures imposed upon Winn. The dungeonous confines of "Lenin's Tomb"—under constant threat of German bombs—also amplified the mental pressures experienced by the analysts. Enemy submarines always added to the stress, as the damp interiors of the Admiralty OIC amplified the unhealthful conditions in which Winn and his team endured. To compensate, Winn "always kept a flask in one pocket and a packet of cigarettes in his other."[20] McDiarmid also noted, "Winn sometimes kept his hands in his pockets, not because it was cold, but because he had a slight tremor whenever he became frustrated."[21]

Mental breakdowns and suicidal tendencies loomed beneath the glorious tales about British and American supremacy in operations and intelligence. Suicides rarely received acknowledgment in official records, although evidence of the plight of the analysts serving in intelligence appeared between the lines of their forced assignments to take leave. Shortly before Christmas 1942, Winn suffered a complete nervous breakdown that was witnessed by McDiarmid and Knowles.[22] Beesly also recalled "vivid recollections of receiving this calamitous news."[23] He temporarily assumed the helm of Section 8S while Winn took an enforced leave.[24] During this fleeting period, the German submarine force achieved "their greatest sustained period of success in the whole course of the war."[25]

SECRETS OF THE SHIP'S SAFE

Overlapping processes often overshadowed fundamental differences among the British and American navies in executing operations with intelligence. Commanders on various fronts also created their own procedures, given their circumstances within their individual spheres of administration and authority. Within the American camp, War Department definitions for governing the flow of information derived from sensitive sources also varied from those used by the Departments of State and Navy.[26] Cryptologic material appeared in various forms and within the subtext of public accounts, although often it originated from documents classified under such caveats as ULTRA and MAGIC. For example, US Army major John H. Gunn highlighted the security problems found in MacArthur's SWPA headquarters. The term "ultra" became commonly used as a shorthand term for intelligence.

Gunn escorted the code and cipher section when MacArthur moved the SWPA headquarters on board ship. In disgust, he reported that the high-grade communications intelligence material "I kept stored in a locked closet in the ship's captain's cabin."[27] He was unable to use more-secure facilities because MacArthur had directed the captain to secure "18 quarts of bourbon whisky in his ship's safe and kept his top-secret battle plans for several operations on top of the desk in his sleeping quarters."[28] The haphazard handling of intelligence by MacArthur's staff caused major problems, as Gunn explained that the "Navy considered 'ULTRA' as a classification, not a code word."[29]

Security breaches provided the British with clear justification to accuse the Americans of being unprepared to collaborate as an equal partner in operations and intelligence. King reacted by making the CominCh chief of staff, Willson, and the assistant CNO, Horne, personally responsible for instituting unprecedented levels of security among headquarters ashore and afloat. Notably, King always left his desk cluttered with papers and classified material. His aide Lt. George Russell observed, "His desk was something of a rat's nest [with] papers stacked six inches deep [and] his incoming basket was always overflowing." Russell noted that, remarkably, King "always knew where everything was."[30]

King's method of cataloging information centered on prioritizing strategic tasks for the purposes of attaining clear ends against the enemy. He envied the British organization for synthesizing operations with intelligence. He always sought as much information as possible from his staff. King also expected technical specialists within the ranks of communications and intelligence to understand their job as being intrinsically tied to the operations and functions of the regular seagoing line. Ten years earlier, King wrote in his Naval War College thesis that commanders require "adequate 'intelligence' about the enemy forces."[31] King thought that "a commander must 'discern' [before] he can have proper basis to 'reason' and to 'decide.'"[32]

THE ATTITUDE OF COMMANDER LAYTON

Given a well-reasoned perspective on the functions of intelligence in naval operations, King expected all regular line officers to serve on brief tours within the specialized subservices of communications and intelligence. King defined the specialties of communications and intelligence as "not a corps but a 'service' into which and out of which people may be detailed according to requirements."[33] He proposed "differentiation of people assigned to duty in these two special operating branches of the Navy [to include] the 'Naval Communication Service' and the 'Naval Intelligence Service,' as they are in reality recognized and appropriate specialties within the Navy."[34] In establishing the new system, King established the office of Navy Inspector General under RAdm. Charles Snyder to "attack this question, in the first instance, from the point of view of requiring full justification of personnel (officer, enlisted, civilian) now available."[35]

King aggressively shattered many bureaucratic kingdoms in overhauling the intelligence organization inside the Navy Department. King empowered Snyder to seek means by which to reduce bureaucratic routines for the purposes of fostering utmost efficiency among headquarters ashore and the seagoing forces afloat. King directed Snyder to "eliminate (1) work that is not clearly essential to the war effort; (2) duplications[;] and (3) overlaps."[36] King emphasized, "My personal conviction is that there is at least 10 percent—in some cases even 20 percent—more personnel than are actually required."[37]

Intelligence requirements tended to outpace the actual abilities of ranking personnel on the active list of the regular line. King directed his chief of staff, Willson, to fix the problem by aggressively replacing regular navy personnel with reservists and newly recruited volunteers with actual expertise.[38] As the inventor of naval cryptologic devices, Willson used the opportunity to purge the Offices of Naval Communications and Intelligence, or alternatively "Op-20" and "Op-16" within the context of OpNav.[39] Throughout 1942, Willson's reign of terror centered on the Communications Security and Cryptographic subdivision, or "Op-20- G." For nearly two decades, Willson harbored a very personal grudge against those affiliated with Cmdr. Lawrence Safford of Op-20-G.[40]

Safford ran Op-20-G like an exclusive fraternity among trusted friends, rather than as an integral function of the operational-planning organization of the Navy Department. He had demonstrated great promise as a qualified submarine line officer. Having developed an amateurish interest in the black arts of codes and ciphers, Safford progressively lost himself in the netherworld of cryptography. Former friends within the seagoing line lamented the demise of Safford. He attained the reputation for being a "mad genius."[41] Early in 1942, Safford perceptively recognized that British critiques of American security were a ruse.

The British no longer had the ability to solve German naval codes and ciphers on a consistent basis, according to Safford. By extension, the handshake agreement to shared American information about the Japanese also seemed uneven.[42] Congressional investigations of Pearl Harbor further complicated the ongoing debates concerning the strategic organization of the Allied high command. During the investigations, Missouri senator Harry S Truman challenged the Roosevelt administration, referring evidence to the Department of Justice accusing the Navy Department of "rapacity, fraud, greed, and negligence."[43]

The Pearl Harbor investigations in Congress revealed the obvious need for changes within the Navy Department. Within this context, King empowered Willson and Horne to break up the communications and intelligence fiefdoms within Main Navy. Following the Battle of Midway, Willson twisted the awards recommendation, as submitted by Nimitz, to decorate Rochefort for his exploits. Willson deeply disliked Rochefort, having previously served as staff officers embarked on the flagship *Pennsylvania*. In addition to their personality differences, Willson considered Rochefort unworthy— having joined the navy as an enlisted sailor.[44] Rochefort became an innocent victim in the bureaucratic infighting.[45]

King simply acted on the recommendations of his immediate subordinates, Willson and Horne. In 1942, Willson arranged orders for US Navy captain Roscoe Hillencoetter and Cmdr. William Goggins to report to Nimitz. Hillencoetter subsequently supervised Layton, and Goggins eased into the desk during the Rochefort's absence in Hawaii.[46] Capt. Joseph R. Redman simultaneously assumed duty as director of naval communications, as part of the regular cycle of rotations. However, he also used his position to arrange the assignment of his brother, Cmdr. John R. Redman, as the replacement for Safford in Op-20-G. Under King's authority, with Willson and Horne working the bureaucratic lines, the Redman brothers subsequently promoted Cmdr. Joseph N. Wenger to lead in Op-20-G.[47]

Coincident with efforts to synthesize transatlantic relations with the Admiralty, King wanted to establish the Navy Department as the worldwide center for maritime operations and intelligence. Under his authority, the Redman brothers abandoned the cozy prewar designations of NEGAT, CAST, and HYPO in the strategic reorganization of Op-20-G. Following the trends, Commanders Jack Holtwick and Bernard Roeder reorganized CAST into the combined Fleet Radio Unit Melbourne (FRUMel) in Australia. The HYPO organization, under Rochefort, likewise received the designation of Fleet Radio Unit–Pacific (FRUPac).

The logical effort to reorganize US naval communications and intelligence organizations unfortunately faded into the mists of rumors and innuendo. The hazy recollections of many junior subordinates many years after the fact also fueled myths and conspiracy theories about Midway and those most directly involved. Indeed, Willson and Redman indirectly maligned Rochefort. Redman described Rochefort as "an ex-Japanese language student (a Lt. Cmdr.)."[48] Continuing, Redman reported that "my feeling is that Radio Traffic Analysis, Deception, and Tracking, etc. are suffering because the importance and possibilities of the phases of Radio Intelligence are not fully realized."[49]

Redman clearly recognized the mandate for injecting fresh blood into the mix of US naval communications and intelligence. Others used the victory at Midway to settle old scores. Willson and Redman harbored personal grudges against Rochefort and Safford. When Nimitz nominated Rochefort for a medal, Willson twisted the decision. Instead of the Distinguished Service Medal, King signed a flag letter of commendation (without ribbon) for Rochefort.[50] Missing in the narrative of what happened was that King arranged orders for Rochefort to secure a seagoing command at the front in the logistical forces of the Pacific Fleet.

For a mustang officer, command at the front provided the opportunity for Rochefort to advance within the regular line ranks of the US Navy. In essence, King put Rochefort on track to attain a higher rank—far beyond the norms of the regular line. King later placed Rochefort in charge of the Pacific Strategic Intelligence Section (PSIS) at the Navy Department planning the reconstruction of Japan.[51] By no means did King fire Rochefort, as was rumored in the hazy recollections of Op-20-G axe grinders. In personal correspondence in 1942, King told the full truth to Nimitz, which was that "Commander Rochefort apparently has contributed a great deal to the results obtained by the radio intelligence unit in Honolulu [but] appears to have been the main obstacle to full coordination."[52] King further warned Nimitz that the "attitude of Commander Layton also seems not to have been very helpful."[53]

The victory at Midway caused significant competition among the various headquarters in their efforts to claim credit. Heroics in combat always tended to fuel the organizational politics of administration. "This will be a long war," King noted; "we cannot be too hasty about going down the road with Napoleon by soiling the uniform with sashes and colorful bobbles."[54] "In this war," King thought, "decorations won in the face of the enemy will become familiar enough."[55] "You can see officers at any Washington cocktail party," another associate noted, "whose chests are covered with ribbons." Gaudy decorations implied heroism, although such displays by those serving primarily in administrative functions struck King's men as having a "strong odor of dead fish."[56]

CARRYING THE TORCH

King replicated the British model of combining operations with intelligence by synthesizing strategic planning with intelligence. He selected Capt. Carl Holden to relieve Redman as director of naval communications and simultaneously replaced the younger Redman with Capt. Earle E. Stone. The two Redman brothers subsequently served as advisers to

Nimitz in the Pacific, helping to synthesize communications and cryptanalysis procedures with the Navy Department in Washington. Standardization sparked an ongoing debate within the CCS and JCS, particularly as the British pressed American counterparts on the questions of strategy, operations, and tactical command. "The American people have got to learn to swallow some very heavy losses in this war," King explained; this "is a war as we have never known war and the 1917 war is a summer breeze besides what this one will ultimately be."[57]

King balanced requirements to support the Anglo-American strategy in Europe and Asia, which enabled Nimitz to concentrate on the tactical execution of the Pacific campaign.[58] King's strategic intent always informed the actions of Nimitz's actions in orchestrating the operations of the Pacific Fleet. After frequent meeting with Ingersoll in Washington, King customarily flew to San Francisco or beyond approximately every three months for summits with Nimitz.

Occasionally, both King and Nimitz placed themselves in harm's way for their meetings. Throughout the war, King and Nimitz maintained rigorous traveling schedules to coordinate operations with intelligence. King flew in a luxury-fitted Lockheed Lodestar. Lt. Cmdr. John J. Hyland received an offer to become King's personal pilot. Hyland explained that "nobody really wanted the job, I was too stupid to realize it then."[59] Hyland noted, "The Admiral was a passenger as much as I was [and] I had a job that put me in a place to see how [King] managed the war [and] it was like having a front[-]row seat to the world series."[60]

King's globetrotting required the CominCh staff to plot his whereabouts in the same manner as they tracked enemy targets. He maintained a constant rotation for meetings with subordinate commanders on multiple fronts. Nimitz shared in the burdens of serving in King's court, frequently traveling vast distances for meetings with his boss. Usually, Nimitz flew to San Francisco to meet King. On one occasion, June 30, 1942, the Sikorsky XPBS-1 flying boat carrying Nimitz crashed on an unmarked submerged object off the Naval Air Station at Alameda, California.[61] Nimitz stayed on board the aircraft until all hands embarked the lifeboat, assisting in efforts to salvage the wreck. The only casualty in the accident, Lt. Thomas Roscoe, died on impact. Nimitz later reflected upon the incident. He kept the service dress blue uniform he was wearing at the time of the accident as a good-luck charm.[62]

King reminded Nimitz about the overarching strategic objectives for planning branch operations in the Pacific. MacArthur's campaign outlook naturally focused on avenging the humiliations of Pearl Harbor. His egotistical desires also factored into the division between the army and navy in the gray areas of what became known as the "MacPac."[63] Having studied the problem for his entire career, King understood the limitations of enemy capabilities. He pushed Nimitz to focus on managing the "Fleet Train" network by establishing forward and advanced bases leading across the central Pacific to culminate at the future "Union Station" in Formosa. Naval War College studies consistently placed priority on Formosa—rather than the Philippines—as the key to solving Mahan's "problem of Asia."[64]

The heaviest burdens of coalition warfare generally fell to King for the purposes of setting the strategic course for future operations. Logistics planning required King to strike the balance in managing two basic subfunctions, as defined under the broad phrases "producer logistics" and "consumer logistics."[65] Among other major problems in the first phases of actual wartime operations, King had to make do while the civil-military machine retooled for offensive operations. Armchair admirals frequently excoriated King for failing to attack in any given theater, as the enemy exploited fleeting opportunities to assault weaknesses. Thankfully, the enemy never developed a coherent global strategy. On the Allied side, close observers of the debates within the CCS and JCS noted that had "King not argued so persistently, it is possible that the [JCS] might have left the Pacific so stripped that the Japanese could have become firmly established and it would have taken years to dislodge them."[66]

Nimitz had the comparably simple task of executing the directives of the CCS and JCS, which by implication filtered from King's CNO/CominCh headquarters. For the purposes of fixing the Japanese in the MacPac, King directed Nimitz to execute operations at Guadalcanal. He recalled the situation in 1942 that "our means were extremely limited in the Pacific at that time, and we were apprehensive of threats to break the lifeline to Australia." He explained that the "first place the Japanese tried it, we discovered, [was] Guadalcanal."[67] He noted that "while we only had a shoestring to operate on [the JCS] after some deliberation, decided that the threat of Japanese occupation in Guadalcanal was one which we had to take action on, limited though our means were."[68]

Unable to focus solely on the vast strategic challenges inherent in naval operations in the Pacific, King also faced challenges in executing the comparably simple strategy for defeating the enemy in the Atlantic. Churchill and Roosevelt indulged their whimsical approach to BOLERO—the broad offensive concept for winning in Europe. In June 1942, King had already committed major efforts to support the TORCH landings in North Africa. However, the British lacked resources, and the Americans still lacked resources to meet the great expectations of Churchill and Roosevelt. During those desperate months, King stood largely alone in fighting the CCS assumptions about restricting offensive efforts to the "essential minimum" in the Pacific.[69] In the vicious fights among the JCS, King also fought withering verbal battles against Marshall and Arnold while fighting for "adequate forces" to thwart the enemy along critical lines of communication with Australia.[70]

Having considered the strategic alternatives, King understood the strategic risk in pushing forces into Guadalcanal. He reasoned that the operations served the bloody purpose for fixing the enemy in the farthest reaches of the Pacific, which enabled efforts to repurchase time for concurrent operations in the Atlantic.[71] King stated that MacArthur's drive from Australia through New Guinea and naval operations in the Solomons had the desired effect of holding the Japanese far from American shores. He explained that the "Navy has studied that whole area for many years but we have always come to the same conclusion that the Marianas, Guam[,] and Saipan are the keys to the Pacific."[72] To these ends, King explained that "first of all we had to take the Gilberts, which brought about the very bitter battle of Tarawa [and] it was bitter, but some of the other later points were bitterer."[73]

To coordinate global planning for maritime expeditionary operations, King organized the Amphibious Warfare Section within the CominCh headquarters. He consulted the president of the Naval War College, Kalbfus, in setting up the organization. In turn, he recommended Admirals Daniel Barbey and Donald P. Moon for the task of coordinating amphibious operations with logistics and intelligence. King later explained that the task always required subordinate commanders to work in tandem by following the rule of thumb with "one hand washing the other."[74] Given responsibilities to support other allies on other fronts in Europe, King highlighted the point by explaining strategy in Asia, that "while Nimitz was working westward, he was covering the flank of MacArthur's advance along northern New Guinea and staving off any operations of the Japanese fleet."[75]

Given the individual strategic responsibilities of various operational commanders, King remained firm on fixing logistical priorities to two basic lines of offensive effort that extended from America to the island citadels of Formosa and the British Isles. Among trusted friends in the media, King complained about subordinate commanders "who suffered from what he called 'Localitis.'"[76] King described this as a "'disease,' which each commander has and makes him believe that his own sphere is the one which should have all the materials." "The worst case of localitis is Australia," King explained, and that he "does not have much use for MacArthur [or] his demands for naval forces."[77] King chastised MacArthur as having "recently discovered the airplane!"[78] During meetings held inside the Citadel in London in July 1942, King argued with Churchill about the realities of supply and logistics. "Mister Churchill did not like the word 'logistics,'" King said, and explained that Churchill preferred the British notion of "supply." Churchill barked in a drunken haze, "Logistics'—what is that!"[79]

TAKING THE CITADEL

The British and American navies operated in tandem to deliver critical supplies to the continental fronts of Europe and Asia. In speeches, Roosevelt explained the strategy by describing the "four policemen" as the Soviet Union, China, and the Anglo-American powers. He also envisioned the brighter future.[80] King followed the strategic vision of a postimperial order in organizing offensive operations against the Axis Tripartite. His strategy transcended the war effort. Peacetime reconstruction strategy making coincided with operational planning. To win, King understood the mandate for conducting the war to win as quickly as possible, for the purposes of reconstructing former enemies as future partners in maintaining sustainable peacetime ends under the United Nations.[81]

Always keeping the future of Britannia in mind, Churchill pressured the Joint Staff mission in Washington to assert British priorities. Churchill still curated the traditions of the British Empire. Imperial strategy was slightly at odds with American visions of the future under the United Nations. Taking the role of intermediary on the British Joint Staff in Washington, Dill nurtured the special relationship with the Americans on the JCS. King described Dill as the "one British leader who really accepted the facts of what was actually needed to win the war."[82] When Dill died suddenly, King and the other members of the JCS sponsored his burial with full military honors at Arlington National Cemetery. Dill received special recognition with an equestrian statue overlooking the hallowed grounds of Arlington.[83]

Personal relationships among key leaders within the Allied high command proved decisive in the war at sea. Yet, Royal Navy liaisons girded heavy bureaucratic seas inside the Navy Department. From June to October 1942, Admiral Sir Andrew B. Cunningham served as head of the BAD. Given his reputation, Cunningham greatly elevated the stature of BAD and immediately commanded the respect of American counterparts. He had orchestrated Royal Navy operations in the Mediterranean, punctuated by the masterful use of the Fleet Air Arm against Axis forces at Taranto and off Cape Matapan. Given

Cunningham's reputation as a fighting admiral, the Admiralty sent him to engage more closely with King's navy.

Cunningham experienced great frustration in the assignment to represent the Admiralty in the bureaucratic battles with the Navy Department. Shortly after taking charge within the BAD in Washington, he observed, "We are only liaison officers with no power to order a man or a dinghy to move."[84] Having faced the enemy at the front, Cunningham challenged King. "When I had something to say against the British," King recalled that Cunningham griped, "I don't like that!" Kindred spirits with similar personalities, Cunningham and King fought ferociously in executing the wills of their superiors. American journalists explained that Cunningham believed "there should be one commander of all antisubmarine operations, air, and sea, with absolute authority."[85] The German submarine menace once again provided the British means to manipulate the Americans, since "Sir Andrew believes there is enough shipping available now to open a major second front in France [but] doesn't think the Allies are handling the submarine question very well."[86]

The differences between Churchill and Roosevelt complicated King's effort to set strategic priorities within the Navy Department. "You have expressed the view," King reminded Roosevelt, that "we should determine on a very few lines of military endeavor and concentrate our efforts on these lines."[87] King criticized Churchill for diluting Allied resources with operations in the Mediterranean and the Indian Ocean.[88] King argued that the Royal Navy lacked any means to "hold the citadel and arsenal of Britain itself."[89] King suggested that British operations in Asia "will absorb its proportion of our (US) munitions."[90]

The CCS struggled to balance the aspirations of Churchill with the policies of the Roosevelt administration, which defined JCS priorities. In efforts to synchronize procurement requirements, King wrote that the "solution can always appear easy on paper, but our problem is not paper."[91] He circulated a memorandum to "All Bureaus and Offices of the Navy Department," addressing the basic question of "Combatting the Submarine Menace: Building Merchant Ships vs. Building Anti-Submarine Craft."[92] "Shall we continue to try to build merchant ships faster than enemy submarines can sink them," King asked, "or shall we build anti-submarine craft of such character and in such numbers that we can sink submarines faster than the enemy can build them?"[93] King concluded that the answer appeared "obvious."[94] He suggested the "construction of combatant ships wherewith to overcome enemy means for the destruction of merchant shipping unless duly opposed by combatant ships of appropriate characteristics in adequate numbers in integrated combinations."[95]

King reveled in Churchill's unique ability to conjure spellbinding prose when angling for any given goal. King told his lawyer, Bull, that it "must never be forgotten that Churchill is first, last[,] and all the time for the British and that is as it should be—but one should never forget it when talking to him."[96] King explained, "Churchill is a very persuasive talker." [97] King admitted that he always "'has a hand on his watch' when Churchill is talking and trying to 'sell' a point."[98] King harbored a "real personal fondness for Churchill."[99] King conversely recognized Churchill as a bad influence on Roosevelt.

Churchill mesmerized Roosevelt with personal anecdotes, as punctuated by dramatic flourishes about the special relationship. Churchill always claimed to have a naval perspective, which resonated with Roosevelt. Conversely, Churchill truly had an imperial view with an aim to conquer. Roosevelt had no intention of conquering enemies. Rather, he wanted to win the sustainable end to war by rebuilding the future under the United Nations. King always followed up with Harry Hopkins to clean up whenever Churchill and Roosevelt struck a bargain without prior coordination by the CCS and JCS. King credited Hopkins for holding American policy on course, "especially when Churchill is doing some of his most persuasive talking [and] Hopkins has been of great assistance to the Army and Navy."[100]

The British dominated CCS discussions through superior administration, which was in stark contrast to the ad hoc organization of the JCS. Roosevelt administration policy always defined the strategy, although King frequently stood alone in advancing the American naval point of view. King observed that the "British Chiefs [were] assisted by two or three secretaries who had been trained in that kind of work for several years [and] these secretaries belonged to a kind of corps which they called 'Civil Servants' and had worn Army (British) uniforms, usually with the grade of 'brigadier[,]' which is the same grade as 'commodore.'"[101] King often reminded Roosevelt that establishing the "common aim of the United Nations must be the defeat of the Axis Powers."[102] King pressed to "concentrate our efforts and avoid dispersion."[103] He refuted Churchill's "eccentric operations that [seemed] attractive but do not fit into a sound military plan."[104] King noted that "Churchill has read the books on strategy while Roosevelt has them read to him."[105]

Roosevelt accepted King's view of the campaign in Europe as being inextricably tied to ongoing offensive efforts in Asia. King and Marshall agreed on this point, as they stood together in unified support of an amphibious campaign to retake the European continent through a direct assault across the English Channel.[106] To these ends, basic plans for Operations ROUNDUP and SLEDGEHAMMER later served as the basis for what evolved into Operation OVERLORD and NEPTUNE. King recalled Churchill's reluctance to cross the English Channel when he delivered a "long and tiresome lecture about Basil H. Liddell Hart, J. F. C. Fuller, and T. E. Lawrence."[107]

The CCS and JCS operated in the uppermost altitudes of bureaucracy, as the principal members maneuvered pins and paper armies on map boards to fight the war. Marshall and King frequently intervened to remind fellow strategists of the human costs. "The British seem to favor what might be called an 'opportunist war,' that is, striking when and where the circumstances seem to dictate at a given moment." He explained that Americans "plan and fight by that plan and not run a hit-or-miss war."[108] King told journalists that the

> "Soft Under-belly" will not prove so soft after all. When we have Italy—should we conquer that country—we shall have a liability rather than asset. We shall have to feed the Italians and carry coal in our ships. This burden of carrying the Italians should be left on Hitler's shoulders and not placed on ours [while] Italy might like to get out of the war, she is as much an occupied country as is France and Holland [as] Germany controls Italy's destinies for most of the Italian troops are not in Italy.[109]

King blamed airpower theorists for the foray into North Africa. King kept ahead of his bureaucratic rivals inside the War Department through his unrelated brother-in-law and son-in-law—both being US Army brigadier generals—sharing the same surname, Smith.

Airpower theorists within the War Department constantly fought for their place at the tables of grand strategy. General Freddy Smith often discussed airpower with his father-in-law, King. Amused by the army airpower point of view, King joked with his chief planner, Cooke, that "'goddamnit, Savvy, I've got an upstart young Army Air Force brigadier who treats me like a contemporary.'"[110] In their debates over the dinner table, King traded notes with his son-in-law Freddy. Behind closed doors, King worried about the US Army Air Force under the influence of the "'Royal Air Force Psychology,' namely the proposition that airpower all by itself can and will win the war—they must come to <u>earth</u> sometimes."[111]

King viewed the oceans as the key geographical feature on the planet, rather than the continental landscapes ashore. In contrast, the Royal Navy had largely relied upon a worldwide network of fortified shore facilities and supply bases.[112] King frequently ran afoul of Marshall in discussions concerning the seizure of terrain ashore. Marshall's director of war plans, Brig. Gen. Dwight D. Eisenhower, noted in his diary that "one thing that might help win this war is to get someone to shoot King."[113] Eisenhower described King as the "antithesis of cooperation, a deliberately rude person, which means he's a mental bully."[114] At first, Eisenhower considered King petty. He recalled a story told by Arnold. After he sent an official letter to King—referring to him in the lower permanent rank of rear admiral—King returned the letter *unopened* with an arrow scrawled on the envelope leading to the word "rear?" As the story circulated, Eisenhower joked that King "ought to be a big help winning this war."[115]

CHAPTER 23

So What, Old Top!

Strategic differences within the CCS about the future sequence of global operations amplified the divisions among the key American commanders within the JCS. Given nuances of policy between Churchill and Roosevelt, strategic differences of perspective hindered relations between Marshall and King. Politics after Pearl Harbor and the bubbling unification debate influenced discussions concerning American strategy against the German submarine menace. Seeking a clear decision from Roosevelt on questions of strategic command, King submitted an implied ultimatum in October 1942. Invoking Navy Regulations, King dutifully informed Roosevelt about his impending transfer to the retired list in November—upon reaching the mandated age of sixty-four. Roosevelt returned the memorandum to King. In blue ink, Roosevelt scribbled the note "So what, old top—I may even buy you a birthday present."[1]

Roosevelt arguably made the most consequential decision of the entire war by holding King in place. Under the unified authorities of CNO and CominCh, King held the additional burdens associated with being the highest-ranking American naval representative *on active service* in dealings with the CCS and JCS. That King had also surpassed the mandatory age of retirement also provided a mechanism for Roosevelt to hold the reins of high command. King always served at the pleasure of Roosevelt—and he knew it.[2] In examining the calculus of the JCS, Leahy held ex officio status and served as a retiree without formal authority—always at the pleasure of Roosevelt.[3] Although Leahy always had Roosevelt's ear, King always retained the actual authority as the ranking naval member of the JCS. The other ex officio member, Arnold, served the purpose only of mitigating the power of Marshall—from King's perspective. Leahy naturally favored King and the Navy Department perspective in deliberations with the CCS and JCS, whereas Marshall and Arnold worked together to push the War Department agenda. King generally discounted Arnold as the "joker in the whole deck."[4]

In the competition to set strategic objectives, King developed an intricate network of trusted associates within the American government and Allied command. King nurtured alliances with Marshall's trusted subordinates inside the planning division of the Army General Staff. His brother-in-law, Brig. Gen. Walter D. Smith, assisted King in these efforts. Smith helped King identify army officers with the requisite "pull" to get things done. Among others, King subjected Eisenhower to a tough interview before supporting his appointment to command the amphibious campaign in North Africa—Operation TORCH.[5] In their brief meeting, Eisenhower chose to stretch "my luck, or my neck."[6] Eisenhower accused King of failing to do "much to assure co-operation between the two services."[7] In the end, Eisenhower impressed King sufficiently enough for him to admit that "I sometimes wonder whether in making decisions I depend too much on naval customs, disciplines, prejudices—or whether I'm really thinking problems through."[8] Eisenhower thought, "From that time on, I had a friend in the Navy."[9]

King presented an unapproachable façade, which served the intended purpose of fostering the presence of command. Discipline dominated the carefully governed personality of King. Playing his part on the theatrical stage of war, King also set standards for fellow Allied commanders to follow. Once he firmly established control over any given relationship, King showed himself in a different way. Cmdr. George Dyer recalled that "once an officer gained King's confidence and respect[, King] would drop his rigid demeanor and could be delightfully informal."[10] King's aide Lt. George Russell thought, "Woe betide the culprit who fell down on the job."[11] Russell credited King for providing "some well[-]founded principles of leadership which he passed on[, one being] never 'give an order to obey an order.'"[12] Russell remembered RAdm. Donald "Wu" Duncan's observation that the "old man was the 'maddest' whenever he was wrong."[13] From a British perspective, Brigadier Sir Ian Jacob shared similar recollections that King's "manners are good as a rule, but he is angular and stiff and finds it difficult, if not impossible, really to unbend."[14] "I am convinced," Jacob continued, "there is much more to him than appears on the surface, and that if one could . . . [and] one would be surprised at what one would find beneath."[15]

King's hardtack approach to command served as another means to challenge superiors and fellow commanders to meet the highest standards in meeting their collective responsibility to make sound military decisions. In so doing, he arguably saved lives and shortened the war.[16] He explained his rationale that "through World War II, as we as in World War I, Churchill was always trying to use some easy way to win the war."[17] King continued to explain that "Stalin got onto him in time and insisted there should be not more than two available fronts at anytime, although he, himself, wanted to carry on the 'Second Front.'"[18] King lamented that Stalin failed to consider "any other 'fronts,' just as Churchill wanted to carry on with Rhodes, etc., and even at Norway."[19] King accused Churchill of letting the "Pacific 'go to the devil.'"[20]

WEAPONS, OR FUNCTIONS?

King empowered Stark to act as an intermediary between Churchill and the Admiralty in efforts to synthesize regional strategy with operations. King similarly used Nimitz as a counterbalance against MacArthur and other Allied commanders to focus on the central Pacific offensive. King also rejected the tribalistic culture of technical specialization within the ranks of the army and navy. Rather, he focused on the broader policy objectives to formulate opinions about future strategy. Armed forces always had the function of creating conditions for peacetime commercial interests. For these reasons, King rejected the "bomber command" mentality that permeated the army focus on tactical targets ashore.[21] He also rejected the singular focus and tribal dynamics that existed in the seagoing line and shore establishment of the American sea services.

King fully believed in an integrated approach in describing the future vision of unified command within the American armed services. He reemphasized the differences between land and sea in characterizing the fundamental question of airpower. "'Battleship Admiral' connotes an officer who does not comprehend the use of anything but a battleship," King stated, emphasizing that naval officers are "'first of all,' a naval officer and a specialist afterwards."[22] King criticized the army concept that the "*weapon* should be the basis of organization."[23] He observed that the US Army Air Corps doctrine claimed control over "all aircraft and should perform all functions of which aircraft were capable; that the Navy should control and operate all ships."[24]

Military doctrines for operations ashore rarely translated for naval operations within the fluid context of the global maritime arena. Environmental realities frequently failed to resonate with the hierarchical minds of many military thinkers. In contrast, King explained the fundamental view that in naval doctrine, "*function* should be the basis of organization."[25] He argued that the "fundamental objective of all military services is the same: to strike the enemy whenever and wherever he can be reached, and that no service should be artificially restricted in the employment of weapons."[26] He characterized the US Army Air Force concept as a "purely military one, devised by the authorities of the German Army and Royal Air Force."[27] King lambasted the acolytes of airpower, like Arnold, by telling journalists that "those 'born with wings' in the RAF and our own Air Forces [suffered from] cockeyed thinking."[28] Instead, he pressed the idea that "Air Power is like Artillery, Cavalry, Infantry—another good weapon which has its uses and limitations [and] it must work as part of a team."[29]

Testing theories within the context of an actual war, Arnold manipulated Marshall to advocate the Army Air Force theory of strategic airpower.[30] Marshall, in turn, used Arnold to counter King. King thought, "Hell, Arnold didn't know what he was talking about."[31] He refuted the notion that the "RAF and USAAF knows everything there is to be known about the use of airpower—certainly no more than any other well-rounded general or admiral who is supposed to know the uses of all of the arms he must use."[32] "To stay up around 30,000 feet—above anti-aircraft range—and bomb from this height," King argued, "is not good technique to hit a small moving target."[33] He observed that "land targets which are stationary are all right[,] but a small moving ship cannot be hit by this method."[34]

Framing offensive military strategy within the broader context of the maritime arena, King characterized naval aviation as all encompassing. Unlike the tactical focus of army concepts, the US Navy system fully integrated airpower to fall within the context of the task at hand for the purpose of attaining clearly defined results.[35] "Strategic airpower will never be anything other than tactical," King argued, and that "bombers are useless without a target."[36] As Arnold manipulated Congress through the political influence Research ANd Development (RAND), Marshall told King that airpower enthusiasts within the US Army created "virtually another Army, in the shape of the Marines." Marshall suggested that "naval commanders will feel that they can work more efficiently if they have the Naval, Air, and Marine units, as a homogenous force, and undoubtedly, they can. But on the other hand, if this argument is carried to its conclusion then it means the consolidation of the Army and Navy."[37]

Marshall and King shared concerns about the underlying debates concerning the military focus of airpower and the maritime focus of American sea power. The antisubmarine problem put the debate between army and naval aviators into full focus.[38] Arnold wanted US Army commanders to command the antisubmarine operations by placing the US Navy in a supporting role. Capt. Francis S. Low recalled that army pilots generally "wanted to attack and get medals and never did understand that except in fortuitous circumstances of availability of accurate intelligence."[39] Given the general location of a prospective target, the act of finding a submarine required patience—like searching for the proverbial "needle in a haystack."[40]

Having served in submarines, both King and Low understood the fundamental advantages of stealth and surprise. In antisubmarine operations, King and Low knew that "attack generally was the product of previous search."[41] Army pilots proved too impatient for antisubmarine operations. King therefore directed RAdm. Mark Bristol and Capt. Robert B. Carney to study the problem. Bristol and Carney recommended standardization in antisubmarine doctrine and training standards. In turn, King created the Atlantic Fleet Antisubmarine Warfare (ASW) Unit by February 6, 1942. He selected a submariner, Capt. Wilder D. Baker, to move from commanding the ROTC unit at Yale to establish the Fleet ASW Unit in Boston. The ASW Unit helped coordinate convoy procedures and identify doctrinal means to combat enemy submarines.

LOOKING FROM 30,000 FEET

Army and air force methods emphasized geographical lines of demarcation between areas of operations. Within the CCS, Roosevelt empowered Leahy to speak on his behalf as a trusted "leg man" after his return to Washington in July 1942. Conversely, Leahy held retired status. He had influence though carried no actual authority over the sitting members of the JCS—Marshall and King. Similarly, Arnold operated as an ex officio observer in deliberations among the JCS. King also mused that the JCS proved "decidedly preferable to the unified deportment urged by the Ground and Air Forces against Navy opposition."[42] The old unification debate and the associated specter of navalism—as a policy—diverted the solution for the strategic task of unifying military strategy with naval operations. The false god of unification infected the debates among CCS and JCS. Memories of the past also influenced Marshall's underhanded surprise tactic of proposing an "Army-Navy merger" during a period of significant turmoil within the Allied high command.[43]

The committee system of the CCS required the Americans of the JCS to maintain a unified front in negotiating combined strategy. The internal disputes within the JCS similarly required constant negotiation and the willingness to make compromises. Under the circumstances, Marshall and Arnold kept Leahy and King on their toes in negotiating maritime strategy. Marshall constantly challenged the authority of King. Marshall regularly encroached upon King's authority. On one occasion, Marshall conspired with Leahy to place King in check by putting a decision on naval construction to a vote. After a show of hands, Leahy remarked to King that "it looked as though the vote is three to one."[44] In turn, King peered accusingly into Leahy's eyes before leveling the full broadside that the JCS "is not a voting organization on any matter in which interests the Navy."[45]

Leahy and Arnold never held authority to overrule Marshall and King in making recommendations to Roosevelt. King later recalled that "matters of major import [requiring] presentation to the President could be counted on the fingers of one hand."[46] Conversely, King thought, "Leahy had a little bark, but no bite [and he] wants to seem tough but isn't."[47] For his part, Leahy often provided top cover for King. As Marshall and Arnold conspired to advance the concept of service unification, Leahy sided with King about setting strategic priorities. Among other major problems he faced, King constantly competed for procurement priorities in competition with Marshall and Arnold. For example, King highlighted differences between land and sea logistics in supporting aviation requirements of the Departments of War and Navy.

Naval aviators understood the benefits of constructing airframes with air-cooled engines for operations over water. Army procurement priorities centered on water-cooled engines, which required facilities well stocked with specialized personnel, spare parts, and precision mechanical gadgetry. King further highlighted the differences in training requirements for seaborne operations, which greatly contrasted with the high-altitude-mission requirements of army theories concerning the future of strategic airpower. Above all, King fought Marshall to win the war against the enemies at hand. He discounted counterarguments within the CCS and JCS concerning prospective Soviet enemies of the future. Through sheer willpower and obstinance, King essentially forced his counterparts to follow his lead.[48]

Marshall and King balanced strategic requirements through constant negotiation, which enabled the utmost flexibility in shaping bureaucratic procurement priorities for winning the war at hand. Airpower theorists like Arnold conversely—if not perversely—used the war as a forum for creating the political mandate for the future armed-service unification under the wild blue yonder. In frustration, King told journalists that "anyone who has ever studied military history knows that you can't win battles from 30,000 feet."[49] As German submarines roved American waters, Air Marshal John Slessor encouraged the Americans to replicate the Western Approaches Command in Liverpool. Given the British model, Andrews acted on his own in establishing the Army-Navy Joint Control and Information Center (JCIC) in his New York City headquarters of the Eastern Sea Frontier.[50]

Andrews encroached upon the prerogatives of the Atlantic Fleet commander by issuing detailed directives to forces operating in the Eastern Sea Frontier. King grew tired of Andrews for failing to follow the chain of command. Lt. Alan R. McFarland recalled King's reaction to the lengthy dispatch that Andrews issued. McFarland watched the fireworks when King "practically hit the ceiling."[51] McFarland subsequently drafted King's directive to Andrews for the entire fleet to read: "Do not presume you are on the bridge of every ship."[52] McFarland prepared the directive as released by King for all navy commands to "transfer ten percent of your personnel to the nearest receiving station for further assignment and turn in fifty percent of your typewriters."[53]

British concepts of airpower influenced American experiments in coordinating naval operations with intelligence from headquarters ashore.[54] The relationships between the RAF Coastal Command and the Royal Navy antisubmarine organizations appeared to serve as a model for the Americans to replicate.[55] Air Marshal Philip Joubert de la Ferté advocated for a unified antisubmarine command in the Atlantic.[56] Under such an organization, the British claimed full control over transatlantic convoys and antisubmarine operations in the Atlantic. Following the trends, Marshall convinced the secretary of war, Stimson, to establish a "Super Air Officer Commander in Chief" to coordinate "unified air control of the Atlantic."[57] Having joined forces on questions of airpower, the RAF sent liaisons to serve under Andrews to coordinate the "Special Air Task Force" to conduct land-based air antisubmarine operations.[58] Marshall concurrently organized a separate US Army Air Force Antisubmarine Command (AAFAC).

Marshall used the question of airpower as a negotiating tool in extracting concessions from counterparts in the Navy Department. Debates over American airpower and the future of the US Marine Corps influenced the dynamics of discussion among JCS members. As chief of staff of the US Army Air Forces, Arnold successfully lobbied for ex officio status on the JCS. His appointment coincided with an arrangement allowing the US Navy to control land-based reconnaissance aircraft. Problems among the JCS leadership exacerbated personality differences within the CCS.[59] Fighting for air, King concurrently fought Marshall for access to US Army long-range bombers. King sought land-based bombers for antisubmarine patrols and for coastal convoy operations.

The personality dynamics on the JCS reflected the traditional rivalries between the branches of the American military. From its inception, Marshall considered the JCS to be lopsided in favor of the Navy Department. Following Stark's departure for London in March, the JCS essentially comprised Marshal and King as the only full members. The addition of Arnold again put the balance of power into question. King fought with Marshall, competing to counteract Arnold through the appointment of the commandant of the Marine Corps, Gen. Thomas Holcomb, as an ex officio member of the JCS. Marshall complained to Roosevelt about the idea, hoping to quash the expanding role of the Marine Corps in American strategy. Roosevelt shrewdly used Leahy as a referee in the fights between King and Marshall. In explaining relationships to journalists, Roosevelt emphasized his constitutional authorities as the commander in chief of the Army and Navy. He then announced Leahy as the chief of staff to the commander in chief and special adviser to the president of the United States. Roosevelt reemphasized Marshall's role as Army chief of staff and King's equivalent roles under the paramount authorities as established in EO 9096.

The nuances of administrative status and lines of authority influenced transatlantic relationships within the CCS and JCS. King relied heavily upon Stark in London. Royal Navy admiral Sir Andrew Cunningham noted that "Stark's task of smoothing over Admiral King's abrupt methods was sometimes invidious and difficult [and] he was a great friend and ally."[60] Leahy assumed the similar role as Roosevelt's "leg man" within the context of the CCS and JCS. Leahy held the personal trust of Roosevelt, as did many European allies.[61] King described relationships among the CCS and JCS to journalists. He explained that the "limits of their spheres of command are fluid and not fixed [and] 'borders' are matters of convenience only and this should be remembered."[62]

King discussed the internal workings of the CCS and JCS in freewheeling discussions with selected journalists. Leahy and King worked together in balancing the personality dynamics within the CCS and JCS. In discussing the nature of transatlantic collaboration, King discussed the importance of sharing information. He often discussed the enemy point of view, as derived from high-grade intelligence sources. "Thankfully, the Japanese think they can go it alone," King noted, "or the Germans might have a chance against Russia."[63] He respected the "natural fighting spirit of the Japanese." Shortly after the apparent victory at Guadalcanal, he thought that the "Japanese Command is not dumb and we can expect a healthy smack on some other point."[64] "It will be Chinese manpower which will beat Japan," King thought, and that the "situation is pretty much the same as the use of Russian manpower to beat Germany."[65]

King viewed the Atlantic campaign as intertwined with the Arctic convoys to Britain and beyond to the Soviet Union. Offensive operations in the Mediterranean sapped resources from the Indian Ocean shipping lanes, which became vulnerable as Allied forces flowed through India to support offensive operations through Burma into China, which simultaneously affected offensive timetables for the Pacific.[66] King described the requirement for the US Navy to enable the "delivery of supplies to allies and our own men all over the world."[67] "Commitments to Russia alone are extremely heavy," King explained. "China is demanding more and more supplies and Australia is clamoring for more and more supplies and munitions; in fact Australia is the most vociferous of the lot."[68] He feared that the "Japanese will decide to call in their troops from the far-away fronts and go all-out against China [and] it will raise hell with our plans to help China."[69]

Taking the maritime view of strategy, King considered that the key to Allied victory ashore fell primarily upon the soldiers of Russia and China. He noted that "Russia, while suffering terrific losses, is bleeding Germany white."[70] "The Russians allow no military observers on their front and we are completely in the dark about what is going on," King complained. "They are 'standing on the dock with their hands out' waiting for us to deliver the goods."[71] King criticized fellow members of the JCS for failing to force the CCS to improve coordination between Russian efforts against Germany and Chinese efforts against Japan. "It will be Chinese manpower which will beat Japan," King contended; "we cannot deliver the goods [and] everything goes in by air and the planes which fly in must carry the gas to fly them out again."[72]

King considered the air supply campaign in China unsustainable in the absence of a seaborne port of entry. "Giving China 500 planes is ridiculous," he said. King explained that the "China problem is not made any easier because the Russians are demanding lots of transport planes for use on their front and on the Persian Gulf supply line."[73] King predicted the keys to victory in secret off-the-record conversations with journalists. "We shall fight one of the major campaigns in the Pacific," King explained. "We shall find use for the 225 ships which will be released when we gain control in the Mediterranean."[74] Once, King explained it in this way:

> We gain access to China, the whole Japanese force in the Dutch East Indies is cut off because the [enemy] supply lines will have to operate within range of our landbased planes. But the chief advantage of our possessing airfields near the China Coast is the bombing of Japan by our big bombers. With the Chinese armies to protect our airfields Japan would have a very tough time . . . the supply lines to Japan's Dutch East Indies are beginning to suffer badly because of the terrible beating the [enemy] is taking at the hands of our submarines.[75]

King wanted to synchronize the Pacific campaign to establish China as the Allied center of gravity in Asia, with the simultaneous campaign in the Atlantic to launch the decisive drive for victory in Europe first. He thought that China provided the key front to sustain a naval blockade, since "Japan will have to withdraw from her positions in the East Indies and some of her islands through sheer inability to supply them." Ultimately, King based his strategy on the notion that "Russia will do nine-tenths of the job of defeating Germany."[76]

Strategic shortfalls in the production of Allied merchant shipping deeply concerned King and the CominCh staff. Within the headquarters, offensive operations on all the various global fronts always hinged on the correct allocation of merchant shipping. Logistics defined operations planned with intelligence, as King pressed efforts to "maintain unrelenting antisubmarine warfare in the Atlantic."[77] Taking a global view, he explained that "we covered the seaways to the British Islands via Iceland, Greenland, [and] the Azores and via the North and South of Ireland [then] via Murmansk and North Russia all seasons of the year, by Archangel when ice permitted, clear around South of Africa and up the Persian Gulf."[78] King mused that his staff coordinated interlocking efforts on other oceanic fronts with the convoys from the West Coast of America to "Vladivostok, right through the Japanese Islands."[79] He concluded that "I never understood how in the world the Japanese allowed the shiploads of materiel (at one time there were 125 ships operating in trade between our northwest ports and Vladivostok) to pass."[80]

Given the global scope of operations, King struggled to balance strategic requirements to support allies with shipping and sufficiently trained personnel. He placed highest priority on organizing efforts on the home front to enable the rapid mobilization of industrial resources. King wanted to fill the wartime ranks of the sea services with able-bodied volunteers, leaving the War Department to hold priority for training draftees for service in the army ranks. While consolidating his authorities as CNO and ComInCh and simultaneously fighting among friends on the CCS and JCS, King also focused on manning and equipping the seagoing forces. Within this context, King recognized the national imperative of incorporating all hands in the quest to win the sustainable peace in the global maritime arena after 1942.

CHAPTER 24

The Navy Team

The American sea services evolved with the requirements for winning the future peace under the future United Nations. Given the Four Freedoms, an idea that was extended further by the theoretical concept of freedom of the seas within the global maritime arena, the Roosevelt administration set policies by which Allied forces fought the Axis with the strategic purpose of creating the future "Four Policemen" to patrol the planet to end all future wars before they could happen. Familial connections with the Opium Wars of the nineteenth century also influenced Roosevelt's personal understanding of the Chinese concept of the "Century of Humiliation" as exemplified by the military adventurism of the twentieth century.[1] Resolute in the task of renegotiating the old imperial systems for the purposes of advancing humanity into a new global order, Roosevelt leaned very heavily on King to keep the dream of the United Nations alive during the war.[2]

Noble humanistic principles combined with the practical purposes behind the Roosevelt administration's racial policies, which coincided with the strategic directives issued by King. Beginning in 1942, he pushed able-bodied males to sea and filled their places ashore with women. King progressively opened opportunities for women and other minorities to volunteer for assignments to combat areas. He fully supported the policies of the Roosevelt administration by forcing changes within the ranks of the American fleet—opening the hatches for women and minorities to take their places at the front. His life in ships had also defined King's views concerning the role of minorities. Once again, he applied the principle of functionality being the basis for organization. In this respect, King had an open view about using able-bodied human beings to perform the tasks inherent with victory in war—notwithstanding sexual or racial considerations.

King's personal views of gender and racial equality reflected the trends in American culture at the time. His aide and biographer, Whitehill, jotted notes about a conversation with King about issues of race. In the notes, Whitehill included such loaded terms as "darkey" and "massa."[3] Whitehill's unbecoming racism reflected the casual assumptions of intellectual superiority that characterized the unspoken classism within the culture among the Brahmins of New England. Whiethill made jokes and often spiced their informal conversations with racial epithets, which went unchecked by King. Unfortunately, this fact overshadows the deeper complexity of King's views on issues of race. His deeds spoke much louder than words in an era defined by Jim Crow laws and segregation within American society.

Having served alongside Black Americans and other racial minorities at sea and ashore, King progressively celebrated democratic ideals of social equality. His approach in handling racial questions followed those of Theodore and Franklin Roosevelt. Traditions of white supremacy in American society persisted under the law and classist culture of the government and within the monoculture of the armed services. Interestingly, King's personal library included Booker T. Washington's *My Larger Education* and *The Man Farthest Down: A Record of Observation and Study in Europe*.[4] According to an aide, King also read "Octavus Roy Cohen's stories [and] expressed his enthusiasm for the Negro spirituals and for the play *Green Pastures*, which he saw several times while at the Naval War College."[5]

Green Pastures was the first Broadway show to feature an entirely Black cast and drew strong reviews at the time. Many critics considered the play insulting and that the white playwright failed to understand the nuances in characterizing religious culture among the Black American community. Conversely, the great American historian William E. B. DuBois argued at the time that "all art is propaganda and without propaganda there is no true art."[6] He added that in "*Green Pastures*, Marc Connelly has made an extraordinarily appealingly beautiful play based on the folk religion of Negroes."[7] DuBois believed that "some whites will not like it because it is too human and tragic with all its humor."[8] DuBois considered the play as the "beginning of an era."[9] DuBois also anticipated the trends leading to global war along racial lines. He warned that the "awakening of the yellow races is certain [and] the awakening of the brown and black races will follow in time."[10]

Eugenic theories fueled the underlying racism that appeared between the logical justifications provided by Mahan in articulating the case for American sea power. Entrepreneurialism replaced old models of European imperialism within the context of American strategy.[11] King recognized racism as a major future vulnerability for the Allied war effort. He took measured steps to turn the American sea services into the model of a free society. The historical conclusions of DuBois informed King's perspective in framing future strategic objectives for American sea power. For King, the unresolved problem of superficial racial divisions in American society increasingly seemed counterproductive in efforts to win the future peace.

American propaganda certainly featured equally ugly portrayals of the enemy, which tended to highlight racial divisions. Racial hierarchies also ran against the idealized American vision of the "Four Freedoms" under the future United Nations. Thus, the Roosevelt administration set course for full integration after 1942. Under the direction of Secretary Knox, Assistant Secretary of the Navy Ralph Baird empowered King to form a special subcommittee on the General Board of the Navy, which included Capt. Francis Whiting, Marine colonel Thomas Watson, Lt. Cmdr. Alvin D. Chandler, and Mr. Addison Walker—a Black civil servant representing Baird as a liaison to the Navy General Board. In addition to these preliminary steps, King supervised the Navy inspector general, Snyder, in planning the phased integration of racial minorities into the seagoing ranks.[12]

Efforts to integrate the wartime ranks of the American armed services coincided with the publicity campaign to highlight the broader humanistic vision of the future United Nations. Under the Roosevelt administration, King understood the importance of fostering the image of unity among all Americans in the propaganda war.[13] Drawing from his strategic understanding of history, King thought that the "attitude of men—and women—in the countries that have been overtaken by the Axis [was] a very considerable factor."[14] King instituted policies within the American sea services to coincide with the constitutional aspiration for all humanity to have the unalienable rights to "life, liberty[,] and the pursuit of happiness."[15] The high humanistic ideals embedded in the American Constitution inspired King to emphasize these principles as being the "cause that [we] are fighting for, that is morale."[16]

WE CAN ALL BE PROUD

Racial integration served as a potent weapon to counter the overtly racist propaganda of the Nazis. To this end, King recruited a former publicist for DuPont Corporation, reserve lieutenant commander Arthur Newmeyer, to recast the US naval services into the model for future American cultural unity. King assigned Newmeyer as an adviser for Captains George Dyer and Leland Lovette—both simultaneously carrying intelligence functions within CominCh—to coordinate public affairs from within the headquarters at the Navy Department.[17] In setting up the effort, King noted that propaganda "is used to inform, to guide, to inspire the home front."[18] In addition, propaganda "was beamed overseas to discourage the enemy in their objectives."[19]

American democratic principles served as foundations in efforts to mobilize fresh recruits for combat in the global maritime arena. After the shock of Pearl Harbor, peacetime professionals held the line in the Atlantic and Pacific to enable the mobilization of civilians and American industry. Civilian volunteers began filtering into the ranks as the peacetime professionals fought the withering early battles in the Atlantic to North Africa and around the globe in the Java Sea, Wake, Coral Sea, Midway, and Guadalcanal.[20]

King set the course for building the future US Navy into a true reflection of American principles of democracy. For practical reasons, King recognized the strategic imperative of replenishing the ranks with fresh recruits—requiring all hands to pull together.[21] Characterizing the rapid expansion of American sea services in wartime, King reported to Congress that "only about ten percent were in service before Pearl Harbor."[22] As the ranks swelled in wartime, King noted that reservists had demonstrated "continued professional improvement and excellent performance of duty[, which] have made them not only an indispensable but an integral part of the Navy team."[23] In explaining his rationale to seagoing commanders in the fleet, King emphasized the "old rule of working one's way out of a job[,] and once it is done well, then we can all be proud."[24]

Minorities traditionally served in the enlisted ranks of the fleet, which provided King's navy with an ideal starting point for recruiting prospective officers from within. Invoking practical requirements for waging war, King instituted programs designed to facilitate integration, such as at Hampton Institute in Virginia or Great Lakes near Chicago.[25] He justified these efforts in conjunction with wartime requirements.[26] King pushed the chief of naval personnel, RAdm. Randall Jacobs, to review the policies of BuNav. Recalling past experiences, King derided Jacobs as a "fixer," along with Leahy and Nimitz.[27] Naval traditions died very hard within the bureaucracy ashore and within the seagoing ranks of the American fleet. Circumventing resistance within BuNav, King overhauled the naval personnel system. He replaced the old bureaucracy by replacing civilians with uniformed loyalists under the Bureau of Naval Personnel (BuPers), as redesignated in April 1942.[28]

Although sailors always operated in close quarters, the personnel system within the naval services still amplified the classist divides between officers and enlisted sailors. Given the influence of Jim Crow in American culture, the idea of integrating the sea services proved very difficult to achieve—even with the wartime mandate after Pearl Harbor. Early in the war, controversy followed with efforts to decorate Petty Officer First Class Doris Miller for his heroic service at Pearl Harbor. King supported the idea, although he faced significant resistance within the Awards Board. Eventually, Miller received a Navy Cross.[29] Miller subsequently appeared on war bond tours and in US naval propaganda.

During operations to take Makin and Tarawa, he was killed in combat off Makin when a Japanese submarine torpedoed USS *Liscome Bay* (CVE-56) in November 1943.[30]

Given the heroic service of Miller and many other Black servicemen, the war provided a clear mandate for placing American sea services on a direct course for full integration.[31] King issued the requisite directives to achieve this goal as early as 1942. He consulted Black leaders, including DuBois and Lester Granger—the chairman of the National Urban League. King told Granger directly that the "past is not our present enemy."[32] King then turned dramatically to look thoughtfully out of his office window in Main Navy. The Lincoln Memorial stood around the corner. After a brief pause, King remarked, "We say that we are a democracy, and a democracy ought to have a democratic navy."[33]

Granger pressed King to explain the extent of his commitment to integrate the American sea services. In response, King assured him that he was prepared to go "all the way."[34] However, the chief of BuNav, Jacobs, delayed in executing the order.[35] Thus, King ordered Jacobs to place his signature under the introduction in the "Guide to Command of Negro Naval Personnel."[36] The directive emphasized that "any avoidable waste of manpower can only be viewed as material aid to the enemy."[37] Commanding officers received warning that "restriction, because of racial theories, of the contribution of any individual to the war effort is a serious waste of human resources [and the] Navy accepts no theories of racial differences in inborn ability."[38]

Commanding officers held responsibility for integrating racial minorities within the American sea services. King's guidance stipulated that "every man wearing the uniform be trained and used in accordance with his maximum individual capacity determined on the basis of individual performance."[39] He added, "Navy Department policy is clear that Negroes are to be rated on the same basis as white personnel and that Negro ratings shall move upwards in the same manner as any other ratings."[40] The guide reflected King's by-the-book approach that all hands act with "rigid and impartial adherence to Naval regulations, in which no distinction is made between the color of individuals wearing the uniform."[41]

In the race to win the future unification fights ongoing between the Departments of War and Navy, King seized wartime opportunities to expand naval aviation. On King's watch, Lt. Oscar Holmes persevered to become the first Black American to earn the golden wings of a US naval aviator.[42] When addressing the midshipmen at the Naval Academy, King explained, "Traditions are, of themselves, no more than testimonials to the successes of our predecessors."[43] He offered an optimistic message in telling aspirant naval officers to "do the best you can with what you've got—don't worry about water that has already gone over the dam."[44] He concluded that "'[d]ifficulties' is the name given to things which it is our business to overcome."[45] King's son, Joe, returned from sea duty to complete studies in Annapolis when Midshipman Wesley A. Brown joined the brigade to become the first Black American to earn his commission at the Naval Academy.[46] Concurrently, Ens. Thomas J. Hudner graduated from Annapolis—later earning the Medal of Honor for attempting to save his Black wingman, Ens. Jesse Brown, as enemy forces closed on their downed aircraft on the frozen mountains of Korea.[47]

The heroic exploits of Black American sailors helped King's efforts to rebuild the sea services into a better reflection of American sea power. Race riots and other disasters in ports and shipyards caused King to take direct action in driving integration efforts. Often, racial minorities carried the dangerous mission of handling ordnance. When massive explosions occurred in naval weapons facilities in Virginia and California, King reemphasized the importance of integration to subordinate commanders. The war enabled King to push the mandate with such reluctant figures as the commandant of the Marine Corps, Lt. Gen. Thomas Holcomb. With losses mounting, King pushed Holcomb to understand that "fighting a war was not a job for the white people of the country alone."[48] Holcomb eventually experienced a great epiphany that "Negro Marines had made very good troops."[49]

OVERTAKEN BY WAVES

King supervised the rapid expansion of the naval ranks, using the practical requirements of the war in the slow battle to open opportunities for racial minorities. He similarly justified the reassignment of male personnel to sea duty, noting the nascent capacity of women to serve in strategic functions within the ranks of the American sea services. Concentrating on the immediate wartime mission, King used the superadministrative powers of CNO and CominCh to destroy various bureaucratic fiefdoms within the Navy Department. Given the shortage of personnel aboard US Navy ships, King questioned males ashore in Main Navy about their seagoing experience. "It is noticeable," King wrote, that "there are on duty in Washington—and at headquarters elsewhere a very considerable number of young able-bodied men."[50] He ordered male personnel to the front.

Women served in various capacities since the earliest establishment of the US Navy, but rarely in the uniformed ranks. Acting on the recommendation of his longtime associate Joy Bright Hancock, King recruited the president of Wellesley College, Mildred McAfee, to organize the Women Accepted for Voluntary Emergency Service (WAVES). McAfee and Hancock worked with Josephine Forrestal, the wife of the undersecretary of the Navy, to develop the WAVES uniform with the assistance of *Vogue* magazine and the best fashion designers of New York. King placed priority on replacing men with women on the home front. As war requirements allowed, King progressively expanded the ranks with women and ethnic minorities—radically changing traditional monoculture of the American naval services.[51]

King expected the WAVES to meet the highest traditions and elite standards of the American sea services. With King presiding at the ceremony, McAfee formally launched the WAVES on July 30, 1942.[52] King also recalled his former secretary at BuAer, Hancock, for active service with the WAVES. Past service as a yeomanette during the First World War provided justification for King to recommend her for direct appointment as an officer in the rank of lieutenant. She initially felt awkward wearing an officer's uniform. Hancock also recalled feeling unsure about herself after receiving a summons from King. Setting the tone for Hancock as she crossed the transom into his office, King asked in low, stern tones, "Why aren't you wearing your World War I ribbon?"[53] Hancock struggled to muster a coherent response. King smirked and said, "I have one for you."[54] Hancock remembered the moment when King fixed the decoration on her jacket that "I practically wept, I was so touched with the damned thing."[55]

King certainly proved himself as a true ladies' man with such gestures of actual respect for women. Hancock, among many other close observers, celebrated King's approach to command.[56] After 1942, King rapidly expanded the WAVES program, directing the commandants of the Coast Guard and Marine Corps to follow the example. Working closely with McAfee to establish personnel standards, Lt. Cmdr. Dorothy C. Stratton adapted from the Coast Guard motto, Semper Paratus, to establish the "SPARS" in the summer of 1942. In November, Maj. Ruth Cheney Streeter reported for duty as the skipper of the Marine Corps Women's Reserve. Alternatively, Marines referred to their female counterparts as "BAMS," as explained by the wartime *Time* magazine to mean "Broad Axle Marines."[57] Marines in the field used other demeaning terms to describe the BAMS.[58]

Yeomanettes set the precedence for the rapid recruitment of women into the ranks of King's navy. Women assumed many functions previously performed by male sailors. King replaced males with women in performing specialized strategic functions, such as in operational planning, logistics, communications, and intelligence. The WAVES of intelligence secretly enabled King's navy to gain the advantage in the solution of German naval codes and ciphers.[59] He highlighted the expanding role of women in discussions with journalists. "The navy seems to have no difficulty in getting WAVES into service," King explained. "[There] will be about 90,000 when the requirements are filled."[60] King worked in conjunction with McAfee and Hancock to rotate WAVES with ComInCh staff experience to assist operations within subordinate headquarters under Nimitz, Ingersoll, and Stark.[61]

REALISTIC THINKING

Women and social minorities improved the potential of King's navy in the quest to win the future of American sea power. When asked about the burgeoning roles for racial minorities and women, King told journalists that "we shall have to determine the kind of world we want to have and work for that."[62] Looking outward, King continued that "realistic thinking warrants the assumption that we shall have to set up governments in the conquered countries."[63] King argued that "we shall have to deal with these same governments for we cannot utterly destroy any country."[64] In essence, the task centered on convincing current enemies to recognize the collective humanistic purpose of achieving a sustainable peace at the end of the war.

In the battle to win the future, King struggled to advance the cause of American sea power. Concurrently, he navigated the political undercurrents on the Washington battlefield. The crosswinds of strategic-airpower theory threatened the dream of American sea power. From their newly constructed offices at the Pentagon, War Department propagandists vastly outpaced their counterparts inside the crumbling halls of the wartime Navy Department. The War Department propaganda organization far outclassed equivalents within the Navy Department. Among other manipulators of information, Maj. Gen. William "Wild Bill" Donovan aided from within the Office of Strategic Services (OSS). The Office of War Information (OWI) included a variety of prominent journalists, including Elmer Davis and Arthur Schlesinger Jr. British operatives, including William Stephenson, served with the Americans of OWI. The general's brother, Milton S. Eisenhower, contributed to the propaganda operations of the OWI, which connected with those of the OSS.

King stood above his counterparts as a strategic thinker, although he failed to measure against his immediate counterparts, Marshall and Arnold, on the public stage. King envied Marshall for having the seemingly natural ability to speak without notes.[65] King's memories of the feuds between Sampson and Schley after the Spanish-American War and then of Daniels and Sims after the First World War further clouded King's perspective in handling the media during the Second World War.[66] Fascist extremism fused with Nazi fanaticism to enable Allied propagandists to exploit the "apathy in Italy."[67] Drawing from successes on the European front, King credited Zacharias for cajoling the Japanese to "give up when they did."[68]

King conceded the success of War Department propagandists, which often twisted the story lines of successes primarily achieved by the American sea services. Fearing the consequences, Secretaries Knox and Forrestal pushed King to participate in press engagements. Forrestal disliked King's stiff delivery, gruff voice, and deep midwestern drawl. Forrestal ordered King to fix the propaganda strategy of the Navy Department. King relied upon his lawyer, Bull, to devise plans for the Navy Department to fight the media war without giving away high-grade intelligence secrets. Over drinks, Bull worked the lines with journalist Glenn Perry and the publicist for DuPont Corporation, Arthur Newmeyer. With Bull pulling the requisite strings, Newmeyer received a direct commission in the Naval Reserve to serve as an adviser within the CominCh staff.[69]

Bull operated behind closed doors with King to frame strategy and make the case for the American sea power in the court of public opinion. Bull invited King to meet *informally* with *trusted* members of the media during regular meetings held in the safe confines of Bull's home on Princess Street in downtown Alexandria, Virginia. Among many others, journalists Hanson Baldwin and Walter Lippmann regularly met with King. Glenn Perry claimed to have conceived the idea of holding the clandestine meetings, although he applauded Bull for making all the key arrangements. Later, when Bull died, Phelps Adams rallied fellow journalists to form the "Arlington County Commandos" in his home, across from the Washington Golf and Country Club in Arlington, Virginia.[70]

King always avoided hyperbole and never apologized for making clear strategic decisions. Fellow journalists appreciated the clarity of King's explanation that a fleet "was something you actually fight with, if you could get the enemy to join the fray, and if you figured your chances for winning were good."[71] Journalists also respected King for telling the hard truths.[72] The clandestine meetings proved highly effective, particularly when operations seemed to go badly. On one occasion, during operations to seize Guadalcanal, Lippmann challenged King about risking the fleet on such a seemingly far-flung adventure to the other side of the world. King told Lippmann that the Guadalcanal scenario "served the purpose of fixing the enemy on the other side of the planet so that we can focus on the enemy on the opposite side." King recognized the potential risks of committing the fleet to battle, though he emphasized the fact by asking, "That's what it is for, isn't it?"[73]

King spoke frankly with trusted journalists to explain the interrelationships of the future policy objectives of the Roosevelt administration and the global strategy being executed by the combined forces of the King's British navy and his American variant. King always limited the conversations to last no longer than the time required to drink a six-pack of beer. He relaxed, smoking cigarettes and sipping on beer as he recounted the tumultuous battles and bureaucratic infighting within the CCS and JCS, the problems of personality among key politicians and commanders, and the critical necessity of keeping sensitive intelligence sources fully secured. King joked about having the direct line to J. Edgar Hoover. The journalists fully understood King's implication.[74]

Arlington County Commandos consistently pressed King to explain the German submarine menace. He always provided facts about the limits of submarine technology. King also reassured journalists about US naval operations and intelligence capabilities.[75] King also characterized the Nazi admirals Erich Raeder and Karl Dönitz as worthy adversaries. He applauded Raeder's wily employment of the battleships *Tirpitz* and *Scharnhorst* in "those Norwegian fjords—safe from British bombs and submarines."[76] "This 'Fleet in Being'" King characterized as a "thorn in our side for just by its very existence it ties up a lot of fighting ships of ours which could be very useful elsewhere—and the German knows this very well."[77] "The British Home Fleet has to be kept on the alert and ready at all times," he explained, so that "American ships act as a 'safety man' in case any of the Germans should get by the British line."[78] "While our submarines are good, they are definitely not as good as German submarines." King observed, "We are learning an awful lot from the Germans in this respect."[79] King referred to the commander of German submarines, Dönitz, as a "keen U-boat man!"[80]

Although King respected the German and Italian naval threat in the Atlantic, the Japanese presented the superior challenge to Allied command at sea. He considered the presence of a few German submarines along the American coast in the Atlantic as secondary to the greater strategic problem of the Imperial Japanese Navy in the Pacific. Most significantly, the US Navy simply lacked forces. King later explained, "I think—and believe—that the great delay in getting along with the anti-submarine war was because we (the United States) were not ready for war in December 1941." According to King, the US Navy

> had to build ships that hadn't even been designed at that time, to say nothing about fitting out merchant ships [and] then try to deal with two wars, which were already underway. Another factor that added to the "troubles" of the United States in the anti-submarine campaign during 1942–43 was the transfer of 50 old destroyers to Great Britain. These ships could have been used to great advantage by ourselves.[81]

"I naturally did everything I could to go after the Japanese," King later explained, and that "is where I ran afoul of the British."[82] His friend since the First World War who served as the First Sea Lord, Pound, offered to assume tactical control over US Navy forces in the Atlantic. While he appreciated the offer, King refused to "revisit the problems we experienced in the war of 1917 when Sims had the ear of the Admiralty, but Rodman and Wilson used their own ears to command their ships."[83]

King recognized the value in replicating the British model of forming OICs to synthesize naval operations with intelligence. However, he rejected the British proposal to established combined naval commands. "Mixed naval commands are not good," King stated, noting that differences in "habits, language, and training all militate against efficiency and prevent close coordination."[84] He emphasized the point in his congressional testimony, "Do not be misled by the slogan 'unity of command.'"[85] In all respects, King viewed the concept of "unity of command" as an alternative form of the airpower "unification" concept—fusing military and naval services under a future centralized bureaucracy. When pressed by Democratic Party congressmen Clarence Cannon of Missouri and James G. Scrugham of Nevada to explain concepts of command within the context of naval appropriations debates, King tersely responded, "It seems to me, Mr. Chairman, in the course of what I have said I have answered the question."[86]

German submarine operations in American waters provided convenient means for rivals to undercut King within the media. Talking realistically about war, King told journalists that "you're going to lose something, but you've got to take that loss in order to get the job done."[87] King lambasted the army propaganda surrounding the Civil Air Patrol as "essentially a political gesture."[88] He had a similar view of the so-called "Donald Duck" or "Hooligan Navy."[89] Private aviators, fishermen, and yachtsmen attempted to defend American coastal waters in the vast area between Newfoundland to Cape Hatteras and the Florida Keys.[90] King considered the citizen hordes of the Hooligan Navy as being untrained, inadequately armed, and unnecessarily vulnerable to German submarine attackers. King considered the Hooligan Navy a hazard to navigation, since they operated beyond the control of US Navy authorities.[91] Notably, King consoled journalists about the German submarine menace by confiding that the "Navy knows where they are from day to day within fairish limits of accuracy."[92]

In conversations with trusted journalists, King applauded the efforts of the Royal Navy and acknowledged the limitations of the US Navy in the Atlantic campaign. Given limited resources, he envisioned a role for the British in the Pacific.[93] The First Sea Lord, Pound, likewise augmented American naval forces in the Atlantic and participated in the early US Navy amphibious operations in the Pacific. Pound confided that the "Russian convoys are becoming a regular millstone round our necks and cause a steady attrition[, and the] whole thing is a most unsound operation with the dice loaded against us in every direction."[94] Weary of the losses sustained in efforts to support the Soviet Union, Pound threatened to abandon support for the Russians and focus on the Mediterranean campaign.[95] King similarly characterized the Soviet attitude as "incomprehensible as to doing their part in getting the convoys in and out[, and] they will accept no help and yet do little or nothing themselves—to help themselves!"[96]

The presence of enemy submarines along the Eastern Sea Frontier amplified American media concerns about the overall situation in the Atlantic.[97] King advised journalists to view the global enemy submarine threat as a "menace."[98] He reassured them by describing enemy naval capabilities as a singular whole. The enemy lacked surface and air forces to fully threaten oceanic lines of communication in the Atlantic, as Allied forces built up for the anticipated invasion of Europe.[99] King framed Royal Navy and US Navy collaboration by explaining that "if the British wanted some of our ships to carry out a mission in conjunction with British ships,"

> then the American fleet will do the entire job without British ships or to have the British withdraw their ships from other station to make up the task force and we, the American navy, would replace the ships the British had to withdraw. But having both British and American ships in on one job—that is out. At times we have patrolled British waters while British ships have been away on other missions, and this has worked out very well.[100]

Having experienced the debacles of ABDA and Dieppe, King set the rules in November 1942. "We have had enough of 'mixed command,'" he explained to journalists, saying that it "does not work."[101] The early 1942 Battles of the Java Sea stood out for King, as he described the operations as "a magnificent display of very bad strategy."[102]

Multinational strategy often produced unfocused objectives in preparing operational plans, which caused greater tactical losses in actual combat. On this point, King frequently sparred with Churchill for pressuring Roosevelt as an indirect means to rebuild the British

Empire with American forces. King explained that "its really hard to get to Berlin or Tokyo through India."[103] He emphasized the role of Anglo-American navies in enabling the Soviet and Chinese forces to defeat the Axis ashore. Conversely, King described fears of communism as the basis for British reluctance to support Soviet and Chinese forces.[104]

King rejected land operations on the fringes of the main line of strategic effort while conversely supporting the efforts of Anglo-American naval forces to employ Soviet and Chinese forces in an indirect campaign to secure victory ashore in Europe and Asia. He mused, "There is a lot more equipment available in India[,] but getting troops out by air is slow business and it is only relatively recently that Chiang has consented to do this." "For any large-scale help," King complained, "China will just have to wait until some road or port can be opened through which supplies can come."[105]

King complained about the backlog of strategic supplies and the failure of the CCS and JCS to manage logistics. King complained that the "British are hoarding war materials."[106] He admitted that "this can be understood for Britain is under the guns of the Luftwaffe and Britain does not want to be caught without plenty of war materials in case of attack."[107] He acknowledged that the JCS "has not opposed this because, after all, Britain is the forward citadel and the materials will always be used."[108] King thought that there "are inevitable points of difference between the British and ourselves."[109] He warned journalists to remember that "Churchill is for the British first and the war afterward!"[110] As examples in making the point, King explained the problem of sending "men to England and then on to the Middle East while we could simply send them to the Middle East."[111] King grumbled that we "send planes (fighters) to England, and England sends fighter planes to Russia—a great waste of shipping space."[112] Marshall agreed with King that "we have a war to win and that is the first consideration always."[113]

King pressed the JCS and CCS to focus on the buildup for the English Channel crossing to retake Europe. Churchill preferred to focus on other options, such as Norway and Italy. Given these diversions, King fought against delaying offensive operations in the Pacific. He explained to journalists on November 30, 1942, that we "sent thousands of invasion barges to England [and] the British wanted to store and keep the barges [and] we said[,] 'nothing doing.'"[114] King argued that operations in the Atlantic required the same "barges for use in the Pacific and elsewhere where they would find instant use."[115] In the war at sea, King grew tired of being "besieged by all and sundry for help."[116]

King described his formula as centering on making the suppliant show what effort that country is making to help itself. He reasoned that whenever an ally appeared to simply be stretching "out its hand and not doing anything to help itself—no help."[117] King reasoned that his methodology "stimulates every country to really get busy and do something before it can demand that we give more aid."[118] Taking Brazil as one example, King "paid high tribute to Admiral Jonas Ingram[, who] 'has the Brazilian Navy actually going to sea—and liking it!'" King portrayed the efforts in Brazil as a "real achievement."[119]

In clandestine meetings over six-packs of beer, King told journalists to tell the truth about the actual capabilities and limitations of the enemy. King refuted unfounded rumors about enemy saboteurs operating from Nazi submarines off the Atlantic coast. Allied propagandists amplified the actual threat for the purposes of keeping civilians engaged in the war effort.[120] He particularly disliked the suppositions and unfounded assertions by journalists after the accidental fire on board SS *Normandie* at Pier 88 on the west side of Manhattan. Journalists spread rumors that "some Nazi agents set the fire."[121] King assured journalists about security in American shipyards. But King failed to defend the reputation of his former roommate at the Naval Academy, Andrews, in the aftermath of the *Normandie* fire. King observed that Andrews burned many bridges, and that "no one liked him at all."[122] King explained that Andrews "got into trouble there as commandant of the Third Naval District over the fire in the steamship *Normandie*—it was his district."[123]

The *Normandie* fire fueled the appearance of security problems verging on the edges of incompetence in American shipyards. King failed to recognize the potential ramifications in shaping the views of the taxpaying public. He regretted setbacks like the *Normandie*, although he essentially left it to smolder as a disaster beyond anyone's actual control. He rarely lingered upon disasters and continually looked forward to meeting the challenges of the next. King's mechanical approach sometimes undercut his ability to recognize the role of the media in fighting wars and in winning the peacetime battles beyond the horizon.

BATTLE STARS

King utterly failed to spin the story of American sea power in wartime propaganda, which later carried major consequences. Navy secretary Knox and his undersecretary, Forrestal, constantly prodded King to take a more active role in highlighting the wartime victories of American sea power. In turn, he dug in his heels and avoided Knox and Forrestal as much as possible. His intelligence officer within the CominCh headquarters, Smedberg, explained that "King's views were that the Navy's performance would speak for itself [and] we did not have to sing our own praises or blow our own horn."[124] The propaganda front perplexed King, since other Allied commanders claimed credit for victories achieved primarily by American sea power. King rewarded successes with simple handshakes and, occasionally, a signed letter stating, "Well done." When other services issued decorations, King refused to endorse recommendations to issue medals for individuals "simply doing their job."[125]

The decorations controversy regarding Daniels and Sims after the First World War lingered in the back of King's mind. He worried about the proliferation of medals, ornaments, and other accoutrements in the Second World War.[126] When Navy secretary Knox approved Forrestal's proposals to establish an equivalency to the newly established Army Commendation Medal for the navy, King immediately complained to Roosevelt that such decorations had no place on an American naval uniform. The green ribbons for army and naval commendation medals looked too similar for King's tastes. The decorations feud between Daniels and Sims also loomed in the memory of Roosevelt when Forrestal issued the decoration on his own authority. Like the gold-laced gentlemen of the fleet, Roosevelt "was so vexed at not having been consulted that he was only with difficulty dissuaded from abolishing it."[127]

Because of his phobic view of media and politics, King completely failed to recognize opportunities to look beyond the immediate task of winning the war to sway voting taxpayers to joining the future peacetime cause of American sea power.[128] For example, the exploits of reserve lieutenant Robert Montgomery and another Hollywood actor, Lt. Douglas Fairbanks Jr., served without significant notice by the American media. They earned their stripes as Motor Torpedo Boat skippers in combat.[129] The sons of the former ambassador, Lieutenants Joseph P. and John F. Kennedy, had significant potential to draw media attention for the US Navy. King completely ignored their heroics or at least cut a wide berth from the Kennedy family.

King initially accepted the presence of the media in warships, although he concluded that their function failed to justify the benefits.[130] He questioned the value of Lt. Cmdr. Samuel Eliot Morison's networking with historians among the reserve ranks of the fleet. King complained about the activities of the Hollywood filmmaker and US naval reserve commander John Ford. Commanding the Naval Field Photographic Unit of the OSS, Ford globetrotted to various scenes of battle. Ford portrayed the drama of battle and viscerally highlighted the heroism of the American sea services. Blood appeared red, since he frequently filmed in full color. Ford had an eye for action, although his most dramatic wartime films portrayed the US Navy as embattled or victimized, or in a subordinate supporting role in relation to the other armed services.

The blood and guts of battle mixed with the salty humor of soldiers and sailors at the front, which appealed to King. Despite his cold façade, King frequently exhibited his wry sense of humor among friends and family. He particularly enjoyed works by the army combat cartoonist Sgt. Bill Mauldin. King cut out the *Stars & Stripes* cartoon in which Mauldin depicted a combat-seasoned GI and boyish Army Air Force colonel with the simple title "Uncle Willie." King sent a copy of the cartoon to his son-in-law Col. Freddy Smith. The cartoon also appeared on King's bulletin board inside the vestibule leading into his office at the CominCh headquarters.[131]

King similarly appreciated Mauldin's depictions of sailors, since he placed them in the same category as the infantry among the working-class heroes of the war. To contrast with the comparably luxurious existence of air force pilots and other ranking martinets like Gen. George S. Patton, the "dogfaces" of the army and tattooed "squids" of the navy carried the visceral burdens of battle "up front."[132] King preferred honest portrayals of war, and he feared the corrosive influence of wartime propaganda on American society. In particular, he criticized the carefully manipulated the image of USAAF pilots in American propaganda. They appeared in wartime media as dashing silk-scarfed knights of the wild blue yonder. The fighter aces of the First World War influenced the popular image of USAAF of the Second World War.

MADMAN

The USAAF used propaganda with a viciousness comparable to the strategic-bombing campaign against the enemy. Indeed, USAAF propagandists arguably achieved greater demonstrated success than the bomber wings at the front. By 1943, Arnold unleashed the remarkable creativity of Capt. Stephen F. "Steve" Leo, USAAF. Before the war, Leo had made his name as a journalist with Guy Gannett Communications. Leo also made a small fortune as an advertising executive on Madison Avenue in New York City. Ultimately, Leo had no actual loyalties and worked as a hired gun for the highest bidder, supporting political campaigns as a spin doctor for candidates of both the Republican and Democratic Parties. In these efforts, Leo assisted Democratic senator Harry S Truman. His portfolio also featured the Republican governor of Maine, Sumner Sewell. Through these connections, Leo attained significant influence in the swampy political battleground of Washington, DC.[133]

Immediately following the Pearl Harbor attack, Leo offered his expertise as a publicist to the Navy Department. His overtures to the Navy Department went unanswered in the early months of 1942. Previous associations with Charles Lindbergh and the fighter ace Eddie Rickenbacker had also put Leo into the orbit of Gen. Henry A. Arnold. Coincident with the Battles of the Coral Sea and Midway, Leo received an offer for an officer's commission in the USAAF. Leo received the plum assignment to Arnold's staff. Shortly after reporting to the War Department, Leo worked himself into the assignment as Arnold's congressional liaison to the Truman Committee.[134]

From within the War Department, Arnold empowered Leo to execute an unscrupulous wartime campaign against the Navy Department. Leo manipulated facts to highlight USAAF achievements—often at the expense of the American sea services.[135] Like a spider at the center of the publicity web, Leo coordinated the story lines with a worldwide network of journalists on all the various fronts. His USAAF media organization blossomed to a reported 120 personnel.[136] He earned the reputation for having the ability for "keeping things out of print as he is getting them in."[137] In an exposé, Guy Richards observed in the *Washington Star* that Leo suffered from a "morbid passion for anonymity."[138] Leo believed that "truth, like water, seeks its own level—and, in a democracy, that level is the people [and] it's our job in information to speed that undeniable flow of truth to Americans inside and outside the Air Force."[139]

The truth rarely hindered Leo in framing the future vision of strategic airpower for public consumption. Leo studied the Nazi propagandist Dr. Josef Goebbels, telling his sparring partner inside the Navy Department that "you know, we have a lot to learn from the Nazis . . . Goebbels had a doctorate after all."[140] In 1941, Goebbels observed that the "English follow the principle that when one lies, one should lie big, and stick to it [and] they keep up their lies, even at the risk of looking ridiculous."[141] Leo used similar tactics by spinning headlines about the "Doolittle Raid," among other examples in which the role of USAAF forces supposedly proved to be decisive in such turning points as the Battle of Midway. The successes of air forces under MacArthur's bomber command in the MacPac held similar long-term influence over the future of American sea power. Leo later spun the phrase "Revolt of the Admirals," for the specific purpose of discrediting the Navy Department.

Leo held significant influence at the War Department and used the Navy Department as a foil for creating an image of the future in the air. He generally avoided wearing his army uniform to work and more frequently appeared in civilian clothing on the stages of Washington, New York, and Hollywood.[142] Lt. Col. Robert McNamera worked closely with Leo in advancing the airpower agenda.[143] Leo portrayed the Eighth Air Force in Europe as proof for the unproven theory of strategic airpower. The glamour of the "Mighty Eighth" gushed with color in American cinemas—with dramatic footage of bombing missions flown over Nazi Europe by such familiar celebrities as Jimmy Doolittle, Clark Gable, and Jimmy Stewart.[144] The air war over the Himalayas and the "Flying Tigers" in China also featured in Leo's propaganda portfolio.

The USAAF propaganda campaign successfully drew from the best elements in selling American sea power on the public stage. Old narratives of American sea power as a peacemaker inspired Leo to turn the tables by using the naval peacemaker argument of Teddy Roosevelt as the foundation for strategic airpower propaganda.[145] In an exposé, a rival journalist at *US News and World Report*, David Lawrence, observed that Leo had made "propagandizing [a] respectable profession, even transcending lobbying or ghostwriting."[146]

Leo exploited the centralized hierarchy of the War Department to control the public-affairs campaign with simple and compelling story lines. With so many other fronts to worry about, King placed secrecy ahead of publicity within the Navy Department. As a result, navy publicists fell short in telling the story of sea power in the global war at sea. The untold victories held consequences for King's navy. Internal rivalries within the Navy Department further obscured the fundamental role of American sea power. The propaganda image of the US Marine Corps also overshadowed the equally compelling sacrifices of sailors in King's navy.[147] The heroic narrative of airpower intermixed with the gritty heroism of the soldiers and marines in combat ashore, which overshadowed the equally notable exploits of sailors like Robert Montgomery, Douglas Fairbanks, and Henry Fonda. In addition, John F. Kennedy received a downgraded medal for heroism in combat, and Joseph P. Kennedy died in a ridiculously dangerous stunt with a radio-controlled bomber rigged with explosives. Baseball stars like Ted Williams and Bob Feller served largely unsung within the ranks of King's navy.

The feats of King's navy on simultaneous fronts went missing in action, as victory in Europe overshadowed equivalent efforts ongoing in Asia. The debacles of North Africa and Italy faded into the myths of Normandy with the smiling image of Gen. Dwight D. Eisenhower—as fleets delivering the troops and goods to far-off fronts from the Arctic to the Indian Ocean and beyond to the MacPac. Leo continued spinning tales about the future of airpower when the USAAF shifted the propaganda focus from the strategic-bombing campaign over Germany to Japan. Leo combined forces with the airpower statistical analysis of McNamara during their service together in the CBI theater.[148] Leo and McNamara carried their wartime work forward with the Strategic Bombing Survey. Gaming the numbers to tell the story, Leo and McNamera helped in the long march for separating air forces within the ironic logic of the future unified defense military-industrial establishment.[149]

King failed to develop a coherent strategy to deal with the truly remarkable sophistication of the USAAF publicity organization. He faced withering criticism from Navy secretary Knox and his immediate subordinate, Forrestal, for failing to counter the airpower narrative. In an uncharacteristically lethargic response, King solicited the General Board of the Navy, as chaired by Admiral Arthur Hepburn, to examine the publicity issue. King also directed his team on the CominCh staff to coordinate efforts with retired captain Dudley W. Knox and RAdm. Aaron "Tip" Merrill. He also recruited Capt. Leland Lovette into the campaign to win the hearts and minds of the public. Leo left no challenge unanswered in the publicity war, and King's publicity organization "was disbanded and the Navy public[-]relations men were spanked for trying to present the Navy side."[150]

King's constant effort to balance operational security against publicity hindered chances to sell the triumph of American sea power. He later admitted that "I had a little trouble in the early days of the war because so many of my newspaper friends said that my motto was—tell 'em nothing and don't give a damn whether they like it or not."[151] King reasoned that the "trouble was [that] in telling you, my fellow citizens, what went on, we would also be telling the enemy something he very much wanted to know, and we could not afford to do that."[152] One trusted associate observed that if King "had his way, the Navy would issue only one communiqué to cover the whole war [and] it would be released the day after the surrender and would read, 'We Won.'"[153]

PART III
"MAKE BEST WITH WHAT YOU HAVE"

CHAPTER 25
Fighting in the War Room

Churchill and Roosevelt struck alliances with such divergent strategic partners as the Soviet Union and various nationalist forces in China. The arrangement sparked major disagreements among the CCS. In discussions with Churchill, British leaders used King as their favorite foil. For example, Field Marshal Sir Alan Brooke characterized the Americans of the JCS by describing the "tough and stubborn King, the old crustacean as one of his countrymen called him, the ablest strategist on the American Chiefs of Staff."[1] Brooke disliked King on a personal level. At the same time, Brooke respected King's singular capabilities as a global strategic thinker. Brooke wrote in his memoirs that King had been "overshadowed in statesmanship and grandeur of character by the great Virginian, Marshall."[2]

The policies set by the Roosevelt administration provided the basis for King to stand so strongly against other Allied commanders by interpreting the Europe First principle as phase 1 of a grander global strategy to rebuild Asia as another key foundation in the future United Nations. King sought speedy victory in Europe by advocating plans to execute a cross-channel amphibious route from the British home islands into Nazi-occupied France. To these ends, King pushed the CCS to focus on deepwater ports like Cherbourg, and along coastal areas with the limit of advance being the Rhine River valley. King had no intention of pushing inland beyond the Rhine—leaving the task of defeating Germany to the Soviets. Furthermore, King personally had no intention of executing a full-scale amphibious campaign against the Japanese home islands.

The idea of sending American troops to die on German and Japanese soil seemed as unnecessary as the costly forays into Italy. The ongoing fights within the CCS and JCS also extended to the question of retaking Singapore, or the Philippines. In these debates, King always asked, "To what end?"[3] King's entire strategy for the Atlantic centered on the island waystations leading to the British Isles and similarly along island routes to Formosa in the Pacific. Given the strategic position of the British Isles for the strategic-bombing campaign in Europe, King explained that American bombers "struck Japan and Manchuria from that pace way up north of Chungking, which always meant long-range flights, but they did hit industrial targets in Kyushu [as] far up as Tokyo."[4] King characterized strategic airpower as being inextricably interlocked with American sea power that "you can't say one dominates one time and one another."[5]

Logistical lines of communication from the western ports of America to the eastern ports of Asia always defined King's strategy in the Pacific. King had a very simple way of thinking globally about strategy and in prioritizing the sequence of global amphibious operations. The British Isles and Formosa always served as the focal points for Allied naval forces to concentrate along island lines of communications in the Pacific and Atlantic. The British Isles and Formosa always stood out for King as the island gateways to continental Europe and Asia. Like his views about the priorities in continental Europe, King wanted to take a few deepwater ports along the continental coast of Asia to support Soviet and Chinese ground forces to win the final victory over Japan. King considered the liberation of the Philippines unnecessary. He similarly characterized army plans for the invasion of Japan as an opportunity to build ships. However, he intended to divert those ships to serve his priorities—always holding the right to pull his support for the final decision to execute plans still under development, such as those associated with Operation DOWNFALL, the amphibious campaign to take Japan.[6]

The priorities for both fronts first required American forces to maintain oceanic lines of communications to Australia and to the embattled shores of the British home isles. King characterized his maritime strategy as being focused on inflicting "cumulative pain on the enemy" through "unrelenting pressure."[7] King modified the phrase in communications by describing his strategy as inflicting "unremitting pressure."[8] He intended to support continental operations through maritime means from the "citadels" of Britain and Formosa.[9] Thus, King focused American sea power on the task of opening the key lines of oceanic communications to these island citadels of Europe and Asia—often frustrating counterparts on the CCS and JCS.

Fighting a war of wits, King seized the leading role in coordinating operations with intelligence in the global maritime arena. Intelligence enabled King to understand the enemy perspective, which allowed him to use limited operational resources to maximum effect. King defined the mission of American naval intelligence as "knowing what the enemy is actually doing from day to day, what he is able to do, and what he probably will do, as disclosed by his day-to-day movements."[10] King expected intelligence analysts to understand what "our final practical, concrete objective is, what our own forces is, what our geographical position is, what major strategic practical plans we can make[, and] what we can actually do in view of all of our commitments."[11]

In the competition to control strategic resources, the CCS tended to fixate on Europe at the collective expense of operations ongoing in Asia. Within the JCS, King constantly reasserted the obvious challenge of dealing with the truly profound imperial Japanese fleet, at large in the Pacific. The ongoing debates about the German submarine menace in American waters further complicated strategic discussions about setting key priorities for *future* procurement, training, and personnel.[12] Propaganda about the enemy also carried the double edge of misleading civilians into fearing the actual threat, particularly when the Truman Committee publicized estimates that German submarines sank 1,000,000 deadweight tons of Allied shipping.[13]

Such wildly inflated estimates about the true capabilities of the enemy submarine threat created actual problems for strategic thinkers to consider within the CCS and JCS.

King worried about the strategic ramifications of making such assertions in public. He attempted to solve his problems with the media by engaging selected journalists during secret meetings with beer and cigarettes with the Arlington County Commandos.[14] The war of perceptions and propaganda always perplexed King, which he fully admitted at the time. He simply lacked the interest in manipulating facts for the purposes of influencing people into a false understanding of the truth. King simply told the truth as he understood it, so he "chose to tell the truth, but only in the right doses, under the right circumstances, and to just the right people."[15]

King struggled to understand the strategic task of dealing with the media for the purposes of influencing popular perceptions of American sea power. His past status as a minor celebrity as the Nemo-like submariner and then as dashing naval aviator on the cutting edges of technology in the 1920s and 1930s had vanished. King completely lacked the homespun familiarity of Nimitz or Eisenhower, the hard-edged warrior image of Halsey, the statuesque persona of MacArthur, or the stately reputation of Marshall. Within the inner circle of the Roosevelt administration, Leahy also stood more comfortably in the limelight. Meanwhile, King's cold façade began to wear thin, as Republican Party rivals and aspirant politicians in the Democratic Party anticipated the election of 1944. King had also alienated himself by nurturing the pack mentality among the CominCh staff. Subordinates of King acted with confidence, which often seemed cocky.[16]

King monitored the careers of younger officers among the seagoing ranks, frequently pulling them for duty in Washington without sufficient warning or advanced administrative coordination. He customarily transmitted orders to hand-selected individuals without going through intermediaries. His chief of staff, Edwards, explained, "All the early CominCh officers came from the Atlantic Fleet [and] later officers were picked based on where they had been."[17] "People were brought in who had been successful in all theaters," Edwards continued; "people who would not get cockeyed about one ocean."[18] He explained that "King insisted on turnover of people who had been here (to avoid Headquarters acquiring a Washington mentality)."[19] King sought to escape the routines of Washington by taking refuge on board his flagship, *Dauntless*.

King committed himself completely to the strategic task of fighting the war for the purposes of winning the sustainable peace. Immediately after he assumed global command, King focused exclusively on defeating the enemy as quickly and efficiently as possible—and at minimal cost in American lives and treasure. As King carried the burdens of war, his family likewise understood their role in keeping their elderly patriarch on the job. After 1942, members of his personal staff grew very close to members of the King family. Given his responsibilities, King also accepted the traditional perks of being CNO. His aides maintained the calendars for both the admiral and Mrs. King. Weekly Sunday junkets to visit his ailing wife, Mattie, at the Naval Observatory inspired "joking at the lower staff level."[20] Dyer mused about the authority carried by Mattie that "we know who was really in charge of the whole operation and it wasn't King."[21]

THE DOMESTIC STAFF

When King assumed office as CNO, Mattie and members of the extended King family moved from their private residence to the Naval Observatory. King kept a regular schedule to visit the family during the war. His grandson Egerton "Liath" van den Berg recalled, "The admiral was a typical grandfather, but he had a presence about him—you just knew he was a great man."[22] Whenever the war allowed, the King family gathered at the Naval Observatory for the Sunday rituals of buffet lunch, card games, and evening dinners. King hosted the wedding of his daughter Mildred to US Army captain James Oliver McReynolds at the Naval Observatory. Along with other sons-in-law within the extended ranks of the King family, McReynolds had earned qualifications as a US Army Air Force pilot. His uncle James Clark McReynolds served as an associate justice on the Supreme Court.

Family connections extended to the highest levels of the American government and armed services, which further amplified King's influence in Washington. Muckrakers like Drew Pearson kept a close watch on King—hoping to get a scoop. One of his daughters, Eleanor, struggled in her marriage with a US Army Air Force pilot who happened to serve on Arnold's staff. Rumors of alcohol-fueled fights instigated by his son-in-law eventually reached King through the Washington grapevine. King worked with Arnold to banish the misbehaving son-in-law to an assignment away from the limelight. King's attorney, Cornelius Bull, assisted Eleanor in obtaining a divorce. King subsequently installed his daughter and the grandchildren with Mattie at the Naval Observatory.

King's daughters and grandchildren used the Naval Observatory and their other home in Washington as the patriarch himself assumed watch on his flagship, *Dauntless*. The warship largely stayed tied to the pier at the Washington Navy Yard during the war, serving primarily as a receiving ship for new recruits. Symbolically, *Dauntless* held status as the flagship of the US Navy with King's flag flying above.[23] In theory, *Dauntless* always stood at the ready to carry King into battle. In practice, the warship performed occasional secret missions to spirit dignitaries in and out of Washington by sea. Journalists later caught on and began monitoring the movements of *Dauntless*—hoping to catch a scoop. King sometimes ordered *Dauntless* to sea for no particular purpose—just to keep the journalists guessing.[24] The CominCh staff secretary, Cmdr. George Russell, described King's standard routine:

> Every morning he went aft on board the *Dauntless* for morning colors, walked to his car, proceeded to the Navy Department on Constitution Avenue, stopped near the Washington Monument, walked the rest of the way. We could practically tell time by him. He quit about four o'clock, went for a ride somewhere, then to the navy yard for dinner on board *Dauntless*. He was a flag secretary's dream as far as paperwork was concerned, that is he acted at once on everything that came to his desk, wasn't afraid to sign his name, didn't have to have a conference every time he made a decision. His desk, however, was something of a rat's nest—he wasn't a so-called "clean desk" man.[25]

Russell explained that King "found it too hard to concentrate with his family around him and, as he once said, with grandchildren crawling through his legs, so, in effect, he lived on his flagship."[26] Given the rigors of commanding a multifront war, King sought the traditional solitude of life on board a warship—with the smells of coffee and fuel together with the fresh sea breeze, the firm steel decks rolling with the sea, and the familiar sounds of the boatswain's whistle marking the regular routines of the day. On board *Dauntless*, King found a refuge to become relatively calm.

SEA DUTY ON *DAUNTLESS*

King carried the responsibility of command by providing clear strategic objectives and planning guidance, which empowered subordinate commanders to carry responsibility for executing operations at the tactical level. King observed that the "ranking officer [is] only as good as the lowest ratings[,] and teamwork is required by all hands from the topmasts to the keel—from port to starboard and stem to stern."[27] With the weight of the world war at sea, King relied upon the junior officers in CominCh to keep watch on his personal schedule. In particular, the duty for keeping watch on King fell to Lieutenant Commanders George Russell, Charles Lanman, Neil Dietrich, and Charles M. Keyes. As a perk, personnel assigned to CominCh technically stood watch on *Dauntless*, which qualified them for extra sea pay.

Rivals in the media and within Congress used *Dauntless* to engage in an indirect attack against the Roosevelt administration. Senator Harry S Truman visited King on board *Dauntless*. Truman subsequently asked King for a cost estimate for maintaining a flagship tied to the pier. Five days before Christmas, Congressman Harry R. Sheppard launched a formal investigation. Truman loomed in the background when Sheppard told Navy secretary Knox that the cost of operating the "vessel during fiscal year 1943 [was] the tidy sum of $252,077."[28] Secretary Knox asked King to explain the costs of keeping *Dauntless* and those associated with maintaining separate residences for the King family at the Naval Observatory. In typical naval style, King acknowledged the query as being "noted."[29] After a brief investigation, King wrote Knox, "We have confirmed the tidy sum, $252,077, and agree that there are opportunities to cut future expenditures by a tidy sum, $77.00."[30]

Secretary Knox passed King's response to the Truman Committee, copying the findings to Leahy. Upon reading King's meticulous breakdown to quantify the cost-cutting savings of $77.00, Roosevelt laughed out loud. Roosevelt then told RAdm. Wilson Brown, the battle-hardened commander of the First Naval District, that "it would be undignified and plain wrong for Ernie to go without his barge—I may even take it for myself."[31] Roosevelt quipped, "If Saint George [Marshall] and his warhorse can keep our boys pitching dung and polishing his boots over there at Fort Myer[,] then our Ernie should get to keep his toys too."[32] Brown subsequently told King about Roosevelt's evaluation of the situation concerning *Dauntless*. King closed the debate with a handwritten memo to Secretary Knox: "As to *Dauntless* becoming the President's yacht, it is clear that the President understands and is satisfied with the status quo."[33]

King used *Dauntless* as the symbolic flagship of the US Navy, which provided a seagoing postal address for officers associated with the CominCh headquarters. The *Dauntless* skipper, Grisham, explained the inestimable value of the arrangement. He noted that former members of the crew earned high honors in combat after their initial service in the flagship. "One officer, though super educated, was unsuited for shipboard duty," Grisham explained. "He has however a fine statistical mind as is now doing that kind of duty in the Philadelphia Navy Yard—I understand very successfully."[34] The individual in question, reserve lieutenant L. Sprague DeCamp, engaged in synthesizing technical developments in radar, sonar, and direction finding within a centralized layout inside warships under construction.[35]

Rigorous traditions of good order and discipline served as the foundation for King's navy to push the superficial boundaries to attain the highest levels of creativity and technical innovation. Among other freewheeling thinkers within the ranks of King's navy, DeCamp worked with retired lieutenant Robert A. Heinlein. As a navy civil servant, Isaac Asimov also worked in close collaboration with DeCamp and Heinlein at the Philadelphia Naval Shipyard. Cmdr. Cal Laning also corresponded with Heinlein about futuristic concepts. Laning held command on destroyers in the Pacific. Combining wild ideas with practical experience, Laning and Heinlein—along with their associates—helped conceptualize the Combat Information Center (CIC) system. In essence, CIC placed warship skippers at the center of all the various sources of tactical information.[36]

HISTORY AS AN INTELLIGENCE FUNCTION

Ideas for fusing strategic intelligence with imperfect speculations about enemy intentions, as derived from high-grade sources, reminded King of past efforts to glean knowledge from widely scattered points of fact. His old shipmate Knox invoked Corbett's earlier success with the Historical Section. As the officer in charge of the Historical Section at ONI, or Op-16-E, Knox submitted his recommendation to King on July 6, 1942. The following day, King directed the president of the Naval War College, Kalbfus, to collaborate with Knox to infuse the work of the Historical Section of ONI with future strategic planning at the Naval War College.

Upon entering his second tenure as president of the Naval War College, Kalbfus received the collateral duty under the authority of the CNO to serve simultaneously as the Director of Naval History with Knox serving as his deputy director in the retired rank of captain. Under King's authority, Kalbfus and Knox received the task of organizing historical functions for applied operational purposes. Kalbfus carried the traditional educational responsibilities at the Naval War College with the added task of mobilizing historical resources in anticipation of wartime requirements. He had the responsibility for fusing the operational analysis functions of ONI with the unique capabilities of the Naval War College. From 1942, Kalbfus and Knox worked together to fuel the development of the Office of Naval History (ONH) as a coequal function to ONI under the CNO. Kalbfus and Knox also pioneered efforts to develop plans for postwar reconstruction, which also extended to using publicity and propaganda for the purposes of advancing the vision of American sea power.

The *predictive* task of ONI required an administrative separation from broader studies of the past with an *applied* view. This point of view originated with Knox or, more correctly, his recollection of the First World War model provided by the Historical Section of the Imperial War Staff under Sir Julian Corbett. The derivations established by Sims and then Knox provided foundation for the Americans to exploit the past for the purposes of promulgating relevant studies of interest to contemporary commanders. The definition provided by Royal Navy Volunteer Reserve commander Donald MacLachlan also inspired the Americans in their definition: "Intelligence is no more than information about events or people [but with] a capital letter and it stands for a vast area of state activity, both in peace and war."[37]

Constantly grappling with the question of intelligence within the Navy Department, King staged an unprecedented bureaucratic revolution from above. Recalling the circumstances, Gallery explained that "on paper the Navy Department is the most cockeyed organization that ever happened to grow up and survive [and it is] both horizontal and vertical at the same time [where] overlapping responsibility and authority are normal, and everybody has his nose stuck into everybody else's business."[38] Lt. Cmdr. Walter Muir Whitehill similarly described the cultural revolution within Main Navy under King:

[It was] an immense building in which unadorned offices of standard size stretched interminably along dreary corridors. When built as a temporary structure in 1918 it seemed a model of efficient use of space, but the additions and alterations of a quarter of a century—coupled with wartime crowding—had turned it into a curiously chaotic rabbit warren. In few places short of the palace of Versailles before 1789 could such widely divergent characters have jostled elbows in corridors. In most parts of the building, flag officers enroute to vital conferences collided with whistling messengers delivering mail by tricycle, ensign's wives bringing babies to the dispensary, plumbers with tools, civil servants in search of a cup of coffee, and laborers engaged in the perennial pastime of shifting somebody's desk and filing cases from one place to another.[39]

Whitehill discovered another world, saying, "On the front corridor of the third deck, between the fifth and eighth wings, there was a subtle difference in the atmosphere [and] there was a brisk sea-going air to the officers and enlisted men who were to be seen." "No sign or barrier marked the boundaries of CominCh Headquarters, yet they were plainly discernible." Whitehill also noted that "in some inexplicable manner it suggested being afloat rather than ashore."[40]

The seagoing culture of the CominCh headquarters inspired members of the staff to seek opportunities for command at the front. King's intelligence officer, Dyer, hoped to escape the bureaucratic battlefields of the Navy Department. He conspired with RAdm. Richard Conolly to send a personal note for Dyer to report for combat duty in the Mediterranean. King agreed, but only on the condition that Dyer first had to find a "qualified officer to take his place."[41] Dyer asked the director of naval intelligence, RAdm. Harold C. Train, for permission to recruit Capt. Henri Smith-Hutton as a replacement in the CominCh headquarters. Smith-Hutton had just arrived in Washington after nearly six months of internment in the former American embassy in Tokyo.[42]

Specialists with experience found a secure home with King inside the CominCh organization. Japanese-language officers drew King's attention. Among others, he recruited Smith-Hutton for service in CominCh. Dyer made the initial recommendation, although Smith-Hutton recalled that RAdm. Charles M. "Savvy" Cooke Jr. "had been gunnery officer of the battleship *Idaho* when I had turret four and apparently, he suggested [to King] that I might be interested." The endorsements of Cooke and Dyer proved sufficient, since King selected Smith-Hutton as the "F-35" within CominCh. He reported to King for duty in command of the War Room on December 18, 1942.[43]

Smith-Hutton offered significant experience in examining imperial Japanese strategy from an enemy perspective. Smith-Hutton was released with 1,400 other Americans and foreign nationals. The Japanese-flagged SS *Asama Maru* transported the American delegation through waters patrolled by US Navy and Allied submarines. Smith-Hutton recalled that the Japanese failed to provide sufficient food and other provisions for the lengthy voyage to Portuguese East Africa. Smith-Hutton then accompanied Ambassador Joseph

Grew to Rio de Janeiro on the neutral Swedish-flagged SS *Gripsholm*. Smith-Hutton hitched a ride in a US Navy cruiser bound for New York. He then traveled by train and reported to the Navy Department.[44] He immediately requested assignment for sea duty in a combat zone. Within hours of reporting to the Navy Department, Smith-Hutton received summons to meet King.

SPEAKING JAPANESE

Smith-Hutton offered an informed perspective on the interrelationships of strategy and intelligence from an enemy point of view. For this reason, King denied Smith-Hutton's request for immediate assignment to sea duty. Instead, King directed Smith-Hutton to take charge of reorganizing the intelligence subdivisions of the CNO and CominCh staffs. To these ends, he collaborated with McCollum to fuse administrative connections between ICPOA, SWPA, and ComNavEu intelligence organizations. Smith-Hutton and McCollum meanwhile assisted their Naval Academy classmate William J. Sebald and another Japanese linguist, Marion Case "Mike" Cheek. As Naval Academy graduates, Sebald and Cheek had resigned from the service to pursue their fortunes as civilians.[45] In 1942, McCollum and Smith-Hutton assisted secured civil-service appointments for Sebald and Cheek. However, Capt. Samuel Moore fought against recruiting the "dud rounds" like Sebald and Cheek. Moore went so far as to accuse Sebald and his wife of being sympathetic to the enemy. Sebald explained that Moore thought that "many of my clients were Japanese firms for whom I acted as a sort of conduit."[46]

Americans of Asian heritage suffered many humiliations in the aftermath of the imperial Japanese attack on Pearl Harbor. Sebald's wife, Edith Frances DeBecker, was of mixed British and Japanese heritage. Her mother was descended from a distinguished Japanese family. At one point, the FBI raided their apartment and threatened to arrest Edith. "They searched high and low," Sebald explained that the "net result of their search was that they found, first of all, my Naval Academy sword [and] there was no question that it was mine because it had my name on it."[47] The skeptical G-men continued questioning Sebald and his wife. "The peculiar thing," Sebald noted, was that "some months later my wife was asked to join OSS as a consultant on Japanese psychology." Sebald remembered that Edith "told me at times that it was almost pathetic to see what juvenile ideas they had in OSS as to operations they planned."[48]

Firsthand knowledge of Japanese language and culture ran in short supply within the ranks of the US Navy. Smith-Hutton recruited Sebald to join the CominCh headquarters. Changes in bureaucratic titles often coincided with the movements of individuals, as King instituted radical organizational changes within the Navy Department. He directed Smith-Hutton to overhaul the War Room, as earlier established by Dyer. In turn, Smith-Hutton recruited Sebald from ONI to replace Lane, or "F-352," in the CominCh Pacific Section. Smith-Hutton further envisioned the merger of the F-35 "War Room" with the similar functions performed inside the spaces housing the ONI tracking room, "Op-16-B/8," under Lt. Cmdr. Charles W. Baldwin. Smith-Hutton recalled Knowles from London as the prospective replacement for Laird, as "F-353," in the CominCh Atlantic Section.[49] After their rotations out of the CominCh headquarters, Lane and Laird served with distinction in combat service in American submarines in the Pacific.[50]

The pins marking the tactical locations of enemy ships and the strings showing the routes of convoys provided means for King to see the strategic picture in clear terms.

Political cartoon depicting Adm. Sims shooting holes in US naval propaganda, as propagated by Secretary of the Navy Daniels and the Navy Department after the First World War. *Library of Congress*

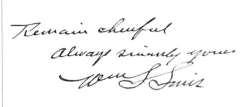

The secret password, as used in personal correspondences among acolytes of Sims

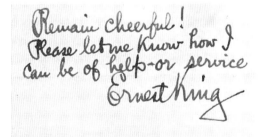

Making best with the 1920s, RAdm. William Moffett stands second from left as chief of BuAer while unveiling the plan to transform Lexington-class battle cruiser hulls into aircraft carriers in 1922. *US Navy photograph*

The battle force and scouting forces off the Panama Canal during Fleet Problems. *US Navy photograph*

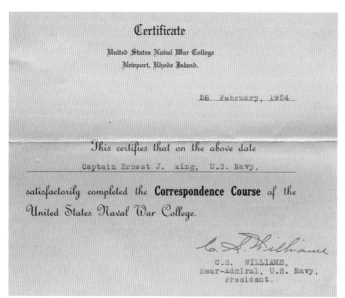

While in command at sea, King encouraged his subordinates to complete the Naval War College curriculum by implementing the "War College Afloat" philosophy of his mentor, Sims. Having earlier qualified in the "Staff Course" of the Naval War College, King set the example by rallying his officers to complete the War College Correspondence Course in 1924. He later completed the curriculum for a third time in 1933.

Treaty limits be damned in the scouting forces of the US Navy with USS *Lexington* (CV-2) and an American airship during Fleet Problems of the 1920s. *US Navy photograph*

Lexington maneuvers into position to strike the simulated "enemy" during seagoing fleet problems in 1929. *US Navy photograph*

King navigating *Lexington* into the Panama Canal during Fleet Problems. *Courtesy of Thomas King Savage and the King family*

King as the victorious trophy winner in command of *Lexington* during Fleet Problems. *US Navy photograph*

President Roosevelt with Navy secretary Swanson to the left
and ambassador Josephus Daniels with the CNO, Standley,
under the guns of *Indianapolis*. *US Navy photograph*

The graduate—three times over—King strolling along
the seaside path from the Naval War College, where
the past intermixes with the future along the
Narragansett Bay. *Courtesy of Thomas Savage King
and the King family*

The interrelationships of history and innovation as developed in the classroom setting and gaming floors of the Naval War College in the 1930s. *Naval War College*

Capt. Adolphus "Dolly" Andrews assumed interim duty as president of the Naval War College, having attempted to slow King's progress during graduation exercises in 1933. *US Navy photograph*

Cartoon presented to King by members of the CominCh staff depicting his surprisingly quick rise to hold unprecedented unified authorities of CNO and CominCh. *Library of Congress*

America's newest star, temporary RAdm. King sitting for his portrait as chief of BuAer in June 1933. *US Navy photograph (King Personnel File)*

Innovators of aviation on May 23, 1934, *from left to right*, are Charles A. Lindbergh, US Navy captain Arthur B. Cook, secretary of the Smithsonian Institution Charles G. Abbot, Dr. Joseph S. Ames, Orville Wright, Edward P. Warner, acting chief of BuAer, and King. *Library of Congress*

From the left, Orville Wright, US Army major general Benjamin Foulis, King, and Eugene Vidal observing an aerial parade in 1934. *Courtesy of Janvier King Smith and the King family*

The chief of BuAer, King, fitted out in the finest suits from the cutters at Brooks Brothers of New York during testimony in Congress between 1934 and 1936. *Courtesy of Janvier King Smith and the King family*

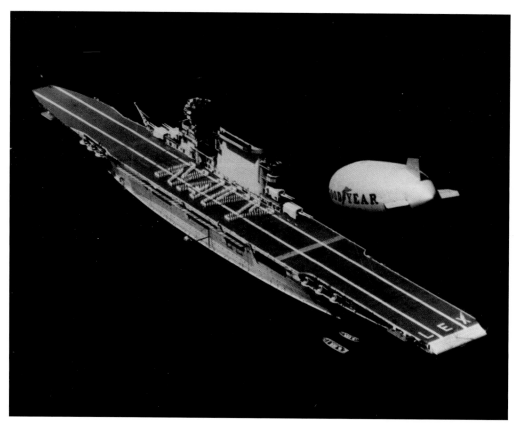

Goodyear blimp closing on *Lexington* after King concluded the contract for LTA forces for the fleet in 1935—such versatile assets proved useful in long-range scouting, air-sea rescue, convoy escort, and antisubmarine operations. *US Navy photograph*

King sits at center with the first Consolidated flying boat, or "Catalina," having circumvented War Department restrictions on land-based HTA airframes. *Courtesy of Janvier King Smith and the King family*

Having previously served as president of the Naval War College until 1936, Adm. Edward C. Kalbfus served as commander, Battle Force, with VAdm. King as his subordinate commander, Scouting Force, before returning for a second tour at the War College in 1939. *US Navy photograph*

In this remarkable snapshot, President Roosevelt looks up at the smiling King on the decks of *Houston* among fellow admirals including Kimmel, Stark, Halsey, Leahy, and Pye—coincident with the nominations of Stark and Richardson to become CNO and CinCUS. *Library of Congress*

Roosevelt with his consigliore, retired Cdre. Dudley W. Knox, as they communicate to American taxpayers about the role of sea power with the publication of *Naval Documents Related to the "Quasi-War" with France: Naval Operations February 1797–October 1798. US Navy photograph*

Lord Louis Mountbatten of the BAD stands between Short and Kimmel with Bellinger in trail during meetings in Hawaii that coincided with the Atlantic Charter meetings in August 1941. Later, Mountbatten nearly killed King with a pistol in Quebec. *US Navy photograph*

The secret seaborne meeting of Roosevelt and Churchill, with King and Stark attending, during the Atlantic Charter discussions in August 1941. *US Navy photograph*

Adm. Ernest J. King carries the weight of being the
newly appointed CominCh with Secretary Knox and the
CNO, Stark, at the White House on December 31, 1941.
US Navy photograph

Likeminded old salts, King conspires
with his opposite number, Pound,
during CCS debates at the pivotal
Casablanca Conference of 1943. *US
Navy photograph*

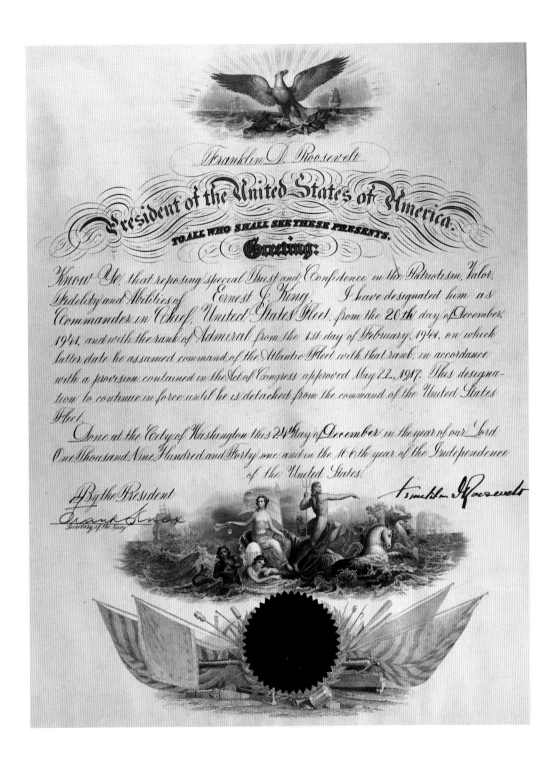

Commander in chief US fleet commissioning certificate for King, as signed by President Roosevelt on December 24, 1941. *Courtesy of Egerton van den Berg and the King family*

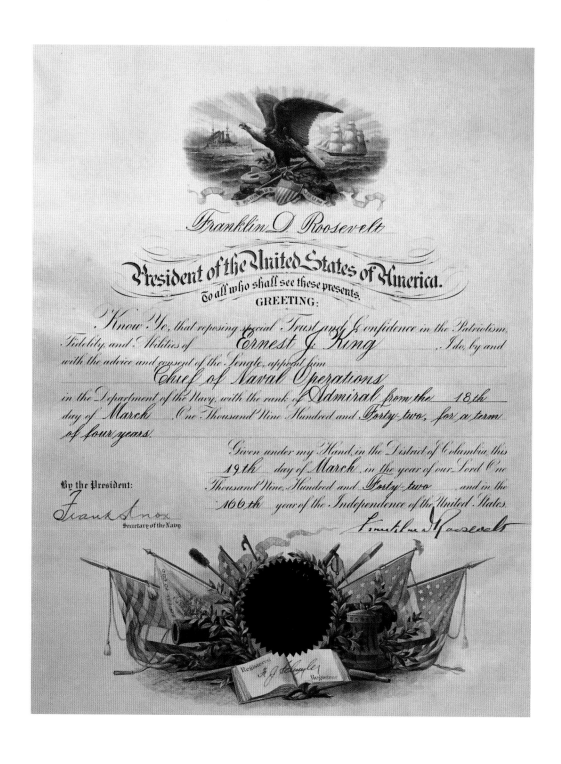

Chief of naval operations commissioning certificate for
King, as signed by President Roosevelt on March 18, 1942.
Courtesy of Egerton van den Berg and the King family

Adm. Harold R. Stark with Lt. Cmdr. Tracy Barrett Kittredge trailing along upon arriving in London in 1942—notably, Stark remained the senior admiral by lineal standing and was by no means in exile as commander, US naval forces in Europe. *US Navy photograph*

With unrestricted submarine warfare already authorized, Adm. Chester W. Nimitz symbolically takes command in the Pacific on the deck of the submarine USS *Grayling* (SS-209), as Adm. Husband E. Kimmel observes from the far right on December 31, 1941. *US Navy photograph*

Nimitz sits with Ghormley overlooking, as MacArthur's generals Richard K. Sutherland (*left*) and Millard F. Harmon (*right*) look on. *Library of Congress*

Vice Admirals Frederick C. Horne and Russell Willson listen to King as RAdm. Richard S. Edwards takes notes over a map of Midway Island in the CominCh headquarters in 1942. *US Navy photograph*

Unwilling to allow a few German submarines to continue harassing Allied shipping, King drew from British methods in organizing the American naval campaign to defeat the enemy with their own words. King placed RAdm. Ellis Zacharias in charge of executing a global psychological-warfare campaign against the enemy.[51] He had studied the methods of Royal Navy Volunteer Reserve lieutenant commander Donald MacLachlan and his associates, including the Hungarian-born journalist Ladislas Faragó. In 1942, MacLachlan and Faragó assisted Zacharias in organizing the "Special Activities Branch," or OP-16-Z, within the ONI table of organization. Zacharias also recruited US Navy commander John L. Riehldaffer to lead efforts within Op-16-Z.[52]

King fully embraced the offensive concept of psychological warfare against enemy combatants, although he missed the point of synthesizing these efforts with propaganda aimed at the general population. Under Zacharias, the Special Warfare Branch provided opportunities for Faragó and Riehldaffer to talk the Germans into surrendering through music, radio shows, and patriotic dreams of American concepts of freedom and democracy.[53] Psychological warfare further reflected the unseen wireless war against the enemy. In 1942, King opened all channels to facilitate speedy solutions for the enigmatic challenge of enemy codes and ciphers. British cryptologic methods and technical innovations also provided inspiration for American innovation on an industrial scale. Setting aside the bureaucrats, King recruited the best magicians and puzzle solvers in the secret war to destroy the enemy in the global maritime arena.

NAVY CONTRACT NXS7892

The earlier exploits of Bletchley Park and the Admiralty OIC inspired King to develop superior capabilities in equivalent organizations within the Navy Department. To this end, he endorsed the Office of Naval Communications plan to contract with the National Cash Register Company (NCR). Cmdr. Howard Engstrom and Lt. Cmdr. Ralph Meader supervised the work inside Building 26 on the NCR campus in Dayton, Ohio. With some assistance from Alan Turing of Bletchley Park, an NCR engineering team under Joe Desch improved upon British designs to develop uniquely American machines, known in some circles as Bombe.[54] One of the WAVES, Lt. Judy [Potter] Parsons, refuted the term, since she and her fellow WAVES cryptanalysts referred to the Bombe *only* as "machines."[55]

British cryptanalysts enjoyed the solitude of the grounds at Bletchley Park, and the War Department secured emergency funding to establish a similar facility. In turn, King empowered the director of naval communications, Holden, and his assistant, Stone, to coordinate efforts with the War Department in organizing the center at Arlington Hall Station in Virginia. Not to be outdone by the British or by the US Army, King wanted the US Navy organization to outpace the others. Stone recalled:

> My assignment was to find a place to move Op-20-G out of the Navy Department and set them up in a spacious establishment where we could have a rapid and rather great expansion of personnel. We looked at some 31 places in Washington. Old schools, an old jail, and any old building that looked like it might serve our purpose and finally decided that the best one was to buy the Mount Vernon Seminary for Women and the Navy bought the old establishment; a 35-acre place for about a million dollars.[56]

Stone added that "we were recruiting not only male personnel, but WAVES at that time [and] we recruited over 4,000 WAVES and built 40 barracks to house them across from what is now the Naval Communication Annex on Nebraska Avenue."[57] In essence, Bletchley Park lost the monopoly on German naval communications with King driving the ship at Nebraska Avenue.

King approved funding to acquire the Mount Vernon Seminary on Nebraska Avenue, near the Navy Department. As communications officers, Holden and Stone relied upon Cmdr. Joseph N. Wenger. In building the new organization at Nebraska Avenue, Stone described, "Wenger was the senior technical man."[58] Stone explained that Wenger "devoted himself to running the cryptographic side of Op-20-G. [And] I devoted myself almost entirely to finding the new location, recruiting the many, many new people we were after."[59] Stone thought that Wenger "was my right-hand man[, but] it wasn't too long after we were nicely set up on Nebraska Avenue that Joe had a heart attack."[60]

The stresses associated with service in headquarters ashore differed from the more visceral consequences of failure in combat. In the war of wits, King sought full domination against the enemy. In 1942, Secretary Knox approved King's request to provide funding for "Navy Contract NXs7892." Knox had no need to know the full details, since King directed Op-20-G to use the funding to procure "components which heretofore did not exist."[61] Otherwise known as the Bombe among British cryptanalysts, such machines required the best minds, significant amounts of precious materials, and individually designed components from roughly 12,000 suppliers across the United States.[62]

King's effort to support the research and development of an American Bombe drew attention from the War Production Board and the Truman Committee in Congress. At the same time that King sought support for the Bombe projects within the Navy Department, the War Department struggled for the same resources for Project MANHATTAN—the Army cover name for efforts surrounding the atomic bomb. Within the US Navy, "Operation Manhattan" had traditionally signified among many sailors a reference to liberty call in ports surrounding the New York City waterfront.[63]

Navy Department requirements to develop Bombe technology sparked a bureaucratic procurement fight with the War Department. The Bletchley Park example inspired Marshall to seek the same capability for the army at Arlington Hall Station. He then submitted a proposal to merge the Navy Department efforts already happening at Nebraska Avenue with those of the War Department at Arlington Hall.[64] The chairman of the War Production Board (WPB), Donald M. Nelson, endorsed Marshall's proposal. Nelson then questioned King about the details surrounding "Navy Contract NXs7892," or the program to build a cryptologic Bombe.[65]

Navy Department requirements for Bombe pulled significant amounts of copper and other precious metals from the War Department's Project MANHATTAN. The War Department failed to share key information with the Navy Department, and vice versa, about such projects.[66] In the competition for control, Marshall questioned the costs associated with King's program under NXs7892. Eventually, the Truman Committee called King to explain the costs. Given the highly sensitive nature of NXs7892, King outright refused to discuss the contract in an open forum such as Congress. Instead, King sent Leahy a memorandum featuring all the details about Navy Contract NXs7892.[67]

The report enclosed by King outlined consequences for failing to continue efforts surrounding the Bombe. He told Leahy that "all existing devices both here and in England for breaking the [M4 Enigma] cipher have been rendered obsolete." King continued that the British, lacking sufficient "material needed in the development and production of equipment designed for their special intelligence purposes, be given an absolutely clear right of way over everything else."[68] King asked Leahy to "please endeavor to personally present this correspondence to the President [to] obtain his authority to give Navy Contract NXs7892 the highest possible preference rating."[69] In explaining the issue, King advised Leahy that the purpose "is to secure an AAA preference rating for NXs7892 from the Chairman of the War Production Board."[70] King requested the highest priority of "A-1 precedence rating from the Army and Navy officers on the Procurement Precedence of Supplies, Materials and Equipment Committee of the Joint Communications Board."[71]

Unlike the War Department, the Navy Department sought complete control over the collection *and dissemination* of information about the enemy. British cryptologists enjoyed the relative calm of Bletchley Park. In 1942, Bletchley Park possessed only ten Bombe machines.[72] Bletchley Park muddled along with three-rotor models, which proved inefficient at solving German naval communications, particularly those encrypted on the M4 Enigma.[73] When German submarines created havoc in American waters, King's man Weeks talked about the sounds of sheep and picturesque landscapes in the area surrounding Bletchley Park. Such vivid descriptions of the British approach certainly annoyed King. In reorganizing the Office of Naval Communications in Washington, King insisted on an unfettered industrial approach to solving enemy codes and ciphers with the establishment of Nebraska Avenue.[74] Meanwhile, King opened the coffers to quickly construct 121 four-rotor "high-speed" Bombe machines.[75]

King's personal network of spies provided remarkable access to other parts of the combined Anglo-American intelligence bureaucracy. Among many others, Cmdr. Robert Weeks kept King fully apprised of British capabilities as the CominCh liaison for cryptologic strategy on the CCS and JCS. From his offices at Nebraska Avenue, Weeks also maintained liaison with the BAD, the War Department, and the wartime offices of naval intelligence and communications. By 1942, Weeks joined forces with Wenger to arrange a summit between GC&CS and Op-20-G at the Navy Department. The director of naval communications, Capt. Carl Holden, took charge of the effort.[76] Having focused on battleships, Holden knew virtually nothing about the black arts of cryptography or naval intelligence.[77] However, the arrangement concluded under his supervision became known as the "Holden Agreement," resetting the administrative relationships between GC&CS and Op-20-G.[78] The Holden agreement became a monumental waypoint in negotiations culminating in the British–United States Agreement (BrUSA), defining transatlantic collaboration for the duration of the war and beyond.[79]

CHAPTER 26
Building 26 versus TRITON

King seized strategic control over the transatlantic intelligence relationship in the solution of German naval codes and ciphers. After 1943, epic cryptologic battles quietly unfolded behind closed doors in the pastoral solitude on the campuses of Bletchley Park and Nebraska Avenue. Academics worked within the impatient atmosphere of the wartime bureaucracy. The information provided by these faceless heroes established the transatlantic "special relationship."[1] Intelligence collaboration served as the keystone in transatlantic collaboration in the global maritime arena—through both world wars and beyond into the uncertain waters of unsettled peace. Past British intelligence triumphs received due attention as the Americans progressively assumed full control of the helm in setting course for the future United Nations after 1943.

The operations subdivisions within the CominCh headquarters swelled with information from multiple sources, which required specialized personnel. Given the seagoing orientation of the US Navy, few among the active ranks had the education—or requisite intellectual openness—to consider ideas exceeding the constraints of naval regulations and the maritime rules of the road. Entering the salty arena of bureaucratic gladiators within the wartime ranks of the US Navy, Yale University professor of mathematics Howard T. Engstrom spearheaded the cryptologic campaign against enemy codes and ciphers. Previous reserve affiliations with the Office of Naval Communications influenced Engstrom's assignment to Commanders Joseph Wenger and Bernard Roeder in organizing Nebraska Avenue. Engstrom supervised the ongoing technical work of the civilian engineer Joe Desch at NCR in Dayton, Ohio.[2]

British experience provided a foundation for American innovation, which defined the industrial approach required for solving enemy codes and ciphers. Engstrom explained that the "ultimate desire is to be able to run synchronously a series of machines initially set and thereafter run in such a fashion that their settings are always at fixed intervals."[3] "The outposts of each machine would be wired to the inputs of its neighbors in a fashion to be determined by the cryptanalysts," and the report continued that it would then be "required to discover and record those settings and wheel combinations for which circuits established by these cross wirings were active."[4] The original memorandum *did not* feature caveats like ULTRA or MAGIC, and it carried the relatively low classification of secret.[5]

Beyond the Enigma, Engstrom required a separate team to focus on the short-signal procedures employed by the Germans. The brevity codes used to transmit tactical signals presented a significant problem. The German Naval Grid Chart cipher presented another layer of security in identifying the locations of enemy submarines. Even during periods when they had unfettered access to intercepted Enigma messages, the German Naval Grid obscured the actual geographic references found in the enemy text. With Engstrom's recommendation, Wenger placed Cmdr. Bernard Roeder in charge of connecting the Atlantic Section and Pacific Section within Op-20-G with those organizations of the same name within the operational headquarters of CominCh. Roeder subsequently installed reserve lieutenant commander Randolph Church and Lt. (j.g.) Willard Van Orman Quine to focus on the German commerce-raiding problem within the Atlantic Section of Op-20-G.

Close connections among individual personalities within Op-20-G extended to the higher levels of command within the Navy Department. Working for the Goodyear company as a senior executive, Ward Van Orman provided a personal endorsement for his cousin Quine to secure a reserve commission in the US Navy. Van Orman's close friendship with the King family in Lorain extended to the familial connections with the Quine branch in Akron, Ohio. Quine brought significant experience and educational credentials from his advanced academic studies in philosophy and mathematics. Upon reporting to the Navy Department, Quine considered his doctorate and academic awards to be completely inadequate as preparation for service in the US Navy. He later remembered Roeder as a "guy who got it, that we were just a bunch of hired guns who did not take well to the whole navy thing[, and he] just let us do our jobs with or without ties and buttoned[-]up navy jackets."[6]

Accustomed to the serenity and intellectual freedom of academic life, Quine was amused by the hierarchical tribal culture of the US Navy. The novelty of receiving notice of his "promotion" to the rank of a lieutenant—on the basis of his PhD from Harvard—inspired Quine to think that he "should have preferred to have been appointed to the rank of admiral."[7] He explained that the "pattern of work was an abrupt departure, consisting of imposed tasks in a clean[-]cut eight-hour day."[8] He described the Op-20-G Atlantic Section as "a bright and congenial group, thirty-four all told." His team ultimately included "two professors of philosophy, one of English, one of German, one of Greek, along with half a dozen young college graduates whose careers had not crystallized. The cipher people downstairs were largely mathematicians, two of whom divided their time with us."[9]

With Engstrom concentrating on a mechanical solution to the Enigma cipher, Quine and Carson focused on other aspects of German communications. Quine nurtured a loose atmosphere within the Atlantic Section of Op-20-G, which contrasted with the regimented framework of the US Navy. Having recruited some of the brightest minds in American academe, Quine worked very closely with Neil Carson to solve the German Navy Grid Chart cipher. Another Harvard scholar with a PhD in music, Carson first examined British information. Quine attempted to guess the locations of German submarines and brush up on maritime geography while Carson solved the German navy's grid charts.[10] "There would be days on end when the cryptanalysts would labor in vain," Quine recalled. "I would sit through the lonely midwatch hoping for news from them. Lounging back with our feet on our desks and a Mercator projection of the world on the wall at one side, we would try each other on latitudes and longitudes. '55N, 63W: wet or dry?'"[11]

The solution of German naval codes and ciphers required an ongoing process of pooling multiple sources. Information provided weeks after the fact appeared irrelevant to many seagoing commanders. For this reason, King decided to reorganize the CominCh headquarters once again. King established the US Navy cryptologic organization at Nebraska Avenue to mirror the operational functions of the CominCh headquarters at the Navy Department. The Op-20-G subsections known as the Pacific Section (or Op-20-G/P, under Safford) and Atlantic Section (Op-20-G/A, under Quine) provided direct support to the broader operational missions performed by the Pacific Section, under Sebald, and Atlantic Section, under Knowles, within CominCh. Under the overall supervision of Smith-Hutton, the F-35 organization blossomed into a fully functional OIC within King's navy.

Many specialists within the cryptologic branches of naval communications resisted oversight from King's organization in Washington. Regular line officers like the Redman brothers, Holden, and Stone engaged in a campaign against the communications and intelligence fiefdoms under Safford and his associates within Op-20-G. In Hawaii, Layton and Rochefort also failed to change their habits. Ultimately, King made clear his intentions after directing Nimitz to expand collaboration between the army and naval intelligence functions. ICPOA thereafter added the "J" for "Joint" under the acronym "JICPOA."[12]

DREAM WORLDS

The war at sea followed the ebbs and flows of logistics on the singular oceanic front, within which King's navy operated in conjunction with other Allied forces against their common Axis enemy. The unresolved fight for air between the Departments of War and Navy further soured Marshall and King's relationship.[13] War secretary Stimson also influenced Marshall in his relationship with King, as Roosevelt openly tilted the bureaucratic scales in favor of unifying the armed services under the amalgamated vision of enforcing the sustainable future peace through American sea power. Alternative military and airpower concepts for future reconstruction ran squarely against the views of Roosevelt and his primary *naval* strategist—King.

Army and air force leaders within the CCS had no means to fight the enemy without the direct involvement of King's navy, which hemmed the transatlantic alliance together within the global maritime arena. Stimson and his generals recognized King as one means to hold the Navy Department in check. The unseen bureaucratic knife fights on the Washington battlefield also appeared between the lines of headlines about the ongoing congressional hearings concerning the Pearl Harbor disaster. Stimson also pressed Democratic congressman Clifton A. Woodrum to study the problems of unification by framing airpower as the future for unifying the military and naval services into a single bureaucratic entity. Professor Ferdinand Eberstadt of Princeton University chaired the study concerning the future of American service unification.[14]

British allies exploited the unresolved unification debates within the American camp, which caused major problems between Marshall and King. The airpower debate placed them in opposite corners of the bureaucratic boxing ring. Arnold stood behind Marshall and Leahy periodically coached King, as other members of the CCS observed the bout unfold. In November 1943, Marshall preempted King with another memo for the JCS, "Single Department of War in the Post-war Period."[15] As the JCS read the memo, Leahy was silent when King erupted with the ferocity of Neptune himself—subjecting Marshall to a tirade punctuated by deeply personal insults. King thought, "Marshall is really a reptile."[16]

The unification fight bubbled beneath the surface of strategic discussions within the CCS and JCS. By 1943, King's navy stood ready to unleash simultaneous offensive operations on a worldwide scale. Yet, counterparts on the CCS and JCS often refuted King's views about the sequence of global offensive priorities for operations against the Axis Tripartite.[17] "What a hell of a fight we had about it," King recalled. "Churchill's basic idea was that the troops and ships scheduled for the invasion of France should be kept to go up into Yugoslavia."[18] King dismissed such forays as "eccentric operations."[19]

Churchill and Roosevelt faced a potential impasse about the future strategic sequence of offensive operations against the enemies of Europe and Asia. The campaign in North Africa still lingered, as debates within the CCS erupted about the problem of Asia. Operations in China proved very difficult, as various factions engaged in civil war rather than fighting the Japanese. Chiang Kaishek's nephew and adopted son, Chiang Wei-Quo, also served in the Nazi armed forces. Chinese Nationalist armies wore Nazi *Stahlhelmen* and Fascist uniforms, which further pushed Chiang under a cloud. Describing this rich cast of characters to journalists, King explained, "Chiang is pretty well 'set' in his opinions and—this is humorous—Chiang is also a naval strategist and knows exactly how the American fleet should be run and maneuvered."[20] Observing King's interactions with Chiang from afar, Smith-Hutton suggested, "Chiang Kai-Shek seemed to live in a dream world [and] Chinese staff officers showed that they had no real grasp of modern military problems."[21]

The influence of China on American strategy stood among the most significant disconnects in the transatlantic relationship between Churchill and Roosevelt. With the Humphrey Bogart movie appearing in theaters in the fall of 1942, Roosevelt made the inspired choice of setting the next showdown of the CCS in the Moroccan crossroads of Casablanca.[22] During the flight to Casablanca, King flew with Cooke, US Army general Albert Coady Wedemeyer, and Col. Brehon B. Somervell. Capt. Milo Campbell flew a Trans-World Airlines "Skyliner" to Puerto Rico and then southward to refuel in Brazil before turning eastward, across the Atlantic, toward Africa. During the flight, King explained that he "crossed the equator for the first time in his sixty-four years."[23] Campbell released the aircraft controls for King to cross the line by air. Wedemeyer later wrote that all were left astonished by King's admission that the "trip was the first in his long seadog's life that had ever taken Admiral King across the Equator."[24] Campbell arranged for special "shellback" certificates for King and all the passengers on board when they crossed the line.[25]

On the flight to Casablanca, King anticipated trouble concerning the future focus of combined strategy. He traded notes with Dill on the flight. King recalled Dill telling stories about service in Palestine and India. Dill then told the biblical story of Adam as a predictive analogy for deliberations in Casablanca. He told King that the "Lord, when almost finished with the creation of animals, agreed to allow Adam to try his hand with a little leftover clay—Adam did not do very well [and] that is how camels came into being."[26] Upon reaching the designated place, Churchill and Roosevelt kept their differences behind closed doors in a separate compound—negotiating policy disagreements over martinis and Pol Roger champagne.

Churchill and Roosevelt presented a unified front, taking on the role of referees in managing the bitter battles among the CCS. The fights among British and American staffs at the Anfa Hotel in Casablanca took on the aura of a bloody boxing match. From a JCS perspective, King recalled, "[We] went into a huddle and decided what could be done in a military way and [then] had our dope sheet drawn up and presented it to Roosevelt and Churchill."[27] Much to the frustration of King, Churchill and Roosevelt insisted that the

"Combined Chiefs had to do <u>much</u> better."[28] King explained, "So, we sharpened our pencils and worked like beavers [and] then Churchill and Roosevelt patted each other on the back and congratulated each other on what expert needlers they were!"[29]

Broadly, the British wanted to focus on the Mediterranean and Atlantic fronts, whereas the Americans fought for offensive options in the Indian Ocean and the Pacific. In essence, the army thinkers of the CCS slovenly wanted to focus on the European front, and the naval thinkers wanted to exploit opportunities ashore in Asia. King's aide Lt. Cmdr. Frederick H. Schneider recalled the heated debates:

> The most important result of the Casablanca Conference [was] that Admiral King, alone and unaided, by his individual personal forcefulness—prevented the Combined Chiefs of Staff, the Prime Minister, and the President from committing ourselves to numerous piecemeal unrelated actions because of the lack of a global strategic plan.[30]

Schneider later reflected upon the significance of Casablanca as he went on to fight with distinction in the Pacific. Observing the strategic consequences of decisions from the subordinate point of view, Schneider characterized King's contributions at Casablanca as fundamental to the future victory at sea.

Taking the global perspective, King pushed the CCS to utilize collective British and American resources with greater efficiency to limit Anglo-American losses while enabling Soviet and Chinese efforts against common Axis enemies ashore. King vocally insisted on an amphibious campaign across the English Channel through France, rather than from Italy or Yugoslavia.[31] As one of the key architects of the Europe First strategy, King viewed victory over the Nazis as a prerequisite for winning the future in Asia. He explained that "one story that has gone around is that the US chiefs of staff would pull out of Europe altogether if the British did not 'play ball.'"[32] King admitted that "such rumors may have passed around at these conferences [but] there was no real intention in them."[33]

British and American differences about strategic priorities in the global maritime arena frequently unfolded in the skies above. During the critical convoy battles of March and April 1943, the German submarine force initially experienced success.[34] Coincidentally, the RAF coastal commander, Joubert, and his successor, Air Marshal Sir John Slessor, collaborated with their American counterparts in framing the case for an overarching Atlantic antisubmarine command.[35] Secretary of War Stimson endorsed the concept of a "Super Air Officer Commander in Chief," to coordinate "unified air control of the Atlantic."[36] King noted that the "Royal Air Force wanted to manage the carriers of the Royal Navy [and] the Air Force of the United States were copycats."[37] The USAAF favored strategic bombing doctrine and claimed control over aviation assets capable of delivering heavy ordnance on a worldwide scale.[38] Arnold suggested that "'<u>unity of air power</u>' must be employed to suit its peculiar character rather than borrowed from older military theory."[39]

Arnold annoyed King by portraying technological advances as proof about the unproven success of airpower theory. King blamed the British for stoking the airpower conflict between the War Department and Navy Department.[40] Arnold shrewdly reevaluated the historical foundations of American sea power to recast airpower as the future. In these efforts, Arnold collaborated with the Douglas Aircraft Company and its affiliated RAND

Project. MIT professor Edmund Bowles helped draft the RAND analysis of airpower organization. Together, Arnold and Bowles produced a carefully constructed operational research study featuring a series of colorful charts and graphs. Arnold envisioned a unified command to solve the overall problem of submarines. King laughed at Arnold for describing the "20th Air Force" as a central headquarters to coordinate army and naval aviation.[41] "Hell, Arnold didn't know what he was talking about," King said. He belittled Arnold as "just a yes man for Marshall."[42]

Bureaucratic infighting reflected the personal goals and professional experience of individual personalities within the War Department and Navy Department. King argued the differences between "unity of effort" and "unity of command."[43] He thought, "Under no circumstances [should] the air forces of a Fleet be placed under the command of anyone except the commander of that Fleet."[44] He rationalized that "every Naval aviator is, first of all, a Naval officer [and] knows ships and what they can do as well as what they cannot do."[45] Unlike army pilots indoctrinated to focus on securing air supremacy to raze fixed targets, a naval aviator "learned in ships what he will do in the air."[46]

King refused to allow army aircraft to operate independently in missions clearly falling under the responsibility of the US Navy.[47] He also exploited the opportunity to consolidate naval aviation. In essence, King flipped Marshall's logic about unifying antisubmarine operations within the prewar provisions of joint army-navy agreements for aviation forces. King emphasized that antisubmarine tactics required the synthesis of surface with subsurface operations and that "Army aviation, if it comes into the picture, is to be added to a naval force already in being."[48] Missing at the debate table in the critical moment, Arnold lost the chance to thwart King after a series of heart attacks in the spring of 1943. Convinced by the logic of King's argument, Marshall agreed to transfer shore-based USAAF bomber aircraft to expand the arsenal of long-range PBY and blimp forces within the US naval services.

Heavy army bombers provided additional space for weapons and specialized gear for long-range antisubmarine operations over deep-blue waters. US naval aviators with specialized training for antisubmarine operations further enhanced chances for success against elusive enemy submarine targets.[49] Unlike the army configuration of the Consolidated B-24 "Liberator," King's variant of the same airframe became known as the PB4Y-1 "Privateer." King purposely antagonized Arnold by offering to train USAAF pilots to serve as naval aviators at Pensacola. He further irked counterparts in the USAAF by recalling that the majority of the original "Flying Tigers" in China had first volunteered from the aviation ranks of the American sea services.[50]

Army pilots largely disappeared from the antisubmarine squadron flight lines with the arrival of specially trained US naval aviators. Marines and Coast Guardsmen also worked within navy antisubmarine composite squadrons. All naval aviators attended specialized training together in the individual schools of the Atlantic Fleet Operational Training Command (COTCLant). King placed RAdm. Donald B. Beary in overall command, with Captains Aurilius B. Voseller, John L. Holloway, and Dashiell L. Madeira assigned from the CominCh staff to assist. In essence, Beary and his team coordinated the various individual shore activities associated with the various subfields under what he called the "antisubmarine university."[51]

British antisubmarine schools inspired efforts under Beary to organize various subcommands for various technical subfields inherent with the task. The antisubmarine mission rapidly blossomed into a fully recognized element of fleet operations. Unlike the past, scouting and reconnaissance functions came together under the broader functional auspices of antisubmarine fleets, task forces, and the more tactically focused "task units" and "task groups." Sensing the future threat to army airpower, Marshall warned King that aviation had been a

> continuing problem in the Army since 1917[,] but I think the Navy has had little of it to contend with until this question of air striking forces has arisen and virtually another Army, in the shape of Marines, is in process of being established. Naval commanders will feel that they can work more efficiently if they have the Naval, Air, and Marine units, as a homogenous force, and undoubtedly, they can. But on the other hand, if this argument is carried to its conclusion, it means the consolidation of the Army and Navy.[52]

Marshall and King feared the divisions fostered by an airpower cabal within the US Army Air Force, which amplified differences between the War Department and Navy Department. Marshall grew weary of King in the wartime interservice fight for air.[53]

JEEPS AFLOAT AND ASHORE

Following the bargain to allow the US Navy to fly land-based aircraft on antisubmarine operations, Marshall and King predicted a future showdown on the issue between the Departments of War and Navy. King warned that "it is important to realize that there can be no hard[-]and[-]fast rule for setting up commands in the field."[54] Since the army held responsibility in land operations, King explained the role of the navy by emphasizing that aviation, "though a specialty, is much more closely interwoven with the rest of the fleet than is the submarine branch of the Navy."[55] King imagined "an efficient modern fleet in which there is not a complete welding of aviation and surface elements [that is] accomplished by requiring aviators to rotate in other duties in the same manner as do submarine officers."[56]

Staffers frequently carried the burden of grooming ruffled feathers in the wake of the vicious verbal duels between Marshall and King. In memoirs, Wedemeyer criticized Marshall and praised King.[57] As Marshall's chief planning officer, Wedemeyer observed that in "my judgement King was the strongest man on the [JCS]."[58] Wedemeyer observed that King "had a keen analytical mind [and] was incisive and direct in his approach to the solution of a problem [and] did not understand and could not engage in small talk."[59] At one point, he recalled Cooke mumbled, "Nuts," when Brooke began lecturing King about strategy.[60] Together with Cooke in the battles for transatlantic control over future strategy, Wedemeyer characterized the British as "particularly stuffy."[61] Wedemeyer explained that "King had talked to me, and at great length, to Admiral Cooke about the build-up of Allied forces in North Africa." King characterized the British strategy for operations to cross the Mediterranean as a vast waste of resources in Europe. King asked the piercing question of what purpose would be "served if we were to continue operations in that area?"[62]

The differences between Churchill and Roosevelt bubbled beneath the surface of debates ongoing within the CCS and JCS. Marshall and King used their subordinates to negotiate unity of effort in relations with their British counterparts.[63] Both frequently worked together to mitigate the meddling of Churchill on the focus of American policy. Among the biggest examples, which prompted Marshall and King to complain together, Churchill convinced Roosevelt to build escort "jeep" carriers, otherwise known as "CVE" in the US Navy.[64] Among sailors, CVE meant "Combustible, Vulnerable, and Expendable."[65] Sailors also combined the reference with general-purpose (GP) vehicles, known as "jeeps" among the landlubber troops, which emphasized simplicity for the sake of speedy production, portability, and expediency.[66] King discounted the idea of building cheaply constructed jeep carriers as unnecessarily wasteful. Larger fast carriers had proven King's prewar theories against the enemy in the Pacific. By comparison, jeep carrier designs lacked sufficient range and air-wing strike capacity to keep up with deep-blue oceanic fleet operations—such as in the Pacific. In considering the procurement priorities, King warned that the jeeps "will distract from our effort to combat the enemy submarines."[67] King protested that the "British have asked for more destroyer escorts, which we do not yet have."[68]

Roosevelt simply smiled and changed the subject, which Marshall and King recognized as being the end of debate. American shipyards produced roughly 151 aircraft carriers, including 122 jeeps—thirty-nine of which sailed under the British ensign after commissioning in American shipyards.[69] Jeep carriers became a key antisubmarine platform—having a direct role in sinking an estimated fifty-five Axis submarines after 1943.[70] King later admitted, "F.D.R. was right about the jeeps."[71] British efforts to control American aircraft carriers inspired King to solicit recommendations from US Navy captain Marshall R. Greer. Having served with the Fleet Air Arm of the Royal Navy, Greer characterized British naval aviation that because of

inexperience the inability of the officers to efficiently operate the carriers is deplorable, even though the young captains in command are, and have been, exceptionally fine young gunnery and submarine officers; and I now can better understand why it is necessary to run the carriers from Headquarters ashore like a puppet show instead of giving them complete freedom of action which we are successfully employing. It is my opinion that we must continue to accept the unpleasant truth that we cannot expect much from British CVEs [aircraft carriers] in the anti-submarine warfare in the near future. This, to my mind, results directly from the fact that they have not our good fortune of able leadership in Naval Aviation.[72]

Greer suggested that the "US Navy could put these assets to better use in the Atlantic."[73] The British corroborated Greer's conclusions.[74] Making the best with what he had, King directed his staff to consider the potential use of jeep carriers for offensive fleet operations.

King insisted on clear results in efforts to coordinate fleet operations with those focused on solving the unique enigma of antisubmarine warfare. For King, fleet operations were always interconnected with convoy tactics. He failed to accept separations between the functions of such seagoing basics. Sharing the similar view, King put Capt. Wilder D. Baker in charge of studying the issue of jeep carriers in conjunction with ongoing efforts to defeat the enemy submarine menace.[75] In turn, Baker created the Antisubmarine Warfare

Section, or "F-25," within the CominCh organization.[76] From offices in Boston, Baker's team included chiefs René B. Chevalier and Roy Hanna, Yeoman First Class Samuel P. Livecchi, and Harvard professor William E. Schevill.[77]

The Boston team under Baker used Schevill's oceanographic research on whale migration to make improvements on British ASDIC technology. Baker's team helped perfect the American variant, known as sound, navigation, and ranging (SONAR). Baker's team also featured MIT professors Jacinto Steinhardt and George E. Kimball. Princeton University physicist Philip M. Morse then took charge of organizing these research efforts under the Antisubmarine Warfare Operations Research Group (ASWORG). In the spring of 1943, the longhairs of ASWORG advised King's directive to fuse the CIC concept with SONAR, RADAR, HF/DF, and magnetic-anomaly detection (MAD).[78]

ASWORG personnel operated independently within the antisubmarine subsections of the CominCh headquarters. Witnessing the comedy unfolding within the CominCh headquarters, Low observed that the "scientific people, mostly individualists and unacquainted with Naval procedures and discipline, were quite different and required most careful handling."[79] With ASWORG fully functional within CominCh by February 1943, King organized its extensions closer to the front with the establishment of the Antisubmarine Development Detachment (ADD) at the Naval Air Station in Quonset, Rhode Island.[80]

King enlisted civilians into the effort to exploit technological innovations, as exemplified by the ASWORG. Working in conjunction with the mad scientists of CominCh, Commanders Mahlon S. Tisdale and Joseph C. Wylie concurrently supervised efforts to install CIC on board warships, which integrated air and sea sensors to hasten the flow of tactical information among warships operating in tandem under combat conditions.[81] King's man, retired lieutenant Robert A. Heinlein, worked with the ASWORG to perfect CIC from the shipyards at Philadelphia and New York.[82] Isaac Asimov, Theodore Sturgeon, and US Navy lieutenants L. Ron Hubbard and Sprague de Camp also contributed wild ideas with Heinlein in efforts to refine the CIC concept.[83] The skipper of USS *Hutchins* (DD-475), Lt. Cmdr. Cal Laning, also provided Heinlein with recommendations from the front line.[84]

The motley cast of naval professionals and mad scientists within King's immediate orbit demonstrated unbridled creativity. CIC evolved from early inspirations found in the science fiction writings of E. E. Smith, which particularly inspired Laning and Heinlein. Their classified wartime work later inspired Heinlein and his associates to fictionalize their personal experiences. Heinlein's fictional characters resembled the towering persona of King as well as members of his family and the CominCh staff.[85] Heinlein explained that "King was always an innovator."[86] Heinlein explained, "What King wanted was possible, but highly improbable at the state of the art [at the time]."[87] Heinlein thought, "King always had a driving, intelligent interest in developing new and better means of naval warfare."[88]

HUNTER-KILLERS

The development of CIC on board warships coincided with King's strategic efforts to reorganize the CominCh headquarters into the worldwide center of American naval operations. He envisioned CominCh as the hub for synthesizing planning and logistics within subordinate headquarters ashore—like CinCPac/POA and ComNavEu—with the seagoing task force commands afloat. With the special intelligence linkages fully established between London and Washington and beyond to Hawaii and Melbourne, the CominCh headquarters thereafter served as the central strategic clearinghouse to coordinate operations with intelligence at the front.[89] Within areas of command responsibility falling under King, the messages transmitted from CominCh headquarters prompted tactical action at the front.[90]

There were differences between the British and American systems for synthesizing strategic decisions. Admiralty procedures for coordinating convoy and aircraft carrier operations served as one basis for combined operations, whereas King's navy progressively operated autonomously within areas falling under American control. King's submarines attacked enemy targets with precision, since the CominCh headquarters essentially operated as a global CIC for offensive submarine operations after 1943. King naturally carried the CIC concept to another level by forming task groups comprising jeep carriers and destroyer escorts to operate in tandem against enemy submarines.

Wireless communications enabled King's CominCh headquarters to evolve into the unparalleled flagship for American sea power in the global maritime arena. In 1943, King approved plans developed by Beary and Capt. Aurelius B. Vosseller to implement "hunter-killer" antisubmarine tactics. King directed Vosseller to take the initiative in putting theories to practice in combat as the commander, Task Group (CTG) on board USS *Bogue* (CVE-9). Vosseller whipped his crew into shape with the assistance of battle-seasoned refugees from aircraft carriers lost in combat, such as *Lexington* and *Yorktown*. Greenhands recently arriving from basic training quickly adapted to their new homes at sea. Unlike the salty veterans—many of whom reminisced about the ways of the old navy—the new boots embraced the newly constructed jeep carriers.[91]

British convoy escort group doctrine inspired American experimentation with existing US Navy procedures. Task group tactics evolved from prewar experimentation at the Naval War College and in seagoing fleet problems. Thus, in the summer of 1943, King gave full approval when Vosseller used the CIC concept to maneuver *Bogue* as a floating headquarters for antisubmarine operations. He broke from British procedures by operating *Bogue* as a roving antisubmarine task group—apart from the convoys under escort. The tactics employed by Vosseller proved the concept for future "hunter-killer" aircraft carrier operations. After the spring of 1943, the *Bogue* task group alone tallied thirteen Axis submarines in the Atlantic—including the Japanese submarines *RO-501* and *I-52*.[92] Such aggressive American tactics caused rumblings at the higher levels of strategic command within the CCS after 1943.

CHAPTER 27
Fly by Night

The Casablanca Conference provided the mandate for King to stage the ultimate showdown over the question of airpower. By the spring of 1943, King insisted that "any individual action must fit into the over-all picture."[1] Exploiting the opportunity to advance his American agenda, King joined forces with Canadian rear-admiral Victor-Gabriel Brodeur.[2] The senior Canadian naval representative in Washington, Brodeur collaborated with King to organize the Atlantic Convoy Conference. Brodeur influenced the Canadian chief of the Naval Staff, Vice-Admiral Percy W. Nelles, to suggest a conference to frame Anglo-American strategy and command relations in the Atlantic.[3] Recognizing an opportunity to renegotiate the transatlantic relationship, Nelles and King collaborated in organizing the Atlantic Convoy Conference—drawing the Admiralty into accepting the American navies as coequal partners in the global maritime arena.

The situation hindered collective efforts to coordinate strategy with ongoing operations and intelligence. Furthering efforts to coordinate dissimilar tactical objectives among Allied naval commanders, King championed the recommendations of the Western Approaches chief of staff, Royal Navy rear admiral Sir John M. Mansfield, to establish a Western Atlantic Antisubmarine Command. In January 1943, King assigned RAdm. James L. Kauffman to study the various options. Working together, Mansfield and Kauffman advised Cooke and Edwards that the Royal Navy and US Navy should establish uniform training standards to implement the "group system of operating antisubmarine forces [to be] universally adopted and the integrity of groups maintained."[4]

The Admiralty employed aircraft carriers to create an air umbrella over transatlantic convoys. Royal Navy captain Stephen W. Roskill explained that the "protagonists of powerful convoy escorts and evasive routing—far to the north in the case of the Atlantic convoys—obtained their way in general."[5] King considered fast-moving large convoys preferable to smaller formations, enabling fewer escorts to safeguard more merchant ships. He explained that a "slow convoy proceeds at six and a 'fast' one at nine knots."[6] He continued, "This so burdened the US–UK route that we had to increase the interval from the usual six to eight days in order to get a supply of escort vessels sufficient to protect the convoy."[7]

From within the Admiralty, Pound encouraged King to clarify debates concerning transatlantic command at the Atlantic Convoy Conference in Washington. "I am very glad you have arranged this conference about the North Atlantic," Pound wrote King in February 1943. "I am sure things can be simplified a good deal, particularly the air question."[8] Pound encouraged King to organize the Washington Convoy Conference of March 1943. Pound struggled with his health, so he sent his vice chief of the Naval Staff, Royal Navy rear-admiral Sir Henry Ruthven Moore. King wrote Pound, "[I am] heartily glad that

Moore has come over—he has done much to help 'quell' the 'fly-by-night' ideas which are all too many."[9] "I dare say," Pound responded, "you might be able to get away with this with your pair of wings."[10]

Strategic airpower theorists failed to prove their point in waging concerted efforts against German submarines during the Biscay offensive. Always the skeptic of army notions about airpower, King directed Professors Philip M. Morse and George E. Kimball of the Massachusetts Institute of Technology to study the Biscay campaign. Kimball and Morse applied operational-research theory to demonstrate the failure of air force pilots and the relative success of naval aviators in antisubmarine operations.[11] Morse and Kimball concluded that the sinking of an individual enemy submarine helped the Allies attain the rough "net savings of about eight ships."[12] Pleased by the results of the Atlantic Convoy Conference of 1943, the Admiralty staff used the findings to unify Royal Navy aviation and antisubmarine efforts with their American counterparts. The Atlantic Convoy Conference also provided momentum for British efforts to prepare for operations with American forces in the Pacific, particularly in anticipation of planned amphibious campaigns into continental Asia and pursuant to Anglo-American postwar global reconstruction objectives.[13]

UNITY OF EFFORT

British representatives in Washington faced few alternatives in negotiating geographic areas of oceanic control as proposed by the Canadians and the United States. The Canadians, under Brodeur, set the tone for the Atlantic Convoy Conference at the Navy Department in the spring of 1943.[14] Brodeur stated, "I wish to impress this most important fact about Canada[,] which appears to be so little understood."[15] He stipulated, "All Canadian armed forces are under the control of one, only one, higher authority[,] which is the Canadian Government."[16] Brodeur set the limits of negotiation, saying, "If all sub-committees studying the present agenda will remember that very important factor, a great deal of time will be saved and many misunderstandings avoided."[17]

From their close collaboration with the US Navy in American waters, the Royal Canadian Navy sought their own capacity to control operations in the North Atlantic. King conspired with the Royal Canadian Navy to enable NSHQ to assume separate responsibility for operations within a designated area in the Northwest Atlantic.[18] This would expand the scope of responsibility for Rear-Admiral Leonard W. Murray in the MOEF. In anticipation of assuming command as commander in chief of Canadian Northwest Atlantic (CinCCNA) in April 1943, Murray worked with NSHQ to synthesize relations with the OIC and the CominCh headquarters to coordinate Canadian operations with intelligence.[19]

Overlapping British and American security procedures frequently failed to synthesize with those of the Canadians. The cryptologic capacity of Bletchley Park and Nebraska Avenue also far outpaced the capabilities of equivalent Canadian efforts. During the Atlantic Convoy Conference, the leading intelligence expert at NSHQ, de Marbois, explained that a major problem in the relationship between the OIC in London and NSHQ in Ottawa centered on time delays in the dissemination of intelligence.[20] Admiralty estimates reached Ottawa after roughly seven hours, whereas those from the Navy Department arrived within two hours.[21]

The challenge at hand hinged on the strategic question of security in disseminating tactical intelligence among forces directly engaged against the enemy. Various headquarters transmitted information to the forces at sea, which caused significant confusion in coordinating antisubmarine and convoy escort operations. King addressed the problem in clear terms in his keynote remarks for the Atlantic Convoy Conference in March of 1943. King argued that

> what we seek is unification of effort. <u>I hope this conference will be able to suggest the best way to effect unity</u>. I think you all know in a general way the meaning of unified effort, but when it comes to details of organization, there is bound to be divergence of opinion . . . May I caution you not to think that unity (of command) is a panacea for military difficulties or that it is the *sin qua non* of—unity of effort. Unity of command, in appropriate circumstances, does unify the effort. But inappropriate centralization of command produces only the form—not the substance—of unified effort . . . A point upon which I have very strong (personal) opinion is the avoidance of mixed forces. It is a great pleasure to work with our allies, and we can always learn something from each other, but nevertheless, I have had what to me is conclusive proof that these advantages are more than nullified by the ~~lack of unity~~ (handicap) of effort that ~~results~~ (is inherent) when forces of different nations, with different customs and systems of command, are brigaded together.[22]

King rejected the concept of mixing multinational forces with such loaded phrases as "handicap" and "brigaded together."[23] "Even after the Air Force got out of antisubmarine warfare," King explained, "there were still troubles with the British who wanted to run everything all the time [while] I was thinking about the situation in the Pacific."[24] King mused that if the "Japanese had really understood about submarines we would have had a hard time."[25]

GET LOW

The Allied campaign in Europe intertwined with operations ongoing in Asia, which informed the strategy of King's navy in the global maritime arena. Seeking to launch a central Pacific offensive while balancing priorities for the Atlantic, King also rotated personnel between the various naval fronts. Every twelve to eighteen months, he rewarded individuals within CominCh with orders to sea duty. His friend Capt. Knox described King's approach within the CominCh headquarters that "as a general rule, young and able sea-going officers who came in from combat zones for brief periods of duty, and were sent back there pretty fast."[26] King's lawyer, Bull, recalled watching as the elder admiral joined a younger officer on the floor. Bull described King scouring the details with an ensign "on their hands and knees on an officer floor carpeted with blueprints."[27] After the young officer left, King chuckled while telling his lawyer, "I like that kid [because] he wasn't afraid of me."[28]

King planned an unrelenting offensive by using the CominCh headquarters to coordinate hunter-killer operations with intelligence. He wanted fresh blood to lead the charge. King reviewed the combat records of various candidates before gravitating to the selection board results—noting the familiar name Low appearing on the list for prospective two-star promotion. Since his earlier service in the CominCh headquarters, Low accrued a combat record worthy of Nelson himself. During the amphibious operations in North Africa, Low attacked French battleships and barely escaped a German torpedo. Low then took *Wichita* through the Panama Canal to support operations against the Japanese. During operations off Guadalcanal, Low maneuvered into the shallows to provide direct support for the Marines ashore. Later joining RAdm. Robert C. "Ike" Giffen with Task Force 14 to drive a reinforcement convoy through the Japanese defenses, Low demonstrated remarkable seamanship on *Wichita*—damning the torpedoes to escape the ugly fate of *Chicago*. Low thrived in combat.

Having earned battle stars in two oceans, Low impressed Nimitz in anticipation of the amphibious campaign to retake the Aleutians. Assisting the planning staff in Hawaii, Giffen provided another stage for Low to win the hearts of Admirals Ghormley, Rockwell, and Kincaid. Having expected stiff Japanese resistance, Low recalled that the "Japanese had performed the extraordinary feat of evacuating over 5,000 people in less than an hour."[29] He sent a situation report, which circulated all the way up the chain to Washington that "we landed on Kiska to find [only] dogs and hot coffee."[30]

Low had the right combination of combat seasoning, which sharpened his ability to solve complex problems with an appropriately acute sense of levity. He had the ability to make his shipmates chuckle under the most-challenging circumstances. Upon receiving this report in Washington, Navy secretary Knox impatiently questioned King by inquiring, "Admiral, what does this mean?"[31] Stupid questions also inspired King's wry sense of humor. King calmly responded, "Mr. Secretary, what it means is that for the first time in recorded military history, dogs have been known to prepare coffee."[32]

The battle record of *Wichita* reflected the excellence of the skipper, which Low humbly failed to recognize. During the return voyage to Hawaii, Low was flummoxed when the ship's runner reported from the radio shack with flash orders from CominCh. King directed Low to detach upon reaching Hawaii. Low left his executive officer, Lt. Cmdr. Howard E. Orem, in temporary command. Low also rewarded Orem with a shared fate. Within weeks, Orem received orders, as reviewed for release by Low under the signature of King, to report from *Wichita* to *Dauntless*. From 1943, Orem served among the flag secretaries in the office immediately connected to King's.[33]

Combat experience in the Pacific provided the key justification for rotating seasoned Atlantic veterans from duty in CominCh. King placed great value on keeping officers from settling into any given front. For this reason, King modified Low's detachment orders. Nimitz was left helpless whenever King pulled an officer from the Pacific. During a brief exchange, Nimitz simply passed an itinerary for Low to fly from Hawaii to Australia. Nimitz asked Low to keep him apprised of any information gathered during meetings with MacArthur and Halsey.

MacArthur treated Low as an unnecessary distraction, whereas Halsey extended a welcoming hand and a smile over drinks. Returning to Hawaii to debrief Nimitz about the situation in the Southwest Pacific, Low channeled MacArthur's concerns about the clandestine operations of Commodore Miles in China. Nimitz happened to agree with MacArthur. Conversely, Halsey recommended an aggressive campaign to maneuver aircraft carrier raids along the Philippines and China coast, circling up to Japanese waters, and then repeating the cycle on the southbound voyage. Low duly explained the general situation to King upon reporting to CominCh in February 1943.[34]

King listened intently to Low's firsthand impressions of the strategic situation in the Pacific. Notably, Low channeled Halsey's backhanded criticism of Nimitz that "everyone and his aunt were getting out instructions."[35] King asked Low for an opinion, which reinforced Halsey's point. In turn, King ordered Low to provide a solution. Low considered British and American organizational doctrines to establish super seagoing task force organizations. The system also provided means for CominCh to communicate strategic information to designated fleet commanders at sea with the purpose-specific "X-Com" circuit, which was encrypted in Electronic Code Machine—Mark II (ECM MKII), or alternatively in the army as SIGABA.[36] Low drafted the historic order for geographic fleet commanders to organize "numbered fleets."

These super task organizations all received fleet intelligence officers especially trained and equipped to handle high-grade special intelligence sources on board ship. King released the message directing subordinate commanders to establish numbered fleets at 2200 on February 19, 1943, saying that "each fleet commander shall allocate at least one task force number to the equivalent of 'miscellaneous force' for assignment of task force numbers to small groups operating directly under [the] fleet commander."[37] Thereafter, King used the CominCh headquarters as the mechanism for disseminating information from the highest levels of strategic command to the lowest-possible echelons closest to the enemy at the front.[38] On March 15, 1943, King further clarified the numbered fleets by designating even numbers for the Atlantic and odd numbers for the Pacific.[39]

Under King's ingenious concept, numbered fleets existed only for the tasks assigned and then dissolved immediately upon achieving the purposes of executing any given mission. Mission specialization provided the critical edge, as King configured forces to perform individual tasks for the purposes of achieving clear results. In reorganizing the seagoing forces, King sent RAdm. Forest Sherman to replace Spruance as chief of staff, Pacific Fleet and Ocean Areas. Having suffered from medical problems during operations at Guadalcanal, Ghormley reported for duty in Hawaii to assist another of King's men, Turner, in planning the amphibious drive across the central Pacific. Admirals McCain, Duncan, and Barbey arrived from Washington to assist Nimitz in executing King's will in the Pacific and beyond to Asia.

King surrounded Nimitz with trusted operatives to keep the Pacific strategy focused on the citadel of Formosa and the future reconstruction of Asia. To this end, Towers acted as expected in relations with Nimitz. Conversely, King refereed problems between Towers and Spruance. Aviators followed Towers in criticizing Spruance's abilities. Whenever Nimitz complained about Towers, King advised Nimitz to fire Towers.[40] Nimitz refused to remove Towers, and so the cycle continued. King observed that Nimitz surrounded himself "with too many damned yes men."[41] King also warned Nimitz to assert greater control over subordinates "who customarily surprised Nimitz more than the enemy when issuing directives."[42] King complained, "Nimitz just seemed to sort of follow along."[43] King noted that CominCh staffers "believed that the brains of the Pacific Fleet was [Rear Admiral] Forrest Sherman [and] Nimitz would not make a move without asking Sherman."[44]

A DISH BEST SERVED COLD: VENGEANCE

The strategy employed by Grant in the Vicksburg Campaign during the Civil War inspired King's vision for the Pacific. Given the situation on the Atlantic front, King used the Guadalcanal Campaign to fix the Japanese into stalemate. Following the summit at Casablanca, King organized the CominCh headquarters to serve as the primary clearin-house for offensive operations and intelligence. In April 1943, King directed subordinate commanders to follow directives issued by CominCh. King wrote to Nimitz that

> experience has shown both in London (since 1939) and in Washington (since 1941) that the natural centers of information and of control are in the Admiralty and in the Navy Department, and that the relaying of operating information in connection with the delegation of control to outlying agencies require[s] constant situation and supervision in order to act in time to take effective counter-measures [; if] additional very-long-range aircraft are available for allocation to anti-submarine warfare, every consideration of unity of effort and efficiency requires that they should be under the operational control of the Headquarters, Commander in Chief, US Fleet, in those areas under the strategical control of the UNITED STATES.[45]

King emphasized security in handling sensitive *sources* of intelligence. Conversely, he consistently used information derived from high-grade strategic intelligence to enable subordinate commanders to take direct tactical action against the enemy closer to the front.

Considering the influence of intelligence on operations, cryptographers solved enemy codes and ciphers to provide key perspectives from an enemy's point of view. Yet, they generally *did not* have the authority to *direct* tactical action at the front. Intelligence analysts serving within higher headquarters, such as CominCh, had the ability to *inform* key decisions. However, the operational directives always originated under the *authority* of King. This dynamic is perhaps best exemplified with the assassination of Admiral Yamamoto Isoroku. By April 1943, Yamamoto ultimately faced the reality of defeat in the Guadalcanal area. He ordered Japanese forces to withdraw to the north. To boost Japanese morale, he decided to make personal appearances with the troops at the front. His staff transmitted these travel plans.

Information derived from the solution of Imperial Japanese Navy tactical communications enabled the Americans to put the hit on Yamamoto. Since the plan required coordination with the US Army Air Force, King and Marshall worked key details within the JCS. Nimitz and MacArthur clearly knew about the plan. Under the circumstances, the key members of the CCS possibly had advanced knowledge of the plan to kill Yamamoto.[46] Churchill and Roosevelt certainly celebrated the assassination as just vengeance for the deprivations of Singapore, Pearl Harbor, and Bataan.[47] The ultimate decision to execute assassination operations against key enemy targets usually required the blessings of Churchill and Roosevelt. Ultimately, the joint tactical plan to kill Yamamoto received approval under the cover name Operation VENGEANCE.[48]

Allied listening posts throughout the greater East Asia region intercepted the initial indications and warnings of Yamamoto's intentions in the Southwest Pacific. Broken translations of intercepted Japanese traffic filtered up the Allied chains of command, which ultimately revealed Yamamoto's plan to visit the embattled troops during the evacuation of Guadalcanal. As early as April 14, US Navy analysts in Hawaii and Washington collaborated to pool information derived from various enemy communications sources to fill the gaps in the original Japanese message as encoded in JN-25D.[49] Analysts in Britain and Australia contributed to the US Navy assessment. Along with many others, Lt. John Paul Stevens assisted in compiling all the information flowing from FRUMEL in Australia and from the Main Navy in Washington during service under Layton at JICPOA in Hawaii. Reflecting upon this experience after service as an associate justice on the Supreme Court, Stevens later pondered the legality of his role in planning the assassination of Yamamoto.[50]

Analysts serving under the immediate authority of King in Washington directly participated in the decision to assassinate Yamamoto. Capt. Ellis Zacharias and his team in Washington endorsed the plot to assassinate Yamamoto by noting historical examples, which highlighted the value of removing such an important enemy leader. Typically, analysts serving under Nimitz with Layton in Hawaii often failed to recall the overarching role of their counterparts in Washington and in Australia in efforts to kill Yamamoto.

The decision to execute Operation VENGEANCE reflected supreme coordination between all the various commanders and within a very short window of opportunity. Intelligence informed the whole operation, from the very highest levels of American strategic command to the most tactical perspective of the pilots, as they peered through the gunsight and zeroed in on Yamamoto's aircraft. The aircraft with Yamamoto crashed in a dramatic trail of flames into the dense jungle near Buin on Bougainville. Roughly one month after Japanese troops fished the mangled bodies of Yamamoto and members of his staff from the wreckage, Roosevelt feigned surprise with a twinkle in his eye during a press conference on May 22, 1943.[51]

ALL THE DISMEMBERED HEADS

The assassination of Yamamoto perhaps stands out as a turning point in the debate between Marshall and King about questions of joint wartime command in the air. The precision attack reflected the supremacy of King's naval intelligence organization. The operation to kill Yamamoto also demonstrated the clear mandate for collaboration between the army and naval air forces. From King's point of view, Operation VENGEANCE proved the point for aviation forces to perform *naval* missions. Marshall anticipated King's strategy for the future of armed-service unification. Marshall knew that King made clear functional distinctions between the hierarchical organization of air forces. Broadly, King reserved the term "military" for references to land forces, whereas "naval" served as a catchall for both civil and armed seagoing forces in the global maritime arena.[52] Marshall worried about the efforts of his naval counterparts, Leahy and King, in shaping the strategic vision of Roosevelt on the question of unification. For this reason, Marshall used Arnold to balance the ongoing debates concerning the future of empires and airpower theory among the wartime CCS and JCS.[53]

German submarines provided the ideal point of reference for King's competitors to divert the strategic focus of the CCS. Debates concerning the allocation of resources to serve key operational priorities often drifted into the endless disagreements about the methods employed in fighting the war for the purposes of building future foundations for the strategic end. Staff officers generally sat as silent witnesses to the epic battles going on between the principal members of the CCS and JCS. Whenever King seemed to attain the upper hand in these debates, Churchill and his henchmen frequently joined forces with those of Marshall and Arnold to divert the conversation to focus on the alleged failure of King's navy in the antisubmarine campaign—particularly in the Atlantic and more specifically involving Nazi U-boats. In fact, King refused to let the enemy find refuge anywhere in the global maritime arena. It was apparent that he fully understood the scope of the enemy submarine menace in explaining, "I am afraid I am a hard-boiled skeptic, but I am always glad to be disappointed in my pessimism [but] the U-boat situation looks very encouraging <u>for the time being</u>."[54]

Behind closed doors, King and the CominCh staff quietly orchestrated operations with intelligence. Just as Arlington Hall provided Marshall with high-grade intelligence advantages, Nebraska Avenue enabled King to use the CominCh headquarters as the clearinghouse for intelligence. The numbered fleet system enabled King to empower geographic area commanders or directly influence operations with intelligence. Capt. Dudley W. Knox joined forces with the Naval War College staff to develop a series of recommendations, which King used to make the case for merging army and naval aviation for *offensive* hunter-killer antisubmarine operations on all fronts. Knox also collaborated with Stark's trusted confidant in the Intelligence Division of ComNavEu, Kittredge, in pushing the American concept of hunter-killer operations with the British.[55]

The British struggled to keep pace with the rapid rise of King's navy in coordinating operations with intelligence.[56] Under constant strain, Winn collapsed from exhaustion at Christmas in 1942. Beesly took his place, relying on his American understudies to perform the work within the dungeons of Lenin's Tomb. McDiarmid and Knowles viewed their work as another form of combat.[57] Aerial reconnaissance and agents on the ground suggested that the Germans maintained roughly 100 protected berths for submarines. Just before Christmas, all the evidence suggested a major German submarine offensive in the North Atlantic in the spring of 1943.[58] Stark filled the gap created by the departure of Knowles at the OIC by assigning Kittredge and Follmer as ComNavEu liaisons.[59]

Beesly had to make best with a bad situation at the OIC when McDiarmid and Knowles received orders recalling them back to America shortly before Christmas. In the spring of 1943, McDiarmid subsequently established the submarine-tracking room designated as "OIC-5" at NSHQ in Ottawa.[60] Knowles returned for duty in the War Room of the CominCh headquarters.[61] Following the Holden agreement, King sent Sebald to assist Nimitz in fusing army and naval intelligence functions under the JICPOA. McDiarmid and Knowles returned fully conditioned to replicate the OIC system within their respective headquarters in Ottawa and Washington.

Knowles reported to Smith-Hutton, the F-352 within the context of the CominCh headquarters. Given recent OIC experience, Knowles assumed duty as the antisubmarine officer, the "F-353." Knowles drafted a report with recommendations for reorganizing the antisubmarine functions of CominCh, which returned with a handwritten note on a yellow slip, "O.K. K." Knowles explained, "King was a man of quick perception and intellect [but he] was not the brainy type—there was too much action in his makeup." "He could not abide mediocrity or less than superior staff work," Knowles explained that "it was said with some truth that each morning upon arriving at CominCh Headquarters that one could see heads of newly dismembered staffers rolling down the corridors."[62]

Knowles returned to the Navy Department to assist the reorganization of the operations and intelligence subdivisions of the CominCh headquarters. Ongoing debates surrounding control in the air inspired King to take personal control over worldwide submarine and antisubmarine operations. He established individually numbered fleets to coordinate Allied submarine operations and for antisubmarine efforts. Reacting to these moves, Arnold organized the 20th Air Force as a unified strategic command for USAAF operations—including a plot to monitor naval efforts. From the War Department perspective, Secretary Stimson thought "King has retreated [on the issue of] antisubmarine warfare and is now placing it in the hands of a young admiral named [Low]."[63]

Numbered fleet organization enabled King to maneuver forces to support tactical operations. The idea originated with the fight between King and Marshall, which centered on the naval requirement to employ army bombers from airfields ashore to support antisubmarine operations. "Boy, we had a fight, but we won," King explained. "Air Corps people were just as tricky as they could be."[64] King drafted a handwritten outline titled "Set-up for antisubmarine warfare will include the 9th Fleet—R. Adm. Low temp. in command." King initially designated that the

COMMANDER NINTH FLEET shall, on his own initiative or on representation by CinCLant and/or Sea Frontier Commanders, be assigned operational control of such commanders for temporary operations either to reinforce convoys under attack or coming under attack or as striking groups against known or predicted submarine concentrations.[65]

Low later explained that "the idea of numbering fleets was his and had been borrowed from Army nomenclature[; the] odd numbers were assigned to the Pacific and the even to the Atlantic."[66] At first, the Ninth Fleet served antisubmarine efforts in the Pacific. Similarly, the Tenth Fleet focused on the Atlantic.[67] At first, King envisioned two separate numbered fleets to coordinate antisubmarine operations in the Pacific and Atlantic. King changed his mind by designating Tenth Fleet as the singular clearinghouse for _global_ antisubmarine operations.[68]

THE TENTH FLEET

Tenth Fleet served as the administrative lens through which the operational and intelligence subdivisions _within_ the CominCh headquarters achieved unity of effort for all antisubmarine operations in the global maritime arena. The concept initially confused seagoing skippers to describe the organization as a "fleet without ships."[69] To the contrary, King viewed Tenth Fleet as the mechanism for achieving "unity of effort for the Allied powers to concentrate fleet operations against enemy submarines."[70] In essence, Tenth Fleet influenced all Allied naval operations on the sea, below the surface, and in the air. From within the CominCh headquarters, Tenth Fleet essentially comprised the warships of all the Allied navies by synthesizing strategy with operations through the dissemination of intelligence _after_ 1943.

Given the ongoing competition for strategic control within the CCS and JCS, King anticipated challenges to the directive establishing the Tenth Fleet as the overarching authority for US Navy antisubmarine operations. On May 18, 1943, King circumvented bureaucratic resistance to the idea that "all bureaus and offices of the Navy Department were notified that, effective 1200Z on May 20, there is established the Tenth Fleet, with

Headquarters in the Navy Department to exercise unity of control over US antisubmarine operations."[71] He established clear separations by defining the area of primary responsibility for the Tenth Fleet focused in that "part of the Atlantic under US strategic control."[72]

King's artfully framed explanation overshadowed the underlying point in restricting the British from asserting strategic control over American warships in the Atlantic and on other fronts. His concept for the Tenth Fleet also set clear lines of demarcation among his competitors on the CCS and JCS. As expected, Marshall wrote King with a strong rebuttal against the idea of using the Tenth Fleet as the overarching worldwide headquarters for air and surface antisubmarine operations. Marshall paraphrased Arnold that the "elimination of the submarine menace is a task which requires the full effort of a joint force, under the guidance of the Joint Chiefs of Staff with the principles of a unified command."[73] Marshall then suggested USAAF lieutenant general Willis H. Hale to command the air component of the Tenth Fleet. In turn, King asked Low to provide recommendations.

Drawing from years of service in submarines, Low examined the antisubmarine mission as a fundamental function of the naval services that required coordination from headquarters ashore. Low advised King that "regardless of the outcome of present conversations with the Army as to status of air for the Tenth Fleet[, the] effectiveness of the Fleet per se will be improved as will our position vis-à-vis the Army [by] the appointment forthwith of a separate Tenth Fleet Commander in the person of a Naval Aviator."[74] For these reasons, Low identified two aviation-qualified admirals as prospective commanders for the Tenth Fleet, Charles A. Pownall and John S. McCain. King rejected both, believing that Pownall lacked aggressiveness while McCain was "a fighter but not very much in the way of brains."[75]

Given the stakes involved in establishing the Tenth Fleet, King struggled with the decision of naming its commander. "Finally, one day in desperation," Low recalled that King "simply named himself as the commander."[76] Failing to request permission, King formally identified himself as the commander, with Low serving as his deputy for all matters concerning the operations of the Tenth Fleet.[77] Always ready for a duel, King put his most junior-ranking two-star in daily command of the Tenth Fleet. Thereafter, King's handle appeared in message traffic as "CominCh," with the added title of "FX." Low likewise acted under King's authority as the assistant chief of staff, FX-01. King later elaborated on the circumstances by saying that Low "was a junior rear admiral and with the trouble with Marshall and Arnold about antisubmarine matters it was preferable for King to be Commander and Low to be Chief of Staff."[78]

Marshall was administratively helpless when King assumed personal responsibility for synthesizing strategy with the operations of the numbered fleets, such as the Tenth Fleet. Marshall viewed the numbered fleet organizations as a bureaucratic gauntlet thrown down by King. In organizing the Tenth Fleet within the CominCh headquarters, Low recruited Captains William D. Sample and Arnold J. Isbell from the CominCh Operations Division, giving them the additional designation of FX-30. Both had served as aircraft carrier hunter-killer skippers in the Atlantic. Sample earned distinction as the skipper of USS *Santee* (CVE-29), by intercepting the German blockade runner *Kota Nopan*. Isbell earned distinction as the task group commander aboard USS *Card* (CVE-11), claiming a confirmed eleven German submarines. Sample and Isbell advised Metcalf in the Convoy and Routing Division / FX-37. Meanwhile, submarine-qualified captains John M. Haines and Harold C. Fitz took charge in the Antisubmarine Measures Division / FX-40.

King progressively assumed overall strategic command over the global operations of numbered fleets from within the CominCh headquarters. Under his authority, the various subdivisions of CominCh filtered information from the highest strategic levels to the tactical forces at the front. Numbered-fleet commanders individually served under the singular pleasure of King, under his unique unified authorities as CominCh/CNO. This arrangement completely undercut the traditional prerogatives of the SecNav, as well as the subordinate geographic fleet organizations of the Pacific and Atlantic. Each of the numbered-fleet commanders had collateral administrative functions that fell under the immediate responsibility of subordinate headquarters, such as those of Nimitz, Ingersoll, and Stark. However, King and his CominCh headquarters always retained strategic control.

Setting the original precedence for numbered-fleet organizations, the Tenth Fleet enabled the CominCh headquarters to achieve unity of effort in all the key areas of tactical focus for global antisubmarine operations. After May 1943, the Tenth Fleet also kept training current with new enemy surprises through the ASWORG and COTCLant. Keeping with the tactical trends, Tenth Fleet provided specialized antisubmarine training for Patrol Composite (VC) squadrons. Among the most effective, VC-13 used a logo of an alley cat showing paws with two middle fingers. German submariners always dreaded the insulting logo of VC-13, which greatly enhanced morale among the American naval aviators.[79]

LOST IN ACTION AT SEA

Aircraft-carrier-based VC squadrons operated in tandem with the first land-based antisubmarine squadrons. Marshall and King's gentlemen's agreement to allow the US Navy to operate land-based bombers for maritime missions paid significant dividends in the antisubmarine war. In June 1943, King's trusted associates from the PBY squadrons before the war helped organize the Patrol Bomber (VB) squadrons of PB4Y-1 "Privateers." Among the first to the front, Lt. Cmdr. Bertram Prueher demonstrated the full potential of the Privateers as the VB-107 skipper. From the Brazilian naval base near Natal, Prueher and his squadron ran regular patrols to Ascension Island and the surrounding waters. Flying on cues provided by King's staff at CominCh in Washington, Prueher interrupted the rendezvous of three German submarines in a remote area of the South Atlantic off the coast of Brazil.

Prueher proved the full potential of integrating tactical operations with the strategic precision provided by intelligence. Among the first naval aviators to complete the Antisubmarine University, Prueher understood the interrelationship between operations and intelligence. Information provided from CominCh served as the basis for attacking enemy targets with precision. Prueher chose to act upon the information rather than request permission to act. Having flown under King in the ranks of the patrol bomber squadrons, Prueher rallied VB-107 into a potent weapon against Axis submarines in Brazilian waters. Armed with intelligence provided by CominCh, he flew at long range in a Privateer christened as the "Spirit of 83" to interrupt the refueling of *U-604*. Prueher damaged the submarine.

Intercepted enemy communications provided opportunities for Prueher to launch additional attacks. Upon returning to the scene of *U-604*, Prueher reported that the German submariners had already scuttled the boat. He observed two other enemy submarines with crews huddled on deck and other sailors in the water. Survivors from

U-604 treaded water while awaiting rescue from *U-172* and *U-185*.[80] Swooping in for the kill, Prueher handled the aircraft like an attack fighter—barreling into the barrage of German 20- and 40-millimeter antiaircraft fire. As Prueher's aircraft flew by the submarines, it suddenly banked at a high angle, stalled, and then plunged into the water. There were no survivors.[81] German sailors photographed Prueher's aircraft during the battle. Prueher's son, Adm. Joseph Prueher, also kept the aviator's flight log of his late father. Neatly scratched block letters in red pencil noted, "LOST IN ACTION AT SEA."[82]

Monitoring the enemy transmissions between headquarters ashore and the submarines, the CominCh headquarters continued pressing the battle. After the loss of Prueher and his crew, Knowles filtered intelligence through the Tenth Fleet to maneuver USS *Core* (CVE-13) into position to sink *U-185*—with the *U-604* survivors embarked. Knowles and Low subsequently avenged Prueher by maneuvering USS *Bogue* (CVE-9) to sink *U-172*. By 1943, King's navy dominated in the Atlantic. The bankruptcy of German strategy in the war at sea foundered under the supremacy of King's navy—often to the chagrin of some British counterparts.[83] After 1943, the CominCh headquarters served as the hub of antisubmarine operations—using intelligence to destroy enemy targets with surgical precision in conjunction with King's strategy of "unremitting pressure."[84]

CHAPTER 28

Combat Intelligence

The CominCh headquarters synthesized the policy war aims of the Roosevelt administration with strategic efforts in the global maritime arena. After 1943, the British and American navies achieved "unity of command" by dividing global responsibilities under the principle of "unity of effort."[1] To this end, King directed Kalbfus to assume collateral duty as the first director of the Office of Naval History (ONH) in two stars as president of the Naval War College. Pye subsequently served in three stars when Kalbfus transferred to the retired list in 1943. Navy secretary Knox subsequently approved King's novel arrangement for keeping Pye on active service as president of the Naval War College—in three stars—with Kalbfus acting with equivalent authority in *retired* four-star rank as the director of Naval History.

Coalition strategy required nuanced coordination, balancing the traditions and expectations of foreign partners against those of the Roosevelt administration. King understood the strategic purposes of the Naval War College—as the key forum for thinking about the future through applied historical research. To this end, King organized ONH to operate under Kalbfus as a *coequal* in collaboratively producing "Battle Studies" with ONI.[2] In prefacing these efforts, King wrote that the studies provided an applied historical assessment of "battles in which our Fleets have engaged in the current war [to] form a basis for a broader understanding which will result in ever more successful operations."[3]

Fusing history with intelligence, King synthesized the historical functions of the Naval War College with the coequal analytical functions of ONH and ONI. By examining message traffic from recent combat operations, analysts scrutinized the decisions made by friendly and enemy forces. Reconstructing past battles on the gaming floors of Newport also enabled historians to examine alternative scenarios, thereby producing recommendations for future commanders to consider in the heat of combat. Kalbfus and Pye supervised these studies on the wartime campus of the Naval War College as Knox served in wartime one-star rank as deputy director of Naval History from within the ONI spaces at the Navy Department. Harkening back to the Historical Section of Sir Julian Corbett and then that of Sims after the First World War, King made applied methods in historical analysis a fundamental operational function in the grander effort to gain intelligence supremacy against the enemy in the Second World War.[4]

History always held strategic relevance within the ranks of King's navy, as operations unfolded with intelligence in the global maritime arena. Kalbfus and Knox stood among King's closest compatriots, as did his classmate Pye. King explained that "Kalbfus knew how to think[,] and when he set out to do something, he never failed."[5] King also thought that "Knox is the best naval officer I have known [and he] knows what has happened and knows how to make things happen."[6] King thought that "Pye looks things over very carefully [and] he looks everything over and cannot make up his mind rapidly."[7] "I knew that Pye would measure everything and might come out with the answer—too late," King recalled. "Pye operated in something of an ivory tower and was always unable to condense his ideas into reasonable dimensions."[8]

Pye mobilized the resources of the Naval War College to examine the problems of multinational strategy. He also focused on the nexus between operations and intelligence functions within naval headquarters. King credited Pye for suggesting the "establishment of a fourth division, of Combat Intelligence, which [King] put into effect at once."[9] In June, King decreed the establishment of the Combat Intelligence Division, to appear as "F-2" within the CominCh table of organization. He clarified functions by specifying that

> Combat Intelligence is the term applied to information of enemy forces, strength, disposition, and probable movements. With personnel now assigned to Combat Intelligence, institute rigorous, continuous examination of enemy capabilities and potentialities, thereby getting the utmost value out of information of the enemy and enabling our forces to be used with the greatest effectiveness. It is particularly important to comprehend the enemy point of view in all aspects.[10]

King fused operations and intelligence. In June 1943, he reorganized the CominCh headquarters to reflect the situation at the time. The Plans Division, or "F-1," fell under Cooke. The F-2 became the Combat Intelligence Division, which coincidentally fell under the DNI/Op-16, RAdm. Roscoe E. Schuirmann. The Operations Division, or "F-3," fell under RAdm. Walter S. DeLany. Finally, RAdm. Arthur C. Davis ran the "F-4" Readiness Division within the CominCh headquarters.

King fused operations with intelligence by designating trusted subordinates with the requisite authority to implement his will. King shattered bureaucratic rice bowls to merge operations with intelligence. Before the reforms instituted by King, the ONI essentially functioned as a "post office charged with forwarding Intelligence reports and other data to the activity in the Navy Department most likely to need and make use of the information."[11] King instructed Smith-Hutton to fix the problem, along with the new title of assistant chief of staff for Combat Intelligence. Smith-Hutton subsequently carried the administrative code of F-20. He absorbed the functions of F-35 by creating the new F-2 organization, as comprising an Atlantic Section, or F-21; the Pacific Section, or F-22; the Operational Summaries Section, or F-23; the security officer, or F-24; and the publicity security officer, or F-25.[12]

King empowered intelligence analysts within the Main Navy building to participate directly in actions at the front. Under the overall supervision of Schuirmann as the DNI, the F-2 Combat Intelligence revolved around the close collaboration of Smith-Hutton as F-20, Knowles as F-21, and Sebald as F-22.[13] From room 3509 on the third deck of Main Navy, Smith-Hutton assumed the duties of F-20 and worked with Knowles inside the Atlantic Section, which now carried the designation of F-2 in room 3509. Through a connecting suite housing teleprinters, room 3402 served as the home of the Pacific Section, or F-22, under Sebald. High-grade special intelligence arrived through teletype from Nebraska Avenue through the F-21 subsidiary, as designated as F-211 and otherwise known as the "Secret Room."[14]

Knowles carried the onerous responsibility of managing the flow of intelligence from within the CominCh headquarters, which was transmitted to forces at the front. He reconfigured the chart storage locker within room 3509 inside the CominCh headquarters to serve as the Secret Room. On December 27, 1942, Knowles then assigned US Navy Reserve lieutenant John E. Parsons to supervise the analysts assigned to the Secret Room.[15] Parsons supervised reserve lieutenant (j.g.) John V. Boland with two enlisted sailors, Chevalier and Livecci. During their service in the Secret Room, Chevalier and Livecci later rose from the enlisted ranks to earn status as commissioned officers.[16]

The Secret Room quickly developed into the central clearinghouse for information derived from high-grade special intelligence sources. Knowles concentrated on the strategic efforts, while Parsons focused on tactical operations within the Secret Room. In addition, Parsons had personal connections with Roosevelt and others inside the White House—being the grandson to the New York assistant district attorney and president of the New York Bar. Having earlier earned a reserve commission at Yale University in 1925, Parsons followed the family tradition upon receiving his law degree in 1928. Parsons clerked for Chief Justice William Howard Taft. Later, David Sarnoff hired Parsons to handle the legal portfolios for Radio-Keith-Orpheum (RKO) and Radio Corporation of America (RCA). In this role, Parsons enabled the film productions on such critically acclaimed films as *King Kong* and *Citizen Kane*.[17]

Hollywood credentials and past business connections among the highest levels of American industry and the government made Parsons an invaluable asset of the CominCh headquarters. While organizing the Secret Room, Knowles sent Parsons to London to earn Winn's trust.[18] Parsons returned in May 1943, during the reorganization of the CominCh organization, the formal establishment of numbered fleets, and the related effort to synthesize global offensive operations on all maritime fronts. The relatively simple task of fighting the war was second to the far more complicated purposes of winning sustainable victory in the global maritime arena. For this reason, the CominCh headquarters focused on the systematic deconstruction of the enemy's ability to fight and *not* on wholesale destruction for the purposes of future conquest.[19]

King's staff adopted his views for supporting Soviet and Chinese armies with the combined maritime strength of Britain and America. To these ends, Smith-Hutton acted as the senior analyst. Knowles and Sebald coordinated operations with intelligence from the Atlantic and Pacific Sections. Knowles and Sebald shared the assistance of Parsons. In addition, Chief Petty Officer (Supply) Charles J. Falcone and Chief Roy Hanna joined the team as the senior enlisted leaders.[20] With the exception of the Secret Room, WAVES assigned to the CominCh headquarters shared watches in the various subdivisions of F-20, F-21, and F-22.[21] All hands also learned to correlate information from all sources for the following reason:

> The picture [that "Special Intelligence"] supplied was highly detailed and yet very incomplete. From this it resulted that the task of handling it operationally was onerous and responsible—onerous because the inductive process of building up from fragments is necessarily slow, and responsible because the gaps in knowledge had to be supplied by deduction and for practical purposes deductions had to be used as though they were known facts.[22]

Analysts noted that "one of the lesser but still very valuable points of Special Intelligence [was] its use in assessing the value of intelligence from other sources."[23]

The alchemistic art of analysis required unfettered access to the primary sources of enemy information. This task similarly required analysts to develop a mature familiarity with the operational focus of intelligence. Thus, Knowles and Parsons were completely chagrined when Chavalier suddenly received orders to sea duty. Knowles complained that "it is of utmost importance [that] personnel of the Tracking Room be permanently assigned there."[24] He continued that the "familiarity with enemy thought processes as applied to his operations and the characteristics of individual U/Boat commanders can only be developed with long practice [and] such intangible factors frequently are invaluable in the process of U/Boat tracking."[25]

King took such observations in stride, fully expecting all hands to remain cheerful in making do with what they had. He expected men serving inside the CominCh headquarters to seek orders for sea duty, fully recognizing the capacity of women to serve in the same capacity. Among other perks, junior officers and enlisted members had opportunities to earn qualifications and collect sea pay during weekly voyages on *Dauntless* along the shores of the Potomac and into the Chesapeake Bay.[26]

Still, King's austere persona always lingered. He empowered subordinates to do their job—and he expected them to do so with confidence. Smith-Hutton characterized King as a "very strict disciplinarian, but there weren't any special discipline problems in the headquarters."[27] Smith-Hutton described King as being

quite simple and straightforward in his manner. He thought clearly. He was extremely intelligent[,] and the things he said or wrote were brief and to the point. I think he had tremendous ability, but at the same time he seemed to be modest, and[,] although he didn't always follow them, always open to advice and suggestions. On the surface, he appeared to be cold and austere, but I believe this was only his manner, although I must say he didn't make friends easily.[28]

After Smith-Hutton, Knowles briefed King on nearly a daily basis but thought that "he wasn't one to be familiar with in any way."[29] Knowles noted that King "possessed little warmth or charisma but captured one's loyalty and zeal by his own superior conduct and performance."[30] Knowles described King as "just plain cold armor-plated steel."[31]

Knowles operated in very close quarters as the key spokesman for King in coordinating antisubmarine operations with intelligence. His immediate counterparts in London and Ottawa, Winn and McDiarmid, provided Knowles with information concerning British and Canadian efforts. In turn, Knowles shared details missing between the lines of official messages in regular morning briefings with King. During these ritualistic gatherings, King sometimes smoked while drinking a cup of coffee. He usually sat silently like a statue. King rarely asked questions because he usually studied raw reports on his own. King attended briefings to provide direction, or what Knowles called "rudder orders."[32] Running the CominCh staff like a shipboard bridge team, King provided course and speed, quizzed them to ensure that they knew what he knew, and always expected his team to take appropriate action on his authority.[33]

King understood the value of keeping a predictable daily routine, which enabled his team to work with utmost efficiency. Like clockwork, King appeared every morning at 0900 in room 3509 of Main Navy. One of King's aides, Capt. Malcolm Schoeffel, explained that "you could set your watch bill by the schedule King kept even when he was travelling for meetings[, and] you always knew where he would be whenever he was in town."[34] Schoeffel thought King "was not one of those 'unnecessary night owls,' he was all business all the time."[35] Schoeffel considered King to be "a master of concise precision in writing and speech."[36] King gave succinct directives, such as "and you'd better jump to it forthwith!"[37] "One deviation from exact precision of direction," Schoeffel explained, "was his handling of correspondence sent to him for release."[38] "If he didn't like it," Schoeffel recalled,

> it might come back with a single question mark in blue [ink]. This meant that he wanted it reworded but it was up to you to find out how. Two question marks meant he didn't like it at all [and] some exclamation points could be translated as "drop this whole foolishness, you idiot!"[39]

Schoeffel understood that "King could on occasion get very angry [and] a vein on his right forehead stood out as a sign of his wrath."[40] Schoeffel remembered an occasion when "King sent for me and was either the maddest man in the world or the best actor I have ever seen."[41]

Always seeking the unvarnished truth in all circumstances, King expected his team to provide facts unemotionally. Whenever the enemy successfully delivered an unanticipated surprise, Knowles explained that King "wasn't a man of snap judgments [and] approached serious problems in a coldly analytical manner."[42] Among King's men, Knowles keenly observed the hierarchy among the inner circles of the CominCh headquarters. Knowles knew King appreciated his work but understood King's highest praise as simply being a verbal "Well done."[43] Knowles occasionally saw the man behind the façade. Knowles remembered that "King had a very warm heart for Admiral Low[,] and I did attend a few cocktail parties [where] I did see Admiral King in his more reposed situation."[44] Knowles's immediate boss, Smith-Hutton, similarly joined King at "very few cocktail parties and receptions[, which] he thought they were a waste of time, and he was busy."[45] In the end, Knowles concluded that nobody "could have come anywhere near King in competence for the job of CominCh."[46]

THERE'LL ALWAYS BE AN *ENGLAND* IN THE US NAVY

Women orchestrated the operations of King's navy with intelligence, acting in secrecy with unparalleled knowledge of combat at the front. The wartime cocktail culture in Washington stood in stark contrast to the tense combat environment within the CominCh headquarters.

Below the windows overlooking the Washington Mall—on the third deck of the Navy Department—the Atlantic Section of CominCh relentlessly killed the enemy with intelligence. Their files contained all the message traffic, historical chronologies, and photographic records used in sinking individual enemy submarines. Photographs often depicted the floating flesh and dismembered heads of young enemy submariners among the flotsam and debris, along with the clinically written narratives submitted in action reports. Within CominCh, the Antisubmarine Survey Board adjudicated these reports to confirm "credit" for the "kill." Once the evidence had been adjudicated, it was placed in the Atlantic Section file, which analysts called the "morgue."[47]

King's navy set new precedents by enabling headquarters ashore to exploit the advantages of electronic communications. On a personal level, he also felt the rigors of age creeping into his daily routines. The war took a personal toll on all hands, regardless of rank. One aide, McFarland, described the manner in which King carried on under the pressures of high command. McFarland described King as "a strong character, ethically correct[, and he] always obeyed rules, laws, and regulations."[48] McFarland noted that King "was inclined to be abrupt, at times he was a great humorist, a great storyteller, a great conversationalist on many subjects."[49] McFarland described King as "an avid reader and historian and was very knowledgeable in art and music [and] a better[-]than[-]average sports fan."[50] Junior officers viewed King as a role model, which McFarland quantified by noting that "his capacity to read, learn, and discuss a wide range of subjects was absolutely tremendous."[51]

King avoided the temptation of making close friendships with subordinates, recognizing the inevitable pitfall of allowing familiarity to breed contempt among the crew. He maintained the Age of Sail tradition of being seen and immediately understood. "There is no doubt that the Admiral was a brilliant man," his aide noted, and "there was no one more qualified to direct the entire Naval establishment."[52] Although King maintained an objective distance in relations with immediate subordinates, he demonstrated great compassion for them and their families. Assisting McFarland as an aide, Lt. Lawrence Cook suffered from polio, and his wife struggled with a difficult pregnancy. "I was on the critical list and my condition was being influenced by my worry over my wife's problem," Cook recalled, and that King personally intervened by ordering "provisions be made for the delivery of our child [and] it was the first dependent's delivery [at Bethesda Naval Hospital] and set the stage for thousands to follow." "Ernest King did this," Cook concluded. "Anyone says he was cold and indifferent I tell them this story."[53]

King inspired subordinates to recognize the purpose of naval traditions by establishing a familiar wardroom routine. "The mess was noticeable for a fixed custom," Schoeffel recalled, and that King presided as "Edwards and Cook carried on an animated and informative conversation [as] the rest of us confined ourselves to 'please pass the butter' or answering when spoken to."[54] Schoeffel explained that "King's personality so dominated us[, and this] was noted and reported by the Britishers who lunched with us."[55] The presence of Royal Navy liaisons from BAD provided means for the CominCh staff to encourage close collaboration between the operations and intelligence subdivisions. Few knew the actual identities of the men and women of the Combat Intelligence Division.[56] Schoeffel recalled that "King was a great believer in a 'need to know' for dissemination of information."[57]

Direct communications between CominCh and forces at the front reveal the strategic interrelationships between operations and intelligence. After 1943, the US Navy numbered fleets enabled the CominCh headquarters to communicate with individual fleet intelligence officers and numbered-fleet commanders. Subordinate intelligence centers, such as JICPOA and ComNavEu, shared information with the Combat Intelligence Division within CominCh.

All messages featuring the address "CominCh" always referred to King individually by implication. By extension, messages transmitted from the CominCh headquarters also carried the personal authority of King himself.[58]

FIRST AND TEN

Through the First Fleet, King and his staff provided intelligence to coordinate submarine offensive operations through the submarine force commanders of the geographic area and seagoing fleet organizations. Under the auspices of the Tenth Fleet, King and his staff provided the information required in the same manner to facilitate antisubmarine operations. "I have used the term 'package' to convey the idea of areas and commands necessary to manage a worldwide set-up," King explained, the "arrangement of having the job 'parceled out' in a few large packages, and I was clearly against a 'one package' anti-U-boat campaign."[59]

US Navy submarine and antisubmarine forces operated under the overall control of CominCh. Subordinate commanders assumed temporal authority in executing numbered-fleets operations, akin to supersized task forces. King outlined this system in message traffic, which clarified the concept of numbered fleets in March 1943. In June, Nimitz adapted from the original ideas of King by issuing his own tactical concept in "Current Tactical Orders and Doctrine, US Pacific Fleet," or "PAC-10."[60] After much confusion among the seagoing forces, King further clarified the basics of the numbered-fleet system in "Naval Directives and the Order Form (CominCh P-1)."[61] Numbered fleets existed only for finite purposes—they were *not* supposed to ossify into standing bureaucratic entities under King's original vision.

King held overarching strategic command over all the forces at sea as the CominCh, always having the prerogative of communicating directly with operational headquarters and individual numbered-fleet commanders at the tactical levels. The CominCh headquarters provided means to orchestrate global operations with the precision of special intelligence. Under the immediate authority of King, the First Fleet served as the mechanism by which the US Navy orchestrated submarine operations with precision against targets. Conversely, the Tenth Fleet provided information for Allied antisubmarine forces to destroy enemy submarines—not just in the Atlantic, but globally.[62]

Individual commanders carried primary duties and operated as numbered fleets only for missions of finite focus and duration. For example, Ingersoll carried double responsibility for the Atlantic Fleet and as the commander, Second Fleet. Falling subordinate to Ingersoll from headquarters in Brazil, Ingram carried tactical responsibility to cover the South Atlantic as commander, Fourth Fleet. Geographically fixed with headquarters ashore as commander in chief, Northwest Africa, Hewitt held tactical responsibility for amphibious operations in the greater Mediterranean as commander, Eighth Fleet. Given responsibilities as ComNavEu, Stark assumed tactical command as commander, Twelfth Fleet. The commandant of the Coast Guard, Waesche, held responsibility for operations in the North Atlantic, Alaskan, and Arctic waters. He occasionally acted as the commander, Sixth Fleet.[63]

Flagships associated with the locations of individual numbered-fleet commanders enabled King to assert control over worldwide operations. The Third Fleet staff of Halsey specialized in sweeping aircraft carrier strike operations designed to keep the Japanese high command guessing as to the focus of future American offensive operations. As Halsey swept island strongholds and fortified positions along the Japanese-occupied China coast, Nimitz empowered the Pacific Fleet chief of staff, VAdm. Raymond A. Spruance, to plan following amphibious operations. In these efforts, King had sent Turner to coordinate amphibious and logistical forces in the Pacific. King pressed Nimitz to put Turner in command of a numbered fleet. Yet, King recalled Nimitz as being tepid about Turner.[64]

King envisioned Turner as the natural choice for keeping offensive momentum while Halsey and Spruance prepared for their spot in the numbered-fleet rotation. King based his idea on the baseball concept of a pitching rotation. King prodded Nimitz to organize the Turner-Halsey-Spruance cycle for numbered-fleet operations throughout the Pacific. Unfortunately, Turner lived up to his nickname, "Terrible." He frequently butted heads with Nimitz. King regularly pushed Nimitz to give Turner a numbered fleet during the central Pacific drive. King eventually relented because "Nimitz did not like the idea."[65] On reflection, King felt that if Turner "could get along with other people, he would be a good one."[66]

The elements of ego and aspiration frequently defined the competition among the admirals of King's navy. Churchill and Roosevelt were in the backdrop of higher command, while King managed his subordinates closer to the front. He largely left Stark and Ingersoll to focus on collaboration with the British. Concurrently, King always kept a tight rein on Nimitz, as Halsey had collateral duty as Third Fleet and Spruance assumed Fifth Fleet. With MacArthur in the SWPA, the Seventh Fleet of VAdm. Thomas Kinkaid featured warships from the Royal Navy and Dominions, along with warships manned by French and Dutch sailors in exile. Kinkaid carried the simultaneous function as US Navy commander, Western Pacific Area. Although the Ninth Fleet existed primarily on paper, VAdm. Frank Jack Fletcher was prepared to operate in that capacity as the commander, Northwest Pacific Ocean Area. Similarly, VAdm. Francis E. M. Whiting, as commander, Eastern Pacific Ocean Area, theoretically carried double duty as the Eleventh Fleet commander.[67]

King and Nimitz progressively standardized procedures for rotating numbered-fleet commanders in conjunction with combined operations in the greater Pacific and beyond to Asia. Halsey and Spruance developed a razzle-dazzle cycle after 1943, both alternating their commands over the same warships to execute sequential offensive operations. Halsey planned the next cycle of aircraft carrier strikes whenever Spruance presided over amphibious operations. In general, Halsey and Spruance shared the flagships *Indianapolis* and *New Jersey* during the central Pacific drive to Formosa. Meanwhile, Whiting supplied Kinkaid with logistical support for MacArthur's operations in SWPA, beyond to Miles with SACO, and then Mountbatten's forces in the China-Burma-India (CBI) area of combined operations.

From Europe to Asia, King stood at the strategic top of the pyramid of numbered-fleet operations. Low recalled, "I have repeatedly seen [King] allow unit commanders and captains of private ships to work themselves into situations from which there seemed to be little hope of extrication and then turn his back when they sought help."[68] At the same time, he added, "I never saw one case where the individual was not able to work himself out of his troubles."[69] Low remembered King nearly fired Ingersoll for muddling in the Atlantic. "Only on one occasion was this authority ever seriously considered," Low explained. "King became exceedingly angry (which was effortless) at what he considered a dereliction of duty on the part of the commander-in-chief, Atlantic Fleet."[70]

The antisubmarine campaign in the Atlantic always remained directly tied to similar offensive operations in the Pacific. King stipulated that these operations "stemmed from the submarine plot, maintained by F-21 in the Combat Intelligence Division."[71] After the reforms instituted by King in 1943, the US Navy operated as a well-oiled machine that held the sole function of defeating the Axis Tripartite while setting the foundations for postwar reconstruction. Knowles explained the infusion of operations with intelligence. He described the messages transmitted from CominCh to the numbered fleets as appearing to be "more right than wrong and, therefore, they listened very carefully to everything we sent out."[72]

PURPOSEFULLY RUDE

US Navy submarines operating from Scotland stood poised to attack German targets in European waters. King solicited opinions about using submarines for hunter-killer operations in the Atlantic. The idea resonated among the key submariners on the CominCh staff, Cooke, Edwards, and Low.[73] For the mission, King selected Capt. Norman S. Ives to establish Submarine Squadron 50 in New London, Connecticut. Establishing the tender USS *Beaver* (AS-5) as the flagship, he organized SubRon 50 with six newly commissioned Gato-class submarines—including USS *Barb* (SS-220), USS *Blackfish* (SS-221), USS *Gunnel* (SS-253), USS *Gurnard* (SS-254), USS *Herring* (SS-233), and USS *Shad* (SS-235). After supporting the landings in North Africa, Ives established the permanent headquarters of SubRon 50 at Rosneath near Faslane in Scotland. Augmenting this group, USS *Haddo* (SS-255) and USS *Hake* (SS- 256) sailed for operations in European waters by the spring of 1943.

German naval intelligence analysts monitored the movements of American submarines as they prepared to conduct an aggressive campaign to sink Axis targets in European waters. In a message transmitted from headquarters ashore, German submarine skippers received this warning on May 27, 1943: "American [submarine] in position AK 5445 at 2100/24/5 on passage to patrol area near AK 7657—further American [submarine] on patrol near AK 7182 at 2100/24/5 both submerged by day."[74] As the ComNavEu liaison to the submarine operations subdivision within the OIC in London, Follmer supplied Ives with enemy targets.[75] The CominCh headquarters supplied Follmer with targets. He then relayed the information to SubRon 50.

The scheme to employ American submarines in hunter-killer operations caused significant controversy. In the spring of 1943, Admiral Sir Andrew Cunningham served as chief of the BAD in Washington. He delivered a dossier of complaints from the Admiralty about the plan to use SubRon 50 for hunter-killer operations in the Atlantic. Cunningham later characterized King as "a man of immense capacity and ability, quite ruthless in his methods, he was not easy to get on with."[76] Cunningham observed, "We are only liaison officers with no power to order a man or a dinghy to move."[77]

Cunningham and King shared similar personalities and competed to protect their respective services. Cunningham believed that the Admiralty should control operations in European waters. He explained, "We had some straight speaking over the trifling matter of four or five American submarines for work on our side of the Atlantic."[78] Cunningham regarded King's position as "offensive, and I told him what I thought of his method of advancing Allied unity and amity. We parted friends."[79] From another point of view, King considered "Cunningham's query as a 'needle' directed at me[, and] I was indeed very abrupt (rude) with him—and purposely so!"[80]

The central issue hinged on the differences between Admiralty protocols for handling special intelligence sources as compared with those of King's navy. Cunningham argued that American hunter-killer ambushes would inevitably "result in our shipping losses going up by anything from 50 to 100 percent."[81] King responded, "I am equally concerned with you as to the security of [Special Intelligence;] it is my belief we are not deriving from it the fullest value."[82] King observed that given the "risk of compromise it would be a matter of lasting regret to all if [Special Intelligence] security were jeopardized in some less worthy cause."[83] To avoid an unnecessary argument with Cunningham and the Admiralty, King simply dissolved Submarine Squadron 50 and sent the individual submarines to the Pacific.[84]

Hunter-killer operations enabled naval forces to clear oceanic shipping lanes in advance of convoys and other operational forces in contested waters. Always seeking means to engage the enemy in decisive battle, King used intelligence to maximum effect. He gambled on American industrial supremacy to wage an unrelenting war of attrition against the enemy. He ignored critics by unleashing American hunter-killer task forces, coordinated through the First and Tenth Fleets. Messages originating from CominCh through to the numbered fleets enabled American hunter-killer operations to hit the enemy with extreme precision on a worldwide scale. Among other dramatic examples, King noted the operations of USS *England* (DE-635) during operations culminating in the destruction of six Japanese submarines within a fortnight off Bougainville.[85] King wryly remarked, "There'll always be an *England* in the US Navy."[86]

CHAPTER 29
Someone to Shoot King

The unified armadas of Britain and America were unprecedented in the global maritime arena. After 1943, the historical King's navy of Britain stood in the shadows of the American variant under King. Meanwhile, Prime Minister Mackenzie King asserted Canadian sovereignty in the competition for strategic influence among the Allies, along with his counterparts from Australia, New Zealand, and other commonwealth leaders of the British Empire. Political outliers, including General Charles de Gaulle, insisted upon holding an equal seat at the table with Churchill and Roosevelt. Stalin further complicated the strategic debates by providing clear ultimatums about the importance of opening another front in Europe. Chiang Kai-shek made similar demands upon the Allies from Asia. Knowing the ramifications, Churchill attempted to recast the British Empire as the future foundation for Roosevelt's vision of the United Nations.[1]

The CCS was divided about the focus of strategy, which hindered progress in setting procurement priorities. During the QUADRANT Conference in the historic setting of Le Château Frontenac, King joined with Pound and Nelles in balancing the discussions about naming a prospective commander for the invasion of Europe. In advance of the meetings, Marshall told Leahy and King about Roosevelt and Churchill's decision to inform the Canadians about the atomic bomb.[2] King rejected atomic weapons as outlandish and unnecessary. He preferred to use precious resources associated with atomic experimentation. King required warships—and particularly landing craft—immediately for operations already underway in upcoming weeks.[3]

Experimental weapons of arguably dubious value similarly also appealed to Churchill's sometimes childish whims. For example, Churchill sponsored an experimental form of concrete known as Pykrete. The concept originated with the British adventurer and amateur military theorist Geoffrey Pyke. Given Pyke's surname, Professor John D. Bernal of the University of London subsequently produced prototypes of Pykrete. In turn, references to Pykrete received classification as MOST SECRET under the classification, HABAKKUK. By mixing ninety-five parts wood pulp with 5 percent water, the British proposed to create large floating islands of Pykrete—or "Project HABAKKUK."[4]

King focused on proven methods for defeating enemies in war while keeping an open mind about technological innovations. Many ideas seemed overly crazy and outright impractical. Projects MANHATTAN and HABAKKUK seemed interesting as theoretical curiosities. Goaded by Churchill and fascinated by the novelty, Mountbatten insisted upon demonstrating the potential of Pykrete for the amusement of the CCS. He made special arrangements to bring an example for display in the grand ballroom of Le Château Frontenac.[5] King complained about the "damned fool [and] those 'nuts' brought into the room a revolver and made a shot at the 'mush.'"[6] The bullet ricocheted, and enraged King when it "nicked the leg of his trousers."[7]

The undertones of a black comedy appear in the various CCS accounts about the Pykrete demonstration. The ongoing verbal duels between British and American leaders suddenly stopped when the sound of pistol shots echoed within the halls of Le Château Frontenac. Field Marshal Sir Alan Brooke agreed with King on the stupidity of the Pykrete episode, noting that the "bullet rebounded out of the block and buzzed around our legs like an angry bee!"[8] Brooke wryly observed that "when our original meeting had become too heated, we had cleared the room of all the attending staff [when] the revolver shots were heard, [and] the wag of the party shouted: Good heavens, they've started shooting now!!"[9] Captain Ruthven Libby stood in the hallway outside the room when he heard the pistol shot, the gasps of witnesses, and then a pregnant silence. "King got really riled up," Libby recalled. "I've seen him mad before, but that ice thing topped it all like a cherry on the cake."[10]

PRO-AMERICAN

The Pykrete incident highlighted key divisions within the CCS about the future role of new technologies. King generally followed traditional views in focusing on the transcendent historical foundations of strategy. King warned fellow strategists to focus on the human dimension of war, the importance of eroding the enemy's will to fight, and the strategic purpose of fighting wars—under the fundamental principle of the "attainment of the sustainable end." To achieve wartime strategic objectives against the Axis Tripartite, King emphasized the policies of the Roosevelt administration in setting reconstruction priorities for the eventual development of the United Nations. In turn, Churchill purposely mischaracterized King's strategy as being overly focused on the Pacific and overly confident about the situation in the Atlantic.

King emphasized the point by noting the tenuous position of Chiang Kai-shek and the importance of providing sufficient logistical support to operations in China. Royal Navy admirals Louis Mountbatten and James Somerville endorsed King's proposal to conduct Operation RAVENOUS—to open the Chindwin Valley in Malaya as a precursor for the ANAKIM offensive into China. King envisioned simultaneous efforts to plan an amphibious crossing of the English Channel under the ROUNDUP and SLEDGEHAMMER plans. Marshall's assistant Wedemeyer observed that King "visibly annoyed the British."[11] Wedemeyer noted that King "is often depicted as anti-British [but] actually he was simply pro-American in the same way that Churchill was pro-Empire."[12] Wedemeyer credited King for keeping transatlantic strategy on schedule and focused on the ultimate objectives. Wedemeyer thought that "if it hadn't been for the operations of the American navy under Admiral King, the Japanese might have moved on India and toward the Mediterranean."[13] Observing from the corners of the CCS and JCS, Wedemeyer said, "Frankly I was surprised that Admiral King's position was not reinforced by supporting statements on the part of Marshall and Arnold."[14]

The sporadic presence of German submarines in the Atlantic factored into the mix of transatlantic strategy among the Anglo-American navies. Churchill constantly invoked the specter of "U-boats" to keep King in check. Reflecting upon the question from service in Tenth Fleet, Low explained that King "was sometimes apprehensive [whenever] the

British would try to take over both strategic and tactical direction [but] anti-British—he was <u>not</u>."[15] He refuted British characterizations by describing German submarines as simply being "a menace."[16] Churchill influenced Roosevelt to pressure Marshall and King by pushing the concept of a unified command, falling under the British, for all forces in the Atlantic.

Marshall demurred by proposing the unification of army and naval air forces, and the associated convoy-routing shore establishment, to fall under the War Department. King flipped the argument by suggesting that the "navy is all inclusive as a 'joint' service which is already one package." King went on to suggest that the army should fall under the Navy Department. In critiquing the British RAF and American army equivalents, King mused, "The Germans never understood that airplanes are not tanks and the guys flying in them are not soldiers."[17] He continued explaining this mindset to the Arlington County Commandos that the "Japanese use their fleet only when it will help carry out some plan of the Army [and it] is an adjunct to the Army."[18] He boasted, "We'd <u>like</u> them to come out."[19] King mused that the Japanese "have had a taste of what a wallop the American Navy packs and does not like the taste."[20]

King applauded Roosevelt for setting the strategic Allied objectives as being focused on the establishment of the United Nations. For similar reasons, King praised Walter Lippmann for doing a "great service by writing his book on Foreign Policy [and] everyone should read it."[21] Continuing, he explained that at the Naval War College, "officers have first to determine a foreign policy and then go on from there into war games."[22] King explained that "knowing foreign policy means knowing who your enemy is."[23] King worried that "Field-Marshal Alan Brooke and General Marshall had no idea about 'sea power,'" and King complained that "they just saw things as fixed forts to be bombarded, reduced, seized, reinforced, and then defended in perpetuity."[24] King lambasted the airpower clique surrounding Arnold that the "proponents of Air-Power-winning-the-war have oversold themselves." He explained to journalists that

> Air Power is another magnificent weapon, but it is to be coordinated with all other arms and integrated into the scheme of battle. It is "flying artillery" and without it we cannot win, but by and of itself it will not win the war and whoever thinks this is kidding himself—and others. A great deal of harm has been done to the people of this country by writers who have preached that air power could win the war. The war will be won by a bloody series of battles on the continent of Europe, the Russians on one front and we on the other.[25]

King applauded MacArthur in the interests of supporting the heroic imagery surrounding the notion of "I shall return," in Allied propaganda. Among trusted friends, King contradicted himself by admitting, "MacArthur did not know how to use naval power and, as a matter of fact, wasn't using what he already had and would never learn."[26]

King viewed strategy with a distinctly maritime focus, aiming for speedy and decisive results in the war effort by using naval forces to render fortified enemy positions ashore irrelevant. "We shall not waste the lives of our men in taking all the islands the Jap[anese] have garrisoned," King explained, and he continued that "there is no reason to attack islands we shall not need, so we'll just let them starve to death—or commit suicide."[27] He warned about the possibility of a dramatic Japanese show of force by putting on a "show some-where[,] and we are always on the alert for that move."[28] Ever supportive of the Europe First concept in executing operations in the Atlantic, King observed, "Japan is not doing a lot of things they might do to embarrass us." He expected that the Japanese might "pull another stunt—maybe Midway."[29] King mused, "It seems incredible that the Jap[anese] would accept the loss of face in the losses in the Solomons[,] and we expect a real blow-off."[30] Summing up his strategy in the fall of 1943, King assured journalists, saying, "Our heavy ships are out in the Pacific looking for trouble [and] all hell will break loose out there for these heavy ships are on the warpath!"[31]

Support to the Soviet Union in Europe and Chinese forces in Asia defined the strategy of King's navy. He lambasted the British for indulging in various fringe strategies, from Norwegian waters to the Indian Ocean. King applauded the efforts of Harry Hopkins to keep Roosevelt on track to victory. King explained that Hopkins "sits with the President, especially when Churchill is doing some of his persuasive talking[, and] Hopkins has been of great assistance to the Army and Navy in his job."[32] King claimed that "eighty-five percent of our war effort is being made in Europe and fifteen percent in the Pacific."[33] King mused, "We are way ahead of schedule in the Pacific."[34]

Journalists asked critical questions about Marshall and MacArthur to press King to explain the dynamics of personality within the JCS. King thought, "Marshall had a grasp of the global aspects of the war and his activities should not be narrowed to a particular front."[35] In anticipation of Christmas in 1943, King revealed to journalists the secret deci-sion to hold Marshall in place in Washington. "Eisenhower has had command in the Mediterranean and Middle East," King divulged, adding, "Eisenhower will shift his com-mand to England sometime in January, the exact time to be left to him."[36] King told journalists that he "thinks the world of Marshall." Out of respect, King explained that the "announcement about Eisenhower will not be made until he leaves for London."[37]

King told journalists about the importance of taking the German rocket and submarine bases on the European coast. He warned that the "Germans have in contemplation the use of bacteria against England[, and there exists] no known cure for some of the dis-eases."[38] "That the Germans will use such a weapon is a safe assumption," King warned. "That there is something new in German hands is fairly certain[,] and it is better than an even bet that the mystery weapon is bacteria."[39] This shocking statement inspired journal-ists to speculate about the potential threat of German submarines and the prospective use of rockets for chemical and biological attacks against the United States.[40]

King reassured journalists by emphasizing the difficulties involved with penetrating Allied defenses to deliver such weapons by submarine. He admitted that the Germans "are developing devices that will neutralize our radar[,] and they will soon equip their U-boats with it [and] we shall have more headaches."[41] Assessing the situation for jour-nalists in the fall of 1943, King thought that the "U-boats will return and although they are always trouble, we have an unbeatable system; the carrier and the escort vessel working as a team."[42] He explained that the "initial decision to keep pressure on the Jap[anese] is still in full swing[,] and everything is being done to keep this pressure[; if] a move is made it must be one which increases pressure—otherwise it is not made, no matter how attrac-tive it might appear."[43] King reasoned that the Japanese relied upon "intermediate points from which they ship supplies down to their troops in wooden barges so that they will not have to risk their ships[, and] the Japanese are in a bad way for tonnage."[44] King wondered "why the Jap[anese] U-boats have not caused us more trouble than they have."[45]

Enemy submarines lost the strategic advantage within the global context of Anglo-American convoy operations. American hunter-killer tactics proved particularly untenable for the enemy. King knowingly violated his own security restrictions by telling journalists, "Our planes locate a U-boat and escort vessels maintain constant contact by the 'pinging' device [and] when the U-boat dives with a full can—with the batteries fully charged—she must eventually come to the surface and when she does, the escort vessel is there waiting for her."[46] King thought, "We have not had the good luck to capture any U-boats recently, but we have captured crews, quite a lot of them[, and] we can sink U-boats faster than the Germans can build them."[47] King mused that the "U-boat picture has been too darkly painted [and the] high ship losses were for the most part piled up at the very beginning of the war when we did not have the tools."[48.] King consoled journalists that the "U-boats are under control and will be kept in that state[, and] U-boats surrender more easily than they formerly did due to the inept and green crews."[49]

This remarkable statement by King coincided with his tacit approval of operations then underway in the Atlantic. In April 1944, he knew that his wingman from Pensacola, Gallery, declared his full intention to capture a German submarine. King fully understood the value of capturing enemy ships in naval warfare. King told journalists, "We always try to guess what the enemy is doing, or at least what he is trying to do."[51] To this end, King gave full approval for the Combat Intelligence Division to inform the antisubmarine training centers about enemy submarines. Individual task group skippers, like Gallery, also met with King before and after their deployments to the front. Monitoring their progress every morning at 0900, King received updates about ongoing offensive operations at sea. On the afternoon of June 4, Gallery sent the message to CominCh—requesting assistance to bring *U-505* under tow to a friendly port.

The *U-505* capture stood among the most dramatic milestones in the antisubmarine campaign in the Atlantic. British information derived from such previous captures as the *U-110* and *U-570* enabled the equally important American capture of *U-505*—especially in the final months of offensive operations in Europe. The capture happened just two days preceding the landings on Normandy and in close conjunction with other amphibious "D-days" along multiple fronts from the Atlantic to the Indian Ocean and beyond to the Pacific.[50] In full command of operations and intelligence, King successfully balanced American forces to conduct almost simultaneously the D-day operations NEPTUNE, at Normandy, and FORAGER, on Saipan.

Trusted journalists took detailed notes as King outlined deep reservations about the differences of British and American strategy. He thought, "There is no use getting into this Italian proposition any deeper than we are now."[52] He advised that the "most that we should do with respect to the Balkans is a landing on the Dalmatian Coast in order that we might have ports which the Chetniks should be supplied."[53] King noted, "Churchill likes the Balkan idea and thinks the natives would give us a tremendous amount of aid by keeping the Germans terrorized."[54] King gave a warning, saying, "We shall be tied up in the most unfavorable country and under circumstances far from favorable [it] would be terribly slow going and cost a lot of men [and] in the end, we would profit little."[55]

DAMN THE TORPEDOES

American morale suffered under the anxiety of war, further punctuated by assertions made in Congress. In 1943, King corrected the record: "Admiral Horne had not said that we'd win the war against Japan in 1949, but that we should be prepared to fight that long if necessary."[56] King argued that the "only method of succeeding is to literally blast a way into France with our air power, pouring men and materials through the breach and then utilizing our air forces [at] a terrible cost, of course[,] but the job has to be done."[57] King warned journalists that the Japanese "are digging in."[58] King used the campaign in Asia as leverage to force the CCS into reaching consensus about the strategic priorities for Europe. He forced the JCS to set clear target dates for decisive operations in the Atlantic to synchronize offensive efforts in the Pacific and other oceanic fronts.

The British reacted to American advances in operations and intelligence with anguish and begrudging envy. Two world wars had undermined the foundations of the empire upon which the sun never set, as the Americans filled the vacuum with strange assumptions about their own claims to cultural supremacy. Among the old salts, the past still provided context for mutual respect. On this point, King was deeply saddened by the slow suffering of his friend—First Sea Lord Pound. Complications from a hip injury hindered Pound. Then Pound suffered a series of minor strokes forcing him to resign in September 1943. Within weeks, Pound died of a brain tumor. "Dudley was first rate," King lamented; "toward the end of his life he would sit in a meeting and you would think he was asleep, but when some important point came along he would hit it at once."[59] "His loss was keenly deplored," King recalled, "both in the United States and England."[60] King emphasized the "need, for the peace of the world, of assuring the permanence of the Anglo-American alliance."[61]

Pound possessed the rare ability to cajole King into treating Anglo-American solidarity as the topmost priority in the global war at sea. Pound inspired King to acknowledge that "English is the language of empires[,] and Pound spoke it better than anyone, even Churchill." Pound's death possibly set the British at a disadvantage in dealings with King. On the other hand, Pound's successor, Cunningham, proved worthy of the task. Cunningham fleeted up from presiding over the BAD in Washington. Knowing the Americans, Cunningham and King also shared similar personalities. Cunningham struck King as a "real man."[62] Cunningham seemed to fit the definition of a leader for King, as the "spiritual successor to the Earl of St. Vincent."[63]

Cunningham faced the very real strategic problem of managing Churchill, while King carried an equal burden with Roosevelt. Somehow, King always stayed a few steps ahead. His personal family network and their associates proved decisive in keeping ahead of the bureaucratic trends. His brother-in-law, Gen. Smith, shared information about the goings-on from within the War Department. His sons-in-law similarly kept King well apprised. Trusted associates like Ghormley and Turner kept King apprised of the situation in Hawaii. King remained in firm control of the tiller during bimonthly visits with Nimitz in San Francisco. King similarly relied upon Stark to stay focused on the campaign to seize a deepwater port on the European continent.[64]

King's priorities for the Atlantic campaign to Europe tied with operations already underway in the Pacific and ashore in Asia. His carefully synchronized strategy frequently drew amateurish criticism from fellow members of the CCS and JCS. On one occasion, Churchill made snide remarks about the Pacific being "King's Ocean."[65] He simply stood up and walked out of the discussion—leaving Churchill free to subject Marshall to an all-night lecture about the merits of prospective expeditions to Norway, the Levant, and the Balkans.[66] Alcohol fueled Churchill's vision for a campaign through Rhodes and ashore into Greece.

The specter of Gallipoli came to mind when Marshall discounted operations against fortified enemy positions in the mountainous terrain ashore in Greece. Having given Churchill silence out of respect, Marshall calmly delivered the last word in stating, "Not one American soldier will die on that goddamned beach."[67] The whimsical tendencies of Churchill forced Roosevelt to make equally dramatic gestures to bring coherence to transatlantic strategy. Having chosen to sail on the newly commissioned battleship USS *Iowa* (BB-61), Roosevelt agreed to meetings held in Cairo and Tehran. Much to Churchill's chagrin, Roosevelt made special arrangements to meet with Chiang Kai-shek and Stalin. The SEXTANT Conference in Cairo—followed by EUREKA in Tehran—pressed Roosevelt to the physical brink. His cheerful façade camouflaged his failing health during the 1944 election year.[68] Earlier, King advised Roosevelt to make a symbolic point by "holding court with the allies somewhere here in America."[69] King explained his complex views about the British and American connection:

> I personally felt that the "Allies" would lose the war against the Japanese unless we stopped them in a few weeks or months, that the "Allies" should provide troops, planes, and ships as soon as possible, and that they must stop the Japanese at the earliest possible time. It seemed to me that the British "egged" the US on to accept their ideas since they were already fighting the Nazi's when the US entered the war and also since the Nazi's were close by and the Pacific was far away. . . . I can't get over the idea that most of the US People had been sold a "pig in a poke" at that time and were in the well-known situation of having been worked into a concept (even a real obsession) of British origin rather than to look out for the basic interests of the USA throughout the entire world![70]

King viewed the Axis as a single threat comprising three dissimilar factions. The best path to complete victory centered on supporting the Soviets in defeating the Axis in Europe first. In the meantime, King had a similar view of supporting the Chinese in efforts to win the war in Asia. He characterized the Pacific campaign as "being one part of the larger whole."[71]

King was among the key authors of the Europe First principle, which always stood out as phase 1 to solving the Mahanian problem of Asia. The immediate challenge of defeating the Axis Tripartite was subordinate to the broader peacetime agenda set by Roosevelt. Often with a smile and sometimes with a drink in hand, Roosevelt unleashed King upon the CCS and JCS to establish the Americas as the future center of the United Nations. King discussed his role on the CCS and JCS with his friend—the skipper on *Iowa*, Capt. John L. McCrea. The pair monitored the messages transmitted from the CominCh headquarters to *Iowa*.

With Roosevelt carousing with *Iowa* sailors on the decks below, King continued looking outward toward the sea. McCrea recalled a moment in which King was standing with binoculars and a cigarette dangling out of his mouth during the transatlantic passage of Roosevelt to North Africa in 1943. McCrea frequently joined King on the bridgewing with a cup of coffee. Nearby, destroyer escorts orbited *Iowa*, prepared for any possibility. At one point, USS *William D. Porter* (DD-579) accidentally fired a torpedo at *Iowa* during an exercise. Roosevelt reveled in the drama when *Iowa* suddenly turned hard, and the friendly torpedo passed harmlessly in the wake. He joked with sailors about the incident.

King erupted with the ferocity of Neptune and other monsters of the deep while chain-smoking on the flying bridge. King summoned the skipper, Cmdr. Wilfred A. Walter. Expecting to be relieved, Walter maneuvered *Porter* to board *Iowa*. Walter reported to the flying bridge to find King chain-smoking and looking out over the sea. An aide stood by as a witness. King then turned to ask, "Well?" Walter offered no excuses and took full responsibility for his ship. Contrary to myth, King left Walter in command, and he continued serving with distinction in combat. King certainly had the ability to sideline Walter, but he did not. Walter ended the war in good standing—working directly under Nimitz on the Pacific Fleet staff. Walter retired as a two-star rear admiral. The *William D. Porter* incident illustrated King's approach in enabling subordinates to rise above failure and develop into excellent leaders. While still at sea, King told McCrea, "I regard you as a good officer, but you could be a lot better [but] your big weakness, McCrae, is that you are not a son of a bitch."[72] In response, McCrea said, "Admiral King, you are a good naval officer and universally regarded as such."[73] McCrea fibbed in telling King, "I have never heard anyone refer to you as a son of a bitch."[74]

King forcibly synthesized the global priorities as established by the CCS to drive the strategic negotiations within the JCS. By 1943, the JCS had matured into an effective forum for Marshall and King. Unhappy with his lot in managing global continental operations, Marshall yearned for the opportunity to follow in the heroic footsteps of Generals Washington and Lee. The gritty myth of Grant and the polished image of Pershing further influenced Marshall. He knew the sting of cold steel after being wounded with a bayonet during a stupid hazing ritual among fellow "Keydets" at the Virginia Military Institute (VMI)—an embarrassing incident known among friends within the ranks of the US Army. Marshall conversely earned the reputation for being strong enough to take an unanticipated jab from the likes of King.[75]

Marshall grew deeply frustrated with the monotony of fighting in the swampy political battles of Washington. Above all, Marshall sought the opportunity to chisel his name into the annals of American popular myth and memory—standing alongside the statues of his underlings, like MacArthur and Eisenhower. When Marshall articulated his desires for transfer to the front, Roosevelt asked Leahy and King for their opinions during the voyage to the Cairo Conference.

Leahy and King separately voiced the same recommendation to hold Marshall in place. Should Roosevelt satisfy Marshall's request, Leahy and King feared the likelihood of MacArthur filling the void left by Marshall on the JCS. The delicate CCS arrangement also stood in the balance.

Roosevelt held his silence with implied support when King clapped bureaucratic shackles around Marshall's ankles. Sightseeing the ancient battlefields at Carthage, Marshall was stone faced when King told Eisenhower of his prospective appointment to form the Supreme Headquarters, Allied Expeditionary Force (SHAEF) in Europe.[76] As

King predicted, Eisenhower formally assumed responsibility for planning the amphibious campaign in Europe in January 1944.[77] To assist this work, King installed RAdm. Alan Goodrich Kirk to coordinate American naval planning. King kept additional tabs on Eisenhower through his naval liaisons, including Capt. John A. "Jack" Moreno with reserve commanders Harry C. Butcher and McGeorge Bundy.[78]

King's internal family network of spies within Marshall and Eisenhower's bureaucratic camp had to stay ahead of the trends within the Allied command. Among the US Army brigadier generals, the elder Walter D. Smith collected information as a participant in the ongoing feuds within the Pentagon. Unrelated to the elder other than their mutual familial connections with King, the younger Freddy Smith flew in from MacArthur's SWPA to join SHAEF in planning the amphibious assault on Normandy and beyond onto continental Europe. Together, the Smiths kept King's court fully apprised of strategic discussions for operations ashore in the global maritime arena. For his work before Normandy, Freddy Smith earned the honorary designation as Commander of the Most Excellent Order of the British Empire.[79]

OUR PAL JOEY

King fully understood the corrosive ideological influence of Bolshevism, and he always remained guarded in dealings with Soviet allies. He advised reporters that "Stalin is too damn smart to want to take over Europe[,] for that would be laying up trouble for Russia[,] which would have to try to control unwilling subjects." He thought that "Stalin will take over part of Poland and the Baltic States." King predicted that Stalin "would be willing to draw a line down through occupied Poland to the Baltic Sea." King envisioned Soviet control in the maritime provinces of Siberia and Manchuria as the key to the future commercial success of the United Nations. King thought that such concessions "would give Russia what she wants and with no additional danger to Peace."[80] King told journalists, "Stalin is a stark realist [and] there is very little hocus-pocus about him and he is not given to rhetorical outbursts."[81]

Having witnessed the scene at Tehran, King recalled how Roosevelt and Churchill presented long and laudatory remarks about the future of Allied collaboration. "After these two had finished, it was the turn of Stalin to speak," King recalled. Stalin said, "quite simply, that the remarks just made by Roosevelt and Churchill seemed appropriate to the occasion, that he subscribed to them and then remarked—'and now let's get down to business.'"[82] King observed of Stalin that "there is no foolishness about him."[83]

Stalin exhibited cold confidence in dealings with Churchill and Roosevelt, which greatly impressed King. Bolshevism appeared to be nothing more than a flawed philosophy. King thought that czars "Ivan and Peter would have liked Stalin."[84] King told journalists that "Stalin almost always used the terms 'Russ' and 'Ruski'; not 'Soviet.'"[85] Stalin doodled on small pieces of paper during negotiations before folding them up into tiny squares. At one point, King attempted to take one as a souvenir. Stalin used an interpreter named Pavlov for discussions with Churchill and Roosevelt. The interpreter demonstrated proficiency, although sometimes he acted as though he misunderstood certain words. King observed the tactics at the table of negotiation, as "Stalin professed not to understand English."[86]

Whenever an adversary provided the opportunity, Stalin suddenly seemed to understand English. He customarily pounced with the ferocity of an angry Siberian bear. Having witnessed Stalin's tactics, King was also impressed by the Soviet troops of the personal guard. Stalin's entourage added to the aura of quiet confidence among the Soviet representatives. The crisp discipline of the Soviets deeply impressed King. In addition, the Soviet uniforms added to the show—with distinctive mixes of blues, reds, and olive drab. King noticed the bespoke uniform, as uniquely worn by Stalin, which gave a slimming effect and appeared to glow in the sunlight.[87] King enjoyed the aura of unbridled power that filled the room and emanated from Stalin. King thought that the "Russians are hell to get committed to any given proposition[,] but once having given their word they will deliver—they do deliver."[88]

Churchill and Stalin indulged in verbal duels, while Roosevelt used charm to soothe the lions and bears among the CCS. The characters surrounding the so-called Big Three amused King.[89] He explained that the "Russians are tough traders."[90] Behind closed doors, King told journalists that the "British had to be pitchforked into the coming invasion [and] our pal Joey applied the pitchfork."[91] King warned that the Russians "do not become angry at the most direct talk or the toughest attitude on our part[, but] if we are soft, they regard us as fools and they expect the other fellow to look out for himself—fully—if he doesn't it is his own fault."[92]

King optimistically predicted a bright future for the Anglo-American coalition with the Soviets and Chinese allies. China emerged at the center of focus. King explained that "we do not propose to 'take the Philippines' before proceeding to the Japanese islands [and] any move to retake Luzon is an 'eccentric operation' and is to be avoided."[93] He stunned journalists with the emphatic declaration that it is "our intention to take Formosa."[94] "While somewhat over-simplified," he explained, "China manpower and geographical position would be the factor in beating Japan."[95]

King's entire strategy for the Atlantic centered on the British Isles; likewise, Formosa provided the ultimate destination for operations in the Pacific. He viewed the British Isles as the key naval advanced base from which to supply forces ashore on the European continent. Similarly, Formosa provided means to facilitate and the reconstruction in Asia.[96] British counterparts on the CCS naturally focused on the immediate problem of continental Europe—often at the expense of concurrent plans for operations in Asia. Taking the global view of the maritime battlefield, King worked the lines in supporting the appointment of Lord Louis Mountbatten as supreme Allied commander, South-East Asia Command (SEAC). King told journalists during one of his regular secret meetings, "Now that Mountbatten is there, maybe we can get things moving in China."[97] King also chuckled when journalists asked him about the alternative definition of the SEAC being "Supreme Example of Allied Confusion."[98]

King clearly understood the British perspective on the whimsical strategic influence of Mountbatten. As a member of the royal family, he had influence beyond the limits of his naval rank. From Churchill to Brooke, the Mountbatten question plagued the British Joint Staff. By shipping Mountbatten to the relative exile of the SEAC, the British essentially attempted to remove the joker card from the deck while playing bureaucratic poker with the Americans. Conversely, Mountbatten enhanced King's political hand in making the case for offensive operations in China. Mountbatten served as King's counterbalance in debates with Churchill about his proposals for future operations in Norway, into the Balkans, along the Levant, and beyond to the Middle East. Through their subordinates, King and Marshall also worked the bureaucratic angles to force the British to accept the Americans as equal partners in debates of combined strategy and command. In this respect, King and Marshall were the most responsible on the CCS for keeping the Europe First principle on schedule.[99]

Decisions to execute any given operation customarily required *unanimous* consent among the CCS and JCS. Yet, Churchill often violated the rules—pushing the British staff to execute operations without the full American consent of the JCS. Caught between Churchill and Roosevelt, the First Sea Lord and his subordinates struggled for resources to execute operations in the Adriatic. At Churchill's insistence, the Royal Navy drew from the amphibious assistance of US Navy vice admiral Henry Kent Hewitt, performing the double functions of commander, Northwest African Waters, and commander, Eighth Fleet. In addition, the operations reflected Churchill's underhandedness—using American forces for operations specifically rejected by the unanimous consent of the CCS after the QUADRANT and SEXTANT conferences.[100]

British commanders strongarmed the effort to divert American warships for operations along Greek shores. As a result, American ships remained in European waters, delaying the strategic schedules for offensive operations in Asia. Notably, Roosevelt had personally assured Chiang about Operation BUCCANEER—the plan to drive Allied offensives in China. BUCCANEER proved impossible after the British delayed the American warships for Mediterranean operations. Disgusted by the apparent scheming of the British to control American forces, King issued direct orders to his commanders to stop operations in Greek waters.

King failed to ask permission before issuing the order to cease all American naval support for operations along the Levant and into the Adriatic. He specifically based the order on Roosevelt administration policy. Secretary of State Edward R. Stettinius Jr. also played his double-edged part as a diplomat by acting surprised while secretly supporting King's gambit in having a showdown with British counterparts. Although the precipitous decree from King put the commander, Hewitt, in the middle of an inter-Allied world war for command at sea, King successfully drew a very clear line about future control over American naval strategy. King sharpened his point by accusing the British of fighting a war that "does not appear to be a war in which the United States is participating."[101]

Diplomatic troubles with Churchill prompted Roosevelt to seek an elegant solution for clarifying the role of King's navy in combined operations. Roosevelt used Leahy as the middleman, pushing King to relent by reflagging US Navy warships under the Union Jack for the short-term purposes of the Greek adventure. British scheming to control American assets greatly upset relations among the staffs. In correspondence, King complained to Stark that the "seeming helplessness of our cousins strikes me as amusing when it is not annoying."[102] King mused, "I am sure that what they wish in their hearts is that we would haul down the Stars and Stripes and hoist the White Ensign in all of our ships."[103] King admitted, "What particularly irks me is their strong liking for mixed forces, which you know approached anathema to me."[104] King reasoned, "I cannot be expected to agree to help them cling to tasks that they themselves say they are unable to do unless we lend them our ships and other forces."[105]

Churchill occasionally proposed plans for combining British and American forces simply to watch King's predictable reaction. King referred to "Mr. Churchill" in explaining the proposal for sending British forces to operate in the Pacific "because Great Britain wished to help the United States."[106] Faced with such an outlandish interpretation of the actual relationship between Britain and America, King angrily stood up and looked down at Churchill—squarely locking eyes. King then pointed his finger at Churchill. In low grinding tones, King defiantly declared that the "Royal Navy was _not_ needed and would only cause trouble."[107] Remembering the tense quiet that settled over the negotiating table, King recalled, "Even FDR looked me over."[108] At that point, King explained, "Mr. President, that's exactly what I mean [because] the Royal Navy knows too little about logistics and naval aviation—that the United States would have to get supplies for them—that it would take six months to get anything out of them."[109] At that point, Churchill impishly chided King with a smile, saying, "Yes, but the Royal Navy wants to have some little 'fun' too with the Japanese."[110]

CHAPTER 30
The Problem of Asia

On the basic questions of British and American policy, Chuchill's views about the future of the empire and Roosevelt's contradictory vision for the future United Nations left the strategic planners on the CCS on opposite ends of the operational debates, which simultaneously extended to the divisive perspectives among the British Joint Staff and the American JCS. On these issues, Mahan's timeless book *The Problem of Asia* greatly influenced King's views about the future of the British Empire and the United States. Given the Europe First strategy, King recognized that the key to future peace existed in Asia. For this reason, King elevated his man in China, Miles, from the lower rank of commander to the newly established one-star flag rank of "commodore" for the purposes of organizing US naval operations in Asia. By 1943, Miles had successfully negotiated strategic relationships with various Chinese factions under the SACO agreement. Miles fully understood King's intent, which centered on using Chinese forces—not American combat troops—to defeat the Japanese in Asia.[1]

Under the SACO agreement with Chiang's regime, the Roosevelt administration fully supported King's strategy for Asia. Miles had relative autonomy to operate as he deemed fit in China. King allowed Miles to operate as an extension of the CominCh headquarters. The US Naval Group in China therefore operated with relative autonomy in relations with CinCPAC/POA of Nimitz in Hawaii. King fully approved the decisions made by Miles after the American naval mission fell subordinate within the Chinese National Army hierarchy. King gambled that the Chinese lacked resources to assert full authority over Miles, thus enabling the Americans to hold true control over operations ashore in Asia. King also assumed that the Chinese Communist forces of Mao also required direct American assistance in efforts to defeat their common enemies of Japan. King envisioned the future role of British and American sea power as being the key governing influence for the future reconstruction of Europe and Asia under the Roosevelt's Four Policemen concept for the United Nations.

The future of China played into the strategic debates between Marshall and King, which shaped the priorities for simultaneous efforts in Europe and Asia. Having served in China earlier in his career, Marshall also worried about King's strategy for Asia. Meanwhile, MacArthur's vision for the Philippines directly conflicted with King's efforts to drive the amphibious focus on Formosa. King recalled that the "Naval War College had long agreed that if we could get into the Marianas[,] the Japanese fleet would have to fight."[2] "It took me three months to educate Marshall about the importance of the Marianas," King continued, "but any educated naval officer would have understood it."[3] King thought, "Strategy is not an exact science and you have to use horse sense."[4] King complained, "It always seemed to me that the Navy was better equipped with strategic insight than the Army—the Air Corps didn't know a damned thing about it."[5]

King's navy prepared for the final offensives against the Axis Tripartite by focusing on the postwar reconstruction objectives for Europe and Asia. King warned journalists about the misleading influence of airpower propagandists. King told the media to expect amphibious campaigns in Europe and Asia, which were prerequisite to defeating the Axis Tripartite and the eventual development of the United Nations. He mused that "there have been persistent rumors in Washington all to the effect that there will be no invasion at all."[6] King assured the media, saying that "there will be an invasion [against] the 'Rocket-Coast' of France."[7] He explained the bloody future by paraphrasing Dr. Josef Goebbels: "Should the German people have to leave the stage, they will slam the door so hard as to shake the world and cause civilization to topple."[8] King reflected on the situation and, with grim determination, said that

> we are now moving into the grimmer aspects of war. The casualties will be higher, and the overall picture is a little blacker than it was some time ago. The war in Europe is going well on the Russian Front and badly in Italy. It is going well in the Pacific and very badly—or not at all—in Burma. The bombings of German industry are getting results at not-too-high a cost in planes and men. The Luftwaffe is undoubtedly being hurt and has to save some of its fighting strength for the days of the invasion.[9]

King envisioned equally bleak times in warning that "nobody should be surprised if we get a bloody nose in the Pacific."[10] "Should Japan withdraw into the inner defenses this war would prolong indefinitely." King warned that the Japanese defensive barrier ranged from north of the "Yangtze, through Manchuria, Korea, and around the Sea of Japan and the inner rim of the Japanese Islands." He explained that the only road to victory appeared to lead through China, although regarding the prospect of ground operations in "this inner area[,] there are few roads, [and] attacking in such country is going to be a hard task and a job of the first magnitude."[11]

Sea power provided the keys for an ultimate Allied victory, with the navies of Britannia and Columbia enabling Chinese guerrillas in Asia and the Red Army of the Soviet Union in Europe. King emphasized the importance of close collaboration in secret meetings with journalists.[12] "Churchill is enthusiastic about perpetuating the CCS after the war," King told reporters, and that Churchill "wants this to continue for a period of ten years after the war with the right of either party to discontinue on three years['] notice."[13] Churchill pressured Brooke to prod King about the Mediterranean strategy. In response, King angrily argued that the "Italians should be left to ride the shoulders of Hitler and a constant drain [and] Germany will have to feed and supply Italy."[14] King anticipated that the conquest of Italy required the Allies to "supply Italy with all food, coal, and other supplies—taking American shipping." King mused that "Hannibal and Napoleon crossed the Alps [but] the times are now different!"[15]

Under the Churchillian thumb, Brooke dutifully advocated for future offensive operations in Norway and the Balkans. Silently witnessing heated exchanges between Brooke and King across the table, Leahy sat stone faced as Brooke condescendingly insulted King for pushing alternative plans for India and China.[16] Gen. Joseph Stilwell observed, "Brooke got nasty, and King got good and sore [and] King almost climbed over the table at Brooke." "God, he was mad." Stilwell wished that King "had socked him."[17] Stilwell concluded,

"Brooke is an arrogant bastard."[18] Leahy played his part on the cleanup crew after King had done his part in dealings with the CCS and JCS. Leahy observed that King "lives up to his reputation of being a tough you know what, and in dealing with the British, he sometimes shocks me."[19] Leahy admitted, "Thank god he does, because he takes care of it for both of us."[20] King later admitted to trusted journalists, "Relations between the British and American members of the CCS have not always flowed smoothly."[21]

Balancing the wild strategic visions of Churchill against Roosevelt's dreamy outlook in the global maritime arena, King carried the burden of taking the point in the CCS negotiations. Leahy and Marshall had the diplomatic role of rebuilding bridges within the CCS. King was alone on the JCS, since Leahy frequently joined Marshall in using Arnold as the joker in the joint fights for command in the air. King recalled that "my friends seemed to enjoy hearing about new gadgets [and] were always looking for excuses to avoid punching the Nazis right in the face."[22] He laughed aloud that "Arnold also bought the line that we could win the war without putting our boys on the beach."[23] King thought Arnold "was so painfully dense."[24]

NO MORE DELAYS!

The airpower debates were tied to the War Department proposals to develop the vision of armed-service unification. Within the Navy Department, King agreed with the general concept of unification. The death of Secretary Knox in April 1944 also rekindled contentious debates about the future of airpower when Forrestal assumed duty as Navy secretary.[25] Although King shared Forrestal's view of unification, the pair failed to get along. Forrestal also challenged King's authority, under EO 9096. Questions concerning future unification were complicated with civil-military debates. Within the Roosevelt administration, measures enacted in the interests of necessity after Pearl Harbor—such as EO 9096— seemed increasingly unnecessary as the war progressed and victory became tangible. Having participated in discussions involving Roosevelt and his closer advisers, Leahy asked King to stop using the "customary term Commander in Chief, both in respect to the United States Fleet and the Pacific and Atlantic Fleet."[26] King refused to act in the absence of a presidential directive.[27] Leahy sheepishly explained that the "president did not wish to issue a definite order, but simply would like to have it done."[28]

King recognized the unspoken indications of shifting tides and changing winds within the Roosevelt administration. Another election year lay just beyond the horizon. King anticipated the politics as he raced to ensure that global strategy remained on schedule within the CCS and JCS. Racing to hold the course, King grew impatient with subordinates for failing to act as planned or on established timelines. Capt. George C. Dyer recalled that "Admiral Nimitz recommending delaying this and delaying that."[29] Within the CominCh staff, the offensive in Europe required planning staffs in the Pacific to prepare for the final push in Asia. Dyer remembered King "constantly saying, 'no more delays.'"[30] Cmdre. Dudley W. Knox similarly thought that

there were many things that he, and he alone could do[, and] it is difficult, in a naval hierarchy, for the top man to be on terms of intellectual equality with people younger than himself, and junior in rank, but the Admiral certainly kept the place free of apple-polishers and, in my view, kept only those lines of naval administration in his own hands that he could not conceivably put in those of someone else.[31]

To spark action within the subordinate headquarters of Nimitz and other commanders, King injected trusted veterans of the CominCh staff in a regular rotation between the headquarters in Washington and other fronts. "One of his best practices," RAdm. Alan Edward Smith noted, "was sending the planners out to sea to execute the plans they had written."[32] This practice forced commanders to plan with a "realistic view of problems and solutions."[33] Smith described how the CominCh planning division had "charts which showed the next four operations, each with about six items displaying the state of readiness for execution—logistics, supply, ships, aircraft, timetables, and the like."[34]

King often surprised younger officers with frontline experience when he ordered them to report for duty on the staff. He preferred to use submariners as his closest junior-ranking aides. For example, he shanghaied Lt. Cmdr. Robert "Dusty" Dornin from command on USS *Trigger* (SS-237) after a series of successful combat patrols along the China coast. Dornin had served on the staff of VAdm. Charles Lockwood, using intelligence to maneuver American submarines with precision in critical chokepoints and key lines of communication. As the skipper on *Trigger*, Dornin earned the reputation as an "ace" submarine commander.[35] Dornin set the record for sinking the highest tonnage in a previous patrol and had demonstrated the novel tactic of attacking targets with radar.[36] To his surprise, Dornin observed Nimitz and Lockwood waiting at the pier as *Trigger* set lines and shifted colors upon returning to port.

The success of *Trigger* along the Chinese coast drew the attention of King and the CominCh headquarters staff. Nimitz and Lockwood were surprised with orders for Dornin to report immediately for duty with CominCh in Washington. Dornin refused, hoping to stay with *Trigger*. Nimitz was silent when Lockwood consoled Dornin to "shut up and get back there in Washington sitting at the right hand of King." Lockwood emphasized that Dornin had the responsibility to provide "proper information to them about submarine warfare in the Pacific."[37]

King surprised the bureaucrats within the Navy Department by transmitting orders detaching Dornin in a personal message to Nimitz. King's aide and a fellow submariner, Cmdr. Charles Kirkpatrick, was surprised when Dornin suddenly arrived with the order to report to CominCh. Kirkpatrick accompanied Dornin into the initial meeting with King. At that time, "King gave a big smile and told [Kirkpatrick] you are fired."[38] King then turned to Dornin with a gruff tone and said, "You relieve [Kirkpatrick], now get to work."[39] King arranged orders for Kirkpatrick to a frontline command in the Pacific, where he suffered severe wounds in combat. With King's endorsement, Kirkpatrick subsequently earned a promotion to flag rank.

Dornin hated the bureaucratic humdrum of the Navy Department and quickly grew frustrated with the grind of managing King's rigorous schedule. Among the first surprises, Dornin received the frantic telephone directive from the White House—directing King to leave immediately to escort General Charles de Gaulle from the Washington National Airport. King responded with insulting remarks aimed at Dornin. As King stopped doing what he was doing, Dornin recalled, "I was hopping goddamn mad, and I remembered that I never wanted the job in the first place."[40] In the rush to meet de Gaulle at the airport, Dornin recognized King's growing frustration as they sat together in the backs eat of their car, "which was hot as hell, no air conditioning[,] and Admiral King didn't say a word."[41]

King deeply disliked de Gaulle on a personal level, which amplified the frustration of being summoned by Roosevelt. Cajoling foreign partners always riled King. Having lost a working day because of de Gaulle's visit, King seemed particularly gruff to Dornin. The following day, Dornin recalled the buzzer on his desk when King summoned him into the office. "I went in and stood in front of Admiral King at rigid attention," and Dornin also remembered that King "peeled off his glasses and looked at me with a little twinkle in his eye."[42] King then reassured Dornin that "you and I have to come to an understanding—I didn't want to meet that goddamn Frenchman [and] I wasn't mad at you yesterday."[43]

With ground rules established, Dornin recognized the nature of war at the high command level in which King existed. Dornin understood that King "didn't want anybody kowtowing to him—you just did your job and you worked like hell [and] you could have a lot of fun and feel like you accomplished something."[44] Dornin explained that King "told me what to do, and to the best of my ability, I did it [but] I'd stand up to him if necessary."[45] Having served in the Pacific, Dornin was surprised about King's frustration with Nimitz and MacArthur. Behind the closed doors of the CCS and JCS, Dornin was shocked when King barked across the table at his British counterparts. Edwards similarly witnessed King's legendary temper when he told the British that "you cannot stash and hoard if you expect to win the goddamned war."[46] King threatened them, saying, "If you don't use what you have, I will!"[47] Dornin applauded King for reminding fellow leaders about the human costs involved with "eccentric operations."[48]

The stakes always seemed too high for King whenever Churchill convinced Roosevelt to indulge in an unplanned strategic tangent against the enemy. When Churchill announced plans to execute a wild operation into Nazi-occupied Yugoslavia after he requested additional American assets to reinforce the British Eastern Fleet in the Indian Ocean to expand operations into the Pacific, King completely lost his composure by tersely telling Churchill, "NO!"[49] In the presence of Roosevelt and the CCS, King directly told Churchill that the British fleet "would be on their own."[50] In essence, he refused to offer the requisite support for the British to sustain operations in the Pacific. Edwards noted that King "MADE HIS POINT."[51] Edwards thought Churchill respected King for his staunch rebuke, which prompted the "Prime Minister's wisecrack referring to the Pacific as 'King's Ocean.'"[52]

The combined maritime forces of Britain and America dominated at sea, which enabled the armies of China and the Soviet Union to exert unrelenting pressure upon the enemy ashore. Within less than four years, King held command over nearly 7,000 warships sailing under the Stars and Stripes. King presided over the rapid strategic transformation of American sea power, which enabled the Allied navies to support worldwide operations ashore on an unprecedented scale. By initiating the process of opening ranks to ethnic minorities and women, King forever changed the culture of the American sea services. In addition, King also expanded the US Navy from roughly 383,150 to 3,408,347 total personnel.[53] To keep morale high among his forces, King and his chief planner, Cooke, set strategic priorities for the logistical staffs to figure out. Cooke issued the challenge of delivering arms and supplies by balancing the percentages against the concurrent requirements for sustained operations—essentially keeping sailors satisfied with a steady stream of ice cream, cigarettes, and beer.[54]

Logistical planners in the CominCh headquarters aspired to provide one case of beer to each serviceman at the front in planning logistical requirements for sustained operations at sea. Each sailor was to receive a steady flow of two cans of beer for each day at the front. Given this seemingly superfluous goal, King formed the Logistics Organizational

Planning Unit (LOPU) to coordinate the naval supply chain infrastructure. King's man, Capt. Paul Pihl, took charge in figuring out procedures for matching merchant ships and military transports with the beans, bullets, black oil, coffee, cigarettes, hot dogs, ice cream, and beer.[55] Pihl then calculated the flow of supplies from railheads in America to the forces engaged against the enemy in the global maritime arena. As an informal rule of thumb, Pihl calculated that each sailor required roughly two beers and an equal number of cigarette cartons for each day spent in a designated combat area—along with everything else required to kill the enemy.[56]

UNREMITTING PRESSURE

Pihl used the British Isles and Formosa as the end points for planning the flow of supplies across the oceanic highways to Europe and Asia. Sailors rotated on a regular schedule between ports, which enabled them to anticipate opportunities for rest and relaxation. This enabled commanders to have another mechanism to govern morale among their crews. The geographic fleets and area commands—amplified by the numbered-fleet system— similarly enabled King and the CominCh headquarters to regulate the offensive operations on a worldwide scale. To these ends, King unleashed the full potential of Special Intelligence by empowering the Combat Intelligence Division to coordinate precision attacks against known targets.[57]

By recruiting personnel with recent experience into the CominCh headquarters, King kept a seagoing focus on strategy. In the same manner, seasoned veterans of the CominCh headquarters frequently rotated from combat duty to bring King's spark to the staffs of his key subordinates—like Stark and Nimitz. The amphibious offensive along the coast of Europe coincided with similar operations of comparable scale along the island-hopping route to Asia. The landings on Normandy happened in concert with those conducted on Saipan in June 1944. King employed whatever means necessary to win decisive results. US Navy hunter-killer groups operated freely and with precision to sweep the path forward for amphibious forces. Submarine and aircraft carrier hunter-killer groups plowed the Pacific and the Atlantic with a series of highly aggressive and overtly executed attacks in April and May 1944, including the remarkable capture of German submarine *U-505* in June 1944—just two days preceding the "D-day" landings at Normandy.

The aggressive tactics required in efforts to capture enemy submarines originated with the British. In the weeks following the capture of *U-505,* tensions reached a breaking point in the relationship between the Admiralty and CominCh. In separate communications on a secure line between the submarine-tracking rooms, Winn signaled Knowles, "Your 1157/9, too true to be good."[58] The British complained about the American tactics by noting the sinkings of U-boat-refueling vessels and rapid destruction of enemy submarines at rendezvous locations, which seemed only to amplify concerns about the capture of *U-505.* British analysts hoped to study the captured enemy warship, which sat in American custody in Bermuda. Reflecting upon the difficult summer of 1944, Knowles explained that Winn

had the feel of the British, naturally, of protecting ULTRA at all costs. So, they were very cautious in utilizing ULTRA. They made very indirect moves in order to support it with an operational program so that it was completely submerged in this operation. Whereas, over in my area, being younger at the game and also being somewhat aggressive[,] we were using ULTRA more aggressively. There's quite a difference in philosophy here.[59]

Winn and Knowles discussed their opinions and resolved problems during daily conversations on their scrambled telephone system, which Knowles considered "so necessary for insuring [sic] full and complete exchange of ideas, comments, and information."[60] In a double-edged gesture of friendship, King sent a personal note of congratulations to Winn upon his promotion to captain. The note included a box containing a set of sterling silver US Navy captain's-rank insignia.[61]

From the Admiralty's perspective, the transatlantic relationship had fallen out of balance with King's navy dominating at sea. Within twenty-four months after 1943, hunter-killer operations in the Atlantic provided the foundations for decisive victory over the enemy—with seventeen enemy surface vessels (fifteen blockade runners and two U-tankers) and the "liquidation" of more than ninety-three Axis submarines (fifty-four by the US Navy).[62] King's lead antisubmarine coordinator in CominCh, Knowles, concluded that the U-tankers were "the pivots which, upon being dislodged, made of B.d.U.'s moving structure a disjointed frame, sagging here, hastily bolstered there, gradually crumbling to inevitable collapse."[63]

The Allied landings on the Normandy coastline coincided with the US Navy hunter-killer operations in the Atlantic, as Nimitz supervised the amphibious offensive of King's navy in the Pacific. King accompanied Marshall and Arnold on a quick tour of the Normandy beachhead. With Nazi snipers at large in the area, the commander of the US Navy amphibious forces, RAdm. Alan G. Kirk, offered a sidearm to King. "Why do I need that," King barked. "Don't you have control here?"[64] King returned from Normandy to Portsmouth to meet with the former head of the BAD, Admiral Sir Charles Little. In memoirs, King specifically referred to Little as a very good "friend."[65] Churchill instead hijacked King—forcibly providing Pol Roger champagne to celebrate the success at Normandy.[66]

High spirits in Normandy temporarily distracted the CCS and JCS from the simultaneous operations of King's navy in the Pacific. He recalled the discussions over a formal celebratory dinner with King George VI at 10 Downing Street on June 14, 1944, during which Churchill "had a great deal to say about everything and was in good form."[67] "He again complained about a new word that everyone was using that he did not understand": King recalled the amusement of King George VI as Churchill lambasted the Americanism "'logistics,' which he rather preferred to call 'supplies.'"[68] King recalled the surreal scene with alcohol flowing and German buzz bombs flying overhead. British spirits ran high when King shared reports from Nimitz about the simultaneous success of operations in the Pacific.

The personality dynamics among American flag officers provided another means for King to influence subordinates. Nimitz had an excellent working relationship with Spruance, although sometimes he struggled with Halsey. Given the complexity of the Pacific front, King likewise harbored his own concerns about Nimitz but had great confidence in Halsey, while characterizing Spruance as "the best flag officer in the Navy in every way."[69] Following the success of Normandy, King increasingly reduced the number of American naval forces in the Atlantic to focus on the decisive phases of the Pacific campaign. As Churchill subjected King to an unrelenting barrage of champagne in Normandy, King turned his focus toward maintaining "unremitting pressure" throughout the Pacific and ashore in Asia.[70]

NOSES OUT OF JOINT

As the troops consolidated the beachhead at Normandy, American naval forces on the other side of the planet seized Saipan. King's aviators also won decisive victory in the air over the Philippine Sea—thereafter the Imperial Japanese Navy never fully recovered in the air. The American Fifth Fleet took Saipan and engaged in the great Marianas "Turkey Shoot" during the Battle of the Philippines Sea in June 1944. Following these successes, however, the deputy commander, Pacific Fleet (Air), VAdm. John H. Towers, accused Spruance of incompetence. Nimitz failed to suppress Towers and his associates in defense of Spruance after the Battle of the Philippines Sea.

Nimitz dutifully reported the divergent opinions of key subordinates in the Pacific, which riled King on the other side of the planet. Deeply frustrated, King flew from Normandy, across the American continent, and beyond to the other side of the planet, to Saipan.[71] King chastised Nimitz for surrounding himself with "too many damned yes men and glory seekers issuing directives in his name[, and] Nimitz just seemed to sort of follow along."[72] King later shared that "a lot of people believed that the brains of the Pacific Fleet was [Rear Admiral] Forrest Sherman."[73] King recalled, "Nimitz would not make a move without asking Sherman."[74]

King maintained continual communications with Nimitz to ensure compliance with operational priorities in the Pacific and an ultimate strategy for Asia. King worried about Nimitz's leadership style. At one point, King nearly lost complete confidence in Nimitz when Towers gossiped about Spruance. Towers sparked rumors among aviators about Spruance being a coward during the Battle of the Philippines Sea.[75] King intervened upon arriving in Saipan on July 17, 1944. King explained, "His first act on stepping ashore was to tell Spruance that he had done exactly the right thing with the Fifth Fleet in the Battle of Philippine Sea, no matter what anyone else might say."[76] King recalled:

> Towers had been in command of Pacific Fleet Aviation, but he was then made a vice admiral and Nimitz made him his deputy for logistics, which Towers didn't like. Nimitz and Towers did not agree about anything. When King went to Saipan, he had to say something to Towers at Nimitz' request, and while King and Towers were driving across the island of Oahu, King said to him, "You have to do the job, and you are the man to do it. Go ahead and do it!" Various friends of King told him that Towers hated Nimitz and vice versa.[77]

"Towers was an able man," King thought, "but hard to work with."[78] More annoyingly, King observed that Nimitz "would frequently use some circumlocution to avoid saying unpleasant things."[79] King dismissed Nimitz as a "fixer."[80] King derided Nimitz for failing to "take appropriate action without first asking permission."[81]

King made his presence known among commanders and their troops close to the frontline action. Having visited Normandy just a few days earlier, King rallied American troops with unannounced appearances in areas still contested on Kwajalein and Saipan. His aide recalled flying over Tinian when Japanese antiaircraft batteries opened fire. Dornin felt uncomfortable when the percussion "shook the hell out of the plane, and it scared me."[82] "I'll never forget." Dornin continued that King had mumbled, "Coming this close, I think, is entirely unnecessary."[83]

The lingering enemy presence on Saipan caused major concern for members of the ComInCh staff. Dornin recalled Japanese snipers picking off nearby American troops on Saipan. However, King outwardly acted unconcerned. King continued wearing his four stars when Nimitz suggested taking them off. Both continued wearing their four-star insignia on their collars during the tour of the front. Dornin recalled the passing jeep: "Dead Japanese soldiers, killed during the banzai attack[, and] all of a sudden, gunfire came whisking by us."[84] "I knew we were being shot at," Dornin complained, and that "I didn't like being shot at."[85] Marine general "Howlin' Mad" Smith accompanied King. "Our cavalcade came dangerously near sniper haunts," Smith later recalled. He added, "Nobody has ever accused Ernie King or Chester Nimitz of a lack of guts, or equilibrium."[86] At that time, King endorsed Smith's decision to fire US Army major general Ralph C. Smith. The decision later sparked serious fights between Marshall and King about the future of the US Marine Corps.[87]

Meetings in Saipan were followed by a sudden surprise diversion to the American submarine bases in the Marshall Islands. Dornin introduced King to his former submarine squadron comrades. As King and Cooke rekindled their connection to the submarine force, Dornin followed along in the entourage. Suddenly, Cooke turned to Dornin and said, "Hey, Dusty, see if you can find a bar and open it up and we'll have a brew or two."[88] Through his submarine connections, Dornin found a bar being run by a seasoned "old chief, who said, Sir, I've got some 100 proof forty-year-old Old Grand Dad [whiskey]. How about having that instead of the lousy green beer we got down here."[89] With Cooke sitting at his side, Dornin noticed King departing in a barge for the airfield. "'Oh, Christ,' we thought," Dornin explained. "When Admiral King arrived in a plane ready to take off, he didn't wait for anybody."[90] Cooke and Dornin quickly finished their drinks and secured a fast launch—just making the flight home.

Dornin recalled that the trip enabled King to make sweeping decisions about the quality of commanders at the front. King returned to the Navy Department and issued a target list. "I want all these squadron commanders that haven't made a war patrol relieved," Dornin remembered King saying. "Frankly I think a lot of them are not too hot."[91] The purpose of the whirlwind inspection tours of the fronts in Europe and Asia centered on debates surrounding the strategy in the Pacific. King applied unremitting pressure on Nimitz—always focusing on the grander prize of victory in Asia through Formosa, as envisioned in the campaign plans for CAUSEWAY and its branch operations along the China coast.[92] Extending this vision, Admirals Willson and Cooke supervised JWPC branch planning for Operation LONGTOM. Spruance and the Fifth Fleet staff envisioned LONGTOM as an amphibious seizure of the Chosun Island group, followed by the seizure of Shanghai in the approaches to the Yangtze River.[93]

King kept American naval planners focused on the coordinated amphibious campaign across the central Pacific to synchronize with efforts in China.[94] Variants of CAUSEWAY and LONGTOM later informed operations during the Chinese Civil War and subsequent conflicts in the region.[95] King always kept the longer strategic view in mind, looking beyond the ultimate Allied victory in anticipation of the requirements for reconstruction. During meetings in Saipan, Spruance and Turner advised King to placate army strategists by scheduling Iwo Jima as the next stepping-stone in the Pacific.[96] Nimitz and Spruance favored the Iwo Jima plan.[97] Spruance further suggested operations to take Okinawa.[98] King relented in allowing Nimitz and Spruance to develop plans for Iwo Jima.[99] China still remained on the far shores for King.

The main effort in Asia centered on enabling the Indigenous forces of China to defeat the Japanese army ashore. King pressed his CominCh staff to focus on Operations RAVENOUS and ANAKIM, augmented by Operation CULVERIN—the amphibious landings by British and other Allied forces in Sumatra. King planned supporting operations against the Andaman Islands with Operation BUCCANEER.[100] Under these plans, King wanted the British to have virtually autonomous command authority in executing combined operations in the Southwest Pacific and into the South China Sea.[101] He wanted to execute Operation CARBONADO—a plan calling for commando raids, aerial strike, and limited amphibious landings to establish a port in China. He later expanded the concept under the Cooke plan code-named Operation BETA.[102] On assignment from CominCh, RAdm. Dan Barbey assisted Nimitz in coordinating these operations.

CominCh staffers overheard King's efforts to promote Nimitz away from the front and into a different role. Sherman was at the top of the list of prospective replacements, although King considered Ingersoll and RAdm. Aubrey Fitch as potential candidates to replace Nimitz in the Pacific.[103] Admirals Edwards and Cooke stopped King from making any rash decisions about Nimitz. On one close call, King summoned Nimitz for a meeting in San Francisco. King then told Edwards to prepare a list of prospective replacements for Nimitz. When King embarked the aircraft, Edwards followed him on board to "hash it out."[104] He recalled that "my wife had no idea that I had inadvertently gone to California with the Admiral."[105] In San Francisco, King received an ultimatum from Forrestal.

Forrestal held King in bureaucratic check in managing the rotation of flag officers and key commanders within the American naval command.[106] Nimitz had also attained popular status as the hero of the Pacific war in the American media, which constrained King. Unable to make the changes desired in the Pacific, King quietly held Nimitz on course by reorganizing the logistical organization on the West Coast. King pushed Nimitz to anticipate operations beyond the oceanic limits of the Pacific to prepare the fleet for sustained operations ashore on the Asian continent. Within the CominCh staff, Bieri supervised Capt. Paul Pihl in framing plans to shake up routines on the Pacific front.[107] Cmdr. Jerauld Wright and Lt. Cmdr. Richard D. Shepard added their expertise.[108] With all the pieces in place by November 1944, King sent Ingersoll from the Atlantic to the Pacific. By placing Ingersoll on the West Coast, King awaited an opportunity to rotate Nimitz.[109]

King failed to request permission in rearranging logistical pathways to the Pacific and beyond to the Asian continent. He filled flag positions on the West Coast and Pacific fleets with trusted agents. For example, RAdm. James L. Kauffman reported to Hawaii to assist planning for the assault on Formosa and following operations into China as the prospective commander, Philippine Sea Frontier. Admirals John H. Hoover and Donald B. Beary followed to assume command in mobile logistics forces tied to the Third and Fifth Fleets. The naval service squadrons and forward bases along the island route across the central Pacific all fell immediately subordinate to Nimitz. All also owed their assignments to King. In reorganizing the Western Sea Frontier to support future operations in Asia, King considered Ingersoll "possibly ahead of Spruance in ability"—telling Ingersoll that "things had gotten all bawled up out there [and] the army just wanted to stockpile everything and the whole machine didn't run right."[110] King reasoned, "I thought Ingersoll could handle it[, but] Ingersoll hated the job and took it as a demotion."[111] King noted that Ingersoll "never came to Washington unless I sent for him [and that] his nose was always out of joint and would buck about this and that."[112]

THROWING A HAYMAKER

King intended to use sea power by establishing coastal logistical hubs to support operations along the China coast. He also intended to limit the footprint of American and other Allied ground forces by enabling the Indigenous armies of continental Asia to fight the Japanese ashore. King knew about the alternative strategy of Marshall and MacArthur, which focused on the Philippines and then the Japanese home islands.[113] Within the CCS and JCS, the differing strategies of King and MacArthur caused significant debate. American commanders on the ground, including Joseph Stilwell and Miles, added their endorsements of King's view.[114] British commanders on the Indian Ocean front, Mountbatten and Somerville, added their endorsements. In addition, Field Marshal William Slim added his support by proposing an offensive to open the Burma Road to China.[115]

Marshall hedged on the maritime strategy of supporting the Indigenous armies of continental Asia against their common Japanese enemy. He was trapped between the logic of King and the hubris of MacArthur. Marshall's chief planning officer, Wedemeyer, sided with King about the China strategy. Wedemeyer surmised, "We would have no difficulties in bringing about an efficient, carefully coordinated employment of American and Chinese forces against the Japanese."[116] He warned Marshall to recognize China as the key to opening other strategic options in the Pacific. In memoirs, Wedemeyer recalled being "eased out to Asia."[117] Marshall sent Wedemeyer on a fact-finding mission to India, which was followed by orders to relieve Stilwell in China by the fall of 1944.[118]

Marshall and King continued debating the merits of the China strategy within the CCS and JCS. Marshall continued acknowledging the MacArthur plan to retake the Philippines, whereas King focused on Formosa.[119] For the sake of fixing Marshall's support for the China strategy, King amplified the authorities of Wedemeyer. King placed Miles, his man in China, under the overall army command of Wedemeyer. Concurrently, King sent Capt. Wilfred Painter on a fact-finding tour of the Asian continent. With King's blessing to do wherever was required to attain the goal, Painter organized what became known as the "Painter Expedition" in June 1944.[120] Painter's presence in China somewhat upset Miles.

Miles and Painter operated separately under King's singular authority, which caused problems among all involved. Miles assumed superiority, since he was a Naval Academy line officer with longer lineal standing. As a civilian expert with an exceptionally fast rise to the rank of captain of the naval reserves, Painter essentially ignored Miles to get the job done. The senior-ranking commander of the Civil Engineer Corps (CEC), Adm. Ben Moreell, sided with Miles. King trumped all and supported Painter. Thus, the SACO organization under Miles and the CEC under Moreell had almost nothing to say about the activities of the Painter expedition. For the mission, Painter did whatever he needed to do under the authority of King. In so doing, Miles and Moreell controlled the resources. Chinese officials supported the Americans but also wondered about Painter's exact connection with the US Naval Group in China.[121]

The Painter expedition along the China coast and Formosa provides clear evidence of King's actual strategy against Japan and the bigger objective of solving the problem of Asia. As a member of the CominCh staff, Painter also operated under King's personal authority.[122] The SACO organization under Miles assisted Painter in completing beach surveys along the coast. Painter also explored key land routes from the beaches to the interior of China.[123] The Painter expedition proceeded in conjunction with the victory at Saipan. Thereafter, King focused on seizing the island chains south of Shanghai. King also envisioned amphibious landings on the Korean Peninsula for the purposes of opening seaports to support the Chinese ground offensive against the Japanese.

King resisted the decision to pursue the amphibious operations against Iwo Jima and then Okinawa. He thought that "Iwo served no useful naval purpose whatsoever[, and] its only value was as a fighter base."[124] In discussions with his team in Saipan, King described MacArthur's drive from the south and into the mountainous jungles of the Philippines as being a "diversion from the main effort in Asia."[125] Unforeseen circumstances influenced King's perspective. First the July 1944 disaster at the Naval Munitions Facility at Port Chicago and then the mutiny of Black American sailors hindered logistical planning for operations against Formosa.[126] At that time, the US Navy lacked procedures for rearming warships at sea. Given its proximity on the island-hopping route to Formosa, King acknowledged the prospective value of Iwo Jima as a forward base for munitions, supply, and floating drydocks. Before leaving Saipan, King approved Nimitz's proposals—and particularly Spruance—to add Iwo Jima to the target list.

Logistics proved decisive for sustained amphibious operations on the maritime battlefields of the Pacific. Buying time to build up the requisite logistical capacity for the drive to Formosa, King took MacArthur's aspirations for the Philippines into consideration during meetings in Saipan and Honolulu. Information provided by the Combat Intelligence Division at CominCh also shaped King's views. Enemy efforts to reinforce Formosa provided clear indication of Japanese expectations in anticipation of future American amphibious operations. As the Japanese focused on Formosa, King used the boxing analogy to explain that "we could deliver the unexpected body blow and then 'knock 'em out.'"[127]

King wanted to focus first on taking islands in the northern Philippines along the maritime route to Formosa. He initially discounted other potential landing spots, like Leyte, as being too far off the central Pacific path to Formosa. Army planners in the JCS and SWPA staffs wanted to focus on a southern route up through the Philippines along the mountainous jungle pathways to Japan. Taking the broader strategic view, King outright discounted the concept as being logistically unsustainable and tactically unnecessary. King also noted the example of the Balkan War of 1912–13 to highlight the problems of multinational command, which inevitably created challenges in supporting logistical requirements among the various foreign forces.[128] Under the circumstances, King encouraged Nimitz to anticipate prospective orders to support MacArthur during their meetings in Saipan and Formosa. Meanwhile, King placed the higher priority on Formosa—and the strategy to support the Indigenous populations of China to carry the burden of defeating the enemy ashore in Asia.[129]

CHAPTER 31
Suicide Is Painless

King set an unrelenting pace globetrotting to various fronts for direct meetings with his commanders. He specifically flew from the Normandy beachhead to meet with Nimitz on the Saipan beachhead for the purposes of outlining the China strategy. King pushed Nimitz to use his influence in avoiding unnecessary operations in the Philippines. In memoirs, King expressed regret for his failure to push this vision more strongly or to "give Nimitz any definite orders."[1] Rather, King simply requested that Nimitz "think the matter over very carefully before he was called upon to speak."[2] Following the meetings with Nimitz and his team, King flew from Hawaii to Washington on July 22, 1944. Two days later, Roosevelt and MacArthur arrived in Honolulu. King later explained that with the "timing of the trip in relation to the Democratic National Convention, [it was] suggested to King that the President wished to emphasize his role as Commander in Chief of the Army and Navy."[3]

Roosevelt's cheerful façade obscured the crippling pain as he traveled along the West Coast for election year events. He had already achieved a lasting place by winning an unprecedented third term. Just three years before, he had fought to earn a fourth term in office with American forces on the offensive on all fronts. Without consulting the JCS in advance, Roosevelt summoned MacArthur and Nimitz to meet in Honolulu. He then shanghaied USS *Baltimore* (CA-68) and sailed to Hawaii—as King flew along the same oceanic route above the Pacific on his return flight to the West Coast. Upon landing in San Francisco, King received a telephone call from Cooke in Hawaii. At that time, King learned that Leahy also arrived with Roosevelt in Hawaii. Asia stood in the balance during the meetings in Honolulu, which King fully understood.[4]

The entire Pacific strategy evolved from the gaming floors of the Naval War College, which centered on the issue of logistics. The overextended supply lines leading to Australia remained vulnerable to enemy forays, whereas the incremental seizure of the central Pacific islands along the path to Formosa enabled King's navy to dominate the enemy. Despite the logic, King understood the political calculus when Roosevelt undercut the JCS—even with Leahy in the room—by going to Hawaii for the pivotal meetings with Nimitz and MacArthur. In memoirs, King later explained that the "President was particularly swayed by MacArthur's appeal to the moral commitments of the United States to the Philippines."[5] Leahy also vexed King by explaining how Nimitz had hedged about the "necessity for occupation of the Manila area [and that] he had sufficient forces to carry out either operation."[6]

Leahy and Nimitz completely failed to do their part in managing Roosevelt's expectations, at least from King's perspective. King gathered information from his other spies in the room.[7] Towers thought that MacArthur dominated the discussions and that "Nimitz wilted like a flower."[8] Cooke tempered his portrayal in saying, "Nimitz made some remark as 'Mr. President, if you want to go into the Philippines rather than Formosa[,] we can work that out.'"[9] Whatever was said in Honolulu, King berated Nimitz for having "that kind of mind to manage personnel [and] promise anything."[10] King described Nimitz as the type of naval officer that "I dislike the most, a fixer."[11] Recalling the debacle in Honolulu, King grumbled that Nimitz "let me down."[12]

Nimitz clearly failed to fight for King's strategy against imperial Japan and the future reconstruction of Asia. Whether or not Nimitz had the obligation to do so shall likely inspire future discussion about the question of his leadership style. Nimitz had the easygoing ability to inspire subordinates. His superior ability to use bureaucratic backchannels also frustrated King.[13] The pair stood on opposite sides of personality extremes, since King's firm approach also inspired success. Close associates recognized King as a "man toward whom no one who knew him felt indifferent [and] aroused either extreme dislike (often mixed with begrudging admiration) or he inspired liking so extreme that his admirers tended to worship the deck he trod."[14]

King's subordinates aimed to please their boss, which sometimes came at a very heavy price. Such pressure took a toll on some of the most trusted among King's men.[15] For example, RAdm. Donald P. Moon committed suicide in August 1944.[16] The incident greatly disappointed King. King recalled how "Moon did an excellent piece of work in the UTAH beach landings."[17] Recognizing the toll taken upon his former assistant in the CominCh headquarters, he said that Moon "was the type of officer who wished to have everything correctly done and was prone to worry."[18] King understood the pressure. King thought that Moon felt overly responsible for the losses sustained under his command. King explained that Moon's responsibilities "weighed so heavily upon him that he took his own life."[19] King recalled with sadness that Moon "had abilities that could have brought him to the top of his profession."[20]

King's subordinates within CominCh headquarters and closer to the front felt the unrelenting pressures of war. The scope of operations required King to make constant visits with subordinate commanders between the various fronts. After Saipan, King stayed briefly in Washington before another transatlantic visit to meet Stark in London and after American forces took Paris. King relied upon updates from Kirk, his man ashore with Patton's forces in Europe. Knowing Marshall's intentions of sending Eisenhower beyond the Rhine into Germany, King also remembered that "General Patton had no intention of sitting on his thumbs."[21]

King preferred to leave the burdens of fighting the continental war in Europe for the Soviets, thereby allowing Anglo-American and French forces to fortify in anticipation of picking up the pieces after the inevitable collapse of the Third Reich. King understood the politics behind the decisions to proceed with land offensives on the various fronts in anticipation of the 1944 election. The image of triumphant Allied armies on the move against the enemy had the added benefit of obscuring underlying problems within the transatlantic alliance.[22]

War Department plans for the occupation of Europe coincided with the Navy Department strategy of attrition in Asia. Knowing the political considerations, King accepted the logic for diverting forces for an election year gesture. He mused that the "attitude of the Filipinos in resisting the Jap[anese] was a factor in the decision to go into the Philippines instead of Formosa."[23] King acknowledged "not only the fighting spirit of the Filipinos but their friendliness to us, where in Formosa, they were all enemies, every last one of them."[24] He knew that the "Japanese were studying our moves as we were studying theirs[, and] they started piling troops into Formosa."[25] Under the circumstances, King observed that the "factor that turned the scale in favor of going into the Philippines first was the resistance of the Filipinos [versus] the hostile characters in Formosa."[26]

War Department plans essentially focused on the major land routes from Australia through the Philippines and north to Japan. Conversely, King followed the maritime logic of Navy Department priorities by focusing on the oceanic lines of communication between the West Coast of America to Asia. King dutifully diverted logistical priorities from supporting the advance to Formosa for the purposes of placing MacArthur ashore in the Philippines.[27] In planning the beachhead operations for Leyte, King changed the subject by telling Marshall that following "land operations for the seizure of Formosa should be an army officer[, and] the amphibious part of such an operation should remain under the command of the navy."[28]

The diversion to the Philippines always appeared in the shadows of King's vision for Formosa and the future reconstruction of Asia. Marshall saw things differently, although King attempted to manipulate the discussion by nominating Gen. Joseph Stilwell and VAdm. Raymond A. Spruance as the key commanders for the future campaign in Asia.[29] King later explained his rationale: "You have to be just as cold blooded as you can be about it—just as there was not enough dividends in a military sense to make us try to land in Norway and push an offensive there, so might it have been in the Philippines."[30]

British aspirations to participate in the Pacific campaign further complicated the planning for operations in the Philippines. The festering problems of command, like those experienced in Europe, similarly influenced efforts to plan amphibious operations involving foreign forces in Asia. Divisions between the CinCPac/PoA of Nimitz and the SWPA of MacArthur also created problems within the MacPac. To avoid future conflict, Nimitz proposed using the 159th east meridian as a line of demarcation between CinCPac/POA and SWPA. This arbitrary geographic reference became known within the US Navy as the "Pope's Line," referring to the old line of demarcation as established centuries ago by Popes Alexander VI and Julius II between the empires of Portugal and Spain under the treaties of Tordesillas and Zaragoza.[31]

King worried about making such clear lines of demarcation between naval and army commanders. He supported Nimitz's recommendation although disliked the idea of allowing MacArthur to have a free rein over naval forces assigned to the SWPA area of operations. King sent RAdm. Dan Barbey and Capt. Wilfred Painter to SWPA for the purposes of evaluating the situation under Kinkaid.[32] Within the context of SWPA, the Seventh Fleet staff under Kinkaid grew bloated with more than 405 personnel—to King's chagrin.[33] Under MacArthur's tactical control, the Seventh Fleet of Kinkaid hung in the balance in the competition between other Allied commanders for control. Kinkaid reported concurrently to Nimitz for operations and, ultimately, to King. Under the established policy, the JCS approved all plans before execution. King expected his subordinate commanders to act first in accordance with the approved provisions of an operational plan. He also expected his commanders to take appropriate action in combat, adapt to the circumstances at hand, and make sound military decisions to defeat the enemy.

WHAT THE HELL???

Intelligence requirements increased the numbers of specialists engaged in crucial analytical work within various naval headquarters ashore.[34] Given the stage upon which CominCh performed, King reluctantly carried a total staff of 625 at a highpoint in the war—the majority being from the WAVES. Staffs created for the temporal purposes of the war drew personnel from the armed services to assist the work of the CCS and JCS.[35] King was dissatisfied with how the "systems of command [were] placed in effect to meet a specific condition imposed by the characteristics of the current situation in the theater of operations."[36] He further clarified, "It is important to realize that there can be no hard[-]and[-]fast rule for setting up commands in the field."[37] King noted that "integration and unification characterized every amphibious operation [entered on] paramount capability."[38]

Through intelligence, King fully understood the Japanese strategy to defend Formosa and the Philippines. Americans operating with Filipino guerrilla forces captured a copy of the imperial Japanese "Z-Plan," which provided full details of the enemy's perspective.[39] Among other veterans of the CominCh staff, Cmdr. George H. Laird maneuvered USS *Blackfin* (SS-322) in direct support of operations under Miles in China. Laird secured recently captured Japanese codes and ciphers. Given the persistent surveillance of US Navy forces in China, Miles and Laird indirectly contributed to the American plans for the Philippines—providing queuing information about the locations of Imperial Japanese Navy forces.[40]

Special intelligence sources confirmed the authenticity of the captured Japanese plan. Under the circumstances, the JCS hastened the schedule for operations to establish a foothold in Luzon in the Philippines. Within the Pacific Section of CominCh, Sebald characterized the Luzon operation as having the primary objective of putting MacArthur ashore, attrite imperial Japanese naval forces in Philippine waters, and ultimately set the stage for taking Formosa.[41] The JCS delegated planning for these operations to the staffs of Nimitz and MacArthur in developing joint schemes for the amphibious operations in the Philippines and Formosa.[42]

King always kept Formosa on the top of the list of strategic priorities within the CominCh headquarters. Edwards ran the staff as Cooke supervised the operational planning teams under Capt. Ralph F. Good, serving as the F-31 in the CominCh headquarters. His planners mimicked the Combat Intelligence Division, with the F-31A being associated with Knowles's F-21 Atlantic Section and the F-31P working in close collaboration with Sebald in the F-22 Pacific Section.[43] In anticipation of the drive across the Rhine and the simultaneous assaults on Luzon, King injected fresh blood into the planning efforts within CominCh headquarters in the summer of 1944.

REPORT IMMEDIATELY COMINCH

King avoided bureaucratic stagnation by rotating personnel with recent combat experience from the front to the CominCh headquarters. Among others, he arranged orders for his leading intelligence officer, Smith-Hutton, to assume command as commodore of Destroyer Squadron 14. Much to his surprise, Smith-Hutton received a Legion of Merit for establishing the Combat Intelligence Division and by demonstrating "highly specialized knowledge, together with his effective plans for the prompt dissemination of intelligence."[44] Smith-Hutton essentially invented the Combat Intelligence Division.

Having served on shore duty for nearly a decade, however, Smith-Hutton's chances for promotion seemed bleak. For this reason, King personally arranged for Smith-Hutton to receive command of a cruiser division in the Pacific within weeks preceding the Luzon operation. In this capacity, Smith-Hutton attained the temporary title—along with an acting rank—of commodore.

King failed to coordinate the assignments of individuals for whom he had taken a personal interest in managing the rotations among key positions within the CominCh headquarters. On his personal authority, King transmitted the message to RAdm. Robert W. Hayler—ordering the immediate detachment of his chief of staff in Cruiser Division 12, Smedberg. Upon receiving the summons from CominCh, Hayler requested clarification by noting Smedberg's key role in preparing for the upcoming Philippines campaign. King simply responded, "SMEDBERG TO REPORT IMMEDIATELY COMINCH."[45] Smedberg explained, saying that "I was in a boat within a couple of hours, in a big PBM shortly thereafter[,] and hitch-rode my way to Washington in a variety of freak rides, part of it on top of a cargo of aircraft engines." He recalled, "When I reported to Admiral King's office three days later, I asked the dumbfounded flag secretary, George Russell, what it was all about."[46] Russell suggested that the "old man must have written the dispatch himself."[47] "What took you so long to get here?" King barked as Smedberg entered the office. He responded, "I thought I had broken all records."[48]

Smedberg initially struggled to understand King's personality and his seemingly distant leadership style. As a member of the Class of 1926, Smedberg had dated King's neighbor Nan Ferrell. Many decades later, Smedberg recalled that King had a reputation among midshipmen at the time as a "'garter snatcher' because of his under[-]the[-]table work."[49] Smedberg tempered his characterization that King "had a wife, six, daughters[,] and [a son] who I never met in all the years I knew him[, but] with a brood like that, I guess that qualifies him as a lady's man."[50] Working in close quarters, Smedberg increasingly admired King's unique style of command. Personnel assigned to CominCh pulled together like a well-oiled bureaucratic machine—King's style matching that of the fabled "Nelson touch."[51]

Smedberg had mentally prepared himself for combat in anticipation of the Philippines Campaign. He felt deeply disappointed about the assignment to CominCh. Having reported from the Pacific in 1944, Smedberg recalled sitting in a morning CominCh staff briefing. Still suffering from the time zone changes, Smedberg realized that "I was the only one present in khaki: all the others were in the King Grey that I detested." Continuing, he said, "Savvy Cooke took me aside and said, Smeddy, have you noted the Admiral's look when he sees your khaki." Cooke warned that it "won't be long until King explodes."[52] Given fair warning, Smedberg purchased a navy-gray uniform "off the rack" to avoid King's wrath.[53] Struggling to understand the reasoning for his assignment to the CominCh staff, Smedberg considered himself a "fish out of water."[54]

King had good reason to dragoon Smedberg from the Pacific front for duty on the Washington battlefield. Smedberg had participated in staff discussions with Royal Navy counterparts in the Eastern Fleet for British operations in the South China Sea. In anticipation of British forces arriving in the Pacific, King withdrew US naval forces from SWPA for rest and refits in anticipation of operations under development for the central Pacific. Smedberg worked closely with Sebald to study the Z-Plan in detail to deduce the most likely enemy response to the invasion of the Philippines. Given all these factors, King directed Nimitz to seize all opportunities to fix the Japanese fleet in a final decisive battle. With the earlier Battle of Philippines Sea providing additional context, Nimitz directed Halsey to support the landings at Luzon, with the caveat "In case opportunity for [the] destruction of major portion of enemy fleet is offered or can be created, such destruction becomes the primary task."[55]

The task of delivering MacArthur to the beaches at Leyte served the primary political purpose of the Roosevelt administration. The propaganda value of picturing MacArthur with wet pants on the beaches of Luzon provided opportunity to reset the conversation about the future strategy in the Pacific.[56] Once again, propaganda interests overshadowed the true objectives in Asia.[57] Coincident with the Philippines campaign, Forrestal forced King to assign Smedberg to handle the public-affairs strategy. Smedberg explained, "I was called to the CominCh's office one day, to find a very red-faced Ernie King in his inner office, apparently angry at a calm Secretary of the Navy."[58] Smedberg saw King give "one of the looks that caused naval officers near-heart failure, but which effected [sic] Mr. Forrestal not a whit, and said, aye-aye sir—he will do it."[59]

Smedberg carried the double-duty burdens of handling classified information in the Combat Intelligence Division while providing daily unclassified briefings to the press during the operations at Leyte Gulf. Smedberg felt "aghast," saying, "I was privy to every single item of intelligence of, and from, the enemy[, and I] was the last officer in the US Navy who could possibly carry out such an assignment."[60] Smedberg left "in about as depressed a mood as I have ever felt."[61] He wondered, "How in the world I, whose 16–24-hour-a-day effort was devoted to enemy intelligence and probably intentions, could possibly deal with the press."[62]

Behind closed doors, King provided an unseen hand on the propaganda front by engaging the Arlington County Commandos. Sharing details with journalists with a beer in hand, King dramatically surprised his audience after looking at his watch and declaring, "Gentlemen, in forty minutes we will be landing on the beach at Leyte and starting to retake the Philippines."[63] King saw the opportunity to seize the quick publicity victory of putting MacArthur ashore in Leyte.[64] King's primary target for the Philippines centered on fixing the Imperial Japanese Navy in a decisive battle.[65]

Putting MacArthur ashore provided the propaganda victory, whereas the carnage unfolding in the waters surrounding Leyte proved King's strategic concerns about the long logistical diversion to the Philippines. In briefings with the media, Smedberg wryly commented, "One of the worst moments of my life [as] I was explaining the decoy force which had drawn Halsey and his carriers to the north, away from San Bernadino and Surigao Straits, I mentioned the 'old battleships' *Ise* and *Hyuga*." Smedberg recalled:

Admiral King interrupted me, turned to the other Chiefs[,] and said that Captain Smedberg was quite new in his job; that the two battleships *Ise* and *Hyuga* were new, powerful ships. I thought a long, hard few moments about whether to let Admiral King leave a wrong statement with his contemporaries, or to correct him. I finally said it was the Admiral who was mistaken . . . King pierced me with that frigid look of his and said, "Proceed[,] Captain Smedberg."[66]

After the briefing, Smedberg recalled sitting at his desk, "awaiting the guillotine."[67] A few hours later, King called Smedberg into his chambers. "I have never stood more rigidly at attention before his desk awaiting sentence," he recalled. King "merely said, 'I have checked *Ise* and *Hyuga* [and I] was mistaken—you were correct, but god help you if you ever correct me again without being 100% correct."[68] The lead planner in CominCh, Cooke, later told Smedberg that "you are a lucky man in that you apparently caught the admiral in just the right mood!"[69] Smedberg thought highly of King in noting that a "lesser man would have crucified me."[70]

WITNESS TO THE CRUCIFIXION

King was at the nexus between strategy and tactical command in coordinating operations with intelligence. He articulated his strategic desires and allowed subordinates to carry the responsibility for planning operations. His CominCh staff provided the information required for tactical commanders to act with intelligence at the front. Before the landings at Leyte, the Americans held all the advantages. Armed with a complete copy of the Japanese Z- Plan, Sebald added to the intelligence picture by monitoring intercepted enemy communications. Special intelligence revealed the latest updates to the Japanese strategy.[71] From the CominCh perspective, Sebald recalled, "We had that entire [Japanese] plan—so there was no question but that the Third Fleet, Halsey, had this plan."[72]

The Americans knew the enemy's strategy for defending the waters surrounding the Philippines and Formosa. Within the context of operations in Leyte Gulf, Halsey carried the radio call sign of commander, Third Fleet—but he was not acting in that capacity while operating in support of the officer in tactical command (OTC) of the main effort. Rather, he operated as the subordinate commander of Task Force 38—falling in support of the landing forces of the Seventh Fleet, under Kinkaid. Both Halsey and Kinkaid had full knowledge of the Japanese plan.[73] The flow of intelligence from the highest pinnacles of command within the CominCh headquarters in Washington, the CinCPac headquarters in Hawaii, and the tactical commanders at the front had also matured into an efficient machine.[74]

Between the CominCh and JICPAC headquarters, Sebald traded information with Layton in direct communications. Through the "HICom" and "X-Com" circuits, Sebald and Layton maintained close communications with the individual numbered-fleet intelligence officers at the front. Sebald and Layton shared the same information as their friend on the Third Fleet staff, Cmdr. Marion "Mike" Cheek. In recalling the Battle of Leyte Gulf, Sebald kept in constant contact with the key fleet intelligence officers at the scene. He explained that the "principal ones with whom I communicated were [Captain Edward] Layton and [Commander Jaspar] Holmes at CinCPac, [Commander Arthur] McCollum in the Seventh Fleet[, and] the intelligence officers of the Third [Cheek] and Fifth Fleets [Commander Charles H. Murphy]."[75]

All the numbered-fleet intelligence officers had served in the CominCh headquarters with King at the Navy Department. Thus, they had a good understanding of King's expectations as they faced the enemy in combat.[76] All the major commanders, including MacArthur and Nimitz, had full knowledge of the Japanese plan. All the key task force commanders, including Kinkaid and Halsey, had the same information. Ultimately, the purpose of the operations centered on MacArthur wading ashore to declare, "I have returned."[77] True to form, MacArthur claimed personal credit for the landings at Leyte. Meanwhile, the Japanese navy provided the ideal opportunity for Halsey to secure complete maritime supremacy by maneuvering against the Leyte beachhead.

Following the landings at Leyte, members of the CominCh staff witnessed King's anger about MacArthur's treatment of sailors on the scene. He refused to put soldiers on the job of offloading supplies. King received a report that MacArthur "in his high-handed manner refused to 'demean' his numerous troops by having them assist in the unloading."[78] Messages transmitted between King and the commanders at the front in Leyte fail to reflect significant difficulty after MacArthur shifted from the flagship to advanced headquarters ashore.[79] Recalling the CominCh headquarters perspective in Washington, Lt. Cmdr. Richard D. Shepard recalled drafting a personal message from King to MacArthur saying, "Unless you so order and provide troop labor under your command for unloading ships filled with supplies for forces operating under you within the next twelve hours, I will order all ships to sea immediately to provide much[-]needed supplies for other scheduled operations."[80]

From King's perspective, the landings at Leyte were a large-scale raid to divert the enemy from reinforcing positions in Formosa. For King, the liberation of the Philippines held secondary importance to the primary objective in the Pacific—the final destruction of the Imperial Japanese Navy. The destruction of enemy naval capability enabled all other strategic contingencies from King's perspective.[81] With MacArthur safely ashore at Leyte, American naval commanders became restless. Chomping at the bit, King's salt horse on the Pacific front—Halsey—seized the opportunity to meet the enemy in decisive fleet engagement to destroy the Imperial Japanese Navy. Demonstrating sound military decision-making under difficult circumstances, Halsey took the opportunity to destroy the enemy fleet once and for all.[82]

SWALLOWING THE BAIT

The CominCh staff in Washington monitored communications to plot the locations of friendly and enemy forces at Leyte. Within the headquarters, the situation at Leyte unfolded like a sports tournament—with observers keeping score.[83] Sebald recalled watching the WAVES moving the pins, with the Japanese plan pinned to the wall. Sebald stated in horror, "My god, I hope Halsey doesn't swallow the bait and go north."[84] Another CominCh staffer reassured Sebald that Halsey "wouldn't be that foolish."[85] Sebald described the tension building among the Combat Intelligence Division analysts: "We were also pulling our hair out when we saw that Halsey was heading north."[86] Sebald reasoned, "Everyone in authority, certainly above me[,] had available to them [the Japanese plan] and I made no effort to go to my boss [Smedberg] or to Admiral King or to Admiral Cooke." "I knew it would be considered as interfering with operations," Sebald recalled. "In any event it was routine procedure to transmit all operational intercepts of this kind to CinCPac."[87]

King monitored the worldwide situation with American naval forces decisively engaged in the battles simultaneously unfolding off the Philippines. Tensions among his staff ran particularly high as they tried to confirm the newspaper headlines about the apparent death of German field marshal Erwin Rommel. Meanwhile, Patton's Third Army drove into the heart of the Nazi heartland—with American troops marching in the streets of Metz. The strategic-bombing campaign in Europe continued, although air force planners increasingly complained about lacking suitable targets. Perhaps ironically, Hap Arnold voiced his support for King's ongoing focus on taking Formosa for the purposes of expanding the strategic-bombing campaign in Asia. Setting the stage for the Philippines, American long-range bombers struck the Japanese strongholds from Okinawa to Iwo Jima and along the shores of Formosa. These operations unfolded in conjunction with sweeping naval task group raids against the same targets.

The global strategic offensive provided the broader framework for King to focus on the Leyte beachhead, which stood out on the CominCh war room charts like a giant bull's eye. Analysts in Washington kept King fully apprised as Nimitz monitored from Hawaii. The Seventh Fleet of Kinkaid focused on fixing the logistical problems ashore—with MacArthur pushing troops forward and expanding the beachhead. Halsey appeared in message traffic by his callsign, "Third Fleet," although Kinkaid had responsibility for the overall operation. Halsey served in the supporting role as commander of Task Force 38. Kinkaid failed to respond when Halsey announced intentions to steam northward against the Japanese, which he fully understood as being an essentially unarmed decoy force.[88]

Intelligence supremacy lulled the Americans into a false sense of security about the situation at Leyte. During the unfolding battle, Sebald exchanged messages with Layton in Hawaii. Just as King's men kept the plots updated in Washington, Nimitz and Spruance monitored the battle with the Fifth Fleet intelligence officer, Cmdr. Charles Murphy, in Hawaii.[89] The fluidity of combat at the front outpaced the intelligence reflected in the headquarters plotting rooms in Hawaii and Washington.[90]

King followed the strategic rule of allowing commanders at the scene to make decisions on their own—with full authority to adapt to unforeseen tactical circumstances. Nimitz initially followed the same rule, as Spruance provided play-by-play analysis in Hawaii. Messages among the commanders at the scene in Leyte indicated no significant surprises. Knowing the personalities, Spruance pointed at the San Bernardino Strait. Nimitz acknowledged Spruance when Spruance stated, "If I were there I would keep my force there."[91] In contrast, Halsey preferred to maneuver against the enemy rather than running back and forth for no particular reason other than to guard the straits.

The tactical commanders on the scene at Leyte had the same information as King and Nimitz. Halsey monitored the three pincers of the imperial Japanese naval forces, which conformed to the Z-Plan. King had directed Nimitz to seize opportunities to destroy the enemy fleet. In turn, Nimitz also understood the Philippines to be a diversion in the grander plan to take Formosa.[92] The naval commanders on scene, Kinkaid and Halsey, also understood the strategy. Within the context of tactical operations, Kinkaid focused on his immediate responsibility to supply MacArthur's troops ashore. Thus, Halsey transmitted fair warning to all the major commanders at the scene in advance of maneuvering against an enemy force—known by all to be a decoy.[93] Sailing with Halsey on the flagship, *New Jersey*, Cheek worried about the chances for an enemy surprise. Cheek dutifully articulated his concerns to Halsey.[94]

Cheek's intuition proved correct after a series of unconnected accidents and confused orders among the Japanese forces. The Japanese uncharacteristically broke from their Z-Plan, and the battleships of the imperial Japanese fleet steamed into a surprised American force, which put up a vicious defense. With Halsey driving northward, the Americans were suddenly out of position to engage the enemy at Leyte Gulf.[95] The shocking losses sustained among the American forces in the battles off Samar—with simultaneous melees in the Sibuyan Sea and Surigao Strait—became known in the singular as the Battle of Leyte Gulf.[96] After the battle, Nimitz reported that it "never occurred to me that Halsey, knowing the composition of the ships in the Sibuyan Sea, would leave the San Bernardino Strait unguarded."[97]

King was absolutely dumbfounded, particularly after the message Nimitz transmitted to Halsey and the other commanders at the scene in which the damning phraseology seemed perfectly designed to cause trouble.[98] In the heat of battle, Nimitz transmitted a message, of which all the major world commanders received a copy, asking for Halsey's actual location in proximity to Surigao Straits. Controversy followed when Nimitz's staff included the seemingly meaningless phrase that the "WORLD WONDERS TURKEY TROTS TO WATER." Halsey misunderstood the message from Nimitz as a personal insult. Whether by accident or design, Nimitz humiliated Halsey with a few meaningless words. From afar, King was very angry with Nimitz for making matters worse by inserting himself into the message traffic of the battle. Summarizing the postmortem conclusions on the Battle of Leyte Gulf, King observed, "Halsey had fixed ideas about what the Japanese were doing."[99] King vindicated Halsey because "he thought the strikes on the Japanese in the Sibuyan Sea had caused them to quit, and he could go up north—we knew they had three or four carriers somewhere—to make a killing."[100]

THE TRAFALGAR OF KING'S NAVY

American naval forces scored a decisive victory against the Imperial Japanese Navy during the melee at Leyte. Intelligence supremacy provided means for King's navy to anticipate the strategic intentions of the enemy. Conversely, knowing enemy plans also influenced American naval commanders to become overconfident in their estimate of the situation on many occasions in the war at sea. Always worried about the element of chance, King joined Halsey in guessing that the enemy might "do what they had done at Guam."[101] Nimitz made similar assumptions from afar. Armed with the Japanese plan, Halsey fixated on destroying the "decoy force."[102]

After the battle, King began making preliminary moves to promote Nimitz to a future assignment away from the front. King sent Ingersoll to the West Coast in November 1944, explaining, "It's a hard job you've got[, and] if anything happens to Nimitz you will be in line for that command."[103] King allowed Nimitz to stand in the limelight of victory after the Battle of Leyte Gulf. Working the lines through the Arlington County Commandos of the media, King quietly vindicated Halsey by observing that Kinkaid and the forces of Seventh Fleet "had failed to take reasonable precaution that would have discovered the approach of the Japanese Central Force."[104] King blamed losses sustained by brave US Navy destroyer sailors off Samar on "Kinkaid's failure to use his own air squadrons for search at a critical moment."[105] King told his chief of staff, Edwards, that the "answer is simple[; the] Japanese were not observed because nothing was done except to send out two so-called 'snoopers' through the all-important area, or if any other escort planes were sent they didn't go in the proper (or correct) direction."[106]

King grew particularly annoyed with Kinkaid about the whole controversy surrounding Halsey's actions off the San Bernardino Straits. King thought that Kinkaid made matters worse on purpose. Halsey had fired Kinkaid during the Guadalcanal Campaign two years earlier. King thought that Kinkaid unnecessarily undercut Halsey at Leyte Gulf. "From all the available information that I have gleaned," King wrote to Kinkaid,

I have to conclude that, except for the five patrol planes available as "snoopers," no proper orders were given by you to say of the three escort carrier groups to search the whole area of the Sibuyan Sea down through the rest of the important strait to the entrance of the open sea. Had such planes been on "search" even only from the earliest dawn, such planes could not have missed the Japanese "middle" group if it were there[,] or could have remained aloft long enough to report nothing important was to be seen. With your kindly help, I'll have to let the matter drop unless more information should become available. I'm sorry to seem so insistent on these points[,] but they are rather important to understanding what happened the night of October 24–25, 1944.[107]

Attempting to explain his decisions, Kinkaid wrote a long and detailed letter to King. "I believe Halsey made a serious mistake," Kinkaid explained. "I regret that he did not acknowledge it [given] his shabby references to me." "I have refused to be drawn into a controversy on the subject," Kinkaid explained, "because no good can come of it."[108]

Reputations became the focus as the world wondered about key decisions by commanders at the scene in the aftermath of the Battle of Leyte Gulf. Halsey's trusted friend and intelligence officer, Cheek, made the correct assumptions about Japanese movements. Later, Halsey recommended Cheek for the Legion of Merit for service at Leyte. Halsey shepherded Cheek to attain promotion to the rank of a reserve rear admiral. Halsey's friendship with Cheek continued to flourish long after the Battle of Leyte Gulf. Many myths have since appeared around Halsey's decisions at Leyte, including those spun many decades after the fact by Ens. Carl Solberg. As a very inexperienced young officer without detailed knowledge of special intelligence, Solberg's recollections must be understood as having been formulated over many decades after the fact.[109] Like other great naval actions in history, Halsey's reasoned decisions at Leyte Gulf have instead been lambasted by armchair admirals and airpower propagandists as the "Battle of Bull's Run."[110]

CHAPTER 32
The Devil's Language

China became more problematic for King's navy, under the setting sun of imperial Japan in the Pacific. Immediately following the Battle of Leyte Gulf, King explained his perspective to trusted journalists, over a six-pack of beer. He also highlighted the purpose behind subsequent operations under Halsey. Tales of glory mesmerized the journalists, as King spoke about roving aircraft carrier strikes ongoing in the western Pacific and along the Asian coast. The pathway to Formosa and beyond seemed clear. King explained how American sailors embraced their mission to "haul ass with Halsey."[1] Always driving close to the wind, Halsey pushed his forces to the brink in achieving maximum results. King applauded Halsey's hard-driving approach. From King and down to Nimitz, all hands recognized Halsey as a commander willing to do whatever was necessary to kill the enemy.

Halsey embraced his popular image as a salt-encrusted warrior, which likewise inspired the sailors under his command. In executing this task in the winter of 1944, weather forecasts failed to change the operational timelines for Nimitz's CinCPAC/POA headquarters. Turning into the winds of war, Halsey maneuvered from the China coast and plotted a course to meet Spruance for turnover in December 1944. Weather forecasts transmitted from Saipan and Hawaii indicated the probable presence of a major typhoon. Under the operational circumstances, Halsey acted with the information he had in driving forward through the storm. As a result, American forces suffered major damage—with three warships sunk and many others damaged, with an estimated toll of 790 sailors. Typhoon COBRA became known as "Halsey's Typhoon" in popular memory.[2]

Per Navy regulations, Nimitz was required to conduct a formal investigation after the damages sustained by the American fleet. He attended the proceedings held in Ulithi. As the one who was most responsible for operations in the Pacific area, Nimitz shared in the outcome of the investigation into Halsey's decisions. Operational requirements for the upcoming landings at Luzon stood out as a major factor. Halsey kept the wartime mission at the center of focus and, in the process, followed the old and widely accepted naval tradition of weathering the storm. Nimitz once again took his place in the backdrop when his subordinate Halsey faced the ramifications of war.

Readers grew weary of the war and the heavy casualty figures associated with the loss of warships in combat. Headlines about ships foundering in stormy seas sometimes drew attention in peacetime. Back in Washington, King was fit to be tied about Typhoon COBRA. King's aides Whitehill and Dornin remembered when Halsey suddenly appeared in the vestibule outside King's office in the CominCh headquarters. Dornin explained that King summoned Halsey without filtering the message through the staff. Dornin recalled that Halsey arrived from Ulithi in his gray navy uniform "in a short time, believe me, a very short time."[3] After a brief exchange, Dornin escorted Halsey into King's lair. Dornin remembered King scolding Halsey. Many years later, Dornin mused, "Talk about reprimands, bawling outs [and] boy, it was insulting, not foul, but the devil's language[, and I] never heard anything in the world like it."[4]

King subjected Halsey to an epic tongue-lashing session for the cumulative series of decisions culminating in unnecessary losses. King still recognized Halsey as the type of naval officer who knew how to win. Dornin recalled that "King was very fond of Halsey."[5] Letting the past fade into memory, King invited Halsey to join him at a reception held at the Army and Navy Club in Washington. King held a glass of sherry and Halsey had a stiff drink in his hand when they were pictured together in American newspapers. Both appeared very confident about the future. King's navy had essentially won the war in 1944. The gradual influence of British and American sea power appeared sufficient to ensure an inevitable collapse of Germany and Japan. Looking outward to 1945, King regarded Soviet and Chinese ground forces as the primary means to win ashore in Europe and Asia. He hoped to avoid unnecessary losses through the cumulative victory of British and American sea power.

APPALACHIAN SACRIFICES

Maritime strategy afloat and aloft occasionally conflicted with the continental focus of military operations ashore. British and American naval units frequently intermixed with army commands ashore in Europe and Asia. Although Anglo-American forces spoke in similar terms, their procedures and doctrinal routines often failed to correspond during operations at the front. In the fall of 1944, King arranged orders for Adm. Ghormley to transfer from the Pacific to address problems of combined command in anticipation of reconstruction operations ashore in occupied Germany. In this role, he supervised forces falling under the broad tactical control of Cmdre. Henry Schade in Europe.[6] As the war lingered across the Rhine, King also began shifting forces from Europe for operations ongoing in Asia.

The naval campaign in the Indian Ocean influenced the focus of operations, since the sea lines of communication in the region provided the connections to oil and other critical resources required for the reconstruction of Europe and Asia.[7] King had provided direct intelligence support through his representative to Mountbatten and the SEAC, Comdr. Clark Lawrence Green.[8] Having assisted Cooke as a planning officer in the CominCh headquarters, Green advised British naval forces during Operations COCKPIT and TRANSOM. Green embarked with Royal Navy admiral Sir Bruce Fraser in the Eastern Fleet after Somerville left for duty in Washington to preside with the BAD.[9] For Christmas in 1944, King uncharacteristically participated in a welcome party with cocktails and holiday music to welcome Somerville to the Navy Department. Working together, Somerville and King supervised the plans of subordinate headquarters to unify the efforts of British task forces operating with the numbered fleets of King's navy in the Pacific in the spring of 1945.

King fully supported the introduction of Royal Navy forces by setting clear lines of demarcation between Allied commands in Asia. The First Sea Lord, Cunningham, fought fire with fire by accusing King of having "a rooted antipathy to placing United States naval forces under British command, though he raised no objection to British forces and units being under United States command wherever he thought it fit and proper."[10] Intermixing naval forces under a coherent organization, elements of the British Pacific Fleet fell in with US naval forces of Fifth Fleet to take key objectives along the route to Formosa.

Spruance begrudgingly accepted the presence of Allied warships by stipulating clear delineations between foreign task forces and US naval areas of responsibility. Knowing the difficulties of managing mixed forces, King invited his old friend Admiral Roger Keyes, 1st Baron Keyes of Zeebrugge and Dover, to assist Spruance in planning the seizure of Luzon. As a liaison, Keyes embarked the amphibious command ship USS *Appalachian* (AGC-1) to coordinate the assault on Luzon. Given his experience in organizing combined British and American commando forces, Keyes offered a seasoned hand in fusing Anglo-American forces at the front. He later died from complications associated with smoke inhalation after a Japanese kamikaze struck *Appalachian*.

When Keyes succumbed to his injuries, King also lost a very good ally in his ongoing campaign to carry the Pacific strategy ashore in Asia. The old China hands of the Anglo-American navies understood where King wanted to go in anticipation of the continental battles in Asia. Like-minded British naval officers helped King's campaign for Asia in the swampy fog of the wartime battlefield in Washington. Having recently served with US naval forces in the Pacific, Royal Navy commander Stephen W. Roskill assisted Somerville in planning the anticipated operations of the British Pacific Fleet. He reported to the BAD while recovering from wounds suffered during the Solomon Islands campaign. In combined operations with the US Navy, Roskill offered firsthand experience as the former skipper in the light cruiser HMNZS *Leander*. Wartime service with the BAD later influenced Roskill in describing the character of Anglo-American collaboration in war at sea.[11]

The spirit of collaboration took root as King's navy combined the traditions of Britannia with the innovations of her American cousins. Members of BAD in Washington celebrated the arrival of Somerville there. Roskill observed that Somerville used "his peculiar brand of bawdy humor, and his repartee heavily laden with obscenities, tedious and overdone, he [proved] the most successful of all British Admirals in handling 'Ernie' King."[12] Somerville supported King on the question of control as Royal Navy forces assembled in Australia for following operations into the Pacific.[13] At the same time, King advised Nimitz with wry humor that the British "are not accustomed to speaking American."[14]

King's navy blockaded Axis forces in Asia while seeking decisive battle against the Imperial Japanese Navy. To these ends, King assisted the British by delivering US Army forces to help keep oil pipelines flowing in greater Persia. Sailing under the Royal Navy ensign, US naval assets enabled simultaneous offensive operations in the greater Indian Ocean area. The ship that had been constructed as USS *Altamaha* (ACV-6) was rechristened as HMS *Battler*, and the British drew from American methods to suppress enemy submarines operating in the Indian Ocean. King dispatched USS *Saratoga* (CV-3) to support the combined offensive strikes against enemy forces in striking Japanese targets in the area surrounding Java. Sailing together with Australian and Dutch submarines, US Navy submarines in the Malacca Strait cleared routes from the Indian Ocean into the Southwest Pacific to support operations between Singapore to Indochina.

!!! ??? ***

China stood out as the key to victory against Japan and as the primary foundation for lasting peace in Asia. Early in the war, King established forward outposts under Miles at Chungking. King empowered Miles to operate at his discretion under the immediate authority of ComInCh to foster collaboration among the Chinese forces—rallying efforts to fix the Japanese in a war of attrition in continental Asia. In addition, Miles and his forces set key foundations for US Army Air Forces to conduct long-range operations against the Japanese home islands. Generals Stilwell and Chennault worked very closely with Miles to coordinate clandestine offensive operations ashore in Asia. Among this colorful cast of American characters, Miles had special notoriety for superimposing the "What the Hell" logo (or alternatively, "!!! ??? ***") over the blue-sun insignia of the Kuomintang with the US Navy eagle insignia.[15]

Miles developed a very sophisticated intelligence collection and weather-reporting organization ashore on the Asian continent that directly influenced naval operations in the Pacific.[16] SACO provided immediate assistance to Chiang in operations against the Japanese in China. Miles provided similar assistance to the Communist forces of Mao Tse Tung.[17] Yet, Miles struggled to retain control over the naval forces of SACO following Wedemeyer's expansion of OSS operations on the ground in Asia. The friction between Wedemeyer and Miles in China fueled problems between Marshall and King, which then extended to Churchill and Roosevelt.[18] Staunchly anticommunist and highly critical of the Roosevelt administration, Wedemeyer accused Miles of sympathizing with Maoist forces.[19] Wedemeyer and Miles traded indirect insults in their parallel complaints to Marshall and King. Wedemeyer accused Miles of being too close to the Chinese. In addition, Wedemeyer suspected Mao of murdering British and American prisoners for the purpose of discrediting Chiang.[20]

Miles criticized Wedemeyer for failing to ban American servicemen from indulging themselves in brothels on US Army facilities in China. Early in the development of SACO, Miles placed heavy restrictions on American sailors in China.[21] Marshall and King agreed to send Cooke to inspect the situation in China. He flew around the planet to India, then traversed the Himalayas into China. Cooke arrived at the SACO base camp at "Happy Valley" for meetings with Wedemeyer and Miles.[22] Cooke met the key Chinese leaders, including Chiang and Dai Li. Mao sent representatives to meet with Cooke. Wedemeyer and Miles disagreed about the chain of command ashore in China. Capt. Wilfred Painter also provided an estimate of the situation.[23]

As an indication of their intentions on the Asian continent, King empowered Painter to act on the authority of ComInCh to collect the requisite information for future operations into China. In June 1944, King launched the so-called Painter expedition to survey prospective amphibious landing locations, port facilities, railroads, interior waterways, and roads. Painter and his teams also collected images of fortified enemy positions, airfields, and communications targets. Painter mapped the locations of Chinese "puppet armies," which frequently included turncoats and guerrilla forces operating on whatever side happened to be winning in the moment. Above all, Painter provided clear information about the overlapping interests and dynamics of personality, which influenced problems within the command organization among Allied forces ashore in China.[24]

Painter's report influenced King to reconsider the command organization for naval operations ongoing ashore and in Chinese waters. Wedemeyer and Miles struggled for strategic control, as all operations hinged on enabling the Indigenous forces to fight the battle against Japan. Having pioneered efforts under SACO, Miles also considered Wedemeyer unqualified to make decisions concerning efforts to prepare for future amphibious operations. In turn, Wedemeyer thought that Miles failed to understand the bigger picture in Asia. Wedemeyer further accused Miles of becoming too close with the local Chinese leaders Chiang and Dai Li. In addition, Wedemeyer thought that Miles failed to recognize Mao as the future threat. Wedemeyer characterized Mao's strategy as "Chinese Communists were simply engaged in raiding the Japanese [and] played the role of jackal or hyena against the wounded and suffering Chinese elephant who would not submit to his enemy."[25]

Mao's forces assassinated supporters of Chiang and Dai Li, who responded by arranging the arrests and untimely disappearances of suspected Chinese Communist sympathizers. Both Mao and Chaing indulged in betraying individuals suspected of holding divided loyalties to the imperial Japanese.[26] Mao's guerrilla tactics provided sufficient disarray within the enemy interior lines, which enabled Chiang's conventional military operations. Taking the longer view, King overlooked the fragility of the pseudo-coalition of Chiang and Mao in framing plans centered on Formosa and the postwar reconstruction plan.[27] In some respects, King looked too far beyond the horizon—leaving his subordinates to worry about fighting the enemy at hand.

Marshall and King agreed to place Wedemeyer in overall command over Miles and the SACO organization. Having been in China under rigorous conditions, Miles struggled to understand the decision. However, the bargain with Marshall also reflected King's willingness to compromise for the purpose of attaining higher strategic ends. The appointment of Wedemeyer provided additional impetus for an amphibious campaign against Formosa, as was being followed by Allied operations along the Chinese coast. In addition, King designated Kinkaid, the commander of the Seventh Fleet, with the responsibility of leading the planning of future operations in Chinese waters. King and Nimitz made similar arrangements to assign foreign naval forces to Kinkaid. These moves also reflected King's effort to leave MacArthur behind as his campaign bogged down in the Philippines.[28]

The CCS and JCS were also divided on the strategic priorities, as Churchill and Roosevelt haggled over the future reconstruction vision for Asia. Along with other Allied naval commanders, King compromised with army counterparts in planning the amphibious campaign against Japan under the overall concept for Operation DOWNFALL. King continued developing similar plans for CAUSEWAY to Formosa and beyond to China. These plans required Marshall and King to haggle over the allocation of forces. Summarizing the basic issue, King told journalists of strategic shortages of ships and personnel.[29] King explained, "We own the oceans, but the Japanese army has dug-in [sic], and they won't quit anytime soon."[30] "Chinese manpower will fix them," King thought. He figured that the "Russians can cleanup [sic]."[31]

DYER RETURNS

Disputes between the army and King's navy influenced pettiness in efforts to unify the efforts of forces ashore with those afloat. The ongoing debates concerning the war in

China also directly influenced planning for victory in Europe. During the final drive into Germany, Eisenhower applauded the contributions of Kirk. Eisenhower recommended Kirk for an *Army* Distinguished Service Medal for service in combat from Normandy to the Rhine.[32] War secretary Stimson failed to process the recommendation. Marshall advised King to endorse Kirk for a *Navy* Distinguished Service Medal. In turn, King angrily pushed Marshall to arrange an *Army* Distinguished Service Medal by arguing that "not one of your generals would have made it to the damned beach without my boys putting them there!"[33]

Success in operations also propelled figures like Eisenhower into the spotlight, which overshadowed the roles performed by figures like Kirk and King in organizing the naval requirements to execute and then sustain operations ashore in Europe.[34] King insisted that Marshall give navy participants equal credit in the form of medals and decorations equating—or exceeding—those issued to army personnel.[35] "Some people felt King had favored old friends in promotion," Capt. Malcolm Schoeffel suggested. "I know he rather regretted some of the promotions that were made, but he never _de_-moted anyone."[36] Schoeffel admitted, "I feel this was something of a weakness[, and the] worst King did was send a man to undesirable duty."[37] King strived to place subordinates in positions to succeed. Another close confidant noted that King "had a blind spot for personnel in that he had several friends that he stuck with through thick and thin who were just not worth sticking with."[38]

King struggled to maintain a small organization within the context of a war of unprecedented scale. Dyer accurately predicted the requirements in 1942, although King initially dismissed the notion of creating an organization like that of Sims and the London Flagship of the First World War. Wounded severely during the landings at Salerno, Dyer recalled returning to the CominCh headquarters. "Ah," King chided Dyer, "the returning war hero!" He wore the newly minted Bronze Star Medal with a Combat "V" along with a Purple Heart ribbon. As Dyer limped into the office, King explained that the aide had just "laid a piece of paper on my desk and I wanted you to see it." Both had a laugh about the fact that CominCh headquarters tallied in at 416 personnel assigned.[39]

Dyer characterized King as the quintessential naval warrior with a single weakness of personality that centered on the basic question of loyalty. Dyer explained that King suffered from "very distinct blind spots: he had great loyalty to sometimes quite unworthy people in my humble opinion." Dyer illustrated the point by highlighting King's efforts to help Capt. Jesse L. Kenworthy, a naval aviator and survivor of the earlier disasters in the airship crash of *Macon,* to become the de facto commanding officer of the battleship USS *Oklahoma* (BB-37) during the attack at Pearl Harbor. Kenworthy suffered a nervous breakdown and was committed to a psychiatric hospital near the Philadelphia Navy Yard. Kenworthy frequently used the direct telephone connection to King at the Navy Department. Dyer recalled, "I was sitting in a mass of papers and trying to do a thousand things and here would come this long-winded call [from Kenworthy]. I would finally say[,] 'I cannot talk to you another instant.'"[40] Dyer recalled, "King kept trying to get [Kenworthy] out of the hospital[, and] that's one of the reasons why I told him that his blind spot was personnel."[41]

King maintained the hardened façade in dealings with government officials and among his subordinates. His public image contrasted with the actual personality of King. Among friends and family, King revealed himself to be a warmhearted family man. His daughters and son recalled how King enjoyed chasing the grandchildren on the lawn of the Naval Observatory during his Sunday visits. He rarely allowed the war to become a topic of discussion, since his extended family included various sons-in-law serving in all the various branches of the service. Having served as a personal aide to King in the CominCh headquarters, Capt. Neil K. Dietrich characterized King as a "man who dedicated himself to winning the war[, and] I only saw him chuckle whenever he told stories about his grandkids."[42]

King's taut demeanor fueled his public image, which obscured the true personality at the center of the CominCh headquarters. Lt. Cmdr. Alan R. McFarland noted that the "Admiral was always tough, but fair[,] and [he] had a great sense of humor." McFarland illustrated his point with an anecdote. When Adm. Jonas Ingram visited CominCh headquarters, McFarland characterized King's sense of humor. McFarland explained:

> Ingram was a man who spoke very loudly, a real extrovert and a wonderful man—very capable. Ingram was sitting in the outer office with me making a telephone call to New York in his usual loud voice. All of a sudden, Admiral King appeared from his office and said, "Jonas, you don't need a telephone. They can hear you all the way to New York without it!"[43]

King's closest associates held their boss in great esteem. "[King] had dinner at my apartment on a few occasions," McFarland explained. "We witnessed the Army-Navy game together in Washington over television, a novelty then."[44]

Young naval associates of King mimicked the cocky confidence of their leader within the headquarters. Whitehill recounted the "rumor that Admiral King occasionally dined on raw ensigns[, which] undoubtedly sprang from a misunderstanding of his teasing."[45] Whitehill recalled that King "enjoyed making disconcerting remarks, partly for the fun involved and partly as a test of the person he was dealing with."[46] His protégés served him well as CominCh liaisons among other headquarters and on Capitol Hill. As the old unification debates bubbled beneath the surface of debates concerning the war, congressmen and their staffers acknowledged King's influence on liaisons like Orem, Saunders, Russell, and Shepard.[47]

Veterans of the CominCh headquarters recalled how King used humor to foster trust among younger officers. Capt. Malcolm Schoeffel recalled that King "could yarn very pleasantly and [his] personality so dominated us."[48] Whitehill remembered taking a moment to relax with a book at his desk. King suddenly appeared, looking down sternly at Whitehill and asking, "Loafing on the job again?"[49] Whitehill responded by ignoring the question with a non sequitur, saying, "I had always understood that in the Navy it was well thought of to take any opportunity of going to sea."[50] Walking away, King conceded with a laugh, "You win."[51]

The CominCh staff vicariously endured the rigors of combat by monitoring the progress of operations and by anticipating enemy actions with intelligence. The mind-numbing administrative routines also strained the nerves. Combat veterans rotated from the front for shore duty in the CominCh headquarters, leaving no real time for rest. Setting the pace, Edwards regulated King's schedule. Younger aides, including Lt. Charles M. Keyes, remained in King's constant presence. The chief petty officers on the CominCh staff also maintained a twenty-four-hour watch with duty drivers assigned to King.[52] The firsthand recollections of individuals closest to towering personalities like King often provide critical insight to *why* decisions were made and events unfolded as they ultimately did in history.

Historical distractions concerning the motivations and personal behavior of individuals sometimes provide the keys to unlocking the treasure chests, which sometimes lead to other widely overlooked documentary sources. Just as Horatio Nelson's personal correspondence with Lady Hamilton tantalized historians in the past, the personal correspondences of figures operating at analogous levels of strategic command provide invaluable insights. Looking beyond a key personality such as King's in order to consider the recollections of closer associates often highlights the uncertainties inherent with carrying the responsibilities that come with high command in war.

The tribal culture among the American armed services centered on hierarchical order among various chieftains and their close circles of subordinates. Given ongoing debates concerning other historical figures of King's era—from Roosevelt to Eisenhower—the human dimension often fades into the hazy realm of myth and popular memory. For example, biographers of Eisenhower naturally focused on his wartime chauffeur, US Army lieutenant Kay Summersby. The Red Cross nurse Jean Gordon also became a close confidant of Patton.[53]

The past lives of fellow human beings who have long since departed provide unlimited opportunity for ongoing discussion, although behavioral questions often result in irrelevant conclusions about human motivations in both peace and war. As with other major commanders among the high command, King's trust in a longtime family friend illustrated the monumental pressures inherent with high command in war. King's relentless wartime schedule unfolded between the lines in letters written to Nan Ferrell between 1940 and 1945. Having lived in the media spotlight for most of his naval career, King confided in Ferrell, telling him, "I am constantly 'tied down' or 'on call' so that I have almost no time to do things that I want, personally."[54] King complained, "Such is the rule for those engaged in the work of the 'high command.'"[55]

RING OF FIRE

King existed at the center of a very tight-knit family circle, which extended into the ranks of the armed services through marriage and associated friendships. Having had a longtime acquaintance, and since they were all from the Franklin Street neighborhood in Annapolis, the King and Ferrell families kept especially close connections. The Ferrell family lived at 18 Franklin Street, nearby the main anchorage of the King family at 45 Franklin Street. Ferrell's elder brother, William, served as a professor of aeronautics at the Naval Academy, served as museum curator on the yard, and maintained his naval commission on the reserve list. The Ferrell brothers also stood at the center of an expanding social network among younger Naval Academy graduates of the Prohibition era. Joseph and Edwin pursued their commissions with Arthur, thus establishing the Ferrell family as the first to have three brothers among the brigade of midshipman at the same time. Arthur graduated with the US Naval Academy Class of 1925, qualified as an aviator by 1932, and then served on King's staff at BuAer.

The Ferrell family had much influence in the local naval culture of Annapolis and among King's close circle of young aviator proteges. After ten years on active service, Ferrell was killed when his aircraft crashed into a fence adjacent to the San Diego Naval Air Station on the estate of the humorist Will Rogers in April 1936. Tragedy reinforced the long connections between the Ferrell and King families within the close-knit naval community on Franklin Street in Annapolis, just outside the south gate of the Naval Academy. The King family rallied to assist whenever tragedy struck. Such was the case when the Ferrell family endured the most-extreme consequences of voluntary naval service in peacetime.

The Ferrell and King families operated within the same close circles among the naval culture of Annapolis and Washington. Knowing the price of readiness for war, King especially respected the tragic heroism of those quietly risking everything while relying on cutting-edge technology. Aviation and submarine duty were among the most dangerous assignments in the fleet. Whenever one of his sailors died, King and his growing mafia of submariners and naval aviators followed the unspoken rule of keeping very close contact with the families of the bereaved. In various letters, King wrote about his own ailments and constantly feeling overwhelmed. Under unremitting pressure, King felt completely worn out—just as he reached the highest summits of his power and political influence in 1943.[56]

King sought shelter from the raging wartime maelstrom by keeping steady correspondence with Nan Ferrell. Having been an old family friend, Ferrell joined the so-called Lipstick Brigade as a resident at the Meridian Park Hotel for Women during wartime service on the fringes of clandestine activities within the Department of State in Washington.[57] Ferrell also visited the Naval Observatory after Mattie suffered from a series of heart attacks in 1943. Interestingly, Nan and King kept regular handwritten correspondence during the war—though they both lived within very close proximity in the Washington metropolitan area. The letters filtered through official mail—sometimes stamped by Navy Department censors.

Letters from Nan to King remain unavailable, although his responses to her letters provide firsthand perspectives on the bureaucracy of war. Ferrell earned formal qualifications as a librarian. After Pearl Harbor, she left the Annapolis Public Library to work as a Red Cross volunteer. Through King's assistance, Nan reported for duty in the classified- records subdivision of the Navy Department Library under Capt. Knox. She subsequently served in the Department of State and eventually the Library of Congress before retiring after twenty-two years in the federal civil service.[58] Ferrell was much younger than the admiral but was clearly a very close friend of King. In July 1943, for example, King complained that the "doctors insist on 'checking' me about twice a month—all they find is that I tend to tire[,] and urge me to rest all I can, which I do!—as I certainly do lead 'the simple life.'"[59]

King established residence within the closely regulated bubble of the CominCh headquarters. He wrote to Ferrell that "I may have much to do with the progress of the war—it is true that I am one of the 'wheels' of the 'machine' but it is the 'machine' that is producing results."[60] King complained about flying on a constant rotation between the various fronts of Europe and Asia. He said, "I am 'tied down' more than ever to 'the job.'"[61] Given his celebrity media status in wartime propaganda, King described himself as a "finely preened bird in an gilded cage[, which] rather hampers my going where I would wish to go."[62] King also thought that "I am fortunate to be called upon to do the work that I have striven to be fitted to do—and hope (pray) that I may do it well!"[63]

Navy doctors warned King to relax as much as possible in executing the duties of running the war at sea. His diagnosis of high blood pressure and the aftereffects of two hernia surgeries caused persistent pain. Shoulder damage sustained during his previous seaplane crash stiffened King's already taut demeanor.[64] Doctors threatened to disqualify King from continued active service. At sixty-six years old by the fall of 1944, King rarely admitted to the chronic pains of simply being an old man at war.[65] King also felt somewhat helpless when Mattie suffered a series of heart attacks. Unlike the tangential observations of staff and family, King spoke in very open terms about the pressures and unique challenges of being in the spotlight of war in personal letters to Ferrell.[66.]

King confided in Ferrell about the challenges of balancing the home front against the unfathomable responsibilities of high command in the global maritime arena. Occasionally, Ferrell joined the King family for weekend luncheons. In addition to old friends, the King family also relied upon their navy stewards who had been officially assigned to the official residence of the CNO. Chief Steward's Mate Lazario Dorio assisted King's daughters Eleanor and Florie in coordinating the mess within the Naval Observatory.[67] With their assistance, Mattie kept an even pace as the matriarch of the household. With all her daughters married to servicemen and with a son in the navy, she strived to reduce the stress by spending time with her fourteen grandchildren. Given the stresses of war, King played his part in assisting Mattie in her role as the family matriarch. Like Mattie, King managed the burdens and health problems associated with old age.

King found solitude in the naval routines that characterized the orderly atmosphere on board *Dauntless*. Navy doctors constantly attempted to throw King off *Dauntless,* threatening to deem him unfit for sea duty. In turn, King threatened his doctor. During an annual checkup, King brought orders "all typed up for the doc to be sent to China[, and] all King had to do was sign the order."[68] King thrived in the chaos, but Leahy whispered in Roosevelt's ear. After a phone call from the White House, King directed Edwards to manage a monthly rest schedule. In turn, Captains Dick Matter, Stan Dunlap, and Paul Pihl, along with their wives; Betsy Matter and her sister Abby Dunlap; and Charlotte Pihl regularly hosted King at their family farms. He also joined Secretary of State Edward Stettinius Jr. at his rural home.[69]

The CominCh staff tracked enemy forces in the same manner as they monitored King's exact location. His aides worked together to keep contact, as one manned the office, one stood watch on *Dauntless*, and another accompanied the man himself. His hobby of keeping chickens became somewhat of a running joke. On Thanksgiving, he arrived with a live turkey at the Naval Observatory, rendered the bird in front of his grandchildren, and then passed the cooking chores to the chef.[70] Mattie joked that King referred to the turkey as just another "chicken he grabbed from the coop."[71] Whenever he went to the countryside, King simply sipped scotch on the front porch, listened to Gene Autry music on the radio, and rested—as ordered.[72]

In many respects, King had the status of a Mafia boss among a very large and interesting circle of a highly accomplished family and their friends. The matriarch of the family, Mattie, stood watch with her daughters and grandchildren at the Naval Observatory. King's daughters—all married to servicemen and stationed at various military bases around the United States—also did their bit for the war effort by hosting foreign guests in their homes.[73] King and Mattie acted as surrogate grandparents of Eugenie Matter and Rowan Dunlap, daughters of Stan and Betsy and Dick and Abby. The Pihls and Matters babysat King's grandchildren after the war.[74]

The war dominated the lives of the King family, as they collectively accepted the burden of being related to the only American in history to hold the double-edged wartime responsibilities of CNO and CominCh. Such responsibility drew significant scrutiny among the gossipy ranks of the Washington battlefield. Many years after the fact, Charlotte Pihl, the forty-three-year-old wife of King's most trusted logistician, Capt. Paul Pihl, explained, "My being the sister of Wendell Willkie caused great rumor and gossiping in Washington."[75] Rejecting inevitable comparisons to the historical infidelities of Lord Nelson and Lady Emma Hamilton, Pihl emphasized, "If you knew Paul Pihl, if anything was going on between his wife and any man, King included, that Paul would of course kick him out of the house immediately."[76] The director of naval intelligence, RAdm. Leo Hewlett Thebaud, directly refuted rumors of marital infidelity of King, saying, "If he had any quiet little affairs on the side, they were ADMIRALTY CONCEALED."[77]

The King family rallied to the cause of supporting the war effort, enabling their top-ranking commander to focus on the tasks at hand for the purposes of winning the peace. King's daughters weathered the storm, taking care of Mattie while their father, brother, and husbands fought in uniformed military and naval services. King and Mattie also demonstrated great humanity.[78] When King's daughter Claire and her Naval Academy graduate husband, John Howard, adopted their orphaned daughter, Amanda, the admiral and Mrs. King also added their names to the paperwork—making Amanda their legal grandchild.[79]

Whenever King was in port with *Dauntless* at the Washington Navy Yard, he regularly joined the family at the Naval Observatory. On Sundays, he attended buffet luncheons followed by a late-afternoon dinner with his wife and family. These visits were cherished in the memories of King's grandchildren.[80] His grandson Egerton recalled spending his wartime weekends building a stone fence at the family home with his grandfather. Egerton recalled sitting at the feet of his grandfather as King listened to music and read the newspaper.[81] The unremitting pressures of commanding global operations in war seemed unapparent to King's family, although the physical strains silently took their toll as he approached age sixty-seven. In the meantime, the bloody war continued progressing to an uncertain end as the corrosive unification debate seeped through the armor plating of King's navy.

CHAPTER 33
The Family Business

The King family understood the implied responsibility of pulling together as a team, each performing their role as port of a tight-knit unit. Familial ties proved useful for King. He maintained an intricate and widely unacknowledged network of trusted friends and loyalists within the interconnected bureaucracies of the CCS and JCS. His key spies in the War Department both carried the ubiquitous surname Smith. Both being well-placed army generals, they came from different and unrelated branches of the Smith family tree. Another son-in-law, Col. Oliver Wolcott van den Berg, commanded army amphibious forces in the Pacific. Having been wounded in combat, van den Berg attended the Naval War College. He then served as an instructor with the establishment of the Army-Navy Staff College (ANSCOL).[1] Ranking representatives from foreign navies joined the discussions in Newport as they completed the ANSCOL curriculum.[2]

The unification debate bubbled below the surface when King preempted the debate to unify the war colleges of the army and the navy under a single entity. King failed to request permission in establishing ANSCOL. Army officers joined British and Commonwealth forces in Newport to frame a coalition strategy for the reconstruction.[3] In an address at the Naval War College, King warned, "As to wars of the future[, in] World War I we were under no apprehension of the security of the United States or of the Western Hemisphere."[4] Given recent experience in the war at sea, he concluded, "I have only one proposal to offer about future warfare as planned—first use sea power to limit the options of your adversary and secondly keep it away from the United States—keep it overseas."[5]

King reflected upon the importance of maintaining the wartime fusion of authority in anticipation of victory in the war at sea. "In logistics the Navy has adopted a differentiation that some of you may not be familiar with," King explained to a Naval War College audience. He added, "Producer logistics are not strictly the business of the military[; that] is chiefly on the civilian side of the Army-Navy[,] with some help."[6] "There is a no-man['] s land" between civilian and military command, although King observed, "Since it is all under the control of the Secretary of the Navy we are sure it will work out."[7] King frequently turned to his friends in the Naval War College to study such issues.[8] He ordered the president of the Naval War College, Kalbfus, to "'infiltrate' capable reserve officers into staff and other duties to get the most effective <u>distribution</u>, of the 'leaven' of regular officers."[9] King thought that the "quality of the 'leaven' should be kept up—by due assignments to the War College!"[10] In 1945, King planed to retain reserve personnel on active service "who will be sent to [ANSCOL] for one year after the end of the war, after which they will be assigned to the fleet on an equal basis with Academy graduates."[11]

King used the Naval War College for the purposes of educating practitioners about the longer strategic trends in wartime fleet operations. Twenty-five years after the original

K-P-K Report, Knox and King worked with Pye to form the "Pye Board" for the purposes of defining national standards for future education, which included studies in military and maritime history, military science, and engineering. After Pye relieved Kalbfus in Newport, the Naval War College and the ONH in Washington developed plans to revitalize historical education in civilian colleges and universities after the war. The Pye Board advocated for the "national education" plan, requiring Americans to complete national service as a prerequisite for studies at civilian trade schools and institutions of higher education.[12]

The radical ideas found in the Pye Board Report informed strategic plans for the future organization of the US Navy. King appointed VAdm. James Holloway II to consider the Pye Board recommendations for the purposes of reorganizing Reserve Officer Training Corps and Officer Candidate School programs.[13] King agreed with the conclusions of Pye and Holloway about the fundamental importance of national service.[14] The Pye and Holloway studies coincided with the deliberations ongoing about future service unification.[15] For King, the best means to achieve the full benefits of unification centered on using the regimental system of the army as the basis for "universal military training" for American citizens.[16] In King's view, all citizens had to complete military training in the army before embarking on naval service, beginning education at the elite Naval Academy, or seeking a civilian education.[17]

King used the Naval War College as a sounding board to examine the strategic priorities for future reconstruction. As part of the discussion, King asked the president of the Naval War College, Pye, to consider the strategic outlook for operations in the Pacific through 1945. King recalled that "Iwo Jima was a nuisance to our occupation of the Marianas [, and] we wanted to get rid of that."[18] King also highlighted the interrelationships of strategic airpower with amphibious planning:

> We also wanted to stage fighters out of there, army fighters to escort the B-29s[,] and we also found out that after the B-29s realized that they could land on Iwo Jima, if necessary, on their way from their long flight up there, their performance went up. I say that in no disparagement to anyone, I am relating a fact, which perhaps it will help you to understand why Iwo Jima was so important, even at such a great cost. Then came Okinawa [and] that enabled us to control by sea and by air the seaways to China as well as definitely cutting off what little traffic the Japanese had with those large number of troops that were left hanging on the vine in the Philippines and the East Indies, and all the rest of them.[19]

King further argued that "Okinawa was important because Army fighter aircraft based there could cover Kyushu, which is the largest of the southernmost main islands of Japan."[20] King noted that the army planners hoped to use Kyushu as the future "base for land-based aircraft for going up into the Tokyo plain."[21] King kept an open mind about the prospective amphibious assault on Kyushu, since such a position provided opportunity to "control the Japanese sea ways to Manchuria and Korea definitely."[22] He mused, "Thank god we didn't have to do it, but that was the military strategy."[23]

Operations in preparation of an anticipated amphibious assault against Japan still resulted in heavy losses, which bothered King on a personal level. The tragic loss of Lt. Cmdr. John Pye struck very close to home for King. Having served in the CominCh headquarters, Pye had the option of serving in Washington for the duration.[24] He refused to stay tied to a desk. Pye specifically volunteered for hazardous duty in submarines. Pye then earned the Navy Cross while serving as the temporary skipper and then as executive officer on USS *Swordfish* (SS-193). During his thirteenth combat patrol on a reconnaissance mission off Okinawa, Pye drowned with all hands on *Swordfish*.[25]

The wrenching duty of telling the Pye family about another lost son fell squarely upon King's shoulders.[26] With great sadness, King personally took the helm in flying his Lockheed Lodestar from Washington to Quonset, Rhode Island. King then boarded a launch and sailed across the Narragansett Bay to Newport, walked up the hill to the Naval War College, and met Pye at his office on the second deck of Luce Hall. There, King told Pye about the loss of his second son in the spring of 1945. True to form, Pye stoically continued manning the watch as president of the Naval War College, and his wife, Anne, exemplified the values she articulated in her manual, *The Navy Wife*.

SPARING NO EFFORT

The death of a family friend in combat required all hands to assist as King worked the lines to support Pye. Among others, Mattie and King's daughters helped console the Pye family.[27] Admiral and Mrs. Pye focused on raising the children of their lost sons and never spoke of their tragedy in public.[28] Such personal tragedies deeply bothered King. In reflection, he felt "sorry for all the families, but we could not announce the loss or say anything about a submarine overdue for two or three months after she was lost [and] we never said when she was lost, we never said where."[29] King disliked the hardships associated with clandestine operations at sea and ashore, but, as he said, "That is what we call security."[30]

King acted with stoic confidence about the inevitable defeat of the Axis Tripartite in outlining the tragic cost of winning the sustainable end of war. His aide Lt. Cmdr. Walter Muir Whitehill assisted in writing the reports to the secretary of the Navy and Congress. King used the reports to highlight the bloody costs of war.[31] "In terms of total naval strength," King explained, the "total death rate from all causes is estimated at 5.8 per thousand for the year 1944 against the final figure of 5.4 per thousand in 1943." "Experience in this war indicates that of the wounded men who live until they receive medical attention," King noted, "98 out of every 100 survive." He emphasized that they "are sparing no effort."[32]

King's view of sea power further highlighted the importance of continued Anglo-American collaboration under the future United Nations. To these ends, King accompanied Roosevelt in the cruiser USS *Quincy* (CA-39) to join the CCS for meetings in Europe. Arriving at Malta, Roosevelt joined King in trading signals with the younger ensign Ernie "Joe" King Jr., since he had the deck on board USS *Savannah* (CL-42) as the American cruisers entered port at Malta. That evening, Joe joined his father for dinner with the CCS.[33] The two traded jokes with Churchill and Roosevelt during visits to the historic sites of Malta.[34] Whenever Churchill and Roosevelt came together, Harry Hopkins stood out for King as the key to managing transatlantic strategy. King described Hopkins as the "man who would get into the 'root of the matter.'"[35] King observed that many times the President and Prime Minister would talk without looking over the real situation[,] and Hopkins would say, "Mr. President, do you remember what we were talking about? It seems to me that what you want is, etc." There was a great difference. Mr. Churchill was always remembering about his work during World War I, and also, about World War II. After the US entered the war, he was always giving "whatfor" [*sic*] to the British Chiefs-of-Staff, when they wouldn't agree with him. Also, he would try to get the US Chief's [*sic*] of staff to agree with some of his pet ideas. . . . I don't remember of any time when President Roosevelt didn't agree with his own (US) Chiefs-of-Staff although we, usually, took note of his special ideas.[36]

Keeping with the policies of the Roosevelt administration, King framed strategy to realize the "Four Policemen" dream in anticipation of the reconstruction in Europe and Asia.[37] In public speeches, King began asking American listeners to ponder the "question I know is close to the hearts of us all—WHAT SHALL BE THE GRAND STRATEGY OF PEACE?"[38]

Being realistic about the future, King discounted the likelihood of a lasting alliance among the major Allied powers. As insurance, he hoped to fix the Russians into supporting ongoing plans for the reconstruction of Europe and Asia during the ARGONAUT Conference at Yalta in the Crimea on the Black Sea. At Yalta, King emphasized the ongoing importance of Russian forces in efforts to defeat the Japanese through operations on mainland China. King reasoned that the "Ruskis would be too tired to fight for quite some time [and] anyway they won't be able to do much anyway without our assistance."[39] He also told journalists about open debates within the CCS and JCS about plans for Japan. King warned of "a tremendous shortage of troops in the Pacific."[40]

King conversely believed in the prospective success of lasting partnerships between the maritime powers of Britain and America. He considered sea power key to the future reconstruction of Europe and Asia under the future United Nations. King observed that "if there were to be an aggressor in the future, Russia was the most likely candidate."[41] However, King characterized Stalin "as less potent as a leader [and] the military and the political had 'caught up with him.'"[42] For these reasons, King supported efforts to recruit Russia into the war against Japan. King predicted, "Since the occupation of Japan will be almost at the same strength planned as if it had been an actual invasion."[43] Looking outward to victory, King fully embraced the United Nations as the best possible mechanism for sustaining future peace.[44]

With victory in Europe and Asia apparently closer, King worried about the future ability of fellow Americans to ensure the sustainable end of war. In speeches, King warned, "I am afraid we are too prone to think of peace as a 'do nothing' state of affairs."[45] He further pressed the point, saying, "I can say to you as one American citizen to his fellow citizens that it does not seem to me that a 'do nothing' attitude about peace is going to get us anywhere."[46] King argued that "we must do our part, not only in a military but in an economic and political sense to make the United Nations work—we must be ready to support it[,] and may I say by deeds as well as words."[47] Pondering the reconstruction of Europe and Asia, King mused, "I am sure you will not be surprised if, after forty years in the service, I say that I believe in those words attributed to Theodore Roosevelt, 'speak softy, but carry a big stick.'"[48]

TWINKLING STARS FOR CHRISTMAS

Wartime conditions forced major changes in American civil-military relationships, as Congress enabled the Roosevelt administration to act as required to meet the enemy in battle and win. Constitutional constraints on the executive branch balanced policy negotiations between the legislative and judiciary branches. Roosevelt always demurred whenever Marshall and King pushed to formalize the existence of the JCS through legislation.[49] This implies that Roosevelt likely intended to restore the traditional arrangements for civilian control within the Departments of State, Navy, and War. Roosevelt diverted debates concerning the permanent establishment of the JCS by floating the idea of creating wartime ranks equivalent to those carried by foreign allies on the CCS.

Roosevelt had tabled King's idea of higher five-star ranks for the American army and navy during the ARCADIA discussions. To King's surprise, Roosevelt floated six-star and five-star rank in conjunction with debates concerning the future relationship of the Departments of War and Navy.[50] In these contentious debates, Roosevelt favored Navy Department concepts for future unification—essentially rendering the landed military and services in a secondary role while American sea power took hold in the global maritime arena.[51] To these ends, Roosevelt quietly worked plans with Leahy to create five-star ranks for the JCS. At that time, Leahy had no actual authority as a retired officer. The pecking order as indicated within the Naval Register also included Stark as technically the most senior naval officer by lineal standing, and King had temporary supremacy as the CNO/CominCh. Under the circumstances, Roosevelt reintroduced the idea of six- and five-star ranks to clarify his intention of placing the navy on top of the bureaucratic hierarchy in anticipation of the future unification debate.[52]

Churchill and Roosevelt retained strategic authorities over the deliberations within the CCS and JCS. For this reason, Anglo-American strategy always remained subject to heated debate behind closed doors. Among the key American commanders, Leahy had influence but no actual authority as an ex-officio presidential liaison the CCS and JCS. In addition, Marshall faced his mandatory retirement at age sixty-four under the legislative statutes. Arnold rarely appeared after 1943, constantly suffering from a chronic heart condition. King had already broken the barrier of mandatory retirement by three years. Only Roosevelt stood between Marshall's and King's inevitable transfer to the retired list.[53] Roosevelt also recognized the gathering storms concerning the future transatlantic alliance, which coincided with the bubbling unification debates between the Departments of State, Navy, and War.[54]

The long-term implications of wartime expediency concerned the Roosevelt administration, which complicated deliberations concerning the future of American sea power. King's efforts to make the merger of the CNO and CominCh permanent under the provisions of EO 9096 had also upset the political balance.[55] Among other key civilian bureaucrats, Forrestal used political backchannels to hold King in check. Forrestal intended to restore the prewar separations between the functions of CNO and CominCh. To this end, Forrestal groomed Senator Harry S Truman during ongoing unification debates about the postwar organization of the American defense establishment.[56]

Efforts to rescind EO 9096 inspired King to maneuver by making constant changes within the organization of the Navy Department. "General Motors got out a new organization chart every three months to avoid the dangers of static organization," King explained.

He added that he "was doing the same sort of thing throughout the war."[57] Observing from the White House, Roosevelt complained that "Ernie should stop trying to reorganize the navy and concentrate on winning the war."[58] In addition to administrative problems within the Navy Department, within shore establishments, and among the seagoing fleets, King constantly faced the prodding scrutiny of various congressional committees.

Overlapping investigations within Congress sparked ongoing media attention, which fueled continued troubles for the Roosevelt administration on the public stage. The Pearl Harbor investigations carried particular importance within the context of concurrent unification debates and the proposal to establish a separate US Air Force *during* the war.[59] In these discussions, Roosevelt and Leahy discouraged King from constantly reminding fellow commanders about the fact that "Kimmel and Stark were hung out to dry and nobody wants to talk about Marshall and Arnold also having the watch on that day."[60] In Congress, the Pearl Harbor investigations served as the bellwether for anticipating the future of American sea power. Throughout the war, King regularly lobbied through the Woodrum Committee and the Richardson Commission to support the naval agenda of the Roosevelt administration.[61]

Roosevelt frequently used King like a broadsword to cut through the wartime politics. Roosevelt always sent King a Christmas gift. As time passed, the quality of the gifts and the cheerfulness of the greetings from Roosevelt progressively decreased.[62] Bureaucratic intermediaries inserted themselves into the ongoing conversation between Roosevelt and the JCS. Civilian leaders like Forrestal particularly worried about the prospective threats posed by uniformed strongmen—like King and MacArthur. King remembered that Forrestal "would make dirty cracks at me."[63] Republican senator Leverett Saltonstall recalled Forrestal stating, "King had the brains all right, but I hated his guts [but] King had the brains in the JCS."[64] Forrestal then continued, "But still, I didn't like him."[65]

Forrestal and King's acrimonious relationship reflected the tensions that were building within the CCS and JCS. Had the provisions of EO 9096 been dissolved during the war, King thought, "Forrestal would have tried to manage the whole thing."[66] Close observers on the CominCh staff witnessed the tension between Forrestal and King. During an awards ceremony at the Navy Department, King executed the classic bureaucratic power play of making Forrestal wait. Lt. Richard "Dick" Shepard stood with other staff members awaiting King's arrival, as Forrestal fidgeted and kept checking his watch. Shepard recalled the drama when "in slowly strode the tall Ernie King[,] who nodded while saying[,] 'Mr. Secretary.'"[67] Shepard noted, "Forrestal appeared to me to be noticeably annoyed because of King's cool manner, because of his promptness to a fault, and because of Forrestal's having to wait in embarrassment for the on-the-second appearance of his subordinate."[68]

The tension between Forrestal and King hindered their shared vision for American sea power. Observing in close quarters from within the ONH at the Navy Department, Robert G. Albion recalled the frustration of Forrestal and other civilian bureaucrats in relations with "King's 'CominCh-CNO' henchmen."[69] Among other fringe battles ongoing within the Navy Department, Forrestal wrested control from King over the acquisitions process.[70] He explained that Forrestal hindered efficiency by inserting himself into the "three broad phases of naval logistics—planning of requirements, procurement, and distribution."[71] Forrestal bifurcated these functions under his coconspirators in the plan, Horne and RAdm. Samuel M. Robinson—after his appointment in the newly established

Office of Procurement and Management (OP&M). Forrestal attempted to nullify King by inserting verbiage into the draft executive order to cancel EO 9096. Forrestal intended to promote King into political oblivion with the rarified five-star title of "Admiral of the Navy and Commander United States Fleets."[72]

Forrestal demonstrated a masterful understanding of bureaucratic gamesmanship by playing the part of being a strong supporter of King. Being equally pugilistic, King discounted the five-star idea as an "outdated solution for an administrative problem that had already been solved."[73] King thought, "Forrestal wanted to manage everything, especially the bureaus and material."[74] Working behind closed doors, King outflanked Forrestal.[75] Acting before asking permission, King summarily appointed Edwards as deputy CNO and deputy CominCh, which corresponded to a recommendation for an accelerated promotion. In turn, King promoted Cooke to replace Edwards as chief of staff, and RAdm. Bernhard Bieri to replace Cooke as deputy chief of staff. Equally shrewd in the political games of Washington, King created the title of deputy CNO (DCNO)—with Horne shouldered with the unglamorous duties of working with Congress, naval administration, and logistics.[76] King explained that the "duties now assigned to Vice Admiral Edwards do not constitute a demotion of Vice Admiral Horne or of anyone else."[77]

The ongoing feud for control within the Navy Department centered on the tribal associations surrounding Forrestal's and King's personalities. Caught between the two, Horne attempted to strike a balance in managing the civil-military divide. King eventually lost trust in Horne. In memoirs, King artfully explained his concerns about "Horne's skill in making things as they were work."[78] King then admitted that he "was always concerned with improving the organization."[79] King described Horne as "a yes man, but a very able man all the same."[80] King thought and said that Horne "always wanted to run with the hares and the hounds too."[81] "I never liked him and never knew why." King thought that Horne "would have liked to have been Chief of Naval Operations—who wouldn't?"[82]

Forrestal disliked the temporary measures of EO 9096, constantly seeking opportunities to reestablish the traditional authority of the secretary of the Navy by again subdividing the functions of CNO and CominCh. To these ends, Forrestal groomed Horne to replace King as CNO. The bureaucratic feud between Forrestal and King proved cancerous for the future of American sea power. Forrestal warned King about the threat of airpower, which bubbled under the simmering heat of the unification debate. Perhaps feeling overly confident in the vision of American sea power, King turned a blind eye when he should have paid greater attention during the pivotal months leading to victory. He joked with journalists, saying, "[The] bomber people rarely see that their way of looking at strategy is taking us all back to the stone-age."[83] He told Walter Lippmann, "Our Air Force friends can go to the birds, but I assure you that your Navy will not give the enemy 'aid and comfort' by telling them what we are doing."[84]

BULL SESSIONS

Journalists pressed King to explain propaganda narratives and to clarify rumors about other key personalities within the Allied command. Derogatory information about fellow naval officers circulated around key media circles. For example, the muckraker Drew Pearson and the airpower propagandist Leo circulated rumors about Halsey's favorite chief of staff, Capt. Miles R. Browning. King characterized Browning as potentially gifted as a US naval officer. King praised Browning for remarkable performances in the early operations following Pearl Harbor and during the pivotal Battle of Midway. Journalists told King about stories of Browning's infidelity with another officer's wife. Browning had attempted to cover up details about the accidental death of sailors under his command while in port. King ultimately felt betrayed by Browning and thought "he was no damned good at all."[85]

King proved to be a feeble spokesman in advocating for the future of American sea power. He later credited Forrestal for recognizing the importance of propaganda in wartime. Forrestal forced King to continue his clandestine meetings with journalists after King's lawyer, Bull, passed away. Under Forrestal's direct orders, King dutifully continued the secret meetings at the home of Phelps Adams of the *New York Sun*. Adams later explained that King "spoke his mind forthrightly [and] the language of diplomacy was a tongue utterly foreign to him."[86] The "Bull sessions" continued after Adams rallied his trusted contacts within the Washington press corps to gather at his home across from the Washington Golf and Country Club. Among the others associated with the "Arlington County Commandos," Adams recalled how his wife customarily prepared the battlefield for King, as she filled "a washtub full of cracked ice and bottled beer in front of the fireplace [and] arranged all the chairs we possessed around it."[87]

Perry described that the ritual followed in the same manner as previous Bull sessions, where King used beer to keep the time. Perry explained King's "unvarying custom to drink two bottles during a 2½- or 3-hour session, mount the stairs for a trip to the head, return to his chair for a question period and informal discussion with one more beer as a nightcap."[88] Perry noted that the "beer had not the slightest effect on him."[89] In his secret meetings with journalists, King often provided the macadamia nuts and took his "place in an overstuffed armchair we had reserved for him, [and] thanked me for the glass of beer I placed on the end table."[90] He always told the truth and ensured that the journalists understood the ramifications, should classified information appear in the media. "And so it went," Adams explained. "King would finish five glasses of beer[, then] go upstairs to the 'head,' and return for one more glass of beer."[91] King smoked an average of eight cigarettes while sipping on beer and telling the unedited tales of his navy in the war at sea. Among those attending the meetings at the Adams family home, his fellow New York journalist Perry observed, "King was not only a great officer but a great guy."[92]

YOUR WARSHIP

King always relied upon a tight-knit circle of friends and family to hold the line in shaping the future of American sea power. The debates concerning the question of airpower and the unification of the armed services again distracted King from the more immediate problem of war when Senator Harry S Truman published an article in *Collier's* magazine under the title "Our Armed Forces Must Be Unified." Retired admiral Harry E. Yarnell endorsed unification, although he made the counterpoint against Truman's argument. Yarnell portrayed the American naval services as already being configured as a fully integrated military force with capacity to exert command ashore, at sea, and in the air.[93] Truman's and Yarnell's assertions in the context of the 1944 presidential election caused major headaches for Roosevelt.

The ongoing feud between the American armed services about the questions of unification and airpower lingered beneath the surface of strategy in the war at sea. Churchill exploited the divisions to insert himself into the political mix, which greatly frustrated Roosevelt. Recalling the situation at that time, Leahy observed that Roosevelt was never "in favor either of a unification of the armed forces, or of an independent air force separate from the Army and Navy."[94] King disagreed with Truman's untimely assertions. In correspondence with fellow members of the JCS, King explained that

> I think it inadvisable for authority over the armed forces of the United States to be vested in any one person, civil or military, other than the President of the United States, who is constitutionally Commander in Chief of the Army and Navy[, and the] Government of the United States is inherently premised on the principle of "checks and balances." I do not wish this statement to be construed too literally but rather as proposing that friendly competition and differing viewpoints will obtain better all-around results at the cabinet level than regimented administration and military control.[95]

Unification politics coincided with efforts to make the temporary wartime organization of the JCS as a single entity permanent, thereby nullifying the traditional authorities of the civilian secretaries of war and Navy.

The British model of civil-military command seeped into the debates concerning the future of American sea power. Ongoing efforts to build equities among the "Four Policemen" of the United Nations rekindled debates to establish of higher ranks within the American armed services. In earlier negotiations to establish the CCS, King suggested the prospective titles of "Captain-Admiral" or "Arch-Admiral."[96] When the idea of five-star rank resurfaced in memos circulated by Forrestal and Stimson to Roosevelt, Leahy pretended ignorance about the politics of rank by joking that the title of captain-admiral seemed confusing, and that arch-admiral sounded like a religious rank.[97] King chuckled when an aide told him, "If they make you an Arch-Admiral, I'll call you 'Your Warship.'"[98] Leahy pressed the point in telling King that Roosevelt "wanted to reward us with another star."[99] Jocularity turned deadly serious when King made the argument that "Dewey and Pershing carried six stars or so[, and] five-stars were probably a good idea for this war, but not now."[100] King asked, "What the hell are they supposed to do when there is not a war to win?"[101]

Five-star rank carried the double-edged function of fueling the broader wartime propaganda campaign, simultaneously subordinating the JCS and other key commanders under a clear lineal hierarchy of command. King saw the rank for what it was. He joked that his army counterpart would be "Marshal Marshall."[102] When Congress passed the legislation to establish five-star rank, King told the media that "he too was not the least interested in 'gathering a new title.'"[103] Georgia congressman Carl Vinson advised King to anticipate six-star rank, to which he retorted, "I have no desire for the '6-star rank' unless and until a '5-star rank' is provided for—and further, that I think it advisable that any promotion in connection with CominCh-CNO should first be '5-star rank.'"[104] King observed that "Marshall was against it, but he didn't kick when he got it."[105]

The establishment of a five-star rank completely changed the hierarchical routines of the CCS and JCS. Leahy returned to active status to push Stark off the number 1 position in the Naval Register. King subsequently held his place at number 2, although in the order of five-star precedence, Marshall was senior when King fell in as the third, and MacArthur as the fourth. In December, the hierarchy on the JCS rebalanced, with Leahy holding formal seniority over Marshall and, by extension, King. Junior to the other five-stars in lineal standing, Nimitz and Eisenhower received promotions before Arnold's on December 21, 1944. The five-star ranks also expanded the number of four- and three-star ranks within the military and naval services. By implication, King understood his new place in the upcoming hierarchical battles within transatlantic strategy and unification politics.[106]

King used debates concerning military and naval rank equivalencies to reframe relations between American army and naval services. He advocated for reductions in the number of rear admirals by creating the operational—or temporary—one-star rank of commodore. King recalled that Roosevelt "approved the idea, but the Senate, which was very jealous about its right to confirm any promotion[,] was quite unwilling that it should be so used[,] and insisted that all officers promoted to that rank should be confirmed."[107] King complained that "lots of people became rear admirals who might have been tested and found wanting in the rank of commodore."[108]

Congress failed to pass the requisite legislation to establish the permanent *rank* of commodore. Under executive wartime authorities, Roosevelt empowered King to designate worthy officers with the formal *rank* with one star. King also used the informal *title* of commodore for officers on special assignments. For example, Knox served informally as a commodore as the deputy director of Naval History until he received formal approval for the rank in the closing months of the war. During operations in China, Miles was elevated from his permanent rank of commander to serve with designation as a commodore before attaining a temporary wartime designation of two stars. Similarly, Painter held the title of commodore and wore the rank while acting on the authority of King during reconnaissance expeditions in the Pacific, Formosa, and beyond to China.[109]

Army commanders frequently struggled to understand the American naval tradition of simply doing the job at hand in the absence of clear guidance from above. For example, Wedemeyer commended his naval counterparts for their ability to adapt and overcome. He applauded Miles for setting the foundations for victory in China. On the other hand, Wedemeyer thought Miles needed to go—after nearly four years under harsh conditions and the constant stress of having the target for assassination by the Japanese. Wedemeyer asked King for assistance in reorganizing the American mission in China. In turn, King sent Capt. Wilfred Painter to serve on Wedemeyer's staff in July 1945. In the weeks following, Wedemeyer recommended Painter for promotion to the rank of rear admiral.[110]

The influx of reserve personnel with unique expertise and experience often frustrated the routines of the monoculture of the Naval Academy alumni and the admirals of King's navy. Notably, King purposely attempted to break up the tribal atrophy within the ranks. He noted that the "Naval Academy yachting club needs a good shake[-]up every five years or so."[111] When Wedemeyer recommended Painter for promotion to flag rank in the summer of 1945, Miles and Nimitz complained to King. Just three years earlier, Painter had carried the reserve rank of a junior-grade lieutenant. As a result, Miles and Nimitz provided backhanded compliments about Painter's performance in communications to King. In addition, Miles complained about Painter's failing to provide notification of his presence on the higher command staff of Wedemeyer in China. In response, King gave permission for Painter to use the positional title of commodore while on the staff with Wedemeyer. Annoyed with Miles and Nimitz, King also questioned their criticism of both Wedemeyer and Painter on September 10, 1945.[112]

Hostilities had subsided with the surrender of Axis forces in Europe and Asia, although King anticipated troubled waters in China and Russia. He wanted to solve the problem of Asia while concurrently fighting the decision to withdraw forces from Europe. Within this context, King wanted to reduce the number of roughly 300 flag officers in the sea services to peacetime numbers. Just three years earlier, the US Navy sailed with confidence under the command of fewer than eighty-four admirals on active service—all but two had completed the Naval War College curriculum.[113] Among other measures, King fixed ANSCOL as a postwar promotion requirement to qualify for flag rank in *all* branches of the American armed services. This enlightened measure quickly faded into the mire of joint bureaucracy.[114]

King sensed the shifting currents in the closing phases of the war as being early signs of stormy conditions lurking over American sea power. "In the latter days of the war," Dyer thought that King anticipated Roosevelt's death and worried about the potential consequences. After one meeting at the White House, King confided in Dyer that he felt as though Roosevelt's condition was like his being courted by the grim reaper. King treated Roosevelt with sorrowful compassion. During their last few meetings with Roosevelt, Dyer observed that King was "looking as you do when you look at someone and feel that he's about to pass on, not necessarily tomorrow or three weeks from tomorrow."[116]

CHAPTER 34

Gray King

The ramifications of Roosevelt's impending death threatened the delicate strategic balance within the CCS. Churchill maneuvered to reestablish British imperial claims as the JCS debated the offensive sequence for the final phases of offensive operations and into the transition for reconstruction in Europe and Asia.[1] Anticipating changes under the prospective Truman administration, Marshall greatly annoyed King by rekindling bureaucratic fires about the question of unification between the Departments of War and Navy. Army concepts of a unified military establishment ran against the prevailing winds of American sea power.[2] To Marshall's complete surprise, King preemptively requested space inside the Pentagon.[3] In addition, King provided plans to install a dock to accommodate *Dauntless* beside the Pentagon.[4]

Unification spread like a mushroom cloud over the bureaucratic détente between the various personalities within the CCS and JCS. British and American diplomats already set the foundations for the transatlantic alliance to thrive under the United Nations. Giving due respect to the British, King argued that American sea power "was directed to operations against land objectives [in] a continuous battle which for sustained intensity has never been equaled in naval history."[5] King directly influenced Assistant Secretary of the Navy Gates in making the argument in Congress that the "Navy itself could serve as a framework for merger [since it] can operate on the sea, under the sea, in the air, in amphibious operations, on land."[6] With American sea power alone, Gates argued that the US Navy "can by itself police the world."[7]

King proposed an American maritime patrol force operating in concert with other navies under the United Nations. Looking back on what was required after Pearl Harbor, King characterized the US Navy as a "complete organization that is able and ready to preserve peacetime preventative measures which might keep war from starting anywhere in the entire world."[8] King admitted,

> I've been one of those people who, for almost thirty years, have been advocating that the Coast Guard should be put under the Navy permanently, in order for the Navy, Marine Corps, and Coast Guard to be ready to manage any situation around the whole world under the secretary of the Navy—whether the Army and Air Force shall pass away or not.[9]

In making the argument, he refuted studies produced by the Strategic Bombing Survey and RAND project. He shrewdly recast the debate by listing the fallacies found in assertions made by Stimson, Marshall, and other insiders within the War Department.[10]

Airpower propagandists undercut American naval traditions as quaint and essentially outdated. Bell-bottomed sailors in cracker jack uniforms had become a vulnerability for the American sea services, as compared with the dashingly futuristic image of the US Army Air Force. King recognized the vulnerabilities inherent in outdated traditions. Looking to the future of American sea power, King attempted to beat the army by redesigning the uniforms of sea services. He pushed his subordinates among the US naval services—including the marines and coast guard as well as the civil-naval merchant marine—to adopt a single US naval look. He wanted the maritime services to lead the way in setting the course for the inevitable unification fights of the future.[11]

Uniforms stand among the many trivialities of military culture, which have often reflected bigger strategic trends of the past. King joked with staff about the image of Field Marshal Sir Bernard L. Montgomery and his concocted look. King observed that Montgomery's "beret was somewhat dramatic, but hardly more so than MacArthur's gold[-]embroidered cap and corncob pipe, or Patton's two pearl-handled pistols."[12] King noted that Halsey "could hardly have been considered constrained [in] style."[13] In considering questions of military fashion, King confided that his "own taste did not run to such personal exuberance."[14]

OUR AMERICAN PRINCIPLES

King celebrated the modest example set by Eisenhower in adapting existing military fashions to his own liking. British military fashions influenced "Ike" to adopt the jacket widely known as the "Eisenhower jacket." King designed an Eisenhower jacket variation of the naval uniform.[15] Given the looming questions concerning the future of unification, King championed the idea of creating a single uniform for all the American armed services.[16] Gray uniforms traditionally appeared on the parade grounds of West Point and at Marshall's alma mater, VMI. Various hues of gray appeared on the painted broadsides of American warships. For these reasons, King proposed gray as the best choice for uniforms for the purposes of unification.

King hoped to preempt the unification debate by opening an offensive campaign on the wartime fashion front. He always hated the white naval uniforms. Navy denim dungarees seemed too like prison uniforms. King also considered army khaki as being too closely reminiscent of British military traditions. He liked the aviator greens but thought the uniform seemed unmistakably like the US Marine Corps variant. Seeking alternatives, King concocted a design featuring navy-blue cotton braiding, black Bakelite buttons, and gray herringbone "jungle cloth" canvas.[17] He first appeared in the prototype version in the fall of 1942.[18] After 1943, he forced his immediate staff to wear the gray uniform. King described the bluish-gray naval uniform as being "consistent with democratic traditions [and] our American principles."[19]

Allies on all sides tended to prefer the classic blue-and-white uniforms of the naval services. By design, King's gray uniforms stood out on the wartime sea of multinational and interservice fashion. Gray uniforms reflected the practical character of King. Upon seeing the uniform for the first time, Churchill wryly offered to help King by soliciting bespoke assistance from his personal tailors on Saville Row in London. Churchill said chidingly, "Poole's has braiding in stock and we may be able to get a nicer fit for you at Gieves."[20] Churchill then suggested, "You might add a bit of gold—you know we wouldn't want to confuse you with the Germans."[21]

King soldiered on in gray gabardine in a personal campaign to win the unification battles looming just over the horizon. Unfortunately, American sailors universally rejected the gray uniform. Aides of King generally hated the uniform. Lt. Alan R. McFarland recalled hearing the "remarks about looking like a bus driver or a door-man."[22] Smedberg recalled a "fresh-faced young supply corps Lt. (j.g.) reported on board[, and] I took one look at him and told him never to wear that thing on my ship again."[23] Unwilling to appear in gray, Nimitz authorized personnel in the Pacific to wear army khaki—invoking logistical delays in shipping the gray uniforms to Hawaii. King recalled seeing Nimitz in the uniform only once during the war.[24] During meetings in San Francisco, King debuted the drab navy grays when Nimitz appeared in the classic service dress blues. King stood with Nimitz in the drizzling rain while awaiting their car. Nimitz later recalled that a newspaper photographer yelled, "Get out of my way, chief, [I] want to get a picture of Admiral Nimitz."[25]

Gray uniforms proved wildly unpopular within the seagoing ranks of the US Navy and US Coast Guard. Marines simply ignored the uniform. Individuals assigned to CominCh headquarters slowly swallowed the anchor—embracing their distinctive gray uniforms as a mark for being among the select few elites of King's navy. The unique design proved exceedingly practical. The black Bakelite buttons and black cotton piping on the insignia required no polish. The herringbone "jungle cloth" fabric in the original design proved serviceable for wear out of a seabag, and it produced sharp creases without ironing. Compared with the traditional blue-and-white uniforms, the gray uniform proved reasonably priced. Lt. Richard D. Shepard recalled wearing the outfit upon reporting to CominCh headquarters at Main Navy:

> Up to my third-deck office and often, around 0745[,] would see in a long corridor a tall, thin figure striding towards me, dressed in the drab gray "bus driver" uniform, complete with black plastic buttons and dreary plain (no gold) black thin chin strap, black chicken[-]guts cap that Ernie had prescribed as a seagoing officer's uniform [and] here would approach not only [my] boss but one of the most powerful commanders in the world—this tall, remote, preoccupied man would notice me, nod briefly in return, and stride on without a word and without breaking his step.[26]

Shepard admitted, "I really liked the gray uniform, especially when we were able to add the gold buttons and standard navy braid."[27] Gray uniforms also resonated among SeaBees, amphibious forces, and Motor Torpedo Boat squadrons.[28]

TEARDROPS IN VICTORY

Looking outward and into the hazy, gray world of the future, King envisioned the unified navies of Britain and America as the counterforce in future relations with Soviet and Chinese allies. Leahy agreed with King in suggesting that the army commanders failed "to be able to understand that the Navy, with some Army air assistance[,] had already defeated Japan."[29] Characterizing the situation, Leahy was concerned that the army "not only was planning a huge land invasion of Japan, but was convinced that we needed Russian assistance as well to bring the war against Japan to a successful conclusion."[30] Working on the fringes, King endorsed plans championed by Miles to expand intelligence collaboration with the Chinese. To these ends, Capt. John "Jack" Holtwick arrived from FRUMEL in Australia to establish an advanced station in Chungking in 1944.[31] His assignment with Miles in China reflected the focus of King's navy in the Pacific, as the US Navy conducted a maritime war of attrition against Japan.

King again overhauled the CominCh headquarters in anticipation of the Allied victory in Europe. He expected to shift forces rapidly from the Atlantic to the Pacific in keeping with the Formosa strategy for Asia.[32] He therefore merged the First and the Tenth Fleets under his personal authority within the CominCh headquarters—sending Low to the Pacific as the commander, Cruiser Division 16. King then dragooned the skipper of the battleship USS *Iowa* (BB-61), Capt. Alan R. McCann, to assume Low's multiple functions within the CominCh headquarters—and particularly as the coordinator for Allied submarine operations under the First Fleet and conversely the antisubmarine functions of Tenth Fleet.[33]

McCann offered significant experience in conducting offensive submarine operations at the front. Conversely, he failed to understand his assignment to replace Low in the Tenth Fleet during the decisive phases of the antisubmarine campaign. McCann protested to King, "I am a submarine officer and not an antisubmarine officer." "King chuckled" and McCann recalled him responding, "Well, McCann, I am setting up a thief to catch a thief."[34] McCann recalled meeting the analysts in the Combat Intelligence Division. Smedberg and Sebald educated McCann about the vision for Asia and the nuances of tracking the Imperial Japanese Navy in the Pacific. McCann described Knowles as being an officer with the unique ability to think like a German submarine skipper. McCann described Knowles as "particularly outstanding [at briefing] the Admiral every morning at 0900, emphasizing the locations of various German submarines as he knew their locations, at least we made believe [that he did]."[35]

King challenged his analysts to prove the actual capabilities of the enemy, rather than simply focus on the intentions of the enemy. In the spring of 1945, the CominCh headquarters staff suffered from an uneasy fear of an unexpected Nazi presence in the Atlantic as German U-boats appeared to break for the Indian Ocean. Captured enemy prisoners and other intelligence flowing in from the European front indicated Nazi plans to send missile-launching U-boats with chemical weapons to attack the American coast. Newspapers fueled popular fear about a surprise Nazi attack as the Third Reich spiraled to defeat in Europe.[36]

McCann and Knowles continued working with Sebald in executing the antisubmarine mission of the Tenth Fleet. Intercepts from the Japanese naval attaché in Berlin, Rear-Admiral Kojima Hideo, included detailed reports about German navy experimentation with snorkel technology, antidetection countermeasures, and high-speed submarine propulsion. Kojima described the Type XXI and Type XXIII designs in detail—suggesting submerged speeds of more than 16 knots. British and American cryptanalysts struggled to solve the intercepted messages until June 1944—well after Allied forces went ashore at Normandy and coinciding with the assault on Saipan and the Battle of the Philippine Sea.[37]

American cryptographers solved the Japanese naval attaché dispatch six months after its original transmission drew significant attention among the analysts within the submarine-tracking rooms.[38] Their discussions centered on the prospective ramifications of the new German U-boat innovations.[39] Fears then amplified with the solution of a separate Japanese description, this time transmitted by the ambassador in Berlin, Ōshima Hiroshi.[40] On July 26, 1944, he reported great expectations for the Type XXI in suggesting that "its effect will first be felt from about September; and by November or December [the German navy expects] greater results by its use in great quantity."[41]

Indications of German technical advances and the potential transfer of such innovations to the Japanese held the additional prospect of prolonging the war at sea. In response, King directed Edwards and Cooke to mobilize the CominCh/CNO headquarters planning staff to develop a layered antisubmarine defense within American coastal waters—Operation BUMBLEBEE.[42] In turn, Cooke and McCann planned operations to force a decisive result in the Atlantic—aimed at "liquidating" the German submarine force altogether.[43] These plans became the basis for Operation TEARDROP. In a three-pronged assault, multiple hunter-killer groups combed the Atlantic in a systematic offensive to destroy German submarines.

TEARDROP aligned the hunter-killer groups in a line running from north to south and running back and forth from west to east to drag the bottom for indications of enemy targets. King envisioned the Tenth Fleet as the central authority for coordinating TEARDROP with Royal Navy, Royal Canadian Navy, and US Navy forces operating in unison.[44] Thus, it is perhaps ironic that King had earlier stood so firmly against such a centralized organization during negotiations among the Admiralty, NSHQ, and Navy Department.[45] The unified command under Tenth Fleet in the Atlantic was not established when King authorized CominCh to transmit the TEARDROP execution orders to the Atlantic Fleet in April.[46]

Captured enemy prisoners and other intelligence flowing in from the European front suggested the possibility of Nazi plans to send missile-launching U-boats with chemical weapons to attack the American coast.[47] Royal Navy and US Navy commandos provided reports highlighting German advances in submarine snorkel propulsion, hydrogen peroxide fuels, acoustic homing torpedoes, and jet aircraft. German radio burst transmission technology threatened Allied intelligence. The possibility of rogue Nazi submarines with deck-launched missiles inspired Knowles to conclude that "it would be touch-and-go all over again."[48]

KEELBLOCKS OR DOWNFALL?

The final collapse of the Third Reich failed to mark the end of operations for King's navy in the Atlantic and ashore on the European continent. In the spring of 1945, he progressively shifted strategy to focus on stabilization and reconstruction operations in Europe. King simultaneously continued debating with Marshall and MacArthur about the strategy for Asia. Diplomatic foundations, which had been negotiated at the Moscow Conference two years earlier, provided inroads for CCS planners to adjoin the four-phased operational concept for synthesizing Soviet operations into China and Japan. Under the general designations for Operations KEELBLOCKS 1 through 4, the JCS approved the phased inclusion of Soviet army and naval forces in combined efforts to seize control in Asia. Once again, the CCS and JCS were divided about the strategic priorities for planning operations to invade the Japanese home islands, or DOWNFALL.[49]

Various planning staffs fought for control over future strategic priorities, with forces already settling into the routines of reconstruction in Europe while combat operations intensified in Asia. Playing a bureaucratic shell game, King earmarked equipment and personnel requirements slated for DOWNFALL for the alternative purposes of Operations KEELBLOCKS and the associated plan to take Formosa under CAUSEWAY.[50] King explained his plan to Admirals Walter S. DeLany and William H. P. "Spike" Blandy. Within the context of DOWNFALL, CCS planners referred to the Kyushu assault under the code name OLYMPIC and Honshu as CORONET. The associated strategic air campaign, MATTERHORN, was split among KEELBLOCKS, CAUSEWAY, and DOWNFALL.[51] DeLany and Blandy were confused when King approved a series of "nutty" requests from MacArthur to procure equipment for DOWNFALL.[52] In essence, King used the overall plans for DOWNFALL as a bureaucratic bluff.[53]

As was done in Europe, all the various plans under development for Asia provided rich opportunities for King to make the case for building more ships.[54] King told his staff that "MacArthur is about to conduct the greatest amphibious operations in history [and] will have tremendous difficulties of his own."[55] King reassured DeLany and Blandy that "it is not for us to add to his difficulties by raising technical objections."[56] All the while, King planned to use the ships allocated for an invasion of Japan for the alternative purpose of taking Formosa. Any invasion of Japan also failed to synchronize with broader reconstruction strategies in the Pacific and beyond to Asia.[57]

King often agreed to the unanimous rulings of the JCS to divert resources from the War Department to the Navy Department to pursue US naval plans.[58] Observing from the wings, Edwards recalled that the "'democratic' system [and] processes leading to unanimous vote in the wartime JCS were sometimes slow—that was one shortcoming[,] but the decisions when finally made that way stood up in action."[59] Considering the debate over a direct assault on Kyushu and Honshu under Operation DOWNFALL, King thought the "defeat of Japan could be accomplished by sea-air power, without the necessity of invasion."[60] "As the planning of amphibious operations is a slow and painstaking process," King anticipated the "future contingencies."[61] "Thus," King reasoned, "he concurred in the majority decision of the Joint Chiefs to make plans for the invasion and seizure of objectives in the Japanese home islands without sharing the conviction that such operations were necessary."[62]

King had no intention of pursuing an amphibious campaign beyond Kyushu, which happened to provide the ideal position for supporting sustained operations ashore on the Asian continent. King provided endorsements with caveats only for DOWNFALL plans in Japan. Always holding the priority for future operations in China, King shrewdly used the requirements for Japan to play a bureaucratic shell game in gaining JCS approvals for diverting industrial resources from the War Department to the Navy Department.[63] King explained:

We were very anxious to get a seaway into China in order to bring to bear their manpower and geographic position. I spoke about our intentions at one time, our serious consideration of the occupation of Formosa that would enable us to get hold of Amoy and possibly Hong Kong and Canton. Then, later in the war, after we had decided we had to go into Okinawa, we had an alternative of going into Kyushu or what is called the Chusan Archipelagoes below the Yangtse River in China.[64]

King reasoned with the CCS and JCS by using empirical logic. He explained, "[To] go into Kyushu, we had to get the means from Europe, to get the troops moved to the western Pacific in time."[65] King stipulated, "We could do Kyushu if we gathered up everything we had in the Pacific."[66] To emphasize, he said, "Kyushu and the Tokyo plain would have had to wait."[67] The prospective invasion of Japan by the Red Army served as King's gambit to refocus the CCS strategy on China. He reasoned that the Soviets and Chinese forces on the Asian continent "would be bogged down for decades in the mountains and swamps."[68] In June 1945, King strongly endorsed the CCS proposal to assign the Royal Navy into the Pacific for the purpose of taking Indonesia, Malaya, and areas along the southern coast of China.[69]

At that time, King also directed the Combat Intelligence Division to predict the conditions required to impel a Japanese surrender. In anticipation of impending meetings with the CCS in Potsdam, King told Smedberg, "I want you and your staff [to] tell me when you think the Japanese will surrender if the most awful thing you can imagine happens to them in, say, the next two or three months."[70] At that time, plans under discussion by Rochefort and Sebald in the PSIS included several crazy ideas. King recalled proposals to "drop salt or some other substance into the Japanese rice paddies when the rice was ripe, to spoil the crops."[71] King recalled another proposal to "trap bats, numb them, take them to Japan and attach firebombs to them[,] and drop them over Japanese cities, and there was a magnificent scheme proposed by a Texan for taking great numbers of Texas jackrabbits to Europe and tuning them loose on the battlefields to explode land mines."[72]

The general concept of an amphibious campaign against the Japanese home islands seemed unnecessary among the analysts within the CominCh headquarters. Smedberg supervised the studies of Rochefort and Sebald in efforts to determine the optimal conditions required for the Japanese to accept surrender.[73] Sebald submitted a detailed analysis and anticipated that the Japanese were prepared to surrender on the condition of Emperor Hirohito as figurehead.[74] Sebald thought the Imperial War Staff sought an event to save face to justify surrender. Sebald suggested that the Japanese may surrender in the aftermath of a lunar eclipse, a major tsunami, or some other form of natural disaster.[75]

King invoked the examples of Napoleon and the Balkan Wars to highlight the problems with invading the Japanese home islands. He placed responsibility for defeating Japanese forces on the Asian continent on the Soviets and Chinese armies ashore. In July 1945, King met Nimitz in San Francisco before flying to the other side of the globe for meetings with the CCS.[76] King flew to New York to join Leahy on the transatlantic flight to Paris. There, Stark arrived from London to travel with Leahy and King from Paris to Berlin on July 14, 1945.

The scars of war appeared on the faces of civilians, which made a clear impression upon King. The smoldering cities and charred moonscapes of Europe inspired the observation that "there was nothing left to fix[;] it all had to be rebuilt."[77] Before the Potsdam meetings, King visited the devastated area surrounding the Brandenburg Gate and then traveled in a limousine under Red Army escort to the historic Sanssouci Palace of Frederick the Great. The discipline of the Red Army greatly impressed King, although he was amused by the obvious presence of the Soviet secret police.

The CCS meetings at Potsdam provided opportunity for King to press the concept of a China strategy. Between July 16 and 24, 1945, his primary effort centered on convincing the CCS to support a Red Army offensive into Manchuria to crush the Japanese in a grand pincer. This was to be executed with a northward drive into the central and northern provinces of China by the Communist armies of Mao in conjunction with those of Generalissimo Chiang Kai-shek.[78] Having won CCS support for this concept of operations at Potsdam, King received the news of the first successful atomic bomb test on July 16, in the New Mexican desert. Marshall used the opportunity to pursue DOWNFALL. Still reluctant about an invasion of Japan, King encouraged the Royal Navy to focus on offensive operations in Burma and Malaysia and into Indochina, thereby clearing the path to Formosa under Operation CAUSEWAY.

"CALL ME ERNIE"

Deliberations at Potsdam initially centered on bringing the Soviets into the war against Japan in Asia. King watched Stalin carefully during these discussions. Having previously resisted the idea, Stalin suddenly announced his decision to declare war on Japan. The announcement threw a wrench into the works of other ongoing discussions between Churchill and Truman.[79] On the final day of meetings at Potsdam, Churchill stood nearby when Truman told Stalin about the atomic bomb on July 24. Stalin simply shrugged off the news by telling Truman to "make good use of it against the Japanese."[80] Churchill and other observers at the scene were surprised by Stalin's nonchalant response.[81]

CCS and JCS estimates suggested the likelihood of heavy casualties among American forces in anticipation of the assault on Japan. The projections horrified Truman.[82] The unknown ramifications of using the atomic bomb caused concern among the key members of the CCS at Potsdam. The order circulated within the army staff on the day after Truman told Stalin about the weapon.[83] Once Truman had made the decision at Potsdam, Cunningham noted in his diary that Leahy and King appeared uncharacteristically drunk. Cunningham described King as so unburdened from the stress that he "fell on my neck and besought me to call him Ernie."[84]

After Potsdam, King nursed his hangover in the back of a limousine, visiting historical attractions around Berlin. He then turned southward to visit Nazi landmarks in Bavaria. The commander, US Naval Forces in Germany, Ghormley, also briefed King about the status of Nazi outlaws—to include SS-Sturmbannführer (Major) Wernherr von Braun. King then traveled farther south to the ruins at Berchtesgaden.[85] There, King caroused with the American troops with Gen. George S. Patton. King recalled that "Patton had raised hell against the Air [Force] because they did not help the ground troops."[86] During their exchange, Patton asked King to facilitate orders for transfer to the Asiatic front. In memoirs, Wedemeyer recalled Patton's name in describing plans for future operations in China.[87]

Atomic weapons influenced debates about influence of sea power on the military policy of the United States. King warned journalists that the "scientists have most of the information still in their heads concerning the future use of the new weapon."[88] King admitted "frankly that he did not know how it would affect future naval warfare."[89] Since the deed had been done, King kept his personal feelings about the bomb opaque in discussions with the media. Advisers at the Navy Department, like RAdm. Ellis M. Zacharias, articulated their collective disgust about the amateurish decision to drop the bomb. Zacharias reasoned, "Japan would have accepted our surrender terms even without the prodding which the two atomic bombs provided."[90] "The atomic bomb, as did the bombings at Pearl

Harbor and the bombing of London," Zacharias argued, "could have strengthened instead of destroying morale."[91]

Airpower propagandists weaponized King's honest, professional arguments in their effort to defeat the Navy Department. King lambasted the airpower clique, saying that their "target is always tactical, and the effects are always strategic when everybody else has to clean up their mess."[92] On the atom bomb, King asked rhetorically, "Who would have guessed that the damned thing would have worked?"[93] King rejected the atomic bomb in observing that "you can't win a war with gizmos and weird ideas like the Air Force people [thought] and that's why they are so damned dangerous."[94] US Army Air Force propagandists quickly claimed credit for the naval victory in the summer of 1945.[95] After the atomic bomb, Admirals Cooke and Sherman both refuted the airpower advocates in testimony to Congress.[96] King formally characterized the atom bomb as a weapon of "limited purpose."[97] Indeed, the full strategic success of American sea power became crystal clear when Allied forces went ashore in Japan, seeing the problems of mass starvation, fouled supply lines, and famine among the war-weary people of Japan. MacArthur's pleas for help, as amplified by King and Sebald, sparked significant debate within the Truman administration.

CROSSROADS

The rising sun over imperial Japan suddenly brightened with two atomic flashes, which outlined the silhouettes of King's navy in the waters below. "Apart from the humanitarian arguments [against] *using* the atomic bomb," reserve rear admiral Samuel Eliot Morison argued, "was it not the *possession* of atomic weapons that contributed to the international tensions following the war?"[98] He continued, "It was probably unfortunate that the war in the Pacific ended so abruptly [before] proper preparations could have been made for the surrender of the Japanese army in China."[99] Morison ultimately laid the blame for the tensions between the Anglo-American and Soviet allies at the feet of Truman and the atomic bomb by arguing, as "it happened, the Communists profited by the confusion in China."[100]

Forrestal stood with Leahy and King in full opposition against using the atomic bomb over civilian populations in Japan. Forrestal and King preferred other options, including a demonstration of the bomb at sea.[101] Truman ignored the alternatives.[102] As the first atomic bombs fell from US Army Air Force bombers over Hiroshima and Nagasaki, King and the CominCh staff continued work on the DOWNFALL and CAUSEWAY plans.[103] King's team planned DOWNFALL simultaneously with CAUSEWAY.[104] The logistics plans for executing wartime operations simultaneously served as the basis for reconstruction operations in peacetime. Despite Marshall and MacArthur's vision for an invasion of Japan, King never planned to allow Operation DOWNFALL to happen. He agreed to a "D-day" only to procure the resources required for Operation CAUSEWAY and the development of Formosa as the springboard for the reconstruction of Asia.[105] The fights to establish conditions for the sustainable peace further informed King's vision for the future of American sea power. King's men, wearing their gray uniforms, and civilian diplomats in gray flannel suits gathered at the picturesque Mount Washington Hotel in Bretton Woods, New Hampshire. The Bretton Woods agreement set the foundations for reconstruction under the United Nations. In theory, the American dollar provided steady foundations for all humanity to pursue happiness under the protection of Roosevelt's dream of the "Four Policemen" Russian and Chinese forces ashore and Anglo-American navies afloat. These negotiations fell into the shadow of the sudden atomic victory over imperial Japan in 1945.[106]

As Japanese forces ceded control in China, Mao's operatives murdered British and American prisoners of war. In a pivotal turn, Chinese Communists kidnapped and tortured an OSS team headed by US Army Air Force captain John M. Birch. The Chinese mutilated Birch's body in a gambit to discredit Chiang's Kuomintang and disrupt British and American efforts to reconstruct China. Mao denied involvement in Birch's kidnapping and other OSS forces, later shifting blame to Chiang during a direct conversation with Marshall.[107] The uncertainties inherent in King's vision for operations in China precluded the CCS and JCS from making firm strategic commitments ashore on the Asian continent.

The administrative crown weighed heavily upon King's head as he managed the transition from war to peace. He faced the reality of civilian control. With the surrender of imperial Japan, the Allied victory set into motion the six-month sunset clause to rescind the emergency war powers given by Congress to Roosevelt after Pearl Harbor. King anticipated the end of EO 9096 with the victory in 1945.[108] Still, his strategy for winning the peace through China defined early phases of reconstruction in Asia. Among the first to step ashore in Korea in August 1945, RAdm. Francis S. Low found the Japanese forces completely demoralized, starving, and very accommodating.[109] Smith-Hutton concurrently arrived in Japan in time to witness the surrender ceremonies held in Tokyo Bay on board the battleship USS *Missouri* (BB-63) in September.[110]

Shortly after these rituals, King's navy received orders to reverse course to bring home American service personnel from the fronts under Operation MAGIC CARPET. The ironic twist in crossing the nexus from war to peace centered on the plans originally designed for killing the enemy. DOWNFALL and CAUSEWAY plans provided a framework for bringing combatant forces home. Thus, the reverse plan—MAGIC CARPET—enabled Truman to claim full responsibility for bringing the troops home.[111] King anticipated disaster looming as the reconstruction strategy diverted from its planned course under the United Nations. Observing the trends from below within the ONH at the Navy Department, Professor Robert G. Albion observed that Truman's people thought that during the "Roosevelt administration, the White House was a Navy wardroom; we're gonna fix all that!"[112]

SWIMMING WITH SHARKS

Airpower propagandists seized opportunities to embarrass King's navy in anticipation of the postwar fight for American sea power. The loss of a warship due to enemy action or by accident always carried special significance for many American taxpayers. The losses of tanks and bombers in combat ashore paled in comparison with the sinking of an American warship at sea.[113] On the day following Truman's decision to use the atomic bomb, a Japanese submarine torpedoed USS *Indianapolis* (CA-35) on July 26, 1945—just after the warship delivered the Hiroshima bomb to the remote airfield on Tinian in the central Pacific.

Headlines about the atomic bombings of Japan appeared with the equally shocking reports about *Indianapolis*. Horrific details soon leaked into the media. Concurrent with

Indianapolis's sinking, Generals James Doolittle and Carl Spaatz referred to the mass casualties inherent with the warship losses.[114] Doolittle overlooked the role of naval aviation in enabling the famous raid over Tokyo, which had become manufactured by the airpower propagandists. Popular myths surrounded the heroic image of Doolittle when he argued that "the battleship has been obsolescent for the past twenty years and obsolete for the last ten."[115] He embraced the atomic bomb as the solution for all future scenarios in arguing that "there will be no future use for aircraft carriers."[116]

The sinking of *Indianapolis* and the subsequent surrender of Japan after the atomic bomb seemingly provided an exclamation point to the strategic-airpower argument in the court of public opinion. Putting a face on the *Indianapolis* disaster, Capt. Charles B. McVay III paid a heavy price for the sin of surviving in the media. In the bureaucratic kabuki dances within navy lifelines, Nimitz had also completed a formal review of all available evidence in accordance with Navy Regulations. The facts revealed fundamental problems in the standard operating procedures of CinCPac/POA, which rendered McVay to fall victim to the unforeseeable circumstances of war. Mistakes made in the CinCPAC/POA Combat Intelligence Division resulted in miscommunications about the estimated locations of the enemy submarine threats in the vicinity of *Indianapolis*.[117] Estimates available to McVay appeared to indicate minimal probability of encountering an enemy combatant along the route between Tinian and the Philippines.

Like many other skippers throughout history in either peace or war, the element of chance placed McVay on an unexpected course in the annals of American sea power. McVay made the reasoned decision to cease the laborious tactic of zigzagging and instead gambled on reaching safe harbor at best speed along a straight course. Unfortunately, *Indianapolis* encountered the imperial Japanese submarine *I-58*. The enemy skipper, Lieutenant-Commander Hashimoto Mochizura, gave the order, and after the torpedoes struck he observed his target sink very quickly under the stars into the inky waters of the Pacific.[118] The investigation conducted by Nimitz resulted in an obligatory letter of reprimand—a predictable outcome when McVay admitted to exercising his prerogative to abandon zigzag as prescribed in CinCPAC/POA standing orders. Within the seagoing ranks of King's navy, the issue of culpability for *Indianapolis*'s sinking was closed. McVay accepted the facts and focused on making his physical recovery to pass the medical retention board and qualify for future active service in the seagoing ranks.[119]

Newspaper headlines and the grieving parents of *Indianapolis* sailors still demanded heads to roll for the disaster. Forrestal acknowledged the wildest allegations in personal correspondence to families, which subsequently leaked into the press. Taking a different tack, King referred all inquiries concerning the loss of *Indianapolis* sailors to BuNav. Standard procedure dictated a slow and methodical approach governing the release of information, in accordance with the existing wartime security protocols. The standard timing between a given individual being *officially* declared missing in action had not yet met the mark to issue the requisite confirmation of being killed in action.[120]

Leaks to the media and letters from families inspired Congress to demand action, which trickled through the Truman administration to Forrestal's desk. With his hands tied, Forrestal formally ordered King to reopen the investigation of *Indianapolis*. McVay was also *not* the only American skipper to be court-martialed after suffering the loss of a command in combat, as had been alleged in the original investigation.[121] In numerous cases, King himself participated by chairing administrative court-martial proceedings after the loss of warships in both peace and war. In one case, King ruled against a fellow captain with the double-edged observation that "his only fault had been a lack of toughness in checking on the ability of his subordinates, but that as captain is personally responsible for his ship."[122]

Subsequent accounts about the grave misfortunes of *Indianapolis* have left many dubious interpretations to blossom in popular memory. Many accounts propagate the myth that King personally wanted to humiliate McVay and Nimitz for their "sins of omission."[123] More egregiously, there were unsubstantiated tales about a fictitious grudge between King and McVay's father. According to the sea story, the elder, RAdm. Charles B. McVay Jr., supposedly found King with "women aboard his ship."[124] Two decades earlier, the elder McVay indeed filed a report about King. Contrary to myth, the elder McVay characterized King as being "one of the most capable officers of his grade."[125]

The McVay family primarily operated in a completely different orbit among the surface fleet, while King went into the depths with submarines and beyond to aviation. As the younger McVay successfully completed multiple surface commands, King welcomed him onto the OpNav staff in 1943 and 1944. Having made the grade with King at OpNav, McVay received orders to command *Indianapolis* in the first place. Under the circumstances prevailing in 1945, McVay won personal commendations for superior performance as the skipper of *Indianapolis*—earning the noteworthy distinction of commanding Spruance's favorite flagship during operations from Saipan to Okinawa.

Documentary evidence fails to substantiate the conspiracy theories surrounding the sinking of *Indianapolis*. Opening the McVay case would only undercut King's primary effort, since the failures of the CinCPAC/POA Combat Intelligence Division fell under Nimitz. Thus, the actual fault for the sinking of *Indianapolis* arguably centered on the CinCPAC/POA staff under Nimitz.[126] Such highly classified details hung in the balance, and King wanted to keep those details out of the newspapers. Behind closed doors, negotiations had already commenced for what became the United States–United Kingdom Agreement (UKUSA).

The politics surrounding efforts to establish a unified defense establishment appeared alongside the announcements surrounding the sinking of *Indianapolis*. Under direct orders from Forrestal, Navy Department bureaucrats expunged the Nimitz letter of reprimand for McVay along with orders for court-martial. Behind the scenes, King put Cmdre. Wilder D. Baker in charge of chairing the court-martial at the Washington Navy Yard—in a building adjacent to King's flagship, *Dauntless*. This location also put King at the center of an unhelpful spectacle, which unfolded when Hashimoto appeared to testify on behalf of McVay.[127]

King characteristically strived to stay out of the media spotlight throughout the court-martial of McVay. The timing of the court-martial itself also reflected the politics when the proceedings began on December 3, 1945. At that time, King had already vacated his offices in the Navy Department as his relief, Nimitz, prepared to assume the chair as the CNO. Behind the scenes, King also stacked the tribunal with Baker as the presiding member to govern the proceedings. Admirals Sprague and Denfeld also assisted by ordering friends of McVay to serve on the court-martial panel. King officially left office as CNO when Baker promulgated the findings of McVay's court-martial to the media on December 19.

The punishments awarded to McVay for the *Indianapolis* episode fulfilled the broader purposes of allowing King's navy to pass with a clean bureaucratic slate for Nimitz to serve as the CNO. McVay completely understood his mission *at that time*. Yet, the sinking of *Indianapolis* had captured the American imagination. McVay's court-marshal caused indelible scars in the record of American sea power. The complexities of the carefully orchestrated verdict also backfired when Forrestal refused to accept mitigating evidence. As a result, McVay suffered a standard "sentence" under Navy Regulations to "lose one hundred (100) numbers in his temporary grade of captain and one hundred (100) numbers in his permanent grade of commander."[128]

Missing in the deeper analysis of the story, McVay's court-martial essentially resulted in no punishment in bureaucratic terms. In essence, McVay retained his *temporary* rank as a captain. His reduction by 100 in lineal standing kept him on pace to compete for a two-star assignment. In the summary ruling, a direct recommendation from King in *support* of McVay noted that the "sentence was remitted in its entirety."[129] Within the bureaucratic lifelines of King's navy, McVay continued serving in good standing as the chief of staff to the newly appointed commander of the Eastern and Gulf Sea Frontier, Adm. Thomas C. Kinkaid. In 1948, McVay received formal notice of his selection to the permanent rank of captain—ahead of other Naval Academy classmates and officers of comparable time in service.[130]

Promotion to the permanent rank of captain normally provided McVay another five years in the rank, to earn a chance for competitive promotion to flag rank. McVay suffered from spinal injuries and other maladies associated with wounds sustained in combat, years of hard driving on steel decks, and basic melancholy. Unsurprisingly, McVay received notification of his forced transfer to retired status in January 1949. After an administrative retention board's review, as appointed by Forrestal, and with the final verdict of BuMed, McVay dutifully transferred to retired status in the "tombstone" rank of rear admiral with an effective date of June 30, 1949.[131] Nineteen years later, King's navy had also sunk into the murky bureaucratic malaise of the postwar era when McVay committed suicide.

CHAPTER 35
King's Henchmen

Headlines heralding McVay's court-martial overshadowed the internal feuding within the Navy Department. Forrestal fought King for control over the proverbial helm. Emergency wartime measures like EO 9096 featured a sunset clause—dissolving the merger of CominCh and CNO within six months of the final defeat of the Axis Tripartite in 1945. Victory over Germany in May and then Japan in September set the clock running, as Forrestal anticipated King's five-star passage to lame-duck status by March 1946. In a blatant power play, Forrestal rejected the flag selection board results that were submitted by VAdm. Patrick N. L. Bellinger. Working behind closed doors, Forrestal overruled the promotion board with Truman's endorsement.[1] King anticipated the underlying political currents. King then lamented the deaths of Knox and then Roosevelt, saying, "I had a great deal of trouble with Mr. Forrestal [since] I wanted to have no one above me except the President himself."[2]

King characteristically acted without requesting higher approval by preemptively dissolving the position of CominCh. He alone was CNO—essentially daring Forrestal to respond. King admitted, "I never went to talk to the President about it because he might not agree."[3] King further explained, "I have always felt that the CominCh concept was a mistaken one."[4] King referred to the examples provided by the number of generals serving in the American ranks of the Civil War, the ambiguous role of Dewey before the CNO, and, "more recently, Pershing—whose functions developed into a fifth[-]wheel status because there was no real need for the position."[5] King further explained that

> I think we must realize that CNO (CominCh ex officio) cannot allow himself to be moored (2 anchors down) in Washington—he must get out and around. Above all he cannot allow himself to get submerged in material details—the precedents of 1916–1941 are bad in this respect and must be changed.[6]

His experiencing two world wars inspired King's unilateral decision to dissolve the CominCh organization under the singular authority of the CNO on October 10, 1945. He failed to request permissions from Forrestal before informing Truman of the decision.

Truman remained unsure of Forrestal and the Navy Department hierarchy, which extended to the seagoing ranks of King's navy. Anticipating the unification battles to come, King explained, "I studied [the] overall organization for years [and] by the latter part of 1944 my ideas began to jell."[7] In a preemptive strike, King announced the appointment of Edwards to serve in the new title of vice chief of naval operations. Still focused on winning the peace in China, King appointed Cooke as the commander, Western Pacific.

In this role, he had the responsibility to support the future development of China under the wartime strategy for reconstruction in Asia. Concurrently, King reduced Horne to perform the inglorious duty of "special assistant."[8] King released the news to the media without consulting Forrestal. King considered Forrestal unworthy of the position of Navy secretary. King and Forrestal also worked hard to keep their differences private—both keenly aware of their lingering memories of Sims and Daniels's feud.[9]

King disagreed with the policy changes during the transition from the Roosevelt era into the Truman administration, since the unification debates affected the established strategy for reconstruction in Europe and Asia. Having assembled a war-winning team at CominCh, King initially nominated Edwards as a successor, followed by Cooke. In turn, Forrestal maligned Edwards and Cooke as King's "henchmen."[10] Setting personal misgivings aside, King surprised Forrestal by telling Truman that the "time had come for me to give up[,] and [I] stated that in my view Admiral Nimitz [is] the proper relief for me."[11] At the time, King also told Edwards that "I believe that 'Savvy' Cooke (after you) should have been made CNO."[12] Forrestal had other ideas about potential replacements for King. Knowing Nimitz's reputation for being an equally savvy political animal, Forrestal had other ideas about potential replacements for King. Forrestal complained about Nimitz—prompting Truman to suggest, "Sometimes you have to give the show horse a kiss!"[13]

In nominating Nimitz for the responsibility of being the future CNO, King calculated that Nimitz had the ability to navigate the uncharted waters of unification in advancing the future of American sea power for sustained peacetime operations in the global maritime arena. When Marshall's smiling face was to be replaced by Eisenhower's, Nimitz's reputation for being easygoing provided an equally appealing counterforce in shaping the image of American sea power. In October 1945, Nimitz returned from the Pacific to make speeches at tickertape parades in raising money for the Seventh War Loan.[14] King's men Topper and Schoeffel met Nimitz and Sherman at the airport.[15] As they drove on Pennsylvania Avenue, Nimitz dutifully took his position on the back seat of the convertible limousine and started waving to the thrilled crowd. King's aviators provided additional flair with grumbling engines roaring overhead, flying in close formation to create the letters "N–I–M–I–T–Z."[16]

Forrestal and King continued maneuvering for the advantage in shaping the future of American sea power. The political chess master Forrestal trumped the salty naval strategist King. Behind closed doors, Forrestal inserted verbiage in legislation to set a two-year sunset on the appointment of Nimitz as CNO. This legislation passed on November 26, 1945. The *Indianapolis* court-martial commenced the following week. Changing the subject for publicity reasons, Forrestal presided over the five-star promotion ceremony for Halsey on December 11, 1945.[17] Visibly perturbed during the proceedings in the flag meeting room of the Navy Department, King can be seen sneering at Nimitz in film footage of the Halsey promotion ceremony. The strained smile on Forrestal's face balanced Halsey's famous grin. Four days later, Nimitz assumed duty as CNO, on December 15, 1945, and King signed the directive for the Atlantic and Pacific Fleets to dissolve all numbered fleets, with an effective date of January 1, 1946.

King carried on in five-star rank on the presidential select committee, with the task of examining the issues with armed-services unification. Roosevelt administration affiliates like King slowly lost influence in the unification debate. He also understood the decision to implement a forced unification of the army and naval services as a fait

Admiral of the Fleet David Beatty, 1st Earl Beatty, looking the part. *US Navy photograph*

Fleet Admiral King, "pulling his Beatty" and looking the part. *Library of Congress*

The global flagship for the US Navy, *Dauntless,* traversing the brown waters of the Potomac with King's flag aloft along the shores of the Washington battlefield. *US Navy photograph*

Funeral caisson of Secretary Knox passing Main Navy as King's navy wages peace with unremitting pressure within the global maritime arena in 1944. *US Navy photograph*

King's lair on the third deck of Main Navy. *Courtesy of Janvier King Smith and the King family*

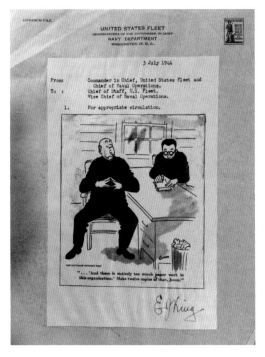

King's wry sense of humor about the bureaucracy of war, as circulated among the CominCh headquarters staff. *Courtesy of Janvier King Smith and the King family*

King standing with Capt. Mildred McAfee and Forrestal during wartime celebration following the establishment of the WAVES. *US Navy photograph*

Forrestal decorated his wartime adviser Lester Granger, with King and his staff attending ceremonies held in the Main Navy conference room. *US Navy photograph*

"Future history" being the mission for King's men, Lt. L. Sprague DeCamp, Isaac Asimov, and Lt. Robert Heinlein, USN (Ret.) at the Philadelphia Naval Yard. *Heinlein Archives, University of California, Santa Cruz*

Bletchley Park on an industrial scale at the US naval communications annex on Nebraska Avenue in Washington, DC. *US Navy photograph*

WAVES analyst solving encrypted enemy communications with a four-rotor "high-speed Bombe" at Nebraska Avenue. *US Navy photograph*

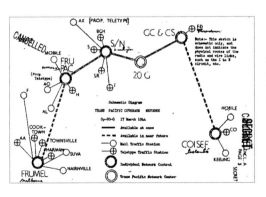

Global special intelligence communications network, otherwise known as "X-Com" within CominCh headquarters, which fused British and American organizations after 1943. *National Archives*

Leahy referees the verbal duels between Arnold and Marshall (*at left*), as King leans forward in advocating the global maritime view to synchronize strategy with operations. *FDR Library*

King's chief planning officer Cooke always shared the vision for taking Formosa in order to facilitate sustainable peacetime ends in Asia with a focus on the future of China. *FDR Library*

Mountbatten stands in the middle between Churchill and Roosevelt during a CCS meeting—Arnold and King sit to far left with Marshall, Pound, and Brook sitting from far right. *FDR Library*

Admiral of the Fleet Sir Andrew Cunningham became First Sea Lord upon Pound's passing in 1943. King deeply respected Cunningham as a "real man." *US Navy photograph*

UNITED STATES FLEET

October 23, 1942

My dear Mr. President:

It appears proper that I should bring to your notice the fact that the record shows that I shall attain the age of 64 years on November 23d next - one month from today.

I am, as always, at your service.

Most sincerely yours,

Ernest J. King
Admiral, U.S. Navy

E.J.K.

So what, old Top ?! I may even send you a Birthday present !

After 1942, FDR expected King to be his "blowtorch" in the epic transatlantic battles to control the course of American sea power—vesting King with unprecedented authority to win the future for the United Nations. *Courtesy of Janvier King Smith and the King family*

(*Below*) Fighting the global war, Cmdr. Daniel V. Gallery Jr. stands third from left under the aluminum palm trees, as constructed in Iceland to welcome King (*at center*) during his frequent transatlantic flights to the European front. *Gallery Papers, Nimitz Library*

Among the key architects of the US Navy "numbered fleet" task force organizations within King's navy, RAdm. Francis S. "Frog" Low also synthesized operations with intelligence as the assistant chief of staff for submarine operations and, conversely, antisubmarine operations within the CominCh headquarters after 1943. *US Navy photograph*

WAVES of intelligence take charge in the antisubmarine division within the CominCh headquarters after 1943. *US Navy photograph*

Two days preceding the landings on Normandy, King's headquarters staff enabled the capture of German submarine *U-505* during operations unfolding between April and June 1944. The following year, *U-505* symbolized victory in the Atlantic when juxtaposed to the triumphant flag raising on Mount Suribachi in the Pacific. *US Navy photograph*

King risking German sniper fire with Marshall and Eisenhower with the troops immediately following the landings at Normandy on June 6, 1944. *US Navy photograph*

King dodging bullets with Japanese snipers in the area as Gen. Holland M. "Howlin Mad" Smith and Nimitz ride along on Saipan in June 1944. *US Navy photograph*

Roosevelt sharing secrets with King in the White House Oval Office in August 1944. *Courtesy of the King family*

Mission accomplished on the circular path to Formosa, as MacArthur is photographed with his pants wet during the landings on Leyte in the Philippines in October 1944. *National Archives*

Secretary Forrestal holding court with Admirals
Spruance, King, Cooke, Jacobs, Nimitz, and Sherman in
1944. *US Navy photograph*

King's trusted operative in coordinating amphibious planning in the Pacific, VAdm. Richmond Kelly "Terrible" Turner. *US Navy photograph*

President of the Naval War College, VAdm. William S. Pye, explains forward base construction to Secretary Knox with admirals Ben Morell (*left*) and Randall Jacobs (*right*) in Davisville, Rhode Island. *US Navy photograph*

Nimitz to the left and VAdm. Robert Ghormley to the right of King's old friend Admiral of the Fleet Roger Keyes, who later died of wounds after combined amphibious landings on Luzon in January 1945. *National Archives*

King's unsung hero at "Happy Valley" in China, VAdm. Milton Miles set the stage for the reconstruction of China, only to be thwarted by the atomic bomb and politics, as later explained in his posthumous memoir, *Another Kind of War*. *US Navy photograph*

Gen. Albert Coady Wedemeyer stands to left after he coordinated global CCS and JCS plans, which culminated in his assignment for overall command in anticipation of the offensive campaign in China, only to be thwarted by the atomic bombs of 1945, as he later explained in his memoir, *Wedemeyer Reports! National Archives*

Halsey taking his medicine for making poor decisions during the disastrous Typhoon COBRA, which later inspired Herman Wouk's novel *The Caine Mutiny*, as seen in his cups at a party in Washington following an epic tongue lashing from King. *US Navy photograph*

The infamous "King Gray" service dress uniform evolved from the admiral's personal effort to define the future of Army–Navy debates concerning service unification during the Second World War. *US Navy photograph*

Racing ahead of the future in Army-Navy relations, King blended in with civilians by removing his "King Gray" uniform jacket during his frequent wartime visits to the Jet Propulsion Laboratories—always looking beyond the horizon to the stars. *NASA photograph*

King's unsung heroes of intelligence from the Office of Naval History, *from the left*, are Professor Robert G. Albion; Col. John Potts, USMC; Capt. Dudley W. Knox (Ret.); and Adm. Edward C. Kalbfus (Ret.). *US Navy photograph*

King observes from the left as the new CNO, Nimitz, receives a decoration from President Harry S Truman as Edwards witnesses from the right on the White House grounds. *Truman Presidential Library*

Gone in a flash and then lost in the atomic mists, King's navy under the cloud of strategic airpower during postwar unification battles after 1946. *US Navy photograph*

(*Below*) German V-1 rocket launches from a US Navy submarine during postwar weapons testing in the aftermath of the atomic bomb. *US Navy photograph*

Feeling old and in the way, King quickly faded into the bureaucratic mists of the early atomic era following a series of debilitating strokes. *Courtesy of Thomas King Savage and the King family*

(*Below*) Old and in the way, Leahy stands in uniform with former CNOs Stark and Denfeld at King's funeral in 1956. *Courtesy of Janvier King Smith and the King family*

accompli within the Truman administration. King tried to turn the proverbial ship out of the shallows of militarism and back out into the deeper waters of American sea power.[18] Unfortunately, the airpower clique won the war of public opinion by twisting the old Rooseveltian idea of "Our Navy, the Peacemaker" into the Truman-era US Air Force variant, "Peace is our Profession."[19] King laughed out loud when his son-in-law Gen. Freddy Smith announced the slogan.[20] Newspapers, meanwhile, warned that "King Foresees Dictator Threat in Unification."[21]

King's slow fade from center stage in the intensifying heat of unification debates coincided with concerns about the factionalized character of the Truman administration. The mismanagement that followed the "Roosevelt-Knox-King period" also defined the disasters of the "Truman-Forrestal-Nimitz combination."[22] Backchannel dealmaking, however, failed to measure against the tsunami of peacetime that was rising, which overwhelmed Nimitz as the CNO. Tired from wartime service under King's forceful hand, Nimitz fumbled along as the CNO. King often derided Nimitz as a "fixer."[23] King's favorite missive in describing colleagues like Nimitz perhaps overshadowed the more fundamental problem—politics always trumped strategic logic in peacetime battles for bureaucratic control in the two-party system of American governance.[24]

The historical question of American sea power hung in the balance when the Truman administration turned into the rocks and shoals of continentalist strategy. Running the ship aground within the muddy shallows of an unsettled peace, the ruins of Europe still smoldered as American forces waded ashore and beyond to the rugged mountains and darkest jungles of Asia. Along with Stimson's other friends, Marshall and MacArthur had their way as the airpower clique shaped the future within the Truman administration. Foreseeing the disasters to come, Forrestal gained a new understanding of the laws of bureaucratic gravity within the context of the Truman administration, which likewise hobbled Nimitz in his brief tenure as the CNO.

King remained cheerful in making best with a very bad situation for the future of American sea power. His wide smile failed to draw equal attention to others, as King George VI bestowed upon King the honorary titles with the Knight Grand Cross in the Order of the Bath. Not to be outdone, de Gaulle fulfilled King's childhood dreams of receiving the Napoleonic decoration of the Légion d'Honneur along with a Croix de Guerre. King politely declined the Order of Ushakov from Stalin following inquiries made at Potsdam. Perhaps notably, he conversely accepted the Order of Pao Ting from Generalissimo Chiang Kai-shek. In semiretirement, King received a constant barrage of honors from international friends, former enemies, and innumerable civic organizations like the Masons, the Shriners, and veterans' organizations. Congress also passed a special joint resolution to grant Truman the honor of presenting singular gold medals, as issued to Marshall and King, "on behalf of a grateful nation."[25]

Foreign allies recognized an unprecedented problem of historical proportions when King's navy and the dream of American sea power faded into the stormy mists that followed the mushroom clouds of the atomic bomb. The unproven theory of strategic airpower destroyed the legacy of King's navy, as Forrestal and Nimitz lost headway after 1946. Awaiting his fifth star as president of the Naval War College, Spruance instead faced mandatory retirement as a four-star. Meanwhile, Halsey drank himself into oblivion and lost his edge in as a semiretired five-star. Leahy dutifully fought to right the ship behind the bureaucratic scenes. Stark also did his part in keeping King engaged after a series of physical ailments forced his silence after 1947. Nimitz kept his cheerful façade upon leaving his successor, Admiral Louis Denfeld, ill equipped for the heavy seas ahead. The smiling Texan arguably failed to measure against the haberdasher from Missouri, Truman, and the happy warrior from Abilene, Eisenhower.[26]

INFAMY AND HISTORY

Having inherited victory, the Truman administration pursued a radically different strategy in which land forces and naval fleets fell under the cloudy vision of airpower. The Pearl Harbor investigations provided an opportunity for advocates of unification to highlight the problems of maintaining separate Departments of War and Navy. The battleships of the Pacific Fleet symbolized American prestige and power, rendering the burning image of the Japanese attacks indelible in popular memory. As predicted by Roosevelt, the singular date of December 7, 1941, lived in infamy—particularly on Capitol Hill. Kimmel and Stark endured undue humiliation in the media during postwar congressional hearings.[27] King made best with a bad situation in offering the double-edged conclusion that "dereliction[s] on the part of Admiral Stark and Admiral Kimmel were those of omission rather than those of commission [and were] errors of judgement as distinguished from culpable inefficiency."[28]

King was among other major Allied leaders who considered Stark to be the man most responsible for setting the stage for victory in the war at sea. The First Sea Lord, Cunningham, agreed that "Stark's task of smoothing over Admiral King's abrupt methods was sometimes invidious and difficult." Cunningham respected King as an honest partner in the global war but considered Stark a "great friend and ally."[29] For this service, King George VI vested Stark with the honorary title of commander, British Empire. Marshall endorsed Eisenhower's recommendation for Stark to receive the Army Distinguished Service Medal. King similarly recommended Stark for a second Navy Distinguished Service Medal. King later noted that "Betty won this war in his own way."[30]

King lambasted journalists for propagating the strategic-airpower narrative, which twisted the history about Pearl Harbor. The ongoing investigations in Congress coincided with the controversial vision of unification and the strangely disconnected idea of creating a separate air force.[31] In discussions with journalists, King issued the surprising warning to "guard against assuming that a Navy of quantity was equal to one of quality."[32] He disagreed with Forrestal's saying that the "number of ships was impressing the important individuals, when in reality the retention of many of the old battleships and the old cruisers built during the period of the Navy 5-5-3 ration was useless."[33] King wanted to prune the wartime fleet for peacetime purposes. King had his plan for using the American sea services as an elite force under the United Nations, and he pressed Marshall on the idea of establishing a singular "superman" to run American strategy.[34] King blamed Marshall for spreading an "appalling amount of misinformation."[35]

To set the record straight for the American public, King strongly supported efforts within the Navy Department to recruit historians into the service to perform original documentary research. Professional military education fused with the requirement for public education about the future of American sea power. To coordinate these efforts, King placed retired captain Dudley W. Knox up for wartime promotion to the one-star rank of commodore. In explaining the nomination, King noted that Knox had been forced to the retired list since "1921 (for physical disability) [and] he has been continually employed on active duty."[36] King emphasized that during

> those twenty-five years, he has not only assembled the documentary sources for the entire history of the Navy, published the records of our early wars (thanks to President Roosevelt's interest), written extensively and authoritatively on naval history and its interpretations—often being likened to Admiral Mahan, but has made a host of friends for the Navy in universities, colleges, libraries—and other organizations—throughout the country. It can be said, also, that he is well known abroad for his writings. [The] whole scope and caliber of his work during the twenty-five years—from 1921 to 1946—[should] be recognized by the award of the Distinguished Service Medal.[37]

King continued working with Knox in mobilizing history as an unclassified means to pursue the vision of a United Nations navy. Having a shared appreciation for the strategic role of history in shaping future strategy, King assumed the chairmanship of the Naval Historical Foundation. In this role, King assisted the fundraising efforts to restore the pride of former enemies in the interests of creating future allies.[38] Among other initiatives, King arranged funding for the restoration of the German Naval Memorial at Laboe. He joined forces with Nimitz to raise the money to overhaul and display the historic battleship *Mikasa*, which symbolized the victory of imperial Japan in the Russo-Japanese War.[39]

Veterans of the CominCh headquarters continued fighting for the reconstruction strategy of King. Edwards coordinated logistics to support ongoing global peacetime operations. Adm. Lynde McCormick reported for duty to focus on European reconstruction when Cooke left for similar operations as commander, Western Pacific.[40] McCormick focused on the reconstruction of the German and Italian navies as strategic partners while Cooke concentrated on naval partnerships in the greater Asiatic.[41] The US Navy relied heavily upon former enemies to achieve their desired ends in attempting to solve the problem of Asia.[42] Similarly in Europe, anticommunist ideology fueled the development of new lines of demarcation. Captains Henri Smith-Hutton and Kenneth A. Knowles assisted clandestine operations in the Soviet sectors of occupation as members of the Central Intelligence Group—ostensibly assigned on temporary duty with the Department of State to assist in the reconstruction, war crimes investigations, and data gathering for use in official histories.[43]

Postwar operations for reconstruction coincided with secret efforts by historians assigned to intelligence functions within the ranks of the US Navy. Kalbfus and Knox supervised these efforts from within ONH in close collaboration with the Battle Studies Group at the Naval War College.[44] Crafting an official narrative, historians assisted the effort to restrict access to details about the organization and character of Allied intelligence collaboration well into the postwar era. Historians wore the "King Gray" naval uniforms until they donned gray flannel business suits to complete the work of the ONH and ONI in the early postwar effort to glean applicable historical lessons from the world wars. Knox supervised the historians in a systematic effort to blur the role of cryptography and special intelligence in the historiography of the Cold War era.[45]

Younger scholars serving in reserve status bridged the functions of the Offices of Naval Intelligence and of Naval History. Fusing intelligence with historical analysis, King's men included young scholars like reserve lieutenants James Michener, Philip Lundeberg, and Elting E. Morison. Their graduate work as young historians in the university setting prepared them for the arduous analytical drudgery of compiling disheveled documents, gleaning information from captured enemy sources, and then drafting operational studies, staff histories, and classified recommendations for higher-level action. Analysts at ONH joined together with the Battle Studies Group at the Naval War College to produce roughly 300 bound volumes, which became the basis for the earliest semiofficial histories. War college personnel studied the ULTRA and MAGIC secrets of Special Intelligence for the purpose of meeting future challenges in the global maritime arena. For the purpose of educating the public, reserve historians on active duty also proved ONH's value by creating official narratives that blurred the truth about analytical methods and sensitive sources.[46]

Intelligence veterans faced the consequences of maintaining strict oaths of secrecy by attaining the desired end objective of defeating the enemy. Women veterans lacked opportunities to build upon their wartime experience. Many suffered the disappointing reality of being left to perform secretarial work or simply return to being housewives. Recalling their collective sense of deflated importance, Sebald described feeling a "sense of futility."[47] "Although important work remained to be done, the tasks seemed minor and meaningless without the goad of war," Sebald explained. "Whole offices lost their personnel overnight."[48]

The disappearance of fellow intelligence analysts contrasted with the reappearance of combat veterans returning home from fronts. For these personnel, King considered the reserves best suited to maintain the future of American sea power. In 1946, King explained, "In the Navy [we] had two general classes of officers—temporary (Regular Navy with temporary promotions) and reserve (enrolled in USNR)."[49] "Personally," King said, "I think that the Reserves did so well and made such a name for USNR that I incline to view that 'USNR' is a badge of distinction."[50]

ATOMIC HISTORY

Postwar testing of new technologies and captured enemy equipment required significant assistance from subject matter experts in the reserves. Since the authority to establish numbered fleets required the approval of the CNO, Nimitz approved the requests to establish the 16th and 19th Fleets by March 1946. Using mostly reserve personnel, the 16th and 19th Fleets performed mothballing chores, accounted for lost equipment, and supported atomic bomb testing.[51] Having fallen from King's graces after the Battle of Leyte Gulf, VAdm. Thomas Kinkaid held command of the 16th Fleet in the Atlantic. Among other chores, he focused on the postwar tests on captured German submarines. RAdm. Walter K. Kilpatrick held command in the 19th Fleet, supporting the atomic bomb tests of Operation CROSSROADS. Among others, Capt. Hyman G. Rickover served under Kilpatrick in the 19th Fleet to examine the futuristic questions surrounding the potential role of atomic power in the US Navy.

King always considered navies engaged in continuous operations at sea relatively safe from attack by high-altitude bombers. Fleets sailing in widely dispersed formations enabled individual warships to maneuver and evade bombs. These tactics proved exceedingly successful in combat. To test the theory, the derelict fleet off Bikini Atoll stood in various formations when the atomic bombs exploded from above and below the surface of the sea. Among these derelict targets, the venerable battlewagon *Nevada* and the flattop *Saratoga* met unworthy fates.

Most of the warships anchored off Bikini Atoll had weathered the divine winds of the kamikaze only to be irradiated by the atomic bomb. Sailors had the duty of going aboard the ships to scuttle after the bomb failed to sink them. Nevertheless, the shadows cast over King's navy by the atomic bomb lingered well after the tests at Bikini Atoll. Many of King's men at the scene later struggled with long-term medical problems, including the on-scene commander for CROSSROADS, VAdm. William H. P. "Spike" Blandy. Spry at age fifty-six in 1946, Blandy died of cancer at age sixty-three.[52] Reflecting upon CROSSROADS, King stipulated, "I didn't like the atom bomb, or any part of it."[53]

King anticipated peacetime political wars of an atomic scale closing in on American sea power. He attempted to prepare Nimitz for the battles to come as the new CNO. Like during the arrival of King and his trusted team from the Atlantic Fleet five years before, Nimitz installed veterans of the Pacific Fleet in key positions within the Navy Department in April 1946.[54] Capt. Thomas F. McDill recalled the shifting tides of personality among the staff. McDill recalled "going into Admiral Edwards office and finding him surrounded by papers." McDill offered to assist Edwards. In frustration with the new regime at the Navy Department, Edwards barked, "I am trying to un-sink the *Indianapolis*."[55]

British concepts of organization inspired the Americans in envisioning the future of airpower. The RAF nurtured the heroic imagery of the Battle of Britain, and the USAAF made false claims about the success of strategic bombing. Transatlantic collaboration had influenced British efforts to influence American bureaucracy during the transition from peace to war. Behind closed doors, airpower theorists pressed the service unification concept within the context of secret negotiations between London and Washington. Records relating to postwar reconstruction later revealed significant mission creep within the Anglo-American intelligence bureaucracies. In efforts to reconstruct former enemies into future allies under the United Nations, the Central Intelligence Agency turned a blind eye—and sometimes provided direct assistance—for such despotic Nazi war criminals as Otto Skorzeny, Adolf Eichmann, Klaus Barbie, and Joseph Mengele. The Stuka pilot Hans Ulrich Rudel consulted with the US Air Force, and the rocket scientist Wernher von Braun forgot his SS rank after becoming an American citizen during service at the National Aeronautics and Space Administration.[56]

The establishment of centrally organized British and American intelligence bureaucracies evolved from secret wartime agreements. Given the Holden agreement of 1942, the BrUSA of 1943 served as the foundation for UKUSA. Civilian control over the quasi-civilian ranks of the Anglo-American intelligence services eroded with the UKUSA agreement of March 5, 1946—the same day that Churchill spoke, with Truman listening, at Westminster College in Fulton, Missouri. Churchill refused to relinquish the dream of an Anglo-American "special relationship" when he described the ominous specter of the Communist "Iron Curtain."[57] The English language again served as the weapon of choice for Churchill in framing the vision of an "intelligence community."[58]

British imperial traditions provided a foundation for American sea power, which King recognized in pursuit of Roosevelt's dream of United Nations. As one of many original architects of Plan DOG and the whole concept of "Europe First," King executed the strategy he outlined in his writings at the Naval War College more than ten years preceding his triumphant performance at the highest levels of global command in the Second World War. King always remained true to the Europe First concept, since it always represented the first phase in the grander strategy to solve Mahan's "problem of Asia." Mahan agreed with the British concept of an "Imperial Federation," which influenced Sims's generation to embrace the League of Nations concept of the First World War, which ultimately evolved into King's mandate to realize the American dream of the United Nations in the Second World War.

The simple act of collaboration proved deeply difficult in balancing the fundamental challenges of multinational command. King observed, "[The] British had known a great deal more about the world situation than did the Americans before World War I."[59] King recognized that the ramifications of Pearl Harbor caused a "great change to take place since it was the United States who had the forces, the material, and especially the money."[60] King criticized the British for assuming "they had their own ideas 'sewed up.'"[61] Old Prussian ideas of military organization influenced British airpower theories to undercut the original genius of American sea power.

Physical ailments precluded King from fighting the peacetime battles that coincided with the final phases of winning victory in Europe First. His persistent effort to remind fellow commanders about problems of equal concern in Asia likewise fell upon deaf ears after 1945. King was helpless as the Truman administration succumbed to the anticommunist politics and the false promises of strategic-airpower theory. His son-in-law Freddy Smith channeled King somewhat by acknowledging the capabilities and limitations of airpower. In 1947, Smith also spoke honestly in response to probing questions about the defense-industrial establishment.[62]

Defense proved highly lucrative for entrepreneurs outside the uniformed ranks and some select few among the services. The ironies within the airpower argument against the naval services appeared in clear terms when advocates for the establishment of a *separate* US air force predicted significant budgetary savings through the unification of the military and naval services under the unified Department of Defense. Airpower propagandists exploited American fears of a future Pearl Harbor scenario; meanwhile, Europe was divided and Stalin had fortified positions around Berlin and southward to the Balkans. Asia concurrently dissolved with the rise of Mao and the ingenious strategy of waging the long war against foreign exploitation.[63]

The historical legacies of past European wars intermixed with the perceived menace of Communist ideology and ongoing conflict among the war lords of Asia. Within this context, Churchill's vision of a "special relationship" among English-speaking peoples resonated with King in the aftermath of two world wars. Like Sims at Cambridge two decades earlier, King accompanied his friend Stark to accept his honorary degree at All Souls College at the University of Oxford in June 1946. King and Stark appeared in their service blue uniforms with academic regalia during the ceremonies—steeped in British tradition.[64] King and Stark lunched with King George VI. The future queen, Elizabeth II, introduced herself to King in her British army uniform.[65] Following their audience with the royal family, the honorary Oxons—King and Stark—flew together on the transatlantic flight back to America. Following this last overseas journey, King fought a withering campaign to wage peace.

The xenon flashed in the moment when the atomic bomb destroyed the fleeting histori-cal achievement of American sea power. When the combined navies of Britain and America were completely unchallenged in the global maritime arena, the politics of peace created the ironically divided Department of Defense bureaucracies in which the *separate* US Air Force came into being. The visions of Theodore and Franklin Roosevelt ended with King's influence after 1945. Predicting the future, the First Sea Lord, Cunningham, confided that "on the whole I think Ernest King was the right man in the right place, though one could hardly call him a good co-operator."[66] Cunningham characterized King as "a man of im-mense capacity and ability, quite ruthless in his methods[;] he was not easy to get on with."[67] In considering the future of Anglo-American naval collaboration, Cunningham envisioned the necessity for having "a supreme commander [and] he should be British."[68]

IN A BAD WAY

King attempted to guide the Truman administration in a failed effort to avoid conflict among former allies in Europe and Asia. His wartime favorites also struggled to keep the vision of Anglo-American naval collaboration on course in the development of global maritime alliances under the United Nations. Politics always remained the fundamental question as Mountbatten went on to preside over the death of the Admiralty when the Ministry of Defense (MoD) emerged with the swinging sixties and the last British invasion of America in the form of the Beatles. The death of King's wartime logistics planner, Adm. Lynde McCormick, also marked a major turning point after his postwar term as president of the Naval War College. McCormick invoked King's model for organizing the multinational headquarters as the first supreme Allied commander, Atlantic (SACLant).[69]

Multinational naval commands ultimately faded into the jungles and atomic winds of the nuclear-charged space race to the moon. The Soviets predictably stood against the Anglo-American military presence ashore in Europe. Chinese Communist forces broke from their tenuous alliance with Generalissimo Chiang Kai-shek to threaten the future of Asia. As predicted by King, the sudden defeat of Japan sparked the explosion of civil war between the forces of Chiang and Mao. King's man Miles returned from China to the Navy Department completely exhausted. King had sent Miles to China in the perma-nent grade of commander nearly three years earlier. King then arranged for Miles to receive the temporary wartime rank of captain.[70] Soon thereafter, King arranged a temporary two-star appointment for Miles. Service in China took a profound physical toll on Miles—he stood nearly 50 pounds lighter upon reporting to King. When Miles reported after nearly three years of constant stress in China, King told Edwards to "get this man a steak!"[71]

Miles suffered from ailments associated with hard-driving combat service in the mountainous terrain of China. Negotiating deals in the opium dens of warlords, along with the constant pressure of operating with a bounty on his head, took a remarkable toll. Miles initially served as an assistant to King—compiling a comprehensive study of the situation in China. He then received temporary assignment with Knox in ONH. He cin-cidentally worked with CIG to produce strategic studies of the situation in China, the Korean Peninsula, and in the newly restored European colonies of Indochina, Burma, and India. After 1946, Miles predicted very heavy seas.[72] Junior in lineal standing to others, Miles "remoted" from two stars to the rank of captain. King continued taking care of Miles by arranging his assignment to command USS *Columbus* (CA-74). He sailed back to the contested waters of Asia during the early phases of the Chinese Civil War, watching in disappointment as American forces bogged down in the marshes, jungles, and mountainous terrain of Asia.[73]

King's men struggled to solve the problems of Asia as Communist forces rushed to fill the vacuum of former European empires. With the Chinese Civil War ongoing, Cooke rushed to the scene in response as the commander, Western Pacific. In November, Nimitz approved the request for Cooke to assume operational control as the commander, Seventh Fleet—coordinating offensive tactical efforts by US Navy warships supporting clandestine operations along the Chinese coast. He again dissolved the Seventh Fleet after assisting the withdrawal of the Chinese National Army to Formosa, which Chiang changed to the Republic of China on Taiwan. Writing from Bethesda Naval Hospital while recovering from a stroke, King complained to Edwards, "I suppose you read about Formosa and perhaps can recall when the <u>Navy</u> wanted to go into that island as the sure way to cut down Japan." "Roosevelt decided (with MacArthur and the Army) to go up through the Philippines and now look at the damn thing."[74] "In fact," King continued, "I would like to know what MacArthur and the Army is thinking (if anything) about the situation as it has turned out to be."[75]

King and MacArthur struggled to strike the balance between their differing strategies and operational priorities in the global war at sea. King had fought the establishment of the supreme commander, Allied Powers (SCAP), and "was much disturbed by MacArthur's demand to be designated Supreme Commander Japan."[76] King worried about MacArthur turning Japan into another personal fiefdom as he had attempted to do in the Philippines. King worried about MacArthur's kingdom building in greater Asia. His protégé Schoeffel recalled that "King was adept at and a believer in the efficacy of semantics."[77] Schoeffel explained that King "solved the problem, at least in his own mind, by insisting that the title should be 'Supreme Commander <u>IN</u> Japan' [to ensure] that Navy forces outside Japan should be independent of MacArthur."[78]

King further contained MacArthur by installing trusted operatives within the SCAP headquarters. Among King's other men, Sebald proved an ideal candidate to serve as a regulating influence to assist MacArthur. Given personal connections established in Kobe and Tokyo before the war, Sebald's wife, Edith, added her familial ties with prominent Japanese families. Her sister, Marie Antoinette DeBecker, married MacArthur's chief of intelligence and close friend, Lt. Gen. Charles A. Willoughby.[79] Once again, familial connections among key individuals influenced future strategy. King certainly assisted in rigging the lines for Sebald to serve on MacArthur's staff in organizing the occupation of Japan. In this role, Willoughby and Sebald worked together to align reconstruction policies with MacArthur's peacetime stabilization strategy for Asia.

Sebald departed from the CominCh headquarters with little fanfare and an autographed portrait of King. Arriving in Japan, Sebald subsequently helped MacArthur in organizing the SCAP headquarters. In this role, Sebald earned the appointment to serve as the first postwar ambassador to Emperor Hirohito's court in shaping the diplomatic future of imperial Japan. Technically, Sebald transformed from being MacArthur's bureaucratic subordinate into being the most senior diplomat in Japan. He customarily circumvented MacArthur and spoke directly with Truman about the problems of Asia.[80] Sebald kept King apprised of the actual strategic situation unfolding in Asia. As had been predicted, civil war among the various warlords in China spilled from the Asian continent and onto the global stage.[81]

King received regular updates about the worsening situation in Asia from former subordinates. "'Savvy' Cooke has been in Washington for some time apparently trying to help <u>China</u> against the 'Reds,'" King reported. He added that Cooke stood firmly "in a discussion on whether to recognize the Chinese 'Reds' and he was <u>against</u> it."[82] Having formally retired from active service, Cooke established Commerce International China Incorporated, with headquarters based in New York City.[83] Ostensibly acting as a private businessman, Cooke flew to Taiwan under the pretense of selling fertilizer.[84] He then helped establish the Ingalls Taiwan Shipbuilding and Dry Dock Company, ostensibly using his navy connections to make money as a private businessman.[85] Operating under a thin veil, Cooke blended with the CIG in Asia and became heavily involved with organizing the Republic of China navy. Edwards wrote King, "I concur in Savvy's enthusiasm for holding Formosa but doubt that the military advantages of so doing will prevail."[86]

American involvement in China proved deeply counterproductive when the US Army seized strategic control over American efforts ashore on the Asian continent. The poisonous relationship between Wedemeyer and Miles also undermined prospects for success. On reflection, King blamed Marshall for bungling the postwar strategy for China. Congressional investigations revealed fundamental differences between King's naval concept and Marshall's military views about the question of Formosa. King felt vindicated when Maoist forces pushed those of Chiang offshore to Formosa, which soon became known as Taiwan with the establishment of the Republic of China.[87]

King concluded that China's problems erupted after Marshall failed to marshal the divergent policies of Anglo-French imperialists with American concepts of Chinese sovereignty. On reflection, King thought that Marshall "never understood, or bothered to hear about, the problem of Asia." King further pointed an accusing finger at the British for making "such a great mistake in trying to get along with the Red Chinese in order to save their large holdings in China—they should have known that they could not do business with the Reds while employing conventional methods."[88]

NO DOGMA

Atomic weapons appeared to render the historical lessons of past wars irrelevant in the new context of strategic airpower. Countering the technological trends, King used the Naval War College to refute the airpower clique within the War Department. King worked behind the scenes within the Truman administration to save the Naval War College. King sent Spruance to the Naval War College for two primary reasons. First, King encouraged Spruance to retool the curriculum to synthesize the historical analysis of ONH with the forward-thinking work of ONI. Second, King placed Spruance in Newport to await promotion to five-star rank. Reporting to Newport in the spring of 1946, Spruance told the Naval War College staff that there is "no dogma, nor doctrine, nor any set of rules by which campaigns can be conducted or battles won."[89] He directed the staff to study, saying, "[Study] history for the lessons it has to teach us, but we must not expect necessarily to obtain from history the correct answers to future problems."[90]

History served as the foundation for educating American naval practitioners to think strategically about the future of sea power in both peace and war. Among King's men, Spruance acted upon recommendations from Professors Edward Meade Earle, Bernard Brodie, and Robert G. Albion.[91] Retired on active service, Cmdre. Dudley W. Knox joined forces with reserve captain Samuel Eliot Morison to work with the staff at the Naval War College. Cmdre. Richard S. Bates established the Battle Studies Group to produce applied historical studies of the Second World War. Among others, retired captain Joseph Rochefort served under Bates on the staff of the Naval War College. Captains Joseph Wenger, Kenneth A. Knowles, and Robert Weeks assisted Bates in the Battle Studies Group. Spruance organized the logistical-planning curriculum under Capt. Henry Eccles. Concurrently, Capt. Joseph C. Wylie assisted in synthesizing operational histories with discussions of future strategy.[92]

The Naval War College thrived as a forum for practitioners, since Spruance reexamined the events of past wars to inform then-current discussions of American sea power. Given the politics surrounding unification, Spruance stood out as a figure of stature within the ranks of the US Navy. He also served as the most senior four-star admiral in waiting for a five-star appointment as the president of the Naval War College. Politics within the Truman administration snuffed chances for Spruance to attain a fifth star, although Congress provided special provisions in the retirement package designed specifically for Spruance. Upon hearing the news, King wrote to Spruance, "I hoped that Congress would make a fifth five[-]star admiral[, and] I hope you will carry on in the [Naval] War College for several years."[93] Responding on June 28, 1948, Spruance wrote King that the "fourth five-star went where it belonged when Bill Halsey got it. I am retiring on July 1."[94]

Politics influenced debates concerning the role of professional education within the ranks of the military and naval services. Having replaced Spruance as the president of the Naval War College, VAdm. Donald B. Beary continued pressing King's agenda. During the war, Beary had participated in the development of the CominCh organization, numbered fleets, and procedures for planning. His role in establishing the Antisubmarine University System provided an impetus for his declaration to King in 1949 that the institution was in "appreciation and gratitude for your unfailing interest in the affairs of the Naval War College."[95]

The Naval War College was central to King's campaign to defeat the War Department vision for service unification. With funding provided personally by King, the Naval War College recruited Yale University professor Thomas C. Mendenhall for temporary duty as the Fleet Admiral Ernest J. King Chair of Maritime History.[96] Other than the Gardiner Professorship of Oceanic History at Harvard, the King Chair of Maritime History stood out as the only such chair in the United States.

Writing histories of the war at sea coincided with the airpower debates within the Departments of War and Navy. King defined the issue by observing, "There are two—and only two—surfaces of the earth—land and water—and 'air power' cannot exist if it has no surface to take off from or to alight on whether it be land or water."[97] He lectured about the fallacy of airpower by explaining that the "simple law of gravity" proved

> it is impossible to hold a line of battle in the air. It is futile therefore to classify air as a separate entity, or as to the surface from which it operates. It is more important to classify air as to the forces it must operate *with*. Control of the air is only a momentary thing unless a superior force is kept continually aloft. It is necessary to hold the surface in order to *hold* the air.[98]

Dismissing the whole concept of a separate US Air Force on basic scientific grounds, King drew from personal experience at the highest levels of command in efforts to educate the Truman administration about American sea power.

King continued operating behind the scenes in semiretired status as a five-star adviser to the Truman administration and Congress. He aligned with the subcommittees chaired by Vinson and Woodrum. Associate Justice McReynolds on the Supreme Court—the uncle of King's son-in-law—challenged the notion of unification as being inconsistent with the Constitution. When Truman pushed Congress to unify the American armed services, King wondered "whether the rule in the field of sports applies—why tinker with a winning team?"[99] Senator Vinson observed that the "very phraseology of the scheme smacks of the German of the Kaiser and Hitler [and] of Japanese militarism."[100] Vinson added that the decisions of the Truman administration "would sink the Navy."[101]

As the Truman administration rolled with the political tides in managing the ebbing flow of wartime operations, King strongly reminded fellow commanders about the unfinished task of winning the peace. Whether in peace or war, King emphasized the responsibility for naval thinkers to understand the "necessity of arriving at some decision and not upon individual influence."[102] King drew from his past experience in arriving at the conclusion that "every war has its causes and every war is about making the enemy accept the outcome."[103] King explained that we learned a lot from our failure to "win the peace after the last war."[104] He then admitted, "You know, I have great respect for the Japanese, and I had occasion to work with them in the last war."[105] King encouraged fellow Americans to embrace their responsibility for past failures by arguing, "In whatever situation we found ourselves at the time of Pearl Harbor, in the last analysis it comes down to the citizens of this country who are represented in Congress which speaks and acts for all of us."[106]

Looking outward in anticipation of semiretirement in five-star rank, King continued operating at the center of a network of trusted friends and well-positioned family within the bureaucracies on the Washington battlefield. He listened carefully over glasses of beer at family gatherings. His brother-in-law and his son-in-law, the unrelated generals Smith, assisted King in anticipating the debates concerning unification. The two generals Smith kept King apprised as the army airpower clique aimed high in pursuit of the wild blue horizon. His extended network of spies also connected to loyalists embedded on congressional committees and within CCS and JCS, and among old shipmates and veterans of his ComInCh headquarters.

Few noticed the intricate network of close family affiliates within the bureaucracy of the American armed services, which enabled King to keep ahead of rivals. King's protégé Schoeffel served on the Richardson Committee in the temporary rank of rear admiral. Schoeffel recalled that King "was never unkind to me[,] although late in World War II, I gave him reason to be very upset with me."[107] Schoeffel explained that the

Army was strong for unification and so was the Air Corps provided they were split off from the Army and set up independently as the Air Force. The Navy, from Secretary Forrestal on down, was almost unanimously against it. Nevertheless, I felt the Congressional and public clamor for unification was so great that it was inevitable. We prepared a report favoring three-way unification, though very different from what was finally put into effect.[108]

The senior member of the Joint Board, Adm. James O. Richardson, refused to sign the report and wrote a separate dissenting recommendation.[109] By contrast, Schoeffel explained, "I signed this report [and] I fully expected King's wrath to fall upon me, but it did not." Schoeffel recalled that King instead "accepted my position more in sorrow than in anger."[110]

King's men continued working the lines in the interservice fight for air and for the future of American sea power. Having served as the senior analyst in the wartime Combat Intelligence Division, Smedberg reported for duty in peacetime as the aide to the Navy secretary, Forrestal. The peacetime political battles proved as lethal as those in war. Smedberg witnessed Forrestal grappling with the interservice question. Forrestal disagreed with the Truman administration decision to establish the Department of Defense (DoD). In a perverse twist, Forrestal became the first secretary of defense. In this role, Forrestal endured unrelenting pressure under the atomically charged airpower clouds of the Truman administration.[111]

CHAPTER 36
"I Hope It Isn't That!"

Forrestal and King were united against the vision of service unification within a centralized Defense Department. The fingerprints of Marshall and Arnold appeared on the final recommendations submitted to Truman, which recommended the establishment of DoD. Among the historians closest to the problem, Albion succinctly observed that the example set in the "Roosevelt-Knox-King period would have to be altered considerably to explain the Truman-Forrestal-Nimitz combination."[1] Having earlier participated in the debates surrounding DoD, King criticized the idea by noting the differences between "unification and integration," and, he said, "Now it seems to me that what they are working out is integration."[2] Schoeffel paraphrased King's comment that DoD should have been a "small policymaking body, rather than the detailed controlling monster that it has since become."[3]

The Truman administration ran the original vision of American sea power into the rocks and shoals of the military-industrial establishment. As the first defense secretary, Forrestal suffered a complete physical and mental breakdown. King wrote Edwards, saying, "I suppose that you have seen in the 'newspapers' [that] Mr. Forrestal entered Bethesda last weekend, but no one can see him except one doctor and one nurse." King explained that Forrestal "has 'nervous exhaustion' brought on by his work for the last two years." In conclusion, King advised that the doctors treating Forrestal: "Don't call it a 'nervous breakdown'—yet—and I hope it isn't that!"[4]

King disliked Forrestal for being overly political about making decisions about the future of American sea power. Among friends, King admitted with full-throated conviction about Forrestal, "I didn't like him, and he didn't like me."[5] On the other hand, King respected Forrestal for fighting a withering peacetime battle against the airpower lobby within DoD.[6] Having relieved Nimitz as the CNO, Denfeld endured the humiliation of being fired for telling the truth about the myths of airpower to Congress and the Truman administration. His testimony later symbolized what was called "Revolt of the Admirals" in airpower propaganda. In fact, this was no "revolt" at all. Denfeld acted far more honorably than did his airpower rivals. He still suffered consequences for doing his job as CNO. Observing from afar, King applauded Denfeld, stating, "What he had to say was correct and [it] had to be said."[7]

The Truman administration turned definitively in favor of the atomic mirage of airpower, thereby compromising the original vision of American sea power. Forrestal felt isolated and betrayed within the Truman administration. After he resigned, Louis Johnson assumed office as secretary of defense. Johnson purposely humiliated the US Navy by outright dismissing the CNO, Denfeld. Demoralized by the whole spectacle, Forrestal committed suicide by attempting to hang himself from the top-floor window of his hospital suite at Bethesda Naval Hospital in January 1949. Following Forrestal's tragic end, King sent a framed card with gracious condolences for his wife, Josephine.[8]

The death of Forrestal coincided with the resurgence of King's navy, as the rise of Mao in China provided the pretext for additional disasters on the Korean Peninsula and French Indochina. King monitored the situation through trusted agents. Edwards reported about the pathetic scene in correspondence with King that the "Man on Horseback [was] given a long day in court and then thrown out, along with the Prussian version of the general staff."[9] Edwards said, "The process of unhorsing the military Buddha did result in strengthening civilian control." He suggested that it was "too much to the disadvantage of military authority in military matters."[10] King's man Gallery blamed strategic airpower as the cause when American forces "were very nearly run out of Korea by a rabble of communist stooges!"[11] King simply thought, "MacArthur's in a bad way today."[12]

Soviet and Chinese military forces under Mao supported the armies of Kim Il-Sung in achieving a stalemate on the Korean Peninsula. King understood why "'Stalin and Co.' decided to 'welch' on their agreements with Allies and carry on their own ideas."[13] King told his aide Whitehill that "from a military point of view—the Allies should press the issue in Korea until the Red Chinese and Red Koreans are forced to stop their fighting against the Allies' principle of non-aggression."[14] "Our entire object lesson in Korea has been to put down aggression on the part of the Communist-inspired North Koreans who overran South Korea by force of arms." King continued, "The basic trouble has been (and still is) the fact that the Russians won't 'play ball' with another country nor with the whole world."[15] As the war spun out of control, King argued, "Once committed to war it is best to carry on until one's 'enemy' has had <u>enough</u>!"[16]

Communism provided a handy nemesis for the atomic-powered American military and airpower strategists to dominate the DoD. King observed that "a number of people are convinced that the United States Air Force equipped with an atom bomb [and] long-range planes is capable of delivering such a knockout punch that we no longer need an Army or a Navy."[17] He worried that "Congress is being asked to reduce the Army and cripple the fleet in favor of a powerful Air Force which can supposedly win a war with a single technique—mass atomic bombing of enemy population and resources."[18] King and his associates argued that atomic bombs employed against "civil populations [would] identify the cause of the Russian people with the cause of the Soviet government more effectively than the Communist party has ever been able to do."[19] Pressing the point, King thought that the "fortification of the Russian spirit by atomic ordeal would progress concurrently with [a] brooding sense of guilt in the soul of each American citizen who lent his support to such a betrayal of simple humanity."[20]

Noting the tactics employed by the Nazis against civilian populations, King implicated the US Air Force with an overly simplistic strategy for securing victory in war through genocide. King argued, "If Hitler had followed a humane policy [he] might have defeated Stalin[, since] whole Red Army divisions surrendered without a fight [and] the Russian people at first looked upon Germany as a liberator from the Stalinist terror."[21] King lambasted the concept of strategic airpower as essentially tactical in focus, morally bankrupt, and essentially un-American. Again, referring to Hitler and the Nazis, King encouraged fellow naval officers to adopt the view that the "[Third] Reich's cold-blooded slaughter of native Russians could not compare with the mass murder caused by the successful atomic bombing of Russian cities." He predicted that the "heat from atomic blasts would weld the Russian people together in bonds of adamant hatred against a brutal enemy[, and] neutral peoples, viewing this cataclysm with horror, would be reluctant to cooperate with a savagely demented United States."[22]

Recalling perspectives derived from earlier Naval War College studies, King revisited the question of technology as a strategic variable within the human context of war. Reasserting the ideas articulated in his thesis as submitted in 1932, King warned about the "false assumption about progress in technology."[23] King sarcastically noted the "recurrent desire of the land airmen to have his cake and eat it too" and added, "[The] United States Air Force doesn't like the way God put oceans on this planet."[24] Emphasizing the role of sea power in peacetime, King thought that geography "determines where the game of war shall be played and to a significant extent depends how the game shall be played."[25] King observed that

> following World War I the British tried the experiment of clipping the wings of their fleet. Naval aviation was turned over to the Royal Air Force. Results were nearly disastrous. Midway in the war naval aviation was hurriedly returned to the Navy. The lethargic control and dim appreciation of sea-air power of the RAF brought the British Navy into the war tragically unprepared. British aircraft carriers imported US planes and techniques wholesale. Without the benefit of American planes and know-how, the British carrier effort would not have succeeded.[26]

King wrongly assumed that the "English are too intelligent of a people to commit the same mistake twice."[27] He thought the "Royal Navy has no fears about again losing its wings."[28] "Only in America is there an extremist group urging us to learn the fool's way—by our own blunders [and] by repeating the mistakes of others.[29]

The airpower debates within DoD inspired King to focus on the future of historical education for all American citizens. In advocating his point, King pressed Congress to recognize the role of public education on issues of military and maritime policy. Pushing his point, King argued that "military strategy almost exclusively, and quite appropriately, requires sound military tactics, ways and means to seize the superior position, and defeat the enemy through force."[30] King warned that in the "absence of a sound maritime policy, naval strategy cannot exist."[31] He concluded that the "Nazis found this out the hard way."[32] When King testified in Congress, he said, "Successful application of our sea power [has] been the flexibility and balanced character of our naval forces."[33] King pressed his point by observing that "Japanese sea power was hampered by army control, and Japanese naval officers lacked freedom of initiative so necessary to gain and exercise command of the seas."[34]

The mission of educating future generations of maritime thinkers and naval professionals dominated King's thoughts. As a semiretired adviser to the Truman administration, King stipulated that the "distinction should be made between Universal Military Training in peacetime and Universal Military Service during a state of emergency declared by Congress."[35] King emphasized that his desired strategic objective centered on civilian education, establishing national requirements for public benefits, and ensuring interests "by retaining a Draft System and by requiring those who complete Universal Military Training to join one of the Reserve Components of the Armed Forces."[36] "Universal Military Training is a democratic process," King argued, "the better to provide for the 'common defense.'"[37]

Service unification under the overarching auspices of DoD blended with airpower theory, which, ironically, resulted in bureaucratic expansion. King worried about the changes associated with technology as the armed services reorganized to accommodate specialized technological developments and professional subfields. In 1950, King complained about the number of flag-ranking staff officers on active service "by remarking with some asperity that there were now four dentists who were rear admirals[, and] there is now only one lawyer who is a rear admiral but in for or five years there will probably be a number of them."[38] King thought, "No officer should be promoted to flag rank in the naval service without first having the benefit of command as a regular line officer."[39] He joked, "If I can do it, I am sure that a dentist, a doctor, an engineer, or anybody else can do it too with the right mix of education and experience[, but] the lawyers will always debate the point."[40]

Overspecialization in conjunction with the ongoing changes associated with innovations in technology always presented themselves as problematic trends in the back of King's mind. Having served in two world wars, King kept a steady pace until suffering a heat stroke in Los Angeles in 1947. He then grew very angry during testimony on Capitol Hill in the summer of 1948, after which King walked outside and sat on a park bench with a distant look in his eye—unable to speak. Following testimony in Congress, King lost the ability to speak after a debilitating stroke. His grandson later recalled how his grandfather fought to regain his voice "through sheer force of will."[41] King protested orders to the retired list, stating, "I do not wish to be retired because it does not make any change in my pay[,] and allowances by law [and] the technical language of the report of the Board of Medical Survey seems to me to imply a much[-]greater primary speech disability than that which I believe I experienced."[42] The old salt added, "From the tone of this memorandum it should be clear to the reviewers that my ability to express myself is not greatly impaired at the present time."[43]

King never actually retired from active service in the rarified five-star rank of fleet admiral. Physical ailments, nevertheless, forced him to slowly fade away. From his hospital bed in Bethesda Naval Hospital, King drafted the request of September 15, 1948, that read, "I would like to be retired for physical reasons at the pleasure of the President."[44] Continuing, King asked that "I be retired on November 23, 1948, after more than fifty-one years in the Naval service, and on my seventieth birthday."[45] "The last time I saw Admiral King," Schoeffel later recalled, "he was in the hospital at Bethesda after his stroke."[46] Schoeffel remembered when the elevator doors opened: "And there was King [and] he immediately recognized me at once and gave me a big smile and pat on the back, although he couldn't say a word."[47]

King despised the halfhearted strategy of using American military forces in games for control over land geography. Following Forrestal's suicide in 1949, King cuttingly observed that US Army and US Air Force "leaders did not understand sea power."[48] In response, Edwards advised King about the key political trends after the clandestine meetings of the rich and powerful at Bohemia Grove in California. "Most of the lakeside talks were about the international situation," Edwards reported, and the "most radical bird was Mr. [Herbert] Hoover[,] who developed at some length the thesis of kicking Russia out of the UN."[49] Edwards was disappointed by the failure of American strategy, referring to the "leap in the Korean dark."[50] "Eisenhower appeared for a few days and made a very deep impression," Edwards reported, adding, "Bohemia has him earmarked as the next President."[51]

CHAPTER 37
A Naval Record

Looking outward, King anticipated heavy seas within the global maritime arena. Airpower appeared in propaganda as the next phase to escape the terrestrial problems of war. Well-anchored philosophical foundations of "sea power," by extension, appeared antiquated in the advertising campaign of Capt. Steve Leo, USAAF, and his handlers in the War Department.[52] Having a hand in it all, Secretary of War Stimson lambasted the "peculiar psychology of the Navy Department, which frequently retired from the realm of logic into a dim religious world in which Neptune was God, Mahan his prophet, and the United States Navy the only true church."[53] After reading this quotation, King laughed aloud and said, "That's just about right."[54] King thought Stimson "lived in an ivory tower high on the slopes of Olympus, as befitted an elder statesman, and his voice was as the mutter of distant thunder."[55] King decided to allow Stimson's assertions to go unchecked, reasoning that any response "might lead to a general mudslinging contest between Army and Navy which would be bad for both."[56]

The fading influence of the Roosevelt administration provided opportunity for War Department partisans to settle old scores against their counterparts inside the Navy Department. As the Truman administration took form, Stimson helped advance the narrative of Generals Arnold, Spaatz, Doolittle, and LeMay and their favorite propagandist, Leo. The RAND Corporation assisted in the gaming, along with McNamara, Leo, and others associated with the Strategic Bombing Survey. Miscasting the facts with empirically framed datap oints in the halls of Congress, Gen. Omar N. Bradley declared that "large[-]scale amphibious operations will never occur again." Such irresponsible predictions reflected the bombastic confidence of other militarists within the postwar American bureaucracy. Wedemeyer, by contrast, was opposed to the prevailing attitude within the War Department that "America fought the war like a football game after which the winner leaves the field and celebrates."[57] Maritime history faded into the atomic mists when the watery mushroom erupted from the depths. The older warships of King's navy stood unmanned and at anchor—weathering the blast. Sailors experienced the irradiated consequences as airpower took flight in the American defense-industrial complex. Coincident with the Forrestal suicide, King fought for strength to regain a voice in the debates following Denfeld's demise, the unification of DoD, and the apparent subordination of sea power to the brave new world of airpower. Under these circumstances, King decided to contribute to the narrative written primarily by his aide Whitehill. By 1952, King and Whitehill published *Fleet Admiral King: A Naval Record.*[58]

In writing this history, Whitehill interviewed fellow veterans of CominCh and other close associates of King. In his research, Whitehill collected King's official papers—including classified records featuring high-grade caveats like ULTRA and MAGIC. Whitehill enjoyed five-star access to King.[59] In the writing process, Whitehill frequently commuted from Boston to work in residence at the King family home at 2919 West 43rd Street in northwestern Washington, DC. King also stayed in the Whitehill home during his regular sojourns to New England. King frequently visited his grandson among the corps of cadets at West Point before heading through his old stomping grounds by the Naval War College. He kept a private suite at the Portsmouth Naval Hospital as he grappled with health problems following a series of strokes.[60]

Whenever he stayed at the Whitehill home, King proofread the latest drafts of the memoir. Under King's supervision, Whitehill wrote a factual naval record from original documentary sources. Working together, Whitehill and King finished the manuscript by 1950, and Norton Publishing finished the final editing process for what became *Fleet Admiral King: A Naval Record* by 1952. One close associate, Adm. Robert "Mick" Carney, remembered that King was very proud. King declared that his memoir "would blow the lid off the deliberations of the Joint Chiefs of Staff." Carney recalled, "Well, it never did . . . he had something bugging him that never came out in the book."[61]

King simply told the truth by describing the work in the subtitle, *A Naval Record*. Past media controversies likely influenced King, since he had witnessed the damage done to the cause of American sea power after the Samson and Schley controversy after the Spanish-American War, the Daniels and Sims duels after the First World War, and then the disputes between Halsey and Kinkaid after the Second World War. In the early 1950s, the Department of Defense bureaucracy blossomed as King had predicted. Worried about the ramifications, he failed to say so in clear terms within the narrative of *Fleet Admiral King*. He left the bigger story on the cutting-room floor. Whitehill kept all the notes and draft manuscripts along with King's personal papers in the original navy filing cabinets. Whitehill guarded these papers, and so they sat dormant in a barn behind his house outside Boston, Massachusetts.

Whitehill recalled that King reduced entire paragraphs into single sentences, or strategically planted words. King wanted to state his case in coldly delivered facts. He synthesized the material to the point of being impenetrable for unindoctrinated readers. Looking for the smoking gun between the lines of *Fleet Admiral King*, one sympathetic associate recalled that "King himself was such a frigid machine that his prose was not easy to read."[62] Unsatisfied with King's "just the facts" approach, Hanson Baldwin provided a balanced assessment for the *New York Times Book Review.* He complained that the "reader finds himself trying to break through the dull recital of events to find out what manner of man King was and to determine his personal relationships with his associates."[63] Baldwin explained that *Fleet Admiral King* fell short of the objective as a "biography or history or memoir [since it] lacks sparkle and presents only half a portrait."[64] In the final evaluation, *Fleet Admiral King* provided "some idea of the fierce rectitude and integrity and unswerving purpose of the least known member of our Joint Chiefs of Staff—a man whom succeeding generations may call either stubborn or strong, but a man too rare in any age, a man who could not be had."[65]

The publication of *Fleet Admiral King* coincided with the end of a remarkable era in the history of American sea power. King fought to speak as he struggled to recover from a series of strokes, and his family rallied around the patriarch. Eventually, the physical toll forced him to weather the storm under the watchful eyes of his flag assistant and a staff of medical caretakers in the naval hospitals at Bethesda and in Portsmouth, New

Hampshire. He continued the weekend visits to their home and frequently made surprise appearances to visit his grandson Liath, who was earning his commission at the Military Academy at West Point in New York at that time. King rode in the back of his limousine, adorned with the five-star flag mounted on the front bumper.[66] Another grandson, Jan, had fond memories of his grandfather. In the years following, he recalled the circumstances of learning of the quiet departure of King for the final voyage:

> In June of 1956 we had just visited Washington and stayed with Mattie[, and] Ernie was up in his summer quarters at the Portsmouth Naval Hospital. The next morning, we took off for Japan, with a refueling stop at Wake Island. We were in the air about 2 hours when a message came over the radio that my grandfather King had died. [General Smith] came back from the radio compartment and told my mother the news. He said we could turn the plane around and go back to Washington for the funeral, but she said no, there would be plenty of family there to represent her, and she did not want to disrupt the plans for my father's turnover and change of command in Nagoya.[67]

King died in the same hospital suite as his personal hero, Mayo, at the Portsmouth Naval Hospital on June 25, 1956. Just as in life, King followed his old mentors to find his own place among the stars of the past. The uncharted waters of the future were there for others to chart, which King happily accepted in his final years.

The funeral rituals surrounding King's five-star coffin reflected the remarkable stature of the old sailor resting within. Among other international leaders, Queen Elizabeth II and Churchill sent personal condolences to the King family. Emperor Hirohito and Chiang Kai-shek sent personal notes to mark the passing of King. The old soldier Marshall eulogized King during ceremonies at the National Cathedral. Admirals Leahy and Stark stood with Mattie, along with Pye, Low, and Cmdre. Dudley W. Knox. Missing but accounted for among King's most trusted associates, Edwards passed away shortly before King in June 1956. Cooke characteristically joked with wry humor that "Edwards just did what any good chief of staff does [in death] by getting things ready for the boss."[68]

Representatives of the various military branches and sea services participated in King's five-star funeral. President Eisenhower spoke glowingly about King for the media as members of Congress appeared on the steps of the US Capitol to render a final salute as King's coffin was transferred from the horse-drawn caisson to a hearse. The pallbearers and color guard included enlisted men from all branches. The funeral procession then proceeded to Hospital Point, near the yard at the Naval Academy, where his wife, a daughter, and son later joined King. Final eulogizing remarks by the CNO, Adm. Arleigh A. Burke, emphasized the "extraordinary brilliance of King."[69] In addition, Burke observed that King "was blessed with complete intellectual integrity and the undeviating courage of his convictions[, his] conclusions were logical and his beliefs unshakeable."[70] Burke concluded that King "adhered doggedly to his reasoned beliefs in the face of tremendous opposition[, but] no pressure except the pressure of logic could make him back down."[71]

For a brief and shining moment, King successfully realized the dream of American sea power. His generation carried the British visions of "Imperial Federation" and "League of Nations Navy" in the First World War era to set foundations for the "United Nations

Navy" with American sea power during the Second World War. Airpower theory and the atomic bomb subsequently destroyed the vision of American sea power. The old foundations of imperialism seeped into American society under the "Truman Doctrine," which Walter Lippmann warned about in his ironically titled book *The Cold War*. In 1947, Lippmann characterized Truman's decisions as a "strategic monstrosity." He then concluded with a warning for Americans to return focus on the key objective in war as being the attainment of a peacetime end. Lippmann referred to this vision as "our oldest and best tradition—to be the friend and champion of nations seeking independence and an end to the rule of alien powers."[72]

American sea power evolved through an unprecedented era of global transformation and rapid technological innovation to reach its zenith under the able supervision of King. With his slow demise after fifty years on active service, American sea power also quickly faded into the bureaucratic malaise of the DoD. The atomic winds of airpower further undercut the dream of American sea power as codified in the Truman Doctrine after the Second World War. The old specters of militarism and navalism appeared in the backdrop of British and American propaganda about Soviet and Chinese communism in the Cold War era and into the space age. By the 1960s, the rise of American sea power during the earlier generations of Sims and King faded into the realm of heroic myth and popular memory.

Unification debates bubbled below the surface of Anglo-American politics when Soviet forces developed the technological means to launch preemptive atomic strikes. Airpower theorists of the era also made truly dangerous assumptions about the capacity of atomic weapons to win wars without having to fight battles.[73] The image of atomic mushroom clouds amplified tensions in the global maritime arena, as King's navy fell under the spell of atomic weapons and then nuclear technology. Preemptive-strategic-strike theories were inserted into poorly framed strategic justifications to conduct undeclared "small wars."[74] Having been one of the architects of the bureaucratic machine envisioned by the War Department before the Second World War, President Dwight David Eisenhower increasingly lamented past dreams of American sea power in the era of King's navy. Eisenhower predicted heavy seas under the darker clouds of airpower in his warnings about the "Military-Industrial Complex" within the subtext of his farewell address of January 1961.[75] Former torpedo boat skipper and then-current president John F. Kennedy proclaimed that "any man who may be asked in this century what he did to make his life worth while, I think can respond with a good deal of pride and satisfaction: 'I served in the United States Navy.'" Given the proud assertions of President Kennedy, it should be noted that Kennedy served in the unique wartime culture of American sea power as exemplified when Ernest J. King and his associates created "King's Navy" during the first fifty years of the twentieth century.[76]

WAR AND REMEMBRANCE

Lost in the mountains and jungles on foreign shores, American naval professionals drifted into the intellectual desert under the windy skies of airpower theory. Recognizing the strategic vulnerability, US Navy commander Thomas B. Buell began writing semiofficial histories of key American naval commanders as a member of the Naval War College staff in the 1970s. The president of the Naval War College, Adm. Stansfield Turner, provided funding and the administrative mandate for Buell to gain access to previously unseen documentary collections. From 1971 to 1973, Turner supervised Buell in securing interviews with the closest living associates of such past luminaries as Sims, Leahy, King, Nimitz, Spruance, and Halsey.[77] Turner also convinced King's former aide and seasoned historian Whitehill to assist the aspirant novice Buell in researching the great American naval captains of the past.[78]

By revisiting the history of the institution, Turner attempted to use the Naval War College as a platform for revitalizing American sea power in the aftermath of undeclared wars in Korea and Vietnam. The counterculture movement inspired Turner to restore the original purpose of the Naval _War_ College as an open forum for practitioners to recapture the sustainable end of war. As in the past, the Naval War College used history as the foundation for applied discussion of issues of American policy and future strategy. Drawing from the examples of Sims and Kalbfus in organizing historical efforts, Turner assembled a small group of bright young naval officers to rekindle the mission of the Historical Section of the Naval War College.

Original research in documentary sources served as one means to restore the original vision of American sea power. To secure this fundamental goal, Turner joined forces with retired rear admiral Richard S. Bates and the former assistant secretary of the Navy (Air) John Nicholas Brown II. Together, Bates and Brown filed the paperwork to establish the Naval War College Foundation in 1969. Turner validated the Articles of Association to formally incorporate the Naval War College Foundation in 1972.[79] The organization subsequently served as a gateway for collecting "money but also of intangible personal property such as stocks and bond, of memorabilia and artifacts, memoirs, art such as naval paintings and portraits, and other archival material from both military and civilian sources."[80]

Through the Naval War College Foundation, Turner placed Buell in charge of assisting historians in writing new biographical studies of key figures from the institutional history of the Naval War College. During this period, several scholars rotated for temporary appointments at the Naval War College as the King Chair in Maritime History, to include Gerald B. Wheeler, Stephen Ambrose, and Martin Blumenson. The presence of civilian scholars provided means by which to educate serving naval practitioners about documentary methods of historical research. Among others, Buell stood among a contingent of young and promising naval officers on the staff at the Naval War College. The former marine Kenneth McDonald also worked closely with Buell alongside Lt. John B. Hattendorf and Ens. Craig Symonds. With Turner backing their educations, all earned their doctoral degrees in history. Buell chose to pursue other avenues of historical scholarship.[81]

Turner planned to expand the Naval War College campus, which coincided with his effort to broaden the curriculum by reducing the number of active-service instructors. He found inspiration in the Oxford model, seeking to recruit civilian academics for short-term appointments. Turner pushed his agenda by adapting the traditional naval staff organization by superimposing titles like dean, professor, and faculty on the places where terms like department head, instructor, and staff traditionally appeared in the Naval War College table of organization.

Turner had dreams of establishing the Naval War College as the international model for the future of joint professional education. Building from his predecessors, Turner pushed construction for new buildings later christened in honor of Admirals Spruance, Conolly, and Hewitt. As construction began, Turner envisioned the publication of new biographies about these personalities. Turner wanted these books to be published under the name of a serving naval officer, like Buell, and to appear on bookshelves. Buell took up the task of writing a new biography of Adm. Raymond A. Spruance. In research, retired rear admiral Henry E. Eccles introduced Buell to King's former aide Whitehill.[82] Other historians assisted Buell—including Wheeler, Elmer B. Potter, Paolo Coletta, and Lloyd J. Graybar. In addition, Buell began regular correspondence with Robert A. Heinlein and Hermann Wouk on a variety of projects.

Heinlein and Wouk frequently extrapolated their futuristic story lines by fictionalizing actual historical events and personalities. Both referred to the singular personality of King in developing their fictional characters. Along with Heinlein and Wouk, historians affiliated with the Naval War College coached Buell in developing his writing skills. Buell had significant assistance in writing the biography *The Quiet Warrior*, as published commercially in 1974 by Little, Brown.[83] Just as Buell won his reputation for writing the Spruance biography, he received orders to take command in the destroyer escort USS *Joseph Hewes* (DE-1078).

Buell balanced the success of *Quiet Warrior* with the responsibilities inherent with command at sea. He maintained steady correspondence with Heinlein and Wouk. Buell also traveled to various archives conducting oral-history interviews and exchanged letters with closer associates of King—*all while in command*. Perhaps looking beyond his naval career, Buell drew inspiration from the storytelling styles of Heinlein and Wouk while attempting to write the epic saga of King. In correspondence, Wouk encouraged Buell to get "behind the careful Whitehill façade [and] disclose many of the warts and wrinkles of the man."[84] In the same letter, Wouk warned Buell to recognize that "you are taking a shot at one of the most demanding and exasperating of human endeavors." Wouk advised Buell that writing "can be exalting fun, but usually after a lot of missteps and agony."[85]

In chasing the story, Buell demonstrated great tenacity in gathering original documentary sources and firsthand perspectives on King. He gave appropriate credit to all the key contributors, as well as associates of King and members of his immediate family. Notably, Buell frequently visited the Whitehill home in Massachusetts. Buell recalled, "I slept in King's bed, sat in his chair, ate at his table, and talked for hours with [Whitehill] about Fleet Admiral King."[86] Whitehill allowed Buell to study King's papers, out in the barn. Among the first to open the file cabinets after King's death nearly two decades before, Buell discovered "magic in those papers [as] King's soul and spirit permeated every page that I read."[87] He decided at that moment that "I wanted to write a biography of Ernest J. King."[88]

Whitehill allowed Buell to take the massive collection of documents, which he later passed to the Naval War College Foundation for the future benefit of all. Many of the original documents still feature Buell's handwritten annotations. Clearly, he found inspiration in the seagoing environment as the skipper of a warship while writing about King in his stateroom. In 1975, Buell received detachment orders to an assignment ashore. He requested orders for duty at the Naval War College. Instead, Buell received a staff assignment to the Military Academy at West Point in New York. Buell had the Whitehill papers with him while writing about King during his tenure at West Point. Buell completed a rough draft of his King biography in 1977.

As a naval officer, Buell naturally struggled with the challenge of writing for the uninitiated, general reader. Heinlein and Wouk again lent a hand to Buell during the process of writing about King. Wouk's 1971 novel *The Winds of War* inspired Buell to mimic the narrative style. While writing the King biography, Buell, in turn, shared his technical expertise with Wouk, who was writing *War and Remembrance*. In these flowing tales of the navy, Wouk based his fictional character Commander Victor "Pug" Henry on the actual experiences of King's close associates, including Admirals Smedberg and Pihl and Pihl's first wife, Charlotte.

Buell progressively drifted from writing a straight biography of King from contemporaneous documentary sources. He began writing a story about King, which more closely resembled the fictional characters found in the stories told by Wouk. In separate recorded interviews, for example, retired captain John A. "Jack" Moreno recalled his younger days as a freshly minted ensign. He remembered meeting the much-elder King during a poker game in a wardroom.[89] In passing, Moreno then recalled fellow aviators telling wild sea stories about King's younger days. Moreno provided no clear evidence when retelling sea stories about King's younger days in the navy—alleging that he had been a "boudoir athlete."[90]

In recordings, Moreno sounded like a seasoned radio broadcaster with a gift for spinning colorful tales of adventure on the high seas. When Moreno graduated from the Naval Academy with the Class of 1930, King was in command of *Lexington*. He had already raised six daughters, and he had an eight-year-old son living in their very happy home in Long Beach. His wife, Mattie, regularly held court with the wives of King's officers on *Lexington*. In fact, Moreno did not know King until he reported for duty at the Navy Department four years later, in 1934. At that time, Moreno served briefly for King before reporting to flight school. Ten years later, Moreno served as a liaison assigned from the ComInCh staff to ComNavEu to assist in planning the OVERLORD/NEPTUNE operations—primarily based in London.[91]

Moreno's sea stories inspired Buell to dig more deeply into the family life and personal behavior of King. In this quest, Buell surprised Paul and Charlotte Pihl with questions about King's relationship with his wife and family. In a recorded interview, Buell coaxed Charlotte Pihl into suggesting, "Of course [King] had affairs."[92] She then waxed poetic about King in recalling him dancing with the wives of subordinate officers on board *Lexington*. Pihl recalled:

> The most aggravating part [about] King's ability to drink off duty was that he could go to a party and stay up most of the night, drink more whiskey than the junior officers, dance longer than any of them, and yet the next morning when the junior officers were all suffering from the grandmother of all hangovers [he] would appear on duty bright eyed and bushy tailed, and ready for work.[93]

"Let me be very careful about this," Charlotte Pihl then mused. "I *think* I know of two, and probably three that he had affairs with."[94] Pihl then qualified her statement by stating, "I don't think—it wasn't the kind of affair where he would take them out to dinner or let them around or something like that—because that would insult his wife [and] he wouldn't do that."[95]

Buell coaxed his interview subjects with carefully crafted questions about King's behavior and personality. In correspondence and recorded audio interviews, associates of King told their recollections many decades after the fact. Turning every rock for evidence, Buell asked leading questions in interviews with key associates of King, including the widow of the late admiral John J. Ballentine, Catherine. Ballentine provided a confused answer about King's character when asked by Buell. In recorded comments made after the interview, Buell recorded himself stating that Mrs. Ballentine spoke in opaque terms about alleged affairs with other women.[96] Buell fixated on questions of character and personality, seeking to provide a glimpse behind King's towering façade. In the process, Buell added unnecessary spice and diverted his analysis of King away from the key historical issues at hand.[97] He also fueled superfluous historiographical debates about King's family, with oblique references to his interconnected inner circle of close friends like the Pihls, Matters, and Dunlaps.

Losing sight of the bigger story, Buell possibly fell under the spell of the commercial publishing industry. Seeking a career beyond the naval service in the 1970s, Buell became nostalgic about King's era. When Buell completed the draft manuscript in 1977, he sent it for review among trusted associates—many of whom had assisted Buell in writing *The Quiet Warrior* during his previous assignment at the Naval War College. Buell sought to follow in the reputation of the sailor and scholar Morison. Buell wanted to write the definitive biography, although he struggled with his writing. He mimicked the writing styles of his favorite historians while writing drafts of what became *Master of Sea Power* while in command on board *Hewes*. Having worked very hard on the manuscript while at sea, Buell felt disappointed with the feedback provided by trusted friends and mentors. Among other scholars, Coletta simply advised Buell to "burn this."[98] Potter asked Buell, "What the hell are you trying to do?"[99] Wheeler warned Buell, telling him, "You might be compromising your own future."[100]

Buell cast King in the role of an epic figure in the historical narrative of American sea power. He simultaneously wanted to achieve the popularity and financial success of Heinlein and Wouk. Having evaluated the manuscript, Heinlein wrote Buell, "I served with King and the guy you are talking about is not anything like him."[101] Similarly, Wouk characterized the Buell manuscript as "absolutely unpublishable."[102] "I've made some harsh, almost Kingian comments on your writing," Wouk told Buell. "I don't know how else to drive home your weaknesses to you[, but] it is really awful."[103] Wouk attempted to show Buell an alternative in examining his subject by suggesting that King's tale had

lapsed into almost total obscurity, more so than Nimitz, Spruance, or Halsey. There is no Ernest King Library like the Marshall Library. Maybe there should be, but there isn't. The man came and went, unsung except in journalism that did the "steely-eyed" cliché and then forgot him.[104]

Wouk advised Buell to focus on King as the singular naval strategist of the Second World War by answering this basic question: "How does such a creature get formed?"[105] Wouk suggested that the truth "lies in the nature of the United States Navy, as it affected a very powerful and rather complicated personality."[106] "My Pug Henry," Wouk warned, "could never become an Ernest King."[107] Wouk advised Buell that King was an "absolutely quintessential military man, the kind you couldn't be if you tried."[108]

Wouk warned Buell to rewrite the King biography, or perhaps to abandon the manuscript altogether. He chastised Buell, saying, "You promise more than you deliver about his peccadilloes [with] sly hints and disagreeable touches like the hands under the table, I was disappointed in this part; and not because I was drooling for hot stuff."[109] Whether or not King had extramarital affairs seemed an unnecessary diversion from the point of Buell's work. On this specific question, Wouk was completely unconvinced. Providing some seasoned editorial advice, Wouk told Buell that tales about King's "visits to Charlotte Pihl and those two sisters, as the book stands, are right out of Louisa May Alcott."[110]

Buell faced a terrible dilemma, having already accepted a financial advance and a contract from Little, Brown, on the King biography. He made minor editorial corrections by 1978 before submitting the final manuscript to Little, Brown. Buell simply lacked sufficient time to start over. With the publication of *Master of Sea Power* in 1980, the King family felt deeply betrayed by Buell. Retired commander Janvier King Smith recalled, "Buell interviewed my mother (Martha) at my parents' home in San Antonio in the 1970s [and] she was so angry she invited him to leave."[111] Buell's work was also panned by Smith's father, US Air Force general Freddy Smith. In addition, King's only son, Joe, dismissed the Buell biography as "deeply unfortunate." Under the circumstances, the King family asked the Naval Historical Foundation to make inquiries about the tales told by Buell for the purposes of correcting the record. In response, retired vice admiral Walter S. DeLany responded on behalf of others, including Admirals Robert Carney, Jerauld Wright, Elliot Strauss, and Arleigh Burke. Writing in July 1980, DeLany reassured the King family, saying that *Master of Sea Power* "is a story about him but not a biography of him[, and] I find it difficult to evaluate the author's real intent."[112]

LOOKING OUTWARD

The conclusions offered by Buell in *Master of Sea Power* caught King's family by complete surprise. Many of those to whom Buell attributed the racier allegations also wrote strongly worded letters in protest after the publication of *Master of Sea Power.* Among others, Smedberg, van Deurs, and Madeira—along with Charlotte and Paul Pihl—also lambasted Buell's account. Indeed, there exists no conclusive—or necessarily convincing—evidence of bad behavior on King's part within official or unofficial documentary records, in the media, or in other potential sources. In reviewing *Master of Sea Power*, Lloyd J. Graybar correctly accused Buell of falsifying the historical record. Graybar had also scoured original documents while gathering material for a biography of King. Having seen the same sources and spoken to the same associates of King, Graybar fired a full broadside that "Buell's study thus gives the appearance of careful research."[113]

Graybar condemned Buell for taking too many methodological shortcuts in the rush to tell King's story. While Graybar should have continued writing his own biography, he did provide sufficient warning for future historians to treat Buell's biography as fundamentally unreliable as a historical reference. Graybar aptly noted the "failure of Buell and his publisher to provide documentation."[114] He condemned Buell for making veiled accusations concerning King's alcoholic habits and lecherous behavior toward women. Graybar discounted Buell for his "casual handling" of the evidence. Graybar concluded that Buell's "failure to provide satisfactory documentation for the weak case he does make [also] needlessly raises doubts about the reliability of his portrayal of King."[115]

Graybar's corrective warnings failed to set the record straight when Buell spun unsubstantiated tales, which resonated in popular media and among historians. Many failed to follow Graybar's advice in considering the evidence, as historians deferred to the Buell narrative. After the publication of *Master of Sea Power*, Buell also retained the original papers he had inherited from Whitehill. As a result, Graybar had no definitive means to refute Buell's evaluation of the evidence. Upon his retirement from active service, Buell deposited the Whitehill papers with the Naval War College Foundation in 1979. He imposed restrictions requiring his personal approval for other historians to access the files. Under the circumstances, Graybar abandoned his effort to write his own biography of King.[116] The disclosures associated with the slow declassification of Special Intelligence sources also opened many new questions, as historians sought to be the first to publish tantalizing secrets about the world wars.

Historians in the generation of Graybar and Buell faced the building historiographical tidal wave of ULTRA and MAGIC. While nothing was new in broad historical terms, the details found in original Special Intelligence sources provided the means to crawl into the minds of key decision makers like King as they made decisions *at the time*. The work required to understand these records proved too daunting for many historians in the 1980s and 1990s. During this period, Buell drifted far off course in navigating the uncertain seas after his retirement from the US Navy. As a researcher, Buell's exacting attention to detail also reflected the seasoning acquired after many hours on the deck as a career naval officer. His ability to uncover and then hunt down the original sources stands as his greatest contribution. With all the material he had acquired after nearly a decade of work, Buell aspired to continue working as a historian on the civilian faculty of the Naval War College. He fostered old ties with the Naval War College Foundation, Naval Historical Foundation, and Naval Institute, and at the Naval Academy.

In the ongoing quest to find suitable civilian employment after a career in the US Navy, Buell parlayed his treasure trove of research papers by donating them in small batches to various institutions. Beyond his documentary collections at the Naval War College, the Special Collections at Nimitz Library at the Naval Academy interconnected with the collection he later donated to the University of North Carolina at Chapel Hill. Buell never realized his dream of securing a faculty appointment as a historian. Resigned to a career at 3M in Minnesota, Buell eventually lifted restrictions governing access to the papers donated to the Naval War College Foundation, in 1992. At that time, Dr. Evelyn Cherpak produced a listing of boxes and general themes, which sat largely unnoticed in the original organization as received from Buell.[117]

Future historians must respect Buell's foresight in saving the King-Whitehill papers from oblivion. Along with other Naval War College documentary collections, the materials deposited by Buell sat dormant for many decades. Indeed, future historians still have much work to do. Unfortunately, the Naval War College historical collections were moved to deep storage under the cover of the COVID-19 pandemic in 2020. At that time, the director of historical functions at the Naval War College unsuccessfully argued, "History is an operational function of intelligence[,] and any decision to restrict access to our singular institutional collections is akin to telling the intelligence community that they can no longer have access to spies or satellites."[118]

CONCLUSION

The global maritime arena shaped the gladiatorial fight for control among empires of the past, which by extension defined the vision of American sea power. Given this longer saga, the full story of King's navy shall never truly be written. The era of such figures as Sims and King has now forever passed into the mists of popular myth and memory. Both lived in a very dangerous era of world wars punctuated by the relentless advance of technologies—from wireless to the atomic bomb—during careers spanning the first fifty years of the twentieth century. From this perspective, the ramifications of the War of Independence and the Civil War cannot be ignored in considering the period in which Sims influenced King's generation.

The world wars of the twentieth century are equally intertwined with the contemporaneous questions we all face together in the twenty-first. As this work has demonstrated, King's navy provides a useful foundation for contemporary maritime thinkers to continue looking outward. In the twenty-first century, old problems have continued to cloud debates concerning the future role of navies. In this, King's navy may inform our discussions concerning the vacuous maritime environment of space. As he advised so well in private correspondence in May 1941,

> My experience in life has been that things come "right" the more one is steadfast in the belief that they will—and never gives up in the belief—no matter what delays and discouragements may intervene[, so] don't let anything get you down—hold fast to the belief that you'll get what you want if you stick to it—work for it—plan for it and don't take "no" for an answer.[1]

With these words of encouragement to a close confidant, King went on to win the future of American sea power in the Second World War. Had he remained physically able in the aftermath, the rise of airpower under the bureaucracy of DoD may have taken a completely different course. History, nevertheless, unfolded as we now know it after 1947. King's silence after the publication of his memoirs in 1952 has subsequently been filled by other narratives, which defined King's place in the historiography. Yet, few have acknowledged his education in the First World War era as he evolved into becoming the boss of all American naval efforts on the global stage of the Second World War. Many gaps must still be filled in this fifty-year chronology, since documents relating to this history are still largely inaccessible or otherwise difficult to access into the twenty-first century.

Looking outward and across the still largely unknown oceanic commons, future historians still have much work to do in addressing problems of myth and popular memory. Just as Mahan fueled historical debates concerning the future of American sea power, Corbett used original archival sources to advance our collective understanding of maritime strategy in both peace and war. Drawing from those historical ideas, Sims and Mayo grappled with strategic problems of combined command after the First World War—thereby educating the younger generation to continue working the lines to pull together the nexus between American policy and naval strategy. By consistent review of original documentary sources, future researchers will discover new perspectives on such popular myths as War Plan ORANGE, the primacy of Bletchley Park, and the actual genius of individuals muddling along long enough for a chance to open unforeseeable variables into the unwritten future.

Future historians must constantly interrogate contemporaneous sources to consider the mythologies found in historiography. Among other mythologized figures in history, King has been widely caricatured in secondary literature. His personal past often appears in the distant mirrors of the Second World War. In the current work, his longer view becomes clear after fifty years on the deck. Just as Sims was an Anglophile in his times, King was *not* an Anglophobe in navigating the uncharted waters of coalition naval operations in peace and in war. From their studies at the Naval War College, the generation of Sims and King always recognized the strategic primacy of "Europe First" in the longer effort to stabilize Asia—using the influence of Britannia to enhance the role of American sea power to attain the sustainable end of war. The policies of Theodore Roosevelt, which later influenced those of his cousin Franklin, shaped this global strategic outlook in anticipation of the Second World War. For King, defeating the Axis Tripartite through Europe before Asia also provided critical foundations for realizing the dream of American sea power under the future United Nations.

The history of King's navy leaves us with the current question of American sea power. When the US Navy completely overlooked King's pioneering role by commissioning an entire class of nuclear-powered aircraft carriers after his subordinate—a submariner named Nimitz—mythology and misguided traditions had clearly taken hold. As in the past, collective historical ignorance is among humanity's greatest challenges in navigating the uncharted waters of the future. To this point, King mused in 1946 that "we read about robot-controlled planes which we are going to set up and knock out the enemy's planes out of the air, but he, of course, is going to have robot-controlled plans and knock our planes out of the air."[2] King asked, "What is gained if our robot-controlled planes meet the enemy's robot-controlled planes, and they destroy one another?"[3] King concluded that the "point I want to make is—the important thing is not the machines, but the men who man them and give them life."[4]

Technology rarely proved decisive in historical wars, which King fully understood in shaping American sea power. Among the most tangible reminders of King's navy, the captured German submarine *U-505* stands out as a most remarkable war trophy of the Second World War. Technologically, the Type IXC submarine proved completely inadequate by comparison with comparable American designs. King's CominCh staff directly enabled the task group under his protégé Gallery to capture the enemy submarine. Having become popularly recognized as the American "face" of victory in the Atlantic, Gallery later recast the former German warship as a monument to King's navy in 1954. He mused, "I look on this U-boat in Chicago as a memorial, of a sort, to our misguided enemies."[5] He portrayed *U-505* as "direct proof of war's futility that now, only eleven years after VJ-Day, we are wooing the Germans and the Japs, and arming them to help protect the western world against our former allies, the communists."[6] Gallery thought, "Hitler's ghost must cackle sardonically over that one!"[7]

The human dimension far exceeded variables of technology in advancing the historical future of American sea power when King's generation stood on the deck. Fighting for the end of war by attaining sustainable peacetime ends, King stood out as "reputed to be cold and tough."[8] His protégé Low thought King placed on "himself a suit of armor in his early days and rarely stepp[ed] out of it."[9] In his own explanation, King characterized himself as a byproduct of American sea power. After his many decades on the deck, the First World War informed King's evaluation of his role in the Second World War: "From the Argentia Conference of August 1941 to the Potsdam Conference in July 1945—for that stretch of time, about four years, I can echo him who said, 'all of which I saw, and a part of which I was.'"[10]

Looking outward and beyond the troubled future in the twenty-first century, the history of King's navy provides means to reimagine the future of sea power. The first Americans into space—from John Glenn to Alan Shepard—later followed King's legacy to the stars. His contributions to naval aviation similarly appeared when Neil Armstrong left the first footprints on the face of the moon. The exploits of King and his associates later inspired other feats in deep-sea exploration, such the exploits of Don Walsh and Jacques Picard in the bathyscaph *Trieste*. From 1897 to 1947, King pursued similar adventures on the cutting edges of futuristic technology. Always well tethered to the past, King studied history to develop his own course in navigating the uncharted waters of the future.

King's navy is now gone, and the dream of American sea power has perhaps disappeared into the wild blue yonder and cloudy theoretical assumptions of airpower. Nuclear technology also irradiated the second fifty years of the twentieth century—and now into the twenty-first century. Looking outward, King warned contemporary naval thinkers that "no matter how ingenious the war machines—no matter how marvelous the developments of science[, we] must always remember, without fail, that the wars of the future—if more wars there must be—will be similar to the wars of the past."[11] Reflecting upon the experience of two world wars, he warned American listeners: "Our fellow citizens, yours and mine, decry war, hate everything about it, which is right, but is not realistic, and funds were not appropriated by your representatives and mine."[12] Carrying the torch of the Roosevelts, Sims, and other mentors of his generation, King pondered the timeless question about the fundamental mission of American sea power in the global maritime arena in asking, "Why should we not 'wage peace'?"[13]

In history, the future is still to be written . . .

Appendixes

The following transcriptions of key archival documents are provided, since few other histories have featured information found within. The author transcribed the original documents, which generally followed grammatical and spelling conventions employed within the Admiralty and Navy Department during the Second World War. While the author has attempted to replicate exactly the original documents in detail, minor changes were required for the purposes of grammatical clarity and overall consistency. The general rules employed in transcribing the following documents reflect the dissertation standards of King's College London and are also in keeping with those of the *Chicago Manual of Style*, as applied from the guidelines provided in the seventh edition of Kate Turabian's *A Manual for Writers of Term Papers, Theses, and Dissertations*. The standards established by the Navy Records Society provided additional guidance for the transcriber.

Documents provided herein were generally found in the British National Archives (formerly the Public Record Office) at Kew near London and the National Archives at College Park, Maryland, in the United States. Although duplicates of these documents may be obtained in various other collections, the author has used the first editions and original drafts of the documents featured on the following pages. Editorial changes have been kept to an absolute minimum and have been generally indicated with the square brackets, or "[ ]." Wherever readers may find parentheses, or "( )," these markings appear in the original documents. Wherever readers may find words that have been stricken with lines or other such editorial notes, these annotations also appear in the original documents. Any errors found in this work are, of course, the responsibility of the author and not of the reader.

APPENDIX A

Previously unpublished First World War Chronology
Atlantic Fleet and Captain Ernest J. King movements to European Front
(1916–19)
Ernest J. King Papers
Naval War College MSC 37

Room 3046
Navy Department
Washington 25, DC,
17 November 1948.

Admiral Leigh Noyes, USN (Ret.),
2301 Connecticut Avenue, N.W.,
Washington 8, DC.

Dear Noyes,

Of course, I need your fine notes that you gave me but I wonder if you have the correct times written down? I'm trying to write up our two trips to Europe in World War I, and it seems to me that perhaps, you as well as myself don't just remember the exat times that we were there. For instance, I don't remember when Admiral Mayo and party left Paris in <u>1917</u> to go back to London unless it was at the time of the incident of 'the other five' at Boulogne when some of the party couldn't go to Calais and Dunkerque and went on board the BROKE and crossed to Dover. If not at that time then when was the incident about the BROKE? I remember clearly when we left Paris in <u>1918</u> and crossed in a new USA destroyer commanded by Vernou. If I'm not right about <u>1917</u>, what time was it that we left France to go to England? Again, I remember that we crossed the Channel in <u>1918</u> from Southampton to Havre but I don't seem to remember our crossing the Channel twice in <u>1918</u>.

Please help me with my poor memory especially times.

Of course, I can try to change things after I've written up my notes but I'm one of those people who has to get the 'dope' at once and correctly.

Faithfully yours,
King

OUTLINE OF IMPORTANT INCIDENTS OF CRUISE
OF ADMIRAL MAYO AND STAFF
DURING WORLD WAR I

1916

Sept.   Interned *Kronprinz Wilhelm* & *Prinz Eitel Friedrich*

1917

Jan.   Fleet to Guantanamo, thence to Guacanyabo Bay

Feb.   Diplomatic relations with Germany severed

Fleet prepared for surprise attack

Armed Guards—gun crews & communication personnel

Furnished merchant vessels

Training for gun crews, engineers, and communication personnel for entire fleet

March   Fleet to Hampton Roads

April   War declared. Fleet to Yorktown (Base 2)

Base defense system inaugurated

June   Estimate of Situation made re[garding] visit of C-in-C & Staff to Europe. (Copy available). Approved.

July   C-in-C & Staff to Europe, leaving incognito in SS *St. Louis*, while Fleet shifted to Base 10. Arrived Liverpool thence to London.

Conferences with Admiralty. Visits to Grand Fleet

And Light Forces at Harwich. Visit to our DD's at Queenstown

Aug.   Inspection trip to France

Inspected our Air Base at Autaing. Visited Allies' Front Line—Albert, Soissons, Arras, St. Quentin, Cambrai, Reims, Comiegne, Chateau Thierry, Put up by French Govt. at Hotel Crillon.

Admiral Mayo conference in Paris with General Pershing particularly on subject of Brigading our troops with Allies.

Jackson, Sayles & Bingham inspected our Marines. Injured in auto accident. King acting Chief of Staff.

Inspected our forces at Brest

Unable to visit GIB[ralter] as planned on account of Spanish neutrality

[*Handwritten November*]

~~Sept.~~ C-in-C & Staff (less Jackson) returned to Fleet at Base 2. Improved security measures, including Defensive Sea Areas.

1917 (con)

Sept.   As result of European Inspection Trip Ad. Mayo made the following recommendations to SecNav:

> 1. North Sea Mine Barrage be proceeded with
> 2. Division of coal-burning BBs be sent to join Grand Fleet
> 3. Increase our DD's for escort duty on other side. Also our [submarines]
> 4. Unified communications with British & French
> 5. Establish US Air Stations for [antisubmarine] work

1918

Fleet at Base 2

British worried that capital ships might escape from North Sea as raiders in spite of North Sea Barrage. Decision made to send three BB's to base on Bantry Bay.

June

Utah, Florida & [blank] sailed to Bantry Bay, C-in-C and operational staff taking passage in *Utah.*

Inspected our [submarines] at Bantry Bay, DD's at Queenstown, our Air at Loch Foyle, Loch Swilley, Wexford. By Irish Mail Packet to Holley Head, thence to London. [U-boat] fired at us.

Conferences at Admiralty.

Visited Grand Fleet at Firth of Forth. Shifted base with them to Scapa Flow.

July

King, Noyes & [blank] witnessed laying of North Sea Barrage by Mine Force from *San Francisco* with Captain Belknap.

Ad. Mayo, Sims, King, Whiting, Noyes & [blank] together with Ad. Jellicoe and other British admirals, from HMS *Broke* witnessed bombardment of Ostend by HMS *Puritan*. Air raid passed over while returning to London via Dover.

Aug.   Inspected Killinshome. Conference on future Air operations.

Sept.   Confidential "news" that "Big Push" will start 12 October.

Hanrahan requests delay in starting operation so that he can bomb his objective (Thiers) before it is captured by land forces.

[*Handwritten: "Southampton inspect 'ferries' cross the Channel"*]

Inspection trip to France. Inspected all our Air Stations on French Coast; including Belle Isle, Paimbeuf, Quiberon, St. Nazire, Paulliac, Archachon. Ad. Mayo was please to find that crews always had pie for dinner.

[Handwritten: "sal-ammoniac plug]

Visited Argonne Forest, Mont Faucon, and Verdun. Inspected our Railroad Battery.

1918 (cont)

Oct.   Inspection Trip to Italy.

Special Italian Train meets us at boarder. To Rome. Inspected our Sea plane Stations in Italy, near Rome & Venice.

Nov.   Visited Italian Front. Climbed Monte Grappa.

Audience and dinner with King of Italy at his Chateau near Padua at Front.

Dinner with Marshall Badoglio at Army H.Q. Cable received during dinner stating Armistice had been signed.

C-in-C & Staff sailed from Liverpool to New York.

Dec.

1   Arrived New York

4   Sailed in *Pennsylvania* to Brest escorting President Wilson to Peace Conference

14   Sailed from Brest with our returning BB's of 6th [Battle Squadron]

24   Arrived off Scotland Light Ship

1919

Jan.   Return of troops from Europe. Rest of Fleet to Guantanamo.

June

30   Admiral Mayo hauled down his flag as C-in-C.

APPENDIX B

Naval War College Thesis
"The Relationship in War of Naval Strategy, Tactics and Command"
Library of Congress, Box 35

THESIS III—Senior Class—1933

The Relationship in War of Naval Strategy, Tactics and Command
by
Captain Ernest J. King, US Navy

I. FOREWORD

1. In order that there may be clear understanding of the scope of this paper it must be noted that the subject stated to be "relationship in war." This limitation permits, if it does not impose, orientation of peace (pre-war) considerations except insofar as matters of preparatory to effectiveness in war may require action.

2. We thus exclude consideration of the relationship of strategy to national policy and to national economies. We assume that the national policy has brought about a state of war and that certain economic factors obtain. We assume that the armed forces have come into action in accordance with a directive of national policy—which involves and includes political and economic considerations.

3. We assume that, while national policy has given the directive to the employment of the armed forces—has said "What" and "Why"—and retains power to alter them, it has left to the armed forces themselves the "how" and largely the "where" and the "when" of the actual conduct of the war. We are, then, concerned with a state of war.

II. DEFINITIONS

4. It is also essential to state just what is to be understood by use of the terms—Strategy, Tactics, Command. Brief definitions are:

> (a) <u>Strategy</u> is the conduct of war.
> (b) <u>Tactics</u> is the conduct of battle.
> (c) <u>Command</u> is the conduct of the armed forces employed in strategy and/or tactics.

5. These brief definitions may well be elaborated somewhat in order to gain clearer and more specific ideas of their several and relative scopes. For this purpose it is helpful to make use of the estimate of the situation system of stating the "decision"—what, how, why.

6. (a) <u>Strategy</u> involves the conduct of war by the management of the armed forces in such manner as to ensure situations favorable for battle, in order to gain advantage in war.

(b) <u>Tactics</u> involves the conduct of battle by the management of armed forces in such manner as to ensure victory in battle, in order to make strategy effective in war.

(c) Command involves the management of the armed forces in such a manner that they are responsive to the will of the commander, in order to make strategy and/or tactics effective in war.

III. STRATEGY VS TACTICS

7. In our first thesis we defined strategy as:—"in the general sense, the science or art of military position and the combination of 'ways and means' on a broad scale (in the theater of war, differentiated from tactics which is concerned with the theater of battle) for gaining advantage in war. It is a science in its theory and in that it involves measurable considerations of mass, velocity, space and time; it is an art in its practical application to a given war, to general situations in that war, and to the resulting specific situations. It makes use of the available, and potential "ways and means" in that manner, to the degree, and in the combination, that will best ensure the successful outcome of the war. Briefed, it may well be expressed in paragraph 4 (a)—"Strategy in the conduct of war."

8. Since strategy merges into tactics in practice—the same armed forces are involved, the same people are in command—but battle is imminent and, presumably, not to be avoided. We may paraphrase the definition of strategy in paragraph 7 above to read, for definition of tactics (parentheses indicate changes): "in the general sense, the science or art of military position and of the combination and employment of "ways and means" (in a battle situation) for gaining the advantage in (strategy). It is a science in its theory and in that it involves measurable considerations of mass, velocity, space and time; it is an art in its practical application to a given (battle), to general situations in that (battle), and to the resulting specific situations. It makes use of the available "ways and means" in the manner, to the degree, and in the combination, that will best ensure the successful outcome of the (battle)." Briefed, it may well be expressed as in paragraph 4 (b)—Tactics is the conduct of battle.

9. It is essential to appreciate the conception that strategy may be effective in gaining advantage in war without the use of battle (tactics) but it is imperative to realize that advantage so gained depends on position, readiness, and dispositions which require the enemy to engage in battle on terms so unfavorable to himself that he yields the advantage rather than dispute the issue.

10. It may be said that battle (tactics) is an element of strategy—perhaps the principle element but none-the-less inferior and subordinate to strategy itself, almost an incident in strategy. On the other hand, battle (tactics) is so important an element of strategy that strategy requires to make sure that resort to battle (tactics) can only occur under conditions so favorable to permit the attainment of the aim of strategy—to gain advantage in war.

IV. COMMAND in THEORY

11. In the definitions of strategy (paragraph 7) and of Tactics (paragraph 8) we used the expressions "combination and employment of "ways and means" and "it makes use of the available "ways and means" in the manner, to the degree, and in the combination, that will best ensure the successful outcomes of . . . In these expressions lies our conception of "command"—the combination and employment of the available "ways and means." What are the "ways and means"—what can they be but the conduct of the armed forces? What do we mean by "armed forces"? What can they be but the personnel and its attached material?

13. (*sic.*) Thus we look on command—see paragraph 3 (c) above—as "Command is the conduct of armed forces employed in strategy and/or tactics." We have also to keep in mind, as noted in the beginning of paragraph 6, that strategy merges into tactics—the same armed forces are involved, the same people are in command, the same "means" are employed even though "ways" differ. It is the function of "command" to make the armed forces responsive to the will of the commander whether it be in the field of strategy (conduct of war) or the field of tactics (conduct of battle).

14. What does the commander require in order to have the armed forces responsive to his will? Obviously, he requires the nearest possible approach to being able to control each individual of the armed forces and each piece of material, as if he himself were any given individual or were making use of any given piece of material.

15. The ideal condition may be considered analogous to the commander's control of himself—as to his ideas, his capacity to discern, to reason and to decide—as to his body, his control and direction of his locomotion (mobility) and of his arms and legs, head and torso—and last but not least, the necessity that his body has for food and water and for rest. How can this be done? It is the function of command so to do it, that the armed forces respond, as nearly may be, as does the body of the commander.

16. As to the control and direction of the "body"—the armed forces—the means available and employed is called "organization."

> As to the "food, water and rest" for the "body"—the armed forces—the means available and employed are called "administration."
>
> As to the control and direction of locomotion—mobility—the means available and employed is called "logistics."
>
> As to the ideas—the ability to discern, to reason and decide—the means available is called "staff work."

17. Organization employs the "group and leader" system of subdivision and combination so that the armed forces of whatever size or composition or purpose, is a group of groups each under its own leader. Each of the leaders of a group—large or small—has to exercise "command" which differs chiefly only in degree from that of the commander.

18. Such "group and leader" organization is the basis, and chiefly the means, of administration and of the measures whereby logistics are controlled and directed. The armed forces—when adequately organized are, then, in such condition as to permit the commander to control and direct their movements (logistics) and their supply (administration).

19. Assuming that the organization is suitable and adequate for control and direction of movements, and of supply, that is that the armed forces are capable of being controlled and directed—and assuming that, as armed forces they are suitably armed (prepared to fight)—yet they are inert and ineffective unless and until they are actually made to move and/or to fight.

20. The crux of any system of command lies in its effectiveness in conveying the "ideas" of the Commander to the individuals of the armed forces—for this is the essence of command. It will by no means suffice to attempt this after war begins, no mat[ter] how detailed orders and/or instructions may be. It is essential that the armed forces be prepared by training (education, practice) before war begins. Such training is itself an indispensable element of any sound system of command.

21. Here is where the "ideas" of the commander—his ability to discern, to reason and to decide—become of most effect. Not but what his "ideas" have had their due effect in details (great and small) of organization, of administration, and of armament, but the time has come to make us o the armed forces which are assumed to be duly prepared for movements, for supply, and for fighting but have, as yet, made no movements and have done no fighting.

V. COMMAND in PRACTICE

22. The first requirement among the "ideas" of the commander is as to just what he is to do. If national policy—see paragraph 3—has not said "what" and "why" he must deduce them from the existing circumstances—the political and/or economic situation. It is essential that he shall not direct his armed forces in their movements or in their fighting without a clear-cut task to effect a definite aim. This is called "mission"—"Task" and "purpose."

23. It is clear that before directing the movements and/or fighting of the armed forces, the commander must arrange to know certain things. It is obvious that the commander must "discern" before he can have proper basis to "reason" and to "decide." The means which enable him to "discern" are commonly called "information" or "intelligence" and includes not only that relating to the enemy but that relating to the commander's own forces. These latter are one of the chief means of obtaining enemy information by observation and/or by contact. It is an important part of "staff work" to receive, classify and analyze information, to condense it into usable form and to promulgate such parts of it as may be essential. It is to be noted that this function is, again, essential to the group leaders in adequate degree. This is called the consideration of "relative strength."

24. Since the commander can count with certainty on the "information" about his own forces—their numbers, disposition, and condition—and must have more or less adequate similar "intelligence" about the enemy forces—and so has been able to "discern" as far as he can, he is ready for the next step—"to reason" and "to decide."

25. With his "mission" firmly in mind, and with a clear view of "relative strengths" he then "considers what the enemy can do and what the enemy probably will do, giving due weight to that enemy action which will be called reviewing the "enemy probable intentions." This, again, is a necessary function to be done by group leaders to the extent adequate to their several groups.

26. With "mission," "relative strengths" and "enemy probably intentions" duly surveyed, the commander may then weigh the pros and cons of the "courses of action open to him" in their several stages of application, choosing that one which promises to be most effective in fulfilling the "what" and "why" of his mission. This choice is called the "decision." This is also an essential procedure for all group leaders in their respective spheres of activity.

27. The commander having "decided" what to do, how he will do it and why (to accomplish the "task" of his "mission") is then in readiness to direct his armed forces in their movements and/or in their fighting. It is necessary for him not only to have means for expressing himself in clear and definite terms but indispensible that he shall be able to transmit his "wishes." The first requirement is not by employing the "order form" whether or not the wishes actually are "orders" or "plans" or "instructions." The second requirement is met by means of various means of "communication"—voice, letter, dispatch, etc.

28. At this point it is well to summarize the "ways and means" which it is the function of command to combine and employ in the manner and to the degree that will best ensure the successful outcome of war (strategy) and/or of battle (tactics):

First: organization of the armed forces into groups under group leaders

Second: administration (supply) of the organization (groups)

Third: logistics—mobility of the armed forces and of their supplies

Fourth: Control and direction—clear and definite "views" as to what to do, how to do it and why it is done

Fifth: Transmission of such "views" to the armed forces—Communications

VI. STRATEGY versus TACTICS versus COMMAND

29. Reverting now to paragraph 15, we see that command has thus furnished a practical approach to the ideal condition. The commander's "ideas"—duly discerned, reasoned and decided—reach the armed forces. His "body"—include groups—his arms and legs, head and torso. The needs of his body as to sustenance (supply) and rest are met by means of administration and logistics on the basis of the groups (organization).

30. It does not matter, except chiefly in degree, whether the armed forces are engaged in strategical or tactical operations, command thus furnishes an efficient and adequate means whereby the commander may, as nearly as possible, control each individual and each piece of materiel—see paragraph 14.

31. Again, as to strategy, command provides the ways and means not only of managing the armed forces in such manner as to ensure situations favorable for battle but also, as to tactics, command provides similar (if not identical) was and means of managing the same armed forces in such manner as to ensure victory in battle. Command, then, is the effective instrumentality whereby strategy gains advantage in war and also whereby tactics makes strategy effective in war.

VII. NAVAL APPLICATIONS

32. The prescribed subject is the relationship in war of naval strategy, naval tactics, and naval command. If the foregoing development may be considered sound, little remains to be done but to insert the adjective "naval" at discretion. The principles are the same in naval (sea) as in Army (land) strategy, tactics and/or command; it is only this application of the principles that differ and for the same reason that armies and navies differ. Chiefly as to available "ways and means" on land as compared with those available at sea.

33. However, it may be well to point out that the minimum unit concerned in naval strategy and tactics is the ship and that we are therefore not here concerned with the internal affairs and arrangements of a ship.

34. Again, terrain, of primary importance in land warfare, is largely incidental in naval warfare. Bases of supply and hence logistics are of a similar degree of importance to both in strategy whereas in tactics naval forces are not concerned with replenishment of munitions and other supplies but do have to give heed to the expenditures—such heed being an essential to proper command.

35. A most striking difference between land and naval warfare is the relatively (*sic.*) mobility of land and naval forces. The advantage of navies in this respect is, however, offset by the limitations imposed by fuel expenditures. An army can stop and hold; a navy must, relatively, be able to move in order to hold. An army campaign or battle may require, respectively, months and days whereas a naval campaign or battle will usually require, respectively, weeks and hours. An army reverse may be counter-acted/; a naval reverse usually is final.

VIII. SUMMARY

36. The best available summary of the relationship in war of naval strategy, tactics, and command appears to lie in making "naval" paraphrases of the definitions in paragraph 6 above.

> (a) Naval Strategy involves the conduct of naval war by the management of the naval forces in such manner as to ensure situations favorable for naval battle, in order to gain advantage in naval war.
>
> (b) Naval tactics involves the conduct of naval battle by the management of the naval forces in such manner as to ensure victory in battle, in order to make naval strategy effective in naval war.
>
> (c) Naval Command involves the management of the naval forces in such manner that they are responsive to the will of the Admiral, in order to make naval strategy and/or naval tactics effective in war.

APPENDIX C

Library of Congress, King Papers, Box 21
Commander in Chief, Atlantic Fleet (1941)

(Serial 053) "Exercise of Command—Excess of Detail in Orders and Instructions"
and (Serial 328) "Exercise of Command—Correct Use of Initiative"
CINCLANT SERIAL (053) OF JANUARY 21, 1941

Subject: Exercise of Command—Excess of Detail in Orders and Instructions.

1. I have been concerned for many years over the increasing tendency—now grown almost to "standard practice"—of flag officers and other group commanders to issue orders and instructions in which their subordinates are told "how" as well as "what" to do to such an extent and in such detail that the "Custom of the service" has virtually become the antithesis of that essential element of command—"initiative of the subordinate."

2. We are preparing for—and are now close to—those active operations (commonly called war) which require the exercise and the utilization of the full powers and capabilities of every officer in command status. There will be neither time nor opportunity to do more than prescribe the several tasks of the several subordinates (to say "what", perhaps "when" and "where," and usually, for their intelligent cooperation, "why"), leaving to them—expecting and requiring of them—the capacity to perform the assigned tasks (to do the "how").

3. If subordinates are deprived—as they now are—of that training and experience which will enable them to act "on their own"—if they do not know, by constant practice, how to exercise "initiative of the subordinate"—if they are reluctant (afraid) to act because they are accustomed to detailed orders and instructions—if they are not habituated to think, to judge, to decide and to act for themselves in their several echelons of command—we shall be in sorry case when the time of "active operations" arrives.

4. The reasons for the current state of affairs—how did we get this way?—are many but among them are four which need mention: first, the "anxiety" of seniors that everything in their commands shall be conducted so correctly and go so smoothly, that none may comment unfavorably; second, those energetic activities of staffs which lead to infringement of (not to say interference with) the functions for which the lower echelons exist; third, the consequent "anxiety" of subordinates lest their exercise of initiative, even in their legitimate spheres, should result in their doing something which may prejudice their selection for promotion; fourth, the habit on the one hand and the expectation on the other of "nursing" and "being nursed" which lead respectively to the violation of command principles known as "orders to obey orders" and to that admission of incapacity or confusion evidenced by "request instructions."

5. Let us consider certain facts: first, submarines operating submerged are constantly confronted with situations requiring the correct exercise of judgment, decision and action; second, planes, whether operating singly or in company, are even more often called upon to act correctly; third, surface ships entering or leaving port, making a landfall, steaming in thick weather, etc., can and do meet such situations while "acting singly" and, as well, the problems involved in maneuvering in formations and dispositions. Yet these same people—proven competent to do these things without benefit of "advice" from higher

up—are, when grown in years and experience to be echelon commanders, all too often are not made full use of in conducting the affairs (administrative and operative) of the several echelons—echelons which exist for the purpose of facilitating command.

6. It is essential to extend the knowledge and the practice of "initiative of the subordinate" in principle and in application until they are universal in the exercise of command throughout all the echelons of command. Henceforth, we must all see to it that full use is made of the echelons of command—whether administrative (type) or operative (task)—by habitually framing orders and instructions to echelon commanders so as to tell them "what to do" but not "how to do it" unless the particular circumstances demand.

7. The corollaries of paragraph 6 are:

(a) adopt the premise that the echelon commanders are competent in their several command echelons unless and until they themselves prove otherwise;

(b) teach them that they are not only expected to be competent for their several command echelons but that it is required of them that they be competent;

(c) train them—by guidance and supervision—to exercise foresight, to think, to judge, to decide and to act for themselves;

(d) stop "nursing" them;

(e) finally, train ourselves to be satisfied with "acceptable solutions" even though they are not "staff solutions or other particular solutions that we ourselves prefer.

CINCLANT SERIAL (0328) OF APRIL 22, 1941

Subject: Exercise of Command -- Correct Use of Initiative.

Reference: My confidential memorandum, serial 053, dated January 21 1941 -- Subject "Exercise of Command -- Excess of Detail in Orders and Instructions."

1. In the three months that have elapsed since the promulgation of the reference, much progress has been made in improving the exercise of command through the regular echelons of command—from forces through groups and units to ships. It has, however, become increasingly evident that correct methods for the exercise of initiative are not yet thoroughly understood—and practiced—by many echelon commanders.

2. The correct exercise of the principle of the initiative is essential to the application of the principle of decentralization. The latter, in turn, is premised on the basic principle known as "division of labor," which means that each does his own work in his own sphere of action or field of activity.

3. What seems to have been overlooked is that the exercise of initiative as involved in "division of labor" (as embodied in "decentralization") not only requires *labor* on the part of those who exercise any degree of command, but, as well and even more particularly, on the part of those who exercise initiative. It also seems to have been overlooked that the correct exercise of initiative is applicable not only to operations but to administration and, as well, to personnel and material matters.

4. (a) Initiative means freedom to act, but it does not mean freedom to disregard or to depart *unnecessarily* from standard procedures or practices or instructions. There is no degree of being 'independent' of the other component parts of the whole—the Fleet.

(b) It means freedom to act only after all of one's resources in education, training, experience, skill and *understanding* have been brought to bear on the work in hand.

(c) It requires intense application in order that what is to be done shall be done as a *correlated part of a connected whole*—much as the link of a chain or a gear-wheel in a machine.

5. In order that there may be clearer understanding—and better practice—in the exercise of initiative, the following paraphrase of certain passages in the reference, together with appropriate additions, are enjoined as a guide upon all those concerned in the exercise of initiative:

"... active operations (commonly called war) require the *exercise* and the utilization of the *full powers and capabilities* of every officer in command status."

"Subordinates are to become 'habituated to *think*, to *judge*, to *decide* and to *act* for themselves'";

It requires *hard work*—concentration of powers—to exercise command effectively and, frequently, even harder work to exercise initiative *intelligently*;

When told "what" to do—make sure that "how" you do it is effective not only in itself but as an *intelligent, essential* and *correlated* part of a *comprehensive and connected whole.*

APPENDIX D

Library of Congress, King Papers, Box 21
Delineations of command functions of Stark as CNO and King as CominCh
(Administratively fused under EO 9096 in March of 1942)

DEPARTMENT OF THE NAVY
GENERAL BOARD
WASHINGTON

G.B. NO. 446
February 9, 1942

I am enclosing herewith a memorandum showing the definition of duties between the Chief of Naval Operations and the Commander in Chief, US Fleet. There may be some minor matters which are not covered and it is possible that some further adjustments will be made, but in the main I believe that the definition of duties shown in the enclosure is correct.

/s/ W.R. SEXTON.

Definition of duties as between the Chief of Naval Operations and theCommander in Chief, United States Fleet.

1. Executive Order No. 8984, of December 18, 1941, assigned certain duties to the Commander in Chief, United States Fleet and directed that subject thereto the duties and responsibilities of the Chief of Naval Operations remain unchanged. The definition of duties between the Chief of Naval Operations and the Commander in Chief, United States Fleet is shown hereunder.

DEPARTMENT OF THE NAVY
GENERAL BOARD
WASHINGTON

G.B. NO. 446.   **February 9, 1942**

I am enclosing herewith a memorandum showing the definition of duties between the Chief of Naval Operations and the Commander in Chief, U.S. Fleet. There may be some minor matters which are not covered and it is possible that some further adjustments will be made, but in the main I believe that the definition of duties shown in the enclosure is correct.

/s/ W.R. SEXTON.

<u>Definition of duties</u> as between the <u>Chief of Naval Operations and the Commander in Chief, United States Fleet.</u>

1. Executive Order No. 8984, of December 18, 1941, assigned certain duties to the Commander in Chief, United States Fleet and directed that subject thereto the duties and responsibilities of the

Under Chief of Naval Operations		Under Commander in Chief, U.S. Fleet
Issues orders for commissioning and initial assignment of vessels and aircraft units. Issues orders for decommissions vessels. Performs certain administrative functions – in liaison with Commander in Chief – regarding operating forces. Allocates floating equipment to yards and stations.	(a)	Organization, assignment and operation of the several fleets, the special task forces and the sea frontier forces. Operation and escort of allied vessels in United States waters. Information to other departmental offices and agencies concerning location and address of ships under the Commander in Chief. Outside correspondence concerning movement, location and operation of vessels of forces under the Commander in Chief. Review of courts and boards involving important units or personnel.
Operations naval local defense forces and district craft; has cognizance of other naval district matters as regard general policy, military administration and defensive measures.		
Prepares war planes from the long range point of view.	(b)	Prepares and executes plane for current war operations.
Directs training of naval local defense forces.	(c)	Directs training and readiness essential to carrying out operations.
Keeps Commander in Chief informed as to extent to which logistic and other needs of the forces under his command can be met.	(d)	Keeps Chief of Naval Operations informed as to logistic and other needs of the fleets and forces under the Commander in Chief.

Advises the Secretary of the Navy on all business of the department in regard to insular governments and foreign relations.

Has direction of Office of Naval Intelligence which office furnishes information to Commander in Chief.

Has direction of Naval Communication Service.

Coordinates all repairs and alterations to vessels and the supply of personnel and material thereto; controls docking and overhaul of vessels, preparing schedules and issuing orders in regard thereto. Keeps commander in chief informed.

The formation of convoys and their routing, in close liaison with Commander in Chief.

Operates the Naval Transportation Service, in close liaison with Commander in Chief.

Advises the Secretary of the Navy in regard to the military features and design of all new ships and as to any alterations of a ship which may affect her military value; as to the location, capacity, and protection of navy yards and naval stations, including all features which affect their military value; also, as to matters pertaining to fuel reservations and depots, the allocation of radio stations, reserve of ordnance and ammunition, fuel, stores, and other supplies of whatsoever nature with a view to meeting effectively the demands of the fleet.

(e) Makes recommendations to the Secretary of the Navy through Chief of Naval Operations.

(f) Maintains a fleet intelligence section in close contact with the Office of Naval Intelligence and other sources of information.

(g) Maintains a fleet communication section in close connection with the Director of Naval Communications.

(h) Maintains liaison.

(i) Maintains liaison, furnishes escorts.

(j) Maintains liaison, furnishes escorts.

(k) Makes recommendations to the Secretary of the Navy through Chief of Naval Operations.

APPENDIX E

EO 9096

Office of the President of the United States
Franklin Delano Roosevelt
Executive Order 9096
12 March 1942

By virtue of the authority vested in me by Title I of the First War Powers Act, 1941, approved December 18, 1941 (Public Law 354, 77th Congress), and other applicable statutes, and as Commander in Chief of the Army and Navy and as President of the United States, it is hereby ordered as follows:

1. The duties of the Commander in Chief, United States Fleet, and the duties of the Chief of Naval Operations, may be combined and devolve upon one officer who shall have the title "Commander in Chief, United States Fleet, and Chief of Naval Operations," and who shall be the principal naval adviser to the President on the conduct of the war, and the principal naval adviser and executive to the Secretary of the Navy on the conduct of the activities of the naval establishment. While so serving he shall have the rank and title of Admiral and shall receive the pay and allowances provided by law for an officer serving in the grade of Admiral.

2. As Commander in Chief, United States Fleet, the officer holding the combined offices as herein provided shall have supreme command of the operating forces comprising the several fleets, seagoing forces, and sea frontier forces of the United States Navy and shall be directly responsible, under the general direction of the Secretary of the Navy, to the President therefor[e].

3. The Staff of the Commander in Chief, United States Fleet, shall be composed of

   (a) A Chief of Staff, who shall while so serving have the rank, pay, and allowances of a Vice Admiral, and who, in the temporary absence or incapacity of the "Commander in Chief, United States Fleet, and Chief of Naval Operations," shall act as Commander in Chief, United States Fleet;
   (b) Such deputy and assistant Chiefs of Staff as may be necessary; and
   (c) Such other officers as may be appropriate and necessary to enable the "Commander in Chief, United States Fleet, and Chief of Naval Operations" to perform as Commander in Chief, United States Fleet, the duties prescribed in Executive Order No. 8984 of December 18, 1941.

4. As Chief of Naval Operations, the officer holding the combined offices as herein provided shall be charged, under the direction of the Secretary of the Navy, with the preparation, readiness, and logistic support of the operating forces comprising the several fleets, seagoing forces, and sea frontier forces of the United States Navy, and with the coordination and direction of effort to this end of the bureaus and offices of the Navy Department except such offices (other than bureaus) as the Secretary of the Navy may specifically exempt. Duties as Chief of Naval Operations shall be contributory to the discharge of the paramount duties of Commander in Chief, United States Fleet.

5. The staff of the Chief of Naval Operations shall be composed of –

(a) A Vice Chief of Naval Operations, who shall while so serving have the rank, pay, and allowances of a Vice Admiral. The Vice Chief of Naval Operations shall have all necessary authority for executing the plans and policies of the "Commander in Chief, United States Fleet, and Chief of Naval Operations" so far as pertains to the duties herein prescribed for the Chief of Naval Operations. In the temporary absence or incapacity of the "Commander in Chief, United States Fleet, and Chief of Naval Operations," he shall act as Chief of Naval Operations.

(b) An Assistant to the Chief of Naval Operations with the title of Sub Chief of Naval Operations, who shall have the rank of Rear Admiral and while so serving shall receive the pay and allowances of a Rear Admiral, upper half, and such additional assistant Chiefs of Naval Operations as may be required; and

(c) Such other officers as may be considered to be appropriate and necessary for the performance of the duties at present prescribed for the Chief of Naval Operations.

6. During the temporary absence of the Secretary of the Navy, the Under Secretary of the Navy, and the Assistant Secretaries of the Navy, the "Commander in Chief, United States Fleet, and Chief of Naval Operations" shall be next in succession to act as Secretary of the Navy. In the temporary absence of all of these officers, the Vice Chief of Naval Operations and the Chief of Staff, United States Fleet, respectively, shall be next in succession to act as Secretary of the Navy.

APPENDIX F
Dates of formally scheduled meetings between Roosevelt and King

President Franklin D. Roosevelt Library

Naval visitors to the White House according to the President's daily appointment schedule, as documented by George M. Elsey and Grace Tully between 1941–1945. Note, Secretary of the Navy Frank Knox is the person referenced, unless otherwise identified as a different Knox.

Naval Visitors to the White House		
George M. Elsey and Grace Tully comps.		
1941	**Time**	**NOTES**
Monday, 1 December	12 Noon	Hull, Stark
Tuesday, 2 December	12 Noon	Stimson, Knox, Stark
Thursday, 3 December	2:00 p.m.	Capt. Dudley W. Knox
Friday, 5 December	12 Noon	Marshall, Stark
6–7 December, NO RECORD		
Tuesday, 9 December		Stimson, [Frank] Knox, and a large group of people about Supplies, Priorities, and Allocation Board
Saturday, 12 December	12:30	Forrestal (undersecretary), Stark, Adm. S.M. Robinson, Rr. Adm. Sexton, Rr.Admiral Nimitz
Tuesday, 16 December	4:30	Knox, Stark, King
Thursday, 18 December	3:15	Stimson, Knox, Marshall, Stark, King
Tuesday, 23 December	5:00	Harry Hopkins, Stimson, Marshall, Arnold, Knox, Stark, King, Churchill, Lord Beverbrook, Pound, Portal
Monday, 29 December	1:00	King for lunch
Tuesday, 30 December		Memorandum initialed "G.T." [Grace Tully stating 'The President would like to have Admiral King for lunch with him tomorrow, Wednedsy -- if he hasn't told someone else already
Wednesday, 31 December	1:00	King for lunch
1942		
Friday, 2 January	5:00	Stimson, Marshall, Arnold, Knox, Stark, King, Minister of the Netherlands
Wednesday, 28 January	2:00	Marshall, Stark, King, Arnold, Dill, Gen. Coville Weymss, Air Marshal Harris, Adm. Sir Chas. Little
Friday, 6 February	1:00	King, Marshall, Hopkins
Saturday, 14 February	11:00	Knox, Stimson, Stark, King, Marshall, Arnold, Hopkins, Dill, Weymss, Air Marshal Evill, Adm. Sir Chas. Little, Brigadier Dykes
Tuesday, 17 February	11:30	King, Stark, Marshall, Arnold
Thursday, 5 March	2:00	Stimson, Marshall, King, Stark, Hopkins
Saturday, 7 March	12:00	Stimson, Knox, Marshall, Arnold, Stark, King
Tuesday, 10 March	12:00	King, Adm. Thomas C. Hart

Wednesday, 18 March	11:15	Adm. Wm. H. Standley, King
20 March		Memorandum for General Watson, initialled "GCT" states that "The president wants to have lunch in the Cabinet Room on next Wednesday (March 25th) with the following people: 1. Secretary of War 4. General Marshall 2. Secretary of the Navy 5. Harry Hopkins 3. Admiral King 6. Gen. Arnold
Monday, 23 March	2:00	King, [Adolphus] Andrews
Wednesday, 25 March	1:00	(Lunch) Secretary of War, Secretary of the Navy, King, Marshall, Hopkins, Arnold
Thurday, 16 April	2:00	King, Gen. Joseph T. McNarney
Saturday, 18 April		Memorandum signed "G.C.T." stating that "The President desires meeting with Secretary of the Navy and King before arrival of Mrs. and Lt. E. H. O'Hare for ceremony on April 21st.
Thursday, 7 May	10:45	Marshall, King, Arnold
Tuesday, 19 May	1:00	King, Hopkins
Friday, 22 May	11:00	Secretary of the Navy, King, Hart
Tuesday, 9 June	2:00	Secretary of War, Secretary of the Navy, Marshall, King, Arnold
Tuesday, 21 June	11:20	King, R.Adm. S.M. Robinson, Rr.Adm. Emory S. Land, Rr.Adm. Howard L. Vickery, Hon. Lewis Douglas (Former Democratic Representative and Deputy to Adm. Land in the War Shipping Administration)
Sunday, 23 June	9:30	Prime Minister Churchill
		King -- 11:15
		Little -- 11:15
		Cdre. Wilfred Patterson, RN -- 11:35
		Marshall -- 12:15
		Arnold -- 12:15
		Gen. Hastings Ismay -- 1:00
		Gen. Brooke -- 1:00
		Gen. Dill -- 1:00
		Mr. Hopkins -- 1:00
Tuesday, 25 June	11:40	Prime Minister Churchill, Sir Arthur Salter, Adm. Little, Adm. Darling, Col. Jacob, Hon. Harry Hopkins, Mr. A. Harriman, King, Robinson, Farber, Land, Vickery, Hon. L. Douglas
Friday, 28 July	12:00	Marshall, Leahy, King
Tuesday, 28 August	2:00	Marshall, King, Arnold, Leahy, Hon. Donald Nelson (War Production Board), Hopkins
Friday, 2 October	12:30	Hon. James V. Forrestal, King
22–Oct		Memorandum for General Harold E. Watson [USAAF], initialed "H.L.H" [Hopkins] says, "You will recall yesterday the President said he would see King, Marshall, Leahy, Hon. Donald M. Nelson, Land, Vickery, Douglass, and myself Friday morning. I think if possiblet the time should be fixed and these people asked today because some of them might otherwise go out of town"
Friday, October 23	3.00	Leahy, King
Monday, 9 November	2:30	Leahy, Marshall, King

20 November		Memorandum signed "McCrea [Capt. John L. McCrea, USN] stating that "The President requests suitable birthday cake for King
Wednesday, 23 November	2:30	Leahy, Marshall, King, Arnold, Hopkins
1943		
5 January		Memorandum for General Watson, signed by McRea, contains following paragraphs: "The President has further indicated that he desires to see Admiral Leahy, General Marshall, Admiral King, and General Arnold at 2:30 p.m., Thursday, January 7, 1943. "Both of the above appointments to be 'on the record.'"
Thursday, 7 January	3:00	Leahy, Marshall, King, Arnold
Thursday, 4 February	11:00	Gen. [Alexander A.] Vandegrift, USMC, Mrs. A.A. Vandegrift, Major A.A. Vandegrift, Jr., USMC, Adm. E.J. King, Gen. Thomas Holcomb, USMC, Commandant, USMC
Saturday, 14 February	12:00	Leahy, Marshall, King, Rr.Adm. Wilson Brown, Maj. Gen. Watson
Wednesday, 24 March	11:30	Maj. Robert E. Caler, USMC, Mrs. Kenneth D Baily, Mrs. Fred C. Galer, The Secretary of the Navy, King, Holcomb, Rr.Adm. John S. McCain, Maj.Gen. Robert J. Mitchell, USMC, Lt. George Allison, USMC, Mrs. John M. Speissegger, Mrs. John Flynn
Tuesday, 10 August	2:00	Leahy, Marshall, Arnold, King
Friday, 29 October	1:00	(Lunch) Adm. E.J. King
Monday, 8 November	2:45	Marshall, King, Arnold
1944		
Thursday, 10 February	12:30	Adm. E.J. King
Friday, 11 February	12:00	Marshall, Leahy, King, Arnold
Monday, 21 February	2:00	Marshall, Leahy, King, Arnold, [pencil notation states] "added at official request of Adm. W.D. Leahy a.m. 21st"
Wednesday, 1 March	2:00	Marshall, Leahy, King, Arnold
Tuesday, 6 June	11:30 [pencil note] "D-Day"	Memorandum initialed by, "G.C.T.," says, "The President desires meeting
Thursday, 22 June	12:15	Marshall, King, Arnold
Friday, 8 September	11:15	Marshall, Leahy, King, Arnold
Wednesday, 4 October	3:30	Marshall, Leahy, King, Arnold
Friday, 17 November	11:45	Secretary of the Navy, King
Friday, 22 December	4:00	Leahy, Marshall, King for Christmas gifts from the President [five-star rank]
1945		
Tuesday, 16 January	10:30	Marshall, King, Sen. Elbert D. Thomas, Sen. Warren R. Austin, Congressman Andrew J. May, Walter G. Andrws, and R. Ewing Thomson
Thursday, 12 April	1:00	FDR suffered cerebral hemorrage
	4:45	FDR pronounced dead
	7:10 p.m.	Oath of Office administered to President Harry S. Truman [pencil annotation] "The President desires to see Secretary of War, Secretary of the Navy, King, Leahy, Marshall, Arnold at earliest convenience

APPENDIX G

Author's reconstruction of key strategic meetings and King's global travels (1941–1945)			
1941	**CODENAME**	**LOCATION**	**PARTICIPANTS**
29 January–27 March	ABC-1	Washington, DC	Army-Navy Staffs
21–27 April	ADB	Singapore	Army-Navy Staffs
8–10 August	RIVIERA	Placentia Bay (Newfoundland)	Churchill, FDR, and Army-Navy Staffs
1942			
22 December–14 January	ARCADIA	Washington, DC	CCS/JCS
23 January–19 May	Post-ARCADIA	London and Washington, DC	CCS/JCS
25–27 April	King-Nimitz with staffs	San Francisco	CominCh/MacPac Staffs
19–25 June	Washington II	Washington, DC	CCS/JCS
4–5 July	King-Nimitz with staffs	San Francisco	CominCh/MacPac Staffs
17–25 July	"July Conference"	London	CCS/JCS
October	Holden Agreement	Washington, DC	GC&CS, CominCh, and Op-20
1943			
14–23 January	SYMBOL	Casablanca	CCS/JCS with French and other allied representatives
19 February	CominCh "numbered fleet" concept issued		CCS/JCS
21–23 February	King-Nimitz with staffs	San Francisco	CominCh/MacPac Staffs
1–12 March	"Atlantic Convoy Conference"	Washington, D.C.	CCS/JCS
April–May	British-US Agreement (BRUSA)	London and Washington, DC	CCS/JCS
12–25 May	TRIDENT	Washington, DC	CCS/JCS
20 May	CominCh "Tenth Fleet" announced	Washington, DC	CCS/JCS
29 May–3 June	King-Stark-Kirk with staffs	Algiers	CCS/JCS
30 July–1 August	King-Nimitz with staffs	San Francisco	CominCh/MacPac Staffs
17–24 August	QUADRANT	Quebec, Canada	CCS/JCS
19 August	QUADRANT	Quebec, Canada	Churchill-Roosevelt secret atomic weapons agreement
25–26 September	King-Nimitz with staffs	San Francisco	CominCh/MacPac Staffs
22–26 November	SEXTANT	Cairo	CCS/JCS with Chinese Nationalist Representatives
28 November–1 December	EUREKA	Tehran	CCS/JCS with Soviet Representatives
1944			
1 January			Eisenhawer reports as SHAEF
2–5 January	King-Nimitz with staffs	Pearl Harbor	CominCh/MacPac Staffs

11 March	King-Nimitz with staffs	Washington, DC	FDR meeting with King and Nimitz
5 May	King-Nimitz with staffs	San Francisco	King, Nimitz, Spruance, Halsey, and staffs with representatives from U.S. Naval Group China
8–15 June	JCS Battlefield Tour	London and Normandy	CCS/JCS
13 July	King-Nimitz with staffs	Pearl Harbor	King, Nimiz, and Halsey with numbered fleet staffs
14 July	King-Nimitz with staffs	Kwajalein	King, Nimitz, with staffs
17–21 July	King-Nimitz with staffs	Saipan	King, Nimitz, Spruance, and staffs
22 July	King-Nimitz with staffs	Pearl Harbor	King, Nimitz, Halsey, and staffs
26–29 July	"Honolulu Conference"	Pearl Harbor	FDR with Leahy and MacPac staffs
12–16 September	OCTAGON	Quebec, Canada	CCS/JCS
26-28 October			Wedemeyer reports as Allied commander in China
29 September–1 October	King-Nimitz with staffs	San Francisco	King, Nimitz, Spruance, and staffs
24–26 November	King-Nimitz with staffs	San Francisco	King, Nimitz, and staffs
1945			
30 January–3 February	CRICKET	Malta	CCS/JCS
4–11 February	ARGONAUT	Yalta	CCS/JCS with Soviet Representatives
5 March	King-Nimitz with staffs	Washington, DC	JCS with Nimitz
3 July	King-Nimitz with staffs	San Francisco	King, Nimitz, and staffs
16–26 July	TERMINAL	Potsdam, Germany	CCS/JCS

APPENDIX H
CominCh in Global Command through Numbered Fleets

FROM: COMINCH   RESTRICTED
ACTION: U.S. FLEET   FEB. 19, 1943.
INFO: VCNO, BUREAUS, AND OFFICES

192200
EFFECTIVE NOON GCT MARCH 15 US FLEET WILL COMPRISE NUMBERED FLEETS WITH TASK FORCE ORGANIZATION CONFORMING TO FOLLOWING ALLOCATIONS OF TASK FORCE NUMBERS:

(A)   U.S. FLEET 00 TO 09 AND 9TH FLEET 90 TO 99.

(B)   PACIFIC (1ST) FLEET 10 TO 19, 3RD FLEET NOW SOPACFOR 30 TO 39 AND 5TH FLEET 50 TO 59 FOR ASSIGNMENT BY CINCPAC AS DESIRED FOR FORCES OPERATING IN CENTRAL AND NORTH PACIFIC

(C)   ATLANTIC (2ND) FLEET 20 TO 29, 4TH FLEET NOW SOLANTFOR 40 TO 49 AND 6TH FLEET 60 TO 69 FOR ASSIGNMENT BY CINCLANT AS DESIRED FOR FORCES OPERATING IN CENTRAL AND NORTH ATLANTIC

(D)   7TH FLEET NOW SOWESTPACFOR 70 TO 70

(E)   8TH FLEET NOW NORTHWEST AFRICA FORCE 80 TO 89

U.S. FLEET TASK FORCES ARE:
- (A)   00, 01 FOR ASSIGNMENT BY COMINCH
- (B)   02 ESTERN SEA FRONTIER
- (C)   03 GULF SEA FRONTIER
- (D)   04 CARRIBEAN SEA FRONTIER
- (E)   05 PANAMA SEA FRONTIER
- (F)   06 WESTERN SEA FRONTIER
- (G)   07 NORTHWEST SEA FRONTIER

9TH FLEET TASK FORCES ARE:
- (A)   90, 91 BLANK
- (B)   92 FORCES IN EUROPEAN WATERS
- (C)   93 SOUTHEAST PACIFIC FORCE
- (D)   94 NAVAL TRANSPORTATION SERVICE
- (E)   95 TO 99 FOR ASSIGNMENT BY COMINCH

EACH FLEET COMMANDER SHALL ALLOCATE AT LEAST ONE TASK FORCE NUMBER TO THE EQUIVALENT OF MISCELLANEOUS FORCE FOR ASSIGNMENT OF TASK FORCE NUMBERS TO SMALL GROUPS OPERATING DIRECTLY UNDER FLEET COMMANDER

APPENDIX I

<table>
<tr><td colspan="4">Author's reconstruction of Numbered Fleet Organization (1943–1945)</td></tr>
<tr><td colspan="4" align="center">First Fleet (15 March 1943-1 January 1946)</td></tr>
<tr><td>Commander</td><td>Chief of Staff</td><td>Fleet / Special Intelligence Officer</td><td>Flagship and Assigned Staff</td></tr>
<tr><td>King/Nimitz</td><td>Low</td><td>Layton/Laird/Price</td><td>CominCh Headquarters</td></tr>
<tr><td colspan="4" align="center">Second Fleet (15 March 1943–1 January 1946)</td></tr>
<tr><td>Commander</td><td>Chief of Staff</td><td>Fleet / Special Intelligence Officer</td><td>Flagship and Assigned Staff</td></tr>
<tr><td>Ingersoll (Ingram from November 1944)</td><td>Hustvet</td><td>Baldwin</td><td>Constellation and Prarie with nominally 15 personnel embarked on numbered fleet staff</td></tr>
<tr><td colspan="4" align="center">Third Fleet (16 June 1944–1 January 1946)</td></tr>
<tr><td>Commander</td><td>Chief of Staff</td><td>Fleet / Special Intelligence Officer</td><td>Flagship and Assigned Staff</td></tr>
<tr><td>Halsey</td><td>Carney</td><td>Cheek</td><td>New Jersey and Saratoga with nominally 60 personnel embarked for numbered fleet staff</td></tr>
<tr><td colspan="4" align="center">Fourth Fleet (1 June 1943–1 November 1944)</td></tr>
<tr><td>Commander</td><td>Chief of Staff</td><td>Fleet / Special Intelligence Officer</td><td>Flagship and Assigned Staff</td></tr>
<tr><td>Ingram until relieved by Munroe in November of 1944</td><td>Braine</td><td>Moore</td><td>Natal Headquarters with USS Bib Pebble designated with nominally 25 personnel assignd to numbered fleet staff</td></tr>
<tr><td colspan="4" align="center">Fifth Fleet (26 April 1944–1 January 1946)</td></tr>
<tr><td>Commander</td><td>Chief of Staff</td><td>Fleet / Special Intelligence Officer</td><td>Flagship and Assigned Staff</td></tr>
<tr><td>Spruance</td><td>Moore</td><td>Murphy</td><td>Indianapolis and New Jersey with nominally 29 personnel on staff</td></tr>
<tr><td colspan="4" align="center">Sixth Fleet (1 June 1943–1 January 1946)</td></tr>
<tr><td>Commander</td><td>Chief of Staff</td><td>Fleet / Special Intelligence Officer</td><td>Flagship and Assigned Staff</td></tr>
<tr><td>King/Waesche</td><td>as required</td><td>CominCh Headquarters</td><td>as required</td></tr>
<tr><td colspan="4" align="center">Seventh Fleet (1 June 1943–1 January 1946)</td></tr>
<tr><td>Commander</td><td>Chief of Staff</td><td>Fleet / Special Intelligence Officer</td><td>Flagship and Assigned Staff</td></tr>
<tr><td>Kinkcaid</td><td>van Hook</td><td>McCollum</td><td>USS Wasatch (AGC-9) with nominally 41 personnel designated for numbered fleet staff</td></tr>
</table>

Eighth Fleet (1 July 1943–1 January 1946)			
Commander	**Chief of Staff**	**Fleet / Special Intelligence Officer**	**Flagship and Assigned Staff**
Hewitt until relieved by Glassford in April of 1945	Lewis	Bachman	Mediterranean Theater with nominally 30 personnel designated for numbered fleet staff

Ninth Fleet (18 November 1943–1 January 1946)			
Commander	**Chief of Staff**	**Fleet / Special Intelligence Officer**	**Flagship and Assigned Staff**
Fletcher	Capt. Robert E. Robinson Jr.	CominCh Headquarters	no change

Tenth Fleet (20 May 1943–1 January 1946)			
Commander	**Chief of Staff**	**Fleet / Special Intelligence Officer**	**Flagship and Assigned Staff**
King	Low until November of 1944	Smith-Hutton until September of 1944	CominCh Headquarters

Eleventh Fleet (Task Organized for MacPac and China, as required)			
Commander	**Chief of Staff**	**Fleet / Special Intelligence Officer**	**Flagship and Assigned Staff**
Ingersoll	Whiting	Pihl	San Francisco

Twelfth Fleet (1 January 1944-1 January 1946)			
Commander	**Chiefs of Staff**	**Fleet / Special Intelligence Officers**	**Flagship and Assigned Staff**
Stark	Kirk and Shelly	Kittredge, Butcher, and Price	ComNavEu Headquarters-London

CominCh Naval Group China / Sino-American Cooperation Organization (SACO)			
Commander	**On Scene Liaison**	**Fleet / Special Intelligence Officers**	**Flagship and Assigned Staff**
King	Miles	McCollum and Holtwick	CominCh Headquarters / Chungking China

APPENDIX J
King to Marshall Concerning Five-star Rank
21 January 1944
UNITED STATES FLEET
HEADQUARTERS OF THE COMMANDER IN CHIEF
NAVY DEPARTMENT, Washington, DC.

January 21, 1944

Dear Marshall,

This matter of advanced rank is getting rather "complicated."

To my mind, the creation of the grades of "General of the Armies" (as I understand the War Department view) and "Admiral of the Navy"—with a limitation on two officers in the grade—provides for what may be called a "6-star" rank.

There should be a "5-star" rank, for which the navy can use "Fleet Admiral" or Admiral of the Fleet" or even "Captain Admiral"—the Army will have to work out its own ideas of title but I suggest that "Colonel General" matches "Captain Admiral."

What I am seriously concerned about is that there are in prospect many promotions in Washington which will have serious repercussions in the Forces overseas unless provision is made for proportionate promotion in the operating forces—such as would be attained by the "5-star" rank hereinbefore mentioned.

Mr. Vinson (Chairman of the House Naval Committee) has been advised of the foregoing views and appears to be agreeable to the inclusion of a "5-star" rank but insistant on a "6-star rank." I have got word to him that, personally, I have no desire whatever for the "6-star rank" unless and until a "5-star rank is provided for—and further, that I think it advisable that any promotion in prospect in connection with CominCh-CNO should first be "5-star rank."

       [Signed]

       E. J. King

Copies to:

       Adm. Leahy

       Chief of Naval Personnel

General G.C. Marshall, USA,

       Chief of Staff, US Army

       War Department, Washington

APPENDIX K
King Address about "Waging Peace"
The basis for his Valedictory Speeches (as delivered in 1946 and 1947)

I appreciate the opportunity of addressing you at this annual convention of the National Exchange Club. My appreciation arises, in part, from the fact that I am a member of The Exchange Club. It arises, also in part from the fact that I am mindful of my privilege of speaking to you members of The National Exchange Club at your annual convention in Cincinnati some twelve years ago. Again it arises, in part, from the fact that The National Exchange Club is incorporated and chartered under the laws of the State of Ohio—and that its headquarters are in Toledo (Ohio)—all of which makes it appropriate that I—a native of Ohio—should be addressing you.

There is not, here and now, time to review and to comment on all of the many and worthy activities which engage the attention and the interest of The National Exchange Club. However, I do want to say that your interests and your attention are directed to matters which cannot fail to pay dividends to the nation which we all are—as citizens—pledged to uphold, and to defend. The National Exchange Club—and all local Exchange Clubs—stand for an intense, sincere loyalty to the United States, its traditions and its ideals. You advocate a strong educational program designed to reveal and eradicate all elements known to menace the fundamentals of the American way of life. It is certain that the decisions and policies of this body will have an important influence on our national welfare.

Such power and influence always carry with them great responsibility. The exercise of such responsibility must always be accompanied by the closest scrutiny of all available information, by the benefit of the wisest counsel and by the utmost deliberation.

I wish to say something to you today on the matter of the relationship of the citizen to the "common defense"—by way, perhaps, of that education in civic responsibility which The National Exchange Club fosters. I note that it was in 1924 that it originated its National Defense Program.

I raise the question that I know is close to the hearts of all—HOW SHALL THE PEACE BE KEPT? We always contrast in our own minds, not alone peace and war, but peace and strife. But what I am most afraid of is that we are too prone to think of peace as a "do nothing" state of affairs. I can say to you, as one American citizen to his fellow citizens that it does not seem to me that a "do nothing" attitude about peace is going to get us anywhere. We must, if you like, paraphrase the phrase "waging war." Why should we not "wage peace?" Why should we not make as much effort to win the peace as we do to win the war? Why should there not be militant peace, and not for a few weeks or a few months, or a few years but always. Can we not wage the peace under the United Nations Charter, which is the adopted policy of this country? I raise the the question again, "How shall the peace be kept?"

All American citizens hope and expect that, through the operations of the United Nations there will come a lasting world peace. However, in this world of realism we must keep ourselves prepared to support by realistic methods, if necessary, our idealistic hopes and efforts, looking toward enduring peace throughout the world.

The first and foremost obligation of the "common defense" of the people of America is our own national defense. Our own national defense is directly affected by a second obligation—the security of the Western Hemisphere. A third obligation is to cooperate with other freedom loving nations in the maintenance of world peace, which in turn supports the defense of our country and the security of neighboring countries of the Western Hemisphere. To fulfill these obligations it is vitally necessary to provide an adequate postwar establishment. It must be capable of prompt expansion from peacetime to wartime strength.

It is always well, I think, to go back to original sources. No matter how many times we refer to them there is always profit, and even inspiration, to be gained. I have, therefore, to commend to your attention this extract from the Declaration of Independence drafted in 1776: "We hold these truths to be self-evident that all men are created equal hat they are endowed by their Creator with certain unalienable rights; that among those are life, liberty and the pursuit of happiness. That, to secure these rights, governments are instituted among men deriving their Just powers from the consent of the governed."

Take note of the words "deriving their just powers from the consent of the governed" for therein lies our first duty as citizens—to participate in government—local, state, national. Inform yourself—discuss with your fellow citizens—local, state and national affairs. Then, having informed yourselves, take an active part in your government—local, state and national.

At this point I wish to proffer the advice of the fellow citizen and fellow taxpayer—advice that you inform yourself as to the principles of government that are in effect in other countries. Acquaint yourselves with the meanings of communism, socialism, fascism and other "isms." Do not emulate the ostrich—and ignore or decry them—for they are living forces in the world today. Study them—ascertain their merits, if any, and demerits—the better to understand and appreciate the benefits of the democracy that is synonymous with "United States of America." I number myself among those that believe that our democracy must be a militant democracy for we are, beyond any doubt, in contrast—in competition, perhaps even in conflict—with militant political creeds such as communism—and you should know, as citizens, that our cause in the late war was not won by assuming a "do nothing" attitude.

The second reference which I commend to your attention—as citizens, many of whom are veterans, is the preamble to the Constitution of the United States, drafted in 1787:

"We, the people of the United States, in order to form a more perfect union, establish justice, ensure domestic tranquility, provide for the common defense, promote the general welfare, and secure the blessings of liberty to ourselves and our posterity, do ordain and establish this Constitution for the United States of America."

How are we—who are all of us, citizens and, some of us, veterans—to do our part to "provide for the common defense?" Well here are the words of a great citizen who was also a veteran:

I cannot recommend to your notice measures for the fulfillment of our duties to the rest of the world without again pressing upon you the necessity of placing ourselves in a condition of complete defense, and of exacting from them fulfillment of their duties toward us. There is a rank due to the United States among nations, which will be withheld, if not absolutely lost, by the reputation of weakness. If we desire to avoid insult, we must be able to repel it; if we desire to secure peace, one of the most powerful instruments of our rising prosperity, it must be known that we are at all times ready for war.

The words are those of George Washington in one of his messages to Congress dated December 3, 1793. I leave it to you to judge how clearly those words apply to the world situation in which the United States finds itself today. Please note that Washington's oft quoted maxim, "In time of peace, prepare for war," must not be interpreted that we should seek war, but rather that we should seek to prevent war by being ready for war. Theodore Roosevelt said the same thing in another way when he said, "speak softly, but carry a big stick!"

No matter how ingenious the war machines—no matter how marvelous the developments of science—we must always remember, without fail, that the wars of the future—if more wars there must be—will be similar to the wars of the past, in that they comprise the endeavors of one lot of men to impose their will on another lot of men. War will be—as it has been—men against men.

Now, it seems to me that it is the role of The National Exchange Club particularly to deal with this matter of men. The Club is composed of men -it deals with men -it is set up to guide and influence the ideas—and the ideals—of men. How then, can we of the Exchange Clubs do our part in providing for the "common defense" by guiding and influencing our fellow citizens of the United States?

It always is to be remembered that the Army and Navy of the United States are distinctly servants of the people. In our democracy it has never been, nor will it ever be, the prerogative of the armed forces to formulate national policy. It is their duty to support national policies established by the executive and legislative branches of our Government. It is their duty to advise the Congress of the naval and military needs necessary to enforce national policies.

Adequate measures of preparedness—political, economic, military, industrial—are essential measures of national insurance with worldwide effects. Such insurance means we must be ready to expand quickly our overseas line of defense, such as the Navy, in time of national emergency. It follows that, in addition to the regular armed forces, we must have a citizen reserve, and that it must be trained before the emergency is upon us. An efficient trained citizen, naval and military reserve can be obtained—and maintained— only through universal military training. While it is true that our fellow citizens who are recent veterans are available in time of need in the immediate future, Old Man Time like Ol' Man River—will go rolling along! Their successors in the lower age groups should be made ready to answer the call of their country—which is your country and mine.

As a fellow citizen and fellow taxpayer, as well as a naval officer of over forty years service, I emphasize the democratic nature of universal military training. I believe that every man and woman is obligated to assist in the maintenance of our national security—as some ten million veterans have already done. In addition, we would all profit by the individual's better understanding of his responsibilities to his country, his family and himself. Universal military training is a democratic process aimed at that end. The primary purpose of a year of universal military training is to provide additional national security—the better to provide for the "common defense."

The waging of war is not the concern of the Army and Navy only; it involves even more perhaps, political (that is to say diplomatic), economic and industrial factors as well.

There are three things that are to be done if we are to be prepared—first, to see to it that we are ready with manpower—second, to see to it that we are ready with "ways and means"—third, to see to it that we are ready with the organization to wage war, that is, the combination of manpower with "ways and means." In the endeavor to indicate practicable solutions, I will be as brief and concise as may be.

The first objective—readiness of men—can, to my mind, best be attained by support of the continuation of selective service and of the institution of universal military training.

The second objective—readiness of "ways and means"—can, to my mind, best be attained by support of the continuation of the activities of the War Production Board, the Defense Transportation Administration, the War Shipping Administration and other like agencies, transposed into permanent appropriate peacetime form.

The third objective—readiness to wage war—can, to my mind, best be attained by the creation of what may well be called the "National Security Council." The Council should comprise all those officers and agencies of the government who have to do with the political, the military, the economic, and the industrial factor, involved in the "common defense." The President should be chairman *ex-officio*. The membership should include the Secretary of State, the Secretary of War, the Secretary of the Navy, the head of the counterpart of the War Manpower Commissioner, the head of the counterpart of the War Production Board, and, perhaps, the Secretary of the Treasury.

Such a group is eminently fitted to survey and to correlate and to coordinate all the primary factors of the "common defense". From the deliberations and conclusions of such a group can come the legislation and, indeed, the action when needed, to make our "common defense" the integrated entity which is essential to our national security. I urge upon The National Exchange Club full consideration of this vital matter which will, I hope and believe lead to your active support of it. By so doing, The National Exchange Club will add one more important item to its long list of achievements whereby it fulfills that purpose whereby it stands for an intensely sincere loyalty to the United States, its traditions, and its ideals.

May you—one and all—profit by your membership in the Exchange Clubs. May the Exchange Clubs profit by your membership. But, above all, may our Country profit from your patriotism as citizens -not only in words, but in deeds.

Author's note: King delivered variations of this speech in various venues across the United States, to include national gatherings of the American Legion, Veterans of Foreign Wars, and Naval Order of the United States. He delivered a similar address at the Naval Academy, Naval War College, and Military Academy at West Point. In the fall of 1947, King suffered a stroke and generally declined additional opportunities to speak publically about his views concerning national service, professional education, the influence of history upon sea power, and other matters of particular concern in the military policy of the United States.

APPENDIX L
Edwards rebuttal against assertions by Stimson

25 Josepha Avenue
San Francisco, California
7 June 1948

Commander Walter Muir Whitehill, USNR
The Boston Anthenauem,
10 Beacon Street, Boston 8 Massachusettes.

Dear Commander,

My comments on Mr. Stimson's biography are as follows:

The book introduces the reader to a great man and a wise statesman, a man strong in his likes and dislikes and, in his later years, a nurser of grudges. He took office as Secretary with an ancient grudge against "the Admirals" to which grudge he clung throughout the war. He appears to have been favorably impressed with the few US Admirals he met and met abroad, and his mentions of Admiral King though infrequent indicate admiration, but his position as to the admirals in general was one of aloof mistrust.

Mr. Stimson's opinion of generals, except General Marshall, is not wholly flattering. They were better than Admirals, having been elevated to a higher spiritual plan by the sacrament of comeuppance (p. 506), but the military mind, in blue or khaki, impressed the Secretary as immature and addicted to petty wrangles. This is evident throughout the discussion of interservice relations. Mr. Stimson attributes differences mostly to jealousy on both sides, particularly the Navy side, but to some extent on the Army side, too. He ignores the existence of logical basis for difference of opinion. It is a fact that there were enthusiasts in both Army and Navy who stirred up a considerable froth of emotional discussion, but this was a consequence and not the cause of differences. Underneath the froth there was always to be found a solid kernel of rational division of opinion. Emotional approach to interservice problems is a bad thing and Mr. Stimson does well to condemn it. But to pretend that the problems were in themselves merely figments of emotion is still worse, because differences can never be settled rationally unless the core of the fact is recognized and explored. I think Mr. Stimson's attitude is unfortunate. If he had chosen to analyze objectively the matters in dispute, during the war or in his book, it would have helped to arrive at the solutions all concerned are seeking. As it is, he merely adds fuel to the embers of controversy by saying it amounts to nothing but petty squabbling. I think you will find that most of the Secretary's comments on interservice relations, or rather interservice differences—he calls attention to the fact that he discusses only differences—are colored by his mistrust of all things naval, and/or by his blindness to the facts that formed the basis of dispute.

As an example of biased view, take the discussion of the Navy's refusal to share the Pentagon Building (p. 506). Mr. Knox was persuaded to refuse on the ground that the space the Army could make available was insufficient for Naval personnel who needed to be physically close to the Secretary and CominCh. It may be that Mr. Knox was badly advised, but even so there is no excuse for the outburst about "Bureau of Admirals." (p. 507)

Another example is the negro problem (pp. 461–464, 507). The inference to be drawn from the book is that the Navy was stupid and stubborn in not copying the Army plan of accepting negroes in large numbers and segregating them. The fact is that the Navy could not segregate negroes at sea because of the way people live on board ship; the Navy had to go at the problem more cautiously. It may be that the Army was right and the Navy wrong or vice versa (in view of recent unfavorable public reaction to the Army scheme it looks like vice versa), but the point is that in discussing this difference Mr. Stimson gives no heed to the reasons behind the naval course of action.

Now take the statement on page 507 "the Navy's extraordinary bitterness against him (General MacArthur) seemed childish." The truth is that the General had traits of character, euphemistically called lack of tact by Mr. Stimson, which at times made difficulties for the Joint Chiefs. But Admiral King, like General Marshall, never let irritation get the better of his confidence in the outstanding military ability of the colorful soldier. Moreover, the naval personnel assigned to his command never lacked in loyalty to General MacArthur and most of those who knew him personally liked him. On the other hand, it must be admitted that there was indignation in the Navy over the General's spoken and implied criticism of Nimitz' conduct of operations and the fighting ability of the Marines (p. 234 "On to Westward" by Robert Sherrod), and in the Navy as well as in Army and civilian circles, there was a tendency, difficult to check, to discuss the less orthodox facets of the Genera's characters with lack of respect. All this adds up to something other than the childish bitterness alleged by Mr. Stimson.

The Secretary's discussion of the antisubmarine war is of particular importance. He says (p. 508) that he has chosen to examine the disagreement in this matter in some detail, so as to look behind disagreements toward their causes, in order to prevent or minimize their future occurrence. This is a laudable intent, but I think intent outruns performance in this as in other instances I have cited. Mr. Stimson's examination of the ASW dispute is a superficial study of some aspects of the U-boat war considered without any reference to their relation to the antisubmarine campaign as a whole, and without ever getting down to the real basis of the argument—the difference between the Army and Navy concepts of air power.

It is perhaps worthwhile to discuss the Secretary's discussion (pp. 508–518) at some length.

The compelling fact about the U-boat campaign is that it was carried through to success under Admiral King by methods adopted in the beginning and never in essence changed.

It is an obvious fact that we took a beating from the U-boats in 1942, but this was due to the shortage of means, not to defect in method. When we got the means we achieve success as even Mr. Stimson admits. We entered the war totally unprepared for the problem of dealing with enemy submarines throughout the Pacific and in the Western Atlantic. It took time to build ships and planes and to procure and train personnel to man them. While we were building up our forces the U-boats had a field day, but acquisition of adequate forces put an end to this. Of course, great improvement in antisubmarine weapons and devices played a considerable part in the matter, as did also improvement in staff planning and in operational technique as we gained combat experience. The point is, however, that the principles and methods criticized by Mr. Stimson proved sound by test of success.

Mr. Stimson's criticism is principally concerned with the scheme of command, particularly command over aviation. The system throughout the war was this. Admiral King (at first as CominCh, later in his dual capacity as CominCh and Commander Tenth Fleet) exercised command, as executive agent for the Joint Chiefs of Staff, over area commanders

(CinC Atlantic Fleet, and Sea Frontier Commanders) who were responsible for operations. Admiral King's exercise of command consisted of assignment of missions, allocation of forces, and formalization of standard tactical instructions. The operating commanders were responsible for carrying out the missions with the forces assigned to them. This was the system used not only by Admiral King, but also by General Marshall for the several campaigns which each directed as executive agent of the Joint Chiefs.

The Army Air Force and Mr. Stimson's civilian advisers took exception to this system as applied to the U-boat war primarily in the matter of air command. They considered it unsound to assign air to the Sea Frontier Commanders; they believed it would be better to segregate all shore-based air (Army and Navy) into a command of its own independent of area commanders. They thought Admiral King did not use air to the best advantage. They believed he laid too much stress on the importance of air cover for convoys and that air could be better employed for other purposes. All these ills could, so they believed, be remedied only by giving an Air Force General command of shore-based air with the understanding that he would employ it as an autonomous force subject only to the general direction of Admiral King.

Such was the substance of the three proposals referred to on pages 512 and 513. The reasoning behind them according to Mr. Stimson was this. The Air Force people were unhappy under naval control, they did not like Admiral King's system of command over air units and his method of employing aviation, so they advocated transfer of antisubmarine aviation to Air Force command. Mr. Sitmson claims that this would have centralized command responsibility. Actually, as is obvious, it would have had the opposite effect. It would have resulted in two antisubmarine wars, one conducted by the Navy with ships and carrier planes, the other conducted by the Air Force with shore-based air. There would have been little connection between the two, since the demand was for autonomy for aviation. Actually, in the Air Force plan Admiral King was asked to accept as his antisubmarine air commander (the Arnold proposal, p. 513) a general who would take office with the avowed intention of fighting Admiral King's method of fighting U-boats.

The War Department stand in the matter was, I think, obviously unsound. But regardless of whether or not one believes that Army ideas might have turned out all right if they had been put into effect, the pragmatic fact is that the principles actually followed—Admiral King's principles—proved successful.

The antisubmarine dispute was a collision, or rather two collisions, between opposing concepts. One set of concepts related to air command; the Army regards air as an entirely separate element of warfare which should be autonomous administratively and operationally, while the Navy holds that air should be integrated with other arms. The second collision occurred between opposing concepts as to how to fight submarines; in this matter the Air Force knowing about air and nothing else naturally did not see eye to eye with the Navy which understood not only air, but also ships and submarines and the potency of air—sea power from the submarine point of view.

As an example of unobjective reporting I take Mr. Stimson's treatment of unification (pp. 518–523). He implies that a sound merger plan, eventually adopted, was blocked for three years by a contumacious Navy solely because naval approval died with the premature death of Mr. Knox. Mr. Stimson oversimplifies. In the first place, Mr. Knox did not approve of the merger plan as presented to the Woodrum Committee just before he died, and in the second place that plan never was adopted. The facts, as I saw them, were these. The merger plan in its nascent state was a proposal by General Marshall to join the War and Navy Departments in order to facilitate the cure of certain ills of duplication. The Marshall proposal was regarded favorably not only by Secretary Knox and Admiral King, but also by most senior officers in the Navy Department. It seemed a good idea in principle, but we all wanted to look into it a bit to see if the good idea could be hatched out into a workable arrangement. When the egg of unity hatched it turned out to be not a simple departmental merger, but a complicated business involving among other things, divorce of the Air Force from the Army, and [the] creation of a fourth service—an autonomous service of Supply. Naval enthusiasm cooled off—the expanded plan did not appear sound, and sound or not it involved dislocations that could not be tolerated while the war was in progress. The Navy Department took the stand that study was in order, but that no drastic reorganization could be placed in effect until after the end of the war. I am quite sure that this was the view of Mr. Knox just before he died, but this should be checked with Mr. Forrestal. The merger as finally effected in 1947 after much study was quite different from that advocated by Mr. Stimson in 1944.

My general impression of the book is that it is an excellent character study of Secretary Stimson, that it deals in an interesting and enlightening manner with his part in world affairs, and that it gives a vivid picture of the prominent men with whom he came in contact. But in the matter of interservice relations bias has got the better of sober judgement with the result that what is intended to be objective study of service differences degenerates into [an] acrimonious attack on the Navy.

This attack should, I think, be answered, but I do not think a direct answer would do any good. In the first place Mr. Stimson's arguments are so vague in many instances that it is hard to get your teeth into them. In the second place dispute with him might lead to a general mudslinging contest between Army and Navy which would be bad for both. And in the tird place I think the Navy's case can be presented best by giving the whole story of matters at issue without trying to orient the presentation with specific reference to specific criticism on the part of Mr. Stimson or anyone else.

My suggestion is that you use Mr. Stimsons biography as a check-off list to ensure that your treatment covers the Navy's side of matters wherein Mr. Stimson fails to do justice to the Navy, but that you do not make any specific reference to Mr. Stimson or his criticism.

I think that the following are the more important items to be covered:

(1) Admiral King's views as to the role of air power.
This is the major point of difference between Army and Navy and it should be fully explored. The Naval concept of air integrated with other areas should be explained and compared with the Army concept of air autonomy, and the British concept which was as disastrous to the Royal Navy. I think disputes with the Army in this matter should be discussed frankly and freely, but care should be used to avoid undue emphasis on the emotional phases of disputes; the Army should be given credit for having arrived at its stand by due, if not entirely logical, process of thought.

(2) Admiral King's views as to the Combined and Joint Chiefs of Staff. Mr. Stimson pays well deserved tribute to these organizations in Chapter XVII, but he ignores Admiral King's great part in the top-level management of the war and, as usual, does not go into the background to find the factors that made top-level war management a success. Admiral King's analysis would be of great historical value.

(3) <u>Admiral King's views as to merger</u>. This should include presentation of the Admirals ideas for unification of the whole war effort of the nation.

(4) <u>The U-boat campaign</u>. This should have extensive treatment not only because of Mr. Stimson's criticism, but also because it was the only phase of the war that was fought on our door step and therefore aroused great public interest. I tentatively suggest the following outline:

<u>a</u>. Pre-war awareness of the U-boat menace. Pre-war research and training in antisubmarine measures. Pre-war scientific research and development of antisubmarine weapons and devices. Failure to provide adequate antisubmarine forces prior to our entry into the war.

<u>b</u>. The U-boat situation when we entered the war. Our need for large antisubmarine forces and our lack of them. I suggest that you point this up by comparing the number of sea-going antisubmarine vessels (destroyers, DEs, CVEs. PCs, SCs, sea-going Coast Guard cutters and converted yachts) and planes assigned to antisubmarine operations (including Army planes and planes on escort carriers, but excluding planes on regular carriers) in the Atlantic commands (Atlantic Fleet; Eastern, Gulf, Caribbean and Panama Sea Frontiers) on 1 January 1942 and 1 July 1944, the latter date being selected as the time when our means approached our needs.

<u>c</u>. Outline of results (condensation of "US Fleet Antisubmarine Summary").

<u>d</u>. System of command and staff control. Full story of establishment of Tenth Fleet, and explanation of what Tenth Fleet was. Story of disputes with Army over antisubmarine matters.

<u>e</u>. Explnation of reasons behind insistence on the convoy system. Remarks on the lost opportunity (the bombing of U-boat bases and building yards which, despite Admiral King's urging, was delayed until 1944 when it turned out to be a devastating blow to the U-boats as set forth in enemy by Admiral Doenitz dated 24 September 1945).

<u>f</u>. Lessons. The submarine is a potent element in war. The submarine menace can be dealt with in two ways (1) By destroying bases and building yards by bombing, and (2) by destroying submarines at sea. Neither measure can be fully effective by itself. We must be prepared to use both methods in case of another war. We cannot again wait for war to begin before building up antisubmarine forces because next time submarines will be a threat not only to shipping, but also to coastal cities which can be attacked disastrously with rocket bombs if submarines are permitted to get near them.

I am sending a copy of this letter to Admiral King who doubtless will put you right as to any matters in which I have incorrectly set forth his ideas.

Sincerely yours,
[signed]
R. S. Edwards
Admiral, USN, Retired

Copy: Fleet Admiral King

APPENDIX M

Letter from King to Betsy Matter, 3 August 1948

Courtesy family of Fleet Admiral Ernest J. King, USN

[Handwritten]

Naval Medical Center

Bethesda, Maryland

August 3, 1948

Dear Betsy,

I can't believe that it's been two months since your letter of June 3rd.

I was very glad that Admiral Spruance's change in his situation was made although I had hoped that he would carry on at the War College. I could have wished that there was another "five star" for him!

About two months ago I went to Cleveland for a ten-day visit to see my brother and had a very good time with them.

Mrs. King is now permanently invalided—her heart trouble is, the doctors say, incurable. But she seems quite comfortable—had a spell about a month ago during some very hot weather. She goes out only on little shopping trips and to see her sister who lives in Arlington. Florie is keeping the watch and her sisters are doing their bit too. Joe is doing fine and keeping the navy running smooth.

Since that time it has been so hot in Washington that I don't like the weather and I don't flourish. It was just about a year ago that my illness began; it stated with what looked like a small sun stroke in Los Angeles and then with another one when I returned to Washington—so I have to watch myself during the next month or so.

I hope—and expect—that Eugenie is running all over the place but when she will be talking?

Since Dick was to go to sea in June, I suppose that you are staying in Newport at least until the autumn. Please say "hello" to Abby and Stan.

Hoping that you and your baby are fine.

Love,
Ernest King

APPENDIX N

Admiral William S. DeLany rebuttal against assertions by Buell
Courtesy the family of Fleet Admiral Ernest J. King, USN

1 July 1980

Dear Lieutenant Smith,

I have your letter of 24 June in which you ask me about the historical accuracy of the content of the Buell book about your distinguished grandfather.

My first comment would be that it is a story about him but not a biography of him.

I am sure you have read the author's 44 pages of Bibliography including sources and notes. You will have noted, I am sure, that they are rarely specific as to content or sources. Quotes are used extensively and again they are rarely identified with or attributed to listed published or unpublished sources. For these reasons it is almost impossible to verify many quotes and statements in the book's contents. Regarding the notes, once on page 580 and twice on page 583 which refer to information obtained from me, I may tell you that my discussions with the author were unrecorded and lasted only a short time. Regarding the CominCh organization I found he had not yet read Furer's book, and I showed him my copy and suggested he read it and then I would answer his questions. I note his "grand divisions" of the staff mentioned on page 235 do not agree with the officially shown components in the Furer book, even though it is included in his sources. I recall no conversation with the author regarding 1945 shipbuilding programs nor wartime personnel policies. The incident reported on page 312 relates to a matter with an Under Secretary and on a different subject than noted in the book.

There is no way I know to verify the so-called Knox-King incident mentioned on page 234. It has no attribution and the author himself questions its truthfulness. With reference to the incident on page 232, between Edwards and King, certainly in view of the very close relations which the author himself repeatedly mentions, needs confirmation if the reader is to be satisfied. The same is true of the Knox-King discussion covered on page 237 and the undocumented statement regarding the Knox suggestion that King go to sea to command the fleet. Much emphasis is placed on the King-Horne disagreements. Again they are undocumented. A reading of the Walter Whitehill book, *Fleet Admiral King*, especially 476, 477, 573, 574, show clearly the high regard in which King held Horne in all his relations (the author has had access to these papers). No one can deny there were differences between these two in those very tense days.

They were common to intra- and inter-service and allied decisions.

I had them with the Admiral myself. Certainly the emphasis which the author has chosen to place on them to develop his composite to match the public version of the Admiral's toughness, needs to be given further documentation to make them authentic.

I can understand your concern about the book. I find it difficult to evaluate the author's real intent. I trust the above may be of help to you.

Sincerely,
[Signed]
W. S. DeLany
President

Author's note: Among those listed on the letterhead as senior leaders within the Naval Historical Foundation, Admirals DeLany, Carney, Dietrich, Strauss, and Wright served in the CominCh Headquarters of the Second World War and their personal correspondences regarding their experience in close quarters with King is available at the Naval War College.

Endnotes

Prologue

1. Washington, DC, Library of Congress (LC), Ernest J. King Papers (King Papers), Box 39, speech file, "Town Hall Meeting—March 21st, 1946—Pottstown, Penna.," 31.

2. Samuel Eliot Morison, *History of US Naval Operations in the Second World War: The Battle of the Atlantic, September 1939–May 1943* (Boston: Little Brown, 1947), Vol. I, 3–113.

3. LC, King Papers, Box 39, Town Hall Meeting, 31.

4. Ibid. 8.

5. Ibid.

6. Ibid.

7. Newport, Rhode Island, Naval War College (NWC), Manuscript Register Series 22, Walter M. Whitehill and Thomas B. Buell comps., Fleet Admiral Ernest J. King Papers (King Papers), Box 8, "A Discussion of the Authority Exercised by the Secretary of the Navy, with Reference to Military Operations," George L. Russell (comp.), 25 May 1945, 3.

8. Gerald E. Wheeler, *Admiral William Veazie Pratt, US Navy: A Sailor's Life* (Washington, DC: Naval History Division, 1974), 107, fn. 21.

9. NWC, King papers, Box 5, Atlantic Fleet Confidential Memorandum 2CM-41, "Making the Best of What We Have," 24 March 1941.

10. John B. Hattendorf, B. Mitchell Simpson III, and John R. Wadleigh, *Sailors and Scholars: The Centennial History of the US Naval War College* (Newport, RI: Naval War College Press, 1984), 137–210.

11. NWC, King Papers, Box 7, Folder 9, "Miscellaneous notes of conversation with Fleet Admiral King," August 1946, 4.

12. Edward C. Kalbfus, ed., *Sound Military Decision* (Newport, RI: Naval War College, 1942), 25–26 and 41.

13. United Kingdom, London (Kew), the National Archives (TNA), HW 8/49, "History of Liaison with OP-20-G (Washington) as carried out by Representatives of Naval Section, GC&CS," 50–53. TNA, HW 57/2, "Monthly letters from Colonel O'Connor (GC&CS representative in Washington) to the Director, GC&CS, attaching monthly notes and reports from other GC&CS liaison officers 1943 Dec 26–1944 Dec 31," reports dated 2nd July, 1944, 2. Very special thanks to Ralph Erskine for providing material found in these documents.

14. Stephen Maffeo, *US Navy Codebreakers, Linguists, and Intelligence Officers against Japan, 1910–1941* (Washington, DC: Rowan and Littlefield, 2016), 27, 78, 117, 148, 174, 177, 284, and 409.

15. LC, King Papers, Box 39, speech file, "Town Hall Meeting," 2. Handwritten underline in original.

16. Ibid.

17. Ibid.

18. NWC, Manuscript Collection 155 (MSC-155), B. Mitchell Simpson Research Papers (Simpson Papers), Box 18, Commander, ComNavEu monograph, "United States British Naval Relations, 1939–1942," Tracy B. Kittredge (comp.), part I, "Office of Naval Attaché Organization," 19.

19. Ibid.

20. Ibid., 19.

21. Ibid.

22. Ibid.,17.

23. Ibid.

24. Ibid.

25. Ibid.

26. Ibid.

27. Glenn C. H. Perry, *Dear Bart: Washington Views of World War II* (Westport, CT: Greenwood Press, 1982), 13.

28. Ibid.

29. Ibid.

30. Anon., "Stormy Man, Stormy Weather," in *Time* magazine, vol. 37, no. 22 (2 June 1941): 17.

31. Ibid.

32. Perry, *Dear Bart*, xii.

33. Ibid, 81.

34. Ibid. 92.

35. Ibid.

36. Ibid., xii and 325–328.

37. Ibid., 327.

38. Joseph J. Thorndike Jr., "King of the Atlantic: America's Triple Threat Admiral is Americas Stern, Daring Model of a War Commander," in *Life* magazine, vol. 11, no. 21 (27 November 1941), 93–108.

39. NWC, King Papers, Box 18, Message, From Chief of Naval Operations for Action of fleet commanders in the Asiatic and Pacific fleets and for the information of the Atlantic Fleet and Special Naval Observer in London, Naval District Commanders, and Army Commanders, as transmitted on 27 November 1941. An amplification message was sent on 28 November 1941.

40. Ibid., 96.

41. Tyler Field, comp., *Newport Reading Room Sesquicentennial History* (Newport, RI: Newport Reading Room, 2003), 72; and McBurney, *Untold Stories*, 20–25. King was in the Reading Room when the message arrived, although other accounts suggest otherwise. See Thomas B. Buell, *Master of Sea Power: A Biography of Fleet Admiral Ernest J. King* (Boston, MA: Little Brown, 1980), 150–52. Given Buell's story about King, Lloyd J. Graybar provides an excellent corrective analysis in "Ernest J. King: Commander of the Two-Ocean Navy," in *Quarterdeck and Bridge: Two Centuries of American Naval Leaders*, ed. James C. Bradford (Annapolis, MD: Naval Institute Press, 1997), 307–26.

42. Field, *Newport Reading Room*, 1–10.

43. NWC, Low Papers, Box 1, "A Personal Narrative of Association with Fleet Admiral Ernest J. King, US Navy" (Personal Narrative), 23.

44. NWC, Low Papers, Box 1, Low Diary, 7–8 December 1941.

45. NWC, King Papers, Box 2, Russell to Buell, 18 November 1974.

46. Ibid.

47. Ibid.

48. Perry, *Dear Bart*, 19.

49. Ibid.

50. Clark G. Reynolds, "Admiral Ernest J. King and the Strategy for Victory in the Pacific," in *Naval War College Review*, vol. 28, no. 3 (Winter, 1976), 57–64.

51. Alfred Thayer Mahan, *The Problem of Asia and its Effect on International Policies* (Boston, MA: Little, Brown, 1900), 38, 62, 125, and 175.

52. NWC, King Papers, Box 6, Diary of Cornelius Bull (Bull Diary), 6 November 1942, p. 15; LC, King Papers, Box 35, thesis, "The Influence of the National Policy on the Strategy of a War," 7 November 1932, 21; and Ernest J. King with Walter Muir Whitehill, *Fleet Admiral King: A Naval Record* (New York: W.W. Norton, 1952), 400, 487, and 504.

53. Perry, *Dear Bart*, 328.

54. LC, Box 39, "An address by Fleet Admiral Ernest J. King, at the National Exchange Club Convention," in *The Exchangite*, vol. 26, no. 11 (November, 1947): 4.

Chapter 1

1. Grace Tully, *FDR: My Boss* (New York: Scribners, 1949), 255–57.

2. William Roy Smith, "British Imperial Federation," in *Political Science Quarterly*, vol. 36, no. 2 (June 1921): 274–297.

3. Jesse Tumblin, *The Quest for Security: Sovereignty, Race, and the Defense of the British Empire, 1898–1931* (New York: Cambridge University Press, 2020), 78, 102–8, 116–19, and 271–81.

4. Winston S. Churchill, *History of the Second World War* (New York: Houghton Mifflin, 1948–53), vols. III and IV.

5. Winston S. Churchill, *History of the English-Speaking Peoples*, (London: Cassel, 1957), Vol. III, 281–85.

6. Andrew Lambert, *The British Way of War. Julian Corbett and the Battle for a National Strategy* (New Haven, CT: Yale University Press, 2021), 25–26, 281, 345–56, 370, and 409–11; Louis Halewood, "Peace throughout the Oceans and Seas of the World: British Maritime Strategic Thought and World Order, 1892–1919," in *Historical Research* Vol. 94, No. 265 (August 2021): 554–57; and Kevin McCranie, "The War of 1812: Historical Justification for Roosevelt's Naval Advocacy," in *Forging the Trident: Theodore Roosevelt and the United States Navy*, eds John B. Hattendorf and William P. Leeman (Annapolis, MD: Naval Institute Press, 2020), 32–55.

7. Wyman H. Packard, *A Century of US Naval Intelligence* (Washington, DC: Office of Naval Intelligence and Naval Historical Center, 1996), 204–14. Note: this work was a SECRET training document as originally compiled in August 1974. After its public release, this widely cited volume has served as a useful reference. Unfortunately, future historians must recognize that innumerable errors of omission appear between the lines of this work and key historical details are unprecise by design.

8. Christopher M. Bell, *Churchill and Sea Power* (New York: Oxford, 2013), 198–200, 220–25, 246–65, and 294–97; William T. Johnsen, *Origins of the Grand Alliance: Anglo-American Military Collaboration from the* Panay *Incident to Pearl Harbor* (Lexington: University Press of Kentucky, 2016), 23–25 and 37–39; and H. M. Brands, *Traitor to His Class: The Privileged Life and Radical Presidency of Franklin Delano Roosevelt* (New York: Doubleday, 2008), 1–10, 17–38, 447, 680–682, 727.

9. FDR, Fireside Chat, 27 May 1941, "Announcing Unlimited National Emergency."

10. Harvey G. Johnston, *The Haraldry of the Murrays* (Edinburgh, Scotland: Johnston, 1910), 67–71.

11. John Gunther, *Roosevelt in Retrospect: A Profile in History* (New York: Harper Brothers., 1950), 45 and 81.

12. Ibid.

13. Ibid.

14. King, *Fleet Admiral King*, 412 and 628.

15. Henry L. Stimson and McGeorge Bundy, *On Active Service in Peace and War* (New York: Harper, 1947), 506.

16. Ibid.

17. Ibid.

18. Rexford G. Tugwell, "The 'Looking Outward' of the Americans," in *Antioch Review*, vol. 9 no. 3 (Autumn 1949), 340–53.

19. LC, King Papers, Box 39, speech file, "Town Hall Meeting," 33–34.

20. Bell, *Churchill and Sea Power*, 258.

21. Ralph Ingersoll, *Top Secret* (New York: Harcourt and Brace, 1946), 64–66, 74, and 75.

22. NWC, King Papers, Box 7, folder 13, "Whitehill notes for verification."

23. Samuel Eliot Morison, *History of US Naval Operations in World War II* (Boston: Little Brown, 1947), vol. II, 17.

24. King, *Fleet Admiral King*, 445–86.

25. LC, King Papers, Box 39, speech file, "Town Hall Meeting," 33–34. Emphasis in original.

26. Ibid.

27. Ibid.

28. Ibid., 34.

29. Ibid.

30. Perry, *Dear Bart*, 11.

31. Ibid.

32. Arthur Bryant, ed., *The Turn of the Tide: A History of the War Years Based on the Diaries of Field-Marshal Lord Alanbrooke, Chief of the Imperial General Staff* (New York: Doubleday, 1957), 279.

33. Ibid.

34. Patrick Beesly, *Very Special Intelligence: The Story of the Admiralty's Operational Intelligence Centre, 1939–1945* (London: Hamish Hamilton, 1977), 107.

35. Stephen Roskill, *Naval Policy between the Wars: The Period of Anglo-American Antagonism, 1919–1929* (New York: Walker, 1968), 20.

36. Stephen Roskill, *The War at Sea* (London: HMSO, 1960), Vol. III, Pt. I, 6.

37. Harry Sanders, "King of the Oceans," in Naval Institute *Proceedings*, vol. 100, no. 8 (August, 1974), 52–59.

38. Theodore Roosevelt, *America and the World War—Fear God and Take Your Own Part* (New York: Charles Scribner's Sons, 1926), 122–35.

39. Ibid.

40. Ibid.

41. LC, King Papers, Box 20, "Report of Board of Medical Survey," 3 August 1942.

42. The label associated with King as, "Triple Threat," dates from 1939. See King, *Fleet Admiral King*, 304–05.

43. Craig L. Symonds, *American Naval History: A Very Short Introduction* (New York: Oxford University Press, 2018), 80; Albert A. Nofi, *To Train the Fleet for War: The US Navy Fleet Problems, 1923–1940* (Newport, RI: Naval War College Press, 2010), 1–55, 132–35, 143–54, and 160–64; and Michael D. Besch, *A Navy Second to None: A History of US Navy Training in World War I* (Westport, CT: Greenwood, 2002), 1–15; Trent Hone, *Learning War: The Evolution of Fighting Doctrine in the US Navy, 1898–1945* (Annapolis, MD: Naval Institute Press, 2018), 34–54, 56–64, 87–91.

44. Perry, *Dear Bart*, 82.

45. James O. Richardson, *On the Treadmill to Pearl Harbor: The Memoirs of Admiral James O. Richardson as Told to George C. Dyer* (Washington, DC: Naval Historical Center, 1974), 5.

46. King, *Fleet Admiral King*, 412 and 628.

47. NWC, King Papers, Box 7, Whitehill notes, "Five-Stars"; NWC, King Papers, Box 7, Whitehill notes, "Rank of Commodore"; and NWC, King Papers, Box 8, "Chief of Naval Operations Organization," 3.

48. LC, King Papers, Box 39, "Naval Strategy and Tactics," unpublished by Ernest J. King, 30 July 1940, 3.

49. Ibid., pp. 3–4.

50. Roger Keyes, *Amphibious Warfare and Combined Operations* (Cambridge, United Kingdom: Cambridge University Press, 1943). Special thanks to Thomas King Savage for sharing access to some books kept within the family by King. Other works owned by King may be found in the libraries of the Naval Academy and the Naval War College. He also gave several books to the Newport Reading Room and Bowdoin College.

51. Mahan, *Problem of Asia*, 38, 62, 125, and 175.

52. Books from King's personal library with thanks to Thomas King Savage.

53. LC, King Papers, Box 20, King to Keeper of Records, 9 November 1946.

54. LC, King Papers, Box 20, Registrar General in Edinburgh, Scotland, 18 February 1946.

55. King, *Fleet Admiral King*, 635. For their gracious assistance in providing access to keepsakes held by the family, the author is particularly indebted to King's grandsons, Edgerton van den Berg, Janvier King Smith, and Tom King Savage.

56. NWC, King Papers, Box 2, Howard Orem to Buell, 12 December 1974.

57. Santa Cruz, California, University of California Library (UCL), Robert A. Heinlein Archives, Box 316, Heinlein to Buell, "Subject: FADM E.J. King, USN, Deceased," (Heinlein Memoir), 60.

58. Smith email to author, 29 March 2019.

59. Smith email to author, 9 June 2021.

60. Ibid.

61. Perry, *Dear Bart*, 80.

62. Ibid.

63. NWC, King Papers, Box 2, Russell to Buell, 18 November 1974.

64. LC, King Papers, Box 39, speech file, "Principles Relating to Command."

65. NWC, RG 4, Box 20, Harold R. Stark, comp., "Extracts from Books Read in Connection with War College Reading Courses," vol. II, 116–17.

66. LC, King Papers, Box 39, speech file, "Town Hall Meeting," 32–33.

67. Ibid.

68. Ibid.

69. Ibid., 62–63.

70. Alfred Thayer Mahan, *From Sail to Steam: Recollections of Naval Life* (New York: Harper and Brothers, 1907), 324.

71. LC, King Papers, Box 39, "An address by Fleet Admiral Ernest J. King, at the National Exchange Club Convention" in *The Exchangite*, vol. 26, no. 11 (November 1947), 4.

72. Ibid.

73. Ibid., 26–27.

74. Robert O'Connell, *Sacred Vessels: The Cult of the Battleship and the Rise of the US Navy* (New York: Oxford University Press), 1993, 60–64; Peter Karsten, *The Naval Aristocracy: The Golden Age of Annapolis and the Emergence of Modern American Navalism* (New York: Free Press), 1972, 5–7; and Hattendorf, *Sailors and Scholars*, 38–65.

75. Walter Muir Whitehill, "A Postscript to 'Fleet Admiral King: A Naval Record,'" in *Proceedings of the Massachusetts Historical Society*, 3rd series, vol. 70 (October 1950–May 1953), 203–226; King, *Fleet Admiral King*, 3–19; and Buell, *Master of Sea Power*, 1–17.

76. NWC, King Papers, Box 10, Buell interview with RAdm. and Mrs. Boynton Brown, 8 December 1974.

77. NWC, King Papers, Box 3, Whitehill notes, undated.

78. King, *Fleet Admiral King*, 14.

79. Author's copy, Ernest J. King to Nan Ferrell, 4 May 1941. Special thanks to the descendants of Nancy Ferrell, which King sent on a regular basis between 1940 and 1945. Ferrell worked most of her professional career at the Library of Congress and in this role also worked with the Office of Naval History and Naval Historical Foundation in handling the acquisition of the King Papers at the Library of Congress. Her previously unknown collection of roughly 100 personal correspondences became available to the author just before the present manuscript was completed.

80. Karsten, *Naval Aristocracy*, 5–7.

81. O'Connell, *Sacred Vessels*, 1–8.

82. Robert G. Albion and Rowena Reed, eds., *Makers of Naval Policy, 1798–1947* (Annapolis, MD: Naval Institute Press, 1980), 1–111.

83. King, *Fleet Admiral King*, 14. Note: the train ticket remains in the King family collections.

84. Whitehill, "A Postscript to 'Fleet Admiral King: A Naval Record,'" 203–226.

85. NWC, King Papers, Box 5, Walter Muir Whitehill Notes, "Memorandum of Conversation with Commodore D. W. Knox," 31 May 1946.

86. King, *Fleet Admiral King*, 16–34.

87. Ibid.

88. NWC, King Papers, Box 3, Whitehill notes, undated.

89. King, *Fleet Admiral King*, 106.

90. Ibid.

91. Scott Mobley, *Progressives in Navy Blue: Maritime Strategy, American Empire, and the Transformation of US Naval Identity, 1873–1898* (Annapolis, MD: Naval Institute Press, 2018), 1–19; O'Connell, *Sacred Vessels*, 9–101; and Karsten, *The Naval Aristocracy*, 1–15 and 50–81.

92. King, *Fleet Admiral King,* 76–77.

93. Ibid.

94. LC, Theodore Roosevelt Papers (TR), "Brief Summary of Lieut. Sims' Criticisms Contained in his Reports from the Asiatic Station," 8.

95. LC, Sims Papers, correspondence files, Box 145, Niblack to Sims, 20 June 1901.

96. Benjamin Armstrong, ed., *Twenty-First-Century Sims: Innovation, Education, and Leadership in the Modern Era* (Annapolis, MD: Naval Institute Press, 2015), vii.

97., NWC, King Papers, Box 3, Whitehill notes, "Naval Academy."

98. NWC, King Papers, Box 8, Whitehill notes, "The Roosevelts."

99. NWC, King Papers, Box 3, Whitehill notes, "Naval Academy."

100. NWC, King Papers, Box 7, "Comments on Flag Officers, US Navy," 31 July 1949, 6.

101. Ibid.

102. Ernest J. King, ed., *The Lucky Bag: Class of 1901* (Philadelphia, PA: Franklin Printing, 1901), 13–35 and 121–64.

103. Ibid., 13.

104. Craig Symonds, *Nimitz at War: Command Leadership from Pearl Harbor to Tokyo Bay* (New York: Oxford University Press, 2022), 1–19.

105. NWC, King Papers, Box 7, Whitehill random notes, November 1946.

106. Ibid.

107. Mahan, *Problem of Asia*, 111.

108. Ibid., 40.

109. Ibid.

110. Ibid.

111. King, *Fleet Admiral King*, 35–37.

112. Jason W. Smith, *To Master the Boundless Sea: The US Navy, The Marine Environment, and the Cartography of Empire* (Chapel Hill: University of North Carolina Press, 2018), 157–91.

113. Juan Estrigas Rodrigas, *La inteligencia en las Operaciones Navales de 1898 Consecuencias de una Estrategia Improvisada* (Madrid: Iberdrola, 2022), 1–10; Michel Laguerre Kliemann, *US Naval War College & Escuela Superior de Guerra Naval del Perú* (Lima, Peru, Escuela Superior de Guerra Naval del Perú / Naval War College, 2017), 81–82; and David Kohnen, "El Americano:Las Aventuras del Capitán de la Reserva Naval de los Estados Unidos—Harold Bartley Grow en Perú, 1923–1930," *Revista de Marina* , fall 2021, 103–17.

114. Charles Johnson, *A General History of the Pyrates from First Rise and Settlement in the Island of Providence to the Present Time* (London: Charles Rivington, 1724). Inscribed copy in King family.

115. St. Louis, Missouri, National Archives and Records Administration (NARA), National Personnel Records Center (NRPC), Record Group 24 (RG 24), Records of the Bureau of Naval Personnel, 1798–2007, Official Military Personnel Files, 1885–1998, File Unit: King, Ernest J., "Officer Record of Fitness" (King Service Record).

116. NWC, King Papers, Box 7, Whitehill random notes, November 1946.

117. NARA, NRPC, RG 24, King Service Record.

118. NWC, King Papers, Box 13, "Naval Personalities," Admiral E. C. Kalbfus, 30 July 1950.

119. Ibid.

120. NWC, King Papers, Box 8, Officer's Record of Fitness, June 1904.

121. Annapolis, Maryland, US Naval Institute (USNI), John T. Mason Oral History Program, "Reminiscences of John C. Neidermair" (Neidermair Oral History), 118–20.

122. King, *Fleet Admiral King*, 35–37.

123. Ibid.

124. Ibid.

125. Ibid.

126. NARA, NRPC, RG 24, King Service Record.

127. Ibid.

128. Ibid.

129. Ibid.

130. NWC, King Papers, Box 2, Charles A. Focht correspondence.

131. Ibid.

132. King, *Fleet Admiral King*, 232.

133. Ibid.

134. Ibid.

135. Ibid., 623.

Chapter 2

1. John Hattendorf, "Rear Admiral Charles H. Stockton, the Naval War College, and the Law of Naval Warfare," in *International Law Studies Blue Book Series—the Law of Armed Conflict: Into the New Millennium*, Michael N. Schmitt and Leslie C. Green, eds. (Newport, RI: Naval War College Press, 1980), vol., 71, xvii–xxii.

2. NARA, NRPC, RG 24, King Service Record, correspondence concerning unfavorable performance, May to September 1906.

3. NWC, King Papers, Box 3, Whitehill notes.

4. King, *Fleet Admiral King*, 63–72.

5. NWC, King Papers, Box 8, "Fleet Organization, 1919–1941," Lieutenant Dr. Richard W. Leopold, USNR, comp., 1945.

6. LC, King Papers, Box 17, King to Admiral Arthur W. Radford, 15 April 1949.

7. David Kohnen, *Feeding Greyhounds: Fueling the US Navy "Second to None" in the First World War Era* (Naval War College Foundation, 2021), 1–55.

8. Stephen Wertheim, "Reluctant Liberator: Theodore Roosevelt's Philosophy of Self-Government and Preparation for Philippine Independence" in *Presidential Studies Quarterly*, vol. 39, no. 3 (September 2009), 494–518.

9. Ibid.

10. Roosevelt, "Self-Defense without Militarism" in *America and the World War*, 87–104.

11. Ibid., "The Japanese in Korea," 406–13.

12. See King's profile in *The Lucky Bag*.

13. King, *Fleet Admiral King*, 64.

14. Ibid.

15. NWC, Low Reminiscences, 13–14.

16. King, *Fleet Admiral King*, 74.

17. Ibid.

18. NWC, King Papers, Box 8, "General MacArthur."

19. King, *Fleet Admiral King*, 74.

20. NWC, King Papers, Box 2, Charles D. Griffen to Buell, 19 December 1974.

21. Author's copy, King to Ferrell, 4 May 1941.

22. "Green Bowlers Investigation," in *Army-Navy Journal*, vol. 48, no. 3386 (2 August 1947), 1,265.

23. Drew Pearson, "Washington Merry-Go-Round," in *Cumberland News* (12 August 1947), 4.

24. NWC, MSC-183, Charles P. Snyder Papers, Box 42, "The Green Bowlers."

25. NWC, RG 4, folder 22, Captain Ernest J. King, "Education of Naval Officers, 16 May 1925."

26. Ibid., 72.

27. David Kohnen, "Alan Goodrich Kirk," in *Nineteen Gun Salute*, John B. Hattendorf and Bruce Elleman, eds. (Newport, RI: Naval War College Press, 2010), 77–84.

28. NWC, Low Papers, Box 1, "Personal Narrative," 2.

29. Ibid.

30. James C. Bradford, *John Paul Jones and the American Navy* (New York: Rosen Publishing Group, 2002), 92–100; Evan Thomas, *John Paul Jones: Sailor, Hero, Father of the American Navy* (New York: Simon and Schuster, 2003), 1–13 and 299–312; Samuel Eliot Morison, *John Paul Jones: A Sailor's Biography* (Boston, MA: Little Brown, 1959); Charles Stewart West, *John Paul Jones Commemoration at Annapolis—April 24, 1906* (Washington, DC: Government Printing Office, 1906), 9–21; and O'Connell, *Sacred Vessels*, 9–101 and 302–22.

31. Sarah M. Goldberger, "An Indissoluble Union: Theodore Roosevelt, James Bulloch, and the Politics of Reconciliation," in John B. Hattendorf and William P. Leeman, eds., *Forging the Trident: Theodore Roosevelt and the United States Navy* (Annapolis, MD: Naval Institute Press, 2020), 14–31.

32. James R. Soley, "The Effect on American Commerce of an Anglo-Continental War," *Scribner's*, vol. 6, no. 5 (November 1889), 543–45.

33. FDR Library, inscribed copy of James R. Soley, *The Blockade and the Cruisers* (New York: Scribner's and Sons, 1898).

34. Hattendorf, *Forging the Trident*, 149–76.

35. Peter V. Nash, *The Development of Mobile Logistic Support in Anglo-American Naval Policy, 1900–1953* (Gainesville, FL: University Press of Florida), 1–77; Volkan S. Ediger and John V. Bowlus, "A Farewell to King Coal: Geopolitics, Energy Security, and the Transition to Oil, 1898–1917," in *The Historical Journal*, vol. 62, no. 2 (June, 2019), 427–49; and Besch, *Navy Second to None*, 1–15.

36. Albion, *Makers of Naval Policy*, 12, 93–94, 211–16, 334–38, 358, and 379.

37. Ibid., 379.

38. Woodrow Wilson, *Addresses of President Wilson, January 27–February 3, 1916* (Washington, DC: Government Printing Office, 1916).

39. Albion, *Makers of Naval Policy*, 77–78 and 377–419.

40. Ibid., 212.

41. Donald Chisholm, *Waiting for Dead Men's Shoes: Origins and Development of the US Navy's Officer Personnel System* (Stanford, CA: Stanford University Press, 2001), 514–16 and 681–94; Philip Crowl, "Alfred Thayer Mahan: The Naval Historian," in *Makers of Modern Strategy: From Machiavelli to the Nuclear Age*, Peter Paret, ed. (Princeton, NJ: Princeton University Press, 1994), 448; and Anthony Nicolosi, "The Spirit of McCarty Little," in Naval Institute *Proceedings*, vol. 110, no. 9 (September, 1984), 72–80.

42. King, *Fleet Admiral King*, 78.

43. David Kohnen, "Checking the Wake While Looking beyond the Horizon," in *Forging the Trident: Theodore Roosevelt and the United States Navy*, John B. Hattendorf and William P. Leeman, eds. (Annapolis, Maryland: Naval Institute Press, 2020), 149–76.

44. Alfred Thayer Mahan, "Britain and Imperial Germany—Admiral Mahan's Warning," reprinted from *The Daily Mail* (1910), 2.

45. Ibid.

46. William Roy Smith, "British Imperial Federation," in *Political Science Quarterly*, vol. 36, no. 2 (June 1921), 274–297.

47. Morison, *Admiral Sims*, 176–200.

48. LC, Sims Papers, Box 48, folder 1909–1916, Benson to Sims, March 1909.

49. NWC, unpublished typescript by Joseph Strauss, *As I Recall It: Being the Recollections of Forty-Four Years Spent in the US Navy*, undated, p. 172.

50. Ibid.

51. LC, Sims Papers, Box 68, folder 1906–1918, Jellicoe to Sims, 3 February 1909.

52. Roosevelt, *America and the World War*, 122–35.

53. LC, King Papers, Box 39, "Design for Pye-King Range Machine," 1909.

54. King, *Fleet Admiral King*, 77.

55. John T. Kuehn, *America's First General Staff: A Short History of the Rise and Fall of the General Board of the Navy, 1900–1950* (Annapolis, MD: Naval Institute Press, 2017), 1–138.

56. NWC, King Papers, Box 8, "A Discussion of the Authority," 2.

57. Ibid.

58. Ibid.

59. Ibid.

60. King, *Fleet Admiral King*, 79.

61. LC, Sims Papers, Box 101, Menu and seating arrangements for Thanksgiving dinner at Savoy Hotel in 1910.

62. Ibid.

63. NWC, King Papers, Box 2, Whitehill notes.

64. King, *Fleet Admiral King*, 78.

65. LC, Sims Papers, Box 101, "Reception of Seamen of United States Atlantic Fleet, Guildhall—Saturday, 3rd December, 1910."

66. Morison, *Admiral Sims*, 281.

67. NWC, King Papers, Box 13, "Staff Duty," 31 July 1949.

68. LC, Sims Papers, Box 68, Sims to Jellicoe, 25 December 1910.

69. LC, Sims Papers, Box 101, Invitation from the Commander and Officers of the Third Division—US Atlantic Fleet to "Mrs. E. A. Hitchcock and the whole St. Louis Family Push."

70. LC, Sims Papers, Box 68, Sims to Jellicoe, 25 December 1910.

71. "Sims' Chief Bo'sun for an Alliance Too: British Heard from Man Before the Mast at that Guildhall Love Fest," in *New York Times*, vol., LX, no. 19,322 (19 December 1910), 2.

72. Ibid.

73. Ibid.

74. Morison, *Admiral Sims*, 282.

75. Erik Larson, *Dead Wake: The Last Voyage of the Lusitania* (New York: Crowne, 2015), 10–11.

76. NWC, MSC-356, Box 19, "A Comparative Analysis of Problems and Methods of Coalition Action in Two World Wars," Historical Section, by Captain Tracy Barrett Kittredge USNR (Ret.) for the International Relations Section, JCS, during the Annual Meeting of the American Political Science Association (Comparative Analysis).

77. Ibid.

78. Ibid.

79. Ibid.

80. Armstrong, *Twenty-First-Century Sims*, 135–45.

81. George C. Dyer, *The Amphibians Came to Conquer: The Story of Admiral Richmond Kelly Turner* (Washington, DC: Naval Historical Center, 1972), 123.

82. LC, Sims Papers, Box 68, Sims to Knox, 14 August 1914.

Chapter 3

1. King, *Fleet Admiral King*, 91.

2. Ibid., 92.

3. Ibid., 85.

4. Ibid.

5. Henry C. Dinger, "Some Notes on Naval Needs and Requirements," in Naval Institute *Proceedings*, vol. 30, no. 1 (January, 1904), 91.

6. LC, Sims Papers, Box 68, Sims to King, 20 February 1914.

7. Rodney P. Carlisle, *Where the Fleet Begins: A History of the David Taylor Research Center* (Washington, DC: Naval Historical Center, 1998), 89–207; Timothy S. Wolters, *Information at Sea: Shipboard Communication in the US Navy from Mobile Bay to Okinawa* (Baltimore, MD: Johns Hopkins University Press, 2013), 72–76 and 92–97; Jonathan Winkler, *Nexus: Strategic Communications and American Security in World War I* (Boston, MA: Harvard University Press, 2008), 1–33, 61–100, 124–25,

and 206–66; and Aitor Anduaga, *Wireless & Empire: Geopolitics, Radio Industry and Ionosphere and the British Empire, 1918–1939* (London: Oxford University Press, 2009), 1–48 and 54–120.

8. Chester W. Nimitz, "Military Value and Tactics of Modern Submarines," in Naval Institute *Proceedings*, vol. 38, no. 4 (December 1912), 1,192.

9. King, *Fleet Admiral King*, 92.

10. Wolters, *Information at Sea*, 72–74, 94–96, and 185; and Linwood S. Howeth, *History of Communications-Electronics in the United States Navy* (Washington, DC: Navy Department, 1963), 189–95, 267, and 524.

11. Clark G. Reynolds, *Admiral John Towers: The Struggle for Naval Air Supremacy* (Annapolis, MD: Naval Institute Press, 1991), 56.

12. NARA, NRPC, RG 24, King Service Record.

13. LC, Sims Papers, Box 68, Sims to King, 20 February 1914.

14. King, *Fleet Admiral King*, 92.

15. Bradley Fiske, *The Navy as a Fighting Machine* (New York: Scribners, 1916), i.

16. Ibid.

17. Ibid.

18. Albion, *Makers of Naval Policy*, 171–77.

19. Ibid., 172–73.

20. Ibid., 220–67.

21. Kuehn, *America's First General Staff*, 17–23.

22. Richardson, *On the Treadmill*, 5.

23. LC, Sims Papers, Box 68, Sims to King, 20 February 1914.

24. NWC, Kittredge, "Comparative Analysis."

25. Guy Gaunt, *The Yield of the Years: A Story of Adventure Afloat and Ashore* (London: L. Hutchinson, 1940); and Anthony Delano, *Guy Gaunt: The Boy from Ballarat Who Talked America into the Great War* (Kew, Victoria: Australian Scholarly Publishing, 2016); Franz Kleist von Rintelen, *The Dark Invader: Wartime Reminiscences of a German Naval Intelligence Officer* (London: Lovat Dickson Ltd., 1933), 79–186; and Chad Millman, *The Detonators: The Secret Plot to Destroy America and an Epic Hunt for Justice* (New York: Little, Brown, 2006), 352–60.

26. Michael C. Meyer, "The Arms of the *Ypiranga*," in *The Hispanic American Historical Review*, vol. 50, no. 3 (August 1970), 543–556.

27. Ibid.

28. Robert E. Quirk, *An Affair of Honor: Woodrow Wilson and the Occupation of Veracruz* (Lexington: University of Kentucky Press, 1962), 1–5.

29. James C. Bradford, ed., *Admirals of the New Steel Navy: Makers of the American Naval Tradition, 1880–1930* (Annapolis, MD: Naval Institute Press, 1990), 253–81.

30. Albion, *Makers of Naval Policy*, 274–75.

31. Ibid.

32. Kuehn, *America's First General Staff*, 81–97.

33. NARA, NRPC, RG 24, King Service Record, orders and associated correspondences, April to July 1914.

34. NARA, NRPC, RG 24, King Service Record, telegram from Daniels, 25 April 1914.

35. NWC, King Papers, Box 17, folder 2, Whitehill notes, "Veracruz."

36. Albion, *Makers of Naval Policy,* 338–41

37. Linda Lumsden, "Socialist Muckraker John Kenneth Turner," in *American Journalism*, vol. 32, no. 3 (July 2015), 282–306.

38. NWC, King Papers, Box 7, Whitehill notes, "Grape Juice War."

39. Ibid.

40. LC, Sims Papers, Box 68, Knox to Sims, 13 February 1914.

41. LC, Sims Papers, Box 68, Sims to Knox, 14 August 1914.

42. LC, Sims Papers, Box 68, King to Sims, 3 July 1914.

43. LC, Sims Papers, Box 68, Sims to King, 20 February 1914

44. NARA, NRPC, RG 24, King Service Record, telegram from King to Sims, 2 July 1914.

45. LC, Sims Papers, Box 68, Sims to King, 6 July 1914.

46. Ibid.

47. David Kohnen, ed., *Twenty-First-Century Knox: Influence, Sea Power, and History for the Modern Era* (Annapolis, MD: Naval Institute Press, 2016), 1–15, 107–1.

48. NWC Museum, Model, USS *Sims*, courtesy of Dr. Nathaniel Sims and the Sims family. See the picture in Kohnen, *Feeding Greyhounds*, 25. Note: the model presented by the flotilla skippers is not USS *Sims* (DD-409).

49. Ibid., 2.

50. Ibid.

51. Ibid.

52. Ibid.

53. NWC, King Papers, Box 13, Miscellaneous notes, "Radio Traffic," 29 August 1949.

54. Hattendorf, *Sailors and Scholars*, 89.

55. Wheeler, *Pratt*, 74–75.

56. Hattendorf, *Sailors and Scholars*, 89.

57. David Kohnen, "Charting a New Course: The Knox-Pye-King Board and Naval Professional Education, 1919–23" in *Naval War College Review*, vol. 71, no.3 (Summer 2018), 126–27.

58. Land, *Winning the War with Ships*, 96–97.

59. Wheeler, *Pratt*, 83–88.

60. Morison, *Admiral Sims*, 3–14, 280, 289–312, and 389–92; Trent Hone, *Learning War: The Evolution of Fighting Doctrine in the US Navy, 1898–1945* (Annapolis, MD: Naval Institute Press, 2018): 34–54, 56–64, 87–91, and 115–16; and Kohnen, "The US Navy Won the Battle of Jutland," 126–31.

61. King, *Fleet Admiral King*, 91.

62. NWC, RG 8, Series 1, Op-F, folder 4, file 2656, "Fueling at Sea," 29 August 1919.

63. Kohnen, *Feeding Greyhounds*, 38–55.

64. King, *Fleet Admiral King*, 84–110.

65. NWC, King Papers, Box 1, Whitehill notes of interview, undated.

66. Ibid.

67. Wheeler, *Pratt,* 107, fn. 21.

68. King, *Fleet Admiral King*, 95.

69. Ibid.

70. Ernest J. King, trans., "A German View of the Strategic Importance of the Panama Canal," in *Naval Institute Proceedings*, vol. 40, no. 3 (May–June 1914), 803–09.

71. King, *Fleet Admiral King*, 16–17.

72. NWC, King Papers, Box 5, Atlantic Fleet Confidential Memorandum 2CM-41, "Making the Best of What We Have," 24 March 1941.

73. NWC, King Papers, Box 5, Knox to Morison, 19 November 1946.

74. NARA, NRPC, RG 24, King Service Record.

75. On this point, the author is indebted for the assistance of King's granddaughter, Ellie, and his great-grandsons, Tom Savage and Janvier King Smith.

76. Morison, *Admiral Sims*, 313–36.

77. William S. Sims, "Cheer Up!! There Is No Naval War College," in Naval Institute *Proceedings*, vol. 42, no. 3/163 (May–June 1916), 856.

78. King, *Fleet Admiral King*, 106.

79. NWC, RG 4, Box 23, William S. Sims, "The Practical Character of the Naval War College," 1.

80. NWC, King Papers, Sims to King, 22 December 1914.

81. Ibid.

82. Howard Blum, *Dark Invasion—1915: Germany's Secret War and the Hunt for the First Terrorist Cell in America* (New York: Harper, 2014), 279–331; Thomas J. Tunney and Paul M. Hollister: *Throttled! The Detection of the German and Anarchist Bomb Plotters* (New York: Small, Maynard, 1919); Howard Blum, *Dark Invasion: 1915: Germany's Secret War and the Hunt for the First Terrorist Cell in America* (New York: Harper, 2014); and Ron Chernow, *The House of Morgan: An American Banking Dynasty and the Rise of Modern Finance* (New York; Grove, 2001).

83. Charles C. Marsh, Dudley W. Knox, Tracy Barrett Kittredge (comps.), *German Submarine Activities on the Atlantic Coast of the United States of America*, publication no. 1 (Washington, DC: Navy Department, 1920), 9–119.

84. NWC, King Papers, Box 3, typescript, "LCDR, Commander."

85. Julius A. Furer, *Administration of the Navy Department in World War II* (Washington, DC: Naval Historical Division, 1959), 29–30. Note: emphasis added by author.

86. Henry P. Beers, *The Bureau of Navigation, 1862–1942* (Washington, DC: National Archives, 1942), 1–118; Ronald Specter, *The Professors of War: The Naval War College and the Development of the Naval Profession* (Newport, RI: Naval War College Press, 1977), 1–101; and Hattendorf, *Sailors and Scholars*, 16–111.

87. Wheeler, *Pratt*, 89–135; Furer, *Administration of the Navy Department,* 102–17; and Kohnen, *Twenty-First-Century Knox,* 1–15.

88. Albion, *Makers of Naval Policy*, 170–71, 220–25, and 358–74.

89. Ibid., 172.

90. Albion, *Makers of Naval Policy* 362.

91. Morison, *Admiral Sims*, 313–36; Armstrong, *Twenty-First-Century Sims*, 154–57; and Chisholm, *Waiting for Dead Men's Shoes*, 681–94.

92. NWC, King Papers, Box 3, typescript, "LCDR, Commander."

Chapter 4

1. NWC, King Papers, Box 8, "Fleet Organization," 6.

2. Boyd, *British Intelligence*, 101–249.

3. Cambridge, Massachusetts, Harvard University, Houghton Library (HL), Walter Hines Page Papers (Page Papers), Series IV, Diaries and embassy notebooks, 1913–1918, "Sims to Command," Box 1.

4. Nicholas A. Lambert, "Strategic Command and Control for Maneuver Warfare: Creation of the Royal Navy's "War Room" System, 1905–1915," in *The Journal of Military History* 69, no. 2 (April 2005), 361–410; Thomas Boghardt, *The Zimmerman Telegram: Intelligence, Diplomacy, and America's Entry into World War I* (Annapolis, MD: Naval Institute Press, 2012), 33–159; Patrick Beesly, "British Naval Intelligence in Two World Wars: Some Similarities and Differences," in *Intelligence and International Relations, 1900–1945*, Christopher Andrew and Jeremy Noakes, eds. (Exeter, UK: University of Exeter, 1987), 253–73; David Ramsay, *"Blinker" Hall: Spymaster—the Man Who Brought America into World War I* (Brimscome Port, UK: History Press, 2010), 163–64; Patrick Beesly, *Room 40: British Naval Intelligence, 1914–1918* (New York: Harcourt, Brace, 1982), 1–45; David Kahn, *The Code-Breakers: The Story of Secret Writing* (New York: Macmillan, 1967), 282–97; and Barbara Tuchman, *The Zimmermann Telegram: America Enters the War, 1917–1918* (New York: Random House, 1958), 61–97, 125–40, and 168–86.

5. James J. Lopach and Jean A. Luchowski, *Jeanette Rankin: A Political Woman* (Boulder: University of Colorado, 2005), 1–10; Charles Chatfield, "World War I and the Liberal Pacifist in the United States," in *American Historical Review* Vol. 75 No. 7 (December, 1970), 1920–1937; and Walter D. Kaemphoefner, "Language and Loyalty among German Americans in World War I," in *Journal of Austrian-American History*, vol. 3, no. 1 (January 2019): 1–25.

6. David F. Trask, *Captains & Cabinets: Anglo-American Naval Relations, 1917–1918* (Columbia: University Press of Missouri, 1972), 63–65 and 141–42; David F. Trask, *The AEF and Coalition Warmaking, 1917–1918* (Lawrence: University Press of Kansas, 1993), 55–56; and William N. Still, *Crisis at Sea: The United States Navy in European Waters in World War I* (Pensacola, FL: University Press of Florida, 2006), 379–408.

7. King, *Fleet Admiral King*, 114–17: Taussig, *Queenstown Patrol*, 5–35: Still, *Crisis at Sea*, 25–33; and Paul Halpern, *A Naval History of World War I* (London: University College Press, 1994), 354–62.

8. Washington, DC, Library of Congress (LC), Ernest J. King Papers (King Papers), Box 2, "Confidential Mobilization Plan of 21 March 1917."

9. Josephus Daniels, *Our Navy at War* (Washington, DC: Pictorial Bureau, 1922), 36–39.

10. Wheeler, *Pratt*, 92.

11. Ibid.

12. Kittredge, Comparative Analysis, 4.

13. Ibid.

14. *The New York Times,* 2 February 1920, "Broke Law for Navy—F. D. Roosevelt Says Committed Enough Illegal Acts to Put Him in Jail for 999 Years, He Adds 'Didn't Wait for Congress."

15. Ibid.

16. Ibid.

17. Ibid.

18. Morison, *Admiral Sims*, 340.

19. LC, Sims Papers, Box 10, Percy Foote to Sims, 7 November 1918.

20. King, *Fleet Admiral King*, 101.

21. Ibid.

22. King, *Fleet Admiral King*, 103 and 114–45.

23. Washington, DC., Naval History and Heritage Command (NHHC), Navy Department Library (NDL), Microfilm, Reel 1, ME-11, "Memorandum from Henry T. Mayo to Josephus Daniels about questions regarding organization of fleet after mobilization," 9 April 1917.

24. LC, Sims Papers, Box 142, Orders to Duty, formal appointment, and commission to rear admiral, 19 March 1917. Sims annotated formal receipt of promotion on 21 March.

25. Daniels, *Our Navy at War*, 39.

26. "Naval Investigation: Hearings before the Subcommittee on Naval Affairs," vol. II, pages 1,883–1,893, 1,917–19, 1,992, 3,139. The quotation attributed to Benson in testimony by Sims became a point of contention between the two.

27. Daniels, *Our Navy at War*, 36–40.

28. William Sowden Sims, *Victory at Sea* (New York: Doubleday, Page, & Co., 1920), 240–43.

29. LC, Sims Papers, Box 142, Orders to Duty, "Subject: Special Duty," 28 March 1917.

30. John Milton Cooper Jr., *Reconsidering Woodrow Wilson: Progressivism, Internationalism, War, and Peace* (Washington, DC: Wilson Center Press, 2008), 15–16 and 226–28.

31. Ibid.

32. United States Congress, Senate, "Awarding of Medals in the Naval Service: Hearing before a Subcommittee on Naval Affairs" (Washington, DC: Government Printing Office, 1920), 563.

33. Ibid., 5.

34. Boyd, *British Intelligence*, 96, 102, 130, 204–19, and 222.

35. Morison, *Admiral Sims*, 289–312; Wheeler, *Pratt*, 71–88; and Kohnen, "The US Navy Won the Battle of Jutland," 126–31.

36. King, *Fleet Admiral King,* 103.

37. Ibid.

38. Ibid., 115.

39. NARA, NRPC, RG 24, King Service Record.

40. Newport, Rhode Island, Naval War College Archives (NWC), Record Group 4 (RG 4), Captain Frank N. Schofield Lecture, "Estimate of the Situation and Formulation of Orders," 1.

41. Michael Simpson, ed., *Anglo-American Naval Relations, 1917–1919* (Brookfield, VT: Navy Records Society—Scholar Press, 1991), 76–123.

42. TNA, Records of the Foreign Office (FO), Book 4, "Cabinet Memorandum 738," 21 August 1917.

43. Sarah M. Goldberger, "Challenging the Interest and Reverence of All Americans: Preservation and the Yorktown National Battlefield," in *Destination Dixie: Tourism and Southern History*, ed. Karen L. Cox (Gainesville: University Press of Florida, 2012), 185–203.

44. TNA, Admiralty Records (ADM) 137, Book 1436, 179–81.

45. TNA, ADM 137, Book 1436, Grasset Instructions, April 1917.

46. Trask, *Captains & Cabinets*, 63–65 and 141–42; Trask, *AEF*, 11–12 and 55–56; and Still, *Crisis at Sea*, 379–408.

47. King, *Fleet Admiral King*, 113–14.

48. Cooper, *Reconsidering Woodrow Wilson*, 15–16 and 226–28. See Michael Simpson, ed., *Anglo-American Naval Relations, 1917–1919* (Aldershot, UK: Scholar Press for the Navy Records Society, 1991), 60–95: and King, *Fleet Admiral King*, 114–17.

49. King, *Fleet Admiral King*, 114–18.

50. LC, King Papers, Box 1, "Orders to Duty," 13 April 1917, "Temporary Duty, Boston." See Thomas Wildenberg, *Grey Steel and Black Oil* (Annapolis, MD, Naval Institute Press, 1996), 9–13; King, *Fleet Admiral King* 114–17; and Potter, *Nimitz*, 125–27.

51. LC, King Papers, Box 1, "Orders to Duty," 19 April 1917, "Temporary Duty, Washington, DC."

52. Joseph K. Taussig with William Still, ed., *The Queenstown Patrol, 1917—the Diary of Commander Joseph Knefler Taussig, US Navy* (Newport, RI: Naval War College Press, 2010), 9 and 206.

53. Evelyn Cherpak, ed., *Three Splendid Little Wars: The Diary of Joseph K. Taussig* (Newport, RI, Naval War College Press, 2009), 134–36; Sims, *Victory at Sea*, 5; and Morison, *Admiral Sims*, 377.

54. Lewis Bayly, *Pull Together! The Memoirs of Admiral Sir Lewis Bayly* (London: George C. Harrop, 1929), 221–25.

55. Taussig, *Queenstown Patrol*, 20.

56. Michael Simpson, "Admiral William S. Sims, US Navy, and Admiral Sir Lewis Bayly, Royal Navy: An Unlikely Friendship and Anglo-American Cooperation, 1917–1919," in *Naval War College Review*, vol. 41, no. 2 (Spring 1988), 66–80.

57. Bayly, *Pull Together*, 57 and 269; Sims, *Victory at Sea*, 71 and 219; and Taussig, *Queenstown Patrol*, 21–22, 25–26, 205, and 222.

58. Sims, *Victory at Sea*, 71.

59. NHHC, Kittredge Papers, Box 8, "A Brief Summary of the United States Naval Activities in European Waters with Outline of the Organization of Admiral Sims' Headquarters," Tracy Barrett Kittredge, comp., 3 August 1918, 3–9.

60. LC, Sims Papers, Box 142, Orders to Duty, Woodrow Wilson signed orders to Sims, 26 May 1917.

61. Ibid., Daniels order to Sims, 4 June 1917.

62. Kohnen, *Feeding Greyhounds*, 1–55.

63. Ibid., 30–45.

64. Sims, *Victory at Sea*, 204–22.

65. LC, Sims Papers, Box 142, Orders to Duty, "Subject: Detached Commandant Naval Station Newport; to command certain destroyers, etc.," 28 April 1917.

66. Tracy Barrett Kittredge, *Naval Lessons of the Great War: A Review of the Senate Naval Investigation of the Criticisms by Admiral Sims of the Policies and Methods of Josephus Daniels* (New York: Doubleday, Page, 1921), 3–117, 255–79, and 407–50; and John Langdon Leighton, *SIMSADUS-London: The American Navy in Europe* (New York: Henry Holt, 1920), 352–55, and 3–23, 59–62, and 150–58.

67. King, *Fleet Admiral King*, 144.

68. Sims, *Victory at Sea*, 68.

69. Liam Nolan and John E. Nolan, *Secret Victory: Ireland and the War at Sea, 1914–1918* (Blackrock-Dublin, Ireland: Mercier, 2009), 150–85, 195–230, 250–301; Steve R. Dunn, *Bayly's War: The Battle for the Western Approaches in the First World War* (Barnsley, UK: Seaforth, 2018), 133–52, 160–62, 263–66, and 276; Steve R. Dunn, *Securing the Narrow Sea: The Dover Patrol, 1914–1918* (Barnsley, UK: Seaforth, 2017), 149–50; and Charles Townshend, *The British Campaign in Ireland, 1919–1921* (New York: Oxford University Press, 1975), 1–72 and 96.

70. Trask, *Captains and Cabinets*, 63–67; Trask, *AEF*, 11–12; Still, *Crisis at Sea*, 25–33; and Cooper, *Reconsidering Woodrow Wilson*, 15–16 and 226–28.

71. King, *Fleet Admiral King*, 144.

72. Ibid.

73. Ibid.

74. King and Whitehill, *Fleet Admiral King*, 114.

75. Sarah M. Goldberger, "Challenging the Interest and Reverence of All Americans," 185–203.

76. Ibid.

77. "Russians Arrive—Special Mission to Confer with Experts," in *The News Newport* (21 September 1917).

78. Carl J. Richard, *When the Americans Invaded Russia: Woodrow Wilson's Siberian Disaster* (Lanham, MD: Rowman and Littlefield, 2012), 10 and 180.

79. Henry P. Beers with Robert G. Albion, *Administrative Reference Service Report No. 5—US Naval Forces in Northern Russia* (Washington, DC: Navy Department, 1943), 1–58.

80. Henry P. Beers with Robert G. Albion, *Administrative Reference Service Report No. 2—US Naval Detachment in Turkish Waters, 1919–1924* (Washington, DC: Navy Department, 1943), 1–29.

81. Wheeler, *Pratt*, 130–31.

82. Nicholas Lambert, *Planning Armageddon: British Economic Warfare and the First World War* (Cambridge, MA: Harvard University Press, 2012), 325–506.

83. NWC, King Papers, Box 7, Keynote address by King, as compiled by Admiral Charles M. Cooke on 28 February 1943, "ASW Conference 1 March 1943 Remarks by Admiral King."

84. Ibid.

85. Branden Little, "Tarnishing Victory? Contested Histories and Civil-Military Discord in the US Navy, 1919–24," in *Defense & Security Analysis*, vol. 36, no. 1 (Spring, 2020), 1–29.

86. Hugh Rodman, *Yarns of a Kentucky Admiral* (Indianapolis, IN: Bobbs-Merrill Company, 1928), 261–311; Albert Gleaves *A History of the Transport Service: Adventures and Experiences of United States Transports and Cruisers in the World War* (New York: George H. Doran Company, 1921), 237; and Simpson, "An Unlikely Friendship," 66–80.

87. Frank A. Blazich Jr., "The Ablest Men: American Naval Planning Section London and the Adriatic, 1917–1918," in *The Northern Mariner/Le Marin du Nord* XXVI, no. 4 (October 2016), 383–406.

88. NWC, RG 4, Box 20, Harold R. Stark (comp.), "Extracts from Books Read in Connection with War College Reading Courses," vols. 1 and 2.

89. Simpson, "An Unlikely Friendship," 66–80.

90. Little, "Tarnishing Victory," 1–29.

91. LC, King Papers, Box 2, "Estimate of the Situation with Regard to the Efficient Development of Operations of the Atlantic Fleet."

92. NWC, King Papers, Box 3, "World War I," typescript circa 1948.

93. NWC, King Papers, Box 7, Memorandum, 12 November 1946.

94. Ibid.

95. LC, King Papers, Box 2, "Organization of Fleet after mobilization," 9 April 1917.

96. Ibid.

97. Taussig, The Queenstown Patrol, 9 and 206.

98. LC, King Papers, Box 2, "Organization of Fleet after mobilization," 9 April 1917.

99. Ibid.

100. Tracy Barrett Kittredge, The History of the Commission for Relief in Belgium, 1914–1917 (unknown Publisher, 1918), 1–6, 187–96, 224–35, and 414–25.

101. "Naval Officer and His Italian Bride Are Visiting at Berkley," in Oakland Tribune, 6 October 1919.

102. NHHC, Kittredge, Box 1, folder "Miscellaneous."

103. Stanford, California, Hoover Institute Archives (HIA), Tracy Barrett Kittredge Papers (Kittredge Papers), materials relating to the activities of Kittredge in Europe and at Oxford are found in Boxes 7 and 8.

104. Henry Edgerton Chapin, ed., "Tracy Barrett Kittredge," in The Tomahawk of Alpha Sigma Phi, vol. 17, no. 1 (December 1919), 15–16.

105. HIA, Kittredge Papers, "Naval Orders," 1917–1957, Box 47.

106. Simpson, Anglo-American Naval Relations, 76–123.

107. NHHC, Kittredge Papers, Box 8, "A Brief Summary of the United States Naval Activities in European Waters with Outline of the Organization of Admiral Sims' Headquarters" (Outline of Organization), Tracy Barrett Kittredge, comp., 3 August 1918, 3.

108. King, Fleet Admiral King, 115.

109. LC, King Papers, Box 2, "Organization of Fleet after mobilization," 9 April 1917.

110. Taussig, Queenstown Patrol, 95.

111. John V. Babcock obituary in Los Angeles Times, 10 March, 1955, 37.

112. NWC, King Papers, Box 2, Chronology of European visits 1917–19, Noyes and King comps., 17 November 1918.

113. LC, King Papers, Box 2, "Estimate of the Situation with Regard to the Efficient Development of Operations of the Atlantic Fleet."

114. Ibid.

115. NHHC, Sims Papers, Box 29, Sims to Anne Sims, 25 February 1918.

116. Ibid.

117. NHHC, Kittredge Papers, "Outline of Organization," 6–7. William Sowden Sims, Victory at Sea (New York: Doubleday, Page, & Co., 1920), 240.

118. Dudley W. Knox, "The Elements of Leadership," in Naval Institute Proceedings, vol. 46, no. 12 (December 1920), 1895.

119. Wheeler, Pratt, 71–88.

120. Andrew Boyd, British Naval Intelligence Through the Twentieth Century (Barnsley, United Kingdom: Seaforth Publishing, 2020), 222.

121. Dudley W. Knox, comp., The American Naval Planning Section London (Washington, DC: Navy Department, 1923), 231, 297, 505–07.

122. NWC, King Papers, Box 3, "World War I," typescript circa 1948.

123. NHHC, Kittredge Papers, "Outline of Organization," 1.

124. Ibid., 2.

125. Ibid.

126. Elizabeth B. Drury, "Historical Units of Agencies in the First World War, in Bulletins of the National Archives No. 4 (Washington, DC: National Archives and Records Administration, 1942), 1–31.

127. NHHC, Kittredge Papers, "Outline of Organization, 1–12.

128. King, Fleet Admiral King, 121.

129. Jerry W. Jones, US Battleship Operations in World War I (Annapolis, MD: Naval Institute Press, 1998), 1–51.

130. Hugh Rodman, Yarns of a Kentucky Admiral (Indianapolis, IN: Bobbs-Merrill, 1928), 261–311.

Chapter 5

1. Albert Gleaves A History of the Transport Service: Adventures and Experiences of United States Transports and Cruisers in the World War (New York: George H. Doran, 1921), 237; and Sims, Victory at Sea, 350.

2. LC, King Papers, Box 2, "Estimate of the Situation with Regard to the Efficient Development of Operations of the Atlantic Fleet"; NWC, King Papers, Box 5, "Radio Traffic"; and NHHC, Kittredge Papers, "Outline of Organization."

3. Raymond P. Schmidt, "From Code-Breaking to Policy-Making: Four Decades in the Memorable Career of Russel Willson," in Prologue, vol. 49, no. 2 (Summer, 2016), 25–35; James L. Gilbert and John P. Finnegan, US Army Signals Intelligence in World War II (Washington, DC: Army Center of Military History, 1993), 3–47; and Knox, American Naval Planning Section, 231 and 297.

4. Julian Corbett, League of Peace and a Free Sea (London: Hodder Stoughton, 1917), 1–15.

5. King, Fleet Admiral King, 121.

6. Andrew Gordon, Neptune's Admiral: The Life of Sir Bertram Ramsay—Commander of Dunkirk and D-Day (Cambridge, MA: Harvard University Press, 2023).

7. King, Fleet Admiral King, 121.

8. Knox, American Naval Planning Section, 231, 297, 505–07; Wheeler, Pratt, 104 and 120–22; and King, Fleet Admiral King, 130.

9. LC, King Papers, Box 35, "Thesis III—Senior Class—1933: The Relationship in War of Naval Strategy, Tactics, and Command," 3.

10. NWC, King Papers, Box 3, typescripts and annotated notes, "World War I, 1917–19."

11. King, Fleet Admiral King, 113–45.

12. NWC, King Papers, Box 3, "World War I."

13. King, *Fleet Admiral King*, 120.

14. Ibid.

15. Wheeler, *Pratt,* 107, fn. 21.

16. King, *Fleet Admiral King*, 130.

17. David Kohnen, *Grippe Caught Us Quicker Than U-boats: The Lingering Sickness of War and the Pandemic of 1918–1920* (Newport, RI: Naval War College Foundation, 2020), 1–27.

18. Christopher North (aka John Wilson), "Noctes Ambrosianae" in *Blackwood's Edinburgh Magazine*. vol. 25, no. 42 (April, 1829), 527.

19. Roosevelt, *Fear God and Take Your Own Part*, 185.

20. Geoffrey C. Ward, "FDR's Western Front Idyll," in *Experience of War*, Robert Cowley, ed. (New York: Doubleday, 1992), 352.

21. James Tertius DeKay, *Roosevelt's Navy: The Education of a Warrior President, 1882–1920* (New York: Pegasus, 2012), 251.

22. Morison, *Admiral Sims*, 425–26.

23. NWC, King Papers, Box 7, "Random Notes," circa 1945.

24. NWC, King Papers, Box 3, Whitehill notes.

25. Morison, *Admiral Sims*, 467.

26. LC, Sims Papers, Box 10, Sims to Sims, 20 January 1918.

27. Ibid.

28. Ibid.

29. NWC, King Papers, Box 3, Whitehill notes.

30. Trask, *AEF*, 55–56.

31. King, *Fleet Admiral King*, 127 and 137.

32. NWC, King Papers, Box 7, "Five-Stars."

33. John B. Hattendorf, "The United States Navy in the Mediterranean during the First World War and Its Immediate Aftermath. 1971–23," in *The First World War in the Mediterranean and the Role of Lemnos*, Zisis Fotakis, ed., (Athens: Editions Hêrodotos, 2018), 173–192; Joseph Husband, *On the Coast of France: The Story of US Naval Forces in France* (Chicago, IL: A.C. McClurg & Co., 1919), 26; and Francis T. Hunter, *Beatty, Jellicoe, Sims, and Rodman: Yankee Gobs and British Tars, as Seen by an "Anglomaniac"* (New York: Doubleday, Page, 1919), 16–33.

34. Louis Halewood, "Peace Throughout the Oceans and Seas of the World: British Maritime Strategic Thought and World Order, 1892–1919," in *Historical Research*, vol. 94, no. 265 (August 2021), 554–577.

35. London, British Library, MS 49045, vol. 58, Correspondence and Papers of Jellicoe concerning the Empire Naval Mission, 1918–1920, "League Navy;" Halewood, "Peace throughout the Oceans and Seas of the World," 554–577; and Sims, *Victory at Sea*, 240–43 and 255–65; and Wheeler, *Pratt*, 130–31 and 142.

36. King, *Fleet Admiral King*, 136.

37. Winston S. Churchill, "The Third Great Title-Deed of Anglo-American Liberties," in *Winston Churchill: His Complete Speeches 1897–1963*, Robert Rhodes James, ed. (London: Chelsea House Publishers, 1974), vol. III, 2614.

38. LC, Sims Papers, Box 10, Sims to Sims, 6 July 1918.

39. Ibid.

40. Ibid.

41. Ibid.

42. Jim Leeke, *Nine Innings for the King: The Day Wartime London Stopped for Baseball, July 4, 1918* (Jefferson, NC: McFarland, 2015), 130–74.

43. David Kohnen and Sarah Goldberger, *Remain Cheerful: Baseball, Britannia, and American Independence, 4 July 1918* (Newport, RI: Naval War College Foundation, 2022), 1–63; Sims, *Victory at Sea*, 240–43; *The Daily Mirror*, 5 July 1918, 7–8; and Leeke, *Nine Innings for the King*, 130–74.

44. King, *Fleet Admiral King*, 134.

45. Ibid.

46. NWC, King Papers, Box 7, "ASW Conference of 1 March 1943, Remarks by Admiral King," 2.

47. LC, Records of the Queenstown Association, Boxes 1–3.

48. LC, Sims Papers, Box 80, Queenstown Association, folder contains Sims correspondence and keepsakes. Additional original records relating to the Queenstown Association are available in the Sims and Taussig papers at the Naval War College.

49. NWC, King Papers, Box 3, Whitehill notes on World War I.

50. Sims, *Victory at Sea*, 240–43 and 255–65.

51. NWC, King Papers, Box 3, Whitehill notes on World War I, probably taken in 1948.

52. Nicholas Jellicoe, *The Last Days of the High Seas Fleet: From Mutiny to Scapa Flow* (Barnsley, UK: Seaforth, 2019), 119–135.

53. NWC, Kittredge, Comparative Analysis, 4.

54. NWC, King Papers, Box 8, "Fleet Organization."

55. Ibid.

56. Woodrow Wilson, "Peace without Victory," speech concerning the establishment of a "League for Peace," in 64th Congress, Senate Document No. 685.

57. Morison, *Admiral Sims*, 179. Original in LC, Sims Papers, Box 10, Sims to Herbert Dunn, January 1919.

58. Wheeler, *Pratt*, 130–31.

59. London, British Library, MS 49045, vol. 58, Correspondence and Papers of Jellicoe concerning the Empire Naval Mission, 1918–1920, "League Navy;" Halewood, "Peace Throughout the Oceans and Seas of the World," 554–577; and Sims, *Victory at Sea*, 240–43 and 255–65.

60. NWC, King Papers, Box 8, "Fleet Organization."

61. NWC, Kittredge, Comparative Analysis, 8–9.

62. Harold Sprout and Margaret Sprout, *Toward a New Order of Sea Power: American Naval Policy and the World Scene, 1918–1922* (Princeton, NJ: Princeton University Press, 1940, 140–53; Thomas H. Buckley, The United States and the Washington Conference, 1921–1922 (Knoxville, TN: University of Tennessee Press, 1970), 53–54; and Morison, *Admiral Sims*, 430–70.

63. Albion, *Makers of Naval Policy*, 223–25.

64. Wheeler, *Pratt*, 130–31; Morison, *Admiral Sims*, 430–32, 463–69; and Knox, *The American Naval Planning Section*, 231, 297, 505–07.

65. LC, Benson Papers, Box 42, "Memorandum No. 67: Building Programme," Captains Dudley W. Knox, Frank Schofield, and Luke McNamee, comps., 6–7. Special thanks to my friends Ryan Peeks and Frank Blazich for providing this document for this study.

66. Ibid.

67. Wheeler, *Pratt*, 108.

68. Henry P. Beers with Robert G. Albion, *Administrative Reference Service Report No. 5—US Naval Forces in Northern Russia* (Washington, DC: Navy Department, 1943), 1–58.

69. Knox, *American Naval Planning Section London*; Wheeler, *Pratt*, 104 and 120–22; and King, *Fleet Admiral King*, 130.

70. Kohnen, *Grippe,* 1–27.

71. Jellicoe, *The Last Days*, 119–135.

72. Kittredge, *Naval Lessons*, 360–90.

73. Morison, *Admiral Sims*, 467.

74. Kenneth J. Hagen, "Radical but Right: William Sowden Sims (1878–1936)," in *Nineteen-Gun Salute: Case Studies of Operational, Strategic, and Diplomatic Leadership during the Twentieth and Early Twenty-First Centuries*, John B. Hattendorf with Bruce Elleman, eds., (Newport, RI: Naval War College Press, 2010), 1–12; Deane C. Allard, "Anglo-American Differences during World War I" in *Military Affairs* 45 (April 1980), 75–81; and David F. Trask, "The American Navy in a World at War, 1914–1918," in *In Peace and War: Interpretations of American Naval History, 1775–1978*, Kenneth J. Hagen, ed. (New York: Greenwood Press, 1978), 169–81.

75. Little, "Tarnishing Victory," 1–29.

76. Ryan D. Wadle, *Selling Sea Power: Public Relations and the US Navy* (Norman, OK: University of Oklahoma, 2019), 3–41.

77. Josephus Daniels, "Report of the Secretary of the Navy," in *Annual Report of the Navy Department for Fiscal Year 1913* (Washington, DC: Government Printing Office, 1914), 6.

78. Ibid.

79. Morison, *Admiral Sims,* 289–312; Wheeler, *Pratt*, 71–88; Trent Hone, *Learning War: The Evolution of Fighting Doctrine in the US Navy, 1898–1945* (Annapolis, MD: Naval Institute Press, 2018), 34–54, 56–64, 87–91, and 115–16; and Kohnen, "The US Navy Won the Battle of Jutland," 126–31.

80. LC, Sims Papers, Box 69, Sims to Knox, 22 June 1922.

81. Hattendorf, *Sailors and Scholars*, 113.

82. Anne E. Hitchcock Sims private typescript for an unpublished memoir, as provided by her grandson, Dr. Nathaniel Sims, with permission granted to the author in 2021.

83. Ibid.

84. Trask, *Captains & Cabinets*, 63–65 and 141–42; Trask, *AEF,* 11–12 and 55–56; Still, *Crisis at Sea*, 25–33; and Cooper, *Reconsidering Woodrow Wilson*, 15–16 and 226–28

85. Trask, *AEF*, 55–56 and 166–77.

86. Morison, *Admiral Sims*, 334.

87. Little, "Tarnishing Victory?," 1–29; Wadle, *Selling Sea Power*, 25–53; and Kohnen, "Charting a New Course," 126–27.

88. Lawrence R. Murphy, *Perverts by Official Order: The Campaign against Homosexuals by the United States Navy* (New York: Harrington Park Press, 1988), 154, 162, and 251–99; John Loughery, *The Other Side of Silence: Men's Lives and Gay Identities—a Twentieth-Century History* (New York: Henry Holt, 1998), 1–16; and Ryan Wadle, *Selling Sea Power: The US Navy and Public Relations, 1917–1941* (Norman: University of Oklahoma, 2019), 3–62.

89. USNI, Reminiscences of George Van Deurs, vol. I, 326–7.

90. Wadle, *Selling Sea Power*, 3–62.

91. Ibid.

92. King, *Fleet Admiral King*, 91.

93. NWC, King Papers, Box 13, Whitehill miscellaneous notes on King's recollections of fellow naval officers, 29 August 1949.

94. NWC, King Papers, Box 13, "Staff Duty," 31 July 1949.

95. LC, Leahy Papers, Diary, 29 September 1936.

Chapter 6

1. NWC, King Papers, Box 3, typescripts and annotated notes, "World War I, 1917–19."

2. NWC, unpublished manuscript, "History of the Naval War College to 1937," 97–98.

3. Ibid., 98.

4. NWC, RG 9, Records of the Library Officer, Box 20, "Officer in Charge Historical Section," 1919–23.

5. Drury, "Historical Units," 1–31.

6. LC, Sims Papers, Box 69, Sims to Knox, 22 June 1922.

7. Drury, "Historical Units," 1–31.

8. Holloway H. Frost, *The Conduct of an Overseas Naval Campaign* (Washington, DC: Navy Department, 1920), 1–60.

9. Wheeler, *Pratt*, 74–75.

10. Morison, *Admiral Sims*, 425; Knox, *American Planning Section*, 203–04; and King, *Fleet Admiral King*, 156.

11. Little, "Tarnishing Victory?" 1–29; Wadle, *Selling Sea Power*, 25–53; and Kohnen, "Charting a New Course," 126–27.

12. Ernest J. King, "Some Ideas about the Effects of Increasing the Size of Battleships," in *Proceedings* vol. 45, no. 3 (March 1919), 387–406.

13. Kohnen, "Charting a New Course," 126–27.

14. LC, King Papers, Box 2, BuNav Letter 0839-198, "Report and Recommendations of a Board Appointed by the Bureau of Navigation Regarding the Instruction and Training of Line Officers," 16 October 1919, Supporting Annex, p. 3.

15. Kohnen, *Twenty-First Century Knox*, 1–19.

16. Dudley W. Knox, *The Eclipse of American Sea Power* (New York: Army and Navy Journal, 1922), 1.

17. London, British Library, MS 49045, vol. 58, Correspondence and Papers of Jellicoe concerning the Empire Naval Mission, 1918–1920, "League Navy;" Halewood, "Peace throughout the Oceans and Seas of the World," 554–577; Sims, *Victory at Sea*, 240–43 and 255–65; and Wheeler, *Pratt*, 130–31 and 142.

18. John Maurer and Christopher M. Bell, *At the Crossroads between Peace and War—the London Naval Conference of 1930* (Annapolis, MD: Naval Institute Press, 2014), 1–3, 180–83, and 234–34.

19. David Kahn, *The Code-Breakers: The Story of Secret Writing* (New York: Palgrave Macmillan, 1967),

350–60, 360–64, and 367–68; and David Kahn, *The Reader of Gentlemen's Mail: Herbert O. Yardley and the Birth of American Codebreaking* (New Haven, CT: Yale University Press, 2004), 126–36.

20. Ibid., 94.

21. Ibid., 200–41; Timothy Wilford, *Canada's Road to the Pacific War: Intelligence, Strategy, and the Far East Crisis* (Vancouver: University of British Columbia Press, 2011), 10–12 and 42–50; and Kurt F. Jensen, *Cautious Beginnings: Canadian Foreign Intelligence—1939–51* (Vancouver: University of British Columbia Press, 2008), 40–48.

22. Maochun Yu, *OSS in China: Prelude to Cold War* (Annapolis, MD: Naval Institute Press, 1996), 47.

23. Hector C. Bywater, *Sea-Power in the Pacific: A Study of the American-Japanese Naval Problem* (London: Constable, 1921).

24. NWC, RG 8, folder 5, News clippings and selected articles, Captain Dudley W. Knox, comp., "The Next Great Naval War: Criticism of Hector Bywater's Book, *The Great Pacific War*" (27 August 1925). Also see William H. Honan, *Visions of Infamy: The Untold Story of How Journalist Hector C. Bywater Devised the Plans That Led to Pearl Harbor* (New York: St. Martin's Press, 1991), 143–216; and Gordon W. Prange, *At Dawn We Slept: The Untold Story of Pearl Harbor* (New York: Penguin Books, 1991), 287, 601, 630–31, and 739–56.

25. For a commentary on the seedy culture of Fleet Street journalism from the interwar period, see Evelyn Waugh, *Scoop* (London: Chapman and Hall, 1938).

26. Knox, *Eclipse*, x.

27. Wadle, *Selling Sea Power*, 50–55.

28. Edward Marolda, *Theodore Roosevelt, The US Navy, and the Spanish-American War* (New York: Palgrave Macmillan, 2001), 67–70.

29. Washington, DC, Smithsonian Institution (SI), National Museum of American History (NMAH), Recruiting Posters, 59744-N(16), "Join the Navy and *Free* the World," circa 1942.

30. SI, NMAH, Posters, ZZRSN79679W52, "Join the Navy and *Save* the World," circa 1945.

31. Albion, *Makers of Naval Policy,* 271.

32. Ibid.

33. NWC, King Papers, Box 13, "Adolphus Andrews," 3 November 1949.

34. Ibid.

35. Lafayette, University of Louisiana (UL), Collection No. 25, John M. Caffrey Papers (Caffrey Papers), Series B, Box 2, Caffrey to King letters.

36. King, *Fleet Admiral King*, 158.

37. Special thanks to Edgerton van den Berg for providing access to original envelope and associated documentation.

38. NWC, King Papers, Whitehill notes, "World War I."

39. King, *Fleet Admiral King*, 104–10.

40. Anne Cipriano Venzon, ed., *General Smedley Darlington Butler: Letters of a Leatherneck—1898–1931* (New York: Praeger, 1992), 163.

41. Kittredge, *Naval Lessons*, 42.

42. King, *Fleet Admiral King*, 106.

43. Wadle, *Selling Sea Power*, 7, 17, 174, 179–80, and 185.

44. UL, Caffrey Papers, Caffrey to King.

45. NWC, King Papers, Whitehill notes, "World War I."

46. Morison, *Admiral Sims*, 434–52.

47. Amy Kaplan and Donald E. Pease, *Cultures of United States Imperialism* (Durham, NC: Duke University Press, 1991), 41–58, 85–108, and 219–36.

48. Anon, "The Navy Decorations," in *The New York Times*, 12 November 1920, 14.

49. King, *Fleet Admiral King*, 147.

50. NWC, RG 4, folder 22, Captain Ernest J. King, "Education of Naval Officers, 16 May 1925."

51. LC, King Papers, Box 35, thesis, "The Influence of the National Policy on the Strategy of a War," 7 November 1932, 1–32; LC, King Papers, Box 35, "History of Year's Work—Senior and Junior Classes of 1933," Van Auken and W. C. Wickham, comps., 1–8; and NWC, RG 4, Box 20, Harold R. Stark, comp., "Extracts from Books Read in Connection with War College Reading Courses," vols. 1 and 2.

52. NWC, King Papers, Whitehill notes, "World War I," 74.

53. Ibid.

54. King, *Fleet Admiral King*, 641.

55. Dennis D. Nelson, *The Integration of the Negro into the US Navy* (New York: Farrar, Strauss, and Young, 1951), 1–26; Moriss J. McGregor Jr., *Integration of the Armed Forces, 1940–1965* (Washington, DC: Center of Military History, 1981), 88–89; and NHHC, Navy Department Library, Bureau of Naval Personnel, "Guide to Command of Negro Naval Personnel—NAVPERS-15092 (February 1945).

56. NWC, King Papers, Box 9, Whitehill notes, "Race Relations."

57. NWC, King Papers, Box 7, Whitehill notes, "Five-Stars."

58. Ibid.

59. NWC, King Papers, Box 1, Whitehill Notes, 4 May 1948.

60. King, *Fleet Admiral King*, 170.

61. NARA, NRPC, RG 24, King Service Record, telegram to King, 9 September 1921.

62. King, *Fleet Admiral King*, 156.

63. Ibid.

64. Ibid., 155.

65. Ibid.

66. Ibid.

67. Ibid.

68. Ibid., 156.

69. Ibid., 157.

70. Ibid.

71. NWC, King Papers, Box 2, Schoeffel to Buell, 9 September 1974.

72. Ibid.

73. NARA, NRPC, RG 24, King Service Record, Fitness Report, 1 April 1922.

74. LC, King Papers, Box 35, "Thesis III—Senior Class—1933: The Relationship in War of Naval Strategy, Tactics, and Command," 3.

75. NWC, King Papers, Box 2, Schoeffel to Buell, 9 September 1974.

76. Thomas Wildenberg, *All the Factors of Victory: Admiral Joseph Mason Reeves and the Origins of Carrier Airpower* (Washington, DC: Potomac Books, 2003), 132–33, 170–83, and 214–15; William F. Trimble, *Admiral William A. Moffett: Architect of Naval Aviation* (Washington, DC: Smithsonian Institution Press, 1994), 41–87; and King, *Fleet Admiral King*, 185–88, 206–13, and 240–41.

77. Albion, *Makers of Naval Policy*, 371–74.

78. Kittredge, "Comparative Analysis," 9–10; Knox, *A History of the United States*, 430–35; and Albion, *Makers of Naval Policy*, 178–236.

79. Albion, *Makers of Naval Policy*, 372.

80. Ibid.

81. Laton McCartney, *The Teapot Dome Scandal: How Big Oil Bought the Harding White House and Tried to Steal the Country* (New York: Random House, 2009), 85–143.

82. Ibid., 29, 84–88, 105–12, and 209–28.

83. Wildenberg, *Factors of Victory*, 100–128; 172, 219–23, 260, and 264–66.

84. NWC, Sims Papers, Box 2, Newspaper Clippings.

85. NWC, King Papers, Box 7, Whitehill notes, "Five-Stars."

86. Ibid.

87. Brian McAllister Linn, *The Echo of Battle: The Army's Way of War* (Cambridge, MA: Harvard University Press, 2007), 122–28; Wildenberg, *Billy Mitchell's*, 60–62, 100–10, 121, 149–53, and 167–69; and Alfred Hurley, *Billy Mitchell: Crusader for Air Power* (Bloomington: University of Indiana Press, 1964), 43–48.

88. NWC, King Papers, Box 7, Whitehill notes, "Billy Mitchell," 2 June 1949, 2–3.

89. Brian McAllister Linn, *The Echo of Battle: The Army's Way of War* (Cambridge, MA: Harvard University Press, 2007), 122–28; Wildenberg, *Billy Mitchell's*, 60–62, 100–10, 121, 149–53, and 167–69; and Alfred Hurley, *Billy Mitchell: Crusader for Air Power* (Bloomington: University of Indiana Press, 1964), 43–48.

90. Albion, *Makers of Naval Policy*, 373–76.

91. John T. Kuehn, *Agents of Innovation: The General Board and the Design of the Fleet That Defeated the Japanese Navy* (Annapolis, MD: Naval Institute Press, 2008), 1–22; Trimble, *Moffett*, 45–60; and Wheeler, *Pratt*, 71–88.

92. Albion, *Makers of Naval Policy*, 272.

93. See *Proceedings* vol. 52, no. 3 (March 1926).

Chapter 7

1. Gary E. Weir, *Building American Submarines, 1914–1940* (Washington, DC: Naval Historical Center, 1991), 35–59 and 70–80.

2. United States Congressional Record, House of Representatives, Seventieth Congress, First Session, Report No. 1438 to accompany H.R. 10274, 1 May 1928, "House Committee on Naval Affairs," Francis James Cleary, Resolution for the retroactive promotion of Cleary to the permanent rank of captain, pp. 1–30. Note: Cleary never received his promotion to captain because of the politics of the Navy Department and because of his earlier role in the ongoing disputes with the Electric Boat Company between 1916 and 1927.

Cleary continued serving in the rank of commander on the retired list and remained a trusted adviser to King into the Second World War.

3. Gary E. Weir, *Building American Submarines, 1914–1940* (Washington, DC: Naval Historical Center, 1991), 35–59 and 70–80.

4. Perry, *Dear Bart*, 80–95.

5. Kuhn, *General Staff*, 1–4.

6. Weir, *Building American Submarines*, 35–59.

7. NARA, NRPC, RG 24, King Service Record, Appointment, 1 July 1922.

8. NWC, Low Reminiscences, 2–3.

9. NWC, King Papers, Box 10, "Sinking of *S-5*."

10. NARA, RG 80, General Correspondence of the Secretary of the Navy (SECNAV), Box 2835, folder, "Findings of Investigation," memorandum from King to Taylor with additional recommendations provided to Bureau of Engineering and Bureau of Construction & Repair.

11. NARA, NRPC, RG 24, King Service Record, Fitness Report, 1 October 1922.

12. NARA, NRPC, RG 24, 20 November 1922.

13. LC, King Papers, Box 16, King to Forrestal, 25 January 1946.

14. LC, King Papers, Box 23, Naval War College Correspondence Course materials, 1919–23.

15. NWC, King Papers, McCann Reminiscences, 1–3; NWC, Low Reminiscences, 2–3; and NWC, King Papers, Box 3, Whitehill notes of interview with King, undated.

16. NWC, King Papers, Box 5, Dudley W. Knox to Samuel Eliot Morison, 19 November 1946; and NWC, King Papers, Box 5, Walter Muir Whitehill Notes, "Memorandum of Conversation with Commodore D. W. Knox," 31 May 1946.

17. Ibid.

18. Ibid.

19. NWC, King Papers, Box 3, Whitehill notes of interview with King, undated.

20. Ibid.

21. King, *Fleet Admiral King*, 168–70 and 587; and Buell, *Master of Sea Power*, 67–70 and 156–58.

22. NWC, King Papers, Box 1, "Sinking of *S-5*."

23. NWC, King Papers, Box 1, Memorandum to Bureau of Navigation, Submarine Qualification, 23 February 1923.

24. Ibid.

25. NWC, King Papers, Box 1, Memorandum to Bureau of Navigation, Submarine Qualification, 23 February 1923.

26. NWC, Low Reminiscences, 2–3.

27. King, *Fleet Admiral King*, 167.

28. Ibid.

29. NWC, Low Reminiscences, 3.

30. NWC, King Papers, Box 1, New London Naval Station Newspaper, 1 July 1923.

31. Seymour, *Baseball*, 290–362.

32. US Naval Institute, "Reminiscences of Vice Admiral George C. Dyer" (Dyer Reminiscences), 465.

33. Ibid.

34. NWC, McCann Reminiscences, 1 and 3.

35. King, *Fleet Admiral King*, 166–67.

36. NWC, King Papers, Box 10, Buell Transcription of Taped Interview, "Vice Admiral Alan R. McCann, September 1974," (McCann Reminiscences), 2.

37. Buell, *Master of Sea Power*, 223.

38. Ibid., 3.

39. Ibid.

40. Ibid.

41. Ibid.

42. Ibid.

43. Ibid.

44. NWC, King Papers, McCann Reminiscences, 1–3.

45. Ibid., 13.

46. Ibid.

47. Ibid.

48. Ibid., 6.

49. Ibid.

50. Ibid.

51. Nofi, *Train the Fleet*,1–55 and 56.

52. King, *Fleet Admiral King*, 161.

53. NWC, King Papers, McCann Reminiscences, 1–3.

54. Nofi, *Train the Fleet*, 1–56.

55. NARA, NRPC, RG 24, King Fitness Reports, 30 September 1923.

56. Ibid.

57. NWC, Low Reminiscences, 2–3; McCann Reminiscences, 1–3; and USNI, Neidermair Oral History, 68–120.

58. King, *Fleet Admiral King*, 171.

59. Ibid.

60. Ibid.

61. LC, King Papers, Boxes 24 and 25, "Savaging the Submarine *S-51* and *S-4*"; NWC, King Papers, Box 2, "King Family;"

62. King, *Fleet Admiral King*, 172.

63. Wadle, *Selling Seapower*, 144–47, 170–85, and 215–17

64. LC, King Papers, Boxes 24 and 25, "Savaging the Submarine *S-51* and *S-4*."

65 USNI, Neidermair Oral History, 68–120.

66. King, *Fleet Admiral King*, 173–85.

67. NWC, RG 28, Box 2, Presidents Records, Miscellany, Lynde McCormick.

68. NWC, King Papers, Box 5, Knox to Morison, 19 November 1946.

69. USNI, Neidermair Oral History, 68–120.

70. Ibid.

71. King, *Fleet Admiral King*, 173–85.

72. Edward Ellsberg, *On the Bottom* (New York, Dodd, Meade, and Co., 1929), 1–20; Edward Ellsberg, *Pigboats* (New York: Dodd, Meade, 1930), 1–10; Edward Ellsberg, *Thirty Fathoms Deep* (New York: Harrop, 1941), 12; and King, *Fleet Admiral King*, 173–85.

73. NARA, NRPC, RG 24, King Fitness Reports, 1 April 1926.

74. Ibid.

75. Ibid.

76. Wadle, *Selling Seapower*, 170–85.

77. King, *Fleet Admiral King*, 126–27.

78. NWC, King Papers, Box 7, Whitehill notes, "Admiral Leahy."

79. Ibid.

80. LC, King Papers, King to Johnson (undated), Box 3.

81. NWC, King Papers, Box 3, King to Moffett, August 1926.

Chapter 8

1. NWC, King Papers, Box 18, newspaper clipping, "King's Daughter to Wed Army Pilot."

2. NWC, King Papers, Box 7, Whitehill notes, "Billy Mitchell," 2 June 1949, 2–3.

3. Kohnen, "El Americano," 103–17

4. Wildenberg, *Billy Mitchell's War*, 60–62, 100–10, 121, 149–53, and 167–69.

5. King, *Fleet Admiral King*, 186–214.

6. NWC, King Papers, Box 2, Bidwell to Buell, 2 June 1974, 2.

7. NARA, NRPC, RG 24, King Service Record, ComAirSquadrons, Scouting Fleet to BuAer, 12 October 1926.

8. NARA, NRPC, RG 24, King Service Record, Raby to BuAer, BuNav, ComAirSquadrons, Scouting Fleet, 8 October 1926.

9. NARA, NRPC, RG 24, King Service Record, Moffett to BuNav, 22 October 1926.

10. Ibid.

11. Ibid.

12. NARA, NRPC, RG 24, King Service Record, Chief of BuMed to Chief of BuNav, 21 October 1926.

13. NARA, NRPC, RG 24, King Service Record, Kurtz to Shoemaker, 26 October 1926.

14. Ibid.

15. Thomas Wildenberg, *Destined for Glory: Dive Bombing, Midway, and the Evolution of Carrier Air Power* (Annapolis, MD: Naval Institute Press, 1998), 28–31; William Trimble, *Admiral William A. Moffett: Architect of Naval Aviation* (Washington, DC: Smithsonian Institution Press, 1994), 93–96; Norman Friedman, Thomas C. Hone, and Mark Mandeles, *American and British Aircraft Carrier Development, 1919–1941* (Annapolis, MD: Naval Institute Press, 1999), 145–147; and Kuehn, *Agents of Innovation*, 114–15.

16. Clark G. Reynolds, *On the Warpath in the Pacific: Admiral Jocko Clark and the Fast Carriers* (Annapolis, MD: Naval Institute Press, 2005), 72–73.

17. Ibid.

18. Ibid.

19. Joseph J. Clark with Clark G. Reynolds, *Carrier Admiral* (New York: David McKay Company, Inc., 1967), 3–88.

20. NWC, King Papers, Box 2, Gallery to Buell, 21 August 1974, 1–2.

21. Ibid.

22. Ibid.

23. Ibid.

24. William F. Trimble, *Admiral John S. McCain and the Triumph of Naval Air Power* (Annapolis, MD: Naval Institute Press, 2019), 27.

25. USNI, Reminiscences of Daniel V. Gallery Jr. (Gallery Reminiscences), 23.

26. NWC, King Papers, Box 7, "Comments on Flag Officers, US Navy," 31 July 1949, "Admiral R. K. Turner," 2–3.

27. Ibid., 24.

28. NWC, King Papers, Box 2, Gallery to Buell, 2 August 1974.

29. Ibid., 2.

30. NWC, King Papers, Box 2, Gallery to Buell, 2 August 1974.

31. King, *Fleet Admiral King*, 407–08 and 554–55.

32. USNI, van Deurs Reminiscences, 173.

33. Ibid.

34. Ibid.

35. NWC, King Papers, Box 2, Baker to Buell, 5 August 1974, 1.

36. Ibid.

37. Ibid., 2.

38. Ibid. Emphasis in original.

39. NWC, King Papers, Box, 2, Gallery to Buell, 21 August 1974, 1.

40. USNI, Gallery Reminiscences, 24.

41. USNI, van Deurs Reminiscences, 174–75.

42. Ibid.

43. Ibid.

44. Ibid., 175.

45. USNI, Gallery Reminiscences, 24.

46. NARA, NRPC, RG 24, King Fitness Reports, 1 April 1927.

47. NARA, NRPC, RG 24, King Fitness Reports, 6 June 1927.

48. Ibid., Identification Card, Captain Ernest J. King, USN, 8 December 1927.

49. King, *Fleet Admiral King*, 407–08 and 554–55.

50. NWC, King Papers, Box 2, Whitehill notes on BuAer.

51. Ibid.

52. Joseph A. Williams, *Seventeen Fathoms Deep: The Saga of the Submarine S-4 Disaster* (Chicago: Review Press, 2015), 82 126, 157, 180, and 197.

53. King, *Fleet Admiral King*, 211.

54. Ibid.

55. NWC, King Papers, Box 2, Whitehill notes on BuAer.

56. Ibid.

57. Ibid.

58. Ibid.

59. Rondell R. Rice, *The Politics of Air Power: From Confrontation to Cooperation in Army Aviation Civil-Military Relations* (Lincoln: University of Nebraska Press, 2004), 100–30.

60. NWC, King Papers, Box 13, folder 7, "Comments on Joint Chiefs of Staff," 30–31 July 1949.

61. Rear Admiral J. M. Reeves, "Aviation in the Fleet," US Naval Institute *Proceedings*, 55 (October 1929), 868–69.

62. Wildenberg, *Factors of Victory*, 100–128, 172, 219–23, 260, and 264–66.

63. NWC, King Papers, Box 2, Whitehill notes, undated.

64. Ibid.

65. Ibid.

66. NWC, King Papers, Box 7, "Air Force Bombing," 2.

67. NWC, King Papers, Box 2, Whitehill notes, undated.

68. King, *Fleet Admiral King*, 207.

69. Ibid.

70. Clark, *Carrier Admiral*, 30.

71. Ibid., 211.

72. Ibid.

73. NARA, NRPC, RG 24, King Fitness Reports, 6 August 1928.

74. Ibid.

75. Ibid.

76. NWC, Box 18, Gallery to Buell, 2 August 1974, 2

77. NWC, Manuscript Collection, 308, John H. Hoover Papers (Hoover Papers), Series I, Box 1, Naval Orders, 1930–33.

78. Phil Keith, *Stay the Rising Sun: The True Story of USS* Lexington*, Her Valiant Crew, and Changing the Course of World War II* (Minneapolis: Zenith, 2015), 1–41; Anon., *The Observer: The Queen of the Flattops as We Remember Her: USS* Lexington *CV-2 "Sit Tibi Mare Libis"* (The Minutemen Club / Lexington Veterans, 1998), 1–139; and Nofi, *Train the Fleet*, 173–74.

79. UCL, Heinlein Memoir, 9.

80. William H. Patterson Jr., *In Dialogue with His Century: An Authorized Biography of Robert A. Heinlein—Learning Curve, 1907–1948* (New York: Tor Books, 2010), 126–43; Keith, *Stay the Rising Sun*, 11–35; and UCL, Heinlein Memoir, 1–10.

81. UCL, Heinlein Papers, Box 1, *The Observer*, vol. III, no. 22 (6 September 1930), 2.

82. Clark, *Carrier Admiral*, 45.

83. NWC, King Papers, Box 2, Clark to Buell, 3 September 1974, 2.

84. NWC, King Papers, Box 2, Gallery to Buell, 2 August 1974, 2.

85. Ibid.

86. Ibid.

87. Ibid.

88. Patterson, *In Dialogue with His Century*, 126–43.

89. Ibid.; Edward M. Wysocki Jr., *The Great Heinlein Mystery: Science Fiction, Innovation, and Naval Technology* (Scotts Valley, CA: Create Space Independent Publishing, 2012), 78–79, 98–99, 150–57, 216–17, and 240; Robert Dedman, *May the Armed Forces Be with You: The Relationship between Science Fiction and the United States Military* (Jefferson, NC: McFarland, 2016), 190–95; Michael Okuda, Denise Okuda, and Debbie Mirek, *The Star Trek Encyclopedia: A Reference Guide to the Future* (New York: Simon and Schuster, 1994), 173 and 357; and David Alexander, *Star Trek Creator: The Authorized Biography of Gene Roddenberry* (New York: Penguin, 1996).

Chapter 9

1. Patterson, *In Dialogue with His Century*, 126–70.

2. Trimble, *McCain*, 27.

3. UCL, Heinlein Memoir, 43.

4. UCL, Heinlein Papers, Heinlein to Laning, 8 August 1930.

5. Ibid.

6. Ibid.

7. Ibid.

8. Ibid.

9. UCL, Heinlein Memoir, 43.

10. Ibid.

11. Ibid.

12. Ibid.

13. Ibid., 40–44.

14. NWC, King Papers, Box 2, Heinlein Memoir, 43.

15. Ibid.

16. Ibid.

17. Ibid.

18. Ibid.

19. UCL, Heinlein Memoir, 27.

20. UCL, Heinlein Papers, Box 1, *The Observer*, vol. III, no. 22 (6 September 1930), 2.

21. Ibid.

22. Ibid.

23. Ibid. Emphasis in original.

24. UCL, Heinlein Papers, Box 1, *The Observer*, vol. III. no. 36 (20 December 1930), 3.

25. Ibid.

26. Seymour, *Baseball*, 354 and 359.

27. UCL, Heinlein Memoir, 27. Emphasis in original.

28. Ibid. Emphasis in original.

29. Clark, *Carrier Admiral*, 44.

30. Ibid., 44.

31. Ibid., 45.

32. Ibid., 16.

33. Ibid., 16.

34. UCL, Heinlein Papers, Box 1, *The Observer (of the) US Aircraft Carrier* Lexington, vol. III, no. 22 (6 September 1930), 2.

35. Franklin H. Bruce, *Robert A. Heinlein: America as Science Fiction* (New York: Oxford University Press, 1980), 12, 170–73, and 213.

36. UCL, Heinlein Papers, Box 1, *The Observer* (6 September 1930), 2.

37. UCL, Heinlein Memoir, 37.

38. Ibid.

39. Ibid., 1–65.

40. Ibid., 5.

41. Ibid.

42. Ibid.

43. UCL, Heinlein Memoir, 16.

44. Ibid.

45. NWC, King Papers, Box 2, King to LaChance, 8 June 1938.

46. UCL, Heinlein Memoir, 25–26.

47. Ibid.

48. Ibid.

49. UCL, Heinlein Memoir, 13.

50. Ibid.,10–11.

51. Ibid, 2–3.

52. Ibid.

53. Ibid.

54. NWC, King Papers, Box 2, Whitehill notes, undated.

55. King, *Fleet Admiral King,* 223.

56. NWC, King Papers, Box 13, "Admiral J. H. Towers."

57. Ibid.

58. LC, Papers of John H. Towers (Towers Papers), Box 10, "Henry Harley Arnold."

59. Clark G. Reynolds, "John H. Towers and the Origins of Strategic Flexibility in the Central Pacific Offensive, 1941," in *Naval War College Review*, vol. 40, no. 2 (Spring 1987); 28–36; Reynolds, *John H. Towers*, 457–89; 479–91; and Miller, *War Plan Orange,* 267–85.

60. UCL, Heinlein Memoir, 36.

61. Nofi, *Train the Fleet,* 45.

62. Walter Muir Whitehill, "A Postscript to '*Fleet Admiral King—a Naval Record,*'" in *Proceedings of the Massachusetts Historical Society*, series III, vol. 70 (October 1950–May 1953), 203–22.

63. Ibid.

64. McCrae, *McCrea's War*, 77.

65. Ibid.

66. UCL, Heinlein Memoir, 49–53; NWC, Box 18, King Papers, Scoles to Buell, August 1974; and King, *Fleet Admiral King*, 220–24.

67. Nofi, *Train the Fleet*,143.

68. UCL, Heinlein Memoir, 49–53; NWC, Box 18, King Papers, Scoles to Buell, August 1974; and King, *Fleet Admiral King*, 220–24.

69. King, *Fleet Admiral King*, 222.

70. Ibid., 221–22.

71. UCL, Heinlein Memoir, 46.

72. Ibid.

73. Robert Heinlein, "Searchlight," in *Scientific American*, vol. 207, no. 2 (August 1962), 88–89.

74. UCL, Heinlein Memoir, 46.

75. Ibid., 57. Emphasis in original.

76. NWC, King Papers, Box 2, Whitehill notes, undated.

77. Ibid.

78. King, *Fleet Admiral King*, 219.

Chapter 10

1. UCL, Heinlein Papers, Box 1, *The Observer*, vol. IV, no. 47 (20 February 1932), 4.

2. NWC, King Papers, Box 2, Schoeffel to Buell, 9 September 1974.

3. Ibid.

4. Ibid.

5. Ibid.

6. Ibid.

7. Ibid.

8. Ibid.

9. John T. Kuehn, *A Military History of Japan: From the Age of the Samurai to the Twenty-First-Century* (New York: Praeger, 2014), 192–226.

10. Ibid., 57. Emphasis in original.

11. Patterson, *In Dialogue with His Century*, 162–76, 184, and 217–18.

12. Albion, *Makers of Naval Policy*, 372–73.

13. Ibid., 266–67.

14. Kohnen, "El Americano," 103–17.

15. King, *Fleet Admiral King*, 226.

16. Ibid., Wheeler, *Pratt*, 345–52; and Albion, *Makers of Naval Policy*, 344–45 and 372–73.

17. Nofi, *Train the Fleet*, 58.

18. UCL, Heinlein Memoir, 44.

19. Ibid.

20. Ibid.

21. Ibid.

22. Ibid.

23. King, *Fleet Admiral King*, 226.

24. UCL, Heinlein Memoir, 31.

25. King, *Fleet Admiral King*, 233.

26. UCL, Heinlein Memoir, 22. Emphasis in original.

27. Ibid., 32.

28. Henry H. Adams, *Witness to Power: The Life of Fleet Admiral William D. Leahy* (Annapolis, MD: Naval Institute Press, 1985), 60.

29. UCL, Heinlein Memoir, 35.

30. Ibid., 36.

31. Ibid.

32. Ibid.

33. Ibid., 16–17.

34. Ibid., 17.

35. Ibid.

36. Ibid.

37. Ibid.

38. Ibid., 18.

39. Ibid.

40. Ibid.

41. Ibid.

42. Ibid.

43. UCL, Heinlein Papers, Box 1, *The Observer*, vol. III, no. 44 (28 February 1931), 3.

44. NWC, King Papers, Box 10, McCann Oral History, page 3.

45. Harry Sanders, "King of the Oceans," in Naval Institute *Proceedings*, vol. 100, no. 8 (August 1974), 52–59.

46. Ibid.

47. Ibid.

48. USNI, van Deurs Reminiscences, 322.

49. Frank A. Blazich Jr., "Neptune's Oracle: Admiral Harry E. Yarnell's Wartime Planning, 1918–20 and 1943–44," in *Naval War College Review*, vol. 73, no. 1 (Winter 2020), 107–34.

50. Nofi, *Train the Fleet*, 152.

51. USNI, van Deurs Reminiscences, 325–30.

52. UCL, Heinlein Memoir, 33.

53. Nofi, *Train the Fleet*, 145–52.

54. Clark, *Carrier Admiral*, 48.

55. NWC, King Papers, Box 2, Gallery to Buell, 2 August 1974, 4–5.

56. Nofi, *Train the Fleet*, 154.

57. King, *Fleet Admiral King*, 231.

58. Ibid., 159–60.

59. Kuehn, *Agents of Innovation*, 22–23, 33–38, 123, 171; Wheeler, *Pratt*, 169–214 and 281–376; and Richard S. MacAlpine, *Admiral Frank H. Schofield: A Portrait in Letters of an American Navy Family* (Orange, CA: Infinity Publishing, 2016).

60. Rebecca Wohlstetter, *Pearl Harbor: Warning and Decision* (Stanford, CA: Stanford University Press, 1962), 170–277; Nofi, *Train the Fleet*, 145–52; and McCallister, *Guardians of Empire*, 81–96, 169–87, and 203–31.

61. NARA, NRPC, RG 24, Secretary of the Navy Letter of Commendation and CinCUS Memorandum for Record (issued in 1933).

62. Albion, *Makers of Naval Policy*, 374.

63. Ibid.

64. UCL, Heinlein Papers, Box 1, *The Observer*, vol. III, no. 30 (1 November 1930), 1.

65. Ibid.

66. Ibid.

67. UCL, Heinlein Papers, Box 1, *The Observer*, vol. IV, no. 21 (8 August 1931), 1.

68. Janvier King Smith to author, including examples of personal letters to family signed "Daddy" by King.

69. UCL, Heinlein Memoir, 26.

70. Ibid., 38.

71. Ibid.

72. Ibid.

73. Ibid.

74. Ibid.

75. Ibid., 39.

76. NWC, King Papers, Box 2, Clark to Buell, 3 September 1974, 2. Note: Clark later served as aide to Fleet Admiral William D. Leahy—working with King daily during the Second World War.

77. Janvier King Smith email correspondence with author, 30 November 2020.

78. UCL, Heinlein Memoir, 3–4.

79. Ibid., 4.

80. Ibid.

81. Ibid.

82. UCL, Heinlein Memoir, 40–43.

83. LC, King Papers, Box 35, "Commendation for Communications Efficiency, 1,931–32, USS *Lexington*," 12 September 1932.

84. Ibid., 1.

85. Ibid., 16.

86. UCL, Heinlein Memoir, 14–15.

87. Ibid.

88. UCL, Heinlein Memoir, 14–15.

89. NWC, King Papers, Box 2, Whitehill notes, "The *Lexington* Farewell Party."

90. Ibid., 14–15.

91. Ibid.

92. Email to author from Egerton and Nikki van den Berg, 9 March 2018.

93. NWC, King Papers, Box 7, Whitehill notes, "Naval War College"; and NWC, King Papers, Box 3, Whitehill notes, "Assignment to BuAer."

94. Albion, *Makers of Naval Policy*, 374.

Chapter 11

1. Wheeler, *Pratt, US Navy,* 71.

2. NWC, King Papers, Box 7, Whitehill notes, "Naval War College;" and NWC, King Papers, Box 3, Whitehill notes, "Assignment to BuAer.".

3. King, *Fleet Admiral King,* 242.

4. NARA, NRPC, RG 24, "Last Will and Testament of Ernest J. King."

5. Wildenberg, *Billy Mitchell's War,* 148–88.

6. NWC, RG 4, Box 32, "Memorandum to all Ships and Stations: Naval Air Operating Policy," 28 November 1930.

7. James P. Tate, *The Army and Its Air Corps: Army Policy toward Aviation, 1919–1941* (Maxwell Air Force Base, AL: Air University Press, 1998), 71–78; Kuehn, *Agents of Innovation,* 88–124; and Wildenberg, *Billy Mitchell's War,* 160–61.

8. Albion, *Makers of Naval Policy,* 373–76.

9. Jonathan Katz, *Gangsters of Capitalism: Smedley Butler, the Marines, and the Making and Breaking of America's Empire* (New York: Macmillan, 2022), 1–5, 248, and 316–25.

10. Arthur W. Schlessinger Jr., *The Politics of Upheaval, 1935–36* (Boston, MA: Houghton Mifflin, 2003), 83–85; Smedley Butler, *War Is a Racket* (New York: Roundtable, 1935), 1–52; Felix Morrow, *The Bonus March,* International Pamphlets, no. 31. (New York: International Publishers, 1932), 1–31; and Dorris Clayton James, *The Years of MacArthur: 1880–1941* (New York: Houghton Mifflin, 1970), 391–92.

11. Alfred Thayer Mahan, *The Influence of History upon "Sea Power"* (Boston, MA: Little, Brown, 1890), 11.

12. NWC, RG 4, Box 20, Harold R. Stark, comp., "Extracts from Books Read in Connection with War College Reading Courses," vols. 1 and 2.

13. LC, King Papers, Box 38, "What It Takes to Win a War," 9.

14. Anne Briscoe Pye and Nancy Shea, *The Navy Wife* (New York: Harper, 1942), 193.

15. Ibid.

16. Thorndike, "King of the Atlantic," 100.

17. Ibid.

18. Ibid.

19. Ibid.; Author's interview notes with Egerton van den Berg, 1 March 2018; and Connie Connolly, "The Tall Grandfather in Uniform," *Star Democrat* (7 December 2016).

20. Jim Cheevers with Sharon Kennedy, ed., "The United States Naval Academy, 1845–2020," (Annapolis, MD: Naval Academy Pamphlet), 1–20.

21. Elizabeth Kauffman Bush, *America's First Frogman: The Draper Kauffman Story* (Annapolis, MD: Naval Institute Press, 2004), 16–24.

22. Thorndike, "King of the Atlantic," 100.

23. Janvier King Smith email correspondence with author, 21 June 2019.

24. Connolly, "The Tall Grandfather in Uniform."

25. Author's interview notes with Egerton van den Berg, 1 March 2018.

26. Ibid.

27. Ibid.

28. Connolly, "The Tall Grandfather in Uniform."

29. Author's interview notes with Egerton van den Berg, 1 March 2018.

30. King, *Fleet Admiral King,* 242.

31. LC, King Papers, Box 35, "History of Year's Work—Senior and Junior Classes of 1933," Van Auken and W. C. Wickham, comps., 1–8.

32. Ibid.

33. Hattendorf, *Sailors and Scholars,* 138–61.

34. NWC, RG-4, Box 64, folder 27, "Introductory Remarks—Tactics Course," Commander Roscoe C. MacFall, July 1933.

35. NWC, Low Papers, Box 1, "Orders and Scrap Book."

36. Phillips Payson O'Brian, *The Second Most Powerful Man in the World: The Life of Admiral William D. Leahy, Roosevelt's Chief of Staff* (New York: Random House, 2019), 64–65.

37. King, *Fleet Admiral King,* 242.

38. LC, King Papers, Box 35, "History of Year's Work—Senior and Junior Classes of 1933," Van Auken and W. C. Wickham, comps., 1–8.

39. LC, King Papers, Box 35, thesis, "The Influence of the National Policy on the Strategy of a War," 7 November 1932, 21.

40. Ibid.

41. NWC, RG 15, Box 6, lectures as presented by visiting scholars in 1932 and 1933.

42. NWC, RG 3, Box 119, File P 11-3, "Stoddard, Lathrop."

43. NWC, King Papers, Box 9, "Race Relations."

44. NHHC, "Guide to Command of Negro Naval Personnel"; Nelson, *Integration of the Negro,* 1–26; and McGregor, *Integration of the Armed Forces,* 88–89.

45. Philip S. Foner, ed., *W.E.B. DuBois Speaks: Speeches and Addresses, 1920–1963* (New York: Pathfinder, 1970), vol. 1, 59–67; Carol M. Taylor, "W.E.B. DuBois's Challenge to Scientific Racism," in *Journal of Black Studies,* vol. 11, no. 4 (Winter 1981), 449–460; and Stefan Kühl, *The Nazi Connection: Eugenics, American Racism, and German National Socialism* (New York: Oxford University Press, 1994), 59–62.

46. LC, King Papers, Box 35, "History of Year's Work," 1–8.

47. NWC, King Papers, Box 9, "Race Relations."

48. LC, King Papers, Box 35, thesis, "The Influence of the National Policy on the Strategy of a War," 7 November 1932, 21.

49. NWC, RG 15, Box 6, Lecture, Gordon W. Allport, "Psychology of Propaganda in Peace and War."

50. NWC, RG 15, Box 6, Lecture, Sevellon Brown, "Collection and Dissemination of News."

51. Katheryn S. Olmstead, *The Newspaper Axis: Six Press Barons who Enabled Hitler* (New Haven, CT: Yale University Press, 2022), 116.

52. LC, King Papers, Box 35, thesis, "The Influence of the National Policy on the Strategy of a War," 7 November 1932, 21.

53. Ibid., 22–23.

54. Ibid.

55. Ibid., 24–25.

56. Ibid.

57. Ibid., 26–27.

58. Ibid., 27.

59. Ibid., 4.

60. Ibid., 10.

61. Ibid., 3.

62. Ibid.

63. Ibid.

64. Ibid.

65. Ibid.

66. Ibid., 25.

67. LC, King Papers, Box 35, "Thesis III," 6.

68. Tate, *The Army and Its Air Corps*, 71–78; Kuehn, *Agents of Innovation*, 88–124; and Wildenberg, *Billy Mitchell's War*, 160–61

69. NWC, King Papers, Box 7, King's remarks delivered at the Seattle Athletic Club, 7 August 1934.

70. LC, King Papers, Box 38, "What It Takes to Win a War," 9. Emphasis in original.

71. Ibid.

72. Ibid., 9.

73. NWC, King Papers, Box 7, rough interview notes, 4 July 1950.

74. LC, King Papers, Box 35, "Thesis III," 1–8.

75. LC, King Papers, Box 35, "RED-ORANGE Solution."

76. Ibid.

77. USNI, van Deurs Reminiscences, 236.

78. Ibid.

79. LC, King Papers, Box 35, "RED-ORANGE Solution."

80. LC, King Papers, Box 39, speech file, "Town Hall Meeting," 18.

81. Ibid.

82. LC, King Papers, Box 35, "RED-ORANGE Solution."

83. Henry G. Gole, *The Road to Rainbow: Army Planning for Global War, 1934–1940* (Annapolis: MD: Naval Institute Press, 2002), 1–35 and 40–103; Christopher M. Bell, "Thinking the Unthinkable: British and American Naval Strategies for an Anglo-American War, 1918–1931," in *The International History Review*, vol. 19, no. 4 (November 1997), 789–808; Edward S. Miller, *War Plan Orange: The US Strategy to Defeat Japan, 1897–1945* (Annapolis, MD: Naval Institute Press, 2001), 2–3, 11–13, 263–71, and 364–66; and Nofi, *Train the Fleet*, 220–67.

84. Ibid.

85. Ibid.

86. Ibid.

87. Gole, *The Road to Rainbow*, 1–35 and 40–103.

88. LC, King Papers, Box 35, thesis, "The Influence of the National Policy on the Strategy of a War," 31–33.

89. Ibid.

90. Ibid., 33.

91. Hattendorf, *Sailors and Scholars*, 145.

92. Gerald E. Wheeler, "The War College Years of Admiral Harris Laning, US Navy," in *Naval War College Review* Vol. 22, No. 3 (March, 1969), 69–87.

93. Alan D. Zimm, "The USN's Flight Deck Cruisers," in *Warship International*, vol. 16, no. 3 (1979) 216–45; R. D. Layman and Stephen McLachlan, *The Hybrid Warship: The Amalgamation of Big Guns and Aircraft* (London: Conway Maritime, 1990), 50–62; and Malcolm Muir, *The Iowa Class Battleships: Iowa, New Jersey,*

Missouri, and Wisconsin (New York: Sterling, 1989), 8–41 and 129–30.

94. NWC, MSC-116, Caleb Laning Papers, Box 1; UCL, Heinlein Memoir, 14–15, 40–50, and 58–61; Patterson, *In Dialogue with His Century*, 126–43; and Wysocki, *The Great Heinlein Mystery*, 78–79, 98–99, 150–57, 216–17, and 240.

95. NWC, King Papers, Box 7, Whitehill notes, "Naval War College"; and NWC, King Papers, Box 3, Whitehill notes, "Assignment to BuAer."

96. NWC, RG 13, Box 157, Henry T. Mayo, "Modification of US Strategy Towards Latin America"; LC, Henry T. Mayo Papers, Box 15, Speeches, 1922–1934, "Atlantic Fleet Operations in the Great War"; LC, King Papers, Box 35, "History of Year's Work—Senior and Junior Classes of 1933," Van Auken and W. C. Wickham, comps., 1–8; and LC, King Papers, Box 26, Commander in Chief, Atlantic Fleet to the Bureau of Navigation (Mayo to Washington), "Education and the Training of Officers for Staff Duty," 20 February 1919.

97. LC, Sims Papers, Box 48, Sims to Fullam, March 1922.

98. United States Congress, 68th Congress, House of Representatives, "Hearings before the Select Committee of Inquiry into the Operations of the United States Air Services," Sims testimony, 2,959–3,015.

99. M. Ernest Marshall, *Rear Admiral Herbert V. Wiley: A Career in Airships and Battleships* (Annapolis, MD: Naval Institute Press, 2019), 1–20.

100. LC, King Papers, Box 35, Flight Certificate and Schedule, USS *Akron,* 4 November 1932.

101. NWC, King Papers, Box 3, Whitehill notes, "Assignment to BuAer."

102. Ibid.

103. Ibid.

104. LC, King Papers, speech file, Box 39, "Principles Relating to Command, Organization, Administration." Of note, the draft handwritten notes from 1934 are appended to a 1946 document about King's dissenting opinion about the establishment of the US Air Force.

105. Ibid.

106. Ibid.

107. Ibid.

Chapter 12

1. Dudley W. Knox, "Introduction: The United States Navy between World Wars," in *History of United States Naval Operations in World War II—the Battle of the Atlantic*, Samuel Eliot Morison, ed. (Boston, MA: Little, Brown, 1947), xxxiv–lxii.

2. Gole, *The Road to Rainbow*, 1–35 and 40–103; Bell, "Thinking the Unthinkable," 789–808; Miller, *War Plan Orange*, 2–3, 11–13, 263–71, and 364–66; and Nofi, *Train the Fleet*, 220–67.

3. King, *Fleet Admiral King*, 317.

4. Tate, *The Army and Its Air Corps*, 71–78; Kuehn, *Agents of Innovation*, 88–124; and Wildenberg, *Billy Mitchell's War*, 160–61.

5. Albion, *Makers of Naval Policy*, 373.

6. Trimble, *McCain*, 27.

7. Newport, Rhode Island, Naval War College (NWC), Manuscript Register Series 22, Walter M. Whitehill and

Thomas B. Buell comps., Fleet Admiral Ernest J. King Papers (King Papers), Box 4, Topper to Buell, 27 September 1974.

8. Franklin D. Roosevelt, "Inaugural Address, March 4, 1933," in Samuel Rosenman, ed., *The Public Papers of Franklin D. Roosevelt, Volume Two: The Year of Crisis, 1933* (New York: Random House, 1938), 11–16.

9. Edward C. Kalbfus, "The Naval War College: Bright Officers Fight Imaginary Battles," in *Life* magazine, vol. 9, no. 18 (28 October 1940), 60.

10. Ibid.

11. Ibid.

12. Clark G. Reynolds, *The Fast Carriers: The Forging of an Air Navy* (New York: McGraw Hill, 1968), 1–3, 39–50, and 361.

13. Trimble, *McCain*, 27.

14. LC, King Papers, Box 1, "Orders to Duty," 1 May 1933, from Chief of Bureau of Navigation to Captain Ernest J. King via the president of the Naval War College.

15. LC, King Papers, Box 1, "Report by Committee on Agenda," 24 May 1933.

16. Ibid.

17. NWC, King Papers, Box 4, Whitehill notes, 3 May 1947.

18. USNI, van Deurs Reminiscences, 318–28.

19. King, *Fleet Admiral King*, 242.

20. NWC, King Papers, Box 5, Pratt to Swanson, 28 April 1933

21. Albion, *Makers of Naval Policy*, 266–68, 373, and 512–46.

22. LC, King Papers, Box 4, King to Babcock, 15 May 1933.

23. LC, King Papers, Box 1, "Orders to Duty," 1 May 1933, from Chief of Bureau of Navigation to Captain Ernest J. King via the president of the Naval War College.

24. NWC, King Papers, Box 7, Whitehill typewritten notes.

25. LC, King Papers, Box 4, Cook to King, 21 April 1933.

26. Ibid.

27. NWC, King Papers, Box 7, "Comments on Flag Officers, US Navy," 31 July 1949, 6.

28. Ibid.

29. Ibid.

30. NWC, King Papers, Box 7, Whitehill typewritten notes.

31. Ibid.

32. NWC, King Papers, Box 1, "Miscellaneous Notes," undated.

33. NWC, King Papers, Box 7, "Comments on Flag Officers, US Navy," 31 July 1949, 6.

34. NWC, King Papers, Box 13, "Adolphus Andrews," 3 November 1949.

35. LC, King Papers, Box 4, King to Babcock, 1 May 1933.

36. Ibid.; and King to Cook, 24 April 1933.

37. LC, King Papers, Box 35, "History of Year's Work," 8.

38. Perry, *Dear Bart*, 328.

39. Ibid.

40. Dudley W. Knox, "Bases Mean Ships," *Marine Corps Gazette*, vol. 18, no. 1 (February 1934): 5; NWC,

King Papers, Box 1, "Advanced Bases West of Hawaii," 21 September 1939; and Jennifer Muzzara, *Shared Experience Organization Culture and Ethos at the Marine Corps Basic School, 1924–1941* (Quantico, VA: Marine Corps University Press, 2023), 111–15.

41. Albion, *Makers of Naval Policy,* 542–45.

42. Craig L. Symonds, *American Naval History: A Very Short Introduction* (New York: Oxford University Press, 2018), 80.

43. Theodore Roosevelt, *America and the World War—Fear God and Take Your Own Part* (New York: Charles Scribner's Sons, 1926), 122–35.

44. Wildenberg, *Billy Mitchell's War with the Navy*, 167–70.

45. NARA, RG 72, Records of BuAer, Entry 67, King to the General Board, 27 March 1934.

46. Ibid.

47. Ibid.

48. Wildenberg, *Billy Mitchell's War with the Navy*, 167–70.

49. LC, King Papers, Box 4, King to Babcock, 15 May 1933.

50. NWC, King Papers, Box 1, Whitehill Notes.

51. NWC, King Papers, Box 8, Chief of Naval Operations Organization, 1.

52. Janvier King Smith email correspondence with author, 21 June 2019.

53. Perry, *Dear Bart*, 11.

54. Ibid.

55. Ibid.

56. Ibid., 48.

57. Ibid.

58. Thorndike, "King of the Atlantic," 100.

59. Ibid.

60. NWC, King Papers, Box 1, Whitehill Notes.

61. NWC, King Papers, Box 8, Chief of Naval Operations Organization, 1.

62. Ibid., 2.

63. NWC, King Papers, Box 8, "Admiral Nimitz," 31 July 1949.

64. *Time*, "Stormy Man, Stormy Weather," 17.

65. Independence, Missouri, Harry S Truman Presidential Library and Museum, Oral History with John H. Tolan Jr. (March 1970), 12–13, 127–28, 135–39.

66. Chisholm, *Waiting for Dead Men's Shoes*, 681–94.

67. USNI, van Deurs Reminisences, 276–79.

68. Ibid.

69. NWC, King Papers, Box 8, "Admiral Nimitz," 31 July 1949.

70. Ibid.

71. King, *Fleet Admiral King,* 693–95.

72. Ibid.

73. NWC, King Papers, Box 8, "Admiral Nimitz," 31 July 1949.

74. James M. Merrill, *A Sailor's Admiral: A Biography of William F. Halsey Jr.* (New York: Crowell, 1976), 11.

75. Ibid.

76. USNI, van Deurs Reminiscences, 279.

77. NWC, King Papers, Box 13, "Admiral J. H. Towers"; and LC, Papers of John H. Towers (Towers Papers), Box 3, "Eye Care, 1933–1939."

78. Ibid.

79. King, *Fleet Admiral King*, 262–63.

80. Ibid., 262.

81. NWC, King Papers, Box 8, "Admiral Nimitz."

82. Ibid.

83. Ibid.

84. Buell, *Master of Seapower*, 50–80.

85. Trimble, *McCain*, 33–40.

86. Ibid.

87. Clark, *Carrier Admiral*, 44.

88. NWC, King Papers, Box 9, Whitehill notes, "Race Relations."

89. King, *Fleet Admiral King*, 322.

90. Ibid.

91. McGregor, *Integration*, 88–89; NARA, RG 24, Records of the Bureau of Naval Personnel, Entry 93, Cards, Location Reference NAI, 19E-4 7/13/05, Box 62, "Use of Negroes for Aviation Assignments, 1935"; NARA, RG 80, General Records of the Department of the Navy, 80 /3/2, "Negro Spindle File, 1942;" and NWC, King Papers, Box 9, Whitehill notes, "Race Relations."

92. King, *Fleet Admiral King*, 221.

93. Rice, *The Politics of Air Power*, 100–30.

94. Wildenberg, *Billy Mitchell's War*, 168.

95. Miller, *War Plan Orange*, 177.

96. King, *Fleet Admiral King*, 247–66.

97. James P. Duffy, *Lindbergh vs. Roosevelt: The Rivalry That Divided America* (Washington, DC: Regnery, 2010), 26–41; Arthur Herman, *Freedom's Forge: How American Business Produced Victory in World War II* (New York: Random House, 2012), 292–99, 305; Dana Parker, *Building Victory: Aircraft Manufacturing in the Los Angeles Area in World War II*. Cypress, CA: Dana Parker Enterprises, 2013), 40–43; and Tate, *Army and Its Air Corps*, 138–150.

98. Wildenberg, *Billy Mitchell's War*, 168–69; Wildenberg, *Destined for Glory*, 120–23; and King, *Fleet Admiral King*, 266–78.

Chapter 13

1. Albion, *Makers of Naval Policy*, 603.

2. Kuehn, *Agents of Innovation*, 58. Special thanks to John Kuehn for showing the differences between the official script and the extemporaneous remarks, as filmed and recorded at the Naval Academy in 1933.

3. Douglas MacArthur, *Reminiscences* (New York: McGraw Hill, 1964), 101.

4. Ibid.

5. Kohnen, *Twenty-First-Century Knox*, 1–2, 107–10, and 121–44.

6. Bayly, *Pull Together*, 222.

7. Annapolis, Maryland, US Naval Academy, Nimitz Library, William J. Sebald Papers, Boxes 1–70.

8. Special thanks to retired Rear Admiral Katsuya Yamamoto and Captain Riyuji Honmyo for their assistance in accessing Japanese Maritime Self-Defense Force (JMSDF) files on Sebald.

9. NARA, RG 38, Entry 48-A, Box 4, Naval Mission to Peru, "Operations for the Month of May," Pye to ONI, 29 May 1929. See Kliemann, *US Naval War College & Escuela Superior de Guerra Naval del Perú*, 81–82.

10. Clayton, *The Years of MacArthur*, 479–506.

11. Franklin D. Roosevelt, "Shall We Trust Japan?," *Asia: The American Magazine on the Orient*, vol. 23, no. 7 (July, 1923), 475–78.

12. Albion, *Makers of Naval Policy*, 344–45.

13. MacArthur, *Reminiscences*, 99–106.

14. Herbert Hoover with George H. Nash, ed., *Freedom Betrayed: Herbert Hoover's Secret History of the Second World War and Its Aftermath* (Stanford, CA: Hoover Institution, 2011), 759–65 and 832–35.

15. NWC, Manuscript Collection MSC-141, Charles P. Snyder Papers (Snyder Papers), Series VI, Box 8, Task Force/Fleet Organization, "Organization, Battle Force, Efficiency of."

16. King, *Fleet Admiral King*, 255–65.

17. United States Congress, Seventy-Fourth Congress, House Document No. 342, "Register of Commissioned and Warrant Officers of the United States Navy and Marine Corps—1 July 1936" (Washington, DC: Government Printing Office, 1936), 14–17.

18. Ibid.

19. Julian Corbett, *England in the Seven Years War* (London: Longman's, Green, 1918), Vol. I, 3–4.

20. King, *Fleet Admiral King*, 255–65.

21. Miller, *War Plan Orange*, 179.

22. King, *Fleet Admiral King*, 260–78. Borneman, *Admirals*, 174–75; and Buell, *Master of Sea Power*, 108–09.

23. Chisholm, *Waiting for Dead Men's Shoes*, 181, 223, 305–06, 664, 670, 684, 689, 715–18, and 733.

24. NWC, King Papers, Box 3, "Admiral Leahy's Successor as Chief of Naval Operations—1939," 3.

25. Charleston, South Carolina Historical Society (SCHS), Collection #0598.00, Admiral Paul E. Pihl Papers (Pihl Papers), Aviators Flight Logbook (1 April 1935 to 12 April 1938), Box 1, folder 1.

26. King, *Fleet Admiral King*, 264–78.

27. Ibid., "Standard Diary," 1 January 1938 to 9 January 1939, Box 1, folder 4.

28. King, *Fleet Admiral King*, 269.

29. King, *Fleet Admiral King*, 272.

30. NWC, King Papers, Box 6, King to Bull, 3 April 1937.

31. King, *Fleet Admiral King*, 264–78.

32. Lawrence Safford with Cameron A. Warren and Robert R. Payne, eds., *Earhart's Flight into Yesterday: The Facts without the Fiction* (McLean, VA: Paladwr Press, 2003), 57–70, 148–59, and 163–96.

33. NARA, RG 38, Entry 81, General Correspondence, 1929–1942, Box 70, File A4-3/Earhart; RG 38, NARA Identifier 305240, "Report of the Search for Amelia Earhart, July 2–18, 1937," 1–91; USNI, Oral History of Thomas H. Dyer, 194; and USNI, Oral History of Stephen Jurika Jr. (Jurika Oral History), vol. 1, 282–84.

34. Safford, *Earhart's Flight into Yesterday*, 148–59 and 163–96.

35. NWC, King Papers, Box 5, Whitehill notes, 5 November 1946.

36. NWC, King Papers, Box 10, oral history transcript, Rear Admiral Paul Pihl and Charlotte Willkie Pihl.

37. Ibid. See NWC, King Papers, Box 18, correspondences from the individuals listed and interview notes as collected by Buell, dating from 1974 to 1975.

38. Gallery, *Clear the Decks*, 96.

39. Ibid.

40. Ibid.

41. NWC, King Papers, Box 2, Gallery to Buell, 21 August 1974.

42. Gallery, *Clear the Decks*, 96.

43. Ibid.

44. Author's interview with Lena Bunch (Townsend), 18 May 2022.

45. Eric Larrabee, *Commander in Chief: Franklin Delano Roosevelt, His Lieutenants, and Their War* (Annapolis, MD: Naval Institute Press, 1987), 171–75; Jonathan W. Jordan, *American Warlords: How Roosevelt's High Command Led Americans to Victory in World War II* (New York: Penguin Random House, 2015), 283; and Buell, *Master of Seapower*, 106–08.

46. NWC, King Papers, Box 18, correspondences from the individuals listed and interview notes as collected by Buell, dating from 1974–1975.

47. NWC, King Papers, Box 10, Buell interview with RADM and Mrs. Boynton Brown, 8 December 1974.

48. Richard B. Frank, *Tower of Skulls: A History of the Asia-Pacific War, July 1937–May 1942* (New York: Norton, 2020), 59–61, 88–89, 99–102, 409, 495–501; Iris Chang, *The Rape of Nanking: The Forgotten Holocaust of World War II* (New York: Penguin, 1997), 35–105 and 159–168; and Hans-Joachim Krug, Yoichi Hirama, Berthold J. Sander-Nagashima, and Axel Niestlé, *Reluctant Allies: German-Japanese Naval Relations in World War II* (Annapolis, MD: Naval Institute Press, 2001), 9–12 and 80–82.

49. Hamilton Darby, *The Panay Incident: Prelude to Pearl Harbor* (New York: Macmillan, 1969), 1–20.

50. Murfett, *Fool-Proof Relations*, xiii–xv, 3–26, 104–08, 120–25, and 286–296.

51. Albion, *Makers of Naval Policy*, 88.

52. NWC, King Papers, Box 7, "Memorandum of conversation with Admiral E. C. Kalbfus, USN (ret.), 18 February 1946 concerning relations of CNO and CinCUS in peacetime."

53. William D. Leahy, *I Was There: The Personal Story of the Chief of Staff to Presidents Roosevelt and Truman, Based on His Notes and Diaries Made at the Time* (New York: Whittlesey House, 1950), 64.

54. In US naval vernacular of the time, "Tare" is the phonetic term for the letter "T." See Morison, *US Naval Operations*, Vol. I, 16.

55. King, *Fleet Admiral King*, 244–94.

56. Nofi, *Train the Fleet*, 287.

57. Walter Lippmann, *US Foreign Policy: Shield of the Republic* (Boston, MA: Little, Brown, 1943), 27–77, 81–113, 119–36, and 161–77.

58. Ibid., 176–77.

59. Lippmann, *US Foreign Policy*, 176.

60. Gole, *The Road to Rainbow*, 1–35 and 40–103; Bell, "Thinking the Unthinkable," 789–808; Miller, *War Plan Orange*, 2–3, 11–13, 263–71, and 364–66; and Nofi, *Train the Fleet*, 220–67.

61. Nofi, *Train the Fleet*, 229.

62. NWC, King Papers, Box 3, "Admiral Leahy's Successor as Chief of Naval Operations—1939," 3.

63. Ibid.

64. Nofi, *Train the Fleet*, 229–237.

65. Logan C. Ramsey, "Aerial Attacks on Fleets at Anchor," in Naval Institute *Proceedings*, vol. 63, no. 8 (August, 1937), 1,126–40.

66. Stephen Jurika Jr., "Pilots, Man Your Planes," in *Saturday Evening Post*, vol. 211, issue 30 (21 January 1939), 23–30.

67. Nofi, *Train the Fleet*, 240.

68. NWC, RG-4, Box 64, folder 27, "Introductory Remarks—Tactics Course," Commander Roscoe C. MacFall, July 1933.

69. Norman Friedman, *Winning a Future War: War Gaming and Victory in the Pacific War* (Washington, DC: Naval History and Heritage Command, 2019), 2; Douglas Smith, *Carrier Battles: Command Decision in Harm's Way* (Annapolis, MD: Naval Institute Press, 2006), 9; and Nofi, *Train the Fleet*, 52.

70. NWC, MSC-364/MSI024, Nimitz to Charles L. Melson, 14 September 1965, page 2.

71. NWC, RG-4, Box 64, folder 27, "Introductory Remarks—Tactics Course," Commander Roscoe C. MacFall, July 1933, LC, King Papers, Box 35, "History of Year's Work," 1–8.

72. Kuehn, *America's First General Staff*, 187–88, 192–93, 195–98, and 200–224.

73. NWC, King Papers, Box 5, Whitehill notes, 5 November 1946.

74. Nofi, *Train the Fleet*, 240.

75. James D. Hornfischer, *Ship of Ghosts: The Story of USS Houston. FDR's Legendary Lost Cruiser and the Epic Saga of Her Survivors* (New York: Bantam, 2006), 5–65.

76. Borneman, *The Admirals*, 171–80; Nofi, *Train the Fleet*, 143–54 and 160–64; and NWC, King Papers, Box 3, "Admiral Leahy's Successor as Chief of Naval Operations—1939," 2.

77. Albion, *Makers of Naval Policy*, 88.

78. Carl Boyd, *Hitler's Japanese Confidant: General Ōshima Hiroshi and MAGIC Intelligence, 1941–1945* (Lawrence: University Press of Kansas, 1993), 18–19, 57–74; Carl Boyd, "How Not to Cooperate: National Socialist Germany and Imperial Japan," in Dennis E. Showalter, *Future Wars: Coalition Operations in Global Strategy* (Chicago: Imprint Publications, 2002), 79–88; and John W. M. Chapman, *The Price of Admiralty: The War Diary of the German Naval Attaché in Japan, 1939–1943* (Ripe-Sussex, UK: Saltire, 1982), vol. I, 80–111.

79. Greg Kennedy, *Anglo-American Strategic Relations and the Far East, 1933–1939: Imperial Crossroads* (Portland, OR: Frank Cass, 2002), 1–50 and 211–67.

80. LC, King Papers, Box 39, "An Address by Fleet Admiral Ernest J. King, at the National Exchange Club Convention," in *The Exchangite*, vol. 26, no. 11 (November 1947), 4.

Chapter 14

1. Richard B. Frank, "Picking Winners?" in *Naval History* magazine, vol. 25, no. 3 (May, 2011), 24–30.

2. King, *Fleet Admiral King*, 103 and 114–45.

3. *Time*, "Stormy Man, Stormy Weather," 17.

4. Richardson, *On the Treadmill*, 1–12.

5. Thorndike, "King of the Atlantic," 93–108; *Time*, "Stormy Man, Stormy Weather," 19–18; and King, *Fleet Admiral King*, 304–5.

6. NWC, King Papers, Box 3, "Admiral Leahy's Successor as Chief of Naval Operations—1939," 3.

7. NARA, NRPC, RG 24, Service Record, Personal Characteristics, King, Ernest J.

8. Gallery, *Clear the Decks*, 96.

9. Ibid., 212; Borneman, *Admirals*, 156–57; and Trimble, *McCain*, 27.

10. NWC, King Papers, Box 3, "Admiral Leahy's Successor as Chief of Naval Operations—1939," 2.

11. LC, King Papers, Box 17, Kalbfus to King, 19 June 1939.

12. Ibid.

13. Ibid.

14. Ibid.

15. Ibid.

16. Ibid.

17. E. B. Potter, *Bull Halsey: A Biography* (Annapolis, MD: Naval Institute Press, 1985), 142–43.

18. NWC, King Papers, Box 3, "Admiral Leahy's Successor as Chief of Naval Operations—1939," 2.

19. Thorndike, "King of the Atlantic," 93–108; *Time*, "Stormy Man, Stormy Weather," 19–18; and King, *Fleet Admiral King*, 304–5.

20. John Gunther, *Roosevelt in Retrospect: A Profile in History* (New York: Harper Brothers, 1950), 45 and 81.

21. King, *King's Navy*, 291.

22. Ibid.

23. Ibid.

24. NWC, King Papers, Box 8, "Admiral Nimitz," 31 July 1949.

25. NWC, King Papers, Box 3, "Admiral Leahy's Successor as Chief of Naval Operations—1939," 1.

26. Ibid.

27. William D. Leahy, *I Was There: The Personal Story of the Chief of Staff to Presidents Roosevelt and Truman, Based on His Notes and Diaries Made at the Time* (New York: Whittlesey House, 1948), 4.

28. Alfred W. McCoy and Francisco A. Scarano, eds., *Colonial Crucible: Empire in the Making of the Modern American State* (Madison: University of Wisconsin, 2009), 435–40.

29. Albion, *Makers of Naval Policy*, 56, 171, and 175–77.

30. NWC, King Papers, Box 3, "Admiral Leahy's Successor as Chief of Naval Operations—1939.

31. Albion, *Makers of Naval Policy*, 175.

32. Ibid., 512–22 and 545–569.

33. Ibid., 175.

34. King, *Fleet Admiral King*, 293.

35. Ibid, 291.

36. NWC, King Papers, Box 3, "Admiral Leahy's Successor as Chief of Naval Operations—1939.

37. Ibid.

38. King, *Fleet Admiral King*, 291.

39. LC, King Papers, Box 20, King to Keeper of Records, 9 November 1946; Smith email to author, 8 February 2023; and King, *Fleet Admiral King*, 292.

40. King, *Fleet Admiral King,* 293–94.

41. NWC, King Papers, Box 3, "Admiral Leahy's Successor as Chief of Naval Operations—1939.

42. Ibid.

43. Ibid.

44. Ibid.

45. Ibid.

46. NWC, King Papers, Box 2, Schoeffel to Buell, 9 September 1974.

47. Ibid.

48. Corbett, *League of Peace*, 1–15.

49. LC, King Papers, Box 39, "Naval Strategy and Tactics," 3.

50. Perry, *Dear Bart*, 79–81 and 325–30.

51. King, *Fleet Admiral King*, 291–94.

52. Ibid., 317.

53. Albion, *Makers of Naval Policy,* 88, 391–94, and 430–60.

54. Ibid., 549.

55. LC, King Papers, Halsey to King, 22 June 1939.

56. Ibid.

57. Bruce Orriss, *When Hollywood Ruled the Skies: The Aviation Film Classics of World War II* (Los Angeles, CA: Aero, 1985), 26–7.

58. King, *Fleet Admiral King*, 285.

59. Ibid., 116.

60. Ibid.

61. NWC, Kittredge, "Comparative Analaysis," 13.

62. Ibid.

63. Maochen Yu, *OSS in China: Prelude to Cold War* (New Haven, CT: Yale University Press, 1996), 50.

64. Samuel J. Cox, "The China Theater, 1944–45: A Failure of Joint and Combined Operations Strategy," Master's thesis, US Army Command and General Staff College (Fort Leavenworth, KS, 1993), 37–40.

65. Winston S. Churchill, *While England Slept: A Survey of World Affairs, 1932–1938* (New York: Putnam, 1938), 350–404.

66. NWC, King Papers, Box 7, "Admiral of the Fleet Sir Dudley Pound;" King, *Fleet Admiral King*, 74; and Robin Broadhurst, *Churchill's Anchor: The Biography of Admiral of the Fleet Sir Dudley Pound* (London: Pen and Sword, 2000), 22–52, 186, 205–7, and 216–238.

67. FDR, Great Britain Diplomatic Files, Diplomatic Correspondence, chronologically arranged by personality, Roosevelt to Chamberlain, 11 September 1939, and Roosevelt to Churchill, 11 September 1939.

68. David Reynolds and Vladimir Pechatonov, *The Kremlin Letters: Stalin's Wartime Correspondence with Churchill and Roosevelt* (New Haven, CT: Yale University Press, 2019); Jon Meacham, *Franklin and Winston: An Intimate Portrait of an Epic Friendship* (New York: Random House, 2003); and David Kennedy, *Freedom from Fear: The American People in Depression and War, 1929–1945* (New York: Oxford University Press, 1999), 381–515.

69. TNA, ADM 205, vol. 9, "Correspondence with British Admiralty Delegation, Washington. United States Naval Co-operation," (ADM 205/9), part 2—April–December 1941, Letter from Little to Pound, 15 July 1941.

70. Abbazia, *Mr. Roosevelt's Navy*, 119–23 and 141–42.

71. NARA, RG 313, Records of the Operating Forces, Atlantic Squadron and Patrol Force (Atlantic Squadron), Dispatches, Box 23, dispatch of 26 October 1939.

72. For one account, see Otto Giese and James Wise, *Shooting the War: The Memoir and Photographs of a U-boat Officer in World War II* (Annapolis, MD: Naval Institute Press, 1994), 3–48.

73. Abbazia, *Mr. Roosevelt's War*, 30–31.

74. Beesly, *Very Special Intelligence*, 152.

75. Ibid., 30–31, 52–59, 65, and 92.

76. NWC, Henry C. Eccles Library, Office of Naval Intelligence, "Engagement between *Admiral Graf Spee* and the British Cruisers *Exeter*, *Ajax*, and *Achilles* off Uruguay, 13 December 1939," shelf reference D772.G7 U5 1940.

77. Eric Grove, *The Price of Disobedience: The Battle of the River Plate Reconsidered* (Annapolis, MD: Naval Institute Press, 2000), 151.

78. Abbazia, *Mr. Roosevelt's Navy*, 48.

79. NWC, Low Reminiscences, 8.

80. Ibid.

81. Ibid.

82. Ibid.

83. USNI, Neidermair Oral History, 239.

84. Leahy, *I Was There*, 4.

85. Carlisle, *Where the Fleet Begins*, 89–207.

86. Thorndike Jr., "King of the Atlantic," 93–108.

87. Kuehn, *America's First General Staff*, 187–88, 192–93, 195–98, and 200–224.

88. Perry, *Dear Bart*, 86.

89. Kuehn, *America's First General Staff*, 194–206.

90. Albion, *Makers of Naval Policy*, 83.

Chapter 15

1. Herbert Feis, *Churchill-Roosevelt-Stalin: The War They Waged and the Peace they Sought* (Princeton, NJ: Princeton University Press, 1957), 3–46; William Hardy McNeill, *America, Britain, and Russia: Their Co-operation and Conflict, 1941–1946* (New York: Johnson Reprint, 1970), 1–79; and Robert Dallek, *Franklin D. Roosevelt and American Foreign Policy, 1932–1945* (New York: Oxford University Press, 1979), 23–233.

2. King, *Fleet Admiral King*, 295–309; Kuehn, *Agents of Innovation*, 125–79; and Mark A. Stoler, *Allies and Adversaries: The Joint Chiefs of Staff, the Grand Alliance, and US Strategy in World War II* (Chapel Hill, NC: University of North Carolina, 2006), 58–63 and 103–22.

3. Marriner Eccles, *Beckoning Frontiers* (New York: Arthur Knopf, 1951), 336.

4. NWC, King Papers, Box 5, Whitehill to Albion, 17 June 1946.

5. Abbazia, *Mr. Roosevelt's War*, 97–106.

6. LC, King Papers, Box 20, King's notes from "Atlantic Charter Conference;" James Leutze, *Bargaining for*

Supremacy: Anglo-American Naval Collaboration, 1937–1941 (Chapel Hill, NC: University of North Carolina, 1977), 219–31; and Miller, *War Plan Orange*, 264–88.

7. David C. Fuquea, "Advantage Japan: The Imperial Japanese Navy's Superior High Seas Refueling Capability," *Journal of Military History*, vol. 84, no. 1 (January 2020), 213–35.

8. Abbazia, *Mr. Roosevelt's War*, 23–31.

9. NWC, Low Reminiscences, 13–14.

10. Abbazia, *Mr. Roosevelt's Navy*, 97–106.

11. Drew Pearson, "The Daily Washington Merry-Go-Round," in *Chicago Tribune* (10 April 1934).

12. Holland M. Smith with Percy Finch, *Coral and Brass* (New York: Scribner's, 1949), 65–68.

13. Kuehn, *America's First General Staff*, 1–138; Kuehn, *Agents of Innovation*, 1–22; and Kohnen, *Twenty-First Century Knox*, 1–19.

14. NWC, King Papers, Box 4, General Board, Whitehill notes.

15. Albion, *Makers of Naval Policy*, 433–65.

16. NWC, King Papers, Box 1, Notes on conversation, 13 June 1946.

17. Ibid.

18. Kuehn, *Agents of Innovation*, 13; Kuehn, *America's First General Staff*, 172–95; and Muir, *Iowa Class Battleships*, 15, 17, 42, and 59.

19. Robert Coram, *Brute: The Life of Victor H. Krulak, US Marine* (Boston: Little, Brown, 2010), 53–94.

20. NWC, King Papers, Box 1, "Advanced Bases west of Hawaii," 21 September 1939.

21. Ibid.

22. Ibid.

23. King, *Fleet Admiral King*, 295–309.

24. NWC, King Papers, Box 7, rough interview notes by Walter Muir Whitehill 4 July 1950.

25. NWC, King Papers, Box 8, "Fleet Organization," 24–25.

26. NWC, King Papers, "Comments on Flag Officers of US Navy," 6.

27. Brian McAllister, *Guardians of Empire: The US Army and the Pacific, 1902–1940* (Chapel Hill: University of North Carolina, 1997), 123; John P. Rosa, *Local Story: The Massie-Kahahawai Case and the Culture of History* (Honolulu: University of Hawaii, 2014); and Nofi, *To Train the Fleet for War*, 154.

28. Yates Stirling, *Sea Duty: The Memoirs of a Fighting Admiral* (New York: Putnam, 1939), 244–71.

29. Ibid.

30. NWC, King Papers, "Comments on Flag Officers of US Navy," 6.

31. NWC, King Papers, Box 8, "Fleet Organization," 24–25.

32. Ibid.

33. Ibid.

34. Richardson, *On the Treadmill*, 12 and 380–82.

35. LC, King Papers, Box 39, "Naval Strategy and Tactics."

36. Ibid., 6.

37. Ibid.

38. Ibid., 7.

39. Ibid.

40. Ibid.

41. USNI, "Reminiscences of Vice Admiral William R. Smedberg, III," (Smedberg Reminiscences), vol. I, 131.

42. NWC, King Papers, Box 7, "Comments by Fleet Admiral E. J. King on Chapter II of J.C.S. 'History of the War against Japan,'" 1.

43. Ibid.

44. NWC, Manuscript Collection (MSC-050), Edward C. Kalbfus (Kalbfus Papers), Box 1, King to Kalbfus and Kalbfus to King, 4 and 6 January 1940.

45. Ibid. Emphasis in original.

46. David Reynolds, *The Creation of the Anglo-American Alliance, 1937–1941: A Study in Competitive Cooperation* (Chapel Hill, NC: University of North Carolina Press, 1982), 108–86; William T. Johnsen, *Origins of the Grand Alliance: Anglo-American Military Collaboration from the* Panay *Incident to Pearl Harbor* (Lexington: University Press of Kentucky, 2016), 23–25, 37–39, and 161–87, and Abbazia, *Mr. Roosevelt's Navy*, 119–24, 133–51.

47. NWC, King Papers, Box 7, comments regarding "'The War against Japan.'"

48. Richardson, *On the Treadmill*, 386.

49. NWC, King Papers, Box 8, Chief of Naval Operations Organization, 3.

50. NWC, King Papers, Box 8, "Fleet Organization," 24–25.

51. Richardson, *On the Treadmill*, 1–12 and 370–72.

52. Ibid., 372.

53. Ibid., 372.

54. NWC, King Papers, "Comments on Flag Officers of US Navy," 6.

55. Ibid.

56. NWC, King Papers, Box 1, Notes on conversation, 13 June 1946.

57. Ibid.

58. NWC, King Papers, Box 1, "Memorandum for the President," Edison to Roosevelt, 24 June 1940.

59. Ibid.

60. NWC, King Papers, Box 7, "Secretaries Knox and Forrestal."

61. Ibid.

62. Ibid.

63. Ibid.

64. Ibid.

65. Perry, *Dear Bart*, 11–13.

66. NWC, King Papers, Box 10, oral history transcript, Rear Admiral Paul Pihl and Charlotte Willkie Pihl.

67. TNA, ADM 199/1236, "History of British Admiralty Delegation to the USA" (BAD History), 1–18.

68. TNA, ADM 199 1236, "Naval Background of US Naval Officers," paragraph 45.

69. David Nutting and James Glanville, ed., *Attain by Surprise: The Story of 30 Assault Unit—Royal Navy / Royal Marine Commando* (Burgess Hill, UK: Selwood, 1997), 224–35.

70. SCHC, Pihl Papers, "Standard Diary," 1 January 1938 to 9 January 1939, Box 1, folder 4.

71. New York, Columbia University, Collection 2770, James M. McHugh Papers, Boxes 2 and 3.

72. LC, Knox Papers, Memorandum for Admiral Stark, 6 January 1940.

73. Ibid.

74. Ibid.

75. Drury, "Historical Units and Agencies," 13–18.

76. LC, Knox Papers, Memorandum for Admiral Stark, 6 January 1940.

77. Ibid.

78. Ibid.

79. Ibid.

80. Gerald E. Wheeler, *Kinkaid of the Seventh Fleet—a Biography of Thomas C. Kinkaid, US Navy* (Annapolis, MD: Naval Institute Press, 1996), 105–22.

81. William J. Sebald, *With MacArthur in Japan: A Personal History of the Occupation* (New York: W. W. Norton), 1965), 24; USNI OH, "Reminiscences of Captain Henri Smith-Hutton" (Smith-Hutton Reminiscences), vol. 1, 310–17; and Ellis M. Zacharias, *Secret Missions: The Story of an Intelligence Officer* (New York: Putnam, 1946), 1–60.

82. Ibid, page 2, paragraph 5, "First Step Towards a Naval Staff Representation."

83. BNS, part I, page 1, paragraph 3, "First Step towards a Naval Staff Representation."

84. United Kingdom, Portsmouth, Royal Navy Historical Branch, Key Subject-Matter File, Wartime Administration, History of the British Naval Staff, "World War II: The British Naval Staff in the USA" (BNS); and Simpson Papers, Box 18, ComNavEu monograph, "United States British Naval Relations, 1939–1942."

85. TNA, ADM 199 1236, "Naval Background of US Naval Officers," paragraph 45.

86. Ibid., paragraph 53.

87. Ibid.

88. Ibid.

89. Ibid.

90. Ibid.

91. Ibid., paragraph 85.

92. NHHC, Paul H. Bastedo Papers, Box 2, Memorandum to Assistant Chief of Naval Operations, 13 February 1941.

93. TNA, ADM 199/1236, BAD History, 12 18 and 280–81.

94. Ibid.

95. Larrie Ferreiro, *Churchill's American Arsenal: The Partnership behind the Innovations That Won World War Two* (New York: Oxford University Press, 2022), 63–66, 78–86, 133–37, and 256–62.

96. John Ferris, *Behind the Enigma: The Authorized History of GCHQ, Britain's Secret Cyber-intelligence Agency* (New York: Bloomsbury 2020), 174–80, 179–81, 196–213, 241–42, 255–62, and 330–45.

97. Churchill, *English-Speaking Peoples*, 281.

Chapter 16

1. BNS, vol. I, page 4, paragraph 13, "Rainbow Plan."

2. Ibid.

3. BNS, part I, paragraph 11, page 3, "Singapore Conference."

4. NWC, ComNavEu, Administrative History, part I, "US Naval Representation in the United Kingdom," page 4.

5. BNS, part I, page 4, paragraph 14, "Differing Strategic Concepts."

6. Ibid., page 4, paragraph 13, "Rainbow Plan."

7. Ibid., part I, page 5, paragraph 16, "Approach to Anglo-American Staff Conversations."

8. Ibid.

9. TNA, ADM 199 1236, "Naval Background of US Naval Officers," paragraph 45.

10. LC, King Papers, Box 39, speech file, "Town Hall Meeting," 2–8.

11. Steven T. Ross, *American War Plans 1890–1939* (New York: Frank Cass, 2000), xi; Gole, *The Road to Rainbow*, 1–35 and 40–103; Bell, "Thinking the Unthinkable," 789–808; Miller, *War Plan Orange*, 2–3, 11–13, 263–71, and 364–66; and Nofi, *Train the Fleet*, 220–67.

12. NWC, King Papers, Box 7, "Memorandum of conversation with Admiral E. C. Kalbfus, USN (ret.), 18 February 1946 concerning relations of CNO and CinCUS in peacetime."

13. FDR, Safe Files, Box 4, Plan Dog, "Memorandum for the Secretary," 12 November 1940.

14. Ibid.

15. Ibid.

16. Abbazia, *Mr. Roosevelt's Navy*, 119–24, 133–35, and 138–51.

17. Miller, *War Plan Orange*, 216–80; Waldo H. Heinrichs, *Threshold of War: Franklin D. Roosevelt and American Entry into World War II* (New York: Oxford University Press, 1988), 64–70; and Abbazia, *Mr. Roosevelt's Navy*, 119–24, 133–35, and 138–51.

18. Ibid.

19. Dyer, *Amphibians Came to Conquer*, 166–77.

20. BNS, part I, page 3, paragraph 10, "Contact with the United States Naval War Plans Division."

21. Edwin Layton with John Costello and Roger Pineau, *And I Was There: Pearl Harbor and Midway—Breaking the Secrets* (New York: William Morrow, 1985), 96.

22. Richardson, *On the Treadmill*, 5.

23. Ibid.

24. Ibid., 436.

25. Ibid.

26. Richardson, *On the Treadmill*, 372.

27. NWC, King Papers, Box 5, "Pacific vs. Sickle—the Urgency of the Anti-U-boat War," 1946, 1–2.

28. LC, King Papers, Box 39, speech file, "Town Hall Meeting," 1–38.

29. Ibid.

30. King, *Fleet Admiral King*, 305–46.

31. NWC, King Papers, Box 7, "Comments on Flag Officers," 31 July 1949, "Admiral J. O. Richardson."

32. Ibid.

33. Ibid.

34. Ibid.

35. Furer, *Administration of the Navy Department*, 178.

36. NWC, King Papers, Box 8, "Fleet Organization," 5.

37. Ibid.

38. Ibid.

39. Richardson, *On the Treadmill,* 436.

40. Ibid., 9.

41. NWC, King Papers, "Comments on Flag Officers of US Navy," "Admiral J. O. Richardson," p. 6.

42. NWC, King Papers, Box 7, "Admiral T. C. Hart."

43. NWC, King Papers, Box 5, Nimitz to Secretary of the Navy, 8 January 1941.

44. Malcolm Murfett, *Fool-Proof Relations: The Search for Anglo-American Naval Cooperation during the Chamberlain Years, 1937–1940* (Kent Ridge: Singapore University Press 1984), xiii–xv, 3–26, 104–08, 120–25, and 286–296.

45. NWC, King Papers, Box 7, "Admiral Ingersoll," 4 July 1950.

46. NWC, "Reminiscences of Royal E. Ingersoll," 70.

47. NHC, Chief of Naval Operations Double Zero Files (CNO Double Zero), Royal E. Ingersoll memorandum, 3 January 1938.

48. NWC, King Papers, Box 2, Schoeffel to Buell, 9 September 1974.

49. Ibid.

50. LC, King Papers, Box 39, "Naval Strategy and Tactics," 19–20.

51. Ibid., 4.

52. NWC, King Papers, Box 1, Whitehill notes of 27 April 1948.

53. Ibid.

54. NWC, King Papers, Box 7, "Comments on Flag Officers, US Navy," Admiral R. E. Ingersoll.

55. Ibid.

56. Furer, *Administration of the Navy Department*, 178–79 and 363–65; Richardson, *On the Treadmill*, 380–82 and 402; and King, *Fleet Admiral King*, 318.

57. Ibid., 308.

58. NWC, King Papers, Box 5, Andrews to King, 15 November 1940.

59. LC, King Papers, King to J. D. P. "Dale" Hodapp, 21 December 1940.

60. NWC, King Papers, Box 5, "Speech on Taking Command," handwritten date of 15 November 1940.

61. Ibid.

62. LC, King Papers, correspondence files, Box 38, Rear Admiral Thomas B. Inglis to King, 2 August 1948. Emphasis in original.

63. Navy Register of 1941. By lineal precedence, these were Hart, Richardson, Stark, and Snyder.

64. NWC, King Papers, Box 5, "Pacific vs. Sickle—The Urgency of the Anti-U-boat War," 1946, 1–2.

65. NWC, King Papers, Box 5, Memorandum from Chester W. Nimitz, 8 January 1941.

66. Ibid.

67. Ibid.

68. NWC, King Papers, Box 5, King to Gibbs, 12 January 1941. Note, in memoirs, King wrote "frosting on the cake." King, *Fleet Admiral King*, 318.

69. LC, King Papers, Box 8, Knox to King, 9 January 1941.

70. NWC, King Papers, Box 2, James R. Topper to Buell, 27 September 1974.

71. King, *Fleet Admiral King*, 339.

72. BNS, part I, page 7, paragraph 22, Note 5, "Difficulties Encountered."

73. Ibid.

74. Ibid.

75. BNS, part I, page 8, paragraph 24, "Dominion Representation."

76. Ibid.

77. Ibid.

78. Beesly, *Very Special Admiral*, 173–75.

79. NWC, Kirk Reminiscences, 210–11.

80. Ibid., 261–63 and 265.

81. See the foreword by Roskill in Beesly, *Very Special Admiral*, xv–xvi.

82. NWC, "Reminiscences of Alan Goodrich Kirk," 210–11. Emphasis in original 1962 transcript.

83. Ibid. Emphasis in original.

84. Ibid.

85. NARA, RG 313, ComNavEu, "Sub/Anti-sub ETOUSA Operations," Box 12, "Rough Draft—Submarine and Anti-submarine Section," May 1945, p. 3.

86. TNA, ADM 205, vol. 9, "Correspondence with British Admiralty Delegation, Washington. United States Naval Co-operation," (ADM 205/9), part 2—April–December 1941, Letter from Little to Pound, 15 July 1941.

87. TNA, ADM 205/9, Letter from Little to Pound, 6 November 1941.

88. Ibid., "Conclusion," paragraph 277.

89. Ibid.

90. Ibid.

91. Ibid.

92. Ibid.

93. Ibid.

94. Ibid.

95. NWC, King Papers, Box 7, comments regarding "'The War against Japan,'" 1.

96. Christopher M. Bell, "The View from the Top: Churchill, British Grand Strategy, and the Battle of the Atlantic," in Faulkner and Bell, *Decision in the Atlantic*, 20–45.

97. Morison, *History of US Naval Operations*, vol. I, 27–74.

98. Wilford, *Canada's Road to the Pacific War*, 56–77.

99. NWC, King Papers, ABC-1, Annex II.

100. Mark Milner, "The Atlantic War: 1939–1945: The Case for a New Paradigm," in Faulkner and Bell, *Decision in the Atlantic*, 5–19.

101. LC, King Papers, King to Stark, Box 5, 14 January 1941.

102. Ibid.

103. Ibid.

104. Abbazia, *Mr. Roosevelt's Navy*, 69–68, 97–117, 142–46, and 243–46.

105. Ibid.

106. Ibid.

107. Marc Milner, *North Atlantic Run: The Royal Canadian Navy and the Battle for the Convoys* (Toronto: University of Toronto Press, 1985), 60.

108. Malcolm Llewellyn-Jones, *The Royal Navy and Anti-submarine Warfare, 1917–49* (New York: Routledge, 2006), 35–45.

109. E. F. Gueritz, "Nelson's Blood: Attitudes and Actions of the Royal Navy, 1939–45," in *Journal of Contemporary History*, vol. 16, no. 3 (July 1981), 497.

110. Nicholas Monserrat, *The Cruel Sea* (New York: Alfred A. Knopf, 1951), 214.

111. Ibid.

112. Donald MacIntyre, *U-boat Killer: Fighting the U-boats in the Battle of the Atlantic* (New York: W.W. Norton, 1957), 94–95.

113. Ibid.

114. Llewellyn-Jones, *Royal Navy and Anti-Submarine Warfare*, 42.

115. Ibid.

116. Roskill, *The War at Sea*, vol. I, 132–35.

117. Stephen Budiansky, *Blackett's War: The Men Who Defeated the Nazi U-boats and Brought Science to the Art of Warfare* (New York: Alfred Knopf, 2013), 94–99, 163–219, and 225; Timothy P. Mulligan, *Neither Sharks nor Wolves: The Men of Nazi Germany's Submarine Arm, 1939–1945* (Annapolis, MD: Naval Institute Press, 1999), 35–38, 56–64, 73–83, and 198–201; and Erich Grove, ed., *The Defeat of the Enemy Attack on Shipping, 1939–1945* (Brookfield, VT: Ashgate, 1997), ix–lxii.

118. Milner, *North Atlantic Run*, 60.

119. FDR, Safe Files, Box 3, Navy Department, Denfeld to Stark, "Convoy System as established by the British and Recommended Changes if the United States enters the War," 12 May 1941.

120. Ibid. Emphasis in the original.

121. Ibid.

122. Ibid.

Chapter 17

1. LC, King Papers, Box 8, King to Harold R. Stark, 7 May 1941.

2. LC, King Papers, Box 8, King to Drake, 24 October 1941.

3. NWC, King Papers, Box 5, "Atlantic Fleet Commissioning Address," 1 February 1941.

4. Ibid.

5. Ibid.

6. Ibid.

7. Ibid.

8. NWC, King Papers, Box 5, "Atlantic Fleet Confidential Memorandum 2CM-41," 24 March 1941.

9. NWC, King Papers, "Neutrality Instructions, US Navy, 1940," 1–117.

10. NWC, King Papers, Box 2, Topper to Buell, 27 September 1974.

11. Ibid.

12. Ibid.

13. Ibid.

14. Ibid.

15. Ibid.

16. Ibid.

17. Ibid.

18. Ibid.

19. NWC, King Papers, Box 2, Beakly to Buell, 19 December 1974

20. Ibid.

21. Ibid.

22. Ibid.

23. Ibid.

24. Ibid.

25. NWC, Low Papers, Box 1, "Personal Narrative," ii.

26. NWC, King Papers, Box 4, David Kline letter to Buell, February 1974.

27. NWC, King Papers, Box 4, Whitehill notes, 3 May 1947.

28. Greg Denning, *Mr. Bligh's Bad Language: Passion, Power and Theatre on the Bounty* (New York: Cambridge University Press, 1994), 42.

29. Thorndike, "King of the Atlantic," 100.

30. Ibid.

31. Thorndike, "King of the Atlantic," 96.

32. Ibid.

33. Ibid.

34. Ibid.

35. NWC, King Papers, Box 10, Pfeiffer interview with Buell.

36. NWC, King Papers, Box 2, Topper to Buell, 27 September 1974.

37. Thorndike, "King of the Atlantic," 96–100.

38. NWC, King Papers, Box 2, Russell to Buell, 18 November 1974.

39. United Kingdom, London (Kew), the National Archives (TNA), HW 8/49, "History of Liaison with OP-20-G (Washington) as Carried Out by Representatives of Naval Section, GC&CS," 50–53: and TNA, HW 57/2, "Monthly letters from Colonel O'Connor (GC&CS representative in Washington) to the Director, GC&CS, attaching monthly notes and reports from other GC&CS liaison officers 1943 Dec 26–1944 Dec 31," reports dated 2nd July, 1944, 2. Very special thanks to Ralph Erskine for providing material found these documents.

40. Ferris, *Behind the Enigma*, 328 and 343–44.

41. College Park, Maryland, National Archives and Records Administration, Archives II (NARA), Record Group (RG) 457, Box 1123, "A Chronology of Cooperation Between the SSA and GC&CS," Section 1, "Prewar Cooperation Established."

42. Prescott H. Currier, "My PURPLE Trip to England," *Cryptologia* (vol. 20, no. 3, 1996), 193–201; Ralph Erskine, "What Did the Sinkov Mission Receive from Bletchley Park?," in *Cryptologia*, vol. 24, no. 2 (2000), 97–109; Ralph Erskine, Colin Burke, and Philip Marks, "Memorandum to OP-20 G on Naval Enigma (c. 1941)" in *The Essential Turing*, Jack Copeland (ed.) (Oxford: Clarendon, 2004), 341–352; and Joel Greenberg, *Alastair Denniston: Code-Breaking from Room 40 to Berkley Street to Bletchley Park* (Barnsley, UK: Frontline Books, 2017), 150–53.

43. NWC, King Papers, Box 7, Letter from King to Ingram, 20 September 1941.

44. NWC, RG 28, President's Correspondence File, King to Kalbfus, 1 February 1941.

45. Ibid.

46. LC, King Papers, Boxes 7 and 12, various correspondences between Kalbfus and King.

47. Kalbfus, *Sound Military Decision*, 25–26 and 41.

48. Potter, *Nimitz*, 221–22. Potter relies upon a speech delivered in 1973 by Admiral Isaac Kidd in describing the desktop "rules of thumb" and "principles of war," as written out on a notecard by Nimitz. Although he did have the "rules of thumb," no evidence proves that Nimitz listed the "principles of war" on a notecard. See the detailed description provided by Noel F. Busch in the 10 July 1944 issue of *Life* magazine, p. 84.

49. Thomas B. Buell, "Admiral Edward C. Kalbfus and the Naval Planner's 'Holy Scripture': *Sound Military Decision*," in *Naval War College Review*, vol. 26, no. 3 (May–June 1973), 31–41.

50. Kohnen, *Twenty-First-Century Knox*, 107–21.

51. NWC, King Papers, Box 2, Madiera to Buell, 9 August 1974.

52. Johnsen, *Origins of the Grand Alliance*, 131–87, 195–204, and 245–53.

53. Murfett, *Fool-Proof Relations*, xiii–xv, 3–26, 104–08, 120–25, and 286–296.

54. MacArthur, *Reminiscences*, 101; Ronald K. Edgerton, "General Douglas MacArthur and the American Military Impact in the Philippines," in *Philippine Studies*, vol. 25, no. 4 (Winter 1977): 420–40; and B. Mitchell Simpson III, *Admiral Harold R. Stark: Architect of Victory, 1939–1945* (Columbia: University of South Carolina Press, 1989), 76–81 and 104–10.

55. NWC, Pratt Papers, Box: 2, Nomura correspondence.

56. Washington, DC, Central Intelligence Agency (CIA), Center for Intelligence History, Office of Strategic Services—Research and Analysis Branch, "R&A 33378—the Greater East Asia Co-prosperity Sphere," 10 August 1945 (Released in January 2002).

57. Hull, *Peace and War*, 124–25.

58. Simpson, *Stark*, 76–81 and 104–10.

59. Hull, *Peace and War*, 124–25.

60. Ibid., 700.

61. Ibid.

62. King, *Fleet Admiral King*, 331.

63. NWC, Low Papers, Box 1, "Journal, 1941."

64. King, *Fleet Admiral King*, 331–37.

65. Ibid.

66. Ibid., 506–10.

67. NWC, King Papers, Box 7, Letter from King to Ingram, 20 September 1941.

68. Perry, *Dear Bart*, 13.

69. Ibid., 15.

70. NWC, King Papers, Box 8, "Fleet Organization."

71. Craig M. Cameron, *American Samurai: Myth, Imagination, and the Conduct of Battle in the First Marine Division, 1941–1951* (New York: Cambridge University Press, 1994), 55.

72. Ibid.

73. O'Brian, *Powerful Man,* 165–76.

74. BBC Photographic Library, Lieutenant Draper Kauffman, RNVR, at Trafalgar Square on 4 July 1941. See Bush, *America's First Frogman*, 1–57; and Erich Dietrich-Berryman, Charlotte Hammond, and R. E. White, *Passport Not Required: US Volunteers in the Royal Navy, 1939–1941* (Annapolis, MD: Naval Institute Press), 93.

75. Daniel V. Gallery, "U-boat War from Iceland to Murmansk to the Coasts of Africa," in John T. Mason,

ed., *The Atlantic War Remembered: An Oral History Collection* (Annapolis, MD: Naval Institute Press, 1990), 115. See the original interview transcript in Annapolis, Maryland, United States Naval Institute, Oral History Department, Reminiscences of Rear Admiral Daniel V. Gallery Jr., US Navy (retired), John T. Mason interviews with Gallery conducted between 1970 and 1974 (Gallery Reminiscences), 32–35 and 41–63.

76. NARA, RG 38, CominCh, War Diaries, Box 1, NND 968133, CominCh for Action US Fleet, 192200 February 1943, effective 15 March 1943.

77. *Time*, "Stormy Man, Stormy Weather," 17.

78. Perry, *Dear Bart*, 315–30.

79. Emory S. Land, *Winning the War with Ships—Land, Sea, and Air* (New York: McBride, 1959), 39–41, 65, 76, 102, 126, 137, 144–45, 172–76, 227, 236, 241–42, and 249–49.

80. Reg Ingraham, *First Fleet: The Story of the US Coast Guard at War* (New York: Bobbs-Merrill, 1944), 15–119.

81. John A. Tilly, *The US Coast Guard in World War II: The Coast Guard and the Greenland Patrol* (Washington, DC: US Coast Guard, 1992), 1–17; Robert Erwin Johnson, *Coast Guard Manned Naval Vessels in World War II* (Washington, DC: US Coast Guard, 1993), 1–17; and Morison, *Battle of the Atlantic*, 59–63.

82. Ibid.

83. Perry, *Dear Bart*, 79–115.

84. Philips Payson O'Brian, *How the War Was Won: Air-Sea Power and Allied Victory in World War II* (New York: Cambridge University Press, 2015), 237; Symonds, *Nimitz at War*, 78–80; and Williamson Murray and Alan Millett, *A War to Be Won: Fighting in the Second World War* (Cambridge, MA: Belknap Press of Harvard University Press, 2000), 337.

Chapter 18

1. John B. Hattendorf, "The Idea of a 'Fleet in Being' in Historical Perspective," in *The Naval War College Review*, vol. 67, no. 1 (Winter, 2014), 44–60.

2. Robert Switky, *Wealth of an Empire: The Treasure Shipments that Saved Britain and the World* (Lincoln: University of Nebraska Press, 2013), 1–84.

3. Blair, *Hitler's U-boat War—the Hunters*, 375–76.

4. Morison, *Battle of the Atlantic*, 3–108.

5. Kennedy, *Freedom from Fear*, 494.

6. FDR, Speeches and Statements, "President Franklin Delano Roosevelt Message to the Congress on the Sinking of the *Robin Moor*, 20 June 1941."

7. Ibid.

8. FDR, Fireside Chat, 27 May 1941, "Announcing Unlimited National Emergency."

9. Ibid.

10. Ibid.

11. Ibid.

12. NWC, Low Reminiscences, 22–23.

13. NARA, RG 313, ComNavEu, "Sub/Anti-sub ETOUSA Operations," Box 12, "Rough Draft—Submarine and Anti-submarine Section," May 1945, 3.

14. Hattendorf, *On His Majesty's Service*, 40.

15. NWC, Low Reminiscences, 22–23.

16. Kirk Reminiscences, 182.

17. USNI, Smedberg Reminiscences, vol. I, 131.

18. HIA, Kittredge Papers, Box 19, Rockefeller Foundation, Papers and Records.

19. LC, Knox Papers, Box 7, Kittredge letter to Knox and appended letter from Knox to Stark, June and August 1941.

20. HIA, Kittredge Papers, materials relating to Kittredge and his role in establishing an intelligence organization are found in Boxes 39–41.

21. NARA, RG 38, Records of the Tenth Fleet, Organization, Box AMS-35, folder A7(2), 12 April 1941, SpeNavO, Report of Lieutenant Commander C. F. Baldwin, USNR, Observations of Admiralty Operational Intelligence Organization.

22. NHC, "United States Naval Administration in World War II," Robert G. Albion, comp., 486–89.

23. NARA, RG 38, Records of the Tenth Fleet, Organization, Box AMS-35, folder A7(2), 12 April 1941, SpeNavO, Report of Lieutenant Commander C. F. Baldwin, USNR, Observations of Admiralty Operational Intelligence Organization.

24. USNI, McCollum Reminiscences, 309.

25. NWC, King Papers, Box 5, "Dyer interview of 1 August 1945," p. 3.

26. NWC, King Papers, Box 7, Letter from King to Ingram, 20 September 1941.

27. Ibid.

28. NWC, King Papers, Box 5, King to Stark, 5 November 1941.

29. Ibid.

30. Ibid.

31. USNI, "Reminiscences of Vice Admiral Ruthven E. Libby," (Libby Reminiscences), 220–45.

32. NWC, Low Papers, Box 1, "Personal Narrative," 13–15.

33. Ibid., 15.

34. Ibid.

35. Ibid.

36. Ibid.

37. Quantico, Virginia, Archives Branch, Marine Corps History Division (MHD), Advanced Base Problems, Advanced Base Problem V–VIII (1939), remarks of Lieutenant Colonel Alfred H. Noble, "Conclusion."

38. NWC, King Papers, Box 8, Pfeiffer to Buell.

39. Holland M. Smith with Percy Finch, *Coral and Brass* (New York: Scribner's, 1949), 86–100; Jeter A. Isely and Philip A. Crowl, *The US Marines and Amphibious War: Its Theory and Its Practice in the Pacific* (Princeton, NJ: Princeton University Press, 1951), 1–20; and Bernard E. Trainor, "School for Doctrine," Marine Corps Gazette, vol. 51, no. 11 (1967), 66.

40. NWC, student thesis, Jake Hubbard, "Advanced Base Problems: 1933–1939," unpublished, submitted for the Graduate Certificate in Maritime History, Naval War College (Class of 2020), 2–46.

41. NWC, King Papers, Box 2, Topper to Buell, 27 September 1974.

42. Ibid.

43. Ibid.

44. Ibid.

45. Ibid.

46. Ibid.

47. Ibid.

48. NWC, King Papers, Box 8, Krulak to Buell, May 1974.

49. Theodore Roscoe, *United States Submarine Operations in World War II* (Annapolis, MD: Naval Institute Press, 1949), 85–86; and Clay Blair, *Silent Victory: The US Submarine War against Japan* (New York: J.B. Lippencott, 1975), 78–80.

50. NARA, RG 38, CominCh, Crane Files, SSIC 3840/2, Box 37, "F-21 Memoranda Regarding Submarine Tracking and Operations, June 1943–June 1945," memorandum titled "Offensive Action against U-boats," 3.

51. NWC, King Papers, Box 5, 5 November 1941.

52. Ibid.

53. NWC, King Papers, Box 5, "Pacific vs. Sickle—the Urgency of the Anti-U-boat War," 1946, 1–2.

54. NWC, King Papers, Box 5, King to Stark, 5 November 1941.

55. Ibid.

56. NWC, King Papers, Box 6, Bull Diary, 6 November 1942, 15; LC, King Papers, Box 35, thesis, "The Influence of the National Policy on the Strategy of a War," 7 November 1932, 21; and King, *Fleet Admiral King*, 487 and 504.

57. Abbazia, *Mr. Roosevelt's Navy*, 3–33, 114–151, and 183–360; Kohnen, *Twenty-First-Century Knox*, 1–15 and 107–10; and Christian McBurney, Norman Desmaris, and Varoujan Karentz, *Untold Stories from World War II Rhode Island* (Charleston, SC: History Press, 2019), 7–25.

58. Joseph J. Thorndike Jr., "King of the Atlantic: America's Triple Threat Admiral Is Americas Stern, Daring Model of a War Commander," in *Life* magazine, vol. 11, no. 21 (27 November 1941), 94.

59. Abbazia, *Mr. Roosevelt's Navy*, 293–312.

60. Ibid., 346–49.

61. NWC, King Papers, Box 5, King to Stark, 5 November 1941.

62. Ibid.

63. Ibid.

64. Ibid.

65. Ibid.

66. NWC, Low Reminiscences, 21.

67. Ibid.

68. NWC, King Papers, Box 5, King to Stark, 28 November 1941.

69. TNA, CO 968/231, "Western Pacific (Denial Plans) Canton Island."

70. Alibion, *Makers of Naval Policy*, 517.

71. Perry, *Dear Bart*, 13.

72. Ibid.

73. Ibid.

74. Ibid.

75. Ibid., 19.

76. USNI, Oral History, Captain Willard G. Triest, CEC, USNR.

77. TNA, WO 106/3393, "Christmas and Canton Island from 31/10/41 to 07/4/44"; CAB 122/114, "Christmas and Canton Island"; CO 968/231, "Western Pacific (Denial Plans) Canton Island;" and ADM 178/223, "US Pacific Fleet Reports of R.N. Observers."

78. TNA, WO 106/3393, "Christmas and Canton Island from 31/10/41 to 07/4/44."

79. NHHC, COLL 307, Logan C. Ramsey Papers, Box 3, Pearl Harbor Messages and Letters, 7 December 1941.

80. Perry, *Dear Bart*, 19–84.

81. Stanly E. Hilton, *Hitler's Secret War in South America, 1939–1945: German Military Espionage and American Counterespionage in Brazil* (Baton Rouge: Louisiana State University, 1981), 1–11; María Emilia Paz Salinas, *Strategy, Security, and Spies: Mexico and the US as Allies in World War II* (University Park: Pennsylvania State University Press, 1997), 61–90, 160–188, and 190–220; and Francis MacDonnell, *Insidious Foes: The Axis Fifth Column and the American Homefront* (New York: Oxford University Press, 1995), 95–100, 208–10, and 240–43.

82. Christopher M. Bell, "The 'Singapore Strategy' and the Deterrence of Japan: Winston Churchill, the Admiralty and the Dispatch of Force Z," in *English Historical Review*, vol. 116, no. 467 (June 2001), 604–34; Spector, *Eagle against the Sun*, 19–24, 93–100, 128; and Martin Middlebrook and Patrick Mahoney, *Battleship: The Sinking of the Prince of Wales and Repulse* (New York: Scribner's, 1977), 257–68.

83. Perry, *Dear Bart*, 19.

84. NWC, King Papers, Box 4, "Some Aspects of the High Command in World War II," 8–9.

85. NWC, King Papers, Box 2, Topper to Buell, 27 September 1974.

86. Annapolis, Maryland, Naval Institute Oral Histories, Vice Admiral Olaf M. Hustvedt, 1975, 167–210.

87. Harry Sanders, "King of the Oceans," in Naval Institute *Proceedings*, vol. 100, no. 8 (August 1974): 52–59.

88. Ibid.

89. Ibid.

90. Whitehill, "Postscript," 205.

91. NWC, King Papers, Box 7, "Pearl Harbor in Reverse."

Chapter 19

1. NWC, "Nimitz Graybook," vol. I, entries for 7 December 1941, 5.

2. Scott H. Bennett, "American Pacifism, the 'Greatest Generation,' and World War II," in *The United States and the Second World War: New Perspectives on Diplomacy, War, and the Home Front, World War II: The Global, Human, and Ethical Dimension*, G. Kurt Piehler and Sidney Pash (eds.) (New York: Fordham University Press, 2010), 259–92.

3. NARA, RG 313, ComNavEu, Blue Finding Aid, Box 32, folder A9/8 (16) "Far Shore."

4. NWC, Box 6, Bull Diary, 30 November 1942, 13.

5. Ibid.

6. NWC, King Papers, Box 7, "Pearl Harbor in Reverse."

7. Walter Muir Whitehill, "Admiral King and the Naval High Command," in *Proceedings*, vol. 78, no. 10 (October 1952), 1,073–80.

8. NWC, King Papers, Box 7, "Admiral Stark."

9. James E. Hewes Jr., *From Root to McNamera: Army Organization and Administration* (Washington, DC: Center of Military History, 1975), 53–120.

10. King, *Fleet Admiral King,* 350; NWC, Bull Diary, 30 November 1942, 2; and NWC, King Papers, Box 7, Memorandum, 12 November 1946.

11. NWC, King Papers, Box 7, Memorandum, 12 November 1946.

12. Ibid.

13. Ibid.

14. Ibid.

15. Ibid.

16. Shalett, "Admiral King Hits a Single Command," *New York Times*, 13 February 1946.

17. NWC, King Papers, Box 7, "Admiral Stark."

18. John B. Hattendorf and Pelham Boyer, eds., *To the Java Sea: Diary, Letters and Reports of Commander Henry E. Eccles, 1940–1942* (Newport, RI: Naval War College Press, 2021), 197.

19. NWC, King Papers, Box 8, "Chief of Naval Operations Organization," 3.

20. Ibid.

21. Perry, *Dear Bart*, 27.

22. Trent Hone, *Mastering the Art of Command: Admiral Chester W. Nimitz and Victory in the Pacific* (Annapolis, MD: Naval Institute Press, 2022), 19–24, 41, 44, 59, 69, 70.

23. NWC, King Papers, Box 7, "Admiral Ingersoll," 4 July 1950.

24. NWC, RG 16, Box 2, Nimitz Address, 2 December 1941. Also see Albion, *Makers of Naval Policy*, 519.

25. NWC, King Papers, Box 7, "Fixers."

26. NWC, King Papers, Box 7, "Admiral Ingersoll," 4 July 1950.

27. Ibid. Emphasis in original.

28. David J. Bercuson and Holger H. Holweg, *One Christmas in Washington: Churchill and Roosevelt Forge the Grand Alliance* (London: Widenfeld & Nicolson, 1985), 181–265; Robert G. Albion with Jeannie Barnes Pope, *Forrestal and the Navy* (New York: Columbia University Press, 1962), 132; and Stoler, *Allies and Adversaries*, 58–63 and 103–22.

29. Albion, *Makers of Naval Policy*, 381.

30. Harold H. Sprout and Margaret T. Sprout, *The Rise of American Naval Power, 1776–1918* (Princeton, NJ: Princeton University, 1942), 15; Demetrios Caraley, *The Politics of Military Unification: A Study of Conflict and the Policy Process* (New York: Columbia University Press, 1966), 3–122; and Kuehn, *America's First General Staff*, 8.

31. NWC, King Papers, Box 8, "Chief of Naval Operations Organization," 3.

32. NWC, King Papers, Box 7, Whitehill notes, "Five-Stars"; NWC, King Papers, Box 7, Whitehill notes, "Rank of Commodore"; and NWC, King Papers, Box 8, "Chief of Naval Operations Organization," 3.

33. NWC, King Papers, Box 6, Bull Diary, 30 November 1942, pages 15–16.

34. Albion, *Makers of Naval Policy*, 539.

35. Ibid., Albion, *Makers of Naval Policy*, 500–10.

36. Perry, *Dear Bart*, 82.

37. Ibid.

38. NWC, King Papers, Box 8, "Chief of Naval Operations Organization," 3.

39. Ibid.

40. Ward, "FDR's Western Front Idyll," 352.

41. Albion, *Makers of Naval Policy*, 400–05.

42. LC, King Papers, Box 39, speech file, "Town Hall Meeting," 15.

43. Ibid.

44. Sydney Shalett, "Admiral King Hits a Single Command," in *New York Times* (13 February 1946).

45. Ibid.

46. Ibid.

47. NWC, King Papers, Box 6, Bull Diary, 30 November 1942, 15–16.

48. Ibid.

49. Ibid.

50. NWC, King Papers, Box 6, Bull Diary, 6 November 1942, 2.

51. Albion, *Makers of Naval Policy*, 382.

52. McCrea, *McCrea's War*, 25–32.

53. Gilbert, *Signals Intelligence,* 159–71.

54. Albion, *Makers of Naval Policy*, 579.

55. Ibid.

56. Ibid.

57. King, *Fleet Admiral King*, 482–90, 499–512, and 523–26; Stoler, *Allies and Adversaries*, 15–122; and Rigby, *Allied Master Strategists,* 9–67.

58. NWC, King Papers, Box 8, "Chief of Naval Operations Organization," 3.

59. Alan D. Zimm, *Attack on Pearl Harbor: Strategy, Combat, Myths, Deceptions* (Philadelphia: Casemate, 2011), 15–52, 71–130, 289–26, and 355–86.

60. NWC, King Papers, Box 7, "Comments on Flag Officers, US Navy," 31 July 1949, "Vice Admiral W. S. Pye," 8.

61. AHC, Husband Kimmel Papers (Kimmel Papers), Box 3, folder J-F 1942, King to Kimmel, 27 February 1942.

62. Ibid.

63. Ibid.

64. Husband E. Kimmel, *Admiral Kimmel's Story* (Chicago: Henry Regnery, 1954), 16.

65. King, *Fleet Admiral King*, 356.

66. NWC, King Papers, Box 7, "Admiral T. C. Hart."

67. Brian Bond, ed., *Chief of Staff: The Diaries of Lieutenant-General Sir Henry Pownall* (London: Leo Cooper, 1972), vol. II, 83.

68. Morison, *Atlantic Battle Won*, vol. X, 17.

69. Frank, *Tower of Skulls,* 376–77.

70. Shalett, "Admiral King Hits a Single Command."

71. Ibid.

72. LC, King Papers, Box 39, speech file, "Town Hall Meeting," 23.

73. Perry, *Dear Bart*, 82.

74. NWC, King Papers, Box 7, "Admiral Ingersoll."

75. Ibid.

76. Ibid.

77. Perry, *Dear Bart*, 81, 304, 313, and 322.

78. King, *Fleet Admiral King*, 353–54.

79. Symonds, *Nimitz at War*, 20–61.

80. Ibid., 79–95.

81. NWC, King Papers, Box 5, "Memorandum of conversation with Captain George C. Dyer, USN, 1 August 1945."

82. NWC, King Papers, Box 5, "Memorandum, Edwards, 30 January 1946."

83. NWC, King Papers, Box 7, "Miscellaneous Notes," 4 July 1950.

84. Ibid.

85. Ibid.

86. Ibid.

87. NWC, King Papers, Box 5, "Memorandum, Edwards, 30 January 1946."

88. NWC, King Papers, Box 7, Letter from King to Ingram, 20 September 1941.

89. NWC, King Papers, Box 2, Murphy to Buell, 18 September 1974.

90. NWC, Low Papers, Box 1, Personal Diary, 7 January 1942.

91. NWC, Low Papers, Box 1, Personal Narrative, 25–26.

92. Oral histories of key participants provide significant insight beyond the secondary histories. Among other sources, USNI oral histories with Jurika, Duncan, Doolittle, Schoeffel, Libby, Smith-Hutton, and Sebald.

93. King, *Fleet Admiral King*, 376. See Paolo Coletta, "Launching the Doolittle Raid on Japan, April 18, 1942," *Pacific Historical Review*, vol. 63, no. 1, (February 1993), 73–86; Quinton Reynolds, *The Amazing Mr. Doolittle: A Biography of Lieutenant General James H. Doolittle* (New York: Appleton, Century and Crofts, 1953), 160–72; and Gordon W. Prange, Donald M. Goldstein, and Katherine V. Dillon. *Miracle at Midway* (New York: McGraw-Hill, 1982), 23–27.

94. NWC, King Papers.

95. USNI, Smith-Hutton Reminiscences, vol. II, 405.

96. Joseph C. Grew, *Ten Years in Japan: A Contemporary Record Drawn from the Diaries and Official Papers of Joseph C. Grew—United States Ambassador to Japan, 1932–1942* (New York: Simon and Schuster, 1944), 293–95, 480, and 493–538.

97. USNI, Smith-Hutton Reminiscences, vol. II, 456.

98. King, *Fleet Admiral King*, 381–413.

99. NWC, King Papers, Box 7, "Comments on Flag Officers, US Navy—Additional notes," "Rear Admiral Robert A. Theobald," 2.

100. Whitehill, Postscript, 216.

101. NWC, King Papers, Box 7, "Early Days—42."

Chapter 20

1. Perry, *Dear Bart,* 145–46.

2. NWC, King Papers, Box 8, "Admiral Nimitz," 31 July 1949.

3. Ibid.

4. Perry, *Dear Bart*, 92.

5. Trimble, *Admiral John S. McCain*, 104–53.

6. NWC, King Papers, Box 7, "Additional notes on flag officers," 14 August 1942, 1 and 2.

7. Ibid.

8. NWC, King Papers, Box 5, "Memorandum of Conversation with Admiral Edwards, 30 January 1946."

9. Ibid.

10. NWC, Box 7, Whitehill notes, "Admiral Edwards, 1/5/44."

11. Ibid.

12. Ibid.

13. NWC, King Papers, Box 7, "Additional notes on flag officers," 14 August 1942, 1 and 2.

14. NWC, King Papers, Box 7, "Various Personalities."

15. Ibid.

16. NWC, Box 7, Whitehill notes, "Admiral Edwards, 1/5/44."

17. NWC, King Papers, Box 5, "Memorandum," Edwards, 30 January 1946"; NWC, King Papers, Box 7, "Admiral Ingersoll;" and King, *Fleet Admiral King*, 567–68.

18. Stoler, *Allies and Adversaries*, 103–22; Charles F. Brower, *Defeating Japan: The Joint Chiefs of Staff and Strategy in the Pacific War, 1943–1945* (New York: Palgrave Macmillan, 2012); David Rigby, *Allied Master Strategists: The Combined Chiefs of Staff in World War II* (Annapolis, MD: Naval Institute Press, 2012), 91, 116, 128–32 138–41; and Doug M. McLean, "Muddling Through: Canadian Anti-submarine Doctrine and Practice, 1942–1945," in *A Nation's Navy: In Quest of Canadian Naval Identity*, Michael Hadley, Rob Huebert, and Fred W. Crickard, eds. (Montreal: McGill-Queen's University Press, 1996), 173–89.

19. NWC, Box 7, Whitehill notes, "Admiral Edwards, 1/5/44."

20. NWC, King Papers, Box 7, "F.D.R. and the Joint Chiefs of Staff."

21. Ibid.

22. Whitehill, "Postscript," 206.

23. NWC, Box 7, Whitehill notes, "Admiral Edwards, 1/5/44."

24. Bryant, *The Turn of the Tide*, 614.

25. Andrew Cunningham, *A Sailor's Odyssey: The Autobiography of Admiral of the Fleet Viscount Cunningham of Hyndhope* (New York: E.P. Dutton, 1951), 471.

26. NWC, King Papers, Box 7, "Statue of Sir John Dill," statement by King, November 1950.

27. Ibid.

28. Ibid.

29. NWC, King Papers, Box 5, "Comments on Joint Chiefs of Staff," 30–31 July 1949.

30. Ibid.

31. NWC, King Papers, Box 7, "Admiral Stark."

32. LC, King Papers, Box 39, speech file, "Town Hall Meeting," 19.

33. Ibid., 16.

34. Ibid.

35. Ibid., 18.

36. Ibid., 27.

37. Ibid., 10.

38. Ibid.

39. Ibid.

40. Ibid., 37.

41. James Leutze, *A Different Kind of Victory: A Biography of Admiral Thomas C. Hart* (Annapolis, MD: Naval Institute Press, 1981), 252–82.

42. Albion, *Makers of Naval Policy*, 386.

43. Ibid., 377.

44. Ibid., 386.

45. NWC, King Papers, Box 7, "Emory S. Land."

46. L. A. Sawyer and W. H. Mitchell, *The History of the Long-Range Merchant Shipbuilding Programme of the United States Maritime Commission, 1937–1952* (London: World Ship Society, 1981), vol. 2.

47. NWC, King Papers, Box 7, "Memorandum of Conversation," November 1946. Emphasis in original.

48. Ibid.

49. Ibid. See the US Navy Manual, "Boxing," as released under King's authority by the Bureau of Aeronautics in the "Naval Aviation Physical Training Series" in 1943.

50. LC, King Papers, Box 35, Memorandum from Stark to King, 12 February 1942.

51. Ibid.

52. Ibid.

53. LC, King Papers, Box 35, Memorandum for Admiral Stark, 13 February 1942.

54. Ibid.

55. Ibid.

56. Albion, *Makers of Naval Policy*, 87–92.

57. NHC, "CominCh Administrative History," 205–10.

58. NWC, King Papers, Box 7, King to Cooke, 7 January 1942.

59. Richardson, *On the Treadmill*, 441–42 and 450–51.

60. Ibid., 442.

61. King, *Fleet Admiral King*, 352–57.

62. NWC, King Papers, Box 7, "Memorandum of Conversation," April 1948, 3.

63. NWC, King Papers, Box 7, "Memorandum of Conversation," November 1946.

64. Ibid.

65. NWC, King Papers, Box 7, "Admiral Stark."

66. Albion, *Makers of Naval Policy*, 482–511.

67. NWC, King Papers, Box 7, "Admiral Stark."

68. Perry, *Dear Bart,* 324.

69. NHHC, Papers of Admiral Harold R. Stark (Stark Papers), Box 23, Series II, "Admiral H. R. Stark Fitness Reports, 1905–1945," Distinguished Service Medal Certificate.

70. Ibid.

71. Independence, Missouri, Harry S Truman Presidential Library and Museum, Oral History with John H. Tolan Jr. (March 1970), 12–13, 127–28, 135–39.

72. Albion, *Makers of Naval Policy*, 534–46.

73. Ibid., 382–85.

74. McCrea, *McCrea's War*, 81.

75. Whitehill, Postscript, 219.

76. LC, King Papers, Box 17, Kalbfus to King, 1 April 1942.

77. Ibid.

78. Albion, *Makers of Naval Policy*, 87–92.

79. Albion, *Forrestal and the Navy*, 102.

80. LC, George C. Dyer Papers, Box 7, Orders.

81. Ibid.

82. Ibid.

83. NWC, King Papers, Box 5, "Memorandum of conversation with Captain George C. Dyer, USN, 1 August 1945."

84. Potter, "Command Personality," 20–21.

85. Ibid.

86. Ibid.

87. NWC, King Papers, Box 5, "Dyer interview of 1 August 1945," 3.

88. Ibid.

89. Ibid.

90. Ibid.

91. NHHC, CominCh Administrative History, 59.

92. NWC, King Papers, Box 5, "Memorandum of conversation with Captain George C. Dyer, USN, 1 August 1945."

93. Ibid.

94. NSA, Knowles Oral History, 4.

95. NWC, King Papers, Box 5, "Memorandum of conversation," Dyer.

96. NWC, King Papers, Box 4, George Russell to Buell, 18 November 1974.

97. Ibid.

98. NWC, King Papers, Box 5, "Memorandum of conversation with Captain George C. Dyer, USN, 1 August 1945."

99. Ibid.

100. Ibid.

101. Potter, "The Command Personality," 21.

102. Author's copy, King to Ferrell, 21 April 1941.

103. Author's copy, King to Ferrell, 4 May 1941.

104. Whitehill, "Postscript," 208.

105. NWC, King Papers, Box 4, George Russell to Buell, 18 November 1974.

106. NHC, "CominCh Administrative History," 210.

107. NARA, RG 38, Records of the Tenth Fleet, Organization, Box AMS-35, folder A /(5), 12 February 1942, "Merchant Marine Officers of the Naval Reserve, Request for," Commander George Dyer, USN to Rear Admiral Richard S. Edwards, Deputy Chief of Staff, CominCh.

108. NARA, RG 38, CominCh, Crane Files, SSIC 5750/24, Box 37, "F-21 (Atlantic Section of Combat Intel) War Report on U-boat Tracking, 15 May 1945," Commander Kenneth A. Knowles, comp. (F-21 War Report), 3; NARA, RG 38, Crane Files, F-22 War Report (F-22 War Report), 1; and NWC, King Papers, Box 7, "Dyer interview of 1 August 1945," 2.

109. NWC, King Papers, Box 5, "Admiralty Anti-U/B Org."

110. Laramie, University of Wyoming, American Heritage Center (AHC), Clay Blair Papers, Box 170, Knowles, Kenneth A.

111. NWC, King Papers, Box 5, "Dyer interview of 1 August 1945," 1–4; NARA, RG 38, CominCh, Crane Files, SSIC 5750/24, Box 37, F-21 War Report, 3; and NARA, RG 38, CominCh, SSIC 5750/24, Box 37, F-22 War Report, 1.

112. USNI, Smith-Hutton Reminiscences, vol. I, 388–89.

113. AHC, Box 170, Knowles.

114. Nofi, *Train the Fleet*, 207–37.

115. NSA, Knowles Oral History, 1–4.

116. Ibid, 3.

117. Ibid, 4.

118. Ibid.

Chapter 21

1. NWC, King Papers, Box 6, Bull Diary, 30 November 1942, 16.

2. Ibid.

3. Ibid.

4. Ibid.

5. Ibid.

6. Ibid.

7. TNA, ADM 223/107, Godfrey Papers, "Collaboration," 22 June 1942.

8. TNA, ADM 223/107, Godfrey Papers, "Submitted herewith the following account of my recent visit to Washington made with the object of establishing an effective U/B tracking room" (Winn Report), 3 June 1942.

9. Jürgen Rohwer, *Die U-Boot Erfolge der Achsenmachte: 1939–1945* (Munich: J.F. Lehmann, 1968), 73–120; and Blair, *Hitler's U-boat War*, vol. I, 727–32.

10. Ibid., 110.

11. Beesly, *Very Special Intelligence*, 157–59.

12. TNA, ADM 1 114207, Personal to ACNS (H) to ACNS (F), via ACNS (UT) and (25L), folder dated 30 October 1943, "Recommendation for Promotion, Ship N.I.D., Station Admiralty, Period of Report 28 Nov. 1942 to 2 Nov. 1943," confidential service report, "Charles Rodger Noel Winn, OBE, Seniority date of 1 February 1941."

13. TNA, ADM 223/286, "The Americans, The Navy Department and Anti U/Boat Warfare."

14. Ibid.

15. Ibid.

16. Beesly, *Very Special Intelligence*, 108.

17. Ibid.

18. Ibid.

19. Ibid.

20. Ibid.

21. Ibid.

22. Ibid.

23. Ibid.

24. TNA, ADM 223/286, "The Americans." Note the handwritten annotations by Winn.

25. Ibid.

26. Ibid.

27. Ibid.

28. Ibid.

29. Ibid.

30. Ibid.

31. TNA, ADM 223/286, "The Americans."

32. NWC, MSC 354, Sims Papers, William S. Sims Jr., papers.

33. Gregory M. Pfitzer, *Samuel Eliot Morison's Historical World: In Quest of a New Parkman* (Boston: Northeastern University Press, 1991), 171–296.

34. NWC, Box 7, Pound letter to King, 18 May 1942.

35. Kirk Reminiscences, 265.

36. Ibid.

37. Dwight D. Eisenhower, *Crusade in Europe* (New York: Doubleday, 1948), 173.

38. Christopher D. Yung, *Gators of Neptune: Naval Amphibious Planning for the Normandy Invasion* (Annapolis, MD, 2006), 228.

39. Yu, *OSS in China*, 48–53.

40. LC, King Papers, Box 39, speech file, "Town Hall Meeting," 19.

41. Ibid.

42. Milton E. Miles, *A Different Kind of War: The Little-Known Story of the Combined Guerrilla Forces Created in China by the US Navy and Chinese in World War II* (New York: Doubleday, 1967), 16–24, 110–17, and 260–63.

43. King, *Fleet Admiral King*, 541; Michael Schaller, "The United States Navy's Secret War in China," in *Pacific Historical Review*, vol. 44, no. 4 (November 1975); 527–33; and Yu Shen, "SACO in History and Histories: Politics and Memory," in *Journal of American East-Asian Relations*, vol. 5, no. 1 (Spring 1996); 37–55.

44. USNI, Kauffman Reminiscences, 285; and USNI, Reminiscences of Rear Admiral Ernest M. Eller, vol. II, 486.

45. King, *Fleet Admiral King*, 541.

46. Miles, *Different Kind of War*, 16–24, 110–17, and 260–63.

47. King, *Fleet Admiral King*, 541.

48. NWC, King Papers, Box 10, Buell transcript of interview with Charlotte Pihl, 16 March 1974.

49. Elmer B. Potter, "The Command Personality," in Naval Institute *Proceedings*, vol. 95, no. 2 (January 1969); 20.

50. Benson, *History of US Communications Intelligence*, 21, 23, 43, 47, and 63; Packard, *Century of US Naval Intelligence*, 228–35; Carlson, *Joe Rochefort's War*, 64–85, 390–93, and 472–75; Layton, *And I Was There*, 49–50; and Maffeo, *US Navy Codebreakers*, 191–92.

51. Raymond P. Schmitt, "From Code-Making to Policy-Making: Four Decades in the Memorable Career of Russell Willson," in *Prologue*, Summer 1916, 25–35.

52. NWC, "Graybook," vol. II, 26 May 1942, 532.

53. Ibid., 543.

54. Symonds, *Nimitz at War*, 57–60.

55. Benson, *History of US Communications Intelligence*, 21, 23, 43, 47, 63, and 64.

56. Ibid, 21, 23, 43, 47, 63, and 64.

57. Ibid., 64.

58. Layton, *And I Was There*, 465–70.

59. Packard, *Century of US Naval Intelligence*, 228–35.

60. Frederick D. Parker, "How Op-20-G Got Rid of Joe Rochefort," in *Cryptologia*, Vol. 24 No. 3 (July, 2000), 212–234.

61. Cited in Allan Haris Bath, *Tracking the Axis Enemy: The Triumph of Anglo-American Intelligence* (Lawrence: University Press of Kansas, 1998), 171; John B. Lundstrum,

"Confrontation in the Coral Sea: Admiral Nimitz's Plan for a Decisive Battle in the South-West Pacific," in *Kokoda: Beyond the Legend*, Karl James, ed. (New York: Australian War Memorial / Cambridge University Press, 2017), 59; and Borneman, *The Admirals*, 245.

62. USNI, Dyer Reminiscences, 469; NWC, King Papers, Box 8, "Admiral Nimitz," 31 July 1949; and NWC, King Papers, Box 7, Whitehill notes, "Leyte Gulf."

63. NWC, King Papers, Box 8, "Admiral Nimitz," 31 July 1949.

64. Prados, *Combined Fleet Decoded,* 299–305.

65. John B. Lundstrom, *Black Shoe Carrier Admiral: Frank Jack Fletcher at Coral Sea, Midway, and Guadalcanal* (Annapolis, MD: Naval Institute Press, 2006), 496–516; John B. Lundstrom, *The First Team: Pacific Naval Air Combat From Midway to Pearl Harbor* (Annapolis, MD: Naval Institute Press, 1984), 35–59, 84–87, 121–24, 155–60, 292–97, and 434–35; and Prados, *Combined Fleet Decoded,* 299–305.

66. Buell, *Master of Sea Power*, 194–204 and M. E. Butcher, "Admiral Frank Jack Fletcher: Pioneer Warrior or Gross Sinner?," *Naval War College Review*, vol. 40, no. 1 (Winter, 1987), 69–79.

67. Lundstrom, *Black Shoe Carrier Admiral*, 496–516.

68. NWC, King Papers, Box 8, "Admiral Nimitz," 31 July 1949.

69. Frank A. Blazich Jr., *An Honorable Place in American Air Power: Civil Air Patrol Coastal Patrol Operations, 1942–1943* (Montgomery, AL: Air University Press, 2021), 11–30, 39–79, and 100–63.

70. NWC, King Papers, Box 7, "Circumstances leading to the appointment of Vice Admiral F. J. Horne as Vice Chief of Naval Operations."

71. NWC, King Papers, Box 7, "Secretaries Knox and Forrestal," 3.

72. Ibid.

73. Ibid.

74. NWC, "Nimitz Graybook," vols. I and II, including numerous entries between December 1941 and July 1942. See pp. 433, 453, 468, 489, 490, 492, 499, 500, 506–21, 543, 548–74.

75. NWC, Low Papers, Box 1, "Personal Narrative," 25–26.

76. NWC, "Nimitz Graybook," vol. I, 492.

77. Ibid.

78. Ibid.

79. Ibid.

80. NWC, King Papers, Box 6, Bull Diary, 6 November 1942, 4. See NWC," Nimitz Graybook," vol. I, 433, 453, 468, 489, 490, 492, 499, 500, 506–21, 543, 548–74.

81. NWC, King Papers, Box 6, Bull Diary, 6 November 1942, 4.

82. Ibid.

83. Ibid.

84. Ibid.

85. Ibid.

Chapter 22

1. Eliot Carlson, *Stanley Johnston's Blunder: The Reporter Who Spilled the Secret behind the US Navy's Victory at Midway* (Annapolis, MD: Naval Institute Press, 2017), 77–80, 85–88, 156–57, 174–77; Larry J. Frank, "The United States Navy vs. the *Chicago Tribune*," *The Historian* (February 1980), 284–303; Dina Goren, "Communications Intelligence and the Freedom of the Press: The *Chicago Tribune's* Battle of Midway Dispatch and the Breaking of the Japanese Naval Code," *Journal of Contemporary History* 16, no. 4 (October 1981), 663–690; and B. Nelson MacPherson, "The Compromise of US Navy Cryptanalysis after the Battle of Midway," *Intelligence and National Security* 2, no. 2 (April 1987), 320–323.

2. TNA, ADM 116/5418/NID 001669/42, "Categories of Security."

3. NARA, RG 38, Records of the Tenth Fleet, Organization, Box AMS-35, folder A7(2), 12 April 1941, SpeNavO, Report of Lieutenant Commander C. F. Baldwin, USNR, Observations of Admiralty Operational Intelligence Organization.

4. Catherine E. Allan, "A Minute Bletchley Park: Building a Canadian Naval Operational Intelligence Centre, 1939–1943," in Hadley, et. al., *A Nation's Navy: In Quest of Canadian Naval Identity*, 157–72; Douglas, *No Higher Purpose*, vol. II, pt. 1, 59–65; and Timothy Wilford, *Canada's Road to the Pacific War: Intelligence, Strategy, and the Far East Crisis* (Vancouver: University of British Columbia Press, 2011), 34–53.

5. Wesley K. Wark, "The Evolution of Military Intelligence in Canada," in *Armed Forces & Society*, vol. 16, no. 1, (Fall 1989), 77–98.

6. LAC, DND, OIC Canada, 5 March 1943, "Recommendations of the Sub-committee on Communications and Operational Intelligence."

7. NARA, RG 38, Records of the Tenth Fleet, Organization, Box AMS-35, folder A7(2), 12 April 1941, SpeNavO, Report of Lieutenant Commander C. F. Baldwin, USNR, Observations of Admiralty Operational Intelligence Organization.

8. McDiarmid letters to author, 14 November 1999 and 22 April 2000. Also see Douglas, *No Higher Purpose*, vol. II, part 1, 59–65.

9. McDiarmid to author, 12 August 2000.

10. McDiarmid letters to author, 22 April 2000.

11. Beesly, *Very Special Intelligence,* 158.

12. Douglas, *Blue Water Navy*, 60.

13. TNA, ADM 223/88, 48–49.

14. Beesly, *Very Special Intelligence*, 105.

15. NSA, Knowles Oral History, 4–5.

16. Ibid., 2–3 and 21.

17. NARA, F-21 War Report, 23.

18 Ibid.

19. Douglas, *A Blue Water Navy*, 58–62; and Beesly, *Very Special Intelligence*, 60.

20. McDiarmid letters to author, 14 November 1999, and 22 April 2000.

21. McDiarmid, letter to author, 22 April 2000.

22. Beesly, *Very Special Intelligence*, 117–21 and 157–59.

23. Ibid., 158.

24. TNA, ADM 223/286, "Submarine Tracking and Anti-U/Boat Warfare, NID 8S," Lieutenant-Commander Patrick Beesly, comp., 151–53.

25. Hinsley, *British Intelligence*, vol. II: 228–29.

26. Ibid.

27. Original trans., Gilbert, *Signals Intelligence,* 155–57.

28. Ibid.

29. Ibid.

30. NWC, King Papers, Box 2, Russell to Buell, 18 November 1974.

31. LC, King Papers, Box 35, "Thesis III," 4.

32. Ibid.

33. NWC, King Papers, Box 8, Memorandum to Rear Admiral Randall Jacobs," January 1942. Emphasis in original.

34. Ibid.

35. NWC, King Papers, Box 5, "Navy Department Office Space in Washington, DC," 15 March 1944.

36. Ibid.

37. Ibid.

38. NARA, RG 457, SRH 149, "A Brief History of Communications Intelligence in the United States," Lawrence F. Safford, comp., 6.

39. Schmitt, "From Code-Making to Policy-Making," 25–35.

40. Matt Zullo, *The US Navy's On-the-Roof-Gang: Prelude to War* (Chambersburg, PA: ZooHaus Books, 2020), 7–38, 258–95, and 315–415.

41. Layton, *And I Was There,* 32.

42. Ralph Erskine, Colin Burke, and Philip Marks, "Memorandum to OP-20-G on Naval Enigma (c. 1941)," in *The Essential Turing,* Jack Copeland, ed. (Oxford: Clarendon, 2004), 341–352.

43. Washington, DC, US Congress, Senate Report no. 10, (78th Cong., 2d sess.), 271.

44. Carlson, *Joe Rochefort's War,* 64–85, 390–93, and 472–75; Layton, *And I Was There,* 49–50; and Maffeo, *US Navy Codebreakers,* 191–92.

45. TNA, ADM 223/107, Observations from visit to Washington and Ottawa by John Henry Godfrey, September to October 1942, submitted on 1 November 1942.

46. Benson, *History of US Communications Intelligence,* 47.

47. NARA, RG 457, SRH 403, "Selections from the Cryptologic Papers Collection of Rear Admiral J. N. Wenger, USN."

48. NARA, SRH 268, "Advanced Intelligence Centers in the US Navy," Redman memorandum to Horne, 20 June 1942.

49. Ibid.

50. Parker, "How Op-20-G Got Rid of Joe Rochefort," 230–34.

51. USNI, Sebald Reminiscences, 290–340.

52. NARA II, RG 38, CNSG Library, Box 92, File 5750/49, King to Nimitz, 28 October 1942.

53. Ibid.

54. NWC, King Papers, Box 13, King to Jacobs, 10 August 1942.

55. Ibid.

56. Gallery, *Clear the Decks,* 7.

57. LC. King Papers, Box 39, speech file, "Town Hall Meeting," 25.

58. Simpson, *Cunningham,* 127–72; Roskill, *Churchill and the Admirals,* 117–93; and King, *Fleet Admiral King,* 349–413.

59. Buell, *Master of Seapower,* 354.

60. NWC, King Papers, Box 2, Hyland to Buell, 2 August 1974.

61. Potter, *Nimitz,* 109–12.

62. Newport News, Virginia, the Mariners' Museum Library and Archives, Nimitz to Lieutenant Robert Saunders, 12 July 1948.

63. Albion, *Makers of Naval Policy,* 577.

64. NWC, MSC-52, Henry C. Eccles Papers, Box 31, "Theater Logistics Planning."

65. Albion, *Makers of Naval Policy,* 543.

66. Ibid.

67. LC, King Papers, Box 39, speech file, "Town Hall Meeting," 25.

68. Ibid.

69. Albion, *Makers of Naval Policy,* 579.

70. Ibid.

71. NWC, King Papers, Box 8, "Admiral Nimitz," 31 July 1949.

72. LC, King Papers, Box 39, speech file, "Town Hall Meeting," 26.

73. Ibid.

74. Ibid.

75. Ibid., 27.

76. NWC, King Papers, Box 6, Bull Diary, 5 April 1943.

77. Ibid.

78. Ibid.

79. NWC, King Papers, Box 7, "London Visit," 4.

80. John Lewis Gaddis, *The United States and the Origins of the Cold War* (New York: Columbia University Press, 1972), 23–27.

81. Robert W. Coakley and Richard M. Leighton, *Global Logistics and Strategy, 1943–45* (Washington, DC: US Army Center of Military History, 1986), 297–354, 391–433, and 462–91.

82. NWC, King Papers, Box 7, "Statue of Sir John Dill," Statement by King, November 1950.

83. Ibid.

84. Michael A. Simpson, ed., *The Cunningham Papers: Selections from the Private and Official Correspondence of Admiral of the Fleet Viscount Cunningham of Hyndhope* (Aldershot, UK: Scholar Press of the Navy Records Society—Ashgate Publishing, Ltd., 2006), vol. II, 14.

85. Perry, *Dear Bart,* 52.

86. Ibid.

87. NARA, FDR, Safe Files, Box 3, "King, Ernest J.," King to Roosevelt, 5 March 1942. Emphasis in original.

88. Christopher M. Bell, *Churchill and Seapower* (New York: Oxford University Press, 2013), 258, 295–300.

89. NARA, FDR, Safe Files, Box 3, "King, Ernest J.," King to Roosevelt, 5 March 1942.

90. Ibid.

91. NWC, King Papers, Box 7, "Combatting the Submarine Menace—Building Merchant Ships vs. Building Anti-submarine Craft."

92. Ibid.

93. Ibid

94. Ibid.

94. Ibid.

96. NWC, King Papers, Box 6, Bull Diary, 24 July 1943, 42.

97. Ibid.

98. Ibid.

99. Ibid.

100. Ibid.

101. NWC, King Papers, Box 7, "Pacific vs. Sickle," 2.

102. FDR, Safe Files, Box 3, folder "King, Ernest J.," "Instructions for London Conference—July, 1942."

103. Ibid.

104. Ibid., 34.

105. Ibid.

106. Stoler, *Allies and Adversaries*, 103–22; Brower, *Defeating Japan*, 18–22, 29–32, 74–93, 112–20, 139, 144, 149–51; and Rigby, *Allied Master Strategists*, 91, 116, 128–32, 138–41.

107. NWC, King Papers, Box 6, Bull Diary, 6 June 1943, 33.

108. NWC, King Papers, Box 6, Bull Diary, 24 July 1943, 44.

109. Ibid.

110. Maxwell Air Force Base, Alabama, United States Air Force Oral History Program, Interview of Frederic H. Smith Jr. (released in 1976).

111. NWC, King Papers, Box 6, Bull Diary, 30 November 1942, 16.

112. Duncan S. Ballentine, *US Naval Logistics in the Second World War* (Princeton, NJ: Princeton University Press, 1949), 100–296; Worrall R. Carter, *Beans, Bullets, and Black Oil: The Story of Fleet Logistics Afloat in the Pacific during World War II* (Annapolis, MD: Naval Institute Press, 1952), 1–20; George C. Dyer, *Naval Logistics* (Annapolis, MD: Naval Institute Press, 1960), iii–x, 2–30, and 40–60; and William L. McGee with Sandra McGee, eds., *Pacific Express: The Critical Role of Military Logistics in World War II* (Tiburen, CA: BMC Press, 2009), vol. III, 93–235 and 439–55.

113. Robert H. Ferrell, ed., *The Eisenhower Diaries* (New York: Norton, 1981), 50–51

114. Ibid.

115. Ibid.

Chapter 23

1. King, *Fleet Admiral King*, 412 and 628.

2. Ibid.

3. O'Brian, *Powerful Man in the World*, 299–300.

4. NWC, King Papers, Box 7, "Hap Arnold," 1 March 1949.

5. Dwight D. Eisenhower, *At Ease: Stories I Tell to Friends* (New York: Doubleday, 1967), 252.

6. Ibid.

7. Ibid.

8. Ibid.

9. Ibid.

10. Potter, "Command Personality," 20.

11. NWC, King Papers, Box 4, George Russell to Buell, 18 November 1974.

12. Ibid.

13. Ibid.

14. Whitehill, "Postscript," 216.

15. Ibid.

16. Ibid., 209.

17. LC, King Papers, Box 17, King to Morison, 27 October 1948.

18. Ibid.

19. Ibid.

20. Ibid.

21. NWC, King Papers, Box 6, Bull Diary, 6 November 1942, 9.

22. Ibid.

23. King, *Fleet Admiral King*, 465.

24. Ibid.

25. Ibid.

26. Ibid.

27. Ibid.

28. NWC, King Papers, Box 6, Bull Diary, 12 September 1943, 48.

29. Ibid.

30. NWC, King Papers, Box 7, "Hap Arnold," 1 March 1949.

31. NWC, King Papers, Box 7, interview notes, 4 July 1950.

32. NWC, King Papers, Box 6, Bull Diary, 12 September 1943, 49.

33. NWC, King Papers, Box 6, Bull Diary, 6 November 1942, 5.

34. Ibid.

35. Blazich, *An Honorable Place*, 11–30, 39–79, and 100–63.

36. NWC, King Papers, Box 6, Bull Diary, 12 September 1943, 49.

37. NWC, King Papers, Box 13, "Memorandum for Admiral King from General Marshall (1 July 1943)."

38. Ibid.

39. NWC, Low Papers, Box 1, "Personal Narrative," 34.

40. NWC, King Papers, Box 5, King to Stark, 5 November 1941

41. NWC, Low Papers, Box 1, "Personal Narrative," 34.

42. Sterett, "Admiral King Hits a Single Command," *New York Times*, 13 February 1946.

43. Ibid.

44. William Frye, *Marshall: Citizen Soldier* (New York: Bobbs-Merrill, 1947), 325.

45. Ibid.

46. United States Congress, Hearings before the Senate Committee on Military Affairs, 79th Congress, 1st Session (1945), 142.

47. NWC, King Papers, Box 5, "Admiral Leahy," November 1950.

48. Stimson, *On Active Service*, 505–15.

49. NWC, King Papers, Box 7, rough interview notes by Walter Muir Whitehill, 4 July 1950.

50. NWC, Archives Reading Room, Robert G. Albion and Elting E. Morison, comps., "History of the Eastern Sea Frontier (Organizational and Operational)," unpublished manuscript prepared for the Navy Department (1946), vol. I, 1–53.

51. NWC, King Papers, Box 2, Alan R. McFarland to Buell, 3 September 1974.

52. Ibid.

53. Ibid.

54. King, *Fleet Admiral King,* 448–49; Buell, *Master of Sea Power,* 284; and Abbazia, *Mr. Roosevelt's Navy,* 32–47.

55. TNA, ADM 223/107, Godfrey Papers, "Collaboration," 22 June 1942; TNA, ADM 223/107, Godfrey Papers, "submitted herewith the following account of my recent visit to Washington made with the object of establishing an effective U/B tracking room" (Winn Report), 3 June 1942; and TNA, ADM 223/286, "The Americans, the Navy Department and Anti U/Boat Warfare."

56. Roskill, *War at Sea,* vol. I, 360; Philip Joubert de la Ferté, *Birds and Fishes: The Story of Coastal Command* (London: Hutchinson, 1960); and William S. Chalmers, *Max Horton and the Western Approaches* (London: Hodder and Stoughton, 1954), 277 and 179.

57. Roskill, *War at Sea,* vol. II, 361.

58. NHC, "United States Naval Administration in World War II," vol. I, 1–53.

59. Stoler, *Allies and Adversaries,* 41–123.

60. Cunningham, *A Sailor's Odyssey,* 654.

61. Leahy, *And I Was There,* 85, 117–127, 221–41, 249–50, 338, and 351–54; Adams, *Witness to Power,* 222–23; and O'Brian, *Powerful Man,* 172, 178–79, 188–89, 194, 196, 199, and 285–90.

62. NWC, Box 6, Bull Diary, 6 November 1942, 2.

63. Ibid., 19 February 1943, 21.

64. Ibid., 5 April 1943, 27.

65. Ibid., 19 February 1943, 20.

66. Samuel Eliot Morison, *History of United States Naval Operations in World War II* (Boston, MA: Little Brown, 1947), vol. I, 46–49; Maurice Matloff and Edwin M. Snell, *Strategic Planning for Coalition Warfare, 1941–1942* (Washington, DC: US Army Center of Military History, 1953), vol. I, 32–51 and 97–113; and David Reynolds, *From World War to Cold War: Churchill, Roosevelt, and the International History of the 1940s* (New York: Oxford University Press, 2006), 42–58.

67. NWC, King Papers, Box 6, Bull Diary, 6 November 1942, 3.

68. Ibid.

69. Ibid., 16 April 1944, 68.

70. Ibid., 3 November 1942, 10.

71. Ibid.

72. Ibid.

73. Ibid., 19 February 1943, 21.

74. Ibid., 21.

75. Ibid.

76. Ibid., 20.

77. LC, King Papers, Box 39, speech file, "Town Hall Meeting," 18.

78. Ibid.

79. Ibid.

80. Ibid.

Chapter 24

1. James L. Hevia, , "Remembering the Century of Humiliation: The Yuanming Gardens and Dagu Forts Museums," in *Ruptured Histories: War, Memory, and the Post-Cold War in Asia,* Sheila Jager (ed.) (Cambridge, MA: Harvard University Press), 192–208; Gaddis, *Origins of the Cold War,* 23–27; and Kennedy, *Freedom from Fear,* 380.

2. Kennedy, *Freedom from Fear,* 380.

3. NWC, King Papers, Box 9, Whitehill notes, "Race Relations."

4. King's signature indicating his ownership appears in books held by the family.

5. NWC, King Papers, Box 9, Whitehill notes, "Race Relations."

6. Amherst, Massachusetts, University of Massachusetts—Amherst (UMA), Special Collections and University Archives, Manuscript Collections (MS-312), William E. B. DuBois Papers (DuBois Papers), "Green Pastures," circa 1930.

7. Ibid.

8. Ibid.

9. Ibid.

10. William E. B. DuBois, "The Color Line Belts the World," in *W.E.B. DuBois: A Reader,* David Levering Lewis, ed. (New York: Henry Holt, 1995), 43.

11. Nahum Dimitri Chandler, ed., *The Problem of the Color Line at the Turn of the Twentieth Century: The Essential Early Essays of W.E.B. DuBois* (New York: Fordham University Press, 2015), 111–37.

12. McGregor, *Integration,* 77, 82, 85–94, and 166.

13. NWC, King Papers, Box 7, rough interview notes by Walter Muir Whitehill 4 July 1950.

14. LC, King Papers, Box 39, speech file, "Town Hall Meeting," 8.

15. Ibid.

16. Ibid.

17. Paolo Coletta, *The United States Navy and Defense Unification, 1947–1953* (East Brunswick, NJ: Associated University Press, 1981), 93–95, 104–05, 186–88; Barlow, *Revolt of the Admirals,* 26–28, 50–52, 61–62, 68–69, 77–78, 163–64, 180; and Herman S. Wolk, *Planning and Organizing the Postwar Air Force, 1943–1947* (Washington, DC: Office of US Air Force History, 1984), 91–95 and 186.

18. LC, King Papers, Box 39, speech file, "Town Hall Meeting," 9.

19. Ibid.

20. Lundstrom, *The First Team,* 35–59, 84–87, 121 24, 155–60, 292–97, and 434–35.

21. Furer, *Administration,* 567–69; King, *US Navy at War,* 151–57; and Cameron, *American Samurai,* 60–62.

22. King, *US Navy at War,* 152.

23. Ibid.

24. Ibid.

25. NHHC, "Guide to Command of Negro Naval Personnel."

26. NHHC, Administrative Histories, Historical Section, *The Negro in the Navy of World War II* (Washington, DC: Navy Department, 1945), 22–39.

27. NWC, King Papers, Box 8, "Admiral Nimitz."

28. McGregor, *Integration*, 77, 82, 85–94, and 166.

29. NARA, NRPC, RG 24, correspondence associated with Navy Cross Medal for Petty Officer First Class Doris Miller, King to Jacobs, 20 March 1942.

30. Thomas W. Cutler, *Doris Miller, Pearl Harbor, and the Civil Rights Movement* (College Station: Texas A&M Press, 2017), 69–70, 80–82, 87, and 100.

31. Nelson, *Integration of the Negro,* 184–233.

32. NWC, King Papers, Box 9, "Race Relations."

33. McGregor, *Integration*, 77, 82, 85–94, and 166.

34. NHHC, "Guide to Command of Negro Naval Personnel."

35. NWC, King Papers, Box 9, "Race Relations."

36. Ibid.

37. Ibid.

38. Ibid.

39. Ibid.

40. Ibid.

41. Ibid.

42. Robert J. Schneller Jr., "Oscar Holmes: A Place in Naval Aviation," in *Naval Aviation News* (January–February, 1998), 26–27.

43. Ernest J. King, "Responsibilities of Leadership," in *The Naval Officer's Guide*, Arthur A. Ageton, comp. (New York: Whittlesey House, 1943), 499–502.

44. Ibid.

45. Ibid.

46. Robert J. Schneller Jr., *Breaking the Color Barrier: The US Naval Academy's First Black Midshipmen and the Struggle for Racial Equality* (New York: New York University Press, 2005), 153–61; Paul Stillwell, *The Golden Thirteen: Recollections of the First Black Naval Officers* (Annapolis, MD: Naval Institute Press, 2003); and Cameron, *American Samurai*, 30, 42, 65, 71, 89–91, 123, 214–15, and 271.

47. Adam Makos, *Devotion: An Epic Story of Friendship, Heroism, and Sacrifice* (New York: Bantam Books, 2015), 3–35 and 297–395.

48. King, *Fleet Admiral King*, 322.

49. Ibid.

50. NWC, King Papers, Box 5, Admiral King memorandum to the Chief of Naval Personnel, Commandant of the Marine Corps, and Commandant of the Coast Guard, 16 September 1942.

51. John T. Mason Jr., *The Atlantic War Remembered: An Oral History Collection* (Annapolis, MD: Naval Institute Press, 1990), 1–39.

52. Elizabeth G. Hendricks, "Mildred McAfee Horton (1900–1994): Portrait of a Pathbreaking Christian Leader," in *Journal of Presbyterian History*, vol. 76, no. 2 (Summer 1998): 159–174.

53. NWC, King Papers, Box 5, USNI, "Joy Bright Hancock (Oftsie)," vol. I, 37–38.

54. Ibid.

55. Ibid.

56. Joy Bright Hancock, *Lady in the Navy: A Personal Reminiscence* (Annapolis, MD: Naval Institute Press, 1972), 64, 121, 148–49, and 154.

57. Anon., "Army & Navy—Marines: BAMS," *Time* magazine, 4 October 1943.

58. In truth, marines generally referred to women marines as "Broad Assed Marines." See Cameron, *American Samurai*, 63–75 and 243–45.

59. Jim DeBrosse and Colin Burke, *The Secret in Building 26: The Untold Story of America's Ultra War Against the U-boat Enigma Codes* (New York: Random House, 2004), 5–7, 10–11, 85–87, and 189–92.

60. NWC, King Papers, Box 6, Bull Diary, 16 April 1944, 69.

61. NWC, King Papers, Box 3, "Mildred McAfee and Joy Hancock-Oftsie."

62. NWC, King Papers, Box 6, Bull Diary, 6 June 1943, 35.

63. Ibid.

64. Ibid.

65. NWC, King Papers, Box 3, Whitehill notes, undated.

66. LC, King Papers, Box 39, speech file, "Town Hall Meeting," 8–9.

67. Ibid.

68. Ibid.

69. Ibid.

70. Perry, *Dear Bart*, xii, 6, 10, 80, 85, and 329.

71. Ibid.

72. Lloyd J. Graybar, "Admiral King's Toughest Battle," *Naval War College Review*, vol. 32, no. 1 (February 1979), 38–47.

73. Ibid., 107–08.

74. NWC, King Papers, Box 2, Adams to Buell.

75. NWC, King Papers, Box 6, Bull Diary, 30 November 1942, 16.

76. Ibid.

77. Ibid., 5 April 1943, 24.

78. Ibid.

79. Ibid., 6 November 1942, 7.

80. Ibid., 19 February 1943, 23.

81. NWC, King Papers, Box 7, "Pacific vs. Sickle," circa 1946, 1–2.

82. NWC, King Papers, Box 7, "Random Notes," written by King, circa 1950.

83. Ibid.

84. Ibid.

85. Navy Department Appropriations Bill for 1943 in "Hearings before the Subcommittee on Appropriations in the House of Representatives (77th Congress, 2nd Session), 8–10.

86. Ibid.

87. Perry, *Dear Bart*, 49.

88. Ibid.

89. Blair, *Hitler's U-boat War*, vol. I, 461–62; Farago, *Tenth Fleet*, 54, 117, and 143; and Love, "Ernest Joseph King," 137–79.

90. Blazich, *An Honorable Place*, 11–30, 39–79, and 100–63.

91. King, *Fleet Admiral King*, 355–57; Farago, *Tenth Fleet*, 83–86; and Robert William Love Jr., "Ernest Joseph King, 26 March 1942–15 December 1945," in *The Chiefs of Naval Operations*, Robert W. Love Jr., ed. (Annapolis, MD: Naval Institute Press, 1980), 146.

92. Perry, *Dear Bart*, 49.

93. Coles, "Ernest King and the British Pacific Fleet," 127; Max Hastings, *Nemesis: The Battle for Japan, 1944–45* (London: Harper, 2007), 112–113 and 400–402; and Roskill, *The War at Sea*, vol. II, 37, 97, 102–3, 130, 222, and 229–31.

94. NWC, King Papers, Box 7, Pound to King, 18 May 1942.

95. NWC, King Papers, Box 7, Pound to King, 2 February 1943.

96. NWC, King Papers, Box 7, King to Pound, 5 March 1943.

97. Ralph Erskine and Frode Weierud, "Naval Enigma: M4 and Its Rotors," *Cryptologia*, 9 (1987), 235; and Ralph Erskine, "The First Naval ENIGMA Decrypts of World War II," 44.

98. NWC, King Papers, Box 6, Bull Diary, 30 November 1942, 13.

99. Ibid.

100. NWC, King Papers, Box 6, Bull Diary, 30 November 1942, 9.

101. Ibid.

102. Ibid.

103. NWC, King Papers, Box 7, "Random Notes," written by King, circa 1950.

104. Herbert Feis, *The China Tangle: The American Effort in China from Pearl Harbor to the Marshall Mission* (Princeton, NJ: Princeton University Press, 1953), vii, 3–13, 56–58, and 115–44.

105. NWC, King Papers, Box 6, Bull Diary, 30 November 1942, 13.

106. Ibid.

107. Ibid.

108. Ibid., 5.

109. Ibid.

110. Ibid.

111. Ibid.

112. Ibid.

113. Ibid.

114. Ibid.

115. Ibid.

116. Ibid., 10.

117. Ibid.

118. Ibid.

119. Ibid.

120. MacDonnell, *Insidious Foes*, 20–31 and 157–84.

121. Gannon, *Operation Drumbeat*, 413–16.

122. NWC, King Papers, Box 7, "Miscellaneous notes of conversation with Admiral King," 4 July 1950.

123. Ibid.

124. NWC, King Papers, Box 2, Smedberg to Buell, 6 February 1975.

125. NWC, King Papers, Box 6, "Awards."

126. NWC, King Papers, Box 5, King to Stark.

127. Albion, *Makers of Naval Policy*, 386.

128. Coletta, *Navy and Defense Unification*, 26–53.

129. James Wise with Anne Collier Rehil, *Stars in Blue: Movie Actors in America's Sea Services* (Annapolis, MD: Naval Institute Press, 1997), 20–27, 50–57, and

133; Renehan, *The Kennedys at War*, 104, 187, and 191–94; and Albion, *Forrestal and the Navy*, 132.

130. Carlson, *Stanley Johnston's Blunder*, 77–80, 85–88, 156–57, 174–77; and Frank, "The United States Navy vs. the *Chicago Tribune*," 284–303.

131. Bill Mauldin, *Up Front* (Cleveland, OH: World Publishing, 1945), 100.

132. Ibid., 162 and 195–202.

133. David Lawrence, "Master of Propaganda: Stephen Leo Gets Navy Service Award," in *The Marion Star* (16 June 1950), 1.

134. Maxwell Air Force Base, Alabama, Center for Air Force History (AFH), George M. Watson Interview with Stephen F. Leo (Leo Reminiscences), August 1982, 21–25, 48–52, 67–80; Obituary, Stephen F. Leo, *New York Times* (3 October 1983), 15; and Jeffrey G. Barlow, *Revolt of the Admirals: The Fight for Naval Aviation 1945–1950* (Washington, DC: US Government Printing Office, 2001), 3–40 and 50–62.

135. Lawrence, "Master of Propaganda."

136. Ibid.

137. Guy Richards, "Air Force Drum-Beater Keeps Feet on the Ground," *Washington Star* (18 September 1948), 10.

138. Ibid.

139. AFH, Leo Reminiscences, 1–30.

140. Chicago, Illinois, Museum of Science and Industry (MSI), Daniel V. Gallery Jr., *U-505* Papers, Box 2, Stephen F. Leo, "The Information Program through the Years."

141. Joseph Goebbels, *Die Zeit ohne Beispiel* (Munich: Zentralverlag der NSDAP, 1941), 364.

142. Robert L. McLaughlan and Sally Perry, *We'll Always Have the Movies: American Cinema during World War II* (Lexington: University Press of Kentucky, 2006), 53–55, 84–85, and 297–98; Mark Harris, *Five Came Back: A Story of Hollywood and the Second World War* (New York: Penguin, 2014); and Eric Mills, "John Ford, USN," in *Naval History*, vol. 27, no. 2 (April, 2013), 48–55.

143. Wolk, *Planning and Organizing*, 36–38, 87–95, and 154; George M. Watson Jr., *The Office of the Secretary of the Air Force 1947–1965* (Washington, DC: Government Printing Office, 1992), 56, 60, 79, 90–91, and 112; and Gian Peri Gentile, "Advocacy or Assessment? The United States Strategic Bombing Survey of Germany and Japan," *Pacific Historical Review*, vol. 66, no. 1 (February 1997): 53–79.

144. Robert Matzen, *Mission: Jimmie Stewart and the Fight for Europe* (Pittsburgh, PA: GoodNight Books, 2016), 1–3, 29–30, 77–79, and 262–64; Starr Smith, *Jimmie Stewart: Bomber Pilot* (Saint Paul, MN: Zenith, 2005), 25 and 210; and Alan J. Vick, *Force Presentation in Air Force History and Airpower Narratives* (Santa Clara, CA: RAND, 2018), 1–41; and Wolk, *Planning and Organizing*, 62–64, 126–31, 160–62, 183–85, 289–91, and 312–13.

145. Coletta, *Navy and Defense Unification*, 92–93.

146. Lawrence, "Master of Propaganda."

147. Cameron, *American Samurai*, 15–16 and 89–129.

148. George M. Watson Jr. and Herman S. Wolk, "'Whiz Kid:' Robert S. McNamara's World War II Service," in *Air Power History*, vol. 50, no. 4 (Winter, 2003), 4–15.

149. Wolk, *Planning and Organizing*, 36–38, 87–95, and 154.

150. Lawrence, "Master of Propaganda."

151. LC, King Papers, Box 39, speech file, "Town Hall Meeting," 8–9.

152. Ibid.

153. Gallery, *Clear the Decks*, 96.

Chapter 25

1. Arthur Bryant, *Turn of the Tide: A History of the War Years Based on the Diaries of Field-Marshal Lord Alanbrooke, Chief of the Imperial General Staff* (New York: Doubleday, 1957), 504.

2. Ibid.

3. NWC, Box 6, Bull Diary, 30 November 1942, 13.

4. LC, King Papers, Box 39, speech file, "Town Hall Meeting," 30.

5. Ibid.

6. NWC, King Papers, Box 5, "Admiral Edwards, 1 May 1946."

7. NWC, King Papers, Box 6, Bull Diary, 19 February 1943, 18.

8. King, *Fleet Admiral King*, 428, 441, and 589.

9. NWC, Box 6, Bull Diary, 30 November 1942, 13.

10. LC, King Papers, Box 35, from Assistant Chief of Staff (Plans) to CominCh, "Proposed formation of 'Strategic Planning Group,'" 13 February 1942.

11. Ibid.

12. Donald H. Riddle, *The Truman Committee: A Study in Congressional Responsibility* (New Brunswick, NJ: Rutgers University Press, 1964), 59, 78, 87, 113–18; and David McCullogh, *Truman* (New York: Simon and Schuster, 1992), 304–35, 435, and 536. See Harold D. Smith, comp., *The United States at War Development and Administration of the War Program by the Federal Government* (Washington, DC: Government Printing Office, 1946), 140–45.

13. "US At War: Truman v. Knox" *Time* magazine, vol. XLI, no. 19 (10 May 1943), 5. In the same edition of *Time*, see the article "World Battle Fronts: Doenitz of the Sub-Atlantic: Germany's First Defense in the Atlantic Moat," 28–30.

14. Perry, *Dear Bart*, xii.

15. NWC, Box 2, Whitehill notes, "Walter Lippmann."

16. Stoler, *Allies and Adversaries*, 57–63.

17. NWC, King Papers, Box 5, "Memorandum," Edwards, 30 January 1946."

18. Ibid.

19. Ibid.

20. Ibid.

21. Ibid.

22. Author's telephone interview with Egerton van den Berg, March 2018.

23. Ibid.

24. NWC, King Papers, Box 5, USNI Oral History Extract, "Reminiscences of Vice Admiral George C. Dyer," (Dyer Reminiscences), 465.

25. NWC, King Papers, Box 4, George Russell to Buell, 18 November 1974.

26. Ibid.

27. NWC, King Papers, Box 2, Griffen to Buell, 19 December 1974.

28. LC, King Papers, Box 8, Sheppard to Knox, 20 December 1943.

29. Ibid.

30. LC, King Papers, Box 8, King to Knox, 31 December 1943.

31. LC, King Papers, Box 8, Brown to King, 30 December 1943.

32. NWC, King Papers, Box 5, *Dauntless*, Whitehill interview with Grisham.

33. Ibid.

34. LC, King Papers, Box 8, Grisham to King, 22 December 1943.

35. Wolters, *Information at Sea*, 170–219, 220, 221–25.

36. NWC, MSC-116, Caleb Laning Papers, Box 1; UCL, Heinlein Memoir, 14–15, 40–50, and 58–61; Patterson, *In Dialogue with His Century*, 126–43; and Wysocki, *The Great Heinlein Mystery*, 78–79, 98–99, 150–57, 216–17, and 240.

37. Ibid.

38. Gallery, *Clear the Decks*, 94.

39. King, *Fleet Admiral King*, 647–48.

40. Ibid.

41. NWC, King Papers, Box 5, USNI Oral History Extract, "Reminiscences of Vice Admiral George C. Dyer," (Dyer Reminiscences), 465.

42. USNI, Smith-Hutton Reminiscences, vol. II, 456.

43. Ibid., 388–89.

44. USNI, Reminiscences of Captain Henri Smith-Hutton (Smith-Hutton Reminiscences), 352–79.

45. USNI, Smith-Hutton Reminiscences, 319–20.

46. USNI, Sebald Reminiscences, 250.

47. Ibid., 318.

48. Ibid., 319.

49. NWC, King Papers, Box 5, "Dyer interview of 1 August 1945," 1–4; NARA, RG 38, CominCh, Crane Files, SSIC 5750/24, Box 37, F-21 War Report, 3; and NARA, RG 38, CominCh, SSIC 5750/24, Box 37, F-22 War Report, 1.

50. USNI, Smith-Hutton Reminiscences, vol. I, 388–89.

51. Ibid.

52. NARA, RG 38, Records of the Chief of Naval Operations (CominCh), Office of Naval Intelligence, Special Warfare Branch (OP-16-W), Box 12, "Grossadmiral Karl Doenitz: A Charecterological Study," 2–6. An interesting wartime monograph prepared by Ladislas Farrago while assigned the Op-16-Z / Special Activities Branch.

53. MacLachlan, *Room 39*, 163–81; Ladislas Farago, *The Tenth Fleet: The Untold Story of the Submarine and Survival* (New York: Obolensky, 1962), 65–81, 145–52, 156, 228, and 247; and Kenneth A. Knowles, review of *The Tenth Fleet*, in *Central Intelligence Agency Journal*, vol. 7, no. 2 (Fall 1962), approved for release, CIA Historical Review Program (September 1993).

54. DeBrosse, *The Secret in Building 26*, 5–7, 10–11, 85–87, and 189–92.

55. Judy Parsons email to author, 9 June 2020. Her interview with the author appeared on the Cable News

Network in August 2020. Her interview appears on the internet https://www.cnn.com/2020/08/04/us/world-war-ii-women-codebreakers-nebraska-avenue/index.html.

56. NSA, Oral History (NSA-OH-03-83), R. D. Farley interview with Earl E. Stone (Stone Reminiscences), p. 3. Released under FOIA by Jimmie Collins after the request by the author of 15 December 2010.

57. Ibid.

58. Ibid.

59. Ibid.

60. Ibid.

61. NARA, RG 38, Crane Files, Box 74, Meader report to Wenger, 21 January 1949.

62. Ibid.

63. NWC, King Papers, Box 7, "Hap Arnold," 1 March 1949.

64. NARA, RG 457, Box 808, "Final Report on Patent Matters at Naval Communication Annex."

65. NSA, Random Analytical Machine (RAM) File, "Navy Contract NXs7892," King to Leahy, 17 March 1943.

66. DeBrosse, Secret in Building 26, 88–110.

67. NSA, Random Analytical Machine (RAM) File, "Navy Contract NXs7892," King to Leahy, 17 March 1943.

68. Ibid.

69. Ibid.

70. Ibid.

71. Ibid.

72. NARA, RG 80, Box 287, folder A6-2/A8 (April 6–17), "Final Report: British-Canadian-American Radio Intelligence Discussions."

73. Ibid.

74. NARA, RG 457, Box 1414, "Memorandum for the Director of Naval Communications: History of the Bombe Project, 30 May 1944," (Bombe History), Howard Engstrom, Joseph Wenger, and Ralph Meader comps.; and NARA, RG 457, Box 1424, GC&CS Naval History Correspondence, "History of Hut 8," chapter 9, "Four Wheel Bombe Policy and the Contributions of OP-20-G," unpublished manuscript by A. Patrick Mahon, circa 1946. This is a duplicate copy of TNA, "HW 25/2."

75. NARA, RG 457, File 35701, "Op-20-G Memorandum," Captain Joseph N. Wenger, comp., 12 February 1945.

76. McGinnis, Naval Cryptologic Veterans Association, 16 and 20–37.

77. Ralph Erskine, "The Holden Agreement on Naval SigInt: The First BrUSA?" in Intelligence and National Security, vol. 14, no. 2 (1999), 187–97.

78. Ibid.

79. Ibid.

Chapter 26

1. Henry B. Ryan, "A New Look at Churchill's 'Iron Curtain' Speech," in The Historical Journal, vol. 22, no. 4 (December, 1979): 895–920.

2. Jennifer Wilcox, Solving the Enigma: History of the Cryptanalytic Bombe (Washington, DC: Center for Cryptologic History, 2006), 1–55.

3. NARA, RG 38, Box 54, CNSG 3200/1, "Op-20-G Memorandum describing Enigma analog."

4. Ibid.

5. Ibid.

6. Author's Collection, Quine to Jeffrey Bray, 3 August 1991. Special thanks to Carl Boyd and Jeffrey Bray for sharing their research, which was used in compiling the edited volumes as published by Aegean Park Press, Ultra in the Atlantic.

7. Ibid.

8. Willard Quine, The Time of My Life: An Autobiography (Cambridge, MA: Massachusetts Institute of Technology Press, 1985), 181–82.

9. Ibid.

10. Ibid.

11. Quine, Time of My Life, 184.

12. Packard, Century of US Naval Intelligence, 229–35.

13. King, Fleet Admiral King, 356.

14. Caraley, Unification, 23–122.

15. Larry I. Bland and Sharon Ritenour Stevens, eds., The Papers of George Catlett Marshall: Aggressive and Determined Leadership, June 1, 1943–December 31, 1944 (Baltimore, MD: Johns Hopkins University Press, 1996), vol. 4, 416.

16. NWC, King Papers, Box 7, Whitehill notes, 4 July 1950.

17. Eisenhower, Crusade in Europe, 1–49 and 387–404; Stoler, Allies and Adversaries, 10–41, 64–103, and 231–70; and Winston S. Churchill, The Second World War: The Grand Alliance (New York: Houghton and Mifflin, 1950): vol. III, 315–53, 465–77, and 604–18.

18. NWC, King Papers, Box 7, "Comments on Flag Officers of US Navy"; comment on Churchill appears in discussion of Henry Kent Hewitt.

19. NWC, King Papers, Box 6, Bull Diary, 19 February 1943, 18.

20. Ibid., 24 July 1943, 40.

21. USNI, Smith-Hutton Reminiscences, vol. II, 218.

22. LC, King Papers, Box 35, "Mr. Roosevelt versus Chiang Kai-shek."

23. King, Fleet Admiral King, 415.

24. Albert C. Wedemeyer, Wedemeyer Reports! (New York: Henry Holt, 1958): 171–72.

25. Ibid.

26. King, Fleet Admiral King, 415.

27. NWC, King Papers, Box 6, Bull Diary, 5 April 1943, 25.

28. Ibid.

29. Ibid.

30. NWC, King Papers, Box 8, 12 January 1951 Memorandum from Schneider to Historical Section, JCS.

31. Stoler, Allies and Adversaries, 71–83.

32. LC, King Papers, Box 17, King to Morison, 27 October 1948.

33. Ibid.

34. Rohwer, Critical Convoy Battles, 195–200.

35. Denis Richards and Hilary Saunders, The Royal Air Force 1939–1945: The Fight Avails (London: HMSO, 1953), vol. II, 106–08; Sir Philip Joubert de la Ferté, Birds and Fishes: The Story of Coastal Command (London: Hutchinson, 1960); and Roskill, War at Sea, vol. II, 361–63.

36. Roskill, *War at Sea*, Vol. II, 361.

37. NWC, King Papers, Box 7, "Air Force."

38. Henry Harley Arnold, *Global Mission* (New York: Harper, 1949), 216 and 300–18.

39. NWC, King Papers, Box 7, "Hap Arnold," 1 March 1949.

40. Ibid., 452–55.

41. Charles Schrader, *History of Operations Research in the United States Army: 1942–62* (Washington, DC: US Army Center of Military History, 2008), 58–62.

42. NWC, King Papers, Box 7, Whitehill notes, 4 July 1950.

43. NWC, King Papers, Box 7, "ASW Conference 1 March 1943 Remarks by Admiral King."

44. NWC, King Papers, Box 6, Bull Diary, 12 September 1943, 49.

45. Ibid.

46. Ibid.

47. King, *Fleet Admiral King*, 452–71.

48. NWC, King Papers, Box 13, King to Marshall, 5 June 1943.

49. Wolk, *Planning and Organizing*, 17–21, 41–44, and 85–90.

50. Daniel Ford, *Flying Tigers: Claire Chennault and His American Volunteers, 1941–1942* (New York: Harper Collins, 2007), 6–92.

51. Morison, *Atlantic Battle Won*, 45–52.

52. NWC, King Papers, Box 13, "Memorandum for Admiral King from General Marshall (1 July 1943)."

53. Ibid.

54. King, *US Navy at War*, 172.

55. Ibid., 170.

56. Ibid.

57. Wedemeyer, *Wedemeyer Reports*, 184.

58. Ibid.

59. Ibid.

60. Ibid.

61. Ibid.

62. Ibid., 174.

63. Nicholas Reynolds, *Need to Know: World War II and the Rise of American Intelligence* (New York: Marriner, 2022), 234–43.

64. NWC, King Papers, Box 7, "1943 File, "Combustible, Vulnerable, and Expendable": King's thoughts on the CVE in the Battle of the Atlantic."

65. Ibid.

66. Ibid.

67. NWC, King Papers, Box 7, "Tenth Fleet."

68. Ibid.

69. William T. Y'Blood, *Hunter-Killer: US Escort Carriers in the Battle of the Atlantic* (Annapolis, MD: Naval Institute Press, 1983), 1–10.

70. Ibid., 280–83.

71. NWC, King Papers, Box 7, "King's thoughts on the CVE in the Battle of the Atlantic."

72. Ibid.

73. Ibid.

74. TNA, ADM 199/1048, "US Navy Escort Carrier Operations," 12 February 1944.

75. NWC, King Papers, Box 7, "Tenth Fleet."

76. NHC, "ComInCh Administrative History," 143.

77. Author's notes from interviews with René B. "Chevy" Chevalier and Samuel P. Livecchi conducted in 1998, 2001, and 2002.

78. Gary E. Weir, *An Ocean in Common: American Naval Officers, Scientists, and the Ocean* (College Station: Texas A&M University Press, 2001), 141–95.

79. NWC, Low Reminiscences, 34.

80. Ferreiro, *Churchill's American Arsenal*, 180–200; Reynolds, *Need to Know*, 234–43; and Tilden, *Operations Evaluation Group*, 60–61.

81. Wolters, *Information at Sea*, 193–235.

82. Ibid., 207–10.

83. Ibid., 208, 210–11, and 220–21.

84. NWC, MSC-116, Caleb Laning Papers, Box 1; UCL, Heinlein Memoir, 14–15, 40–50, and 58–61; Patterson, *In Dialogue with His Century*, 126–43; Wysocki, *The Great Heinlein Mystery*, 78–79, 98–99, 150–57, 216–17, and 240.

85. Patterson, *Heinlein*, vol. 1, 333–37.

86. UCL, Heinlein Memoir, 35.

87. Ibid.

88. Ibid.

89. King, *Fleet Admiral King*, 462–78; Farago, *Tenth Fleet*, 157–293; and David Kohnen, *Commanders Winn and Knowles: Winning the U-boat War with Intelligence* (Kraków: Enigma, 1999), 75–138.

90. King, *Fleet Admiral King*, 462–78.

91. Y'Blood, *Hunter-Killer*, 215–19 and 239–40.

92. Ibid. See Carl Boyd, "US Navy Radio Intelligence during the Second World War and the Sinking of the Japanese Submarine *I-52*," in *The Journal of Military History*, vol. 63, no. 2 (April 1999), 339–54. Note: the *RO-501* was a German Type IXC/40 submarine with a Japanese crew sailing from Europe to Asia.

Chapter 27

1. NWC, King Papers, Box 8, 12 January 1951 Memorandum from US Navy Commander F. H. Schneider to US Army colonel G. Dohyns, executive, Historical Section, JCS.

2. Gilbert Norman Tucker, *The Naval Service of Canada: Its Official History* (Ottawa, ON, King's Printer, 1952), vol. II, 412–51; and Michael Whitby, Richard H. Gimblett, and Peter Haydon, *The Admirals: Canada's Senior Naval Leadership in the Twentieth Century* (Toronto: Dundurn Press, 2006), 69–72 and 89–92.

3. W. A. B. Douglas, *The Creation of a National Air Force: The Official History of the Royal Canadian Air Force* (Toronto: University of Toronto Press, 1986), vol. II, 546–49; Sherry, *The Rise of American Airpower*, 90–110; and Barlow, *Revolt of the Admirals*, 3–40.

4. NARA, RG 218, Box 6, 3 June 1948, manuscript by Captain Tracy Barrett Kittredge, USNR, and Lieutenant Abbott Smith, USNR, comps. "History of the Joint Chiefs of Staff: The War against Germany," 114–20.

5. Ibid., 252–53.

6. NWC, King Papers, Box 6, Bull Diary, 19 February 1943, 18.

7. Ibid.

8. NWC, King Papers, Box 7, Pound to King, 18 February 1943.

9. NWC, King Papers, Box 7, "King to Pound," 5 March 1943.

10. NWC, King Papers, Box 7, "Pound to King," 18 February 1943.

11. Brian McCue, *U-boats in the Bay of Biscay: An Essay in Operations Analysis* (Washington, DC: National Defense University Press, 1990), 8–19, 109–43, and 153–78.

12. Philip M. Morse and George E. Kimball, *Methods of Operational Research* (Cambridge, MA: Technology Press, 1951), 49–50.

13. Robin Broadhurst, *Churchill's Anchor: The Biography of Admiral of the Fleet Sir Dudley Pound* (London: Pen and Sword, 2000), 22–52, 186, 205–7, and 216–238.

14. McLean, "Muddling Through," 174–75 and 187–89.

15. DND, Directorate of History, 181.009 (D-268), "Atlantic Convoy Conference Washington, DC. (1–12 March 1943), Brodeur remarks.

16. Ibid.

17. Ibid.

18. LAC, RG 24, vol. 11928, file 8740-102/1, Nelles, "Operational Control of Northwest Convoy Lanes West of 35 Degrees West," 17 December 1942.

19. LAC, Collection MG30 E207, Admiral Leonard W. Murray Papers.

20. Ibid., addendum, "Recommendations of the Sub-committee on Communications and Operational Intelligence," 5 March 1943.

21. LAC, RG 24, vol. 3805, file 1008-75-10, DDSD(Y) to DSD, "Lt. Cdr. John (Jock) de Marbois, Memorandum, 17 May 1943.

22. NWC, King Papers, Box 7, keynote address by King, prepared on 28 February 1943, "ASW Conference 1 March 1943 Remarks by Admiral King." This typescript document was amended by King with handwritten notations. The parenthesis appears in the original notes written in King's hand.

23. Ibid.

24. NWC, King Papers, Box 7, "Tenth Fleet."

25. Ibid.

26. Ibid.

27. Perry, *Dear Bart*, 142–43.

28. Ibid.

29. NWC, Low Reminiscences, 28.

30. Ibid.

31. Ibid., 29.

32. Ibid.

33. NWC, King Papers, Box 2, Howard Orem to Buell, 12 December 1974.

34. Ibid., 28–35.

35. NARA, RG 38, CominCh, Tenth Fleet, Box AMS-35, 19 September 1944, "Memorandum of Conversation with Rear Admiral F. S. Low (FX-01)."

36. NSA, Library, Operating Instructions for ECM Mark 2 (CSP 888/889) and CCM Mark 1 (CSP 1600), May 1944.

37. NARA, RG 38, CominCh, War Diaries, Box 1, NND 968133, CominCh for Action US Fleet, 192200 February 1943, effective 15 March 1943.

38. Ibid.

39. NARA, RG 38, CominCh, Tenth Fleet, Box AMS-35, 10 February 1943, King handwritten annotation on yellow memo pad that is appended to the recommendation by Low, "Fleet Headquarters and Task Force Organization."

40. King, *Fleet Admiral King*, 532–35.

41. NWC, King Papers, Box 7, Miscellaneous Notes, 4 July 1950.

42. Ibid.

43. Ibid.

44. Ibid.

45. NARA, RG 38, Tenth Fleet, Box AMS-35, "Anti-submarine Warfare," King to Nimitz, 4 April 1943.

46. Edward Drea, *MacArthur's ULTRA: Codebreaking and the War against Japan* (Lawrence: University of Kansas, 1992), 73; Boyd, *Hitler's Japanese Confidant*, 107–08; Layton, *And I Was There*, 474–76; Potter, *Nimitz*, 284–85; and Holmes, *Double-Edged Secrets*, 129–36.

47. Dan Hampton, *Operation Vengeance: The Astonishing Aerial Ambush That Changed World War II* (New York: William Murrow, 2020), 75–77, 87–88, 162–78, 185–91, 236–39, 274–75, 298–300, and 358–67.

48. John Prados, *Combined Fleet Decoded: The Secret History of American Intelligence and the Japanese Navy in World War II* (New York: Random House, 1995), 459–61.

Morison, *History of US Naval Operations*, vol. VI, 127–29; Maffeo, *US Navy Codebreakers*, 202, 268, 302, and 493–94; Drea, *MacArthur's ULTRA*, 73; and Potter, *Nimitz*, 233–34.

49. NARA, RG 457, SRH-288, 336.

50. John Paul Stevens, *The Making of a Justice: Reflections on My First 94 Years* (Boston: Little Brown, 2019).

51. Hiroyuki Agawa with John Bester, trans., *The Reluctant Admiral: Yamamoto and the Imperial Japanese Navy* (Tokyo: Kodansha International, 1982), 347–67.

52. NWC, King Papers, Box 7, Whitehill notes, 4 July 1950.

53. Ibid.

54. NWC, King Papers, Box 5, King to Andrews, 7 June 1943.

55. Morison, *Atlantic Battle Won*, 17–19.

56. Boyd, *British Naval Intelligence*, 421–552

57. Beesly, *Very Special Intelligence*, 152.

58. Ibid.

59. NARA, RG 38, Records of the Tenth Fleet, Organization, Box AMS-35, folder A7(2), 12 March 1942, Lieutenant Commander P. L. Hammond, USNR, to Captain Wilder DuPuy Baker, USN, with enclosure of a 11 March 1942 report submitted by Commander John P. W. Vest, USN, to Captain Charles Lockwood, USN, Enclosure A, Organization of the Royal Navy Division of Anti-submarine Warfare and Attached Thereto a Memo Amplifying Each Officer's Job," (SpeNavO Report on NID Organization and Functions).

60. Ottawa, Library and Archives of Canada (LAC), National Defence Headquarters, Directorate of History and Heritage, Reference 1440-18 "History and Activities

of Operational Intelligence Centre, N.H.Q. (ca. 1945)," memoranda files, 11 July 1945, "History of O.I.C. 5," John B. McDiarmid, comp.

61. NHC, "CominCh Administrative History," 210.

62. NWC, King Papers, Box 2, Knowles to Buell, 22 September 1974.

63. New Haven, Connecticut, Yale University Archives (YUA), Henry Lewis Stimson Papers, Diaries, vol. 43, 28 April 1943.

64. NWC, King Papers, Box 7, "Comments on Chapter V."

65. NARA, RG 38, World War II Operational Records, Records of the Tenth Fleet, Box AMS-35, 26 April 1943, "Memorandum for the Joint Chiefs of Staff."

66. NWC, King Papers, Box 7, "Tenth Fleet."

67. Ibid.

68. Kohnen, "The Cruise of *U-188*," in *Decision in the Atlantic*, 252–88; Kohnen, *Twenty-First-Century Knox,* 1–19; and Kohnen, "Seizing German Naval Intelligence from the Archives of 1870–1945," 133–71.

69. NWC, King Papers, Box 2, Knowles to Buell, 22 September 1974.

70. Ibid.

71. NHC, "CominCh Administrative History," 167.

72. Ibid.

73. NARA, CominCh, Records of the Tenth Fleet, Box AMS-35, 8 May 1943, Memorandum for Admiral King, "Air Offensive against the Submarine."

74. Ibid.

75. NWC, King Papers, Box 7, "Comments on Flag Officers," 31 July 1949, "Admiral John S. McCain," 8.

76. NWC, Low Reminiscences, 31.

77. Ibid.

78. NWC, King Papers, Box 7, "Tenth Fleet."

79. NWC, King Papers, Box 2, Gallery to Buell, 21 August 1974, 1–2.

80. Morison, *US Naval Operations*, vol. X: 219–23.

81. Ibid.

82. The author wishes to extend very special thanks to Admiral Joseph Prueher, former ambassador to China and the son of Commander Bertram Prueher, 17 May 2018.

83. Chalmers, *Western Approaches*, 277 and 179.

84. King, *Fleet Admiral King*, 428, 441, and 589.

Chapter 28

1. NWC, King Papers, Box 7, ASW Conference 1 March 1943.

2. NWC, Manuscript Collection Number 2, Richard W. Bates Papers, Combat Narratives, "Battle of Midway, 3–6 June 1942—US Confidential-British Secret," Office of Naval Intelligence Publication (March 1943).

3. Ibid.

4. NWC, King Papers, Box 7, keynote address by King, as compiled by Admiral Charles M. Cooke on 28 February 1943, "ASW Conference 1 March 1943 Remarks by Admiral King."

5. NWC, King Papers, Box 7, Whitehill notes, "Cdre. Knox."

6. Ibid.

7. NWC, King Papers, Box 7, "Comments on Flag Officers, US Navy," 31 July 1949, "William S. Pye," 8.

8. Ibid.

9. Ibid.

10. NHHC, "CominCh Administrative History," 143.

11. Furer, *Administration of the Navy Department*, 119–20.

12. NHHC, CominCh Administrative History, 145.

13. Ibid., 142–45.

14. NARA, RG 457, SRMN-038, Box 35, "Functions of the Secret Room (F-211) of CominCh Combat Intelligence, Atlantic Section," 1–10; NARA, RG 38, CominCh, Crane Files, SSIC 5750/24, Box 37, F-21 War Report, 3; and NARA, RG 38, CominCh, SSIC 5750/24, Box 37, F-22 War Report, 4.

15. YUA, MS 792, John E. Parsons Papers (Parsons Papers).

16. NARA, RG 457, SRMN-38, 1–10.

17. Ibid.

18. Ibid.

19. Ibid.

20. NHC, "CominCh Administrative History," 143–247.

21. NARA, RG 457, SRMN-038, SRMN-38; NARA, RG 38, Box 37, F-21 War Report, 3; and NARA, RG 38, Box 37, F-22 War Report, 4.

22. TNA, HW 50/94, "U/B Tracking," Section IV, Subparagraph (i), 15.

23. Ibid., Section V, Subparagraph (d), 20.

24. NARA, RG 38, Crane Files, F-21 War Report, 14.

25. Ibid.

26. Author's notes from interviews with Chevalier and Livecchi conducted in 1998, 2001, and 2002.

27. USNI, Smith-Hutton Reminiscences, vol. II, 458.

28. NSA, Knowles Reminiscences, 14–15.

29. Ibid.

30. NWC, King Papers, Box 2, Knowles to Buell, 22 September 1974.

31. Ibid.

32. Ibid.

33. Ibid.

34. NWC, King Papers, Box 2, Schoeffel to Buell, 9 September 1974.

35. Ibid.

36. Ibid.

37. Ibid.

38. Ibid.

39. Ibid.

40. Ibid.

41. Ibid.

42. NWC, King Papers, Box 2, Knowles to Buell, 22 September 1974.

43. Ibid.

44. Ibid.

45. USNI, Smith-Hutton Reminiscences, vol. II, 456–57.

46. Ibid.

47. NARA, RG 457, SRMN-038, 6.

48. NWC, King Papers, Box 2, McFarland to Buell, 8 August 1974.

49. Ibid.

50. Ibid.

51. Ibid.

52. Ibid.

53. NWC, King Papers, Box 2, Lawrence B. Cook to Buell, 5 August 1974.

54. NWC, King Papers, Box 2, Schoeffel to Buell, 9 September 1974.

55. Ibid.

56. Gallery, *Clear the Decks*, 93–95.

57. Ibid.

58. NHC, "CominCh Administrative History," 99–100.

59. LC, King Papers, Box 17, King to Edwards, 22 April 1949.

60. Hone, *Mastering the Art of Command*, 165.

61. NWC, MSC-107, Thomas C. Shaw Papers, Box 17, "CominCh P-1: Naval Directives and the Order Form," Ernest J. King, comp., 1 April 1944.

62. NWC, King Papers, Box 7, "Admiral Ingersoll"; NWC, King Papers, Box 8, "Fleet Organization," 2; Roscoe, *Submarine Operations*, 85–86; and Blair, *Silent Victory*, 78–80.

63. NWC, King Papers, Box 8, "Fleet Organization."

64. NWC, King Papers, Box 7, "Additional notes on flag officers," 14 August 1942, 2.

65. Ibid.

66. NWC, King Papers, Box 7, "Comments on Flag Officers, US Navy," 31 July 1949, "Admiral R. K. Turner," 2–3.

67. NARA, RG 38, CominCh, War Diaries, Box 1, NND 968133, CominCh for Action US Fleet, 192200 February 1943, effective 15 March 1943.

68. NWC, Low Reminiscences, 32.

69. Ibid.

70. Ibid.

71. NHHC, "CominCh Administrative History," 169.

72. NSA, Knowles Reminiscences, 14.

73. NARA, RG 38, CominCh, Crane Files, SSIC 3840/2, Box 37, "F-21 Memoranda Regarding Submarine Tracking and Operations, June 1943–June 1945," undated memorandum, "Offensive Action against U-boats," submitted to Captain George C. Dyer in OpNav for transmittal to CNO Chief of Staff, 3.

74. TNA, DEFE 3/719, 413; and NARA, RG 457 Entry 9020, SRMN 054, Op-20-GI Special Studies Relating to U-boat Activity, enclosure D.

75. NARA, RG 313, ComNavEu, Box 12, "Sub/Anti-sub ETOUSA Operations," 3–4.

76. Ibid.

77. Simpson, *The Cunningham Papers*, vol. II, 14.

78. Cunningham, *A Sailor's Odyssey*, 466.

79. Ibid.

80. NWC, King Papers, Box 7, "Memorandum for the Record," April 1951.

81. NARA, RG 38, CominCh, Tenth Fleet, Box 33, 27 April 1943/281628, CominCh to Admiralty.

82. Ibid.

83. Ibid.

84. NHHC, "United States Naval Administrative Histories of World War II, Appendices Collection," Command Files, Low Report, Francis F. Low, *A Study of Undersea Warfare*, TOP SECRET Annex, Draft submitted on 1 January 1946.

85. Carl Boyd, *The Imperial Japanese Submarine Force and World War II* (Annapolis, MD: Naval Institute Press, 1994), 149–52; Theodore Roscoe, *United States Destroyer Operations in World War II* (Annapolis, MD: Naval Institute Press, 1953), 398–401; and Morison, *History of US Naval Operations*, vol. VIII, 228.

86. Morison, *History of US Naval Operations*, vol. VIII, 228.

Chapter 29

1. Lambert, *The British Way of War*, 435–39; Stoler, *Allies and Adversaries*, 103–22; Brower, *Defeating Japan*, 18–22, 29–32, 74–93, 112–20, 139, 144, 149–51; and Rigby, *Allied Master Strategists*, 91, 116, 128–32 138–41.

2. Richard G. Hewlett and Oscar E. Anderson, Jr, *The New World, 1939/1946, A History of the United States Atomic Energy Commission* (University Park: Pennsylvania State University Press, 1962), vol. I, 278–327 and 456–64.

3. King, *Fleet Admiral King*, 620–21; Rearden, *Council of War*, 47; and Stoler, *Allies and Adversaries*, 213–16.

4. Edward Terrell, *Admiralty Brief: The Story of Inventions That Contributed to Victory in the Battle of the Atlantic* (London: Harrop, 1958), 26–27.

5. Buell, *Master of Seapower*, 397; Jordan, *American Warlords*, 283; and Borneman, *The Admirals*, 329.

6. NWC, King Papers, Box 9, Whitehill notes, 31 July 1949.

7. King, *Fleet Admiral King*, 487: Leahy, *I Was There*, 177–79; and Arnold, *Global Mission*, 443–44.

8. Alex Danchev, ed., *Field Marshal Lord Alanbrooke: War Diaries—1939–1945* (London: Weidenfeld and Nicholson, 2001), 446.

9. Ibid.

10. NWC, King Papers, Box 5, Whitehill notes of interview with Rear Admiral Libby.

11. Wedemeyer, *Wedemeyer Reports!*, 181.

12. Ibid.

13. Ibid., 183.

14. Ibid.

15. NWC, Low Reminiscences, 43.

16. NWC, King Papers, Bull Diary, 18 December 1943, 55.

17. NWC, King Papers, Box 8, Whitehill notes, "Combined Chiefs."

18. Ibid.

19. Ibid. Emphasis in original.

20. Ibid.

21. Ibid., 24 July 1943, 42.

22. Ibid.

23. Ibid.

24. NWC, King Papers, Box 8, Whitehill notes, "Combined Chiefs."

25. NWC, King Papers, Box 6, Bull Diary, 18 December 1943, 54.

26. Ibid., 5 April 1943, 26.

27. Ibid., 18 February 1944, 58.

28. Ibid.

29. Ibid., 6 June 1943, 32.

30. Ibid.

31. Ibid., 12 September 1943, 47.

32. Ibid., 24 July 1943, 42.

33. Ibid.

34. Ibid., 18 February 1944, 59.

35. NWC, King Papers, Box 6, Bull Diary, 18 December 1943, 53.

36. Ibid.

37. Ibid.

38. Ibid., 16 April 1944, 63.

39. Ibid., 18 February 1944, 62.

40. Ibid., 16 April 1944, 63.

41. NWC, King Papers, Box 6, Bull Diary, 6 June 1943, 31.

42. Ibid., 47–48.

43. Ibid.

44. Ibid., 12 September 1943, 48.

45. Ibid.

46. Ibid.

47. Ibid., 48.

48. Ibid.

49. Ibid., 16 April 1944, 63.

50. David Kohnen, "Tombstone of Victory: Tracking the *U-505* from German Commerce Raider to American War Memorial 1944–1954," *Journal of America's Military Past*, vol. 32, no. 3 (Winter 2007): 5–33.

51. NWC, King Papers, Box 6, Bull Diary, 12 September 1943, 45.

52. Ibid.

53. Ibid.

54. Ibid.

55. Ibid., 44.

56. Ibid.

57. Ibid., 45.

58. Ibid., 40.

59. NWC, King Papers, Box 5, rough interview notes by Walter Muir Whitehill from July 1950.

60. King, *Fleet Admiral King*, 483.

61. Ibid., 646.

62. NWC, King Papers, Box 5, rough interview notes by Walter Muir Whitehill from 14 August 1949.

63. King, *Fleet Admiral King*, 409.

64. NARA, RG 38, ComInCh Serials, multiple boxes. Specifically see serial 02200 (18 Jun 42); ComInCh letter to ComNavEu, Serial 001915 (9 September 1943); ComInCh dispatch 111902 (12 August 43); ComInCh Serial 03683 (24 October 1943); BuPers dispatch 281439 (28 October 43); ComInCh Serial 03800 (4 November 1943); ComInCh Serial 04350 (24 Dec 1943); ComInCh Serial 0400 (1 Feb 1944); and ComInCh Serial 01200 (12 April 1944).

65. Ibid.

66. Nicolas Jellicoe, *George Jellicoe: SAS and SBS Commander* (Philadelphia, PA: Pen and Sword, 2021), 61–128.

67. Forrest C. Pogue, *George C. Marshall—Organizer of Victory, 1943–1945* (New York: Viking Press, 1973), 307.

68. Heiferman, *The Cairo Conference*, 76–82.

69. NWC, King Papers, Box 7, "Command of OVERLORD."

70. NWC, King Papers, Box 7, comments regarding "The War against Japan," 2.

71. Ibid.

72. John L. McCrea with Julia C. Tobey, eds., *Captain McCrea's War: The World War II Memoir of Franklin D. Roosevelt's Naval Aide and USS Iowa's First Commanding Officer* (New York: Skyhorse, 2016), 189–90.

73. Ibid.

74. Ibid.

75. Greg Behrman, *A Most Notable Adventure: The Marshall Plan and the Time When America Helped Save Europe* (New York: Free Press / Simon and Schuster, 2007), 10.

76. NWC, King Papers, Box 7, "Command of OVERLORD."

77. Robert H. Ferrell, ed., *The Eisenhower Diaries* (New York: Norton, 1981), 50–51.

78. Harry C. Butcher, *My Three Years with Eisenhower: The Personal Diary of Captain Harry C. Butcher, USNR—Naval Aide to General Eisenhower, 1942–1945* (New York: Simon and Schuster, 1946), 561–79.

79. King's grandchildren still hold the family secrets about the unrelated Generals Walter D. and Freddie Smith. For sharing these materials and for helping to map out the internal workings of King's familial network of trusted friends and families on the Washington battlefield, the author is particularly indebted to Janvier King Smith, Thomas King Savage, and the late Egerton van den Berg.

80. Ibid., 24 July 1943, 35–36.

81. NWC, King Papers, Box 6, Bull Diary, 18 December 1943, 51.

82. Ibid.

83. Ibid.

84. NWC, King Papers, Box 8, Whitehill notes, "Combined Chiefs."

85. NWC, King Papers, Box 6, Bull Diary, 18 December 1943, 51.

86. King, *Fleet Admiral King*, 516

87. NWC, King Papers, Box 6, Bull Diary, 18 December 1943, 51–52.

88. Ibid., 52.

89. Ibid., 512–24, 588–95, 608–10, and 614.

90. NWC, King Papers, Box 6, Bull Diary, 18 December 1943, 52.

91. NWC, King Papers, Box 11, Whitehill notes.

92. NWC, King Papers, Box 6, Bull Diary, 18 December 1943, 52.

93. Ibid., 67.

94. Ibid., 67.

95. Ibid., 24 July 1943, 40.

96. LC, King Papers, Box 35, "Roosevelt versus the Philippines and Formosa."

97. NWC, King Papers, Box 6, Bull Diary, 18 February 1944, 61–62.

98. Albion, *Makers of Naval Policy*, 574.

99. Nigel Hamilton, *War and Peace: FDR's Final Odyssey—D-day to Yalta, 1943–1945* (New York:

Houghton-Mifflin, 2019), 63–64, 334, 344, and 353–57.

100. King, *Fleet Admiral King*, 482–90, 499–512, and 523–26; Stoler, *Allies and Adversaries*, 15–122; and Rigby, *Allied Master Strategists*, 9–67.

101. NWC, King Papers, Box 7, King directives to Hewitt regarding Greek operations.

102. NWC, Simpson Papers, Box 9, King to Stark, November 1943.

103. Ibid.

104. Ibid.

105. Ibid.

106. NWC, King Papers, Box 8, Chief of Naval Operations Organization.

107. NWC, King Papers, Box 8, Whitehill notes, "Combined Chiefs." Emphasis in original.

108. Ibid.

109. Ibid.

110. Ibid., 2.

Chapter 30

1. Zach Fredman, *The Tormented Alliance: American Servicemen and the Occupation of China* (Chapel Hill: University of North Carolina, 2022), 14–15, 91–93, 148, and 157–67.

2. NWC, King Papers, Box 7, "Strategy after the Marianas."

3. Ibid.

4. Ibid.

5. Ibid.

6. NWC, King Papers, Box 6, Bull Diary, 18 February 1944, 61–62.

7. Ibid.

8. Ibid.

9. Ibid.

10. Ibid., 57.

11. Ibid., 59.

12. Michael Coles, "Ernest King and the British Pacific Fleet: The Conference at Quebec, 1944 (Octagon)," in *The Journal of Military History*, vol. 65, no. 1 (January 2001), 105–129.

13. NWC, King Papers, Box 6, Bull Diary, 12 September 1943, 50.

14. NWC, King Papers, Box 6, Bull Diary, 6 June 1943, 30.

15. Ibid.

16. Ronald Ian Heiferman, *The Cairo Conference of 1943: Roosevelt, Churchill, Chiang Kai-Shek, and Madame Chiang* (Jefferson, NC: McFarland, 2011), 76–82.

17. King, *Fleet Admiral King*, 511.

18. Stanford, California, Hoover Institution Archives (HIA), Diaries of General Joseph W. Stilwell (1941–1945), 23 November 1943 [online] https://digitalcollections. hoover.org/images/Collections/51001/1943_stilwell_diary_rev.pdf.

19. NHHC, Oral History, Vice Admiral John V. Smith, 139.

20. Ibid.

21. NWC, King Papers, Box 6, Bull Diary, 12 September 1943, 44.

22. NWC, King Papers, Box 6, Whitehill notes, 3 March 1947.

23. Ibid.

24. Ibid.

25. Leahy, *And I Was There*, 85, 117–127, 221–41, 249–50, 338, and 351–54; Adams, *Witness to Power*, 222–23; and O'Brian, *Powerful Man*, 172, 178–79, 188–89, 194, 196, 199, and 285–90.

26. King, *Fleet Admiral King*, 567.

27. NWC, King Papers, Box 8, Chief of Naval Operations Organization.

28. Ibid.

29. USNI, Dyer Reminiscences, 469.

30. Ibid.

31. NWC. King Papers, Box 5, Knox to Morison, 19 November 1946.

32. NWC, King Papers, Alan Edward Smith to Buell, 19 August 1974.

33. Ibid.

34. Ibid.

35. Roscoe, *Submarine Operations*, 237–39, 290–92, and 310.

36. Ibid, 292.

37. USNI, Captain Robert E. Dornin Reminiscences (Dornin Reminiscences), 2.

38. NWC, King Papers, Kirkpatrick to Buell, 2 August 1974.

39. USNA, Dornin Reminiscences, 3.

40. Ibid., 3.

41. Ibid., 6.

42. Ibid.

43. Ibid.

44. Ibid.

45. Ibid., 7.

46. NWC, King Papers, Box 7, folder 14, Whitehill notes, "Memorandum of Conversation with Admiral R. S. Edwards—30 January 1946." Emphasis in the original.

47. Ibid.

48. Ibid.

49. Ibid. Emphasis in original.

50. Ibid.

51. Ibid.

52. Ibid.

53. Ernest J. King, comp., *The US Navy at War, 1941–45—Official Reports to the Secretary of the Navy* (Washington, DC: Navy Department, 1946), 217.

54. James J. Cooke, *Chewing Gum, Candy Bars, and Beer: The Army PX in World War II* (Columbia: University of Missouri Press, 2009), vol. 1, 77–104.

55. Ballentine, *US Naval Logistics*, 172–77, 183–85, 210–15; Carter, *Beans, Bullets, and Black Oil*, 1–20; Dyer, *Naval Logistics*, iii–x, 2–30, and 40–60; and McGee, *Pacific Express*, 439–55.

56. NWC, RG-15, Box 11, "Sea Frontier Organization and Problems," Pihl lecture, 1950.

57. NARA, RG 38, ComInCh, Atlantic Section War Report, 4.

58. NARA, RG 38, Records of ComInCh, Tenth Fleet, Box 33, 5 June 1944/1159/9, Admiralty to ComInCh.

59. NSA, Knowles Oral History, 5–6.

60. NARA, RG 38, CominCh, Atlantic Section War Report, 4.

61. NWC, King Papers, Box 2, Knowles to Buell, 22 September 1974.

62. NARA, RG 457, SRMN-051A, vol. II, "OP-20-GI Memoranda to CominCh F21 on German submarine Activities," appendix I, "Submarines Sunk by US Forces with the Aid of Radio Intelligence."

63. NSA, CCH, GC&CS Naval History, part 6, 344.

64. NWC, King Papers, Box 8, Whitehill notes of King's recollections of Normandy.

65. King, *Fleet Admiral King*, 550.

66. Ibid.

67. Ibid., 552.

68. Ibid.

69. NWC, King Papers, Box 7, "Comments on Flag Officers," 2.

70. Ibid, 428, 441, and 589.

71. Potter, *Nimitz*, 90 and 175.

72. NWC, King Papers, Box 8, "Admiral Nimitz," 31 July 1949.

73. NWC, King Papers, Box 7, Miscellaneous Notes, 4 July 1950.

74. Ibid.

75. King, *Fleet Admiral King*, 563.

76. Ibid, 560–65.

77. NWC, King Papers, Box 13, "Admiral J. H. Towers."

78. Ibid.

79. NWC, King Papers, Box 8, "Admiral Nimitz," 31 July 1949.

80. Ibid.

81. Ibid.

82. USNI, Dornin Reminiscences, 7.

83. Ibid.

84. Ibid., 8.

85. Ibid.

86. Smith, *Coral and Brass*, 192.

87. Caraley, *Unification*, 68.

88. USNI, Dornin Reminiscences, 9.

89. Ibid.

90. Ibid.

91. Ibid., 10–11.

92. LC, King Papers, Box 35, "Roosevelt versus the Philippines and Formosa."

93. Hone, *Mastering the Art of Command*, 309–40.

94. King, *Fleet Admiral King*, 604–23.

95. LC, King Papers, Box 17, correspondence files, King to Edwards, 1 August 1950.

96. MHD, "Iwo Jima Project," Commander Amphibious Forces (CTF 51) Operation Plan, A25-44 (CTF 51 Operation Plan), Annex A.

97. Potter, *Nimitz*, 325–27.

98. MHD, Historical Amphibious Files, Box 11B, folder 255, *Amphibious Operations: Capture of Iwo Jima, 16 February–16 March 1945* (COMINCH P-0012).

99. Richard B. Frank, *Downfall: The End of the Imperial Japanese Empire* (New York: Penguin, 2001), 303–06.

100. King, *Fleet Admiral King*, 604–23.

101. Ibid.

102. Ibid.

103. Ibid.

104. Ibid.

105. Ibid.

106. NWC, King Papers, Box 8, "Western Sea Frontier—1944."

107. NWC, RG-15, Box 11, Rear Admiral Paul Pihl, "Sea Frontier Organization and Problems" (1948).

108. NWC, King Papers, Box 2, Sheppard to Buell, 4 August 1974.

109. NWC, King Papers, Box 8, "Western Sea Frontier—1944."

110. Ibid., 1–2.

111. Ibid.

112. Ibid.

113. Ibid.

114. Ibid.

115. William Slim, *Defeat into Victory: Battling Japan in Burma and India, 1942–1945* (London: Cassel, 1956), 199–347.

116. Wedemeyer, *Wedemeyer Reports*, 278.

117. Ibid., 248.

118. Ibid.

119. LC, King Papers, Box 35, "Roosevelt versus the Philippines and Formosa."

120. NARA, RG 38, Records of the Far Eastern Section, Foreign Intelligence, records relating to the Painter Expedition to the China Coast, 1944–45, multiple boxes (Painter Expedition). The author thanks retired US Navy command master chief Mark Fiorey and Painter's son, Bill, for sharing details of their research.

121. Miles, *Different Kind of War*, 591–607.

122. George van Deurs, "Engineering in Reconnaissance," in *The Navy Civil Engineer*, August 1967, 14–17.

123. Anon, "Sower of Invasions: Capt. W. L. Painter, CEC, USNR one of the CECR's Outstanding Officers was Recently Killed in a Yachting Accident," in *Civil Engineer Corps*, vol. 3 no. 35 (October 1949); 25–27; William Bradford Huie, *From Omaha to Okinawa: The Story of the Seabees* (New York: Dutton, 1946), 157–63; Miles, *Different Kind of War*, 591–607; and Wedemeyer, *Wedemeyer Reports!*, 248–365.

124. NWC, King Papers, Box 7, "Strategy after the Marianas."

125. Ibid.

126. Robert L. Allen, *The Port Chicago Mutiny: The Story of the Largest Mass Mutiny Trial in US Naval History* (Berkeley, CA: Heyday Books, 2006), 21–55; Robert J. Schneller Jr., *Breaking the Color Barrier: The US Naval Academy's First Black Midshipmen and the Struggle for Racial Equality* (New York: New York University, 2005), 160–63; and Buell, *Master of Sea Power*, 333–35.

127. NWC, King Papers, Box 7, "Strategy after the Marianas."

128. King, *Fleet Admiral King*, 645.

129. LC, King Papers, Box 35, "Roosevelt versus the Philippines and Formosa."

Chapter 31

1. King, *Fleet Admiral King*, 567.

2. Ibid., 566–67.

3. Ibid.

4. O'Brian, *Powerful Man*, 280–90.

5. Ibid., 568.

6. Leahy, *And I Was There*, 250–51.

7. King, *Fleet Admiral King*, 566–67.

8. NWC, King Papers, Box 13, "Naval Personalities."

9. NWC, King Papers, Box 5, "Naval Promotions."

10. Ibid.

11. NWC, King Papers, Box 13, "Naval Personalities."

12. NWC, King Papers, Box 8, "1944 Pearl Harbor Conference."

13. NWC, King Papers, Box 13, "Naval Personalities."

14. UCL, Heinlein Memoir, 1.

15. Yung, *Gators of Neptune*, 174–78 and 222–23.

16. Jonathan P. Alter with Daniel Crouch, eds., *My Dear Moon: A Literary Collection—Life, Death, and the Untold Story* (Charleston, SC: Booksurge, 2005).

17. King, *Fleet Admiral King*, 552.

18. Ibid.

19. Ibid.

20. Ibid.

21. NWC, King Papers, Box 7, "Generals Eisenhower, Truscott, and Patton."

22. LC, King Papers, Box 35, "Roosevelt versus the Philippines and Formosa."

23. LC, King Papers, Box 39, speech file, "Town Hall Meeting," 8–9.

24. Ibid.

25. Ibid., 27.

26. Ibid.

27. King, *Fleet Admiral King*, 566–67.

28. Ibid., 540.

29. Ibid., 538–43.

30. LC, King Papers, Box 39, speech file, "Town Hall Meeting," 28.

31. Hughes, *Halsey*, 258; Solberg, *Decision and Dissent*, 7; and Nathan Miller, *The War at Sea: A Naval History* (New York: Oxford University Press, 1995), 232.

32. Anon, "Sower of Invasions," 25–27.

33. NARA, RG 38, CominCh, War Diaries, Box 1, NND 968133, "Roster of Officers, Staff of the Seventh-Fleet, United States Fleet, 1 September 1944."

34. Christopher Ford and David Rosenberg, *The Admiral's Advantage: US Navy OPINTEL in World War II to the Cold War* (Annapolis, MD: Naval Institute Press, 2005), 26–29.

35. NHHC, "CominCh Administrative History," 244–47; NWC, ComNavEu, Administrative History, part I, "US Naval Representation in the United Kingdom," 1–10; and NWC, King Papers, Box 8, Navy Department Organization."

36. King, *US Navy at War*, Third Report, 172.

37. Ibid.

38. Ibid., 171.

39. John Prados, *Storm over Leyte: The Philippine Invasion and the Destruction of the Japanese Navy* (New York: Caliber, 2016), 10–20, 57–50, 60–66, 91–92, 96–100, 104, and 117–23.

40. Ibid., 320–25.

41. USNI, Sebald Reminiscences, 309.

42. LC, King Papers, Box 35, "Roosevelt versus the Philippines and Formosa."

43. NHC, CominCh Administrative History, 95–97.

44. NWC, King Papers, Box 2, Smith-Hutton to Buell, 19 September 1974.

45. NWC, King Papers, Box 2, Smedberg to Buell, 6 February 1975.

46. Ibid., 3.

47. Ibid.

48. Ibid.

49. Ibid., 5.

50. NWC, King Papers, Box 2, Smedberg to Buell, 5.

51. Smedberg to Ernest J. "Joe" King Jr. concerning publication of the book *Master of Sea Power*, 23 March 1981. Copy provided to author by Egerton van Den Burg then donated to NWC.

52. Ibid.

53. Ibid.

54. Ibid.

55. Prados, *Storm Over Leyte*, 219–20.

56. Perry, *Dear Bart*, 197–98.

57. LC, King Papers, Box 35, "Roosevelt versus the Philippines and Formosa."

58. NWC, King Papers, Box 2, Smedberg to Buell, 5.

59. Ibid.

60. Ibid.

61. Ibid.

62. Ibid.

63. Perry, *Dear Bart*, 326.

64. LC, King Papers, Box 35, "Roosevelt versus the Philippines and Formosa."

65. Perry, *Dear Bart*, 303.

66. NWC, King Papers, Box 2, Smedberg to Buell, 5.

67. Ibid.

68. Ibid.

69. Ibid.

70. Ibid.

71. Carl Solberg, *Decision and Dissent: With Halsey at Leyte Gulf* (Annapolis, MD: Naval Institute Press, 1995), 10, 27, 100, 118–25, 151, and 156.

72. USNI, Sebald Reminiscences, 309.

73. Prados, *Storm over Leyte*, 96–98; Solberg, *Decision and Dissent*, 120–25; and Sebald, Reminiscences, 309–12.

74. Hone, *Mastering the Art of Command*, 282–86.

75. USNI, Sebald Reminiscences, 309–12.

76. NWC, King Papers, Box 2, Murphy to Buell, 18 September 1974.

77. Edgerton, "MacArthur and the American Military Impact," 420–40.

78. NWC, King Papers, Box 2, Sheppard to Buell, 4 August 1974.

79. NWC, "Nimitz Graybook," vol. 5, Entries for October 1944, pages 2,100–110 and 2,243.

80. Ibid.

81. NWC, RG-15, Box 11, Rear Admiral Paul Pihl, "Sea Frontier Organization and Problems" (1948).

82. Thomas A. Hughes, *Admiral Bill Halsey: A Naval Life* (Cambridge, MA, Harvard University Press, 2016), 109–13; John Wukovitz, *Admiral "Bull" Halsey: The Life and Wars of the Navy's Most Controversial Commander* (New York: St. Martin's Press, 2010), 32–35; Potter, *Bull Halsey*, 286–307; and Alan Rems, "Seven Decades of Debate," *Naval History* vol. 31, no. 5 (October 2017).

83. Prados, *Storm over Leyte*, 11–19, 43–44, 57–60, 83, 91–92, 96–99, 310, and 338.

84. USNI, Sebald Reminiscences, 310.

85. Ibid.

86. Ibid.

87. USNI, Sebald Reminiscences, 310–11.

88. Prados, *Storm over Leyte*, 221–25, 269–74, and 344–52.

89. NWC, King Papers, Box 2, Murphy to Buell, 18 September 1974.

90. Edward Drea, *In the Service of the Emperor: Essays on the Imperial Japanese Army* (Lincoln: University of Nebraska, 1998), 126–44.

91. Edward P. Forrestel, *Admiral Raymond A. Spruance: A Study in Command* (Washington, DC: Department of the Navy, 1966), 167.

92. LC, King Papers, Box 35, "Roosevelt versus the Philippines and Formosa."

93. Potter, *Nimitz*, 321–23.

94. Ibid.

95. Hanson W. Baldwin, *Sea Fights and Shipwrecks: True Tales of the Seven Seas* (Garden City, NY: Hanover House, 1955), 165–82; Gerald E. Wheeler, *Kinkaid of the Seventh Fleet—A Biography of Thomas C. Kinkaid, US Navy* (Annapolis, MD: Naval Institute Press, 1996), 389–415; and William F. Halsey Jr. with Joseph Bryan III, *Admiral Halsey's Story* (New York: Whittlesey House, 1947), 210–23.

96. James D. Hornfisher, *The Last Stand of the Tin Can Sailors: The Extraordinary World War II Story of the US Navy's Finest Hour* (New York: Bantam Books, 2004), 406–27.

97. NWC, King Papers, Box 7, Nimitz to King, 28 October 1944.

98. NWC, King Papers, Box 7, Whitehill notes, "Leyte Gulf."

99. NWC, King Papers, Box 7, "Halsey's Five-Stars—1944."

100. Ibid.

101. Ibid.

102. Prados, *Storm over Leyte*, 221–25, 269–74, and 344–52.

103. NWC, King Papers, Box 8, "Western Sea Frontier—1944," 1–2.

104. King, *Fleet Admiral King*, 580.

105. Ibid.

106. LC, King Papers, Box 17, King to Edwards, 30 August 1949.

107. LC, King Papers, Box 17, King to Kinkaid, 22 August 1949.

108. LC, King Papers, Box 17, Kinkaid to King, 2 September 1949.

109. Solberg, *Decision and Dissent*, 30–95, 114, 120–25, and 149–57.

110. Prados, *Storm over Leyte*, 221–25, 269–74, and 344–52.

Chapter 32

1. Potter, *Nimitz,* 47.

2. Hughes, *Halsey*, 352–97; Morison, *History of US Naval Operations*, vol. XIII, 70–71; and Bob Drury and Tom Clavin, *Halsey's Typhoon: The True Story of a Fighting Admiral, an Epic Storm, and an Untold Rescue* (New York: Grove, 2007), 93–196.

3 USNI, Dornin Reminiscences, 15–16.

4. Ibid.

5. Ibid.

6. Kohnen, "Seizing German Naval Intelligence," 133–71.

7. David Kohnen, "The Cruise of *U-188*: Special Intelligence and the 'Liquidation' of Group Monsoon,' in *Decision in the Atlantic: The Allies and the Longest Campaign of the Second World War*, Christopher Bell and Markus Faulkner, eds. (Lexington: University of Kentucky/Andarta-Brecourt Academic, 2019), 226–52.

8. Ibid.

9. Reynolds, *From World War to Cold War*, 29–68; Beesly, "British Naval Intelligence in Two World Wars," 257; Stephen Roskill, *Naval Policy between the Wars: The Period of Anglo-American Antagonism, 1919–1929* (New York: Walker, 1968), 20; and Simpson, *Somerville Papers*, 589–98.

10. Andrew Cunningham, *A Sailor's Odyssey: The Autobiography of Admiral of the Fleet Viscount Cunningham of Hyndhope* (New York: E.P. Dutton, 1951), 471.

11. Stephen W. Roskill, *Churchill and the Admirals* (London: William Collins, 1977), 210–71.

12. Ibid., 271.

13. Michael Coles, "Ernest King and the British Pacific Fleet: The Conference at Quebec, 1944 (Octagon)" in *The Journal of Military History*, vol. 65, no. 1 (January 2001), 127; Max Hastings, *Nemesis: The Battle for Japan, 1944–45* (London: Harper, 2007), 112–13 and 400–02; and Roskill, *The War at Sea*, vol. II, 37, 97, 102–12, 130, 222, and 229–31.

14. NWC, King Papers, Box 8, Chief of Naval Operations Organization, 3.

15. Miles, *Different Kind of War*, 16–24, 110–17, and 260–63.

16. Yu, *OSS in China*, 48–53; Fredman, *Tormented Alliance*, 14–15, 91–93, 148, and 157–67; and Miles, *Different Kind of War*, 16–24, 110–17, and 260–63.

17. Carolle J. Carter, *Mission to Yenan: American Liaisons with the Chinese Communists* (Lexington: University Press of Kentucky, 1997), 16–36, 63–88, and 177–226; Rana Mitter, *Forgotten Ally: China's World War II* (New York: Mariner, 2013), 335–50; and John Paton Davies Jr., *Dragon by the Tail: American, British, Japanese, and Russian Encounters with China and One Another* (New York: Norton, 1972), 305–430.

18. Wedemeyer, *Wedemeyer Reports*, 317–21.

19. Ibid.

20. Ibid.

21. Yu, *OSS in China*, 48–53; Fredman, *Tormented Alliance*, 14–15, 91–93, 148, and 157–67; and Miles, *Different Kind of War*, 16–24, 110–17, and 260–63.

22. Miles, *Different Kind of War*, 591–607.

23. Ibid.

24. NARA, RG 38, Painter Expedition.

25. Wedemeyer, *Wedemeyer Reports*, 284.

26. Ibid., 317–21; Miles, *Different Kind of War*, 591–607; Carter, *Mission to Yenan*, 16–36, 63–88, and 177–226; Mitter, *Forgotten Ally: China's World War II* (New York: Mariner, 2013), 335–50; and Davies, *Dragon by the Tail*, 305–430.

27. Yu, *OSS in China*, 48–53; Fredman, *Tormented Alliance*, 14–15, 91–93, 148, and 157–67; and Miles, *Different Kind of War*, 16–24, 110–17, and 260–63.

28. NWC, Box 11, Whitehill notes, "Yalta."

29 Perry, *Dear Bart*, 322.

30. NWC, Box 11, Whitehill notes, "Yalta."

31. Ibid.

32. Buell, *Master of Sea Power*, 382–83; Yung, *Gators of Neptune*, 174–78 and 222–23; and Kohnen, *Alan Goodrich Kirk*, 75–92.

33. NWC, King Papers, Box 7, "Command of OVERLORD."

34. Adrian R. Lewis, *Omaha Beach: A Flawed Victory* (Chapel Hill: University of North Carolina Press, 2001).

35. NWC, King Papers, Box 7, "Command of OVERLORD."

36. NWC, King Papers, Box 2, Schoeffel to Buell, 9 September 1974. Emphasis in original.

37. Ibid.

38. USNI, Dyer Reminiscences, 469.

39. Potter, "Command Personality," 21.

40. USNI, Dyer Reminiscences, 471.

41. Ibid.

42. NWC, King Papers, Box 2, Dietrich to Buell, 4 September 1974.

43. NWC, King Papers, Box 2, McFarland to Buell, 5 August 1974.

44. Ibid.

45. Whitehill, "Postscript," 222.

46. Ibid.

47. Albion, *Makers of Naval Policy*, 177, 409, 454, 472, and 601–24.

48. NWC, King Papers, Box 2, Schoeffel to Buell, 9 September 1974.

49. Whitehill, "Postscript," 223.

50. Ibid.

51. Ibid.

52. NWC, King Papers, Box 2, ComInCh/CNO, interview transcript, observations of Charles M. Keyes, August of 1974.

53. Stephen E. Ambrose, *Eisenhower: Soldier, General of the Army, President-Elect—1890–1952* (New York: Simon&Schuster, 1983), vol. I, 224 and 418; Martin Blumenson, *The Patton Papers—1940–1945* (Boston, MA, DaCapo, 1994), 855–57; and Carlo D'Este, *Patton: A Genius for War* (New York: Harper, 1996), 743–45, 805–8, and 924–25.

54. Author's copy, King to Ferrell, 8 September 1942.

55. Ibid.

56. Author's copy, King to Ferrell, 20 June 1940.

57. Cindy Gueli, *Lipstick Brigade: The Untold True Story of Washington's World War II Government Girls* (Washington, DC: Tahoga, 2015), 1–66; Lisa Mundy, *Code Girls: The Untold Story of Women Code Breakers in World War II* (New York: Hachette, 2017), 137–38; and NHHC, "ComInCh Administrative History," 244–47.

58. "Staff Notes," Nan Ferrell retirement notice in "Commerce Library Bulletin," (17 August 1972), 4.

59. Author's copy, King to Ferrell, 11 July 1943.

60. Author's copy, King to Ferrell, 6 December 1942.

61. Author's copy, King to Ferrell, 28 February 1943.

62. Author's copy, King to Ferrell, 11 July 1943.

63. Author's copy, King to Ferrell, 30 March 1941.

64. LC, King Papers, Box 20, "Report of Board of Medical Survey," 3 August 1942.

65. Ibid, 20 February 1945.

66. Ibid.

67. NWC, Box 5, Whitehill notes of discussion with Lozario Dorio.

68. NWC, King Papers, Box 2, Howard Orem to Buell, 12 December 1974.

69. Ibid.

70. Email to author from Egerton and Nikki van den Berg, 9 March 2018.

71. NWC, King Papers, Box 2, Howard Orem to Buell, 12 December 1974.

72. NWC, King Papers, Box 2, McFarland to Buell, 5 August 1974.

73. Author's interview notes with Egerton van Den Berg, 1 March 2018.

74. NWC, King Papers, Box 10, oral history transcript, Rear Admiral Paul Pihl and Charlotte Willkie Pihl.

75. NWC, King Papers, Box 10, Buell interview transcripts with Charlotte Pihl.

76. NWC, King Papers, Box 10, Buell interview transcripts with Paul Pihl, Charlotte Pihl, and Betsy Matter.

77. NWC, King Papers, Box 2, Thebaud to Buell, 1 August 1974 (emphasis in original).

78. Author's interview notes with King's grandchildren Amanda Downing and Eleanor Savage; his great-grandchildren Janvier King Smith, Tom Savage, Meg van Den Berg, and Elizabeth (King); and her husband Harry Slaughter III.

79. NARA, NRPC, RG 24, "Last Will and Testament of Ernest J. King."

80. Email to author from Egerton and Nikki van Den Berg, 9 March 2018; Janvier King Smith email to author, 29 March 2019; and Tom Savage email to author, 30 November 2020.

81. Author's interview notes with Egerton van Den Berg, 1 March 2018.

Chapter 33

1. Hattendorf, *Sailors and Scholars*, 164–78.

2. Ibid., 171–210.

3. NWC, RG 3, Box 2, William S. Pye, comp, "Report of Board to Study the Methods of Educating Naval Officers, 3 March 1944."

4. NWC, King Papers, Box 4, "Some Aspects of the High Command in World War II," 8–9.

5. Ibid.

6. Ibid., 17–18.

7. Ibid.

8. Bernard Brodie, *A Layman's Guide to Naval Strategy* (Princeton, NJ: Princeton University Press, 1943), 1–16, 84–147, and 257–84; Joseph C. Wylie, *Military Strategy: A General Theory of Power Control* (New Brunswick, NJ: Rutgers University Press, 1967), 23–29, 39–64, and 99–111; Caraley, *Unification*, 23–122; and Lambert, *Seapower States*, 1–44, 204–26, and 266–331.

9. LC, King Papers, Box 17, King to Jacobs, 3 April 1942.

10. Ibid.

11. Perry, *Dear Bart,* 323.

12. NWC, RG 3, Box 2, William S. Pye, comp, "Report of Board to Study the Methods of Educating Naval Officers, 3 March 1944."

13. LC, King Papers, Box 35, Naval War College Prospectus, Beary to King, 29 December 1949.

14. NWC, RG 3 Box, 2, Memorandum from the Holloway Board to the Secretary of the Navy, "Study of Proper Form, System, and Method of Instruction of United States Naval Officers of the Post-War United States Navy, 15 September 1945." See John L. Holloway Jr., "The Holloway Plan—A Summary View and Commentary," in Naval Institute *Proceedings*, vol. 73, no. 11 (November 1947), 1,303.

15. Hattendorf, *Sailors and Scholars*, 164–208; John Wesley Masland and Lawrence I. Radway, *Soldiers and Scholars* (Princeton, NJ: Princeton University Press, 1957), 128–35. and Peter D. Feaver and Richard Kohn, *Soldiers and Civilians: The Civil-Military Gap and National Security* (Cambridge, MA: Harvard University Press, 2001), 1–13, 215–74, 327–60, and 429–74.

16. NWC, RG 3, Box 2, William S. Pye, comp., "Report of Board to Study the Methods of Educating Naval Officers, 3 March 1944."

17. Ibid.

18. LC, King Papers, Box 39, speech file, "Town Hall Meeting," 28.

19. Ibid.

20. Ibid.

21. Ibid.

22. Ibid.

23. Ibid.

24. NWC, King Papers, Box 4, "Pye."

25. Roscoe, *Submarine Operations*, 446–47.

26. NWC, King Papers, Box 4, "Pye."

27. Ibid.

28. Ibid.

29. LC, King Papers, Box 39, speech file, "Town Hall Meeting," 10.

30. Ibid.

31. Whitehill, "Postscript," 208.

32. Ernest J. King, comp., *Second Report to the Secretary of the Navy: Covering Combat Operations, 1 March 1944 to 1 March 1945* (Washington, DC: Department of the Navy, 1945), 157.

33. King, *Fleet Admiral King*, 586–87.

34. NWC, Box 11, Whitehill notes, "Yalta."

35. NWC, King Papers, Box 4, "Some Aspects of the High Command in World War II," President of the Naval War College Addendum, "Questions for Fleet Admiral King, 22 June 1948."

36. Ibid.

37. Gaddis, *Origins of the Cold War*, 23–27.

38. LC, King Papers, Box 39, speech file, "Town Hall Meeting," 31. Emphasis in original.

39. NWC, Box 11, Whitehill notes, "Yalta."

40. Perry, *Dear Bart*, 322.

41. Ibid., 323.

42. Ibid.

43. Ibid., 322.

44. Brodie, *Layman's Guide*, 148–74; Samuel Eliot Morison, *Strategy and Compromise: A Reappraisal of the Crucial Decisions Confronting the Allies in the Hazardous Years, 1940–1945* (Boston: Little Brown, 1955), 3–35, 78–106, and 111–20.

45. LC, King Papers, Box 39, speech file, "Town Hall Meeting," 31.

46. Ibid., 32.

47. Ibid., 32.

48. Ibid., 32.

49. Robert G. Albion with Jeannie Barnes Pope, *Forrestal and the Navy* (New York: Columbia University Press, 1962), 1, 8, 142, 200–24, and 284–86; Caraley, *Unification*, 23–122; Coletta, *Navy and Defense Unification*, 93–95, 104–05, 186–88; Barlow, *Revolt of the Admirals*, 26–28, 50–52, 61–62, 68–69, 77–78, 163–64, 180; Wolk, *Planning and Organizing*, 36–38, 86–89, 91–95, and 186; and O'Brian, *Powerful Man*, 222.

50. Albion, *Forrestal and the Navy*, 92–93, 96–103, 124–27, 232–35, and 259–62; Connery, *The Navy and Industrial Mobilization in World War II*, 415–18; and Caraley, *Unification*, 3–56.

51. Albion, *Makers of Naval Policy*, 592–624.

52. Ibid., 539.

53. Ibid., 512–46.

54. Ibid., 378–80, 539, and 545.

55. NWC, King Papers, Box 8, "Horne."

56. Albion, *Makers of Naval Policy*, 105–10, 483–84, 495, and 593–618.

57. King, *Fleet Admiral King*, 477.

58. Robert Connery, *The Navy and Industrial Mobilization in World War II* (Princeton, NJ: Princeton University Press, 1951), 415.

59. Caraley, *Unification*, 3–56.

60. NWC, King Papers, Box 7, "Admiral Stark."

61. Albion, *Forrestal and the Navy*, 92–93, 96–103, 124–27, 232–35, and 259–62; Connery, *The Navy and Industrial Mobilization in World War II*, 415–18; Caraley, *Unification*, 3–56.

62. Jan Smith, email to author, 9 March 2021.

63. NWC, King Papers, Box 7, "Mr. Forrestal."

64. Ibid.

65. Ibid.

66. NWC, King Papers, Box 8, "Chief of Naval Operations Organization."

67. NWC, King Papers, Box 2, Shepard to Buell, 7 August 1974.

68. Ibid.

69. Ibid., 102.

70. Dyer, *Naval Logistics*, 160–67; Henry E. Eccles, *Operational Naval Logistics* (Newport, RI: Naval War College, 1950), 1–25; and Alan Gropman, ed., *The Big "L": American Logistics in World War II* (Washington, DC: National Defense University Press, 1997), 97–144 and 393–412.

71. NWC, King Papers, Box 7, "Secretaries Knox and Forrestal," 3.

72. Albion, *Makers of Naval Policy*, 539.

73. NWC, King Papers, Box 7, "Secretaries Knox and Forrestal," 3.

74. Ibid.

75. Albion, *Forrestal and the Navy*, 101–06.

76. NWC, King Papers, Box 8, 5 September 1944 Memorandum from King to the SecNav, "Deputy Cominch-Deputy CNO."

77. NWC, King Papers, Box 8, 4 October 1944, press release, "Statement by Admiral King."

78. King, *Fleet Admiral King*, 477.

79. Ibid.

80. NWC, King Papers, Box 7, "Secretaries Knox and Forrestal," 3.

81. NWC, King Papers, Box 8, "Chief of Naval Operations Organization."

82. Ibid.

83. NWC, King Papers, Box 9, Whitehill notes.

84. NWC, King Papers, Box 5, Whitehill notes of discussion with Lippmann.

85. NWC, King Papers, Box 7, "Comments on Flag Officers, US Navy—Additional Notes," "Rear Admiral Miles R. Browning." Note: Browning was retroactively promoted to the tombstone rank of a two-star rear admiral. His grandson became a famous American comedian and movie star, Cornelius Crane "Chevy" Chase.

86. NWC, King Papers, Box 2, Adams to Buell.

87. Ibid.

88. Perry, *Dear Bart*, 80.

89. Ibid.

90. Ibid., 325.

91 Ibid., 326.

92. NWC, King Papers, Box 2, Perry to Buell.

93. Caraley, *Unification*, 31.

94. Ibid.

95. NWC, King Papers, Box 7, King to Marshall, 21 January 1944.

96. Ibid.

97. NWC, King Papers, Box 7, Knox to King, January 1944.

98. NWC, King Papers, Box 7, Whitehill notes, undated.

99. Ibid.

100. Ibid.

101. Ibid.

102. Ibid.

103. Leo Cullinane, "Marshall Asks That New Rank Bill Be Shelved," in *Herald Tribune*, 4 April 1944.

104. NWC, King Papers, Box 7, King to Marshall, 21 January 1944.

105. NWC, King Papers, Box 7, Whitehill notes, "Five-Stars."

106. Albion, *Makers of Naval Policy*, 539–624.

107. NWC, King Papers, Box 7, Whitehill notes, "Rank of Commodore."

108. Ibid., 45; King, *Fleet Admiral King*, 433; Kohnen, *Twenty-First-Century Knox*, 121–52; Anon., "Sower of Invasions," 25–27; Miles, *Different Kind of War*, 591–607; and Wedemeyer, *Wedemeyer Reports!*, 248–365.

109. NARA, RG 38, FESFI, CominCh to CinCPac, 10 September 1945.

110. NARA, RG 38, FESFI, , 25 July 1945.

111. NWC, King Papers, Box 7, Whitehill notes, "Rank of Commodore."

112. Ibid.

113. NWC, King Papers, Box 7, "CominCh," 11 September 1945.

114. Wolk, *Planning and Organizing*, 85–90.

115. USNI, "Dyer Reminiscences," 469.

116. Ibid.

Chapter 34

1. LC, King Papers, Box 35, "Roosevelt versus the Philippines and Formosa."

2. King, *Fleet Admiral King*, 593–657.

3. Steve Vogel, *The Pentagon: The Untold Story of the Wartime Race to Build the Pentagon—and to Restore It Sixty Years Later* (New York: Random House, 2007), 278–88 and 332–34.

4. NWC, King Papers, Box 8, Whitehill notes.

5. Albion, *Forrestal and the Navy*, 260.

6. Ibid.

7. Ibid.

8. LC, King Papers, Box 17, King to Admiral Arthur W. Radford, 15 April 1949.

9. Ibid.

10. Gentile, "Advocacy or Assessment?" 53–79.

11. King, *Fleet Admiral King*, 612.

12. Ibid.

13. Ibid.

14. Ibid.

15. Anon., *Battle Stations!: Your Navy in Action—a Photographic Epic of the Naval Operations of World War II Told by the Great Admirals Who Sailed the Fleet from Norfolk to Normandy and from the Golden Gate to the Inland Sea* (New York: William H. Wise, 1946), 385.

16. Paul Fussell, *Uniforms: Why We Are What We Wear* (New York: Houghton Mifflin, 2002), 21–34.

17. Albion, *Forrestal and the Navy*, 124.

18. NWC, King Papers, Box 9, Whitehill notes, "Uniforms."

19. NWC, King Papers, Box 9, King to Jacobs, 27 June 1942.

20. NWC, King Papers, Box 2, Smith to Buell, 5 October 1974.

21. NWC, King Papers, Box 9, Whitehill notes, "Uniforms."

22. NWC, King Papers, Box 2, McFarland to Buell, 3 September 1974.

23. NWC, King Papers, Box 2, Smedberg to Buell, 6 February 1975.

24 NWC, King Papers, Box 7, Whitehill notes, "gray uniform."

25. Potter, *Nimitz*, 186.

26. NWC, King Papers, Box 2, Sheppard to Buell, 7 August 1974.

27. Ibid.

28. NWC, King Papers, Box 7, Whitehill notes, "gray uniform."

29. Leahy, *And I Was There*, 304–05.

30. Ibid.

31. Maffeo, *US Navy Codebreakers*, 96–104.

32. LC, King Papers, Box 35, "Roosevelt versus the Philippines and Formosa."

33. Carl LaVo, *Pushing the Limits: The Remarkable Life and Times of Vice Admiral Allan R. McCann, USN* (Annapolis, MD: Naval Institute Press, 2013), 136–224.

34. NWC, King Papers, Box 10, McCann Oral History, page 9.

35. Ibid.

36. King, *Fleet Admiral King*, 601–57.

37. NARA, SRH 025, 42–43.

38. Llewellyn-Jones, *The Royal Navy and Anti-submarine Warfare*, 68–69.

39. Ibid., 79–103.

40. Packard, *Century of US Naval Intelligence*, 128; Boyd, *Hitler's Japanese Confidant*, 102, 106, and 110; and Carl Boyd and Akihiko Yoshida, *The Japanese Submarine Force and World War II* (Annapolis, MD: Naval Institute Press, 1995), 44, 117, 129–33, and 163–65.

41. NARA, SRH 025, 45.

42. NARA, RG 38, ComInCh Plans Division (F-1), Box 25, Operations Files, folder 10, OPlan 2-44. Note: the wartime plans for Operation BUMBLEBEE should not be confused with the postwar submarine rocket testing conducted with the same cover name under the supervision of the first ACNO for Guided Missiles, Daniel V. Gallery Jr., between 1946 and 1948.

43. NARA, RG 38, Box 35, SRMN-38, 9.

44. NARA, RG 38, ComInCh Plans Division (F-1), Box 25, Operations Files, folder 10, OPlan 2-44.

45. Philip Lundeburg, "Operation TEARDROP Revisited," in Runyan, ed., *To Die Gallantly*, 215–30.

46. NARA, RG 38, ComInCh Plans Division (F-1), Box 25, Operations Files, folder 10, OPlan 2-44.

47. King, *Fleet Admiral King*, 601–57.

48. Knowles, "Special Intelligence and the Battle of the Atlantic," 449.

49. Special thanks to Dennis Giangreco for sharing his pioneering research on Operations KEELBLOCKS 1–4.

50. King, *Fleet Admiral King*, 605. See the footnote explanation, as provided by King.

51. Frank, *Downfall*, 126–27, 142–48, 212–13, and 240–41; Dennis M. Giangreco, *Hell to Pay: Operation Downfall and the Invasion of Japan—1945–47* (Annapolis, MD: Naval Institute Press, 2009), 105–10, and 187–89; and Tim Maga, *America Attacks Japan: The Invasion That Never Was* (Lexington: University Press of Kentucky, 2002), 79–82, 87, 123–24, and 134–53.

52. NWC, King Papers, Box 2, Schoeffel to Buell, 9 September 1974.

53. NWC, King Papers, Box 5, "Admiral Edwards, 1 May 1946."

54. NWC, Box 6, Bull Diary, 30 November 1942, 13; Stoler, *Allies and Adversaries*, 15–122; and Rigby, *Allied Master Strategists*, 9–67.

55. NWC, King Papers, Box 2, Schoeffel to Buell, 9 September 1974.

56. Ibid.

57. King, *Fleet Admiral King*, 605. See the footnote explanation, as provided by King.

58. NWC, Box 6, Bull Diary, 30 November 1942, 13; Stoler, *Allies and Adversaries*, 15–122; and Rigby, *Allied Master Strategists*, 9–67.

59. NWC, King Papers, Box 5, "Admiral Edwards, 1 May 1946."

60. Ibid., 604–23.

61. Ibid.

62. Ibid.

63. Ibid.

64. LC, King Papers, Box 39, speech file, "Town Hall Meeting," 35.

65. Ibid.

66. Ibid.

67. Ibid.

68. NWC, Box 11, Whitehill notes, "Invasion of Kyushu."

69. King, *Fleet Admiral King*, 605. See the footnote explanation, as provided by King.

70. NWC, King Papers, Box 11, Buell interview notes, Smedberg, 9 June 1976.

71. NWC, Box 11, Whitehill notes, "Invasion of Kyushu."

72. Ibid.

73. USNI, Smedberg Reminiscences, 289–90.

74. NWC, King Papers, Box 2, Schoeffel to Buell, 9 September 1974; USNI, Sebald Reminiscences, 326–28 and 363–66; and USNI, Smedberg Reminiscences, 289–90.

75. Sebald Reminiscences, 326–28 and 363–66.

76. King, *Fleet Admiral King*, 639–46.

77. NWC, Box 11, Whitehill notes, "Invasion of Kyushu."

78. King, *Fleet Admiral King*, 609–12.

79. Ibid.

80. Harry S. Truman, *Year of Decisions* (Garden City, NY: Doubleday, 1955), 416.

81. Winston Churchill, *Triumph and Tragedy* (Boston, MA: Houghton-Mifflin, 1953), 669–70; James F. Byrnes, *Speaking Frankly* (New York: Harper, 1947), 263; and Georgii Konstantinovich Zhukov, *The Memoirs of Marshal Zhukov* (New York: Delacorte Press, 1971), 674–675.

82. Jacob Darwin Hamblin, *Arming Mother Nature: The Birth of Catastrophic Environmentalism* (New York: Oxford University Press, 2013), 3–85 and 151–97.

83. Arnold A. Offner, *Another Such Victory: President Truman and the Cold War, 1945–1953* (Stanford, CA:

Stanford University Press, 2002), 1–125; Denise M. Bostdorff, *Proclaiming the Truman Doctrine: The Cold War Call to Arms* (College Station: Texas A&M University Press, 2008), 1–30; Gar Alperovitz, *The Decision to Use the Atomic Bomb* (New York: Random House, 1995), 329 and 334–39; and James Parton, *Air Force Spoken Here: General Ira Eaker and Command of the Air* (Air Force Base, AL: Air University Press, 2000), 440–45.

84. Roskill, *Churchill and the Admirals*, 266.

85. King, *Fleet Admiral King*, 609–12.

86. NWC, King Papers, Box 7, "Unification."

87. Wedemeyer, *Wedemeyer Reports*, 331.

88. Perry, *Dear Bart*, 322.

89. Ibid.

90. Ellis M. Zacharias, *Secret Missions: The Story of an Intelligence Officer* (New York: Putnam, 1946), 388.

91. Ibid.

92. NWC, King Papers, Box 7, interview notes by Walter Muir Whitehill, 4 July 1950.

93. Ibid.

94. Ibid.

95. Coletta, *Navy and Defense Unification*, 93–95, 104–05, 186–88; Barlow, *Revolt of the Admirals*, 26–28, 50–52, 61–62, 68–69, 77–78, 163–64, 180; and Wolk, *Planning and Organizing*, 91–95 and 186.

96. Caraley, *Unification*, 88–89.

97. NWC, King Papers, Box 7, interview notes by Walter Muir Whitehill, 4 July 1950.

98. Morison, *Strategy and Compromise*, 116.

99. Ibid.

100. Ibid.

101. Albion, *Forrestal and the Navy*, 172–78.

102. Frank, *Downfall*, 126–27, 142–48, 212–13, and 240–41; Giangreco, *Hell to Pay*, 105–10 and 187–89; and Maga, *America Attacks Japan*, 79–82, 87, 123–24, and 134–53.

103. Lawrence Freedman, *The Future of War: A History* (New York: Public Affairs, 2017), 68–73; Lawrence Friedman, *Strategy: A History* (New York: Oxford University Press, 2013) 143–57; and Peter Paret, ed., *Makers of Modern Strategy: From Machiavelli to the Nuclear Age* (Princeton, NJ: Princeton University Press, 1986), 3–10, 186–216, 481–597, and 677–816.

104. LC, King Papers, Box 35, "Roosevelt versus the Philippines and Formosa."

105. King, *Fleet Admiral King*, 604–10. See the footnote explanation by King on page 605.

106. Benn Stiel, *The Battle of Bretton Woods: John Maynard Keynes, Harry Dexter White, and the Making of a New World Order* (Princeton, NJ: Princeton University Press, 2013), 1–19 and 330–48; Benn Stiel, *The Marshall Plan: Dawn of the Cold War* (New York: Simon and Schuster, 2018), 315–18; and Ed Conway, *The Summit: Bretton Woods, 1944: J. M. Keynes and the Reshaping of the Global Economy* (New York: Pegasus, 2014), 21–53, 201–63, and 365–85.

107. Terry Lautz, *John Birch: A Life* (New York: Oxford University Press, 2016), 122–28, 151–55, and 173–84; Miles, *Different Kind of War*, 434–36, 442, 446, 453, 457–59, and 490–91; and Wedemeyer, *Wedemeyer Reports*, 317–21.

108. Hamilton, *War and Peace*, 50–53, 56, 205–07, 304–10, 343–44, 353–55, 425–26, 435–38, 449, 457, and 469–71.

109. NWC, Low Papers, Box 1, "Autobiography," 35–38.

110. NWC, King Papers, Box 2, Smith-Hutton to Buell, September 1974.

111. NWC, King Papers, Box 7, interview notes by Walter Muir Whitehill, 4 July 1950.

112. Ibid, 261.

113. Richard Hulver and Peter Lubeke, eds., *A Grave Misfortune: The* Indianapolis *Tragedy* (Washington, DC: Naval History and Heritage Command, 2018), 297.

114. Caraley, *Unification*, 49.

115. United States Congress, Hearings before the Senate Committee on Military Affairs, 79th Congress, 1st Session (1945), 290.

116. Ibid., 308.

117. Hulver and Lubeke, *A Grave Misfortune*, 217–42, 263–85, and 297.

118. Hashimoto Mochitsura, *Sunk: The Story of the Japanese Submarine Fleet 1942–1945* (London: Cassell, 1954), 162–69.

119. Hulver and Lubeke, *A Grave Misfortune*, 217–42, 263–85, and 297.

120. NARA, NRPC, RG 24, File Unit, McVay, Charles B. III, BuNav Notification of Survival, sent separately various next of kin, August 1945.

121. Michael Junge, "From Pillar to Pillory: US Navy Crimes of Command 1945–2015," doctoral dissertation, Salve Regina, 2018. Special thanks to Junge for sharing his very detailed research, which has since been published as an electronic book under the title *Crimes of Command in the United States Navy, 1945–2015*.

122. King, *Fleet Admiral King*, 170.

123. Ibid., xxxi.

124. Hulver and Peter, eds., *A Grave Misfortune: The* Indianapolis *Tragedy* (Washington, DC: Naval History and Heritage Command, 2018), 297.

125. NWC, King Papers, Box 8, Officer Record of Fitness, Captain Charles B. McVay Jr., September 1923.

126. Hulver and Lubeke, *A Grave Misfortune*, 217–42, 263–85, and 297.

127. Hashimoto, *Sunk*, 162–69; Boyd, *Japanese Submarine Force*, 178–79, 181–84, and 241; and Hulver and Lubeke, *A Grave Misfortune*, 217–42, 263–85, and 297;

128. NARA, NRPC, RG 24, File Unit, McVay, Charles B. III, Judge Advocate General to McVay, 26 February 1946.

129. Ibid.

130. Ibid., Chief of Naval Personnel, Permanent Appointment, 31 March 1948.

131. Ibid., Permanent Appointment, Retired List, 30 June 1949.

Chapter 35

1. Ibid.; and King, *Fleet Admiral King,* 631–35.

2. Ibid.

3. Ibid.

4. NWC, King Papers, Box 7, "ComInCh" 11 September 1945.

5. Ibid.

6. Ibid.

7. NWC, King Papers, Box 8, Navy Department Organization, 30 July 1949.

8. NWC, King Papers, Box 7, "Mr. Forrestal."

9. King, *Fleet Admiral King*, 634.

10. Albion, *Forrestal and the Navy*, 102.

11. NWC, King Papers, Box 8, "Admiral Nimitz."

12. LC, King Papers, King to Edwards, 30 January 1950.

13. NWC, King Papers, Box 2, Perry to Buell.

14. Potter, *Nimitz*, 400–52.

15. NWC, King Papers, Box 2, Topper to Buell, 10 September 1974.

16. Ibid., 399–401.

17. NWC, King Papers, Box 7, "Halsey's Five-Stars."

18. LC, King Papers, Box 35, Comments by King on War Histories, 1946–50, "Reorganization of National Defense."

19. John Campbell, Donna Campbell, and Mike Hill, *Peace Was Their Profession: Strategic Air Command—a Tribute* (Atglen, PA: Schiffer, 1997); Melvin Deale, *Always at War: Organizational Culture in Strategic Air Command, 1946–62* (Annapolis, MD: Naval Institute Press, 2018), 1–25; and Trevor Albertson, *Winning Armageddon: Curtis LeMay and Strategic Air Command, 1948–1957* (Annapolis, MD: Naval Institute Press, 2019), 1–4.

20. Author interview with Egerton van Den Berg, March 2018.

21. Albion, *Makers of Naval Policy*, 609.

22. Ibid., 378–80.

23. NWC, King Papers, Box 8, "Admiral Nimitz," 31 July 1949.

24. Albion, *Makers of Naval Policy*, 609.

25. King, *Fleet Admiral King*, 637–46.

26. O'Brian, *Powerful Man*, 386–448; Hughes, *Halsey*, 228–39; and Symonds, *Nimitz at War*, 403–10.

27. Coletta, *Navy and Defense Unification*, 17–87; Barlow, *Revolt of the Admirals*, 20–78, 163–64, 180; and Wolk, *Planning and Organizing*, 36–95.

28. King, *Fleet Admiral King*, 632–35.

29. Cunningham, *A Sailor's Odyssey*, 654.

30 NWC, King Papers, Box 6, Whitehill interview notes.

31. Sterett, "Admiral King Hits a Single Command," *New York Times*, 13 February 1946.

32. Perry, *Dear Bart*, 323.

33. Ibid.

34. Sterett, "Admiral King Hits a Single Command," *New York Times*, 13 February 1946.

35. Ibid.

36. LC, King Papers, Box 16, King to Forrestal, 3 August 1946 "Award to Commodore D. W. Knox (Ret.), USN."

37. Ibid.

38. NARA, RG 313, ComNavEu, Box 1, folder 4, A 12-2 (6)(9), "History and Accomplishments of the ComNavEu Special Intelligence Unit," Tully Shelly comp., circa June 1945.

39. Special thanks to Dr. David Winkler for providing special access to the private historical records of the Naval Historical Foundation, located at the Washington Navy Yard.

40. NWC, RG 28, Box 2, Presidents Records, Miscellany, Lynde McCormick.

41. Janvier King Smith, *Affirming the Bond: US-Japan Security in the Post-Cold War Age—Strategic Research Department Report 2-94* (Newport, RI: Naval War College Press, 1994), 3–71.

42. Agawa Naoyuki with Hiraku Yabuki trans., *Friendship across the Seas: The US Navy and the Japan Maritme Self-Defense Force* (Tokyo: Japan Publishing Industry for Culture, 2019), 109–242 and 261–98.

43. NARA, RG 38, ComInCh, Crane Files, Box 37, "F-21 Memoranda Regarding U-boat Tracking and Operations, June 1943–June 1945," 22 May 1945 assessment of German navy messages; NARA, RG 313, "Report of Special Mission Regarding Correlation of Historical Documentation on Naval Operations in the Atlantic Theater," 23 October 1945 Memorandum from Kenneth A. Knowles to the director of Naval History, 11; NARA, RG 313, ComNavEu, Box 10, folder 53, "Axis Archives," serial A-12 (9), "Microfilming Facilities, Survey of," memorandum from F. L. Carr, USN, to Shelley of 28 May 1945; and NARA, RG 313, ComNavEu, Box 10, folder 53, "Axis Archives," serial A-12 (9), "Germany—Naval Archives at Tambach," Shelley memorandum to Kittredge derived from the original report by Earle of 3 July 1945, 1–4.

44. Kohnen, *Twenty-First-Century Knox,* 1–19; and Kohnen, "Seizing German Naval Intelligence from the Archives of 1870–1945," 133–71.

45. TNA, Cabinet Office and Predecessors (CAB 103), Historical Section Registered Files (CAB 103/288), "Official Histories of the War, 1939–45: Use of Special Intelligence by Historians," memorandum "General Directive to Chief of Historians," Top Secret Ultra Annex, entry of 11 February 1948.

46. NHHC, Library, Administrative Histories of the World War II, Edwin B. Hooper, comp., v–ix.

47. Sebald, *With MacArthur in Japan*, 15.

48. Ibid.

49. LC, King Papers, Box 17, King to Morison, 22 July 1946.

50. Ibid.

51. NARA, RG 38, ComInCh, War Diaries, Box 1, NND 968133, ComInCh for Action US Fleet, 192200 February 1943, effective 15 March 1943.

52. Jonathan Weisgall, *Operation CROSSROADS: The Atomic Tests at Bikini Atoll* (Annapolis, MD: Naval Institute Press, 1994), 1–69.

53. NWC, King Papers, Box 7, Miscellaneous notes, 4 July 1950.

54. LC, King Papers, Box 17, correspondence files, Edwards, various correspondence from 1946 to 1954.

55. NWC, King Papers, Box 7, "Admiral R. S. Edwards."

56. Washington, DC, Department of Justice, Office of Special Investigations, Criminal Division, Judy Feigin, comp., "Striving for Accountability in the Aftermath of the Holocaust" (December 2006); Brian E. Crim, *Our Germans: Project Paperclip and the National Security State* (Baltimore, MD: Johns Hopkins University Press, 2018), 32–33, 45–46, 139–46, and 150–90; Robert Coram, *Boyd: The Fighter Pilot Who Changed the Art of War*

(Boston, MA: BackBay / Little Brown, 2004), 234–36; Stephan Robinson, *The Blind Strategist: John Boyd and the American Way of War. Stephen Robinson* (Dunedin, New Zealand: Exisle Publishing, 2021), 1–10; Grant T. Hammond, *The Mind of War: John Boyd and American Security* (Washington, DC: Smithsonian Institution Press, 2004), 1–30; and Ray Bonds, *Modern Military Weapons* (New York: Crescent Books, 1985), 4–6.

57. Reginald Whitaker, "Cold War Alchemy: How America, Britain and Canada Transformed Espionage into Subversion," *Intelligence and National Security* vol. 15, no. 2 (June, 2000), 177–210; Reynolds, *From World War to Cold War*, 259–84; Ryan, "A New Look at Churchill's 'Iron Curtain' Speech," 895–920; and Robert Dallek, *Harry S. Truman: The American Presidents Series* (New York: Time-Warner, 2008), 43–46.

58. Tyrus G. Fain with Katherine C. Plant and Ross Milloy, eds., *The Intelligence Community: History, Origin, and Issues* (New York: Bowker, 1977), 1–36, 215–305, 675–93, and 817–946; Michael Warner, ed., *Central Intelligence: Origin and Evolution* (Washington, DC: Center for the Study of Intelligence, Central Intelligence Agency, 2001), 6; David Stafford and Rhodri Jeffreys-Jones, eds., *American-British-Canadian Intelligence Relations, 1939–2000* (London: Frank Cass, 2000), 5–20, 49–73, and 74–94; David Rudgers, *Creating the Secret State: Origins of the Central Intelligence Agency, 1943–1947* (Lawrence: University Press of Kansas, 2000), 93–186; and Stafford T. Thomas, *The US Intelligence Community* (Lanham, MD: University Press of America, 1983), 1–102.

59. NWC, King Papers, Box 7, Random Notes.

60. Ibid.

61. Ibid.

62. John Caratola, *Autumn of Our Discontent: Fall 1949 and the Crises in American National Security* (Annapolis, MD: Naval Institute Press, 2022), 81–94, 145–50, and 182–83.

63. Morison, *Strategy and Compromise*, 115–20; and Daniel Kurz-Phelan, *The China Mission: George Marshall's Unfinished War, 1945–1947* (New York: W.W. Norton, 2018), 9–126, 205–65, and 335–57.

64. LC, King Papers, Box 17, Oxford University Correspondence, *Encaena* instructions, 1946.

65. NWC, King Papers, Box 13, "King George VI," Whitehill notes, June 1950.

66. Simpson, *Cunningham Papers*, Vol. I, 130.

67. Ibid.

68. NWC, King Papers, Box 7, folder 7, newspaper clipping, *Evening Star* (1 April 1951), book review citing a Cunningham letter to the *London Times*, in "Lord Cunningham's Book Calls Admiral King Rude, Ruthless."

69. NWC, RG 28, Box 2, Presidents Records, Miscellany, Lynde McCormick.

70. Miles, *Different Kind of War*, 490, 562, 573–87; Miles, *Billy*, 165–202; and Richard Bernstein, *China 1945: Mao's Revolution and America's Fateful Choice* (New York: Knopf, 2014), 155–66, 192–94, and 258.

71. NWC, MSC-026, Wilma S. Miles Papers, Box 12, correspondence file, King.

72. Jonathan Marshall, "Opium, Tungsten, and the Search for National Security," *Journal of Policy History*, vol. 3, no. 4 (October 1991), 89–116.

73. NWC, RG-15, Box 13, folder 2, Milton Miles, comp., "A Rice Paddy Navy."

74. LC, King Papers, Box 17, correspondence files, Edwards, King to Edwards, 30 January 1950.

75. Ibid.

76. NWC, King Papers, Box 2, Schoeffel to Buell, 9 September 1974.

77. Ibid.

78. Ibid. Emphasis in original.

79. Charles A. Willoughby and John Chamberlain, *MacArthur: 1941–1951* (New York: McGraw Hill, 1954), 284–327.

80. Sebald, *With MacArthur in Japan*, 20–23, 55–89, 95, 115–22, 140, 155–71, 177–210, and 211–20.

81. NWC, King Papers, Box 2, notes and correspondences from Captain James R. Topper, Commander Walter Muir Whitehill, and Commander Eric E. Hopley.

82. LC, King Papers, Box 17, King to Edwards, 12 December 1949.

83. Sebald, *With MacArthur in Japan*, 20–24.

84. Ibid.; Willoughby, *MacArthur*, 378–422; Hsiao-ting Lin, *Accidental State: Chiang Kaishek, the United States, and the Making of Taiwan* (Cambridge, MA: Harvard, 2016); and Shu Guang Zhang, *Deterrence and Strategic Culture: Chinese-American Confrontations, 1949–1958* (New York: Cornell University Press, 1992), 56–58.

85. HIA, Charles M. Cooke Jr., (Cooke Papers), Boxes 26–30.

86. LC, King Papers, Box 17, correspondence files, Edwards to King, 30 November 1950.

87. McLean, Virginia, CIA, Center for the Study of Intelligence, "Possible Investigation by the Senate Internal Security Subcommittee Affecting the Central Intelligence Agency, 21 March 1957," document released under FOIA in 2003 and then posted for public disclosure in 2016; and "From the Record of the Senate Internal Security Subcommittee—Chief Counsel Robert Morris deposition of Admiral Charles M. Cooke Jr., USN (Ret.)," document released under FOIA in 2004 and posted for public release in 2016.

88. NWC, King Papers, Box 7, "Additional Remarks," 1 October 1951.

89. Hattendorf, *Sailors and Scholars*, 184.

90. Ibid., 164–78.

91. NWC, RG 3, Box 141, Morison to Beary, 27 April 1948.

92. Hattendorf, *Sailors and Scholars*, 201–02.

93. LC, King Papers, Box 17, King to Spruance, 21 June 1948.

94. LC, King Papers, Box 17, Spruance to King, 24 June 1948.

95. LC, King Papers, Box 17, Beary to King, 29 December 1949.

96. NWC, RG 3, Box 144, Ernest J. King Chair of Maritime History, duties and functions, 26 April 1954.

97. Ibid., 643.

98. Ibid.

99. LC, King Papers, Box 17, Edwards to Whitehill, 7 June 1948.

100. Louis Denfeld, ed., "The Month's News," *All Hands* no. 346 (January, 1946), 42.

101. LC, King Papers, Box 17, Edwards to Whitehill, 7 June 1948.

102. Washington, DC, Library of Congress (LC), Ernest J. King Papers (King Papers), Box 39, speech file, "Town Hall Meeting—March 21st, 1946—Pottstown, Penna.," 35.

103. NWC, King Papers, Box 3, "World War I."

104. Ibid.

105. Ibid.

106. LC, King Papers, speech file, "Town Hall Meeting," 34.

107. NWC, King Papers, Box 2, Schoeffel to Buell, 9 September 1974.

108. Ibid.

109. Wolk, *Planning and Organizing*, 85–90.

110. NWC, King Papers, Box 2, Schoeffel to Buell, 9 September 1974.

111. Albion, *Forrestal and the Navy*, 1, 8, 142, 200–24, and 284–86; Caraley, *Unification*, 23–122. Coletta, *Navy and Defense Unification*, 93–95, 104–05, 186–88; Barlow, *Revolt of the Admirals*, 26–28, 50–52, 61–62, 68–69, 77–78, 163–64, 180; and Wolk, *Planning and Organizing*, 36–38, 86–89, 91–95, and 186.

Chapter 36

1. Albion, *Makers of Naval Policy*, 378.

2. NWC, King Papers, Box 7, "Unification."

3. NWC, King Papers, Box 2, Schoeffel to Buell, 9 September 1974.

4. LC, King Papers, Box 17, correspondence files, Edwards, King to Edwards, 11 April 1949.

5. NWC, King Papers, Box 7, "Secretaries Knox and Forrestal."

6. Arnand Toprani, "Budgets and Strategy: The Enduring Legacy of the Revolt of the Admirals," in *Political Science Quarterly*, vol. 134, no. 1 (2019), 117–46.

7. NWC, King Papers, Box 7, "Miscellaneous notes of conversation with Admiral King," 4 July 1950.

8. NWC, King Papers, Box 7, "Secretaries Knox and Forrestal."

9. LC, King Papers, Box 17, correspondence, Edwards to King, 19 September 1949.

10. Ibid.

11. Gallery, *Clear the Decks*, 105.

12. NWC, King Papers, Box 7, "Unification."

13. NWC, King Papers, Box 7, "Random Notes."

14. NWC, King Papers, Box 7, "Additional Remarks," 1 October 1951.

15. Ibid.

16. Ibid.

17. LC, King Papers, Box 38, Unattributed Point Paper for Op-23, "What It Takes to Win a War," 16 February 1949.

18. Ibid.

19. Ibid., 3–4.

20. Ibid., 4.

21. Ibid.

22. Ibid.

23. Ibid. Note, emphasis in original.

24. Ibid.

25. Ibid., 14.

26. Ibid., 26.

27. Ibid.

28. Ibid.

29. Ibid.

30. LC, King Papers, Box 26, "Universal Military Training," King to Werdel, 12 September 1951.

31. Ibid.

32. Ibid.

33. King, *US Navy at War*, Third Report, 169.

34. Ibid.

35. Ibid.

36. Ibid.

37. LC, King Papers, Box 39, "An address by Fleet Admiral Ernest J. King, at the National Exchange Club Convention," in *The Exchangite*, vol. 26, no. 11 (November 1947), 4.

38. NWC, King Papers, Box 5, "Sea Duty and Admiral C. M. Cooke."

39. Ibid.

40. Ibid.

41. Author's interview notes with Egerton and Nikki van Den Berg, 1 March 2018.

42. LC, King Papers, Box 20, "Report of Board of Medical Survey," first draft by Admiral King, 29 April 1948.

43. Ibid.

44. LC, King Papers, Box 20, "Retirement for Medical Reasons," 16 September 1948.

45. Ibid.

46. NWC, King Papers, Box 2, Schoeffel to Buell, 9 September 1974.

47. Ibid.

48. NWC, King Papers, Box 7, "Random Notes."

49. LC, King Papers, Box 17, correspondence files, King to Edwards, 1 August 1950.

50. Ibid.

51. Ibid.

52. Lawrence, "Master of Propaganda," 1.

53. Stimpson, *On Active Service*, 506.

54. NWC, King Papers, Box 7, "Random Notes."

55. King, *Fleet Admiral King*, 469.

56. LC, King Papers, Box 17, Edwards to Whitehill, 7 June 1948.

57. Robert D. Heinl, "The Inchon Landing: A Case Study in Amphibious Planning," in *Naval War College Review*, vol. 51, no. 2 (Spring 1998), 118.

58. Gregory M. Pfitzer, *Samuel Eliot Morison's Historical World: In Quest of a New Parkman* (Boston: Northeastern University Press, 1991), 171–296; Benjamin W. Laberee with William E. Baker, eds., *The Atlantic World of Robert G. Albion* (Middletown, CT: Wesleyan University Press, 1975); William R. McClintock, "Clio Mobilizes: Naval Reserve Historians during the Second World War," in *The Public Historian* 13, 1 (Winter 1991), 25–46; and Edward Drea, "Change Becomes Continuity: The Start of the US Army's Green Book Series," in Jeffrey Grey, *The Last Word: Essays on Official History in the United States and British Commonwealth*, 83–104.

59. Whitehill, "Postscript," 206.

60. Author's telephone interview with Egerton van Den Berg, March 2018.

61. William B. Hayler and Betty Taussig Carney, *A Warrior for Freedom* (Manhattan, KS: Sunflower University Press, 1995), 85.

62. Ibid.

63. Hanson Baldwin, "The Admiral Preferred a Taut Ship: Ernest King's Story Casts New Light on the Fateful Events of World War II," *New York Times Book Review* (23 November 1952).

64. Ibid.

65. Ibid.

66. Telephone interview by author with Egerton van Den Berg, March 2018.

67. Janvier King Smith email to the author, 9 May 2020.

68. NWC, King Papers, Box 7, "Admiral R. S. Edwards."

69. Whitehill, "Postscript," 206.

70. Ibid.

71. Ibid.

72. Walter Lippmann, *The Cold War: A Study in US Foreign Policy* (New York: Harper, 1947), 62.

73. Paul Fussell, *Thank God for the Atomic Bomb and Other Essays* (New York: Summit, 1988), 11, 20–26, and 36; Kohnen, *Twenty-First-Century Knox*, 131–51; and Coletta, *The United States Navy and Defense Unification,* 92–93.

74. Beatrice Heuser, *NATO, Britain, France, and the FRG: Nuclear Strategies and Forces for Europe, 1949–2000* (New York: St. Martins, 1997); Beatrice Heuser, "Small Wars in the Age of Clausewitz: The Watershed between Partisan War and People's War," *Journal of Strategic Studies*, vol. 33, no. 1, (February 2010), 139–32; and Beatrice Heuser, *The Evolution of Strategy: Thinking War from Antiquity to Present* (Cambridge, UK: Cambridge University Press, 2010), 313–82.

75. NARA, President Dwight D. Eisenhower Library, Speech Series, Box 38, Papers of Dwight D. Eisenhower as President, 1953–61, 17 January 1961, "Farewell Address."

76. James Ledbetter, *Unwarranted Influence: Dwight D. Eisenhower and the Military Industrial Complex* (New Haven, CT: Yale University Press, 2011).

77. Buell produced the biographies of Spruance and King, as well as two separate studies exploring the leadership qualities of Civil War generals and Korean War naval commanders.

78. NWC, MSC-037.2, Thomas B. Buell and Walter M. Whitehill Collection on Ernest J. King (Buell-Whitehill Papers), Box 1.

79. Robert M. Edsall and Brett Witter, *The Monuments Men: Allied Heroes, Nazi Thieves and the Greatest Treasure Hunt in History* (New York: Center Street Publishers, 2009), 16–70.

80. NWC, MSC 030 (02-18-09-01), brochures and correspondence, "Naval War College Foundation, Inc."

81. Kenneth McDonald, Craig Symonds, and John Hattendorf told the author in separate interviews conducted from 2017 through 2022 that Turner gave Buell full freedom to write the biography of Spruance while serving on the Naval War College staff.

82. Buell, *Master of Sea Power*, xxi.

83. MHS, Whitehill Papers, Carton 34, "Buell, Thomas B., USN."

84. NWC, Buell-Whitehill Papers, Box 1, Wouk to Buell, 28 August 1978.

85. Ibid., 5 July 1978.

86. Buell, *Master of Sea Power*, xxi.

87. Ibid.

88. Ibid.

89. NWC, Buell-Whitehill Papers, Box 21, audio recordings, John A. Moreno to Buell, 18 August 1976.

90. Ibid.

91. Ibid.

92. NWC, Buell-Whitehill Papers, audio recording, Buell interview with Charlotte Pihl, digital recordings, interviews with Paul and Charlotte Pihl in 1974.

93. NWC, King Papers, Box 8, Whitehill notes of interview with the Pihls from 1949.

94. Ibid.

95. Ibid.

96. NWC, Buell-Whitehill Papers, audio recording, Box 21, Buell verbal notes of interview with Catherine Ballentine, digital recordings. Similar leading questions appear in Buell's recorded interviews with Boynton and Mary Braun.

97. Ibid.

98. NWC, Buell-Whitehill Papers, Box 1, Coletta to Buell, 10 September 1978.

99. Ibid., Potter to Buell, 23 July 1978.

100. Ibid.

101. Ibid., Heinlein to Buell, 2 July 1978.

102. Ibid., Wouk to Buell, 28 August 1978.

103. Ibid.

104. Ibid., 3.

105. Ibid., 5.

106. Ibid.

107. Ibid.

108. Ibid.

109. Ibid., 6.

110. Ibid.

111. Janvier King Smith email to author, 29 March 2019.

112. Original 1 July 1980 letter from DeLany provided by Janvier King Smith in an email to author, 29 March 2019.

113. Lloyd J. Graybar, "Master of Sea Power: A Biography of Fleet Admiral Ernest J. King," *Naval War College Review*, vol. 33, no. 6 (November–December, 1980), 100–2.

114. Ibid., 102.

115. Ibid.

116. NHHC, Lloyd J. Graybar Papers (Collection 500), Box 1.

117. Evelyn Cherpak, comp., "Register of the Ernest J. King Papers" in the Naval Historical Collection (1992), 1–17.

118. NWC, Director, Hattendorf Historical Center (HHC) to President of the Naval War College, "Utilization documentary collections of NWC," 8 May 2020. Author's copy.

Chapter 37

1. Author's copy, King to Ferrell, 4 May 1941.

2. LC, King Papers, Box 39, speech file, "Town Hall Meeting," 8.

3. Ibid.

4. Ibid.

5. Ibid.

6. Gallery, *Twenty Million Tons*, 328.

7. Ibid.

8. NWC, Low Reminiscences, 1.

9. Ibid.

10. LC, King Papers, Box 39, speech file, "Town Hall Meeting," 1.

11. LC, King Papers, Box 39, "An address by Fleet Admiral Ernest J. King, at the National Exchange Club Convention," in *The Exchangite*, vol. 26, no. 11 (November 1947), 4.

12. LC, King Papers, speech file, "Town Hall Meeting," 33.

13. LC, King Papers, Box 39, speech file, "National Exchange Club," 4; and "Town Hall Meeting," 32.

Bibliography

ARCHIVES

Canada
Ottawa

National Defence Headquarters, Directorate of History and Heritage

Library and Archives of Canada

> Department of National Defence, Record Group 24
>
> Records of the Department of External Affairs, Record Group 25

Germany
Cuxhaven, U-Boot-Archiv

Freiburg, Bundesarchiv-Militärarchiv

United Kingdom
Cambridge, Churchill College, Churchill Archives Centre

British Naval Intelligence Papers, mainly of Donald McLachlan and Patrick Beesly

London (Kew), The National Archives (Formerly The Public Record Office)

> Papers of the Government Communications Headquarters (GCHQ) / Government Code and Cypher School (GC&CS)
>
> Admiralty Records

London, King's College London (Strand), Liddell Hart Centre for Military Archives

United States
Boston University, Howard Gottlieb Archival Research Center, Massachusetts

Center for Naval Analysis (CNA), Washington, DC

Center of Military History, Washington, DC

Columbia University, Oral History Research Office (OHRO), New York

Congress, Washington, DC

East Carolina University, Joyner Library, Manuscript Collections, Greenville, North Carolina

Hoover Institution Archives, Stanford, California

Military History Institute, Carlisle, Pennsylvania

Museum of Science and Industry, Chicago, Illinois

National Archives and Records Administration (NARA), College Park, Maryland

> Record Group 19. Bureau of Ships Correspondence Files
>
> Record Group 24. Records of the Bureau of Naval Personnel
>
> Record Group 38. Records of the Office of the Chief of Naval Operations (CNO), World War II files of the Commander in Chief, US Navy (CominCh)

Record Group 80. Records of the Secretary of the Navy and Chief of Naval Operations

Record Group 165. Records of the War Department, General Staff

Record Group 242. Foreign Records Seized After 1945

Record Group 226. Office of Strategic Services, Central Files

Record Group 313. Records of the Naval Operating Forces

Record Group 331. Supreme Headquarters, Allied Expeditionary Force

Record Group 389. Enemy POW Information Bureau

Record Group 457. Records of the National Security Agency, Special Research Histories and Studies

National Archives and Records Administration, Franklin Delano Roosevelt Presidential Library and Museum, Hyde Park, New York

National Security Agency, Center for Cryptologic History, Fort Meade, Maryland

Library of Congress, Manuscript Collections Division, Washington, DC

Naval Academy, Chester W. Nimitz Memorial Library, Annapolis, Maryland

Naval History and Heritage Command (Naval Historical Center), Operational Archives, Washington, DC

Naval Institute Oral History Collection, Annapolis, Maryland

Naval War College, Archives, Newport, Rhode Island

University of Colorado at Boulder, University Libraries

University of Maryland, Library and Archives, Maryland Room, College Park

University of Wyoming, American Heritage Center, Laramie

Wisconsin Historical Society, Madison, Wisconsin

Yale University Library and Archives, New Haven, Connecticut

SECONDARY SOURCES

Abbazia, Patrick. *Mr. Roosevelt's Navy: The Private War of the US Atlantic Fleet, 1939–1942.* Annapolis: Naval Institute Press, 1975.

Agawa, Hiroyuki with John Bester (trans.). *The Reluctant Admiral: Yamamoto and the Imperial Japanese Navy.* Tokyo: Kodansha International, 1982.

Agawa Naoyuki with Hiraku Yabuki trans., *Friendship across the Seas: The US Navy and the Japan Maritime Self-Defense Force.* Tokyo: Japan Publishing Industry for Culture, 2019.

Albion, Robert Greenhalgh with Rowena Reed, eds., *The Makers of Naval Policy, 1798–1947.* Annapolis: Naval Institute Press, 1980.

Albion, Robert Greenhalgh and Jeannie Barnes Pope. *Forrestal and the Navy.* New York: Columbia University Press, 1962.

Aldrich, "Policing the Past: Official History, Secrecy and British Intelligence since 1945," *English Historical Review*, September 2004.

Allard, Dean C. "A United States Overview," in Steven Howarth and Derek Law, eds., in *The Battle of the Atlantic, 1939–1945: The 50th Anniversary International Naval Conference*. Annapolis: Naval Institute Press, 1994.

Allen, Robert L. *The Port Chicago Mutiny: The Story of the Largest Mass Mutiny Trial in US Naval History*. Berkeley: Heyday Books, 2006.

Alperovitz, Gar. *The Decision to Use the Atomic Bomb*. New York: Random House, 1995.

Alter, Jonathan P. with Daniel Crouch, eds. *My Dear Moon: A Literary Collection—Life, Death, and the Untold Story*. Charleston: Booksurge Publishing, 2005.

Andrew, Christopher. *For the President's Eyes Only: Secret Intelligence and the American Presidency from Washington to Bush*. New York: Harper Perennial, 1995.

Andrew, Christopher and Jeremy Noakes. *Intelligence and International Relations, 1900–1945*. Exeter, UK: University of Exeter, 1987.

Andrew, Christopher. *Codebreaking and Signals Intelligence*. London: Frank Cass, 1986.

Anduaga, Aitor. *Wireless & Empire: Geopolitics, Radio Industry and Ionosphere and the British Empire, 1918–1939*. London: Oxford, 2009.

Anon. *Battle Stations!: Your Navy in Action—a Photographic Epic of the Naval Operations of World War II Told by the Great Admirals Who Sailed the Fleet from Norfolk to Normandy and from the Golden Gate to the Inland Sea*. New York: William H. Wise, 1946.

Anon. "Sower of Invasions: Capt. W. L. Painter, CEC, USNR One of the CECR's Outstanding Officers Was Recently Killed in a Yachting Accident," *Civil Engineer Corps*, 3, 35 (October 1949).

Armstrong, Benjamin A. ed. *Twenty-First-Century Sims: Innovation, Education, and Leadership in the Modern Era*. Annapolis: Naval Institute Press, 2015.

Atha, Robert I. "Bombe! 'I could hardly believe it!,'" *Cryptologia*, IX, 4 (October 1985).

Aylen, I. G. "Jan " "Recollections of 30 Assault Unit," *Naval Review*, 65, 4 (October 1977).

Baily, Thomas A. and Paul B. Ryan. *Hitler and Roosevelt: The Undeclared Naval War*. New York: Free Press, 1979.

Baldwin, Hanson W. *Sea Fights and Shipwrecks: True Tales of the Seven Seas*. Garden City: Hanover House, 1955.

———, "The Admiral Preferred a Taut Ship: Ernest King's Story Casts New Light on the Fateful Events of World War II," *New York Times Book Review* (23 November 1952).

Bamford, James. *Bodyguard of Secrets: Anatomy of the Ultra-Secret National Security Agency*. New York: Anchor Books, 2002.

Banks, Arthur. *Wings of the Dawning: The Battle for the Indian Ocean, 1939–1945*. Upton-upon-Severn, Great Britain: Malvern Publishing, 1999.

Barlow, Jeffery G. *Revolt of the Admirals: The Fight for Naval Aviation, 1945–1950*. Washington, DC: Naval Historical Center, 1994.

Barnett, Correlli. *Engage the Enemy More Closely*. London: Hodder & Stoughton, 1991.

Bath, Alan Harris. *Tracking the Axis Enemy: The Triumph of Anglo-American Naval Intelligence*. Lawrence: University of Kansas Press, 1998.

Bauer, Hermann. *Als Führer der Unterseeboote im Weltkrieg, 1914–1918*. Leipzig: Köhler und Amelang, 1942.

———, *Das Unterseeboot*. Berlin: Mittler & Sohn, 1931.

Bayly, Lewis. *Pull Together! The Memoirs of Admiral Sir Lewis Bayly*. London: George C. Harrap & Co., 1929.

Beach, Edward L. *Salt and Steel: Reflections of a Submariner*. Annapolis: Naval Institute Press, 1999.

Beers, Henry P., with Robert G. Albion, *Administrative Reference Service Report No. 5: US Naval Forces in Northern Russia*. Washington, DC: Navy Department, 1943.

———, with Robert G. Albion, *Administrative Reference Service Report No. 2: US Naval Detachment in Turkish Waters, 1919–1924*. Washington, DC: Navy Department, 1943.

Beesly, Patrick. *Room 40: British Naval Intelligence, 1914–1918*. London: Hamish Hamilton, 1982.

———, "British Naval Intelligence in Two World Wars: Some Similarities and Differences," in Christopher Andrew and Jeremy Noakes, eds., *Intelligence and International Relations, 1900–1945*. Exeter: University of Exeter, UK, 1987.

———, *Very Special Admiral: The Life of Admiral J. H. Godfrey, C. B.* London: Hamish Hamilton, 1980.

———, "Special Intelligence and the Battle of the Atlantic: The British View," in Robert W. Love Jr., ed. *Changing Interpretations and New Sources in Naval History: Papers from the Third United States Naval Academy History Symposium*. New York: Garland, 1980.

———, *Very Special Intelligence: The Story of the Admiralty's Operational Intelligence Centre, 1939–1945*. London: Hamish Hamilton, 1977.

Bell, Christopher M. *Churchill and Seapower*. New York: Oxford University Press, 2013.

———, "Thinking the Unthinkable: British and American Naval Strategies for an Anglo-American War, 1918–1931," *The International History Review*, 19, 4 (November 1997).

Bell, Wiley I. *Historical Program of the US Army, 1939 to Present*. Washington, DC: Department of the Army, 1945.

Benson, Robert Lewis. *A History of US Communications Intelligence during World War II: Policy and Administration*. Fort Meade: National Security Agency, 1997.

Bennett, Ralph. *Ultra in the West*. Hutchinson, London, 1979.

———, *Ultra and Mediterranean Strategy*. New York: William Morrow, 1989.

Bercuson, David J. and Holger H. Holweg. *One Christmas in Washington: Churchill and Roosevelt Forge the Grand Alliance*. London: Widenfeld & Nicolson, 1985.

Bernstein, Richard. *China 1945: Mao's Revolution and America's Fateful Choice*. New York: Knopf, 2014.

Besch, Michael D. *A Navy Second to None: A History of US Navy Training in World War I.* Westport: Greenwood Press, 2002.

Beyer, Kenneth M. *Q-Ships Versus U-Boats: America's Secret Project.* Annapolis: Naval Institute Press, 1999.

Biddlescombe, Perry. *The Last Nazis: SS Werwolf Guerilla Resistance in Europe, 1944–1945.* Toronto: University of Toronto Press, 1998.

Bird, Keith W. *Erich Raeder: Admiral of the Third Reich.* Annapolis: Naval Institute Press, 2008.

Blair, Clay. *Hitler's U-Boat War: The Hunted, 1942–1943.* New York: Random House, 1998.

———, *Hitler's U-Boat War: The Hunters, 1939–1942.* New York: Random House, 1996.

———, *Silent Victory: The US Submarine War Against Japan.* New York: J.B. Lippencott, 1975.

Bland, Larry I. and Sharon Ritenour Stevens, eds. *The Papers of George Catlett Marshall: Aggressive and Determined Leadership, June 1, 1943–December 31, 1944.* Baltimore: Johns Hopkins University Press, 1996.

Blazich, Frank A. Jr. *An Honorable Place in American Air Power: Civil Air Patrol Coastal Patrol Operations, 1942–1943.* Montgomery: Air University Press, 2021.

———, "Neptune's Oracle: Admiral Harry E. Yarnell's Wartime Planning, 1918–20 and 1943–44," *Naval War College Review*, 73, 1 (Winter 2020).

Bloch, Gilbert, and Ralph Erskine. "Enigma: The Dropping of the Double Encipherment," and "Exploit the Double Encipherment Flaw in Enigma," *Cryptologia*, 10, 3 (July 1986).

Boghardt, Thomas. *The Zimmerman Telegram: Intelligence, Diplomacy, and America's Entry into World War I.* Annapolis: Naval Institute Press, 2012.

Bonatz, Heinz. *Seekrieg im Äther.* Herford: Mittler & Sohn, 1981.

Bond, Brian. *Chief of Staff: The Diaries of Lieutenant-General Sir Henry Pownell.* London: Leo Cooper, 1972.

Borneman, Walter R., *The Admirals: Nimitz, Halsey, Lahey, and King—The Five Star Admirals Who Won the War at Sea.* New York: Little Brown, 2012.

Bostdorff, Denise M. *Proclaiming the Truman Doctrine: The Cold War Call to Arms.* College Station: Texas A&M University Press, 2008.

Boyd, Andrew. *British Naval Intelligence Through the Twentieth Century.* Barnsley, UK: Seaforth Publishing, 2020.

Boyd, Carl. "How Not to Cooperate: National Socialist Germany and Imperial Japan," in Dennis E. Showalter, *Future Wars: Coalition Operations in Global Strategy.* Chicago: Imprint Publications, 2002.

———, "US Navy Radio Intelligence During the Second World War and the Sinking of the Japanese Submarine *I-52*," *The Journal of Military History*, 63, 2 (April 1999).

———, and Akihiko Yoshida. *The Japanese Submarine Force and World War II.* Annapolis: Naval Institute Press, 1995.

———, *American Command of the Sea through Carriers, Codes, and the Silent Service: World War II and Beyond.* Newport News: The Mariners Museum, 1995.

———, *Hitler's Japanese Confidant: General Ōshima Hiroshi and MAGIC Intelligence, 1941–1945.* Lawrence: University Press of Kansas, 1993.

———, *The Extraordinary Envoy: General Hiroshi Ōshima and Diplomacy in the Third Reich, 1934–1939.* Washington, DC: University Press of America, 1980.

Boutier, James A. *The RCN in Retrospect, 1910–1968.* Vancouver: Univeristy of British Columbia Press, 1982.

Bradford, Richard. "Learning the Enemy's Language: US Navy Officer Language Students in Japan, 1920–1941," *International Journal of Naval History*, 1, 1 (April 2002).

Brands, H. W. *Traitor to His Class: The Privileged Life and Radical Presidency of Franklin Delano Roosevelt.* New York: Doubleday, 2008.

Brennecke, Jochen. *Haie im Paradies: Der Deutsche U-Boote in Asiens Gewässern, 1943–1945.* Preez-Holstein: Ernst Gerdes, 1961.

Brodie, Bernard. *A Layman's Guide to Naval Strategy.* Princeton: Princeton University Press, 1943.

Brower, Charles F. *Defeating Japan: The Joint Chiefs of Staff and Strategy in the Pacific War, 1943–1945.* New York: Palgrave McMillan, 2012.

Brice, Martin. *Axis Blockade Runners of World War II.* Annapolis: Naval Institute Press, 1981.

Broadhurst, Robin. *Churchill's Anchor: The Biography of Admiral of the Fleet Sir Dudley Pound.* London: Pen and Sword, 2000.

Brown, Anthony Cave. *"C:" The Secret Life of Sir Stewart Graham Menzies, Spymaster to Winston Churchill.* New York: Palgrave MacMillan, 1987.

Bryant, Arthur. *Turn of the Tide: A History of the War Years Based on the Diaries of Field-Marshal Lord Alanbrooke, Chief of the Imperial General Staff.* New York: Doubleday, 1957.

Budiansky, Stephen. *Blackett's War: The Men Who Defeated the Nazi U-Boats and Brought Science to the Art of Wafare.* New York: Alfred A. Knopf, 2013.

———, *Battle of Wits: The Complete Story of Codebreaking in World War II.* London: Viking, 2000.

Buell, Thomas. *Master of Sea Power: A Biography of Fleet Admiral Ernest J. King.* Boston: Little Brown & Co., 1980.

———, *Quiet Warrior: A Biography of Admiral Raymond A. Spruance.* Boston: Little Brown & Co., 1974.

———, "Admiral Edward C. Kalbfus and the Naval Planner's 'Holy Scripture': *Sound Military Decision*," *Naval War College Review*, 26, 3 (May–June 1973).

Burdick, Charles. "The Tambach Archive—A Research Note," *Military Affairs*, 31, 4 (December 1972).

Butcher, Harry C. *My Three Years with Eisenhower: The Personal Diary of Captain Harry C. Butcher, USNR—Naval Aide to General Eisenhower, 1942–1945.* New York: Simon and Schuster, 1946.

Butler, Smedley D. *War is a Racket.* New York: Roundtable Press, 1935.

Bush, Elizabeth Kauffman. *America's First Frogman: The Draper Kauffman Story.* Annapolis: Naval Institute Press, 2004.

Busch, Reiner and Hans-Joachim Röll, *German U-Boat Commanders of World War II.* Annapolis: Naval Institute Press, 1999.

Butler, J. R. M. *Grand Strategy (vol. 2): September 1939–June 1941.* London: HMSO, 1957, 1964.

————, *Grand Strategy (vol. III, pt. 2): June 1941–August 1942.* London: HMSO, 1964.

Byrnes, James F. *Speaking Frankly.* New York: Harper, 1947.

Bywater, Hector C. Bywater and H. C. Ferraby, *Strange Intelligence: Memoirs of Naval Secret Service.* London: Constable & Co. Ltd., 1931.

————, *The Great Pacific War: A History of the American-Japanese Campaign of 1931–33.* Boston: Houghton Mifflin, 1925.

Cabell, Craig. *Ian Fleming's Secret War.* London: Pen and Sword, 2008.

Cairncross, John. *The Enigma Spy.* London: Century, 1997.

Calvocoressi, Peter. *Top Secret Ultra.* New York: Pantheon, 1980.

Cameron, Craig M. *American Samurai: Myth, Imagination, and the Conduct of Battle in the First Marine Division, 1941–1951.* New York: Cambridge, 1994.

Cameron, John. *War Crimes Trials: The Pelius Trial.* London: William Hodge and Company, 1948.

Caraley, Demetrios. *The Politics of Military Unification: A Study of Conflict and the Policy Process.* New York: Columbia University Press, 1966.

Caratola, John. *Autumn of Our Discontent: Fall 1949 and the Crises in American National Security.* Annapolis: Naval Institute Press, 2022.

Carlisle, Rodney P. *Where the Fleet Begins: A History of the David Taylor Research Center.* Washington, DC: Naval Historical Center, 1998.

Carlson, Elliot. *Stanley Johnston's Blunder: The Reporter who Spilled the Secret Behind the US Navy's Victory at Midway.* Annapolis: Naval Institute Press, 2017.

————, *Joe Rochefort's War: The Odyssey of the Codebreaker Who Outwitted Yamamoto at Midway.* Annapolis, Naval Institute Press, 2011.

Carter, Carolle J. *Mission to Yenan: American Liaisons with the Chinese Communists.* Lexington: University Press of Kentucky, 1997.

Carter, Frank. *Codebreaking with the Colossus Computer.* Milton Keynes: Bletchley Park Trust, 1996.

Carter, Worrall R. *Beans, Bullets, and Black Oil: The Story of Fleet Logistics Afloat In the Pacific During World War II.* Annapolis: Naval Institute Press, 1952.

Casey, William. *The Secret War Against Hitler.* Washington: Regnery-Gateway, 1988.

Chalmers, William S. *Max Horton and the Western Approaches.* London: Hodder and Stoughton, 1954.

Chang, Iris. *The Rape of Nanking: The Forgotten Holocaust of World War II.* New York: Penguin, 1997.

Chapin, Henry Edgerton, ed. "Tracy Barrett Kittredge," *The Tomahawk of Alpha Sigma Phi*, 17, 1 (December 1919).

Chapman, John W. M. *The Price of Admiralty: The War Diary of the German Naval Attaché in Japan, 1939–1943.* Ripe-Sussex, UK: Saltire Press, 1982.

Chatfield, Charles. "World War I and the Liberal Pacifist in the United States," *American Historical Review*, 75, 7 (December 1970).

Cheevers, James W. "Use of Historic Warships as Museum Settings," in Daniel Masterson, ed., *Naval History: The Sixth Symposium of the US Naval Academy.* Wilmington: Scholarly Resources, 1987.

————, with Sharon Kennedy, ed. "The United States Naval Academy, 1845–2020," Annapolis: Naval Academy pamphlet.

Cherpak, Evelyn, ed. *Three Splendid Little Wars: The Diary of Joseph K. Taussig.* Newport: Naval War College, 2009.

Chisholm, Donald. *Waiting for Dead Men's Shoes: Origins and Development of the US Navy's Officer Personnel System, 1793–1941.* Stanford: Stanford University Press, 2001.

Churchill, Winston S. *A History of the English-Speaking Peoples: The Age of Revolution.* New York: Bantam Books, 1957.

————, *While England Slept: A Survey of World Affairs, 1932–1938.* New York: Putnam, 1938.

————, *The Second World War: The Gathering Storm.* Boston: Houghton Mifflin, 1948.

————, *The Second World War: Their Finest Hour.* Boston: Houghton Mifflin, 1949.

————, *The Second World War: The Grand Alliance.* Boston: Houghton Mifflin, 1950.

————, *The Second World War: The Hinge of Fate.* Boston: Houghton Mifflin, 1950.

————, *The Second World War: Closing the Ring.* Boston: Houghton Mifflin, 1951.

————, *The Second World War: Thriumph and Tragedy.* Boston: Houghton Mifflin, 1953.

————, "The Third Great Title-Deed of Anglo-American Liberties," in Robert Rhodes James, ed. *Winston Churchill: His Complete Speeches 1897–1963.* London: Chelsea House Publishers, 1974.

Clark, Joseph J., with Clark G. Reynolds. *Carrier Admiral.* New York: David McKay Company, Inc., 1967.

Coakley, Robert W., and Richard M. Leighton. *Global Logistics and Strategy, 1943–45.* Washington, DC: US Army Center of Military History, 1986.

Coles, Michael. "Ernest King and the British Pacific Fleet: The Conference at Quebec, 1944 (Octagon)," *The Journal of Military History*, 65, 1 (January 2001).

Coletta, Paolo. *The United States Navy and Defense Unification, 1947–1953.* East Brunswick: Associated University Press, 1981.

Connery, Robert. *The Navy and Industrial Mobilization in World War II.* Princeton: Princeton University Press, 1951.

Conway, Ed. *The Summit: Bretton Woods, 1944: J. M. Keynes and the Reshaping of the Global Economy.* New York: Pegasus, 2014.

Copeland, Jack, ed. *The Essential Turing.* Oxford: Clarendon, 2004.

Coram, Robert. *Brute: The Life of Victor H. Krulak, US Marine.* Boston: Little Brown, 2010.

Corbett, Julian and H. J. Edwards, eds. "Staff Histories" in *Naval and Military Essays: Being Papers Read in the Naval and Military Section at the International Congress of Historical Studies—1913.* Cambridge: Cambridge University Press, 1914.

————, *England in the Seven Years War.* London: Longman's, Green & Co., 1918.

————, *Some Principles of Maritime Strategy.* London: Longman's, Green & Co., 1911.

Costello, John. *The Pacific War.* New York: Quill, 1981.

Cox, Samuel J. "The China Theater, 1944–45: A Failure of Joint and Combined Operations Strategy," master's thesis, US Army Command and General Staff College (Fort Levenworth, Kansas, 1993).

———, with Terry Hughes. *The Battle of the Atlantic.* New York: Dial, 1977.

Cross, Robert F. *Sailor in the White House: The Seafaring Life of FDR.* Annapolis: Naval Institute Press, 2003.

Cunningham, Andrew. *A Sailor's Odyssey: The Autobiography of Admiral of the Fleet Viscount Cunningham of Hyndhope.* New York: E.P. Dutton & Company, Inc., 1951.

Currier, Prescott H. "My PURPLE Trip to England," *Cryptologia*, 20, 3 (1996).

Dallek, Robert. *Franklin D. Roosevelt and American Foreign Policy, 1932–1945.* New York: Oxford, 1979.

Danchev, Alex. ed. *Field Marshal Lord Alanbrooke: War Diaries—1939–1945.* London: Weidenfeld and Nicholson, 2001.

———, *Alchemist of War: The Life of Basil Liddell Hart.* London: Orion, 1998.

Daniels, Josephus. *Our Navy at War.* Washington, DC: Pictorial Bureau, 1922.

Darby, Hamilton. *The Panay Incident: Prelude to Pearl Harbor.* New York: MacMillan, 1969.

Davies, Donald W. "The Bombe: A Remarkable Logic Machine," *Cryptologia*, 23, 2 (February 1999).

Davies, John Paton Jr. *Dragon by the Tail: American, British, Japanese, and Russian Encounters with China and One Another.* New York: Norton, 1972.

Day, Michael H. *Maritime Domain Awareness: A Modern Maginot Line?* Newport: Naval War College, 2003.

Deavours, Cipher A., "Lobsters, Crabs, and the Abwehr Enigma," *Cryptologia*, XXI, 3 (July 1997).

———, "How the British Broke Enigma," *Cryptologia*, IV, 3 (July 1980).

Debrosse, Jim and Colin Burke. *The Secret in Building 26: The Untold Story of America's ULTRA War Against the U-Boat Enigma Codes.* New York: Random House, 2004.

Dedman, Robert. *May the Armed Forces be With You: The Relationship between Science Fiction and the United States Military.* Jefferson: McFarland & Co., 2016.

DeKay, James Tertius. *Roosevelt's Navy: The Education of a Warrior President, 1882–1920.* New York: Pegasus, 2012.

Delmer, Sefton. *Black Boomerang: The Spectacular Story of "Black" Radio in World War II.* New York: Viking, 1962.

Denniston, Alistair G. "The Government Code and Cypher School Between the Wars," *Intelligence and National Security*, 1, 1 (January 1986).

Dietrich-Berryman, Eric, Charlotte Hammond, and R. E. White, *Passport Not Required: US Volunteers in the Royal Navy, 1939–1941.* Annapolis: Naval Institute Press.

Dinger, Henry C. "Some Notes on Naval Needs and Requirements," Naval Institute *Proceedings*, 30, 1 (January 1904).

Dockrill, Michael and David French. *Strategy and Intelligence: British Policy During the First World War.* London: Hambledon Press, 1996.

Dönitz, Karl. *Memoirs: Ten Years and Twenty Days* (with introduction and afterword by Jürgen Rohwer). Annapolis: Naval Institute Press, 1990.

———, *Zehn Jahre und Zwanzig Tage.* Frankfurt am Main: Bernard & Graefe, 1957.

———, *Die Fahrten der Breslau im Schwarzen Meer.* Berlin: Ullstein, 1917.

Douglas, W. A. B., with Roger Sarty, Michael Whitby with Robert H. Caldwell, William Johnson, and William G. P. Rawling, eds. *No Higher Purpose: The Official Operational History of the Royal Canadian Navy in the Second World War, 1939–1945*, vol. II, pt. 1. Ontario, Canada: Vanwell Press, 2002.

———, with Roger Sarty, Michael Whitby with Robert H. Caldwell, William Johnson, and William G. P. Rawling, eds. *A Blue Water Navy: The Official Operational History of the Royal Canadian Navy in the Second World War, 1939–1945*, vol. II, pt. 2. Ontario, Canada: Vanwell Press, 2007.

———, *The Creation of a National Air Force: The Official History of the Royal Canadian Air Force.* Toronto: University of Toronto Press, 1986.

Dorwart, Jeffrey M. *Eberstadt and Forrestal: A National Security Partnership, 1909–1949.* College Station: Texas A&M University Press, 1991.

———, *Conflict of Duty: The US Navy's Intelligence Dilemma, 1919–1945.* Annapolis: Naval Institute Press, 1983.

———, *The Office of Naval Intelligence: The Birth of America's First Intelligence Agency 1865–1918.* Annapolis: Naval Institute Press, 1979.

Drewry, Elizabeth B. "Historical Units of Agencies in the First World War, in *Bulletins of the National Archives*, no. 4. Washington, DC: National Archives and Records Administration, 1942.

Drea, Edward. *In the Service of the Emperor: Essays on the Imperial Japanese Army.* Lincoln: University of Nebraska, 1998.

———, *MacArthur's ULTRA: Codebreaking and the War Against Japan, 1942–1945.* Lawrence: University Press of Kansas, 1993.

———, "Change Becomes Continuity: The Start of the US Army's Green Book Series," in Jeffrey Grey, *The Last Word: Essays on Official History in the United States and British Commonwealth.*

Drummond, John D. *H.M. Submarine.* London: W.H. Allen, 1958.

Drury, Bob and Tom Clavin. *Halsey's Typhoon: The True Story of a Fighting Admiral, an Epic Storm, and an Untold Rescue.* New York: Grove, 2007.

Drury, Elizabeth B. "Historical Units of Agencies in the First World War," in *Bulletins of the National Archives*, no. 4. Washington, DC: National Archives and Records Administration, 1942.

Duffy, James P. *Lindbergh vs. Roosevelt: The Rivalry That Divided America.* Washington, DC: Regnery Publishing, 2010.

Dunn, Steve R. *Bayly's War: The Battle for the Western Approaches in the First World War.* Barnsley, UK: Seaforth, 2018.

———, *Securing the Narrow Sea: The Dover Patrol, 1914–1918.* Barnsley, UK: Seaforth, 2017.

Dyer, George C. *The Amphibians Came to Conquer: The Story of Admiral Richmond Kelly Turner.* Washington, DC: Naval Historical Center, 1972.

———, *Naval Logistics.* Annapolis: Naval Institute Press, 1960.

Earle, Hubert P. *Blackout: The Human Side of Europe's March to War.* New York: Lippencott, 1940.

Eccles, Henry E. *Operational Naval Logistics.* Newport: Naval War College, 1950.

Eccles, Marriner. *Beckoning Frontiers.* New York: Arthur Knopf, 1951.

Edgerton, Ronald K. "General Douglas MacArthur and the American Military Impact in the Philippines," *Philippine Studies*, 25, 4 (Winter 1977).

Ediger, Volkan S. and John V. Bowlus. "A Farewell to King Coal: Geopolitics, Energy Security, and the Transition to Oil, 1898–1917," *The Historical Journal*, 62, 2 (June 2019).

Ehrman, John. *Grand Strategy (vol. V): August 1943–September 1944.* London: HMSO, 1956.

———, *Grand Strategy (vol. VI): October 1944–August 1945.* London: HMSO, 1956.

Ehrmann, Howard M. "German Naval Archives (Tambach)," in Robert Wolfe, ed. *Captured German and Related Records: A National Archives Conference.* Athens: Ohio University Press, 1974.

Eisenhower, Dwight D. *Crusade in Europe.* Garden City: Doubleday, 1948.

———, *At Ease: Stories I Tell to Friends.* New York: Doubleday, 1967.

Eller, Ernest M. "United States Navy Microfilm of German Naval Archives," in Robert Wolfe, ed. *Captured German and Related Records: A National Archives Conference.* Athens: Ohio University Press, 1974.

Ellsburg, Edward. *Pigboats.* New York: Dodd, Meade, and Co., 1930.

———, *On the Bottom.* New York, Dodd, Meade, and Co., 1929.

Erskine, Ralph. "The Holden Agreement on Naval SigInt: The First BrUSA"? *Intelligence and National Security,* 14, 2 (1999).

———, "ULTRA and Some US Navy Carrier Operations," *Cryptologia ,* 19, 1 (1995).

———, and Weierud, Frode, "Naval Enigma: M4 and Its Rotors," *Cryptologia,* 11, 4 (January 1991).

———, "Naval Enigma, The Breaking of Heimisch and Triton," *Intelligence and National Security,* 3, 1 (January 1988).

Evans, David C. and Mark R. Peattie. *Kaigun: Strategy, Tactics, and Technology in the Imperial Japanese Navy, 1887–1941.* Annapolis: Naval Institute Press, 1997.

Fain, Tyrus G., Katherine C. Plant, and Ross Milloy. *The Intelligence Community: History, Organization, and Issues.* New York: R.R. Bowker, 1977.

Fairbanks, Charles. "The Origins of the Dreadnought Revolution: A Historiographical Essay," *The International History Review*, 13 (May 1991).

Farago, Ladislas. *The Game of the Foxes.* New York: Hodder and Stoughton, 1972.

———, *The Broken Seal: "Operation MAGIC" and the Secret Road to Pearl Harbor.* New York: Random House, 1967.

———, The *Tenth Fleet: The Untold Story of the Submarine and Survival.* New York: Obelensky, 1962.

———, *Burn After Reading.* New York: Walker and Company, 1961.

———, *War of Wits.* New York: Funk & Wagnalls, 1954.

Faulkner, Marcus and Christopher M. Bell. *Decision in the Atlantic: The Allies and the Longest Campaign of the Second World War.* Lexington: Andarta/University Press of Kentucky, 2019.

Feaver, Peter D. and Richard Kohn, *Soldiers and Civilians: The Civil-Military Gap and National Security.* Cambridge: Harvard University Press, 2001.

Feis, Herbert. *Churchill-Roosevelt-Stalin: The War They Waged and the Peace they Sought.* Princeton: Princeton University Press, 1957.

———, *The China Tangle: The American Effort in China from Pearl Harbor to the Marshall Mission.* Princeton: Princeton University Press, 1953.

Ferrell, Robert H., ed. *The Eisenhower Diaries.* New York: Norton, 1981.

Ferreiro, Larrie. *Churchill's American Arsenal: The Partnership Behind the Innovations that Won World War Two.* New York: Oxford, 2022.

Ferris, John. *Behind the Enigma: The Authorized History of GCHQ, Britain's Secret Cyber-Intelligence Agency.* New York: Bloomsbury Publishing, 2020.

Foner, Philip S., ed. *W.E.B. DuBois Speaks: Speeches and Addresses, 1920–1963.* New York: Pathfinder, 1970.

Ford, Christopher and David Rosenberg. *The Admiral's Advantage: US Navy OPINTEL in World War II to the Cold War.* Annapolis: Naval Institute Press, 2005.

Ford, Corey. *Donovan of OSS: The Untold Story of William J. ("Wild Bill") Donovan and America's top-secret agency for intelligence, espionage, and unorthodox warfare in World War II.* Boston: Little Brown, 1970.

Ford, Daniel. *Flying Tigers: Claire Chennault and His American Volunteers, 1941–1942.* New York: Harper Collins, 2007.

Forrestal, James V. *The Navy: A Study in Administration.* Chicago: Public Administration Service Publication, 1945.

Forrestel, Edward P. *Admiral Raymond A. Spruance: A Study in Command.* Washington, DC: Department of the Navy, 1966.

Fotakis, Zisis, ed. *The First World War in the Mediterranean and the Role of Lemnos.* Athens: Editions Hêrodotos, 2018.

Frank, Larry J. "The United States Navy vs. the *Chicago Tribune.*" *The Historian* (February 1980).

Frank, Richard B. *Tower of Skulls: A History of the Asia-Pacific War, July 1937–May 1942.* New York: Norton, 2020.

———, *Downfall: The End of the Imperial Japanese Empire.* New York: Penguin, 2001.

Freedman, Lawrence. *The Future of War: A History.* New York: Public Affairs, 2017.

———, *Strategy: A History.* New York: Oxford, 2013.

Friedman, Norman. *Winning a Future War: War Gaming and Victory in the Pacific War.* Washington, DC: Naval History and Heritage Command, 2019.

———, Thomas C. Hone, and Mark Mandeles. *American and British Aircraft Carrier Development, 1919–1941.* Annapolis: Naval Institute Press, 1999.

Frost, Holloway H. *The Conduct of an Overseas Naval Campaign.* Washington, DC: Navy Department, 1920.

Frye, William. *Marshall: Citizen Soldier.* New York: Bobbs-Merrill, 1947.

Furer, Julius Augustus. *Administration of the Navy Department in World War II.* Washington, DC: Naval Historical Center, 1959.

Fussell, Paul. *Uniforms: Why We Are What We Wear.* New York: Houghton Mifflin, 2002.

———, *Wartime: Understanding and Behavior in the Second World War.* New York: Oxford, 1986.

———, *The Great War and Modern Memory.* New York: Oxford, 1975.

Gaddis, John L. *The Landscape of History: How Historians Map the Past.* New York: Oxford, 2004.

———, *Strategies of Containment: A Critical Appraisal of Postwar American National Security.* New York: Oxford, 1982.

Gallery, Daniel V. *Twenty Million Tons Under the Sea.* Chicago: Henry Regnery, 1956.

———, *Clear the Decks!* New York: William Morrow, 1951.

Gannon, Michael. *Black May : The Epic Story of the Allies" Defeat of the German U-Boats in May 1943.* New York: Dell, 1999.

———, *Operation Drumbeat: The Dramatic True Story of Germany's First U-Boat Attacks Along the American Coast in World War II.* New York: Harper and Row, 1990.

Gardiner, Philip. *The Bond Code: The Dark World of Ian Fleming and James Bond.* Franklin Lakes, 2008.

Gardner, W. J. R. *Decoding History: The Battle of the Atlantic and Ultra.* Annapolis: Naval Institute Press, 2000.

Garlinski, Joseph. *Intercept: The Enigma War.* London: J.M. Dent & Sons, 1979.

Giangreco, Dennis M. *Hell to Pay: Operation Downfall and the Invasion of Japan—1945–47.* Annapolis: Naval Institute Press, 2009.

Gibbs, Norman H. *Grand Strategy (vol. I), Rearmament Policy.* London: HMSO, 1976.

Gibson, R. H. and Maurice Prendergast, *The German Submarine War, 1914–1918.* London: Constable and Co. Ltd., 1931

Giese, Otto and James E. Wise. *Shooting the War: The Memoir and Photographs of a U-Boat Officer in World War II.* Annapolis: Naval Institute Press, 2003.

Gill, G. Hermon. *Australia in the War of 1939–1945: Royal Australian Navy*, vols. I–II. Canberra: Australian War Memorial, 1957–1968.

Gleaves, Albert. *A History of the Transport Service: Adventures and Experiences of United States Transports and Cruisers in the World War.* New York: George H. Doran Company, 1921.

Godson, Susan H. *Serving Proudly: A History of Women in the US Navy.* Annapolis: Naval Institute Press, 2001.

Goldrick, James and John B. Hattendorf, eds., *Mahan is Not Enough: The Proceedings of a Conference on the Works of Sir Julian Corbett and Admiral Sir Herbert Richmond.* Newport: Naval War College Press, 1993.

Good, Jack I. "Early Work on Computers at Bletchley," *Cryptologia*, 3:2 (April 1979).

Goebler, Hans and John Vanzo. *Steel Boat, Iron Hearts: A U-Boat Crewman's Life Aboard U-505.* New York: Savas-Beatie, 2004.

Goldberger, Sarah M. "An Indissoluble Union: Theodore Roosevelt, James Bulloch, and the Politics of Reconciliation," in John B. Hattendorf and William P. Leeman, eds., *Forging the Trident: Theodore Roosevelt and the United States Navy.* Annapolis: Naval Institute Press, 2020.

———, "Challenging the Interest and Reverence of All Americans: Preservation and the Yorktown National Battlefield," in Karen L. Cox, *Destination Dixie: Tourism and Southern History.* Gainesville: University Press of Florida, 2012.

Gole, Henry G. *The Road to Rainbow: Army Planning for Global War, 1934–1940.* Annapolis: Naval Institute Press, 2002.

Gordon, Michael R. and Bernard E. Trainor. *Cobra II: The Inside Story of the Invasion and Occupation of Iraq.* New York: Pantheon, 2006.

Goren, Dina. "Communications Intelligence and the Freedom of the Press: The Chicago Tribune's Battle of Midway Dispatch and the Breaking of the Japanese Naval Code." *Journal of Contemporary History*, 16, 4 (October 1981).

Gough, Barry. *Historical Dreadnaughts: Arthur Marder, Stephen Roskill, and Battles for Naval History.* Barnsley, UK: Seaforth Publishing, 2010.

Graybar, Lloyd J. "Admiral King's Toughest Battle," *Naval War College Review*, 32, 1 (February 1979).

———, "Ernest J. King: Commander of the Two-Ocean Navy," James C. Bradford, ed., *Quarterdeck and Bridge: Two Centuries of American Naval Leaders.* Annapolis: Naval Institute Press, 1997.

Greenberg, Joel. *Alastair Denniston: Code-Breaking from Room 40 to Berkley Street to Bletchley Park.* Barnsley South Yorkshire, UK: Frontline Books, 2017.

Grew, Joseph C. *Ten Years in Japan: A Contemporary Record Drawn From the Diaries and Official Papers of Joseph C. Grew—United States Ambassador to Japan, 1932–1942.* New York: Simon and Schuster, 1944.

Grey, Jeffrey. *The Last Word? Essays on Official History in the United States and British Commonwealth.* Westport: Praeger, 2003.

Gropman, Alan, ed. *The Big "L": American Logistics in World War II.* Washington, DC: National Defense University Press, 1997.

Grove, Eric. *The Price of Disobedience: The Battle of the River Plate Reconsidered.* Annapolis: Naval Institute Press, 2001.

———, "The Modern View: The Battle and Post-War British Naval Policy," in Stephen Howarth and Derek Law, *The Battle of the Atlantic, 1939–1945: The 50th Anniversary International Naval Conference.* Annapolis: Naval Institute Press, 1994.

———, *Vanguard to Trident: British Naval Policy Since World War II.* Annapolis: Naval Institute Press, 1987.

———, *The Defeat of the Enemy Attack on Shipping, 1939–1945.* Brookfield: Ashgate, 1998.

Gueli, Cindy. *Lipstick Brigade: The Untold True Story of Washington's World War II Government Girls.* Washington, DC: Tahoga, 2015.

Gucritz, E. F. "Nelson's Blood: Attitudes and Actions of the Royal Navy, 1939–45," *Journal of Contemporary History,* 16, 3 (July 1981).

Gunther, John. *Roosevelt in Retrospect: A Profile in History.* New York: Harper Bros., 1950.

Gunton, Dennis. *The Penang Submarines.* Penang, Malaysia: City Council of Georgetown, 1970.

Gwyer, J. M. A. *Grand Strategy (vol. III, pt. 1: June 1941–August 1942.* London: HMSO, 1964.

Hackmann, Willem. *Seek & Strike: Antisubmarine Warfare and the Royal Navy, 1914–1954.* London: HMSO, 1984.

Hadley, Michael L. with Rob Huebert, and Fred W. Crickard, eds., *A Nation's Navy: In Quest of Canadian Naval Identity.* Montreal: McGill-Queen's University Press, 1996.

———, *Count Not the Dead: The Popular Image of the German Submarine.* Canada, Montreal: McGill-Queens University Press, 1995.

———, and Roger Sarty. *Tin Pots and Pirate Ships: Canadian Naval Forces and German Sea Raiders, 1880–1918.* Montreal, Canada: McGill-Queens, 1991.

Hagan, Kenneth J. *This People's Navy: The Making of American Seapower.* New York: Free Press (1991).

Halsey, William F. and Joseph Bryan. *Admiral Halsey's Story.* New York: McGraw-Hill, 1947.

Halewood, Louis. "Peace Throughout the Oceans and Seas of the World: British Maritime Strategic Thought and World Order, 1892–1919," *Historical Research,* 94, 265 (August 2021).

Halpern, Paul. *A Naval History of World War I.* London: University College Press, 1994.

Hamblin, Jacob Darwin. *Arming Mother Nature: The Birth of Catastrophic Environmentalism.* New York: Oxford, 2013.

Hamer, David H. "G-312: An *Abwehr* Enigma," *Cryptologia,* XXIV, 1. (January 2000).

Hamilton, C. Ian. "The Character and Organization of the Admiralty Operational Intelligence Centre during the Second World War," *War In History* (July 2000).

Hamilton, Nigel. *War and Peace: FDR's Final Odyssey—D-Day to Yalta, 1943–1945.* New York: Houghton-Mifflin, 2019.

Hampton, Dan. *Operation Vengeance: The Astonishing Aerial Ambush That Changed World War II.* New York: William Murrow, 2020.

Hancock, Joy Bright. *Lady in the Navy: A Personal Reminiscence.* Annapolis: Naval Institute Press, 1972.

Hara, Tameichi. *Japanese Destroyer Captain: Pearl Harbor, Guadalcanal, Midway—The Great Naval Battles as Seen Through Japanese Eyes.* Annapolis: Naval Institute Press, 2011.

Harper, Stephen. *Capturing Enigma: How HMS Petard Seized the German Naval Codes.* London: Sutton, 2000.

Harris, Mark. *Five Came Back: A Story of Hollywood and the Second World War.* New York: Penguin, 2014.

Hashimoto Mochitsura. *Sunk: The Story of the Japanese Submarine Fleet 1942–1945.* Cassell, London, 1954.

Hastings, Max. *Nemesis: The Battle for Japan, 1944–45.* London: Harper, 2007.

Hattendorf, John B., and William P. Leeman, eds., *Forging the Trident: Theodore Roosevelt and the United States Navy.* Annapolis: Naval Institute Press, 2020.

———, with Pelham Boyer. *To The Java Sea: Selections from the Diary, Reports, and Letters of Henry E. Eccles, 1940–1942.* Newport: Naval War College Press, 2021.

———, "The Idea of a 'Fleet in Being' in Historical Perspective," *The Naval War College Review,* 67, 1 (Winter 2014).

———, and Bruce Elleman. *Nineteen Gun Salute.* Newport: Naval War College Press, 2010.

———, *Naval History and Maritime Strategy: Collected Essays.* Malabar: Krieger Publishing, 2000.

———, *Doing Naval History: Essays Toward Improvement.* Newport: Naval War College Press, 1995.

———, with B. Mitchell Simpson and John R. Wadleigh. *Sailors and Scholars: The Centennial History of the US Naval War College.* Newport: Naval War College Press, 1984.

———, *On His Majesty's Service: Observations of the British Home Fleet from the Diary, Reports, and Letters of Joseph H. Wellings, Assistant US Naval Attaché London 1940–41.* Newport: Naval War College Press, 1983.

———, "Rear Admiral Charles H. Stockton, the Naval War College, and the Law of Naval Warfare," in Michael N. Schmitt and Leslie C. Green, eds., *International Law Studies Blue Book Series—The Law of Armed Conflict: Into the New Millennium,* vol. 71. Newport: Naval War College Press, 1980.

Haydon, Peter. *The Admirals: Canada's Senior Naval Leadership in the Twentieth Century.* Toronto: Dundurn Press, 2006.

Heiferman, Ronald Ian. *The Cairo Conference of 1943: Roosevelt, Churchill, Chiang Kai-shek, and Madame Chiang.* Jefferson: McFarland & Co., 2011.

Heimdahl, William C. and Edward J. Marolda. *Guide to United States Naval Administrative Histories of World War II.* Washington, DC: Naval History Division, 1976.

Heinlein, Robert. *Rocket Ship Gallileo.* New York: Scribners, 1947.

———, *Starman Jones.* New York: Scribners, 1953.

———, *Starship Troopers.* New York: Putnam, 1959.

———"Searchlight," *Scientific American,* 207, 2 (August 1962).

Heinrichs, Waldo H. *Threshold of War: Franklin D. Roosevelt and American Entry Into World War II.* New York: Oxford University Press, 1988.

Heinsius, Paul. "Der Verbleib des Aktenmaterials der deutschen Kriegsmarine," *Der Archivar,* VIII, 2 (April 1955).

Hendricks, Elizabeth G. "Mildred McAfee Horton (1900–1994): Portrait of a Pathbreaking Christian Leader," *The Journal of Presbyterian History,* 76, 2 (Summer 1998).

Herf, Jeffrey. *Nazi Propaganda for the Arab World.* New Haven: Yale Universtiy Press, 2009.

Herman, Arthur. *Freedom's Forge: How American Business Produced Victory in World War II.* New York: Random House, 2012.

Herwig, Holger H. *Politics of Frustration: The United States in German Naval Planning: 1889–1941.* Boston: Little Brown, 1976.

———, *The German Naval Officer Corps: A Social and Political History, 1890–1918.* New York: Oxford University Press, 1973.

———, "From Kaiser to Führer: The Political Road of a German Admiral, 1923–33," *Journal of Contemporary History*, 9, 2 (April 1974).

Hessler, Günter, et al. *Ministry of Defense (Navy): The U-Boat War in the Atlantic, 1939–1945.* London: HMSO, 1989.

Heuser, Beatrice. *The Evolution of Strategy: Thinking War from Antiquity to Present.* Cambridge: Cambridge University Press, 2010.

———, *NATO, Britain, France, and the FRG: Nuclear Strategies and Forces For Europe, 1949–2000.* New York: St. Martins Press, 1997.

Hewlett, Richard G. and Oscar E. Anderson Jr. *The New World, 1939/1946: A History of The United States Atomic Energy Commission.* University Park: Pennsylvania State University, 1962.

Hickam, Homer H. *Torpedo Junction: U-Boat War Off America's East Coast, 1942.* Annapolis: Naval Institute Press, 1989.

Hilton, Stanly E. *Hitler's Secret War in South America, 1939–1945: German Military Espionage and American Counterespionage in Brazil.* Baton Rouge: Louisiana State University, 1981.

Hinsley, Francis H. and Alan Stripp, eds. *Codebreakers: The Inside Story of Bletchley Park.* New York: Oxford, 1993.

———, E. E. Thomas, C. F. G. Ransom, and R. C. Knight. *British Intelligence in the Second World War: Its Influence on Strategy and Operations.* London: HMSO, I–III, 1979–1988.

———, E. E. Thomas, C. F. G. Ransom, and R. C. Knight. *British Intelligence in the Second World War: Security and Counter-Intelligence.* London: HMSO, IV, 1990.

Hirschmann, Werner with Donald E. Graves. *Another Place, Another Time.* Annapolis: Naval Institute Press, 2004.

Hobbs, David. *The British Pacific Fleet: The Royal Navy's Most Powerful Strike Force.* Annapolis: Naval Institute Press, 2011.

Hodges, Andrew. *Alan Turing: The Enigma.* New York: Simon & Schuster, 1983.

Holmes, W. J. *Double-Edged Secrets: US Naval Intelligence in the Pacific during World War II.* Annapolis: Naval Institute Press, 1979.

Holloway, John L. Jr., "The Holloway Plan—A Summary View and Commentary," Naval Institute *Proceedings*, 73, 11 (November 1947).

Hone, Trent. *Learning War: The Evolution of Fighting Doctrine in the US Navy, 1898–1945.* Annapolis: Naval Institute Press, 2018.

Hornfischer, James D. *The Last Stand of the Tin Can Sailors: The Extraordinary World War II Story of the US Navy's Finest Hour.* New York: Bantam Books, 2004.

———, *Ship of Ghosts: The Story of USS Houston. FDR's Legendary Lost Cruiser and the Epic Saga of Her Survivors.* New York: Bantam, 2006.

Hougen, John. *History of the Famous 34th Infantry Division: Attack, Attack, Attack.* Nashville: Battery Press, 1949.

Howard, Michael. *The Lessons of History.* New Haven: Yale University Press, 1994.

———, *British Intelligence in the Second World War: Strategic Deception.* London: HMSO, 1990.

———, *The Causes of War: Revised and Enlarged Edition.* Cambridge: Harvard University Press, 1984.

———, *Grand Strategy: September 1942–August 1943.* London: HMSO, 1970.

Howarth, Stephen and Derek Law, eds. *The Battle of the Atlantic, 1939–1945: The 50th Anniversary International Naval Conference.* Annapolis: Naval Institute Press, 1994.

Howeth, Linwood S. *History of Communications-Electronics in the United States Navy.* Washington, DC: Government Printing Office, 1963.

Hughes, Thomas A. *Admiral Bill Halsey: A Naval Life.* New York, Harvard University Press, 2016.

Huie, William Bradford. *From Omaha to Okinawa: The Story of the Seabees.* New York: Dutton, 1946.

———, *Can Do! The Story of the Seabees.* New York: Dutton, 1944.

Hulver, Richard and Peter Lubeke, eds. *A Grave Misfortune: The Indianapolis Tragedy.* Washington, DC: Naval History and Heritage Command, 2018.

Hunter, Francis T. *Beatty, Jellicoe, Sims, and Rodman: Yankee Gobs and British Tars, As Seen by an "Anglomaniac."* New York: Doubleday, Page & Company, 1919.

Hurley, Alfred. *Billy Mitchell: Crusader for Air Power.* Bloomington: University of Indiana Press, 1964.

Husband, Joseph. *On the Coast of France: The Story of US Naval Forces in France.* Chicago: A.C. McClurg & Co., 1919.

Ingersoll, Ralph. *Top Secret.* New York: Harcourt and Brace, 1946.

Ingraham, Reg. *First Fleet: The Story of the US Coast Guard at War.* New York: Bobbs-Merrill, 1944.

Isely, Jeter A. and Philip A. Crowl, *The US Marines and Amphibious War: Its Theory and Its Practice in the Pacific.* Princeton: Princeton University Press, 1951.

James, Dorris Clayton. *The Years of MacArthur: 1880–1941.* New York: Houghton Mifflin, 1970.

James, Karl, ed. *Kokoda: Beyond the Legend.* New York: Australian War Memorial / Cambridge University Press, 2017.

James, Robert Rhodes, ed. *Winston Churchill: His Complete Speeches 1897–1963.* London: Chelsea House Publishers, 1974.

Jellicoe, Nicholas. *George Jellicoe: SAS and SBS Commander.* Philadelphia: Pen and Sword, 2021.

———, *The Last Days of the High Seas Fleet: From Mutiny to Scapa Flow.* Barnsley, UK: Seaforth, 2019.

———, *Jutland: The Unfinished Battle: A Personal History of a Naval Controversy.* Barnsley, UK: Seaforth, 2016.

Jensen, Kurt F. *Cautious Beginnings: Canadian Foreign Intelligence, 1939–51*. Toronto: University of British Columbia Press, 2008.

Johnsen, William T. *Origins of the Grand Alliance: Anglo-American Military Collaboration from the* Panay *Incident to Pearl Harbor.* Lexington: University Press of Kentucky, 2016.

Johnson, Charles. *A General History of the Pyrates from First Rise and Settlement in the Island of Providence to the Present Time.* London: Charles Rivington, 1724.

Johnston, Harvey G. *The Haraldry of the Murrays.* Edinburgh, Scotland: Johnston, 1910.

Jones, Reginald V. *Most Secret War: British Scientific Intelligence, 1939–1945.* London: Hamish Hamilton, 1978.

Jordan, Jonathan. *American Warlords: How Roosevelt's High Command Led Americans to Victory in World War II.* New York: Penguin-Random House, 2015.

Joubert de la Ferté, Phillip. *Birds and Fishes: The Story of Coastal Command.* London: Hutchinson, 1960.

Jurika, Stephen Jr. "Pilots, Man Your Planes," *Saturday Evening Post*, 211, 30 (21 January 1939).

Kahn, David. *The Reader of Gentleman's Mail: Herbert O. Yardley and the Birth of American Codebreaking.* New Haven: Yale University Press, 2004.

———, *Seizing the Enigma: The Race to Break the German U-Boat Codes, 1939–1943.* Boston: Houghton Mifflin, 1991.

———, *Hitler's Spies.* New York: Palgrave MacMillan, 1978.

———, *The Codebreakers: The Story of Secret Writing.* New York: MacMillan, 1967.

Kalbfus, Edward C., ed. *Sound Military Decision.* Newport: Naval War College, 1942.

———, "The Naval War College: Bright Officers Fight Imaginary Battles," *Life* magazine, 9, 18 (28 October 1940).

Kaplan, Amy and Donald E. Pease. *Cultures of United States Imperialism.* Durham: Duke University Press, 1991.

Karsten, Peter. *Naval Aristocracy: The Golden Age of Annapolis and the Rise of American Navalism.* Annapolis: Naval Institute Press, 2008.

Keegan, John. *The Face of Battle.* New York: Viking Press, 1976.

Kemp, Peter. *Key to Victory: The Triumph of British Seapower in World War II.* New York: Little, Brown, 1957.

Kent, Sherman. *Strategic Intelligence for American World Policy.* Princeton: Princeton University Press, 1949.

Kennedy, David M. *Freedom from Fear: The American People in Depression and War, 1929–1945.* New York: Oxford University Press, 2000.

Kennedy, Greg. *Anglo-American Strategic Relations and the Far East, 1933–1939: Imperial Crossroads.* Portland: Frank Cass, 2002.

Kennedy, John F. *Why England Slept.* New York: Wilfred Funk, 1940.

Kennedy, Paul M. *Engineers of Victory: The Problem Solvers Who Turned the Tide in the Second World War.* New York: Random House, 2013.

———, *The Rise and Fall of British Naval Mastery.* London: Allan Lane, 1983.

Keith, Phil. *Stay the Rising Sun: The True Story of USS Lexington, Her Valiant Crew, and Changing the Course of World War II.* Minneapolis: Zenith Press, 2015.

Keyes, Roger. *Amphibious Warfare and Combined Operations.* Cambridge, UK: Cambridge University Press, 1943.

Kimmel, Husband E. *Admiral Kimmel's Story.* Chicago: Henry Regnery, 1954.

King, Ernest J. and Walter Muir Whitehill. *Fleet Admiral King: A Naval Record.* New York: Norton, 1952.

———, "An address by Fleet Admiral Ernest J. King, at the National Exchange Club Convention," *The Exchangite*, 26, 11 (November 1947).

———, comp. *The US Navy at War, 1941–45—Official Reports to the Secretary of the Navy.* Washington, DC: Navy Department, 1946.

———, "Responsibilities of Leadership," in Arthur A. Ageton, comp., *The Naval Officer's Guide.* New York: Whittlesley House, 1943.

———, trans., "A German View of the Strategic Importance of the Panama Canal," Naval Institute *Proceedings*, 40, 3 (May–June 1914)

Kirby, S. Woodburn, et al. *History of the Second World War: War Against Japan*, vols. 1–5. London: HMSO, 1957–1969.

Kittredge, Tracy Barrett. *Naval Lessons of the Great War: A Review of the Senate Naval Investigation of the Criticisms by Admiral Sims of the Policies and Methods of Josephus Daniels.* New York: Doubleday, Page & Co., 1921.

———, *The History of the Commission for Relief in Belgium, 1914–1917.* Unknown publisher, 1918.

Kliemann, Michel Laguerre. *US Naval War College & Escuela Superior de Guerra Naval del Perú.* Lima, Peru: Escuela Superior de Guerra Naval del Perú/ Naval War College, 2017.

Knowles, Kenneth A. "Ultra and the Battle of the Atlantic: The American View," in Robert W. Love Jr., ed. *Changing Interpretations and New Sources in Naval History: Papers from the Third United States Naval Academy History Symposium.* New York: Garland, 1980.

———, "Review of *The Intelligence Community: History, Organization, and Issues*, by Tyrus G. Fain" in collaboration with Katherine C. Plant and Ross Milloy comps., Naval Institute *Proceedings* (November 1978).

———, "Review of *The Tenth Fleet: The Untold Story of the Submarine and Survival* by Ladislas Farago," *Central Intelligence Agency Journal*, 7, 2 (Fall 1962).

Knox, Dudley Wright. *The Naval Genius of George Washington.* Boston: Houghton Mifflin, 1932.

———, *The Eclipse of American Sea Power.* New York: Army and Navy Journal, 1922.

Koelshbach, Heinz. *Der Blockadebrecher mit der glück-lichen Hand.* Herford, Germany: Koehlers, 1958.

Kohn, Richard, ed. *The United States Military under the Constitution of the United States, 1789–1989.* New York: New York University Press, 1991.

———, *Eagle and the Sword: The Federalists and the Creation of the Military Establishment in America, 1783–1802.* New York: The Free Press, 1975.

Kohnen, David. *Remain Cheerful: Baseball, Britannia, and American Independence, 4 July 1918.* Naval War College Foundation, 2022.

———, "El Americano:Las Aventuras del Capitán de la Reserva Naval de los Estados Unidos—Harold Bartley Grow en Perú, 1923–1930," in *Revista de Marina* (Fall 2021).

———, *Feeding Greyhounds: Fueling the US Navy 'Second to None' in the First World War Era.* Naval War College Foundation, 2021.

———, *Grippe Caught us Quicker than U-Boats: The Lingering Sickness of War and the Pandemic of 1918–1920.* Naval War College Foundation, 2020.

———, Charting a New Course: The Knox-Pye-King Board and Naval Professional Education, 1919–23" *Naval War College Review*, 71, 3 (Summer 2018).

———, *Twenty-First Century Knox: Influence, Sea Power, and History for the Modern Era.* Annapolis: Naval Institute Press, 2016.

———, with Nicholas Jellicoe and Nathaniel Sims. "The US Navy Won the Battle of Jutland," *Naval War College Review*, 69, 4 (Autumn 2016).

———, "Alan Goodrich Kirk," in John B. Hattendorf and Bruce Elleman. *Nineteen Gun Salute.* Newport: Naval War College Press, 2010.

———, "F-21 and F-211: A Fresh Look into the Secret Room" in Randy Bolano and Craig Symonds, ed., *New Sources in Naval History: Selected Papers from the Fourteenth Naval History Symposium.* Annapolis: Naval Institute Press, 2001.

———, *Commanders Winn and Knowles: Winning the U-Boat War with Intelligence, 1939–1943.* Kraków, Poland: Enigma Press, 1999.

Kühl, Stefan. *The Nazi Connection: Eugenics, American Racism, and German National Socialism.* New York: Oxford, 1994.

Kuehn, John T. *America's First General Staff: A Short History of the Rise and Fall of the General Board of the Navy, 1900–1950.* Annapolis: Naval Institute Press, 2017.

———, *A Military History of Japan: From the Age of the Samurai to the Twenty-First Century.* New York: Praeger, 2014.

———, *Agents of Innovation: The General Board and the Design of the Fleet that Defeated the Japanese Navy.* Annapolis: Naval Institute Press, 2008.

Kurz-Phelan, Daniel. *The China Mission: George Marshall's Unfinished War, 1945–1947.* New York: W.W. Norton, 2018.

Krug, Hans-Joachim, Yōichi Harama, Berthold J. Sander-Nagashima, and Axel Niestlé. *Reluctant Allies: German-Japanese Naval Relations in World War II.* Annapolis: Naval Institute Press, 2001.

Laberee, Benjamin W. with William E. Baker. *The Atlantic World of Robert G. Albion.* Middletown: Wesleyan University Press, 1975.

Lambert, Andrew. *The British Way of War: Julian Corbett and the Battle for a National Strategy.* New Haven: Yale University Press, 2021.

———, *The Challenge: Britain Against America in the Naval War of 1812.* London: Faber & Faber, 2012.

———, *The Admirals: The Naval Commanders who Made Britain Great.* London: Faber & Faber, 2008.

———, *The Foundations of Naval History: John Knox Laughton, The Royal Navy, and the Historical Profession.* London: Chatham Publishing, 1998.

Lambert, Nicholas A. *Planning Armageddon: British Economic Warfare and the First World War.* Boston: Harvard University Press, 2012.

———, "Strategic Command and Control for Maneuver Warfare: Creation of the Royal Navy's "War Room" System, 1905–1915," *The Journal of Military History*, 69, 2 (April 2005).

Land, Emory S. *Winning the War with Ships—Land, Sea, and Air.* New York: McBride, 1959.

Larrabee, Eric. *Commander in Chief: Franklin Delano Roosevelt, His Lieutenants, and Their War.* Annapolis: Naval Institute Press, 1987.

Lautz, Terry. *John Birch: A Life.* New York: Oxford University Press, 2016.

LaVo, Carl. *Pushing the Limits: The Remarkable Life and Times of Vice Admiral Allan R. McCann, USN.* Annapolis: Naval Institute Press, 2013.

Layman, R. D. and Stephen McLachlan. *The Hybrid Warship: The Amalgamation of Big Guns and Aircraft.* London: Conway Maritime Press, 1990.

Layton, Edwin T., Roger Pineau, and John Costello. *"And I Was There": Pearl Harbor and Midway—Breaking the Secrets.* New York: Quill, 1985.

Leahy, William D. *I Was There: The Personal Story of the Chief of Staff to Presidents Roosevelt and Truman, Based on His Notes and Diaries Made at the Time.* New York: Whittlesey House, 1948.

Lebra-Chapman, Joyce C. *Japan's Greater East Asia Co-Prosperity Sphere in World War II: Selected Readings and Documents.* New York: Oxford University Press, 1975.

Ledbetter, James. *Unwarrented Influence: Dwight D. Eisenhower and the Military Industrial Complex.* New Haven: Yale University Press, 2011.

Leeke, Jim. *Nine Innings for the King: The Day Wartime London Stopped for Baseball, July 4, 1918.* Jefferson: McFarland & Co., 2015.

Leighton, John Langdon. *SIMSADUS-London: The American Navy in Europe.* New York: Henry Holt, 1920.

Leutze, James R. *A Different Kind of Victory: A Biography of Admiral Thomas C. Hart.* Annapolis: Naval Institute Press, 1981.

———, *Bargaining for Supremacy: Anglo-American Naval Collaboration, 1937–1941.* Chapel Hill: University of North Carolina Press, 1977.

Lewin, Ronald. *The American Magic: Codes, Ciphers and the Defeat of Japan.* New York: Farrar, Straus, Giroux, 1982.

Lewis, Adrian R. *Omaha Beach: A Flawed Victory.* Chapel Hill: University of North Carolina Press, 2001.

Liddell Hart, Basil H. *Reputations: Ten Years After.* New York: Little Brown, 1928.

Lin, Hsiao-ting. *Accidental State: Chiang Kaishek, the United States, and the Making of Taiwan.* Cambridge: Harvard, 2016.

Linenthal, Edward T. and Tom Engelhardt, eds. *History Wars: The Enola Gay and Other Battles for the American Past.* New York: Metropolitan, 1996.

Linn, Brian McAllister. *The Echo of Battle: The Army's Way of War.* Cambridge: Harvard University Press, 2007.

Lippmann, Walter. *The Cold War: A Study in US Foreign Policy.* New York: Harper, 1947.

———, *US Foreign Policy: Shield of the Republic.* Boston: Little, Brown, & Co., 1943.

Little, Branden. "Tarnishing Victory? Contested Histories and Civil–Military Discord in the US Navy, 1919–24," *Defense & Security Analysis*, 36, 1 (Spring 2020).

Llewellyn-Jones, Malcolm. *The Royal Navy and Anti-Submarine Warfare, 1917–49.* New York: Routledge, 2006.

Longden, Sean. *T-Force: The Race for Nazi Secrets, 1945.* London: Conatable, 2009.

Lockwood, Charles A. *Sink 'Em All: Submarine Warfare in the Pacific.* New York: E.P. Dutton, 1951.

Lopach, James J. and Jean A. Luchowski, Jeanette Rankin. *A Political Woman.* Boulder: University of Colorado, 2005.

Loughery, John. *The Other Side of Silence: Men's Lives and Gay Identities—A Twentieth Century History.* New York: Henry Holt, 1998.

Love, Robert William Jr., "The US Navy and Operation *Roll of Drums*, 1942," Timothy J. Runyan and Jan M. Copes, eds., *To Die Gallantly: The Battle of the Atlantic.* Boulder: Westview Press, 1994.

———, ed. *Changing Interpretations and New Sources in Naval History: Papers from the Third United States Naval Academy History Symposium.* New York: Garland, 1980.

———, "Ernest Joseph King, 26 March 1942–15 December 1945," in Robert W. Love Jr., ed. *The Chiefs of Naval Operations.* Annapolis: Naval Institute Press, 1980.

Lumsden, Linda. "Socialist Muckraker John Kenneth Turner," *American Journalism*, 32, 3 (July 2015).

Lundeberg, Philip K. "Allied Co-operation." In Stephen Howarth and Derek Law, eds. *The Battle of the Atlantic, 1939–1945: The 50th Anniversary International Naval Conference.* Annapolis: Naval Institute Press, 1994.

———, "Operation TEARDROP Revisited," in Timothy J. Runyan and Jan M. Copes, eds., *To Die Gallantly: The Battle of the Atlantic.* Boulder: Westview Press, 1994.

Lundstrom, John B. *Black Shoe Carrier Admiral: Frank Jack Fletcher at Coral Sea, Midway, and Guadalcanal.* Annapolis: Naval Institute Press, 2006.

———, *The First Team: Pacific Naval Air Combat from Pearl Harbor to Midway.* Annapolis: Naval Institute Press, 1984.

MacArthur, Douglas. *Reminiscences.* New York: McGraw Hill, 1964.

MacDonogh, Giles. *After the Reich: The Brutal History of the Allied Occupation* Philadelphia: Basic Books, 2007.

MacLachlan, Donald. *Room 39: A Study in Naval Intelligence.* New York: Atheneum, 1968.

MacDonnell, Francis. *Insidious Foes: The Axis Fifth Column and the American Homefront.* New York: Oxford, 1995.

MacIntyre, Ben. *For Your Eyes Only: Ian Fleming and James Bond.* London: Bloomsbury, 2008.

MacIntyre, Donald. *The Naval War Against Hitler.* New York: Scribner's, 1971.

MacPherson, B. Nelson. "The Compromise of US Navy Cryptanalysis After the Battle of Midway," *Intelligence and National Security*, 2, 2 (April 1987).

Madsen, Chris. *The Royal Navy and German Naval Disarmament: 1942–1947.* London: Taylor and Francis, 1998.

Maffeo, Stephen. *US Navy Codebreakers, Linguists, and Intelligence Officers against Japan, 1910–1941.* Washington, DC: Rowan and Littefield, 2016.

Maga, Tim. *America Attacks Japan: The Invasion that Never Was.* Lexington: University Press of Kentucky, 2002.

Marsh, Charles C., Dudley W. Knox, and Tracy Barrett Kittredge (comps.). *German Submarine Activities on the Atlantic Coast of the United States of America—Publication no. 1.* Washington, DC: Navy Department, 1920.

Matloff, Maurice and Edwin M. Snell, *Strategic Planning for Coalition Warfare, 1941–1942.* Washington, DC: US Army Center of Military History, 1953.

McCoy, Alfred W. and Francisco A. Scarano, eds. *Colonial Crucible: Empire in the Making of the Modern American State.* Madison: University of Wisconsin, 2009.

McCrea, John L. with Julia C. Tobey, ed. *Captain McCrea's War: The World War II Memoir of Franklin D. Roosevelt's Naval Aide and USS Iowa's First Commanding Officer.* New York: Skyhorse Publishing, 2016.

McCue, Brian. *U-Boats in the Bay of Biscay: An Essay in Operations Analysis.* Washington, DC: National Defense University Press, 1990.

McCullough, David. *Truman.* New York: Simon and Schuster, 1992

McGee, William L. with Sandra McGee, eds. *Pacific Express: The Critical Role of Military Logistics in World War II.* Tiburen: BMC Press, 2009.

McLaughlan, Robert L. and Sally Perry, *We'll Always Have the Movies: American Cinema during World War II.* Lexington: University Press of Kentucky, 2006.

McGregor, Moriss J. Jr. *Integration of the Armed Forces, 1940–1965.* Washington, DC: Center of Military History, 1981.

McLean, Doug M. "Muddling Through: Canadian Anti-submarine Doctrine and Practice, 1942–1945," in Michael Hadley, Rob Huebert, and Fred W. Crickard, eds., *A Nation's Navy: In Quest of Canadian Naval Identity.* Montreal: McGill-Queen's, 1996.

McNeill, William Hardy. *America, Britain, and Russia: Their Co-operation and Conflict, 1941–1946.* New York: Johnson Reprint Corporation, 1970.

McBurney, Christian, Norman Desmaris, and Varoujan Karentz. *Untold Stories from WorldWar II Rhode Island.* Charleston: History Press, 2019.

McClintock, William R. "'Clio Mobilizes:' Naval Reserve Historians During the Second World War," *The Public Historian*, 13, 1 (Winter 1991).

Mahan, Alfred Thayer. *The Influence of History Upon Sea Power.* Boston: Little Brown, 1890.

————, *The Problem of Asia and its Effect on International Policies*. Boston: Little Brown, 1900.

————, *From Sail to Steam: Recollections of Naval Life*. New York: Harper and Brothers, 1907.

————, "Britain and Imperial Germany—Admiral Mahan's Warning," reprinted from *The Daily Mail* (1910).

Marolda, Edward J. ed. *FDR and the US Navy*. New York: Palgrave MacMillan, 1998.

Marshall, M. Ernest. *Rear Admiral Herbert V. Wiley: A Career in Airships and Battleships*. Annapolis: Naval Institute Press, 2019.

Martin, Bernd. *Deutschland und Japan im Zweiten Weltkrieg: Vom Angriff auf Pearl Harbor bis zur deutschen Kapitulation*. Frankfurt: Musterschmidt, 1969.

Marsh, Charles C., Tracy B. Kittredge, and Dudley W. Knox. *German Submarine Activities on the Atlantic Coast of the United States and Canada*. Washington, DC: US Government Printing Office, 1920.

Masland, John Wesley and Lawrence I. Radway. *Soldiers and Scholars*. Princeton: Princeton University Press, 1957.

Mason, John T., ed. *The Atlantic War Remembered: An Oral History Collection*. Annapolis: Naval Institute Press, 1990.

Matzen, Robert. *Mission: Jimmie Stewart and the Fight for Europe*. Pittsburgh: GoodNight Books, 2016.

McAllister, Brian. *Guardians of Empire: The US Army and the Pacific, 1902–1940*. Chapel Hill: University of North Carolina, 1997.

McCartney, Laton. *The Teapot Dome Scandal: How Big Oil Bought the Harding White House and Tried to Steal the Country*. New York: Random House, 2009.

Meacham, Jon. *Franklin and Winston: An Intimate Portrait of an Epic Friendship*. New York: Random House, 2003.

Merrill, James M. *A Sailor's Admiral: A Biography of William F. Halsey Jr.* New York: Crowell, 1976.

Meyer, Michael C. "The Arms of the *Ypiranga*," *The Hispanic American Historical Review*, 50, 3 (August 1970).

Michael-Mallman, Klaus and Martin Cüppers, *Nazi Palestine: The Plan for the Extermination of the Jews in Palestine*. New York: Enigma Books, 2010.

Middlebrook, Martin and Patrick Mahoney, *Battleship: The Sinking of the Prince of Wales and Repulse*. New York: Scribner's, 1977.

Miles, Milton E. *A Different Kind of War*. New York: Doubleday, 1967.

Miles, Wilma S. *"Billy," Navy Wife*. Salt Lake City: Publisher's Press, 1999.

Miller, Edward S. *War Plan Orange: The US Strategy to Defeat Japan*. Annapolis: Naval Institute Press, 1991.

Miller, John and Michael Stone with Chris Mitchell. *The Cell: Inside the 9-11 Plot and Why the FBI and CIA Failed to Stop It*. New York: Hyperion, 2002.

Milner, Marc. *The Battle of the Atlantic*. St. Katherines: Vanwell Press, 2003.

————, *The U-Boat Hunters: The Royal Canadian Navy and the Offensive Against Germany's Submarines, 1943–1945*. Annapolis: Naval Institute Press, 1994.

————, *North Atlantic Run: The Royal Canadian Navy and the Battle for the Convoys* Toronto: University of Toronto Press, 1985.

Mitter, Rana. *Forgotten Ally: China's World War II*. New York: Mariner, 2013.

Mobley, Scott. *Progressives in Navy Blue: Maritime Strategy, American Empire, and the Transformation of US Naval Identity, 1873–1898*. Annapolis: Naval Institute Press, 2018.

Mohr, Ulrich and A. V. Sellwood. *Sea Raider Atlantis*. London: New English Library, 1955.

Mollo, Andrew. *Uniforms and Insignia of the Navies of World War II: A Facsimile Edition of the US Navy Intelligence Manual Published in World War II*. Barnsley–South Yorkshire, Great Britain: Greenhill Books, 1991.

Monserrat, Nicholas. *The Cruel Sea*. New York: Alfred A. Knopf, 1951.

Moran, Christopher R. and Christopher J. Murphy, eds. *Intelligence Studies in Britain and the US Historiography since 1945*. Edinburgh, Scotland, UK: Edinburgh University Press, 2013.

Morison, Elting, E. *Admiral Sims and the Modern American Navy*. Boston: Houghton Mifflin, 1942.

Morison, Samuel E. *History of United States Naval Operations in World War II*. Boston: Little Brown and Company, vols. I–XV, 1947–1962.

————, *The Scholar in American, Past, Present, and Future*. New York: Oxford University Press, 1961.

————, *Strategy and Compromise*. Boston: Little Brown and Company, 1958.

————, *American Contributions to the Strategy of World War II*. New York: Oxford University Press, 1958.

————, *John Paul Jones: A Sailor's Biography*. Boston: Little Brown, 1959.

Morrow, Felix. *The Bonus March*. International Pamphlets, no. 31. New York: International Publishers, 1932.

Morse, Philip M. and Geoge E. Kimball, *Methods of Operational Research*. Cambridge: Technology Press, 1951.

Muggenthaler, Karl August. *German Raiders of World War II*. London: Prentice-Hall, 1977.

Muir, Malcolm. *The Iowa Class Battleships: Iowa, New Jersey, Missouri, and Wisconsin*. New York: Sterling Publishing, 1989.

Mulligan, Timothy P. *Neither Sharks Nor Wolves: The Men of Nazi Germany's U-Boat Arm, 1939–1945*. Annapolis: Naval Institute Press, 1999.

————, *Lone Wolf: The Life and Death of U-Boat Ace Werner Henke*. New York: Praeger, 1993.

Mundy, Lisa. *Code Girls: The Untold Story of Women Code Breakers in World War II*. New York: Hachette, 2017.

Murfett, Malcolm. *Fool-Proof Relations: The Search for Anglo-American Naval Collaboration during the Chamberlain Years, 1937–1940*. Singapore: Singapore University Press, 1984.

Murphy, Lawrence R. *Perverts by Official Order: The Campaign Against Homosexuals by the United States Navy*. New York: Harrington Park Press, 1988.

Nakajima, Tadashi and Roger Pineau. *The Devine Wind: Japan's Kamikaze Force in World War II*. New York: Ballantine Books, 1970.

Nash, Peter V. *The Development of Mobile Logistic Support in Anglo-American Naval Policy, 1900–1953*. Gainesville: University Press of Florida.

Neitzel, Sönke. "Deployment of the U-Boats." In Stephen Howarth and Derek Law, eds. *The Battle of the Atlantic, 1939–1945: The 50th Anniversary International Naval Conference*. Annapolis: Naval Institute Press, 1994.

Nelson, Dennis D. *The Integration of the Negro into the US Navy*. New York: Farrar, Strauss, and Young, 1951.

Newhouse, John. *Imperial America: The Bush Assault on the World Order*. New York: Random House, 2004.

Nimitz, Chester W. "Military Value and Tactics of Modern Submarines," Naval Institute *Proceedings*, 38, 4 (December 1912).

Nofi, Albert A. *To Train the Fleet for War: The US Navy Fleet Problems, 1923–1940*. Newport: Naval War College Press, 2010.

Nolan, Liam and John E. Nolan. *Secret Victory: Ireland and the War at Sea, 1914–1918*. Blackrock-Dublin, Ireland: Mercier, 2009.

Nöldeke, Hartmut and Volker Hartmann. *Der Sanitätsdienst in der deutschen U-Boot-Waffe und bei den Kleinkampfverbänden: Geschichte der deutschen U-Boot-Medizin*. Berlin: Mittler & Sohn, 1996.

Nutting, David with Trevor J. Glanville. *Attain by Surprise: Capturing Top Secret Intelligence in World War II*. Chichester, West Sussex, UK: David Colver, 1997.

O'Brian, Phillips Payson. *The Second Most Powerful Man in the World: The Life of Admiral William D. Leahy, Roosevelt's Chief of Staff*. New York: Dutton/Random House, 2019.

———, *How the War was Won: Air-Sea Power and Allied Victory in World War II*. New York: Cambridge University Press, 2015.

O'Connell, Robert. *Sacred Vessels: The Cult of the Battleship and the Rise of the US Navy*. New York: Oxford University Press, 1993.

Odom, William O. *After the Trenches: The Transformation of US Army Doctrine, 1918–1919*. College Station: Texas A&M, 1999.

Offner, Arnold A. *Another Such Victory: President Truman and the Cold War, 1945–1953*. Stanford: Stanford University Press, 2002.

Orriss, Bruce. *When Hollywood Ruled the Skies: The Aviation Film Classics of World War II*. Los Angeles: Aero Press, 1985.

Packard, Wyman H. *A Century of US Naval Intelligence*. Washington, DC: Naval Historical Center, 1996.

Paret, Peter, ed. *Understanding War: Essays on Clausewitz and the History of Military Power*. Princeton: Princeton University Press, 1992.

———, ed. *Makers of Modern Strategy from Machiavelli to the Nuclear Age*. Princeton: Princeton University Press, 1986.

———, ed. and translator with Michael Howard. Carl von Clausewitz, *On War*. Princeton: Princeton University Press, 1976.

———, *Clausewitz and the State*. New York: Oxford University Press, 1976.

Parker, Dana. *Building Victory: Aircraft Manufacturing in the Los Angeles Area in World War II*. Cypress: Dana Parker Enterprises, 2013.

Parker, Frederick D. "How Op-20-G Got Rid of Joe Rochefort," *Cryptologia*, 24, 3 (July 2000).

Parsons, John E. *West on the 49th Parallel: Red River to the Rockies, 1872–1876*. New York: William R. Murrow, 1963.

———, *Firearms in the Custer Battle*. Harrisbary: Stackpole, 1953.

———, *Henry Derringer's Pocket Pistol*. New York: William R. Murrow, 1952.

———, *Peacemaker and its Rivals*. New York: William R. Murrow, 1950.

Pash, Boris T. *The ALSOS Mission*. New York, Charter Books, 1969.

Parton, James. *Air Force Spoken Here: General Ira Eaker and Command of the Air*. Maxwell: Air University Press, 2000.

Parrish, Thomas. *The ULTRA Americans: The US Role in Breaking the Nazi Codes*. New York: Stein and Day, 1986.

Patterson, Lawrence. *Black Flag: The Surrender of Germany's U-Boat Forces*. Barnsley, UK: Pen & Sword, 2009.

———, *Hitler's Gray Wolves: U-Boats in the Indian Ocean*. Annapolis: Naval Institute Press, 2004.

Patterson, William H. Jr. *In Dialogue with His Century: An Authorized Biography of Robert A. Heinlein—Learning Curve, 1907–1948*. New York: Tor Books, 2010.

Pearson, John. *The Life of Ian Fleming*. London: Companion, 1966.

Perisco, Joseph E. *Roosevelt's Secret War: FDR and World War II Espionage*. New York: Random House, 2001.

Perry, Glen C. H. *"Dear Bart:" Washington Views of World War II*. Westport: Greenwood Press, 1982.

Pfitzer, Gregory M. *Samuel Eliot Morison's Historical World: In Quest of a New Parkman*. Boston: Northeastern University Press, 1991.

Piehler, Gunther-Kurt. *Remembering War the American Way*. Washington, DC: Smithsonian Press, 1995.

Pogue, Forrest C. *George C. Marshall—Organizer of Victory, 1943–1945*. New York: Viking Press, 1973.

Poolman, Kenneth. *Escort Carrier: An Account of British Escort Carriers in Trade Protection*. London: Ian Allan, 1972.

Potter, Elmer B. *Bull Halsey: A Biography*. Annapolis: Naval Institute Press, 1985.

———, *Nimitz*. Annapolis: Naval Institute Press, 1976.

———, *The Command Personality*," Naval Institute *Proceedings*, 95, 2 (January 1969).

Powell, Michael. *The Last Voyage of the Graf Spee*. London, Kimber, 1956.

Prados, John. *Storm over Leyte: The Philippine Invasion and the Destruction of the Japanese Navy*. New York: NAL Caliber, 2016.

———, *Combined Fleet Decoded: The Secret History of American Intelligence and the Japanese Navy in World War II*. New York: Random House, 1995.

Prange, Gordon. *At Dawn We Slept: The Untold Story of Pearl Harbor*. New York: McGraw-Hill, 1981.

Pye, Anne Briscoe and Nancy Shea. *The Navy Wife*. New York: Harper, 1942.

Quine, Willard. *The Time of My Life: An Autobiography.* Boston: Massachusetts Institute of Technology, 1985.

Quirk, Robert E. *An Affair of Honor: Woodrow Wilson and the Occupation of Veracruz.* Lexington: University of Kentucky Press / Norton, 1962.

Rahmlow, Hans-Joachim Rahmlow. "Denn wir fuhren . . . Weisse Flagge auf U-*570?*," *Kristall* (1956).

Ramsay, David. *"Blinker" Hall: Spymaster—The Man Who Brought America into World War I.* Brimscome Port-Gloucestershire, UK: The History Press, 2010.

Ramsey, Logan C. "Aerial Attacks on Fleets at Anchor," Naval Institute *Proceedings*, 63, 8 (August 1937).

Rankin, Nicholas, *Ian Fleming's Commandos: The Story of the Legendary 30 Assault Unit.* New York: Oxford, 2011.

Ratcliff, Rebecca A. "Searching for Security: The German Investigations into Enigma's Security" *Intelligence and National Security*, 14, 1 (Spring 1999).

Rearden, Steven L. *Council of War: A History of the Joint Chiefs of Staff, 1942–1991.* Washington, DC: National Defense University Press, 2012.

Redmond, Kent C. and Thomas M. Smith. *From Whirlwind to MITRE: The R&D Story of the SAGE Air Defense Computer.* Boston: Masachusetts Institute of Technology Press, 2000.

Reynolds, Clark G. *On the Warpath in the Pacific: Admiral Jocko Clark and the Fast Carriers.* Annapolis: Naval Institute Press, 2005.

———, "John H. Towers and the Origins of Strategic Flexibility in the Central Pacific Offensive, 1941," *Naval War College Review*, 40, 2 (Spring 1987).

———, "Admiral Ernest J. King and the Strategy for Victory in the Pacific," *Naval War College Review*, 28, 3 (Winter 1976).

———. *The Fast Carriers: The Forging of an Air Navy.* New York: McGraw Hill, 1968.

Reynolds, David and Vladimir Pechatonov, *The Kremlin Letters: Stalin's Wartime Correspondence with Churchill and Roosevelt.* New Haven: Yale University Press, 2019.

———. *From World War to Cold War: Churchill, Roosevelt, and the International History of the 1940s.* New York: Oxford University Press, 2006.

———, *In Command of History: Churchill Fighting and Writing the Second World War.* New York: Random House, 2005.

———, "A 'Special Relationship'"? America, Britain and the International Order Since the Second World War," *International Affairs (Royal Institute of International Affairs)*, 62, 1 (Winter 1985–86).

———, *The Creation of the Anglo-American Alliance, 1937–1941: A Study in Competitive Cooperation.* Chapel Hill: University of North Carolina Press, 1982.

Reynolds, Nicholas. *Need to Know: World War II and the Rise of American Intelligence.* New York: Marriner, 2022.

Rice, Rondall R., *The Politics of Air Power: From Confrontation to Cooperation in Army Aviation Civil-Military Relations.* Lincoln: University of Nebraska Press, 2004.

Richard, Carl J. *When the Americans Invaded Russia: Woodrow Wilson's Siberian Disaster.* Lanham: Rowman and Littlefield, 2012.

Richards, Denis and Hilary Saunders. *The Royal Air Force 1939–1945: The Fight Avails.* London: HMSO, 1953.

Richardson, James O. *On the Treadmill to Pearl Harbor: The Memoirs of Admiral James O. Richardson as Told to Commander George C. Dyer.* Washington, DC: Naval Historical Center, 1974.

Riddle, Donald H. *The Truman Committee.* New Brunswick: Rutgers University Press, 1964.

Rigby, David. *Allied Master Strategists: The Combined Chiefs of Staff in World War II.* Annapolis: Naval Institute Press, 2012.

Robertson, Terence. *Night Raider of the Atlantic (the Golden Horseshoe).* London: Evans, 1955.

———, *Escort Commander (Walker, R.N.).* London: Evans, 1956.

Rodman, Hugh. *Yarns of a Kentucky Admiral.* Indianapolis: Bobbs-Merrill Company, 1928.

Rodriguas, Juan Estrigas. *La inteligencia en las Operaciones Navales de 1898 Consecuencias de una Estrategia Improvisada.* Madrid: Iberdrola, 2022.

Rohwer, Jürgen. *The Critical Convoy Battles of March 1943: The Battle for HX.229 and SC122.* Annapolis: Naval Institute Press, 1977.

———, *Die U-Boot Erfolge der Achsenmächte: 1939–1945.* Munich: J.F. Lehmann, 1968.

———, "ULTRA and the Battle of the Atlantic: The German View." In Robert W. Love Jr., ed. *Changing Interpretations and New Sources in Naval History: Papers from the Third United States Naval Academy History Symposium.* New York: Garland, 1980.

Roll, David L. *The Hopkins Touch: Harry Hopkins and the Forging of the Alliance to Defeat* New York: Oxford University Press, 2013.

Roosevelt, Theodore. *America and the World War: Fear God and Take Your Own Part.* New York: Charles Scribner's Sons, 1926.

Rosa, John P. *Local Story: The Massie-Kahahawai Case and the Culture of History.* Honolulu: University of Hawaii Press, 2014.

Roscoe, Theodore. *United States Submarine Operations in World War II.* Annapolis: Naval Institute Press, 1949.

Roskill, Stephen W. *Churchill and the Admirals.* London: William Collins, 1977.

———, *Naval Policy Between the Wars: The Period of Anglo-American Antagonism, 1919–1929.* New York: Walker, 1968.

———, *The War at Sea, 1939–1945*, vols. 1–4. London: HMSO; vols. I–III, 1954–1961.

———, *The Secret Capture.* London: Collins, 1959.

Ross, Steven T. *American War Plans 1890–1939.* New York: Frank Cass, 2000.

Rossler, Eberhard. *The U-Boat: The Evolution and Technical History of German Submarines.* Annapolis: Naval Institute Press, 1982.

Rowlett, Frank B. *The Story of MAGIC: Memoirs of an American Cryptologic Pioneer.* Laguna Hills: Aegean Park Press, 1998.

Rudgers, David. *Creating the Secret State: Origins of the Central Intelligence Agency, 1943–1947.* Lawrence: University Press of Kansas, 2000.

Runyan, Timothy J. and Jan M. Copes, eds., *To Die Gallantly: The Battle of the Atlantic.* Boulder: Westview Press, 1994.

Ryan, Henry B. "A New Look at Churchill's 'Iron Curtain' Speech," *The Historical Journal*, 22, 4 (December 1979).

Safford, Lawrence with Cameron A. Warren and Robert R. Payne, eds. *Earhart's Flight into Yesterday: The Facts without the Fiction.* McClean: Paladwr Press, 2003.

Salewski, Michael. "Das Kriegstagebuch der deutschen Seekriegsleitung im Zweiten Weltkrieg," *Marine-Rundschau*, LXIV, 3 (June 1967).

Salinas, María Emilia Paz. *Strategy, Security, and Spies: Mexico and the US as Allies in World War II.* University Park: Penn State University Press, 1997.

Sanders, Harry. "King of the Oceans," Naval Institute *Proceedings*, 100, 8 (August 1974).

Sangster, Andrew. *Alanbrooke: Churchill's Right-Hand Critic—A Reappraisal of Lord Alanbrooke.* London: Casemate, 2021.

Sarty, Roger. *War in the St. Lawrence: The Forgotten U-Boat Battles on Canada's Shores* Toronto: Allen Lane, 2012.

———, "The Nationalization of Military History: Scholarship, Politics and the Canadian War Museum," in Norman Hillmer and Adam Chapnick, eds., *Canadas of the Mind: The Making and Unmaking of Canadian Nationalisms in the Twentieth Century.* Montreal and Kingston: McGill-Queen's University Press, 2007.

Savas, Theodore. *Hunt and Kill: U-505 and the U-Boat War in the Atlantic.* New York: Savas-Beatie, 2004.

Saville, Allison W. "German Submarines in the Far East," Naval Institute *Proceedings*, 87, 8 (August 1961).

Sawyer, L. A. and W. H. Mitchell. *The History of the Long-Range Merchant Shipbuilding Programme of the United States Maritime Commission, 1937–1952.* London: World Ship Society, 1981.

Scalia, Joseph Mark. *Germany's Last Mission to Japan: The Failed Voyage of U-234.* Annapolis: Naval Institute Press, 2000.

Schaeffer, Heinz. *U-Boat 977: The Personal Account of a German U-Boat Commander during World War II.* New York: W.W. Norton, 1952.

Schaller, Michael. "The United States Navy's Secret War in China," *Pacific Historical Review*, 44, 4 (November 1975).

Schrader, Charles. *History of Operations Research in the United States Army: 1942–62.* Washington, DC: US Army Center of Military History, 2008.

Shen, Yu. "SACO in History and Histories: Politics and Memory," *Journal of American East-Asian Relations*, 5, 1 (Spring 1996).

Schlessinger, Arthur W. Jr. *The Politics of Upheaval, 1935–36.* Boston: Houghton Mifflin, 2003.

Schmidt, Raymond P. "From Code-Breaking to Policy-Making: Four Decades in the Memorable Career of Russel Willson," *Prologue*, 49, 2 (Summer 2016).

Schneller, Robert J. Jr. *Breaking the Color Barrier: The US Naval Academy's First Black Midshipmen and the Struggle for Racial Equality.* New York: New York University, 2005.

———, "Oscar Holmes: A Place in Naval Aviation," *Naval Aviation News* (January–February 1998).

Schrijvers, Peter, *The Crash of Ruin: American Combat Soldiers in Europe during World War II.* New York: New York University Press, 1998.

Sebald, William J. *With MacArthur in Japan: A Personal History of the Occupation.* New York: W.W. Norton, 1965.

———, *The Entry, Sojourn, and Departure of Aliens.* Tokyo: Department of Home Affairs, 1939.

———, *A Selection of Japan's Emergency Legislation.* New York: Praeger, 1979.

Sherry, Michael S. *The Rise of American Airpower: The Creation of Armageddon.* New Haven: Yale University Press, 1989.

Shirer, William L. *The Rise and Fall of the Third Reich: A History of Nazi Germany.* New York: Touchstone, 1990.

Simpson, Michael A., ed. *The Cunningham Papers: Selections from the Private and Official Correspondence of Admiral of the Fleet Viscount Cunningham of Hyndhope.* Aldershot, UK: Scholar Press of the Navy Records Society, Ashgate Publishing, Ltd., 2006.

———, ed. *The Somerville Papers: Selections from the Private and Official Correspondence of Admiral of the Fleet Sir James Somerville.* Aldershot, UK: Scholar Press of the Navy Records Society, Ashgate Publishing, Ltd., 1995.

Simpson, B. Mitchell, III. *Admiral Harold R. Stark: Architect of Victory, 1939–1945.* Columbia: University of South Carolina, 1989.

Sims, William Sowden. *The Victory at Sea.* New York: Doubleday, Page, & Co., 1920.

———, "Cheer Up!! There is No Naval War College," Naval Institute *Proceedings*, 42, 3/163 (May–June 1916).

Slavick, Joseph P. *The Cruise of the German Raider Atlantis.* Annapolis: Naval Institute Press, 2003.

Slim, William. *Defeat into Victory: Battling Japan in Burma and India, 1942–1945.* London: Cassel, 1956.

Smith, Bradley. *The Codebreaker's War: The ULTRA-MAGIC Deals.* Novato: Presidio Press, 1993.

Smith, Douglas. *Carrier Battles: Command Decision in Harm's Way.* Annapolis: Naval Institute Press, 2006.

Smith. Harold D., comp. *The United States at War Development and Administration of the War Program by the Federal Government.* Washington, DC: Government Printing Office, 1946.

Smith, Holland M., with Percy Finch, *Coral and Brass.* New York: Scribners, 1949.

Smith, Janvier King. *Affirming the Bond: US-Japan Security in the Post-Cold War Age—Strategic Research Department Report 2-94.* Newport: Naval War College Press, 1994.

Smith, Jason W. *To Master the Boundless Sea: The US Navy, The Marine Environment, and the Cartography of Empire.* Chapel Hill: University of North Carolina Press, 2018.

Smith, Starr. *Jimmie Stewart: Bomber Pilot.* Saint Paul: Zenith Press, 2005.

Smith, Richard Norton. *The Colonel: The Life and Legend of Robert R. McCormick.* New York: Houghton Mifflin, 1997.

Smith, William Roy. "British Imperial Federation," *Political Science Quarterly*, 36, 2 (June 1921).

Smythe, Donald. *Guerilla Warrior: The Early Life of John J. Pershing.* New York: Scribners, 1973.

Solberg, Carl. *Decision and Dissent: With Halsey at Leyte Gulf.* Annapolis: Naval Institute Press, 1995.

Soybel, Phyllis L. *A Necessary Relationship: The Development of Anglo-American Cooperation in Naval Intelligence.* Westport: Praeger, 2005.

Spector, Ronald H. *Eagle Against the Sun: The American War With Japan.* New York: Vintage, 1985.

———, *At War at Sea: Sailors and Naval Combat in the Twentieth Century.* New York: Penguin, 2001.

———, *Professors of War. The Naval War College and the Development of the Naval Profession,* Newport: Naval War College Press, 1977.

Sprout, Harold H. and Margaret T. Sprout. *The Rise of American Naval Power, 1776–1918.* Princeton: Princeton University, 1942.

Stafford, David and Rhodri Jeffreys-Jones, eds. *American-British-Canadian Intelligence Relations, 1939–2000.* London: Frank Cass, 2000.

Stevens, David. *U-Boat Far From Home: The Epic Voyage of U-862 to Australia and New Zealand.* London: Allen & Unwin, 1997.

Stevens, John Paul. *The Making of a Justice: Reflections on My First 94 Years.* Boston: Little Brown, 2019.

Stiel, Benn. *The Marshall Plan: Dawn of the Cold War.* New York: Simon and Schuster, 2018.

———, *The Battle of Bretton Woods: John Maynard Keynes, Harry Dexter White, and the Making of a New World Order.* Princeton: Princeton University Press, 2013.

Still, William N. *Crisis at Sea: The United States Navy in European Waters in World War I.* Pensacola: University Press of Florida, 2006.

Stillwell, Paul. *The Golden Thirteen: Recollections of the First Black Naval Officers.* Annapolis: Naval Institute Press, 2003.

Stimson, Henry L. and McGeorge Bundy. *On Active Service in Peace and War.* New York: Harper, 1947.

Stirling, Yates. *Sea Duty: The Memoirs of a Fighting Admiral.* New York: Putnam,1939.

Stoler, Mark A. *Allies and Adversaries: The Joint Chiefs of Staff, the Grand Alliance, and US Strategy in World War II.* Chapel Hill: University of North Carolina Press, 2006.

Sumida, Jon Tetsuro. *Decoding Clausewitz: A New Approach to On War.* Lawrence: University Press of Kansas, 2008.

Switky, Robert. *Wealth of an Empire: The Treasure Shipments that Saved Britain and the World.* Lincoln: University of Nebraska Press, 2013.

Symonds, Craig. *Nimitz at War: Command Leadership from Pearl Harbor to Tokyo Bay.* New York: Oxford, 2022.

Syrett, David, ed. *The Battle of the Atlantic and Signals Intelligence: U-Boat Situations and Trends, 1941–1945.* Brookfield: Ashgate, 1998.

Tate, James P. *The Army and Its Air Corps: Army Policy Toward Aviation, 1919–1941.* Maxwell: Air University Press, 1998.

Taussig, Joseph K. with William Still, ed. *The Queenstown Patrol, 1917: The Diary of Commander Joseph Knefler Taussig, US Navy.* Newport: Naval War College Press, 2010.

Taylor, Carol M. "W.E.B. DuBois's Challenge to Scientific Racism," *Journal of Black Studies*, 11, 4 (Winter 1981).

Terrell, Edward. *Admiralty Brief: The Story of Inventions that Contributed to Victory in the Battle of the Atlantic.* London: Harrup, 1958.

Theoharis, Athan G. *Chasing Spies: How the FBI failed in Counterintelligence but Promoted the Politics of McCarthyism in the Cold War Years.* Chicago: Ivan R. Dee, 2002.

———, *A Culture of Secrecy: The Government Versus the People's Right to Know.* Lawrence, Kansas: University Press of Kansas, 1998.

Thomas, Charles S. *The German Navy in the Nazi Era.* Annapolis: Naval Institute Press, 1990.

Thomas, Evan. *John Paul Jones: Sailor, Her, Father of the American Navy.* New York: Simon and Schuster, 2003.

Thomas, Stafford T. *The US Intelligence Community.* Lanham: University Press of America, 1983.

Thowsen, Atle. "The Norwegian Merchant Navy in Allied War Transport." In Stephen Howarth and Derek Law, eds. *The Battle of the Atlantic, 1939–1945: The 50th Anniversary International Naval Conference.* Annapolis: Naval Institute Press, 1994.

Thorndike, Joseph J. Jr., "King of the Atlantic: America's Triple Threat Admiral is Americas Stern, Daring Model of a War Commander," *Life* magazine, 11, 21 (27 November 1941).

Tidman, Keith R. *The Operations Evaluation Group: A History of Naval Operations Analysis.* Annapolis: Naval Institute Press, 1984.

Tilly, John A. *The US Coast Guard in World War II: The Coast Guard and the Greenland Patrol.* Washington, DC: US Coast Guard, 1992.

Townshend, Charles. *The British Campaign in Ireland, 1919–1921.* New York: Oxford, 1975.

Topriani, Arnand. "Budgets and Strategy: The Enduring Legacy of the Revolt of the Admirals," *Political Science Quarterly*, 134, 1 (2019).

Trask, David F. *The AEF and Coalition Warmaking, 1917–1918.* Lawrence: University Press of Kansas, 1993.

———, *Captains & Cabinets: Anglo-American Naval Relations, 1917–1918.* Columbus: University Press of Missouri, 1972.

Trimble, William F. *Admiral John S. McCain and the Triumph of Naval Air Power.* Annapolis: Naval Institute Press, 2019.

———, *Admiral William A. Moffett: Architect of Naval Aviation.* Washington, DC: Smithsonian Institution Press, 1994.

Troy, Thomas. *Donovan and the CIA: A History of the Establishment of the Central Intelligence Agency.* Langley: Central Intelligence Agency History Staff, Center for the Study of Intelligence, 1981.

Tucker, Gilbert Norman. *The Naval Service of Canada: It's Official History.* Ottawa: King's Printer, 1952.

Tuchman, Barbara. *The Zimmermann Telegram: America Enters the War, 1917–1918.* New York: Random House, 1958.

Tumblin, Jesse. *The Quest for Security: Sovereignty, Race, and the Defense of the British Empire, 1898–1931.* New York: Cambridge University Press, 2020.

Turabian, Kate L. *A Manual for Writers of Term Papers, Theses, and Dissertations—7th Edition.* Chicago, University of Chicago, 2007.

Turkel, Studs. *The "Good" War: An Oral History of World War II.* New York: Pantheon, 1984.

Turner, L. C. F., et al. *War in the Southern Oceans: 1939–45.* Cape Town, South Africa: Oxford, 1961.

Turner, Michael A. *Why Secret Intelligence Fails.* Dullas: Potomac Books, 2005.

Van Deurs, George. *Wings of the Fleet: A Narrative of Naval Aviation's Early Development.* Annapolis: Naval Institute Press, 1966.

Venzon, Anne Cipriano, ed. *General Smedley Darlington Butler: Letters of a Leatherneck, 1898–1931.* New York: Praeger, 1992.

Vick, Alan J. *Force Presentation in Air Force History and Airpower Narratives.* Santa Clara: RAND, 2018.

Vlahos, Michael. *The Blue Sword: The Naval War College and the American Mission, 1919–1941.* Newport: Naval War College Press, 1980.

Vogel, Steve. *The Pentagon: The Untold Story of the Wartime Race to Build the Pentagon—And to Restore it Sixty Years Later.* New York: Random House, 2007.

Waddington, Conrad Hal. *OR in World War II: Operations Research against the U-Boat.* New York: Harper Collins, 1973.

Wadle, Ryan. *Selling Sea Power: The US Navy and Public Relations, 1917–1941.* Norman: University of Oklahoma, 2019.

Wallerstein, Immanuel Maurice. *The Decline of American Power: The United States in a Chaotic World.* New York: New Press, 2004.

Ward, Geoffry C. "FDR's Western Front Idyll," in Robert Cowley, ed., *Experience of War.* New York: Doubleday, 1992.

Warner, Michael. *Central Intelligence: Origin and Evolution.* Langley: Central Intelligence Agency History Staff, Center for the Study of Intelligence, 2001.

Watson, George M. Jr. *The Office of the Secretary of the Air Force 1947–1965.* Washington, DC: Government Printing Office, 1992.

Webber, Bert. *Retaliation: Japanese Attacks and Allied Countermeasures on the Pacific Coast in World War II.* Corvallis: Oregon State University, 1975.

Wedemeyer, Albert C. *Wedemeyer Reports!* New York: Henry Holt, 1958.

Welchman, Gordon. "From Polish Bomba to British Bombe: The Birth of Ultra," *Intelligence and National Security,* 1, (January 1986).

———, *The Hut Six Story: Breaking the Enigma Codes.* New York: McGraw-Hill, 1982.

Weigley, Russell F. *The American Way of War: A History of United States Military Strategy and Policy.* Bloomington: Indiana University Press, 1973.

———, *The Age of Battles: The Quest for Decisive Warfare from Breitenfeld to Waterloo.* Bloomington: Indiana University Press, 1991.

———, "American Strategy from Its Beginnings through the First World War," in Peter Paret, ed., *Makers of Modern Strategy: From Machiavelli to the Nuclear Age.* Princeton: Princeton University Press, 1986.

Weir, Gary E. *An Ocean in Common: American Naval Officers, Scientists, and the Ocean.* College Station: Texas A&M University Press, 2001.

———, *Building American Submarines, 1914–1940.* Washington, DC: Naval Historical Center, 1991.

Weisgall, Jonathan. *Operation CROSSROADS: The Atomic Tests at Bikini Atoll.* Annapolis: Naval Institute Press, 1994.

Wheeler, Gerald E. *Kinkaid of the Seventh Fleet: A Biography of Thomas C. Kinkaid, US Navy.* Annapolis: Naval Institute Press, 1996.

———, *Admiral William Veazie Pratt, US Navy: A Sailor's Life.* Washington, DC: Naval History Division, 1974.

———, "The War College Years of Admiral Harris Laning, US Navy," *Naval War College Review,* 22, 3 (March 1969).

Whitby, Michael, Richard H. Gimblett, and Peter Haydon. *The Admirals: Canada's Senior Naval Leadership in the Twentieth Century.* Toronto: Dundurn Press, 2006.

White, John F. *U-Boat Tankers, 1941–45: Submarine Suppliers to Atlantic Wolfpack.* Annapolis: Naval Institute Press, 1998.

Whitehill, Walter Muir. "A Postscript to '*Fleet Admiral King: A Naval Record,*'" *Proceedings of the Massachusetts Historical Society,* series III, vol. 70 (October 1950–May 1953).

Wilcox, Jennifer. *The Secret of Adam and Eve.* Fort Meade: National Security Agency, 2003.

———, *Sharing the Burden: Women in Cryptography During World War II.* Fort Meade: National Security Agency, 1998.

Wildenberg, Thomas. *Billy Mitchell's War with the Navy: The Interwar Rivalry over Air Power.* Annapolis: Naval Institute Press, 2014.

———, *All the Factors of Victory: Admiral Joseph Mason Reeves and the Origins of Carrier Airpower.* Washington, DC: Potomac Books, 2003.

———, *Destined for Glory: Dive Bombing, Midway, and the Evolution of Carrier Air Power.* Annapolis: Naval Institute Press, 1998.

Wilford, Timothy. *Canada's Road to the Pacific War: Intelligence, Strategy, and the Far East Crisis.* Vancouver: UBC Press, 2011.

Williams, Joseph A. *Seventeen Fathoms Deep: The Saga of the Submarine S-4 Disaster.* Chicago: Review Press, 2015

Williams, Kathleen Broome. *Grace Hopper: Admiral of the Cyber Sea.* Annapolis: Naval Institute Press, 2005.

———, *Secret Weapon: US High Frequency Radio Direction Finding in the Battle of the Atlantic.* Annapolis: Naval Institute Press, 1996.

Willoughby, Charles A. and John Chamberlain. *MacArthur: 1941–1951.* New York, McGraw Hill, 1954.

Winkler, Jonathan Reed. *Nexus: Strategic Communications and American Security in World War I.* Boston: 2008.

Winterbotham, Frederick W. *The Ultra Secret*. London: Weidenfeld & Nicolson, 1974.

Winton, John. *Ultra in the Pacific*. Annapolis: Naval Institute Press, 1993.

———, *Ultra at Sea*. London, Leo Cooper, 1988.

Wise, James E. Jr. *U-505: The Final Journey*. Annapolis: Naval Institute Press, 2005.

———, with Anne Collier Rehil, *Stars in Blue: Movie Actors in America's Sea Services*. Annapolis: Naval Institute Press, 1997.

Wohlstetter, Roberta. *Pearl Harbor: Warning and Decision*. Palo Alto: Stamford University Press, 1962.

Wolk, Herman S. *Planning and Organizing the Postwar Air Farce, 1943–1947*. Washington, DC: Office of US Air Force History, 1984.

Wolfe, Robert. *Guides to the Microfilmed Records of the German Navy, 1850–1945, no. 1: U-Boats and T-Boats, 1914–1918*. Washington, DC: National Archives and Records Service, 1984.

———, *Captured German and Related Records: A National Archives Conference*. Athens: Ohio University Press, 1974.

Wolters, Timothy. *Information at Sea: Shipboard Command and Control in the US Navy, from Mobile Bay to Okinawa*. Baltimore: Johns Hopkins Studies in the History of Technology, 2013.

Wouk, Herman, *The Caine Mutiny*. New York: Doubleday, 1951.

Wukovitz, John. *Admiral "Bull" Halsey: The Life and Wars of the Navy's Most Controversial Commander*. New York: St. Martin's Press, 2010.

Wylie, Joseph C. *Military Strategy: A General Theory of Power Control*. New Brunswick: Rutgers University Press, 1967.

Wynn, Kenneth. *U-Boat Operations of the Second World War*. Annapolis: Naval Institute Press, 2003.

Wysocki, Edward M. Jr. *The Great Heinlein Mystery: Science Fiction, Innovation, and Naval Technology*. Scotts Valley: Create Space Independent Publishing, 2012.

Y'Blood, William T. *The Little Giants: US Escort Carriers against Japan*. Annapolis: Naval Institute Press, 1999.

———, *Hunter-Killer: US Escort Carriers in the Battle of the Atlantic*. Annapolis: Naval Institute Press, 1983.

Yu, Maochen. *OSS in China: Prelude to Cold War*. New Haven: Yale University Press, 1996.

Yung, Christopher D. *Gators of Neptune: Naval Amphibious Planning for the Normandy Invasion*. Annapolis, 2006.

Zacharias, Ellis. *Secret Missions: The Story of an Intelligence Officer*. New York: Paperback Library, 1961.

———, and Ladislas Farago. *Behind Closed Doors*. New York, McMillan, 1953.

Zhang, Shu Guang. *Deterrence and Strategic Culture: Chinese-American Confrontations, 1949–1958*. New York: Cornell University Press, 1992.

Zhukov, Georgii Konstantinovich. *The Memoirs of Marshal Zhukov*. New York: Delacorte Press, 1971.

Zimm, Alan D. *Attack on Pearl Harbor: Strategy, Combat, Myths, Deceptions*. Philadelphia: Casemate, 2011.

———, "The USN's Flight Deck Cruisers," *Warship International*, 16, 3 (1979).

Zimmerman, David. *Top Secret Exchange: The Tizard Mission and the Scientific War*. Montreal: McGill Queens, 1997.

Zullo, Matt. *The US Navy's On the Roof Gang: Prelude to War*. Chambersburg: ZooHaus Books, 2020.

Index

Army Air Corps, US, 96, 113–17, 148–50

Army Air Corps Mail Operation (AACMO), 173–74

Army Air Force, US, 160–63, 166–68, 171–73, 243, 275, 289, 293, 295, 310, 316, 331, 340, 396, 418–19, 425–26, 496

Army, US (see individual units)

Arnold, Henry A. "Hap," 115, 17–74, 248–50, 252, 256–57, 285, 289, 291, 293–97, 304, 310–12, 316, 327, 329–30, 341–44, 358–59, 371, 375, 388, 409–11, 414, 445, 449, 481–85; 496; King views on Marshall and Arnold's complicity in Pearl Harbor disaster, 410, 248–50, 267, 377, 282, 410–11, 434, 496

Arosemena, Juan Demóstenes, 191

Arras, 464

Asbury, 207

Ascension Island, 345

"Asia for the Asians" (Imperial Japanese concept), 185

Asiatic Fleet, US Naval, 30, 32–33, 36, 38, 79, 81–82, 88, 99, 105, 118, 134–36, 135, 143, 177, 188–91, 206, 209, 211–15, 227, 243, 249, 264–65

Asimov, Isaac, 318, 333

Associated Powers, 61

Astor, Vincent, 91

Atlantic (as maritime area of operations), 7, 13–23, 28, 36, 41–43, 47–75, 78, 80, 82, 88, 90, 98, 104, 159, 179, 182, 192, 194, 197–202, 211–45, 249–53, 256, 261, 270, 273–75, 277–80, 285, 294–97, 301, 306–09, 313–15, 320, 326–59, 361–63, 366, 371, 374–76, 384, 422, 432, 436–40, 460, 463, 473, 484, 486, 496

Atlantic, Battle of (see "Battle of the Atlantic" under propaganda)

Atlantic Charter, 20

Atlantic Charter Conference (Argentia, or RIVIERA conference of August 1941), 20, 202, 218, 227–31, 246, 299, 461, 484

Atlantic Convoy Conference (1943), 335–37, 484

Atlantic Convoy Instructions (ACI), 218

Atlantic Fleet, 7, 13–23, 28, 36, 41–43, 47–75, 78, 80, 82, 88, 90, 98, 104, 158–59, 179, 182, 192, 194, 197–202, 211–45, 249–53, 256, 261, 270, 273–75, 277–80, 285, 294–97, 301, 306–09, 313–15, 320, 326–59, 361–63, 366, 371, 374–76, 384, 420–22, 432, 436–40, 460, 463, 473, 484, 486, 496

Atlantic Fleet, Operational Training Command (COTCLant), 330–33, 345, 442

Atlantic Section (CominCh F-21), 348, 351–53, 384

Atlantic Section (Op-20-G), 326–27

Atlantic Squadron, 194, 197–98, 201, 213–15, 221

atomic bomb, 322, 357, 424–27, 433, 436–41, 445–49, 452, 459, 485

Attainment of the End (see "Fundamental Principle of War")

Augusta, 13

Autaing, 464

aviation, 7–8, 23, 38, 40, 46, 64, 86, 88, 94–97, 105, 107–22, 126–35, 140–41, 147–48, 152, 156–200, 204, 232, 234, 255, 267, 274, 293–94, 302, 329–44,

368, 376, 401, 428, 447, 461, 496

awards (see medals and decorations)

Axis Tripartite, 19, 193, 200, 205, 206, 210, 227, 241, 257, 267, 286, 328, 355, 363, 370, 407, 431, 460

Babcock, John V., 29, 42, 48, 51–52, 61–62, 68–69, 105, 107, 165

Badger, Oscar C., 195, 222

Badoglio, Pietro, 74, 466

Baker, Felix L., 111–12

Baker, Newton D., 49

Baker, Wilder D., 294, 332–33, 428

Baker Island, 179

Balboa, Panama, 190–91

Baldwin, Charles F., 233, 278, 487

Baldwin, Hanson, 305, 320, 450

Balfour, Arthur, 77, 81

Balkans, 82, 361–62, 366, 370, 438

Balkans War, 380

Baltic Sea, 365

Baltimore, 381–82

Bantry Bay, 465

Barb, 355

Barbey, Daniel, 235, 265, 339, 378, 383

Barbie, Klaus, 437

Base 2 (see Hampton Roads), 60–63, 68, 464–65

Base Forces, 177–79

Base Plan 1 (BP-1), 211, 218

baseball, 66, 77, 100, 123, 164, 183, 193, 312, 354

Bastedo House (also see British Admiralty Delegation), 207, 216

Bastedo, Paul, 50, 207, 216, 528

Bates, Richard, S., 442, 453

Battenberg (see Mountbatten)

Battle of the Atlantic (also see under propaganda), 231, 277

Battle Force, 127, 134, 177–78, 181–83, 188–89, 191, 201, 212, 215

Battle Studies Group (see historical section, Naval War College), 435–36, 442

Battler, 395

Battleship Conference, 40

Battleship Divisions, Atlantic Fleet, 41; THREE, 41; NINE, 71, 75

Bayly, Lewis, 64–65, 78

Beary, Donald B., 330, 334, 378, 442, 556, 562

Beasly, F. M., 274

Beatty, David, 71, 78, 99

Beaver, 355

beer, 18, 24, 27, 138, 142, 152, 168, 189, 190–91, 199, 267, 305, 308, 315, 373–74, 377, 386, 393, 412, 443

Beesly, Patrick, 268–80, 342

Belgian Relief Commission, 68, 74

Belknap, Charles, 465

Bell Aircraft Company, 173

219, 224, 225, 232–33, 242, 264–65, 269, 273, 278–80, 286, 320–22, 327, 336, 342, 355

Citadel (military school), 27

circular formations (also task group operations), 152

"Citizen Fixit," (or King's critique of American exceptionalism), 156

City of Rome (also see *S-51*), 102–4

Civil Air Patrol (CAP), 275, 307

Civil War (also see Revolutionary War and War of Independence), 459

Civil War, American, 23, 26–27, 30, 37, 39, 92, 198, 223, 244–45, 328, 340, 377, 431

Civil War, Chinese, 141, 439, 440

Civil War, Spanish, 201

Civil War veterans, 27, 39, 83, 85, 437

Civilian Conservation Corps (CCC), 163

Clark, Jr., Frank H., 36

Clark, Joseph J. "Jocko," 109, 119, 124, 128, 141, 143, 172

Clark, Vincent R., 128

Clarke, Arthur Wellesley, 205–11, 215–18, 225

classes, Naval Academy, (1896), 147; (1897) 27; (1900), 147; (1901), 28–30, 38, 41, 106, 109, 145, 162, 165; (1902), 212; (1903), 212; (1921), 180; (1925), 400; (1926), 385; (1927), 264; (1929), 120; (1930), 455

Clausewitz, Carl von, 13, 149, 155

Clemson, 197

coal (see fueling at sea)

Coast Guard, US, 103, 113, 177, 198, 200, 229, 304, 353, 417–19, 498

Coastal Command (British concept), 275, 295

Coaster's Harbor Island, 17, 225

COBRA (typhoon), 393–95

codebreaking (slang, see cryptography)

Cohen, Roy, 300

Coletta, Paolo, 454

Colombo, 265

Color Plans, 1897–1937 (War Department, albeit joint but not to be confused with naval plans), 23, 41, 49, 55, 66, 79–82, 105, 135, 140, 148, 178, 181–85, 195, 200–11, 214, 216–17, 227–28, 241–42, 250–53, 257, 259, 262–63, 271–72; BLACK, 60–62, 68, 70, 202; BLUE. 128, 157–58, 162–66, 182, 202; BROWN, 128, 157–58, 202; CRIMSON, 157–58, 202; GRAY, 202; JADE, 157, ORANGE, 157–59, 182, 202, 226–27, 459; RED, 157–58; YELLOW, 157–58

Columbia Sugar Company, 90

Columbus (German blockade runner), 194

Columbus (cruiser), 439

Combat Air Patrol tactics (CAP), 129

Combat Information Center (CIC), 318, 333–35

Combat Intelligence Division (CominCh), 233, 247–63, 374, 348, 380–88, 420–23, 427–28, 444

combat narratives (see historical section)

Combined (British concept of multinational or imperial strategy, as defined in American English), 6, 14, 76, 79, 80, 85, 246, 250, 255, 261, 270–74, 278,

283, 294, 306, 334, 348, 367, 380, 395, 418, 438–39, 459, 479, 498

Combined Chiefs of Staff (CCS), 21, 241, 246, 249–50, 255–58, 260–61, 267, 272, 284–85, 287–88, 291, 294–98, 304, 308, 313–14, 323, 327–31, 334, 340–44, 357–58, 362–79, 384, 397, 405, 407–10, 413–17, 421–26, 479, 484–86, 498

CominCh (amalgamated as King, also see commander in chief, US Fleet, CNO, CinCUS)

CominCh "F" staff organization, 263, 348

"CominCh P-1" (also see "Naval Directives and the Order Form" and Sound Military Decision), 353

commandant, Coast Guard, 177, 229, 304, 353

commandant, Marine Corps, 177, 296, 303, 304, 483

commandant, Third Naval District, 309

commandant, Tenth Naval District, 235

commander in chief, Asiatic Fleet (CinCAF), 32–33, 36, 38, 79–82, 88, 99, 105, 118, 134–36, 143, 177, 189, 206, 211–15, 227, 243, 249, 264–65

commander in chief, Atlantic Fleet (CinCLant), 7–17, 23, 28, 36, 40–43, 48, 50, 54–57, 60–80, 90, 98, 104, 212, 215, 221–43, 250, 261, 270, 294–95, 315, 330, 353–54, 371, 421, 437, 463, 473, 496, 498

commander in chief, Canadian Northwest Atlantic (CinCCNA), 217–18, 298, 336, 353–54

commander in chief, Northwest Pacific, 354

commander in chief, Northwest Africa (CinCNWA), 353, 367, 486

commander in chief, Pacific Fleet (CinCPac), 36, 86, 212–17, 238–39, 243–44, 248, 250, 255, 273, 283–84, 339, 353, 364, 376, 395, 434, 437

commander in chief, US Fleet (CinCUS), 23, 61–63, 68–70, 79, 82, 88, 90, 100, 133, 141, 147, 162, 175, 177–78, 182, 187–89, 191, 201–204, 212–15, 232, 241–45

commander in chief, US Fleet (CominCh), 8, 68, 242–45, 250–66, 269, 270–75, 281, 284–86, 291, 297–98, 301, 303–5, 309–12, 315–23, 325–27, 330–34, 336–56, 361, 363, 369, 371–411, 413, 419–25, 431–32, 435, 440–43, 449, 455, 460, 476, 484–89, 495–96

commander in chief (US naval), 175, 371, 381, 413, 473, 476–89

commander in chief, US Navy (CinCUSN), 242

commander, South Atlantic (British), 192

commander, US Naval Forces in China (ComNavForCha), 272

commander, US Naval Forces in Europe (ComNavEu, after 1942, also see SpeNavO), 260, 270–71, 320, 333, 342, 352–55, 455, 489

commander, US Naval Forces in European Waters (after 1917), 65, 73, 79

commander, US Naval Forces in Germany (ComNavForGer), 424

commander, US Navy Destroyers Operating from British Bases (May–June 1917), 64

commander, US Navy Destroyers, in European Waters (after 1917), 64

commander, Task Group (CTG), 141, 183, 334, 344, 361, 389, 460 commander, West Indies Station (British), 63

Commerce International China Incorporated, 441

Committees, Commissions, Boards (as political tool), 68, 86, 91, 96, 231, 258, 406, 434, 451, 493

commodore (functional flag officer), 28, 48, 71, 86, 98, 104, 108, 120, 190, 218, 229, 268, 269, 338, 384–85, 414–15

commodore (as formal US naval rank), 414, 434

communications officers (naval), 73, 125, 238, 273

Compiegne, 464

Comstock, Lewis, 127, 140

Conanicut Island (Rhode Island), 14

Cone, Hutch, 52

Conelly, Marc, 300

Confederates, 39, 41

conference method (command inclusivity applied), 52, 119

Congress (see government, US)

Connecticut, 41–42

Conolly, Richard L., 319, 453

Consolidated Aircraft Company, 167–68, 173, 176, 330

Constitution (US), 23, 39, 55, 59, 91, 95, 115, 146, 161, 169, 175, 206, 228, 241, 246, 259, 261, 296, 300, 316, 409, 413, 443, 492

Continentalists (militaristic mindset), 9, 47, 148, 433

Converse, George A., 32–33

convoy, 21, 73, 218–20, 224–28, 233, 250, 270, 278–79, 294, 296, 329, 332–38, 344, 359–60, 484, 498

Convoy Conference, Atlantic, 335–37, 484

Cook, Arthur B., 163, 187, 188, 229, 233–34, 240, 243

Cook, Harold Earle, 165

Cook, Lawrence, 352

Cooke, Charles M., 38, 99, 211, 253, 259, 264, 271, 278, 289, 319, 328, 331, 335, 348, 355, 373, 377, 381–88, 394–96, 411, 421, 425, 431–35, 440–42, 451

Coolidge, Calvin, 96, 153

Coral Sea, Battle of the, 131, 274–77, 301, 311

Corbett, Julian, 7, 13, 24, 71, 73, 85, 91, 149, 177, 191, 213, 318, 347, 459

Core, 345

Cornwallis, Charles, 66

Corps organization, (also see Army staff organization), 96, 113–17, 117, 133, 150, 160, 163, 166, 168, 171–75, 230, 281, 288, 293, 295–96, 303–04, 312, 343, 369, 379, 406, 417–19, 443

Corps mentality (King's views on), 281

Corps, naval infantry (also see Marine Corps)

Courtenay, Charles, 181

CRICKET (conference in Malta), 484

Crilley, Charles, 99

Cromwell, Oliver, 23, 77

Cromwell, Thomas, 60

cryptography, 15, 205, 224, 269, 273, 279, 282, 321–36, 435, 342, 348

Cuba, 28, 31, 135–36, 225

Culp, Paul N., 264

CULVERIN (see operations and plans)

Cunningham, Andrew, 7, 224–25, 256, 286–87, 296, 355–56, 362, 394, 424, 434, 439

Currier, Prescott, 224–25

Curtis, Glen, 91

Custer, George A., 27

Dalmatian Coast, 361

Danae, 152

Daniels, Josephus, 47–50, 56, 60–92, 237, 305, 309, 432, 450

Daniels-Sims controversy, 450

Dauntless, 99, 251, 315–18, 338, 350, 402–03, 428

Davis, Arthur C., 346

Davis, Jr., Charles H., 36

Davis, Elmer, 304

DeCamp, L. Sprague, 317–18

Deception, 257, 283

Decision Analysis (technique in gaming and experimentation, also see historical section)

deck-load-launch (carrier tactics), 182

decorations, 90–92, 99, 114, 191, 126, 237, 282–83, 293, 301, 309, 328, 398, 410, 433

Deem, Joseph M., 140

De Gaulle, Charles, 357, 372, 433

DeGrey, Nigel, 68

Delano, Francis, 29

Delano, Frederick H., 29

Delano, Harvey, 29, 190

Delano, Warren, 20

Delany, Walter S., 348, 422, 457

Delaware, 42

Democratic party, 43, 88–90, 148–49, 153–54, 162, 169, 193, 204, 241, 245, 250, 299, 302, 306, 310, 315, 327, 381, 418, 422, 447, 482, 493

Denby, Edwin, 97

Denfeld, Louis E., 219–20, 235, 428, 434, 445, 449

Denniston, Alastair, 68, 205, 233

Department of Commerce, 114

Department of Defense, 95, 438–39, 444, 450

Department of Justice (also see Federal Bureau of Investigation), 187, 282

Department of National Defense, 96, 134

Department of the Navy (see Navy Department)

Department of War (see War Department)

Desch, Joe, 321, 325

DeSomer, Abraham, 126

DeSteiguer, Louis R., 94

Destroyers for Bases Deal, 197, 201, 203, 231, 279, 332–24

Destroyer and Torpedo Boat Flotilla, Atlantic Fleet, 46, 48, 50–55, 63–67, 70, 86, 192, 229

Dewar, Alfred, 7

Dewey, George, 44–49, 56, 80, 83, 413, 431

Dewey, Thomas E., 161

105, 141, 158–59, 180, 183–85, 200, 224, 228–30, 234–37, 265, 271, 285, 288, 291, 307, 313–15, 329, 336–39, 353–55, 361, 364–70, 374–75, 377–80, 383–85, 395–96, 405–07, 417, 419, 422–23, 449

"F" staff functions (see CominCh)
Fairbanks, Jr., Douglas, 309, 312
Fala (FDR's dog), 20
Faragó, Ladislas, 320–21
Farber, William S., 482
Falcon, 104
Falcone, Charles J., 346
Falkland Islands, 55, 79, 215
Farragut Attack Force, 198
Farragut, David Glasgow, 83, 198, 202
Fascism, 181, 491
Faslane, 355
Federal Bureau of Investigation (FBI), 187
Ferrell, Edwin, 400
Ferrell, Joseph, 400
Ferrell, Nan, 37, 180, 385, 400–2, 504
Ferrell, William E., 37
Fifth Fleet (also see under numbered fleets), 354, 376–77, 389, 395, 487
Fine Gentlemen (Naval Academy clique), 38
First Fleet (also see under numbered fleets), 353, 420, 487
First Fleet (informal reference, see under US Coast Guard)
First Lord (of Admiralty), 193
First Sea Lord, 59–62, 65, 71, 81, 205, 209, 217, 244–57, 271, 275, 306–07, 362, 367, 394, 434, 439
Fisher, John "Jacky," 42
Fiske, Bradley, 44, 47–48, 60
Fitch, Aubrey, 50, 378
Fitz, Harold C., 344
five-star rank (see fleet admiral)
"Fixers" (King missive), 169–71, 255, 257–65, 301, 376, 382, 433
fleet, purpose of in war (King's view), 305
Fleet in Being (concept), 147, 197, 200–03, 231, 240, 306
Fleet Admiral (rank), 489
Fleet Admiral King (book), 449–51
fleet intelligence officer (FIO), 14, 17, 224, 232, 264, 273, 339, 352, 387, 389, 477–78
Fleet Landing Exercises (FLEX), 185, 195, 200, 235
Fleet Problems (also see Joint Army-Navy Exercises), 102, 140–42, 182–85, 264
Fleet Radio Unit, Melbourne (FRUMEL), 283, 341, 420
Fleet Radio Unit, Pacific (FRUPac), 283
Fleet Train (see logistics), 8, 92–94, 168, 179, 284
Fleet Type submarines, 97–98, 199
Fletcher Class (destroyer), 199

Fletcher, Frank Friday, 37, 56, 199
Fletcher, Frank Jack, 37, 90, 187, 274–75, 354, 488
Fleming, William, 196
Flower Squadron, 198
Flying Tigers, 311, 330
Foch, Ferdinand, 74
Focht, Charles A., 34
Follmer, Lewis D., 216, 278, 342, 365
football, 37, 66, 77, 90, 150, 183, 449
FORAGER (operation), 361
Formosa (also see "Citadels"), 18, 135, 158, 182, 241, 243–49, 251–53, 271, 284–86, 313–14, 339, 354, 366, 377–85, 387–89, 393–95, 397, 414, 420–25, 440–41
Fordney, Chester L., 173
Formosa (Taiwan), 18, 135, 158, 182, 241, 271, 284, 286, 313–14, 339, 354, 366, 369, 374, 377–97, 414, 420, 422–25, 440–42
Forrestal, James N., 199, 204, 237, 260, 275, 303, 305, 309, 312, 371, 378, 386, 409–13, 425–29, 431–34, 443–49, 481, 482, 497
Forth Fleet (also see under numbered fleets), 353, 487
Four Freedoms (FDR conception as applied), 20, 227, 231, 244, 246, 484, 299–300
Four Policemen (FDR conception under United Nations), 8, 286, 299–300, 369, 408, 425
Franklin, Benjamin, 77
Fraser, Bruce, 394
Frawley, Edward R., 113
Freedom of the Seas (concept as strategy), 20, 227, 231, 246, 484, 299–300
French Frigate Shoal, 178
Freud, Sigmund, 154
Friend, Roger C., 224
Frost, Holloway H., 85
fueling (also replenishment at sea), 30, 36, 40, 45, 52, 64, 71, 73, 178, 184, 236, 257, 288, 345, 370, 374, 345, 374, 451, 465
Fuller, John F. C., 288
Funakoshi, Kaijishiro, 80–81
Fundamental Principle of War (the singular Principle of War, also see Sound Military Decision and "CominCh P-1"), 13–14, 47, 86, 149, 185, 201, 226, 244–47, 267, 286–87, 297–98, 304, 315, 327, 358, 380, 407–08, 425, 453, 460
Furer, Julius A., 256

Gaines, Oliver W., 140
Galápagos Islands, 129, 138, 215
Gallery, Jr., Daniel V., 141, 180, 187, 318, 361, 446, 460
Gallipoli (campaign), 363
gaming and experimentation (tactical analysis), 8, 17, 45, 95–96, 133, 141, 149, 151–53, 157–59, 182–84, 191, 201, 312, 334, 347, 357, 381, 449
Gates, Artemis, 199, 417
General Board, Navy, 23, 47–50, 56, 82–83, 91, 97, 109, 159, 178, 181–85, 191–221, 243, 258–59,

Haydon, Elanor, 233
Headley, John T., 91
heavier than air (HTA), 95, 115, 127, 161–73, 179
Heinlein, Robert A., 120–27, 129–30, 134, 136–45, 159, 317–18, 333, 456
Heisman, John, 37
Helena, 194
Hempstead, Edward B., 150
Henderson, 105
Hendrick, Burton, 84
Henry VIII (King), 60
Herbster, Victor, 128
Herring, 355
Hewitt, Henry Kent, 37, 151, 183, 353, 367, 453, 488
Hickam Army Air Field, 140–41
Hickerson, John D., 153
Higgins, Andrew, 195, 200, 235, 258
high-frequency radio direction finder (HF/DF), 333
Hillenkoetter, Roscoe, 282
Himalayas, 311, 396
Hirohito, Emperor, 176, 194, 227, 423, 440, 451
Historical Section (British), 7, 71, 85–87; (Naval War College and Op–16–E) 85–89, 175, 347, 453; (Navy Department, or Op–16–E) 175, 205, 233, 271, 218, 318, 347, 453; and (War Department, or Army War College), 150
Hitler, Adolf, 192, 194, 200, 205, 227, 233, 288, 370, 443, 446, 460
Hobson, Richmond P., 55
Holden Agreement, 342, 437, 484
Holden, Carl, 283, 321–23, 327, 342, 437, 484
Holloway Board (on National Education), 406
Holloway, II, James, 406
Holloway, John L., 330
Holtwick, Jack, 282, 420, 489
Home Islands, British (also see "Citadels"), 18, 73, 135, 158, 182, 241, 243–49, 251–53, 271, 284–86, 313–14, 339, 354, 366, 377–85, 387–89, 393–97, 414, 420–25, 440–41
Hong Kong, 36, 193, 216, 422
Honolulu, 238, 283, 380, 381–82, 485
Honolulu Conference, 381–82, 485
Hoover, Herbert, 68, 117, 134–35, 141, 148–49, 160, 162, 165–67, 175, 448
Hoover, J. Edgar, 187, 305
Hoover, John H., 114, 119, 121–22, 126–29, 183, 188, 378
Hopkins, Harry, 187, 287–88, 360, 407–08, 481–83
Hopkins, John Jay, 196
Hopper, Bruce, 66
Horne, Frederick C., 105, 109, 177–08, 188, 243, 252, 255–56, 275, 282–82, 361, 410–11, 432, 500, 501, 538
Hornet, 252
hospital, naval, 31, 159, 275, 352, 398, 440, 445, 448, 450, 451
Hotel Crillon, 464

Hotel Grafton, 207
Hotel Majestic, 142
Houston, 184–85, 188–90
Howard, John M. B., 150
Howland Island, 179
Hubbard, Lafayette Ronald "L. Ron," 333
humanitarian relief, 136, 139, 209, 425
"Hunter-Killer" (antisubmarine tactics), 219, 334, 337, 342, 344, 355–60, 374–75, 421
Hurricane, 278–79
HUSKY (see operations and plans)
Husting, Eugene E., 264
Hustvedt, Olaf M., 222, 224, 240
Hutchins, 333
Hyde Park (Roosevelt), 36, 227
Hyland, John, J., 284
HYPO, Station, 282–83

I-58 (Japanese submarine), 427–28
ICEBURG (see operations and plans)
Iceland, 194, 228–29, 237, 239, 297
Ickes, Harold, 154, 197, 222
Idaho, 42, 165, 190, 191, 319
Illinois, 31–32, 94, 153
Imperial Federation (British concept), 19, 67, 74, 77–81, 438, 451
Imperial War Staff (British), 7, 67, 71, 209, 318, 423
Imperialism (American), 16, 32, 35–36, 41, 44, 154–58, 161, 176, 314, 388, 406
Impossible, 22
Improvident, 22
Inchon, 36
Indian Ocean (as maritime area of operations), 258, 287, 296, 312, 329, 354, 360–62, 373, 379, 394–96, 420
Indianapolis, 261, 354, 426–29, 432, 437, 487
Infantry Division, 82nd (US Army), 151
Ingalls Taiwan Shipbuilding and Dry Dock Company, 441
Ingersoll, Ralph, 21
Ingersoll, Royal E., 196, 207, 212, 213, 243, 250, 274–75, 284, 304, 345, 353–54, 378, 390, 487, 489
Ingram, Jonas H., 75, 90, 233, 233, 234, 275, 308, 353, 399, 487
"Initiative of the subordinate" (King philosophy), 234, 473–74
inspector general (naval), 281, 300
integration (also see Black personnel and racial policies), 44, 92, 102, 153–54, 170–72, 180, 224, 299–302, 302–02, 367, 380, 445, 495
integration (women), 153, 172, 299, 300, 303, 304, 321, 352, 373, 401, 436, 456–57
Intelligence Center, Pacific Ocean Area (ICPOA), 273–75, 320, 327
intelligence centers (also see individual headquarters), 7, 15, 21, 47, 59–65, 67, 69–74, 78, 193–94, 202, 205–10, 216–25, 232–33, 242, 257, 259, 264–69,

Liscome Bay, 302

Little America (see London Flagship)

Little Big Horn, Battle of, 27

Little, Charles, 71

Livecci, Samuel, 333, 349

Liverpool, England, 216, 264, 279, 295, 464, 466

Lockwood, Charles A., 99, 216, 372

Lodge, Henry Cabot, 88

Logistics Organizational Planning Unit (LOPU), 373

logistics (producer and consumer), 8, 63, 74, 94, 147, 152, 156–58, 166, 232, 272, 284–89, 294, 297, 304, 308, 327, 333, 366–68, 372–74, 378, 380–81, 389, 405, 410–11, 425, 435, 469–71, 478

London Flagship (see US Naval Headquarters, London), 7, 64–65, 69–73, 78–79, 85, 193, 233, 263, 271, 398

London Naval Treaty, 129

Long Beach, California, 139, 142, 142, 455

LONGTOM (see operations and plans)

Lorain, Ohio, 26–28, 173, 326

Los Angeles, 128

Los Angeles, 192, 448, 500

Lothian, Lord, 181

Lovette, Leland, 301, 312

Low, Francis S. "Frog," 17, 36, 99–103, 195, 197, 223–28, 232–36, 238, 243, 251–53, 260–65, 275–78, 293–94, 303, 320, 325, 333, 337–40, 344, 346, 351, 354, 358, 367, 420, 426, 451, 460, 487–88

Luce, Stephen B., 6, 13, 25, 27, 38, 55–57, 80, 88, 92, 146–48, 152, 225–25, 259, 407

Luftwaffe, 308, 370

Lundeberg, Philip, 436

Lusitania, 54

Luzon (also see MIKE under operations and plans), 366, 384–86, 393, 395

MacArthur, III, Arthur, 37

MacArthur, Douglas, 20, 37–38, 50, 76, 148–50, 160–61, 171, 175–76, 188, 227, 242, 264, 272, 280–86, 292, 311, 315, 338, 340, 354, 359–65, 369, 373, 379–90, 397, 410, 414, 421–25, 433, 440, 446, 495

MacIntyre, Donald, 219

MacKinder, Halford, 13

MacLachlan, Donald, 318, 320

"MacPac," (also see SWPA and "Pope's Line"), 284–85, 311–12, 383, 484–85, 488

Madeira, Dashiell L., 201, 226, 330, 457

Maddox, Charles, 11, 46, 152, 238–39

MAGIC (see special intelligence)

MAGIC CARPET (see operations and plans)

magnetic anomaly detector (MAD), 333

Mahan, Alfred Thayer, 6–8, 13, 18, 24–30, 38–44, 47, 54–57, 80, 88, 91, 146–49, 152, 267, 284, 363, 369, 435, 438, 449, 459

Main Navy (building, also see under Navy Department), 7, 12, 15, 17, 20, 27–28, 35, 39, 41, 44–51, 54–56,

60–69, 73, 82–84, 86, 90, 92, 95, 102–05, 107, 110, 113–17, 141, 148, 150, 162–69, 171–77, 190–96, 199, 202–10, 216–19, 224–25, 232–33, 237–38, 240–45, 250–52, 257–62, 270–73, 281–86, 291, 295–96, 302–03, 310–12, 316–18, 320–31, 336, 340–48, 351, 359, 371, 377, 382–83, 387, 394, 398–401, 410–11, 422, 424–28, 431–34, 437, 439, 449, 455, 462–63, 479, 489, 497

"Make Best with What You Have" (King directive), 5, 11, 14, 313

Malacca Strait, 395

Malta (also see CRICKET Conference), 407, 486

Managua (humanitarian relief expedition), 136

Manhattan, Project (see atomic bomb)

Manpower (King's views on continental strategy), 15, 257, 272, 296–97, 302, 366, 397, 422, 493

Mansfield, John M. (Kauffman-Mansfield Board), 22, 335

Mao, Tse Tung (also see Red Chinese forces), 272, 369, 396–97, 424–26, 438–39, 446

map room (White House), 247, 261

Marianas, 285, 369, 376, 406

Marietta, 50

Marine Corps, US, 8, 49, 67, 105, 109, 133, 234–35, 295, 285, 296, 303–04, 312, 417–18

Marine Corps Schools, US, 133, 234

Marine Corps Women's Reserve ("BAMS"), 304

maritime arena, global (defined), 7–8, 13–16, 18, 20–23, 36, 39–45, 60, 65, 67, 73, 78–80, 86, 89, 185, 193, 199, 209, 212–14, 221, 239, 241, 244, 245–47, 265–67, 271, 277, 293, 298–301, 34, 321, 325, 327, 329, 334–35, 337, 342–43, 347, 349, 357, 365, 371, 374, 403, 436, 439, 449, 452, 459, 461

maritime and naval history (King's strategic views about), 14–18, 22–27, 31, 37, 47, 53–55, 63–68, 71, 75, 85–86, 94–95, 100–102, 125, 147, 149–51, 154, 159, 162, 166–67, 176–77, 189, 213–14, 222–26, 241, 244, 252, 260, 263, 271, 277, 300, 318, 338, 347, 391, 400, 403, 406, 141, 417, 422, 427, 434–36, 441–50, 453–54, 458–61, 494

Marlborough, 152

Marshall, George C., 20, 23, 55, 110, 158, 179, 182, 193, 206, 211, 218, 242–60, 264, 285, 289, 291, 293–96, 304, 308, 313, 315, 317, 322, 327, 330–33, 340–45, 357–66, 369, 371, 375, 377–79, 382–84, 396–98, 409–11, 413–15, 417–21, 424–27, 432–35, 441, 445, 451, 456, 466, 482–85, 489–97; King views on Marshall and Arnold's complicity in Pearl Harbor disaster, 248–50, 267, 377, 282, 410–11, 434, 496

Marshall Islands, 55, 158, 179, 182, 211, 250, 252, 313, 357, 359, 366, 377, 379, 396, 421

Marshall Library, 456

Mason, Newton E., 32–33

Masonry, Order of the, 433

Massie, Thomas (Massie Affair), 201

Massachusetts Institute of Technology (MIT), 336, 420

Matter, Alfred "Dick," 180, 402, 403, 410, 500, 507

Matter, Betsy, 180, 402, 403, 499

MATTERHORN (see operations and plans)

Matthews, J. F., 142

Maumee, 64

Mayflower, 36

Mayflower (warship), 89

Mayflower Hotel, 196

Mayo, Claude B., 50

Mayo, Henry T., 6–7, 24, 49–50, 56–57, 60–85, 91–92, 143, 193, 225, 242, 270, 451, 459, 463–66

McAfee, Mildred, 303–04

McCallister, James "Cap'n Jim," 94

McCain, John S., 37, 41, 114, 172, 181, 183, 188, 255, 339, 344, 483

McCann, Alan R., 99, 101–02, 139, 183, 420–21

McCarty Little, William, 39

McCollum, Arthur, 233, 272–73, 320, 387, 488–89

McCord, William J., 113

McCrary, Frank R. 105, 128–29, 140

McCrea, John L., 129, 247, 261, 263, 364, 483

McDiarmid, John B., 278–80, 342, 350

McDill, Thomas F., 437

McDonald, Kenneth, 453

McDougal, William B., 60, 68

McFall, Roscoe C., 152

McFarland, Alan R., 295, 352, 399, 419

McGauley, Carlton, 108

McMorris, Charles H. "Soc," 273

McNair, Lesley, 242

McNamara, Patrick, 152

McNamara, Robert, 312, 449

McNarny, Joseph T., 242, 482

McReynolds, James O., 443

McReynolds, James Clark, 316, 443

McVay, III, Charles B., 98, 427–31

McVay, Jr., Charles B., 98, 134, 427

Meader, Ralph, 321

Medal of Honor, 83, 90, 99, 114

medals (see decorations)

media (King's handling of), 14, 17, 23, 31, 42–46, 59, 62–65, 77, 84, 100, 103–04, 107, 114–16, 128, 135, 139, 150, 154, 169, 175, 179, 196, 237–38, 242, 245, 248, 259, 277–78, 286, 305–11, 215, 317, 370, 378, 390, 394, 400, 410–13, 420, 424, 426–28, 432–24, 445, 451, 457

Mediterranean (campaigns in), 79, 238, 286–97, 296–97, 307, 319, 329, 331, 353, 358, 360, 367, 370, 488

Melbourne (also see FRUMel), 238, 265, 283, 334

Melville, 65, 67, 70

Mengele, Josef, 437

mental health, 274–75, 280, 289, 359, 382, 414, 424, 439, 445, 448–49, 496

Merchant Marines, 103, 177, 229, 264, 418

Merchant Shipping Commission, 258

Meridian Park Hotel, 401

Merrill, Aaron "Tip," 312

Mexico, 48–50, 59, 90, 134

Meyer, George von L., 43, 49

Meyers, William Starr, 153

Michelin Company, 173

Michener, James, 436

Middle East, 24, 45, 64, 114, 175, 308, 360, 366

Mid-Ocean Escort Force (MOEF), 217, 278

Mid-Ocean Meeting Point (MOMP), 217, 336

Midway, 131, 135, 192, 211, 255, 273–78, 282–83, 301, 311, 360, 412, 447

Miles, Milton E., 193, 271–72, 338, 354, 369, 379, 384, 396–97, 411, 414–15, 419–20, 329, 441, 489

military mistory (see naval or maritime mistory)

Military Mission in Washington, British (also see under Joint Staff Mission and BAD), 23, 206–07, 217, 243–47, 257, 286, 366, 369

Military Orders (FDR extralegal action as commander in chief of the Army and Navy), 244

Militia Act, 47

Miller, Doris, 301–02

Mines, 9, 76, 98, 423, 427

Ministry of Defense, 439

Minnesota, 40–44

Mississippi, 42, 95, 109

Missouri, 426

Mitchell, William "Billy," 95–97, 107, 114–15, 156, 159, 252, 483

Mitscher, Marc A., 38, 188, 252

"Mixed forces" (King missive), 78, 306–07, 332

Moffett, William A., 88, 95–97, 105–10, 113–18, 145, 159, 162–63, 166

Momsen, Charles "Swede," 99

Moncy, Bon-Adrien Jennot de, 91–92

Monongahela, 29

Monserrat, Nicholas, 219

Montgomery, Bernard, 418

Montgomery, Robert, 247, 309–12

Montrose, Duke of (see also James Graham), 71, 190

Moon, Donald P., 152, 235, 285, 382

Moore, Henry Ruthven, 320–336

Moore, Samuel, 320, 487

Moreell, Ben, 379–80

Morgue, (U-boat tracking), 352

Morison, Elting E., 271, 436

Morison, Peter E., 271

Morison, Samuel E., 21, 99, 151, 271, 310, 425, 442, 456

Morrow Board, 96

Morrow, Dwight, 96

Mount Vernon Seminary (see Nebraska Avenue Station)

Mount Washington Hotel, 425

Mountbatten, Louis, 354, 357–59, 379, 394, 439

Mozart (music of), 123

mugged (King in Japan), 34

Multinational strategy and operations (see Combined, League Navy, or United Nations Navy)

RAINBOW 5, 195–211, 214, 216–17, 226–30, 241–59, 262–63, 271–72
Orem, Howard E., 338, 399
Ostend (bombardment of), 74, 465
Osterhaus, Hugo, 24, 28, 33–35, 41, 35, 57, 143
Our Navy magazine, 264
"Our Navy, The Peacemaker," 23, 67, 167, 433
OVERLORD (see operations and plans)
Oxford University, 68, 438, 453
Oyster Bay, 36

Pacific (as maritime area of operations), 8–17, 23, 31, 36, 69, 80, 82, 86, 99, 134, 136, 138, 167, 179, 181–84, 189, 193, 197, 201, 211–15, 221, 225, 227, 229, 232, 238–44, 248–51, 255–59, 264, 272–75, 283–85, 297, 306–308, 313–15, 318, 327, 329, 332, 336–41, 343, 345, 348, 353–55, 358, 360–67, 370–95, 405–08, 414, 419–25, 432, 434, 437, 496
Pacific Fleet, British, 394–96
Pacific Fleet, US, 36, 86, 212, 213–16, 238–39, 243–45, 248, 250, 255, 272–73, 283–84, 333, 327, 339, 341–42, 353, 364, 369, 376, 383, 387, 393, 395, 427–28, 434, 437
Pacific Ocean Area (POA), 272–73, 333, 369, 383, 327, 341–42, 387, 393, 427–28
Pacific Strategic Intelligence Section (PSIS), 283, 423
Page, Walter Hines, 59–60
"Painter Expedition" (beach reconnaissance in China), 379–80, 396
Painter, Wilfred, 379–83, 396–97, 414–15
Palmer, Leigh C., 61
Pan-American Neutrality Zone, 7–8, 11, 13–19, 36, 161, 176, 182, 190, 194, 215, 217–18, 228, 237, 241
Panama Canal (and Zone), 50–53, 59, 102, 105, 125, 128, 135, 139, 156, 158, 183–84, 190–91, 202, 211, 215, 264, 338, 486, 498
Panay, 36
Panay, 181, 185, 193, 237
pandemics, 11, 80, 82, 458
Parliament (British), 228, 249
Parsons, John E., 349–51
Parsons, Judy (Potter), 321
Patterson, 53
Patterson, Wilfred, 482
Patton, George S., 49, 211, 310, 382, 388, 418, 424
Paul Jones, 264
Paulding, 114
peacemaker, Navy as (see also Roosevelt, Theodore), 23, 167, 433
Pearl Harbor, 8, 17–23, 140–41, 201, 211, 239–53, 257–71, 277, 282, 284, 301, 310, 320, 327, 340, 371, 398, 401, 410, 412, 417, 426, 434, 438, 443, 485; (King simulated attacks on), 8, 140–41, 183, 199–201, 211, 239
Pearson, Drew, 179, 198, 316, 411
Pennsylvania, 60, 66, 133, 201, 225, 264, 282, 466
Pensacola, 107, 109–13, 170, 330, 361

Pentagon (building), 304, 365, 417, 495
Pepys, Samuel, 23
Perry, Cecil, 206
Perry, George, 224
Perry, Glen C. H., 16, 97, 169, 196, 240, 243, 245, 412
Perry, Matthew, 34
Pershing, John J., 49, 67, 75–78, 83, 148, 182, 193, 242, 364, 413, 431, 464
Persian Gulf, 297
petroleum (see fueling at sea)
Peruvian Navy, 176
Pfeiffer, Oman T., 224, 234
Philadelphia Naval Hospital, 159
Philadelphia Naval Shipyard, 56, 317–18, 398
Philippines, 16, 36, 44, 90, 134–35, 153–61, 176–77, 183, 188, 200, 209, 212, 226–27, 238, 249, 264, 284, 313–15, 338, 366, 369, 376, 379, 380–89, 406, 427, 440
Philippine Sea (Battle of), 376, 386
Philippines Liberation Act, 176–77
Phillips, Tom, 206
Picard, Jacques, 461
Pihl, Charlotte, 180, 204–06, 457
Pihl, Paul, 178, 180, 204–06, 374, 378, 402–03, 455, 457, 489
pirates (or piracy), 28, 30–31, 125, 136, 190, 235
"Plan Dog" (also see RAINBOW Plans), 211
Plunkett, Charles P., 104
"Pope's Line" (also see Treaty of Tordesillas and Zaragoza), 383
Port Arthur, 184, 271
Port Chicago, 380
Portal, Charles, 244, 257, 481
Porter, David Dixon, 151–52
Potsdam (also see TERMINAL conference), 486
Potter, Elmer B., 454, 456
Pound, Dudley, 7, 42, 71, 205, 217–19, 244–45, 257, 271, 276, 306–07, 335–36, 357, 362, 481
Prairie, 417
Pratt-MacArthur Agreement, 148, 171
Pratt, William V., 48, 52, 56, 60, 77, 81, 96, 134–35, 141, 146–48, 159–67, 171, 177, 210, 227, 242
president, Naval War College (also collateral duty as director of naval history from 1939), 11, 14, 35, 38–41, 49, 55, 57, 59, 61, 69, 82–83, 86, 122, 146–47, 153, 157–71, 175, 177, 184, 210–11, 226, 236–37, 318, 347, 405–07, 433, 442
Prince of Wales, 228–29, 239
Princeton (cruiser class), 200
Princeton University, 39, 151, 153, 200, 327, 333
Pringle, Joel R. P., 52, 67, 78, 85, 141
Prinz Eitel Friedrich, 54–55, 464
"Problem of Asia" (Mahanian idea), 5, 8, 18, 24
Proceedings (also see Naval Institute), 46, 53, 86, 96, 104, 458
procurement, 148–51, 166–68, 173, 247, 251, 294–96,

214, 322–33, 323, 332, 357, 410–12

profanity (strategic use of), 81, 123, 130, 180, 235, 252, 283, 393–95, 412, 437, 448

Prohibition, 84, 111–12, 152, 400

Project MANHATTAN (see atomic bomb)

Project RAND (see Research and Development Corporation)

promotion (system), 6–7, 35, 39, 42, 44, 56–57, 69, 75, 78–79, 82–83, 88–90, 94, 98, 104–07, 122, 133, 138, 141, 143, 145–47, 155, 162–64, 167, 171, 176, 187, 211, 215, 145, 326, 338, 372, 375, 385, 391, 398, 311, 414–15, 429, 431, 434, 436, 473, 489

propaganda (King's failure to understand), 14, 17, 23, 31, 42–46, 59, 62–65, 77, 84, 100, 103–04, 107, 114–16, 128, 135, 139, 150, 154, 169, 175, 179, 196, 237–38, 242, 245, 248, 259, 277–78, 286, 305–11, 215, 317, 370, 378, 390, 394, 400, 410–13, 420, 424, 426–28, 432–24, 445, 451, 457; airpower, 8, 21, 96, 115–17, 127, 148, 156, 159–64, 169, 171, 174–77, 200, 213, 260, 275, 288–90, 293, 295, 304, 306, 311–14, 327, 329–31, 335–36, 341, 359, 370–72, 391, 406, 411–13, 418, 425–27, 433–35, 437–38, 441–52, 459, 461; American "sea power," 26–28, 444–51, 459–61; Battle of the Atlantic, 231, 277; also see Leo, Stephen F.

Prueher, Bertram "Bert," 180

Prussianism, (also see general staff system), 39

psychology, 108, 154, 203, 252, 289, 320–21, 449

public affairs (see propaganda)

Puerto Rico, 135, 178, 185, 189, 196, 218, 228, 235, 328

Puget Sound (see under naval shipyards)

"Puppet Armies" (Chinese forces aligned with Japan), 395–96

PURPLE (cipher), 249

Pye, Anne Briscoe, 149

Pye Board (on National Education and Universal Service), 406, 447, 492, 493

Pye, John, 406

Pye, William S., 28–29, 37, 41, 69, 78. 85–86, 149, 165, 176–78, 192, 212, 248, 347–48, 406–07, 451

Pye, Jr., William S., 192

Pyke, Geoffrey, 357

Pykrete, 357–58

QUADRANT (conference in Quebec), 357–58, 486

Quebec, 357–58, 484–86

Queen Elizabeth, 73, 78

Queenstown (Cobh), 63–65, 70, 78, 464–65

Queenstown Association, 87

Quiberon, 465

Quincy, 407

Quine, Willard van Orman, 326–27

Quonset (Rhode Island), 225–26, 333, 407

Raby, John J., 107–08, 113

racial policies (also see Black personnel and integration), 29, 44, 88, 92, 102, 153–54, 170–72, 180, 224, 299–302, 302–02, 367, 380, 495

radar, 264, 317, 333, 360, 372

radio (also see wireless) 13–15, 17, 19, 38, 40, 46, 49–52, 51, 62–63, 65, 70, 80, 83, 86, 94, 96, 136, 142, 147, 152, 156, 159, 161, 194, 199, 216, 222, 225, 232, 234, 279, 283, 312, 321, 334, 338, 349, 387, 400, 402, 421, 451, 455, 459, 478

Radio Corporation of America (RCA), 349

radio direction finder (RDF), 129

Radio-Keith-Orpheum (RKO), 349

Raeder, Erich, 306

RAINBOW (also see WPL-46), 195–211, 214, 216–17, 226–30, 241–59, 262–63, 271–72

Raleigh, 105

Ramsay, Bertram, 7, 74

Ramsey, Dewitt, 38

Ramsey, Logan, 180, 184, 239

RAND, Project (see Research and Development Corporation)

range machine (Pye-King invention), 29

Ranger, 158, 172, 161, 184–85, 198, 229, 302

Rankin, Jeanette, 59, 241

Ratham, John, 84

Reading Room (Newport), 17, 29, 19, 147

reconnaissance, 138–40, 160, 177–80, 235, 331, 342, 407

Red Army (or Soviet Union), 8, 18, 94, 154–59, 185, 205, 210, 227, 238, 241, 267, 271, 286, 295–97, 307–08, 313–15, 329, 349, 360–66, 370–74, 394, 419–25, 435, 439, 446, 452, 485–86

Red Chinese (also see Mao), 272, 369, 396, 424, 426, 438–39, 441, 446

Red Cross, 233, 400–01

Redman, John, 282–83, 327

Redman, Joseph R., 210, 282–83, 327

Reeder, William H., 35

Reeves, Joseph M., 105, 115–16, 127–28, 131, 133, 138, 163

refueling (at sea, also see logistics), 52, 64, 178, 184, 236, 345, 374, 451

Reichmuth, Ferdinand, 229

"Remain Cheerful" (Sims motto), 11, 14, 19, 53, 75, 238, 350

replenishment (see logistics)

Republic of China (also see Kuomintang), 272, 396, 426

Republican Party, 27, 43, 59, 88, 95–96, 134, 148, 154, 161, 165–66, 175, 199, 204, 241–42, 244, 310, 315, 410

Repulse, 239

Research and Development Corporation (RAND), 293, 329–30, 417, 449

Reserve Officer Training Command (ROTC), 265, 294

retired rank (also see promotion system), 11, 18, 39–40, 56, 86, 90, 92, 99, 104, 147, 149, 150–51, 159, 166, 175–70, 182, 190, 218, 226–29, 233–34, 242, 258, 260, 264, 270–71, 291, 294, 312, 218, 222, 247, 364, 409, 412, 429, 441–43, 447–55,

457, 499

retirement (mandatory), 81, 98, 160, 165, 187, 198, 214, 245, 250, 291, 409, 433

Reuben James, 13, 237

Reuterdahl, Henry, 84

Revolutionary War (in popular memory), 14, 26, 28, 47, 53, 63, 77, 83, 125, 264, 269

Ribbentrop, Annaleis von, 233

Ribbentrop, Joachim, 233

Richthoven von, Manfred, 53

Rickenbacker, Eddy, 115, 310

Rickover, Hyman G., 436

Richardson, James O., 183, 187, 189, 191, 198, 201, 203–05, 211–12, 259, 410, 443–44

Richardson Commission, 410

Ridiculous, 22

Rinehart, Carl W., 232

Riviera, the, 76–80

RIVIERA (see Atlantic Charter)

RO-501 (Japanese submarine), 334

Roberts Committee (Pearl Harbor), 248

Roberts, Owen, 248

Robin (see HMS *Victorious*), 257

Robin Moor, 231

Robinson, Douglas, 88

Robinson, Samuel M., 163, 410, 481, 482

Rochefort, Joseph, 252, 264, 273, 282–83, 327, 423, 442

Rockwell, Francis, 338

Rodgers, John, 45–46

Rodman, Hugh, 33, 35, 71–75, 82, 85, 93, 306

Rodney, 232

Roeder, Bernard, 282, 325–26

Rogers, Buck, 116, 125

Rogers, Will, 401

Rome, 74, 80, 103–04, 166, 205–06, 466

Room 40, Old Building (see Admiralty)

Roosevelt family, 7, 29, 38–39, 88, 161

Roosevelt, Franklin D., 6–8, 14–16, 18, 19–23, 29, 47, 56, 57, 60–61, 65, 69–95, 116–17, 141–42, 148–49, 153–54, 160–71, 175–76, 181–215, 217, 221, 226–31, 233, 236–52, 255–75, 282–96, 299–309, 311, 313, 315, 317, 327–29, 330–32, 340–41, 347, 349, 354, 357, 360, 362–69, 371–73, 381, 386, 396–402, 407–10, 412–18, 425–26, 431–37, 439–40, 445, 449, 460–61, 479, 481, 485, 492

Roosevelt, Henry Latrobe, 6, 29, 116, 165, 171

Roosevelt, Theodore, 6–8, 14–16, 23, 27, 29, 36, 38, 40–44, 49, 57, 59, 75, 88, 153, 165, 188, 199, 210, 299, 408, 439, 460, 492

Roscoe, Thomas, 284

Roskill, Stephen, 22, 335, 395

Rosneath, 355

Rosyth, 80

ROUNDUP (see operations and plans)

Royal Air Force, 107, 156, 289, 293, 329, 447

Royal Air Force psychology, 289

Rudel, Hans-Ulrich, 437

"Rules of Thumb" (in naval strategy and planning), 226

Russell, George L., 14, 17, 73, 80, 212, 224, 229, 240, 243, 251, 262, 264, 281, 292, 316–17, 385, 399

Russo-Japanese War, 184, 435

S-4, 114

S-5, 99

S-46, 101

S-51, 103–7, 516

Safford, Laurence, 282–83, 327

St. John Island (Caribbean), 235

St. John's (Newfoundland), 218

St. Louis, 464

St. Nazaire, 465

St. Paul's Rocks, 215

St. Vincent, Lord (John Jervis), 7, 53, 362

Saipan, 277, 285, 361, 374, 376–77, 380–82, 393, 420, 428, 485

Saker, 208

Salinas, 237

Saltenstall, Levertt, 410

salvage divers, 104–07, 114, 144, 284

Sample, William D., 344

Sampson, Richard D., 194

Samson-Schley controversy, 450

San Clementine Island, 184

San Diego, 86, 127–28, 179, 401

San Francisco, 140, 178, 203, 231, 256, 273, 284, 362, 378, 381, 419, 423, 465, 484–89, 494

San Francisco, 28

San Pedro, 135, 139, 192

Sands, James H., 37

Santee, 344

Saratoga, 116, 123, 128–29, 131, 133, 140–42, 170, 181–84, 190, 192, 229, 395, 437, 487, 488

Sarnoff, David, 349

Satō, Kōzō, 74

Savanah, 407

Savoy Hotel, 42

Scalzi, Olympia, 68

Scapa Flow, 75, 79, 80, 82, 465

Schade, Henry, 394

Scharnhorst, 306

Schevill, William E., 333

Schlessinger, Jr., Arthur, 304

Schneider, Frederick H., 329

Schoeffel, Malcolm, 133, 191, 213, 351–52, 398–99, 432, 440–45, 448

Schofield, Frank H., 128, 141, 146–48, 162

Schwab, Charles M., 91

science fiction, 114, 116, 120–21, 125, 159, 333

Scoles, Albert "Buddy," 129–30

scouting force, 178

Scrugham, James G. (senator), 306

SeaBees (also see naval construction battalions), 379, 419

Sea Frontier (Eastern) 275, 295, 307, 343, 378, 429, 477, 479, 486, 488, 496; (Gulf), 275; (Western), 378, 486

Seattle (also see Naval Shipyard, Bremerton), 135, 142–45, 488

Sebald, William J., 176, 320, 327, 342, 348–50, 384–89, 420, 423, 436, 440

Second Fleet (also see under numbered fleets), 353, 487

"Secret Room" (see CominCh "F Staff" functions)

Section 8S (see Admiralty OIC)

Seeadler, 55

Selfridge, Harry Gordon, 42

Sellars, David, 191

Settle, Thomas G. W. "Tex," 173

Seventh Fleet (also see under numbered fleets), 354, 383, 387, 389–90, 397, 440, 488

Sewell, Sumner, 310

SEXTANT (see Cairo Conference), 363–64, 485

Seymour Expedition, 205

Shakespeare, William, 19, 60

Shanghai, 377, 380

Shark, 249

"Shellback" (equator crossing ritual), 138, 328

Shelly, Tully, 38, 489

Shenandoah, 96, 172

Shepard, Alan, 461

Shepard, Richard D., 378, 388, 399, 419

Sheppard, Harry R., 317

Sherman, Forrest, 128, 140, 240, 274, 339, 376, 378, 425, 432

Sherman, Frederick C., 274

Shoemaker, William B., 108–10, 113

shoot on sight (policy), 237

shore establishment, naval, 48, 59, 88, 104, 149, 188–89, 196–98, 228–29, 235, 264, 273, 275, 309, 317, 359, 477

Shriners, the (organization), 433

Siberia, 62, 66, 76, 82, 365

signal intelligence, 54, 247, 269, 279, 322, 334, 339, 348–53, 356, 374, 384, 387, 391, 435–36, 458, 487–89

Sikorsky Aircraft Company, 284

Sims, William S., 6–7, 11, 14, 24, 29, 38, 40–63, 64–65, 66–88, 91–96, 102, 143, 146–59, 164, 176–77, 183–84, 191, 193, 205, 233, 237–40, 259–63, 270–71, 305–06, 309, 318, 347, 398, 432, 438, 450, 452–53, 459–61, 465

"SimsADUS" (also see Sims, William S.), 65

Singapore, 19, 33, 209–12, 216, 226, 238–39, 249, 271, 276, 313, 349, 395, 484

"Sink Us," 61, 68, 242

Sino-American Cooperation Organization (SACO, also see Naval Group, China), 272, 354, 369, 379, 396–97, 489

Sixteenth Fleet (also see under numbered fleet), 436

Sixth Battle Squadron, Grand Fleet, US Navy (also see Battleship Division Nine), 71, 75

Sixth Fleet (also see under numbered fleets), 229, 253, 489

Skorzeny, Otto, 437

SLEDGEHAMMER (see operations and plans)

Slessor, John C., 295, 329

Slim, William, 379

Smedberg, III, William, 17, 232–33, 261, 309, 385–88, 419–23, 444, 455, 457

Smith, Alan E., 372

Smith, E. E., 159, 333

Smith Edward H. "Iceberg," 227–28

Smith, Frederick H. "Freddy," 150, 288, 289, 310, 365, 405, 433, 438, 443, 451

Smith, Holland M. "Howlin Mad," 198, 200, 235, 377

Smith, Janvier "Jan," 451, 457, 500

Smith, Leonard B., 232

Smith, Walter D., 37, 76, 151, 173, 288, 291, 362, 365, 405, 443

Smith-Hutton, Henri, 206, 252–53, 319–20, 327–28, 342, 348–51, 384–85, 426, 435, 488

Snyder, Charles P., 38, 177, 191, 212, 259, 281, 300

"Society for Repression of Ignorant Assumptions," 29

Solace, 35

Soley, James, 39, 57, 506

Solomon Islands, 211, 255–56, 272, 285, 360, 395

Somervell, Brehon B., 242, 328

Somerville, James, 71, 358, 379, 394–95

SONAR (also see ASDIC), 317–18, 333–34

Sound Military Decision, 14, 49, 195, 203, 226, 248, 267, 292, 388

South-East Asia Command (SEAC), 366, 394

Southwest Pacific Area (SWPA), 272, 280, 320, 354, 365, 380, 383, 385

Soviet Union, 8, 18, 94, 154–59, 185, 205, 210, 227, 238, 241, 267, 271, 286, 295–97, 307–08, 313–15, 329, 349, 360–66, 370–74, 394, 419–25, 435, 439, 446, 452, 485–86

Spaatz, Carl, 426, 449

Spanish Armada, 75

Spanish Civil War, 181

SPARS (Coast Guard), 304

special intelligence (SI), 54, 347, 269, 279, 322, 334, 339, 348–53, 356, 374, 384, 387, 391, 435–36, 458, 487, 488–89

special naval observer (SpeNavO), 224, 232–34, 242, 270–75

"Special relationship" (Churchillian concept), 8–9, 169, 205, 279, 286–87, 325, 437–38

Sperry, Charles, 39, 46, 176

Spike Island, 65

Spruance, Raymond A., 37, 151–52, 196, 218, 228, 235, 275, 339, 354, 375–78, 380, 383, 389, 393, 395, 433, 441–42, 453–54, 456

Spurious, 22

Squadron 40-Tare, 181

staff conferences (Anglo-American and associates in world wars), 15, 63, 86–88, 116–19, 157, 205–07, 217–18, 225, 243–47, 249, 256–57, 286–87, 323, 329, 335–37, 341, 352, 355, 357, 362–64, 366, 369, 375, 395, 408, 421, 461, 464–66, 484–85

"Staff Course" (Naval War College), 52, 147

Stamford Bridge (baseball game), 77

Standard Oil Company, 45

Standard-Type battleship, 46

Star Trek, 120

Stark, Harold R., 16–17, 30, 52–53, 78, 149, 183, 187–91, 193, 196, 198, 201–06, 209–16, 227, 229, 232–34, 236, 238, 240–53, 256–64, 270–71, 288, 292, 296, 342, 345, 351, 353–54, 362, 365, 367, 374, 409–10, 414, 423, 433–34, 438, 451, 476, 481, 484, 489

starvation (as strategy), 359, 425

Stettinius, Jr., Edward R., 187, 367, 402

Stilwell, Joseph, 370, 379, 383, 396

Stimson, Henry L., 20, 21, 87, 134, 135, 242, 245, 248–49, 260, 275, 295, 327, 329, 343, 398, 413, 417, 433, 449, 481, 494–98

Stockton, Charles H., 35

Stoddard, Theodore Lotrob, 153

Stoddard-DuBois debate, 153–54

Stone Acres, 144–45

Stone, Earle E., 283, 321–22, 327

stone frigates, 207–08

strategic analysis (see Naval War College, historical section, intelligence)

Stratton, Dorothy, C., 304

Strauss, Elliott, 457

Strauss, Joseph, 40, 76

Streeter, Ruth Cheney, 304

stress, 9, 16, 280, 322, 359, 382, 401–02, 414, 424, 439, 445, 448–49, 496

Stringham (see also wireless tests), 46

Sturdee, Frederick, 78

Submarine Boat Company, 97

submarine qualification insignia, 99

Submarine Squadron 50, 355

suicide, 280, 359, 382, 429, 445, 448–49

Summersby, Kay, 400

Sun Yat–Sen, 272

supply (concept), 289, 366, 372–74, 380–81, 389, 469–71, 478

supply (enemy targets), 236, 276, 286

support group (SG), 218

supreme commander, Allied Forces in Japan, 440

supreme commander, Allied Powers (SCAP), 440

Supreme Court (see government, US)

Supreme Headquarters, Allied Expeditionary Force (SHAEF), 364–65, 485

surrender (versus victory), 415, 423–27

sustainable end (see "Fundamental Principle")

Sutphen, Henry R., 97, 196

Swanson, Claude, 163, 164, 171

Swordfish, 407

Sylph, 63

SYMBOL (see Casablanca Conference), 328–29, 335, 340, 484

Symonds, Craig, 453

tactical analysis (see gaming and experimentation)

"Tactical Masterpiece" (King reference to Pearl Harbor attack), 8, 18, 231, 239, 240

Taft, William H., 41–44, 49, 349

Tampico affair, 49–50

Tanglin Club, 33

Taranto (raid), 286

task group (concept), 102, 141, 183, 185, 188, 198, 218, 326, 331, 334, 339, 344, 361, 389, 436, 460, 470, 473, 474, 487

task organization, 36, 177, 181, 185, 198, 199, 212, 214, 233, 245, 258, 273–75, 281, 285, 294–95, 299, 304, 318, 326, 330, 339, 344, 349, 353, 395, 470, 477, 486–87

Taussig, Joseph K., 52, 63–64, 78, 85, 170, 183

Taylor Board, 109

Taylor, David W., 97

Taylor, Montgomery C., 100, 102, 109

Teapot Dome (scandal), 95

TEARDROP (operation), 421–22

technology (King's views on), 13, 46, 95–99, 105, 110–116, 130, 136, 152, 195, 305, 315, 322, 333, 336, 401, 420, 425, 447–48, 452, 460–61

teetotalers, 59, 100, 111

Tehran (conference, see also EUREKA), 363–65, 485

temporary rank (also see promotion system), 35, 50, 64–65, 69, 78, 86, 89–93, 97–99, 101, 109, 113, 120, 148, 162–64, 201–02, 211, 221, 233, 248, 261, 264, 268, 272–74, 279, 318, 338, 343, 385, 407, 409, 411, 413–15, 429, 435–36, 439, 442–3, 453, 480

Tenth Fleet (also see under numbered fleets), 268, 343–46, 353, 356, 385, 420–22, 484–88, 496–98

TERMINAL (Potsdam conference), 486

terror (as tactic), 231, 282, 361, 446

Terry, 50

Texas, 198, 214, 221, 223, 225

Thebaud, Leo, 38, 403

Theobald, Robert A., 50

Third Fleet (also see under numbered fleets), 353–54, 387, 389, 487

Thorndike, Joseph J., 16, 223

Time magazine, 16, 169, 304

Tines, Samuel, 29

Tirpitz, 306

Tisdale, Mahlon S., 333

Titanic, 46

Tobey, Edward C., 68

Tokyo, 87, 181, 252–53, 308, 314, 319, 406, 423, 426, 440

"Tombstone promotion" (honorary rank granted upon retirement), 39, 86, 90, 93, 176, 178, 196, 429

toothpick for "Blowtorch" (FDR inspired gift), 213

Topper, John R., 222–24, 235, 432

TORCH (see operations and plans)

torpedoes, 12, 39, 179, 236–37, 262, 274, 302, 338, 361, 421, 426–27

Towers, John H., 46, 113, 116, 118, 129, 140, 163, 165, 170–71, 183, 187–88, 255–56, 339, 376, 381

Trafalgar, Battle of, 42, 80, 159, 216, 229, 277, 390

traffic analysis, 283

Train, Charles R., 152

Train, Harold C., 319

Trammel, Park (also see neutrality acts after 1934), 166, 181, 194, 197–98, 217, 221, 229, 231

Trans-Siberian Railway, 62, 66

Trans World Airlines (TWA), 328

treaties, (British way of war), 205; (London Naval), 129, 157; (Tordesillas and Zaragoza), 383; of Versailles, 82, 87–88, 94–95; (Washington Naval), 7, 86–87, 103

Treaty Navy (also see "League Navy" idea), 88

Tremaine, Glenville, 196

Trever, 129

TRIDENT (conference in Washington), 484

Triest, Willard G., 239, 461

Trieste, 461

Trigger, 372

Tripartite Pact, 19, 193, 200, 205, 206, 210, 227, 241, 257, 267, 286, 328, 355, 363, 370, 407, 431, 460

"Triple Threat" (King nom de guerre), 13, 23, 187–88, 196, 198

Truman Committee, 311, 314, 317, 322

Truman, Harry S, 170, 260, 282, 310–11, 314, 317, 322, 409, 412–13, 417, 424–27, 431–34, 437–45, 447, 449, 452, 484

Tsushima Straits, 184

Tully, Grace, 481

Turing, Alan, 321

Turner, Frederick Jackson, 13, 25

Turner, John Kenneth, 50

Turner, Richmond Kelly, 37, 50, 110–11, 114, 151–52, 210–211, 227, 232, 244, 251, 255–56, 271, 339, 353–54, 362, 377

Turner, Stansfield, 452–453

Twelfth Fleet (also see under numbered fleets), 353, 489

"Two Ocean Navy" (concept), 23, 166, 181

type commands, 178

Typhoon ("COBRA"), 393–95

U-boat (British propaganda), 22

U-boat (see German submarines)

U-tankers (targeted), 280, 306, 373–75

ULTRA (see special intelligence)

underwater demolition team (see Draper Kauffman), 228–29, 272

unification (debates concerning joint organization), 71, 95–96, 107, 114–15, 148, 160–61, 164, 260, 294, 302, 306, 327, 341, 359, 371, 384, 399, 403, 405–06, 409, 411–14, 417–19, 431–39, 443–52, 497–98

uniforms, 26, 61–62, 93, 109, 115, 119, 126–27, 136, 145, 163, 199, 223, 237, 288, 328, 365, 418–19, 425, 435, 438

universal education (historical, also see national service as citizenship), 84, 406, 406, 447, 492–94

universal military training (and education), 406, 447

United Nations, 6–8, 18–20, 244, 267, 286–87, 299–300, 313, 325, 358–59, 363, 365, 369–70, 407–08, 413, 417, 425–26, 434–40, 451, 460, 491

United Nations Navy (international navy concept), 435

United States government, (Constitution), 23, 39, 55, 59, 91, 95, 115, 146, 161, 169, 175, 206, 228, 241, 246, 259, 261, 296, 316, 409, 413, 443, 492; (legislative branch), 115, 244, 245, 259–63, 270, 275, 296, 371, 409–11, 426, 431, 476–79; (executive branch), 245, 259–63, 270, 275, 296, 371, 409–11, 426, 431, 476–79 ; (judicial branch), 228, 316, 341, 440, 443

United States-United Kingdom Agreement (UKUSA), 428, 437

Union Station (Washington, DC), 240

"Union Station" (as reference to Formosa), 284

Unity of Command (concept), 6, 21, 67, 148, 306, 330, 337, 347

Unity of Effort (concept), 7, 21, 46, 67, 223, 330–31, 336–37, 340, 343, 345, 347

University of Alabama, 38

University of Greifswald, 53

University of London (King's College), 147, 263

University of North Carolina (Chapel Hill), 458

University of Oxford, 438

Unlimited National Emergency (policy), 231

"Unremitting pressure" (King strategic concept), 8, 241, 314, 346, 374–75, 377, 401, 403

Upham, Frank B., 109, 113, 163

Upton, Emory (inspired Luce to establish war college), 13, 25

Urban League, 302

Utah, 465

UTAH Beach (see operations and plans, NEPTUNE), 382

Van Auken, Wilbur R., 152, 165

van den Berg, Egerton "Liath" (grandson), 315, 403

van den Berg, Oliver (son-in-law), 150, 405

van Deurs, George, 111–12, 140, 157, 457

van Orman, Ward, 172–74

Vandegrift, Alexander, 483

VENGEANCE (Yamamoto assassination), 340–41

Venice, 466

Veracruz, 49–50, 64, 95, 126

Verdun, 466

Vermont, 42